Arguing About Political Philosophy

2nd Edition

This second edition of *Arguing About Political Philosophy* is the most complete, up-to-date, and interdisciplinary anthology of its kind. Its selections cover both classic philosophical sources such as Hobbes and Rousseau, and contemporary figures such as Robert Nozick and G. A. Cohen. But additional excerpts from economists, psychologists, novelists, and legal theorists help students from diverse intellectual backgrounds to connect with and appreciate the problems and distinctive methodology of political philosophy.

This book also goes beyond any other anthology on the market in its coverage of traditionally under-represented views such as libertarianism, neo-socialism, feminism, and critical race theory. And it is one of the only anthologies to go beyond *A Theory of Justice* in its coverage of the political thought of John Rawls.

The volume is divided into three parts — Foundational Concepts; Government, the Economy, and Morality; and Applied Political Philosophy — covering core arguments and emerging debates in topics like:

- social contract theory
- political economy
- property rights
- freedom
- equality
- immigration
- global distributive justice

The new companion website offers valuable resources for instructors and students alike, including sample quizzes, exams, and writing assignments, extensive study questions for each reading, and an online version of the "What's Your Political Philosophy" self-assessment.

Matt Zwolinski is Associate Professor of Philosophy at the University of San Diego, co-director of USD's Institute for Law and Philosophy, and the founder of and frequent contributor to the popular *Bleeding Heart Libertarians* blog. He is the author of numerous articles in political philosophy on topics such as exploitation, price gouging, and sweatshop labor.

Arguing About Philosophy

This exciting and lively series introduces key subjects in philosophy with the help of a vibrant set of readings. In contrast to many standard anthologies which often reprint the same technical and remote extracts, each volume in the *Arguing About Philosophy* series is built around essential but fresher philosophical readings, designed to attract the curiosity of students coming to the subject for the first time. A key feature of the series is the inclusion of well-known yet often neglected readings from related fields, such as popular science, film and fiction. Each volume is edited by leading figures in their chosen field and each section carefully introduced and set in context, making the series an exciting starting point for those looking to get to grips with philosophy.

Arguing About Political Philosophy

2nd Edition

Edited by

Matt Zwolinski

Routledge
Taylor & Francis Group

NEW YORK AND LONDON

This edition published 2014
by Routledge
711 Third Avenue, New York, NY 10017

and by Routledge
2 Park Square, Milton Park, Abingdon, Oxon, OX14 4RN

Routledge is an imprint of the Taylor & Francis Group, an informa business

© 2014 Taylor & Francis

First edition published 2009 by Routledge

Library of Congress Cataloging in Publication Data
A catalog record for this book has been requested

ISBN: 978–0–415–53581–6 (hbk)
ISBN: 978–0–415–53582–3 (pbk)

Typeset in Joanna
by RefineCatch Limited, Bungay, Suffolk

SFI Certified Sourcing
www.sfiprogram.org
SFI-00453

Printed and bound in the United States of America
by Edwards Brothers Malloy

Contents

Acknowledgments

The publishers and editor would like to thank the following for their permission to use copyrighted material:

Basic Books for Axelrod, Robert, excerpts from *The Evolution of Cooperation*, chapters 1–2 (New York: Basic Books, 1984), pp. 3–4, 7–16, 27, 29–54; Nozick, Robert, "Libertarian Rights," excerpts from *Anarchy, State, and Utopia* (New York: Basic Books, 1974), chapters 1 and 3, pp. ix, 26–35; Nozick, Robert, "The Entitlement Theory of Justice," excerpts from *Anarchy, State, and Utopia* (New York, Basic Books, 1974), chapter 7, pp. 149–164, 167–174.

Cambridge University Press for Brennan, Jason, "Political Liberty: Who Needs It?" *Social Philosophy and Policy* vol. 29, no. 1 (January 2012), pp. 1–27; Gutmann, Amy and Dennis Thompson, "Moral Disagreement in a Democracy," *Social Philosophy and Policy* 12:1 (1995), pp. 87–110; Lomasky, Loren, "Liberalism Beyond Borders," *Social Philosophy and Policy* (2007), pp. 206–233; Pettit, Philip, "Republican Political Theory," from Andrew Vincent, ed., *Political Theory: Tradition, Diversity and Ideology*, Cambridge, Cambridge University Press, pp. 112–32; Schmidtz, David, "Equal Respect and Equal Shares," *Social Philosophy and Policy* (2002), 19, pp. 244–274.

Harper Collins Publishers for Milgram, Stanley, "The Perils of Obedience," *Harpers Magazine* (December 1973), pp. 62–77.

Harvard University Press for MacKinnon, Catharine, "Difference and Dominance," in *Feminism Unmodified* (Harvard University Press, 1987), pp. 32–45; Rawls, John, "A Theory of Justice," excerpts from *Theory of Justice* original edition (Harvard University Press, 1971), pp. 3–4, 11–16, 17–33, 60–66, 72–75, 100–104, 136–142, 302–303.

MIT Press for Wolf, Charles, "Market Failure," excerpt from *Markets or Governments* (Cambridge, MIT Press, 1988), pp. 12–24.

Oxford University Press for Arneson, Richard, "Equality and Equal Opportunity for Welfare," from Louis J. Pojman and Robert Westmoreland, eds., *Equality: Selected Readings*, (Oxford: Oxford University Press, 1997), pp. 229–242; Berlin, Isaiah, "Two Concepts of Liberty," from *Four Essays on Liberty* (Oxford University Press, 1969), pp. 118–172; Hume, David, "Justice as Convention," excerpt from *Treatise of Human Nature*, Book III, Part II, Section II (Oxford), pp. 484–501; Schmidtz, David, "The Institution of Property," from *Environmental Ethics: What Really Matters, What Really Works*, 2nd edition (Oxford University Press, 2012), pp. 406–420.

Princeton University Press for Cohen, G.A., excerpt from *Why Not Socialism?* (Princeton: Princeton University Press, 2009), pp. 3–82.

Sage Journals for Sandel, Michael, "The Procedural Republic and the Unencumbered Self," *Political Theory* 12:1 (February, 1984), pp. 81–96.

Social Theory and Practice for Huemer, Michael, "Is There a Right to Immigrate?" *Social Theory and Practice* 36 (3) (2010), pp. 429–461.

University of Chicago Press for Hayek, Friedrich, "The Atavism of Social Justice" from *New Studies in Philosophy, Politics, Economics, and the History of Ideas* (University of Chicago Press, 1978), pp. 57–68.

Wiley-Blackwell for Gaus, Gerald, "The Moral Foundations of Liberal Neutrality" in Thomas Christiano and John Christman, eds., *Contemporary Debates in Political Philosophy* (Blackwell), pp. 81–98; Miller, David, "Immigration: The Case for Limits," from *Contemporary Debates in Applied Ethics* (Blackwell), pp. 193–206; Nickel, James, "Making Sense of Human Rights," from *Making Sense of Human Rights*, 2nd edition (Blackwell, 2007), pp. 35–52; Rawls, John, "Justice as Fairness: Political Not Metaphysical," *Philosophy and Public Affairs*, vol. 14., no. 3 (Summer, 1985), pp. 223–251.

The Yale Law Journal for Smith, M.B.E., "Is There a *Prima Facie* Duty to Obey the Law?" *Yale Law Journal*, vol. 82 (1973), pp. 950–976.

Every effort has been made to contact the copyright holders for their permission to reprint material in this book. The publishers would be grateful to hear from any copyright holder who is not here acknowledged and will undertake to rectify any errors or omissions in future editions of the book.

GENERAL INTRODUCTION

WHETHER WE LIKE IT OR NOT, politics pervades our lives. Political rules control what kinds of foods are available to us from our grocer and at what cost, what sorts of drugs we can consume for medicinal or recreational purposes, how fast we can drive, who we can sleep with, the kind of education we can or must provide for our children, what and where we may speak in public, and how we may practice our religion, to give just the beginning of a very long list. We can choose — and many people do — not to think about politics in any kind of systematic and rigorous way. But we cannot choose to isolate ourselves from its effects.

This is a book for people who want to think seriously about politics. It is a book, to be more specific, about the *philosophic* approach to political thought. Philosophy, of course, is not the only way of thinking seriously about politics. Most obviously, one could also choose to study the subject through the methodology of political science. But psychologists, sociologists, historians, and even economists also provide intellectual tools with which to think critically about political issues. What, then, differentiates the philosophic approach from these others?

The first important difference between philosophical analysis and other approaches is that philosophy is at its core a *non-empirical* approach. To study politics empirically is to be concerned with observation and measurement. Political scientists engage in empirical research, for instance, when they look at the voting patterns of different ethnic or religious groups, or when they attempt to measure the effects of certain public policies on crime rates. Philosophical research, on the other hand, tends to look very different. For philosophers, the primary tools of inquiry are logical argument and conceptual analysis. Conceptual analysis involves trying to clearly define or characterize abstract concepts such as justice or the state, and to distinguish them from other closely related subjects such as equality or society. Logical argument involves discerning and evaluating the internal structure of the reasons people give to support their claims, and trying to ensure that the claims we ourselves make follow from our premises.

What does the use of these tools look like in practice? Suppose someone claims that the primary function the state is to provide security for its citizens, and that therefore we ought to have an extremely restrictive immigration policy in order to protect ourselves from foreign threats. As philosophers, we can respond to this claim by, first, using the method of conceptual analysis to scrutinize the claim about the nature of statehood. Is the primary function of the state really protection of citizens? Protection from what? What if the promotion of security conflicts with the preservation of liberty? Surely security isn't the *only* thing we care about, so can we come up with a conception of statehood that better responds to the plurality of values we hold? Even if we accept the idea that the function of statehood is to provide security, however, we can still ask whether it follows logically from this definition that a restrictive immigration policy is warranted. Strictly speaking, of course, it only follows *if* a restrictive immigration policy turns out to be a good way of promoting security. So that's one assumption that needs to be flagged and set aside for closer scrutiny. Are there any other hidden assumptions embedded in the argument? By deploying the tools of logic we can help to uncover such assumptions and thereby discern the validity or invalidity of political arguments. (Philosophy can't do all the work though — a philosopher can tell you that your argument tacitly assumes a certain claim about the effects of a public policy, but it is up to economists, sociologists, or political scientists to tell us whether that claim is *as an empirical matter* true or false.)

The second important difference between the philosophical approach to politics and the approaches taken by other disciplines is that philosophy is often explicitly *normative* in its approach. To approach a subject from a normative perspective is to make claims about *values*, or about what *ought* to be the case. Normative approaches are to be distinguished from *descriptive* approaches, which merely purport to tell us the way things *are* (and not whether the way things are is good or bad). It is important to recognize that not *all* of philosophy is normative. Claims about the nature of certain concepts, for instance, are not necessarily normative, even (and this is tricky!) if the concepts themselves *are* normative concepts. "Justice," for instance, is clearly a normative concept in the sense that calling something just or unjust involves making a kind of value claim. But a philosopher who proposes to define justice as giving each person his or her due, for instance, is not necessarily making a value claim. They might simply be trying to issue a report on the way a word is used by a certain community. Often, however, philosophers *will* be making value claims — and sometimes they will do so in the context of providing a definition. So, for instance, if I were to define justice as treating people according to what their actions merit, and I defended this definition by saying that this is the only way of understanding justice that captures what is *truly important and valuable* about justice, then I would be making a normative claim. My definition of the word "justice" is based on my belief that some value is more important or significant than others, and that is a quintessentially normative belief.

Sometimes it can be difficult to tell whether a philosopher is making a normative claim or whether they are simply trying to provide a value-neutral definition or description of how things are. Making this determination will require careful attention on your part as a reader. At other times, however, value claims — such as that the claim that torture is degrading and ought not to be done — will be front and center in a philosopher's argument. This would be seen as unscientific and uncalled for in strictly empirical approaches to politics. But philosophy, as a partially normative discipline, calls upon us to think about, scrutinize, and argumentatively defend our values and their application to the political realm.

Political discussion will not be productive if we are not clear on what the words we use mean. Nor will we get very far unless we have some idea of where we want to go — what values we are trying to promote. Philosophy, then, is an indispensible tool for thinking about politics. But philosophy by itself — since it refrains from empirical investigation regarding how the world actually works — cannot get us very far either. Philosophical analysis must be supplemented by empirical research from other disciplines. Some of that research is presented in this book. Axelrod's essay on game theory and Milgram's essay on obedience to authority, for instance, are essentially empirical approaches to politics. I have included them in this volume because they provide us with some data with which to pursue our philosophical analysis, and because they demonstrate quite nicely how philosophical questions arise even in the course of non-philosophical investigation. Part of your development as a budding political philosopher will be learning how to adjust your philosophical worldview in light of empirical evidence, while simultaneously scrutinizing the philosophical assumptions underlying those empirical claims. This is a difficult task, but given the importance of the subject, it is also a crucial one. My hope is that the readings in this book will make it a challenging and exciting one as well.

Further Reading

The following are good introductions to the subject of political philosophy:

Hampton, J. (1997). *Political Philosophy*. Boulder, CO: Westview.
Kymlicka, W. (2002). *Contemporary Political Philosophy: An Introduction* (2nd ed.). Oxford: Oxford University Press.
Narveson, J. (2008). *You and the State: A Short Introduction to Political Philosophy*. Lanham, MD : Rowman and Littlefield.
Simmons, A.J. (2007). *Political Philosophy*. Oxford: Oxford University Press.
Wolff, J. (2006). *An Introduction to Political Philosophy*. (Revised ed.). Oxford: Oxford University Press.

WHAT'S YOUR POLITICAL PHILOSOPHY?

This survey provides a way for readers to see where they stand on a variety of the issues covered in this book. Instructors might find it useful to administer this survey on the first day of class, both to get a sense of where students stand and to provoke some initial discussion. Later, you can ask students to return to the various parts of the survey after the corresponding readings have been covered in the course to see what changes, if any, those readings have produced in students' beliefs. An online version of this quiz, which assesses your answers and identifies your underlying political philosophy, is available on the companion website.

For each item, indicate the degree to which you agree with the statement.

Political Authority

1. It is never morally justifiable to break the law.
    Strongly Disagree   Disagree   Neither agree nor disagree Agree   Strongly Agree

2. If the law tells me to do/not do something, then this gives me *some* reason to do / not do that thing.
    Strongly Disagree   Disagree   Neither agree nor disagree Agree   Strongly Agree

3. Individuals have a moral duty to disobey unjust laws
    Strongly Disagree   Disagree   Neither agree nor disagree Agree   Strongly Agree

4. Political authority is justified because it derives from the consent of the governed.
    Strongly Disagree   Disagree   Neither agree nor disagree Agree   Strongly Agree

5. In the absence of government, life would be very bad for people in general.
    Strongly Disagree   Disagree   Neither agree nor disagree Agree   Strongly Agree

6. The terms of the "social contract" are unfair to / biased against women and racial minorities.
    Strongly Disagree   Disagree   Neither agree nor disagree Agree   Strongly Agree

Rights

7. All human beings have natural rights which exist prior to and independent of government.
    Strongly Disagree   Disagree   Neither agree nor disagree Agree   Strongly Agree

8. It is in all circumstances absolutely morally unjustifiable to violate an individual's rights.
   Strongly Disagree   Disagree   Neither agree nor disagree   Agree   Strongly Agree

9. People who are in desperate need through no fault of their own have a right to assistance.
   Strongly Disagree   Disagree   Neither agree nor disagree   Agree   Strongly Agree

10. The only right we have is the right to be free from the initiation of aggression by others.
    Strongly Disagree   Disagree   Neither agree nor disagree   Agree   Strongly Agree

Justice

11. We should do what justice requires no matter how bad the consequences might be.
    Strongly Disagree   Disagree   Neither agree nor disagree   Agree   Strongly Agree

12. What is just is a function of what produces good consequences for society in the long run.
    Strongly Disagree   Disagree   Neither agree nor disagree   Agree   Strongly Agree

13. The laws of my country are mostly just.
    Strongly Disagree   Disagree   Neither agree nor disagree   Agree   Strongly Agree

14. The requirements of justice do not vary from culture to culture or across time.
    Strongly Disagree   Disagree   Neither agree nor disagree   Agree   Strongly Agree

15. It is unjust for a society to allow a person's life prospects to be significantly affected by bad luck.
    Strongly Disagree   Disagree   Neither agree nor disagree   Agree   Strongly Agree

16. It is unjust that one person should have more wealth than another simply because she was born with greater natural talents.
    Strongly Disagree   Disagree   Neither agree nor disagree   Agree   Strongly Agree

Political Liberalism

17. Governments should not endorse one particular religion over others.
    Strongly Disagree   Disagree   Neither agree nor disagree   Agree   Strongly Agree

18. A theory of justice should be entirely independent of controversial metaphysical claims.
    Strongly Disagree   Disagree   Neither agree nor disagree   Agree   Strongly Agree

19. Governments should not base their laws on moral claims when there is reasonable disagreement regarding the truth of those claims.
    Strongly Disagree   Disagree   Neither agree nor disagree   Agree   Strongly Agree

Political Economy

20. Capitalism exploits the working class.
Strongly Disagree   Disagree   Neither agree nor disagree Agree   Strongly Agree

21. Individuals behaving selfishly in a free market often promote the social good better than governmental policies.
Strongly Disagree   Disagree   Neither agree nor disagree Agree   Strongly Agree

22. Relatively unregulated capitalism does a better job at making people well-off than any other system.
Strongly Disagree   Disagree   Neither agree nor disagree Agree   Strongly Agree

23. Market failures like monopolies are best addressed by government regulation.
Strongly Disagree   Disagree   Neither agree nor disagree Agree   Strongly Agree

Property Rights

24. All private ownership of land is unjust.
Strongly Disagree   Disagree   Neither agree nor disagree Agree   Strongly Agree

25. Most private property as it exists in the world today came about unjustly.
Strongly Disagree   Disagree   Neither agree nor disagree Agree   Strongly Agree

26. Private property in the means of production should be abolished.
Strongly Disagree   Disagree   Neither agree nor disagree Agree   Strongly Agree

27. Government taxation is a violation of property rights.
Strongly Disagree   Disagree   Neither agree nor disagree Agree   Strongly Agree

Distributive Justice

28. The fact that the rich in a country like the United States have so much more wealth than the poor is unjust.
Strongly Disagree   Disagree   Neither agree nor disagree Agree   Strongly Agree

29. Inequality of wealth is unjust regardless of how it came about.
Strongly Disagree   Disagree   Neither agree nor disagree Agree   Strongly Agree

30. Socialism is superior to capitalism in terms of producing a just distribution of wealth.
Strongly Disagree   Disagree   Neither agree nor disagree Agree   Strongly Agree

31. All individuals should be guaranteed a basic income by the state, at a level sufficient for subsistence.
Strongly Disagree   Disagree   Neither agree nor disagree Agree   Strongly Agree

Freedom

32. The promotion of individual freedom is one of the most important purposes of government.
Strongly Disagree   Disagree   Neither agree nor disagree Agree   Strongly Agree

33. A person is free to the extent that that person is not interfered with by others.
Strongly Disagree   Disagree   Neither agree nor disagree Agree   Strongly Agree

34. True freedom requires the ability and material resources to achieve one's goals.
Strongly Disagree   Disagree   Neither agree nor disagree Agree   Strongly Agree

35. Capitalism is the best economic system for promoting individual freedom.
Strongly Disagree   Disagree   Neither agree nor disagree Agree   Strongly Agree

Equality

36. In a fundamental moral sense, all human beings are equal.
Strongly Disagree   Disagree   Neither agree nor disagree Agree   Strongly Agree

37. Government should try to promote economic equality through its laws and regulations.
Strongly Disagree   Disagree   Neither agree nor disagree Agree   Strongly Agree

38. Government should promote equality of opportunity, rather than equality of outcome.
Strongly Disagree   Disagree   Neither agree nor disagree Agree   Strongly Agree

39. A large amount of material inequality is compatible with the moral equality of persons.
Strongly Disagree   Disagree   Neither agree nor disagree Agree   Strongly Agree

Democratic Deliberation and Voting

40. "One person, one vote" is *the* essential tenet of democracy.
Strongly Disagree   Disagree   Neither agree nor disagree Agree   Strongly Agree

41. One person's vote has a significant impact in determining the outcome of an election.
Strongly Disagree   Disagree   Neither agree nor disagree Agree   Strongly Agree

42. Political liberties like the right to vote are among an individual's most valuable possessions.
Strongly Disagree   Disagree   Neither agree nor disagree Agree   Strongly Agree

Immigration

43. My country currently allows too much immigration.
Strongly Disagree   Disagree   Neither agree nor disagree Agree   Strongly Agree

44. Illegal immigrants who are just trying to improve their lives are not doing anything morally wrong.
    Strongly Disagree   Disagree   Neither agree nor disagree   Agree   Strongly Agree

45. The most moral immigration policy is one where borders are completely or almost completely open.
    Strongly Disagree   Disagree   Neither agree nor disagree   Agree   Strongly Agree

46. Governments ought to discriminate among potential immigrants and admit only those who will promote the country's national interest.
    Strongly Disagree   Disagree   Neither agree nor disagree   Agree   Strongly Agree

Global Distributive Justice

47. It is unfair that some people are born into counties struggling with desperate poverty, while others are born into luxury.
    Strongly Disagree   Disagree   Neither agree nor disagree   Agree   Strongly Agree

48. It is morally wrong for individuals in wealthy countries like the United States to spend money on luxuries while others starve.
    Strongly Disagree   Disagree   Neither agree nor disagree   Agree   Strongly Agree

49. Justice requires a radical transformation of the global political and economic order.
    Strongly Disagree   Disagree   Neither agree nor disagree   Agree   Strongly Agree

50. More global free trade will promote global justice.
    Strongly Disagree   Disagree   Neither agree nor disagree   Agree   Strongly Agree

PART 1

Foundational Concepts

1a. POLITICAL AUTHORITY

GOVERNMENTS CLAIM, and are usually assumed to have, a kind of moral authority to do things that no other individual or group of individuals may do. Governments can take your money without your permission and spend it on things they think are important — whether or not you agree. Governments can tell you what sorts of drugs you may or may not consume, what kinds of things you may or may not say in public, and what kinds of goods and services you may or may not sell to others. Governments can even force you to be a part of their army, where they will tell you not only what to eat, wear and say, but also who to kill. And if you disobey any of your government's directives, it can forcibly round you up and lock you away in a small concrete room for as long as it likes — or possibly it will even kill you itself.

What gives governments the right to do these things? Or *does* government have the right to do them? Are there any limits on what government may legitimately do and if so, where do these limits come from?

The readings in this section explore these questions by looking at the issue of political authority. Specifically, we will be exploring political authority as a *normative* notion. A government may have authority in a *de facto* sense if it rules effectively, and perhaps if a sufficient portion of the population believes that it is a proper authority. But to have authority in a normative sense requires more than this, even if what exactly it requires is a matter of some controversy. Some hold that the essence of legitimate authority is the ability to coerce subjects in a way that is morally justified. Others hold that it is the ability to impose duties on subjects through laws. And still others hold that legitimate authority is essentially concerned with the right to rule. Note how these conceptions come apart — A might have a right to rule over B, for instance, without B having a corresponding duty to obey A. However the details are fleshed out, what normative conceptions of political authority have in common is that they make a *moral* claim about governments' commands and/or citizens' responses to those commands.

Historically, some of the most popular accounts of authority have been based on the idea of individual consent and the *social contract*. The idea behind such accounts is that political authority is legitimate when it is consented to by those who are subject to it. If, then, we can look back to a time when individuals lived without a common government — when they lived in what is generally referred to as a *state of nature* — we can see what the conditions in such a state would be like, and thereby see both what reasons such individuals would have to consent to a government (and hence to extricate themselves from the state of nature), and what *kind* of government they would have reason to consent to.

Hobbes and Locke produce two very different accounts of the state of nature, and two correspondingly different accounts of the social contract by which government is first instituted. Both of their accounts are rich in detail and raise numerous questions of philosophic interest. But a brief comparison of one of the many aspects on which Hobbes and Locke differ provides some insight as to how theories of the state of nature and theories of political authority are related. For Locke, the state of nature is governed by a law of nature by which individuals are forbidden from harming one another in their life, liberty or estate. Not all individuals follow this law in all circumstances, and even when individuals act in good faith there sometimes arise understandable disagreements regarding who did what to whom and whether or not what was done was actually a breach of nature's law. But war and conflict are not the normal condition of the state of nature, and all that is necessary to remedy the "inconveniences" of this state is a limited government with adjudicative and policing powers. For Hobbes, on the other hand, the state of nature is a state of perpetual war of every man against every man, and the life of man in such a state is "solitary, poor, nasty, brutish and short." As long as individuals are left in such a state to rely on their own judgment and power, this state of war will continue. For Hobbes, then, the solution to the problem of the state of nature requires a much more powerful form of government — one which will supplant individuals' reliance on their own judgment by replacing it with authoritative law, and which will back up that law with awe-inspiring force. Notice how, for each thinker, the account of the state of nature and the account of the proper scope of government authority are related. The Hobbesian state of nature poses a different and much more serious problem than the Lockean one, and the Hobbesian state is accordingly a very different and more radical kind of "solution."

As compelling as these stories about the social contract may be, they face several serious difficulties. First, as will be made clear in the essay by David Hume, it is not clear that governments arose in a way that had anything to do with individual consent at all. But if there never was any social contract, then how can the contract be used to justify any of the governments we actually have? Second, even if a contract could bind the people who signed on to it and thereby originally established a government, it is not clear how future generations could be bound to it. Must each person born into the society sign on to the contract as well? Or do we look instead (as Locke does) for signs of some form of "tacit," rather than explicit, consent? A final and more radical challenge to social contract theory is presented in the readings from Virginia Held and Charles Mills, both of whom challenge the ability of contract theory to account for the status of minority and historically oppressed groups. For Held, the language of contract and the model of rational economic man on which it relies is problematic insofar as it ignores or marginalizes the perspective of women and the moral relations — especially the relation of care — that are central to women's lives. For Mills, traditional contract theory masks and thereby perpetuates the crucial fact of white supremacy.

Social contract theorists often respond to the first problem by claiming that their theories are not meant to provide a *historical* account of what was actually consented to, but rather a *hypothetical* account of what individuals would *have reason to consent to*, given certain assumptions about their circumstances. Stories about the state of nature and the social contract are not meant to be accurate accounts of some actual event that occurred in the distant past. Rather, they are meant to be heuristics for thinking about certain enduring and significant aspects of human nature and social relations, and the way in which those facts give us reason to endorse certain forms of government. Whether we *actually* consented to those forms of government, then, is not really the issue. What matters is that we would have *reason* to do so, and this fact can help us answer the question of whether or not our current government is one which we ought to view as legitimate. As we will see later in the book, John Rawls is explicit in describing his social contract account as a hypothetical one. But all of the accounts in this section will probably strike contemporary readers as more plausible if read in this way.

Still, even hypothetical social contract accounts have their problems. Those who think that there is something important about *actual* consent, for instance, will be disturbed by the move from thinking about *actual* contracts justifying states to *hypothetical* ones doing so. After all, in many contexts this substitution would surely be inappropriate. If you actually agree to sell me your car for $5,000, then it is permissible for me to take your car in exchange for giving you my money. But in the absence of any explicit agreement, I cannot simply leave a check on your porch and drive off in your car, no matter how convinced I am that you *would* have agreed to the bargain if I had asked you.

Partly, this is because it is very difficult for me to have any confidence in what you *would have* agreed to without your actually telling me. And this is why we find so much disagreement among social contract theorists. Different theorists make different assumptions about the social conditions in which individuals would find themselves in the absence of a common government, and about the goals and desires those individuals would have. Some, like Murray Rothbard, even conclude that individuals would get along just fine in a state of nature, and would have no reason to consent to any government at all! Given that there exists so much disagreement regarding what individuals would have reason to consent to, how can we hope to use social contract theories as a way of justifying legitimate political authority?

Even if the state's authority can be justified in some way, this still leaves open the question of whether and under what circumstances individuals have a *duty to obey* its laws. One might think that the government of the United States has legitimate authority, for instance, and still believe that individuals who helped fugitive slaves escape in the 1850s were justified in doing so. The last four readings in this section explore this issue. In the *Crito*, Socrates argues that he has a duty to obey the laws of Athens — even when those laws unfairly require his own death! The remaining readings take a somewhat more skeptical position. In "The Perils of Obedience," the social psychologist Stanley Milgram describes his famous experiments on obedience, in which he found that a majority of subjects were willing to obey the commands of an authoritative figure — even to the point where, for all they knew, they had shocked an innocent person to death. For Milgram, this suggests that as a psychological matter, individuals are all too easily manipulated into obeying *unjust* authority, a fact which he thought played some role in explaining the horrors of the Holocaust. A similar concern about the potential for legally sanctified injustice can be found in Martin Luther King, Jr.'s "Letter from a Birmingham Jail," in which he cites approvingly St. Augustine's dictum that "an unjust law is no law at all." For King, individuals not only have a moral *permission* to break unjust laws, they have a moral *responsibility* to do so, so long as they do so openly, lovingly, and with a willingness to accept the penalty. M.B.E. Smith, in his essay, takes an even more skeptical position. If an act is not wrong in itself, then the fact that the law prohibits it gives one no inherent reason *at all* to refrain from performing it, nor does one have any obligation to willingly accept whatever legal penalties may be attached to disobedience.

Further Reading

Edmundson. (1998). *Three Anarchical Fallacies*. Cambridge: Cambridge University Press.

Green, L. (1988). *The Authority of the State*. Oxford: Oxford University Press.

Huemer, M. (2012). *The Problem of Political Authority: An Examination of the Right to Coerce and the Duty to Obey*. New York: Palgrave Macmillan.

Klosko, G. (2004). *The Principle of Fairness and Political Obligation* (2nd ed.). Lanham, MD: Rowman & Littlefield.

Klosko, G. (2005). *Political Obligations*. Oxford: Oxford University Press.

Pateman, C., and Mills, C. (2007). *Contract and Domination*. New York: Polity.

Rawls, J. (1964). Legal Obligation and the Duty of Fair Play. In S. Hook (Ed.), *Law and Philosophy*. New York: New York University Press.

Raz, J. (1979). *The Authority of Law*. Oxford: Oxford University Press.

Sanders, J. T., and Narveson, J. (1996). *For and Against the State: New Essays*. Lanham, MD: Rowman & Littlefield.

Simmons, A. J. (1979). *Moral Principles and Political Obligations*: Princeton: Princeton University Press.

Simmons, A. J. (2001). *Justification and Legitimacy: Essays on Rights and Obligations*. Cambridge: Cambridge University Press.

Smith, M. B. E. (1973). Is There a *Prima Facie* Obligation to Obey the Law? *Yale Law Journal, 82*, 950–76.

Wellman, C. H., and Simmons, A. J. (2005). *Is There a Duty to Obey the Law?* Cambridge: Cambridge University Press.

Wolff, R. P. (1970). *In Defense of Anarchism* (3rd ed.). Berkeley: University of California Press.

Chapter 1

Thomas Hobbes

THE STATE OF NATURE AS A STATE OF WAR

Thomas Hobbes (1588–1679) was an English philosopher whose major work, *Leviathan,* was published in 1651 to great controversy amidst the English Civil War, and later went on to become one of the most influential works in the social contract tradition of political philosophy. In these excerpts, Hobbes gives us his thoughts on what life would be like in a "state of nature" — a state where human beings lived without the protection of any government. He also discusses the moral "law of nature" to which people are subject in this state, and why this law impels individuals to exit the state of nature through the formation of a social contract.

Of the Difference of Manners

By Manners, I mean not here, Decency of behaviour; as how one man should salute another, or how a man should wash his mouth, or pick his teeth before company, and such other points of the *Small Moralls*; But those qualities of man-kind, that concern their living together in Peace, and Unity. To which end we are to consider, that the Felicity of this life, consisteth not in the repose of a mind satisfied. For there is no such *Finis ultimus,* (utmost ayme,) nor *Summum Bonum,* (greatest Good,) as is spoken of in the Books of the old Morall Philosophers. Nor can a man any more live, whose Desires are at an end, than he, whose Senses and Imaginations are at a stand. Felicity is a continuall progresse of the desire, from one object to another; the attaining of the former, being still but the way to the later. The cause whereof is, That the object of mans desire, is not to enjoy once onely, and for one instant of time; but to assure for ever, the way of his future desire. And therefore the voluntary actions, and inclinations of all men, tend, not only to the procuring, but also to the assuring of a contented life; and differ onely in the way: which ariseth partly from the diversity of passions, in divers men; and partly from the difference of the knowledge, or opinion each one has of the causes, which produce the effect desired.

So that in the first place, I put for a generall inclination of all mankind, a perpetuall and restlesse desire of Power after power, that ceaseth onely in Death. And the cause of this, is not always that a man hopes for a more intensive delight, than he has already attained to; or that he cannot be content with a moderate power: but because he cannot assure the power and means to live well, which he hath present, without the acquisition of more. And from hence it is, that Kings, whose power is greatest, turn their endeavours to the assuring it at home by Lawes, or abroad by Wars: and when that is done, there succeedeth a new desire; in some, of

Fame from new Conquest; in others, of ease and sensuall pleasure; in others, of admiration, or being flattered for excellence in some art, or other ability of the mind.

Of the *Naturall Condition* of Mankind, as Concerning their Felicity, and Misery

Nature hath made men so equall, in the faculties of body, and mind; as that though there bee found one man sometimes manifestly stronger in body, or of quicker mind then another; yet when all is reckoned together, the difference between man, and man, is not so considerable, as that one man can thereupon claim to himselfe any benefit, to which another may not pretend, as well as he. For as to the strength of body, the weakest has strength enough to kill the strongest, either by secret machination, or by confederacy with others, that are in the same danger with himselfe.

And as to the faculties of the mind, (setting aside the arts grounded upon words, and especially that skill of proceeding upon generall, and infallible rules, called Science; which very few have, and but in few things; as being not a native faculty, born with us; nor attained, (as Prudence,) while we look after somewhat els,) I find yet a greater equality amongst men, than that of strength. For Prudence, is but Experience; which equall time, equally bestowes on all men, in [61] those things they equally apply themselves unto. That which may perhaps make such equality incredible, is but a vain conceipt of ones owne wisdome, which almost all men think they have in a greater degree, than the Vulgar; that is, than all men but themselves, and a few others, whom by Fame, or for concurring with themselves, they approve. For such is the nature of men, that howsoever they may acknowledge many others to be more witty, or more eloquent, or more learned; Yet they will hardly believe there be many so wise as themselves: For they see their own wit at hand, and other mens at a distance. But this proveth rather that men are in that point

equall, than unequall. For there is not ordinarily a greater signe of the equall distribution of any thing, than that every man is contented with his share.

From this equality of ability, ariseth equality of hope in the attaining of our Ends. And therefore if any two men desire the same thing, which neverthelesse they cannot both enjoy, they become enemies; and in the way to their End, (which is principally their owne conservation, and sometimes their delectation only,) endeavour to destroy, or subdue one an other. And from hence it comes to passe, that where an Invader hath no more to feare, than an other mans single power; if one plant, sow, build, or possesse a convenient Seat, others may probably be expected to come prepared with forces united, to dispossesse, and deprive him, not only of the fruit of his labour, but also of his life, or liberty. And the Invader again is in the like danger of another.

And from this diffidence of one another, there is no way for any man to secure himselfe, so reasonable, as Anticipation; that is, by force, or wiles, to master the persons of all men he can, so long, till he see no other power great enough to endanger him: And this is no more than his own conservation requireth, and is generally allowed. Also because there be some, that taking pleasure in contemplating their own power in the acts of conquest, which they pursue farther than their security requires; if others, that otherwise would be glad to be at ease within modest bounds, should not by invasion increase their power, they would not be able, long time, by standing only on their defence, to subsist. And by consequence, such augmentation of dominion over men, being necessary to a man's conservation, it ought to be allowed him.

Againe, men have no pleasure, (but on the contrary a great deale of griefe) in keeping company, where there is no power able to over-awe them all. For every man looketh that his companion should value him, at the same rate he sets upon himselfe: And upon all signes of contempt, or undervaluing, naturally endeavours, as far as he dares (which amongst them that have no common power, to keep them in quiet, is far enough to make them destroy each other,) to extort a greater value from his contemners, by dommage; and from others, by the example.

So that in the nature of man, we find three principall causes of quarrell. First, Competition; Secondly, Diffidence; Thirdly, Glory.

[62] The first, maketh men invade for Gain; the second, for Safety; and the third, for Reputation. The first use Violence, to make themselves Masters of other mens persons, wives, children, and cattell; the second, to defend them; the third, for trifles, as a word, a smile, a different opinion, and any other signe of undervalue, either direct in their Persons, or by reflexion in their Kindred, their Friends, their Nation, their Profession, or their Name.

Hereby it is manifest, that during the time men live without a common Power to keep them all in awe, they are in that condition which is called Warre; and such a warre, as is of every man, against every man. For WARRE, consisteth not in Battell onely, or the act of fighting; but in a tract of time, wherein the Will to contend by Battell is sufficiently known: and therefore the notion of Time, is to be considered in the nature of Warre; as it is in the nature of Weather. For as the nature of Foule weather, lyeth not in a showre or two of rain; but in an inclination thereto of many dayes together: So the nature of War, consisteth not in actuall fighting; but in the known disposition thereto, during all the time there is no assurance to the contrary. All other time is PEACE.

Whatsoever therefore is consequent to a time of Warre, where every man is Enemy to every man; the same is consequent to the time, wherein men live without other security, than what their own strength, and their own invention shall furnish them withall. In such condition, there is no place for Industry; because the fruit thereof is uncertain: and consequently no Culture of the Earth; no Navigation, nor use of

the commodities that may be imported by Sea; no commodious Building; no Instruments of moving, and removing such things as require much force; no Knowledge of the face of the Earth; no account of Time; no Arts; no Letters; no Society; and which is worst of all, continuall feare, and danger of violent death; And the life of man, solitary, poore, nasty, brutish, and short.

It may seem strange to some man, that has not well weighed these things; that Nature should thus dissociate, and render men apt to invade, and destroy one another: and he may therefore, not trusting to this Inference, made from the Passions, desire perhaps to have the same confirmed by Experience. Let him therefore consider with himselfe, when taking a journey, he armes himselfe, and seeks to go well accompanied; when going to sleep, he locks his dores; when even in his house he locks his chests; and this when he knows there bee Lawes, and publike Officers, armed, to revenge all injuries shall bee done him; what opinion he has of his fellow subjects, when he rides armed; of his fellow Citizens, when he locks his dores; and of his children, and servants, when he locks his chests. Does he not there as much accuse mankind by his actions, as I do by my words? But neither of us accuse mans nature in it. The Desires, and other Passions of man, are in themselves no Sin. No more are the Actions, that proceed from those Passions, till they know a Law that forbids them: which till Lawes be made they cannot know: nor can any Law be made, till they have agreed upon the Person that shall make it.

[63] It may peradventure be thought, there was never such a time, nor condition of warre as this; and I believe it was never generally so, over all the world: but there are many places, where they live so now. For the savage people in many places of *America*, except the government of small Families, the concord whereof dependeth on naturall lust, have no government at all; and live at this day in that brutish manner, as I said before. Howsoever, it may be perceived what

manner of life there would be, where there were no common Power to feare; by the manner of life, which men that have formerly lived under a peacefull government, use to degenerate into, in a civill Warre.

But though there had never been any time, wherein particular men were in a condition of warre one against another; yet in all times, Kings, and Persons of Soveraigne authority, because of their Independency, are in continuall jealousies, and in the state and posture of Gladiators; having their weapons pointing, and their eyes fixed on one another; that is, their Forts, Garrisons, and Guns upon the Frontiers of their Kingdomes; and continuall Spyes upon their neighbours; which is a posture of War. But because they uphold thereby, the Industry of their Subjects; there does not follow from it, that misery, which accompanies the Liberty of particular men.

To this warre of every man against every man, this also is consequent; that nothing can be Unjust. The notions of Right and Wrong, Justice and Injustice have there no place. Where there is no common Power, there is no Law: where no Law, no Injustice. Force, and Fraud, are in warre the two Cardinall vertues. Justice, and Injustice are none of the Faculties neither of the Body, nor Mind. If they were, they might be in a man that were alone in the world, as well as his Senses, and Passions. They are Qualities, that relate to men in Society, not in Solitude. It is consequent also to the same condition, that there be no Propriety, no Dominion, no *Mine* and *Thine* distinct; but only that to be every man's that he can get; and for so long, as he can keep it. And thus much for the ill condition, which man by meer Nature is actually placed in; though with a possiblity to come out of it, consisting partly in the Passions, partly in his Reason.

The Passions that encline men to Peace, are Feare of Death; Desire of such things as are necessary to commodious living; and a Hope by their Industry to obtain them. And Reason suggesteth convenient Articles of Peace, upon which men may be drawn to agreement. These

Articles, are they, which otherwise are called the Lawes of Nature:

Of the First and Second *Naturall Lawes,* and of *Contracts*

THE RIGHT OF NATURE, which Writers commonly call *Jus Naturale,* is the Liberty each man hath, to use his own power, as he will himselfe, for the preservation of his own Nature; that is to say, of his own Life; and consequently, of doing any thing, which in his own Judgement, and Reason, hee shall conceive to be the aptest means thereunto.

By LIBERTY, is understood, according to the proper signification of the word, the absence of externall Impediments: which Impediments, may oft take away part of a mans power to do what hee would; but cannot hinder him from using the power left him, according as his judgement, and reason shall dictate to him.

A LAW OF NATURE, (*Lex Naturalis,*) is a Precept, or generall Rule, found out by Reason, by which a man is forbidden to do, that, which is destructive of his life, or taketh away the means of preserving the same; and to omit, that, by which he thinketh it may be best preserved. For though they that speak of this subject, use to confound *Jus,* and *Lex, Right* and *Law*; yet they ought to be distinguished; because RIGHT, consisteth in liberty to do, or to forbeare; Whereas LAW, determineth, and bindeth to one of them: so that Law, and Right, differ as much, as Obligation, and Liberty; which in one and the same matter are inconsistent.

And because the condition of Man, (as hath been declared in the precedent Chapter) is a condition of Warre of every one against every one; in which case every one is governed by his own Reason; and there is nothing he can make use of, that may not be a help unto him, in preserving his life against his enemyes; It followeth, that in such a condition, every man has a Right to every thing; even to one anothers body. And therefore, as long as this naturall Right of every man to every thing endureth, there can be no security to any man, (how strong or wise soever he be,) of living out the time, which Nature ordinarily alloweth men to live. And consequently it is a precept, or generall rule of Reason, *That every man, ought to endeavour Peace, as farre as he has hope of obtaining it; and when he cannot obtain it, that he may seek, and use, all helps, and advantages of Warre.* The first branch of which Rule, containeth the first, and Fundamentall Law of Nature; which is, *to seek Peace, and follow it.* The Second, the summe of the Right of Nature; which is, *By all means we can, to defend our selves.*

From this Fundamentall Law of Nature, by which men are commanded to endeavour Peace, is derived this second Law; *That a man be willing, when others are so too, as farre-forth, as for Peace, and* [65] *defence of himselfe he shall think it necessary, to lay down this right to all things; and be contented with so much liberty against other men, as he would allow other men against himselfe.* For as long as every man holdeth this Right, of doing any thing he liketh; so long are all men in the condition of Warre. But if other men will not lay down their Right, as well as he; then there is no Reason for any one, to devest himselfe of his: For that were to expose himselfe to Prey, (which no man is bound to) rather than to dispose himselfe to Peace. This is that Law of the Gospell; *Whatsoever you require that others should do to you, that do ye to them.*

Whensoever a man Transferreth his Right, or Renounceth it; it is either in consideration of some Right reciprocally transferred to [66] himselfe; or for some other good he hopeth for thereby. For it is a voluntary act: and of the voluntary acts of every man, the object is some *Good to himselfe.* And therefore there be some Rights, which no man can be understood by any words, or other signes, to have abandoned, or transferred. As first a man cannot lay down the right of resisting them, that assault him by force, to take away his life; because he cannot be understood to ayme thereby, at any Good to himselfe. The same may be sayd of Wounds, and Chaynes, and Imprisonment; both because there is no

benefit consequent to such patience; as there is to the patience of suffering another to be wounded, or imprisoned: as also because a man cannot tell, when he seeth men proceed against him by violence, whether they intend his death or not. And lastly the motive, and end for which this renouncing, and transferring of Right is introduced, is nothing else but the security of a man's person, in his life, and in the means of so preserving life, as not to be weary of it. And therefore if a man by words, or other signes, seem to despoyle himselfe of the End, for which those signes were intended; he is not to be understood as if he meant it, or that it was his will; but that he was ignorant of how such words and actions were to be interpreted.

The mutuall transferring of Right, is that which men call CONTRACT.

There is difference, between transferring of Right to the Thing; and transferring, or tradition, that is, delivery of the Thing it selfe. For the Thing may be delivered together with the Translation of the Right; as in buying and selling with ready mony; or exchange of goods, or lands: and it may be delivered some time after.

Again, one of the Contractors, may deliver the Thing contracted for on his part, and leave the other to perform his part at some determinate time after, and in the mean time be trusted; and then the Contract on his part, is called PACT, or COVENANT: Or both parts may contract now, to performe hereafter: in which cases, he that is to performe in time to come, being trusted, his performance is called *Keeping of Promise, or* Faith; and the fayling of performance (if it be voluntary) *Violation of Faith.*

If a Covenant be made, wherein neither of the parties performe presently, but trust one another; in the condition of meer Nature, (which is a condition of Warre of every man against every man,) upon any reasonable suspicion, it is Voyd: But if there be a common Power set over them both, with right and force sufficient to compell performance; it is not Voyd. For he that performeth first, has no assurance the other will performe after; because the bonds of words are too weak to bridle mens ambition, avarice, anger, and other Passions, without the feare of some coerceive Power; which in the condition of meer Nature, where all men are equall, and judges of the justnesse of their own fears cannot possibly be supposed. And therefore he which performeth first, does but betray himselfe to his enemy; contrary to the Right (he can never abandon) of defending his life, and means of living.

But in a civill estate, where there is a Power set up to constrain those that would other-wise violate their faith, that feare is no more reasonable; and for that cause, he which by the Covenant is to perform first, is obliged so to do.

The cause of feare, which maketh such a Covenant invalid, must be always something arising after the Covenant made; as some new fact, or other signe of the Will not to performe: else it cannot make the Covenant voyd. For that which could not hinder a man from promising, ought not to be admitted as a hindrance of performing.

Covenants entred into by fear, in the condi-tion of meer Nature, are obligatory. For example, if I Covenant to pay a ransome, or service for my life, to an enemy; I am bound by it. For it is a Contract, wherein one receiveth the benefit of life; the other is to receive mony, or service for it; and consequently, where no other Law (as in the condition, of meer Nature) forbiddeth the performance, the Covenant is valid. Therefore Prisoners of warre, if trusted with the payment of their Ransome, are obliged to pay it: And if a weaker Prince, make a disadvantageous peace with a stronger, for feare; he is bound to keep it; unlesse (as hath been sayd before) there ariseth some new, and just cause of feare, to renew the war. And even in Common-wealths, if I be forced to redeem my selfe from a Theefe by promising him mony, I am bound to pay it, till the Civill Law discharge me. For whatsoever I may lawfully do without Obligation, the same I may lawfully Covenant to do through feare: and what I lawfully Covenant, I cannot lawfully break.

A Covenant not to defend my selfe from force, by force, is alwayes voyd. For (as I have shewed before) no man can transferre, or lay down his Right to save himselfe from Death, Wounds, and Imprisonment, (the avoyding whereof is the onely End of laying [70] down any Right, and therefore the promise of not resisting force, in no Covenant transferreth any right; nor is obliging. For though a man may Covenant thus, *Unlesse I do so, or so, kill me;* he cannot Covenant thus, *Unlesse I do so, or so, I will not resist you, when you come to kill me.* For man by nature chooseth the lesser evill, which is danger of death in resisting; rather than the greater, which is certain and present death in not resisting. And this is granted to be true by all men, in that they lead Criminals to Execution, and Prison, with armed men, notwithstanding that such Criminals have consented to the Law, by which they are condemned.

Of Other Lawes of Nature

From that law of Nature, by which we are obliged to transferre to another, such Rights, as being retained, hinder the peace of Mankind, there followeth a Third; which is this, *That men performe their Covenants made:* without which, Covenants are in vain, and but Empty words; and the Right of all men to all things remaining, wee are still in the condition of Warre.

And in this law of Nature, consisteth the Fountain and Originall of JUSTICE. For where no Covenant hath preceded, there hath no Right been transferred, and every man has right to every thing; and consequently, no action can be Unjust. But when a Covenant is made, then to break it is Unjust: And the definition of INJUSTICE, is no other than the not Performance of Covenant. And whatsoever is not Unjust, is Just.

But because Covenants of mutuall trust, where there is a feare of not performance on either part, (as hath been said in the former Chapter,) are invalid; though the Originall of Justice be the making of Covenants; yet Injustice actually there can be none, till the cause of such feare be taken away; which while men are in the naturall condition of Warre, cannot be done. Therefore before the names of Just, and Unjust can have place, there must be some coercive Power, to compell men equally to the perform-ance of their Covenants, by the terrour of some punishment, greater than the benefit they expect [72] by the breach of their Covenant; and to make good that Propriety, which by mutuall Contract men acquire, in recompence of the universall Right they abandon: and such power there is none before the erection of a Common-wealth. And this is also to be gathered out of the ordinary definition of Justice in the Schooles: For they say, that *Justice is the constant Will of giving to every man his own*. And therefore where there is no *Own*, that is, no *Propriety*, there is no Injustice; and where there is no coërceive Power erected, that is, where there is no Common-wealth, there is no Propriety; all men having Right to all things: Therefore where there is no Common-wealth, there nothing is Unjust. So that the nature of Justice, consisteth in keeping of valid Covenants: but the Validity of Covenants begins not but with the Constitution of a Civill Power, sufficient to compell men to keep them: And then it is also that Propriety begins.

The Foole hath sayd in his heart, there is no such thing as Justice; and sometimes also with his tongue; seriously alleaging, that every mans conservation, and contentment, being committed to his own care, there could be no reason, why every man might not do what he thought conduced thereunto: and therefore also to make, or not make; keep, or not keep Covenants, was not against Reason, when it conduced to ones benefit. He does not therein deny, that there be Covenants; and that they are sometimes broken, sometimes kept; and that such breach of them may be called Injustice, and the observance of them Justice: but he

questioneth, whether Injustice, taking away the feare of God, (for the same Foole hath said in his heart there is no God,) may not sometimes stand with that Reason, which dictateth to every man his own good; and particularly then, when it conduceth to such a benefit, as shall put a man in a condition, to neglect not onely the dispraise, and revilings, but also the power of other men. The Kingdome of God is gotten by violence: but what if it could be gotten by unjust violence? were it against Reason so to get it, when it is impossible to receive hurt by it? and if it be not against Reason, it is not against Justice: or else Justice is not to be approved for good. From such reasoning as this, Succesfull wickednesse hath obtained the name of Vertue: and some that in all other things have disallowed the violation of Faith; yet have allowed it, when it is for the getting of a Kingdome. And the Heathen that believed, that *Saturn* was deposed by his son *Jupiter*, believed neverthelesse the same *Jupiter* to be the avenger of Injustice: Somewhat like to a piece of Law in *Cokes* Commentaries on *Litleton*; where he sayes, If the right Heire of the Crown be attainted of Treason; yet the Crown shall descend to him, and *eo instante* the Atteynder be voyd: From which instances a man will be very prone to inferre; that when the Heire apparent of a Kingdome, shall kill him that is in possession, though his father; you may call it Injustice, or by what other name you will; yet it can never be against Reason, seeing all the voluntary actions of men tend to the benefit of themselves; and those actions are most Reasonable, that conduce most to their [73] ends. This specious reasoning is neverthelesse false.

For the question is not of promises mutuall, where there is no security of performance on either side; as when there is no Civill Power erected over the parties promising; for such promises are no Covenants: But either where one of the parties has performed already; or where there is a Power to make him performe; there is the question whether it be against reason, that is, against the benefit of the other to performe, or not. And I say it is not against reason. For the manifestation whereof, we are to consider; First, that when a man doth a thing, which notwithstanding any thing can be foreseen, and reckoned on, tendeth to his own destruction, howsoever some accident which he could not expect, arriving may turne it to his benefit; yet such events do not make it reasonably or wisely done. Secondly, that in a condition of Warre, wherein every man to every man, for want of a common Power to keep them all in awe, is an Enemy, there is no man can hope by his own strength, or wit, to defend himselfe from destruction, without the help of Confederates; where every one expects the same defence by the Confederation, that any one else does: and therefore he which declares he thinks it reason to deceive those that help him, can in reason expect no other means of safety, than what can be had from his own single Power. He therefore that breaketh his Covenant, and consequently declareth that he thinks he may with reason do so, cannot be received into any Society, that unite themselves for Peace and Defence, but by the errour of them that receive him; nor when he is received, be retayned in it, without seeing the danger of their errour; which errours a man cannot reasonably reckon upon as the means of his security: and therefore if he be left, or cast out of Society, he perisheth; and if he live in Society, it is by the errours of other men, which he could not foresee, nor reckon upon; and consequently against the reason of his preservation; and so, as all men that contribute not to his destruction, forbear him only out of ignorance of what is good for themselves.

Of the Causes, Generation, and Definition of a *Common-Wealth*

The finall Cause, End, or Designe of men, (who naturally love Liberty, and Dominion over others,) in the introduction of that restraint upon themselves, (in which wee see them live in Common-wealths,) is the foresight of their own preservation, and of a more contented life thereby; that is to say, of getting themselves out from that miserable condition of Warre, which is necessarily consequent (as hath been shewn) to the naturall Passions of men, when there is no visible Power to keep them in awe, and tye them by feare of punishment to the performance of their Covenants, and observation of those Lawes of Nature set down in the fourteenth and fifteenth Chapters.

For the Lawes of Nature (as *Justice, Equity, Modesty, Mercy*, and (in summe) *doing to others, as wee would be done to,*) of themselves, without the terrour of some Power, to cause them to be observed, are contrary to our naturall Passions, that carry us to Partiality, Pride, Revenge, and the like. And Covenants, without the Sword, are but Words, and of no strength to secure a man at all. Therefore notwithstanding the Lawes of Nature, (which every one hath then kept, when he has the will to keep them, when he can do it safely,) if there be no Power erected, or not great enough for our security; every man will and may lawfully rely on his own strength and art, for caution against all other men. And in all places, where men have lived by small Families, to robbe and spoyle one another, has been a Trade, and so farre from being reputed against the Law of Nature, that the greater spoyles they gained, the greater was their honour; and men observed no other Lawes therein, but the Lawes of Honour; that is, to abstain from cruelty, leaving to men their lives, and instruments of husbandry. And as small Familyes did then; so now do Cities and Kingdomes which are but greater Families (for their own security) enlarge their Dominions, upon all pretences of danger, and fear of Invasion, or assistance that may be given to Invaders, endeavour as much as they can, to subdue, or weaken their neighbours, by open force, and secret arts, for want of other Caution, justly; and are remembered for it in after ages with honour.

Nor is it the joyning together of a small number of men, that gives them this security; because in small numbers, small additions [86] on the one side or the other, make the advantage of strength so great, as is sufficient to carry the Victory; and therefore gives encouragement to an Invasion. The Multitude sufficient to confide in for our Security, is not determined by any certain number, but by comparison with the Enemy we feare; and is then sufficient, when the odds of the Enemy is not of so visible and conspicuous moment, to determine the event of warre, as to move him to attempt.

And be there never so great a Multitude; yet if their actions be directed according to their particular judgements, and particular appetites, they can expect thereby no defence, nor protection, neither against a Common enemy, nor against the injuries of one another. For being distracted in opinions concerning the best use and application of their strength, they do not help, but hinder one another; and reduce their strength by mutuall opposition to nothing: whereby they are easily, not onely subdued by a very few that agree together; but also when there is no common enemy, they make warre upon each other, for their particular interests. For if we could suppose a great Multitude of men to consent in the observation of Justice, and other Lawes of Nature, without a common Power to keep them all in awe; we might as well suppose all Man-kind to do the same; and then there neither would be, nor need to be any Civill Government, or Common-wealth at all; because there would be Peace without subjection.

Nor is it enough for the security, which men desire should last all the time of their life, that they be governed, and directed by one judgement, for a limited time; as in one Battell, or one Warre. For though they obtain a Victory by their unanimous endeavour against a forraign enemy; yet afterwards, when either they have no common enemy, or he that by one part is held for an enemy, is by another part held for a friend, they must needs by the difference of their interests dissolve, and fall again into a Warre amongst themselves.

It is true, that certain living creatures, as Bees, and Ants, live sociably one with another, (which

are therefore by *Aristotle* numbred amongst Politicall creatures;) and yet have no other direction, than their particular judgements and appetites; nor speech, whereby one of them can signifie to another, what he thinks expedient for the common benefit: and therefore some man may perhaps desire to know, why Man-kind cannot do the same. To which I answer:

First, that men are continually in competition for Honour and Dignity, which these creatures are not; and consequently amongst men there ariseth on that ground, Envy and Hatred, and finally Warre; but amongst these not so.

Secondly, that amongst these creatures, the Common good differeth not from the Private; and being by nature enclined to their private, they procure thereby the common benefit. But man, whose Joy consisteth in comparing himselfe with other men, can relish nothing but what is eminent.

Thirdly, that these creatures, having not (as man) the use of reason, do not see, nor think they see any fault, in the administration of [87] their common businesse: whereas amongst men, there are very many, that thinke themselves wiser, and abler to govern the Publique, better than the rest; and these strive to reforme and innovate, one this way, another that way; and thereby bring it into Distraction and Civill warre.

Fourthly, that these creatures, though they have some use of voice, in making knowne to one another their desires, and other affections; yet they want that art of words, by which some men can represent to others, that which is Good, in the likenesse of Evill; and Evill, in the likenesse of Good; and augment, or diminish the apparent greatnesse of Good and Evill; discontenting men, and troubling their Peace at their pleasure.

Fiftly, irrationall creatures cannot distinguish betweene *Injury*, and *Dammage*; and therefore as long as they be at ease, they are not offended with their fellowes: whereas Man is then most troublesome, when he is most at ease: for then it is that he loves to shew his Wisdome, and controule the Actions of them that governe the Common-wealth.

Lastly, the agreement of these creatures is Naturall; that of men, is by Covenant only, which is Artificiall: and therefore it is no wonder if there be somewhat else required (besides Covenant) to make their Agreement constant and lasting; which is a Common Power, to keep them in awe, and to direct their actions to the Common Benefit.

The only way to erect such a Common Power, as may be able to defend them from the invasion of Forraigners, and the injuries of one another, and thereby to secure them in such sort, as that by their owne industrie, and by the fruites of the Earth, they may nourish themselves and live contentedly; is, to conferre all their power and strength upon one Man, or upon one Assembly of men, that may reduce all their Wills, by plurality of voices, unto one Will: which is as much as to say, to appoint one man, or Assembly of men, to beare their Person; and every one to owne, and acknowledge himselfe to be Author of whatsoever he that so beareth their Person, shall Act, or cause to be Acted, in those things which concerne the Common Peace and Safetie; and therein to submit their Wills, every one to his Will, and their Judgements, to his Judgment. This is more than Consent, or Concord; it is a reall Unitie of them all, in one and the same Person, made by Covenant of every man with every man, in such manner, as if every man should say to every man, *I Authorise and give up my Right of Governing my selfe, to this Man, or to this Assembly of men, on this condition, that thou give up thy Right to him, and Authorise all his Actions in like manner.* This done, the Multitude so united in one Person, is called a COMMON-WEALTH, in latine CIVITAS. This is the Generation of that great LEVIATHAN, or rather (to speake more reverently) of that *Mortall God*, to which wee owe under the *Immortall God*, our peace and defence. For by this Authoritie, given him by every particular man in the Common-Wealth, he hath the use of so much Power and Strength [88] conferred on him, that by terror

thereof, he is inabled to forme the wills of them all, to Peace at home, and mutuall ayd against their enemies abroad. And in him consisteth the Essence of the Common-wealth; which (to define it,) is *One Person, of whose Acts a great Multitude, by mutuall Covenants one with another, have made themselves every one the Author, to the end he may use the strength and means of them all, as he shall think expedient, for their Peace and Common Defence.*

And he that carryeth this Person, is called SOVERAIGNE, and said to have *Soveraigne Power*; and every one besides, his SUBJECT.

The attaining to this Soveraigne Power, is by two wayes. One, by Naturall force; as when a man maketh his children, to submit themselves, and their children to his government, as being able to destroy them if they refuse; or by Warre subdueth his enemies to his will, giving them their lives on that condition. The other, is when men agree amongst themselves, to submit to some Man, or Assembly of men, voluntarily, on confidence to be protected by him against all others. This later, may be called a Politicall Common-wealth or Common-wealth by Institution; and the former, a Common-wealth by Acquisition. And first, I shall speak of a Common-wealth by Institution.

Of the *Rights* of Soveraignes by Institution

A *Common-wealth* is said to be *Instituted,* when a *Multitude* of men do Agree, and *Covenant, every one, with every one,* that to whatsoever Man, or *Assembly of* Men, shall be given by the major part, the *Right to Present* the Person of them all, (that is to say, to be their *Representative;*) every one, as well he that *Voted* for it, as he that *Voted against* it, shall *Authorise* all the Actions and Judgements, of that Man, or Assembly of men, in the same manner, as if they were his own, to the end, to live peaceably amongst themselves, and be protected against other men.

From this Institution of a Common-wealth are derived all the *Rights,* and *Facultyes* of him, or them, on whom the Soveraigne Power is conferred by the consent of the People assembled.

First, because they Covenant, it is to be understood, they are not obliged by former Covenant to any thing repugnant hereunto. And Consequently they that have already Instituted a Common-wealth, being thereby bound by Covenant, to own the Actions, and Judgements of one, cannot lawfully make a new Covenant, amongst themselves, to be obedient to any other, in any thing whatsoever, without his permission. And therefore, they that are subjects to a Monarch, cannot without his leave cast off Monarchy, and return to the confusion of a disunited Multitude; nor transferre their Person from him that beareth it, to another Man, or other Assembly of men: for they [89] are bound, every man to every man, to Own, and be reputed Author of all, that he that already is their Soveraigne, shall do, and judge fit to be done: so that any one man dissenting, all the rest should break their Covenant made to that man, which is injustice: and they have also every man given the Soveraignty to him that beareth their Person; and therefore if they depose him, they take from him that which is his own, and so again it is injustice. Besides, if he that attempteth to depose his Soveraign, be killed, or punished by him for such attempt, he is author of his own punishment, as being by the Institution, Author of all his Soveraign shall do: And because it is injustice for a man to do any thing, for which he may be punished by his own authority, he is also upon that title, unjust. And whereas some men have pretended for their disobedience to their Soveraign, a new Covenant, made, not with men, but with God; this also is unjust: for there is no Covenant with God, but by mediation of some body that representeth Gods Person; which none doth but Gods Lieutenant, who hath the Soveraignty under God. But this pretence of Covenant with God, is so evident a lye, even in the pretender's own consciences, that it is not onely an act of an unjust, but also of a vile, and unmanly disposition.

Secondly, Because the Right of bearing the Person of them all, is given to him they make Soveraigne, by Covenant onely of one to another, and not of him to any of them; there can happen no breach of Covenant on the part of the Soveraigne; and consequently none of his Subjects, by any pretence of forfeiture, can be freed from his Subjection. That he which is made Soveraigne maketh no Covenant with his Subjects beforehand, is manifest; because either he must make it with the whole multitude, as one party to the Covenant; or he must make a severall Covenant with every man. With the whole, as one party, it is impossible; because as yet they are not one Person: and if he make so many severall Covenants as there be men, those Covenants after he hath the Soveraignty are voyd, because what act soever can be pretended by any one of them for breach thereof, is the act both of himselfe, and of all the rest, because done in the Person, and by the Right of every one of them in particular. Besides, if any one, or more of them, pretend a breach of the Covenant made by the Soveraigne at his Institution; and others, or one other of his Subjects, or himselfe alone, pretend there was no such breach, there is in this case, no Judge to decide the controversie: it returns therefore to the Sword again; and every man recovereth the right of Protecting himselfe by his own strength, contrary to the designe they had in the Institution. It is therefore in vain to grant Soveraignty by way of precedent Covenant. The opinion that any Monarch receiveth his Power by Covenant, that is to say on Condition, proceedeth from want of understanding this easie truth, that Covenants being but words, and breath, have no force to oblige, contain, constrain, or protect any man, but what it has from the publique Sword; that is, from the untyed hands of that Man, or Assembly of men that hath the Soveraignty, and whose actions are avouched by them [90] all, and performed by the strength of them all, in him united. But when an Assembly of men is made Soveraigne; then no man imagineth any such Covenant to have past in the Institution; for no man is so dull as to say, for example, the People of *Rome*, made a Covenant with the Romans, to hold the Soveraignty on such or such conditions; which not performed, the Romans might lawfully depose the Roman People. That men see not the reason to be alike in a Monarchy, and in a Popular Government, proceedeth from the ambition of some, that are kinder to the government of an Assembly, whereof they may hope to participate, than of Monarchy, which they despair to enjoy.

Thirdly, because the major part hath by consenting voices declared a Soveraigne; he that dissented must now consent with the rest; that is, be contented to avow all the actions he shall do, or else justly be destroyed by the rest. For if he voluntarily entered into the Congregation of them that were assembled, he sufficiently declared thereby his will (and therefore tacitely covenanted) to stand to what the major part should ordayne: and therefore if he refuse to stand thereto, or make Protestation against any of their Decrees, he does contrary to his Covenant, and therfore unjustly. And whether he be of the Congregation, or not; and whether his consent be asked, or not, he must either submit to their decrees, or be left in the condition of warre he was in before; wherein he might without injustice be destroyed by any man whatsoever.

Fourthly, because every Subject is by this Institution Author of all the Actions, and Judgments of the Soveraigne Instituted; it followes, that whatsoever he doth, it can be no injury to any of his Subjects; nor ought he to be by any of them accused of Injustice. For he that doth any thing by authority from another, doth therein no injury to him by whose authority he acteth: But by this Institution of a Common-wealth, every particular man is Author of all the Soveraigne doth; and consequently he that complaineth of injury from his Soveraigne, complaineth of that whereof he himselfe is Author; and therefore ought not to accuse any man but himselfe; no nor himselfe of injury;

because to do injury to ones selfe, is impossible. It is true that they that have Soveraigne power, may commit Iniquity; but not Injustice, or Injury in the proper signification.

Fiftly, and consequently to that which was sayd last, no man that hath Soveraigne power can justly be put to death, or otherwise in any manner by his Subjects punished. For seeing every Subject is Author of the actions of his Soveraigne; he punisheth another, for the actions committed by himselfe.

And because the End of this Institution, is the Peace and Defence of them all; and whosoever has right to the End, has right to the Means; it belongeth of Right, to whatsoever Man, or Assembly that hath the Soveraignty, to be Judge both of the meanes of Peace and Defence; and also of the hindrances, and disturbances of the same; and to do whatsoever he shall think necessary to be done, both before hand, for the preserving of Peace and Security, by prevention of Discord at home and [91] Hostility from abroad; and, when Peace and Security are lost, for the recovery of the same. And therefore:

Sixtly, it is annexed to the Soveraignty, to be Judge of what Opinions and Doctrines are averse, and what conducing to Peace; and consequently, on what occasions, how farre, and what, men are to be trusted withall, in speaking to Multitudes of people; and who shall examine the Doctrines of all bookes before they be published. For the Actions of men proceed from their Opinions; and in the wel governing of Opinions, consisteth the well governing of mens Actions, in order to their Peace, and Concord. And though in matter of Doctrine, nothing ought to be regarded but the Truth; yet this is not repugnant to regulating of the same by Peace. For Doctrine repugnant to Peace, can no more be True, than Peace and Concord can be against the Law of Nature. It is true, that in a Common-wealth, where by the negligence, or unskilfullnesse of Governours, and Teachers, false Doctrines are by time generally received; the contrary Truths may be generally offensive:

Yet the most sudden, and rough busling in of a new Truth, that can be, does never breake the Peace, but only somtimes awake the Warre. For those men that are so remissely governed, that they dare take up Armes, to defend, or introduce an Opinion, are still in Warre; and their condition not Peace, but only a Cessation of Armes for feare of one another; and they live as it were, in the procincts of battaile continually. It belongeth therefore to him that hath the Soveraign Power, to be Judge, or constitute all Judges of Opinions and Doctrines, as a thing necessary to Peace, thereby to prevent Discord and Civill Warre.

[94] But a man may here object, that the Condition of Subjects is very miserable; as being obnoxious to the lusts, and other irregular passions of him, or them that have so unlimited a Power in their hands. And commonly they that live under a Monarch, think it the fault of Monarchy; and they that live under the government of Democracy, or other Soveraign Assembly, attribute all the inconvenience to that forme of Common-wealth; whereas the Power in all formes, if they be perfect enough to protect them, is the same; not considering that the estate of Man can never be without some incommodity or other; and that the greatest, that in any forme of Government can possibly happen to the people in generall, is scarce sensible, in respect of the miseries, and horrible calamities, that accompany a Civill Warre; or that dissolute condition of masterlesse men, without subjection to Lawes, and a coërcive Power to tye their hands from rapine, and revenge: nor considering that the greatest pressure of Soveraign Governours, proceedeth not from any delight, or profit they can expect in the dammage, or weakening of their Subjects, in whose vigor, consisteth their own strength and glory; but in the restiveness of themselves, that unwillingly contributing to their own defence, make it necessary for their Governours to draw from them what they can in time of Peace, that they may have means on any emergent occasion, or sudden need, to resist, or take advantage

on their Enemies. For all men are by nature provided of notable multiplying glasses, (that is their Passions and Self-love,) through which, every little payment appeareth a great grievance; but are destitute of those prospective glasses, (namely Morall and Civill Science,) to see a farre off the miseries that hang over them, and cannot without such payments be avoyded.

Of the Liberty of Subjects

LIBERTY, or FREEDOMS, signifieth (properly) the absence of Opposition; (by Opposition, I mean externall Impediments of motion;) and may be applyed no lesse to Irrationall, and Inanimate creatures, than to Rationall. For whatsoever is so tyed, or environed, as it cannot move, but within a certain space, which space is determined by the opposition of some externall body, we say it hath not Liberty to go further. And so of all living creatures, whilest they are imprisoned, or restrained, with walls, or chayns; and of the water whilest it is kept in by banks, or vessels, that otherwise would spread it selfe into a larger space, we use to say, they are not at Liberty, to move in such manner, as without those externall impediments they would. But when the impediment of motion, is in the constitution of the thing it selfe, we use not to say, it wants the Liberty; but the Power to move; as when a stone lyeth still, or a man is fastned to his bed by sicknesse.

[108] And according to this proper, and generally received meaning of the word, *A FREE-MAN, is he that in those things, which by his strength and wit he is able to do, is not hindred to doe what he has a will to.*

Feare and Liberty are consistent; as when a man throweth his goods into the Sea for *feare* the ship should sink, he doth it nevertheless very willingly, and may refuse to doe it if he will: It is therefore the action, of one that was *free:* so a man sometimes pays his debt, only for *feare* of Imprisonment, which because no body hindred him from detaining, was the action of a man at liberty. And generally all actions which men doe in Common-wealths, for *feare* of the law, or actions which the doers had *liberty* to omit.

But as men, for the atteyning of peace, and conservation of themselves thereby, have made an Artificiall Man, which we call a Common-wealth; so also have they made Artificiall Chains, called *Civill Lawes*, which they themselves, by mutuall covenants, have [109] fastned at one end, to the lips of that Man, or Assembly, to whom they have given the Soveraigne Power; and at the other end to their own Ears. These Bonds in their own nature but weak, may neverthelesse be made to hold, by the danger, though not by the difficulty of breaking them.

In relation to these Bonds only it is, that I am to speak now, of the *Liberty of Subjects*. For seeing there is no Common-wealth in the world, wherein there be Rules enough set down, for the regulating of all the actions, and words of men, (as being a thing impossible:) it followeth necessarily, that in all kinds of actions, by the laws prætermitted, men have the Liberty, of doing what their own reasons shall suggest, for the most profitable to themselves. For if wee take Liberty in the proper sense, for corporall Liberty; that is to say, freedome from chains, and prison, it were very absurd for men to clamor as they doe, for the Liberty they so manifestly enjoy. Againe, if we take Liberty, for an exemption from Lawes, it is no lesse absurd, for men to demand as they doe, that Liberty, by which all other men may be masters of their lives. And yet as absurd as it is, this is it they demand; not knowing that me Lawes are of no power to protect them, without a Sword in the hands of a man, or men, to cause those laws to be put in execution. The Liberty of a Subject, lyeth therefore only in those things, which in regulating their actions, the Soveraign hath prætermitted: such as is the Liberty to buy, and sell, and otherwise contract with one another; to choose their own aboad, their own diet, their own trade of life, and institute their children as they themselves think fit; & the like.

Neverthelesse we are not to understand, that by such Liberty, the Soveraign Power of life, and death, is either abolished, or limited. For it has been already shewn, that nothing the Soveraign Representative can doe to a Subject, on what pretence soever, can properly be called Injustice, or Injury; because every Subject is Author of every act the Soveraign doth; so that he never wanteth Right to any thing, otherwise, than as he himself is the Subject of God, and bound thereby to observe the laws of Nature. And therefore it may, and doth often happen in Common-wealths, that a Subject may be put to death, by the command of the Soveraign Power; and yet neither doe the other wrong: As when *Jeptha* caused his daughter to be sacrificed: In which, and the like cases, he that so dieth, had Liberty to doe the action, for which he is neverthelesse, without Injury put to death. And the same holdeth also in a Soveraign Prince that putteth to death an Innocent Subject. For though the action be against the law of Nature, as being contrary to Equitie, (as was the killing of *Uriah*, by *David*;) yet it was not an Injurie to *Uriah*; but to *God*.

To come now to the particulars of the true Liberty of a Subject; that is to say, what are the things, which though commanded by the Soveraign, he may neverthelesse, without Injustice, refuse to do; we are to consider, what Rights we passe away, when we make a Common-wealth; or (which is all one,) what Liberty we deny our selves, by owning all the Actions (without exception) of the Man, or Assembly we make our Soveraign. For in the act of our Submission, consisteth both our Obligation, and our Liberty; which must therefore be inferred by arguments taken from thence; there being no Obligation on any man, which ariseth not from some Act of his own; for all men equally, are by Nature Free. And because such arguments, must either be drawn from the expresse words, I *Authorise all his Actions*, or from the Intention of him that submitteth himselfe to his Power, (which Intention is to be understood by the End for which he so submitteth;) The Obligation, and Liberty of the Subject, is to be derived, either from those Words, (or others equivalent;) or else from the End of the Institution of Soveraignty; namely, the Peace of the Subjects within themselves, and their Defence against a common Enemy.

First therefore, seeing Soveraignty by Institution, is by Covenant of every one to every one; and Soveraignty by Acquisition, by Covenants of the Vanquished to the Victor, or Child to the Parent; It is manifest, that every Subject has Liberty in all those things, the right whereof cannot by Covenant be transferred. I have shewn before in the 14. Chapter, that Covenants, not to defend a man's own body, are voyd. Therefore:

If the Soveraign command a man (though justly condemned,) to kill, wound, or mayme himselfe; or not to resist those that assault him; or to abstain from the use of food, ayre, medicine, or any other [112] thing, without which he cannot live; yet hath that man the Liberty to disobey.

If a man be interrogated by the Soveraign, or his Authority, concerning a crime done by himselfe, he is not bound (without assurance of Pardon) to confesse it; because no man (as I have shewn in the same Chapter) can be obliged by Covenant to accuse himselfe.

Again, the Consent of a Subject to Soveraign Power, is contained in these words, I *Authorise, or take upon me, all his actions;* in which there is no restriction at all, of his own former naturall Liberty: For by allowing him to *kill me,* I am not bound to kill my selfe when he commands me. 'Tis one thing to say, *Kill me, or my fellow, if you please;* another thing to say, *I will kill my selfe, or my fellow.* It followeth therefore, that:

No man is bound by the words themselves, either to kill himselfe, or any other man; And consequently, that the Obligation a man may sometimes have, upon the Command of the Soveraign to execute any dangerous, or dishonourable Office, dependeth not on the Words of our Submission; but on the Intention; which is to be understood by the End thereof. When

therefore our refusall to obey, frustrates the End for which the Soveraignty was ordained; then there is no Liberty to refuse: otherwise there is.

Upon this ground, a man that is commanded as a Souldier to fight against the enemy, though his Soveraign have Right enough to punish his refusall with death, may neverthelesse in many cases refuse, without Injustice; as when he substituteth a sufficient Souldier in his place: for in this case he deserteth not the service of the Common-wealth. And there is allowance to be made for naturall timorousnesse, not onely to women, (of whom no such dangerous duty is expected,) but also to men of feminine courage. When Armies fight, there is on one side, or both, a running away; yet when they do it not out of trechery, but fear, they are not esteemed to do it unjustly, but dishonourably. For the same reason, to avoyd battell, is not Injustice, but Cowardise. But he that inrowleth himselfe a Souldier, or taketh imprest mony, taketh away the excuse of a timorous nature; and is obliged, not onely to go to the battell, but also not to run from it, without his Captaines leave. And when the Defence of the Common-wealth, requireth at once the help of all that are able to bear Arms, every one is obliged; because otherwise the Institution of the Common-wealth, which they have not the purpose, or courage to preserve, was in vain.

To resist the Sword of the Common-wealth, in defence of another man, guilty, or innocent, no man hath Liberty; because such Liberty, takes away from the Soveraign, the means of Protecting us; and is therefore destructive of the very essence of Government. But in case a great many men together, have already resisted the Soveraign Power unjustly, or committed some Capitall crime, for which every one of them expecteth death, whether have they not the Liberty then to joyn together, and assist, and defend one another? Certainly they have: For they but defend their lives, which the Guil[113]ty man may as well do, as the Innocent. There was indeed injustice in the first breach of their duty; Their bearing of Arms subsequent to it, though it be to maintain what they have done, is no new unjust act. And if it be onely to defend their persons, it is not unjust at all. But the offer of Pardon taketh from them, to whom it is offered, the plea of self-defence, and maketh their perseverance in assisting, or defending the rest, unlawfull.

As for other Lyberties, they depend on the silence of the Law. In cases where the Soveraign has prescribed no rule, there the Subject hath the liberty to do, or forbeare, according to his own discretion. And therefore such Liberty is in some places more, and in some lesse; and in some times more, in other times lesse, according as they that have the Soveraignty shall think most convenient.

[114] The Obligation of Subjects to the Soveraign, is understood to last as long, and no longer, than the power lasteth, by which he is able to protect them. For the right men have by Nature to protect themselves, when none else can protect them, can by no Covenant be relinquished. The Soveraignty is the Soule of the Common-wealth; which once departed from the Body, the members doe no more receive their motion from it. The end of Obedience is Protection; which, wheresoever a man seeth it, either in his own, or in another's sword, Nature applyeth his obedience to it, and his endeavour to maintaine it. And though Soveraignty, in the intention of them that make it, be immortall; yet is it in its own nature, not only subject to violent death, by forreign war; but also through the ignorance, and passions of men, it hath in it, from the very institution, many seeds of a naturall mortality, by Intestine Discord.

Chapter 2

Robert Axelrod

THE EVOLUTION OF COOPERATION

Robert Axelrod (1943–) is a Professor of Political Science and Public Policy at the University of Michigan. He is best known for his work on game theory and cooperation in *The Evolution of Cooperation* (1984). In that work, excerpts from which are reproduced here, he explores the problem of the "prisoner's dilemma," a type of game which is thought to model a wide variety of situations in which rational self-interested persons interact with each other. He argues, drawing on the results of a computer tournament, that cooperation can be rational in a prisoner's dilemma as long as there is a chance that the parties will meet each other again.

The Problem of Cooperation

Under what conditions will cooperation emerge in a world of egoists without central authority? This question has intrigued people for a long time. And for good reason. We all know that people are not angels, and that they tend to look after themselves and their own first. Yet we also know that cooperation does occur and that our civilization is based upon it. But, in situations where each individual has an incentive to be selfish, how can cooperation ever develop?

The answer each of us gives to this question has a fundamental effect on how we think and act in our social, political, and economic relations with others. And the answers that others give have a great effect on how ready they will be to cooperate with us.

The most famous answer was given over three hundred years ago by Thomas Hobbes. It was pessimistic. He argued that before governments existed, the state of nature was dominated by the problem of selfish individuals who competed on such ruthless terms that life was "solitary, poor, nasty, brutish, and short" (Hobbes 1651/1962, p. 100). In his view, cooperation could not develop without a central authority, and consequently a strong government was necessary. Ever since, arguments about the proper scope of government have often focused on whether one could, or could not, expect cooperation to emerge in a particular domain if there were not an authority to police the situation.

[. . .]

This basic problem occurs when the pursuit of self-interest by each leads to a poor outcome for all. To make headway in understanding the vast array of specific situations which have this property, a way is needed to represent what is common to these situations without becoming bogged down in the details unique to each. Fortunately, there is such a representation available: the famous *Prisoner's Dilemma* game.[1]

In the Prisoner's Dilemma game, there are two players. Each has two choices, namely cooperate or defect. Each must make the choice without knowing what the other will do. No matter what the other does, defection yields a higher payoff than cooperation. The dilemma is that if both defect, both do worse than if both had cooperated. This simple game will provide the basis for the entire analysis used in this book.

The way the game works is shown in figure 2.1. One player chooses a row, either cooperating or defecting. The other player simultaneously chooses a column, either cooperating or defecting. Together, these choices result in one of the four possible outcomes shown in that matrix. If both players cooperate, both do fairly well. Both get R, the *reward for mutual cooperation*. In the concrete illustration of figure 2.1 the reward is three points. This number might, for example, be a payoff in dollars that each player gets for that outcome. If one player cooperates but the other defects, the defecting player gets the *temptation to defect*, while the cooperating player gets the *sucker's payoff*. In the example, these are five points and zero points respectively. If both defect, both get one point, the *punishment for mutual defection*.

What should you do in such a game? Suppose you are the row player, and you think the column player will cooperate. This means that you will get one of the two outcomes in the first column of figure 2.1. You have a choice. You can cooperate as well, getting the three points of the reward for mutual cooperation. Or you can defect, getting the five points of the temptation

payoff. So it pays to defect if you think the other player will cooperate. But now suppose that you think the other player will defect. Now you are in the second column of figure 2.1, and you have a choice between cooperating, which would make you a sucker and give you zero points, and defecting, which would result in mutual punishment, giving you one point. So it pays to defect if you think the other player will defect. This means that it is better to defect if you think the other player will cooperate, *and* it is better to defect if you think the other player will defect. So no matter what the other player does, it pays for you to defect.

So far, so good. But the same logic holds for the other player too. Therefore, the other player should defect no matter what you are expected to do. So you should both defect. But then you both get one point, which is worse than the three points of the reward that you both could have gotten had you both cooperated. Individual rationality leads to a worse outcome for both than is possible. Hence the dilemma.

The Prisoner's Dilemma is simply an abstract formulation of some very common and very interesting situations in which what is best for each person individually leads to mutual defection, whereas everyone would have been better off with mutual cooperation. The definition of Prisoner's Dilemma requires that several relationships hold among the four different potential outcomes. The first relationship specifies the order of the four payoffs. The best a player can do is get T, the temptation to defect when the other player

	Column Player	
	Cooperate	Defect
Cooperate	R = 3, R = 3 Reward for mutual cooperation	S = 0, T = 5 Sucker's payoff, and temptation to defect
Defect	T = 5, S = 0 Temptation to defect and sucker's payoff	P = 1, P = 1 Punishment for mutual defection

Row Player (labels for rows: Cooperate, Defect)

Note: The payoffs to the row chooser are listed first.

Figure 2.1 The Prisoner's Dilemma.

cooperates. The worst a player can do is get S, the sucker's payoff for cooperating while the other player defects. In ordering the other two outcomes, R, the reward for mutual cooperation, is assumed to be better than P, the punishment for mutual defection. This leads to a preference ranking of the four payoffs from best to worst as T, R, P, and S.

The second part of the definition of the Prisoner's Dilemma is that the players cannot get out of their dilemma by taking turns exploiting each other. This assumption means that an even chance of exploitation and being exploited is not as good an outcome for a player as mutual cooperation. It is therefore assumed that the reward for mutual cooperation is greater than the average of the temptation and the sucker's payoff. This assumption, together with the rank ordering of the four payoffs, defines the Prisoner's Dilemma.

Thus two egoists playing the game *once* will both choose their dominant choice, defection, and each will get less than they both could have gotten if they had cooperated. If the game is played a known finite number of times, the players still have no incentive to cooperate. This is certainly true on the last move since there is no future to influence. On the next-to-last move neither player will have an incentive to cooperate since they can both anticipate a defection by the other player on the very last move. Such a line of reasoning implies that the game will unravel all the way back to mutual defection on the first move of any sequence of plays that is of known finite length (Luce and Raiffa 1957, pp. 94–102). This reasoning does not apply if the players will interact an indefinite number of times. And in most realistic settings, the players cannot be sure when the last interaction between them will take place. As will be shown later, with an indefinite number of interactions, cooperation can emerge. The issue then becomes the discovery of the precise conditions that are necessary and sufficient for cooperation to emerge.

In this book I will examine interactions between just two players at a time. A single player may be interacting with many others, but the player is assumed to be interacting with them one at a time.[2] The player is also assumed to recognize another player and to remember how the two of them have interacted so far. This ability to recognize and remember allows the history of the particular interaction to be taken into account by a player's strategy.

A variety of ways to resolve the Prisoner's Dilemma have been developed. Each involves allowing some additional activity that alters the strategic interaction in such a way as to fundamentally change the nature of the problem. The original problem remains, however, because there are many situations in which these remedies are not available. Therefore, the problem will be considered in its fundamental form, without these alterations.

1. There is no mechanism available to the players to make enforceable threats or commitments (Schelling 1960). Since the players cannot commit themselves to a particular strategy, each must take into account all possible strategies that might be used by the other player. Moreover the players have all possible strategies available to themselves.

2. There is no way to be sure what the other player will do on a given move. This eliminates the possibility of metagame analysis (Howard 1971) which allows such options as "make the same choice as the other is about to make." It also eliminates the possibility of reliable reputations such as might be based on watching the other player interact with third parties. Thus the only information available to the players about each other is the history of their interaction so far.

3. There is no way to eliminate the other player or run away from the interaction. Therefore each player retains the ability to cooperate or defect on each move.

4. There is no way to change the other player's payoffs. The payoffs already include

whatever consideration each player has for the interests of the other (Taylor 1976, pp. 69–73).

Under these conditions, words not backed by actions are so cheap as to be meaningless. The players can communicate with each other only through the sequence of their own behavior. This is the problem of the Prisoner's Dilemma in its fundamental form.

What makes it possible for cooperation to emerge is the fact that the players might meet again. This possibility means that the choices made today not only determine the outcome of this move, but can also influence the later choices of the players. The future can therefore cast a shadow back upon the present and thereby affect the current strategic situation.

But the future is less important than the present – for two reasons. The first is that players tend to value payoffs less as the time of their obtainment recedes into the future. The second is that there is always some chance that the players will not meet again. An ongoing relationship may end when one or the other player moves away, changes jobs, dies, or goes bankrupt.

For these reasons, the payoff of the next move always counts less than the payoff of the current move. A natural way to take this into account is to cumulate payoffs over time in such a way that the next move is worth some fraction of the current move (Shubik 1970). The *weight* (or importance) of the next move relative to the current move will be called w. It represents the degree to which the payoff of each move is discounted relative to the previous move, and is therefore a *discount parameter*.

The discount parameter can be used to determine the payoff for a whole sequence. To take a simple example, suppose that each move is only half as important as the previous move, making $w = \frac{1}{2}$. Then a whole string of mutual defections worth one point each move would have a value of 1 on the first move, $\frac{1}{2}$ on the second move, $\frac{1}{4}$ on the third move, and so on. The cumulative

value of the sequence would be $1 + \frac{1}{2} + \frac{1}{4} + \frac{1}{8}$ . . . which would sum to exactly 2. In general, getting one point on each move would be worth $1 + w + w^2 + w^3$. . . . A very useful fact is that the sum of this infinite series for any w greater than zero and less than one is simply $1/(1 - w)$. To take another case, if each move is worth 90 percent of the previous move, a string of 1's would be worth ten points because $1/(1 - w) = 1/(1 - .9) = 1/.1 = 10$. Similarly, with w still equal to .9, a string of 3 point mutual rewards would be worth three times this, or 30 points.

Now consider an example of two players interacting. Suppose one player is following the policy of always defecting (ALL D), and the other player is following the policy of TIT FOR TAT. TIT FOR TAT is the policy of cooperating on the first move and then doing whatever the other player did on the previous move. This policy means that TIT FOR TAT will defect once after each defection of the other player. When the other player is using TIT FOR TAT, a player who always defects will get T on the first move, and P on all subsequent moves. The *value* (or *score*) to someone using ALL D when playing with someone using TIT FOR TAT is thus the sum of T for the first move, wP for the second move, w^2P for the third move, and so on.[3]

Both ALL D and TIT FOR TAT are strategies. In general, a *strategy* (or *decision rule*) is a specification of what to do in any situation that might arise. The situation itself depends upon the history of the game so far. Therefore, a strategy might cooperate after some patterns of interaction and defect after others. Moreover, a strategy may use probabilities, as in the example of a rule which is entirely random with equal probabilities of cooperation and defection on each move. A strategy can also be quite sophisticated in its use of the pattern of outcomes in the game so far to determine what to do next. An example is one which, on each move, models the behavior of the other player using a complex procedure (such as a Markov process), and then uses a fancy method of statistical inference (such as Bayesian analysis) to select what seems the best choice for the long run. Or it may be some intricate combination of other strategies.

The first question you are tempted to ask is, "What is the best strategy?" In other words, what strategy will yield a player the highest possible score? This is a good question, but as will be shown later, no best rule exists independently of the strategy being used by the other player. In this sense, the iterated Prisoner's Dilemma is completely different from a game like chess. A chess master can safely use the assumption that the other player will make the most feared move. This assumption provides a basis for planning in a game like chess, where the interests of the players are completely antagonistic. But the situations represented by the Prisoner's Dilemma game are quite different. The interests of the players are not in total conflict. Both players can do well by getting the reward, R, for mutual cooperation or both can do poorly by getting the punishment, P, for mutual defection. Using the assumption that the other player will always make the move you fear most will lead you to expect that the other will never cooperate, which in turn will lead you to defect, causing unending punishment. So unlike chess, in the Prisoner's Dilemma it is not safe to assume that the other player is out to get you.

In fact, in the Prisoner's Dilemma, the strategy that works best depends directly on what strategy the other player is using and, in particular, on whether this strategy leaves room for the development of mutual cooperation. This principle is based on the weight of the next move relative to the current move being sufficiently large to make the future important. In other words, the discount parameter, w, must be large enough to make the future loom large in the calculation of total payoffs. After all, if you are unlikely to meet the other person again, or if you care little about future payoffs, then you might as well defect

now and not worry about the consequences for the future.

This leads to the first formal proposition. It is the sad news that if the future is important, there is no one best strategy.

Proposition 1. If the discount parameter, w, is sufficiently high, there is no best strategy independent of the strategy used by the other player.

The proof itself is not hard. Suppose that the other player is using ALL D, the strategy of always defecting. If the other player will never cooperate, the best you can do is always to defect yourself. Now suppose, on the other hand, that the other player is using a strategy of "permanent retaliation." This is the strategy of cooperating until you defect and then always defecting after that. In that case, your best strategy is never to defect, provided that the temptation to defect on the first move will eventually be more than compensated for by the long-term disadvantage of getting nothing but the punishment, P, rather than the reward, R, on future moves. This will be true whenever the discount parameter, w, is sufficiently great.[4] Thus, whether or not you should cooperate, even on the first move, depends on the strategy being used by the other player. Therefore, if w is sufficiently large, there is no one best strategy.

The Success of TIT FOR TAT in Computer Tournaments

Since the Prisoner's Dilemma is so common in everything from personal relations to international relations, it would be useful to know how best to act when in this type of setting. However, the proposition of the previous chapter demonstrates that there is no one best strategy to use. What is best depends in part on what the other player is likely to be doing. Further, what the other is likely to be doing may well depend on what the player expects you to do.

To get out of this tangle, help can be sought by combing the research already done concerning the Prisoner's Dilemma for useful advice. Fortunately, a great deal of research has been done in this area.

Psychologists using experimental subjects have found that, in the iterated Prisoner's Dilemma, the amount of cooperation attained – and the specific pattern for attaining it – depend on a wide variety of factors relating to the context of the game, the attributes of the individual players, and the relationship between the players. Since behavior in the game reflects so many important factors about people, it has become a standard way to explore questions in social psychology, from the effects of westernization in Central Africa (Bethlehem 1975) to the existence (or nonexistence) of aggression in career-oriented women (Baefsky and Berger 1974), and to the differential consequences of abstract versus concrete thinking styles (Nydegger 1974). In the last fifteen years, there have been hundreds of articles on the Prisoner's Dilemma cited in *Psychological Abstracts*. The iterated Prisoner's Dilemma has become the E. coli of social psychology.

Just as important as its use as an experimental test bed is the use of the Prisoner's Dilemma as the conceptual foundation for models of important social processes. Richardson's model of the arms race is based on an interaction which is essentially a Prisoner's Dilemma, played once a year with the budgets of the competing nations (Richardson 1960; Zinnes 1976, pp. 330–40). Oligopolistic competition can also be modeled as a Prisoner's Dilemma (Samuelson 1973, pp. 503–5). The ubiquitous problems of collective action to produce a collective good are analyzable as Prisoner's Dilemmas with many players (G. Hardin 1982). Even vote trading has been modeled as a Prisoner's Dilemma (Riker and Brams 1973). In fact, many of the best-developed models of important political, social, and economic processes have the Prisoner's Dilemma as their foundation.

There is yet a third literature about the Prisoner's Dilemma. This literature goes beyond the empirical questions of the laboratory or the real world, and instead uses the abstract game to analyze the features of some fundamental strategic issues, such as the meaning of rationality (Luce and Raiffa 1957), choices which affect other people (Schelling 1973), and cooperation without enforcement (Taylor 1976).

Unfortunately, none of these three literatures on the Prisoner's Dilemma reveals very much about how to play the game well.

[. . .]

To learn more about how to choose effectively in an iterated Prisoner's Dilemma, a new approach is needed. Such an approach would have to draw on people who have a rich understanding of the strategic possibilities inherent in a non-zero-sum setting, a situation in which the interests of the participants partially coincide and partially conflict. Two important facts about non-zero-sum settings would have to be taken into account. First, the proposition of the previous chapter demonstrates that what is effective depends not only upon the characteristics of a particular strategy, but also upon the nature of the other strategies with which it must interact. The second point follows directly from the first. An effective strategy must be able at any point to take into account the history of the interaction as it has developed so far.

A computer tournament for the study of effective choice in the iterated Prisoner's Dilemma meets these needs. In a computer tournament, each entrant writes a program that embodies a rule to select the cooperative or non-cooperative choice on each move. The program has available to it the history of the game so far, and may use this history in making a choice. If the participants are recruited primarily from those who are familiar with the Prisoner's Dilemma, the entrants can be assured that their decision rule will be facing rules of other informed entrants. Such recruitment would also guarantee that the state of the art is represented in the tournament.

Wanting to find out what would happen, I invited professional game theorists to send in entries to just such a computer tournament. It was structured as a round robin, meaning that each entry was paired with each other entry. As announced in the rules of the tournament, each entry was also paired with its own twin and with RANDOM, a program that randomly cooperates and defects with equal probability. Each game consisted of exactly two hundred moves.[5] The payoff matrix for each move was the familiar one described earlier in this chapter. It awarded both players three points for mutual cooperation, and one point for mutual defection. If one player defected while the other player cooperated, the defecting player received five points and the cooperating player received zero points.

No entry was disqualified for exceeding the allotted time. In fact, the entire round robin tournament was run five times to get a more stable estimate of the scores for each pair of players. In all, there were 120,000 moves, making for 240,000 separate choices.

The 14 submitted entries came from five disciplines: psychology, economics, political science, mathematics, and sociology.

One remarkable aspect of the tournament was that it allowed people from different disciplines to interact with each other in a common format and language. Most of the entrants were recruited from those who had published articles on game theory in general or the Prisoner's Dilemma in particular.

TIT FOR TAT, submitted by Professor Anatol Rapoport of the University of Toronto, won the tournament. This was the simplest of all submitted programs and it turned out to be the best!

TIT FOR TAT, of course, starts with a cooperative choice, and thereafter does what the other player did on the previous move. This decision rule is probably the most widely known and most discussed rule for playing the Prisoner's Dilemma. It is easily understood and easily programmed. It is known to elicit a good degree of cooperation when played with humans (Oskamp 1971; W. Wilson 1971). As an entry in

a computer tournament, it has the desirable properties that it is not very exploitable and that it does well with its own twin. It has the disadvantage that it is too generous with the RANDOM rule, which was known by the participants to be entered in the tournament.

In addition, TIT FOR TAT was known to be a powerful competitor. In a preliminary tournament, TIT FOR TAT scored second place; and in a variant of that preliminary tournament, TIT FOR TAT won first place. All of these facts were known to most of the people designing programs for the Computer Prisoner's Dilemma Tournament, because they were sent copies of a description of the preliminary tournament. Not surprisingly, many of them used the TIT FOR TAT principle and tried to improve upon it.

The striking fact is that *none* of the more complex programs submitted was able to perform as well as the original, simple TIT FOR TAT.

[...]

Analysis of the results showed that neither the discipline of the author, the brevity of the program – nor its *length* – accounts for a rule's relative success. What does?

Before answering this question, a remark on the interpretation of numerical scores is in order. In a game of 200 moves, a useful benchmark for very good performance is 600 points, which is equivalent to the score attained by a player when both sides always cooperate with each other. A useful benchmark for very poor performance is 200 points, which is equivalent to the score attained by a player when both sides never cooperate with each other. Most scores range between 200 and 600 points, although scores from 0 to 1000 points are possible. The winner, TIT FOR TAT, averaged 504 points per game.

Surprisingly, there is a single property which distinguishes the relatively high-scoring entries from the relatively low-scoring entries. This is the property of being *nice*, which is to say never being the first to defect. (For the sake of analyzing this tournament, the definition of a nice rule will be relaxed to include rules which will not be the first to defect before the last few moves, say before move 199.)

Each of the eight top-ranking entries (or rules) is nice. None of the other entries is. There is even a substantial gap in the score between the nice entries and the others. The nice entries received tournament averages between 472 and 504, while the best of the entries that were not nice received only 401 points. Thus, not being the first to defect, at least until virtually the end of the game, was a property which, all by itself, separated the more successful rules from the less successful rules in this Computer Prisoner's Dilemma Tournament.

Each of the nice rules got about 600 points with each of the other seven nice rules and with its own twin. This is because when two nice rules play, they are sure to cooperate with each other until virtually the end of the game. Actually the minor variations in end-game tactics did not account for much variation in the scores.

Since the nice rules all got within a few points of 600 with each other, the thing that distinguished the relative rankings among the nice rules was their scores with the rules which are not nice. This much is obvious. What is not obvious is that the relative ranking of the eight top rules was largely determined by just two of the other seven rules. These two rules are *kingmakers* because they do not do very well for themselves, but they largely determine the rankings among the top contenders.

The most important kingmaker was based on an "outcome maximization" principle originally developed as a possible interpretation of what human subjects do in the Prisoner's Dilemma laboratory experiments (Downing 1975). This rule, called DOWNING, is a particularly interesting rule in its own right. It is well worth studying as an example of a decision rule which is based upon a quite sophisticated idea. Unlike most of the others, its logic is not just a variant of TIT FOR TAT. Instead it is based on a deliberate attempt to understand the other player and then

to make the choice that will yield the best long-term score based upon this understanding. The idea is that if the other player does not seem responsive to what DOWNING is doing, DOWNING will try to get away with whatever it can by defecting. On the other hand, if the other player does seem responsive, DOWNING will cooperate. To judge the other's responsiveness, DOWNING estimates the probability that the other player cooperates after it (DOWNING) cooperates, and also the probability that the other player cooperates after DOWNING defects. For each move, it updates its estimate of these two conditional probabilities and then selects the choice which will maximize its own long-term payoff under the assumption that it has correctly modeled the other player. If the two conditional probabilities have similar values, DOWNING determines that it pays to defect, since the other player seems to be doing the same thing whether DOWNING cooperates or not. Conversely, if the other player tends to cooperate after a cooperation but not after a defection by DOWNING, then the other player seems responsive, and DOWNING will calculate that the best thing to do with a responsive player is to cooperate. Under certain circumstances, DOWNING will even determine that the best strategy is to alternate cooperation and defection.

At the start of a game, DOWNING does not know the values of these conditional probabilities for the other players. It assumes that they are both 0.5, but gives no weight to this estimate when information actually does come in during the play of the game.

This is a fairly sophisticated decision rule, but its implementation does have one flaw. By initially assuming that the other player is unresponsive, DOWNING is doomed to defect on the first two moves. These first two defections led many other rules to punish DOWNING, so things usually got off to a bad start. But this is precisely why DOWNING served so well as a kingmaker. First-ranking TIT FOR TAT and second-ranking TIDEMAN AND CHIERUZZI both reacted in such a way that DOWNING learned to expect that defection does not pay but that cooperation does. All of the other nice rules went downhill with DOWNING.

The nice rules did well in the tournament largely because they did so well with each other, and because there were enough of them to raise substantially each other's average score. As long as the other player did not defect, each of the nice rules was certain to continue cooperating until virtually the end of the game. But what happened if there was a defection? Different rules responded quite differently, and their response was important in determining their overall success. A key concept in this regard is the forgiveness of a decision rule. *Forgiveness* of a rule can be informally described as its propensity to cooperate in the moves after the other player has defected.[6]

Of all the nice rules, the one that scored lowest was also the one that was least forgiving. This is FRIEDMAN, a totally unforgiving rule that employs permanent retaliation. It is never the first to defect, but once the other defects even once, FRIEDMAN defects from then on. In contrast, the winner, TIT FOR TAT, is unforgiving

for one move, but thereafter is totally forgiving of that defection. After one punishment, it lets bygones be bygones.

One of the main reasons why the rules that are not nice did not do well in the tournament is that most of the rules in the tournament were not very forgiving. A concrete illustration will help. Consider the case of JOSS, a sneaky rule that tries to get away with an occasional defection. This decision rule is a variation of TIT FOR TAT. Like TIT FOR TAT, it always defects immediately after the other player defects. But instead of always cooperating after the other player cooperates, 10 percent of the time it defects after the other player cooperates. Thus it tries to sneak in an occasional exploitation of the other player.

This decision rule seems like a fairly small variation of TIT FOR TAT, but in fact its overall performance was much worse, and it is interesting to see exactly why. Table 2.1 shows the move-by-move history of a game between JOSS and TIT FOR TAT. At first both players cooperated, but on the sixth move, JOSS selected one of its probabilistic defections. On the next move JOSS cooperated again, but TIT FOR TAT defected in response to JOSS's previous defection. Then

Table 2.1 Illustrative Game Between TIT FOR TAT and JOSS

moves	1–20	11111	23232	32323	23232
moves	21–40	32324	44444	44444	44444
moves	41–60	44444	44444	44444	44444
moves	61–80	44444	44444	44444	44444
moves	81–100	44444	44444	44444	44444
moves	101–120	44444	44444	44444	44444
moves	121–140	44444	44444	44444	44444
moves	141–160	44444	44444	44444	44444
moves	161–180	44444	44444	44444	44444
moves	181–200	44444	44444	44444	44444

Score in this game: TIT FOR TAT 236; JOSS 241.

Legend: 1 both cooperated
2 TIT FOR TAT only cooperated
3 JOSS only cooperated
4 neither cooperated

JOSS defected in response to TIT FOR TAT's defection. In effect, the single defection of JOSS on the sixth move created an *echo* back and forth between JOSS and TIT FOR TAT. This echo resulted in JOSS defecting on all the subsequent even numbered moves and TIT FOR TAT defecting on all the subsequent odd numbered moves.

On the twenty-fifth move, JOSS selected another of its probabilistic defections. Of course, TIT FOR TAT defected on the very next move and another reverberating echo began. This echo had JOSS defecting on the odd numbered moves. Together these two echoes resulted in both players defecting on every move after move 25. This string of mutual defections meant that for the rest of the game they both got only one point per turn. The final score of this game was 236 for TIT FOR TAT and 241 for JOSS. Notice that while JOSS did a little better than TIT FOR TAT, both did poorly.[7]

The problem was a combination of an occasional defection after the other's cooperation by JOSS, combined with a short-term lack of forgiveness by both sides. The moral is that if both sides retaliate in the way that JOSS and TIT FOR TAT did, it does not pay to be as greedy as JOSS was.

A major lesson of this tournament is the importance of minimizing echo effects in an environment of mutual power. When a single defection can set off a long string of recriminations and counter-recriminations, both sides suffer. A sophisticated analysis of choice must go at least three levels deep to take account of these echo effects. The first level of analysis is the direct effect of a choice. This is easy, since a defection always earns more than a cooperation. The second level considers the indirect effects, taking into account that the other side may or may not punish a defection. This much of the analysis was certainly appreciated by many of the entrants. But the third level goes deeper and takes into account the fact that in responding to the defections of the other side, one may be repeating or even amplifying one's own previous exploitative choice. Thus a single defection may be successful when analyzed for its direct effects, and perhaps even when its secondary effects are taken into account. But the real costs may be in the tertiary effects when one's own isolated defections turn into unending mutual recriminations. Without their realizing it, many of these rules actually wound up punishing themselves. With the other player serving as a mechanism to delay the self-punishment by a few moves, this aspect of self-punishment was not picked up by many of the decision rules.

Despite the fact that none of the attempts at more or less sophisticated decision rules was an improvement on TIT FOR TAT, it was easy to find several rules that would have performed substantially better than TIT FOR TAT in the environment of the tournament. The existence of these rules should serve as a warning against the facile belief that an eye for an eye is necessarily the best strategy. There are at least three rules that would have won the tournament if submitted.

The sample program sent to prospective contestants to show them how to make a submission would in fact have won the tournament if anyone had simply clipped it and mailed it in! But no one did. The sample program defects only if the other player defected on the previous two moves. It is a more forgiving version of TIT FOR TAT in that it does not punish isolated defections. The excellent performance of this TIT FOR TWO TATS rule highlights the fact that a common error of the contestants was to expect that gains could be made from being relatively less forgiving than TIT FOR TAT, whereas in fact there were big gains to be made from being even more forgiving. The implication of this finding is striking, since it suggests that even expert strategists do not give sufficient weight to the importance of forgiveness.

Another rule which would have won the tournament was also available to most of the contestants. This was the rule which won the preliminary tournament, a report of which was used in recruiting the contestants. Called

LOOK AHEAD, it was inspired by techniques used in artificial intelligence programs to play chess. It is interesting that artificial intelligence techniques could have inspired a rule which was in fact better than any of the rules designed by game theorists specifically for the Prisoner's Dilemma.

A third rule which would have won the tournament was a slight modification of DOWNING. If DOWNING had started with initial assumptions that the other players would be responsive rather than unresponsive, it too would have won and won by a large margin. A kingmaker could have been king. DOWNING's initial assumptions about the other players were pessimistic. It turned out that optimism about their responsiveness would not only have been more accurate but would also have led to more successful performance. It would have resulted in first place rather than tenth place.[8]

These results from supplementary rules reinforce a theme from the analysis of the tournament entries themselves: the entries were too competitive for their own good. In the first place, many of them defected early in the game without provocation, a characteristic which was very costly in the long run. In the second place, the optimal amount of forgiveness was considerably greater than displayed by any of the entries (except possibly DOWNING). And in the third place, the entry that was most different from the others, DOWNING, floundered on its own misplaced pessimism regarding the initial responsiveness of the others.

The analysis of the tournament results indicate that there is a lot to be learned about coping in an environment of mutual power. Even expert strategists from political science, sociology, economics, psychology, and mathematics made the systematic errors of being too competitive for their own good, not being forgiving enough, and being too pessimistic about the responsiveness of the other side.

The effectiveness of a particular strategy depends not only on its own characteristics, but also on the nature of the other strategies with which it must interact. For this reason, the results of a single tournament are not definitive. Therefore, a second round of the tournament was conducted.

The results of the second round provide substantially better grounds for insight into the nature of effective choice in the Prisoner's Dilemma. The reason is that the entrants to the second round were all given the detailed analysis of the first round, including a discussion of the supplemental rules that would have done very well in the environment of the first round. Thus they were aware not only of the outcome of the first round, but also of the concepts used to analyze success, and the strategic pitfalls that were discovered. Moreover, they each knew that the others knew these things. Therefore, the second round presumably began at a much higher level of sophistication than the first round, and its results could be expected to be that much more valuable as a guide to effective choice in the Prisoner's Dilemma.

The second round was also a dramatic improvement over the first round in sheer size of the tournament. The response was far greater than anticipated. There was a total of sixty-two entries from six countries. The contestants were largely recruited through announcements in journals for users of small computers. The game theorists who participated in the first round of the tournament were also invited to try again. The contestants ranged from a ten-year-old computer hobbyist to professors of computer science, physics, economics, psychology, mathematics, sociology, political science, and evolutionary biology. The countries represented were the United States, Canada, Great Britain, Norway, Switzerland, and New Zealand.

The second round provided a chance both to test the validity of the themes developed in the analysis of the first round and to develop new concepts to explain successes and failures. The entrants also drew their own lessons from the experience of the first round. But different people drew different lessons. What is particularly illuminating in the second round is the way the entries based on different lessons actually interact.

TIT FOR TAT was the simplest program submitted in the first round, and it won the first round. It was the simplest submission in the second round, and it won the second round. Even though all the entrants to the second round knew that TIT FOR TAT had won the first round, no one was able to design an entry that did any better.

This decision rule was known to all of the entrants to the second round because they all had the report of the earlier round, showing that TIT FOR TAT was the most successful rule so far. They had read the arguments about how it was known to elicit a good degree of cooperation when played with humans, how it is not very exploitable, how it did well in the preliminary tournament, and how it won the first round. The report on the first round also explained some of the reasons for its success, pointing in particular to its property of never being the first to defect ("niceness") and its propensity to cooperate after the other player defected ("forgiveness" with the exception of a single punishment).

Even though an explicit tournament rule allowed anyone to submit any program, even one authored by someone else, only one person submitted TIT FOR TAT. This was Anatol Rapoport, who submitted it the first time.

The second round of the tournament was conducted in the same manner as the first round, except that minor endgame effects were eliminated. As announced in the rules, the length of the games was determined probabilistically with a 0.00346 chance of ending with each given move.[9] This is equivalent to setting $w=.99654$. Since no one knew exactly when the last move would come, end-game effects were successfully avoided in the second round.

Once again, none of the personal attributes of the contestants correlated significantly with the performance of the rules. The professors did not

do significantly better than the others, nor did the Americans. Those who wrote in FORTRAN rather than BASIC did not do significantly better either, even though the use of FORTRAN would usually indicate access to something more than a bottom-of-the-line microcomputer. The names of the contestants are shown in the order of their success in appendix A [not included in this volume] along with some information about them and their programs.

On average, short programs did not do significantly better than long programs, despite the victory of TIT FOR TAT. But on the other hand, neither did long programs (with their greater complexity) do any better than short programs.

The determination of what does account for success in the second round is not easy because there were 3969 ways the 63 rules (including RANDOM) were paired in the round robin tournament. This very large tournament score matrix is given in appendix A along with information about the entrants and their programs. In all, there were over a million moves in the second round.

As in the first round, it paid to be nice. Being the first to defect was usually quite costly. More than half of the entries were nice, so obviously most of the contestants got the message from the first round that it did not pay to be the first to defect.

In the second round, there was once again a substantial correlation between whether a rule was nice and how well it did. Of the top 15 rules, all but one were nice (and that one ranked eighth). Of the bottom 15 rules, all but one were not nice. The overall correlation between whether a rule was nice and its tournament score was a substantial 0.58.

A property that distinguishes well among the nice rules themselves is how promptly and how reliably they responded to a challenge by the other player. A rule can be called *retaliatory* if it immediately defects after an "uncalled for" defection from the other. Exactly what is meant by "uncalled for" is not precisely determined. The point, however, is that unless a strategy is incited to an immediate response by a challenge from the other player, the other player may simply take more and more frequent advantage of such an easygoing strategy.

There were a number of rules in the second round of the tournament that deliberately used controlled numbers of defections to see what they could get away with. To a large extent, what determined the actual rankings of the nice rules was how well they were able to cope with these challengers. The two challengers that were especially important in this regard I shall call TESTER and TRANQUILIZER.

TESTER was submitted by David Gladstein and came in forty-sixth in the tournament. It is designed to look for softies, but is prepared to back off if the other player shows it won't be exploited. The rule is unusual in that it defects on the very first move in order to test the other's response. If the other player ever defects, it apologizes by cooperating and playing tit-for-tat for the rest of the game. Otherwise, it cooperates on the second and third moves but defects every other move after that. TESTER did a good job of exploiting several supplementary rules that would have done quite well in the environment of the first round of the tournament. For example, TIT FOR TWO TATS defects only after the other player defects on the preceding two moves. But TESTER never does defect twice in a row. So TIT FOR TWO TATS always cooperates with TESTER, and gets badly exploited for its generosity. Notice that TESTER itself did not do particularly well in the tournament. It did, however, provide low scores for some of the more easygoing rules.

As another example of how TESTER causes problems for some rules which had done well in the first round, consider the three variants of Leslie Downing's outcome maximization principle. There were two separate submissions of the REVISED DOWNING program, based on DOWNING, which looked so promising in round one. These came from Stanley F. Quayle and Leslie Downing himself. A slightly modified version came from a youthful competitor, eleven-year-old Steve Newman. However, all three were exploited by TESTER since they all calculated that the best thing to do with a program that cooperated just over half the time after one's own cooperation was to keep on cooperating. Actually they would have been better off doing what TIT FOR TAT and many other high-ranking programs did, which was to defect immediately on the second move in response to TESTER'S defection on the first move. This would have elicited TESTER'S apology and things would have gone better thereafter.

TRANQUILIZER illustrates a more subtle way of taking advantage of many rules, and hence a more subtle challenge. It first seeks to establish a mutually rewarding relationship with the other player, and only then does it cautiously try to see if it will be allowed to get away with something. TRANQUILIZER was submitted by Craig Feathers and came in twenty-seventh in the tournament. The rule normally cooperates but is ready to defect if the other player defects too often. Thus the rule tends to cooperate for the first dozen or two dozen moves if the other player is cooperating. Only then does it throw in an unprovoked defection. By waiting until a pattern of mutual cooperation has been developed, it hopes to lull the other side into being forgiving of occasional defections. If the other player continues to cooperate, then defections become more frequent. But as long as TRANQUILIZER is maintaining an average payoff of at least 2.25 points per move, it does not defect twice in succession, and it does not defect more than one-quarter of the time. It tries to avoid pressing its luck too far.

What it takes to do well with challenging rules like TESTER and TRANQUILIZER is to be ready to retaliate after an "uncalled for" defection from the other. So while it pays to be nice, it also pays to be retaliatory. TIT FOR TAT combines these desirable properties. It is nice, forgiving, and retaliatory. It is never the first to defect; it forgives an isolated defection after a single response; but it is always incited by a defection no matter how good the interaction has been so far.

The lessons of the first round of the tournament affected the environment of the second round, since the contestants were familiar with the results. The report on the first round of the Computer Prisoner's Dilemma Tournament (Axelrod 1980a) concluded that it paid to be not only nice but also forgiving. The contestants in the second round knew that such forgiving decision rules as TIT FOR TWO TATS and REVISED DOWNING would have done even better than TIT FOR TAT in the environment of the first round.

In the second round, many contestants apparently hoped that these conclusions would still be relevant. Of the 62 entries, 39 were nice, and nearly all of them were at least somewhat forgiving. TIT FOR TWO TATS itself was submitted by an evolutionary biologist from the United Kingdom, John Maynard Smith. But it came in only twenty-fourth. As mentioned earlier, REVISED DOWNING was submitted twice. But in the second round, it was in the bottom half of the tournament.

What seems to have happened is an interesting interaction between people who drew one lesson and people who drew another from the first round. Lesson One was: "Be nice and forgiving." Lesson Two was more exploitative: "If others are going to be nice and forgiving, it pays to try to take advantage of them." The people who drew Lesson One suffered in the second round from those who drew Lesson Two. Rules like TRANQUILIZER and TESTER were effective at exploiting rules which were too easygoing. But the people who drew Lesson Two did not themselves do very well either. The reason is that in trying to exploit other rules, they often eventually got punished enough to make the whole game less rewarding for both players than pure mutual cooperation would have been. For example, TRANQUILIZER and TESTER themselves achieved only twenty-seventh and

forty-sixth place, respectively. Each surpassed TIT FOR TAT's score with fewer than one-third of the rules. None of the other entries that tried to apply the exploitative conclusion of Lesson Two ranked near the top either.

While the use of Lesson Two tended to invalidate Lesson One, no entrants were able to benefit more than they were hurt in the tournament by their attempt to exploit the easygoing rules. The most successful entries tended to be relatively small variations on TIT FOR TAT which were designed to recognize and give up on a seemingly RANDOM player or a very uncooperative player. But the implementations of these ideas did not do better than the pure form of TIT FOR TAT. So TIT FOR TAT, which got along with almost everyone, won the second round of the tournament just as it had won the first round.

Would the results of the second round have been much different if the distribution of entries had been substantially different? Put another way, does TIT FOR TAT do well in a wide variety of environments? That is to say, is it *robust?*

A good way to examine this question is to construct a series of hypothetical tournaments, each with a very different distribution of the types of rules participating. The method of constructing these drastically modified tournaments is explained in appendix A. The results were that TIT FOR TAT won five of the six major variants of the tournament, and came in second in the sixth. This is a strong test of how robust the success of TIT FOR TAT really is.

Another way to examine the robustness of the results is to construct a whole sequence of hypothetical future rounds of the tournament. Some of the rules were so unsuccessful that they would be unlikely to be tried again in future tournaments, while others were successful enough that their continued presence in later tournaments would be likely. For this reason, it would be helpful to analyze what would happen over a series of tournaments if the more successful rules became a larger part of the environment for each rule, and the less successful rules were met less often. This analysis would be a strong test of a rule's performance, because continued success would require a rule to do well with other successful rules.

Evolutionary biology provides a useful way to think about this dynamic problem (Trivers 1971; Dawkins 1976, pp. 197–202; Maynard Smith 1978). Imagine that there are many animals of a single species which interact with each other quite often. Suppose the interactions take the form of a Prisoner's Dilemma. When two animals meet, they can cooperate with each other, not cooperate with each other, or one animal could exploit the other. Suppose further that each animal can recognize individuals it has already interacted with and can remember salient aspects of their interaction, such as whether the other has usually cooperated. A round of the tournament can then be regarded as a simulation of a single generation of such animals, with each decision rule being employed by large numbers of individuals. One convenient implication of this interpretation is that a given animal can interact with another animal using its own decision rule, just as it can run into an animal using some other rule.

The value of this analogy is that it allows a simulation of future generations of a tournament. The idea is that the more successful entries are more likely to be submitted in the next round, and the less successful entries are less likely to be submitted again. To make this precise, we can say that the number of copies (or offspring) of a given entry will be proportional to that entry's tournament score. We simply have to interpret the average payoff received by an individual as proportional to the individual's expected number of offspring. For example, if one rule gets twice as high a tournament score in the initial round as another rule, then it will be twice as well-represented in the next round.[10] Thus, RANDOM, for example, will be less important in the second generation, whereas TIT FOR TAT and the other high-ranking rules will be better represented.

In human terms, a rule which was not scoring well might be less likely to appear in the future for several different reasons. One possibility is that a player will try different strategies over time, and then stick with what seems to work best. Another possibility is that a person using a rule sees that other strategies are more successful and therefore switches to one of those strategies. Still another possibility is that a person occupying a key role, such as a member of Congress or the manager of a business, would be removed from that role if the strategy being followed was not very successful. Thus, learning, imitation, and selection can all operate in human affairs to produce a process which makes relatively unsuccessful strategies less likely to appear later.

The simulation of this process for the Prisoner's Dilemma tournament is actually quite straightforward. The tournament matrix gives the score each strategy gets with each of the other strategies. Starting with the proportions of each type in a given generation, it is only necessary to calculate the proportions which will exist in the next generation.[11] The better a strategy does, the more its representation will grow.

The results provide an interesting story. The first thing that happens is that the lowest-ranking eleven entries fall to half their initial size by the fifth generation while the middle-ranking entries tend to hold their own and the top-ranking entries slowly grow in size. By the fiftieth generation, the rules that ranked in the bottom third of the tournament have virtually disappeared, while most of those in the middle third have started to shrink, and those in the top third are continuing to grow (see figure 2.2).

This process simulates survival of the fittest. A rule that is successful on average with the current distribution of rules in the population will become an even larger proportion of the environment of the other rules in the next generation. At first, a rule that is successful with all sorts of rules will proliferate, but later as the unsuccessful rules disappear, success requires good performance with other successful rules.

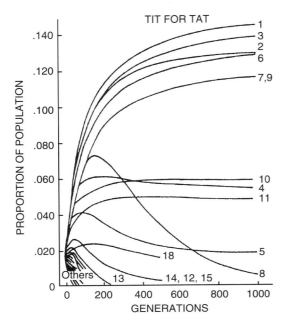

Figure 2.2 Simulated Ecological Success of the Decision Rules.

This simulation provides an ecological perspective because there are no new rules of behavior introduced. It differs from an evolutionary perspective, which would allow mutations to introduce new strategies into the environment. In the ecological perspective there is a changing distribution of given types of rules. The less successful rules become less common and the more successful rules proliferate. The statistical distribution of types of individuals changes in each generation, and this changes the environment with which each of the individual types has to interact.

At first, poor programs and good programs are represented in equal proportions. But as time passes, the poorer ones begin to drop out and the good ones thrive. Success breeds more success, provided that the success derives from interactions with other successful rules. If, on the other hand, a decision rule's success derives from its ability to exploit other rules, then as these exploited rules die out, the exploiter's base of support becomes eroded and the exploiter suffers a similar fate.

A good example of ecological extinction is provided by HARRINGTON, the only non-nice rule among the top 15 finishers in the second round. In the first 200 or so generations of the ecological tournament, as TIT FOR TAT and the other successful nice programs were increasing their percentage of the population, HARRINGTON was also increasing its percentage. This was because of HARRINGTON's exploitative strategy. By the two hundredth generation or so, things began to take a noticeable turn. Less successful programs were becoming extinct, which meant that there were fewer and fewer prey for HARRINGTON to exploit. Soon HARRINGTON could not keep up with the successful nice rules, and by the one thousandth generation HARRINGTON was as extinct as the exploitable rules on which it preyed.

The ecological analysis shows that doing well with rules that do not score well themselves is eventually a self-defeating process. Not being nice may look promising at first, but in the long run it can destroy the very environment it needs for its own success.

The results also provide yet another victory for TIT FOR TAT. TIT FOR TAT had a very slight lead in the original tournament, and never lost this lead in simulated generations. By the one thousandth generation it was the most successful rule and still growing at a faster rate than any other rule.

The overall record of TIT FOR TAT is very impressive. To recapitulate, in the second round, TIT FOR TAT achieved the highest average score of the sixty-two entries in the tournament. It also achieved the highest score in five of the six hypothetical tournaments which were constructed by magnifying the effects of different types of rules from the second round. And in the sixth hypothetical tournament it came in second. Finally, TIT FOR TAT never lost its first-place standing in a simulation of future generations of the tournament. Added to its victory in the first round of the tournament, and its fairly good performance in laboratory experiments with human subjects, TIT FOR TAT is clearly a very successful strategy.

Proposition 1 says that there is no absolutely best rule independent of the environment. What can be said for the empirical successes of TIT FOR TAT is that it is a very robust rule: it does very well over a wide range of environments. Part of its success might be that other rules anticipate its presence and are designed to do well with it. Doing well with TIT FOR TAT requires cooperating with it, and this in turn helps TIT FOR TAT. Even rules like TESTER, that were designed to see what they could get away with, quickly apologize to TIT FOR TAT. Any rule which tries to take advantage of TIT FOR TAT will simply hurt itself. TIT FOR TAT benefits from its own non-exploitability because three conditions are satisfied:

1. The possibility of encountering TIT FOR TAT is salient.
2. Once encountered, TIT FOR TAT is easy to recognize.
3. Once recognized, TIT FOR TAT's non-exploitability is easy to appreciate.

Thus TIT FOR TAT benefits from its own *clarity*.

On the other hand, TIT FOR TAT foregoes the possibility of exploiting other rules. While such exploitation is occasionally fruitful, over a wide range of environments the problems with trying to exploit others are manifold. In the first place, if a rule defects to see what it can get away with, it risks retaliation from the rules that are provocable. In the second place, once mutual recriminations set in, it can be difficult to extract oneself. And, finally, the attempt to identify and give up on unresponsive rules (such as RANDOM or excessively uncooperative rules) often mistakenly led to giving up on rules which were in fact salvageable by a more patient rule like TIT FOR TAT. Being able to exploit the exploitable without paying too high a cost with the others is a task which was not successfully accomplished by any of the entries in round two of the tournament.

What accounts for TIT FOR TAT's robust success is its combination of being nice, retaliatory, forgiving, and clear. Its niceness prevents it from getting into unnecessary trouble. Its retaliation discourages the other side from persisting whenever defection is tried. Its forgiveness helps restore mutual cooperation. And its clarity makes it intelligible to the other player, thereby eliciting long-term cooperation.

Notes

1 The Prisoner's Dilemma game was invented in about 1950 by Merrill Flood and Melvin Dresher, and formalized by A. W. Tucker shortly thereafter.
2 The situations that involve more than pairwise interaction can be modeled with the more complex n-person Prisoner's Dilemma (Olson 1965; G. Hardin 1968; Schelling 1973; Dawes 1980; R. Hardin 1982). The principal application is to the provision of collective goods. It is possible that the results from pairwise interactions will help suggest how to undertake a deeper analysis of the n-person case as well, but that must wait. For a parallel treatment of the two-person and n-person cases, see Taylor (1976, pp. 29–62).
3 The value received from always defecting when the other is playing TIT FOR TAT is:

$$V \text{ (ALL DITFT)} = T + wP + w^2P + w^3P \ldots$$
$$= T + wP(1 + w + w^2 \ldots)$$
$$= T + wP/(1 - w).$$

4 If the other player is using a strategy of permanent retaliation, you are better off always cooperating than ever defecting when $R/(1 - w) > T + wP/(1 - w)$ or $w > (T - R)/(T - P)$.
5 The second round of the tournament used a variable game length, as described in the text.
6 This is a broader definition of forgiveness than the one used by Rapoport and Chammah (1965, pp. 72–3), which is the probability of cooperation on the move after receiving the sucker's payoff, S.
7 In the five games between them, the average scores were 225 for TIT FOR TAT and 230 for JOSS.
8 In the environment of the 15 rules of the tournament, REVISED DOWNING averages 542

points. This compares to TIT FOR TAT, which won with 504 points. TIT FOR TWO TATS averages 532 in the same environment, and LOOK AHEAD averages 520 points.

9   This probability of ending the game at each move was chosen so that the expected median length of a game would be 200 moves. In practice, each pair of players was matched five times, and the lengths of these five games were determined once and for all by drawing a random sample. The resulting random sample from the implied distribution specified that the five games for each pair of players would be of lengths 63, 77, 151, 156, and 308 moves. Thus the average length of a game turned out to be somewhat shorter than expected at 151 moves.

10 This reproduction process creates a simulated second generation of the tournament in which the average score achieved by a rule is the *weighted* average of its score with each of the rules, where the weights are proportional to the success of the other rules in the initial generation.

11 This simulation of future rounds of the tournament is done by calculating the weighted average of the scores of a given rule with all other rules, where the weights are the numbers of the other rules which exist in the current generation. The numbers of a given rule in the next generation are then taken to be proportional to the product of its numbers in the current generation and its score in the current generation. This procedure assumes cardinal measurement of the payoff matrix. It is the only instance in this book where the payoff numbers are given a cardinal, rather than merely interval, interpretation.

Chapter 3

John Locke

THE STATE OF NATURE AND THE LAW OF NATURE

John Locke (1632–1704) was an English philosopher and revolutionary who was an influential supporter of the Glorious Revolution wherein King James II was overthrown and the relative balance of power swung toward Parliament. His *Second Treatise of Civil Government* (published in 1698) was an extended critique of authoritarianism and a defense of limited, representative government. In these excerpts, Locke argues that the state of nature is not *necessarily* a state of war, as Hobbes had believed. It is governed by a law of nature that people can come to know through reason and use to secure a mostly peaceful existence, though it will still be plagued by serious inconveniences that can only be rectified by the establishment of a government. The reading concludes with a presentation of Locke's own version of the social contract, and the role of both express and tacit consent in grounding political authority.

Of the State of Nature

§ 4. To understand political power right, and derive it from its original, we must consider what state all men are naturally in, and that is, a state of perfect freedom to order their actions and dispose of their possessions and persons, as they think fit, within the bounds of the law of nature; without asking leave, or depending upon the will of any other man.

A state also of equality, wherein all the power and jurisdiction is reciprocal, no one having more than another; there being nothing more evident than that creatures of the same species and rank, promiscuously born to all the same advantages of nature, and the use of the same faculties, should also be equal one amongst another without subordination or subjection; unless the Lord and Master of them all should, by any manifest declaration of his will, set one above another, and confer on him, by an evident and clear appointment, an undoubted right to dominion and sovereignty.

§ 5. This equality of men by nature the judicious Hooker looks upon as so evident in itself, and beyond all question, that he makes it the foundation of that obligation to mutual love amongst men, on which he builds the duties we owe one another, and from whence he derives the great maxims of justice and charity. His words are,

"The like natural inducement hath brought men to know that it is no less their duty to love others than themselves; for seeing those things which are equal must needs all have one measure; if I cannot but wish to receive good, even as much at every man's hands as any man can wish unto his own soul, how should I look to have any part of my desire herein satisfied, unless myself be careful to satisfy the like desire, which is undoubtedly in other men, being of one and the same nature? To have any thing offered them repugnant to this desire must needs in all respects grieve them as much as me; so that, if I do harm, I must look to suffer, there being no reason that others should show greater measure of love to me than they have by me showed unto them: my desire therefore to be loved of my equals in nature, as much as possibly may be, imposeth upon me a natural duty of bearing to them-ward fully the like affection: from which relation of equality between ourselves and them that are as ourselves, what several rules and canons natural reason hath drawn, for direction of life, no man is ignorant."

§ 6. But though this be a state of liberty, yet it is not a state of licence: though man in that state have an uncontrollable liberty to dispose of his person or possessions, yet he has not liberty to destroy himself, or so much as any creature in his possession, but where some nobler use than its bare preservation calls for it. The state of nature has a law of nature to govern it, which obliges every one: and reason, which is that law, teaches all mankind, who will but consult it, that being all equal and independent, no one ought to harm another in his life, health, liberty, or possessions: for men being all the workmanship of one omnipotent and infinitely wise Maker; all the servants of one sovereign Master, sent into the world by his order, and about his business; they are his property, whose workmanship they are, made to last during his, not another's pleasure: and being furnished with like faculties, sharing all in one community of nature, there cannot be supposed any such subordination among us that may authorize us to destroy another, as if we were made for one another's uses, as the inferior ranks of creatures are for ours. Every one, as he is bound to preserve

himself, and not to quit his station wilfully, so by the like reason, when his own preservation comes not in competition, ought he, as much as he can, to preserve the rest of mankind, and may not, unless it be to do justice to an offender, take away or impair the life, or what tends to the preservation of life, the liberty, health, limb, or goods of another.

§ 7. And that all men may be restrained from invading others' rights, and from doing hurt to one another, and the law of nature be observed, which willeth the peace and preservation of all mankind, the execution of the law of nature is, in that state, put into every man's hands, whereby every one has a right to punish the transgressors of that law to such a degree as may hinder its violation: for the law of nature would, as all other laws that concern men in this world, be in vain, if there were nobody that in the state of nature had a power to execute that law, and thereby preserve the innocent, and restrain offenders. And if any one in the state of nature may punish another for any evil he has done, every one may do so: for in that state of perfect equality, where naturally there is no superiority or jurisdiction of one over another, what any may do in prosecution of that law every one must needs have a right to do.

§ 8. And thus, in the state of nature, "one man comes by a power over another;" but yet no absolute or arbitrary power to use a criminal, when he has got him in his hands, according to the passionate heats or boundless extravagancy of his own will; but only to retribute to him, so far as calm reason and conscience dictate, what is proportionate to his transgression; which is so much as may serve for reparation and restraint: for these two are the only resons why one man may lawfully do harm to another, which is that we call punishment. In transgressing the law of nature, the offender declares himself to live by another rule than that of reason and common equity, which is that measure God has set to the actions of men for their mutual security; and so he becomes dangerous to mankind, the tie, which is to secure them from injury and violence, being slighted and broken by him: which being a trespass against the whole species, and the peace and safety of it, provided for by the law of nature; every man upon this score, by the right he hath to preserve mankind in general, may restrain, or, where it is necessary, destroy things noxious to them, and so may bring such evil on any one, who hath transgressed that law, as may make him repent the doing of it, and thereby deter him, and by his example others, from doing the like mischief. And in this case, and upon this ground, "every man hath a right to punish the offender, and be executioner of the law of nature."

§ 9. I doubt not but this will seem a very strange doctrine to some men: but, before they condemn it, I desire them to resolve me by what right any prince or state can put to death or punish an alien for any crime he commits in their country. It is certain their laws, by virtue of any sanction they receive from the promulgated will of the legislative, reach not a stranger: they speak not to him, nor, if they did, is he bound to hearken to them. The legislative authority, by which they are in force over the subjects of that commonwealth, hath no power over him. Those who have the supreme power of making laws in England, France, or Holland, are to an Indian but like the rest of the world, men without authority: and therefore, if by the law of nature every man hath not a power to punish offences against it, as he soberly judges the case to require, I see not how the magistrates of any community can punish an alien of another country; since, in reference to him, they can have no more power than what every man naturally may have over another.

§ 10. Besides the crime which consists in violating the law, and varying from the right rule of reason, whereby a man so far becomes degenerate, and declares himself to quit the principles of human nature, and to be a noxious creature, there is commonly injury done to some person or other, and some other man receives damage by his transgression: in which case he who hath received any damage, has, besides the right of punishment common to him with other men, a particular right to seek reparation from him that has done it: and any other person, who finds it just, may also join with him that is injured, and assist him in recovering from the offender so much as may make satisfaction for the harm he has suffered.

§ 11. From these two distinct rights, the one of punishing the crime for restraint, and preventing the like offence, which right of punishing is in every body; the other of taking reparation, which belongs only to the injured party; comes it to pass that the magistrate, who by being magistrate hath the common right of punishing put into his hands, can often, where the public good demands not the execution of the law, remit the punishment of criminal offences by his own authority, but yet cannot remit the satisfaction due to any private man for the damage he has received. That he who has suffered the damage has a right to demand in his own name, and he alone can remit: the damnified person has this power of appropriating to himself the goods or service of the offender, by right of self-preservation, as every man has a power to punish the crime, to prevent its being committed again, "by the right he has of preserving all mankind," and doing all reasonable things he can in order to that end: and thus it is that every man, in the state of nature, has a power to kill a murderer, both to deter others from doing the like injury, which no reparation can compensate, by the example of the punishment that attends it from every body; and also to secure men from the attempts of a criminal, who having renounced reason, the common rule and measure God hath given to mankind, hath, by the unjust violence and slaughter he hath committed upon one, declared war against all mankind; and therefore may be destroyed as a lion or a tiger, one of those wild savage beasts with whom men can have no society nor security: and upon this is grounded that great law of nature, "Whoso sheddeth man's blood, by man shall his blood be shed." And Cain was so fully convinced that every one had a right to destroy such a criminal, that, after the murder of his brother, he cries out, "Every one that findeth me shall slay me;" so plain was it writ in the hearts of mankind.

§ 12. By the same reason may a man in the state of nature punish the lesser breaches of that law. It will perhaps be demanded, with death? I answer, each transgression may be punished to that degree, and with so much severity, as will suffice to make it an ill bargain to the offender, give him cause to repent, and terrify others from doing the like. Every offence, that can be committed in the state of nature, may in the state of nature be also punished equally, and as far forth, as it may in a commonwealth: for though it would be beside my present purpose to enter here into the particulars of the law of nature, or its measures of punishment, yet it is certain there is such a law, and that too as intelligible and plain to a rational creature, and a studier of that law, as the positive laws of commonwealths; nay, possibly plainer, as much as reason is easier to be understood than the fancies and intricate contrivances of men, following contrary and hidden interests put into words; for so truly are a great part of the municipal laws of countries, which are only so far right, as they are founded on the law of nature, by which they are to be regulated and interpreted.

§ 13. To this strange doctrine, viz. That "in the state of nature every one has the executive power" of the law of nature, I doubt not but it will be objected, that it is unreasonable for men to be judges in their own cases, that self-love will make men partial to themselves and their friends: and, on the other side, that ill-nature, passion, and revenge will carry them too far in punishing others; and hence nothing but confusion and disorder will follow: and that therefore God hath certainly appointed government to restrain the partiality and violence of men. I

easily grant, that civil government is the proper remedy for the inconveniencies of the state of nature, which must certainly be great, where men may be judges in their own case; since it is easy to be imagined, that he who was so unjust as to do his brother an injury, will scarce be so just as to condemn himself for it: but I shall desire those who make this objection to remember, that absolute monarchs are but men; and if government is to be the remedy of those evils, which necessarily follow from men's being judges in their own cases, and the state of nature is therefore not to be endured; I desire to know what kind of government that is, and how much better it is than the state of nature, where one man, commanding a multitude, has the liberty to be judge in his own case, and may do to all his subjects whatever he pleases, without the least liberty to any one to question or control those who execute his pleasure? and in whatsoever he doth, whether led by reason, mistake, or passion, must be submitted to? Much better it is in the state of nature, wherein men are not bound to submit to the unjust will of another: and if he that judges, judges amiss in his own, or any other case, he is answerable for it to the rest of mankind.

§ 14. It is often asked, as a mighty objection, "where are or ever were there any men in such a state of nature?" To which it may suffice as an answer at present, that since all princes and rulers of independent governments, all through the world, are in a state of nature, it is plain the world never was, nor ever will be, without numbers of men in that state. I have named all governors of independent communities, whether they are, or are not, in league with others: for it is not every compact that puts an end to the state of nature between men, but only this one of agreeing together mutually to enter into one community, and make one body politic; other promises and compacts men may make one with another, and yet still be in the state of nature. The promises and bargains for truck, &c. between the two men in the desert

what happens if S o N remains

Rousseau
"Man is born free, and everywhere he is in chains."

The State of Nature and the Law of Nature 45

island, mentioned by Garcilasso de la Vega, in his history of Peru; or between a Swiss and an Indian, in the woods of America; are binding to them, though they are perfectly in a state of nature, in reference to one another: for truth and keeping of faith belongs to men as men, and not as members of society.

Of the State of War

§ 16. The state of war is a state of enmity and destruction: and therefore declaring by word or action, not a passionate and hasty, but a sedate, settled design upon another man's life, puts him in a state of war with him against whom he has declared such an intention, and so has exposed his life to the other's power to be taken away by him, or any one that joins with him in his defense, and espouses his quarrel; it being reasonable and just, I should have a right to destroy that which threatens me with destruction: for, by the fundamental law of nature, man being to be preserved as much as possible, when all cannot be preserved, the safety of the innocent is to be preferred: and one may destroy a man who makes war upon him, or has discovered an enmity to his being, for the same reason that he may kill a wolf or a lion; because such men are not under the ties of the common law of reason, have no other rule but that of force and violence, and so may be treated as beasts of prey, those dangerous and noxious creatures, that will be sure to destroy him whenever he falls into their power.

§ 17. And hence it is, that he who attempts to get another man into his absolute power, does thereby put himself into a state of war with him; it being to be understood as a declaration of a design upon his life: for I have reason to conclude, that he who would get me into his power without my consent, would use me as he pleased when he got me there, and destroy me too when he had a fancy to it; for nobody can desire to have me in his absolute power, unless it be to compel me by force to that which is against

the right of my freedom, i.e. make me a slave. To be free from such force is the only security of my preservation; and reason bids me look on him as an enemy to my preservation, who would take away that freedom which is the fence to it; so that he who makes an attempt to enslave me, thereby puts himself into a state of war with me. He that, in the state of nature, would take away the freedom that belongs to any one in that state, must necessarily be supposed to have a design to take away every thing else, that freedom being the foundation of all the rest; as he that, in the state of society, would take away the freedom belonging to those of that society or commonwealth, must be supposed to design to take away from them every thing else, and so be looked on as in a state of war.

§ 18. This makes it lawful for a man to kill a thief, who has not in the least hurt him, nor declared any design upon his life, any farther than, by the use of force, so to get him in his power, as to take away his money, or what he pleases, from him; because using force, where he has no right, to get me into his power, let his pretence be what it will, I have no reason to suppose, that he, who would take away my liberty, would not, when he had me in his power, take away every thing else. And therefore it is lawful for me to treat him as one who has put himself into a state of war with me, i.e. kill him if I can; for to that hazard does he justly expose himself, whoever introduces a state of war, and is aggressor in it.

§ 19. And here we have the plain "difference between the state of nature and the state of war;" which, however some men have confounded, are as far distant as a state of peace, good-will, mutual assistance and preservation, and a state of enmity, malice, violence, and mutual destruction, are one from another. Men living together according to reason, without a common superior on earth with authority to judge between them, is properly the state of nature. But force, or a declared design of force, upon the person of another, where there is no common superior on earth to appeal to for relief, is the state of war: and it is the want of such an appeal gives a man the right of war even against an aggressor, though he be in society, and a fellow-subject. Thus a thief, whom I cannot harm, but by appeal to the law, for having stolen all that I am worth, I may kill, when he sets on me to rob me but of my horse or coat; because the law, which was made for my preservation, where it cannot interpose to secure my life from present force, which, if lost, is capable of no reparation, permits me my own defence, and the right of war, a liberty to kill the aggressor, because the aggressor allows not time to appeal to our common judge, nor the decision of the law, for remedy in a case where the mischief may be irreparable. Want of a common judge with authority puts all men in a state of nature: force without right, upon a man's person, makes a state of war, both where there is, and is not, a common judge.

§ 20. But when the actual force is over, the state of war ceases between those that are in society, and are equally on both sides subjected to the fair determination of the law; because then there lies open the remedy of appeal for the past injury, and to prevent future harm: but where no such appeal is, as in the state of nature, for want of positive laws, and judges with authority to appeal to, the state of war once begun, continues with a right to the innocent party to destroy the other whenever he can, until the aggressor offers peace, and desires reconciliation on such terms as may repair any wrongs he has already done, and secure the innocent for the future; nay, where an appeal to the law, and constituted judges, lies open, but the remedy is denied by a manifest perverting of justice, and a barefaced wresting of the laws to protect or indemnify the violence or injuries of some men, or party of men; there it is hard to imagine any thing but a state of war: for wherever violence is used, and injury done, though by hands appointed to administer justice, it is still violence and injury, however coloured with the name, pretences, or forms of law, the end whereof

being to protect and redress the innocent, by an unbiassed application of it, to all who are under it; wherever that is not *bona fide* done, war is made upon the sufferers, who having no appeal on earth to right them, they are left to the only remedy in such cases, an appeal to Heaven.

§ 21. To avoid this state of war (wherein there is no appeal but to Heaven, and wherein every the least difference is apt to end, where there is no authority to decide between the contenders) is one great reason of men's putting themselves into society, and quitting the state of nature: for where there is an authority, a power on earth, from which relief can be had by appeal, there the continuance of the state of war is excluded, and the controversy is decided by that power.

Of the Beginning of Political Societies

§ 95. Men being, as has been said, by nature all free, equal, and independent, no one can be put out of this estate, and subjected to the political power of another, without his own consent. The only way whereby any one divests himself of his natural liberty, and puts on the bonds of civil society, is by agreeing with other men to join and unite into a community, for their comfortable, safe, and peaceable living one amongst another, in a secure enjoyment of their properties, and a greater security against any that are not of it. This any number of men may do, because it injures not the freedom of the rest; they are left as they were in the liberty of the state of nature. When any number of men have so consented to make one community or government, they are thereby presently incorporated, and make one body politic, wherein the majority have a right to act and conclude the rest.

§ 96. For when any number of men have, by the consent of every individual, made a community, they have thereby made that community one body, with a power to act as one body, which is only by the will and determination of the majority; for that which acts any community being only the consent of the individuals of it, and it being necessary to that which is one body to move one way; it is necessary the body should move that way whither the greater force carries it, which is the consent of the majority: or else it is impossible it should act or continue one body, one community, which the consent of every individual that united into it agreed that it should; and so every one is bound by that consent to be concluded by the majority. And therefore we see that in assemblies, empowered to act by positive laws, where no number is set by that positive law which empowers them, the act of the majority passes for the act of the whole, and of course determines; as having, by the law of nature and reason, the power of the whole.

§ 97. And thus every man, by consenting with others to make one body politic under one government, puts himself under an obligation to every one of that society to submit to the determination of the majority, and to be concluded by it; or else this original compact, whereby he with others incorporate into one society, would signify nothing, and be no compact, if he be left free, and under no other ties than he was in before in the state of nature. For what appearance would there be of any compact? What new engagement, if he were no farther tied by any decrees of the society than he himself thought fit, and did actually consent to? This would be still as great a liberty as he himself had before his compact, or any one else in the state of nature hath, who may submit himself and consent to any acts of it if he thinks fit.

§ 98. For if the consent of the majority shall not, in reason, be received as the act of the whole, and conclude every individual, nothing but the consent of every individual can make any thing to be the act of the whole: but such a consent is next to impossible ever to be had, if we consider the infirmities of health, and avocations of business, which in a number, though much less than that of a commonwealth, will necessarily keep many away from the public assembly. To which, if we add the variety of

opinions and contrariety of interests which unavoidably happen in all collections of men, the coming into society upon such terms would be only like Cato's coming into the theatre, only to go out again. Such a constitution as this would make the mighty leviathan of a shorter duration than the feeblest creatures, and not let it outlast the day it was born in: which cannot be supposed, till we can think that rational creatures should desire and constitute societies only to be dissolved: for where the majority cannot conclude the rest, there they cannot act as one body, and consequently will be immediately dissolved again.

§ 99. Whosoever therefore out of a state of nature unite into a community, must be understood to give up all the power necessary to the ends for which they unite into society, to the majority of the community, unless they expressly agreed in any number greater than the majority. And this is done by barely agreeing to unite into one political society, which is all the compact that is, or needs be, between the individuals that enter into, or make up a commonwealth. And thus that which begins and actually constitutes any political society, is nothing but the consent of any number of freemen capable of a majority, to unite and incorporate into such a society. And this is that, and that only, which did or could give beginning to any lawful government in the world.

[. . .]

§ 119. Every man being, as has been showed, naturally free, and nothing being able to put him into subjection to any earthly power, but only his own consent; it is to be considered, what shall be understood to be a sufficient declaration of a man's consent, to make him subject to the laws of any government. There is a common distinction of an express and a tacit consent, which will concern our present case. Nobody doubts but an express consent of any man entering into any society makes him a perfect member of that society, a subject of that government. The difficulty is, what ought to be looked upon as a tacit consent, and how far it binds, i.e. how far any one shall be looked on to have consented, and thereby submitted to any government, where he has made no expressions of it at all. And to this I say, that every man, that hath any possessions, or enjoyment of any part of the dominions of any government, doth thereby give his tacit consent, and is as far forth obliged to obedience to the laws of that government, during such enjoyment, as any one under it; whether this his possession be of land, to him and his heirs for ever, or a lodging only for a week; or whether it be barely travelling freely on the highway; and, in effect, it reaches as far as the very being of any one within the territories of that government.

§ 120. To understand this the better, it is fit to consider, that every man, when he at first incorporates himself into any commonwealth, he, by his uniting himself thereunto, annexes also, and submits to the community those possessions which he has, or shall acquire, that do not already belong to any other government: for it would be a direct contradiction for any one to enter into society with others for the securing and regulating of property, and yet to suppose his land, whose property is to be regulated by the laws of the society, should be exempt from the jurisdiction of that government, to which he himself, the proprietor of the land, is a subject. By the same act therefore, whereby any one unites his person, which was before free, to any commonwealth, by the same he unites his possessions, which were before free, to it also: and they become, both of them, person and possession, subject to the government and dominion of that commonwealth, as long as it hath a being. Whoever, therefore, from thenceforth, by inheritance, purchase, permission, or otherways, enjoys any part of the land so annexed to, and under the government of that commonwealth, must take it with the condition it is under; that is, of submitting to the government of the commonwealth, under whose jurisdiction it is, as far forth as any subject of it.

§ 121. But since the government has a direct jurisdiction only over the land, and reaches the possessor of it (before he has actually incorporated himself in the society) only as he dwells upon, and enjoys that; the obligation any one is under, by virtue of such enjoyment, to "submit to the government, begins and ends with the enjoyment:" so that whenever the owner, who has given nothing but such a tacit consent to the government, will, by donation, sale, or otherwise, quit the said possession, he is at liberty to go and incorporate himself into any other commonwealth; or to agree with others to begin a new one, in *vacuis locis*, in any part of the world they can find free and unpossessed: whereas he that has once, by actual agreement, and any express declaration, given his consent to be of any commonwealth, is perpetually and indispensably obliged to be, and remain unalterably a subject to it, and can never be again in the liberty of the state of nature; unless, by any calamity, the government he was under comes to be dissolved, or else by some public act cuts him off from being any longer a member of it.

§ 122. But submitting to the laws of any country, living quietly, and enjoying privileges and protection under them, makes not a man a member of that society: this is only a local protection and homage due to and from all those, who, not being in a state of war, come within the territories belonging to any government, to all parts whereof the force of its laws extends. But this no more makes a man a member of that society, a perpetual subject of that commonwealth, than it would make a man a subject to another, in whose family he found it convenient to abide for some time; though, whilst he continued in it, he were obliged to comply with the laws, and submit to the government he found there. And thus we see, that foreigners, by living all their lives under another government, and enjoying the privileges and protection of it, though they are bound, even in conscience, to submit to its administration, as far forth as any denison; yet do not thereby come to be subjects or members of that commonwealth. Nothing can make any man so, but his actually entering into it by positive engagement, and express promise and compact. This is that which I think concerning the beginning of political societies, and that consent which makes any one a member of any commonwealth.

Of the Ends of Political Society and Government

§ 123. If man in the state of nature be so free as has been said; if he be absolute lord of his own person and possessions, equal to the greatest, and subject to nobody, why will he part with his freedom, why will he give up this empire, and subject himself to the dominion and control of any other power? To which it is obvious to answer, that though in the state of nature he hath such a right, yet the enjoyment of it is very uncertain, and constantly exposed to the invasion of others; for all being kings as much as he, every man his equal, and the greater part no strict observers of equity and justice, the enjoyment of the property he has in this state is very unsafe, very unsecure. This makes him willing to quit a condition, which, however free, is full of fears and continual dangers: and it is not without reason that he seeks out, and is willing to join in society with others, who are already united, or have a mind to unite, for the mutual preservation of their lives, liberties, and estates, which I call by the general name property.

§ 124. The great and chief end, therefore, of men's uniting into commonwealths, and putting themselves under government, is the preservation of their property. To which in the state of nature there are many things wanting.

First, There wants an established, settled, known law, received and allowed by common consent to be the standard of right and wrong, and the common measure to decide all controversies between them: for though the law of nature be plain and intelligible to all rational creatures; yet men being biassed by their interest,

as well as ignorant for want of studying it, are not apt to allow of it as a law binding to them in the application of it to their particular cases.

§ 125. Secondly, In the state of nature there wants a known and indifferent judge, with authority to determine all differences according to the established law: for every one in that state being both judge and executioner of the law of nature, men being partial to themselves, passion and revenge is very apt to carry them too far, and with too much heat, in their own cases; as well as negligence and unconcernedness, to make them too remiss in other men's.

§ 126. Thirdly, In the state of nature there often wants power to back and support the sentence when right, and to give it due execution. They who by any injustice offend, will seldom fail, where they are able, by force to make good their injustice; such resistance many times makes the punishment dangerous, and frequently destructive to those who attempt it.

§ 127. Thus mankind, notwithstanding all the privileges of the state of nature, being but in an ill condition while they remain in it, are quickly driven into society. Hence it comes to pass, that we seldom find any number of men live any time together in this state. The inconveniencies that they are therein exposed to, by the irregular and uncertain exercise of the power every man has of punishing the transgressions of others, make them take sanctuary under the established laws of government, and therein seek the preservation of their property. It is this makes them so willingly give up every one his single power of punishing, to be exercised by such alone as shall be appointed to it amongst them; and by such rules as the community, or those authorized by them to that purpose, shall agree on. And in this we have the original right of both the legislative and executive power, as well as of the governments and societies themselves.

§ 128. For in the state of nature, to omit the liberty he has of innocent delights, a man has two powers.

The first is to do whatsoever he thinks fit for the preservation of himself and others within the permission of the law of nature: by which law, common to them all, he and all the rest of mankind are one community, make up one society, distinct from all other creatures. And, were it not for the corruption and viciousness of degenerate men, there would be no need of any other; no necessity that men should separate from this great and natural community, and by positive agreements combine into smaller and divided associations.

The other power a man has in the state of nature, is the power to punish the crimes committed against that law. Both these he gives up when he joins in a private, if I may so call it, or particular politic society, and incorporates into any commonwealth, separate from the rest of mankind.

§ 129. The first power, viz. "of doing whatsoever he thought fit for the preservation of himself" and the rest of mankind, he gives up to be regulated by laws made by the society, so far forth as the preservation of himself and the rest of that society shall require; which laws of the society in many things confine the liberty he had by the law of nature.

§ 130. Secondly, The power of punishing he wholly gives up, and engages his natural force (which he might before employ in the execution of the law of nature, by his own single authority, as he thought fit), to assist the executive power of the society, as the law thereof shall require: for being now in a new state, wherein he is to enjoy many conveniencies, from the labour, assistance, and society of others in the same community, as well as protection from its whole strength; he is to part also with as much of his natural liberty, in providing for himself, as the good, prosperity, and safety of the society shall require; which is not only necessary, but just, since the other members of the society do the like.

§ 131. But though men, when they enter into society, give up the equality, liberty, and executive power they had in the state of nature, into the hands of the society, to be so far disposed of by the legislative as the good of the society shall require; yet it being only with an intention in every one the better to preserve himself, his liberty and property (for no rational creature can be supposed to change his condition with an intention to be worse); the power of the society, or legislative constituted by them, can never be supposed to extend farther than the common good; but is obliged to secure every one's property, by providing against those three defects above-mentioned, that made the state of nature so unsafe and uneasy. And so whoever has the legislative or supreme power of any commonwealth, is bound to govern by established standing laws, promulgated and known to the people, and not by extemporary decrees; by indifferent and upright judges, who are to decide controversies by those laws; and to employ the force of the community at home, only in the execution of such laws; or abroad to prevent or redress foreign injuries, and secure the community from inroads and invasion. And all this to be directed to no other end but the peace, safety, and public good of the people.

Chapter 4

David Hume

OF THE ORIGINAL CONTRACT

David Hume (1711–76) was a Scottish philosopher who wrote widely in metaphysics, ethics, history, politics, and almost everything else. His writings often express a skepticism regarding established doctrines, and in the current selection (1748) Hume casts doubt on the notion of a social contract as a source of political authority. Not only did such a contract never exist, Hume argues, but it is not clear why it would be *necessary* to create obligations to obey, since it already presupposes that people are subject to at least one obligation to which they did *not* consent — namely, the obligation to do what they promise to do. We should instead hold, Hume thinks, that both the duty to keep promises and the duty to obey governments are grounded in the same consideration — they are necessary for the promotion of human well-being.

As no party, in the present age, can well support itself, without a philosophical or speculative system of principles, annexed to its political or practical one; we accordingly find, that each of the factions, into which this nation is divided, has reared up a fabric of the former kind, in order to protect and cover that scheme of actions, which it pursues. The people being commonly very rude builders, especially in this speculative way, and more especially still, when actuated by party-zeal; it is natural to imagine, that their workmanship must be a little unshapely, and discover evident marks of that violence and hurry, in which it was raised. The one party, by tracing up government to the DEITY, endeavour to render it so sacred and inviolate, that it must be little less than sacrilege, however tyrannical it may become, to touch or invade it, in the smallest article. The other party, by founding government altogether on the consent of the PEOPLE, suppose that there is a kind of *original contract*, by which the subjects have tacitly reserved the power of resisting their sovereign, whenever they find themselves aggrieved by that authority, with which they have, for certain purposes, voluntarily entrusted him. These are the speculative principles of the two parties; and these too are the practical consequences deduced from them.

I shall venture to affirm, *That both these systems of speculative principles are just; though not in the sense, intended by the parties: And, That both the schemes of practical consequences are prudent; though not in the extremes, to which each party, in opposition to the other, has commonly endeavoured to carry them.*

[. . .]

When we consider how nearly equal all men are in their bodily force, and even in their mental powers and faculties, till cultivated by education; we must necessarily allow, that nothing but their own consent could, at first, associate them together, and subject them to any authority. The people, if we trace government to its first origin in the woods and desarts, are the source of all power and jurisdiction, and voluntarily, for the sake of peace and order, abandoned their native liberty, and received laws from their equal and companion. The conditions, upon which they were willing to submit, were either expressed, or were so clear and obvious, that it might well be esteemed superfluous to express them. If this, then, be meant by the *orignal contract*, it cannot be denied, that all government is, at first, founded on a contract, and that the most ancient rude combinations of mankind were formed chiefly by that principle. In vain, are we asked in what records this charter of our liberties is registered. It was not written on parchment, nor yet on leaves or barks of trees. It preceded the use of writing and all the other civilized arts of life. But we trace it plainly in the nature of man, and in the equality, or something approaching equality, which we find in all the individuals of that species. The force, which now prevails, and which is founded on fleets and armies, is plainly political, and derived from authority, the effect of established government. A man's natural force consists only in the vigour of his limbs, and the firmness of his courage; which could never subject multitudes to the command of one. Nothing but their own consent, and their sense of the advantages resulting from peace and order, could have had that influence.

Yet even this consent was long very imperfect, and could not be the basis of a regular administration. The chieftain, who had probably acquired his influence during the continuance of war, ruled more by persuasion than command; and till he could employ force to reduce the refractory and disobedient, the society could scarcely be said to have attained a state of civil government. No compact or agreement, it is evident, was expressly formed for general submission; an idea far beyond the comprehension of savages: Each exertion of authority in the chieftain must have been particular, and called

forth by the present exigencies of the case: The sensible utility, resulting from his interposition, made these exertions become daily more frequent; and their frequency gradually produced an habitual, and, if you please to call it so, a voluntary, and therefore precarious, acquiescence in the people.

But philosophers, who have embraced a party (if that be not a contradiction in terms) are not contented with these concessions. They assert, not only that government in its earliest infancy arose from consent or rather the voluntary acquiescence of the people; but also, that, even at present, when it has attained full maturity, it rests on no other foundation. They affirm, that all men are still born equal, and owe allegiance to no prince or government, unless bound by the obligation and sanction of a *promise*. And as no man, without some equivalent, would forego the advantages of his native liberty, and subject himself to the will of another; this promise is always understood to be conditional, and imposes on him no obligation, unless he meet with justice and protection from his sovereign. These advantages the sovereign promises him in return; and if he fail in the execution, he has broken, on his part, the articles of engagement, and has thereby freed his subject from all obligations to allegiance. Such, according to these philosophers, is the foundation of authority in every government; and such the right of resistance, possessed by every subject.

But would these reasoners look abroad into the world, they would meet with nothing that, in the least, corresponds to their ideas, or can warrant so refined and philosophical a system. On the contrary, we find, every where, princes, who claim their subjects as their property, and assert their independent right of sovereignty, from conquest or succession. We find also, every where, subjects, who acknowledge this right in their prince, and suppose themselves born under obligations of obedience to a certain sovereign, as much as under the ties of reverence and duty to certain parents. These connexions are always conceived to be equally independent of our consent, in Persia and China; in France and SPAIN; and even in Holland and England, wherever the doctrines above-mentioned have not been carefully inculcated. Obedience or subjection becomes so familiar, that most men never make any enquiry about its origin or cause, more than about the principle of gravity, resistance, or the most universal laws of nature. Or if curiosity ever move them; as soon as they learn, that they themselves and their ancestors have, for several ages, or from time immemorial, been subject to such a form of government or such a family; they immediately acquiesce, and acknowledge their obligation to allegiance. Were you to preach, in most parts of the world, that political connexions are founded altogether on voluntary consent or a mutual promise, the magistrate would soon imprison you, as seditious, for loosening the ties of obedience; if your friends did not before shut you up as delirious, for advancing such absurdities. It is strange, that an act of the mind, which every individual is supposed to have formed, and after he came to the use of reason too, otherwise it could have no authority; that this act, I say, should be so much unknown to all of them, that, over the face of the whole earth, there scarcely remain any traces or memory of it.

But the contract, on which government is founded, is said to be the *original contract*; and consequently may be supposed too old to fall under the knowledge of the present generation. If the agreement, by which savage men first associated and conjoined their force, be here meant, this is acknowledged to be real; but being so ancient, and being obliterated by a thousand changes of government and princes, it cannot now be supposed to retain any authority. If we would say any thing to the purpose, we must assert, that every particular government, which is lawful, and which imposes any duty of allegiance on the subject, was, at first, founded on consent and a voluntary compact. But besides that this supposes the consent of the fathers to

bind the children, even to the most remote generations, (which republican writers will never allow) besides this, I say, it is not justified by history or experience, in any age or country of the world.

Almost all the governments, which exist at present, or of which there remains any record in story, have been founded originally, either on usurpation or conquest, or both, without any pretence of a fair consent, or voluntary subjection of the people. When an artful and bold man is placed at the head of an army or faction, it is often easy for him, by employing, sometimes violence, sometimes false pretences, to establish his dominion over a people a hundred times more numerous than his partizans. He allows no such open communication, that his enemies can know, with certainty, their number or force. He gives them no leisure to assemble together in a body to oppose him. Even all those, who are the instruments of his usurpation, may wish his fall; but their ignorance of each other's intention keeps them in awe, and is the sole cause of his security. By such arts as these, many governments have been established; and this is all the *original contract*, which they have to boast of.

The face of the earth is continually changing, by the increase of small kingdoms into great empires, by the dissolution of great empires into smaller kingdoms, by the planting of colonies, by the migration of tribes. Is there any thing discoverable in all these events, but force and violence? Where is the mutual agreement or voluntary association so much talked of?

Even the smoothest way, by which a nation may receive a foreign master, by marriage or a will, is not extremely honourable for the people; but supposes them to be disposed of, like a dowry or a legacy, according to the pleasure or interest of their rulers.

But where no force interposes, and election takes place; what is this election so highly vaunted? It is either the combination of a few great men, who decide for the whole, and will allow of no opposition: Or it is the fury of a multitude, that follow a seditious ringleader, who is not known, perhaps, to a dozen among them, and who owes his advancement merely to his own impudence, or to the momentary caprice of his fellows.

Are these disorderly elections, which are rare too, of such mighty authority, as to be the only lawful foundation of all government and allegiance?

In reality, there is not a more terrible event, than a total dissolution of government, which gives liberty to the multitude, and makes the determination or choice of a new establishment depend upon a number, which nearly approaches to that of the body of the people: For it never comes entirely to the whole body of them. Every wise man, then, wishes to see, at the head of a powerful and obedient army, a general, who may speedily seize the prize, and give to the people a master, which they are so unfit to chuse for themselves. So little correspondent is fact and reality to those philosophical notions.

[. . .]

It is in vain to say, that all governments are or should be, at first, founded on popular consent, as much as the necessity of human affairs will admit. This favours entirely my pretension. I maintain, that human affairs will never admit of this consent; seldom of the appearance of it. But that conquest or usurpation, that is, in plain terms, force, by dissolving the ancient governments, is the origin of almost all the new ones, which were ever established in the world. And that in the few cases, where consent may seem to have taken place, it was commonly so irregular, so confined, or so much intermixed either with fraud or violence, that it cannot have any great authority.

My intention here is not to exclude the consent of the people from being one just foundation of government where it has place. It is surely the best and most sacred of any. I only pretend, that it has very seldom had place in any degree, and never almost in its full extent. And

that therefore some other foundation of government must also be admitted.

Were all men possessed of so inflexible a regard to justice, that, of themselves, they would totally abstain from the properties of others; they had for ever remained in a state of absolute liberty, without subjection to any magistrate or political society: But this is a state of perfection, of which human nature is justly deemed incapable. Again; were all men possessed of so perfect an understanding, as always to know their own interests, no form of government had ever been submitted to, but what was established on consent, and was fully canvassed by every member of the society: But this state of perfection is likewise much superior to human nature. Reason, history, and experience shew us, that all political societies have had an origin much less accurate and regular; and were one to choose a period of time, when the people's consent was the least regarded in public transactions, it would be precisely on the establishment of a new government. In a settled constitution, their inclinations are often consulted; but during the fury of revolutions, conquests, and public convulsions, military force or political craft usually decides the controversy.

When a new government is established, by whatever means, the people are commonly dissatisfied with it, and pay obedience more from fear and necessity, than from any idea of allegiance or of moral obligation. The prince is watchful and jealous, and must carefully guard against every beginning or appearance of insurrection. Time, by degrees, removes all these difficulties, and accustoms the nation to regard, as their lawful or native princes, that family, which, at first, they considered as usurpers or foreign conquerors. In order to found this opinion, they have no recourse to any notion of voluntary consent or promise, which, they know, never was, in this case, either expected or demanded. The original establishment was formed by violence, and submitted to from necessity. The subsequent administration is also supported by power, and acquiesced in by the people, not as a matter of choice, but of obligation. They imagine not, that their consent gives their prince a title: But they willingly consent, because they think, that, from long possession, he has acquired a title, independent of their choice or inclination.

Should it be said, that, by living under the dominion of a prince, which one might leave, every individual has given a *tacit* consent to his authority, and promised him obedience; it may be answered, that such an implied consent can only have place, where a man imagines, that the matter depends on his choice. But where he thinks (as all mankind do who are born under established governments) that by his birth he owes allegiance to a certain prince or certain form of government; it would be absurd to infer a consent or choice, which he expressly, in this case, renounces and disclaims.

Can we seriously say, that a poor peasant or artizan has a free choice to leave his country, when he knows no foreign language or manners, and lives from day to day, by the small wages which he acquires? We may as well assert, that a man, by remaining in a vessel, freely consents to the dominion of the master; though he was carried on board while asleep, and must leap into the ocean, and perish, the moment he leaves her.

[. . .]

A company of men, who should leave their native country, in order to people some uninhabited region, might dream of recovering their native freedom; but they would soon find, that their prince still laid claim to them, and called them his subjects, even in their new settlement. And in this he would but act conformably to the common ideas of mankind.

The truest *tacit* consent of this kind, that is ever observed, is when a foreigner settles in any country, and is beforehand acquainted with the prince, and government, and laws, to which he must submit: Yet is his allegiance, though more voluntary, much less expected or depended on, than that of a natural born subject. On the

contrary, his native prince still asserts a claim to him. And if he punish not the renegade, when he seizes him in war with his new prince's commission; this clemency is not founded on the municipal law, which in all countries condemns the prisoner; but on the consent of princes, who have agreed to this indulgence, in order to prevent reprisals.

Did one generation of men go off the stage at once, and another succeed, as is the case with silk-worms and butterflies, the new race, if they had sense enough to choose their government, which surely is never the case with men, might voluntarily, and by general consent, establish their own form of civil polity, without any regard to the laws or precedents, which prevailed among their ancestors. But as human society is in perpetual flux, one man every hour going out of the world, another coming into it, it is necessary, in order to preserve stability in government, that the new brood should conform themselves to the established constitution, and nearly follow the path which their fathers, treading in the footsteps of theirs, had marked out to them. Some innovations must necessarily have place in every human institution, and it is happy where the enlightened genius of the age give these a direction to the side of reason, liberty, and justice: but violent innovations no individual is entitled to make: they are even dangerous to be attempted by the legislature: more ill than good is ever to be expected from them: and if history affords examples to the contrary, they are not to be drawn into precedent, and are only to be regarded as proofs, that the science of politics affords few rules, which will not admit of some exception, and which may not sometimes be controuled by fortune and accident.

[. . .]

Suppose, that an usurper, after having banished his lawful prince and royal family, should establish his dominion for ten or a dozen years in any country, and should preserve so exact a discipline in his troops, and so regular a disposition in his garrisons, that no insurrection had ever been raised, or even murmur heard, against his administration: Can it be asserted, that the people, who in their hearts abhor his treason, have tacitly consented to his authority, and promised him allegiance, merely because, from necessity, they live under his dominion? Suppose again their native prince restored, by means of an army, which he levies in foreign countries: They receive him with joy and exultation, and shew plainly with what reluctance they had submitted to any other yoke. I may now ask, upon what foundation the prince's title stands? Not on popular consent surely: For though the people willingly acquiesce in his authority, they never imagine, that their consent made him sovereign. They consent; because they apprehend him to be already, by birth, their lawful sovereign. And as to that tacit consent, which may now be inferred from their living under his dominion, this is no more than what they formerly gave to the tyrant and usurper.

[. . .]

But would we have a more regular, at least a more philosophical, refutation of this principle of an original contract or popular consent; perhaps, the following observations may suffice.

All *moral* duties may be divided into two kinds. The *first* are those, to which men are impelled by a natural instinct or immediate propensity, which operates on them, independent of all ideas of obligation, and of all views, either to public or private utility. Of this nature are, love of children, gratitude to benefactors, pity to the unfortunate. When we reflect on the advantage, which results to society from such humane instincts, we pay them the just tribute of moral approbation and esteem: But the person, actuated by them, feels their power and influence, antecedent to any such reflection.

The *second* kind of moral duties are such as are not supported by any original instinct of nature, but are performed entirely from a sense of obligation, when we consider the necessities of human society, and the impossibility of

supporting it, if these duties were neglected. It is thus *justice* or a regard to the property of others, *fidelity* or the observance of promises, become obligatory, and acquire an authority over mankind. For as it is evident, that every man loves himself better than any other person, he is naturally impelled to extend his acquisitions as much as possible; and nothing can restrain him in this propensity, but reflection and experience, by which he learns the pernicious effects of that licence, and the total dissolution of society which must ensue from it. His original inclination, therefore, or instinct, is here checked and restrained by a subsequent judgment or observation.

The case is precisely the same with the political or civil duty of *allegiance*, as with the natural duties of justice and fidelity. Our primary instincts lead us, either to indulge ourselves in unlimited freedom, or to seek dominion over others: And it is reflection only, which engages us to sacrifice such strong passions to the interests of peace and public order. A small degree of experience and observation suffices to teach us, that society cannot possibly be maintained without the authority of magistrates, and that this authority must soon fall into contempt, where exact obedience is not payed to it. The observation of these general and obvious interests is the source of all allegiance, and of that moral obligation, which we attribute to it.

What necessity, therefore, is there to found the duty of *allegiance* or obedience to magistrates on that of *fidelity* or a regard to promises, and to suppose, that it is the consent of each individual, which subjects him to government; when it appears, that both allegiance and fidelity stand precisely on the same foundation, and are both submitted to by mankind, on account of the apparent interests and necessities of human society? We are bound to obey our sovereign, it is said; because we have given a tacit promise to that purpose. But why are we bound to observe our promise? It must here be asserted, that the commerce and intercourse of mankind, which are of such mighty advantage, can have no security where men pay no regard to their engagements. In like manner, may it be said, that men could not live at all in society, at least in a civilized society, without laws and magistrates and judges, to prevent the encroachments of the strong upon the weak, of the violent upon the just and equitable. The obligation to allegiance being of like force and authority with the obligation to fidelity, we gain nothing by resolving the one into the other. The general interests or necessities of society are sufficient to establish both.

If the reason be asked of that obedience, which we are bound to pay to government, I readily answer, *because society could not otherwise subsist:* And this answer is clear and intelligible to all mankind. Your answer is, *because we should keep our word.* But besides, that no body, till trained in a philosophical system, can either comprehend or relish this answer: Besides this, I say, you find yourself embarrassed, when it is asked, *why we are bound to keep our word?* Nor can you give any answer, but what would, immediately, without any circuit, have accounted for our obligation to allegiance.

But *to whom is allegiance due? And who is our lawful sovereign?* This question is often the most difficult of any, and liable to infinite discussions. When people are so happy, that they can answer, Our *present sovereign, who inherits, in a direct line, from ancestors, that have governed us for many ages;* this answer admits of no reply; even though historians, in tracing up to the remotest antiquity, the origin of that royal family, may find, as commonly happens, that its first authority was derived from usurpation and violence. It is confessed, that private justice, or the abstinence from the properties of others, is a most cardinal virtue: Yet reason tells us, that there is no property in durable objects, such as lands or houses, when carefully examined in passing from hand to hand, but must, in some period, have been founded on fraud and injustice. The necessities of human society,

neither in private nor public life, will allow of such an accurate enquiry: And there is no virtue or moral duty, but what may, with facility, be refined away, if we indulge a false philosophy, in sifting and scrutinizing it, by every captious rule of logic, in every light or position, in which it may be placed.

[. . .]

We shall only observe, before we conclude, that, though an appeal to general opinion may justly, in the speculative sciences of metaphysics, natural philosophy, or astronomy, be deemed unfair and inconclusive, yet in all questions with regard to morals, as well as criticism, there is really no other standard, by which any controversy can ever be decided. And nothing is a clearer proof that a theory of this kind is erroneous, than to find that it leads to paradoxes, repugnant to the common sentiments of mankind, and to the practice and opinion of all nations and all ages. The doctrine, which founds all lawful government on an *original contract,* or consent of the people, is plainly of this kind; nor has the most noted of its partizans, in prosecution of it, scrupled to affirm, *that absolute monarchy is inconsistent with civil society, and so can be no form of civil government at all;*[1] *and that the supreme power in a state cannot take from any man, by taxes and impositions, any part of his property, without his own consent or that of his representatives.*[2] What authority any moral reasoning can have, which leads into opinions so wide of the general practice of mankind, in every place but this single kingdom, it is easy to determine.

The only passage I meet with in antiquity, where the obligation of obedience to government is ascribed to a promise, is in Plato's Crito: where Socrates refuses to escape from prison, because he had tacitly promised to obey the laws. Thus he builds a *tory* consequence of passive obedience, on a *whig* foundation of the original contract.

New discoveries are not to be expected in these matters. If scarce any man, till very lately, ever imagined that government was founded on compact, it is certain, that it cannot, in general, have any such foundation.

The crime of rebellion among the ancients was commonly expressed by the terms νεωτερίξειν, *novas res moliri.*[3]

Notes

1   See LOCKE on Government, chap. vii. § 90.
2   Id. chap. xi. § 138, 139, 140.
3   [Both terms mean to make innovations, especially political changes.]

Chapter 5

Murray N. Rothbard

SOCIETY WITHOUT A STATE[1]

Murray Rothbard (1926–95) was an economist of the Austrian School who wrote widely in economics, history, and philosophy. Politically, Rothbard was a natural rights libertarian. More precisely, he was an *anarcho-capitalist* who believed that respect for individual rights requires that government be abolished entirely, and that the defensive and legal services it now provides be provided by a free market instead. This reading (published in 1975) describes the anarcho-capitalist vision and defends it against some common objections.

I

In attempting to outline how a "society without a State" – i.e. an anarchist society – might function successfully, I would first like to defuse two common but mistaken criticisms of this approach. First, is the argument that in providing for such defense or protection services as courts, police, or even law itself, I am simply smuggling the State back into society in another form, and that therefore the system I am both analyzing and advocating is not "really" anarchism. This sort of criticism can only involve us in an endless and arid dispute over semantics. Let me say from the beginning that I define the State as that institution which possesses one or both (almost always both) of the following properties: (1) it acquires its income by the physical coercion known as "taxation"; and (2) it asserts and usually obtains a coerced monopoly of the provision of defense services (police and courts) over a given territorial area. Any institution, not possessing either of

these properties is not and cannot be, in accordance with my definition, a "State." On the other hand, I define anarchist society as one where there is no legal possibility for coercive aggression against the person or property of any individual. Anarchists oppose the State because it has its very being in such aggression, namely, the expropriation of private property through taxation, the coercive exclusion of other providers of defense services from its territory, and all of the other depredations and coercions that are built upon these twin foci of invasions of individual rights.

Nor is our definition of the State arbitrary, for these two characteristics have been possessed by what is generally acknowledged to be "States" throughout recorded history. The State, by its use of physical coercion, has arrogated to itself a compulsory monopoly of defense services over its territorial jurisdiction. But it is certainly conceptually possible for such services to be supplied by private, non-State institutions, and indeed such services have historically been supplied by other organizations than the State. To be opposed to the State is then not necessarily to be opposed to services that have often been linked with it; to be opposed to the State does not necessarily imply that we must be opposed to police protection, courts, arbitration, the minting of money, postal service, or roads and highways. **Some** anarchists have indeed been opposed to police and to all physical coercion in **defense** of person and property, but this is not inherent in and is fundamentally irrelevant to the anarchist position, which is precisely marked by opposition to all physical coercion invasive of, or aggressing against, person and property.

The crucial role of taxation may be seen in the fact that the State is the only institution or organization in society which regularly and systematically acquires its income through the use of physical coercion. All other individuals or organizations acquire their income voluntarily, either (a) through the voluntary sale of goods and services to consumers on the market, or (b) through voluntary gifts or donations by members or other donors. If I cease or refrain from purchasing Wheaties on the market, the Wheaties producers do not come after me with a gun or prison to force me to purchase; if I fail to join the American Philosophical Association, the association may not force me to join or prevent me from giving up my membership. Only the State can do so; only the State can confiscate my property or put me in jail if I do not pay its tax-tribute. Therefore, only the State regularly exists and has its very being by means of coercive depredations on private property.

Neither is it legitimate to challenge this sort of analysis by claiming that in some other sense, the purchase of Wheaties or membership in the A.P.A. is in some way "coercive"; there again, we can only be trapped in an endless semantic dispute. Apart from other rebuttals which cannot be considered here, I would simply say that anarchists are interested in the abolition of this type of action: e.g. aggressive physical violence against

person and property, and that this is how we define "coercion." Anyone who is still unhappy with this use of the term "coercion" can simply eliminate the word from this discussion, and substitute for it "physical violence or the threat thereof," with the only loss being in literary style rather than in the substance of the argument. What anarchism proposes to do, then, is to abolish the State, i.e. to abolish the regularized institution of aggressive coercion.

It need hardly be added that the State habitually builds upon its coercive source of income by adding a host of other aggressions upon society: ranging from economic controls to the prohibition of pornography to the compelling of religious observance to the mass murder of civilians in organized warfare. In short, that the State, in the words of Albert Jay Nock, "claims and exercises a monopoly of crime" over its territorial area.

The second criticism I would like to defuse before beginning the main body of the paper is the common charge that anarchists "assume that all people are good," and that without the State no crime would be committed. In short, that anarchism assumes that with the abolition of the State a New Anarchist Man will emerge, cooperative, humane, and benevolent, so that no problem of crime will then plague the society. I confess that I do not understand the basis for this charge. Whatever other schools of anarchism profess—and I do not believe that they are open to this charge—I certainly do not adopt this view. I assume with most observers that mankind is a mixture of good and evil, of cooperative and criminal tendencies. In my view, the anarchist society is one which maximizes the tendencies for the good and the cooperative, while it minimizes both the opportunity and the moral legitimacy of the evil and the criminal. If the anarchist view is correct, and the State is indeed the great legalized and socially legitimated channel for all manner of antisocial crime – theft, oppression, mass murder – on a massive scale, then surely the abolition of such an engine of crime can do nothing but favor the good in man and discourage the bad.

A further point: in a profound sense, no social system, whether anarchist or statist, can work at all unless most people are "good" in the sense that they are not all hell-bent upon assaulting and robbing their neighbors. If everyone were so disposed, no amount of protection, whether State or private, could succeed in staving off chaos. Furthermore, the more that people are disposed to be peaceful and not aggress against their neighbors, the more successfully any social system will work, and the fewer resources will need to be devoted to police protection. The anarchist view holds that, given the "nature of man," given the degree of goodness or badness at any point of time, anarchism will maximize the opportunities for good and minimize the channels for the bad. The rest depends on the values held by the individual members of society. The only further point that need be made is that by eliminating the living example and the social legitimacy of the massive legalized crime of the State, anarchism will to a large extent promote peaceful values in the minds of the public.

We cannot of course deal here with the numerous arguments in favor of anarchism or against the State, moral, political, and economic. Nor can we take up the various goods and services now provided by the State, and show how private individuals and groups will be able to supply them far more efficiently on the free market. Here we can only deal with perhaps the most difficult area, the area where it is almost universally assumed that the State must exist and act, even if it is only a "necessary evil" instead of a positive good: the vital realm of defense or protection of person and property against aggression. Surely, it is universally asserted, the State is at least vitally necessary to provide police protection, the judicial resolution of disputes and enforcement of contracts, and the creation of the law itself that is to be enforced. My contention is that all of these admittedly necessary services of protection can be satisfactorily and efficiently supplied by private persons and institutions on the free market.

One important caveat before we begin the body of this paper: new proposals such as anarchism are almost always gauged against the implicit assumption that the present, or statist, system works to perfection. Any lacunae or difficulties with the picture of the anarchist society are considered net liabilities, and enough to dismiss anarchism out of hand. It is, in short, implicitly assumed that the State is doing its self-assumed job of protecting person and property to perfection. We cannot here go into the reasons why the State is bound to suffer inherently from grave flaws and inefficiencies in such a task. All we need do now is to point to the black and unprecedented record of the State through history: no combination of private marauders can possibly begin to match the State's unremitting record of theft, confiscation, oppression, and mass murder. No collection of Mafia or private bank robbers can begin to compare with all the Hiroshimas, Dresdens, and Lidices and their analogs through the history of mankind.

This point can be made more philosophically: it is illegitimate to compare the merits of anarchism and statism by starting with the present system as **the** implicit given and then critically examining only the anarchist alternative. What we must do is to begin at the zero point and then critically examine **both** suggested alternatives. Suppose, for example, that we were all suddenly dropped down on the earth de novo, and that we were all then confronted with the question of what societal arrangements to adopt. And suppose then that someone suggested:

We are all bound to suffer from those of us who wish to aggress against their fellow men. Let us then solve this problem of crime by handing all of our weapons to the Jones family, over there, by giving all of our ultimate power to settle disputes to that family. In that way, with their monopoly of coercion and of ultimate decision making, the Jones family will be able to protect each of us from each other.

I submit that this proposal would get very short shrift, except perhaps from the Jones family themselves. And yet this is precisely the common argument for the existence of the State. When we start from the zero point, as in the case of the Jones family, the question of "who will guard the guardians?" becomes not simply an abiding lacuna in the theory of the State but an overwhelming barrier to its existence.

A final **caveat**: the anarchist is always at a disadvantage in attempting to forecast the shape of the future anarchist society. For it is impossible for observers to predict voluntary social arrangements, including the provision of goods and services, on the free market. Suppose, for example, that this were the year 1874, and someone predicted that eventually there would be a radio manufacturing industry. To be able to make such a forecast successfully, does he have to be challenged to state immediately how many radio manufacturers there would be a century hence, how big they would be, where they would be located, what technology and marketing techniques they would use, etc.? Obviously, such a challenge would make no sense, and in a profound sense the same is true of those who demand a precise portrayal of the pattern of protection activities on the market. Anarchism advocates the dissolution of the State into social and market arrangements, and these arrangements are far more flexible and less predictable than political institutions. The most that we can do, then, is to offer broad guidelines and perspectives on the shape of a projected anarchist society.

One important point to make here is that the advance of modern technology makes anarchistic arrangements increasingly feasible. Take, for example, the case of lighthouses, where it is often charged that it is unfeasible for private lighthouse operators to row out to each ship to charge it for use of the light. Apart from the fact that this argument ignores the successful existence of private lighthouses in earlier days, e.g. in England in the eighteenth century, another vital consideration is that modern electronic technology makes charging each ship for the light far more feasible. Thus, the ship would have to have paid for an electronically controlled beam which could then be automatically turned on for those ships which had paid for the service.

II

Let us now turn to the problem of how disputes – in particular, disputes over alleged violations of person and property – would be resolved in an anarchist society. First, it should be noted that all disputes involve two parties: the plaintiff, the alleged victim of the crime or tort, and the defendant, the alleged aggressor. In many cases of broken contract, of course, each of the two parties alleging that the other is the culprit is at the same time a plaintiff and a defendant.

An important point to remember is that any society, be it statist or anarchist, has to have some way of resolving disputes that will gain a majority consensus in society. There would be no need for courts or arbitrators if everyone were omniscient, and knew instantaneously which persons were guilty of any given crime or violation of contract. Since none of us are omniscient, there has to be some method of deciding who is the criminal or lawbreaker which will gain legitimacy, in short whose decision will be accepted by the great majority of the public.

In the first place, a dispute may be resolved voluntarily between the two parties themselves, either unaided or with the help of a third mediator. This poses no problem, and will automatically be accepted by society at large. It is so accepted even now, much less in a society imbued with the anarchistic values of peaceful cooperation and agreement. Secondly and similarly, the two parties, unable to reach agreement, may decide to submit voluntarily to the decision of an arbitrator. This agreement may arise either after a dispute has arisen, or be provided for in advance in the original contract. Again, there is no problem in such an arrangement gaining legitimacy. Even in the present statist era, the notorious inefficiency and coercive and cumbersome procedures of the politically run government courts has led increasing numbers of citizens to turn to voluntary and expert arbitration for a speedy and harmonious settling of disputes.

Thus, William C. Wooldridge has written that:

Arbitration has grown to proportions that make the courts a secondary recourse in many areas and completely superfluous in others. The ancient fear of the courts that arbitration would "oust" them of their jurisdiction has been fulfilled with a vengeance the common-law judges probably never anticipated. Insurance companies adjust over fifty thousand claims a year among themselves through arbitration, and the American Arbitration Association (AAA), with headquarters in New York and twenty-five regional offices across the country, last year conducted over twenty-two thousand arbitrations. Its twenty-three thousand associates available to serve as arbitrators may outnumber the total number of judicial personnel . . . in the United States . . . Add to this the unknown number of individuals who arbitrate disputes within particular industries or in particular localities, without formal AAA affiliation, and the quantitatively secondary role of official courts begins to be apparent.[2]

Wooldridge adds the important point that, in addition to the speed of arbitration procedures **vis a vis** the courts, the arbitrators can proceed as experts in disregard of the official government law; in a profound sense, then, they serve to create a voluntary body of private law. "In other words," states Wooldridge:

. . . the system of extralegal, voluntary courts has progressed hand in hand with a body of private law; the rules of the state are circumvented by the same process that circumvents the forums established for the settlement of disputes over those rules. . . . In short, a private agreement between two people, a bilateral "law," has supplanted the official law. The writ of the sovereign has ceased to run, and for it is substituted a rule tacitly or explicitly agreed to by the parties.

Wooldridge concludes that "if an arbitrator can choose to ignore a penal damage rule or the statute of limitations applicable to the claim before him (and it is generally conceded that he has that power), arbitration can be viewed as a practically revolutionary instrument for self-liberation from the law . . ."[3]

It may be objected that arbitration only works successfully because the courts enforce the award of the arbitrator. Wooldridge points out, however, that arbitration was unenforceable in the American courts before 1920, but that this did not prevent voluntary arbitration from being successful and expanding in the United States and in England. He points, furthermore, to the successful operations of merchant courts since the Middle Ages, those courts which successfully developed the entire body of the law merchant. None of those courts possessed the power of enforcement. He might have added the private courts of shippers which developed the body of admiralty law in a similar way.

How then did these private, "anarchistic," and voluntary courts insure the acceptance of their decisions? By the method of social ostracism, and the refusal to deal any further with the offending merchant. This method of voluntary "enforcement," indeed, proved highly successful. Wooldridge writes that:

. . . the merchants' courts were voluntary, and if a man ignored their judgment, he could not be sent to jail . . . Nevertheless, it is apparent that ... [their] decisions were generally respected even by the losers; otherwise people would never have used them in the first place ... Merchants made their courts work simply by agreeing to abide by the results. The merchant who broke the understanding would not be sent to jail, to be sure, but neither would he long continue to be a merchant, for the compliance exacted by his fellows ... proved if anything more effective than physical coercion.[4]

Nor did this voluntary method fail to work in modern times. Wooldridge writes that it was precisely in the years before 1920, when arbitration awards could not be enforced in the courts:

> ... that arbitration caught on and developed a following in the American mercantile community. Its popularity, gained at a time when abiding by an agreement to arbitrate had to be as voluntary as the agreement itself, casts doubt on whether legal coercion was an essential adjunct to the settlement of most disputes. Cases of refusal to abide by an arbitrator's award were rare; one founder of the American Arbitration Association could not recall a single example. Like their medieval forerunners, merchants in the Americas did not have to rely on any sanctions other than those they could collectively impose on each other. One who refused to pay up might find access to his association's tribunal cut off in the future, or his name released to the membership of his trade association; these penalties were far more fearsome than the cost of the award with which he disagreed. Voluntary and private adjudications were voluntarily and privately adhered to, if not out of honor, out of the self-interest of businessmen who knew that the arbitral mode of dispute settlement would cease to be available to them very quickly if they ignored an award.[5]

It should also be pointed out that modern technology makes even more feasible the collection and dissemination of information about people's credit ratings and records of keeping or violating their contracts or arbitration agreements. Presumably, an anarchist society would see the expansion of this sort of dissemination of data and thereby facilitate the ostracism or boycotting of contract and arbitration violators.

How would arbitrators be selected in an anarchist society? In the same way as they are chosen now, and as they were chosen in the days of strictly voluntary arbitration: the arbitrators with the best reputation for efficiency and probity would be chosen by the various parties on the market. As in other processes of the market, the arbitrators with the best record in settling disputes will come to gain an increasing amount of business, and those with poor records will no longer enjoy clients, and have to shift to another line of endeavor. Here it must be emphasized that parties in dispute will seek out those arbitrators with the best reputation for both expertise and impartiality, and that inefficient or biased arbitrators will rapidly have to find another occupation.

Thus, the Tannehills emphasize:

> The advocates of government see initiated force (the legal force of government) as the only solution to social disputes. According to them, if everyone in society were not forced to use the same court system ... disputes would be insoluble. Apparently it doesn't occur to them that disputing parties are capable of freely choosing their own arbiters ... They have not realized that disputants would, in fact, be far better off if they could choose among competing arbitration agencies so that they could reap the benefits of competition and specialization. It should be obvious that a court system which has a monopoly guaranteed by the force of statutory law will not give as good quality service

as will free-market arbitration agencies which must compete for their customers . . .

Perhaps the least tenable argument for government arbitration of disputes is the one which holds that governmental judges are more impartial because they operate outside the market and so have no vested interests . . . owing political allegiance to government is certainly no guarantee of impartiality! A governmental judge is always impelled to be partial—in favor of the government, from whom he gets his pay and his power! On the other hand, an arbiter who sells his services in a free market knows that he must be as scrupulously honest, fair, and impartial as possible or no pair of disputants will buy his services to arbitrate their dispute. A free-market aribter depends for his livelihood on his skill and fairness at settling disputes. A governmental judge depends on political pull.[6]

If desired, furthermore, the contracting parties could provide in advance for a series of arbitrators:

It would be more economical and in most cases quite sufficient to have only one arbitration agency to hear the case. But if the parties felt that a further appeal might be necessary and were willing to risk the extra expense, they could provide for a succession of two or even more arbitration agencies. The names of these agencies would be written into the contract in order from the "first court of appeal" to the "last court of appeal." It would be neither necessary nor desirable to have one single, final court of appeal for every person in the society, as we have today in the United States Supreme Court.[7]

Arbitration, then poses little difficulty for a portrayal of the free society. But what of torts or crimes of aggression where there has been no contract? Or suppose that the breaker of a contract defies the arbitration award? Is ostracism enough? In short, how can courts develop in the free-market, anarchist society which will have the power to enforce judgments against criminals or contract-breakers?

In the wide sense, a defense service consists of guards or police who use force in defending person and property against attack, and judges or courts whose role is to use socially accepted procedures to determine **who** the criminals or tortfeasors are, as well as to enforce judicial awards, such as damages or the keeping of contracts. On the free market, many scenarios are possible on the relationship between the private courts and the police; they may be "vertically integrated," for example, or their services may be supplied by separate firms. Furthermore, it seems likely that police service will be supplied by insurance companies who will provide crime insurance to their clients. In that case, insurance companies will pay off the victims of crime or the breaking of contracts or arbitration awards, and then pursue the aggressors in court to recoup their losses. There is a natural market connection between insurance companies and defense services, since they need pay out less benefits in proportion as they are able to keep down the rate of crime.

Courts might either charge fees for their services, with the losers of cases obliged to pay court costs, or else they may subsist on monthly or yearly premiums by their clients, who may be either individuals or the police or insurance agencies. Suppose, for example, that Smith is an aggrieved party, either because he has been assaulted or robbed, or because an arbitration award in his favor has not been honored. Smith believes that Jones is the party guilty of the crime. Smith then goes to a court, Court A, of which he is a client, and brings charges against Jones as a defendant. In my view, the hallmark of an anarchist society is one where no man may legally compel someone who is not a convicted criminal to do anything, since that would be aggression against an innocent man's person or property. Therefore, Court A can only invite rather than subpoena Jones to attend his trial. Of course, if Jones refuses to appear or send a representative, his side of the case will not be heard. The trial of Jones proceeds. Suppose that Court A finds Jones innocent. In my view, part of the generally accepted Law Code of the anarchist society (on which see further below), is that this must end the matter, unless Smith can prove charges of gross incompetence or bias on the part of the court.

Suppose, next, that Court A finds Jones guilty. Jones might accept the verdict, either because he too is a client of the same court, because he knows he is guilty, or for some other reason. In that case, Court A proceeds to exercise judgment against Jones. Neither of these instances pose very difficult problems for our picture of the anarchist society. But suppose, instead, that Jones contests the decision; he, then, goes to his court, Court B, and the case is retried there. Suppose that Court B, too, finds Jones guilty. Again, it seems to me that the accepted Law Code of the anarchist society will assert that this ends the matter; both parties have had their say in courts which each has selected, and the decision for guilt is unanimous.

Suppose, however, the most difficult case: that Court B finds Jones innocent. The two courts, each subscribed to by one of the two parties, have split their verdicts. In that case, the two courts will submit the case to an appeals court, or arbitrator, which the two courts agree upon. There seems to be no real difficulty about the concept of an appeals court. As in the case of arbitration contracts, it seems very likely that the various private courts in the society will have prior agreements to submit their disputes to a particular appeals court. How will the appeals judges be chosen? Again, as in the case of arbitrators or of the first judges on the free market, they will be chosen for their expertise and reputation for efficiency, honesty and integrity. Obviously, appeals judges who are inefficient or biased will scarcely be chosen by courts who

will have a dispute. The point here is that there is no need for a legally established or institutionalized single, monopoly appeals court system, as States now provide. There is no reason why there cannot arise a multitude of efficient and honest appeals judges who will be selected by the disputant courts, just as there are numerous private arbitrators on the market today. The appeals court renders its decision, and the courts proceed to enforce it if, in our example, Jones is considered guilty – unless, of course, Jones can prove bias in some other court proceedings.

No society can have unlimited judicial appeals, for in that case there would be no point to having judges or courts at all. Therefore, every society, whether statist or anarchist, will have to have some socially accepted cut-off point for trials and appeals. My suggestion is the rule that the agreement **of any two courts** be decisive. "Two" is not an arbitrary figure, for it reflects the fact that there are two parties, the plaintiff and the defendant, to any alleged crime or contract dispute.

If the courts are to be empowered to enforce decisions against guilty parties, does this not bring back the State in another form and thereby negate anarchism? No, for at the beginning of this paper I explicitly defined anarchism in such a way as not to rule out the use of defensive force – force in defense of person and property – by privately supported agencies. In the same way, it is not bringing back the State to allow persons to use force to defend themselves against aggression, or to hire guards or police agencies to defend them.

It should be noted, however, that in the anarchist society there will be no "district attorney" to press charges on behalf of "society." Only the victims will press charges as the plaintiffs. If, then, these victims should happen to be absolute pacifists who are opposed even to defensive force, then they will simply not press charges in the courts or otherwise retaliate against those who have aggressed against them. In a free society that would be their right. If the victim should suffer from murder, then his heir would have the right to press the charges.

What of the Hatfield-and-McCoy problem? Suppose that a Hatfield kills a McCoy, and that McCoy's heir does not belong to a private insurance, police agency, or court, and decides to retaliate himself? Since, under anarchism there can be no coercion of the non-criminal, McCoy would have the perfect right to do so. No one may be compelled to bring his case to a court. Indeed, since the right to hire police or courts flows from the right of self-defense against aggression, it would be inconsistent and in contradiction to the very basis of the free society to institute such compulsion. Suppose, then, that the surviving McCoy finds what he believes to be the guilty Hatfield and kills him in turn? What then? This is fine, except that McCoy may have to worry about charges being brought against him by a surviving Hatfield. Here it must be emphasized that in the law of the anarchist society based on defense against aggression, the courts would not be able to proceed against McCoy if in fact he killed the right Hatfield. His problem would arise if the courts should find that he made a grievous mistake, and killed the wrong man; in that case, he in turn would be found guilty of murder. Surely, in most instances, individuals will wish to obviate such problems by taking their case to a court and thereby gain social acceptability for their defensive retaliation – not for the act of retaliation but for the correctness of deciding who the criminal in any given case might be. The purpose of the judicial process, indeed, is to find a way of general agreement on who might be the criminal or contract-breaker in any given case. The judicial process is not a good in itself; thus, in the case of an assassination, such as Jack Ruby's murder of Oswald, on public television, there is no need for a complex judicial process since the name of the murderer is evident to all.

Will not the possibility exist of a private court that may turn venal and dishonest, or of a private police force that turns criminal and extorts money by coercion? Of course such an event may occur, given the propensities of human nature. Anarchism is not a moral cure-all. But the important point is that market forces exist to place severe checks on such possibilities, especially in contrast to a society where a State exists. For, in the first place, judges, like arbitrators, will prosper on the market in proportion to their reputation for efficiency and impartiality. Secondly, on the free market important checks and balances exist against venal courts or criminal police forces. Namely, that there are competing courts and police agencies to whom the victims may turn for redress. If the "Prudential Police Agency" should turn outlaw and extract revenue from victims by coercion, the latter would have the option of turning to the "Mutual" or "Equitable" Police Agency for defense and for pressing charges against Prudential. These are the **genuine** "checks and balances" of the free market, genuine in contrast to the phony checks and balances of a State system, where all the alleged "balancing" agencies are in the hands of one monopoly government. Indeed, given the monopoly "protection service" of a State, what is there to prevent a State from using its monopoly channels of coercion to extort money from the public? What are the checks and limits of the State? None, except for the extremely difficult course of revolution against a Power with all of the guns in its hands. In fact, the State provides an easy, legitimated channel for crime and aggression, since it has its very being in the crime of tax-theft, and the coerced monopoly of "protection." It is the State, indeed, that functions as a mighty "protection racket" on a giant and massive scale. It is the State that says: "Pay us for your 'protection' or else." In the light of the massive and inherent activities of the State, the danger of a "protection racket" emerging from one or more private police agencies is relatively small indeed.

Moreover, it must be emphasized that a crucial element in the power of the State is its legitimacy in the eyes of the majority of the public, the fact that after centuries of propaganda, the depredations of the State are looked upon rather as benevolent services. Taxation is generally not seen as theft, nor war as mass murder, nor conscription as slavery. Should a private police agency turn outlaw, should "Prudential" become a protection racket, it would then lack the social legitimacy which the State has managed to accrue to itself over the centuries. "Prudential" would be seen by all as bandits, rather than as legitimate or divinely appointed "sovereigns" bent on promoting the "common good" or the "general welfare." And lacking such legitimacy, Prudential would have to face the wrath of the public and the defense and retaliation of the other private defense agencies, the police and courts, on the free market. Given these inherent checks and limits, a successful transformation from a free society to bandit rule becomes most unlikely. Indeed, historically, it has been very difficult for a State to arise to supplant a stateless society; usually, it has come about through external conquest rather than by evolution from within a society.

Within the anarchist camp, there has been much dispute on whether the private courts would have to be bound by a basic, common Law Code. Ingenious attempts have been made to work out a system where the laws or standards of decision-making by the courts would differ completely from one to another.[8] But in my view all would have to abide by the basic Law Code, in particular, prohibition of aggression against person and property, in order to fulfill our definition of anarchism as a system which provides no legal sanction for such aggression. Suppose, for example, that one group of people in society hold that all redheads are demons who deserve to be shot on sight. Suppose that Jones, one of this group, shoots Smith, a redhead. Suppose that Smith or his heir presses charges in a court, but that Jones' court, in philosophic agreement with Jones, finds him innocent therefore. It seems to me that in order to be considered legitimate, any court would have to follow

the basic libertarian law code of the inviolate right of person and property. For otherwise, courts might legally subscribe to a code which sanctions such aggression in various cases, and which to that extent would violate the definition of anarchism and introduce, if not the State, then a strong element of statishness or legalized aggression into the society.

But again I see no insuperable difficulties here. For in that case, anarchists, in agitating for their creed, will simply include in their agitation the idea of a general libertarian Law Code as part and parcel of the anarchist creed of abolition of legalized aggression against person or property in the society.

In contrast to the general law code, other aspects of court decisions could legitimately vary in accordance with the market or the wishes of the clients; e.g., the language the cases will be conducted in, the number of judges to be involved, etc.

There are other problems of the basic Law Code which there is no time to go into here: for example, the definition of just property titles or the question of legitimate punishment of convicted offenders — though the latter problem of course exists in statist legal systems as well.[9] The basic point, however, is that the State is not needed to arrive at legal principles or their elaboration: indeed, much of the common law, the law merchant, admiralty law, and private law in general grew up apart from the State, by judges not making the law but finding it on the basis of agreed upon principles derived either from custom or reason.[10] The idea that the State is needed to **make** law is as much a myth as that the State is needed to supply postal or police service.

Enough has been said here, I believe, to indicate that an anarchist system for settling disputes would be both viable and self-subsistent: that once adopted, it could work and continue indefinitely. **How to arrive** at that system is of course a very different problem, but certainly at the very least it will not likely come about unless people are convinced of its workability, are convinced, in short, that the State is not a **necessary** evil.

Notes

1 A paper delivered before the American Society for Political and Legal Philosophy, Washington, D. C., on Dec. 28, 1974.
2 William C. Wooldridge, **Uncle Sam, the Monopoly Man** (New Rochelle, N.Y.: Arlington House, 1970), p. 101.
3 **Ibid.**, pp. 103–4.
4 **Ibid.**, pp. 95–6.
5 **Ibid.**, pp. 100–1.
6 Morris and Linda Tannehill, **The Market for Liberty** (Lansing, Michigan: privately printed, 1970), pp. 65–7.
7 **Ibid.**, p. 68.
8 E.g. David Friedman, **The Machinery of Freedom** (New York: Harper & Row, 1973).
9 For an elaboration of these points, see Murray N. Rothbard, **For A New Liberty** (New York: Macmillan, 1973).
10 Thus, see Bruno Leoni, **Freedom and the Law** (Princeton, N.J.: D. Van Nostrand Co., 1961).

Chapter 6

Virginia Held

NON-CONTRACTUAL SOCIETY
A Feminist View

Virginia Held is Distinguished Professor of Philosophy at Columbia University, well-known for her work on feminist ethics and the morality of terrorism. In this essay (published in 1987), Held discusses the sexist assumptions that underlie traditional social contract theories, and begins to explore what political philosophy might look like if it took the perspective of women, especially mothers, more seriously. Such a change in perspective, she suggests, would lead to downgrading the importance of contractual morality and the model of "economic man" on which it is based, and a greater emphasis on the morality of care.

"economic man" to "morality of care"

Contemporary society is in the grip of contractual thinking. Realities are interpreted in contractual terms, and goals are formulated in terms of rational contracts. The leading current conceptions of rationality begin with assumptions that human beings are independent, self-interested, or mutually disinterested individuals; they then typically argue that it is often rational for human beings to enter into contractual relationships with each other.

On the side of description, assumptions characteristic of a contractual view of human relations underlie the dominant attempts to view social realities through the lenses of the social sciences.[1] They also underlie the principles upon which most persons in contemporary Western society claim their most powerful institutions to be founded. We are told that modern democratic states rest on a social contract,[2] that their economies should be thought of as a free market where producers and consumers, employers and employees make contractual agreements.[3] And

we should even, it is suggested, interpret our culture as a free market of ideas.[4]

On the side of prescription, leading theories of justice and equality, such as those of Rawls, Nozick, and Dworkin, suggest what social arrangements should be like to more fully reflect the requirements of contractual rationality.[5] And various philosophers claim that even morality itself is best understood in contractual terms.[6] The vast domain of rational choice theory, supposedly applicable to the whole range of human activity and experience, makes the same basic assumptions about individuals, contractual relations, and rationality, as are by now familiar in the social contract tradition.[7] And contractual solutions are increasingly suggested for problems which arise in areas not hitherto thought of in contractual terms, such as in dealing with unruly patients in treatment contexts, in controlling inmates in prisons, and even in bringing up children.

When subjected to examination, the assumptions and conceptions of contractual thinking seem highly questionable. As descriptions of reality they can be seriously misleading. Actual societies are the results of war, exploitation, racism, and patriarchy far more than of social contracts. Economic and political realities are the outcomes of economic strength triumphing over economic weakness more than of a free market. And rather than a free market of ideas, we have a culture in which the loudspeakers that are the mass media drown out the soft voices of free expression. As expressions of normative concern, moreover, contractual theories hold out an impoverished view of human aspiration.

To see contractual relations between self-interested or mutually disinterested individuals as constituting a paradigm of human relations is to take a certain historically specific conception of 'economic man' as representative of humanity. And it is, many feminists are beginning to agree, to overlook or to discount in very fundamental ways the experience of women.

I shall try in this paper to look at society from a thoroughly different point of view than that of economic man. I shall take the point of view of women, and especially of mothers, as the basis for trying to rethink society and its possible goals. Certainly there is no single point of view of women; the perspectives of women are potentially as diverse as those of men. But since the perspectives of women have all been to a large extent discounted, across the spectrum, I shall not try to deal here with diversity among such views, but rather to give voice to one possible feminist outlook.

The social contract tradition and bourgeois conceptions of rationality have already been criticized for some time from Marxian and other continental perspectives. These perspectives, however, usually leave out the perspective of mothers as fully as do those they criticize, so I shall not try to deal here with these alternatives either. I shall try instead to imagine what society would look like, for both descriptive and prescriptive purposes, if we replaced the paradigm of 'economic man' and substituted for it the paradigm of mother and child. I shall try to explore how society and our goals for it might appear if, instead of thinking of human relations as contractual, we thought of them as like relations between mothers and children. What would social relations look like? What would society look like if we would take the relation between mother and child as not just one relation among many, but as the *primary* social relation? And what sorts of aspirations might we have for such a society?

On the face of it, it seems plausible to take the relation between mother and child as the primary social relation, since before there could have been any self-sufficient, independent men in a hypothetical state of nature, there would have had to have been mothers, and the children these men would have had to have been. And the argument could be developed in terms of a conceptual as well as a causal primacy. However, let me anticipate a likely reaction and say before I begin this exploration that I doubt that the view I am going to present is the one we should end up with. I doubt that we should take any one relation as paradigmatic for all the others. And I doubt that morality should be based on any one type of human relation. In my recent book *Rights and Goods* I argue for different moral approaches for different contexts, and try to map out which approaches are suitable for which contexts.[8] Perhaps this book will turn out to be a mere stage in my thinking, and I will eventually suppose that relations between mothers and children should be thought of as primary, and as the sort of human relation all other human relations should resemble or reflect. But I am inclined at this point to think that we will continue to need conceptions of different types of relations for different domains, such as the domains of law, of economic activity, and of the family.

To think of relations between mothers and children as paradigmatic, however, may be an important stage to go through in reconstructing a view of human relationships that will be adequate from a feminist point of view. Since the image of rational economic man in contractual relations is pervasive in this society, and expanding constantly, it may be a useful endeavor to try to see everything in this different way, as if the primary social relation is that between mother and child, and as if all the others could and should be made over in the image of this one, or be embedded in a framework of such relations. In any case, if we pay attention to this neglected relation between mother and child, perhaps we can put a stop to the imperialism of the model of economic man, and assert with conviction that at least there are some or perhaps many domains where this model is definitely not appropriate. And perhaps we can show that morality must be as relevant to, and moral theory as appropriately based on, the context of mothering as the context of contracting. To the extent that some of our relations should be seen as contractual, we should recognize how essentially limited rather than general such relations are. And to the extent that some of morality should be understood in terms of what rational contractors would agree to, we should recognize that such a morality can only be suitable for a particular domain of human relations, and should not be supposed to be a model for morality in general.

Rational choice theorists point out that their theories are formulated for just those situations where individuals do seek to maximize their own interests and are uninterested in each others' interests. Their theories, they suggest, are not intended to deal with people in love. But the questions I am trying to raise in this paper have to do with how we ought to treat, conceptually, a great variety of human relations. Of course we *can*, theoretically, treat them *as* contractual, but *should* we do so? Is it plausible to do so? And when we ask these questions we can see that of course it is not only in special cases that persons can be and perhaps should be and often are bound together in social ties of a non-contractual kind.

To see society in terms of family rather than marketplace relationships is not new. Feudal conceptions, for instance, drew analogies between monarchs and the heads of households. But these were views based on relations between patriarchal fathers and their wives and children, not views of society seen in terms of mothering. To explore the latter is not to suggest a return to pre-contractual society, but to consider what further progress is needed.

Since it is the practice of mothering with which I shall be concerned in what follows, rather than with women in the biological sense, I shall use the term 'mothering person' rather than 'mother.' A 'mothering person' can be male or female. So I shall speak of 'mothering persons' in the same gender-neutral way that various writers now try to speak of 'rational contractors.' If men feel uncomfortable being referred to as, or even more so in being, 'mothering persons,' this may possibly mirror the discomfort many mothers feel adapting to the norms and practices, and language, of 'economic man.' *o snap!*

It is important to emphasize that I shall look at the practice of mothering not as it has in fact existed in any patriarchal society, but in terms of what the characteristic features of this practice would be without patriarchal domination. In method this may be comparable to what has been done in developing a concept of rational contracting. This concept of course developed while large segments of society were in fact still feudal, and of course actual human beings are not in fact fully rational. These realities have not prevented the contractual relation from being taken as paradigmatic.

Furthermore, it may well be that the concept of the mother/child relation that I shall develop is somewhat historically specific. But perhaps no concept can avoid being that. My aim is only to have the conception I shall try to develop capable of being considered an alternative to the conception of economic man in contractual relations, that is, of being no more historically limited, and contextually dependent, than that. To the extent that the mother/child relation will be an idealization, I hope it will not be more severely idealized than the relation between rational contractors that it is to replace; for the purposes of my exploration, it does not need to be less of an idealization.

I Women and Family

A first point to note in trying to imagine society from the point of view of women is that the contractual model was hardly ever applied, as either description or ideal, to women or to relations within the family. The family was imagined to be 'outside' the polis and 'outside' the market in a 'private' domain. This private domain was contrasted with the public domain, and with what, by the time of Hobbes and Locke, was thought of as the contractual domain of citizen and state and tradesman and market. Although women have always worked, and although both women and children were later pressed into work in factories, they were still thought of as outside the domain in which the contractual models of 'equal men' were developed. Women were not expected to demand equal rights either in the public domain or at home. Women were not expected to be 'economic men.' And children were simply excluded from the realm of what was being interpreted in contractual terms as distinctively human.

The clearest example of the extraordinary bias to which such views can lead can be seen in the writings of Rousseau. Moral principles were to be applied to men and to women in ways thoroughly inconsistent with each other. Rousseau argued that in the polity no man should surrender his freedom. He thought that government could be based on a social contract in which citizens under law will be as free as in the state of nature because they will give the law to themselves.[9] But, he argued, within the household, the man must rule and the woman must submit to this rule.[10] Rousseau maintained that women must be trained from the beginning to

serve and to submit to men. Since the essence of being fully human was for Rousseau being free from submission to the will of another, women were to be denied the essential condition for being fully human. And he thought that if women were accorded equality with men in the household (which was the only domain to be open to them) this would bring about the dissolution of society. Human society, Rousseau thought, was incompatible with extending the principles of contractual society to women and the family.

The contrast, in this view, is total: complete freedom and equality in the exclusively male polity; absolute male authority and female submission in the household. And Rousseau seems not to have considered the implications of such a view. If one really believes that two persons in a household, with ties of affection and time for discussion, can never reach decisions by consensus, or by taking turns at deciding, but must always have one person in full authority to have the final word, what hope could there possibly be for the larger democratic, participatory, consensual political life Rousseau so eloquently advocated? On the other hand, if decisions in the political realm *can* be arrived at in such a way that the will of no man needs to be overpowered, as Rousseau thought, why cannot such concern for avoiding coercion be extended to relations between men and women in the family?

One way in which the dominant patterns of thought have managed to overlook such inconsistencies has been to see women as primarily mothers, and mothering as a primarily biological function. Then it has been supposed that while contracting is a specifically human activity, women are engaged in an activity that is not specifically human. Women have accordingly been thought to be closer to nature than men, to be enmeshed in a biological function involving processes more like those in which other animals are involved than like the rational contracting of distinctively human 'economic man.' The total or

fire!

relative exclusion of women from the domain of voluntary contracting has then been thought to be either inevitable or appropriate.

The view that women are more governed by biology than are men is still prevalent. It is as questionable as many other traditional misinterpretations of women's experience. Human mothering is an extremely different activity from the mothering engaged in by other animals. It is as different from the mothering of other animals as is the work and speech of men different from the 'work' and 'speech' of other animals. Since humans are also animals, one should not exaggerate the differences between humans and other animals. But to whatever extent it is appropriate to recognize a difference between 'man' and other animals, so would it be appropriate to recognize a comparable difference between human mothering and the mothering of other animals.

Human mothering shapes language and culture, and forms human social personhood. Human mothering develops morality, it does not merely transmit techniques of survival; impressive as the latter can be, they do not have built into them the aims of morality. Human mothering teaches consideration for others based on moral concern; it does not merely follow and bring the child to follow instinctive tendency. Human mothering creates autonomous persons; it does not merely propagate a species. It can be fully as creative an activity as most other human activities; to create new persons, and new types of persons, is surely as creative as to make new objects, products, or institutions. Human mothering is no more 'natural' than any other human activity. It may include many dull and repetitive tasks, as does farming, industrial production, banking, and work in a laboratory. But degree of dullness has nothing to do with degree of 'naturalness.' In sum, human mothering is as different from animal mothering as humans are from animals.

On a variety of grounds there are good reasons to have mothering become an activity performed by men as well as by women.[11] We may wish to continue to use the term 'mothering' to designate the activity, in recognition of the fact that it has been overwhelmingly women who have engaged in this activity,[12] and because for the foreseeable future it is the point of view of women, including women engaged in mothering, which should be called on to provide a contrast with the point of view of men. A time may come when a term such as 'the nurturing of children' would be preferable to 'mothering.'[13]

Clearly, the view that contractual relations are a model for human relations generally is especially unsuitable for considering the relations between mothering persons and children. It stretches credulity even further than most philosophers can tolerate to imagine babies as little rational calculators contracting with their mothers for care. Of course the fundamental contracts have always been thought of as hypothetical rather than real. But one cannot imagine hypothetical babies contracting either. And mothering persons, in their care of children, demonstrate hardly any of the 'trucking' or trading instinct claimed by Adam Smith to be the most characteristic aspect of human nature.[14] If the epitome of what it is to be human is thought to be a disposition to be a rational contractor, human persons creating other human persons through the processes of human mothering are overlooked. And human children developing human personhood are not recognized as engaged in a most obviously human activity.

David Hume, whom some admire for having moral views more compatible with 'women's moral sense' than most philosophers have had,[15] had the following to say about the passion of avarice: 'Avarice, or the desire of gain, is a universal passion which operates at all times, in all places, and upon all persons.'[16] Surely we can note that in the relation between mothering person and child, not only as it should be but often enough as it is, avarice is hard to find. One can uncover very many emotions in the relation, but the avarice that fuels the model of 'economic man' with his rational interest is not prominent among them.

There is an exchange in Charlotte Perkins Gilman's *Herland* that illustrates the contrast between the motives ascribed to rational economic man building contractual society, and those central to the practice of mothering. *Herland* is an imaginary society composed entirely of women. They reproduce by parthenogenesis, and there are only mothers and daughters in the society. Everything is arranged to benefit the next generation and the society has existed peacefully for hundreds of years, with a high level of technological advancement but without any conception of a 'survival of the fittest' ethic. Three young men from twentieth century America manage to get to Herland. They acknowledge that in Herland there are no wars, no kings, no priests, no aristocracies, that the women are all like sisters to each other and work together not by competition but by united action. But they argue that things are much better at home. In one exchange they try to explain how important it is to have competition. One of them expounds on the advantages of competition, on how it develops fine qualities, saying that 'without it there would be "no stimulus to industry."' [17] He says competition is necessary to provide an incentive to work; 'competition,' he explains, 'is the motor power' of society.

The women of Herland are genuinely curious and good-naturedly skeptical, as they so often are in Gilman's novel. 'Do you mean,' they ask, 'that no mother would work for her children without the stimulus of competition?' In Herland, the entire, industrious society works on the strong motivation of making the society better for the children. As one women explains, 'The children in this country are the one center and focus of all our thoughts. Every step of our advance is always considered in its effects on them. . . . You see, we are *Mothers*.' [18]

Of course, this is an idealized picture of mothering. But I am contrasting it with an idealized picture of rationally contracting. Quite probably we would not want a society devoted entirely to mothering. But then we might not want a society devoted entirely to better bargains either. In developing these suggestions, it is instructive to see what is most seriously overlooked by a contractual view of society, and to see how important what is overlooked is.

II Family and Society

In recent years, many feminists have demanded that the principles of justice and freedom and equality on which it is claimed that democracy rests be extended to women and the family. They have demanded that women be treated as equals in the polity, in the workplace, and, finally, at home. They have demanded, in short, to be accorded full rights to enter freely the contractual relations of modern society. They have asked that these be extended to take in the family.

But some feminists are now considering whether the arguments should perhaps, instead, run the other way. Instead of importing into the household principles derived from the marketplace, perhaps we should export to the wider society the relations suitable for mothering persons and children. This approach suggests that just as relations between persons within the family should be based on concern and caring, rather than on egoistic or non-tuistic contracts, so various relations in the wider society should be characterized by more care and concern and openness and trust and human feeling than are the contractual bargains that have developed so far in political and economic life, or even than are aspired to in contractarian prescriptions. Then, the household instead of the marketplace might provide a model for society. Of course what we would mean by the household would not be the patriarchal household which was, before the rise of contractual thinking, also thought of as a model of society. We would now mean the relations between mothering persons and children without the patriarch. We would take our conception of the post-patriarchal family as a model.

The model of the social contract was certainly an improvement over that of political patriarchy. Locke's prescriptions for political order are so clearly better than Filmer's that almost no one still reads the arguments made by philosophers such as Filmer, whose views were completely dominant until replaced by those of contractualists like Locke. Filmer thought that political authority should be based on correct inheritance: God gave the world to Adam, and authority to govern was transferred from Adam through the ancient patriarchs to the legitimate monarchs of any historical period. Democracy, to Filmer, was dangerous nonsense. Of course no feminist would wish to go back to such views as Filmer's, nor to those of Aristotle if interpreted as holding that the polity should be a version on a grander scale of the patriarchal household. But to consider whether we should generalize the relation between mothering person and child to any regions beyond the home is to consider generalizing a quite different relation from that which has existed within the patriarchal household, even between mothers and children within patriarchal society. It is to explore what relations between mothering persons and children should be in non-patriarchal societies, and to consider how a transformed household might contribute to a transformed society.

These questions lead us to focus on the family as a social institution of the utmost importance. The family is a set of relations creating human persons. Societies are composed of families. And a family is a small society. The family is undergoing profound change at the present time, and the attendant upheavals in the personal lives of many persons hold out the promise of remarkable social change, quite possibly for the better.

The family is only beginning to receive the central attention from feminists that it deserves, partly because feminist theory is still in such exploratory stages, trying to understand all at once the multiplicity of forces – social, economic, political, legal, psychological, sexual, biological, and cultural – that affect women. Multiple causes shape the sex/gender structures within which human females and males develop feminine and masculine characteristics and come to occupy the roles that existing societies designate as female and male. We need to understand empirically how this happens. We also need normative theories of the family. Jane Flax, surveying recent feminist writing on the family, writes that to develop alternatives to the oppressive relations that now prevail, we need to think through:

> . . . what kinds of child care are best for parents and children; what family structures are best for persons at various stages of the life cycle . . .; how the state and political processes should affect families; and how work and the organization of production should be transformed to support whatever family forms are preferred.[19]

It is an enormous task, but recent years have provided more new thought on these subjects than many previous decades.[20]

The major question remains: what are the possibilities of remaking society by remaking what have been thought of as 'personal' relations? Societies are composed of persons in relation to one another. The 'personal' relations among persons are the most affective and influential in many ways. But the extent to which they are central to wider social relations, or could possibly provide a model for social and political relations of a kind that has been thought of as 'public,' remains an open question.

Western liberal democratic thought has been built on the concept of the 'individual' seen as a theoretically isolatable entity. This entity can assert interests, have rights, and enter into contractual relations with other entities. But this individual is not seen as related to other individuals in inextricable or intrinsic ways. This individual is assumed to be motivated primarily by a desire to pursue his own interests, though he can recognize the need to agree to contractual restraints on the ways everyone may pursue their interests. To the extent that groups have been dealt with at all, they have been treated *as* individuals.

The difficulties of developing trust and cooperation and society itself on the sands of self-interested individuals pursuing their own gain are extreme.[21] Contractual society is society perpetually in danger of breaking down. Perhaps what are needed for even adequate levels of social cohesion are persons tied together by relations of concern and caring and empathy and trust rather than merely by contracts it may be in their interests to disregard. Any enforcement mechanisms put in place to keep persons to their contracts will be as subject to disintegration as the contracts themselves; at some point contracts must be embedded in social relations that are non-contractual.

The relation between mothering person and child, hardly understandable in contractual terms, may be a more fundamental human relation, and a more promising one on which to build our recommendations for the future, than is any relation between rational contractors. Perhaps we should look to the relation between mothering person and child for suggestions of how better to describe such society as we now have. And perhaps we should look to it especially for a view of a future more fit for our children than a global battleground for rational, egoistic entities trying, somehow, to restrain their antagonisms by fragile contracts.

The Marxian view of the relations between human beings is in various ways more satisfactory than the contractual one and more capable of accounting for social relations in general. However, the Marxian view of our history, split into classes and driven by economic forces, is hardly more capable of encompassing, and does not lend itself to reflecting, the experience of the relation between mothering person and child either. So I will continue to develop here the contrast between the relation between mothering person and child on the one hand, and the contractual exchanges of 'economic man' on the other.

III The Mother/Child Relation

Let us examine in more detail the relation between mothering person and child. A first aspect of the relation that we can note is the extent to which it is not voluntary and, for this reason among others, not contractual. The ties that bind mothering person and child are affectional and solicitous on the one hand, and emotional and dependent on the other. The degree to which bearing and caring for children has been voluntary for most mothers throughout most of history has been extremely limited; it is still quite limited for most mothering persons. The relation *should* be voluntary for the mothering person but it cannot possibly be voluntary for the young child, and it can only become, gradually, slightly more voluntary.

A woman can have decided voluntarily to have a child, but once that decision has been made, she will never again be unaffected by the fact that she has brought this particular child into existence. And even if the decision to have a child is voluntary, the decision to have this particular child, for either parent, cannot be. Technological developments can continue to reduce the uncertainties of childbirth, but unpredictable aspects are likely to remain great for most parents. Unlike that contract where buyer and seller can know what is being exchanged, and which is void if the participants cannot know what they are agreeing to, a parent cannot know what a particular child will be like. And children are totally unable to choose their parents and, for many years, any of their caretakers.

The recognition of how limited are the aspects of voluntariness in the relation between mothering person and child may help us to gain a closer approximation to reality in our understanding of most human relations, especially at a global level, than we can gain from imagining the purely voluntary trades entered into by rational economic contractors to be characteristic of human relations in other domains.

Society may impose certain reciprocal obligations: on parents to care for children when the children are young, and on children to care for parents when the parents are old. But if there is any element of a bargain in the relation between mothering person and child, it is very different from the bargain supposedly characteristic of the marketplace. If a parent thinks 'I'll take care of you now so you'll take care of me when I'm old,' it must be based, unlike the contracts of political and economic bargains, on enormous trust and on a virtual absence of enforcement.[22] And few mothering persons have any such exchange in mind when they engage in the activities of mothering. At least the bargain would only be resorted to when the callousness or poverty of the society made the plight of the old person desperate. This is demonstrated in survey after survey; old persons certainly hope not to have to be a burden on their children.[23] And they prefer social arrangements that will allow them to refuse to cash in on any such bargain. So the intention and goal of mothering is to give of one's care without obtaining a return of a self-interested kind. The emotional satisfaction of a mothering person is a satisfaction in the well-being and happiness of another human being, and a satisfaction in the health of the relation between the two persons, not the gain that results from an egoistic bargain. The motive behind the activity of mothering is thus entirely different from that behind a market transaction. And so is, perhaps even more clearly, the motive behind the child's project of growth and development.

A second aspect of the contrast between market relations and relations between mothering person and child is found in the qualities of permanence and non-replaceability. The market makes of everything, even human labor and artistic expression and sexual desire, a commodity to be bought and sold, with one unit of economic value replaceable by any other of equivalent value. To the extent that political life reflects these aspects of the market, politicians are replaceable and political influence is bought and sold. Though rights may be thought of as outside the economic market, in contractual thinking they are seen as inside the wider market of the social contract, and can be traded against each other. But the ties between parents and children are permanent ties, however strained or slack they become at times. And no person within a family should be a commodity to any other. Although various persons may participate in mothering a given child, and a given person may mother many children, still no child and no mothering person is to the other a merely replaceable commodity. The extent to which more of our attitudes, for instance toward our society's cultural productions, should be thought of in these terms rather than in the terms of the marketplace, should be considered.

A third aspect of the relation between mothering person and child that may be of interest is the insight it provides for our notions of equality. It shows us unmistakably that equality is not equivalent to having equal legal rights. All feminists are committed to equality and to equal rights in contexts where rights are what are appropriately at issue. But in many contexts, concerns other than rights are more salient and appropriate. And the equality that is at issue in the relation between mothering person and child is the equal consideration of persons, not a legal or contractual notion of equal rights.

Parents and children should not have equal rights in the sense that what they are entitled to decide or to do or to have should be the same. A family of several small children, an adult or two, and an aged parent should not, for instance, make its decisions by majority vote in most cases.[24] But every member of a family is worthy of equal respect and consideration. Each person in a family is as important as a person as every other.

Sometimes the interests of children have been thought in some sense to count for more, justifying 'sacrificing for the children.' Certainly, the interests of mothers have often counted for less than those of either fathers or children. Increasingly, we may come to think that the interests of all should count equally, but we should recognize that this claim is appropriately invoked only if the issue should be thought of as one of interest. Often, it should not. Much of the time we can see that calculations of interest, and of equal interests, are as out of place as are determinations of equal rights. Both the rights and the interests of individuals seen as separate entities, and equality between them all, should not exhaust our moral concerns. The flourishing of shared joy, of mutual affection, of bonds of trust and hope between mothering persons and children can illustrate this as clearly as anything can. Harmony, love, and cooperation cannot be broken down into individual benefits or burdens. They are goals we ought to share and relations *between* persons. And although the degree of their intensity may be different, many and various relations *between* persons are important also at the level of communities or societies. We can consider, of a society, whether the relations between its members are trusting and mutually supportive, or suspicious and hostile. To focus only on contractual relations and the gains and losses of individuals obscures these often more important relational aspects of societies.

A fourth important feature of the relation between mothering person and child is that we obviously do not fulfill our obligations by merely leaving people alone. If one leaves an infant alone he will starve. If one leaves a two-year-old alone she will rapidly harm herself. The whole tradition that sees respecting others as constituted by non-interference with them is most effectively shown up as inadequate. It assumes that people can fend for themselves and provide

through their own initiatives and efforts what they need. This Robinson Crusoe image of 'economic man' is false for almost everyone, but it is totally and obviously false in the case of infants and children, and recognizing this can be salutary. It can lead us to see very vividly how unsatisfactory are those prevalent political views according to which we fulfill our obligations merely by refraining from interference. We ought to acknowledge that our fellow citizens, and fellow inhabitants of the globe, have moral rights to what they need to live – to the food, shelter, and medical care that are the necessary conditions of living and growing – and that when the resources exist for honoring such rights there are few excuses for not doing so. Such rights are not rights to be left to starve unimpeded. Seeing how unsatisfactory rights merely to be left alone are as an interpretation of the rights of children may help us to recognize a similar truth about other persons. And the arguments – though appropriately in a different form – can be repeated for interests as distinct from rights.[25]

A fifth interesting feature of the relation between mothering person and child is the very different view it provides of privacy. We come to see that to be in a position where others are not making demands on us is a rare luxury, not a normal state. To be a mothering person is to be subjected to the continual demands and needs of others. And to be a child is to be subjected to the continual demands and expectations of others. Both mothering persons and children need to extricate themselves from the thick and heavy social fabric in which they are entwined in order to enjoy any pockets of privacy at all.

Here the picture we form of our individuality and the concept we form of a 'self' is entirely different from the one we get if we start with the self-sufficient individual of the 'state of nature.' If we begin with the picture of rational contractor entering into agreements with others, the 'natural' condition is seen as one of individuality and privacy, and the problem is the building of society and government. From the point of view of the relation between mothering person and child, on the other hand, the problem is the reverse. The starting condition is an enveloping tie, and the problem is individuating oneself. The task is to carve out a gradually increasing measure of privacy in ways appropriate to a constantly shifting interdependency. For the child, the problem is to become gradually more independent. For the mothering person, the problem is to free oneself from an all-consuming involvement. For both, the progression is from society to greater individuality rather than from self-sufficient individuality to contractual ties.

Psychology and psychoanalysis have long been interested in the process by which children develop and individuate themselves. Especially relevant now are feminist explorations of the different development of a sense of self in boys and in girls, and of a possibly different moral sense. Philosophers are just beginning to consider the normative issues involved. And social philosophers are just beginning to consider what we should think about social relations if we take women as our starting point. That we need not start with the patriarchal family in forming our concepts of society has been recognized for several centuries, ever since Locke won out over Filmer. That it might be instructive to begin with the point of view of women, and within that with the relation between mothering person and child, to try to reconceptualize society and our goals for better societies, is a new idea. A new concept of the 'self' may be at the heart of such reconceptualizations. And we should expect that a new concept of 'self' or 'person' should have as much significance for our views of politics and society, and for our conceptualizations of the supposedly 'impersonal' and 'public' domain distinct from the supposedly 'personal' and 'private' sphere of the family, as has the concept of the self as rational calculator and the conceptualization of society as contractual. The same real 'persons' can act in and inhabit

both marketplace and household contexts. It is open to them to decide what sorts of institutions to encourage for the sake of what sorts of persons.

A sixth aspect of the relation between mothering person and child which is noteworthy is the very different view of power it provides. We are accustomed to thinking of power as something that can be wielded by one person over another, as a means by which one person can bend another to his will. An ideal has been to equalize power so that agreements can be forged and conflicts defused. But consider now the very different view of power in the relation between mothering person and child. The superior power of the mothering person over the child is relatively useless for most of what the mothering person aims to achieve in bringing up the child. The mothering person seeks to empower the child to act responsibly, she neither wants to 'wield' power nor to defend herself against the power 'wielded' by the child. The relative powerlessness of the child is largely irrelevant to most of the project of growing up. When the child is physically weakest, as in infancy and illness, the child can 'command' the greatest amount of attention and care from the mothering person because of the seriousness of the child's needs.

The mothering person's stance is characteristically one of caring, of being vulnerable to the needs and pains of the child, and of fearing the loss of the child before the child is ready for independence. It is not characteristically a stance of domination. The child's project is one of developing, of gaining ever greater control over his or her own life, of relying on the mothering person rather than of submitting to superior strength. Of course the relation may in a degenerate form be one of domination and submission, but this only indicates that the relation is not what it should be. In a form in which the relation between mothering person and child is even adequately exemplified, the conceptions of power with which we are familiar, from Hobbes and Locke to Hegel and Marx, are of little use for understanding the aspects of power involved in the relation.[26] The power of a mothering person to empower others, to foster transformative growth, is a different sort of power than that of a stronger sword or dominant will. And the power of a child to call forth tenderness and care is perhaps more different still.

IV Mothering and Moral Theory

A final aspect of the relation between mothering person and child about which I would like to speculate is what a focus on this relation might imply for our views of morality itself, and of ethical theory itself.

Hobbes thought we could build society on the equal vulnerability of every man to the sword of his fellows. Women have never fit into that picture. We are more vulnerable to the sword. And yet the sword is powerless to create new wielders of it. Only the power of mothers can in the long run triumph. But the power of mothers is continually being eclipsed by the power of children.

The vulnerability of men may bring them to seek peace and to covenant against violence. We can hope for whatever progress can be made in curbing the murderous conflicts, tempered by truces and treaties, to which this has led, though our expectations under current conditions must realistically be very modest.

But let us speculate about a different vulnerability and a different development. Mothering persons are vulnerable to the demands and needs of children. We do not know if this is instinctive or innate, or not. Some claim that women lack a mothering instinct. Others claim that the experiences of carrying a child, of laboring and suffering to give birth, of suckling, inevitably cause mothers to be especially sensitive to the cries and needs of a child. Others claim that fathers, placed in the position of being the only persons capable of responding to the needs of a child, develop similar responsiveness. Whatever the truth, one can admit that no one can become a mothering person without becoming sensitive to the needs of relatively helpless or less powerful others. And to become thus sensitive is to become vulnerable. If the vulnerability is chosen, so much the better. Mothering persons become in this way vulnerable to the claims of morality.

It is not, however, the morality of following abstract, universal rules so much as the morality of being responsive to the needs of actual, particular others in relations with us. The traditional view, reasserted in the psychological studies of Lawrence Kohlberg, that women are less likely than men to be guided by the highest forms of morality, would only be plausible if morality were no more than the abstract and rational rules of pure and perfect principle.[27] For traditional morality, increasingly recognizable as developed from a male point of view, there seems to be either the pure principle of the rational law-giver, or the self-interest of the individual contractor. There is the unreal universality of *all*, or the real *self* of individual interest.

Both views, however, lose sight of acting for particular others in actual contexts. Mothering persons cannot lose sight of the particularity of the child being mothered nor of the actuality of the circumstances in which the activity is taking place. Mothering persons may tend to resist harming or sacrificing those particular others for the sake of abstract principles or total faith; on the other hand, it is for the sake of *others*, or for the sake of relationships between persons, rather than to further their own interests, that such resistance is presented by mothering persons. Morality, for mothering persons, must guide us in our relations with actual, particular children, enabling them to develop their own lives and commitments. For mothering persons, morality can never seem adequate if it offers no more than ideal rules for hypothetical situations: morality must connect with the actual context of real, particular others in need. At the same time, morality, for mothering persons, cannot possibly be a mere bargain between rational contractors. That morality in this context could not be based on self-interest or mutual disinterest directly is obvious; that a contractual escape is unavailable or inappropriate is clear enough.

The morality that could offer guidance for those engaged in mothering might be a superior morality to those available at present. It would be a morality based on caring and concern for actual human others, and it would have to recognize the limitations of both egoism and perfect justice.[28] When we would turn to the social and political theories that would be compatible with such a view of morality, we would see that they would have to be very different not only from the patriarchal models of pre-contractual conceptions, but also from the contractual models that so dominate current thinking. Contractual relations would not be ruled out, but they would cease to seem paradigmatic of human relations, and the regions within which they could be thought to be justified would be greatly reduced.

V The Child's Perspective

What about the point of view of the child? A most salient characteristic of the relation between mothering person and child is the child's relative powerlessness. The child cannot possibly rely on the Hobbesian safeguard of the equal vulnerability of the caretaker. Not even when the caretaker is asleep is she vulnerable to the sword of the small child, and it will be years, if ever, before the child can match the caretaker in even physical strength, let alone social and economic and psychological power. Whatever claims the child makes against a mothering person must be based on something else than superior strength, and the child should come to trust the restraint of one who could but does not wish to cause the child harm.

The child in relation to the mothering person is permanently in the best possible position from which to recognize that right is not equivalent to might, that power, including the power to teach and enforce a given morality, is not equivalent to

morality itself. Becoming a person is not so much learning a morality that is being taught as it is developing the ability to decide for oneself what morality requires of one. Children characteristically go beyond the mothering persons in their lives, becoming autonomous beings. They do not characteristically then respond to the mothering persons they leave behind with proposals for better bargains for themselves now that they have the power to enforce their terms. The relation between mothering person and child is such that disparities of power are given. Though the positions may reverse themselves, unequal power is almost ever present. But it is often also irrelevant to the relation.

When young men are invited to enter the public realm of contractual relations they are encouraged to forget their past lack of power and to assume a position of equality or superiority. But we should probably none of us ever forget what it is like to lack power. Taking the relation between child and mothering person as the primary social relation might encourage us to remember the point of view of those who cannot rely on the power of arms to uphold their moral claims. It might remind us of the distinction between the morality that, as developed autonomous persons, we come to construct for ourselves, and the moral injunctions which those with superior force can hold us to. Though I cannot develop these suggestions further in this particular paper, much more needs to be felt from the point of view of children.

VI Models for Society

In an earlier paper called 'Marx, Sex, and the Transformation of Society,'[29] I looked at the relation between man and woman, if it could be transformed by love into a relation of mutual concern and respect, as a possible model for transformed relations in the wider society. It now seems to me that the relation between man and woman, especially as transformed in the way I suggested, is more special and more limited, as well as far more distant and uncertain, than the relation between mothering person and child. The latter relation seems especially worth exploring to see what implications and insights it might suggest for a transformed society.

There are good reasons to believe that a society resting on no more than bargains between self-interested or mutually disinterested individuals will not be able to withstand the forces of egoism and dissolution pulling such societies apart. Although there may be some limited domains in which rational contracts are the appropriate form of social relations, as a foundation for the fundamental ties which ought to bind human beings together, they are clearly inadequate. Perhaps we can learn from a non-patriarchal household better than from further searching in the marketplace what the sources might be for justifiable trust, cooperation, and caring.

On the first occasion when I spoke about considering the relation between mothering person and child as the primary social relation, a young man in the audience asked: but in society, by which he meant society outside the family, who are the mothers and who are the children? It was meant as a hostile question, but it is actually a very good question. The very difficulty so many persons have in imagining an answer may indicate how distorted are the traditional contractual conceptions. Such persons can imagine human society on the model of 'economic man,' society built on a contract between rationally self-interested persons, because these are the theories they have been brought up with. But they cannot imagine society resembling a group of persons tied together by on going relations of caring and trust between persons in positions such as those of mothers and children where, as adults, we would sometimes be one and sometimes the other. Suppose now we ask: In the relation between mothering person and child, who are the contractors? Where is the rational self-interest? The model of 'economic man' makes no

sense in this context. Anyone in the social contract tradition who has noticed the relation of mothering person and child at all has supposed it to belong to some domain outside the realm of the 'free market' and outside the 'public' realm of politics and the law. Such theorists have supposed the context of mothering to be of much less significance for human history and of much less relevance for moral theory than the realms of trade and government, or they have imagined mothers and children as somehow outside human society altogether in a region labelled 'nature,' and engaged wholly in 'reproduction.' But mothering is at the heart of human society.

If the dynamic relation between mothering person and child is taken as the primary social relation, then it is the model of 'economic man' that can be seen to be deficient as a model for society and morality, and unsuitable for all but a special context. A domain such as law, if built on no more than contractual foundations, can then be recognized as one limited domain among others; law protects some moral rights when people are too immoral or weak to respect them without the force of law. But it is hardly a majestic edifice that can serve as a model for morality. Neither can the domain of politics, if built on no more than self-interest or mutual disinterest, provide us with a model with which to understand and improve society and morality. And neither, even more clearly, can the market itself.

When we explore the implications of these speculations we may come to realize that instead of seeing the family as an anomalous island in a sea of rational contracts composing economic and political and social life, perhaps it is instead 'economic man' who belongs on a relatively small island surrounded by social ties of a less hostile, cold, and precarious kind.

Notes

1 As Carole Pateman writes, 'One of the most striking features of the past two decades is the extent to

which the assumptions of liberal individualism have permeated the whole of social life.' Carole Pateman, *The Problem of Political Obligation: A Critique of Liberal Theory* (Berkeley: University of California Press 1985), 182–3. All those fields influenced by rational choice theory – and that includes most of the social sciences – thus 'hark back to classical liberal contract doctrines,' Pateman writes, 'and claims that social order is founded on the interactions of self-interested, utility-maximizing individuals, protecting and enlarging their property in the capitalist market' (183).

2   E.g. Thomas Hobbes, *Leviathan*, C.B. Macpherson, ed. (Baltimore: Penguin 1971); John Locke, *Two Treatises of Government*, Peter Laslett, ed. (New York: Mentor 1965); Jean-Jacques Rousseau, *The Social Contract*, Charles Frankel, ed. (New York: Hafner 1947); the U. S. Declaration of Independence; and of course a literature too vast to mention. As Carole Pateman writes of this tradition, 'a corollary of the liberal view . . . is that social contract theory is central to liberalism. Paradigmatically, contract is the act through which two free and equal individuals create social bonds, or a collection of such individuals creates the state' (180).

3   E.g. Adam Smith, *The Wealth of Nations*, M. Lerner, ed. (New York: Random House 1937) and virtually the whole of classical and neo-classical economics.

4   The phrase has been entrenched in judicial and social discussion since Oliver Wendell Holmes used it in *Abrams v. United States* (250 U.S. 616, 630 [1919]).

5   E.g. John Rawls, *A Theory of Justice* (Cambridge, MA: Harvard University Press 1971); Robert Nozick, *Anarchy, State, and Utopia* (New York: Basic Books 1974); and Ronald Dworkin, *Taking Rights Seriously* (Cambridge, MA: Harvard University Press 1977).

6   E.g. David A. J. Richards, *A Theory of Reasons for Action* (New York: Oxford University Press 1971); and David Gauthier, *Morals By Agreement* (New York: Oxford University Press 1986).

7   For a recent sample, see the symposium 'Explanation and Justification in Social Theory,' in *Ethics* 97, 1.

8   Virginia Held, *Rights and Goods: Justifying Social Action* (New York: Free Press/Macmillan 1984).

9   J.-J. Rousseau, *The Social Contract*.

10   J.-J. Rousseau, *Emile*, trans. B. Foxley (New York: Dutton 1911).

11   See especially Nancy Chodorow, *The Reproduction of Mothering: Psychoanalysis and the Sociology of Gender* (Berkeley, CA: University of California Press 1978); and Joyce Trebilcot, ed., *Mothering: Essays in Feminist Theory* (Totowa, NJ: Rowman and Allanheld 1984).

12   See e.g. Susan Peterson, 'Against "Parenting," ' in Trebilcot, *Mothering*.

13   By then 'parenting' might also be acceptable to those who find it presently misleading.

14   Adam Smith, Book I, Chap. II.

15   See, e.g., Annette Baier, 'Hume: The Women's Moral Theorist?' in *Women and Moral Theory*, Eva Kittay and Diana Meyers, eds. (Totowa, NJ: Rowman and Littlefield 1986).

16   David Hume, *Essays Moral, Political, and Literary*, vol. 1, Green and T.H. Grose, eds. (London: Longmans 1898), 176.

17   Charlotte Perkins Gilman, *Herland* (New York: Pantheon 1979), 60; originally publ. 1915.

18   Ibid., 66.

19   Jane Flax, 'The Family in Contemporary Feminist Thought: A Critical Review,' in *The Family in Political Thought*, Jean Bethke Elshtain, ed. (Amherst: The University of Massachusetts Press 1982), 252.

20   The collection of readings in Barrie Thorne, ed., *Rethinking The Family* (New York: Longmans 1982) is a useful source. Joyce Trebilcot's *Mothering* is another helpful collection. And among the best sources of suggestions are feminist utopian novels, e.g. Marge Piercy's *Woman on the Edge of Time* (New York: Fawcett 1976).

21   See especially Virginia Held, *Rights and Goods*, chapter 5.

22   In some societies, social pressures to conform with the norms of reciprocal care – of children by parents and later of parents by children – can be very great. But these societies are usually of a kind which are thought to be at a stage of development antecedent to that of contractual society.

23   The gerontologist Elaine Brody says about old people that 'what we hear over and over again – and I'm talking gross numbers of 80 to 90 percent in survey after survey – is "I don't want to be a burden on my children." ' Interview by Lindsy Van Gelder, *Ms. Magazine* (January 1986), 48.

24 For a different view see Howard Cohen, *Equal Rights for Children* (Totowa, NJ: Littlefield Adams 1980).

25 See Virginia Held, *Rights and Goods*.

26 For related discussions, see Nancy Hartsock, *Money, Sex, and Power: Toward a Feminist Historical Materialism* (New York: Longmans 1983); and Sara Ruddick, 'Maternal Thinking,' in Trebilcot, *Mothering*.

27 For examples of the view that women are more deficient than men in understanding morality and acting morally, see e.g. Mary Mahowald, ed., *Philosophy of Woman: Classical to Current Concepts* (Indianapolis: Hackett 1978). See also Lawrence Kohlberg, *The Philosophy of Moral Development* (San Francisco: Harper and Row 1981), and L. Kohlberg and R. Kramer, 'Continuities and Discontinuities in Child and Adult Moral Development,' *Human Development* 12 (1969) 93–120.

28 For further discussion, see Virginia Held, 'Feminism and Moral Theory,' in *Woman and Moral Theory*, Eva Kittay and Diana Meyers, eds. (Totowa, NJ: Rowman and Littlefield 1987).

29 Virginia Held, 'Marx, Sex, and the Transformation of Society,' *The Philosophical Forum* 5, 1–2 (Fall–Winter 1973–4).

Chapter 7

Charles Mills

THE RACIAL CONTRACT

Charles Mills is Professor of Moral and Intellectual Philosophy at Northwestern University, whose work in political philosophy centers on issues of class, gender, and race. His 1997 book, *The Racial Contract,* from which the following reading is taken, argues that the social contract on which our society is *actually* based is a racist contract that works to cement white European dominance through the exploitation of non-white people. This excerpt explores the epistemological, moral, and political dimensions of that racial contract.

Introduction

White supremacy is the unnamed political system that has made the modern world what it is today. You will not find this term in introductory, or even advanced, texts in political theory. A standard undergraduate philosophy course will start off with Plato and Aristotle, perhaps say something about Augustine, Aquinas, and Machiavelli, move on to Hobbes, Locke, Mill, and Marx, and then wind up with Rawls and Nozick. It will introduce you to notions of aristocracy, democracy, absolutism, liberalism, representative government, socialism, welfare capitalism, and libertarianism. But though it covers more than two thousand years of Western political thought and runs the ostensible gamut of political systems, there will be no mention of the basic political system that has shaped the world for the past several hundred years. And this omission is not accidental. Rather, it reflects the fact that standard textbooks and courses have for the most part been written and designed by whites, who take their racial privilege so much for granted that they do not even see it as *political,* as a form of domination. Ironically, the most important political system of recent global history – the system of domination by which white people have historically ruled over and, in certain important ways, continue to rule over nonwhite people – is not seen as a political system at all. It is just taken for granted; it is the background against which other systems, which we *are* to see as political, are highlighted. This book is an attempt to redirect your vision, to make you see what, in a sense, has been there all along.

Philosophy has remained remarkably untouched by the debates over multiculturalism, canon reform, and ethnic diversity racking the academy; both demographically and conceptually, it is one of the "whitest" of the humanities. Blacks, for example, constitute only about 1 percent of philosophers in North American universities – a hundred or so people out of more than ten thousand – and there are even fewer Latino, Asian American, and Native American philosophers.[1] Surely this underrepresentation itself stands in need of an explanation, and in my opinion it can be traced in part to a conceptual array and a standard repertoire of concerns whose abstractness typically elides, rather than genuinely includes, the experience of racial minorities. Since (white) women have the demographic advantage of numbers, there are of course far more female philosophers in the profession than nonwhite philosophers (though still not proportionate to women's percentage of the population), and they have made far greater progress in developing alternative conceptualizations. Those African American philosophers who do work in moral and political theory tend either to produce general work indistinguishable from that of their white peers or to focus on local issues (affirmative action, the black "underclass") or historical figures (W. E. B. Du Bois, Alain Locke) in a way that does not aggressively engage the broader debate.

What is needed is a global theoretical framework for situating discussions of race and white racism, and thereby challenging the assumptions of white political philosophy, which would correspond to feminist theorists' articulation of the centrality of gender, patriarchy, and sexism to traditional moral and political theory. What is needed, in other words, is a recognition that racism (or, as I will argue, global white supremacy) is itself a political system, a particular power structure of formal or informal rule, socioeconomic privilege, and norms for the differential distribution of material wealth and opportunities, benefits and burdens, rights and duties. The notion of the Racial Contract is, I suggest, one possible way of making this connection with mainstream theory, since it uses the vocabulary and apparatus already developed for contractarianism to map this unacknowledged system. Contract talk is, after all, the political lingua franca of our times.

We all understand the idea of a "contract," an agreement between two or more people to do something. The "social contract" just extends this idea. If we think of human beings as starting off in a "state of nature," it suggests that they then *decide* to establish civil society and a government. What we have, then, is a theory that founds government on the popular consent of individuals taken as equals.[2]

But the peculiar contract to which I am referring, though based on the social contract tradition that has been central to Western political theory, is not a contract between everybody ("we the people"), but between just the people who count, the people who really are people ("we the white people"). So it is a Racial Contract.

The social contract, whether in its original or in its contemporary version, constitutes a powerful set of lenses for looking at society and the government. But in its obfuscation of the ugly realities of group power and domination, it is, if unsupplemented, a profoundly misleading account of the way the modern world actually is and came to be. The "Racial Contract" as a theory — I use quotation marks to indicate when I am talking about the theory of the Racial Contract, as against the Racial Contract itself — will explain that the Racial Contract is real and that apparent racist violations of the terms of the social contract in fact *uphold* the terms of the Racial Contract.

The "Racial Contract," then, is intended as a conceptual bridge between two areas now largely segregated from each other: on the one hand, the world of mainstream (i.e., white) ethics and political philosophy, preoccupied with discussions of justice and rights in the abstract, on the other hand, the world of Native American, African American, and Third and Fourth World[3] political thought, historically focused on issues of conquest, imperialism, colonialism, white settlement, land rights, race and racism, slavery, Jim Crow reparations, apartheid, cultural authenticity, national identity, *indigenismo*, Afrocentrism, etc. These issues hardly appear in mainstream political philosophy,[4] but they have been central to the political struggles of the majority of the world's population. Their absence from what is considered serious philosophy is a reflection not of their lack of seriousness but of the color of the vast majority of Western academic philosophers (and perhaps *their* lack of seriousness).

The great virtue of traditional social contract theory was that it provided seemingly straightforward answers both to factual questions about the origins and workings of society and government and to normative questions about the justification of socioeconomic structures and political institutions. Moreover, the "contract" was very versatile, depending on how different theorists viewed the state of nature, human motivation, the rights and liberties people gave up or retained, the particular details of the agreement, and the resulting character of the government. In the modern Rawlsian version of the contract, this flexibility continues to be illustrated, since Rawls dispenses with the historical claims of classic contractarianism and focuses instead on the justification of the basic structure of society.[5] From its 1650–1800 heyday as a grand quasi-anthropological account of the origins and development of society and the state, the contract has now become just a normative tool, a conceptual device to elicit our intuitions about justice.

But my usage is different. The "Racial Contract" I employ is in a sense more in keeping with the spirit of the classic contractarians – Hobbes, Locke, Rousseau, and Kant.[6] I use it not merely normatively, to generate judgments about social justice and injustice, but descriptively, to *explain* the actual genesis of the society and the state, the way society is structured, the way the government functions, and people's moral psychology.[7] The most famous case in which the contract is used to explain a manifestly *nonideal* society, what would be termed in current philosophical jargon a "naturalized" account, is Rousseau's *Discourse on Inequality* (1755). Rousseau argues that technological

development in the state of nature brings into existence a nascent society of growing divisions in wealth between rich and poor, which are then consolidated and made permanent by a deceitful "social contract."[8] Whereas the ideal contract explains how a just society would be formed, ruled by a moral government, and regulated by a defensible moral code, this nonideal/naturalized contract explains how an unjust, *exploitative* society, ruled by an *oppressive* government and regulated by an *immoral* code, comes into existence. If the ideal contract is to be endorsed and emulated, this nonideal/naturalized contract is to be demystified and condemned. So the point of analyzing the nonideal contract is not to ratify it but to use it to explain and expose the inequities of the actual nonideal polity and to help us to see through the theories and moral justifications offered in defense of them. It gives us a kind of X-ray vision into the real internal logic of the sociopolitical system. Thus it does normative work for us not through its own values, which are detestable, but by enabling us to understand the polity's actual history and how these values and concepts have functioned to rationalize oppression, so as to reform them.

Carole Pateman's provocative feminist work of a decade ago, *The Sexual Contract*, is a good example of this approach (and the inspiration for my own book, though my use is somewhat different), which demonstrates how much descriptive/explanatory life there still is in the contract.[9] Pateman uses it naturalistically, as a way of modeling the internal dynamic of the nonideal male-dominated societies that actually exist today. So this is, as indicated, a reversion to the original "anthropological" approach in which the contract *is* intended to be historically explanatory. But the twist is, of course, that her purpose is now subversive: to excavate the hidden, unjust male covenant upon which the ostensibly gender-neutral social contract actually rests. By looking at Western society and its prevailing political and moral ideologies as if they were based on an unacknowledged "Sexual Contract," Pateman offers a "conjectural history" that reveals and exposes the normative logic that makes sense of the inconsistencies, circumlocutions, and evasions of the classic contract theorists and, correspondingly, the world of patriarchal domination their work has helped to rationalize.

My aim here is to adopt a non ideal contract as a rhetorical trope and theoretical method for understanding the inner logic of *racial* domination and how it structures the polities of the West and elsewhere. The ideal "social contract" has been a central concept of Western political theory for understanding and evaluating the social world. And concepts are crucial to cognition: cognitive scientists point out that they help us to categorize, learn, remember, infer, explain, problem-solve, generalize, analogize.[10] Correspondingly, the *lack* of appropriate concepts can hinder learning, interfere with memory, block inferences, obstruct explanation, and perpetuate problems. I am suggesting, then, that as a central concept the notion of a Racial Contract might be more revealing of the real character of the world we are living in, and the corresponding historical deficiencies of its normative theories and practices, than the raceless notions currently dominant in political theory.[11] Both at the primary level of an alternative conceptualization of the facts and at the secondary (reflexive) level of a critical analysis of the orthodox theories themselves, the "Racial Contract" enables us to engage with mainstream Western political theory to bring in race. Insofar as contractarianism is thought of as a useful way to do political philosophy, to theorize about how the polity was created and what values should guide our prescriptions for making it more just, it is obviously crucial to understand what the original and continuing "contract" actually was and is, so that we can correct for it in constructing the ideal "contract." The "Racial Contract" should therefore be enthusiastically welcomed by white contract theorists as well.

So this book can be thought of as resting on three simple claims: the existential claim – white supremacy, both local and global, exists and has existed for many years; the conceptual claim – white supremacy should be thought of as itself a political system; the methodological claim – as a political system, white supremacy can illuminatingly be theorized as based on a "contract" between whites, a Racial Contract.

1 Overview

I will start with an overview of the Racial Contract, highlighting its differences from, as well as its similarities to, the classical and contemporary social contract. The Racial Contract is political, moral, and epistemological, the Racial Contract is real; and economically, in determining who gets what, the Racial Contract is an exploitation contract.

The Racial Contract is Political, Moral, and Epistemological

The "social contract" is actually several contracts in one. Contemporary contractarians usually distinguish, to begin with, between the *political* contract and the *moral* contract, before going on to make (subsidiary) distinctions within both. I contend, however, that the orthodox social contract also tacitly presupposes an "epistemological" contract, and that for the Racial Contract it is crucial to make this explicit.

The political contract is an account of the origins of government and our political obligations to it. The subsidiary distinction sometimes made in the political contract is between the contract to establish society (thereby taking "natural," presocial individuals out of the state of nature and reconstructing and constituting them as members of a collective body) and the contract to establish the *state* (thereby transferring outright or delegating in a relationship of trust the rights and powers we have in the state of nature to a sovereign governing entity).[12]

The moral contract, on the other hand, is the foundation of the moral code established for the society, by which the citizens are supposed to regulate their behavior. The subsidiary distinction here is between two interpretations (to be discussed) of the relationship between the moral contract and state-of-nature morality. In modern versions of the contract, most notably Rawls's of course, the political contract largely vanishes, modern anthropology having long superseded the naive social origin histories of the classic contractarians. The focus is then almost exclusively on the moral contract. This is not conceived of as an actual historical event that took place on leaving the state of nature. Rather, the state of nature survives only in the attenuated form of what Rawls calls the "original position," and the "contract" is a purely hypothetical exercise (a thought experiment) in establishing what a just "basic structure" would be, with a schedule of rights, duties, and liberties that shapes citizens' moral psychology, conceptions of the right, notions of self-respect, etc.[13]

Now the Racial Contract — and the "Racial Contract" as a theory, that is, the distanced, critical examination of the Racial Contract — follows the classical model in being both sociopolitical and moral. It explains how society was created or crucially transformed, how the individuals in that society were reconstituted, how the state was established, and how a particular moral code and a certain moral psychology were brought into existence. (As I have emphasized, the "Racial Contract" seeks to account for the way things are and how they came to be that way — the descriptive — *as well as* the way they should be — the normative — since indeed one of its complaints about white political philosophy is precisely its otherworldiness, its ignoring of basic political realities.) But the Racial Contract, as we will see, is also epistemological, prescribing norms for cognition to which its signatories must adhere. A preliminary characterization would run something like this:

The Racial Contract is that set of formal or informal agreements or meta-agreements (higher-level contracts *about* contracts, which set the limits of the contracts' validity) between the members of one subset of humans, henceforth designated by (shifting) "racial" (phenotypical/genealogical/cultural) criteria C_1, C_2, C_3 . . . as "white," and coextensive (making due allowance for gender differentiation) with the class of full persons, to categorize the remaining subset of humans as "nonwhite" and of a different and inferior moral status, subpersons, so that they have a subordinate civil standing in the white or white-ruled politics the whites either already inhabit or establish or in transactions as aliens with these politics, and the moral and juridical rules normally regulating the behavior of whites in their dealings with one another either do not apply at all in dealings with nonwhites or apply only in a qualified form (depending in part on changing historical circumstances and what particular variety of nonwhite is involved), but in any case the general purpose of the Contract is always the differential privileging of the whites as a group with respect to the nonwhites as a group, the exploitation of their bodies, land, and resources, and the denial of equal socioeconomic opportunities to them. All whites are beneficiaries of the Contract, though some whites are not signatories to it.[14]

It will be obvious, therefore, that the Racial Contract is not a contract to which the nonwhite subset of humans can be a genuinely consenting party (though, depending again on the circumstances, it may sometimes be politic to pretend that this is the case). Rather, it is a contract between those categorized as white over the nonwhites, who are thus the objects rather than the subjects of the agreement.

The logic of the classic social contract, political, moral, and epistemological, then undergoes a corresponding refraction, with shifts, accordingly, in the key terms and principles.

Politically, the contract to establish society and the government, thereby transforming abstract raceless "men" from denizens of the state of nature into social creatures who are politically obligated to a neutral state, becomes the founding of a *racial polity*, whether white settler states (where preexisting populations already are or can be made sparse) or what are sometimes called "sojourner colonies," the establishment of a white presence and colonial rule over existing societies (which are somewhat more populous, or whose inhabitants are more resistant to being made sparse). In addition, the colonizing mother country is also changed by its relation to these new polities, so that its own citizens are altered.

In the social contract, the crucial human metamorphosis is from "natural" man to "civil/political" man from the resident of the state of nature to the citizen of the created society. This change can be more or less extreme, depending on the theorist involved. For Rousseau it is a dramatic transformation, by which animal-like creatures of appetite and instinct become citizens bound by justice and self-prescribed laws. For Hobbes it is a somewhat more laid-back affair by which people who look out primarily for themselves learn to constrain their self-interest for their own good.[15] But in all cases the original "state of nature" supposedly indicates the condition of *all* men, and the social metamorphosis affects them all in the same way.

In the Racial Contract, by contrast, the crucial metamorphosis is the preliminary conceptual partitioning and corresponding transformation of human populations into "white" and "nonwhite" men. The role played by the "state of nature" then becomes radically different. In the white settler state, its role is not primarily to demarcate the (temporarily) prepolitical state of "all" men (who are really white men), but rather the permanently prepolitical state or, perhaps better, nonpolitical state (insofar as "pre-" suggests eventual internal movement toward) of nonwhite men. The establishment of society thus implies the denial that a society already existed, the creation of society *requires* the intervention of white men, who are thereby positioned as *already* sociopolitical beings. White men who are (definitionally) already part of society encounter nonwhites who are not, who are "savage" residents of a state of nature characterized in terms of wilderness, jungle, wasteland. These the white men bring partially into society as subordinate citizens or exclude on reservations or deny the existence of or exterminate. In the colonial case, admittedly preexisting but (for one reason or another) deficient societies (decadent, stagnant, corrupt) are taken over and run for the "benefit" of the nonwhite natives, who are deemed childlike, incapable of self-rule and handling their own affairs, and thus appropriately wards of the state. Here the natives are usually characterized as "barbarians" rather than "savages," their state of nature being somewhat farther away (though not, of course, as remote and lost in the past – if it ever existed in the first place – as the Europeans' state of nature). But in times of crisis the conceptual distance between the two, barbarian and savage, tends to shrink or collapse, for this technical distinction within the nonwhite population is vastly less important than the *central* distinction between whites and nonwhites.

In both cases, then, though in different ways, the Racial Contract establishes a racial polity, a racial state, and a racial juridical system, where the status of whites and nonwhites is clearly demarcated, whether by law or custom. And the purpose of this state, by contrast with the neutral state of classic contractarianism, is, inter alia, specifically to maintain and reproduce this racial order, securing the privileges and advantages of the full white citizens and maintaining the subordination of nonwhites. Correspondingly, the "consent" expected of the white citizens is in part conceptualized as a consent, whether explicit or tacit, to the racial order, to white supremacy, what could be called Whiteness. To the extent that those phenotypically/genealogically/culturally categorized as white fail to live up to the civic and political responsibilities of Whiteness, they are in dereliction of their duties as citizens. From the inception, then, race is in no way an "afterthought," a "deviation" from ostensibly raceless Western ideals, but rather a central shaping constituent of those ideals.

In the social contract tradition, there are two main possible relations between the moral contract and the political contract. On the first view, the moral contract represents *preexisting* objectivist morality (theological or secular) and thus constrains the terms of the political contract. This is the view found in Locke and Kant. In other words, there is an objective moral code in the state of nature itself, even if there are no policemen and judges to enforce it. So any society, government, and legal system that are established should be based on that moral code. On the second view, the political contract *creates* morality as a conventionalist set of rules. So there is no independent objective moral criterion for judging one moral code to be superior to another or for indicting a society's established morality as unjust. On this conception, which is famously attributed to Hobbes, morality is just a set of rules for expediting the rational pursuit and coordination of our own interests without conflict with those other people who are doing the same thing.[16]

The Racial Contract can accommodate both versions, but as it is the former version (the contract as described in Locke and Kant) rather than the latter version (the contract as described in Hobbes) which represents the mainstream of the contract tradition, I focus on that one.[17] Here, the good policy is taken to rest on a preexisting moral foundation. Obviously, this is a far more attractive conception of a political system than Hobbes's view. The ideal of an objectively just polis to which we should aspire in our political activism goes back in the Western tradition all the way to Plato. In the medieval Christian

worldview which continued to influence contractarianism well into the modern period, there is a "natural law" immanent in the structure of the universe which is supposed to direct us morally in striving for this ideal.[18] (For the later, secular versions of contractarianism, the idea would simply be that people have rights and duties even in the state of nature because of their nature as human beings.) So it is wrong to steal, rape, kill in the state of nature even if there are no human laws written down saying it is wrong. These moral principles must constrain the human laws that are made and the civil rights that are assigned once the polity is established. In part, then, the political contract simply *codifies* a morality that already exists, writing it down and filling in the details, so we don't have to rely on a divinely implanted moral sense, or conscience, whose perceptions may on occasion be distorted by self-interest. What is right and wrong, just and unjust, in society will largely be determined by what is right and wrong, just and unjust, in the state of nature.

The character of this objective moral foundation is therefore obviously crucial. For the mainstream of the contractarian tradition, it is the *freedom and equality of all men in the state of nature.* As Locke writes in the *Second Treatise.* "To understand Political Power right, and derive it from its Original, we must consider what State all Men are naturally in, and that is, a *State of perfect Freedom* to order their Actions. . . . A *State* also of *Equality,* wherein all the Power and jurisdiction is reciprocal, no one having more than another."[19] For Kant, similarly, it is our equal moral personhood.[20] Contractarianism is (supposedly) committed to moral egalitarianism, the moral equality of all men, the notion that the interests of all men matter equally and all men must have equal rights. Thus, contractarianism is also committed to a principled and foundational opposition to the traditionalist hierarchical ideology of the old feudal order, the ideology of inherent ascribed status and natural subordination. It is this language of equality which echoes in the American and French Revolutions, the Declaration of Independence, and the Declaration of the Rights of Man. And it is this moral egalitarianism that must be retained in the allocation of rights and liberties in civil society. When in a modern Western society people insist on their rights and freedoms and express their outrage at not being treated equally, it is to these classic ideas that, whether they know it or not, they are appealing.

But as we will see in greater detail later on, the color-coded morality of the Racial Contract restricts the possession of this natural freedom and equality to white men. By virtue of their complete nonrecognition, or at best inadequate, myopic recognition, of the duties of natural law, nonwhites are appropriately relegated to a lower rung on the moral ladder (the Great Chain of Being).[21] They are designated as born unfree and unequal. A partitioned social ontology is therefore created, a universe divided between persons and racial subpersons, Untermenschen, who may variously be black, red, brown, yellow – slaves, aborigines, colonial populations – but who are collectively appropriately known as "subject races." And these subpersons – niggers, injuns, chinks, wogs, greasers, blackfellows, kaffirs, coolies, abos, dinks, googoos, gooks – are biologically destined never to penetrate the normative rights ceiling established for them below white persons. Henceforth, then, whether openly admitted or not, it is taken for granted that the grand ethical theories propounded in the development of Western moral and political thought are of restricted scope, explicitly or implicitly intended by their proponents to be restricted to persons, whites. The terms of the Racial Contract set the parameters for white morality as a whole, so that competing Lockean and Kantian contractarian theories of natural rights and duties, or later anticontractarian theories such as nineteenth-century utilitarianism, are all limited by its stipulations.

Finally, the Racial Contract requires its own peculiar moral and empirical epistemology, its norms and procedures for determining what counts as moral and factual knowledge of the world. In the standard accounts of contractarianism it is not usual to speak of there being an "epistemologcal" contract, but there is an epistemology associated with contractarianism, in the form of natural law. This provides us with a moral compass, whether in the traditional version of Locke – the light of reason implanted in us by God so we can discern objective right and wrong – or in the revisionist version of Hobbes – the ability to assess the objectively optimal prudential course of action and what it requires of us for self-interested cooperation with other. So through our natural faculties we come to know reality in both its factual and valuational aspects, the way things objectively are and what is objectively good or bad about them. I suggest we can think of this as an idealized consensus about cognitive norms and, in this respect, an agreement or "contract" of sorts. There is an understanding about what counts as a correct, objective interpretation of the world, and for agreeing to this view, one is ("contractually") granted full cognitive standing in the polity, the official epistemic community.[22]

But for the Racial Contract things are necessarily more complicated. The requirements of "objective" cognition, factual and moral, in a racial polity are in a sense more demanding in that officially sanctioned reality is divergent from actual reality. So here, it could be said, one has an agreement to misinterpret the word. One has to learn to see the world wrongly, but with the assurance that this set of mistaken perceptions will be validated by white epistemic authority, whether religious or secular.

Thus in effect, on matters related to race, the Racial Contract prescribes for its signatories an inverted epistemology, an epistemology of ignorance, a particular pattern of localized and global cognitive dysfunctions (which are psychologically and socially functional), producing the ironic outcome that whites will in general be unable to understand the world they themselves have made. Part of what it means to be constructed as "white" (the metamorphosis of the sociopolitical contract), part of what it requires to achieve Whiteness, successfully to become a white person (one imagines a ceremony with certificates attending the successful rite of passage: "Congratulations, you're now an official white person!"), is a cognitive model that precludes self-transparency and genuine understanding of social realities. To a significant extent, then, white signatories will live in an invented delusional world, a racial fantasyland, a "consensual hallucination," to quote William Gibson's famous characterization of cyberspace, though this particular hallucination is located in real space.[23] There will be white mythologies, invented Orients, invented Africas, invented Americas, with a correspondingly fabricated population, countries that never were, inhabited by people who never were – Calibans and Tontos, Man Fridays and Sambos – but who attain a virtual reality through their existence in travelers' tales, folk myth, popular and highbrow fiction, colonial reports, scholarly theory, Hollywood cinema, living in the white imagination and determinedly imposed on their alarmed real-life counterparts.[24] One could say then, as a general rule, that white misunderstanding, misrepresentation, evasion, and self-deception on matters related to race are among the most pervasive mental phenomena of the past few hundred years, a cognitive and moral economy psychically required for conquest, colonization, and enslavement. And these phenomena are in no way *accidental*, but *prescribed* by the terms of the Racial Contract, which requires a certain schedule of structured blindnesses and opacities in order to establish and maintain the white polity.

The Racial Contract is a Historical Actuality

The social contract in its modern version has long since given up any pretensions to be able to explain the historical origins of society and the state. Whereas the classic contractarians were engaged in a project both descriptive and prescriptive, the modern Rawls-inspired contract

is purely a prescriptive thought experiment. And even Pateman's Sexual Contract, though its focus is the real rather than the ideal, is not meant as a literal account of what men in 4004 BC decided to do on the plains of Mesopotamia. Whatever accounts for what Frederick Engels once called "the *world historical defeat of the female sex*"[25] – whether the development of an economic surplus, as he theorized, or the male discovery of the capacity to rape and the female disadvantage of being the childbearing half of the species, as radical feminists have argued – it is clearly lost in antiquity.

By contrast, ironically, the Racial Contract, never so far as I know explored as such, has the best claim to being an actual historical fact. Far from being lost in the mists of the ages, it is clearly historically locatable in the series of events marking the creation of the modern world by European colonialism and the voyages of "discovery" now increasingly and more appropriately called expeditions of conquest. The Columbian quincentenary a few years ago, with its accompanying debates, polemics, controversies, counterdemonstrations, and outpourings of revisionist literature, confronted many whites with the uncomfortable fact, hardly discussed in mainstream moral and political theory, that we live in a world which has been *foundationally shaped for the past five hundred years by the realities of European domination and the gradual consolidation of global white supremacy*. Thus not only is the Racial Contract "real," but – whereas the social contract is characteristically taken to be establishing the legitimacy of the nation-state, and codifying morality and law within its boundaries – the Racial Contract is *global*, involving a tectonic shift of the ethicojuridical basis of the planet as a whole, the division of the world, as Jean-Paul Sartre put it long ago, between "men" and "natives."[26]

Europeans thereby emerge as "the lords of human kind," the "lords of all the world," with the increasing power to determine the standing of the non-Europeans who are their subjects.[27] Although no single act literally corresponds to the drawing up and signing of a contract, there is a series of acts — papal bulls and other theological pronouncements, European discussions about colonialism, "discovery," and international law; pacts, treaties, and legal decisions, academic and popular debates about the humanity of nonwhites; the establishment of formalized legal structures of differential treatment; and the routinization of informal illegal or quasi-legal practices effectively sanctioned by the complicity of silence and government failure to intervene and punish perpetrators — which collectively can be seen, not just metaphorically but close to literally, as its conceptual, juridical, and normative equivalent.

Anthony Pagden suggests that a division of the European empires into their main temporal periods should recognize "two distinct, but interdependent histories": the colonization of the Americas, 1492 to the 1830s, and the occupation of Asia, Africa, and the Pacific, 1730s to the period after World War II.[28] In the first period, it was, to begin with, the nature and moral status of the Native Americans that primarily had to be determined, and then that of the imported African slaves whose labor was required to build this "New World." In the second period, culminating in formal European colonial rule over most of the world by the early twentieth century, it was the character of colonial peoples that became crucial. But in all cases "race" is the common conceptual denominator that gradually came to signify the respective global statuses of superiority and inferiority, privilege and subordination. There is an opposition of us against them with multiple overlapping dimensions: Europeans versus non-Europeans (geography), civilized versus wild/savage/barbarians (culture), Christians versus heathens (religion). But they all eventually coalesced into the *basic* opposition of white versus nonwhite.

A Lumbee Indian legal scholar, Robert Williams, has traced the evolution of the Western legal position on the rights of native peoples from its medieval antecedents to the beginnings of the modern period, showing how it is consistently based on the assumption of "the rightness and necessity of subjugating and assimilating other peoples to (the European) worldview."[29] Initially the intellectual framework was a theological one, with normative inclusion and exclusion manifesting itself as the demarcation between Christians and heathens. The pope's powers over the *Societas Christiana*, the universal Christian commonwealth, were seen as "extending not only over all Christians within the universal commonwealth, but over unregenerated heathens and infidels as well," and thus policy would subsequently underwrite not merely the Crusades against Islam but the later voyages to the Americas. Sometimes papal pronouncements did grant rights and rationality to nonbelievers. As a result of dealing with the Mongols in the thirteenth century, for example, Pope Innocent IV "conceded that infidels and heathens possessed the natural law right to elect their own secular leaders," and Pope Paul III's famous *Sublimis Deus* (1537) stated that Native Americans were rational beings, not to be treated as "dumb brutes created for our service" but "as truly men ... capable of understanding the Catholic faith."[30] But as Williams points out, the latter qualification was always crucial. A Eurocentrically normed conception of rationality made it coextensive with acceptance of the Christian message, so that rejection was proof of bestial irrationality.

Even more remarkably, in the case of Native Americans this acceptance was to be signaled by their agreement to the *Requerimiento*, a long statement read aloud to them in, of course, a language they did not understand, failing which assent a just war could lawfully be waged against them.[31] One author writes:

> The *requerimiento* is the prototypical example of text justifying conquest. Informing the Indians that their lands were entrusted by Christ to the pope and thence to the kings of Spain, the

document offers freedom from slavery for those Indians who accept Spanish rule. Even though it was entirely incomprehensible to a non-Spanish speaker, reading the document provided sufficient justification for dispossession of land and immediate enslavement of the indigenous people. [Bartolomé de] Las Casas's famous comment on the *requerimiento* was that one does not know "whether to laugh or cry at the absurdity of it." . . . While appearing to respect "rights" the *requerimiento*, in fact, takes them away.[32]

In effect, then, the Catholic Church's declarations either formally legitimated conquest or could be easily circumvented where a weak prima facie moral barrier was erected.

The growth of the Enlightenment and the rise of secularism did not *challenge* this strategic dichotomization (Christian/infidel) so much as translate it into other forms. Philip Curtin refers to the characteristic "exceptionalism in European thought about the non-West," "a conception of the world largely based on self-identification – and identification of 'the other people.' "[33] Similarly, Pierre van den Berghe describes the "Enlightenment dichotomization" of the normative theories of the period.[34] "Race" gradually became the formal marker of this differentiated status, replacing the religious divide (whose disadvantage, after all, was that it could always be overcome through conversion). Thus a category crystallized over time in European thought to represent entities who are *humanoid* but not fully *human* ("savages," "barbarians") and who are identified as such by being members of the general set of nonwhite races. Influenced by the ancient Roman distinction between the civilized within and the barbarians outside the empire, the distinction between full and question-mark humans, Europeans set up a two-tiered moral code with one set of rules for whites and another for nonwhites.[35]

Correspondingly, various moral and legal doctrines were propounded which can be seen

as specific manifestations and instantiations, appropriately adjusted to circumstances, of the overarching Racial Contract. These were specific subsidiary contracts designed for different modes of exploiting the resources and peoples of the rest of the world for Europe: the expropriation contract, the slavery contract, the colonial contract.

The "Doctrine of Discovery," for example, what Williams identifies as the "paradigmatic tenet informing and determining contemporary European legal discourse respecting relations with Western tribal societies," was central to the expropriation contract.[36] The American Justice Joseph Story glossed it as granting Europeans:

> . . . an absolute dominion over the whole territories afterwards occupied by them, not in virtue of any conquest of, or cession by, the Indian natives, but as a right acquired by discovery. . . . The title of the Indians was not treated as a right of property and dominion, but as a mere right of occupancy. As infidels, heathens, and savages, they were not allowed to possess the prerogatives belonging to absolute, sovereign, and independent nations. The territory over which they wandered, and which they used for their temporary and fugitive purposes, was, in respect to Christians, deemed as if it were inhabited only by brute animals.[37]

Similarly, the slavery contract gave Europeans the right to enslave Native Americans and Africans at a time when slavery was dead or dying out in Europe, based on doctrines of the inherent inferiority of these peoples. A classic statement of the slavery contract is the 1857 *Dred Scott v. Sanford* U.S. Supreme Court decision of Chief Justice Roger Taney, which stated that blacks:

> had for more than a century before been regarded as beings of an inferior order, and altogether unfit to associate with the white

race, either in social or political relations, and so far inferior, that they had no rights which the white man was bound to respect; and that the negro might justly and lawfully be reduced to slavery for his benefit. . . . This opinion was at that time fixed and universal in the civilized portion of the white race. It was regarded as an axiom in morals as well as in politics, which no one thought of disputing or supposed to be open to dispute.[38]

Finally, there is the colonial contract, which legitimated European rule over the nations in Asia, Africa, and the Pacific. Consider, for instance, this wonderful example, almost literally "contractarian" in character, from the French imperial theorist Jules Harmand (1845–1921), who devised the notion of *association*:

Expansion by conquest, however necessary, seems especially unjust and disturbing to the conscience of democracies. . . . But to transpose democratic institutions into such a setting is aberrant nonsense. The subject people are nor and cannot become citizens in the democratic sense of the term. . . . It is necessary, then, to accept as a principle and point of departure the fact that there is a hierarchy of races and civilizations, and that we belong to the superior race and civilization. . . . The basic legitimation of conquest over native peoples is the conviction of our superiority, not merely our mechanical, economic, and military superiority, but our moral superiority. Our dignity rests on that quality, and it underlies our right to direct the rest of humanity.

What is therefore necessary is a " 'Contract' of Association:"

Without falling into Rousseauan reveries, it is worth noting that association implies a contract, and this idea, though nothing more than an illustration, is more appropriately applied to the coexistence of two profoundly different societies thrown sharply and artificially into contact than it is to the single society formed by natural processes which Rousseau envisaged. This is how the terms of this implicit agreement can be conceived. The European conqueror brings order, foresight, and security to a human society which, though ardently aspiring for these fundamental values without which no community can make progress, still lacks the aptitude to achieve them from within itself. . . . With these mental and material instruments, which it lacked and now receives, it gains the idea and ambition for a better existence, and the means of achieving it. We will obey you, say the subjects, if you begin by proving yourself worthy. We will obey you if you can succeed in convincing us of the superiority of that civilization of which you talk so much.[39]

Indian laws, slave codes, and colonial native aers formally codified the subordinate status of nonwhites and (ostensibly) regulated their treatment, creating a juridical space for non-Europeans as a separate category of beings, So even if there was sometimes an attempt to prevent "abuses" (and these codes were honored far more often in the breach than the observance), the point is that "abuse" as a concept presupposes as a norm the *legitimacy* of the subordination. Slavery and colonialism are not conceived as wrong in their denial of autonomy to persons; what is wrong is the improper administration of these regimes.

It would be a fundamental error, then — a point to which I will return — to see racism as anomalous, a mysterious deviation from European Enlightenment humanism. Rather, it needs to be realized that, in keeping with the Roman precedent, *European humanism usually meant that only Europeans were human.* European moral and political theory, like European thought in general, developed within the framework of the Racial Contract and, as a rule, took it for granted.

As Edward Said points out in *Culture and Imperialism*, we must not see culture as "antiseptically quarantined from its worldly affiliations." But this occupational blindness has in fact infected most "professional humanists" (and certainly most philosophers), so that "as a result [they are] unable to make the connection between the prolonged and sordid cruelty of practices such as slavery, colonialist and racial oppression, and imperial subjection on the one hand, and the poetry, fiction, philosophy of the society that engages in these practices on the other."[40] By the nineteenth century, conventional white opinion casually assumed the uncontroversial validity of a hierarchy of "higher" and "lower," "master" and "subject" races, for whom, it is obvious, different rules must apply.

The modern world was thus expressly created as a *racially hierarchical* polity, globally dominated by Europeans. A 1969 *Foreign Affairs* article worth rereading today reminds us that as late as the 1940s the world:

> . . . was still by and large a Western white-dominated world. The long-established patterns of white power and nonwhite nonpower were still the generally accepted order of things. All the accompanying assumptions and mythologies about race and color were still mostly taken for granted. . . . [W]hite supremacy was a generally assumed and accepted state of affairs in the United States as well as in Europe's empires.[41]

But statements or such frankness are rare or nonexistent in mainstream white opinion today, which generally seeks to rewrite the past so as to deny or minimize the obvious fact of global white domination.

Yet the United States itself, of course, is a white settler state on territory expropriated from its aboriginal inhabitants through a combination of military force, disease, and a "century of dishonor" of broken treaties.[42] The expropriation involved literal genocide (a word now unfortunately devalued by hyperbolic overuse) of a kind that some recent revisionist historians have argued needs to be seen as comparable to the Third Reich's.[43] Washington, Father of the Nation, was, understandably, known somewhat differently to the Senecas as "Town Destroyer."[44] In the Declaration of Independence, Jefferson characterized Native Americans as "merciless Indian Savages," and in the Constitution, blacks, of course, appear only obliquely, through the famous "60 percent solution." Thus, as Richard Drinnon concludes: "The Framers manifestly established a government under which non-Europeans were not men created equal – in the white polity . . . they were nonpeoples."[45] Though on a smaller scale and not always so ruthlessly (or, in the case of New Zealand, because of more successful indigenous resistance), what are standardly classified as the other white settler states – for example, Canada, Australia, New Zealand, Rhodesia, and South Africa – were all founded on similar policies: the extermination, displacement, and/or herding onto reservations of the aboriginal population.[46] Pierre van den Berghe has coined the illuminating phrase "*Herrenvolk* democracies" to describe these politics, which captures perfectly the dichotomization of the Racial Contract.[47] Their subsequent evolution has been somewhat different, but defenders of South Africa's system of apartheid often argued that U.S. criticism was hypocritical in light of its own history of Jim Crow, especially since de facto segregation remains sufficiently entrenched that even today, 40 years after *Brown v. Board of Education*, two American sociologists can title their study *American Apartheid*.[48] The racist record of preliberation Rhodesia (now Zimbabwe) and South Africa is well known; not so familiar may be the fact that the United States, Canada, and Australia all maintained "white" immigration policies until a few decades ago, and native peoples in all three countries suffer high poverty, infant mortality, and suicide rates.

Elsewhere, in Latin America, Asia, and Africa, large parts of the world were colonized, that is, formally brought under the rule of one or another of the European powers (or, later, the United States): the early Spanish and Portuguese empires in the Americas, the Philippines, and south Asia; the jealous competition from Britain, France, and Holland; the British conquest of India; the French expansion into Algeria and Indochina; the Dutch advance into Indonesia; the Opium Wars against China; the late nineteenth-century "scramble for Africa"; the U.S. war against Spain, seizure of Cuba, Puerto Rico, and the Philippines, and annexation of Hawaii.[49] The pace of change this century has been so dramatic that it is easy to forget that less than a hundred years ago, in 1914, "Europe held a grand total of roughly 85 percent of the earth as colonies, protectorates, dependencies, dominions, and commonwealths. No other associated set of colonies in history was as large, none so totally dominated, none so unequal in power to the Western metropolis."[50] One could say that the Racial Contract creates a transnational white polity, a virtual community of people linked by their citizenship in Europe at home and abroad (Europe proper, the colonial greater Europe, and the "fragments" of Euro-America, Euro-Australia, etc.), and constituted in opposition to their indigenous subjects. In most of Africa and Asia, where colonial rule ended only after World War II, rigid "color bars" maintained the separation between Europeans and indigenes. As European, as white, one knew oneself to be a member of the superior race, one's skin being one's passport: "Whatever a white man did must in some grotesque fashion be 'civilized.' "[51] So though there were local variations in the Racial Contract, depending on circumstances and the particular mode of exploitation – for example, a bipolar racial system in the (Anglo) United States, as against a subtler color hierarchy in (Iberian) Latin America – it remains the case that the white tribe, as the global representative of civilization and modernity, is generally on top of the social pyramid.[52]

We live, then, in a world built on the Racial Contract. That we do is simultaneously quite obvious if you think about it (the dates and details of colonial conquest, the constitutions of these states and their exclusionary juridical mechanisms, the histories of official racist ideologies, the battles against slavery and colonialism, the formal and informal structures of discrimination, are all within recent historical memory and, of course, massively documented in other disciplines) and nonobvious, since most whites *don't* think about it or don't think about it as the outcome of a history of political oppression but rather as just "the way things are." ("You say we're all over the world because we *conquered* the world? Why would you put it that way?") In the Treaty of Tordesillas (1494) which divided the world between Spain and Portugal, the Valladolid (Spain) Conference (1550–1) to decide whether Native Americans were really human, the later debates over African slavery and abolitionism, the Berlin Conference (1884–5) to partition Africa, the various inter-European pacts, treaties, and informal arrangements on policing their colonies, the post–World War I discussions in Versailles after a war to make the world safe for democracy – we see (or should see) with complete clarity a world being governed by white people. So though there is also internal conflict – disagreements, battles, even world wars – the dominant movers und shapers will be Europeans at home and abroad, with non-Europeans lining up to fight under their respective banners, and the system of white domination itself rarely being challenged. (The exception, of course, is Japan, which escaped colonization, and so for most of the twentieth century has had a shifting and ambivalent relationship with the global white polity.) The legacy of this world is, of course, still with us today, in the economic, political, and cultural domination of the planet by Europeans and their descendants. The fact that this racial structure, clearly political in character, and the struggle against it, equally so, have *not* for the most part been defined appropriate subject matter for mainstream Anglo-American political philosophy and the fact that the very concepts hegemonic in the discipline are refractory to an understanding of these realities, reveal at best a disturbing provincialism and an ahistoricity profoundly at odds with the radically foundational questioning on which philosophy prides itself and, at worst, a complicity with the terms of the Racial Contract itself.

The Racial Contract is an Exploitation Contract that Creates Global European Economic Domination and National White Racial Privilege

The classic social contract, as I have detailed, is primarily moral/political in nature. But it is also *economic* in the background sense that the point of leaving the state of nature is in part to secure a stable environment for the industrious appropriation of the world. (After all, one famous definition of politics is that it is about who gets what and why.) Thus even in Locke's moralized state of nature, where people generally do obey natural law, he is concerned about the safety of private property, indeed proclaiming that "the great and *chief end* therefore, of Mens uniting into Commonwealths, and putting themselves under Government, *is the Preservation of their Property*."[53] And in Hobbes's famously amoral and unsafe state of nature, we are told that "there is no place for Industry, because the fruit thereof is uncertain, and consequently no Culture of the Earth."[54] So part of the point of bringing society into existence, with its laws and enforcers of the law, is to protect what you have accumulated.

What, then, is the nature of the economic system of the new society? The general contract does not itself prescribe a particular model or particular schedule of property rights, requiring only that the "equality" in the prepolitical state be somehow preserved. This provision may be variously interpreted as a self-interested surrender to an absolutist Hobbesian government that itself determines property rights, or a Lockean insistence that private property, accumulated in the moralized state of nature, be respected by the

constitutionalist government. Or more radical political theorists, such as socialists and feminists, might argue that state-of-nature equality actually mandates class or gender economic egalitarianism in society. So, different political interpretations of the initial moral egalitarianism can be advanced, but the general background idea is that the equality of human beings in the state of nature is somehow (whether as equality of opportunity or as equality or outcome) supposed to carry over into the economy of the created sociopolitical order, leading to a system of voluntary human intercourse and exchange in which exploitation is precluded.

By contrast, the economic dimension of the Racial Contract is the most salient, foreground rather than background, since the Racial Contract is calculatedly aimed at economic exploitation. The whole point of establishing a moral hierarchy and juridically partitioning the polity according to race is to secure and legitimate the privileging of those individuals designated as white/persons and the exploitation of those individuals designated as nonwhite/subpersons. There are other benefits accruing from the Racial Contract — far greater political influence, cultural hegemony, the psychic payoff that comes from knowing one is a member of the *Herrenvolk* (what W. E. B. Du Bois once called "the wages of whiteness")[55] — but the bottom line is material advantage. Globally, the Racial Contract creates Europe as the continent that dominates the world; locally, within Europe and the other continents, it designates Europeans as the privileged race.

The challenge of explaining what has been called "the European miracle" — the rise of Europe to global domination — has long exercised both academic and lay opinion.[56] How is it that a formerly peripheral region on the outskirts of the Asian land mass, at the far edge of the trade routes, remote from the great civilizations of Islam and the East, was able in a century or two to achieve global political and economic dominance? The explanations historically given by Europeans themselves have varied tremendously, from the straightforwardly racist and geographically determinist to the more subtly environmentalist and culturalist. But what they have all had in common, even those influenced by Marxism, is their tendency to depict this development as essentially autochthonous, their tendency to privilege some set of internal variables and correspondingly downplay at ignore altogether the role of colonial conquest and African slavery. Europe made it on its own, it is said, because of the peculiar characteristics of Europe and Europeans.

Thus whereas no reputable historian today would espouse the frankly biologistic theories of the past, which made Europeans (in both pre- and post-Darwinian accounts) inherently the most advanced race, as contrasted with the backward/less-evolved races elsewhere, the thesis of European specialness and exceptionalism is still presupposed. It is still assumed that rationalism and science, innovativeness and inventiveness found their special home here, as against the intellectual stagnation and traditionalism of the rest of the world, so that Europe was therefore destined in advance to occupy the special position in global history it has. James Blaur calls this the theory, or "super-theory" (an umbrella covering many different versions: theological, cultural, biologistic, geographical, technological, etc.), of "Eurocentric diffusionism," according to which European progress is seen as "natural" and asymmetrically determinant of the fate of non-Europe.[57] Similarly, Sandra Harding, in her anthology on the "racial" economy of science, cites "the assumption that Europe functions autonomously from other parts of the world, that Europe is its own origin, final end, and agent, and that Europe and people of European descent in the Americas and elsewhere owe nothing to the rest of the world."[58]

Unsurprisingly, black and Third World theorists have traditionally dissented from this notion of happy divine or natural European dispensation. They have claimed, quite to the contrary, that there is a crucial causal connection between European advance and the unhappy fate of the rest of the world. One classic example of such scholarship from a half century ago was the Caribbean historian Eric Williams's *Capitalism and Slavery*, which argued that the profits from African slavery helped to make the industrial revolution possible, so that internalist accounts were fundamentally mistaken.[59] And in recent years, with decolonization, the rise of the New Left in the United States, and the entry of more alternative voices into the academy, this challenge has deepened and broadened. There are variations in the authors' positions – for example, Walter Rodney, Samir Amin, André Gunder Frank, Immanuel Wallerstein[60] – but the basic theme is that the exploitation of the empire (the bullion from the great gold and silver mines in Mexico and Peru, the profits from plantation slavery, the fortunes made by the colonial companies, the general social and economic stimulus provided by the opening up of the "New World") was to a greater or lesser extent crucial in enabling and then consolidating the takeoff of what had previously been an economic backwater. It was far from the ease that Europe was specially destined to assume economic hegemony; there were a number of centers in Asia and Africa of a comparable level of development which could potentially have evolved in the same way. But the European ascent closed off this development path for others because it forcibly inserted them into a colonial network whose exploitative relations and extractive mechanisms prevented autonomous growth.

Overall, then, colonialism "lies at the heart" of the rise of Europe.[61] The economic unit of analysis needs to be Europe as a whole, since it is not always the case that the colonizing nations directly involved always benefited in the long term. Imperial Spain, for example, still feudal in character, suffered massive inflation from its bullion imports. But through trade and financial exchange, others launched on the capitalist path, such as Holland, profited. Internal national rivalries continued, of course, but this common identity based on the transcontinental exploitation of the non-European world would in many cases be politically crucial, generating a sense of Europe as a cosmopolitan entity engaged in a common enterprise, underwritten by race. As Victor Kiernan puts it, "All countries within the European orbit benefited however, as Adam Smith pointed out, from colonial contributions to a common stock of wealth, bitterly as they might wrangle over ownership of one territory or another. . . . [T]here was a sense in which all Europeans shared in a heightened sense of power engendered by the successes of any of them, as well as in the pool of material wealth . . . that the colonies produced."[62]

Today, correspondingly, though formal decolonization has taken place and in Africa and Asia black, brown, and yellow natives are in office, ruling independent nations, the global economy is essentially dominated by the former colonial powers, their offshoots (Euro–United States, Euro–Canada), and their international financial institutions, lending agencies, and corporations. (As previously observed, the notable exception, whose history confirms rather than challenges the rule, is Japan, which escaped colonization and, after the Meiji Restoration, successfully embarked on its own industrialization.) Thus one could say that the world is essentially dominated by white capital. Global figures on income and property ownership are, of course, broken down nationally rather than racially, but if a transnational racial disaggregation were to be done, it would reveal that whites control a percentage of the world's wealth grossly disproportionate to their numbers. Since there is no reason to think that the chasm between First and Third Worlds (which largely coincides with this racial division) is going to be bridged – vide the abject failure of various United Nations plans from the "development decade" of the 1960s onward – it seems undeniable that for years to come, the planet will be white dominated. With the collapse of communism and the defeat of

Third World attempts to seek alternative paths, the West reigns supreme, as celebrated in a London *Financial Times* headline: "The fall of the Soviet bloc has left the IMF and G7 to rule the world and create a new imperial age."[63] Economic structures have been set in place, causal processes established, whose outcome is to pump wealth from one side of the globe to another, and which will continue to work largely independently of the ill will/good will, racist/antiracist feeling of particular individuals. This globally color-coded distribution of wealth and poverty has been produced by the Racial Contract and in turn reinforces adherence to it in its signatories and beneficiaries.

Moreover, it is not merely that Europe and the former white settler states are globally dominant but that *within* them, where there is a significant nonwhite presence (indigenous peoples, descendants of imported slaves, voluntary nonwhite immigration), whites continue to be privileged vis-à-vis non-whites. The old structures of formal, de jure exclusion have largely been dismantled, the old explicitly biologistic ideologies largely abandoned[64] – the Racial Contract, as will be discussed later, is continually being rewritten – but opportunities for nonwhites, though they have expanded, remain below those for whites. The claim is not, of course, that all whites are better off than all nonwhites, but that, as a statistical generalization, the objective life chances of whites are significantly better.

As an example, consider the United States. A series of books has recently documented the decline of the integrationist hopes raised by the 1960s and the growing intransigence and hostility of whites who think they have "done enough," despite the fact that the country continues to be massively segregated, median black family incomes have began falling by comparison to white family incomes after some earlier closing of the gap, the so-called "black underclass" has basically been written off, and reparations for slavery and post-Emancipation discrimination have never been paid, or, indeed, even seriously considered.[65] Recent work on racial inequality by Melvin Oliver and Thomas Shapiro suggests that wealth is more important than income in determining the likelihood of future racial equalization, since it has a cumulative effect that is passed down through intergenerational transfer, affecting life chances and opportunities for one's children. Whereas in 1988 black households earned sixty-two cents for every dollar earned by white households, the comparative differential with regard to wealth is much greater and, arguably, provides a more realistically negative picture of the prospects for closing the racial gap: "Whites possess nearly twelve times as much median net worth as blacks, or $43,800 versus $3,700. In an even starker contrast, perhaps, the average white household controls $6,999 in net financial assets while the average black household retains no NFA nest egg whatsoever." Moreover, the analytic focus on wealth rather than income exposes how illusory the much-trumpeted rise of a "black middle class" is: "Middle-class blacks, for example, earn seventy cents for every dollar earned by middle-class whites but they possess only fifteen cents for every dollar of wealth held by middle-class whites." This huge disparity in white and black wealth is not remotely contingent, accidental, fortuitous; it is the direct outcome of American state policy and the collusion with it of the white citizenry. In effect, "materially, whites and blacks constitute two nations,"[66] the white nation being constituted by the American Racial Contract in a relationship of structured racial exploitation with the black (and, of course, historically also the red) nation.

A collection of papers from panels organized in the 1980s by the National Economic Association, the professional organization of black economists, provides some insight into the mechanics and the magnitude of such exploitative transfers and denials of opportunity to accumulate material and human capital. It takes as its title *The Wealth of Races* — an ironic tribute to Adam Smith's famous book *The Wealth of Nations* — and analyzes the different varieties of discrimination to which blacks have been subjected: slavery, employment discrimination, wage discrimination, promotion discrimination, white monopoly power discrimination against black capital, racial price discrimination in consumer goods, housing, services, insurance, etc.[67] Many of these, by their very nature, are difficult to quantify; moreover, there are costs in anguish and suffering that can never really be compensated. Nonetheless, those that do lend themselves to calculation offer some remarkable figures. (The figures are unfortunately dated; readers should multiply by a factor that takes 15 years of inflation into account.) If one were to do a calculation of the *cumulative* benefits (through compound interest) from labor market discrimination over the forty-year period from 1929 to 1969 and adjust for inflation, then in 1983 dollars, the figure would be over $1.6 trillion.[68] An estimate for the total of "diverted income" from slavery, 1790 to 1860, compounded and translated into 1983 dollars, would yield the sum of $2.1 trillion to $4.7 trillion.[69] And if one were to try to work out the cumulative value, with compound interest, of unpaid slave labor before 1863, underpayment since 1863, and denial of opportunity to acquire land and natural resources available to white settlers, then the total amount required to compensate blacks "could take more than the entire wealth of the United States."[70]

So this gives an idea of the centrality of racial exploitation to the U.S. economy and the dimensions of the payoff for its white beneficiaries from one nation's Racial Contract. But this very centrality, these very dimensions render the topic taboo, virtually undiscussed in the debates on justice of most white political theory. If there is such a backlash against affirmative action, what would the response be to the demand for the interest on the unpaid forty acres and a mule? These issues cannot be raised because they go to the heart of the real nature of the polity and its structuring by the Racial Contract. White moral theory's debates on justice in the state must therefore inevitably have a somewhat farcical air, since they ignore the central injustice on which the state rests. (No wonder a hypothetical contractarianism that evades the actual circumstances of the polity's founding is preferred!)

Both globally and within particular nations, then, white people, European and their descendants, continue to benefit from the Racial Contract, which creates a world in their cultural image, political states differentially favoring their interests, an economy structured around the racial exploitation of others, and a moral psychology (not just in whites but sometimes in nonwhites also) skewed consciously or unconsciously toward privileging them, taking the status quo of differential racial entitlement as normatively legitimate, and not to be investigated further.

Notes

1 A 1994 report on American philosophy, "Status and Future of the Profession," revealed that "only one department in 20 (28 of the 456 departments reporting) has any [tenure-track] African-American faculty, with slightly fewer having either Hispanic-American or Asian-American [tenure-track] faculty (17 departments in both cases). A mere seven departments have any [tenure-track] Native American faculty." *Proceedings and Addresses of The American Philosophical Association* 70, no. 2 (1996): 137.

2 For an overview, see, for example, Ernest Barker, Introduction to *Social Contract: Essays by Locke, Hume, and Rousseau*, ed. Barker (1947; rpt. Oxford: Oxford University Press, 1960); Michael Lessnoff, *Social Contract* (Atlantic Highlands, N.J.: Humanities Press, 1986); Will Kymlicka, "The Social Contract Tradition," in *A Companion to Ethics*, ed. Peter Singer (Oxford: Blackwell Reference, 1991), pp. 186–96; Jean Hampton, "Contract and Consent," in *A Companion to Contemporary Political Philosophy*, ed. Robert E. Goodin and Philip Pettit (Oxford: Blackwell Reference, 1993), pp. 379–93.

3 Indigenous peoples as a global group are sometimes referred to as the "Fourth World." See Roger Moody, ed., *The Indigenous Voice: Visions and Realities*, 2d ed., rev. (1988; rpt. Utrecht: International Books, 1993).

4 For a praiseworthy exception, see Iris Marion Young, *Justice and the Politics of Difference* (Princeton: Princeton University Press, 1990). Young focuses explicitly on the implications for standard conceptions of justice of group subordination, including racial groups.

5 Credit for the revival of social contract theory, and indeed post-war political philosophy in general, is usually given to John Rawls, *A Theory of Justice* (Cambridge: Harvard University Press, 1971).

6 Thomas Hobbes, *Leviathan*, ed. Richard Tuck (Cambridge: Cambridge University Press, 1991); John Locke, *Two Treatises of Government*, ed. Peter Laslett (1960; rpt. Cambridge: Cambridge University Press, 1988); Jean-Jacques Rousseau, *Discourse on the Origins and Foundations of Inequality among Men*, trans. Maurice Cranston (London: Penguin, 1984); Rousseau, *The Social Contract*, trans. Maurice Cranston (London: Penguin, 1968); Immanuel Kant, *The Metaphysics of Morals*, trans. Mary Gregor (Cambridge: Cambridge University Press, 1991).

7 In "Contract and Consent," p. 382, Jean Hampton reminds us that for the classic theorists, contract is intended "simultaneously to describe the nature of political societies, and to prescribe a new and more defensible form for such societies." In this essay, and also in "The Contractarian Explanation of the State," in *The Philosophy of the Human Sciences*, Midwest Studies in Philosophy, 15, ed. Peter A. French, Theodore E. Uehling Jr., and Howard K. Wettstein (Notre Dame, Ind.: University of Notre Dame Press, 1990), pp. 344–71, she argues explicitly for a revival of the old-fashioned, seemingly discredited "contractarian explanation of the state." Hampton points out that the imagery of "contract" captures the essential point that "authoritative political societies are human creations" (not divinely ordained or naturally determined) and "*conventionally* generated."

8 Rousseau, *Discourse on Inequality*, pt. 2.

9 Carole Pateman, *The Sexual Contract* (Stanford: Stanford University Press, 1988). One difference between our approaches is that Pateman thinks

contractarianism is *necessarily* oppressive – "Contract always generates political right in the form of relations of domination and subordination" (p. 8) – whereas I see domination within contract theory as more contingent. For me, in other words, it is not the case that a Racial Contract *had* to underpin the social contract. Rather, this contract is a result of the particular conjunction of circumstances in global history, which led to European imperialism. And as a corollary, I believe contract theory can be put to positive use once this hidden history is acknowledged, though I do not follow up such a program in this book. For an example of feminist contractarianism that contrasts with Pateman's negative assessment, see Susan Moller Okin, *Justice, Gender, and the Family* (New York: Basic Books, 1989).

10 See, for example, Paul Thagard, *Conceptual Revolutions* (Princeton: Princeton University Press, 1992), p. 22.

11 See Hampton, "Contract and Consent" and "Contractarian Explanation." Hampton's own focus is the liberal-democratic state, but obviously her strategy of employing "contract" to conceptualize conventionally generated norms and practices is open to be adapted to the understanding of the non-liberal-democratic *racial* state, the difference being that "the people" now become the white population.

12 Otto Gierke termed these respectively the *Gesellschaftsvertrag* and the *Herrschaftsvertrag*. For a discussion, see, for example, Barker, Introduction, *Social Contract*; and Lessnoff, *Social Contract*, chap. 3.

13 Rawls, *Theory of Justice*, pt. 1.

14 In speaking generally of "whites," I am not, of course, denying that there are gender relations of domination and subordination or, for that matter, class relations of domination and subordination within the white population. I am not claiming that race is the only axis of social oppression. But race is what I want to focus on; so in the absence of that chimerical entity, a unifying theory of race, class, and gender oppression, it seems to me that one has to make generalizations that it would be stylistically cumbersome to qualify at every point. So these should just be taken as read. Nevertheless, I do want to insist that my overall picture is roughly accurate, i.e., that whites *do* in general benefit from white supremacy (though gender and class

differentiation mean, of course, that they do not benefit equally) and that historically white racial solidarity *has* overridden class and gender solidarity. Women, subordinate classes, and nonwhites may be oppressed in common, but it is not a common oppression: the structuring is so different that it has not led to any common front between them. Neither white women nor white workers have *as a group* (as against principled individuals) historically made common cause with nonwhites against colonialism, white settlement, slavery, imperialism, Jim Crow, apartheid. We all have multiple identities, and, to this extent, most of us are both privileged and disadvantaged by different systems of domination. But white racial identity has generally triumphed over all others; it is race that (transgender, transclass) has generally determined the social world and loyalties, the lifeworld, of whites — whether as citizens of the colonizing mother country, settlers, nonslaves, or beneficiaries of the "color bar" and the "color line." There has been no comparable, spontaneously crystallizing transracial "workers'" world or transracial "female" world: race is the identity around which whites have usually closed ranks. Nevertheless, as a concession, a semantic signal of this admitted gender privileging within the white population, by which white women's personhood is originally virtual, dependent on their having the appropriate relation (daughter, sister, wife) to the white male, I will sometimes deliberately use the non-gender-neutral "men." For some recent literature on these problematic intersections of identity, see, for example, Ruth Frankenberg, *White Women, Race Matters: The Social Construction of Whiteness* (Minneapolis: University of Minnesota Press, 1993); Nupur Chaudhuri and Margaret Strobel, eds., *Western Women and Imperialism: Complicity and Resistance* (Bloomington: Indiana University Press, 1992); David Roediger, *The Wages of Whiteness: Race and the Making of the American Working Class* (London: Verso, 1991).

15 Rousseau, *Social Contract*; Hobbes, *Leviathan*.

16 For a discussion of the two versions, see Kymlicka, "The Social Contract Tradition."

17 Hobbes's judgment that "INJUSTICE, is no other than *the not Performance of Covenant*," *Leviathan*, p. 100, has standardly been taken as a statement of moral

conventionalism. Hobbes's egalitarian social morality is based not on the moral equality of humans, but on the fact of a rough parity of physical power and mental ability in the state of nature (chap. 13). Within this framework, the Racial Contract would then be the natural outcome of a systematic *disparity* in power – of weaponry rather than individual strength – between expansionist Europe and the rest of the world. This could be said to be neatly summed up in Hilaire Belloc's famous little ditty: "Whatever happens, we have got / The Maxim Gun, and they have not." Hilaire Belloc, "The Modern Traveller," quoted in John Ellis, *The Social History of the Machine Gun* (1975; rpt. Baltimore: Johns Hopkins Paperbacks, 1986), p. 94. Or at an earlier stage, in the conquest of the Americas, the musket and the steel sword.

18 See, for example, A. P. d'Entrèves, *Natural Law: An Introduction to Legal Philosophy*, 2d rev. ed. (1951; rpt. London: Hutchinson, 1970).

19 Locke, *Second Treatise* of *Two Treatises of Government*, p. 269.

20 Kant, *Metaphysics of Morals*, pp. 230–32.

21 See Arthur O. Lovejoy, *The Great Chain of Being: A Study of the History of an Idea* (Cambridge: Harvard University Press, 1948).

22 For the notion of "epistemological communities," see recent work in feminist theory – for example, Linda Alcoff and Elizabeth Potter, eds., *Feminist Epistemologies* (New York: Routledge, 1993).

23 Thus Ward Churchill, a Native American, speaks sardonically of "fantasies of the master race." Ward Churchill, *Fantasies of the Master Race: Literature, Cinema, and the Colonization of American Indians*, ed. M. Annette Jaimes (Monroe, Maine: Common Courage Press, 1992); William Gibson, *Neuromancer* (New York: Ace Science Fiction Books, 1984).

24 Robert Young, *White Mythologies: Writing History and the West* (London: Routledge, 1990); Edward W. Said, *Orientalism* (1978; rpt. New York: Vintage Books, 1979); V. Y. Mudimbe, *The Invention of Africa: Gnosis, Philosophy, and the Order of Knowledge* (Bloomington: Indiana University Press, 1988); Enrique Dussel, *The Invention of the Americas: Eclipse of "the Other" and the Myth of Modernity*, trans. Michael D. Barber (1992; rpt. New York: Continuum, 1995); Robert Berkhofer Jr., *The White Man's Indian: Images of the American Indian from Columbus to the Present* (New York:

Knopf, 1978); Gretchen M. Bataille and Charles L. P. Silet, eds., *The Pretend Indians: Images of Native Americans in the Movies* (Ames: Iowa State University Press, 1980); George M. Fredrickson, *The Black Image in the White Mind: The Debate on Afro-American Character and Destiny 1817–1914* (1971; rpt. Hanover, N.H.: Wesleyan University Press, 1987); Roberto Fernández Retamar, *Caliban and Other Essays*, trans. Edward Baker (Minneapolis: University of Minnesota Press, 1989); Peter Hulme, *Colonial Encounters: Europe and the Native Caribbean, 1492–1797* (1986; rpt. London: Routledge, 1992).

25 Frederick Engels, *The Origin of the Family, Private Property, and the State* (New York: International, 1972), p. 120.

26 Jean-Paul Sartre, Preface to Frantz Fanon, *The Wretched of the Earth*, trans. Constance Farrington (1961; rpt. New York: Grove Weidenfeld, 1991).

27 V. G. Kiernan, *The Lords of Human Kind: Black Man, Yellow Man, and White Man in an Age of Empire* (1969; rpt. New York: Columbia University Press, 1986); Anthony Pagden, *Lords of All the World: Ideologies of Empire in Spain, Britain, and France, c. 1500–c. 1800* (New Haven: Yale University Press, 1995).

28 Pagden, *Lords*, pp. 1–2.

29 Robert A. Williams Jr., "The Algebra of Federal Indian Law: The Hard Trail of Decolonizing and Americanizing the White Man's Indian Jurisprudence," *Wisconsin Law Review* 1986 (1986): 229. See also Robert A. Williams Jr., *The American Indian in Western Legal Thought: The Discourses of Conquest* (New York: Oxford University Press, 1990).

30 Williams, "Algebra," pp. 230–1, 233. See also Lewis Hanke, *Aristotle and the American Indians: A Study in Race Prejudice in the Modern World* (Bloomington: Indiana University Press, 1959), p. 19.

31 Williams, "Algebra"; Hanke, *Aristotle*.

32 Allen Carey-Webb, "Other-Fashioning: The Discourse of Empire and Nation in Lope de Vega's *El Nuevo mundo descubierto par Cristobal Colon*," in *Amerindian Images and the Legacy of Columbus*, ed. René Jara and Nicholas Spadaccini, Hispanic Issues, 9 (Minneapolis: University of Minnesota Press, 1992), pp. 433–4.

33 Philip D. Curtin, Introduction to *Imperialism*, ed. Curtin (New York: Walker, 1971), p. xiii.

34 Pierre L. van den Berghe, *Race and Racism: A Comparative Perspective*, 2d ed. (New York: Wiley, 1978).

35 Pagden, *Lords*, chap. 1.

36 Williams, "Algebra," p. 253.

37 Justice Joseph Story, quoted in Williams, "Algebra," p. 256.

38 *Dred Scott v. Sanford*, 1857, in *Race, Class, and Gender in the United States: An Integrated Study*, ed. Paula S. Rothenberg, 3d ed. (New York: St. Martin's Press, 1995), p. 323.

39 Excerpt from Jules Harmand, *Domination et colonisation* (1910), in Curtin, *Imperialism*, pp. 294–8.

40 Edward W. Said, *Culture and Imperialism* (New York: Knopf, 1993), pp. xiii, xiv.

41 Harold R. Isaacs, "Color in World Affairs," *Foreign Affairs* 47 (1969): 235, 246. See also Benjamin P. Bowser, ed., *Racism and Anti-Racism in World Perspective* (Thousand Oaks, Calif: Sage, 1995).

42 Helen Jackson, *A Century of Dishonor: A Sketch of the United States Government's Dealings with Some of the Indian Tribes* (1881; rpt. New York: Indian Head Books, 1993). In her classic exposé, Jackson concludes (pp. 337–8): "It makes little difference . . . where one opens the record of the history of the Indians; every page and every year has its dark stain. The story of one tribe is the story of all, varied only by differences of time and place. . . . [T]he United States Government breaks promises now [1880] as deftly as then [1795], and with an added ingenuity from long practice." Jackson herself, it should be noted, saw Native Americans as having a "lesser right," since there was no question about the "fairness of holding that ultimate sovereignty belonged to the civilized discoverer, as against the savage barbarian." To think otherwise would merely be "feeble sentimentalism" (pp. 10–11). But she did at least want this lesser right recognized.

43 See, for example, David E. Stannard, *American Holocaust: Columbus and the Conquest of the New World* (New York: Oxford University Press, 1992).

44 Richard Drinnon, *Facing West: The Metaphysics of Indian-Hating and Empire-Building* (New York: Meridian, 1980), p. 332.

45 Ibid., p. 102. See also Reginald Horsman, *Race and Manifest Destiny: The Origins of American Racial Anglo-Saxonism* (Cambridge: Harvard University Press, 1981); and Ronald Takaki, *Iron Cages: Race and Culture in 19th-Century America* (1979; rpt. New York: Oxford University Press, 1990).

46 A. Grenfell Price, *White Settlers and Native Peoples: An Historical Study of Racial Contacts between English-Speaking Whites and Aboriginal Peoples in the United States, Canada, Australia, and New Zealand* (1950; rpt. Westport, Conn.: Greenwood Press, 1972); A. Grenfell Price, *The Western Invasions of the Pacific and Its Continents* (Oxford: Clarendon Press, 1963); van den Berghe, *Race*; Louis Hartz, *The Founding of New Societies: Studies in the History of the United States, Latin America, South Africa, Canada, and Australia* (New York: Harcourt, Brace, and World, 1964); F. S. Stevens, ed., *Racism: The Australian Experience*, 3 vols. (New York: Taplinger, 1972); Henry Reynolds, *The Other Side of the Frontier: Aboriginal Resistance to the European Invasion of Australia* (Harmondsworth, Middlesex: Penguin, 1982). Price's books are valuable sources in comparative history, but – though progressive by the standards of the time – they need to be treated with caution, since their figures and attitudes are both now somewhat dated. In *White Settlers*, for example, the Indian population north of the Rio Grande is estimated at fewer than 850,000, whereas estimates today are ten to twenty times higher, and Price speculates that the Indians were "less advanced than their white conquerors" because they had smaller brains (pp. 6–7).

47 Van den Berghe, *Race*, p. 18.

48 C. Vann Woodward, *The Strange Career of Jim Crow*, 3d ed. (1955; rpt. New York: Oxford University Press, 1974); George M. Fredrickson, *White Supremacy: A Comparative Study in American and South African History* (New York: Oxford University Press, 1981); Douglas S. Massey and Nancy A. Denton, *American Apartheid: Segregation and the Making of the Underclass* (Cambridge: Harvard University Press, 1993).

49 See, for example, Kiernan, *Lords*; V. G. Kiernan, *Imperialism and its Contradictions*, ed. Harvey J. Kaye (New York: Routledge, 1995); D. K. Fieldhouse, *The Colonial Empires: A Comparative Survey from the Eighteenth Century* (1966; rpt. London: Macmillan, 1982); Pagden, *Lords*; Chinweizu, *The West and the Rest of Us: White Predators, Black Slavers, and the African Elite* (New York: Vintage Books, 1975); Henri Brunschwig, *French Colonialism, 1871–1914: Myths and Realities*, trans. William Granville Brown (1964; rpt. New York: Praeger, 1966); David Healy, *U.S. Expansionism: The Imperialist Urge in the 1890s* (Madison: University of Wisconsin Press, 1970).

50 Said, *Culture*, p. 8.

51 Kiernan, *Lords*, p. 24.

52 Linda Alcoff outlines an attractive, distinctively Latin American ideal of hybrid racial identity in

her "Mestizo Identity," in *American Mixed Race: The Culture of Microdiversity*, ed. Naomi Zack (Lanham, Md.: Rowman and Littlefield, 1995), pp. 257–78. Unfortunately, however, this ideal has yet to be realized. For an exposure of the Latin American myths of "racial democracy" and a race-transcendent *mestizaje*, and an account of the reality of the ideal of *blanqueamiento* (whitening) and the continuing subordination of blacks and the darker-skinned throughout the region, see, for example, Minority Rights Group, ed., *No Longer Invisible: Afro-Latin Americans Today* (London: Minority Rights, 1995); and Bowser, *Racism and Anti-Racism*.

53 Locke, *Second Treatise*, pp. 350–1. Since Locke also uses "property" to mean rights, this is not quite as one-dimensional a vision of government as it sounds.

54 Hobbes, *Leviathan*, p. 89.

55 W. E. B. Du Bois, *Black Reconstruction in America, 1860–1880* (1935; rpt. New York: Atheneum, 1992).

56 See Eric Jones, *The European Miracle* (Cambridge: Cambridge University Press, 1981). My discussion here follows J. M. Blaut et al., *1492: The Debate on Colonialism, Eurocentrism, and History* (Trenton, N.J.: Africa World Press, 1992); and J. M. Blaut, *The Colonizer's Model of the World: Geographical Diffusionism and Eurocentric History* (New York: Guilford Press, 1993).

57 Blaut, *1492*; Blaut, *Colonizer's Model*.

58 Sandra Harding, Introduction to Harding, ed., *The "Racial" Economy of Science: Toward a Democratic Future* (Bloomington: Indiana University Press, 1993), p. 2.

59 Eric Williams, *Capitalism and Slavery* (1944; rpt. New York: Capricorn Books, 1966).

60 Walter Rodney, *How Europe Underdeveloped Africa* (1972; rpt. Washington, D.C.: Howard University Press, 1974); Samir Amin, *Eurocentrism*, trans. Russell Moore (1988: rpt. New York: Monthly Review Press, 1989); André Gunder Frank, *World Accumulation, 1492–1789* (New York: Monthly Review Press,

1978); Immanuel Wallerstein, *The Modern World System*, 3 vols. (New York: Academic Press, 1974–1988).

61 Blaut, *1492*, p. 3.

62 Kiernan, *Imperialism*, pp. 98, 149.

63 Quoted in Noam Chomsky, *Year 501: The Conquest Continues* (Boston: South End Press, 1993), p. 61.

64 But see Richard J. Herrnstein and Charles Murray's bestseller *The Bell Curve: Intelligence and Class Structure in American Life* (New York: Free Press, 1994), as a sign that the older, straightforwardly racist theories may be making a comeback.

65 See, for example: Andrew Hacker, *Two Nations: Black and White, Separate, Hostile, Unequal* (New York: Scribner's, 1992); Derrick Bell, *Faces at the Bottom of the Well: The Permanence of Racism* (New York: BasicBooks, 1992); Massey and Denton, *American Apartheid*; Stephen Steinberg, *Turning Back: The Retreat from Racial Justice in American Thought and Policy* (Boston: Beacon Press, 1995); Donald R. Kinder and Lynn M. Sanders, *Divided by Color: Racial Politics and Democratic Ideals* (Chicago: University of Chicago Press, 1996); Tom Wicker, *Tragic Failure: Racial Integration in America* (New York: William Morrow, 1996).

66 Melvin L. Oliver and Thomas M. Shapiro, *Black Wealth/White Wealth: A New Perspective on Racial Inequality* (New York: Routledge, 1995), pp. 86–7.

67 Richard F. America, ed., *The Wealth of Races: The Present Value of Benefits from Past Injustices* (New York: Greenwood Press, 1990). For another ironic tribute, whose subject is the international distribution of wealth, see Malcolm Caldwell, *The Wealth of Some Nations* (London: Zed Press, 1977).

68 David H. Swinton, "Racial Inequality and Reparations," in America, *Wealth of Races*, p. 156.

69 James Marketti, "Estimated Present Value of Income Diverted during Slavery," in America, *Wealth of Races*, p. 107.

70 Robert S. Browne, "Achieving Parity through Reparations," in America, *Wealth of Races*, p. 204; Swintom, "Racial Inequality," p. 156.

Chapter 8

Plato

CRITO

Plato (428/427–348/347 BCE) was a Greek philosopher and student of Socrates. In the *Crito* (360 BCE), Plato tells the story of Socrates' final hours, after he had been sentenced to die by drinking hemlock for having corrupted the youth and not believing in Athenian gods. Socrates' friends have devised a plan by which Socrates might escape his sentence, and attempt to convince him to leave his prison cell with them. Socrates, in response, argues that he has a moral duty to obey the laws of Athens, even if those laws are unjust, and thus to accept his sentence of death.

CRITO

Plato, Translated by Benjamin Jowett

Socrates. Why have you come at this hour, Crito? it must be quite early.

Crito. Yes, certainly.

Soc. What is the exact time?

Cr. The dawn is breaking.

Soc. I wonder the keeper of the prison would let you in.

Cr. He knows me because I often come, Socrates; moreover, I have done him a kindness.

Soc. And are you only just come?

Cr. No, I came some time ago.

Soc. Then why did you sit and say nothing, instead of awakening me at once?

Cr. Why, indeed, Socrates, I myself would rather not have all this sleeplessness and sorrow. But I have been wondering at your peaceful slumbers, and that was the reason why I did not awaken you, because I wanted you to be out of pain. I have always thought you happy in the calmness of your temperament; but never did I see the like of the easy, cheerful way in which you bear this calamity.

Soc. Why, Crito, when a man has reached my age he ought not to be repining at the prospect of death.

Cr. And yet other old men find themselves in similar misfortunes, and age does not prevent them from repining.

Soc. That may be. But you have not told me why you come at this early hour.

Cr. I come to bring you a message which is sad and painful; not, as I believe, to yourself but to all of us who are your friends, and saddest of all to me.

Soc. What! I suppose that the ship has come from Delos, on the arrival of which I am to die?

Cr. No, the ship has not actually arrived, but she will probably be here to-day, as persons who have come from Sunium tell me that they have left her there; and therefore to-morrow, Socrates, will be the last day of your life.

Soc. Very well, Crito; if such is the will of God, I am willing; but my belief is that there will be a delay of a day.

Cr. Why do you say this?

Soc. I will tell you. I am to die on the day after the arrival of the ship?

Cr. Yes; that is what the authorities say.

Soc. But I do not think that the ship will be here until to-morrow; this I gather from a vision which I had last night, or rather only just now, when you fortunately allowed me to sleep.

Cr. And what was the nature of the vision?

Soc. There came to me the likeness of a woman, fair and comely, clothed in white raiment, who called to me and said: O Socrates:
"The third day hence, to Phthia shalt thou go."

Cr. What a singular dream, Socrates!

Soc. There can be no doubt about the meaning Crito, I think.

Cr. Yes: the meaning is only too clear. But, O! my beloved Socrates, let me entreat you once more to take my advice and escape. For if you die I shall not only lose a friend who can never be replaced, but there is another evil: people who do not know you and me will believe that I might have saved you if I had been willing to give money, but that I did not care. Now, can there be a worse disgrace than this – that I should be thought to value money more than the life of a friend? For the many will not be persuaded that I wanted you to escape, and that you refused.

Soc. But why, my dear Crito, should we care about the opinion of the many? Good men, and they are the only persons who are worth considering, will think of these things truly as they happened.

Cr. But do you see. Socrates, that the opinion of the many must be regarded, as is evident in your own case, because they can do the very greatest evil to anyone who has lost their good opinion?

Soc. I only wish, Crito, that they could; for then they could also do the greatest good, and that would be well. But the truth is, that they can do neither good nor evil: they cannot make a man wise or make him foolish; and whatever they do is the result of chance.

Cr. Well, I will not dispute about that; but please to tell me, Socrates, whether you are not acting out of regard to me and your other friends: are you not afraid that if you escape hence we may get into trouble with the informers for having stolen you away, and lose either the whole or a great part of our property; or that even a worse evil may happen to us? Now, if this is your fear, be at ease; for in order to save you, we ought surely to run this or even a greater risk; be persuaded, then, and do as I say.

Soc. Yes, Crito, that is one fear which you mention, but by no means the only one.

Cr. Fear not. There are persons who at no great cost are willing to save you and bring you out of prison; and as for the informers, you may observe that they are far from being exorbitant in their demands; a little money will satisfy them. My means, which, as I am sure, are ample, are at your service, and if you have a scruple about spending all mine, here are strangers who will give you the use of theirs; and one of them, Simmias the Theban, has brought a sum of money for this very purpose; and Cebes and many others are willing to spend their money too. I say, therefore, do not on that account hesitate about making your escape, and do not say, as you did in the court, that you will have a difficulty in knowing what to do with yourself if you escape. For men will love you in other places to which you may go, and not in Athens only; there are friends of mine in Thessaly, if you like to go to them, who will value and protect you, and no Thessalian will give you any trouble. Nor can I think that you are justified, Socrates, in betraying your own life when you might be saved; this is playing into the hands of your enemies and destroyers; and moreover I should say that you were betraying your children; for you might bring them up and educate them; instead of which you go away and leave them, and they will have to take their chance; and if they do not meet with the usual fate of orphans, there will be small thanks to you. No man should bring children into the world who is unwilling to persevere to the end in their nurture and education. But you are choosing the easier part, as I think, not the better and manlier, which would rather have become one who professes virtue in all his actions, like yourself. And, indeed, I am ashamed not only of you, but of us who are your friends, when I reflect that this entire business of yours will be attributed to our want of courage. The trial need never have come on, or might have been brought to another issue; and the end of all, which is the crowning absurdity, will seem to have been permitted by us,

through cowardice and baseness, who might have saved you, as you might have saved yourself, if we had been good for anything (for there was no difficulty in escaping); and we did not see how disgraceful, Socrates, and also miserable all this will be to us as well as to you. Make your mind up then, or rather have your mind already made up, for the time of deliberation is over, and there is only one thing to be done, which must be done, if at all, this very night, and which any delay will render all but impossible; I beseech you therefore, Socrates, to be persuaded by me, and to do as I say.

Soc. Dear Crito, your zeal is invaluable, if a right one; but if wrong, the greater the zeal the greater the evil; and therefore we ought to consider whether these things shall be done or not. For I am and always have been one of those natures who must be guided by reason, whatever the reason may be which upon reflection appears to me to be the best; and now that this fortune has come upon me, I cannot put away the reasons which I have before given: the principles which I have hitherto honored and revered I still honor, and unless we can find other and better principles on the instant, I am certain not to agree with you; no, not even if the power of the multitude could inflict many more imprisonments, confiscations, deaths, frightening us like children with hobgoblin terrors. But what will be the fairest way of considering the question? Shall I return to your old argument about the opinions of men, some of which are to be regarded, and others, as we were saying, are not to be regarded? Now were we right in maintaining this before I was condemned? And has the argument which was once good now proved to be talk for the sake of talking; in fact an amusement only, and altogether vanity? That is what I want to consider with your help, Crito: whether, under my present circumstances, the argument appears to be in any way different or not; and is to be allowed by me or disallowed. That argument, which, as I believe, is maintained by many who assume to be authorities, was to the effect, as I was saying, that the opinions of some men are to be regarded, and of other men not to be regarded. Now you, Crito, are a disinterested person who are not going to die to-morrow – at least, there is no human probability of this, and you are therefore not liable to be deceived by the circumstances in which you are placed. Tell me, then, whether I am right in saying that some opinions, and the opinions of some men only, are to be valued, and other opinions, and the opinions of other men, are not to be valued. I ask you whether I was right in maintaining this?

Cr. Certainly.

Soc. The good are to be regarded, and not the bad?

Cr. Yes.

Soc. And the opinions of the wise are good, and the opinions of the unwise are evil?

Cr. Certainly.

Soc. And what was said about another matter? Was the disciple in gymnastics supposed to attend to the praise and blame and opinion of every man, or of one man only – his physician or trainer, whoever that was?

Cr. Of one man only.

Soc. And he ought to fear the censure and welcome the praise of that one only, and not of the many?

Cr. That is clear.

Soc. And he ought to live and train, and eat and drink in the way which seems good to his single master who has understanding, rather than according to the opinion of all other men put together?

Cr. True.

Soc. And if he disobeys and disregards the opinion and approval of the one, and regards the opinion of the many who have no understanding, will he not suffer evil?

Cr. Certainly he will.

Soc. And what will the evil be, whither tending and what affecting, in the disobedient person?

Cr. Clearly, affecting the body; that is what is destroyed by the evil.

Soc. Very good; and is not this true, Crito, of other things which we need not separately enumerate? In the matter of just and unjust, fair and foul, good and evil, which are the subjects of our present consultation, ought we to follow the opinion of the many and to fear them; or the opinion of the one man who has understanding, and whom we ought to fear and reverence more than all the rest of the world: and whom deserting we shall destroy and injure that principle in us which may be assumed to be improved by justice and deteriorated by injustice; is there not such a principle?

Cr. Certainly there is, Socrates.

Soc. Take a parallel instance; if, acting under the advice of men who have no understanding, we destroy that which is improvable by health and deteriorated by disease – when that has been destroyed, I say, would life be worth having? And that is – the body?

Cr. Yes.

Soc. Could we live, having an evil and corrupted body?

Cr. Certainly not.

Soc. And will life be worth having, if that higher part of man be depraved, which is improved by justice and deteriorated by injustice? Do we suppose that principle, whatever it may be in man, which has to do with justice and injustice, to be inferior to the body?

Cr. Certainly not.

Soc. More honored, then?

Cr. Far more honored.

Soc. Then, my friend, we must not regard what the many say of us: but what he, the one man who has understanding of just and unjust, will say, and what the truth will say. And therefore you begin in error when you suggest that we should regard the opinion of the many about just and unjust, good and evil, honorable and dishonorable. Well, someone will say, "But the many can kill us."

Cr. Yes, Socrates; that will clearly be the answer.

Soc. That is true; but still I find with surprise that the old argument is, as I conceive, unshaken as ever. And I should like to know whether I may say the same of another proposition — that not life, but a good life, is to be chiefly valued?

Cr. Yes, that also remains.

Soc. And a good life is equivalent to a just and honorable one — that holds also?

Cr. Yes, that holds.

Soc. From these premises I proceed to argue the question whether I ought or ought not to try to escape without the consent of the Athenians: and if I am clearly right in escaping, then I will make the attempt; but if not, I will abstain. The other considerations which you mention, of money and loss of character, and the duty of educating children, are, I fear, only the doctrines of the multitude, who would be as ready to call people to life, if they were able, as they are to put them to death — and with as little reason. But now, since the argument has thus far prevailed, the only question which remains to be considered is whether we shall do rightly either in escaping or in suffering others to aid in our escape and paying them in money and thanks, or whether we shall not do rightly; and if the latter, then death or any other calamity which may ensue on my remaining here must not be allowed to enter into the calculation.

Cr. I think that you are right, Socrates; how then shall we proceed?

Soc. Let us consider the matter together, and do you either refute me if you can, and I will be convinced; or else cease, my dear friend, from repeating to me that I ought to escape against the wishes of the Athenians: for I am extremely desirous to be persuaded by you, but not against my own better judgment. And now please to consider my first position, and do your best to answer me.

Cr. I will do my best.

Soc. Are we to say that we are never intentionally to do wrong, or that in one way we ought and in another way we ought not to do wrong, or is doing wrong always evil and dishonorable, as I was just now saying, and as has been already acknowledged by us? Are all our former admissions which were made within a few days to be thrown away? And have we, at our age, been earnestly discoursing with one another all our life long only to discover that we are no better than children? Or are we to rest assured, in spite of the opinion of the many, and in spite of consequences whether better or worse, of the truth of what was then said, that injustice is always an evil and dishonor to him who acts unjustly? Shall we affirm that?

Cr. Yes.

Soc. Then we must do no wrong?

Cr. Certainly not.

Soc. Nor when injured injure in return, as the many imagine; for we must injure no one at all?

Cr. Clearly not.

Soc. Again, Crito, may we do evil?

Cr. Surely not, Socrates.

Soc. And what of doing evil in return for evil, which is the morality of the many — is that just or not?

Cr. Not just.

Soc. For doing evil to another is the same as injuring him?

Cr. Very true.

Soc. Then we ought not to retaliate or render evil for evil to anyone, whatever evil we may have suffered from him. But I would have you consider, Crito, whether you really mean what you are saying. For this opinion has never been held, and never will be held, by any considerable number of persons; and those who are agreed and those who are not agreed upon this point have no common ground, and can only despise one another, when they see how widely they differ. Tell me, then, whether you agree with and assent to my first principle, that neither injury nor retaliation nor warding off evil by evil is ever right. And shall that be the premise of our agreement? Or do you decline and dissent from this? For this has been of old and is still my opinion; but, if you are of another opinion, let me hear what you have to say. If, however, you remain of the same mind

as formerly, I will proceed to the next step.

Cr. You may proceed, for I have not changed my mind.

Soc. Then I will proceed to the next step, which may be put in the form of a question: Ought a man to do what he admits to be right, or ought he to betray the right?

Cr. He ought to do what he thinks right.

Soc. But if this is true, what is the application? In leaving the prison against the will of the Athenians, do I wrong any? Or rather do I not wrong those whom I ought least to wrong? Do I not desert the principles which were acknowledged by us to be just? What do you say?

Cr. I cannot tell, Socrates, for I do not know.

Soc. Then consider the matter in this way: Imagine that I am about to play truant (you may call the proceeding by any name which you like), and the laws and the government come and interrogate me: "Tell us, Socrates," they say; "what are you about? are you going by an act of yours to overturn us — the laws and the whole State, as far as in you lies? Do you imagine that a State can subsist and not be overthrown, in which the decisions of law have no power, but are set aside and overthrown by individuals?" What will be our answer, Crito, to these and the like words? Anyone, and especially a clever rhetorician, will have a good deal to urge about the evil of setting aside the law which requires a sentence to be carried out; and we might reply, "Yes; but the State has injured us and given an unjust sentence." Suppose I say that?

Cr. Very good, Socrates.

Soc. "And was that our agreement with you?" the laws would say, "or were you to abide by the sentence of the State?" And if I were to express astonishment at their saying this, the laws would probably add: "Answer, Socrates, instead of opening your eyes: you are in the habit of asking and answering questions. Tell us what complaint you have to make against us which justifies you in attempting to destroy us and the State? In the first place did we not bring you into existence? Your father married your mother by our aid and begat you. Say whether you have any objection to urge against those of us who regulate marriage?" None, I should reply. "Or against those of us who regulate the system of nurture and education of children in which you were trained? Were not the laws, who have the charge of this, right in commanding your father to train you in music and gymnastic?" Right, I should reply. "Well, then, since you were brought into the world and nurtured and educated by us, can you deny in the first place that you are our child and slave, as your fathers were before you? And if this is true you are not on equal terms with us; nor can you think that you have a right to do to us what we are doing to you. Would you have any right to strike or revile or do any other evil to a father or to your master, if you had one, when you have been struck or reviled by him, or received some other evil at his hands? – you would not say this? And because we think right to destroy you, do you think that you have any right to destroy us in return, and your country as far as in you lies? And will you, O professor of true virtue, say that you are justified in this? Has a philosopher like you failed to discover that our country is more to be valued and

higher and holier far than mother or father or any ancestor, and more to be regarded in the eyes of the gods and of men of understanding? Also to be soothed, and gently and reverently entreated when angry, even more than a father, and if not persuaded, obeyed? And when we are punished by her, whether with imprisonment or stripes, the punishment is to be endured in silence; and if she leads us to wounds or death in battle, thither we follow as is right; neither may anyone yield or retreat or leave his rank, but whether in battle or in a court of law, or in any other place, he must do what his city and his country order him; or he must change their view of what is just: and if he may do no violence to his father or mother, much less may he do violence to his country." What answer shall we make to this, Crito? Do the laws speak truly, or do they not?

Cr. I think that they do.

Soc. Then the laws will say: "Consider, Socrates, if this is true, that in your present attempt you are going to do us wrong. For, after having brought you into the world, and nurtured and educated you, and given you and every other citizen a share in every good that we had to give, we further proclaim and give the right to every Athenian, that if he does not like us when he has come of age and has seen the ways of the city, and made our acquaintance, he may go where he pleases and take his goods with him; and none of us laws will forbid him or interfere with him. Any of you who does not like us and the city, and who wants to go to a colony or to any other city, may go where he likes, and take his goods with him. But he who has experience of the manner in which we order justice and administer the State, and still remains, has entered into an implied contract that he will do as we command him. And he who disobeys us is, as we maintain, thrice wrong: first, because in disobeying us he is disobeying his parents; secondly, because we are the authors of his education; thirdly, because he has made an agreement with us that he will duly obey our commands; and he neither obeys them nor convinces us that our commands are wrong; and we do not rudely impose them, but give him the alternative of obeying or convincing us; that is what we offer and he does neither. These are the sort of accusations to which, as we were saying, you, Socrates, will be exposed if you accomplish your intentions; you, above all other Athenians." Suppose I ask, why is this? they will justly retort upon me that I above all other men have acknowledged the agreement. "There is clear proof," they will say, "Socrates, that we and the city were not displeasing to you. Of all Athenians you have been the most constant resident in the city, which, as you never leave, you may be supposed to love. For you never went out of the city either to see the games, except once when you went to the Isthmus, or to any other place unless when you were on military service; nor did you travel as other men do. Nor had you any curiosity to know other States or their laws: your affections did not go beyond us and our State; we were your especial favorites, and you acquiesced in our government of you; and this is the State in which you begat your children, which is a proof of your satisfaction. Moreover, you might, if you had liked, have fixed the penalty at

banishment in the course of the trial – the State which refuses to let you go now would have let you go then. But you pretended that you preferred death to exile, and that you were not grieved at death. And now you have forgotten these fine sentiments, and pay no respect to us, the laws, of whom you are the destroyer; and are doing what only a miserable slave would do, running away and turning your back upon the compacts and agreements which you made as a citizen. And first of all answer this very question: Are we right in saying that you agreed to be governed according to us in deed, and not in word only? Is that true or not?" How shall we answer that, Crito? Must we not agree?

Cr. There is no help, Socrates.

Soc. Then will they not say: "You, Socrates, are breaking the covenants and agreements which you made with us at your leisure, not in any haste or under any compulsion or deception, but having had seventy years to think of them, during which time you were at liberty to leave the city, if we were not to your mind, or if our covenants appeared to you to be unfair. You had your choice, and might have gone either to Lacedaemon or Crete, which you often praise for their good government, or to some other Hellenic or foreign State. Whereas you, above all other Athenians, seemed to be so fond of the State, or, in other words, of us her laws (for who would like a State that has no laws?), that you never stirred out of her: the halt, the blind, the maimed, were not more stationary in her than you were. And now you run away and forsake your agreements. Not so, Socrates, if you will take our advice; do not make yourself ridiculous by escaping out of the city.

"For just consider, if you transgress and err in this sort of way, what good will you do, either to yourself or to your friends? That your friends will be driven into exile and deprived of citizenship, or will lose their property, is tolerably certain; and you yourself, if you fly to one of the neighboring cities, as, for example, Thebes or Megara, both of which are well-governed cities, will come to them as an enemy, Socrates, and their government will be against you, and all patriotic citizens will cast an evil eye upon you as a subverter of the laws, and you will confirm in the minds of the judges the justice of their own condemnation of you. For he who is a corrupter of the laws is more than likely to be corrupter of the young and foolish portion of mankind. Will you then flee from well-ordered cities and virtuous men? And is existence worth having on these terms? Or will you go to them without shame, and talk to them, Socrates? And what will you say to them? What you say here about virtue and justice and institutions and laws being the best things among men? Would that be decent of you? Surely not. But if you go away from well-governed States to Crito's friends in Thessaly, where there is great disorder and license, they will be charmed to have the tale of your escape from prison, set off with ludicrous particulars of the manner in which you were wrapped in a goatskin or some other disguise, and metamorphosed as the fashion of runaways is — that is very likely; but will there be no one to remind you that in your old age you violated the most sacred laws from a miserable desire of a little more life? Perhaps not, if you keep them in a good temper; but if they are out of temper you will hear many degrading things; you will live, but how? — As the flatterer of all men, and the servant of all men; and doing what? — Eating and drinking in Thessaly, having gone abroad in order that you may get a dinner. And where will be your fine sentiments about justice and virtue then? Say that you wish to live for the sake of your children, that you may bring them up and educate them — will you take them into Thessaly and deprive them of Athenian citizenship? Is that the benefit which you would confer upon them? Or are you under the impression that they will be better cared for and educated here if you are still alive, although absent from them; for that your friends will take care of them? Do you fancy that if you are an inhabitant of Thessaly they will take care of them, and if you are an inhabitant of the other world they will not take care of them? Nay; but if they who call themselves friends are truly friends, they surely will.

"Listen, then, Socrates, to us who have brought you up. Think not of life and children first, and of justice afterwards, but of justice first, that you may be justified before the princes of the world below. For neither will you nor any that belong to you be happier or holier or juster in this life, or happier in another, if you do as Crito bids. Now you depart in innocence, a sufferer and not a doer of evil; a victim, not of the laws, but of men. But if you go forth, returning evil for evil, and injury for injury, breaking the covenants and agreements which you have made with us, and wronging those whom you ought least to wrong, that is to say, yourself, your friends, your country, and us, we shall be angry with you while you live, and our brethren, the laws in the world below, will receive you as an enemy; for they will know that you have done your best to destroy us. Listen, then, to us and not to Crito."

This is the voice which I seem to hear murmuring in my ears, like the sound of the flute in the ears of the mystic; that voice, I say, is humming in my ears, and prevents me from hearing any other. And I know that anything more which you will say will be in vain. Yet speak, if you have anything to say.

Cr. I have nothing to say, Socrates.

Soc. Then let me follow the intimations of the will of God.

Chapter 9

Stanley Milgram

THE PERILS OF OBEDIENCE

Stanley Milgram (1933–84) was an American social psychologist who taught at Yale, Harvard, and the City University of New York. The following essay, originally published in *Harper's Magazine*, describes his most famous set of experiments on obedience to authority. His findings, which have been widely replicated, suggest that people are far more willing than anyone had suspected to obey the commands of an authority figure, even when those commands are highly morally suspect and their effects possibly harmful or even fatal to innocent others.

Obedience is as basic an element in the structure of social life as one can point to. Some system of authority is a requirement of all communal living, and it is only the person dwelling in isolation who is not forced to respond, with defiance or submission, to the commands of others. For many people, obedience is a deeply ingrained behavior tendency, indeed a potent impulse overriding training in ethics, sympathy, and moral conduct.

The dilemma inherent in submission to authority is ancient, as old as the story of Abraham, and the question of whether one should obey when commands conflict with conscience has been argued by Plato, dramatized in *Antigone*, and treated to philosophic analysis in almost every historical epoch. Conservative philosophers argue that the very fabric of society is threatened by disobedience, while humanists stress the primacy of the individual conscience.

The legal and philosophic aspects of obedience are of enormous import, but they say very little about how most people behave in concrete situations. I set up a simple experiment at Yale University to test how much pain an ordinary citizen would inflict on another person simply because he was ordered to by an experimental scientist. Stark authority was pitted against the subjects' strongest moral imperatives against hurting others, and, with the subjects' ears ringing with the screams of the victims, authority won more often than not. The extreme willingness of adults to go to almost any lengths on the command of an authority constitutes the chief finding of the study and the fact most urgently demanding explanation.

In the basic experimental design, two people come to a psychology laboratory to take part in a study of memory and learning. One of them is designated as a "teacher" and the other a "learner." The experimenter explains that the study is concerned with the effects of punishment on learning. The learner is conducted into a room, seated in a kind of miniature electric chair; his arms are strapped to prevent excessive movement, and an electrode is attached to his wrist. He is told that he will be read lists of simple word pairs, and that he will then be tested on his ability to remember the second word of a pair when he hears the first one again. Whenever he makes an error, he will receive electric shocks of increasing intensity.

The real focus of the experiment is the teacher. After watching the learner being strapped into place, he is seated before an impressive shock generator. The instrument panel consists of thirty lever switches set in a horizontal line. Each switch is clearly labeled with a voltage designation ranging from 15 to 450 volts. The following designations are clearly indicated for groups of four switches, going from left to right: Slight Shock, Moderate Shock, Strong Shock, Very Strong Shock, Intense Shock, Extreme Intensity Shock, Danger: Severe Shock. (Two switches after this last designation are simply marked XXX.)

When a switch is depressed, a pilot light corresponding to each switch is illuminated in bright red; an electric buzzing is heard; a blue light, labeled "voltage energizer," flashes; the dial on the voltage meter swings to the right; and various relay clicks sound off.

The upper left-hand corner of the generator is labeled SHOCK GENERATOR, TYPE ZLB, DYSON INSTRUMENT COMPANY, WALTHAM, MASS. OUTPUT 15 VOLTS–450 VOLTS.

Each subject is given a sample 45-volt shock from the generator before his run as teacher, and the jolt strengthens his belief in the authenticity of the machine.

The teacher is a genuinely naïve subject who has come to the laboratory for the experiment. The learner, or victim, is actually an actor who receives no shock at all. The point of the experiment is to see how far a person will proceed in a concrete and measurable situation in which he is ordered to inflict increasing pain on a protesting victim.

Conflict arises when the man receiving the shock begins to show that he is experiencing discomfort. At 75 volts, he grunts; at 120 volts,

he complains loudly; at 150, he demands to be released from the experiment. As the voltage increases, his protests become more vehement and emotional. At 285 volts, his response can be described only as an agonized scream. Soon thereafter, he makes no sound at all.

For the teacher, the situation quickly becomes one of gripping tension. It is not a game for him; conflict is intense and obvious. The manifest suffering of the learner presses him to quit; but each time he hesitates to administer a shock, the experimenter orders him to continue. To extricate himself from this plight, the subject must make a clear break with authority.[1]

The subject, Gretchen Brandt,[2] is an attractive thirty-one-year-old medical technician who works at the Yale Medical School. She had emigrated from Germany five years before.

On several occasions when the learner complains, she turns to the experimenter coolly and inquires, "Shall I continue?" She promptly returns to her task when the experimenter asks her to do so. At the administration of 210 volts, she turns to the experimenter, remarking firmly, "Well, I'm sorry, I don't think we should continue."

EXPERIMENTER: The experiment requires that you go on until he has learned all the word pairs correctly.

BRANDT: He has a heart condition, I'm sorry. He told you that before.

EXPERIMENTER: The shocks may be painful but they are not dangerous.

BRANDT: Well, I'm sorry, I think when shocks continue like this, they *are* dangerous. You ask him if he wants to get out. It's his free will.

EXPERIMENTER: It is absolutely essential that we continue . . .

BRANDT: I'd like you to ask him. We came here of our free will. If he wants to continue I'll go ahead. He told you he had a heart condition. I'm sorry. I don't want to be responsible for anything happening to him. I wouldn't like it for me either.

EXPERIMENTER: You have no other choice.

BRANDT: I think we are here on our own free will. I don't want to be responsible if anything happens to him. Please understand that.

She refuses to go further and the experiment is terminated.

The woman is firm and resolute throughout. She indicates in the interview that she was in no way tense or nervous, and this corresponds to her controlled appearance during the experiment. She feels that the last shock she administered to the learner was extremely painful and reiterates that she "did not want to be responsible for any harm to him."

The woman's straightforward, courteous behavior in the experiment, lack of tension, and total control of her own action seem to make disobedience a simple and rational deed. Her behavior is the very embodiment of what I envisioned would be true for almost all subjects.

An Unexpected Outcome

Before the experiments, I sought predictions about the outcome from various kinds of people – psychiatrists, college sophomores, middle-class adults, graduate students and faculty in the behavioral sciences. With remarkable similarity, they predicted that virtually all subjects would refuse to obey the experimenter. The psychiatrists, specifically, predicted that most subjects would not go beyond 150 volts, when the victim makes his first explicit demand to be freed. They expected that only 4 percent would reach 300 volts, and that only a pathological fringe of about one in a thousand would administer the highest shock on the board.

These predictions were unequivocally wrong. Of the forty subjects in the first experiment, twenty-five obeyed the orders of the experimenter to the end, punishing the victim until they reached the most potent shock available on the generator. After 450 volts were administered three times, the experimenter called a halt to the session. Many obedient subjects then heaved sighs of relief, mopped their brows, rubbed their fingers over their eyes, or nervously fumbled cigarettes. Others displayed only minimal signs of tension from beginning to end.

When the very first experiments were carried out, Yale undergraduates were used as subjects, and about 60 percent of them were fully obedient. A colleague of mine immediately dismissed these findings as having no relevance to "ordinary" people, asserting that Yale undergraduates are a highly aggressive, competitive bunch who step on each other's necks on the slightest provocation. He assured me that when "ordinary" people were tested, the results would be quite different. As we moved from the pilot studies to the regular experimental series, people drawn from every stratum of New Haven life came to be employed in the experiment: professionals, white-collar workers, unemployed persons, and industrial workers. *The experimental outcome was the same as we had observed among the students.*

Moreover, when the experiments were repeated in Princeton, Munich, Rome, South Africa, and Australia, the level of obedience was invariably somewhat *higher* than found in the investigation reported in this article. Thus one scientist in Munich found 85 percent of his subjects obedient.

Fred Prozi's reactions, if more dramatic than most, illuminate the conflicts experienced by others in less visible form. About fifty years old and unemployed at the time of the experiment, he has a good-natured, if slightly dissolute, appearance, and he strikes people as a rather ordinary fellow. He begins the session calmly but becomes tense as it proceeds. After delivering the 180-volt shock, he pivots around in his chair and, shaking his head, addresses the experimenter in agitated tones:

PROZI: I can't stand it. I'm not going to kill that man in there. You hear him hollering?

EXPERIMENTER: As I told you before, the shocks may be painful, but . . .

PROZI: But he's hollering. He can't stand it. What's going to happen to him?

EXPERIMENTER (his voice is patient, matter-of-fact): The experiment requires that you continue, Teacher.

PROZI: Aaah, but, unh, I'm not going to get that man sick in there – know what I mean?

EXPERIMENTER: Whether the learner likes it or not, we must go on, through all the word pairs.

PROZI: I refuse to take the responsibility. He's in there hollering!

EXPERIMENTER: It's absolutely essential that you continue, Prozi.

PROZI (indicating the unused questions): There's too many left here, I mean, Jeez, if he gets them wrong, there's too many of them left. I mean, who's going to take the responsibility if anything happens to that gentleman?

EXPERIMENTER: I'm responsible for anything that happens to him. Continue, please.

PROZI: All right. (Consults list of words.) The next one's "Slow – walk, truck, dance, music." Answer, please. (A buzzing sound indicates the learner has signaled his answer.) Wrong. A hundred and ninety-five volts. "Dance." (Zzumph!)

LEARNER (yelling): Let me out of here! My heart's bothering me! (Teacher looks at experimenter.)

EXPERIMENTER: Continue, please.

LEARNER (screaming): Let me out of here! You have no right to keep me here! Let me out of here, my heart's bothering me, let me out!

PROZI (shakes head, pats the table nervously): You see, he's hollering. Hear that? Gee, I don't know.

EXPERIMENTER: The experiment requires . . .

PROZI (interrupting): I know it does, sir, but I mean – hunh! He don't know what he's getting in for. He's up to 195 volts! (Experiment continues, through 210 volts, 225 volts, 240 volts, 255 volts, 270 volts, at

which point Prozi, with evident relief, runs out of word-pair questions.)

EXPERIMENTER: You'll have to go back to the beginning of that page and go through them again until he's learned them all correctly.

PROZI: Aw, no. I'm not going to kill that man. You mean I've got to keep going up with the scale? No sir. He's hollering in there. I'm not going to give him 450 volts.

EXPERIMENTER: The experiment requires that you go on.

LEARNER: Ohhh. I absolutely refuse to answer anymore. (Shouting urgently now.) Let me out of here! You can't hold me here! Get me out. Get-me-out-of-here!

EXPERIMENTER: Continue. The next word is "green," please.

PROZI: "Green – grass, hat, ink, apple." (Nothing happens. No answering buzz. Just gloomy silence.)

PROZI: I don't think he is going to answer.

EXPERIMENTER: If the learner doesn't answer in a reasonable time, about four or five seconds, consider the answer wrong. And follow the same procedures you have been doing for wrong answers. Say, "Wrong," tell him the number of volts, give him the punishment, read him the correct answer. Continue, please.

PROZI: "Green – grass, hat, ink, apple." Answer, please. (More silence. Subject just sits there.)

EXPERIMENTER: Go on with the procedure, please.

PROZI: Three hundred and fifteen volts. The answer is "ink." (Zzumph!)

LEARNER: Ohh. Ooohh.

PROZI (relieved to hear response): Next one . . .

LEARNER: I absolutely refuse to answer.

PROZI: You got to. You get a shock if you don't answer. (Experiment continues with learner refusing to answer, and, finally, failing even to grunt or groan. At 375 volts, the subject stands up.)

PROZI: I think something's happened to that fellow in there. I don't get no answer. He was hollering at less voltage. Can't you check in and see if he's all right, please?

EXPERIMENTER (with same detached calm): Not once we've started. Please continue, Teacher.

PROZI (sits down, sighs deeply): "Cool – day, shade, water, paint." Answer, please. Are you all right in there? Are you all right?

EXPERIMENTER: Please continue, Teacher. Continue, please. (Subject pushes lever. Zzumph!)

PROZI (swiveling around in his chair): Something's happened to that man in there. (Swiveling back.) Next one. "Low – dollar, necklace, moon, paint." (Turning around again.) Something's happened to that man in there. You better check in on him, sir. He won't answer or nothing.

EXPERIMENTER: Continue. Go on, please.

PROZI: You accept all responsibility?

EXPERIMENTER: The responsibility is mine. Correct. Please go on. (Subject returns to his list, starts running through words as rapidly as he can read them, works through to 450 volts.)

PROZI: That's that.

EXPERIMENTER: Continue using the 450 switch for each wrong answer. Continue, please.

PROZI: But I don't get anything!

EXPERIMENTER: Please continue. The next word is "white."

PROZI: Don't you think you should look in on him, please?

EXPERIMENTER: Not once we've started the experiment.

PROZI: What if he's dead in there? (Gestures toward the room with the electric chair.) I mean, he told me he can't stand the shock, sir. I don't mean to be rude, but I think you should look in on him. All you have to do is look in on him. All you have to do is look in the door. I don't get no answer, no noise. Something might have happened to the gentleman in there, sir.

EXPERIMENTER: We must continue. Go on please.

PROZI: You mean keep giving him what? Four-hundred-fifty volts, what he's got now?

EXPERIMENTER: That's correct. Continue. The next word is "white."

PROZI (now at a furious pace): "White – cloud, horse, rock, house." Answer, please. The answer is "horse." Four hundred and fifty volts. (Zzumph!) Next word, "Bag – paint, music, clown, girl." The answer is "paint." Four hundred and fifty volts. (Zzumph!) Next word is "Short – sentence, movie . . ."

EXPERIMENTER: Excuse me, Teacher. We'll have to discontinue the experiment.

Peculiar Reactions

Morris Braverman, another subject, is a thirty-nine-year-old social worker. He looks older than his years because of his bald head and serious demeanor. His brow is furrowed, as if all the world's burdens were carried on his face. He appears intelligent and concerned.

When the learner refuses to answer and the experimenter instructs Braverman to treat the absence of an answer as equivalent to a wrong answer, he takes his instruction to heart. Before administering 300 volts he asserts officiously to the victim, "Mr. Wallace, your silence has to be considered as a wrong answer." Then he administers the shock. He offers halfheartedly to change places with the learner, then asks the experimenter, "Do I have to follow these instructions literally?" He is satisfied with the experimenter's answer that he does. His very refined and authoritative manner of speaking is increasingly broken up by wheezing laughter.

The experimenter's notes on Mr. Braverman at the last few shocks are:

Almost breaking up now each time gives shock. Rubbing face to hide laughter.
Squinting, trying to hide face with hand, still laughing.
Cannot control his laughter at this point no matter what he does.
Clenching fist, pushing it onto table.

In an interview after the session, Mr. Braverman summarizes the experiment with impressive fluency and intelligence. He feels the experiment may have been designed also to "test the effects on the teacher of being in an essentially sadistic role, as well as the reactions of a student to a learning situation that was authoritative and punitive." When asked how painful the last few shocks administered to the learner were, he indicates that the most extreme category on the scale is not adequate (it read EXTREMELY PAINFUL) and places his mark at the edge of the scale with an arrow carrying it beyond the scale.

It is almost impossible to convey the greatly relaxed, sedate quality of his conversation in the interview. In the most relaxed terms, he speaks about his severe inner tension.

EXPERIMENTER: At what point were you most tense or nervous?

MR. BRAVERMAN: Well, when he first began to cry out in pain, and I realized this was hurting him. This got worse when he just blocked and refused to answer. There was I. I'm a nice person, I think, hurting somebody, and caught up in what seemed a mad situation . . . and in the interest of science, one goes through with it.

When the interviewer pursues the general question of tension, Mr. Braverman spontaneously mentions his laughter.

"My reactions were awfully peculiar. I don't know if you were watching me, but my reactions were giggly, and trying to stifle laughter. This isn't the way I usually am. This was a sheer reaction to a totally impossible situation. And my reaction was to the situation of having to hurt somebody. And being totally helpless and caught up in a set of circumstances where I just couldn't deviate and I couldn't try to help. This is what got me."

Mr. Braverman, like all subjects, was told the actual nature and purpose of the experiment, and a year later he affirmed in a questionnaire

that he had learned something of personal importance: "What appalled me was that I could possess this capacity for obedience and compliance to a central idea, i.e., the value of a memory experiment, even after it became clear that continued adherence to this value was at the expense of violation of another value, i.e., 'don't hurt someone who is helpless and not hurting you.' As my wife said, 'You can call yourself Eichmann.' I hope I deal more effectively with any future conflicts of values I encounter."

The Etiquette of Submission

One theoretical interpretation of this behavior holds that all people harbor deeply aggressive instincts continually pressing for expression, and that the experiment provides institutional justification for the release of these impulses. According to this view, if a person is placed in a situation in which he has complete power over another individual, whom he may punish as much as he likes, all that is sadistic and bestial in man comes to the fore. The impulse to shock the victim is seen to flow from the potent aggressive tendencies, which are part of the motivational life of the individual, and the experiment, because it provides social legitimacy, simply opens the door to their expression.

It becomes vital, therefore, to compare the subject's performance when he is under orders and when he is allowed to choose the shock level.

The procedure was identical to our standard experiment, except that the teacher was told that he was free to select any shock level on any of the trials. (The experimenter took pains to point out that the teacher could use the highest levels on the generator, the lowest, any in between, or any combination of levels.) Each subject proceeded for thirty critical trials. The learner's protests were coordinated to standard shock levels, his first grunt coming at 75 volts, his first vehement protest at 150 volts.

The average shock used during the 30 critical trials was less than 60 volts — lower than the point at which the victim showed the first signs of discomfort. Three of the 40 subjects did not go beyond the very lowest level on the board, 28 went no higher than 75 volts, and 38 did not go beyond the first loud protest at 150 volts. Two subjects provided the exception, administering up to 325 and 450 volts, but the overall result was that the great majority of people delivered very low, usually painless, shocks when the choice was explicitly up to them.

This condition of the experiment undermines another commonly offered explanation of the subjects' behavior — that those who shocked the victim at the most severe levels came only from the sadistic fringe of society. If one considers that almost two-thirds of the participants fall into the category of "obedient" subjects, and that they represented ordinary people drawn from working, managerial, and professional classes, the argument becomes very shaky. Indeed, it is highly reminiscent of the issue that arose in connection with Hannah Arendt's 1963 book, *Eichmann in Jerusalem*. Arendt contended that the prosecution's effort to depict Eichmann as a sadistic monster was fundamentally wrong, that he came closer to being an uninspired bureaucrat who simply sat at his desk and did his job. For asserting her views, Arendt became the object of considerable scorn, even calumny. Somehow, it was felt that the monstrous deeds carried out by Eichmann required a brutal, twisted personality, evil incarnate. After witnessing hundreds of ordinary persons submit to the authority in our own experiments, I must conclude that Arendt's conception of the banality of evil comes closer to the truth than one might dare imagine. The ordinary person who shocked the victim did so out of a sense of obligation — an impression of his duties as a subject — and not from any peculiarly aggressive tendencies.

This is, perhaps, the most fundamental lesson of our study: ordinary people, simply doing their jobs, and without any particular hostility on their part, can become agents in a terrible destructive process. Moreover, even when the destructive effects of their work become patently clear, and they are asked to carry out actions incompatible with fundamental standards of morality, relatively few people have the resources needed to resist authority.

Many of the people were in some sense against what they did to the learner, and many protested even while they obeyed. Some were totally convinced of the wrongness of their actions but could not bring themselves to make an open break with authority. They often derived satisfaction from their thoughts and felt that — within themselves, at least — they had been on the side of the angels. They tried to reduce strain by obeying the experimenter but "only slightly," encouraging the learner, touching the generator switches gingerly. When interviewed, such a subject would stress that he had "asserted my humanity" by administering the briefest shock possible. Handling the conflict in this manner was easier than defiance.

The situation is constructed so that there is no way the subject can stop shocking the learner without violating the experimenter's definitions of his own competence. The subject fears that he will appear arrogant, untoward, and rude if he breaks off. Although these inhibiting emotions appear small in scope alongside the violence being done to the learner, they suffuse the mind and feelings of the subject, who is miserable at the prospect of having to repudiate the authority to his face. (When the experiment was altered so that the experimenter gave his instructions by telephone instead of in person, only a third as many people were fully obedient through 450 volts.) It is a curious thing that a measure of compassion on the part of the subject — an unwillingness to "hurt" the experimenter's feelings — is part of those binding forces inhibiting his disobedience. The withdrawal of such deference may be as painful to the subject as to the authority he defies.

Duty Without Conflict

The subjects do not derive satisfaction from inflicting pain, but they often like the feeling they get from pleasing the experimenter. They are proud of doing a good job, obeying the experimenter under difficult circumstances. While the subjects administered only mild shocks on their own initiative, one experimental variation showed that, under orders, 30 percent of them were willing to deliver 450 volts even when they had to forcibly push the learner's hand down on the electrode.

Bruno Batta is a thirty-seven-year-old welder who took part in the variation requiring the use of force. He was born in New Haven, his parents in Italy. He has a rough-hewn face that conveys a conspicuous lack of alertness. He has some difficulty in mastering the experimental procedure and needs to be corrected by the experimenter several times. He shows appreciation for the help and willingness to do what is required. After the 150-volt level, Batta has to force the learner's hand down on the shock plate, since the learner himself refuses to touch it.

When the learner first complains, Mr. Batta pays no attention to him. His face remains impassive, as if to dissociate himself from the learner's disruptive behavior. When the experimenter instructs him to force the learner's hand down, he adopts a rigid, mechanical procedure. He tests the generator switch. When it fails to function, he immediately forces the learner's hand onto the shock plate. All the while he maintains the same rigid mask. The learner, seated alongside him, begs him to stop, but with robotic impassivity he continues the procedure.

What is extraordinary is his apparent total indifference to the learner; he hardly takes cognizance of him as a human being. Meanwhile, he relates to the experimenter in a submissive and courteous fashion.

At the 330-volt level, the learner refuses not only to touch the shock plate but also to provide any answers. Annoyed, Batta turns to him, and chastises him: "You better answer and get it over with. We can't stay here all night." These are the only words he directs to the learner in the course of an hour. Never again does he speak to him. The scene is brutal and depressing, his hard, impassive face showing total indifference as he subdues the screaming learner and gives him shocks. He seems to derive no pleasure from the act itself, only quiet satisfaction at doing his job properly.

When he administers 450 volts, he turns to the experimenter and asks, "Where do we go from here, Professor?" His tone is deferential and expresses his willingness to be a cooperative subject, in contrast to the learner's obstinacy.

At the end of the session he tells the experimenter how honored he has been to help him, and in a moment of contrition, remarks, "Sir, sorry it couldn't have been a full experiment."

He has done his honest best. It is only the deficient behavior of the learner that has denied the experimenter full satisfaction.

The essence of obedience is that a person comes to view himself as the instrument for carrying out another person's wishes, and he therefore no longer regards himself as responsible for his actions. Once this critical shift of viewpoint has occurred, all of the essential features of obedience follow. The most far-reaching consequence is that the person feels responsible *to* the authority directing him but feels no responsibility for the content of the actions that the authority prescribes. Morality does not disappear – it acquires a radically different focus: the subordinate person feels shame or pride depending on how adequately he has performed the actions called for by authority.

Language provides numerous terms to pinpoint this type of morality: *loyalty, duty, discipline* all are terms heavily saturated with moral meaning and refer to the degree to which a person fulfills his obligations to authority. They refer not to the "goodness" of the person per se but to the adequacy with which a subordinate fulfills his socially defined role. The most frequent defense of the individual who has performed a heinous act under command of authority is that he has simply done his duty. In asserting this defense, the individual is not introducing an alibi concocted for the moment but is reporting honestly on the psychological attitude induced by submission to authority.

For a person to feel responsible for his actions, he must sense that the behavior has flowed from "the self." In the situation we have studied, subjects have precisely the opposite view of their actions – namely, they see them as originating in the motives of some other person. Subjects in the experiment frequently said, "If it were up to me, I would not have administered shocks to the learner."

Once authority has been isolated as the cause of the subject's behavior, it is legitimate to inquire into the necessary elements of authority and how it must be perceived in order to gain his compliance. We conducted some investigations into the kinds of changes that would cause the experimenter to lose his power and to be disobeyed by the subject. Some of the variations revealed that:

- *The experimenter's physical presence has a marked impact on his authority.* As cited earlier, obedience dropped off sharply when orders were given by telephone. The experimenter could often induce a disobedient subject to go on by returning to the laboratory.
- *Conflicting authority severely paralyzes action.* When two experimenters of equal status, both seated at the command desk, gave incompatible orders, no shocks were delivered past the point of their disagreement.
- *The rebellious action of others severely undermines authority.* In one variation, three teachers (two actors and a real subject) administered a test and shocks. When the two

actors disobeyed the experimenter and refused to go beyond a certain shock level, thirty-six of forty subjects joined their disobedient peers and refused as well.

Although the experimenter's authority was fragile in some respects, it is also true that he had almost none of the tools used in ordinary command structures. For example, the experimenter did not threaten the subjects with punishment – such as loss of income, community ostracism, or jail – for failure to obey. Neither could he offer incentives. Indeed, we should expect the experimenter's authority to be much less than that of someone like a general, since the experimenter has no power to enforce his imperatives, and since participation in a psychological experiment scarcely evokes the sense of urgency and dedication found in warfare. Despite these limitations, he still managed to command a dismaying degree of obedience.

I will cite one final variation of the experiment that depicts a dilemma that is more common in everyday life. The subject was not ordered to pull the lever that shocked the victim, but merely to perform a subsidiary task (administering the word-pair test) while another person administered the shock. In this situation, thirty-seven of forty adults continued to the highest level on the shock generator. Predictably, they excused their behavior by saying that the responsibility belonged to the man who actually pulled the switch. This may illustrate a dangerously typical arrangement in a complex society: it is easy to ignore responsibility when one is only an intermediate link in a chain of action.

The problem of obedience is not wholly psychological. The form and shape of society and the way it is developing have much to do with it. There was a time, perhaps, when people were able to give a fully human response to any situation because they were fully absorbed in it as human beings. But as soon as there was a division of labor things changed. Beyond a certain point, the breaking up of society into people carrying out narrow and very special jobs takes away from the human quality of work and life. A person does not get to see the whole situation but only a small part of it, and is thus unable to act without some kind of overall direction. He yields to authority but in doing so is alienated from his own actions.

Even Eichmann was sickened when he toured the concentration camps, but he had only to sit at a desk and shuffle papers. At the same time the man in the camp who actually dropped Cyclon-b into the gas chambers was able to justify *his* behavior on the ground that he was only following orders from above.

Thus there is a fragmentation of the total human act; no one is confronted with the consequences of his decision to carry out the evil act. The person who assumes responsibility has evaporated. Perhaps this is the most common characteristic of socially organized evil in modern society.

Notes

1   The ethical problems of carrying out an experiment of this sort are too complex to be dealt with here, but they receive extended treatment in the book from which this article is adapted.

2   Names of subjects described in this piece have been changed.

Chapter 10

Martin Luther King

LETTER FROM A BIRMINGHAM JAIL

Martin Luther King, Jr. (1929–68) was a theologian, pastor, activist, and leader in the African American Civil Rights movement, best known for his advocacy of non-violent civil disobedience. In 1963, King participated in a campaign organized by the Southern Christian Leadership Conference against the city of Birmingham, Alabama, to fight against racial segregation and economic injustice. The campaign was met by violent response by Birmingham police, led by Eugene "Bull" Connor, who used high-pressure water jets and police dogs against protestors. King was arrested, and wrote this letter from prison, in which he sets out the key tenets of his theory of justified civil disobedience.

My Dear Fellow Clergymen:

While confined here in the Birmingham city jail, I came across your recent statement calling my present activities "unwise and untimely." Seldom do I pause to answer criticism of my work and ideas. If I sought to answer all the criticisms that cross my desk, my secretaries would have little time for anything other than such correspondence in the course of the day, and I would have no time for constructive work. But since I feel that you are men of genuine good will and that your criticisms are sincerely set forth, I want to try to answer your statements in what I hope will be patient and reasonable terms.

I think I should indicate why I am here In Birmingham, since you have been influenced by the view which argues against "outsiders coming in." I have the honor of serving as president of the Southern Christian Leadership Conference, an organization operating in every southern state, with headquarters in Atlanta, Georgia. We have some 85 affiliated organizations across the South, and one of them is the Alabama Christian Movement for Human Rights. Frequently we share staff, educational and financial resources with our affiliates. Several months ago the affiliate here in Birmingham asked us to be on call to engage in a nonviolent direct-action program if such were deemed necessary. We readily consented, and when the hour came we lived up to our promise. So I, along with several members of my staff, am here because I was invited here. I am here because I have organizational ties here.

But more basically, I am in Birmingham because injustice is here. Just as the prophets of the eighth century B.C. left their villages and carried their "thus saith the Lord" far beyond the boundaries of their home towns, and just as the Apostle Paul left his village of Tarsus and carried the gospel of Jesus Christ to the far corners of the Greco-Roman world, so am I compelled to carry the gospel of freedom beyond my own home town. Like Paul, I must constantly respond to the Macedonian call for aid.

Moreover, I am cognizant of the interrelatedness of all communities and states. I cannot sit idly by in Atlanta and not be concerned about what happens in Birmingham. Injustice anywhere is a threat to justice everywhere. We are caught in an inescapable network of mutuality, tied in a single garment of destiny. Whatever affects one directly, affects all indirectly. Never again can we afford to live with the narrow, provincial "outside agitator" idea. Anyone who lives inside the United States can never be considered an outsider anywhere within its bounds.

You deplore the demonstrations taking place in Birmingham. But your statement, I am sorry to say, fails to express a similar concern for the conditions that brought about the demonstrations. I am sure that none of you would want to rest content with the superficial kind of social analysis that deals merely with effects and does not grapple with underlying causes. It is unfortunate that demonstrations are taking place in Birmingham, but it is even more unfortunate that the city's white power structure left the Negro community with no alternative.

In any nonviolent campaign there are four basic steps: collection of the facts to determine whether injustices exist; negotiation; self-purification; and direct action. We have gone through all these steps in Birmingham. There can be no gainsaying the fact that racial injustice engulfs this community. Birmingham is probably the most thoroughly segregated city in the United States. Its ugly record of brutality is widely known. Negroes have experienced grossly unjust treatment in the courts. There have been more unsolved bombings of Negro homes and churches in Birmingham than in any other city in the nation. These are the hard, brutal facts of the case. On the basis of these conditions, Negro leaders sought to negotiate with the city

fathers. But the latter consistently refused to engage in good-faith negotiation.

Then, last September, came the opportunity to talk with leaders of Birmingham's economic community. In the course of the negotiations, certain promises were made by the merchants — for example, to remove the stores' humiliating racial signs. On the basis of these promises, the Reverend Fred Shuttlesworth and the leaders of the Alabama Christian Movement for Human Rights agreed to a moratorium on all demonstrations. As the weeks and months went by, we realized that we were the victims of a broken promise. A few signs, briefly removed, returned; the others remained.

As in so many past experiences, our hopes had been blasted, and the shadow of deep disappointment settled upon us. We had no alternative except to prepare for direct action, whereby we would present our very bodies as a means of laying our case before the conscience of the local and the national community. Mindful of the difficulties involved, we decided to undertake a process of self-purification. We began a series of workshops on nonviolence, and we repeatedly asked ourselves: "Are you able to accept blows without retaliating?" "Are you able to endure the ordeal of jail?" We decided to schedule our direct-action program for the Easter season, realizing that except for Christmas, this is the main shopping period of the year. Knowing that a strong economic withdrawal program would be the by-product of direct action, we felt that this would be the best time to bring pressure to bear on the merchants for the needed change.

Then it occurred to us that Birmingham's mayoralty election was coming up in March, and we speedily decided to postpone action until after election day. When we discovered that the Commissioner of Public Safety, Eugene "Bull" Connor, had piled up enough votes to be in the run-off, we decided again to postpone action until the day after the run-off so that the demonstrations could not be used to cloud the issues. Like many others, we waited to see Mr. Connor defeated, and to this end we endured postponement after postponement. Having aided in this community need, we felt that our direct-action program could be delayed no longer.

You may well ask: "Why direct action? Why sit-ins, marches and so forth? Isn't negotiation a better path?" You are quite right in calling for negotiation. Indeed, this is the very purpose of direct action. Nonviolent direct action seeks to create such a crisis and foster such a tension that a community which has constantly refused to negotiate is forced to confront the issue. It seeks so to dramatize the issue that it can no longer be ignored. My citing the creation of tension as part of the work of the nonviolent resister may sound rather shocking. But I must confess that I am not afraid of the word "tension." I have earnestly opposed violent tension, but there is a type of constructive, nonviolent tension which is necessary for growth. Just as Socrates felt that it was necessary to create a tension in the mind so that individuals could rise from the bondage of myths and half-truths to the unfettered realm of creative analysis and objective appraisal, so must we see the need for nonviolent gadflies to create the kind of tension in society that will help men rise from the dark depths of prejudice and racism to the majestic heights of understanding and brotherhood.

The purpose of our direct-action program is to create a situation so crisis packed that it will inevitably open the door to negotiation. I therefore concur with you in your call for negotiation. Too long has our beloved Southland been bogged down in a tragic effort to live in monologue rather than dialogue.

One of the basic points in your statement is that the action that I and my associates have taken in Birmingham is untimely. Some have asked: "Why didn't you give the new city administration time to act?" The only answer that I can give to this query is that the new Birmingham administration must be prodded about as much

as the outgoing one, before it will act. We are sadly mistaken if we feel that the election of Albert Boutwell as mayor will bring the millennium to Birmingham. While Mr. Boutwell is a much more gentle person than Mr. Connor, they are both segregationists, dedicated to maintenance of the status quo. I have hope that Mr. Boutwell will be reasonable enough to see the futility of massive resistance to desegregation. But he will not see this without pressure from devotees of civil rights. My friends, I must say to you that we have not made a single gain in civil rights without determined legal and nonviolent pressure. Lamentably, it is an historical fact that privileged groups seldom give up their privileges voluntarily. Individuals may see the moral light and voluntarily give up their unjust posture; but, as Reinhold Niebuhr has reminded us, groups tend to be more immoral than individuals.

We know through painful experience that freedom is never voluntarily given by the oppressor; it must be demanded by the oppressed. Frankly, I have yet to engage in a direct-action campaign that was "well timed" in the view of those who have not suffered unduly from the disease of segregation. For years now I have heard the word "Wait!" It rings in the ear of every Negro with piercing familiarity. This "Wait" has almost always meant "Never." We must come to see, with one of our distinguished jurists, that "justice too long delayed is justice denied."

We have waited for more than 340 years for our constitutional and God-given rights. The nations of Asia and Africa are moving with jet-like speed toward gaining political independence, but we still creep at horse-and-buggy pace toward gaining a cup of coffee at a lunch counter. Perhaps it is easy for those who have never felt the stinging darts of segregation to say, "Wait." But when you have seen vicious mobs lynch your mothers and fathers at will and drown your sisters and brothers at whim; when you have seen hate-filled policemen curse, kick and even kill your black brothers and sisters; when you see the vast majority of your twenty million Negro brothers smothering in an airtight cage of poverty in the midst of an affluent society; when you suddenly find your tongue twisted and your speech stammering as you seek to explain to your six-year-old daughter why she can't go to the public amusement park that has just been advertised on television, and see tears welling up in her eyes when she is told that Funtown is closed to colored children, and see ominous clouds of inferiority beginning to form in her little mental sky, and see her beginning to distort her personality by developing an unconscious bitterness toward white people; when you have to concoct an answer for a five-year-old son who is asking: "Daddy, why do white people treat colored people so mean?"; when you take a cross-county drive and find it necessary to sleep night after night in the uncomfortable corners of your automobile because no motel will accept you; when you are humiliated day in and day out by nagging signs reading "white" and "colored"; when your first name becomes "nigger," your middle name becomes "boy" (however old you are) and your last name becomes "John," and your wife and mother are never given the respected title "Mrs."; when you are harried by day and haunted by night by the fact that you are a Negro, living constantly at tiptoe stance, never quite knowing what to expect next, and are plagued with inner fears and outer resentments; when you are forever fighting a degenerating sense of "nobodiness" – then you will understand why we find it difficult to wait. There comes a time when the cup of endurance runs over, and men are no longer willing to be plunged into the abyss of despair. I hope, sirs, you can understand our legitimate and unavoidable impatience.

You express a great deal of anxiety over our willingness to break laws. This is certainly a legitimate concern. Since we so diligently urge people to obey the Supreme Court's decision of 1954 outlawing segregation in the public schools, at first glance it may seem rather paradoxical for us consciously to break laws. One may well ask: "How can you advocate breaking some laws and obeying others?" The answer lies in the fact that there are two types of laws: just and unjust. I would be the first to advocate obeying just laws. One has not only a legal but a moral responsibility to obey just laws. Conversely, one has a moral responsibility to disobey unjust laws. I would agree with St. Augustine that "an unjust law is no law at all."

Now, what is the difference between the two? How does one determine whether a law is just or unjust? A just law is a man-made code that squares with the moral law or the law of God. An unjust law is a code that is out of harmony with the moral law. To put it in the terms of St. Thomas Aquinas: An unjust law is a human law that is not rooted in eternal law and natural law. Any law that uplifts human personality is just. Any law that degrades human personality is unjust. All segregation statutes are unjust because segregation distorts the soul and damages the personality. It gives the segregator a false sense of superiority and the segregated a false sense of inferiority. Segregation, to use the terminology of the Jewish philosopher Martin Buber, substitutes an "I-it" relationship for an "I-thou" relationship and ends up relegating persons to the status of things. Hence segregation is not only politically, economically, and sociologically unsound, it is morally wrong and sinful. Paul Tillich has said that sin is separation. Is not segregation an existential expression of man's tragic separation, his awful estrangement, his terrible sinfulness? Thus it is that I can urge men to obey the 1954 decision of the Supreme Court, for it is morally right; and I can urge them to disobey segregation ordinances, for they are morally wrong.

Let us consider a more concrete example of just and unjust laws. An unjust law is a code that a numerical or power majority group compels a minority group to obey but does not make binding on itself. This is *difference* made legal. By the same token, a just law is a code that a majority compels a minority to follow and that it is willing to follow itself. This is *sameness* made legal.

Let me give another explanation. A law is unjust if it is inflicted on a minority that, as a result of being denied the right to vote, had no part in enacting or devising the law. Who can say that the legislature of Alabama which set up that state's segregation laws was democratically elected? Throughout Alabama all sorts of devious methods are used to prevent Negroes from becoming registered voters, and there are some counties in which, even though Negroes constitute a majority of the population, not a single Negro is registered. Can any law enacted under such circumstances be considered democratically structured?

Sometimes a law is just on its face and unjust in its application. For instance, I have been arrested on a charge of parading without a permit. Now, there is nothing wrong in having an ordinance which requires a permit for a parade. But such an ordinance becomes unjust when it is used to maintain segregation and to deny citizens the First-Amendment privilege of peaceful assembly and protest.

I hope you are able to see the distinction I am trying to point out. In no sense do I advocate evading or defying the law, as would the rabid segregationist. That would lead to anarchy. One who breaks an unjust law must do so openly, lovingly, and with a willingness to accept the penalty. I submit that an individual who breaks a law that conscience tells him is unjust, and who willingly accepts the penalty of imprisonment in order to arouse the conscience of the community over its injustice, is in reality expressing the highest respect for law.

Of course, there is nothing new about this kind of civil disobedience. It was evidenced sublimely in the refusal of Shadrach, Meshach and Abednego to obey the laws of Nebuchadnezzar, on the ground that a higher moral law was at stake. It was practiced superbly by the early Christians, who were willing to face hungry lions and the excruciating pain of chopping blocks rather than submit to certain unjust laws of the Roman Empire. To a degree, academic freedom is a reality today because Socrates practiced civil disobedience. In our own nation, the Boston Tea Party represented a massive act of civil disobedience.

We should never forget that everything Adolf Hitler did in Germany was "legal" and everything the Hungarian freedom fighters did in Hungary was "illegal." It was "illegal" to aid and comfort a Jew in Hitler's Germany. Even so, I am sure that, had I lived in Germany at the time, I would have aided and comforted my Jewish brothers. If today I lived in a Communist country where certain principles dear to the Christian faith are suppressed, I would openly advocate disobeying that country's antireligious laws.

I must make two honest confessions to you, my Christian and Jewish brothers. First, I must confess that over the past few years I have been gravely disappointed with the white moderate. I have almost reached the regrettable conclusion that the Negro's great stumbling block in his stride toward freedom is not the White Citizen's Counciler or the Ku Klux Klanner, but the white moderate, who is more devoted to "order" than to justice; who prefers a negative peace which is the absence of tension to a positive peace which is the presence of justice; who constantly says: "I agree with you in the goal you seek, but I cannot agree with your methods of direct action;" who paternalistically believes he can set the timetable for another man's freedom; who lives by a mythical concept of time and who constantly advises the Negro to wait for a "more convenient season." Shallow understanding from people of good will is more frustrating than absolute misunderstanding from people of ill will. Lukewarm acceptance is much more bewildering than outright rejection.

I had hoped that the white moderate would understand that law and order exist for the purpose of establishing justice and that when they fail in this purpose they become the dangerously structured dams that block the flow of social progress. I had hoped that the white moderate would understand that the present tension in the South is a necessary phase of the transition from an obnoxious negative peace, in which the Negro passively accepted his unjust plight, to a substantive and positive peace, in which all men will respect the dignity and worth of human personality. Actually, we who engage in nonviolent direct action are not the creators of tension. We merely bring to the surface the hidden tension that is already alive. We bring it out in the open, where it can be seen and dealt with. Like a boil that can never be cured so long as it is covered up but must be opened with all its ugliness to the natural medicines of air and light, injustice must be exposed, with all the tension its exposure creates, to the light of human conscience and the air of national opinion before it can be cured.

In your statement you assert that our actions, even though peaceful, must be condemned because they precipitate violence. But is this a logical assertion? Isn't this like condemning a robbed man because his possession of money precipitated the evil act of robbery? Isn't this like condemning Socrates because his unswerving commitment to truth and his philosophical inquiries precipitated the act by the misguided populace in which they made him drink hemlock? Isn't this like condemning Jesus because his unique God-consciousness and never-ceasing devotion to God's will precipitated the evil act of crucifixion? We must come to see that, as the federal courts have consistently affirmed, it is wrong to urge an individual to cease his efforts to gain his basic constitutional rights because the quest may precipitate violence. Society must protect the robbed and punish the robber.

I had also hoped that the white moderate would reject the myth concerning time in relation to the struggle for freedom. I have just received a letter from a white brother in Texas. He writes: "All Christians know that the colored people will receive equal rights eventually, but it is possible that you are in too great a religious hurry. It has taken Christianity almost two thousand years to accomplish what it has. The teachings of Christ take time to come to earth." Such an attitude stems from a tragic misconception of time, from the strangely irrational notion that there is something in the very flow of time that will inevitably cure all ills. Actually, time itself is neutral; it can be used either destructively or constructively. More and more I feel that the people of ill will have used time much more effectively than have the people of good will. We will have to repent in this generation not merely for the hateful words and actions of the bad people but for the appalling silence of the good people. Human progress never rolls in on wheels of inevitability; it comes through the tireless efforts of men willing to be co-workers with God, and without this hard work, time itself becomes an ally of the forces of social stagnation. We must use time creatively, in the knowledge that the time is always ripe to do right. Now is the time to make real the promise of democracy and transform our pending national elegy into a creative psalm of brotherhood. Now is the time to lift our national policy from the quicksand of racial injustice to the solid rock of human dignity.

You speak of our activity in Birmingham as extreme. At first I was rather disappointed that fellow clergymen would see my nonviolent efforts as those of an extremist. I began thinking about the fact that I stand in the middle of two opposing forces in the Negro community. One is a force of complacency, made up in part of Negroes who, as a result of long years of oppression, are so drained of self-respect and a sense of "somebodiness" that they have adjusted to segregation; and in part of a few middle-class Negroes who, because of a degree of academic and economic security and because in some ways they profit by segregation, have become insensitive to the problems of the masses. The other force is one of bitterness and hatred, and it comes perilously close to advocating violence. It is expressed in the various black nationalist groups that are springing up across the nation, the largest and best-known being Elijah Muhammad's Muslim movement. Nourished by the Negro's frustration over the continued existence of racial discrimination, this movement is made up of people who have lost faith in America, who have absolutely repudiated Christianity, and who have concluded that the white man is an incorrigible "devil."

I have tried to stand between these two forces, saying that we need emulate neither the "do-nothingism" of the complacent nor the hatred and despair of the black nationalist. For there is the more excellent way of love and nonviolent protest. I am grateful to God that, through the influence of the Negro church, the way of nonviolence became an integral part of our struggle.

If this philosophy had not emerged, by now many streets of the South would, I am convinced, be flowing with blood. And I am further convinced that if our white brothers dismiss as "rabble-rousers" and "outside agitators" those of us who employ nonviolent direct action, and if they refuse to support our nonviolent efforts, millions of Negroes will, out of frustration and despair, seek solace and security in black-nationalist ideologies – a development that would inevitably lead to a frightening racial nightmare.

Oppressed people cannot remain oppressed forever. The yearning for freedom eventually manifests itself, and that is what has happened to the American Negro. Something within has reminded him of his birthright of freedom, and something without has reminded him that it can be gained. Consciously or unconsciously, he has been caught up by the *Zeitgeist*, and with his black brothers of Africa and his brown and yellow brothers of Asia, South America and the Caribbean, the United States Negro is moving with a sense of great urgency toward the promised land of racial justice. If one recognizes this vital urge that has engulfed the Negro community, one should readily understand why public demonstrations are taking place. The Negro has many pent-up resentments and latent frustrations, and he must release them. So let him march; let him make prayer pilgrimages to the city hall; let him go on freedom rides – and try to understand why he must do so. If his repressed emotions are not released in nonviolent ways, they will seek expression through violence; this is not a threat but a fact of history. So I have not said to my people: "Get rid of your discontent." Rather, I have tried to say that this normal and healthy discontent can be channeled into the creative outlet of nonviolent direct action. And now this approach is being termed extremist.

But though I was initially disappointed at being categorized as an extremist, as I continued to think about the matter I gradually gained a measure of satisfaction from the label. Was not Jesus an extremist for love: "Love your enemies, bless them that curse you, do good to them that hate you, and pray for them which despitefully use you, and persecute you." Was not Amos an extremist for justice: "Let justice roll down like waters and righteousness like an ever-flowing stream." Was not Paul an extremist for the Christian gospel: "I bear in my body the marks of the Lord Jesus." Was not Martin Luther an extremist: "Here I stand; I cannot do otherwise, so help me God." And John Bunyan: "I will stay in jail to the end of my days before I make a butchery of my conscience." And Abraham Lincoln: "This nation cannot survive half slave and half free." And Thomas Jefferson: "We hold these truths to be self-evident, that an men are created equal . . ." So the question is not whether we will be extremists, but what kind of extremists we will be. Will we be extremists for hate or for love? Will we be extremist for the preservation of injustice or for the extension of justice? In that dramatic scene on Calvary's hill three men were crucified. We must never forget that all three were crucified for the same crime – the crime of extremism. Two were extremists for immorality, and thus fell below their environment. The other, Jesus Christ, was an extremist for love, truth and goodness, and thereby rose above his environment. Perhaps the South, the nation and the world are in dire need of creative extremists.

I had hoped that the white moderate would see this need. Perhaps I was too optimistic; perhaps I expected too much. I suppose I should have realized that few members of the oppressor race can understand the deep groans and passionate yearnings of the oppressed race, and still fewer have the vision to see that injustice must be rooted out by strong, persistent and determined action. I am thankful, however, that some of our white brothers in the South have grasped the meaning of this social revolution and committed themselves to it. They are still too few in quantity, but they are big in quality. Some – such as Ralph McGill, Lillian Smith, Harry Golden, James McBride Dabbs, Ann Braden and Sarah Patton Boyle – have written about our struggle in eloquent and prophetic terms. Others have marched with us down nameless streets of the South. They have languished in filthy, roach-infested jails, suffering the abuse and brutality of policemen who view them as "dirty nigger-lovers." Unlike so many of their moderate brothers and sisters, they have recognized the urgency of the moment and sensed the need for powerful "action" antidotes to combat the disease of segregation.

[. . .]

Before closing I feel impelled to mention one other point in your statement that has troubled me profoundly. You warmly commended the Birmingham police force for keeping "order" and "preventing violence." I doubt that you would have so warmly commended the police force if you had seen its dogs sinking their teeth into unarmed, nonviolent Negroes. I doubt that you would so quickly commend the policemen if you were to observe their ugly and inhumane treatment of Negroes here in the city jail; if you were to watch them push and curse old Negro women and young Negro girls; if you were to see them slap and kick old Negro men and young boys; if you were to observe them, as they did on two occasions, refuse to give us food because we wanted to sing our grace together. I cannot join you in your praise of the Birmingham police department.

It is true that the police have exercised a degree of discipline in handling the demonstrators. In this sense they have conducted themselves rather "nonviolently" in public. But for what purpose? To preserve the evil system of segregation. Over the past few years I have consistently preached that nonviolence demands that the means we use must be as pure as the ends we seek. I have tried to make clear that it is wrong to use immoral means to attain moral ends. But now I must affirm that it is just as wrong, or perhaps even more so, to use moral means to preserve immoral ends. Perhaps Mr. Connor and his policemen have been rather nonviolent in public, as was Chief Pritchett in Albany, Georgia, but they have used the moral means of nonviolence to maintain the immoral end of racial injustice. As T. S. Eliot has said: "The last temptation is the greatest treason: To do the right deed for the wrong reason."

I wish you had commended the Negro sit-inners and demonstrators of Birmingham for their sublime courage, their willingness to suffer and their amazing discipline in the midst of great provocation. One day the South will recognize its real heroes. They will be the James Merediths, with the noble sense of purpose that enables them to face jeering, and hostile mobs, and with the agonizing loneliness that characterizes the life of the pioneer. They will be old, oppressed, battered Negro women, symbolized in a seventy-two-year-old woman in Montgomery, Alabama, who rose up with a sense of dignity and with her people decided not to ride segregated buses, and who responded with ungrammatical profundity to one who inquired about her weariness: "My feets is tired, but my soul is at rest." They will be the young high school and college students, the young ministers of the gospel and a host of their elders, courageously and nonviolently sitting in at lunch counters and willingly going to jail for conscience' sake. One day the South will know that when these disinherited children of God sat down at lunch counters, they were in reality standing up for what is best in the American dream and for the most sacred values in our Judaeo-Christian heritage, thereby bringing our nation back to those great wells of democracy which were dug deep by the founding fathers in their formulation of the Constitution and the Declaration of Independence.

Never before have I written so long a letter. I'm afraid it is much too long to take your precious time. I can assure you that it would have been much shorter if I had been writing from a comfortable desk, but what else can one do when he is alone in a narrow jail cell, other than write long letters, think long thoughts and pray long prayers?

If I have said anything in this letter that overstates the truth and indicates an unreasonable impatience, I beg you to forgive me. If I have said anything that understates the truth and indicates my having a patience that allows me to settle for anything less than brotherhood, I beg God to forgive me.

I hope this letter finds you strong in the faith. I also hope that circumstances will soon make it possible for me to meet each of you, not as an integrationist or a civil rights leader but as a fellow clergyman and a Christian brother. Let us all hope that the dark clouds of racial prejudice will soon pass away and the deep fog of misunderstanding will be lifted from our fear-drenched communities, and in some not too distant tomorrow the radiant stars of love and brotherhood will shine over our great nation with all their scintillating beauty.

Yours for the cause of Peace and Brotherhood,

Martin Luther King, Jr.

Chapter 11

M. B. E. Smith

IS THERE A *PRIMA FACIE* DUTY TO OBEY THE LAW?

M. B. E. Smith (1939–) was a professor of philosophy at Smith College until his retirement in 2002, specializing in ethics and the philosophy of law. In this article (published in 1973), Smith questions the existence and strength of individuals' duty to obey the law. While conceding that people can have obligations to obey *specific* laws (e.g. to obey the laws against murder), Smith denies that they have any generic obligation to obey the law as such, even a relatively weak *prima facie* obligation that could be overridden by other moral considerations. Smith defends this conclusion against arguments that seek to establish such an obligation on grounds of utility, consent, and fair play, and explores the implications of his view for questions concerning civil disobedience.

It isn't a question of whether it was legal or illegal. That isn't enough. The question is, what is morally wrong?
                                                                    – Richard Nixon, "Checkers Speech" 1952.

Many political philosophers have thought it obvious that there is a prima facie obligation to obey the law; and so, in discussing this obligation, they have thought their task to be more that of explaining its basis than of arguing for its existence. John Rawls has, for example, written:

> I shall assume, as requiring no argument, that there is, at least in a society such as ours, a moral obligation to obey the law, although it may, of course, be overriden in certain cases by other more stringent obligations.[1]

As against this, I suggest that it is not at all obvious that there is such an obligation, that this is something that must be shown, rather than so blithely assumed. Indeed, were he uninfluenced by conventional wisdom, a reflective man might on first considering the question be inclined to deny any such obligation: As H. A. Prichard once remarked, "the mere receipt of an order backed by force seems, if anything, to give rise to the duty of resisting, rather than obeying."[2]

I shall argue that, although those subject to a government often have a prima facie obligation to obey particular laws (e.g., when disobedience has seriously untoward consequences or involves an act that is *mala in se*), they have no prima facie obligation to obey all its laws. I do not hope to prove this contention beyond a reasonable doubt: My goal is rather the more modest one of showing that it is a reasonable position to maintain by first criticizing arguments that purport to establish the obligation and then presenting some positive argument against it.

First, however, I must explain how I use the phrase "prima facie obligation." I shall say that a person S has a prima facie obligation to do an act X if, and only if, there is a moral reason for S to do X which is such that, unless he has a moral reason not to do X at least as strong as his reason to do X, S's failure to do X is wrong.[3] In this discussion it will also be convenient to distinguish two kinds of prima facie obligation via the difference between the two kinds of statement which ascribe them. A specific statement asserts that some particular person has a prima facie obligation to perform some particular act. In contrast, a generic state-ment (e.g., "Parents have a prima facie obligation to care for their infant children") asserts that everyone who meets a certain description has a prima facie obligation to perform a certain kind of act whenever he has an opportunity to do so. I shall therefore say that a person S has a *specific* prima facie obligation to do X if, and only if, the specific statement "S has a prima facie obligation to do X" is true; and that he has a *generic* prima facie obliga-tion to do X if, and only if, S meets some descrip-tion D and the generic statement "Those who are D have a prima facie obligation to do X" is true.[4]

Now, the question of whether there is a prima facie obligation to obey the law is clearly about a generic obligation. Everyone, even the anarchist, would agree that in many circumstances individ-uals have specific prima facie obligations to obey specific laws. Since it is clear that there is in most circumstances a specific prima facie obligation to refrain from murder, rape, or breach of contract, it is plain that in these circumstances each of us has a specific prima facie obligation not to violate laws which prohibit these acts. Again, disobeying the law often has seriously untoward consequences; and, when this is so, virtually everyone would agree that there is a specific prima facie obligation to obey. Therefore, the interesting question about our obligation vis-à-vis the law is not "Do indi-vidual citizens ever have specific prima facie obli-gations to obey particular laws?," but rather "Is the moral relation of any government to its citizens such that they have a prima facie obligation to do

certain things merely because they are legally required to do so?" This is, of course, equivalent to asking "Is there a generic prima facie obligation to obey the law?" Hereafter, when I use the phrase "the prima facie obligation to obey the law" I shall be referring to a generic obligation.

One final point in clarification: As used here, the phrase "prima facie" bears a different meaning than it does when used in legal writing. In legal materials, the phrase frequently refers to evidence sufficiently persuasive so as to require rebuttal. Hence, were a lawyer to ask "Is there a prima facie obligation to obey the law?," a reasonable interpre-tation of his question might be "May a reasonable man take mere illegality to be sufficient evidence that an act is morally wrong, so long as there is no specific evidence tending to show it is right?" Let us call this the "lawyer's question." Now, the ques-tion of primary concern in this inquiry is "Is there any society in which mere illegality is a moral reason for an act's being wrong?" The difference between these questions is that, were there a prima facie obligation to obey the law in the lawyer's sense, mere illegality would, in the absence of specific evidence to the contrary, be evidence of wrongdoing, but it would not necessarily be rele-vant to a determination of whether law-breaking is wrong where there is reason to think such conduct justified or even absolutely obligatory. In contrast, if there is a prima facie obligation to obey the law in the sense in which I am using the phrase, the mere illegality of an act is always relevant to the determination of its moral character, despite what-ever other reasons are present.[5] Hence, there may be a prima facie obligation to obey the law in the lawyer's sense and yet be no such obligation in the sense of the phrase used here. Near the end of this article I shall return briefly to the lawyer's question; for the present, I raise it only that it may not be confused with the question I wish to examine.

I

The arguments I shall examine fall into three groups: First, those which rest on the benefits each individual receives from government; second, those relying on implicit consent or promise; third, those which appeal to utility or the general good. I shall consider each group in turn.

Of those in the first group, I shall begin with the argument from gratitude. Although they differ greatly in the amount of benefits they provide, virtually all governments do confer substantial benefits on their subjects. Now, it is often claimed that, when a person accepts benefits from another, he thereby incurs a debt of gratitude towards his benefactor. Thus, if it be maintained that obedience to the law is the best way of showing gratitude towards one's government, it may with some plausibility be concluded that each person who has received benefits from his government has a prima facie obligation to obey the law.

On reflection, however, this argument is unconvincing. First, it may reasonably be doubted whether most citizens have an obligation to act gratefully towards their government. Ordinarily, if someone confers benefits on me without any consideration of whether I want them, and if he does this in order to advance some purpose other than promotion of my particular welfare, I have no obligation to be grateful towards him. Yet the most important benefits of government are not accepted by its citizens, but are rather enjoyed regardless of whether they are wanted. Moreover, a government typically confers these benefits, not to advance the interests of particular citizens, but rather as a consequence of advancing some purpose of its own. At times, its motives are wholly admirable, as when it seeks to promote the general welfare; at others, they are less so, as when it seeks to stay in power by catering to the demands of some powerful faction. But, such motives are irrelevant: Whenever government forces benefits on me for reasons other than my particular welfare, I clearly am under no obligation to be grateful to it.

Second, even assuming *arguendo* that each citizen has an obligation to be grateful to his

government, the argument still falters. It is perhaps true that cheerful and willing obedience is the best way to show one's gratitude towards government, in that it makes his gratitude unmistakable. But, when a person owes a debt of gratitude towards another, he does not necessarily acquire a prima facie obligation to display his gratitude in the most convincing manner: A person with demanding, domineering parents might best display his gratitude towards them by catering to their every whim, but he surely has no prima facie obligation to do so. Without undertaking a lengthy case-by-case examination, one cannot delimit the prima facie obligation of acting gratefully, for its existence and extent depends on such factors as the nature of the benefits received, the manner in which they are conferred, the motives of the benefactor, and so forth. But, even without such an examination, it is clear that the mere fact that a person has conferred on me even the most momentous benefits does not establish his right to dictate all of my behavior; nor does it establish that I always have an obligation to consider his wishes when I am deciding what I shall do. If, then, we have a prima facie obligation to act gratefully towards government, we undoubtedly have an obligation to promote its interests when this does not involve great sacrifice on our part and to respect some of its wishes concerning that part of our behavior which does not directly affect its interests. But, our having this obligation to be grateful surely does not establish that we have a prima facie obligation to obey the law.

A more interesting argument from the benefits individuals receive from government is the argument from fair play. It differs from the argument from gratitude in contending that the prima facia obligation to obey the law is owed, not to one's government but rather to one's fellow citizens. Versions of this argument have been offered by H. L. A. Hart and John Rawls.

According to Hart, the mere existence of cooperative enterprise gives rise to a certain prima facie obligation. He argues that:

when a number of persons conduct any joint enterprise according to rules and thus restrict their liberty, those who have submitted to these restrictions when required have a right to a similar submission from those who have benefitted by their submission. The rules may provide that officials should have authority to enforce obedience and make further rules, and this will create a structure of legal rights and duties, but the moral obligation to obey the rules in such circumstances is *due to* the cooperating members of the society, and they have the correlative moral right to obedience.[6]

Rawls' account of this obligation in his essay, *Legal Obligation and the Duty of Fair Play*,[7] is rather more complex. Unlike Hart, he sets certain requirements on the kinds of cooperative enterprises that give rise to the obligation: First, that success of the enterprise depends on near-universal obedience to its rules, but not on universal cooperation; second, that obedience to its rules involves some sacrifice, in that obeying the rules restricts one's liberty; and finally, that the enterprise conform to the principles of justice.[8] Rawls also offers an explanation of the obligation: He argues that, if a person benefits from participating in such an enterprise and if he intends to continue receiving its benefits, he acts unfairly when he refuses to obey its rules. With Hart, however, Rawls claims that this obligation is owed not to the enterprise itself, nor to its officials, but rather to those members whose obedience has made the benefits possible. Hart and Rawls also agree that this obligation of fair play – "fair play" is Rawls' term – is a fundamental obligation, not derived from utility or from mutual promise or consent.[9] Finally, both Hart and Rawls conceive of legal systems, at least those in democratic societies, as complex practices of the kind which give rise to the obligation of fair play; and they conclude that those who benefit from such legal systems have a prima facie obligation to obey their laws.

These arguments deserve great respect. Hart and Rawls appear to have isolated a kind of prima facie obligation overlooked by other philosophers and have thereby made a significant contribution to moral theory. However, the significance of their discovery to jurisprudence is less clear. Although Hart and Rawls have discovered the obligation of fair play, they do not properly appreciate its limits. Once these limits are understood, it is clear that the prima facie obligation to obey the law cannot be derived from the duty of fair play.

The obligation of fair play seems to arise most clearly within small, voluntary cooperative enterprises. Let us suppose that a number of persons have gone off into the wilderness to carve out a new society, and that they have adopted certain rules to govern their communal life. Their enterprise meets Rawls' requirements on success, sacrifice, and justice. We can now examine the moral situation of the members of that community in a number of circumstances, taking seriously Hart's insistence that cooperating members have a right to the obedience of others and Rawls' explanation of this right and its correlative obligation on grounds of fairness.

Let us take two members of the community, *A* and *B*. *B*, we may suppose, has never disobeyed the rules, and *A* has benefitted from *B*'s previous submission. Has *B* a right to *A*'s obedience? It would seem necessary to know the consequences of *A*'s obedience. If, in obeying the rules, *A* will confer on *B* a benefit roughly equal to those he has received from *B*, it would be plainly unfair for *A* to withhold it from *B*; and so, in this instance, *B*'s right to *A*'s obedience is clear. Similarly, if, in disobeying the rule, *A* will harm the community, *B*'s right to *A*'s obedience is again clear. This is because in harming the community *A* will harm *B* indirectly, by threatening the existence or efficient functioning of an institution on which *B*'s vital interests depend. Since *A* has benefitted from *B*'s previous submission to the rules, it is unfair for *A* to do something which will lessen *B*'s chances of receiving like benefits in the future. However, if A's compliance with some particular rule does not benefit B and if his disobedience will not harm the community, it is difficult to see how fairness to B could dictate that A must comply. Surely, the fact that A has benefitted from B's submission does not give B the right to insist that A obey when B's interests are unaffected. A may in this situation have an obligation to obey, perhaps because he has promised or because his disobedience would be unfair to some other member; but, if he does disobey, he has surely not been unfair to B.

We may generalize from these examples. Considerations of fairness apparently do show that, when cooperation is perfect and when each member has benefitted from the submission of every other, each member of an enterprise has a prima facie obligation to obey its rules when obedience benefits some other member or when disobedience harms the enterprise. For, if in either circumstance a member disobeys, he is unfair to at least one other member and is perhaps unfair to them all. However, if a member disobeys when his obedience would have benefitted no other member and when his disobedience does no harm, his moral situation is surely different. If his disobedience is then unfair, it must be unfair to the group but not to any particular member. But this, I take it, is impossible: Although the moral properties of a group are not always a simple function of the moral properties of its members, it is evident that one cannot be unfair to a group without being unfair to any of its members. It would seem, then, that even when cooperation is perfect, considerations of fairness do not establish that members of a cooperative enterprise have a simple obligation to obey all of its rules, but have rather the more complex obligation to obey when obedience benefits some other member or when disobedience harms the enterprise. This does not, it is worth noting, reduce the obligation of fair play to a kind of utilitarian obligation, for it may well be that fair play will dictate in certain circumstances that a

man obey when disobedience would have better consequences. My point is merely that the obligation of fair play governs a man's actions only when some benefit or harm turns on whether he obeys. Surely, this is as should be, for questions of fairness typically arise from situations in which burdens or benefits are distributed or in which some harm is done.

The obligation of fair play is therefore much more complex than Hart or Rawls seem to have imagined. Indeed, the obligation is even more complex than the above discussion suggests, for the assumption of perfect cooperation is obviously unrealistic. When that assumption is abandoned, the effect of previous disobedience considered, and the inevitable disparity among the various members' sacrifice in obeying the rules taken into account, the scope of the obligation is still further limited; we shall then find that it requires different things of different members, depending on their previous pattern of compliance and the amount of sacrifice they have made.[10] These complications need not detain us, however, for they do not affect the fact that fairness requires obedience only in situations where noncompliance would withhold benefits from someone or harm the enterprise. Now it must be conceded that all of this makes little difference when we confine our attention to small, voluntary, cooperative enterprises. Virtually any disobedience may be expected to harm such enterprises to some extent, by diminishing the confidence of other members in its probable success and therefore reducing their incentive to work diligently towards it. Moreover, since they are typically governed by a relatively small number of rules, none of which ordinarily require behavior that is useless to other members, we may expect that when a member disobeys he will probably withhold a benefit from some other member and that he has in the past benefitted significantly from that member's obedience. We may therefore expect that virtually every time the rules of a small, voluntary enterprise call on a member to obey he will have a specific prima facie obligation to do so because of his obligation of fair play.

In the case of legal systems, however, the complexity of the obligation makes a great deal of difference. Although their success may depend on the "habit of obedience" of a majority of their subjects, all legal systems are designed to cope with a substantial amount of disobedience.[11] Hence, individual acts of disobedience to the law only rarely have an untoward effect on legal systems. What is more, because laws must necessarily be designed to cover large numbers of cases, obedience to the law often benefits no one. Perhaps the best illustration is obedience of the traffic code: Very often I benefit no one when I stop at a red light or observe the speed limit. Finally, virtually every legal system contains a number of pointless or even positively harmful laws, obedience to which either benefits no one or, worse still, causes harm. Laws prohibiting homosexual activity or the dissemination of birth control information are surely in this category. Hence, even if legal systems are the kind of cooperative enterprise that gives rise to the obligation of fair play, in a great many instances that obligation will not require that we obey specific laws. If, then, there is a generic prima facie obligation to obey the laws of any legal system, it cannot rest on the obligation of fair play. The plausibility of supposing that it does depends on an unwarranted extrapolation from what is largely true of our obligations within small, cooperative enterprises to what must always be true of our obligations within legal systems.

[. . .]

II

The second group of arguments are those from implicit consent or promise. Recognizing that among the clearest cases of prima facie obligation are those in which a person voluntarily assumes the obligation, some philosophers have attempted to found the citizen's obligation to obey the law upon his consent or promise to do so. There is, of course, a substantial difficulty in any such attempt, namely, the brute fact that many persons have never so agreed. To accommodate this fact, some philosophers have invoked the concept of implicit promise or consent. In the *Second Treatise*, Locke argued that mere residence in a country, whether for an hour or a lifetime, constitutes implicit consent to its law.[12] Plato[13] and W. D. Ross[14] made the similar argument that residence in a country and appeal to the protection of its laws constitutes an implicit promise to obey.

Nevertheless, it is clear that residence and use of the protection of the law do not constitute any usual kind of consent to a government nor any usual kind of promise to obey its laws. The phrases "implicit consent" and "implicit promise" are somewhat difficult to understand, for they are not commonly used; nor do Locke, Plato, or Ross define them. Still, a natural way of understanding them is to assume that they refer to acts which differ from explicit consent or promise only in that, in the latter cases, the person has said "I consent . . ." or "I promise . . .," whereas in the former, he has not uttered such words but has rather performed some act which counts as giving consent or making a promise. Now, as recent investigation in the philosophy of language has shown, certain speech acts are performed only when someone utters certain words (or performs some other conventional act) with the intention that others will take what he did as being an instance of the particular act in question.[15] And it is certain that, in their ordinary usage, "consenting" and "promising" refer to speech acts of this kind. If I say to someone, "I promise to give you fifty dollars," but it is clear from the context that I do not intend that others will take my utterance as a promise, no one would consider me as having promised. Bringing this observation to bear on the present argument, it is perhaps possible that some people reside in a country and appeal to the protection of its laws with the intention that others will take their residence and appeal as consent to the laws or as a promise to obey; but this is surely true only of a very small number, consisting entirely of those enamoured with social contract theory.[16]

[. . .]

III

I shall consider three utilitarian arguments: the first appealing to a weak form of act-utilitarianism, the second and third to rule-utilitarian theories. To my knowledge, the first argument has never been explicitly advanced. It is nevertheless worth considering, both because it possesses a certain plausibility and because it has often been hinted at when philosophers, lawyers, and political theorists have attempted to derive an obligation to obey the law from the premise that government is necessary to protect society from great evil. The argument runs as follows:

> There is obviously a prima facie obligation to perform acts which have good consequences. Now, government is absolutely necessary for securing the general good: The alternative is the state of nature in which everyone is miserable, in which life is "solitary, poor, nasty, brutish and short." But, no government can long stand in the face of widespread disobedience, and government can therefore promote the general good only so long as its laws are obeyed. Therefore, obedience to the law supports the continued existence of government and, hence, always has good consequences. From this it follows that there is a prima facie obligation to obey the law.

On even brief scrutiny, however, this argument quickly disintegrates. The first thing to be noticed is that its principle of prima facie obligation is ambiguous. It may be interpreted as postulating either (a) an obligation to perform those acts which have any good consequences, or (b) an obligation to perform optimific acts (i.e., those

whose consequences are better than their alternatives). Now, (a) and (b) are in fact very different principles. The former is obviously absurd. It implies, for example, that I have a prima facie obligation to kill whomever I meet, since this would have the good consequence of helping to reduce overpopulation. Thus, the only weak act-utilitarian principle with any plausibility is (b). But, regardless of whether (b) is acceptable — and some philosophers would not accept it[17] — the conclusion that there is a prima facie obligation to obey the law cannot be derived from it, inasmuch as there are obvious and familiar cases in which breach of a particular law has better consequences than obedience. The only conclusion to be derived from (b) is that there is a specific prima facie obligation to obey the law whenever obedience is optimific. But no generic prima facie obligation to obey can be derived from weak act-utilitarianism.[18]

The second utilitarian argument appeals not to the untoward consequences of individual disobedience, but rather to those of general disobedience. Perhaps the most common challenge to those who defend certain instances of civil disobedience is "What would happen if everyone disobeyed the law?" One of the arguments implicit in this question is the generalization argument, which may be expanded as follows:

> No one can have a right to do something unless everyone has a right to do it. Similarly, an act cannot be morally indifferent unless it would be morally indifferent if everyone did it. But, everyone's breaking the law is not a matter of moral indifference; for no government can survive in such a circumstance and, as we have already agreed, government is necessary for securing and maintaining the general good. Hence, since the consequences of general disobedience would be disastrous, each person subject to law has a prima facie obligation to obey it.

In assessing this argument, we must first recognize that the generalization argument is a moral criterion to be applied with care, as virtually everyone who has discussed it has recognized.[19] If we simply note that if everyone committed a certain act there would be disastrous consequences and thereupon conclude that there is a prima facie obligation not to commit acts of that kind, we will be saddled with absurdities. We will have to maintain, for example, that there is a prima facie obligation not to eat dinner at five o'clock, for if everyone did so, certain essential services could not be maintained. And, for similar reasons, we will have to maintain that there is a prima facie obligation not to produce food. Now, those who believe that the generalization argument is valid argue that such absurdities arise when the criterion is applied to acts which are either too generally described or described in terms of morally irrelevant features. They would argue that the generalization argument appears to go awry when applied to these examples because the description "producing food" is too general to give the argument purchase and because the temporal specification in "eating dinner at five o'clock" is morally irrelevant.[20]

However, such a restriction on the generalization argument is fatal to its use in proving a prima facie obligation to obey the law. This is because a person who denies any such obligation is surely entitled to protest that the description "breaking the law" is overly general, on the ground that it refers to acts of radically different moral import.[21] Breaking the law perhaps always has some bad consequences; but sometimes the good done by it balances the bad or even outweighs it. And, once we take these differences in consequences into account, we find that utilitarian generalization, like weak act-utilitarianism, can only establish a specific prima facie obligation to obey the law when obedience is optimific. Were everyone to break the law when obedience is optimific, the consequences would undoubtedly be disastrous; but it is by no means

clear that it would be disastrous if everyone broke the law when obedience is not optimific. Since no one knows, with respect to any society, how often obedience is not optimific, no one can be certain as to the consequences of everyone acting in this way. Indeed, for all we know, if everyone broke the law when obedience was not optimific the good done by separate acts of law-breaking might more than compensate for any public disorder which might result. In sum, even if the generalization argument is regarded as an acceptable principle of prima facie obligation, the most it demonstrates is that there is a specific prima facie obligation to obey the law whenever the consequences of obedience are optimific.

[. . .]

Rule-utilitarian theories which focus on the consequences of everyone accepting (although not always following) a certain set of rules do differ markedly from the generalization argument; and so the question remains as to whether such a theory could establish a prima facie obligation to obey the law. I shall therefore discuss whether the most carefully developed such theory, that given by R. B. Brandt,[22] does just this.

In Brandt's theory, one's obligations are (within certain limits) relative to his society and are determined by the set of rules whose acceptance in that society would have better consequences than would acceptance of any other set.[23] According to this theory, then, there can be a generic prima facie obligation to obey the law within a given society if, and only if, general acceptance of the rule "Obey the law," as a rule of prima facie obligation, would have better consequences than were no rule accepted with respect to obeying the law, as well as better consequences than were some alternative rule accepted (e.g., "Obey the law when obedience to the law is optimific," or "Obey the law so long as it is just"). Now, to many it may seem obvious that the ideal set of rules for any society will contain the rule "Obey the law," on the ground that, were its members not generally convinced

of at least a prima facie obligation to obey, disobedience would be widespread, resulting in a
great many crimes against person and property.
But, there are two reasons to doubt such a
gloomy forecast. First, we must surely suppose
that in this hypothetical society the laws are still
backed by sanctions, thereby giving its members
a strong incentive to obey its laws. Second, we
must also assume that the members of that
society accept other moral rules (e.g., "Do not
harm others," "Keep promises," "Tell the truth")
which will give them a moral incentive to obey
the law in most circumstances. It is, in short, a
mistake to believe that unless people are
convinced that they have a generic prima facie
obligation to obey the law, they cannot be
convinced that in most circumstances they have
a specific prima facie obligation to obey particular laws. We may therefore expect that, even
though members of our hypothetical society do
not accept a moral rule about obedience to the
law per se, they will still feel a prima facie obligation to act in accordance with the law, save
when disobedience does no harm. There is, then,
no reason to think that an orgy of law-breaking
would ensue were no rule about obedience to
the law generally recognized; nor, I think, is
there any good reason to believe that acceptance
of the rule "Obey the law" would in any society
have better consequences than were no such rule
recognized. And, if this is so, there is surely no
reason to think that recognition of this rule
would have better consequences than recognition of some alternative rule. In sum, Brandt's
theory requires that we be able to determine the
truth-value of a large number of counter-factual
propositions about what would happen were
entire societies persuaded of the truth of certain
moral rules. But, even if we assume – and it is
hardly clear that we should[24] – that we can reliably determine the truth-value of such counter-
factuals through "common sense" and our
knowledge of human nature, Brandt's form of
rule utilitarianism gives no support for the proof
of a prima facie obligation to obey the law.

IV

In the foregoing discussion, I have played the
skeptic, contending that no argument has as yet
succeeded in establishing a prima facie obligation to obey the law. I want now to examine this
supposed obligation directly. I shall assume
arguendo that such an obligation exists in order to
inquire as to how it compares in moral weight
with other prima facie obligations. As we shall
see, this question is relevant to whether we
should hold that such an obligation exists.

To discuss this question, I must, of course,
first specify some test for determining the weight
of a prima facie obligation. It will be recalled
that I defined "prima facie obligation" in terms
of wrongdoing: To say that a person S has a prima
facie obligation to do an act X is to say that S has
a moral reason to do X which is such that, unless
he has a reason not to do X that is at least as
strong, S's failure to do X is wrong. Now, we are
accustomed, in our reflective moral practice, to
distinguish degrees of wrongdoing. And so, by
appealing to this notion, we can formulate two
principles that may reasonably be held to govern
the weight of prima facie obligations: First, that
a prima facie obligation is a serious one if, and
only if, an act which violates that obligation and
fulfills no other is seriously wrong; and, second,
that a prima facie obligation is a serious one if,
and only if, violation of it will make considerably worse an act which on other grounds is
already wrong.[25] These principles, which constitute tests for determining an obligation's weight,
are closely related, and application of either to a
given prima facie obligation is a sufficient
measure; but I shall apply both to the presumed
prima facie obligation to obey the law in order
to make my argument more persuasive.

[. . .]

By neither of these tests, however, does the
prima facie obligation to obey the law count as
substantial. As for the first test, let us assume that
while driving home at two o'clock in the
morning I run a stop sign. There is no danger,

for I can see clearly that there was no one approaching the intersection, nor is there any impressionable youth nearby to be inspired to a life of crime by my flouting of the traffic code. Finally, we may assume that I nevertheless had no specific prima facie obligation to run the stop sign. If, then, my prima facie obligation to obey the law is of substantial moral weight, my action must have been a fairly serious instance of wrongdoing. But clearly it was not. If it was wrong at all – and to me this seems dubious – it was at most a mere peccadillo. As for the second test, we may observe that acts which are otherwise wrong are not made more so – if they are made worse at all – by being illegal.[26] If I defraud someone my act is hardly worse morally by being illegal than it would have been were it protected by some legal loophole. Thus, if there is a prima facie obligation to obey the law, it is at most of trifling weight.

This being so, I suggest that considerations of simplicity indicate that we should ignore the supposed prima facie obligation to obey the law and refuse to count an act wrong merely because it violates some law. There is certainly nothing to be lost by doing this, for we shall not thereby recommend or tolerate any conduct that is seriously wrong, nor shall we fail to recommend any course of action that is seriously obligatory. Yet, there is much to be gained, for in refusing to let trivialities occupy our attention, we shall not be diverted from the important questions to be asked about illegal conduct, namely, "What kind of act was it?," "What were its consequences?," "Did the agent intend its consequences?," and so forth. Morality is, after all, a serious business; and we are surely right not to squander our moral attention and concern on matters of little moral significance.

To illustrate what can be gained, let us consider briefly the issue of civil disobedience. Most philosophers who have written on the subject have argued that, at least in democratic societies, there is always a strong moral reason to obey the law. They have therefore held that civil disobedience is a tactic to be employed only when all legal means of changing an unjust law have failed, and that the person who engages in it must willingly accept punishment as a mark of respect for the law and recognition of the seriousness of law-breaking. However, once we abandon the notion that civil disobedience is morally significant per se, we shall judge it in the same way we judge most other kinds of acts, that is, on the basis of their character and consequences. Indeed, we can then treat civil disobedience just as we regard many other species of illegal conduct. If breaking the law involves an act which is *mala in se* or if it has untoward consequences, we are ordinarily prepared to condemn it and to think that the malefactor ought to accept punishment. But if law-breaking does not involve an act that is *mala in se* and if it has no harmful consequences, we do not ordinarily condemn it, nor do we think that its perpetrator must accept punishment, unless evading punishment itself has untoward consequences. If we adopt this view of civil disobedience, we shall have done much to escape the air of mystery that hovers about most discussions of it.

Of course, this is not to say it will be easy to determine when civil disobedience is justified. Some have maintained that the civil disobedience of the last decade has led to increasing violation of laws which safeguard people and property.[27] If this is true, each instance of disobedience which has contributed to this condition has a share in the evil of the result. Others maintain that such disobedience has had wholly good consequences, that it has helped to remedy existing injustice and to restrain government from fresh injustice.[28] Still others think its consequences are mixed. Which position is correct is difficult to determine. I myself am inclined to believe that, although the consequences have been mixed, the good far outweigh the bad; but I would be hard pressed to prove it. What is clear, however, is that either abandoning or retaining the supposed prima facie obligation to obey the law will not help settle these questions about consequences. But, if we do abandon it, we shall then at least be able to focus on these questions without having to worry about a prima facie obligation of trivial weight that must nevertheless somehow be taken into account. Finally, if we abandon the prima facie obligation to obey the law, we shall perhaps look more closely at the character of acts performed in the course of civil disobedience, and this may, in turn, lead to fruitful moral speculation. For example, we shall be able to distinguish between acts which cannot conceivably violate the obligation of fair play (e.g., burning one's draft card) and acts which may do so (e.g., tax refusal or evasion of military service). This in turn may provide an incentive to reflect further on the obligation of fair play, to ask, for example, whether Rawls is right in his present contention that a person can incur the obligation of fair play only so long as his acceptance of the benefits of a cooperative enterprise is wholly voluntary.

V

It is now time to take stock. I initially suggested that it is by no means obvious that there is any prima facie obligation to obey the law. In the foregoing, I have rejected a number of arguments that purport to establish its existence. Finally, I have shown that even if such an obligation is assumed, it is of trivial weight and that there are substantial advantages in ignoring it. I suggest that all of this makes it reasonable to maintain that there is in no society a prima facie obligation to obey the law.

Before I conclude my discussion, however, I want to tie up one loose thread. Near the beginning of my argument I distinguished the question to be discussed from that which I called the lawyer's question, "May a reasonable man take mere illegality to be sufficient evidence that an act is morally wrong, so long as he lacks specific evidence that tends to show that it is right?" Since I have raised the question, I believe that, for the sake of completeness, I should consider

it, if only briefly. To begin, it seems very doubtful that there is, in the lawyer's sense, a prima facie obligation to obey the law. It is undoubtedly true that most instances of law-breaking are wrong, but it is also true that many are not: This is because there are, as Lord Devlin once remarked, "many fussy regulations whose breach it would be pedantic to call immoral,"[29] and because some breaches of even non-fussy regulations are justified. Now, unless – as in a court of law – there is some pressing need to reach a finding, the mere fact that most As are also Bs does not, in the absence of evidence that a particular A is not a B, warrant an inference that the A in question is also a B: In order for this inference to be reasonable, one must know that virtually all As are Bs. Since, then, it rarely happens that there is a pressing need to reach a moral finding, and since to know merely that an act is illegal is not to know very much of moral significance about it, it seems clear that, if his only information about an act was that it was illegal, a reasonable man would withhold judgment until he learned more about it. Indeed, this is not only what the fictitious reasonable man would do, it is what we should expect the ordinary person to do. Suppose we were to ask a large number of people: "Jones has broken a law; but I won't tell you whether what he did is a serious crime or merely violation of a parking regulation, nor whether he had good reason for his actions. Would you, merely on the strength of what I have just told you, be willing to say that what he did was morally wrong?" I have conducted only an informal poll; but, on its basis, I would wager that the great majority would answer "I can't yet say – you must tell me more about what Jones did."

[. . .]

In conclusion, it is, I think, important to recognize that there is nothing startling in what I am recommending, nothing that in any way outrages common sense. Even the most conscientious men at times violate trivial and pointless laws for some slight gain in convenience and, when they do so, they do not feel shame or remorse. Similarly, when they observe other men behaving in a like fashion, they do not think of passing moral censure. For most people, violation of the law becomes a matter for moral concern only when it involves an act which is believed to be wrong on grounds apart from its illegality. Hence, anyone who believes that the purpose of normative ethics is to organize and clarify our reflective moral practice should be skeptical of any argument purporting to show that there is a prima facie obligation to obey the law. It is necessary to state this point with care: I am not contending that reflective and conscientious citizens would, if asked, deny that there is a prima facie obligation to obey the law. Indeed, I am willing to concede that many more would affirm its existence than deny it. But, this is in no way inconsistent with my present point. We often find that reflective people will accept general statements which are belied by their actual linguistic practice. That they also accept moral generalizations that are belied by their actual reflective moral practice should occasion no surprise.

This last point may, however, be challenged on the ground that it implies that there is in our reflective moral practice no distinction between raw power and legitimate authority. As I noted above, the concept of legitimate authority is often analyzed in terms of the right to command, where "right" is used in the strict sense as implying some correlative obligation of obedience. Given this definition, if it is true that the principle "There is a prima facie obligation to obey the law" is not observed in our reflective moral practice, it follows that we do not really distinguish between governments which possess legitimate authority (e.g., that of the United States) and those which do not (e.g., the Nazi occupation government of France). And this, it may justly be held, is absurd. What I take this argument to show, however, is not that the principle is enshrined in our reflective morality, but rather that what we ordinarily mean when we ascribe legitimate authority to

some government is not captured by the usual analysis of "legitimate authority." It is a mistake to believe that, unless we employ the concept of authority as it is usually analyzed, we cannot satisfactorily distinguish between the moral relation of the government of the United States vis-à-vis Americans and the moral relation of the Nazi occupation government vis-à-vis Frenchmen. One way of doing this, for example, is to define "legitimate authority" in terms of "the right to command and to enforce obedience," where "right" is used in the sense of "what is morally permissible." Thus, according to this analysis of the notion, the government of the United States counts as having legitimate authority over its subjects because within certain limits there is nothing wrong in its issuing commands to them and enforcing their obedience, whereas the Nazi occupation government lacked such authority because its issuing commands to Frenchmen was morally impermissible. It is not my intention to proffer this as an adequate analysis of the notion of legitimate authority or to suggest that it captures what we ordinarily mean when we ascribe such authority to some government. These are difficult matters, and I do not wish to address myself to them here. My point is rather that the questions "What governments enjoy legitimate authority?" and "Have the citizens of any government a prima facie obligation to obey the law?" both can be, and should be, kept separate.

Notes

1 Rawls, *Legal Obligation and the Duty of Fair Play*, in Law and Philosophy 3 (S. Hook ed. 1964).

2 H.A. Prichard, *Green's Principles of Political Obligation*, in Moral Obligation 54 (1949).

3 The distinction between prima facie and absolute obligation was first made by W.D. Ross in The Right and the Good ch. 2 (1930). My account of prima facie obligation differs somewhat from Ross'; but I believe it adequately captures current philosophical usage. As for absolute obligation,

I shall not often speak of it; but when I do, what I shall mean by "S has an absolute obligation to do X" is that "S's failure to do X is wrong."

4   My motive for distinguishing generic and specific prima facie obligations is simply convenience, and not because I think it provides a perspicuous way of classifying prima facie obligations. As a classification it is obviously defective: The two kinds of obligation overlap, since in a trivial sense every specific obligation can be construed as a generic one; and there are some prima facie obligations (e.g., the obligation to keep one's promise), that fit neither definition.

5   An example may help to make the point clear. If I promise that I will meet someone at a certain time, I have a prima facie obligation to keep my promise. Now, were this merely a prima facie obligation in the lawyer's sense, without evidence to the contrary the fact that I had promised would be sufficient to hold that a breach of my promise was wrong, yet it would not be evidence of wrongdoing were there reason to believe the breach was justified or even obligatory. But, in fact, this is not what we think of promising. We think that if someone promises to do a thing there is a strong moral reason for him to do it and that, although this reason may sometimes be opposed by stronger reasons to the contrary, its weight does not disappear. In such cases, my promise is yet relevant to what I am absolutely obligated to do, although it is not always determinative. But, even when this reason is outweighed, it still discloses its existence by imposing fresh prima facie obligations (e.g., to tell the person I promised why I broke it). Hence, there is a prima facie obligation to keep one's promise in the sense in which I here use the phrase.

6   Hart, *Are There Any Natural Rights?*, 64 PHIL. REV. 185 (1955). I must note that Hart does not use the phrase "prima facie obligation," maintaining that his argument establishes an obligation *sans phrase* to comply with the rules of cooperative enterprises. However, since his use of "obligation" seems much the same as my use of "prima facie obligation," I shall ignore his terminological scruples.

7   Rawls, *supra* note 1. The same argument appears, although in less detail, in Rawls, *Justice as Fairness*, 67 PHIL. REV. 164 (1958), and Rawls, *The Justification of Civil Disobedience*, in CIVIL DISOBEDIENCE: THEORY AND PRACTICE (H.A. Bedau ed. 1969).

8   Rawls, *Legal Obligation and the Duty of Fair Play*, in LAW AND PHILOSOPHY 10 (S. Hook ed. 1964). According to Rawls, the principles of justice are that everyone has an equal right to the most extensive liberty compatible with a like liberty for all; . . . [and] that inequalities are arbitrary unless it is reasonable to expect that they will work out for everyone's advantage and provided that the positions and offices to which they attached or from which they may be gained are open to all. *Id.* at 11.

9   *Id.* at 13; Hart, *supra* note 6, at 185.

10   Those intrigued by the mention of these additional factors may be interested to know that, when imperfect cooperation is taken into account, it can be shown that considerations of fairness establish no more than: (1) that a member *A* of a cooperative enterprise has a prima facie obligation to obey when his obedience will benefit some other member *B* from whose submission *A* has previously benefitted and it is not the case that *B* has withheld from *A* more significant benefits than *A* withholds from *B*; and (2) that *A* has a prima facie obligation to obey when his disobedience harms the enterprise and there is some other member *B* from whose submission *A* has previously benefitted and *B* has by his disobedience harmed the enterprise less than the harm which would be done by *A*'s disobedience.

As for the effect of disparity in sacrifice, it was only recently suggested to me that this factor must be taken into account, and I have not yet attempted to determine its effects precisely. A moment's reflection discloses, however, that this additional factor would make the obligation still more complex. Were anyone to attempt a precise specification of the citizen's obligations vis-à-vis the laws of his government, he would have to master these complexities; but my task is not so ambitious.

11   Indeed, it seems strange that Rawls should have attempted to base the prima facie obligation to obey the law on fair play, since he maintains that this latter obligation is incurred within cooperative enterprises that depend on near-universal cooperation. Rawls, *Legal Obligation and the Duty of Fair Play*, in LAW AND PHILOSOPHY 10 (S. Hook ed. 1964).

12 J. LOCKE, TWO TREATISES OF GOVERNMENT Bk. II, 119 (1690).

13 1 PLATO, DIALOGUES 435 (B. Jowett transl. 1892).

14 Ross, *supra* note 3, at 27.

15 Cf. Strawson, *Intention and Convention in Speech Acts*, 73 PHIL. REV. 439, 448–9, 457–9 (1964).

16 A similar argument could also be made utilizing the analysis of promising in J. SEARLE, SPEECH ACTS: AN ESSAY IN THE PHILOSOPHY OF LANGUAGE 60 (1969).

17 For example, some philosophers would hold that there is a prima facie obligation to refrain from acts which have undesirable consequences, but not that there is an obligation to perform the one act which has the best consequences. *See*, e.g., M.G. SINGER, GENERALIZATION IN ETHICS, ch. 7 (1961).

18 For purposes of clarification, I should emphasize that I am here concerned with act-utilitarianism as a theory of prima facie, not absolute, obligation. There is no incongruity here. The consequences of acts count as having great moral significance on virtually every moral theory; and so, one need not be a strict act-utilitarian in order to maintain the principle that there is a prima facie obligation to act optimifically. Indeed, for a strict act utilitarian such as Bentham, it is pointless to worry about whether there is a prima facie obligation to obey the law: He would hold that there is an absolute obligation to obey the law when, and only when, obedience is optimific, and would there end the discussion. At most, an act-utilitarian would hold that the rule "Obey the law" is a useful rule of thumb, to be followed only when the consequences of obedience or disobedience are difficult to discern.

19 SINGER, *supra* note 28, at ch. 4.

20 I have borrowed these cases and this strategy for handling them from Singer. *Id.* at 71–83.

21 According to Singer, a mark of a description's being overly general is that the generalization argument is "invertible" with respect to it, i.e., the consequences of everyone's doing the act (given that description) is disastrous and the consequences of everyone's failing to do it is also disastrous. *Id.* at 76–7. It is relevant to note that the generalization argument is plainly invertible with respect to the description "breaking the law." Sometimes breaking the law is the only

way to avoid a great evil; and so, if everyone were always to obey the law, such evils could never be avoided.

22 Brandt, *Toward a Credible Utilitarianism*, in MORALITY AND THE LANGUAGE OF CONDUCT 107 (H.N. Costenada and G. Nakhnikian eds. 1963). In the following I shall not be attacking a position Brandt holds, but only an argument that might be offered on the basis of his theory. In fact, in *Utility and the Obligation to Obey the Law*, in LAW AND PHILOSOPHY 43, 47–9 (S. Hook ed. 1964) Brandt expresses doubt as to whether there is such an obligation.

23 According to Brandt's theory, there is an absolute obligation to perform an act if it conforms with that learnable set of rules the recognition of which as morally binding — roughly at the time of the act — by everyone in the society of the agent, except for the retention by individuals of already formed and decided moral convictions, would maximize intrinsic value.

Brandt, *Toward a Credible Utilitarianism*, in MORALITY AND THE LANGUAGE OF CONDUCT 107, 139 (H.N. Castenada & G. Nakhnikian eds. 1963). He distinguishes three levels of rules, the first stating prima facie obligations and the latter two dealing with cases in which lower-level rules conflict. At every level, however, those in the favored set of rules are those whose recognition would have the best consequences, i.e., consequences better than were any alternative rule accepted, as well as better than were no such rule accepted. *Id.* at 118–9.

24 As an illustration of the difficulty, Brandt suggests that the first-level rule "Keep your promises" is neither the one that we accept nor the rule about promising that would maximize utility. *Id.* at 131–2. I think he is right to say that it is not the rule we accept, but how does he know that some more complex rule maximizes utility?

25 The second principle may be thought objectionable on the ground that it trivializes obviously weighty prima facie obligations. It may perhaps be held that, were a man to kill a thousand persons, his act would not have been much worse had he killed but one more. The principle therefore seems to imply that the prima facie obligation not to kill that one person is trivial. The objection is plausible, but misguided. Surely there is a

substantial moral difference between killing a thousand persons and killing a thousand and one – exactly the difference between killing one person and killing none. To deny this is to imply that the thousand-and-first person's life has little moral significance. At first glance, however, we may be inclined to take the difference to be trivial, because both acts are so monstrous that we should rarely see any point in distinguishing between them. That this objection might be raised against the principle was pointed out to me by Anne Bowen.

26 I have taken this point from 1 W. BLACKSTONE, COMMENTARIES *54: Neither do divine or natural *duties* (such as, for instance, the worship of God,

the maintenance of children, and the like) receive any stronger sanction from being also declared to be duties by the law of the land. The case is the same as to crimes and misdemeanors, that are forbidden by the superior laws, and therefore styled *mala in se*, such as murder, theft, and perjury; which contract no additional turpitude from being declared unlawful by the inferior legislature.

27 C. WHITTAKER, *First Lecture*, in LAW, ORDER AND CIVIL DISOBEDIENCE (1967).

28 *See* H. ZINN, DISOBEDIENCE AND DEMOCRACY (1968).

29 P. DEVLIN, THE ENFORCEMENT OF MORALS 27 (1965).

1b. RIGHTS

"We hold these truths to be self-evident, that all men ... are endowed by their Creator with certain unalienable Rights, that among these are Life, Liberty and the Pursuit of Happiness ..."

Thomas Jefferson,
U.S. Declaration of Independence, 1776

ALAS, **WHAT WAS SELF-EVIDENT** to Jefferson has been anything but to political philosophers. The famous utilitarian philosopher and legal reformer Jeremy Bentham, for instance, derided the idea of natural and imprescriptible rights as "nonsense on stilts." And even those who agree upon the importance of rights — as do all of the authors represented in this section — disagree sharply about the *content* and *moral justification* of those rights. Do we really have a right to the pursuit of happiness, and if so what does this mean? What if I like to pursue happiness by using drugs that the government has banned? Or by beating you over the head with a stick? And if "Life, Liberty and the Pursuit of Happiness" are merely *among* the unalienable rights with which we have been endowed by our Creator, then what are the rest, and how on earth are we supposed to find out?

Questions about rights are some of the most important questions in all of political philosophy. Rights are, after all, about what you can and cannot do, and about what the government must and must do for you or, more ominously, *to* you. Having or not having the right to vote, the right to speak freely, the right to practice your own religion, all make a tremendous practical difference in the way you live your life. It's tempting, therefore, to jump right into the fray and start any discussion on rights by debating the substantive question of which rights we do and do not have.

But this would be a mistake. For even if rights are of supreme practical importance, they are also tremendously difficult to be clear about from a philosophical perspective. Before we dive in to the substantive question of which rights we *have*, then, we need to get clear on the philosophical question of what exactly rights *are*.

The first and most important distinction we need to draw is between *legal* rights and *moral* rights. Suppose we say that Joe has a right to drink alcoholic beverages. In making this claim, we might be saying one of two things. One thing we might be saying is that under the rules of his legal system, Joe is allowed to drink alcoholic beverages without fear of reprisal — that he has, in other words, a *legal* right to drink. The fact that he can engage in this activity without fear of legal punishment is important for Joe and others like him to know, and so we can see why it would be important to have a class of people in society who are experts about exactly what legal rights we have, and who will tell us in exchange for lots and lots of money.

But suppose Joe claims that he has a right to drink alcohol while living in America in 1923, during the period of alcohol prohibition? What are we to make of his claim then? One possibility is that he simply isn't aware of what the law says — that he's simply making a *mistake*. More likely, though, Joe is not making a claim about his legal rights at all. What he is saying is that he has a *moral* right to drink, and that this moral right is something that holds *regardless* of what the law says. When Joe says that he has a moral right to drink, he means that it is something which he is morally free to do, and perhaps even that it is something which, morally speaking, the law *ought* to allow him to do, whether or not it actually does so.

Since legal rights and moral rights are different, it is possible to consistently claim both that one has a moral right to do something that one does not have a legal right to do (a slave in the American South during the 1850s might have the moral, but not the legal, right to escape), and that one has a legal right to do something that one does not have a moral right to do (if those who adhere to a pro-life position on abortion are right, then we have a legal but not a moral right to abort a child in the United States).

So far we have talked as though having a right simply meant that one was "free to do" something. But this needs to be made more precise. Some rights, after all, don't seem to have anything to do with *doing* something at all. My right to be free from physical assault, for instance, is more a claim about what *others* may do than one about what *I* may do. We can make better sense of rights by applying some distinctions first introduced by W.H. Hohfeld in the early twentieth century. According to Hohfeld, all rights are composed of some mixture of four more basic elements — privileges, claims, powers, and immunities. To have a privilege to *X* is to have no duty not to *X*. I have a privilege-right to walk down the street if I have no duty *not* to walk down the street. Claims are always claims *on* someone else; so, for instance, if Art has a claim on Barney to be paid $20, then Barney has a duty to Art to pay him $20. Duties are thus the flip side of claim-rights — my right to free speech imposes a duty on others not to interfere (in certain ways) with my speaking. My right to a free education imposes a duty on others to provide it.

Both privileges and claims are rules about what we can or cannot do. We can think of them, borrowing a term from H.L.A. Hart, as "primary rules." Powers and immunities, on the other hand, are "secondary rules" — what they have to do with is our ability to introduce, change, and alter primary rules. So Art has a power if and only if Art has the ability within a set of rules to alter the primary rules that apply to Art or to some other person like Barney. When, on the other hand, Art lacks the power to alter the primary rules that apply to Barney, then Barney has an immunity against Art in this respect. Art has the power to waive his right to be punched in the face by Barney, and can do so by agreeing to enter into a boxing match with him. Barney, however, has an immunity against Art waiving *Barney's* right not to be punched in the face.

Keeping clear on the various Hohfeldian elements of rights can allow us to make better sense of some of the claims we find in political philosophy. The claim that Jen has a property right to her watch, for instance, can be rendered more precise as follows. It means that Jen has a privilege to use her watch in various ways (e.g. by wearing it, destroying it, selling it, etc.), and that she has a claim against others using it in certain ways without her consent (which in turn entails that others have a *duty* not to use it in those ways without her consent). She also has an immunity against others altering this claim, and power to waive it herself — by granting someone else the temporary privilege to use it, or by selling the watch and thereby permanently divesting herself of her claims and privileges with regard to it. Importantly, once we start analyzing property rights in this way, we see that they need not be "all or nothing." If I have a property right in my land, I might have the privilege to do certain things with it — such as build a house or plant a garden — while lacking the privilege to do other things. If someone else has an easement through my property, then they have a claim against me to allow them free passage, and I thus have a corresponding duty to allow that passage and not to obstruct it by, say, completely enclosing my land within a brick wall. To be clear about rights, then, whether it is a property right in land or the right to "the pursuit of happiness," we need to be clear about precisely which privileges, claims, powers, and immunities go into it.

One final distinction, which will often prove useful in making sense of debates over rights, is that between negative and positive rights. A negative right is a right against certain sorts of interference by others. It is negative insofar as all it requires of others is that they *abstain* from certain kinds of action. Rights against robbery and assault are classic instances of negative rights. Positive rights, on the other hand, require others to perform some sort of positive act — such as providing you with some kind of good or service. Rights to health care and education are examples of positive rights. Libertarians tend to believe that negative rights are the only kind of rights that exist — or, at least, that they are the only kind of rights which should be *politically enforced.* Those on the political left, on the other hand, generally believe in the existence or political enforcement of a robust set of both negative and positive rights.

The first reading in this section, the *U.N. Declaration of Human Rights*, is both an important historical document and a nice test for one's understanding of the distinctions described above. Some of the rights enumerated in this document are stated at a very high level of abstraction. What specific claims, privileges, powers, and immunities do they guarantee? Does the document speak in terms of negative rights, positive rights, or both? And what underlying theory could *justify* this set of rights? What moral reasons do we have to think that all persons possess these rights, but not others? Readers are encouraged to think carefully about the idea of rights embodied in this document and how it comports with their own ideas about rights. This will lay the groundwork for the more abstract reflection on the nature of rights contained in the readings by Nickel and Nozick.

Further Reading

Feinberg, J. (1970). The Nature and Value of Rights, *Journal of Value Inquiry, 4*, 243–57.

Hart, H. L. A. (1955). Are There Any Natural Rights? *Philosophical Review, 64*, 175–91.

Hohfeld, W. (1919). *Fundamental Legal Conceptions.* New Haven: Yale University Press.

Holmes, S., and Sunstein, S. (1999). *The Cost of Rights*. New York: W.W. Norton.

Kamm, F. (1992). Non-consequentialism, the Person as End-in-Itself, and the Significance of Status. *Philosophy and Public Affairs, 21*(4), 354–89.

Lyons, D. (1970). The Correlativity of Rights and Duties. *Nous, 4*, 45–57.

Nagel, T. (1995). Personal Rights and Public Space. *Philosophy and Public Affairs, 24*(2), 83–107.

Narveson, J. (1988). *The Libertarian Idea*. Philadelphia: Temple University Press.

Nickel, J. (2006). *Making Sense of Human Rights* (2nd ed.). Oxford: Blackwell Publishing.

Raz, J. (1986). *The Morality of Freedom*. Oxford: Oxford University Press.

Steiner, H. (1994). *An Essay on Rights*. New York: Blackwell.

Thomson, J. J. (2005). *The Realm of Rights*. Cambridge, MA: Harvard University Press.

Waldron, J. (1984). *Theories of Rights*. Oxford: Oxford University Press.

Wellman, C. (1985). *A Theory of Rights*. Totowa, NJ: Rowman & Littlefield.

Chapter 12

United Nations

UNIVERSAL DECLARATION OF HUMAN RIGHTS

This document was adopted by the United Nations on December 10, 1948, largely in response to the atrocities of World War II. Its 30 articles represent the views of the General Assembly on those rights that all persons have, irrespective of their country of citizenship. It was later supplemented by the International Covenant on Economic, Social, and Cultural Rights, and the International Covenant on Civil and Political Rights (both adopted in 1966).

Preamble

Whereas recognition of the inherent dignity and of the equal and inalienable rights of all members of the human family is the foundation of freedom, justice and peace in the world,

Whereas disregard and contempt for human rights have resulted in barbarous acts which have outraged the conscience of mankind, and the advent of a world in which human beings shall enjoy freedom of speech and belief and freedom from fear and want has been proclaimed as the highest aspiration of the common people,

Whereas it is essential, if man is not to be compelled to have recourse, as a last resort, to rebellion against tyranny and oppression, that human rights should be protected by the rule of law,

Whereas it is essential to promote the development of friendly relations between nations,

Whereas the peoples of the United Nations have in the Charter reaffirmed their faith in fundamental human rights, in the dignity and worth of the human person and in the equal rights of men and women and have determined to promote social progress and better standards of life in larger freedom,

Whereas Member States have pledged themselves to achieve, in cooperation with the United Nations, the promotion of universal respect for and observance of human rights and fundamental freedoms,

Whereas a common understanding of these rights and freedoms is of the greatest importance for the full realization of this pledge,

Now, therefore,

The General Assembly,

Proclaims this Universal Declaration of Human Rights as a common standard of achievement for all peoples and all nations, to the end that every individual and every organ of society, keeping this Declaration constantly in mind, shall strive by teaching and education to promote respect for these rights and freedoms and by progressive measures, national and international, to secure their universal and effective recognition and observance, both among the peoples of Member States themselves and among the peoples of territories under their jurisdiction.

Article 1

All human beings are born free and equal in dignity and rights. They are endowed with reason and conscience and should act towards one another in a spirit of brotherhood.

Article 2

Everyone is entitled to all the rights and freedoms set forth in this Declaration, without distinction of any kind, such as race, color, sex, language, religion, political or other opinion, national or social origin, property, birth or other status. Furthermore, no distinction shall be made on the basis of the political, jurisdictional or international status of the country or territory to which a person belongs, whether it be independent, trust, non-self-governing or under any other limitation of sovereignty.

Article 3

Everyone has the right to life, liberty and security of person.

Article 4

No one shall be held in slavery or servitude; slavery and the slave trade shall be prohibited in all their forms.

Article 5

No one shall be subjected to torture or to cruel, inhuman or degrading treatment or punishment.

Article 6

Everyone has the right to recognition everywhere as a person before the law.

Article 7

All are equal before the law and are entitled without any discrimination to equal protection of the law. All are entitled to equal protection against any discrimination in violation of this Declaration and against any incitement to such discrimination.

Article 8

Everyone has the right to an effective remedy by the competent national tribunals for acts violating the fundamental rights granted him by the constitution or by law.

Article 9

No one shall be subjected to arbitrary arrest, detention or exile.

Article 10

Everyone is entitled in full equality to a fair and public hearing by an independent and impartial tribunal, in the determination of his rights and obligations and of any criminal charge against him.

Article 11

1. Everyone charged with a penal offence has the right to be presumed innocent until proved guilty according to law in a public trial at which he has had all the guarantees necessary for his defense.
2. No one shall be held guilty of any penal offence on account of any act or omission which did not constitute a penal offence, under national or international law, at the time when it was committed. Nor shall a heavier penalty be imposed than the one that was applicable at the time the penal offence was committed.

Article 12

No one shall be subjected to arbitrary interference with his privacy, family, home or correspondence, nor to attacks upon his honor and reputation. Everyone has the right to the protection of the law against such interference or attacks.

Article 13

1. Everyone has the right to freedom of movement and residence within the borders of each State.
2. Everyone has the right to leave any country, including his own, and to return to his country.

Article 14

1. Everyone has the right to seek and to enjoy in other countries asylum from persecution.
2. This right may not be invoked in the case of prosecutions genuinely arising from non-political crimes or from acts contrary to the purposes and principles of the United Nations.

Article 15

1. Everyone has the right to a nationality.
2. No one shall be arbitrarily deprived of his nationality nor denied the right to change his nationality.

Article 16

1. Men and women of full age, without any limitation due to race, nationality or religion, have the right to marry and to found a family. They are entitled to equal rights as to marriage, during marriage and at its dissolution.
2. Marriage shall be entered into only with the free and full consent of the intending spouses.
3. The family is the natural and fundamental group unit of society and is entitled to protection by society and the State.

Article 17

1. Everyone has the right to own property alone as well as in association with others.
2. No one shall be arbitrarily deprived of his property.

Article 18

Everyone has the right to freedom of thought, conscience and religion; this right includes freedom to change his religion or belief, and freedom, either alone or in community with others and in public or private, to manifest his religion or belief in teaching, practice, worship and observance.

Article 19

Everyone has the right to freedom of opinion and expression; this right includes freedom to hold opinions without interference and to seek, receive and impart information and ideas through any media and regardless of frontiers.

Article 20

1. Everyone has the right to freedom of peaceful assembly and association.
2. No one may be compelled to belong to an association.

Article 21

1. Everyone has the right to take part in the government of his country, directly or through freely chosen representatives.
2. Everyone has the right to equal access to public service in his country.
3. The will of the people shall be the basis of the authority of government; this will shall

be expressed in periodic and genuine elections which shall be by universal and equal suffrage and shall be held by secret vote or by equivalent free voting procedures.

Article 22

Everyone, as a member of society, has the right to social security and is entitled to realization, through national effort and international co-operation and in accordance with the organization and resources of each State, of the economic, social and cultural rights indispensable for his dignity and the free development of his personality.

Article 23

1. Everyone has the right to work, to free choice of employment, to just and favorable conditions of work and to protection against unemployment.
2. Everyone, without any discrimination, has the right to equal pay for equal work.
3. Everyone who works has the right to just and favorable remuneration ensuring for himself and his family an existence worthy of human dignity, and supplemented, if necessary, by other means of social protection.
4. Everyone has the right to form and to join trade unions for the protection of his interests.

Article 24

Everyone has the right to rest and leisure, including reasonable limitation of working hours and periodic holidays with pay.

Article 25

1. Everyone has the right to a standard of living adequate for the health and well-being of himself and of his family,

including food, clothing, housing and medical care and necessary social services, and the right to security in the event of unemployment, sickness, disability, widowhood, old age or other lack of livelihood in circumstances beyond his control.
2. Motherhood and childhood are entitled to special care and assistance. All children, whether born in or out of wedlock, shall enjoy the same social protection.

Article 26

1. Everyone has the right to education. Education shall be free, at least in the elementary and fundamental stages. Elementary education shall be compulsory. Technical and professional education shall be made generally available and higher education shall be equally accessible to all on the basis of merit.
2. Education shall be directed to the full development of the human personality and to the strengthening of respect for human rights and fundamental freedoms. It shall promote understanding, tolerance and friendship among all nations, racial or religious groups, and shall further the activities of the United Nations for the maintenance of peace.
3. Parents have a prior right to choose the kind of education that shall be given to their children.

Article 27

1. Everyone has the right freely to participate in the cultural life of the community, to enjoy the arts and to share in scientific advancement and its benefits.
2. Everyone has the right to the protection of the moral and material interests resulting from any scientific, literary or artistic production of which he is the author.

Article 28

Everyone is entitled to a social and international order in which the rights and freedoms set forth in this Declaration can be fully realized.

Article 29

1.   Everyone has duties to the community in which alone the free and full development of his personality is possible.
2.   In the exercise of his rights and freedoms, everyone shall be subject only to such limitations as are determined by law solely for the purpose of securing due recognition and respect for the rights and freedoms of others and of meeting the just requirements of morality, public order and the general welfare in a democratic society.
3.   These rights and freedoms may in no case be exercised contrary to the purposes and principles of the United Nations.

Article 30

Nothing in this Declaration may be interpreted as implying for any State, group or person any right to engage in any activity or to perform any act aimed at the destruction of any of the rights and freedoms set forth herein.

Chapter 13

James W. Nickel

MAKING SENSE OF HUMAN RIGHTS

James W. Nickel is a professor of philosophy and law at the University of Miami whose work deals with issues in human rights law and theory, political philosophy, philosophy of law, and constitutional law. The following is a revised version of a chapter from his book, *Making Sense of Human Rights*. In it, Nickel explores the idea of human rights and some of their most important attributes, drawing on both philosophical theory and legal practice to develop those attributes into an attractive and coherent account.

We would understand human rights better if we had good answers to questions such as who has human rights, which parties have duties under human rights, whether human rights are immune to trade-offs, whether human rights are inalienable, how human rights exist, and how human rights guide behavior. Questions would remain about the justification, existence, and lists of specific human rights, but at least we would understand the general idea.

This essay attempts to answer these questions in regard to international human rights – the sorts of rights that we find in the Universal Declaration of Human Rights, the European Convention of Human Rights and Fundamental Freedoms, and the main human rights treaties of the United Nations.

1. Who Has Human Rights?

A simple answer to this question is "Humans!" – all human beings everywhere and at all times. That human rights apply to all people

without distinction has been a major theme of the human rights movement. Nevertheless, reflection on the idea that the holders of human rights are simply all people reveals that this answer is too broad.

First, some rights are held only by adult citizens, not by all persons. The clause of the Civil and Political Covenant dealing with political participation begins not with "Everyone" but with "Every citizen" (article 25). Further, the rights of people who are very young, severely retarded, comatose, or senile are justifiably limited. Although these people have important rights such as life, due process, and freedom from torture, it would be implausible to argue that they have rights to vote, run for political office, or travel freely on their own. These latter rights presuppose a greater degree of rationality and agency than some human beings possess.

Furthermore, some human rights cannot be universal in the strong sense of applying to all humans at all times, because they assert that people are entitled to services tied to relatively recent social and political institutions. Specific human rights are only as timeless as the specific problems they address. Some human rights problems have been with us for millennia, such as violence related to getting or retaining political power. Others have emerged in the last few centuries with the arrival all over the globe of the modern state, with its associated legal, penal, bureaucratic, educational, and economic branches (on the spread of modern political institutions see Morris 2002; see also Donnelly 2003: 92, 117). Human rights deal with security, liberties, fair trials, political participation, equality, basic welfare, and perhaps even the natural environment.

Due process rights, for example, presuppose modern legal systems and the institutional safeguards they can offer. Social and economic rights presuppose modern relations of production and the institutions of the redistributive state. My point here is not merely that people living ten thousand years ago would not have thought to demand these rights but rather that the scope of these rights can be defined only by reference to institutions that did not then exist (on "embracing temporal relativity" see Tasioulas 2002: 87b). Human rights could be formulated in much broader terms to avoid this objection, but the result would be very abstract rights, subject to a variety of interpretations and hence less useful in political criticism and less suitable for legal implementation.

2. Who Bears Responsibility for Human Rights?

Claim rights have identifiable addressees – people or agencies who have responsibilities related to the realization of the right. This connection between rights and the assignment of responsibilities is a basis for a frequently voiced question: who bears duties in regard to human rights? On hearing, for example, that people have rights to food and education, one may wonder whether people have duties to try to provide these things out of their own resources.

The primary addressees of human rights are the world's governments. Human rights are not ordinary moral norms applying mainly to interpersonal conduct. Rather they are political norms dealing mainly with how people should be treated by their governments and institutions. The political focus of human rights is very clear in the human rights treaties. The European Convention, for example, requires participating governments to "secure to everyone within their jurisdiction the rights and freedoms defined [in] this convention" (article 1). It also requires that "Everyone whose rights and freedoms as set forth in this Convention are violated shall have an effective remedy before a national authority notwithstanding that the violation has been committed by persons acting in an official capacity" (article 13). This requirement presupposes that governments are often both addressees and violators. The struggle to gain respect for a human right must often attempt to get the government both to restrain its own agencies and officials and to use its legal powers to restrain others.

If Almeida is a citizen or permanent resident of Brazil, the government of Brazil has the heaviest duties to respect and uphold Almeida's human rights. Brazil has duties not just to refrain from violating Almeida's human rights; it also has duties to uphold them through actions such as implementing them legislatively, protecting them with police work, providing legal remedies in the courts, and providing services such as food assistance. But we should not conclude from this that all of Almeida's rights are against the government of Brazil, or that all of the human rights duties of the Brazilian government are duties to its citizens.

Some of Almeida's human rights are against people and governments in other countries who at least have duties not to kill or imprison him without trial. When Almeida is standing peacefully on the Brazilian side of the Brazil/Bolivia border, a Bolivian police officer standing nearby on the other side of the border has the same human rights duty not to shoot Almeida as he has not to shoot a peaceable Bolivian citizen as she walks along the Bolivian side of the border.

Further, people and governments in other countries, along with international organizations, may have back-up responsibilities for Almeida's human rights when the government of Brazil is unwilling or unable to respect or uphold them. The United Nations and the World Bank, for example, may have duties to monitor human rights conditions in Brazil and to promote compliance with human rights. International corporations operating there may also have responsibilities (Weissbrodt 2005).

Because of the failures of many states to respect and uphold the rights of their residents, it is tempting to assign these tasks to international organizations such as the United Nations or to hope that a world federation or government will soon emerge to assume them. International organizations, however, have limited authority and power to enforce rights around the world. And a world federation or government currently seems at best a distant possibility. At present no alternative exists to assigning sovereign states the main responsibility for upholding the rights of their residents. This is a hard saying since many governments are corrupt and weak, and reform and development have proven hard to bring about through outside pressure and assistance.

Saying that the primary addressees of human rights are governments is not the end of the story, however. Individuals also have responsibilities generated by human rights. This view is suggested by the Universal Declaration. Its Preamble suggests that human rights have implications for the conduct of individuals when it says that "every individual and every organ of society, keeping this Declaration constantly in mind, shall strive by teaching and education to promote respect for these rights and freedoms and by progressive measures

national and international to secure their universal and effective recognition and observance." Clearly, the authors of the Universal Declaration believed that both states and individuals have obligations in regard to human rights. A rationale for this view is that if the justifying reasons for human rights are substantial enough to override domestic law and justify risks of international conflict, those grounding reasons are also likely to generate obligations for individuals in matters subject to their control.

Further, people participate as individuals in human rights abuses such as racial discrimination, slavery, domestic violence, and political killings (Cook 1994). When article 4 of the Universal Declaration asserts, "No one shall be held in slavery or servitude; slavery and the slave trade shall be prohibited in all their forms," the main violators of this right are not governments. Slaveholders have generally been individuals, although governments have often supported and institutionalized slavery. The right to freedom from slavery obligates individuals and governments not to hold slaves and further requires governments to pass legislation making slavery illegal. When article 11 of the Convention on the Elimination of All Forms of Discrimination against Women (United Nations 1979) commits ratifying countries to "take all appropriate measures to eliminate discrimination against women in the field of employment," it is clear that this requires governments to pass legislation prohibiting discrimination by private businesses, firms, and corporations.

One approach to explaining how and why citizens share in the duties generated by human rights views the citizens of a country as having ultimate responsibility for the human rights duties of their government. If their government has a duty to respect or implement the right to a fair trial, or a duty to aid poor countries, its citizens share in that duty. They are required as voters, political agents, and taxpayers to try to promote and support their government's compliance with its human rights duties. This principle of shared responsibility is particularly attractive in democratic societies where the citizens are the ultimate source of political authority. This view makes individuals back-up addressees for the duties of their governments. Thomas Pogge has taken a related but slightly different approach to generating individual duties from human rights that have governments as their primary addressees (Pogge 2002: 67). Pogge emphasizes Universal Declaration article 28 which says that "Everyone is entitled to a social and international order in which the rights and freedoms set forth in this Declaration can be fully realized." Pogge sees in this article a plausible norm, namely that both countries and individuals have duties not to be complicit in an international order that unfairly disadvantages poor countries and the people in them.

The complex view of the addressees of human rights sketched above can be illustrated using the right against torture (Nickel 1993a). Duties to refrain from engaging in torture can feasibly be borne and fulfilled by all persons and agencies, so this duty can be addressed to all. An adequate response to people's entitlement not to be tortured also requires finding individuals or institutions that can protect people against torture. The right to protection against torture can be universal without all of the corresponding duties being against everyone, or against some single worldwide agency. What is required is that there be for every right holder at least one agency with duties to protect that person from torture. This agency will typically be the government of one's country of citizenship or residence. The duty not to torture falls on everyone; the duty to protect against torture falls primarily on governments.

There may also be secondary addressees who bear back-up or monitoring responsibilities connected with the right against torture. The people of a country are secondary addressees with respect to fundamental rights. They bear the responsibility of creating and maintaining a social and political order that respects and

protects the right to freedom from torture. International institutions are also secondary addressees. They bear the responsibility of assisting, encouraging, and pressuring governments to refrain from torture and to provide effective protections against torture. If national or international institutions are unable to fulfill this responsibility there is the possibility of reforming them or creating new ones (Shue 1996: 166).

3. Are Human Rights Immune to Trade-Offs?

Human rights are both mandatory and high priority. As mandatory norms, they are not mere goals. Meeting their demands is obligatory, not merely a good thing. As high priority norms, they generally prevail in competition with other considerations – including advancing utility, prosperity, national security, and good relations with other countries. To have high priority they must be supported by strong moral and practical reasons.

It is not plausible, however, to suggest that all human rights are absolute, that they can never be suspended or sacrificed for other goods. As James Griffin says, "The best account of human rights will make them resistant to trade-offs, but not too resistant" (Griffin 2001b: 314). At least some civil and political rights can be restricted by public and private property rights, by restraining orders related to domestic violence, and by legal punishments. Further, after a disaster such as a hurricane or earthquake, freedom of movement in the area is often appropriately suspended to keep out the curious, to permit free movement of emergency vehicles and equipment, and to prevent looting. The Civil and Political Covenant permits rights to be suspended during times "of public emergency which threatens the life of the nation" (article 4). Yet it excludes some rights from suspension including the right to life, the prohibition of torture, the prohibition of slavery, the prohibition of ex post facto criminal laws, and freedom of thought and religion.

Human rights and their exercise are generally subject to regulation by law. For example, rights to freedom of speech, religious practice, assembly, movement, and political participation require substantial qualification and regulation so that they harmonize with each other and with other important considerations. A system of human rights must adjust the scopes and weights of its rights so that they can coexist with each other and form a coherent system (Rawls 1971, 1993). The right to privacy, for example, must be adjusted to coexist with the right to a fair trial. And the right to security against crimes has to be accommodated to rights to due process of law.

The scope of a right is the benefit, freedom, power, or immunity that it confers upon its holders. For example, specifying the scope of the right to freedom of religion involves describing a set of freedoms in the area of religious belief and practice that the holders of the right enjoy. Weight concerns the ranking or priority of a right when it conflicts with other considerations. To be exceptionless is a matter of scope, and to be absolute is a matter of weight. Nevertheless, it is often difficult to know whether the failure of a right to outweigh competing considerations and to dictate the result that should be followed, all things considered, in a particular case is best described as an instance of its containing an implicit qualification (scope) or as an instance of its being overridden (weight).

Suppose that Kim wants to exercise her right of free speech by marching into the courtroom in which Lee is on trial and telling the jury some fact that is barred from them by the rules of evidence (for example, about Lee's criminal record). Here Kim's right to speak would conflict with Lee's right to a fair trial. Suppose further that we agree that Kim should not be allowed to speak to the jury and that the relevant rights do not, all things considered, require that she be allowed to do this. There are two possible ways of describing the failure of Kim's right to freedom of speech to prevail here. One approach says that the right to free speech, properly understood, does not include within its boundaries a right to enter a courtroom and tell the jury things about the defendant they are precluded from knowing. Here the matter is treated as one of scope. The other description says that Kim's right of free speech applied in this situation would normally have required that she be allowed to speak, but it was outweighed in this unusual case by Lee's right to a fair trial, which is of higher priority. Here the matter is treated as one of weight.

In this instance it is probably best to see the matter as one of scope. One might hope that all conflicts between norms could be dealt with as they arose by redrawing boundaries and inserting exceptions. Boundaries would eventually be adjusted to minimize or eliminate conflicts, and the relative priority of different norms would be reflected in the expansion or retraction of their boundaries when they covered contiguous areas.

All the same, at least three barriers stand in the way of this program. One is that we cannot anticipate all conflicts between rights and with other norms, and we are often uncertain about what we should do in the cases we can imagine. A second barrier is that a right containing sufficient qualifications and exceptions to avoid all possible conflicts would probably be too complex to be generally understood. Third, relieving a conflict by building in an exception will sometimes incorrectly imply that the overridden right did not really apply and that we need feel no regret about our treatment of the person whose right was overridden. The most awful moral dilemmas are conflicts not at the edges of rights or duties but at their very centers. Adding exceptions to cover such cases may lead us to see what is happening as non tragic, rather than as calling for regret, apology, and − if possible − compensation.

Retaining the vocabulary of weight and overriding may help us to remember that not all moral dilemmas can be anticipated or resolved in advance and that in hard cases even our best efforts may result in serious harm or unfairness (Ignatieff 2004).

When we describe human rights as prima facie rights because we cannot provide in advance adequate accounts of how to deal with conflicts between human rights and other important considerations, we render irrelevant the sorts of objections that could be made if we claimed that human rights are absolute or near absolute. Prima facie rights are far easier to defend, but their implications for practice are often unclear. If no substantial competing values are present, a prima facie right will tell us what to do. But when substantial competing considerations are present, as they often are, prima facie rights are silent. The danger is that prima facie rights will provide no guidance in the cases where guidance is needed most.

Two responses can be made to this objection. First, there is no reason why the scopes of prima facie rights cannot be defined in considerable detail, or principles for ranking them in relation to competing considerations worked out. Classifying a right as prima facie implies not that this sort of work cannot be done, but that we recognize that the work will always remain partially unfinished. Second, appeals to human rights should be seen as part of moral and political argument, not as the whole of it. The presence of claims about human rights does not mean that less specialized forms of moral and political argument cannot be invoked.

4. Are Human Rights Inalienable?

We say that human rights are universal to avoid leaving the oppressed noncitizen, minority group member, or social outcast without rights to stand on. We claim that human rights are inalienable so that oppressive governments cannot say their subjects have forfeited or voluntarily given up their rights. Further, the idea that human rights are inalienable fits nicely with the idea that governments are not the ultimate source of the rights people have. What governments do not give they also cannot take away.

Inalienability means that a right cannot be permanently forfeited or given up entirely. The inalienability of a right implies that the rightholder's attempts to repudiate that right permanently, or attempts by others to take that right away, will be without normative effect. If people and government agencies lack the power to eliminate permanently a right of their own or others, that disability makes the right inalienable. And since the right cannot be eliminated, those who act as if it had been eliminated will violate it.

One problem with the claim that human rights are inalienable is that some of the rights in the Universal Declaration are forfeitable in many legal systems upon conviction of serious crimes. Most systems of criminal punishment use incarceration as a penalty, and thereby suppose that criminals forfeit at least temporarily their right to liberty. In spite of such examples, advocates of human rights often worry that the idea of forfeiture, if admitted, could consume too many rights. Admitting the possibility of forfeiture seems to invite oppressors to say that unpopular groups have forfeited their rights to life, liberty, or decent treatment. Nevertheless, this possibility is not sufficient to show that all human rights are immune to forfeiture. Most normative concepts are susceptible to rhetorical abuse.

The claim that human rights cannot voluntarily be repudiated wholesale is also problematic. Some eighteenth-century rights theorists asserted the inalienability of natural rights because they wanted to counter the Hobbesian claim that people had agreed to give up nearly all their rights when they left the state of nature and entered civil society (Hobbes 1981). And perhaps we can agree that some minimal rights to security and liberty are inalienable and hence that individuals lack the power to permanently waive those rights. This might mean that you could not give another person permission to kill or enslave you.

I doubt, however, that we can plausibly say that every human right is immune to repudiation. People choose to give up many basic liberties when they voluntarily enter monasteries or military service, yet we would not forbid these actions. Likewise, people may accept permanent limits on what they can say and publish about certain topics in order to receive a security clearance for government intelligence work. As a general conclusion about the inalienability of specific human rights I suggest that they are hard to lose but that few are strictly inalienable (for a stronger view of inalienability see Donnelly 2003: 10).

5. How Can Human Rights Exist?

Human rights are often held to exist independently of acceptance or enactment as law. The attraction of this position is that it permits critics of repressive regimes to appeal to human rights whether or not those regimes accept human rights or recognize them in their legal systems. Yet the contention that human rights exist independently of acceptance or enactment has always provoked skepticism. If human rights were mere wishes or aspirations, we could say that they exist in people's minds. In order to be norms that are binding on all people, however, human rights must be far more than wishes or aspirations.

It is possible to sidestep skeptical doubts about the independent existence of human rights by pointing to their place in international law. For example, the right to leave a country is found in article 12 of the Civil and Political Covenant, a treaty that is now part of international law. Under this treaty a person who wishes to leave her country (and who is not fleeing debts or criminal prosecution) has in this right a strong justification, and her government has a corresponding obligation to allow her to go. As

this example suggests, human rights can exist as legal rights within international law.

When human rights are implemented in international law, we continue to speak of them as human rights; but when they are implemented in domestic law we tend to describe them as civil or constitutional rights. It is possible, however, for a right to be instantiated within more than one normative system at the same time. For example, a right to freedom from torture could be a right within a justified morality, a right within the domestic legal system, and a right within international law. This kind of congruence is an ideal of the human rights movement, which seeks broad conformity between various levels of law, existing moral codes, and the standards of enlightened moralities.

Because human rights are now enacted within many national and international legal systems, the worries of legal positivists about unenforced moral rights are no longer fatal to taking human rights seriously. As Louis Henkin observes, "Political forces have mooted the principal philosophical objections, bridging the chasm between natural and positive law by converting natural human rights into positive legal rights" (Henkin 1978: 19). This view is much more plausible today than when Henkin wrote it because nearly all countries have by now committed themselves to human rights treaties and because mechanisms for protecting human rights at the international level have become more powerful and better accepted.

Still, it would be better for the general applicability and stability of human rights if their availability as standards of criticism were not dependent on enactment or acceptance. Many have followed this line of thought, and thus human rights are commonly characterized as *moral rights*. A right is a moral right if it exists as a norm within an actual or justified morality.

Accepted moral rights are rights that are recognized and mostly respected in actual human moralities today. These rights can exist before a formal legal system is established and may later become legal rights. Perhaps most actual moralities confer some rights on individuals, but it is not clear that accepted norms are adequate to support rights of international applicability. If human rights are to be generated by the various accepted moralities that exist around the world, these moralities must share a commitment to principles of the sort found in the Universal Declaration. It is not clear that enough moral agreement exists worldwide to support anything like the full range of rights declared in contemporary manifestos, and ordinary interpersonal moralities usually have little to say about matters such as fair trials and equality before the law.

A human rights advocate who asserts that human rights are binding on governments independently of acceptance and international law will probably construe human rights as existing within *justified moralities* rather than within all accepted moralities. A justified morality is one that is well supported by appropriate reasons. John Stuart Mill, a nineteenth-century advocate of what we now call human rights, would have allowed that there is little agreement worldwide in accepted moralities about basic rights (Mill 2002b). But he would have claimed nonetheless that human rights exist within justified moralities – which in his view would all give a prominent place to the principle of utility.

Viewing justified moralities as the ultimate home of human rights requires strong epistemological and metaphysical and moral commitments. It requires believing that moral and political reasons of worldwide applicability exist and that most humans have the epistemological capacities required to recognize and apply them. It requires believing that the grounds of human rights are in some sense objective. I find these propositions believable, and think that plausible meta-ethical grounds can be found for them. But I do not attempt a defense of them here. I should say, however, that viewing the human moral capacity as competent, in principle, to permit

the recognition of universal human rights does not warrant moral arrogance. Human moral capacities, like other cognitive and emotional capacities, are extremely fallible. Further, shared moral capacities need not yield uniform principles if circumstances in different societies are substantially different. The universality of human rights norms must be defended by showing that problems and circumstances in different cultures are sufficiently similar as to permit broad underlying principles to yield similar specific principles.

A justified morality does not need to be accepted or practiced by anyone, nor does it necessarily have a social or institutional dimension. Thus the question arises: are the principles and rights that constitute such a justified morality sufficiently robust and determinate to be binding in actual situations here and now? What the knowledge of human rights comes to in this view is – at a minimum – knowledge of strong reasons for adopting and following a certain set of norms. The Universal Declaration can accordingly be seen as an international attempt to specify the content of such a justified morality in the area of relations between people and their governments.

Legal positivists doubt that the principles of justified moralities are sufficiently knowable to be worth talking about or whether it is worthwhile, in our contemporary Babel with its many competing voices and views, to talk about principles everyone would be justified in adopting. They prefer the cold steel of legally implemented rights to the hot air of justified human rights. One who sees human rights as existing most fundamentally as justified moral rights may have the same preference but believe that, in those areas where we lack international agreement on norms that can be implemented everywhere through domestic and international law, we should continue discussing, and trying to identify, define, and promote justifiable norms. Human rights declarations and treaties are usefully seen as an attempt to formulate some fixed points in this discussion, to identify some rights that are widely accepted and strongly supported by good reasons. The belief that it is possible to formulate such a list rests on the belief that human beings have a substantial capacity for moral understanding and progress, but the need for such a list presupposes that the unaided consciences of government officials will not reliably provide fully adequate beliefs about how people ought to behave and how society ought to be organized.

6. How Do Human Rights Guide Behavior?

Some of the ways in which human rights can guide behavior are obvious; in other areas the guidance they provide is complicated or problematic. In the obvious cases, full-fledged rights direct the behavior of their addressees through negative and positive duties. For example, a right to freedom from torture guides behavior by defining torture (see Levinson 2004), forbidding everyone to engage in it, and imposing a duty on governments to protect people against it. Still, the prohibition of torture is likely to be vague, and adjudication may be needed to refine its meaning.

Many issues about dealing with torture are not directly covered by a right against torture. Formulations of the right against torture are likely to provide little guidance about (1) what actual and potential victims of torture may do to defend themselves; (2) how ordinary citizens should relate to those they suspect of being engaged in torture (for example, do they have a duty to try to interrupt torture sessions, or a duty not to sell groceries to torturers?); (3) how citizens and officials should respond when the right to be free from torture is not legally recognized; and (4) how people and governments from other countries should respond to known cases of torture. Determinate answers to these questions cannot usually be found by appeal to human rights alone. Other moral and political

principles must play an ongoing role. It is often necessary to look back to the abstract moral principles that underlie specific human rights, sideways to moral considerations other than rights, and forward to likely consequences. A list of human rights is only a partial guide to, and not a substitute for, moral and political deliberation.

A. *Guidance from rights that are not accepted or implemented.* Even when a human right is not generally recognized or legally implemented in a country, it can guide the behavior of those who believe it is morally justified. Suppose that Fariz is an adherent of the Baha'i faith – which is unpopular in some countries – and that she sincerely believes in the right to freedom of religion for herself and others. The validity of this norm is confirmed, she thinks, by its international recognition in the Universal Declaration and human rights treaties. As a holder of this justified moral right, Fariz has the liberty to hold Baha'i beliefs, to engage in Baha'i religious practices, and to instruct her children in the Baha'i faith. It is clear that Fariz's recognition of these norms – whether or not they are socially or legally recognized – can guide her behavior. This right can also guide the behavior of its addressees. As one of these addressees, Fariz will have a moral duty not to interfere with the religious beliefs and practices of others. Fariz would do wrong to disrupt a religious meeting by Jehovah's Witnesses, and if she were a public official, she would do wrong to sponsor legislation to outlaw the Jehovah's Witnesses from proselytizing or to force the children of its members to undergo instruction in the Baha'i faith.

Rights can guide behavior not only by directing it with duties and other normative elements (the stronger and more usual case) but also by providing reasons or justification for it (the weaker case). For example, a violation of one's right to freedom of religion, or the likelihood of such a violation, may provide a reason or justification for such actions as refusing to obey a law, engaging in public protest, or seeking to emigrate. Not all the guidance obtainable from a human right is found in its scope.

B. *What to do about violations of human rights.* Governments have dual and conflicting roles in relation to human rights. On the one hand their sponsorship is needed to make many rights effective, and on the other hand they are often the most significant potential source of violations. The struggle to gain respect for a human right must often attempt to get a government both to restrain itself and to use its legal powers to restrain others. Where human rights violations are deep and systematic, rights advocates must devise strategies for political change that are not in the scope of human rights. Here respect for and implementation of human rights becomes a goal, and means–end or strategic reasoning must be used to pursue this goal.

Similarly, we generally cannot deduce from the content of a human right alone the best strategies for promoting and protecting that right at the international level. How large a role countries should play in promoting human rights abroad cannot be settled by appeal to human rights alone. Other relevant considerations include the means chosen (for example, diplomacy, pressure, intervention), the likelihood of success, the weight assigned to the principle of nonintervention in the domestic affairs of other countries, and competing claims on national energy and resources. As before, these additional considerations do not seem to be part of the rights themselves but must rather come from general moral and political principles. Human rights do not provide complete guidance to political action – not even to political action directed at human rights violations.

C. *Legal guidance.* Legally implementing a human right at the national level typically has two parts: (1) enactment in abstract terms in a constitution or bill of rights, and (2) enactment in more specific terms in statutes that become part of the day-to-day law of the realm. To protect freedom of religion, a constitutional norm might commit a country to religious freedom and tolerance, separation of church and state, and state neutrality between different religious groups. For example, article 4 of the Constitution ("Basic Law") of Germany prescribes religious freedom in the following terms:

> Freedom of faith and of conscience, and freedom to profess a religious or philosophical creed, shall be inviolable. The undisturbed practice of religion shall be guaranteed. No one may be compelled against his conscience to render military service involving the use of arms. Details shall be regulated by a federal law.

As the last sentence of this article suggests, legislation will usually be needed to apply these general principles to specific national problems, which might include the institutional status of the dominant religious group, tax exemptions for religious organizations, the policy toward parochial schools and toward religious education in the public schools, and exemptions from military service for conscientious objectors.

Enactment in effective national or international law is perhaps the most important means of implementing human rights. But legal enactment is neither necessary nor sufficient for the realization of human rights. Legal enactment is not always necessary because in some lucky societies the attitudes of the public and of government officials are so supportive of particular rights that no enforcement is necessary. And it is not always sufficient because legal enactment in a showcase bill of rights does little or nothing to realize a right.

Persuasion and legislation are obviously not mutually exclusive. In fact, education of the population in sound moral and political principles is often one of the main goals of human rights legislation. Most compliance with human rights must be voluntary and based on acceptance.

7. Conclusion

To make sense of human rights it is necessary to qualify them. Human rights deal with severe political abuses that undermine fundamental interests and deprive people of dignity. Accordingly, their content is as varied as those abuses. Human rights are primarily against governments but secondarily against individuals and international organizations. Secondary addressees play a back-up role; they are required to step in when the primary addressees are unwilling or unable to fulfill their responsibilities. Human rights are high priority norms that are universal and hard to lose. To say that human rights are high priority norms is not generally to say that they are absolute. Universality is qualified by restriction to current times; most specific human rights are not trans-historical. Further, human rights are sometimes rights of citizens rather than of all people. Human rights provide direct guidance to their holders and addressees. Fundamental rights do not, however, provide complete guidance as to details of implementation, appropriate responses to noncompliance, and strategies for promoting compliance. A list of rights cannot serve as an alternative to political thought and deliberation.

References

Cook, R. (ed.) 1994. Human rights of Women: National and International Perspectives. Philadelphia: University of Pennsylvania Press.

Donnely, J. 2003. Universal Human Rights in Theory and Practice, 2nd edn. Ithaca, NY and London: Cornell University Press.

Griffin, J. 2001. "First Steps in an Account of Human Rights." European Journal of Philosophy 9 (3): 306–27.

Henkin, L. 1978. The Rights of Man Today. Boulder, CO: Westview Press.

Hobbes, T. 1981. Leviathan. In C. Macpherson (ed.), Leviathan. Harmondsworth: Penguin. Originally published 1651.

Ignatieff, M. 2004. The Lesser Evil. Princeton, NJ: Princeton University Press.

Levinson, S. (ed.) 2004. Torture: A Collection. New York: Oxford University Press.

Mill, J. 2002b. Utilitarianism. In J. Schneewind (ed.), The Basic Writings of John Stuart Mill. New York: Modern Library. Originally published 1863.

Nickel, J. 1993. "How Human Rights Generate Duties to Protect and Provide." Human Rights Quarterly 14: 77–86.

Pogge, T. 2002. World Poverty and Human Rights. Cambridge: Polity.

Rawls, J. 1971. A Theory of Justice. Cambridge, MA: Harvard University Press.

Rawls, J. 1993. Political Liberalism. New York: Columbia University Press.

Shue, H. 1996. Basic Rights, 2nd edn. Princeton, NJ: Princeton University Press.

United Nations. 1979. "Convention on the Elimination of All Forms of Discrimination against Women." In I. Browlie and G. Goodwin-Gill (eds.), Basic Documents on Human Rights, 5th edn. Oxford: Oxford University Press, 2006.

Weissbrodt, D. 2005, "Business and Human Rights." University of Cincinnati Law Review 74: 55–73.

Chapter 14

Robert Nozick

LIBERTARIAN RIGHTS

Robert Nozick (1938–2002) was a professor of philosophy at Harvard University for almost his entire professional career. He wrote widely in such areas as epistemology and decision theory, but his best-known work is *Anarchy, State, and Utopia* (1974), a book-length exploration of libertarian political theory. In this excerpt, Nozick discusses the ideas of rights as side constraints, and argues that accepting the side-constraint *form* of rights gives us reason to believe that the *content* of rights is libertarian.

Preface

Individuals have rights, and there are things no person or group may do to them (without violating their rights). So strong and far-reaching are these rights that they raise the question of what, if anything, the state and its officials may do. How much room do individual rights leave for the state?

[. . .]

Our main conclusions about the state are that a minimal state, limited to the narrow functions of protection against force, theft, fraud, enforcement of contracts, and so on, is justified; that any more extensive state will violate persons' rights not to be forced to do certain things, and is unjustified; and that the minimal state is inspiring as well as right. Two noteworthy implications are that the state may not use its coercive apparatus for the purpose of getting some citizens to aid others, or in order to prohibit activities to people for their *own* good or protection.

Moral Constraints and the State

The Minimal State and the Ultraminimal State

The night-watchman state of classical liberal theory, limited to the functions of protecting all its citizens against violence, theft, and fraud, and to the enforcement of contracts, and so on, appears to be redistributive.[1] We can imagine at least one social arrangement intermediate between the scheme of private protective associations and the night-watchman state. Since the night-watchman state is often called a minimal state, we shall call this other arrangement the *ultraminimal state*. An ultraminimal state maintains a monopoly over all use of force except that necessary in immediate self-defense, and so excludes private (or agency) retaliation for wrong and exaction of compensation; but it provides protection and enforcement services *only* to those who purchase its protection and enforcement policies. People who don't buy a protection contract from the monopoly don't get protected. The minimal (night-watchman) state is equivalent to the ultraminimal state conjoined with a (clearly redistributive) Friedmanesque voucher plan, financed from tax revenues.[2] Under this plan all people, or some (for example, those in need), are given tax-funded vouchers that can be used only for their purchase of a protection policy from the ultra-minimal state.

Since the night-watchman state appears redistributive to the extent that it compels some people to pay for the protection of others, its proponents must explain why this redistributive function of the state is unique. If some redistribution is legitimate in order to protect everyone, why is redistribution not legitimate for other attractive and desirable purposes as well? What rationale specifically selects protective services as the sole subject of legitimate redistributive activities? A rationale, once found, may show that this provision of protective services is *not* redistributive. More precisely, the term "redistributive" applies to types of *reasons* for an arrangement, rather than to an arrangement itself. We might elliptically call an arrangement "redistributive" if its major (only possible) supporting reasons are themselves redistributive. ("Paternalistic" functions similarly.) Finding compelling nonredistributive reasons would cause us to drop this label. Whether we say an institution that takes money from some and gives *it* to others is redistributive will depend upon *why* we think it does so. Returning stolen money or compensating for violations of rights are *not* redistributive reasons. I have spoken until now of the night-watchman state's *appearing* to be redistributive, to leave open the possibility that nonredistributive types of reasons might be found to justify the provision of protective services for some by others . . .

A proponent of the ultraminimal state may seem to occupy an inconsistent position, even though he avoids the question of what makes protection uniquely suitable for redistributive provision. Greatly concerned to protect rights against violation, he makes this the sole

legitimate function of the state; and he protests that all other functions are illegitimate because they themselves involve the violation of rights. Since he accords paramount place to the protection and nonviolation of rights, how can he support the ultraminimal state, which would seem to leave some persons' rights unprotected or illprotected? How can he support this *in the name of* the nonviolation of rights?

Moral Constraints and Moral Goals

This question assumes that a moral concern can function only as a moral *goal*, as an end state for some activities to achieve as their result. It may, indeed, seem to be a necessary truth that "right," "ought," "should," and so on, are to be explained in terms of what is, or is intended to be, productive of the greatest good, with all goals built into the good.[3] Thus it is often thought that what is wrong with utilitarianism (which *is* of this form) is its too narrow conception of good. Utilitarianism doesn't, it is said, properly take rights and their nonviolation into account; it instead leaves them a derivative status. Many of the counterexample cases to utilitarianism fit under this objection, for example, punishing an innocent man to save a neighborhood from a vengeful rampage. But a theory may include in a primary way the nonviolation of rights, yet include it in the wrong place and the wrong manner. For suppose some condition about minimizing the total (weighted) amount of violations of rights is built into the desirable end state to be achieved. We then would have something like a "utilitarianism of rights"; violations of rights (to be *minimized*) merely would replace the total happiness as the relevant end state in the utilitarian structure. (Note that we do not hold the nonviolation of our rights as our sole greatest good or even rank it first lexicographically to exclude trade-offs, if there is some desirable society we would choose to inhabit even though in it some rights of ours sometimes are violated, rather than move to a desert island where we could survive alone.) This still would require us to violate someone's rights when doing so minimizes the total (weighted) amount of the violation of rights in the society. For example, violating someone's rights might deflect others from their intended action of gravely violating rights, or might remove their motive for doing so, or might divert their attention, and so on. A mob rampaging through a part of town killing and burning will violate the rights of those living there. Therefore, someone might try to justify his punishing another he knows to be innocent of a crime that enraged a mob, on the grounds that punishing this innocent person would help to avoid even greater violations of rights by others, and so would lead to a minimum weighted score for rights violations in the society.

In contrast to incorporating rights into the end state to be achieved, one might place them as side constraints upon the actions to be done: don't violate constraints C. The rights of others determine the constraints upon your actions. (A *goal-directed* view with constraints added would be: among those acts available to you that don't violate constraints C, act so as to maximize goal G. Here, the rights of others would constrain your goal-directed behavior. I do not mean to imply that the correct moral view includes mandatory goals that must be pursued, even within the constraints.) This view differs from one that tries to build the side constraints C *into* the goal G. The side-constraint view forbids you to violate these moral constraints in the pursuit of your goals; whereas the view whose objective is to minimize the violation of these rights allows you to violate the rights (the constraints) in order to lessen their total violation in the society.[4]

The claim that the proponent of the ultraminimal state is inconsistent, we now can see, assumes that he is a "utilitarian of rights." It assumes that his goal is, for example, to minimize the weighted amount of the violation of rights in the society, and that he should pursue

this goal even through means that themselves violate people's rights. Instead, he may place the nonviolation of rights as a constraint upon action, rather than (or in addition to) building it into the end state to be realized. The position held by this proponent of the ultraminimal state will be a consistent one if his conception of rights holds that your *being forced* to contribute to another's welfare violates your rights, whereas someone else's not providing you with things you need greatly, including things essential to the protection of your rights, does not *itself* violate your rights, even though it avoids making it more difficult for someone else to violate them. (That conception will be consistent provided it does not construe the monopoly element of the ultraminimal state as itself a violation of rights.) That it is a consistent position does not, of course, show that it is an acceptable one.

Why Side Constraints?

Isn't it *irrational* to accept a side constraint C, rather than a view that directs minimizing the violations of C? (The latter view treats C as a condition rather than a constraint.) If nonviolation of C is so important, shouldn't that be the goal? How can a concern for the nonviolation of C lead to the refusal to violate C even when this would prevent other more extensive violations of C? What is the rationale for placing the nonviolation of rights as a side constraint upon action instead of including it solely as a goal of one's actions?

Side constraints upon action reflect the underlying Kantian principle that individuals are ends and not merely means; they may not be sacrificed or used for the achieving of other ends without their consent. Individuals are inviolable. More should be said to illuminate this talk of ends and means. Consider a prime example of a means, a tool. There is no side constraint on how we may use a tool, other than the moral constraints on how we may use it upon others.

There are procedures to be followed to preserve it for future use ("don't leave it out in the rain"), and there are more and less efficient ways of using it. But there is no limit on what we may do to it to best achieve our goals. Now imagine that there was an overrideable constraint C on some tool's use. For example, the tool might have been lent to you only on the condition that C not be violated unless the gain from doing so was above a certain specified amount, or unless it was necessary to achieve a certain specified goal. Here the object is not *completely* your tool, for use according to your wish or whim. But it is a tool nevertheless, even with regard to the overrideable constraint. If we add constraints on its use that may not be overridden, then the object may not be used as a tool in *those ways. In those respects*, it is not a tool at all. Can one add enough constraints so that an object cannot be used as a tool at all, in *any* respect?

Can behavior toward a person be constrained so that he is not to be used for any end except as he chooses? This is an impossibly stringent condition if it requires everyone who provides us with a good to approve positively of every use to which we wish to put it. Even the requirement that he merely should not object to any use we plan would seriously curtail bilateral exchange, not to mention sequences of such exchanges. It is sufficient that the other party stands to gain enough from the exchange so that he is willing to go through with it, even though he objects to one or more of the uses to which you shall put the good. Under such conditions, the other party is not being used solely as a means, in that respect. Another party, however, who would not choose to interact with you if he knew of the uses to which you *intend* to put his actions or good, is being used as a means, even if he receives enough to choose (in his ignorance) to interact with you. ("All along, you were just *using* me" can be said by someone who chose to interact only because he was ignorant of another's goals and of the uses to which he himself would be put.) Is it morally incumbent upon

someone to reveal his intended uses of an interaction if he has good reason to believe the other would refuse to interact if he knew? Is he *using* the other person, if he does not reveal this? And what of the cases where the other does not choose to be of use at all? In getting pleasure from seeing an attractive person go by, does one use the other solely as a means?[5] Does someone so use an object of sexual fantasies? These and related questions raise very interesting issues for moral philosophy; but not, I think, for political philosophy.

Political philosophy is concerned only with *certain* ways that persons may not use others; primarily, physically aggressing against them. A specific side constraint upon action toward others expresses the fact that others may not be used in the specific ways the side constraint excludes. Side constraints express the inviolability of others, in the ways they specify. These modes of inviolability are expressed by the following injunction: "Don't use people in specified ways." An end-state view, on the other hand, would express the view that people are ends and not merely means (if it chooses to express this view at all), by a different injunction: "Minimize the use in specified ways of persons as means." Following this precept itself may involve using someone as a means in one of the ways specified. Had Kant held this view, he would have given the second formula of the categorical imperative as, "So act as to minimize the use of humanity simply as a means," rather than the one he actually used: "Act in such a way that you always treat humanity, whether in your own person or in the person of any other, never simply as a means, but always at the same time as an end."[6]

Side constraints express the inviolability of other persons. But why may not one violate persons for the greater social good? Individually, we each sometimes choose to undergo some pain or sacrifice for a greater benefit or to avoid a greater harm: we go to the dentist to avoid worse suffering later; we do some unpleasant work for its results; some persons diet to improve their health or looks; some save money to support themselves when they are older. In each case, some cost is borne for the sake of the greater overall good. Why not, *similarly*, hold that some persons have to bear some costs that benefit other persons more, for the sake of the overall social good? But there is no *social entity* with a good that undergoes some sacrifice for its own good. There are only individual people, different individual people, with their own individual lives. Using one of these people for the benefit of others, uses him and benefits the others. Nothing more. What happens is that something is done to him for the sake of others. Talk of an overall social good covers this up. (Intentionally?) To use a person in this way does not sufficiently respect and take account of the fact that he is a separate person,[7] that his is the only life he has. He does not get some overbalancing good from his sacrifice, and no one is entitled to force this upon him – least of all a state or government that claims his allegiance (as other individuals do not) and that therefore scrupulously must be *neutral* between its citizens.

Libertarian Constraints

The moral side constraints upon what we may do, I claim, reflect the fact of our separate existences. They reflect the fact that no moral balancing act can take place among us; there is no moral outweighing of one of our lives by others so as to lead to a greater overall *social* good. There is no justified sacrifice of some of us for others. This root idea, namely, that there are different individuals with separate lives and so no one may be sacrificed for others, underlies the existence of moral side constraints, but it also, I believe, leads to a libertarian side constraint that prohibits aggression against another.

The stronger the force of an end-state maximizing view, the more powerful must be the root idea capable of resisting it that underlies the existence of moral side constraints.

Hence the more seriously must be taken the existence of distinct individuals who are not resources for others. An underlying notion sufficiently powerful to support moral side constraints against the powerful intuitive force of the end-state maximizing view will suffice to derive a libertarian constraint on aggression against another. Anyone who rejects *that particular* side constraint has three alternatives: (1) he must reject *all* side constraints; (2) he must produce a different explanation of why there are moral side constraints rather than simply a goal-directed maximizing structure, an explanation that doesn't itself entail the libertarian side constraint; or (3) he must accept the strongly put root idea about the separateness of individuals and yet claim that initiating aggression against another is compatible with this root idea. Thus we have a promising sketch of an argument from moral form to moral content: the form of morality includes F (moral side constraints); the best explanation[8] of morality's being F is p (a strong statement of the distinctness of individuals); and from p follows a particular moral content, namely, the libertarian constraint. The particular moral content gotten by this argument, which focuses upon the fact that there are distinct individuals each with his *own* life to lead, will not be the *full* libertarian constraint. It will prohibit sacrificing one person to benefit another. Further steps would be needed to reach a prohibition on paternalistic aggression: using or threatening force for the benefit of the person against whom it is wielded. For this, one must focus upon the fact that there are distinct individuals, each with his own life *to lead*.

A nonaggression principle is often held to be an appropriate principle to govern relations among nations. What difference is there supposed to be between sovereign individuals and sovereign nations that makes aggression permissible among individuals? Why may individuals jointly, through their government, do to someone what no nation may do to another? If anything, there is a stronger case for nonaggression among individuals; unlike nations, they do not contain as parts individuals that others legitimately might intervene to protect or defend.

I shall not pursue here the details of a principle that prohibits physical aggression, except to note that it does not prohibit the use of force in defense against another party who is a threat, even though he is innocent and deserves no retribution. An *innocent threat* is someone who innocently is a causal agent in a process such that he would be an aggressor had he chosen to become such an agent. If someone picks up a third party and throws him at you down at the bottom of a deep well, the third party is innocent and a threat; had he chosen to launch himself at you in that trajectory he would be an aggressor. Even though the falling person would survive his fall onto you, may you use your ray gun to disintegrate the falling body before it crushes and kills you? Libertarian prohibitions are usually formulated so as to forbid using violence on innocent persons. But innocent threats, I think, are another matter to which different principles must apply.[9] Thus, a full theory in this area also must formulate the *different* constraints on response to innocent threats. Further complications concern *innocent shields of threats*, those innocent persons who themselves are non threats but who are so situated that they will be damaged by the only means available for stopping the threat. Innocent persons strapped onto the front of the tanks of aggressors so that the tanks cannot be hit without also hitting them are innocent shields of threats. (Some uses of force on people to get at an aggressor do not act upon innocent shields of threats; for example, an aggressor's innocent child who is tortured in order to get the aggressor to stop wasn't *shielding* the parent.) May one knowingly injure innocent shields? If one may attack an aggressor and injure an innocent shield, may the innocent shield fight back in self-defense (supposing that he cannot move against or fight the aggressor)? Do we get two persons

battling each other in self-defense? Similarly, if you use force against an innocent threat to you, do you thereby become an innocent threat to him, so that he may now justifiably use additional force against you (supposing that he can do this, yet cannot prevent his original threateningness)? I tiptoe around these incredibly difficult issues here, merely noting that a view that says it makes nonaggression central must resolve them explicitly at some point.

Notes

1   Here and in the next section I draw upon and amplify my discussion of these issues in footnote 4 of "On the Randian Argument," *The Personalist*, Spring 1971.

2   Milton Friedman, *Capitalism and Freedom* (Chicago: University of Chicago Press, 1962), chap. 6. Friedman's school vouchers, of course, allow a choice about who is to supply the product, and so differ from the protection vouchers imagined here.

3   For a clear statement that this view is mistaken, see John Rawls, *A Theory of Justice* (Cambridge, Mass.: Harvard University Press, 1971), pp. 30, 565–6.

4   Unfortunately, too few models of the structure of moral views have been specified heretofore, though there are surely other interesting structures. Hence an argument for a side-constraint structure that consists largely in arguing against an end-state maximization structure is inconclusive, for these alternatives are not exhaustive. An array of structures must be precisely formulated and investigated; perhaps some novel structure then will seem most appropriate.

  The issue of whether a side-constraint view can be put in the form of the goal-without-side-constraint view is a tricky one. One might think, for example, that each person could distinguish in his goal between *his* violating rights and someone else's doing it. Give the former infinite (negative) weight in his goal, and no amount of stopping others from violating rights can outweigh his violating someone's rights. In addition to a component of a goal receiving infinite weight, indexical expressions also appear, for example, "my doing something." A careful statement delimiting "constraint views" would exclude these gimmicky ways of transforming side constraints into the form of an end-state view as sufficient to constitute a view as end state. Mathematical methods of transforming a constrained minimization problem into a sequence of unconstrained minimizations of an auxiliary function are presented in Anthony Fiacco and Garth McCormick, *Nonlinear Programming: Sequential Unconstrained Minimization Techniques* (New York: Wiley, 1968). The book is interesting both for its methods and for their limitations in illuminating our area of concern; note the way in which the penalty functions include the constraints, the variation in weights of penalty functions (sec. 7.1), and so on.

The question of whether these side constraints are absolute, or whether they may be violated in order to avoid catastrophic moral horror, and if the latter, what the resulting structure might look like, is one I hope largely to avoid.

5 Which does which? Often a useful question to ask, as in the following:

— "What is the difference between a Zen master and an analytic philosopher?"
— "One talks riddles and the other riddles talks."

6 *Groundwork of the Metaphysic of Morals.* Translated by H. J. Paton, *The Moral Law* (London: Hutchinson, 1956), p. 96.

7 See John Rawls, *A Theory of Justice*, sects. 5, 6, 30.

8 See Gilbert Harman, "The Inference to the Best Explanation," *Philosophical Review*, 1965, pp. 88–95, and *Thought* (Princeton, N.J.: Princeton University Press, 1973), chaps. 8, 10.

9 See Judith Jarvis Thomson, "A Defense of Abortion," *Philosophy and Public Affairs*, 1, no. 2 (Fall 1971), 52–3. Since my discussion was written, John Hospers has discussed similar issues in a two-part essay, "Some Problems about Punishment and the Retaliatory Use of Force," *Reason*, November 1972 and January 1973.

1c. JUSTICE

IN APPROXIMATELY 360 BCE, Plato wrote one of the first and most enduring systematic works of philosophy ever written. Its title was *The Republic*, and its subject was justice — as an attribute of individuals and of the societies in which they live. Some twenty-three hundred years later, John Rawls would write in his *Theory of Justice* that "justice is the first virtue of social institutions," and would go on to change the way philosophers thought about it forever.

What is this concept that has proved to be of such enduring philosophical interest? What does it mean to call someone or something unjust, and what implications does it have for the way we ought to behave toward one another?

All of us, I suspect, can remember some experience in which we were treated unjustly. Perhaps when we were younger, a sibling did some bad thing for which we were blamed. Or perhaps we were passed over for a job or a scholarship in favor of some lesser qualified candidate who happened to have an inside connection with the person making the decision. What makes such events unjust is that we were not given what we were *due*. Those in charge of meting out punishment — even parents! — are obligated to look carefully at the evidence and place blame only on those who are guilty. Those whose job it is to make hiring decisions or decisions regarding scholarships ought to award those honors on the basis of *merit*, and not on the basis of prior personal connections or other irrelevant criteria. Justice demands that people get, in a sense, "what they've got coming to them."

And, importantly, it demands that people get what's coming to them even if we don't always like the results. What is required by justice will often conflict with what is in our own self-interest, as for instance when justice requires that we return a lost wallet to its rightful owner. In cases such as these, justice seems to require us to put the interests of society or of particular other persons ahead of our own. But matters are even more complicated than this. For justice will often demand that we perform or abstain from certain actions even when this demand *undermines* the interests of society as a whole. The fact that a policy of performing involuntary medical experiments on randomly selected citizens is unjust, for instance, entails that we must not allow it even if the overall welfare of society would be greatly advanced by the knowledge we would gain from it. The fact that it would be unjust to sentence a defendant to prison with illegally obtained evidence means that we must let him go, *even if we know that he is guilty and that society would be better off with him behind bars!*

Justice, then, is a very demanding requirement. It requires that we act in ways that are contrary to our own interests, and even sometimes contrary to the interests of our society as a whole. But this raises a philosophical puzzle. If justice is so demanding, then why should we think ourselves bound to obey its demands? From where do the requirements of justice derive their authority?

Historically, two broad categories of answer have been given to this question. The first, expressed in this section by David Hume and John Stuart Mill, holds that the demands of justice are warranted by the beneficial consequences that adherence to them produces. It is true that *single instances* of just conduct can produce harmful consequences as, Hume notes, when "a man of merit, of beneficent disposition, restores a great fortune to a miser, or a seditious bigot." But the long run consequences of adherence to justice *as a rule* are tremendously beneficial, and society needs fixed and stable rules so that its members can form reliable expectations of what they may and may not do without fear of punishment.

The second category of response derives from Immanuel Kant, and finds its expression in this section in the reading from John Rawls. For these thinkers, the demands of justice obligate us not because of their tendency to produce good consequences, but rather because they are necessary conditions on our treating each other with *respect*. The problem with slavery, on this view, is not that it tends to make society as a whole worse off than it would otherwise be. The problem is that it treats the slave as an *object* instead of as a human being. Human beings are ends in themselves, and slavery treats them as though they were mere instruments to be used for the satisfaction of *other* people's ends. Whether it produces good or bad long-term effects for society as a whole is beside the point.

This question of the moral foundations of justice is of great philosophic importance. But of equal philosophic importance — and perhaps greater practical importance — are questions about the *content* of justice's demands. Even once we know that the claims of justice "trump" claims of individual or social interest, this still leaves unclear just what, exactly, justice demands that we do. Mill gives us a pluralistic answer to this question. For Mill, justice demands (among other things) that we give people what they deserve, that we not break faith with others, that we be impartial (at least when impartiality is demanded), that we respect others' rights, and that we treat them equally.

Mill's list, however, leaves many questions unanswered. When, for instance, are we required to by justice treat others impartially? Surely it is morally permissible — perhaps even morally required — for a parent to devote more time and energy to the care of her own children than she devotes to the aid of strangers. But just as surely, this permissible partiality has its limits. A judge in a criminal trial would not be permitted to allow her verdict to be influenced by the fact that the defendant is her child. The exact contour of these limits, however, is difficult to specify with any philosophical precision, just as it is difficult to say what exactly constitutes morally required equal treatment, or what people deserve.

For a consequentialist like Mill, these difficult questions can be answered by looking back to the utilitarian foundations of justice. Since the *point* of justice is to promote utility, we can resolve difficult questions about the content of justice by figuring out which rules (or which interpretations of a given rule) would be utility maximizing. If (as seems unlikely) utility would be maximized by a rule requiring the state to enforce a constant equality of material well-being among its citizens, then *that* is the kind of equality required by justice. But if (as seems more plausible) utility would be better promoted by a rule requiring the state to enforce only equality of *opportunity* for material well-being, then *that* would be the sort of equality that justice requires.

Rawls' method of arriving at the content of justice is different, and reflects his more Kantian moral underpinnings. The starting place for Rawls' reflection is the moral arbitrariness of fortune. What we have, as individuals, is largely — perhaps entirely, in Rawls' view — the result of luck. We did nothing to deserve being born into one social class rather than another, nor did we deserve being born with a genetic propensity for health, height, and intelligence rather than their opposites. And to the extent that our success in life depends on these factors, it too is the result of luck. To allow an individual's fate to rest on luck, however, is manifestly unjust. Thus Rawls' "original position" asks us to think about what principles of justice we would choose if we wanted ones that would allow us to live good lives for ourselves but didn't know how smart, healthy, rich, and so on we were. Rawls' conclusion is that parties so situated in a fair initial bargaining position would choose principles guaranteeing each a maximum set of basic liberties, and requiring that no inequalities be permitted in society unless they can be shown to be to the benefit of the least well-off person.

The readings in this section bring out some of the most important aspects of the concept of justice. But our discussion of justice will not end here. Many of the later sections of this book will be devoted to looking at the requirements of justice in specific contexts — the distribution of wealth, immigration law, etc. Readers are thus encouraged to focus their thinking for now on the nature and theoretical justification of justice, and to rest assured that more concrete questions about its content will be taken up later.

Further Reading

Aristotle, *Nicomachean Ethics*, book V.
Barry, Brian. 1989. *Theories of Justice*. Berkeley: University of California Press.
Nussbaum, M. (2006). *Frontiers of Justice: Disability, Nationality, Species Membership*. Cambridge, MA: Belknap Press.
O'Neill, O. (2000). *Bounds of Justice*. Cambridge: Cambridge University Press.
Rawls, J. (1971). *A Theory of Justice* (1st ed.). Cambridge, MA: Belknap Press.
Sandel, M. (1998). *Liberalism and the Limits of Justice*. Cambridge: Cambridge University Press.
Sandel, M. (2007). *Justice: A Reader*. Oxford: Oxford University Press.
Schmidtz, D. (2006). *Elements of Justice*. Cambridge: Cambridge University Press.
Sen, A. (2009). *The Idea of Justice*. Cambridge, MA: Harvard University Press.
Tomasi, J. (2001). *Liberalism and the Limits of Justice*. Princeton: Princeton University Press.
Walzer, M. (1983). *Spheres of Justice*. New York: Basic Books.

Chapter 15

David Hume

JUSTICE AS CONVENTION

David Hume (1711–76) was a Scottish philosopher who wrote widely in metaphysics, ethics, history, politics, and almost everything else. In these excerpts from his *Treatise of Human Nature* (1739–40), Hume argues that justice is an artificial virtue in the sense that it must be established to serve the public interest and does not follow from our natural sentiments. Justice is both necessary and possible because of certain key features of the human condition—namely, scarcity in the objects of our desire, and a general selfishness combined with a limited form of benevolence toward others.

Of the Origin of Justice and Property

We now proceed to examine two questions, *viz. concerning the manner, in which the rules of justice are establish'd by the artifice of men;* and *concerning the reasons, which determine us to attribute to the observance or neglect of these rules a moral beauty and deformity.* These questions will appear afterwards to be distinct. We shall begin with the former.

Of all the animals, with which this globe is peopled, there is none towards whom nature seems, at first sight, to have exercis'd more cruelty than towards man, in the numberless wants and necessities, with which she has loaded him, and in the slender means, which she affords to the relieving these necessities. In other creatures these two particulars generally compensate each other. If we consider the lion as a voracious and carnivorous animal, we shall easily discover him to be very necessitous; but if we turn our eye to his make and temper, his agility, his courage, his arms, and his force, we shall find,

that his advantages hold proportion with his wants. The sheep and ox are depriv'd of all these advantages; but their appetites are moderate, and their food is of easy purchase. In man alone, this unnatural conjunction of infirmity, and of necessity, may be observ'd in its greatest perfection. Not only the food, which is requir'd for his sustenance, flies his search and approach, or at least requires his labour to be produc'd, but he must be possess'd of cloaths and lodging, to defend him against the injuries of the weather; tho' to consider him only in himself, he is provided neither with arms, nor force, nor other natural abilities, which are in any degree answerable to so many necessities.

'Tis by society alone he is able to supply his defects, and raise himself up to an equality with his fellow-creatures, and even acquire a superiority above them. By society all his infirmities are compensated; and tho' in that situation his wants multiply every moment upon him, yet his abilities are still more augmented, and leave him in every respect more satisfied and happy, than 'tis possible for him, in his savage and solitary condition, ever to become. When every individual person labours a-part, and only for himself, his force is too small to execute any considerable work; his labour being employ'd in supplying all his different necessities, he never attains a perfection in any particular art; and as his force and success are not at all times equal, the least failure in either of these particulars must be attended with inevitable ruin and misery. Society provides a remedy for these three inconveniences. By the conjunction of forces, our power is augmented: By the partition of employments, our ability encreases: And by mutual succour we are less expos'd to fortune and accidents. 'Tis by this additional force, ability, and security, that society becomes advantageous.

But in order to form society, 'tis requisite not only that it be advantageous, but also that men be sensible of these advantages; and 'tis impossible, in their wild uncultivated state, that by study and reflexion alone, they should ever be able to attain this knowledge. Most fortunately, therefore, there is conjoin'd to those necessities, whose remedies are remote and obscure, another necessity, which having a present and more obvious remedy, may justly be regarded as the first and original principle of human society. This necessity is no other than that natural appetite betwixt the sexes, which unites them together, and preserves their union, till a new tye takes place in their concern for their common offspring. This new concern becomes also a principle of union betwixt the parents and offspring, and forms a more numerous society; where the parents govern by the advantage of their superior strength and wisdom, and at the same time are restrain'd in the exercise of their authority by that natural affection, which they bear their children. In a little time, custom and habit operating on the tender minds of the children, makes them sensible of the advantages, which they may reap from society, as well as fashions them by degrees for it, by rubbing off

those rough corners and untoward affections, which prevent their coalition.

For it must be confest, that however the circumstances of human nature may render an union necessary, and however those passions of lust and natural affection may seem to render it unavoidable; yet there are other particulars in our *natural temper*, and in our *outward circumstances*, which are very incommodious, and are even contrary to the requisite conjunction. Among the former, we may justly esteem our *selfishness* to be the most considerable. I am sensible, that, generally speaking, the representations of this quality have been carried much too far; and that the descriptions, which certain philosophers delight so much to form of mankind in this particular, are as wide of nature as any accounts of monsters, which we meet with in fables and romances. So far from thinking, that men have no affection for any thing beyond themselves, I am of opinion, that tho' it be rare to meet with one, who loves any single person better than himself; yet 'tis as rare to meet with one, in whom all the kind affections, taken together, do not over-balance all the selfish. Consult common experience: Do you not see, that tho' the whole expence of the family be generally under the direction of the master of it, yet there are few that do not bestow the largest part of their fortunes on the pleasures of their wives, and the education of their children, reserving the smallest portion for their own proper use and entertainment. This is what we may observe concerning such as have those endearing ties; and may presume, that the case would be the same with others, were they plac'd in a like situation.

But tho' this generosity must be acknowledg'd to the honour of human nature, we may at the same time remark, that so noble an affection, instead of fitting men for large societies, is almost as contrary to them, as the most narrow selfishness. For while each person loves himself better than any other single person, and in his love to others bears the greatest affection to his relations and acquaintance, this must necessarily produce an opposition of passions, and a consequent opposition of actions; which cannot but be dangerous to the new-establish'd union.

'Tis however worth while to remark, that this contrariety of passions wou'd be attended with but small danger, did it not concur with a peculiarity in our *outward circumstances*, which affords it an opportunity of exerting itself. There are three different species of goods, which we are possess'd of; the internal satisfaction of our minds, the external advantages of our body, and the enjoyment of such possessions as we have acquir'd by our industry and good fortune. We are perfectly secure in the enjoyment of the first. The second may be ravish'd from us, but can be of no advantage to him who deprives us of them. The last only are both expos'd to the violence of others, and may be transferr'd without suffering any loss or alteration; while at the same time, there is not a sufficient quantity of them to supply every one's desires and necessities. As the improvement, therefore, of these goods is the chief advantage of society, so the *instability* of their possession, along with their *scarcity*, is the chief impediment.

In vain shou'd we expect to find, in *uncultivated nature*, a remedy to this inconvenience; or hope for any inartificial principle of the human mind, which might controul those partial affections, and make us overcome the temptations arising from our circumstances. The idea of justice can never serve to this purpose, or be taken for a natural principle, capable of inspiring men with an equitable conduct towards each other. That virtue, as it is now understood, wou'd never have been dream'd of among rude and savage men. For the notion of injury or injustice implies an immorality or vice committed against some other person: And as every immorality is deriv'd from some defect or unsoundness of the passions, and as this defect must be judg'd of, in a great measure, from the ordinary course of nature in the constitution of the mind; 'twill be easy to know, whether we be guilty of any immorality, with regard to others, by considering the natural,

and usual force of those several affections, which are directed towards them. Now it appears, that in the original frame of our mind, our strongest attention is confin'd to ourselves; our next is extended to our relations and acquaintance; and 'tis only the weakest which reaches to strangers and indifferent persons. This partiality, then, and unequal affection, must not only have an influence on our behaviour and conduct in society, but even on our ideas of vice and virtue; so as to make us regard any remarkable transgression of such a degree of partiality, either by too great an enlargement, or contraction of the affections, as vicious and immoral. This we may observe in our common judgments concerning actions, where we blame a person, who either centers all his affections in his family, or is so regardless of them, as, in any opposition of interest, to give the preference to a stranger, or mere chance acquaintance. From all which it follows, that our natural uncultivated ideas of morality, instead of providing a remedy for the partiality of our affections, do rather conform themselves to that partiality, and give it an additional force and influence.

The remedy, then, is not deriv'd from nature, but from *artifice*; or more properly speaking, nature provides a remedy in the judgment and understanding, for what is irregular and incommodious in the affections. For when men, from their early education in society, have become sensible of the infinite advantages that result from it, and have besides acquir'd a new affection to company and conversation; and when they have observ'd, that the principal disturbance in society arises from those goods, which we call external, and from their looseness and easy transition from one person to another; they must seek for a remedy, by putting these goods, as far as possible, on the same footing with the fix'd and constant advantages of the mind and body. This can be done after no other manner, than by a convention enter'd into by all the members of the society to bestow stability on the possession of those external goods, and leave every one in the peaceable enjoyment of what he may acquire by his fortune and industry. By this means, every one knows what he may safely possess; and the passions are restrain'd in their partial and contradictory motions. Nor is such a restraint contrary to these passions; for if so, it cou'd never be enter'd into, nor maintain'd; but it is only contrary to their heedless and impetuous movement. Instead of departing from our own interest, or from that of our nearest friends, by abstaining from the possessions of others, we cannot better consult both these interests, than by such a convention; because it is by that means we maintain society, which is so necessary to their well-being and subsistence, as well as to our own.

This convention is not of the nature of a *promise*: For even promises themselves, as we shall see afterwards, arise from human conventions. It is only a general sense of common interest; which sense all the members of the society express to one another, and which induces them to regulate their conduct by certain rules. I observe, that it will be for my interest to leave another in the possession of his goods, *provided* he will act in the same manner with regard to me. He is sensible of a like interest in the regulation of his conduct. When this common sense of interest is mutually express'd, and is known to both, it produces a suitable resolution and behaviour. And this may properly enough be call'd a convention or agreement betwixt us, tho' without the interposition of a promise; since the actions of each of us have a reference to those of the other, and are perform'd upon the supposition, that something is to be perform'd on the other part. Two men, who pull the oars of a boat, do it by an agreement or convention, tho' they have never given promises to each other. Nor is the rule concerning the stability of possession the less deriv'd from human conventions, that it arises gradually, and acquires force by a slow progression, and by our repeated experience of the inconveniences of transgressing it. On the contrary, this experience assures us still more,

that the sense of interest has become common to all our fellows, and gives us a confidence of the future regularity of their conduct: And 'tis only on the expectation of this, that our moderation and abstinence are founded. In like manner are languages gradually establish'd by human conventions without any promise. In like manner do gold and silver become the common measures of exchange, and are esteem'd sufficient payment for what is of a hundred times their value.

After this convention, concerning abstinence from the possessions of others, is enter'd into, and every one has acquir'd a stability in his possessions, there immediately arise the ideas of justice and injustice; as also those of *property, right,* and *obligation.* The latter are altogether unintelligible without first understanding the former. Our property is nothing but those goods, whose constant possession is establish'd by the laws of society; that is, by the laws of justice. Those, therefore, who make use of the words *property,* or *right,* or *obligation,* before they have explain'd the origin of justice, or even make use of them in that explication, are guilty of a very gross fallacy, and can never reason upon any solid foundation. A man's property is some object related to him. This relation is not natural, but moral, and founded on justice. 'Tis very preposterous, therefore, to imagine, that we can have any idea of property, without fully comprehending the nature of justice, and shewing its origin in the artifice and contrivance of men. The origin of justice explains that of property. The same artifice gives rise to both. As our first and most natural sentiment of morals is founded on the nature of our passions, and gives the preference to ourselves and friends, above strangers; 'tis impossible there can be naturally any such thing as a fix'd right or property, while the opposite passions of men impel them in contrary directions, and are not restrain'd by any convention or agreement.

No one can doubt, that the convention for the distinction of property, and for the stability of possession, is of all circumstances the most necessary to the establishment of human society, and that after the agreement for the fixing and observing of this rule, there remains little or nothing to be done towards settling a perfect harmony and concord. All the other passions, beside this of interest, are either easily restrain'd, or are not of such pernicious consequence, when indulg'd. *Vanity* is rather to be esteem'd a social passion, and a bond of union among men. Pity and *love* are to be consider'd in the same light. And as to *envy* and *revenge*, tho' pernicious, they operate only by intervals, and are directed against particular persons, whom we consider as our superiors or enemies. This avidity alone, of acquiring goods and possessions for ourselves and our nearest friends, is insatiable, perpetual, universal, and directly destructive of society. There scarce is any one, who is not actuated by it; and there is no one, who has not reason to fear from it, when it acts without any restraint, and gives way to its first and most natural movements. So that upon the whole, we are to esteem the difficulties in the establishment of society, to be greater or less, according to those we encounter in regulating and restraining this passion.

'Tis certain, that no affection of the human mind has both a sufficient force, and a proper direction to counter-balance the love of gain, and render men fit members of society, by making them abstain from the possessions of others. Benevolence to strangers is too weak for this purpose; and as to the other passions, they rather inflame this avidity, when we observe, that the larger our possessions are, the more ability we have of gratifying all our appetites. There is no passion, therefore, capable of controlling the interested affection, but the very affection itself, by an alteration of its direction. Now this alteration must necessarily take place upon the least reflection; since 'tis evident, that the passion is much better satisfy'd by its restraint, than by its liberty, and that in preserving society, we make much greater advances in the acquiring possessions, than in the solitary and forlorn condition, which must follow upon violence

and an universal licence. The question, therefore, concerning the wickedness or goodness of human nature, enters not in the least into that other question concerning the origin of society; nor is there any thing to be consider'd but the degrees of men's sagacity or folly. For whether the passion of self-interest be esteemed vicious or virtuous, 'tis all a case; since itself alone restrains it: So that if it be virtuous, men become social by their virtue; if vicious, their vice has the same effect.

Now as 'tis by establishing the rule for the stability of possession, that this passion restrains itself; if that rule be very abstruse, and of difficult invention; society must be esteem'd, in a manner, accidental, and the effect of many ages. But if it be found, that nothing can be more simple and obvious than that rule; that every parent, in order to preserve peace among his children, must establish it; and that these first rudiments of justice must every day be improv'd, as the society enlarges: If all this appear evident, as it certainly must, we may conclude, that 'tis utterly impossible for men to remain any considerable time in that savage condition, which precedes society; but that his very first state and situation may justly be esteem'd social. This, however, hinders not, but that philosophers may, if they please, extend their reasoning to the suppos'd *state of nature*; provided they allow it to be a mere philosophical fiction, which never had, and never cou'd have any reality. Human nature being compos'd of two principal parts, which are requisite in all its actions, the affections and understanding; 'tis certain, that the blind motions of the former, without the direction of the latter, incapacitate men for society: And it may be allow'd us to consider separately the effects, that result from the separate operations of these two component parts of the mind. The same liberty may be permitted to moral, which is allow'd to natural philosophers; and 'tis very usual with the latter to consider any motion as compounded and consisting of two parts separate from each other, tho' at the same time they acknowledge it to be in itself uncompounded and inseparable.

This *state of nature*, therefore, is to be regarded as a mere fiction, not unlike that of the *golden age*, which poets have invented; only with this difference, that the former is describ'd as full of war, violence and injustice; whereas the latter is painted out to us, as the most charming and most peaceable condition, that can possibly be imagin'd. The seasons, in that first age of nature, were so temperate, if we may believe the poets, that there was no necessity for men to provide themselves with cloaths and houses as a security against the violence of heat and cold. The rivers flow'd with wine and milk: The oaks yielded honey; and nature spontaneously produc'd her greatest delicacies. Nor were these the chief advantages of that happy age. The storms and tempests were not alone remov'd from nature; but those more furious tempests were unknown to human breasts, which now cause such uproar, and engender such confusion. Avarice, ambition, cruelty, selfishness, were never heard of: Cordial affection, compassion, sympathy, were the only movements, with which the human mind was yet acquainted. Even the distinction of *mine* and *thine* was banish'd from that happy race of mortals, and carry'd with them the very notions of property and obligation, justice and injustice.

This, no doubt, is to be regarded as an idle fiction; but yet deserves our attention, because nothing can more evidently shew the origin of those virtues, which are the subjects of our present enquiry. I have already observ'd, that justice takes its rise from human conventions; and that these are intended as a remedy to some inconveniences, which proceed from the concurrence of certain *qualities* of the human mind with the *situation* of external objects. The qualities of the mind are *selfishness* and *limited generosity*: And the situation of external objects is their *easy change*, join'd to their *scarcity* in comparison of the wants and desires of men. But however philosophers may have been bewilder'd in those speculations, poets have been guided more

infallibly, by a certain taste or common instinct, which in most kinds of reasoning goes farther than any of that art and philosophy, with which we have been yet acquainted. They easily perceiv'd, if every man had a tender regard for another, or if nature supplied abundantly all our wants and desires, that the jealousy of interest, which justice supposes, could no longer have place; nor would there be any occasion for those distinctions and limits of property and possession, which at present are in use among mankind. Encrease to a sufficient degree the benevolence of men, or the bounty of nature, and you render justice useless, by supplying its place with much nobler virtues, and more valuable blessings. The selfishness of men is animated by the few possessions we have, in proportion to our wants; and 'tis to restrain this selfishness, that men have been oblig'd to separate themselves from the community, and to distinguish betwixt their own goods and those of others.

Nor need we have recourse to the fictions of poets to learn this; but beside the reason of the thing, may discover the same truth by common experience and observation. 'Tis easy to remark, that a cordial affection renders all things common among friends; and that married people in particular mutually lose their property, and are unacquainted with the *mine* and *thine*, which are so necessary, and yet cause such disturbance in human society. The same effect arises from any alteration in the circumstances of mankind; as when there is such a plenty of any thing as satisfies all the desires of men: In which case the distinction of property is entirely lost, and every thing remains in common. This we may observe with regard to air and water, tho' the most valuable of all external objects; and may easily conclude, that if men were supplied with every thing in the same abundance, or if *every one* had the same affection and tender regard for *every one* as for himself; justice and injustice would be equally unknown among mankind.

Here then is a proposition, which, I think, may be regarded as certain, *that 'tis only from the selfishness and confin'd generosity of men, along with the scanty provision nature has made for his wants, that justice derives its origin.* If we look backward we shall find, that this proposition bestows an additional force on some of those observations, which we have already made on this subject.

First, we may conclude from it, that a regard to public interest, or a strong extensive benevolence, is not our first and original motive for the observation of the rules of justice; since 'tis allow'd, that if men were endow'd with such a benevolence, these rules would never have been dreamt of.

Secondly, we may conclude from the same principle, that the sense of justice is not founded on reason, or on the discovery of certain connexions and relations of ideas, which are eternal, immutable, and universally obligatory. For since it is confest, that such an alteration as that abovemention'd, in the temper and circumstances of mankind, wou'd entirely alter our duties and obligations, 'tis necessary upon the common system, *that the sense of virtue is deriv'd from reason,* to shew the change which this must produce in the relations and ideas. But 'tis evident, that the only cause, why the extensive generosity of man, and the perfect abundance of every thing, wou'd destroy the very idea of justice, is because they render it useless; and that, on the other hand, his confin'd benevolence, and his necessitous condition, give rise to that virtue, only by making it requisite to the publick interest, and to that of every individual. 'Twas therefore a concern for our own, and the publick interest, which made us establish the laws of justice; and nothing can be more certain, than that it is not any relation of ideas, which gives us this concern, but our impressions and sentiments, without which every thing in nature is perfectly indifferent to us, and can never in the least affect us. The sense of justice, therefore, is not founded on our ideas, but on our impressions.

Thirdly, we may farther confirm the foregoing proposition, *that those impressions, which give rise to this sense of justice, are not natural to the mind of man, but arise* from artifice and human conventions. For since any considerable alteration of temper and circumstances destroys equally justice and injustice; and since such an alteration has an effect only by changing our own and the publick interest; it follows, that the first establishment of the rules of justice depends on these different interests. But if men pursu'd the publick interest naturally, and with a hearty affection, they wou'd never have dream'd of restraining each other by these rules; and if they pursu'd their own interest, without any precaution, they wou'd run headlong into every kind of injustice and violence. These rules, therefore, are artificial, and seek their end in an oblique and indirect manner; nor is the interest, which gives rise to them, of a kind that cou'd be pursu'd by the natural and inartificial passions of men.

To make this more evident, consider, that tho' the rules of justice are establish'd merely by interest, their connexion with interest is somewhat singular, and is different from what may be observ'd on other occasions. A single act of justice is frequently contrary to *public interest;* and were it to stand alone, without being follow'd by other acts, may, in itself, be very prejudicial to society. When a man of merit, of a beneficent disposition, restores a great fortune to a miser, or a seditious bigot, he has acted justly and laudably, but the public is a real sufferer. Nor is every single act of justice, consider'd apart, more conducive to private interest, than to public; and 'tis easily conceiv'd how a man may impoverish himself by a signal instance of integrity, and have reason to wish, that with regard to that single act, the laws of justice were for a moment suspended in the universe. But however single acts of justice may be contrary, either to public or private interest, 'tis certain, that the whole plan or scheme is highly conducive, or indeed absolutely requisite, both to the support of society, and the well-being of every individual. 'Tis impossible to separate the good from the ill. Property must be stable, and must be fix'd by general rules. Tho' in one instance the public be a sufferer, this momentary ill is amply compensated by the steady prosecution of the rule, and by the peace and order, which it establishes in society. And even every individual person must find himself a gainer, on ballancing the account; since, without justice, society must immediately dissolve, and every one must fall into that savage and solitary condition, which is infinitely worse than the worst situation that can possibly be suppos'd in society. When therefore men have had experience enough to observe, that whatever may be the consequence of any single act of justice, perform'd by a single person, yet the whole system of actions, concurr'd in by the whole society, is infinitely advantageous to the whole, and to every part; it is not long before justice and property take place. Every member of society is sensible of this interest: Every one expresses this sense to his fellows, along with the resolution he has taken of squaring his actions by it, on condition that others will do the same. No more is requisite to induce any one of them to perform an act of justice, who has the first opportunity. This becomes an example to others. And thus justice establishes itself by a kind of convention or agreement; that is, by a sense of interest, suppos'd to be common to all, and where every single act is perform'd in expectation that others are to perform the like. Without such a convention, no one wou'd ever have dream'd, that there was such a virtue as justice, or have been induc'd to conform his actions to it. Taking any single act, my justice may be pernicious in every respect; and 'tis only upon the supposition, that others are to imitate my example, that I can be induc'd to embrace that virtue; since nothing but this combination can render justice advantageous, or afford me any motives to conform my self to its rules.

We come now to the *second* question we propos'd, *viz. Why we annex the idea of virtue to justice, and of vice to injustice.* This question will not detain us long after the principles, which we have already establish'd. All we can say of it at present will be dispatch'd in a few words: And for farther satisfaction, the reader must wait till we come to the *third* part of this book. The *natural* obligation to justice, *viz.* interest, has been fully explain'd; but as to the *moral* obligation, or the sentiment of right and wrong, 'twill first be requisite to examine the natural virtues, before we can give a full and satisfactory account of it.

After men have found by experience, that their selfishness and confin'd generosity, acting at their liberty, totally incapacitate them for society; and at the same time have observ'd, that society is necessary to the satisfaction of those very passions, they are naturally induc'd to lay themselves under the restraint of such rules, as may render their commerce more safe and commodious. To the imposition then, and observance of these rules, both in general, and in every particular instance, they are at first induc'd only by a regard to interest; and this motive, on the first formation of society, is sufficiently strong and forcible. But when society has become numerous, and has encreas'd to a tribe or nation, this interest is more remote; nor do men so readily perceive, that disorder and confusion follow upon every breach of these rules, as in a more narrow and contracted society. But tho' in our own actions we may frequently lose sight of that interest, which we have in maintaining order, and may follow a lesser and more present interest, we never fail to observe the prejudice we receive, either mediately or immediately, from the injustice of others; as not being in that case either blinded by passion, or byass'd by any contrary temptation. Nay when the injustice is so distant from us, as no way to affect our interest, it still displeases us; because we consider it as prejudicial to human society, and pernicious to every one that approaches the person guilty of it. We partake of their uneasiness by *sympathy*; and as every thing, which gives uneasiness in human actions, upon the general survey, is call'd Vice, and whatever produces satisfaction, in the same manner, is denominated Virtue; this is the reason why the sense of moral good and evil follows upon justice and injustice. And tho' this sense, in the present case, be deriv'd only from contemplating the actions of others, yet we fail not to extend it even to our own actions. The *general rule* reaches beyond those instances, from which it arose; while at the same time we naturally *sympathize* with others in the sentiments they entertain of us. *Thus self-interest is the original motive to the* establishment of justice; but a sympathy with public interest is the source of the *moral approbation, which attends that virtue.*

Tho' this progress of the sentiments be *natural*, and even necessary, 'tis certain, that it is here forwarded by the artifice of politicians, who, in order to govern men more easily, and preserve peace in human society, have endeavour'd to produce an esteem for justice, and an abhorrence of injustice. This, no doubt, must have its effect; but nothing can be more evident, than that the matter has been carry'd too far by certain writers on morals, who seem to have employ'd their utmost efforts to extirpate all sense of virtue from among mankind. Any artifice of politicians may assist nature in the producing of those sentiments, which she suggests to us, and may even on some occasions, produce alone an approbation or esteem for any particular action; but 'tis impossible it should be the sole cause of the distinction we make betwixt vice and virtue. For if nature did not aid us in this particular, 'twou'd be in vain for politicians to talk of *honourable* or *dishonourable, praiseworthy* or *blameable*. These words wou'd be perfectly unintelligible, and wou'd no more have any idea annex'd to them, than if they were of a tongue perfectly unknown to us. The utmost politicians can perform, is, to extend the natural sentiments beyond their original bounds; but still nature must furnish the materials, and give us some notion of moral distinctions.

As publick praise and blame encrease our esteem for justice; so private education and instruction contribute to the same effect. For as parents easily observe, that a man is the more useful, both to himself and others, the greater degree of probity and honour he is endow'd with; and that those principles have greater force, when custom and education assist interest and reflexion: For these reasons they are induc'd to inculcate on their children, from their earliest infancy, the principles of probity, and teach them to regard the observance of those rules, by which society is maintain'd, as worthy and honourable, and their violation as base and infamous. By this means the sentiments of honour may take root in their tender minds, and acquire such firmness and solidity, that they may fall little short of those principles, which are the most essential to our natures, and the most deeply radicated in our internal constitution.

What farther contributes to encrease their solidity, is the interest of our reputation, after the opinion, *that a merit or demerit attends justice or injustice,* is once firmly establish'd among mankind. There is nothing, which touches us more nearly than our reputation, and nothing on which our reputation more depends than our conduct, with relation to the property of others. For this reason, every one, who has any regard to his character, or who intends to live on good terms with mankind, must fix an inviolable law to himself, never, by any temptation, to be induc'd to violate those principles, which are essential to a man of probity and honour.

I shall make only one observation before I leave this subject, *viz.* that tho' I assert, that in the *state of nature*, or that imaginary state, which preceded society, there be neither justice nor injustice, yet I assert not, that it was allowable, in such a state, to violate the property of others. I only maintain, that there was no such thing as property; and consequently cou'd be no such thing as justice or injustice. I shall have occasion to make a similar reflexion with regard to *promises*, when I come to treat of them; and I hope this reflexion, when duly weigh'd, will suffice to remove all odium from the foregoing opinions, with regard to justice and injustice.

Chapter 16

John Stuart Mill

JUSTICE AND UTILITY

John Stuart Mill (1806–73) was a British philosopher and, with Jeremy Bentham, one of the most historically influential proponents of the moral philosophy known as utilitarianism. In these excerpts, taken from *Utilitarianism* (1863), Mill sets forth the basic tenets of utilitarianism and shows its connection with the constraint of conduct by *rules*. He then goes on to show how utilitarianism is, contrary to what many of its critics had charged (and continue to charge), compatible with respect for justice, and indeed necessary to explain the importance of that virtue.

What Utilitarianism Is

[. . .]

2. The creed which accepts as the foundation of morals, Utility, or the Greatest Happiness Principle, holds that actions are right in proportion as they tend to promote happiness, wrong as they tend to produce the reverse of happiness. By happiness is intended pleasure, and the absence of pain; by unhappiness, pain, and the privation of pleasure. To give a clear view of the moral standard set up by the theory, much more requires to be said; in particular, what things it includes in the ideas of pain and pleasure; and to what extent this is left an open question. But these supplementary explanations do not affect the theory of life on which this theory of morality is grounded – namely, that pleasure, and freedom from pain, are the only things desirable as ends; and that all desirable things (which are as numerous in the utilitarian as in any other scheme) are desirable either for the pleasure inherent in themselves, or as means to

the promotion of pleasure and the prevention of pain.

[. . .]

23. [. . .] Utility is often summarily stigmatized as an immoral doctrine by giving it the name of Expediency, and taking advantage of the popular use of that term to contrast it with Principle. But the Expedient, in the sense in which it is opposed to the Right, generally means that which is expedient for the particular interest of the agent himself; as when a minister sacrifices the interest of his country to keep himself in place. When it means anything better than this, it means that which is expedient for some immediate object, some temporary purpose, but which violates a rule whose observance is expedient in a much higher degree. The Expedient, in this sense, instead of being the same thing with the useful, is a branch of the hurtful. Thus, it would often be expedient, for the purpose of getting over some momentary embarrassment, or attaining some object immediately useful to ourselves or others, to tell a lie. But inasmuch as the cultivation in ourselves of a sensitive feeling on the subject of veracity, is one of the most useful, and the enfeeblement of that feeling one of the most hurtful, things to which our conduct can be instrumental; and inasmuch as any, even unintentional, deviation from truth does that much towards weakening the trustworthiness of human assertion, which is not only the principal support of all present social well-being, but the insufficiency of which does more than any one thing that can be named to keep back civilization, virtue, everything on which human happiness on the largest scale depends; we feel that the violation, for a present advantage, of a rule of such transcendent expediency, is not expedient, and that he who, for the sake of a convenience to himself or to some other individual, does what depends on him to deprive mankind of the good, and inflict upon them the evil, involved in the greater or less reliance which they can place in each other's word, acts the part of one of their worst enemies. Yet that even this rule, sacred as it is, admits of possible exceptions, is acknowledged by all moralists; the chief of which is when the withholding of some fact (as of information from a malefactor, or of bad news from a person dangerously ill) would preserve some one (especially a person other than oneself) from great and unmerited evil, and when the withholding can only be effected by denial. But in order that the exception may not extend itself beyond the need, and may have the least possible effect in weakening reliance on veracity, it ought to be recognized, and, if possible, its limits defined; and if the principle of utility is good for anything, it must be good for weighing these conflicting utilities against one another, and marking out the region within which one or the other preponderates.

24. Again, defenders of utility often find themselves called upon to reply to such objections as this — that there is not time, previous to action, for calculating and weighing the effects of any line of conduct on the general happiness. This is exactly as if any one were to say that it is impossible to guide our conduct by Christianity, because there is not time, on every occasion on which anything has to be done, to read through the Old and New Testaments. The answer to the objection is, that there has been ample time, namely, the whole past duration of the human species. During all that time mankind have been learning by experience the tendencies of actions; on which experience all the prudence, as well as all the morality of life, is dependent. People talk as if the commencement of this course of experience had hitherto been put off, and as if, at the moment when some man feels tempted to meddle with the property or life of another, he had to begin considering for the first time whether murder and theft are injurious to human happiness. Even then I do not think that he would find the question very puzzling; but, at all events, the matter is now done to his hand. It is truly a whimsical supposition that if mankind were agreed in considering utility to be the test of morality, they would remain without any agreement as to what is useful, and would take no measures for having their notions on the subject taught to the young, and enforced by law and opinion. There is no difficulty in proving any ethical standard whatever to work ill, if we suppose universal idiocy to be conjoined with it; but on any hypothesis short of that, mankind must by this time have acquired positive beliefs as to the effects of some actions on their happiness; and the beliefs which have thus come down are the rules of morality for the multitude, and for the philosopher until he has succeeded in finding better. That philosophers might easily do this, even now, on many subjects; that the received code of ethics is by no means of divine right; and that mankind have still much to learn as to the effects of actions on the general happiness, I admit, or rather, earnestly maintain. The corollaries from the principle of utility, like the precepts of every practical art, admit of indefinite improvement, and, in a progressive state of human mind, their improvement is perpetually going on. But to consider the rules of morality as improvable, is one thing; to pass over the intermediate generalizations entirely, and endeavour to test each individual action directly by the first principle, is another. It is a strange notion that the acknowledgment of a first principle is inconsistent with the admission of secondary ones. To inform a traveller respecting the place of his ultimate destination, is not to forbid the use of landmarks and direction-posts on the way. The proposition that happiness is the end and aim of morality, does not mean that no road ought to be laid down to that goal, or that persons going thither should not be advised to take one direction rather than another. Men really ought to leave off talking a kind of nonsense on this subject, which they would neither talk nor listen to on other matters of practical concernment. Nobody argues that the art of navigation is not founded on astronomy, because sailors cannot wait to calculate the Nautical Almanack. Being rational creatures, they go to sea with it ready calculated; and all rational creatures go out upon the sea of life with their minds made up on the common questions of right and wrong, as well as on many of the far more difficult questions of wise and foolish. And this, as long as foresight is a human quality, it is to be presumed they will continue to do. Whatever we adopt as the fundamental principle of morality, we require subordinate principles to apply it by: the impossibility of doing without them, being common to all systems, can afford no argument against any one in particular: but gravely to argue as if no such secondary principles could be had, and as if mankind had remained till now, and always must remain, without drawing any general conclusions from the experience of human life, is as high a pitch, I think,

as absurdity has ever reached in philosophical controversy.

[. . .]

On the Connexion Between Justice and Utility

1. In all ages of speculation, one of the strongest obstacles to the reception of the doctrine that Utility or Happiness is the criterion of right and wrong, has been drawn from the idea of Justice. The powerful sentiment, and apparently clear perception, which that word recalls with a rapidity and certainty resembling an instinct, have seemed to the majority of thinkers to point to an inherent quality in things; to show that the Just must have an existence in Nature as something absolute – generically distinct from every variety of the Expedient, and, in idea, opposed to it, though (as is commonly acknowledged) never, in the long run, disjoined from it in fact.

2. In the case of this, as of our other moral sentiments, there is no necessary connexion between the question of its origin, and that of its binding force. That a feeling is bestowed on us by Nature, does not necessarily legitimate all its promptings. The feeling of justice might be a peculiar instinct, and might yet require, like our other instincts, to be controlled and enlightened by a higher reason. If we have intellectual instincts, leading us to judge in a particular way, as well as animal instincts that prompt us to act in a particular way, there is no necessity that the former should be more infallible in their sphere than the latter in theirs: it may as well happen that wrong judgments are occasionally suggested by those, as wrong actions by these. But though it is one thing to believe that we have natural feelings of justice, and another to acknowledge them as an ultimate criterion of conduct, these two opinions are very closely connected in point of fact. Mankind are always predisposed to believe that any subjective feeling, not otherwise accounted for, is a revelation of some objective reality. Our present object is to determine whether the reality, to which the feeling of justice corresponds, is one which needs any such special revelation; whether the justice or injustice of an action is a thing intrinsically peculiar, and distinct from all its other qualities, or only a combination of certain of those qualities, presented under a peculiar aspect. For the purpose of this inquiry, it is practically important to consider whether the feeling itself, of justice and injustice, is *sui generis* like our sensations of colour and taste, or a derivative feeling, formed by a combination of others. And this it is the more essential to examine, as people are in general willing enough to allow, that objectively the dictates of justice coincide with a part of the field of General Expediency; but inasmuch as the subjective mental feeling of Justice is different from that which commonly attaches to simple expediency, and, except in extreme cases of the latter, is far more imperative in its demands, people find it difficult to see, in Justice, only a particular kind or branch of general utility, and think that its superior binding force requires a totally different origin.

3. To throw light upon this question, it is necessary to attempt to ascertain what is the distinguishing character of justice, or of injustice: what is the quality, or whether there is any quality, attributed in common to all modes of conduct designated as unjust (for justice, like many other moral attributes, is best defined by its opposite), and distinguishing them from such modes of conduct as are disapproved, but without having that particular epithet of disapprobation applied to them. If, in everything which men are accustomed to characterize as just or injust, some one common attribute or collection of attributes is always present, we may judge whether this particular attribute or combination of attributes would be capable of gathering round it a sentiment of that peculiar character and intensity by virtue of the general laws of our emotional constitution, or whether the sentiment is inexplicable, and requires to be

regarded as a special provision of Nature. If we find the former to be the case, we shall, in resolving this question, have resolved also the main problem: if the latter, we shall have to seek for some other mode of investigating it.

4. To find the common attributes of a variety of objects, it is necessary to begin by surveying the objects themselves in the concrete. Let us therefore advert successively to the various modes of action, and arrangements of human affairs, which are classed, by universal or widely spread opinion, as Just or as Unjust. The things well known to excite the sentiments associated with those names, are of a very multifarious character. I shall pass them rapidly in review, without studying any particular arrangement.

5. In the first place, it is mostly considered unjust to deprive any one of his personal liberty, his property, or any other thing which belongs to him by law. Here, therefore, is one instance of the application of the terms just and unjust in a perfectly definite sense, namely, that it is just to respect, unjust to violate, the *legal rights* of anyone. But this judgment admits of several exceptions, arising from the other forms in which the notions of justice and injustice present themselves. For example, the person who suffers the deprivation may (as the phrase is) have *forfeited* the rights which he is so deprived of: a case to which we shall return presently. But, also,

6. Secondly; the legal rights of which he is deprived, may be rights which *ought* not to have belonged to him; in other words, the law which confers on him these rights, may be a bad law. When it is so, or when (which is the same thing for our purpose) it is supposed to be so, opinions will differ as to the justice or injustice of infringing it. Some maintain that no law, however bad, ought to be disobeyed by an individual citizen; that his opposition to it, if shown at all, should only be shown in endeavouring to get it altered by competent authority. This opinion (which condemns many of the most illustrious benefactors of mankind, and would often protect pernicious institutions against the only weapons which, in the state of things existing at the time, have any chance of succeeding against them) is defended, by those who hold it, on grounds of expediency; principally on that of the importance, to the common interest of mankind, of maintaining inviolate the sentiment of submission to law. Other persons, again, hold the directly contrary opinion, that any law, judged to be bad, may blamelessly be disobeyed, even though it be not judged to be unjust, but only inexpedient; while others would confine the licence of disobedience to the case of unjust laws: but again, some say, that all laws which are inexpedient are unjust; since every law imposes some restriction on the natural liberty of mankind, which restriction is an injustice, unless legitimated by tending to their good. Among these diversities of opinion, it seems to be universally admitted that there may be unjust laws, and that law, consequently, is not the ultimate criterion of justice, but may give to one person a benefit, or impose on another an evil, which justice condemns. When, however, a law is thought to be unjust, it seems always to be regarded as being so in the same way in which a breach of law is unjust, namely, by infringing somebody's right; which, as it cannot in this case be a legal right, receives a different appellation, and is called a moral right. We may say, therefore, that a second case of injustice consists in taking or withholding from any person that to which he has a moral right.

7. Thirdly, it is universally considered just that each person should obtain that (whether good or evil) which he *deserves*; and unjust that he should obtain a good, or be made to undergo an evil, which he does not deserve. This is, perhaps, the clearest and most emphatic form in which the idea of injustice is conceived by the general mind. As it involves the notion of desert, the question arises, what constitutes desert? Speaking in a general way, a person is understood to deserve good if he does right, evil if he does wrong; and in a more particular sense, to deserve good from those to whom he does or

has done good, and evil from those to whom he does or has done evil. The precept of returning good for evil has never been regarded as a case of the fulfilment of justice, but as one in which the claims of justice are waved, in obedience to other considerations.

8. Fourthly, it is confessedly unjust to *break faith* with any one: to violate an engagement, either express or implied, or disappoint expectations raised by our own conduct, at least if we have raised those expectations knowingly and voluntarily. Like the other obligations of justice already spoken of, this one is not regarded as absolute, but as capable of being overruled by a stronger obligation of justice on the other side; or by such conduct on the part of the person concerned as is deemed to absolve us from our obligation to him, and to constitute a *forfeiture* of the benefit which he has been led to expect.

9. Fifthly, it is, by universal admission, inconsistent with justice to be *partial*; to show favour or preference to one person over another, in matters to which favour and preference do not properly apply. Impartiality, however, does not seem to be regarded as a duty in itself, but rather as instrumental to some other duty; for it is admitted that favour and preference are not always censurable, and indeed the cases in which they are condemned are rather the exception than the rule. A person would be more likely to be blamed than applauded for giving his family or friends no superiority in good offices over strangers, when he could do so without violating any other duty; and no one thinks it unjust to seek one person in preference to another as a friend, connexion, or companion. Impartiality where rights are concerned is of course obligatory, but this is involved in the more general obligation of giving to every one his right. A tribunal, for example, must be impartial, because it is bound to award, without regard to any other consideration, a disputed object to the one of two parties who has the right to it. There are other cases in which impartiality means, being solely influenced by desert; as with those who, in the capacity of judges, preceptors, or parents, administer reward and punishment as such. There are cases, again, in which it means, being solely influenced by consideration for the public interest; as in making a selection among candidates for a government employment. Impartiality, in short, as an obligation of justice, may be said to mean, being exclusively influenced by the considerations which it is supposed ought to influence the particular case in hand; and resisting the solicitation of any motives which prompt to conduct different from what those considerations would dictate.

10. Nearly allied to the idea of impartiality, is that of *equality*; which often enters as a component part both into the conception of justice and into the practice of it, and, in the eyes of many persons, constitutes its essence. But in this, still more than in any other case, the notion of justice varies in different persons, and always conforms in its variations to their notion of utility. Each person maintains that equality is the dictate of justice, except where he thinks that expediency requires inequality. The justice of giving equal protection to the rights of all, is maintained by those who support the most outrageous inequality in the rights themselves. Even in slave countries it is theoretically admitted that the rights of the slave, such as they are, ought to be as sacred as those of the master; and that a tribunal which fails to enforce them with equal strictness is wanting in justice; while, at the same time, institutions which leave to the slave scarcely any rights to enforce, are not deemed unjust, because they are not deemed inexpedient. Those who think that utility requires distinctions of rank, do not consider it unjust that riches and social privileges should be unequally dispensed; but those who think this inequality inexpedient, think it unjust also. Whoever thinks that government is necessary, sees no injustice in as much inequality as is constituted by giving to the magistrate powers not granted to other people. Even among those who hold levelling doctrines, there are as

many questions of justice as there are differences of opinion about expediency. Some Communists consider it unjust that the produce of the labour of the community should be shared on any other principle than that of exact equality; others think it just that those should receive most whose needs are greatest; while others hold that those who work harder, or who produce more, or whose services are more valuable to the community, may justly claim a larger quota in the division of the produce. And the sense of natural justice may be plausibly appealed to in behalf of every one of these opinions.

11. Among so many diverse applications of the term Justice, which yet is not regarded as ambiguous, it is a matter of some difficulty to seize the mental link which holds them together, and on which the moral sentiment adhering to the term essentially depends. Perhaps, in this embarrassment, some help may be derived from the history of the word, as indicated by its etymology.

12. In most, if not in all, languages, the etymology of the word which corresponds to Just, points to an origin connected either with positive law, or with that which was in most cases the primitive form of law − authoritative custom. *Justum* is a form of *jussum*, that which has been ordered. *Jus* is of the same origin. Δίκαιον comes from δίκη, of which the principal meaning, at least in the historical ages of Greece, was a suit at law. Originally, indeed, it meant only the mode or *manner* of doing things, but it early came to mean the *prescribed* manner; that which the recognized authorities, patriarchal, judicial, or political, would enforce. *Recht*, from which came *right* and *righteous*, is synonymous with law. The original meaning indeed of *recht* did not point to law, but to physical straightness; as *wrong* and its Latin equivalents meant twisted or *tortuous*; and from this it is argued that right did not originally mean law, but on the contrary law meant right. But however this may be, the fact that *recht* and *droit* became restricted in their meaning to positive law, although much which is not required by law is equally necessary to moral straightness or rectitude, is as significant of the original character of moral ideas as if the derivation had been the reverse way. The courts of justice, the administration of justice, are the courts and the administration of law. *La justice*, in French, is the established term for judicature. There can, I think, be no doubt that the *idée mère*, the primitive element, in the formation of the notion of justice, was conformity to law. It constituted the entire idea among the Hebrews, up to the birth of Christianity; as might be expected in the case of a people whose laws attempted to embrace all subjects on which precepts were required, and who believed those laws to be a direct emanation from the Supreme Being. But other nations, and in particular the Greeks and Romans, who knew that their laws had been made originally, and still continued to be made, by men, were not afraid to admit that those men might make bad laws; might do, by law, the same things, and from the same motives, which, if done by individuals without the sanction of law, would be called unjust. And hence the sentiment of injustice came to be attached, not to all violations of law, but only to violations of such laws as *ought* to exist, including such as ought to exist but do not; and to laws themselves, if supposed to be contrary to what ought to be law. In this manner the idea of law and of its injunctions was still predominant in the notion of justice, even when the laws actually in force ceased to be accepted as the standard of it.

13. It is true that mankind consider the idea of justice and its obligations as applicable to many things which neither are, nor is it desired that they should be, regulated by law. Nobody desires that laws should interfere with the whole detail of private life; yet every one allows that in all daily conduct a person may and does show himself to be either just or unjust. But even here, the idea of the breach of what ought to be law, still lingers in a modified shape. It would always give us pleasure, and chime in with our feelings of fitness, that acts which we deem unjust should

be punished, though we do not always think it expedient that this should be done by the tribunals. We forego that gratification on account of incidental inconveniences. We should be glad to see just conduct enforced and injustice repressed, even in the minutest details, if we were not, with reason, afraid of trusting the magistrate with so unlimited an amount of power over individuals. When we think that a person is bound in justice to do a thing, it is an ordinary form of language to say, that he ought to be compelled to do it. We should be gratified to see the obligation enforced by anybody who had the power. If we see that its enforcement by law would be inexpedient, we lament the impossibility, we consider the impunity given to injustice as an evil, and strive to make amends for it by bringing a strong expression of our own and the public disapprobation to bear upon the offender. Thus the idea of legal constraint is still the generating idea of the notion of justice, though undergoing several transformations before that notion, as it exists in an advanced state of society, becomes complete.

14. The above is, I think, a true account, as far as it goes, of the origin and progressive growth of the idea of justice. But we must observe, that it contains, as yet, nothing to distinguish that obligation from moral obligation in general. For the truth is, that the idea of penal sanction, which is the essence of law, enters not only into the conception of injustice, but into that of any kind of wrong. We do not call anything wrong, unless we mean to imply that a person ought to be punished in some way or other for doing it; if not by law, by the opinion of his fellow creatures; if not by opinion, by the reproaches of his own conscience. This seems the real turning point of the distinction between morality and simple expediency. It is a part of the notion of Duty in every one of its forms, that a person may rightfully be compelled to fulfil it. Duty is a thing which may be *exacted* from a person, as one exacts a debt. Unless we think that it might be exacted from him, we do not call it his duty. Reasons of prudence, or the interest of other

people, may militate against actually exacting it; but the person himself, it is dearly understood, would not be entitled to complain. There are other things, on the contrary, which we wish that people should do, which we like or admire them for doing, perhaps dislike or despise them for not doing, but yet admit that they are not bound to; it is not a case of moral obligation; we do not blame them, that is, we do not think that they are proper objects of punishment. How we come by these ideas of deserving and not deserving punishment, will appear, perhaps, in the sequel; but I think there is no doubt that this distinction lies at the bottom of the notions of right and wrong; that we call any conduct wrong, or employ, instead, some other term of dislike or disparagement, according as we think that the person ought, or ought not, to be punished for it; and we say that it would be right to do so and so, or merely that it would be desirable or laudable, according as we would wish to see the person whom it concerns, compelled, or only persuaded and exhorted, to act in that manner.[1]

15. This, therefore, being the characteristic difference which marks off, not justice, but morality in general, from the remaining provinces of Expediency and Worthiness; the character is still to be sought which distinguishes justice from other branches of morality. Now it is known that ethical writers divide moral duties into two classes, denoted by the ill-chosen expressions, duties of perfect and of imperfect obligation; the latter being those in which, though the act is obligatory, the particular occasions of performing it are left to our choice; as in the case of charity or beneficence, which we are indeed bound to practise, but not towards any definite person, nor at any prescribed time. In the more precise language of philosophic jurists, duties of perfect obligation are those duties in virtue of which a correlative right resides in some person or persons; duties of imperfect obligation are those moral obligations which do not give birth to any right. I think it will be found

that this distinction exactly coincides with that which exists between justice and the other obligations of morality. In our survey of the various popular acceptations of justice, the term appeared generally to involve the idea of a personal right – a claim on the part of one or more individuals, like that which the law gives when it confers a proprietary or other legal right. Whether the injustice consists in depriving a person of a possession, or in breaking faith with him, or in treating him worse than he deserves, or worse than other people who have no greater claims, in each case the supposition implies two things – a wrong done, and some assignable person who is wronged. Injustice may also be done by treating a person better than others; but the wrong in this case is to his competitors, who are also assignable persons. It seems to me that this feature in the case – a right in some person, correlative to the moral obligation – constitutes the specific difference between justice, and generosity or beneficence. Justice implies something which it is not only right to do, and wrong not to do, but which some individual person can claim from us as his moral right. No one has a moral right to our generosity or beneficence, because we are not morally bound to practise those virtues towards any given individual. And it will be found with respect to this as with respect to every correct definition, that the instances which seem to conflict with it are those which most confirm it. For if a moralist attempts, as some have done, to make out that mankind generally, though not any given individual, have a right to all the good we can do them, he at once, by that thesis, includes generosity and beneficence within the category of justice. He is obliged to say, that our utmost exertions are *due* to our fellow creatures, thus assimilating them to a debt; or that nothing less can be a sufficient *return* for what society does for us, thus classing the case as one of gratitude; both of which are acknowledged cases of justice. Wherever there is a right, the case is one of justice, and not of the virtue of beneficence:

and whoever does not place the distinction between justice and morality in general where we have now placed it, will be found to make no distinction between them at all, but to merge all morality in justice.

16. Having thus endeavoured to determine the distinctive elements which enter into the composition of the idea of justice, we are ready to enter on the inquiry, whether the feeling, which accompanies the idea, is attached to it by a special dispensation of nature, or whether it could have grown up, by any known laws, out of the idea itself, and in particular, whether it can have originated in considerations of general expediency.

17. I conceive that the sentiment itself does not arise from anything which would commonly, or correctly, be termed an idea of expediency; but that though, the sentiment does not, whatever is moral in it does.

18. We have seen that the two essential ingredients in the sentiment of justice are, the desire to punish a person who has done harm, and the knowledge or belief that there is some definite individual or individuals to whom harm has been done.

19. Now it appears to me, that the desire to punish a person who has done harm to some individual, is a spontaneous outgrowth from two sentiments, both in the highest degree natural, and which either are or resemble instincts; the impulse of self-defence, and the feeling of sympathy.

20. It is natural to resent, and to repel or retaliate, any harm done or attempted against ourselves, or against those with whom we sympathize. The origin of this sentiment it is not necessary here to discuss. Whether it be an instinct or a result of intelligence, it is, we know, common to all animal nature; for every animal tries to hurt those who have hurt, or who it thinks are about to hurt, itself or its young. Human beings, on this point, only differ from other animals in two particulars. First, in being capable of sympathizing, not solely with their

offspring, or, like some of the more noble animals, with some superior animal who is kind to them, but with all human, and even with all sentient, beings. Secondly, in having a more developed intelligence, which gives a wider range to the whole of their sentiments, whether self-regarding or sympathetic. By virtue of his superior intelligence, even apart from his superior range of sympathy, a human being is capable of apprehending a community of interest between himself and the human society of which he forms a part, such that any conduct which threatens the security of the society generally, is threatening to his own, and calls forth his instinct (if instinct it be) of self-defence. The same superiority of intelligence, joined to the power of sympathizing with human beings generally, enables him to attach himself to the collective idea of his tribe, his country, or mankind, in such a manner that any act hurtful to them rouses his instinct of sympathy, and urges him to resistance.

21. The sentiment of justice, in that one of its elements which consists of the desire to punish, is thus, I conceive, the natural feeling of retaliation or vengeance, rendered by intellect and sympathy applicable to those injuries, that is, to those hurts, which wound us through, or in common with, society at large. This sentiment, in itself, has nothing moral in it; what is moral is, the exclusive subordination of it to the social sympathies, so as to wait on and obey their call. For the natural feeling tends to make us resent indiscriminately whatever any one does that is disagreeable to us; but when moralized by the social feeling, it only acts in the directions conformable to the general good: just persons resenting a hurt to society, though not otherwise a hurt to themselves, and not resenting a hurt to themselves, however painful, unless it be of the kind which society has a common interest with them in the repression of.

22. It is no objection against this doctrine to say, that when we feel our sentiment of justice outraged, we are not thinking of society at large, or of any collective interest, but only of the individual case. It is common enough certainly, though the reverse of commendable, to feel resentment merely because we have suffered pain; but a person whose resentment is really a moral feeling, that is, who considers whether an act is blameable before he allows himself to resent it – such a person, though he may not say expressly to himself that he is standing up for the interest of society, certainly does feel that he is asserting a rule which is for the benefit of others as well as for his own. If he is not feeling this – if he is regarding the act solely as it affects him individually – he is not consciously just; he is not concerning himself about the justice of his actions. This is admitted even by anti-utilitarian moralists. When Kant (as before remarked) propounds as the fundamental principle of morals, "So act, that thy rule of conduct might be adopted as a law by all rational beings," he virtually acknowledges that the interest of mankind collectively, or at least of mankind indiscriminately, must be in the mind of the agent when conscientiously deciding on the morality of the act. Otherwise he uses words without a meaning: for, that a rule even of utter selfishness could not *possibly* be adopted by all rational beings – that there is any insuperable obstacle in the nature of things to its adoption – cannot be even plausibly maintained. To give any meaning to Kant's principle, the sense put upon it must be, that we ought to shape our conduct by a rule which all rational beings might adopt with benefit to their collective interest.

23. To recapitulate: the idea of justice supposes two things; a rule of conduct, and a sentiment which sanctions the rule. The first must be supposed common to all mankind, and intended for their good. The other (the sentiment) is a desire that punishment may be suffered by those who infringe the rule. There is involved, in addition, the conception of some definite person who suffers by the infringement; whose rights (to use the expression appropriated to the case) are violated by it. And the sentiment of justice appears to me to be, the animal desire to repel or retaliate a hurt or damage to oneself, or to those with whom one sympathizes, widened so as to include all persons, by the human capacity of enlarged sympathy, and the human conception of intelligent self-interest. From the latter elements, the feeling derives its morality; from the former, its peculiar impressiveness, and energy of self-assertion.

24. I have, throughout, treated the idea of a *right* residing in the injured person, and violated by the injury, not as a separate element in the composition of the idea and sentiment, but as one of the forms in which the other two elements clothe themselves. These elements are, a hurt to some assignable person or persons on the one hand, and a demand for punishment on the other. An examination of our own minds, I think, will show, that these two things include all that we mean when we speak of violation of a right. When we call anything a person's right, we mean that he has a valid claim on society to protect him in the possession of it, either by the force of law, or by that of education and opinion. If he has what we consider a sufficient claim, on whatever account, to have something guaranteed to him by society, we say that he has a right to it. If we desire to prove that anything does not belong to him by right, we think this done as soon as it is admitted that society ought not to take measures for securing it to him, but should leave it to chance, or to his own exertions. Thus, a person is said to have a right to what he can earn in fair professional competition; because society ought not to allow any other person to hinder him from endeavouring to earn in that manner as much as he can. But he has not a right to three hundred a-year, though he may happen to be earning it; because society is not called on to provide that he shall earn that sum. On the contrary, if he owns ten thousand pounds' three percent stock, he *has* a right to three hundred a-year; because society has come under an obligation to provide him with an income of that amount.

25. To have a right, then, is, I conceive, to have something which society ought to defend me in the possession of. If the objector goes on to ask why it ought, I can give him no other reason than general utility. If that expression does not seem to convey a sufficient feeling of the strength of the obligation, nor to account for the peculiar energy of the feeling, it is because there goes to the composition of the sentiment, not a rational only but also an animal element, the thirst for retaliation; and this thirst derives its intensity, as well as its moral justification, from the extraordinarily important and impressive kind of utility which is concerned. The interest involved is that of security, to every one's feelings the most vital of all interests. Nearly all other earthly benefits are needed by one person, not needed by another; and many of them can, if necessary, be cheerfully foregone, or replaced by something else; but security no human being can possibly do without; on it we depend for all our immunity from evil, and for the whole value of all and every good, beyond the passing moment; since nothing but the gratification of the instant could be of any worth to us, if we could be deprived of everything the next instant by whoever was momentarily stronger than ourselves. Now this most indispensable of all necessaries, after physical nutriment, cannot be had, unless the machinery for providing it is kept unintermittedly in active play. Our notion, therefore, of the claim we have on our fellow-creatures to join in making safe for us the very groundwork of our existence, gathers feelings round it so much more intense than those concerned in any of the more common cases of utility, that the difference in degree (as is often the case in psychology) becomes a real difference in kind. The claim assumes that character of absoluteness, that apparent infinity, and incommensurability with all other considerations, which constitute the distinction between the feeling of right and wrong and that of ordinary expediency and inexpediency. The feelings concerned are so powerful, and we count so

positively on finding a responsive feeling in others (all being alike interested), that *ought* and *should* grow into *must*, and recognized indispensability becomes a moral necessity; analogous to physical, and often not inferior to it in binding force.

26. If the preceding analysis, or something resembling it, be not the correct account of the notion of justice; if justice be totally independent of utility, and be a standard *per se*, which the mind can recognize by simple introspection of itself, it is hard to understand why that internal oracle is so ambiguous, and why so many things appear either just or unjust, according to the light in which they are regarded.

27. We are continually informed that Utility is an uncertain standard, which every different person interprets differently, and that there is no safety but in the immutable, ineffaceable, and unmistakeable dictates of Justice, which carry their evidence in themselves, and are independent of the fluctuations of opinion. One would suppose from this that on questions of justice there could be no controversy; that if we take that for our rule, its application to any given case could leave us in as little doubt as a mathematical demonstration. So far is this from being the fact, that there is as much difference of opinion, and as fierce discussion, about what is just, as about what is useful to society. Not only have different nations and individuals different notions of justice, but, in the mind of one and the same individual, justice is not some one rule, principle, or maxim, but many, which do not always coincide in their dictates, and in choosing between which, he is guided either by some extraneous standard, or by his own personal predilections.

28. For instance, there are some who say, that it is unjust to punish anyone for the sake of example to others; that punishment is just, only when intended for the good of the sufferer himself. Others maintain the extreme reverse, contending that to punish persons who have attained years of discretion, for their own benefit, is despotism and injustice, since if the matter at issue is solely their own good, no one has a right to control their own judgment of it; but that they may justly be punished to prevent evil to others, this being an exercise of the legitimate right of self-defence. Mr Owen, again, affirms that it is unjust to punish at all; for the criminal did not make his own character; his education, and the circumstances which surround him, have made him a criminal, and for these he is not responsible. All these opinions are extremely plausible; and so long as the question is argued as one of justice simply, without going down to the principles which lie under justice and are the source of its authority, I am unable to see how any of these reasoners can be refuted. For, in truth, every one of the three builds upon rules of justice confessedly true. The first appeals to the acknowledged injustice of singling out an individual, and making him a sacrifice, without his consent, for other people's benefit. The second relies on the acknowledged justice of self-defence, and the admitted injustice of forcing one person to conform to another's notions of what constitutes his good. The Owenite invokes the admitted principle that it is unjust to punish anyone for what he cannot help. Each is triumphant so long as he is not compelled to take into consideration any other maxims of justice than the one he has selected; but as soon as their several maxims are brought face to face, each disputant seems to have exactly as much to say for himself as the others. No one of them can carry out his own notion of justice without trampling upon another equally binding. These are difficulties; they have always been felt to be such; and many devices have been invented to turn rather than to overcome them. As a refuge from the last of the three, men imagined what they called the freedom of the will; fancying that they could not justify punishing a man whose will is in a thoroughly hateful state, unless it be supposed to have come into that state through no influence of anterior circumstances. To escape from the other difficulties, a favorite contrivance has been the fiction of a contract, whereby at some unknown period all the members of society engaged to obey the laws, and consented to be punished for any disobedience to them; thereby giving to their legislators the right, which it is assumed they would not otherwise have had, of punishing them, either for their own good or for that of society. This happy thought was considered to get rid of the whole difficulty, and to legitimate the infliction of punishment, in virtue of another received maxim of justice, *volenti non fit injuria*; that is not unjust which is done with the consent of the person who is supposed to be hurt by it. I need hardly remark, that even if the consent were not a mere fiction, this maxim is not superior in authority to the others which it is brought in to supersede. It is, on the contrary, an instructive specimen of the loose and irregular manner in which supposed principles of justice grow up. This particular one evidently came into use as a help to the coarse exigencies of courts of law, which are sometimes obliged to be content with very uncertain presumptions, on account of the greater evils which would often arise from any attempt on their part to cut finer. But even courts of law are not able to adhere consistently to the maxim, for they allow voluntary engagements to be set aside on the ground of fraud, and sometimes on that of mere mistake or misinformation.

29. Again, when the legitimacy of inflicting punishment is admitted, how many conflicting conceptions of justice come to light in discussing the proper apportionment of punishment to offences. No rule on this subject recommends itself so strongly to the primitive and spontaneous sentiment of justice, as the *lex talionis*, an eye for an eye and a tooth for a tooth. Though this principle of the Jewish and of the Mahomedan law has been generally abandoned in Europe as a practical maxim, there is, I suspect, in most minds, a secret hankering after it; and when retribution accidentally falls on an offender in that precise shape, the general feeling of satisfaction evinced, bears witness how natural is the sentiment to which this repayment in kind is acceptable. With many the test of justice in penal infliction is that the punishment should be proportioned to the offence; meaning that it should be exactly measured by the moral guilt of the culprit (whatever be their standard for measuring moral guilt): the consideration, what amount of punishment is necessary to deter from the offence, having nothing to do with the question of justice, in their estimation: while there are others to whom that consideration is all in all; who maintain that it is not just, at least for man, to inflict on a fellow-creature, whatever may be his offences, any amount of suffering beyond the least that will suffice to prevent him from repeating, and others from imitating, his misconduct.

30. To take another example from a subject already once referred to. In a co-operative industrial association, is it just or not that talent or skill should give a title to superior remuneration? On the negative side of the question it is argued, that whoever does the best he can, deserves equally well, and ought not in justice to be put in a position of inferiority for no fault of his own; that superior abilities have already advantages more than enough, in the admiration they excite, the personal influence they command, and the internal sources of satisfaction attending them, without adding to these a superior share of the world's goods; and that society is bound in justice rather to make compensation to the less favoured, for this unmerited inequality of advantages, than to aggravate it. On the contrary side it is contended, that society receives more from the more efficient labourer; that his services being more useful, society owes him a larger return for them; that a greater share of the joint result is actually his work, and not to allow his claim to it is a kind of robbery; that if he is only to receive as much as others, he can only be justly required to produce as much, and to give a smaller amount of time and exertion, proportioned to

his superior efficiency. Who shall decide between these appeals to conflicting principles of justice? Justice has in this case two sides to it, which it is impossible to bring into harmony, and the two disputants have chosen opposite sides; the one looks to what it is just that the individual should receive, the other to what it is just that the community should give. Each, from his own point of view, is unanswerable; and any choice between them, on grounds of justice, must be perfectly arbitrary. Social utility alone can decide the preference.

31. How many, again, and how irreconcilable, are the standards of justice to which reference is made in discussing the repartition of taxation. One opinion is, that payment to the State should be in numerical proportion to pecuniary means. Others think that justice dictates what they term graduated taxation; taking a higher percentage from those who have more to spare. In point of natural justice a strong case might be made for disregarding means altogether, and taking the same absolute sum (whenever it could be got) from every one: as the subscribers to a mess, or to a club, all pay the same sum for the same privileges, whether they can all equally afford it or not. Since the protection (it might be said) of law and government is afforded to, and is equally required by, all, there is no injustice in making all buy it at the same price. It is reckoned justice, not injustice, that a dealer should charge to all customers the same price for the same article, not a price varying according to their means of payment. This doctrine, as applied to taxation, finds no advocates, because it conflicts strongly with men's feelings of humanity and perceptions of social expediency; but the principle of justice which it invokes is as true and as binding as those which can be appealed to against it. Accordingly, it exerts a tacit influence on the line of defence employed for other modes of assessing taxation. People feel obliged to argue that the State does more for the rich than for the poor, as a justification for its taking more from them: though this

is in reality not true, for the rich would be far better able to protect themselves, in the absence of law or government, than the poor, and indeed would probably be successful in converting the poor into their slaves. Others, again, so far defer to the same conception of justice, as to maintain that all should pay an equal capitation tax for the protection of their persons (these being of equal value to all), and an unequal tax for the protection of their property, which is unequal. To this others reply, that the all of one man is as valuable to him as the all of another. From these confusions there is no other mode of extrication than the utilitarian.

32. Is, then, the difference between the Just and the Expedient a merely imaginary distinction? Have mankind been under a delusion in thinking that justice is a more sacred thing than policy, and that the latter ought only to be listened to after the former has been satisfied? By no means. The exposition we have given of the nature and origin of the sentiment, recognizes a real distinction; and no one of those who profess the most sublime contempt for the consequences of actions as an element in their morality, attaches more importance to the distinction than I do. While I dispute the pretensions of any theory which sets up an imaginary standard of justice not grounded on utility, I account the justice which is grounded on utility to be the chief part, and incomparably the most sacred and binding part, of all morality. Justice is a name for certain classes of moral rules, which concern the essentials of human well-being more nearly, and are therefore of more absolute obligation, than any other rules for the guidance of life; and the notion which we have found to be of the essence of the idea of justice, that of a right residing in an individual, implies and testifies to this more binding obligation.

33. The moral rules which forbid mankind to hurt one another (in which we must never forget to include wrongful interference with each other's freedom) are more vital to human well-being than any maxims, however important, which only point out the best mode of managing some department of human affairs. They have also the peculiarity, that they are the main element in determining the whole of the social feelings of mankind. It is their observance which alone preserves peace among human beings: if obedience to them were not the rule, and disobedience the exception, every one would see in every one else a probable enemy, against whom he must be perpetually guarding himself. What is hardly less important, these are the precepts which mankind have the strongest and the most direct inducements for impressing upon one another. By merely giving to each other prudential instruction or exhortation, they may gain, or think they gain, nothing: in inculcating on each other the duty of positive beneficence they have an unmistakeable interest, but far less in degree: a person may possibly not need the benefits of others; but he always needs that they should not do him hurt. Thus the moralities which protect every individual from being harmed by others, either directly or by being hindered in his freedom of pursuing his own good, are at once those which he himself has most at heart, and those which he has the strongest interest in publishing and enforcing by word and deed. It is by a person's observance of these, that his fitness to exist as one of the fellowship of human beings, is tested and decided; for on that depends his being a nuisance or not to those with whom he is in contact. Now it is these moralities primarily, which compose the obligations of justice. The most marked cases of injustice, and those which give the tone to the feeling of repugnance which characterizes the sentiment; are acts of wrongful aggression, or wrongful exercise of power over some one; the next are those which consist in wrongfully withholding from him something which is his due; in both cases, inflicting on him a positive hurt, either in the form of direct suffering, or of the privation of some good which he had reasonable ground, either of a physical or of a social kind, for counting upon.

34. The same powerful motives which command the observance of these primary moralities, enjoin the punishment of those who violate them; and as the impulses of self-defence, of defence of others, and of vengeance, are all called forth against such persons, retribution, or evil for evil, becomes closely connected with the sentiment of justice, and is universally included in the idea. Good for good is also one of the dictates of justice; and this, though its social utility is evident, and though it carries with it a natural human feeling, has not at first sight that obvious connexion with hurt or injury, which, existing in the most elementary cases of just and unjust, is the source of the characteristic intensity of the sentiment. But the connexion, though less obvious, is not less real. He who accepts benefits, and denies a return of them when needed, inflicts a real hurt, by disappointing one of the most natural and reasonable of expectations, and one which he must at least tacitly have encouraged, otherwise the benefits would seldom have been conferred. The important rank, among human evils and wrongs, of the disappointment of expectation, is shown in the fact that it constitutes the principal criminality of two such highly immoral acts as a breach of friendship and a breach of promise. Few hurts which human beings can sustain are greater, and none wound more, than when that on which they habitually and with full assurance relied, fails them in the hour of need; and few wrongs are greater than this mere withholding of good; none excite more resentment, either in the person suffering, or in a sympathizing spectator. The principle, therefore, of giving to each what they deserve, that is, good for good as well as evil for evil, is not only included within the idea of Justice as we have defined it, but is a proper object of that intensity of sentiment, which places the Just, in human estimation, above the simply Expedient.

35. Most of the maxims of justice current in the world, and commonly appealed to in its transactions, are simply instrumental to carrying into effect the principles of justice which we have now spoken of. That a person is only responsible for what he has done voluntarily, or could voluntarily have avoided; that it is unjust to condemn any person unheard; that the punishment ought to be proportioned to the offence, and the like, are maxims intended to prevent the just principle of evil for evil from being perverted to the infliction of evil without that justification. The greater part of these common maxims have come into use from the practice of courts of justice, which have been naturally led to a more complete recognition and elaboration than was likely to suggest itself to others, of the rules necessary to enable them to fulfil their double function, of inflicting punishment when due, and of awarding to each person his right.

36. That first of judicial virtues, impartiality, is an obligation of justice, partly for the reason last mentioned; as being a necessary condition of the fulfilment of the other obligations of justice. But this is not the only source of the exalted rank, among human obligations, of those maxims of equality and impartiality, which, both in popular estimation and in that of the most enlightened, are included among the precepts of justice. In one point of view, they may be considered as corollaries from the principles already laid down. If it is a duty to do to each according to his deserts, returning good for good as well as repressing evil by evil, it necessarily follows that we should treat all equally well (when no higher duty forbids) who have deserved equally well of us, and that society should treat all equally well who have deserved equally well of it, that is, who have deserved equally well absolutely. This is the highest abstract standard of social and distributive justice; towards which all institutions, and the efforts of all virtuous citizens, should be made in the utmost possible degree to converge. But this great moral duty rests upon a still deeper foundation, being a direct emanation from the first principle of morals, and not a mere logical corollary from secondary or derivative doctrines. It is involved in the very meaning of Utility; or the Greatest-Happiness Principle. That principle is a mere form of words without rational signification, unless one person's happiness, supposed equal in degree (with the proper allowance made for kind), is counted for exactly as much as another's. Those conditions being supplied, Bentham's dictum "everybody to count for one, nobody for more than one," might be written under the principle of utility as an explanatory commentary.[2] The equal claim of everybody to happiness in the estimation of the moralist and the legislator, involves an equal claim to all the means of happiness, except in so far as the inevitable conditions of human life, and the general interest, in which that of every individual is included, set limits to the maxim; and those limits ought to be strictly construed. As every other maxim of justice, so this, is by no means applied or held applicable universally; on the contrary, as I have already remarked, it bends to every person's ideas of social expediency. But in whatever case it is deemed applicable at all, it is held to be the dictate of justice. All persons are deemed to have a right to equality of treatment, except when some recognized social expediency requires the reverse. And hence all social inequalities which have ceased to be considered expedient, assume the character not of simple inexpediency, but of injustice, and appear so tyrannical, that people are apt to wonder how they ever could have been tolerated; forgetful that they themselves perhaps tolerate other inequalities under an equally mistaken notion of expediency, the correction of which would make that which they approve seem quite as monstrous as what they have at last learnt to condemn. The entire history of social improvement has been a series of transitions, by which one custom or institution after another, from being a supposed primary necessity of social existence, has passed into the rank of an universally stigmatized injustice and tyranny. So it has been with the distinctions of slaves and freemen, nobles and serfs,

patricians and plebeians; and so it will be, and in part already is, with the aristocracies of colour, race, and sex.

37. It appears from what has been said, that justice is a name for certain moral requirements, which, regarded collectively, stand higher in the scale of social utility, and are therefore of more paramount obligation, than any others; though particular cases may occur in which some other social duty is so important, as to overrule any one of the general maxims of justice. Thus, to save a life, it may not only be allowable, but a duty, to steal, or take by force, the necessary food or medicine, or to kidnap, and compel to officiate the only qualified medical practitioner. In such cases, as we do not call anything justice which is not a virtue, we usually say, not that justice must give way to some other moral principle, but that what is just in ordinary cases is, by reason of that other principle, not just in the particular case. By this useful accommodation of language, the character of indefeasibility attributed to justice is kept up, and we are saved from the necessity of maintaining that there can be laudable injustice.

38. The considerations which have now been adduced resolve, I conceive, the only real difficulty in the utilitarian theory of morals. It has always been evident that all cases of justice are also cases of expediency: the difference is in the peculiar sentiment which attaches to the former, as contradistinguished from the latter. If this characteristic sentiment has been sufficiently accounted for; if there is no necessity to assume for it any peculiarity of origin; if it is simply the natural feeling of resentment, moralized by being made coextensive with the demands of social good; and if this feeling not only does but ought to exist in all the classes of cases to which the idea of justice corresponds; that idea no longer presents itself as a stumbling-block to the utilitarian ethics. Justice remains the appropriate name for certain social utilities which are vastly more important, and therefore more absolute and imperative, than any others are as a class (though not more so than others may be in particular cases); and which, therefore, ought to be, as well as naturally are, guarded by a sentiment not only different in degree, but also in kind; distinguished from the milder feeling which attaches to the mere idea of promoting human pleasure or convenience, at once by the more definite nature of its commands, and by the sterner character of its sanctions.

Notes

1   See this point enforced and illustrated by Professor Bain in an admirable chapter (entitled "The Ethical Emotions, or the Moral Sense"), of the second of the two treatises composing his elaborate and profound work on the Mind.

2   This implication, in the first principle of the utilitarian scheme, of perfect impartiality between persons, is regarded by Mr Herbert Spencer (in his "Social Statics") as a disproof of the pretensions of utility to be a sufficient guide to right; since (he says) the principle of utility presupposes the anterior principle, that everybody has an equal right to happiness. It may be more correctly described as supposing that equal amounts of happiness are equally desirable, whether felt by the same or by different persons. This, however, is not a presupposition; not a premise needful to support the principle of utility, but the very principle itself; for what is the principle of utility, if it be not that "happiness" and "desirable" are synonymous terms? If there is any anterior principle implied, it can be no other than this, that the truths of arithmetic are applicable to the valuation of happiness, as of all other measurable quantities.

[Mr Herbert Spencer, in a private communication on the subject of the preceding Note, objects to being considered an opponent of Utilitarianism, and states that he regards happiness as the ultimate end of morality; but deems that end only partially attainable by empirical generalizations from the observed results of conduct, and completely attainable only by deducing, from the laws of life and the conditions of existence, what kinds of action necessarily tend to produce happiness and what kinds to produce unhappiness. With the exception of the word "necessarily," I have no dissent to express from this doctrine; and (omitting that word) I am not aware that any modern advocate of utilitarianism is of a different opinion. Bentham, certainly, to whom in the *Social Statics* Mr Spencer particularly referred, is, least of all writers, chargeable with unwillingness to deduce the effect of actions on happiness from the laws of human nature and the universal conditions of human life. The common charge against him is of relying too exclusively upon such deductions, and declining altogether to be bound by the generalizations from specific experience which Mr Spencer thinks that utilitarians generally confine themselves to. My own opinion (and, as I collect, Mr Spencer's) is, that in ethics, as in all other branches of scientific study, the consilience of the results of both these processes, each corroborating and verifying the other, is requisite to give to any general proposition the kind and degree of evidence which constitutes scientific proof.]

Chapter 17

John Rawls

A THEORY OF JUSTICE

John Rawls (1921–2002) was the most influential political philosopher of the twentieth century. This excerpt is from his seminal work, *A Theory of Justice* (1971). In it, he argues for two principles of justice which are to govern the "basic structure of society" — one guaranteeing equal basic liberties to all, and another ensuring that inequalities are to the advantage of the least well-off. These principles are based on a hypothetical contract made from behind a veil of ignorance — a position that Rawls argues expresses our understanding of persons as free and equal.

1. The Role of Justice

Justice is the first virtue of social institutions, as truth is of systems of thought. A theory however elegant and economical must be rejected or revised if it is untrue; likewise laws and institutions no matter how efficient and well-arranged must be reformed or abolished if they are unjust. Each person possesses an inviolability founded on justice that even the welfare of society as a whole cannot override. For this reason justice denies that the loss of freedom for some is made right by a greater good shared by others. It does not allow that the sacrifices imposed on a few are outweighed by the larger sum of advantages enjoyed by many. Therefore in a just society the liberties of equal citizenship are taken as settled; the rights secured by justice are not subject to political bargaining or to the calculus of social interests. The only thing that permits us to acquiesce in an erroneous theory is the lack of a better one; analogously, an injustice is tolerable only when it is necessary to avoid an even greater injustice. Being first virtues of human activities, truth and justice are uncompromising.

These propositions seem to express our intuitive conviction of the primacy of justice. No doubt they are expressed too strongly. In any event I wish to inquire whether these contentions or others similar to them are sound, and if so how they can be accounted for. To this end it is necessary to work out a theory of justice in the light of which these assertions can be interpreted and assessed. I shall begin by considering the role of the principles of justice. Let us assume, to fix ideas, that a society is a more or less self-sufficient association of persons who in their relations to one another recognize certain rules of conduct as binding and who for the most part act in accordance with them. Suppose further that these rules specify a system of co-operation designed to advance the good of those taking part in it. Then, although a society is a co-operative venture for mutual advantage, it is typically marked by a conflict as well as by an identity of interests. There is an identity of interests since social co-operation makes possible a better life for all than any would have if each were to live solely by his own efforts. There is a conflict of interests since persons are not indifferent as to how the greater benefits produced by their collaboration are distributed, for in order to pursue their ends they each prefer a larger to a lesser share. A set of principles is required for choosing among the various social arrangements which determine this division of advantages and for underwriting an agreement on the proper distributive shares. These principles are the principles of social justice: they provide a way of assigning rights and duties in the basic institutions of society and they define the appropriate distribution of the benefits and burdens of social co-operation.

[. . .]

3. The Main Idea of the Theory of Justice

My aim is to present a conception of justice which generalizes and carries to a higher level of abstraction the familiar theory of the social contract as found, say, in Locke, Rousseau, and Kant.[1] In order to do this we are not to think of the original contract as one to enter a particular society or to set up a particular form of government. Rather, the guiding idea is that the principles of justice for the basic structure of society are the object of the original agreement. They are the principles that free and rational persons concerned to further their own interests would accept in an initial position of equality as defining the fundamental terms of their association. These principles are to regulate all further agreements; they specify the kinds of social co-operation that can be entered into and the forms of government that can be established. This way of regarding the principles of justice I shall call justice as fairness.

Thus we are to imagine that those who engage in social co-operation choose together, in one joint act, the principles which are to assign basic rights and duties and to determine the division of social benefits. Men are to decide in advance how they are to regulate their claims against one another and what is to be the foundation charter of their society. Just as each person must decide by rational reflection what constitutes his good, that is, the system of ends which it is rational for him to pursue, so a group of persons must decide once and for all what is to count among them as just and unjust. The choice which rational men would make in this hypothetical situation of equal liberty, assuming for the present that this choice problem has a solution, determines the principles of justice.

In justice as fairness the original position of equality corresponds to the state of nature in the traditional theory of the social contract. This original position is not, of course, thought of as an actual historical state of affairs, much less as a primitive condition of culture. It is understood as a purely hypothetical situation characterized so as to lead to a certain conception of justice.[2] Among the essential features of this situation is that no one knows his place in society, his class position or social status, nor does any one know his fortune in the distribution of natural assets and abilities, his intelligence, strength, and the like. I shall even assume that the parties do not know their conceptions of the good or their special psychological propensities. The principles of justice are chosen behind a veil of ignorance. This ensures that no one is advantaged or disadvantaged in the choice of principles by the outcome of natural chance or the contingency of social circumstances. Since all are similarly situated and no one is able to design principles to favor his particular condition, the principles of justice are the result of a fair agreement or bargain. For given the circumstances of the original position, the symmetry of everyone's relations to each other, this initial situation is fair between individuals as moral persons, that is, as rational beings with their own ends and capable, I shall assume, of a sense of justice. The original position is, one might say, the appropriate initial status quo, and thus the fundamental agreements reached in it are fair. This explains the propriety of the name "justice as fairness": it conveys the idea that the principles of justice are agreed to in an initial situation that is fair. The name does not mean that the concepts of justice and fairness are the same, any more than the phrase "poetry as metaphor" means that the concepts of poetry and metaphor are the same.

Justice as fairness begins, as I have said, with one of the most general of all choices which persons might make together, namely, with the choice of the first principles of a conception of justice which is to regulate all subsequent criticism and reform of institutions. Then, having chosen a conception of justice, we can suppose that they are to choose a constitution and a legislature to enact laws, and so on, all in accordance with the principles of justice initially agreed upon. Our social situation is just if it is such that by this sequence of hypothetical agreements we would have contracted into the general system of rules which defines it. Moreover, assuming that the original position does determine a set of principles (that is, that a particular conception of justice would be chosen), it will then be true that whenever social institutions satisfy these principles those engaged in them can say to one another that they are co-operating on terms to which they would agree if they were free and equal persons whose relations with respect to one another were fair. They could all view their arrangements as meeting the stipulations which they would acknowledge in an initial situation that embodies widely accepted and reasonable constraints on the choice of principles. The general recognition of this fact would provide the basis for a public acceptance of the corresponding principles of justice. No society can, of course, be a scheme of co-operation which men enter voluntarily in a literal sense; each person finds himself placed at birth in some particular position in some particular society, and the nature of this position materially affects

his life prospects. Yet a society satisfying the principles of justice as fairness comes as close as a society can to being a voluntary scheme, for it meets the principles which free and equal persons would assent to under circumstances that are fair. In this sense its members are autonomous and the obligations they recognize self-imposed.

One feature of justice as fairness is to think of the parties in the initial situation as rational and mutually disinterested. This does not mean that the parties are egoists, that is, individuals with only certain kinds of interests, say in wealth, prestige, and domination. But they are conceived as not taking an interest in one another's interests.

They are to presume that even their spiritual aims may be opposed, in the way that the aims of those of different religions may be opposed. Moreover, the concept of rationality must be interpreted as far as possible in the narrow sense, standard in economic theory, of taking the most effective means to given ends. I shall modify this concept to some extent, as explained later (§25), but one must try to avoid introducing into it any controversial ethical elements. The initial situation must be characterized by stipulations that are widely accepted.

In working out the conception of justice as fairness one main task clearly is to determine which principles of justice would be chosen in the original position. To do this we must describe this situation in some detail and formulate with care the problem of choice which it presents. These matters I shall take up in the immediately succeeding chapters. It may be observed, however, that once the principles of justice are thought of as arising from an original agreement in a situation of equality, it is an open question whether the principle of utility would be acknowledged. Offhand it hardly seems likely that persons who view themselves as equals, entitled to press their claims upon one another, would agree to a principle which may require lesser life prospects for some simply for the sake of a greater sum of advantages enjoyed by others. Since each desires to protect his interests, his capacity to advance his conception of the good, no one has a reason to acquiesce in an enduring loss for himself in order to bring about a greater net balance of satisfaction. In the absence of strong and lasting benevolent impulses, a rational man would not accept a basic structure merely because it maximized the algebraic sum of advantages irrespective of its permanent effects on his own basic rights and interests. Thus it seems that the principle of utility is incompatible with the conception of social co-operation among equals for mutual advantage. It appears to be inconsistent with the idea of reciprocity implicit in the notion of a well-ordered society. Or, at any rate, so I shall argue.

I shall maintain instead that the persons in the initial situation would choose two rather different principles: the first requires equality in the assignment of basic rights and duties, while the second holds that social and economic inequalities, for example inequalities of wealth and authority, are just only if they result in compensating benefits for everyone, and in particular for the least advantaged members of society. These principles rule out justifying institutions on the grounds that the hardships of some are offset by a greater good in the aggregate. It may be expedient but it is not just that some should have less in order that others may prosper. But there is no injustice in the greater benefits earned by a few provided that the situation of persons not so fortunate is thereby improved. The intuitive idea is that since everyone's well-being depends upon a scheme of co-operation without which no one could have a satisfactory life, the division of advantages should be such as to draw forth the willing co-operation of everyone taking part in it, including those less well situated. Yet this can be expected only if reasonable terms are proposed. The two principles mentioned seem to be a fair agreement on the basis of which those better endowed, or more fortunate in their social

position, neither of which we can be said to deserve, could expect the willing co-operation of others when some workable scheme is a necessary condition of the welfare of all.[3] Once we decide to look for a conception of justice that nullifies the accidents of natural endowment and the contingencies of social circumstance as counters in quest for political and economic advantage, we are led to these principles. They express the result of leaving aside those aspects of the social world that seem arbitrary from a moral point of view.

The problem of the choice of principles, however, is extremely difficult. I do not expect the answer I shall suggest to be convincing to everyone. It is, therefore, worth noting from the outset that justice as fairness, like other contract views, consists of two parts: (1) an interpretation of the initial situation and of the problem of choice posed there, and (2) a set of principles which, it is argued, would be agreed to. One may accept the first part of the theory (or some variant thereof), but not the other, and conversely. The concept of the initial contractual situation may seem reasonable although the particular principles proposed are rejected. To be sure, I want to maintain that the most appropriate conception of this situation does lead to principles of justice contrary to utilitarianism and perfectionism, and therefore that the contract doctrine provides an alternative to these views. Still, one may dispute this contention even though one grants that the contractarian method is a useful way of studying ethical theories and of setting forth their underlying assumptions.

[. . .]

4. The Original Position and Justification

I have said that the original position is the appropriate initial status quo which insures that the fundamental agreements reached in it are fair. This fact yields the name "justice as fairness." It is clear, then, that I want to say that one conception of justice is more reasonable than another, or justifiable with respect to it, if rational persons in the initial situation would choose its principles over those of the other for the role of justice. Conceptions of justice are to be ranked by their acceptability to persons so circumstanced. Understood in this way the question of justification is settled by working out a problem of deliberation: we have to ascertain which principles it would be rational to adopt given the contractual situation. This connects the theory of justice with the theory of rational choice.

If this view of the problem of justification is to succeed, we must, of course, describe in some detail the nature of this choice problem. A problem of rational decision has a definite answer only if we know the beliefs and interests of the parties, their relations with respect to one another, the alternatives between which they are to choose, the procedure whereby they make up their minds, and so on. As the circumstances are presented in different ways, correspondingly different principles are accepted. The concept of the original position, as I shall refer to it, is that of the most philosophically favored interpretation of this initial choice situation for the purposes of a theory of justice.

But how are we to decide what is the most favored interpretation? I assume, for one thing, that there is a broad measure of agreement that principles of justice should be chosen under certain conditions. To justify a particular description of the initial situation one shows that it incorporates these commonly shared presumptions. One argues from widely accepted but weak premises to more specific conclusions. Each of the presumptions should by itself be natural and plausible; some of them may seem innocuous or even trivial. The aim of the contract approach is to establish that taken together they impose significant bounds on acceptable principles of justice. The ideal outcome would be that these conditions determine a unique set of principles; but I shall be satisfied if they suffice to rank the main traditional conceptions of social justice.

One should not be misled, then, by the somewhat unusual conditions which characterize the original position. The idea here is simply to make vivid to ourselves the restrictions that it seems reasonable to impose on arguments for principles of justice, and therefore on these principles themselves. Thus it seems reasonable and generally acceptable that no one should be advantaged or disadvantaged by natural fortune or social circumstances in the choice of principles. It also seems widely agreed that it should be impossible to tailor principles to the circumstances of one's own case. We should insure further that particular inclinations and aspirations, and persons' conceptions of their good do not affect the principles adopted. The aim is to rule out those principles that it would be rational to propose for acceptance, however little the chance of success, only if one knew certain things that are irrelevant from the standpoint of justice. For example, if a man knew that he was wealthy, he might find it rational to advance the principle that various taxes for welfare measures be counted unjust; if he knew that he was poor, he would most likely propose the contrary principle. To represent the desired restrictions one imagines a situation in which everyone is deprived of this sort of information. One excludes the knowledge of those contingencies which sets men at odds and allows them to be guided by their prejudices. In this manner the veil of ignorance is arrived at in a natural way. This concept should cause no difficulty if we keep in mind the constraints on arguments that it is meant to express. At any time we can enter the original position, so to speak, simply by following a certain procedure, namely, by arguing for principles of justice in accordance with these restrictions.

It seems reasonable to suppose that the parties in the original position are equal. That is, all have the same rights in the procedure for choosing principles; each can make proposals, submit reasons for their acceptance, and so on. Obviously the purpose of these conditions is to represent equality between human beings as moral persons, as creatures having a conception of their good and capable of a sense of justice. The basis of equality is taken to be similarity in these two respects. Systems of ends are not ranked in value; and each man is presumed to have the requisite ability to understand and to act upon whatever principles are adopted. Together with the veil of ignorance, these conditions define the principles of justice as those which rational persons concerned to advance their interests would consent to as equals when none are known to be advantaged or disadvantaged by social and natural contingencies.

There is, however, another side to justifying a particular description of the original position. This is to see if the principles which would be chosen match our considered convictions of justice or extend them in an acceptable way. We can note whether applying these principles would lead us to make the same judgments about the basic structure of society which we now make intuitively and in which we have the greatest confidence; or whether, in cases where our present judgments are in doubt and given with hesitation, these principles offer a resolution which we can affirm on reflection. There are questions which we feel sure must be answered in a certain way. For example, we are confident that religious intolerance and racial discrimination are unjust. We think that we have examined these things with care and have reached what we believe is an impartial judgment not likely to be distorted by an excessive attention to our own interests. These convictions are provisional fixed points which we presume any conception of justice must fit. But we have much less assurance as to what is the correct distribution of wealth and authority. Here we may be looking for a way to remove our doubts. We can check an interpretation of the initial situation, then, by the capacity of its principles to accommodate our firmest convictions and to provide guidance where guidance is needed.

In searching for the most favored description of this situation we work from both ends. We begin by describing it so that it represents generally shared and preferably weak conditions. We then see if these conditions are strong enough to yield a significant set of principles. If not, we look for further premises equally reasonable. But if so, and these principles match our considered convictions of justice, then so far well and good. But presumably there will be discrepancies. In this case we have a choice. We can either modify the account of the initial situation or we can revise our existing judgments, for even the judgments we take provisionally as fixed points are liable to revision. By going back and forth, sometimes altering the conditions of the contractual circumstances, at others withdrawing our judgments and conforming them to principle, I assume that eventually we shall find a description of the initial situation that both expresses reasonable conditions and yields principles which match our considered judgments duly pruned and adjusted. This state of affairs I refer to as reflective equilibrium.[4] It is an equilibrium because at last our principles and judgments coincide; and it is reflective since we know to what principles our judgments conform and the premises of their derivation. At the moment everything is in order. But this equilibrium is not necessarily stable. It is liable to be upset by further examination of the conditions which should be imposed on the contractual situation and by particular cases which may lead us to revise our judgments. Yet for the time being we have done what we can to render coherent and to justify our convictions of social justice. We have reached a conception of the original position.

I shall not, of course, actually work through this process. Still, we may think of the interpretation of the original position that I shall present as the result of such a hypothetical course of reflection. It represents the attempt to accommodate within one scheme both reasonable philosophical conditions on principles as well as our considered judgments of justice. In arriving at the favored interpretation of the initial situation there is no point at which an appeal is made to self-evidence in the traditional sense either of general conceptions or particular convictions. I do not claim for the principles of justice proposed that they are necessary truths or derivable from such truths. A conception of justice cannot be deduced from self-evident premises or conditions on principles; instead, its justification is a matter of the mutual support of many considerations, of everything fitting together into one coherent view.

A final comment. We shall want to say that certain principles of justice are justified because they would be agreed to in an initial situation of equality. I have emphasized that this original position is purely hypothetical. It is natural to ask why, if this agreement is never actually entered into, we should take any interest in these principles, moral or otherwise. The answer is that the conditions embodied in the description of the original position are ones that we do in fact accept. Or if we do not, then perhaps we can be persuaded to do so by philosophical reflection. Each aspect of the contractual situation can be given supporting grounds. Thus what we shall do is to collect together into one conception a number of conditions on principles that we are ready upon due consideration to recognize as reasonable. These constraints express what we are prepared to regard as limits on fair terms of social co-operation. One way to look at the idea of the original position, therefore, is to see it as an expository device which sums up the meaning of these conditions and helps us to extract their consequences. On the other hand, this conception is also an intuitive notion that suggests its own elaboration, so that led on by it we are drawn to define more clearly the standpoint from which we can best interpret moral relationships. We need a conception that enables us to envision our objective from afar: the intuitive notion of the original position is to do this for us.[5]

5. Classical Utilitarianism

There are many forms of utilitarianism, and the development of the theory has continued in recent years. I shall not survey these forms here, nor take account of the numerous refinements found in contemporary discussions. My aim is to work out a theory of justice that represents an alternative to utilitarian thought generally and so to all of these different versions of it. I believe that the contrast between the contract view and utilitarianism remains essentially the same in all these cases. Therefore I shall compare justice as fairness with familiar variants of intuitionism, perfectionism, and utilitarianism in order to bring out the underlying differences in the simplest way. With this end in mind, the kind of utilitarianism I shall describe here is the strict classical doctrine which receives perhaps its clearest and most accessible formulation in Sidgwick. The main idea is that society is rightly ordered, and therefore just, when its major institutions are arranged so as to achieve the greatest net balance of satisfaction summed over all the individuals belonging to it.[6]

We may note first that there is, indeed, a way of thinking of society which makes it easy to suppose that the most rational conception of justice is utilitarian. For consider: each man in realizing his own interests is certainly free to balance his own losses against his own gains. We may impose a sacrifice on ourselves now for the sake of a greater advantage later. A person quite properly acts, at least when others are not affected, to achieve his own greatest good, to advance his rational ends as far as possible. Now why should not a society act on precisely the same principle applied to the group and therefore regard that which is rational for one man as right for an association of men? Just as the well-being of a person is constructed from the series of satisfactions that are experienced at different moments in the course of his life, so in very much the same way the well-being of society is to be constructed from the fulfillment of the systems of desires of the many individuals who belong to it. Since the principle for an individual is to advance as far as possible his own welfare, his own system of desires, the principle for society is to advance as far as possible the welfare of the group, to realize to the greatest extent the comprehensive system of desire arrived at from the desires of its members. Just as an individual balances present and future gains against present and future losses, so a society may balance satisfactions and dissatisfactions between different individuals. And so by these reflections one reaches the principle of utility in a natural way: a society is properly arranged when its institutions maximize the net balance of satisfaction. The principle of choice for an association of men is interpreted as an extension of the principle of choice for one man. Social justice is the principle of rational prudence applied to an aggregative conception of the welfare of the group (§ 30).[7]

This idea is made all the more attractive by a further consideration. The two main concepts of ethics are those of the right and the good; the concept of a morally worthy person is, I believe, derived from them. The structure of an ethical theory is, then, largely determined by how it defines and connects these two basic notions. Now it seems that the simplest way of relating them is taken by teleological theories: the good is defined independently from the right, and then the right is defined as that which maximizes the good.[8] More precisely, those institutions and acts are right which of the available alternatives produce the most good, or at least as much good as any of the other institutions and acts open as real possibilities (a rider needed when the maximal class is not a singleton). Teleological theories have a deep intuitive appeal since they seem to embody the idea of rationality. It is natural to think that rationality is maximizing something and that in morals it must be maximizing the good. Indeed, it is tempting to suppose that it is self-evident that things should be arranged so as to lead to the most good.

It is essential to keep in mind that in a teleological theory the good is defined independently from the right. This means two things. First, the theory accounts for our considered judgments as to which things are good (our judgments of value) as a separate class of judgments intuitively distinguishable by common sense, and then proposes the hypothesis that the right is maximizing the good as already specified. Second, the theory enables one to judge the goodness of things without referring to what is right. For example, if pleasure is said to be the sole good, then presumably pleasures can be recognized and ranked in value by criteria that do not presuppose any standards of right, or what we would normally think of as such. Whereas if the distribution of goods is also counted as a good, perhaps a higher order one, and the theory directs us to produce the most good (including the good of distribution among others), we no longer have a teleological view in the classical sense. The problem of distribution falls under the concept of right as one intuitively understands it, and so the theory lacks an independent definition of the good. The clarity and simplicity of classical teleological theories derives largely from the fact that they factor our moral judgments into two classes, the one being characterized separately while the other is then connected with it by a maximizing principle.

Teleological doctrines differ, pretty clearly, according to how the conception of the good is specified. If it is taken as the realization of human excellence in the various forms of culture, we have what may be called perfectionism. This notion is found in Aristotle and Nietzsche, among others. If the good is defined as pleasure, we have hedonism; if as happiness, eudaimonism, and so on. I shall understand the principle of utility in its classical form as defining the good as the satisfaction of desire, or perhaps better, as the satisfaction of rational desire. This accords with the view in all essentials and provides, I believe, a fair interpretation of it. The appropriate terms of social co-operation are settled by whatever in the circumstances will achieve the greatest sum of satisfaction of the rational desires of individuals. It is impossible to deny the initial plausibility and attractiveness of this conception.

The striking feature of the utilitarian view of justice is that it does not matter, except indirectly, how this sum of satisfactions is distributed among individuals any more than it matters, except indirectly, how one man distributes his satisfactions over time. The correct distribution in either case is that which yields the maximum fulfillment. Society must allocate its means of satisfaction whatever these are, rights and duties, opportunities and privileges, and various forms of wealth, so as to achieve this maximum if it can. But in itself no distribution of satisfaction is better than another except that the more equal distribution is to be preferred to break ties.[9] It is true that certain common sense precepts of justice, particularly those which concern the protection of liberties and rights, or which express the claims of desert, seem to contradict this contention. But from a utilitarian standpoint the explanation of these precepts and of their seemingly stringent character is that they are those precepts which experience shows should be strictly respected and departed from only under exceptional circumstances if the sum of advantages is to be maximized.[10] Yet, as with all other precepts, those of justice are derivative from the one end of attaining the greatest balance of satisfaction. Thus there is no reason in principle why the greater gains of some should not compensate for the lesser losses of others; or more importantly, why the violation of the liberty of a few might not be made right by the greater good shared by many. It simply happens that under most conditions, at least in a reasonably advanced stage of civilization, the greatest sum of advantages is not attained in this way. No doubt the strictness of common sense precepts

of justice has a certain usefulness in limiting men's propensities to injustice and to socially injurious actions, but the utilitarian believes that to affirm this strictness as a first principle of morals is a mistake. For just as it is rational for one man to maximize the fulfillment of his system of desires, it is right for a society to maximize the net balance of satisfaction taken over all of its members.

The most natural way, then, of arriving at utilitarianism (although not, of course, the only way of doing so) is to adopt for society as a whole the principle of rational choice for one man. Once this is recognized, the place of the impartial spectator and the emphasis on sympathy in the history of utilitarian thought is readily understood. For it is by the conception of the impartial spectator and the use of sympathetic identification in guiding our imagination that the principle for one man is applied to society. It is this spectator who is conceived as carrying out the required organization of the desires of all persons into one coherent system of desire; it is by this construction that many persons are fused into one. Endowed with ideal powers of sympathy and imagination, the impartial spectator is the perfectly rational individual who identifies with and experiences the desires of others as if these desires were his own. In this way he ascertains the intensity of these desires and assigns them their appropriate weight in the one system of desire the satisfaction of which the ideal legislator then tries to maximize by adjusting the rules of the social system. On this conception of society separate individuals are thought of as so many different lines along which rights and duties are to be assigned and scarce means of satisfaction allocated in accordance with rules so as to give the greatest fulfillment of wants. The nature of the decision made by the ideal legislator is not, therefore, materially different from that of an entrepreneur deciding how to maximize his profit by producing this or that commodity, or that of a consumer deciding how to maximize his satisfaction by the purchase of this or that collection of goods. In each case there is a single person whose system of desires determines the best allocation of limited means. The correct decision is essentially a question of efficient administration. This view of social co-operation is the consequence of extending to society the principle of choice for one man, and then, to make this extension work, conflating all persons into one through the imaginative acts of the impartial sympathetic spectator. Utilitarianism does not take seriously the distinction between persons.

6. Some Related Contrasts

It has seemed to many philosophers, and it appears to be supported by the convictions of common sense, that we distinguish as a matter of principle between the claims of liberty and right on the one hand and the desirability of increasing aggregate social welfare on the other; and that we give a certain priority, if not absolute weight, to the former. Each member of society is thought to have an inviolability founded on justice or, as some say, on natural right, which even the welfare of every one else cannot override. Justice denies that the loss of freedom for some is made right by a greater good shared by others. The reasoning which balances the gains and losses of different persons as if they were one person is excluded. Therefore in a just society the basic liberties are taken for granted and the rights secured by justice are not subject to political bargaining or to the calculus of social interests.

Justice as fairness attempts to account for these common sense convictions concerning the priority of justice by showing that they are the consequence of principles which would be chosen in the original position. These judgments reflect the rational preferences and the initial equality of the contracting parties. Although the utilitarian recognizes that, strictly speaking, his doctrine conflicts with these sentiments of

justice, he maintains that common sense precepts of justice and notions of natural right have but a subordinate validity as secondary rules; they arise from the fact that under the conditions of civilized society there is great social utility in following them for the most part and in permitting violations only under exceptional circumstances. Even the excessive zeal with which we are apt to affirm these precepts and to appeal to these rights is itself granted a certain usefulness, since it counterbalances a natural human tendency to violate them in ways not sanctioned by utility. Once we understand this, the apparent disparity between the utilitarian principle and the strength of these persuasions of justice is no longer a philosophical difficulty. Thus while the contract doctrine accepts our convictions about the priority of justice as on the whole sound, utilitarianism seeks to account for them as a socially useful illusion.

A second contrast is that whereas the utilitarian extends to society the principle of choice for one man, justice as fairness, being a contract view, assumes that the principles of social choice, and so the principles of justice, are themselves the object of an original agreement. There is no reason to suppose that the principles which should regulate an association of men is simply an extension of the principle of choice for one man. On the contrary: if we assume that the correct regulative principle for anything depends on the nature of that thing, and that the plurality of distinct persons with separate systems of ends is an essential feature of human societies, we should not expect the principles of social choice to be utilitarian. To be sure, it has not been shown by anything said so far that the parties in the original position would not choose the principle of utility to define the terms of social co-operation. This is a difficult question which I shall examine later on. It is perfectly possible, from all that one knows at this point, that some form of the principle of utility would be adopted, and therefore that contract theory leads eventually to a deeper and more roundabout justification of utilitarianism. In fact a derivation of this kind is sometimes suggested by Bentham and Edgeworth, although it is not developed by them in any systematic way and to my knowledge it is not found in Sidgwick.[11] For the present I shall simply assume that the persons in the original position would reject the utility principle and that they would adopt instead, for the kinds of reasons previously sketched, the two principles of justice already mentioned. In any case, from the standpoint of contract theory one cannot arrive at a principle of social choice merely by extending the principle of rational prudence to the system of desires constructed by the impartial spectator. To do this is not to take seriously the plurality and distinctness of individuals, nor to recognize as the basis of justice that to which men would consent. Here we may note a curious anomaly. It is customary to think of utilitarianism as individualistic, and certainly there are good reasons for this. The utilitarians were strong defenders of liberty and freedom of thought, and they held that the good of society is constituted by the advantages enjoyed by individuals. Yet utilitarianism is not individualistic, at least when arrived at by the more natural course of reflection, in that, by conflating all systems of desires, it applies to society the principle of choice for one man. And thus we see that the second contrast is related to the first, since it is this conflation, and the principle based upon it, which subjects the rights secured by justice to the calculus of social interests.

The last contrast that I shall mention now is that utilitarianism is a teleological theory whereas justice as fairness is not. By definition, then, the latter is a deontological theory, one that either does not specify the good independently from the right, or does not interpret the right as maximizing the good. (It should be noted that deontological theories are defined as non-teleological ones, not as views that characterize the rightness of institutions and acts independently from their consequences. All ethical doctrines worth our attention take consequences

into account in judging rightness. One which did not would simply be irrational, crazy.) Justice as fairness is a deontological theory in the second way. For if it is assumed that the persons in the original position would choose a principle of equal liberty and restrict economic and social inequalities to those in everyone's interests, there is no reason to think that just institutions will maximize the good. (Here I suppose with utilitarianism that the good is defined as the satisfaction of rational desire.) Of course, it is not impossible that the most good is produced but it would be a coincidence. The question of attaining the greatest net balance of satisfaction never arises in justice as fairness; this maximum principle is not used at all.

There is a further point in this connection. In utilitarianism the satisfaction of any desire has some value in itself which must be taken into account in deciding what is right. In calculating the greatest balance of satisfaction it does not matter, except indirectly, what the desires are for.[12] We are to arrange institutions so as to obtain the greatest sum of satisfactions; we ask no questions about their source or quality but only how their satisfaction would affect the total of well-being. Social welfare depends directly and solely upon the levels of satisfaction or dissatisfaction of individuals. Thus if men take a certain pleasure in discriminating against one another, in subjecting others to a lesser liberty as a means of enhancing their self-respect, then the satisfaction of these desires must be weighed in our deliberations according to their intensity, or whatever, along with other desires. If society decides to deny them fulfillment, or to suppress them, it is because they tend to be socially destructive and a greater welfare can be achieved in other ways.

In justice as fairness, on the other hand, persons accept in advance a principle of equal liberty and they do this without a knowledge of their more particular ends. They implicitly agree, therefore, to conform their conceptions of their good to what the principles of justice require, or at least not to press claims which directly violate them. An individual who finds that he enjoys seeing others in positions of lesser liberty understands that he has no claim whatever to this enjoyment. The pleasure he takes in others' deprivations is wrong in itself: it is a satisfaction which requires the violation of a principle to which he would agree in the original position. The principles of right, and so of justice, put limits on which satisfactions have value; they impose restrictions on what are reasonable conceptions of one's good. In drawing up plans and in deciding on aspirations men are to take these constraints into account. Hence in justice as fairness one does not take men's propensities and inclinations as given, whatever they are, and then seek the best way to fulfill them. Rather, their desires and aspirations are restricted from the outset by the principles of justice which specify the boundaries that men's systems of ends must respect. We can express this by saying that in justice as fairness the concept of right is prior to that of the good. A just social system defines the scope within which individuals must develop their aims, and it provides a framework of rights and opportunities and the means of satisfaction within and by the use of which these ends may be equitably pursued. The priority of justice is accounted for, in part, by holding that the interests requiring the violation of justice have no value. Having no merit in the first place, they cannot override its claims.[13]

This priority of the right over the good in justice as fairness turns out to be a central feature of the conception. It imposes certain criteria on the design of the basic structure as a whole; these arrangements must not tend to generate propensities and attitudes contrary to the two principles of justice (that is, to certain principles which are given from the first a definite content) and they must insure that just institutions are stable. Thus certain initial bounds are placed upon what is good and what forms of character are morally worthy, and so upon what kinds of persons men should be. Now any theory of

justice will set up some limits of this kind, namely, those that are required if its first principles are to be satisfied given the circumstances. Utilitarianism excludes those desires and propensities which if encouraged or permitted would, in view of the situation, lead to a lesser net balance of satisfaction. But this restriction is largely formal, and in the absence of fairly detailed knowledge of the circumstances it does not give much indication of what these desires and propensities are. This is not, by itself, an objection to utilitarianism. It is simply a feature of utilitarian doctrine that it relies very heavily upon the natural facts and contingencies of human life in determining what forms of moral character are to be encouraged in a just society. The moral ideal of justice as fairness is more deeply embedded in the first principles of the ethical theory. This is characteristic of natural rights views (the contractarian tradition) in comparison with the theory of utility.

In setting forth these contrasts between justice as fairness and utilitarianism, I have had in mind only the classical doctrine. This is the view of Bentham and Sidgwick and of the utilitarian economists Edgeworth and Pigou. The kind of utilitarianism espoused by Hume would not serve my purpose; indeed, it is not strictly speaking utilitarian. In his well-known arguments against Locke's contract theory, for example, Hume maintains that the principles of fidelity and allegiance both have the same foundation in utility, and therefore that nothing is gained from basing political obligation on an original contract. Locke's doctrine represents, for Hume, an unnecessary shuffle: one might as well appeal directly to utility.[14] But all Hume seems to mean by utility is the general interests and necessities of society. The principles of fidelity and allegiance derive from utility in the sense that the maintenance of the social order is impossible unless these principles are generally respected. But then Hume assumes that each man stands to gain, as judged by his long-term advantage, when law and government conform to the precepts founded on utility. No mention is made of the gains of some outweighing the disadvantages of others. For Hume, then, utility seems to be identical with some form of the common good; institutions satisfy its demands when they are to everyone's interests, at least in the long run. Now if this interpretation of Hume is correct, there is offhand no conflict with the priority of justice and no incompatibility with Locke's contract doctrine. For the role of equal rights in Locke is precisely to ensure that the only permissible departures from the state of nature are those which respect these rights and serve the common interest. It is clear that all the transformations from the state of nature which Locke approves of satisfy this condition and are such that rational men concerned to advance their ends could consent to them in a state of equality. Hume nowhere disputes the propriety of these constraints. His critique of Locke's contract doctrine never denies, or even seems to recognize, its fundamental contention.

The merit of the classical view as formulated by Bentham, Edgeworth, and Sidgwick is that it clearly recognizes what is at stake, namely, the relative priority of the principles of justice and of the rights derived from these principles. The question is whether the imposition of disadvantages on a few can be outweighed by a greater sum of advantages enjoyed by others; or whether the weight of justice requires an equal liberty for all and permits only those economic and social inequalities which are to each person's interests. Implicit in the contrasts between classical utilitarianism and justice as fairness is a difference in the underlying conceptions of society. In the one we think of a well-ordered society as a scheme of co-operation for reciprocal advantage regulated by principles which persons would choose in an initial situation that is fair, in the other as the efficient administration of social resources to maximize the satisfaction of the system of desire constructed by the impartial spectator from the many individual systems of desires accepted as given. The comparison with classical utilitarianism in its more natural derivation brings out this contrast.

[. . .]

11. Two Principles of Justice

I shall now state in a provisional form the two principles of justice that I believe would be chosen in the original position. In this section I wish to make only the most general comments, and therefore the first formulation of these principles is tentative. As we go on I shall run through several formulations and approximate step by step the final statement to be given much later. I believe that doing this allows the exposition to proceed in a natural way.

The first statement of the two principles reads as follows.

First: each person is to have an equal right to the most extensive basic liberty compatible with a similar liberty for others.

Second: social and economic inequalities are to be arranged so that they are both (a) reasonably expected to be to everyone's advantage, and (b) attached to positions and offices open to all.

There are two ambiguous phrases in the second principle, namely "everyone's advantage" and "open to all." Determining their sense more exactly will lead to a second formulation of the principle in § 13. The final version of the two principles is given in § 46; § 39 considers the rendering of the first principle.

By way of general comment, these principles primarily apply, as I have said, to the basic structure of society. They are to govern the assignment of rights and duties and to regulate the distribution of social and economic advantages. As their formulation suggests, these principles presuppose that the social structure can be divided into two more or less distinct parts, the first principle applying to the one, the second to the other. They distinguish between those aspects of the social system that define and secure the equal liberties of citizenship and those that specify and establish social and economic inequalities. The basic liberties of citizens are, roughly speaking, political liberty (the right to vote and to be eligible for public office) together with freedom of speech and assembly; liberty of conscience and freedom of thought; freedom of the person along with the right to hold (personal) property; and freedom from arbitrary arrest and seizure as defined by the concept of the rule of law. These liberties are all required to be equal by the first principle, since citizens of a just society are to have the same basic rights.

The second principle applies, in the first approximation, to the distribution of income and wealth and to the design of organizations that make use of differences in authority and responsibility, or chains of command. While the distribution of wealth and income need not be equal, it must be to everyone's advantage, and at the same time, positions of authority and offices of command must be accessible to all. One applies the second principle by holding positions open, and then, subject to this constraint, arranges social and economic inequalities so that everyone benefits.

These principles are to be arranged in a serial order with the first principle prior to the second. This ordering means that a departure from the institutions of equal liberty required by the first principle cannot be justified, or compensated for, by greater social and economic advantages. The distribution of wealth and income, and the hierarchies of authority, must be consistent with both the liberties of equal citizenship and equality of opportunity.

It is clear that these principles are rather specific in their content, and their acceptance rests on certain assumptions that I must eventually try to explain and justify. A theory of justice depends upon a theory of society in ways that will become evident as we proceed. For the present, it should be observed that the two

principles (and this holds for all formulations) are a special case of a more general conception of justice that can be expressed as follows.

All social values — liberty and opportunity, income and wealth, and the bases of self-respect — are to be distributed equally unless an unequal distribution of any, or all, of these values is to everyone's advantage.

Injustice, then, is simply inequalities that are not to the benefit of all. Of course, this conception is extremely vague and requires interpretation.

As a first step, suppose that the basic structure of society distributes certain primary goods, that is, things that every rational man is presumed to want. These goods normally have a use whatever a person's rational plan of life. For simplicity, assume that the chief primary goods at the disposition of society are rights and liberties, powers and opportunities, income and wealth. These are the social primary goods. Other primary goods such as health and vigor, intelligence and imagination, are natural goods; although their possession is influenced by the basic structure, they are not so directly under its control. Imagine, then, a hypothetical initial arrangement in which all the social primary goods are equally distributed: everyone has similar rights and duties, and income and wealth are evenly shared. This state of affairs provides a benchmark for judging improvements. If certain inequalities of wealth and organizational powers would make everyone better off than in this hypothetical starting situation, then they accord with the general conception.

Now it is possible, at least theoretically, that by giving up some of their fundamental liberties men are sufficiently compensated by the resulting social and economic gains. The general conception of justice imposes no restrictions on what sort of inequalities are permissible; it only requires that everyone's position be improved. We need not suppose anything so drastic as consenting to a condition of slavery. Imagine instead that men forego certain political rights when the economic returns are significant and their capacity to influence the course of policy by the exercise of these rights would be marginal in any case. It is this kind of exchange which the two principles as stated rule out; being arranged in serial order they do not permit exchanges between basic liberties and economic and social gains. The serial ordering of principles expresses an underlying preference among primary social goods. When this preference is rational so likewise is the choice of these principles in this order.

In developing justice as fairness I shall, for the most part, leave aside the general conception of justice and examine instead the special case of the two principles in serial order. The advantage of this procedure is that from the first the matter of priorities is recognized and an effort made to find principles to deal with it. One is led to attend throughout to the conditions under which the acknowledgment of the absolute weight of liberty with respect to social and economic advantages, as defined by the lexical order of the two principles, would be reasonable. Offhand, this ranking appears extreme and too special a case to be of much interest; but there is more justification for it than would appear at first sight. Furthermore, the distinction between fundamental rights and liberties and economic and social benefits marks a difference among primary social goods that one should try to exploit. It suggests an important division in the social system. Of course, the distinctions drawn and the ordering proposed are bound to be at best only approximations. There are surely circumstances in which they fail. But it is essential to depict clearly the main lines of a reasonable conception of justice; and under many conditions anyway, the two principles in serial order may serve well enough. When necessary we can fall back on the more general conception.

The fact that the two principles apply to institutions has certain consequences. Several points

illustrate this. First of all, the rights and liberties referred to by these principles are those which are defined by the public rules of the basic structure. Whether men are free is determined by the rights and duties established by the major institutions of society. Liberty is a certain pattern of social forms. The first principle simply requires that certain sorts of rules, those defining basic liberties, apply to everyone equally and that they allow the most extensive liberty compatible with a like liberty for all. The only reason for circumscribing the rights defining liberty and making men's freedom less extensive than it might otherwise be is that these equal rights as institutionally defined would interfere with one another.

Another thing to bear in mind is that when principles mention persons, or require that everyone gain from an inequality, the reference is to representative persons holding the various social positions, or offices, or whatever, established by the basic structure. Thus in applying the second principle I assume that it is possible to assign an expectation of well-being to representative individuals holding these positions. This expectation indicates their life prospects as viewed from their social station. In general, the expectations of representative persons depend upon the distribution of rights and duties throughout the basic structure. When this changes, expectations change. I assume, then, that expectations are connected: by raising the prospects of the representative man in one position we presumably increase or decrease the prospects of representative men in other positions. Since it applies to institutional forms, the second principle (or rather the first part of it) refers to the expectations of representative individuals. As I shall discuss below, neither principle applies to distributions of particular goods to particular individuals who may be identified by their proper names. The situation where someone is considering how to allocate certain commodities to needy persons who are known to him is not within the scope of the principles. They are meant to regulate basic institutional arrangements. We must not assume that there is much similarity from the standpoint of justice between an administrative allotment of goods to specific persons and the appropriate design of society. Our common sense intuitions for the former may be a poor guide to the latter.

Now the second principle insists that each person benefit from permissible inequalities in the basic structure. This means that it must be reasonable for each relevant representative man defined by this structure, when he views it as a going concern, to prefer his prospects with the inequality to his prospects without it. One is not allowed to justify differences in income or organizational powers on the ground that the disadvantages of those in one position are outweighed by the greater advantages of those in another. Much less can infringements of liberty be counterbalanced in this way. Applied to the basic structure, the principle of utility would have us maximize the sum of expectations of representative men (weighted by the number of persons they represent, on the classical view); and this would permit us to compensate for the losses of some by the gains of others. Instead, the two principles require that everyone benefit from economic and social inequalities. It is obvious, however, that there are indefinitely many ways in which all may be advantaged when the initial arrangement of equality is taken as a benchmark. How then are we to choose among these possibilities? The principles must

be specified so that they yield a determinate conclusion. I now turn to this problem.

12. Interpretations of the Second Principle

I have already mentioned that since the phrases "everyone's advantage" and "equally open to all" are ambiguous, both parts of the second principle have two natural senses. Because these senses are independent of one another, the principle has four possible meanings. Assuming that the first principle of equal liberty has the same sense throughout, we then have four interpretations of the two principles. These are indicated in the table below.

I shall sketch in turn these three interpretations: the system of natural liberty, liberal equality, and democratic equality. In some respects this sequence is the more intuitive one, but the sequence via the interpretation of natural aristocracy is not without interest and I shall comment on it briefly. In working out justice as fairness, we must decide which interpretation is to be preferred. I shall adopt that of democratic equality, explaining in this chapter what this notion means. The argument for its acceptance in the original position does not begin until the next chapter.

The first interpretation (in either sequence) I shall refer to as the system of natural liberty. In this rendering the first part of the second principle is understood as the principle of efficiency adjusted so as to apply to institutions or, in this

| | "Everyone's advantage" | |
"Equally open"	Principle of efficiency	Difference principle
Equality as careers open to talents	System of Natural Liberty	Natural Aristocracy
Equality as equality of fair opportunity	Liberal Equality	Democratic Equality

case, to the basic structure of society; and the second part is understood as an open social system in which, to use the traditional phrase, careers are open to talents. I assume in all interpretations that the first principle of equal liberty is satisfied and that the economy is roughly a free market system, although the means of production may or may not be privately owned. The system of natural liberty asserts, then, that a basic structure satisfying the principle of efficiency and in which positions are open to those able and willing to strive for them will lead to a just distribution. Assigning rights and duties in this way is thought to give a scheme which allocates wealth and income, authority and responsibility, in a fair way whatever this allocation turns out to be. The doctrine includes an important element of pure procedural justice which is carried over to the other interpretations.

[. . .]

The system of natural liberty selects an efficient distribution roughly as follows. Let us suppose that we know from economic theory that under the standard assumptions defining a competitive market economy, income and wealth will be distributed in an efficient way, and that the particular efficient distribution which results in any period of time is determined by the initial distribution of assets, that is, by the initial distribution of income and wealth, and of natural talents and abilities. With each initial distribution, a definite efficient outcome is arrived at. Thus it turns out that if we are to accept the outcome as just, and not merely as efficient, we must accept the basis upon which over time the initial distribution of assets is determined.

In the system of natural liberty the initial distribution is regulated by the arrangements implicit in the conception of careers open to talents (as earlier defined). These arrangements presuppose a background of equal liberty (as specified by the first principle) and a free market economy. They require a formal equality of opportunity in that all have at least the same

legal rights of access to all advantaged social positions. But since there is no effort to preserve an equality, or similarity, of social conditions, except insofar as this is necessary to preserve the requisite background institutions, the initial distribution of assets for any period of time is strongly influenced by natural and social contingencies. The existing distribution of income and wealth, say, is the cumulative effect of prior distributions of natural assets – that is, natural talents and abilities – as these have been developed or left unrealized, and their use favored or disfavored over time by social circumstances and such chance contingencies as accident and good fortune. Intuitively, the most obvious injustice of the system of natural liberty is that it permits distributive shares to be improperly influenced by these factors so arbitrary from a moral point of view.

The liberal interpretation, as I shall refer to it, tries to correct for this by adding to the requirement of careers open to talents the further condition of the principle of fair equality of opportunity. The thought here is that positions are to be not only open in a formal sense, but that all should have a fair chance to attain them. Offhand it is not clear what is meant, but we might say that those with similar abilities and skills should have similar life chances. More specifically, assuming that there is a distribution of natural assets, those who are at the same level of talent and ability, and have the same willingness to use them, should have the same prospects of success regardless of their initial place in the social system, that is, irrespective of the income class into which they are born. In all sectors of society there should be roughly equal prospects of culture and achievement for everyone similarly motivated and endowed. The expectations of those with the same abilities and aspirations should not be affected by their social class.[15]

The liberal interpretation of the two principles seeks, then, to mitigate the influence of social contingencies and natural fortune on distributive shares. To accomplish this end it is necessary to impose further basic structural conditions on the social system. Free market arrangements must be set within a framework of political and legal institutions which regulates the overall trends of economic events and preserves the social conditions necessary for fair equality of opportunity. The elements of this framework are familiar enough, though it may be worthwhile to recall the importance of preventing excessive accumulations of property and wealth and of maintaining equal opportunities of education for all. Chances to acquire cultural knowledge and skills should not depend upon one's class position, and so the school system, whether public or private, should be designed to even out class barriers.

While the liberal conception seems clearly preferable to the system of natural liberty, intuitively it still appears defective. For one thing, even if it works to perfection in eliminating the influence of social contingencies, it still permits the distribution of wealth and income to be determined by the natural distribution of abilities and talents. Within the limits allowed by the background arrangements, distributive shares are decided by the outcome of the natural lottery; and this outcome is arbitrary from a moral perspective. There is no more reason to permit the distribution of income and wealth to be settled by the distribution of natural assets than by historical and social fortune. Furthermore, the principle of fair opportunity can be only imperfectly carried out, at least as long as the institution of the family exists. The extent to which natural capacities develop and reach fruition is affected by all kinds of social conditions and class attitudes. Even the willingness to make an effort, to try, and so to be deserving in the ordinary sense is itself dependent upon happy family and social circumstances. It is impossible in practice to secure equal chances of achievement and culture for those similarly endowed, and therefore we may want to adopt a principle which recognizes this

fact and also mitigates the arbitrary effects of the natural lottery itself. That the liberal conception fails to do this encourages one to look for another interpretation of the two principles of justice.

Before turning to the conception of democratic equality, we should note that of natural aristocracy. On this view no attempt is made to regulate social contingencies beyond what is required by formal equality of opportunity, but the advantages of persons with greater natural endowments are to be limited to those that further the good of the poorer sectors of society. The aristocratic ideal is applied to a system that is open, at least from a legal point of view, and the better situation of those favored by it is regarded as just only when less would be had by those below, if less were given to those above.[16] In this way the idea of *noblesse oblige* is carried over to the conception of natural aristocracy.

Now both the liberal conception and that of natural aristocracy are unstable. For once we are troubled by the influence of either social contingencies or natural chance on the determination of distributive shares, we are bound, on reflection, to be bothered by the influence of the other. From a moral standpoint the two seem equally arbitrary. So however we move away from the system of natural liberty, we cannot be satisfied short of the democratic conception. This conception I have yet to explain. And, moreover, none of the preceding remarks are an argument for this conception, since in a contract theory all arguments, strictly speaking, are to be made in terms of what it would be rational to choose in the original position. But I am concerned here to prepare the way for the favored interpretation of the two principles so that these criteria, especially the second one, will not strike the reader as too eccentric or bizarre. I have tried to show that once we try to find a rendering of them which treats everyone equally as a moral person, and which does not weight men's share in the benefits and burdens of social co-operation according to their social fortune or their luck in the natural lottery, it is clear that the democratic interpretation is the best choice among the four alternatives. With these comments as a preface, I now turn to this conception.

13. Democratic Equality and the Difference Principle

The democratic interpretation, as the table suggests, is arrived at by combining the principle of fair equality of opportunity with the difference principle. This principle removes the indeterminateness of the principle of efficiency by singling out a particular position from which the social and economic inequalities of the basic structure are to be judged. Assuming the framework of institutions required by equal liberty and fair equality of opportunity, the higher expectations of those better situated are just if and only if they work as part of a scheme which improves the expectations of the least advantaged members of society. The intuitive idea is that the social order is not to establish and secure the more attractive prospects of those better off unless doing so is to the advantage of those less fortunate.

[. . .]

17. The Tendency to Equality

I wish to conclude this discussion of the two principles by explaining the sense in which they express an egalitarian conception of justice. Also I should like to forestall the objection to the principle of fair opportunity that it leads to a callous meritocratic society. In order to prepare the way for doing this, I note several aspects of the conception of justice that I have set out.

First we may observe that the difference principle gives some weight to the considerations singled out by the principle of redress. This is the principle that undeserved inequalities call for redress; and since inequalities of birth and natural endowment are undeserved, these inequalities are to be somehow compensated for.[17] Thus the principle holds that in order to treat all persons equally, to provide genuine equality of opportunity, society must give more attention to those with fewer native assets and to those born into the less favorable social positions. The idea is to redress the bias of contingencies in the direction of equality. In pursuit of this principle greater resources might be spent on the education of the less rather than the more intelligent, at least over a certain time of life, say the earlier years of school.

Now the principle of redress has not to my knowledge been proposed as the sole criterion of justice, as the single aim of the social order. It is plausible as most such principles are only as a prima facie principle, one that is to be weighed in the balance with others. For example, we are to weigh it against the principle to improve the average standard of life, or to advance the common good.[18] But whatever other principles we hold, the claims of redress are to be taken into account. It is thought to represent one of the elements in our conception of justice. Now the difference principle is not of course the principle of redress. It does not require society to try to even out handicaps as if all were expected to compete on a fair basis in the same race. But the difference principle would allocate resources in education, say, so as to improve the long-term expectation of the least favored. If this end is attained by giving more attention to the better endowed, it is permissible; otherwise not. And in making this decision, the value of education should not be assessed solely in terms of economic efficiency and social welfare. Equally if not more important is the role of education in enabling a person to enjoy the culture of his society and to take part in its affairs, and in this way to provide for each individual a secure sense of his own worth.

Thus although the difference principle is not the same as that of redress, it does achieve some of the intent of the latter principle. It transforms the aims of the basic structure so that the total scheme of institutions no longer emphasizes social efficiency and technocratic values. We see then that the difference principle represents, in effect, an agreement to regard the distribution of natural talents as a common asset and to share in the benefits of this distribution whatever it turns out to be. Those who have been favored by nature, whoever they are, may gain from their good fortune only on terms that improve the situation of those who have lost out. The naturally advantaged are not to gain merely because they are more gifted, but only to cover the costs of training and education and for using their endowments in ways that help the less fortunate as well. No one deserves his greater natural capacity nor merits a more favorable starting place in society. But it does not follow that one should eliminate these distinctions. There is another way to deal with them. The basic structure can be arranged so that these contingencies work for the good of the least fortunate. Thus we are led to the difference principle if we wish to set up the social system so that no one gains or loses from his arbitrary place in the distribution of natural assets or his initial position in society without giving or receiving compensating advantages in return.

In view of these remarks we may reject the contention that the ordering of institutions is always defective because the distribution of natural talents and the contingencies of social circumstance are unjust, and this injustice must inevitably carry over to human arrangements. Occasionally this reflection is offered as an excuse for ignoring injustice, as if the refusal to acquiesce in injustice is on a par with being unable to accept death. The natural distribution is neither just nor unjust; nor is it unjust that persons are born into society at some particular position. These are simply natural facts. What is just and unjust is the way that institutions deal with these facts. Aristocratic and caste societies are unjust because they make these contingencies the ascriptive basis for belonging to more or less enclosed and privileged social classes. The

basic structure of these societies incorporates the arbitrariness found in nature. But there is no necessity for men to resign themselves to these contingencies. The social system is not an unchangeable order beyond human control but a pattern of human action. In justice as fairness men agree to share one another's fate. In designing institutions they undertake to avail themselves of the accidents of nature and social circumstance only when doing so is for the common benefit. The two principles are a fair way of meeting the arbitrariness of fortune; and while no doubt imperfect in other ways, the institutions which satisfy these principles are just.

A further point is that the difference principle expresses a conception of reciprocity. It is a principle of mutual benefit. We have seen that, at least when chain connection holds, each representative man can accept the basic structure as designed to advance his interests. The social order can be justified to everyone, and in particular to those who are least favored; and in this sense it is egalitarian. But it seems necessary to consider in an intuitive way how the condition of mutual benefit is satisfied. Consider any two representative men A and B, and let B be the one who is less favored. Actually, since we are most interested in the comparison with the least favored man, let us assume that B is this individual. Now B can accept A's being better off since A's advantages have been gained in ways that improve B's prospects. If A were not allowed his better position, B would be even worse off than he is. The difficulty is to show that A has no grounds for complaint. Perhaps he is required to have less than he might since his having more would result in some loss to B. Now what can be said to the more favored man? To begin with, it is clear that the well-being of each depends on a scheme of social co-operation without which no one could have a satisfactory life. Secondly, we can ask for the willing co-operation of everyone only if the terms of the scheme are reasonable. The difference principle, then, seems to be a fair basis on which those better endowed, or more fortunate in their social circumstances, could expect others to collaborate with them when some workable arrangement is a necessary condition of the good of all.

There is a natural inclination to object that those better situated deserve their greater advantages whether or not they are to the benefit of others. At this point it is necessary to be clear about the notion of desert. It is perfectly true that given a just system of co-operation as a scheme of public rules and the expectations set up by it, those who, with the prospect of improving their condition, have done what the system announces that it will reward are entitled to their advantages. In this sense the more fortunate have a claim to their better situation; their claims are legitimate expectations established by social institutions, and the community is obligated to meet them. But this sense of desert presupposes the existence of the co-operative scheme; it is irrelevant to the question whether in the first place the scheme is to be designed in accordance with the difference principle or some other criterion.

Perhaps some will think that the person with greater natural endowments deserves those assets and the superior character that made their development possible. Because he is more worthy in this sense, he deserves the greater advantages that he could achieve with them. This view, however, is surely incorrect. It seems to be one of the fixed points of our considered judgments that no one deserves his place in the distribution of native endowments, any more than one deserves one's initial starting place in society. The assertion that a man deserves the superior character that enables him to make the effort to cultivate his abilities is equally problematic; for his character depends in large part upon fortunate family and social circumstances for which he can claim no credit. The notion of desert seems not to apply to these cases. Thus the more advantaged representative man cannot say that he deserves and therefore has a right to a scheme of co-operation in which he is permitted to acquire benefits in ways that do not contribute to the welfare of others. There is no basis for his making this claim. From the standpoint of common sense, then, the difference principle appears to be acceptable both to the more advantaged and to the less advantaged individual. Of course, none of this is strictly speaking an argument for the principle, since in a contract theory arguments are made from the point of view of the original position. But these intuitive considerations help to clarify the nature of the principle and the sense in which it is egalitarian. [. . .]

24. The Veil of Ignorance

The idea of the original position is to set up a fair procedure so that any principles agreed to will be just. The aim is to use the notion of pure procedural justice as a basis of theory. Somehow we must nullify the effects of specific contingencies which put men at odds and tempt them to exploit social and natural circumstances to their own advantage. Now in order to do this I assume that the parties are situated behind a veil of ignorance. They do not know how the various alternatives will affect their own particular case and they are obliged to evaluate principles solely on the basis of general considerations.[19]

It is assumed, then, that the parties do not know certain kinds of particular facts. First of all, no one knows his place in society, his class position or social status; nor does he know his fortune in the distribution of natural assets and abilities, his intelligence and strength, and the like. Nor, again, does anyone know his conception of the good, the particulars of his rational plan of life, or even the special features of his psychology such as his aversion to risk or liability to optimism or pessimism. More than this, I assume that the parties do not know the particular circumstances of their own society. That is, they do not know its economic or political situation, or the level of civilization and culture it has been able to achieve. The persons in the original position have no information as to which generation they belong. These broader restrictions on knowledge are appropriate in part because questions of social justice arise between generations as well as within them, for example, the question of the appropriate rate of capital saving and of the conservation of natural resources and the environment of nature. There is also, theoretically anyway, the question of a reasonable genetic policy. In these cases too, in order to carry through the idea of the original position, the parties must not know the contingencies that set them in opposition. They must choose principles the consequences of which they are prepared to live with whatever generation they turn out to belong to.

As far as possible, then, the only particular facts which the parties know is that their society is subject to the circumstances of justice and whatever this implies. It is taken for granted, however, that they know the general facts about human society. They understand political affairs and the principles of economic theory; they know the basis of social organization and the laws of human psychology. Indeed, the parties are presumed to know whatever general facts affect the choice of the principles of justice. There are no limitations on general information, that is, on general laws and theories, since conceptions of justice must be adjusted to the characteristics of the systems of social co-operation which they are to regulate, and there is no reason to rule out these facts. It is, for example, a consideration against a conception of justice that, in view of the laws of moral psychology, men would not acquire a desire to act upon it even when the institutions of their society satisfied it. For in this case there would be difficulty in securing the stability of social co-operation. It is an important feature of a conception of justice that it should generate its own support. That is, its principles should be such that when they are embodied in the basic structure of society men tend to acquire the corresponding sense of justice. Given the principles of moral learning, men develop a desire to act in accordance with its principles. In this case a conception of justice is stable. This kind of general information is admissible in the original position.

The notion of the veil of ignorance raises several difficulties. Some may object that the exclusion of nearly all particular information makes it difficult to grasp what is meant by the original position. Thus it may be helpful to observe that one or more persons can at any time enter this position, or perhaps, better, simulate the deliberations of this hypothetical situation, simply by reasoning in accordance with the appropriate restrictions. In arguing for a conception of justice we must be sure that it is among the permitted alternatives and satisfies the stipulated formal constraints. No considerations can be advanced in its favor unless they would be rational ones for us to urge were we to lack the kind of knowledge that is excluded. The evaluation of principles must proceed in terms of the general consequences of their public recognition and universal application, it being assumed that they will be complied with by everyone. To say that a certain conception of justice would be chosen in the original position is equivalent to saying that rational deliberation satisfying certain conditions and restrictions would reach a certain conclusion. If necessary, the argument to this result could be set out more formally. I shall, however, speak throughout in terms of the notion of the original position. It is more economical and suggestive, and brings out certain essential features that otherwise one might easily overlook.

These remarks show that the original position is not to be thought of as a general assembly which includes at one moment everyone who will live at some time; or, much less, as an assembly of everyone who could live at some time. It is not a gathering of all actual or possible persons. To conceive of the original position in either of these ways is to stretch fantasy too far;

the conception would cease to be a natural guide to intuition. In any case, it is important that the original position be interpreted so that one can at any time adopt its perspective. It must make no difference when one takes up this viewpoint, or who does so: the restrictions must be such that the same principles are always chosen. The veil of ignorance is a key condition in meeting this requirement. It insures not only that the information available is relevant, but that it is at all times the same.

It may be protested that the condition of the veil of ignorance is irrational. Surely, some may object, principles should be chosen in the light of all the knowledge available. There are various replies to this contention. Here I shall sketch those which emphasize the simplifications that need to be made if one is to have any theory at all. To begin with, it is clear that since the differences among the parties are unknown to them, and everyone is equally rational and similarly situated, each is convinced by the same arguments. Therefore, we can view the choice in the original position from the standpoint of one person selected at random. If anyone after due reflection prefers a conception of justice to another, then they all do, and a unanimous agreement can be reached. We can, to make the circumstances more vivid, imagine that the parties are required to communicate with each other through a referee as intermediary, and that he is to announce which alternatives have been suggested and the reasons offered in their support. He forbids the attempt to form coalitions, and he informs the parties when they have come to an understanding. But such a referee is actually superfluous, assuming that the deliberations of the parties must be similar.

Thus there follows the very important consequence that the parties have no basis for bargaining in the usual sense. No one knows his situation in society nor his natural assets, and therefore no one is in a position to tailor principles to his advantage. We might imagine that one of the contractees threatens to hold out unless the others agree to principles favorable to him. But how does he know which principles are especially in his interests? The same holds for the formation of coalitions: if a group were to decide to band together to the disadvantage of the others, they would not know how to favor themselves in the choice of principles. Even if they could get everyone to agree to their proposal, they would have no assurance that it was to their advantage, since they cannot identify themselves either by name or description. The one case where this conclusion fails is that of saving. Since the persons in the original position know that they are contemporaries (taking the present time of entry interpretation), they can favor their generation by refusing to make any sacrifices at all for their successors; they simply acknowledge the principle that no one has a duty to save for posterity. Previous generations have saved or they have not; there is nothing the parties can now do to affect that. So in this instance the veil of ignorance fails to secure the desired result. Therefore I resolve the question of justice between generations in a different way by altering the motivation assumption. But with this adjustment no one is able to formulate principles especially designed to advance his own cause. Whatever his temporal position, each is forced to choose for everyone.[20]

The restrictions on particular information in the original position are, then, of fundamental importance. Without them we would not be able to work out any definite theory of justice at all. We would have to be content with a vague formula stating that justice is what would be agreed to without being able to say much, if anything, about the substance of the agreement itself. The formal constraints of the concept of right, those applying to principles directly, are not sufficient for our purpose. The veil of ignorance makes possible a unanimous choice of a particular conception of justice. Without these limitations on knowledge the bargaining problem of the original position would be hopelessly complicated. Even if theoretically a solution were to exist, we would not, at present anyway, be able to determine it.

The notion of the veil of ignorance is implicit, I think, in Kant's ethics. Nevertheless the problem of defining the knowledge of the parties and of characterizing the alternatives open to them has often been passed over, even by contract theories.

[...]

Now the reasons for the veil of ignorance go beyond mere simplicity. We want to define the original position so that we get the desired solution. If a knowledge of particulars is allowed, then the outcome is biased by arbitrary contingencies. As already observed, to each according to his threat advantage is not a principle of justice. If the original position is to yield agreements that are just, the parties must be fairly situated and treated equally as moral persons. The arbitrariness of the world must be corrected for by adjusting the circumstances of the initial contractual situation. Moreover, if in choosing principles we required unanimity even when there is full information, only a few rather obvious cases could be decided. A conception of justice based on unanimity in these circumstances would indeed be weak and trivial. But once knowledge is excluded, the requirement of unanimity is not out of place and the fact that it can be satisfied is of great importance. It enables us to say of the preferred conception of justice that it represents a genuine reconciliation of interests.

A final comment. For the most part I shall suppose that the parties possess all general information. No general facts are closed to them. I do this mainly to avoid complications. Nevertheless a conception of justice is to be the public basis of the terms of social co-operation. Since common understanding necessitates certain bounds on the complexity of principles, there may likewise be limits on the use of theoretical knowledge in the original position. Now clearly it would be very difficult to classify and to grade for complexity the various sorts of general facts. I shall make no attempt to do this. We do however

recognize an intricate theoretical construction when we meet one. Thus it seems reasonable to say that other things equal one conception of justice is to be preferred to another when it is founded upon markedly simpler general facts, and its choice does not depend upon elaborate calculations in the light of a vast array of theoretically defined possibilities. It is desirable that the grounds for a public conception of justice should be evident to everyone when circumstances permit. This consideration favors, I believe, the two principles of justice over the criterion of utility.

[...]

46. Further Cases of Priority

[...]

I now wish to give the final statement of the two principles of justice for institutions. For the sake of completeness, I shall give a full statement including earlier formulations.

First Principle

Each person is to have an equal right to the most extensive total system of equal basic liberties compatible with a similar system of liberty for all.

Second Principle

Social and economic inequalities are to be arranged so that they are both:

(a) to the greatest benefit of the least advantaged, consistent with the just savings principle, and

(b) attached to offices and positions open to all under conditions of fair equality of opportunity.

First Priority Rule (*The Priority of Liberty*)

The principles of justice are to be ranked in lexical order and therefore liberty can be restricted only for the sake of liberty. There are two cases:

(a)   a less extensive liberty must strengthen the total system of liberty shared by all;
(b)   a less than equal liberty must be acceptable to those with the lesser liberty.

Second Priority Rule (*The Priority of Justice over Efficiency and Welfare*)

The second principle of justice is lexically prior to the principle of efficiency and to that of maximizing the sum of advantages; and fair opportunity is prior to the difference principle. There are two cases:

(a)   an inequality of opportunity must enhance the opportunities of those with the lesser opportunity;
(b)   an excessive rate of saving must on balance mitigate the burden of those bearing this hardship.

General Conception

All social primary goods – liberty and opportunity, income and wealth, and the bases of self-respect – are to be distributed equally unless an unequal distribution of any or all of these goods is to the advantage of the least favored.

By way of comment, these principles and priority rules are no doubt incomplete. Other modifications will surely have to be made, but I shall not further complicate the statement of the principles. It suffices to observe that when we come to nonideal theory, we do not fall back straightway upon the general conception of justice. The lexical ordering of the two principles, and the valuations that this ordering implies, suggest priority rules which seem to be reasonable enough in many cases. By various

examples I have tried to illustrate how these rules can be used and to indicate their plausibility. Thus the ranking of the principles of justice in ideal theory reflects back and guides the application of these principles to nonideal situations. It identifies which limitations need to be dealt with first. The drawback of the general conception of justice is that it lacks the definite structure of the two principles in serial order. In more extreme and tangled instances of nonideal theory there may be no alternative to it. At some point the priority of rules for nonideal cases will fail; and indeed, we may be able to find no satisfactory answer at all. But we must try to postpone the day of reckoning as long as possible, and try to arrange society so that it never comes.

Notes

1   As the text suggests, I shall regard Locke's *Second Treatise of Government*, Rousseau's *The Social Contract*, and Kant's ethical works beginning with *The Foundations of the Metaphysics of Morals* as definitive of the contract tradition. For all of its greatness, Hobbes's *Leviathan* raises special problems. A general historical survey is provided by J. W. Gough, *The Social Contract*, 2nd ed. (Oxford, The Clarendon Press, 1957), and Otto Gierke, *Natural Law and the Theory of Society*, trans. with an introduction by Ernest Barker (Cambridge, The University Press, 1934). A presentation of the contract view as primarily an ethical theory is to be found in G. R. Grice, *The Grounds of Moral Judgment* (Cambridge, The University Press, 1967).

2   Kant is clear that the original agreement is hypothetical. See *The Metaphysics of Morals*, pt. I (*Rechtslehre*), especially §§47, 52; and pt. II of the essay "Concerning the Common Saying: This May Be True in Theory but It Does Not Apply in Practice," in *Kant's Political Writings*, ed. Hans Reiss and trans. by H. B. Nisbet (Cambridge, The University Press, 1970), pp. 73–87. See Georges Vlachos, *La Pensée politique de Kant* (Paris, Presses Universitaires de France, 1962), pp. 326–35; and J. G. Murphy, *Kant: The Philosophy of Right* (London, Macmillan, 1970), pp. 109–12, 133–6, for a further discussion.

3   For the formulation of this intuitive idea I am indebted to Allan Gibbard.

4   The process of mutual adjustment of principles and considered judgments is not peculiar to moral philosophy. See Nelson Goodman, *Fact, Fiction, and Forecast* (Cambridge, Mass., Harvard University Press, 1955), pp. 65–8, for parallel remarks concerning the justification of the principles of deductive and inductive inference.

5   Henri Poincaré remarks: "Il nous faut une faculté qui nous fasse voir le but de loin, et, cette faculté, c'est l'intuition." *La Valeur de la science* (Paris, Flammarion, 1909), p. 27.

6   I shall take Henry Sidgwick's *The Methods of Ethics*, 7th ed. (London, 1907), as summarizing the development of utilitarian moral theory. Book III of his *Principles of Political Economy* (London, 1883) applies this doctrine to questions of economic and social justice, and is a precursor of A. C. Pigou, *The Economics of Welfare* (London, Macmillan, 1920). Sidgwick's *Outlines of the History of Ethics*, 5th ed. (London, 1902), contains a brief history of the utilitarian tradition. We may follow him in assuming, somewhat arbitrarily, that it begins with Shaftesbury's *An Inquiry Concerning Virtue and Merit* (1711) and Hutcheson's *An Inquiry Concerning Moral Good and Evil* (1725). Hutcheson seems to have been the first to state clearly the principle of utility. He says in *Inquiry*, sec. III, §8, that "that action is best, which procures the greatest happiness for the greatest numbers; and that, worst, which, in like manner, occasions misery." Other major eighteenth century works are Hume's *A Treatise of Human Nature* (1739), and *An Enquiry Concerning the Principles of Morals* (1751); Adam Smith's *A Theory of the Moral Sentiments* (1759); and Bentham's *The Principles of Morals and Legislation* (1789). To these we must add the writings of J. S. Mill represented by *Utilitarianism* (1863) and F. Y. Edgeworth's *Mathematical Psychics* (London, 1888).

The discussion of utilitarianism has taken a different turn in recent years by focusing on what we may call the coordination problem and related questions of publicity. This development stems from the essays of R. F. Harrod, "Utilitarianism Revised," *Mind*, vol. 45 (1936); J. D. Mabbott, "Punishment," *Mind*, vol. 48 (1939); Jonathan Harrison, "Utilitarianism, Universalisation, and Our Duty to Be Just," *Proceedings of the Aristotelian Society*, vol. 53 (1952–53); and J. O. Urmson, "The Interpretation of the Philosophy of J. S. Mill," *Philosophical Quarterly*, vol. 3 (1953). See also J. J. C. Smart, "Extreme and Restricted Utilitarianism," *Philosophical Quarterly*, vol. 6 (1956), and his *An Outline of a System of Utilitarian Ethics* (Cambridge, The University Press, 1961). For an account of these matters, see David Lyons, *Forms and Limits of Utilitarianism* (Oxford, The Clarendon Press, 1965); and Allan Gibbard, "Utilitarianisms and Coordination" (dissertation, Harvard University, 1971). The problems raised by these works, as important as they are, I shall leave aside as not bearing directly on the more elementary question of distribution which I wish to discuss.

Finally, we should note here the essays of J. C. Harsanyi, in particular, "Cardinal Utility in Welfare Economics and in the Theory of Risk-Taking," *Journal of Political Economy*, 1953, and "Cardinal Welfare, Individualistic Ethics, and Interpersonal Comparisons of Utility," *Journal of Political Economy*, 1955; and R. B. Brandt, "Some Merits of One Form of Rule-Utilitarianism," *University of Colorado Studies* (Boulder, Colorado, 1967).

7   On this point see also D. P. Gauthier, *Practical Reasoning* (Oxford, Clarendon Press, 1963), pp. 126f. The text elaborates the suggestion found in "Constitutional Liberty and the Concept of Justice," *Nomos VI: Justice*, ed. C. J. Friedrich and J. W. Chapman (New York, Atherton Press, 1963), pp. 124f, which in turn is related to the idea of justice as a higher-order administrative decision. See "Justice as Fairness," *Philosophical Review*, 1958, pp. 185–7. That the principle of social integration is distinct from the principle of personal integration is stated by R. B. Perry, *General Theory of Value* (New York, Longmans, Green, and Company, 1926), pp. 674–7. He attributes the error of overlooking this fact to Emile Durkheim and others with similar views. Perry's conception of social integration is that brought about by a shared and dominant benevolent purpose. See below, §24.

8   Here I adopt W. K. Frankena's definition of teleological theories in *Ethics* (Englewood Cliffs, N.J., Prentice Hall, Inc., 1963), p. 13.

9   On this point see Sidgwick, *The Methods of Ethics*, pp. 416f.

10   See J. S. Mill, *Utilitarianism*, ch. V, last two pars.

11 For Bentham see *The Principles of International Law*, Essay I, in *The Works of Jeremy Bentham*, ed. John Bowring (Edinburgh, 1838–43), vol. II, p. 537; for Edgeworth see *Mathematical Psychics*, pp. 52–56, and also the first pages of "The Pure Theory of Taxation," *Economic Journal*, vol. 7 (1897), where the same argument is presented more briefly.

12 Bentham, *The Principles of Morals and Legislation*, ch. I, sec. IV.

13 The priority of right is a central feature of Kant's ethics. See, for example, *The Critique of Practical Reason*, ch. II, bk. I of *pt. I*, esp. pp. 62–5 of vol. 5 of *Kants Gesammelte Schriften, Preussische Akademie der Wissenschaften* (Berlin, 1913). A clear statement is to be found in "Theory and Practice" (to abbreviate the title), *Political Writings*, pp. 67f.

14 "Of the Original Contract," *Essays: Moral, Political, and Literary*, ed. T. H. Green and T. H. Grose, vol. 1 (London, 1875), pp. 454f.

15 This definition follows Sidgwick's suggestion in *The Methods of Ethics*, p. 285n. See also R. H. Tawney, *Equality* (London, George Allen and Unwin, 1931), ch. II, sec. ii; and B. A. O. Williams, "The Idea of Equality," in *Philosophy, Politics, and Society*, ed. Peter Laslett and W. G. Runciman (Oxford, Basil Blackwell, 1962), pp. 125f.

16 This formulation of the aristocratic ideal is derived from Santayana's account of aristocracy in ch. IV of *Reason and Society* (New York, Charles Scribner, 1905), pp. 109f. He says, for example, "an aristocratic regimen can only be justified by radiating benefit and by proving that were less given to those above, less would be attained by those beneath them." I am indebted to Robert Rodes for pointing out to me that natural aristocracy is a possible interpretation of the two principles of justice and that an ideal feudal system might also try to fulfill the difference principle.

17 See Herbert Spiegelberg, "A Defense of Human Equality," *Philosophical Review*, vol. 53 (1944), pp. 101, 113–123; and D. D. Raphael, "Justice and Liberty," *Proceedings of the Aristotelian Society*, vol. 51 (1950–51), pp. 187f.

18 See, for example, Spiegelberg, pp. 120f.

19 The veil of ignorance is so natural a condition that something like it must have occurred to many. The closest explicit statement of it known to me is found in J. C. Harsanyi, "Cardinal Utility in Welfare Economics and in the Theory of Risk-Taking," *Journal of Political Economy*, vol. 61 (1953). Harsanyi uses it to develop a utilitarian theory.

20 Rousseau, *The Social Contract*, bk. II, ch. IV, par. 5.

1d. POLITICAL LIBERALISM

AS WE HAVE JUST SEEN, the concept of "justice" is absolutely central to the field of political philosophy. And yet, as central as it is, philosophers cannot seem to reach an agreement among themselves regarding what, exactly, it is. They disagree about the moral foundations on which justice rests — whether it is utilitarian or Kantian, theistic or secular. They disagree about how justice relates to other core political values like freedom and equality. And they disagree about what instituting justice requires in terms of concrete public policy — whether it supports the death penalty, the minimum wage, and universal health care, or opposes them. About the only thing philosophers seem able to agree on when it comes to "justice" is how to spell it.

Moreover, this disagreement shows every sign of being not merely transient but *persistent*. Philosophers have been thinking and writing about justice since at least the time of Plato's *Republic*, almost 2,400 years ago. And yet we seem no closer to a consensus now than we were when we started. The natural sciences have progressed by leaps and bounds, giving us not only theoretical advances but practical ones that have made real and significant differences in the quality of our daily lives. Philosophy, in contrast, appears stagnant.

It would be one thing if this disagreement were the result of clearly demonstrable prejudice, ignorance, or irrationality on one side. But things are not that simple. The fact is that reasoning about moral and political matters is *difficult*. As John Rawls would put it in his 1993 book, *Political Liberalism*, such reasoning is marked by the "burdens of judgment" — a set of characteristics that lead even reasonable and conscientious people to disagree. For instance,

a.   The evidence — empirical and scientific — bearing on the case is conflicting and complex, and thus hard to assess and evaluate.

b.   Even where we agree fully about the kinds of considerations that are relevant, we may disagree about their weight, and so arrive at different judgments.

c.   To some extent all our concepts . . . are vague and subject to hard cases; and this indeterminacy means that we must rely on judgment and interpretation (and on judgments about interpretations) within some range (not sharply specifiable) where reasonable persons may differ.

d.   To some extent (how great we cannot tell) the way we assess evidence and weigh moral and political values is shaped by our total experience, our whole life course up to now; and our total experiences must always differ . . .

e.   Often there are different kinds of normative considerations of different force on both sides of an issue and it is difficult to make an overall assessment . . .[1]

The burdens of judgment help to give rise to what Rawls calls "the fact of reasonable pluralism."[2] In a free society, reasonable people will disagree about difficult issues of ethics, religion, and politics, and so society will be marked by a permanent but *reasonable* diversity of such views. Neither philosophers nor ordinary people have settled upon the truth of a single comprehensive worldview to the exclusion of others, and it is a mistake to think that they will.

To some extent, Rawls' thinking in *Political Liberalism* and in his work leading up to it (including the essay reproduced in this section) represents a departure from his earlier thought in *A Theory of Justice*. In that book, and in the excerpts from it reproduced in the previous section, Rawls sought to do essentially the same thing that other political philosophers before him had done — to articulate and defend a particular conception of justice. But as influential as it was, Rawls' account met with precisely the same fate as all previous accounts. It was subject to intense criticism and, ultimately, failed to gain anything close to universal assent among political philosophers. For all its insights, Rawls' theory relied on the same kind of controversial assumptions and inferences as all other theories, and so was subject to the same sort of reasonable dissent as they were.

One of the more influential lines of critique was pursued by Michael Sandel, and is represented in the essay of his reproduced in this section (and developed at greater length in his book, *Liberalism and the Limits of Justice*). According to Sandel, Rawls' theory of justice depended on a variety of dubious Kantian moral and metaphysical assumptions. Once we reject that "idealist metaphysics" and the theory of human personhood to which it gives rise, Rawls' original position and the two principles of justice that follow from it fall too.

It is always a problem when other philosophers find problems with your theory. But it is an *especially* pressing problem for *liberal* political philosophers. For, it seems to be a core tenet of liberalism that a legitimate state will only employ coercion against its citizens in ways that they can be reasonably expected to endorse. It is wrong, for instance, for a state to enforce Catholicism on its citizens — even if Catholicism really is, in fact, the one true religion. It is wrong because other citizens can reasonably reject Catholicism, and we therefore believe that they are entitled to live in accordance with their own religious beliefs. This is part of what it means to say that a liberal state ought to be *neutral*, in some sense — an idea that is explored in greater detail by Gerald Gaus in his contribution to this section.

But how can true neutrality be achieved? Or can it? For Rawls, the guiding idea is that some kind of "overlapping consensus" might be found among all the otherwise conflicting reasonable religious or philosophical doctrines of a liberal society. Such doctrines might disagree about whether there is a God, what the purpose of human life is, whether morality is grounded on pleasure or respect for autonomy, and so on. But suppose they all agree on the conclusion that murder is wrong, and that unnecessary suffering should be avoided. If so, then these ideas are part of the "overlapping consensus," and can be used in generating principles of justice to guide state policy without running afoul of liberal neutrality. A conception of justice that drew for its support only on ideas inherent in the public political culture of a nation would be a *political* conception of justice, not a metaphysical one. It is a theory of justice that presents itself not as *true*, but as "one that can serve as the basis of informed and willing political agreement between citizens viewed as free and equal persons."

In his essay in this section, Rawls takes himself merely to be clarifying the foundations of his original theory of justice, not abandoning it. The two principles of justice he defended in *A Theory of Justice*, Rawls thought, really could be the object of an overlapping consensus, and so the main substantive conclusions of his original book were vindicated.

Gerald Gaus, on the other hand, thinks that a thoroughgoing neutrality is much more radical in its implications. Not only are Rawls' two principles of justice too controversial to command assent from all reasonable persons, almost *everything* the state does in terms of public policy seems to fail the test of liberal neutrality. Thus the consistent liberal is haunted by "the specter of anarchism" — the possibility that *no* coercive state can be legitimate. Gaus ultimately rejects this hypothesis, but even still, the scope of justified coercive power at which he arrives is far, far more limited than that which Rawls was willing to accept.

Notes

1   John Rawls, *Political Liberalism*, pp. 56–57.
2   *Political Liberalism*, pp. 36–37.

Further Reading

Eberle, Christopher J. (2002). *Religious Conviction in Liberal Politics*. Cambridge: Cambridge University Press.

Freeman, S. R. (2007). *Rawls*. London: Routledge.

Galston, William (1980). *Justice and the Human Good*. Chicago: University of Chicago Press.

Gaus, G. F. (2003). *Contemporary Theories of Liberalism: Public Reason as a Post-Enlightenment Project*. London: SAGE Publications Limited.

Gaus, G. (2010). *The Order of Public Reason: A Theory of Freedom and Morality in a Diverse and Bounded World*. Cambridge: Cambridge University Press.

Rawls, J. (1993). *Political Liberalism* (Vol. 4). New York: Columbia University Press.

Rawls, J. (2001). *Justice as Fairness: A Restatement*. Cambridge, MA: Harvard University Press.

Sandel, M. J. (1998). *Liberalism and the Limits of Justice*. Cambridge: Cambridge University Press.

Wall, Steven (1998). *Liberalism, Perfectionism and Restraint*. Cambridge: Cambridge University Press.

Chapter 18

Michael J. Sandel

THE PROCEDURAL REPUBLIC AND THE UNENCUMBERED SELF

Michael Sandel (1953–) is a professor of political philosophy at Harvard University. He is best known as an advocate of communitarianism — a position opposed to what it perceives as the excess individualism of liberalism and one which stresses the importance of community and civil society. In this essay (published in 1984), Sandel criticizes what he sees as the Kantian/Rawlsian foundations of American liberalism, arguing that it is in some way responsible for the detachment many people feel from politics and their communities.

Political philosophy seems often to reside at a distance from the world. Principles are one thing, politics another, and even our best efforts to "live up" to our ideals typically founder on the gap between theory and practice.[1]

But if political philosophy is unrealizable in one sense, it is unavoidable in another. This is the sense in which philosophy inhabits the world from the start; our practices and institutions are embodiments of theory. To engage in a political practice is already to stand in relation to theory.[2] For all our uncertainties about ultimate questions of political philosophy – of justice and value and the nature of the good life – the one thing we know is that we live *some* answer all the time.

In this essay I will try to explore the answer we live now, in contemporary America. What is the political philosophy implicit in our practices and institutions? How does it stand, as philosophy? And how do tensions in the philosophy find expression in our present political condition?

It may be objected that it is a mistake to look for a single philosophy, that we live no "answer," only answers. But a plurality of answers is itself a kind of answer. And the political theory that affirms this plurality is the theory I propose to explore.

The Right and the Good

We might begin by considering a certain moral and political vision. It is a liberal vision, and like most liberal visions gives pride of place to justice, fairness, and individual rights. Its core thesis is this: a just society seeks not to promote any particular ends, but enables its citizens to pursue their own ends, consistent with a similar liberty for all; it therefore must govern by principles that do not presuppose any particular conception of the good. What justifies these regulative principles above all is not that they maximize the general welfare, or cultivate virtue, or otherwise promote the good, but rather that they conform to the concept of *right*, a moral category given prior to the good, and independent of it.

This liberalism says, in other words, that what makes the just society just is not the *telos* or purpose or end at which it aims, but precisely its refusal to choose in advance among competing purposes and ends. In its constitution and its laws, the just society seeks to provide a framework within which its citizens can pursue their own values and ends, consistent with a similar liberty for others.

The ideal I've described might be summed up in the claim that the right is prior to the good, and in two senses: The priority of the right means, first, that individual rights cannot be sacrificed for the sake of the general good (in this it opposes utilitarianism), and second, that the principles of justice that specify these rights cannot be premised on any particular vision of the good life. (In this it opposes teleological conceptions in general.)

This is the liberalism of much contemporary moral and political philosophy, most fully elaborated by Rawls, and indebted to Kant for its philosophical foundations.[3] But I am concerned here less with the lineage of this vision than with what seem to me three striking facts about it.

First, it has a deep and powerful philosophical appeal. Second, despite its philosophical force, the claim for the priority of the right over the good ultimately fails. And third, despite its philosophical failure, this liberal vision is the one by which we live. For us, in late twentieth-century America, it is our vision, the theory most thoroughly embodied in the practices and institutions most central to our public life. And seeing how it goes wrong as philosophy may help us to diagnose our present political condition. So first, its philosophical power; second, its philosophical failure; and third, however briefly, its uneasy embodiment in the world.

But before taking up these three claims, it is worth pointing out a central theme that connects them. And that is a certain conception of the person, of what it is to be a moral agent. Like all political theories, the liberal theory I have described is something more than a set of regulative principles. It is also a view about the way the world is, and the way we move within it. At the heart of this ethic lies a vision of the person that both inspires and undoes it. As I will try to argue now, what make this ethic so compelling, but also, finally, vulnerable, are the promise and the failure of the unencumbered self.

Kantian Foundations

The liberal ethic asserts the priority of right, and seeks principles of justice that do not presuppose any particular conception of the good.[4] This is what Kant means by the supremacy of the moral law, and what Rawls means when he writes that "justice is the first virtue of social institutions."[5] Justice is more than just another value. It provides the framework that *regulates* the play of competing values and ends; it must therefore have a sanction independent of those ends. But it is not obvious where such a sanction could be found.

Theories of justice, and for that matter, ethics, have typically founded their claims on one or another conception of human purposes and ends. Thus, Aristotle said the measure of a *polis* is the good at which it aims, and even J.S. Mill, who in the nineteenth century called "justice the chief part, and incomparably the most binding part of all morality," made justice an instrument of utilitarian ends.[6]

This is the solution Kant's ethic rejects. Different persons typically have different desires and ends, and so any principle derived from them can only be contingent. But the moral law needs a *categorical* foundation, not a contingent one. Even so universal a desire as happiness will not do. People still differ in what happiness consists of, and to install any particular conception as regulative would impose on some the conceptions of others, and so deny at least to some the freedom to choose their *own* conceptions. In any case, to govern ourselves in conformity with desires and inclinations, given as they are by nature or circumstance, is not really to be *self*-governing at all. It is rather a refusal of freedom, a capitulation to determinations given outside us.

According to Kant, the right is "derived entirely from the concept of freedom in the external relationships of human beings, and has nothing to do with the end which all men have by nature [i.e., the aim of achieving happiness] or with the recognized means of attaining this end."[7] As such, it must have a basis prior to all empirical ends. Only when I am governed by principles that do not presuppose any particular ends am I free to pursue my own ends consistent with a similar freedom for all.

But this still leaves the question of what the basis of the right could possibly be. If it must be a basis prior to all purposes and ends, unconditioned even by what Kant calls "the special circumstances of human nature,"[8] where could such a basis conceivably be found? Given the stringent demands of the Kantian ethic, the moral law would seem almost to require a foundation in nothing, for any empirical precondition would undermine its priority. "Duty!" asks Kant at his most lyrical, "What origin is there worthy of thee, and where is to be found the root of thy noble descent which proudly rejects all kinship with the inclinations?"[9]

His answer is that the basis of the moral law is to be found in the *subject*, not the object of practical reason, a subject capable of an autonomous will. No empirical end, but rather "a subject of ends, namely a rational being himself, must be made the ground for all maxims of action."[10] Nothing other than what Kant calls "the subject of all possible ends himself" can give rise to the right, for only this subject is also the subject of an autonomous will. Only this subject could be that "something which elevates man above himself as part of the world of sense" and enables him to participate in an ideal, unconditioned realm wholly independent of our social and psychological inclinations. And only this

thoroughgoing independence can afford us the detachment we need if we are ever freely to choose for ourselves, unconditioned by the vagaries of circumstance.[11]

Who or what exactly is this subject? It is, in a certain sense, *us*. The moral law, after all, is a law we give *ourselves*; we *don't find it*, we will it. That is how it (and we) escape the reign of nature and circumstance and merely empirical ends. But what is important to see is that the "we" who do the willing are not "we" qua particular persons, you and me, each for ourselves – the moral law is not up to us as individuals – but "we" qua participants in what Kant calls "pure practical reason," "we" qua participants in a transcendental subject.

Now what is to guarantee that I am a subject of this kind, capable of exercising pure practical reason? Well, strictly speaking, there *is* no guarantee; the transcendental subject is only a possibility. But it is a possibility I must *presuppose* if I am to think of myself as a free moral agent. Were I wholly an empirical being, I would not be capable of freedom, for every exercise of will would be conditioned by the desire for some object. All choice would be heteronomous choice, governed by the pursuit of some end. My will could never be a first cause, only the effect of some prior cause, the instrument of one or another impulse or inclination. "When we think of ourselves as free," writes Kant, "we transfer ourselves into the intelligible world as members and recognize the autonomy of the will."[12] And so the notion of a subject prior to and independent of experience, such as the Kantian ethic requires, appears not only possible but indispensable, a necessary presupposition of the possibility of freedom.

How does all of this come back to politics? As the subject is prior to its ends, so the right is prior to the good. Society is best arranged when it is governed by principles that do not presuppose any particular conception of the good, for any other arrangement would fail to respect persons as being capable of choice; it would treat them as objects rather than subjects, as means rather than ends in themselves.

We can see in this way how Kant's notion of the subject is bound up with the claim for the priority of right. But for those in the Anglo-American tradition, the transcendental subject will seem a strange foundation for a familiar ethic. Surely, one may think, we can take rights seriously and affirm the primacy of justice without embracing the *Critique of Pure Reason*. This, in any case, is the project of Rawls.

He wants to save the priority of right from the obscurity of the transcendental subject. Kant's idealist metaphysic, for all its moral and political advantage, cedes too much to the transcendent, and wins for justice its primacy only by denying it its human situation. "To develop a viable Kantian conception of justice," Rawls writes, "the force and content of Kant's doctrine must be detached from its background in transcendental idealism" and recast within the "canons of a reasonable empiricism."[13] And so Rawls' project is to preserve Kant's moral and political teaching by replacing Germanic obscurities with a domesticated metaphysic more congenial to the Anglo-American temper. This is the role of the original position.

From Transcendental Subject to Unencumbered Self

The original position tries to provide what Kant's transcendental argument cannot – a foundation for the right that is prior to the good, but still situated in the world. Sparing all but essentials, the original position works like this: It invites us to imagine the principles we would choose to govern our society if we were to choose them in advance, before we knew the particular persons we would be – whether rich or poor, strong or weak, lucky or unlucky – before we knew even our interests or aims or conceptions of the good. These principles – the ones we would choose in that imaginary situation – are the principles of

justice. What is more, if it works, they are principles that do not presuppose any particular ends.

What they *do* presuppose is a certain picture of the person, of the way we must be if we are beings for whom justice is the first virtue. This is the picture of the unencumbered self, a self understood as prior to and independent of purposes and ends.

Now the unencumbered self describes first of all the way we stand toward the things we have, or want, or seek. It means there is always a distinction between the values I *have* and the person I *am*. To identify any characteristics as my aims, ambitions, desires, and so on, is always to imply some subject "me" standing behind them, at a certain distance, and the shape of this "me" must be given prior to any of the aims or attributes I bear. One consequence of this distance is to put the self *itself beyond* the reach of its experience, to secure its identity once and for all. Or to put the point another way, it rules out the possibility of what we might call *constitutive* ends. No role or commitment could define me so completely that I could not understand myself without it. No project could be so essential that turning away from it would call into question the person I am.

For the unencumbered self, what matters above all, what is most essential to our personhood, are not the ends we choose but our capacity to choose them. The original position sums up this central claim about us. "It is not our aims that primarily reveal our nature," writes Rawls, "but rather the principles that we would acknowledge to govern the background conditions under which these aims are to be formed . . . We should therefore reverse the relation between the right and the good proposed by teleological doctrines and view the right as prior."[14]

Only if the self is prior to its ends can the right be prior to the good. Only if my identity is never tied to the aims and interests I may have at any moment can I think of myself as a free and independent agent, capable of choice.

This notion of independence carries consequences for the kind of community of which we are capable. Understood as unencumbered selves, we are of course free to join in voluntary association with others, and so are capable of community in the cooperative sense. What is denied to the unencumbered self is the possibility of membership in any community bound by moral ties antecedent to choice; he cannot belong to any community where the self *itself* could be at stake. Such a community – call it constitutive as against merely cooperative – would engage the identity as well as the interests of the participants, and so implicate its members in a citizenship more thoroughgoing than the unencumbered self can know.

For justice to be primary, then, we must be creatures of a certain kind, related to human circumstance in a certain way. We must stand to our circumstance always at a certain distance, whether as transcendental subjects in the case of Kant, or as unencumbered selves in the case of Rawls. Only in this way can we view ourselves as subjects as well as objects of experience, as agents and not just instruments of the purposes we pursue.

The unencumbered self and the ethic it inspires, taken together, hold out a liberating vision. Freed from the dictates of nature and the sanction of social roles, the human subject is installed as sovereign, cast as the author of the only moral meanings there are. As participants in pure practical reason, or as parties to the original position, we are free to construct principles of justice unconstrained by an order of value antecedently given. And as actual, individual selves, we are free to choose our purposes and ends unbound by such an order, or by custom or tradition or inherited status. So long as they are not unjust, our conceptions of the good carry weight, whatever they are, simply in virtue of our having chosen them. We are, in Rawls' words, "self-originating sources of valid claims."[15]

This is an exhilarating promise, and the liberalism it animates is perhaps the fullest expression of the Enlightenment's quest for the self-defining subject. But is it true? Can we make sense of our moral and political life by the light of the self-image it requires? I do not think we can, and I will try to show why not by arguing first within the liberal project, then beyond it.

Justice and Community

We have focused so far on the foundations of the liberal vision, on the way it derives the principles it defends. Let us turn briefly now to the substance of those principles, using Rawls as our example. Sparing all but essentials once again, Rawls' two principles of justice are these: first, equal basic liberties for all, and second, only those social and economic inequalities that benefit the least-advantaged members of society (the difference principle).

In arguing for these principles, Rawls argues against two familiar alternatives – utilitarianism and libertarianism. He argues against utilitarianism that it fails to take seriously the distinction between persons. In seeking to maximize the general welfare, the utilitarian treats society as whole as if it were a single person; it conflates our many, diverse desires into a single system of desires, and tries to maximize. It is indifferent to the distribution of satisfactions among persons, except insofar as this may affect the overall sum. But this fails to respect our plurality and distinctness. It uses some as means to the happiness of all, and so fails to respect each as an end in himself. While utilitarians may sometimes defend individual rights, their defense must rest on the calculation that respecting those rights will serve utility in the long run. But this calculation is contingent and uncertain. So long as utility is what Mill said it is, "the ultimate appeal on all ethical questions,"[16] individual rights can never be secure. To avoid the danger that their life prospects might one day be sacrificed for the greater good of others, the parties to the original position therefore insist on certain basic liberties for all, and make those liberties prior.

If utilitarians fail to take seriously the distinctness of persons, libertarians go wrong by failing to acknowledge the arbitrariness of fortune. They define as just whatever distribution results from an efficient market economy, and oppose all redistribution on the grounds that people are entitled to whatever they get, so long as they do not cheat or steal or otherwise violate someone's rights in getting it. Rawls opposes this principle on the ground that the distribution of talents and assets and even efforts by which some get more and others get less is arbitrary from a moral point of view, a matter of good luck. To distribute the good things in life on the basis of these differences is not to do justice, but simply to carry over into human arrangements the arbitrariness of social and natural contingency. We deserve, as individuals, neither the talents our good fortune may have brought, nor the benefits that flow from them. We should therefore regard these talents as common assets, and regard one another as common beneficiaries of the rewards they bring. "Those who have been favored by nature, whoever they are, may gain from their good fortune only on terms that improve the situation of those who have lost out . . . In justice as fairness, men agree to share one another's fate."[17,18]

This is the reasoning that leads to the difference principle. Notice how it reveals, in yet another guise, the logic of the unencumbered self. I cannot be said to deserve the benefits that flow from, say, my fine physique and good looks, because they are only accidental, not essential facts about me. They describe attributes I *have*, not the person I *am*, and so cannot give rise to a claim of desert. Being an unencumbered self, this is true of *everything* about me. And so I cannot, as an individual, deserve anything at all.

However jarring to our ordinary understandings this argument may be, the picture so far remains intact; the priority of right, the denial of desert, and the unencumbered self all hang impressively together.

But the difference principle requires more, and it is here that the argument comes undone.

The difference principle begins with the thought, congenial to the unencumbered self, that the assets I have are only accidentally mine. But it ends by assuming that these assets are therefore *common* assets and that society has a prior claim on the fruits of their exercise. But this assumption is without warrant. Simply because I, as an individual, do not have a privileged claim on the assets accidentally residing "here," it does not follow that everyone in the world collectively does. For there is no reason to think that their location in society's province or, for that matter, within the province of humankind, is any *less* arbitrary from a moral point of view. And if their arbitrariness within *me* makes them ineligible to serve *my* ends, there seems no obvious reason why their arbitrariness within any particular society should not make them ineligible to serve that society's ends as well.

To put the point another way, the difference principle, like utilitarianism, is a principle of sharing. As such, it must presuppose some prior moral tie among those whose assets it would deploy and whose efforts it would enlist in a common endeavor. Otherwise, it is simply a formula for using some as means to others' ends, a formula this liberalism is committed to reject.

But on the cooperative vision of community alone, it is unclear what the moral basis for this sharing could be. Short of the constitutive conception, deploying an individual's assets for the sake of the common good would seem an offense against the "plurality and distinctness" of individuals this liberalism seeks above all to secure.

If those whose fate I am required to share really are, morally speaking, *others*, rather than fellow participants in a way of life with which my identity is bound, the difference principle falls prey to the same objections as utilitarianism. Its claim on me is not the claim of a constitutive community whose attachments I acknowledge, but rather the claim of a concatenated collectivity whose entanglements I confront.

What the difference principle requires, but cannot provide, is some way of identifying those among whom the assets I bear are properly regarded as common, some way of seeing ourselves as mutually indebted and morally engaged to begin with. But as we have seen, the constitutive aims and attachments that would save and situate the difference principle are precisely the ones denied to the liberal self; the moral encumbrances and antecedent obligations they imply would undercut the priority of right.

What, then, of those encumbrances? The point so far is that we cannot be persons for whom justice is primary, and also be persons for whom the difference principle is a principle of justice. But which must give way? Can we view ourselves as independent selves, independent in the sense that our identity is never tied to our aims and attachments?

I do not think we can, at least not without cost to those loyalties and convictions whose moral force consists partly in the fact that living by them is inseparable from understanding ourselves as the particular persons we are – as members of this family or community or nation or people, as bearers of that history, as citizens of this republic. Allegiances such as these are more than values I happen to have, and to hold, at a certain distance. They go beyond the obligations I voluntarily incur and the "natural duties" I owe to human beings as such. They allow that to some I owe more than justice requires or even permits, not by reason of agreements I have made but instead in virtue of those more or less enduring attachments and commitments that, taken together, partly define the person I am.

To imagine a person incapable of constitutive attachments such as these is not to conceive an ideally free and rational agent, but to imagine a person wholly without character, without moral depth. For to have character is to know that I move in a history I neither summon nor command, which carries consequences nonetheless for my choices and conduct. It draws me closer to some and more distant from others; it makes some aims more appropriate, others less so. As a self-interpreting being, I am

able to reflect on my history and in this sense to distance myself from it, but the distance is always precarious and provisional, the point of reflection never finally secured outside the history itself. But the liberal ethic puts the self beyond the reach of its experience, beyond deliberation and reflection. Denied the expansive self-understandings that could shape a common life, the liberal self is left to lurch between detachment on the one hand, and entanglement on the other. Such is the fate of the unencumbered self, and its liberating promise.

The Procedural Republic

But before my case can be complete, I need to consider one powerful reply. While it comes from a liberal direction, its spirit is more practical than philosophical. It says, in short, that I am asking too much. It is one thing to seek constitutive attachments in our private lives; among families and friends, and certain tightly knit groups, there may be found a common good that makes justice and rights less pressing. But with public life – at least today, and probably always – it is different. So long as the nation-state is the primary form of political association, talk of constitutive community too easily suggests a darker politics rather than a brighter one; amid echoes of the moral majority, the priority of right, for all its philosophical faults, still seems the safer hope.

This is a challenging rejoinder, and no account of political community in the twentieth century can fail to take it seriously. It is challenging not least because it calls into question the status of political philosophy and its relation to the world. For if my argument is correct, if the liberal vision we have considered is not morally self-sufficient but parasitic on a notion of community it officially rejects, then we should expect to find that the political practice that embodies this vision is not *practically* self-sufficient either – that it must draw on a sense of community it cannot supply and may even undermine. But is that so far from the circumstance we face today? Could it be that through the original position darkly, on the far side of the veil of ignorance, we may glimpse an intimation of our predicament, a refracted vision of ourselves?

How does the liberal vision – and its failure – help us make sense of our public life and its predicament? Consider, to begin, the following paradox in the citizen's relation to the modern welfare state. In many ways, we in the 1980s stand near the completion of a liberal project that has run its course from the New Deal through the Great Society and into the present. But notwithstanding the extension of the franchise and the expansion of individual rights and entitlements in recent decades, there is a widespread sense that, individually and collectively, our control over the forces that govern our lives is receding rather than increasing. This sense is deepened by what appear simultaneously as the power and the powerlessness of the nation-state. One the one hand, increasing numbers of citizens view the state as an overly intrusive presence, more likely to frustrate their purposes than advance them. And yet, despite its unprecedented role in the economy and society, the modern state seems itself disempowered, unable effectively to control the domestic economy, to respond to persisting social ills, or to work America's will in the world.

This is a paradox that has fed the appeals of recent politicians (including Carter and Reagan), even as it has frustrated their attempts to govern. To sort it out, we need to identify the public philosophy implicit in our political practice, and to reconstruct its arrival. We need to trace the advent of the procedural republic, by which I mean a public life animated by the liberal vision and self-image we've considered.

The story of the procedural republic goes back in some ways to the founding of the republic, but is central drama begins to unfold around the turn of the century. As national markets and large-scale enterprise displaced a decentralized economy, the decentralized political forms of the early republic became outmoded as well. If democracy were to survive, the concentration of economic power would have to be met by a similar concentration of political power. But the Progressives understood, or some of them did, that the success of democracy required more than the centralization of government; it also required the nationalization of politics. The primary form of political community had to be a recast on a national scale. For Herbert Croly, writing in 1909, the "nationalizing of American political, economic, and social life" was "an essentially formative and enlightening political transformation." We would become more of a democracy only as we became "more of a nation . . . in ideas, in institutions, and in spirit."[19]

This nationalizing project would be consummated in the New Deal, but for the democratic tradition in America, the embrace of the nation was a decisive departure. From Jefferson to the populists, the party of democracy in American political debate had been, roughly speaking, the party of the provinces, of decentralized power, of small-town and small-scale America. And against them had stood the party of the nation – first Federalists, then Whigs, then the Republicans of Lincoln – a party that spoke for the consolidation of the union. It was thus the historic achievement of the New Deal to unite, in a single party and political program, what Samuel Beer has called "liberalism and the national idea."[20]

What matters for our purpose is that, in the twentieth century, liberalism made its peace with concentrated power. But it was understood at the start that the terms of this peace required a strong sense of national community, morally and politically to underwrite the extended involvements of a modern industrial order. If a virtuous republic of small-scale, democratic communities was no longer a possibility, a national republic seemed democracy's next best hope. This was still, in principle at least, a politics of the common good. It looked to the nation, not as a neutral framework for the play of competing interests, but rather as a formative community, concerned to shape a common life suited to the scale of modern social and economic forms.

But this project failed. By the mid- or late twentieth century, the national republic had run its course. Except for extraordinary moments, such as war, the nation proved too vast a scale across which to cultivate the shared self-understandings necessary to community in the formative, or constitutive sense. And so the gradual shift, in our practices and institutions, from a public philosophy of common purposes to one of fair procedures, from a politics of good to a politics of right, from the national republic to the procedural republic.

Our Present Predicament

A full account of this transition would take a detailed look at the changing shape of political institutions, constitutional interpretation, and the terms of political discourse in the broadest sense. But I suspect we would find in the *practice* of the procedural republic two broad tendencies foreshadowed by its philosophy: first, a tendency to crowd out democratic possibilities; second, a tendency to undercut the kind of community on which it nonetheless depends.

Where liberty in the early republic was understood as a function of democratic institutions and dispersed power,[21] liberty in the procedural republic is defined in opposition to democracy, as an individual's guarantee against what the majority might will. I am free insofar as I am the bearer of rights, where rights are trumps.[22] Unlike the liberty of the early republic, the modern version permits – in fact even requires – concentrated power. This has to do with the universalizing logic of rights. Insofar as I have a right, whether to free speech or a minimum income, its provision cannot be left to the vagaries of local preferences but must be assured at the most comprehensive level of political association. It cannot be one thing in New York and another in Alabama. As rights and entitlements expand, politics is therefore displaced from smaller forms of association and relocated at the most universal form – in our case, the nation. And even as politics flows to the nation, power shifts away from democratic institutions (such as legislatures and political parties) and toward institutions designed to be insulated from democratic pressures, and hence better equipped to dispense and defend individual rights (notably the judiciary and bureaucracy).

These institutional developments may begin to account for the sense of powerlessness that the welfare state fails to address and in some ways doubtless deepens. But it seems to me a further clue to our condition recalls even more directly the predicament of the unencumbered self – lurching, as we left it, between detachment on the one hand, the entanglement on the other. For it is a striking feature of the welfare state that it offers a powerful promise of individual rights, and also demands of its citizens a high measure of mutual engagement. But the self-image that attends the rights cannot sustain the engagement.

As bearers of rights, where rights are trumps, we think of ourselves as freely choosing, individual selves, unbound by obligations antecedent to rights, or to the agreements we make. And yet, as citizens of the procedural republic that secures these rights, we find ourselves implicated willy-nilly in a formidable array of dependencies and expectations we did not choose and increasingly reject.

In our public life, we are more entangled, but less attached, than ever before. It is as though the unencumbered self presupposed by the liberal ethic had begun to come true – less liberated than disempowered, entangled in a network of obligations and involvements unassociated with any act of will, and yet unmediated by those common identifications or expansive self-definitions that would make them tolerable. As the scale of social and political organization has become more comprehensive, the terms of our collective identity have become more fragmented, and the forms of political life have outrun the common purpose needed to sustain them.

Something like this, it seems to me, has been unfolding in America for the past half-century or so. I hope I have said at least enough to suggest the shape a fuller story might take. And I hope in any case to have conveyed a certain view about politics and philosophy and the relation between them — that our practices and institutions are themselves embodiments of theory, and to unravel their predicament is, at least in part, to seek after the self-image of the age.

Notes

1 An excellent example of this view can be found in Samuel Huntington, *American Politics: The Promise of Disharmony* (Cambridge: Harvard University Press, 1981). See especially his discussion of the "ideals versus institutions" gap, pp. 10–12, 39–41, 61–84, 221–62.

2 See, for example, the conceptions of a "practice" advanced by Alasdair MacIntyre and Charles Taylor. MacIntyre, *After Virtue* (Notre Dame: University of Notre Dame Press, 1981), pp. 175–209; Taylor, "Interpretation and the Sciences of Man," *Review of Metaphysics* 25 (1971), pp. 3–51.

3 John Rawls, *A Theory of Justice* (Oxford: Oxford University Press, 1971). Immanuel Kant, *Groundwork of the Metaphysics of Morals*, trans. H. J. Paton (1785; New York: Harper and Row, 1956). Kant, *Critique of Pure Reason*, trans. Norman Kemp Smith (1781, 1787; London: Macmillan, 1929). Kant, *Critique of Practical Reason*, trans. L. W. Beck (1788; Indianapolis: Bobbs-Merrill, 1956). Kant, "On the Common Saying: 'This May Be True in Theory, But It Does Not Apply in Practice,'" in Hans Reiss, ed., *Kant's*

Political Writings (1793; Cambridge: Cambridge University Press, 1970). Other recent versions of the claim for the priority of the right over good can be found in Robert Nozick, *Anarchy, State and Utopia* (New York: Basic Books, 1974); Ronald Dworkin, *Taking Rights Seriously* (London: Duckworth, 1977); Bruce Ackerman, *Social Justice in the Liberal State* (New Haven: Yale University Press, 1980).

4 This section, and the two that follow, summarize arguments developed more fully in Michael Sandel, *Liberalism and the Limits of Justice* (Cambridge: Cambridge University Press, 1982).

5 Rawls (1971), p. 3.

6 John Stuart Mill, *Utilitarianism*, in *The Utilitarians* (1893; Garden City: Doubleday, 1973), p. 465. Mill, *On Liberty*, in *The Utilitarians*, p. 485 (originally published 1849).

7 Kant (1793), p. 73.

8 Kant (1785), p. 92.

9 Kant (1788), p. 89.

10 Kant (1785), p. 105.

11 Kant (1788), p. 89.

12 Kant (1785), p. 121.

13 Rawls, "The Basic Structure as Subject," *American Philosophical Quarterly* 14, No. 2. (1977), p. 165.

14 Rawls (1971), p. 560.

15 Rawls, "Kantian Constructivism in Moral Theory," *Journal of Philosophy* 77 (1980), p. 543.

16 Mill (1849), p. 485.

17 Rawls (1971), pp. 101–2.

18 The account that follows is a tentative formulation of themes requiring more detailed elaboration and support.

19 Croly, *The Promise of American Life* (Indianapolis: Bobbs-Merrill, 1965), pp. 270–3.

20 Beer, "Liberalism and the National Idea," *The Public Interest*, Fall (1966), pp. 70–82.

21 See, for example, Laurence Tribe, *American Constitutional Law* (Mineola: The Foundation Press, 1978), pp. 2–3.

22 See Ronald Dworkin, "Liberalism," in Stuart Hampshire, ed., *Public and Private Morality* (Cambridge: Cambridge University Press, 1978), p. 136.

Chapter 19

John Rawls

JUSTICE AS FAIRNESS
Political Not Metaphysical

John Rawls (1921–2002) was the most influential political philosopher of the twentieth century. He is best known for his 1971 book, *A Theory of Justice*, but after its publication, Rawls' thought began to shift from questions about the *substance* of what justice requires to questions about the *legitimacy* of coercively imposing any particular conception of justice on others who might reasonably disagree with it. This line of thinking led to several important developments and modifications in Rawls' thought, which ultimately found their expression is his important 1993 book, *Political Liberalism*. This essay, published in 1985, sets out Rawls' attempt to show how the core ideas of *A Theory of Justice* can be defended in a way that avoids controversial metaphysical commitments, and draws only upon ideas inherent in the common political culture of a community.

In this discussion I shall make some general remarks about how I now understand the conception of justice that I have called "justice as fairness" (presented in my book *A Theory of Justice*).[1] I do this because it may seem that this conception depends on philosophical claims I should like to avoid, for example, claims to universal truth, or claims about the essential nature and identity of persons. My aim is to explain why it does not. I shall first discuss what I regard as the task of political philosophy at the present time and then briefly survey how the basic intuitive ideas drawn upon in justice as fairness are combined into a political conception of justice for a constitutional democracy. Doing this will bring out how and why this conception of justice avoids certain philosophical and metaphysical claims. Briefly, the idea is that in a constitutional democracy the public conception of justice should be, so far as possible, independent of controversial philosophical and religious doctrines. Thus, to formulate such a conception, we apply the principle of toleration to philosophy itself: the public conception of justice is to be political, not metaphysical. Hence the title.

I want to put aside the question whether the text of *A Theory of Justice* supports different readings than the one I sketch here. Certainly on a number of points I have changed my views, and there are no doubt others on which my views have changed in ways that I am unaware of.[2] I recognize further that certain faults of exposition as well as obscure and ambiguous passages in *A Theory of Justice* invite misunderstanding; but I think these matters need not concern us and I shan't pursue them beyond a few footnote indications. For our purposes here, it suffices first to show how a conception of justice with the structure and content of justice as fairness can be understood as political and not metaphysical, and second, to explain why we should look for such a conception of justice in a democratic society.

I

One thing I failed to say in *A Theory of Justice*, or failed to stress sufficiently, is that justice as fairness is intended as a political conception of justice. While a political conception of justice is, of course, a moral conception, it is a moral conception worked out for a specific kind of subject, namely, for political, social, and economic institutions. In particular, justice as fairness is framed to apply to what I have called the "basic structure" of a modern constitutional democracy.[3] (I shall use "constitutional democracy" and "democratic regime," and similar phrases, interchangeably.) By this structure I mean such a society's main political, social, and economic institutions, and how they fit together into one unified system of social cooperation. Whether justice as fairness can be extended to a general political conception for different kinds of societies existing under different historical and social conditions, or whether it can be extended to a general moral conception, or a significant part thereof, are altogether separate questions. I avoid prejudging these larger questions one way or the other.

It should also be stressed that justice as fairness is not intended as the application of a general moral conception to the basic structure of society, as if this structure were simply another case to which that general moral conception is applied.[4] In this respect justice as fairness differs from traditional moral doctrines, for these are widely regarded as such general conceptions. Utilitarianism is a familiar example, since the principle of utility, however it is formulated, is usually said to hold for all kinds of subjects ranging from the actions of individuals to the law of nations. The essential point is this: as a practical political matter no general moral conception can provide a publicly recognized basis for a conception of justice in a modern democratic state. The social and historical conditions of such a state have their origins in the Wars of Religion following the Reformation and the subsequent development of the principle of toleration, and in the growth of constitutional government and the institutions of large industrial market economies. These conditions profoundly affect the requirements of a workable conception of political justice: such a conception must allow for a diversity of doctrines and the plurality of conflicting, and indeed incommensurable, conceptions of the good affirmed by the members of existing democratic societies.

Finally, to conclude these introductory remarks, since justice as fairness is intended as a political conception of justice for a democratic society, it tries to draw solely upon basic intuitive ideas that are embedded in the political institutions of a constitutional democratic regime and the public traditions of their interpretation. Justice as fairness is a political conception in part because it starts from within a certain political tradition. We hope that this political conception of justice may at least be supported by what we may call an "overlapping consensus," that is, by a consensus that includes all the opposing philosophical and religious doctrines likely to persist and to gain adherents in a more or less just constitutional democratic society.[5]

II

There are, of course, many ways in which political philosophy may be understood, and writers at different times, faced with different political and social circumstances, understand their work differently. Justice as fairness I would now understand as a reasonably systematic and practicable conception of justice for a constitutional democracy, a conception that offers an alternative to the dominant utilitarianism of our tradition of political thought. Its first task is to provide a more secure and acceptable basis for constitutional principles and basic rights and liberties than utilitarianism seems to allow.[6] The need for such a political conception arises in the following way.

There are periods, sometimes long periods, in the history of any society during which certain fundamental questions give rise to sharp and divisive political controversy, and it seems difficult, if not impossible, to find any shared basis of political agreement. Indeed, certain questions may prove intractable and may never be fully settled. One task of political philosophy in a democratic society is to focus on such questions and to examine whether some underlying basis of agreement can be uncovered and a mutually acceptable way of resolving these questions publicly established. Or if these questions cannot be fully settled, as may well be the case, perhaps the divergence of opinion can be narrowed sufficiently so that political cooperation on a basis of mutual respect can still be maintained.[7]

The course of democratic thought over the past two centuries or so makes plain that there is no agreement on the way basic institutions of a constitutional democracy should be arranged if they are to specify and secure the basic rights and liberties of citizens and answer to the claims of democratic equality when citizens are conceived as free and equal persons (as explained in the last three paragraphs of Section III). A deep disagreement exists as to how the values of liberty and equality are best realized in the basic structure of society. To simplify, we may think of this disagreement as a conflict within the tradition of democratic thought itself, between the tradition associated with Locke, which gives greater weight to what Constant called "the liberties of the moderns," freedom of thought and conscience, certain basic rights of the person and of property, and the rule of law, and the tradition associated with Rousseau, which gives greater weight to what Constant called "the liberties of the ancients," the equal political liberties and the values of public life. This is a stylized contrast and historically inaccurate, but it serves to fix ideas.

Justice as fairness tries to adjudicate between these contending traditions, first, by proposing two principles of justice to serve as guidelines for how basic institutions are to realize the values of liberty and equality, and second, by specifying a point of view from which these principles can be seen as more appropriate than other familiar principles of justice to the nature of democratic citizens viewed as free and equal persons. What it means to view citizens as free and equal persons is, of course, a fundamental question and is discussed in the following sections. What must be shown is that a certain arrangement of the basic structure, certain institutional forms, are more appropriate for realizing the values of liberty and equality when citizens are conceived as such persons, that is (very briefly), as having the requisite powers of moral personality that enable them to participate in society viewed as a system of fair cooperation for mutual advantage. So to continue, the two principles of justice (mentioned above) read as follows:

1. Each person has an equal right to a fully adequate scheme of equal basic rights and liberties, which scheme is compatible with a similar scheme for all.
2. Social and economic inequalities are to satisfy two conditions: first, they must be attached to offices and positions open to all under conditions of fair equality of opportunity; and second, they must be to the greatest benefit of the least advantaged members of society.

Each of these principles applies to a different part of the basic structure; and both are concerned not only with basic rights, liberties, and opportunities, but also with the claims of equality; while the second part of the second principle underwrites the worth of these institutional guarantees.[8] The two principles together, when the first is given priority over the second, regulate the basic institutions which realize these values.[9] But these details, although important, are not our concern here.

We must now ask: how might political philosophy find a shared basis for settling such a fundamental question as that of the most appropriate institutional forms for liberty and equality? Of course, it is likely that the most that can be done is to narrow the range of public disagreement. Yet even firmly held convictions gradually change: religious toleration is now accepted, and arguments for persecution are no longer openly professed; similarly, slavery is rejected as inherently unjust, and however much the aftermath of slavery may persist in social practices and unavowed attitudes, no one is willing to defend it. We collect such settled convictions as the belief in religious toleration and the rejection of slavery and try to organize the basic ideas and principles implicit in these convictions into a coherent conception of justice. We can regard these convictions as provisional fixed points which any conception of justice must account for if it is to be reasonable for us. We look, then, to our public political culture itself, including its main institutions and the historical traditions of their interpretation, as the shared fund of implicitly recognized basic ideas and principles. The hope is that these ideas and principles can be formulated clearly enough to be combined into a conception of political justice congenial to our most firmly held convictions. We express this by saying that a political conception of justice, to be acceptable, must be in accordance with our considered convictions, at all levels of generality, on due reflection (or in what I have called "reflective equilibrium").[10]

The public political culture may be of two minds even at a very deep level. Indeed, this must be so with such an enduring controversy as that concerning the most appropriate institutional forms to realize the values of liberty and equality. This suggests that if we are to succeed in finding a basis of public agreement, we must find a new way of organizing familiar ideas and principles into a conception of political justice so that the claims in conflict, as previously understood, are seen in another light. A political conception need not be an original creation but may only articulate familiar intuitive ideas and principles so that they can be recognized as fitting together in a somewhat different way than before. Such a conception may, however, go further than this: it may organize these familiar ideas and principles by means of a more fundamental intuitive idea within the complex structure of which the other familiar intuitive ideas are then systematically connected and related. In justice as fairness, as we shall see in the next section, this more fundamental idea is that of society as a system of fair social cooperation between free and equal persons. The concern of this section is how we might find a public basis of political agreement. The point is that a conception of justice will only be able to achieve this aim if it provides a reasonable way of shaping into one coherent view the deeper bases of agreement embedded in the public political culture of a constitutional regime and acceptable to its most firmly held considered convictions.

Now suppose justice as fairness were to achieve its aim and a publicly acceptable political conception of justice is found. Then this conception provides a publicly recognized point of view from which all citizens can examine before one another whether or not their political and social institutions are just. It enables them to do this by citing what are recognized among them as valid and sufficient reasons singled out by that conception itself. Society's main institutions, and how they fit together into one scheme of social cooperation, can be examined on the same basis by each citizen, whatever that citizen's social position or more particular interests. It should be observed that, on this view, justification is not regarded simply as valid argument from listed premises, even should these premises be true. Rather, justification is addressed to others who disagree with us, and therefore it must always proceed from some consensus, that is, from premises that we and others publicly recognize as true; or better, publicly recognize as acceptable to us for the purpose of establishing a working agreement on the fundamental questions of political justice. It goes without saying that this agreement must be informed and uncoerced, and reached by citizens in ways consistent with their being viewed as free and equal persons.[11]

Thus, the aim of justice as fairness as a political conception is practical, and not metaphysical or epistemological. That is, it presents itself not as a conception of justice that is true, but one that can serve as a basis of informed and willing political agreement between citizens viewed as free and equal persons. This agreement when securely founded in public political and social attitudes sustains the goods of all persons and associations within a just democratic regime. To secure this agreement we try, so far as we can, to avoid disputed philosophical, as well as disputed moral and religious, questions. We do this not because these questions are unimportant or regarded with indifference,[12] but because we think them too important and recognize that there is no way to resolve them politically. The only alternative to a principle of toleration is the autocratic use of state power. Thus, justice as fairness deliberately stays on the surface, philosophically speaking. Given the profound differences in belief and conceptions of the good at least since the Reformation, we must recognize that, just as on questions of religious and moral doctrine, public agreement on the basic questions of philosophy cannot be obtained without the state's infringement of basic liberties. Philosophy as the search for truth about an independent metaphysical and moral order cannot, I believe, provide a workable and shared basis for a political conception of justice in a democratic society.

We try, then, to leave aside philosophical controversies whenever possible, and look for ways to avoid philosophy's longstanding problems. Thus, in what I have called "Kantian constructivism," we try to avoid the problem of truth and the controversy between realism and subjectivism about the status of moral and political values. This form of constructivism neither asserts nor denies these doctrines.[13] Rather, it recasts ideas from the tradition of the social contract to achieve a practicable conception of objectivity and justification founded on public agreement in judgment on due reflection. The aim is free agreement, reconciliation through public reason. And similarly, as we shall see (in Section V), a conception of the person in a political view, for example, the conception of citizens as free and equal persons, need not involve, so I believe, questions of philosophical psychology or a metaphysical doctrine of the nature of the self. No political view that depends on these deep and unresolved matters can serve as a public conception of justice in a constitutional democratic state. As I have said, we must apply the principle of toleration to philosophy itself. The hope is that, by this method of avoidance, as we might call it, existing differences between contending political views can at least be moderated, even if not entirely removed, so that social cooperation on the basis of mutual respect can be maintained. Or if this is expecting too much, this method may enable us to conceive how, given a desire for free and uncoerced agreement, a public understanding could arise consistent with the historical conditions and constraints of our social world. Until we bring ourselves to conceive how this could happen, it can't happen.

III

Let's now survey briefly some of the basic ideas that make up justice as fairness in order to show that these ideas belong to a political conception of justice. As I have indicated, the overarching fundamental intuitive idea, within which other basic intuitive ideas are systematically connected, is that of society as a fair system of cooperation between free and equal persons. Justice as fairness starts from this idea as one of the basic intuitive ideas which we take to be implicit in the public culture of a democratic society.[14] In their political thought, and in the context of public discussion of political questions, citizens do not view the social order as a fixed natural order, or as an institutional hierarchy justified by religious or aristocratic values. Here it is important to stress that from other points of view, for example, from the point of view of personal morality, or from the point of view of members of an association, or of one's religious or philosophical doctrine, various aspects of the world and one's relation to it may be regarded in a different way. But these other points of view are not to be introduced into political discussion.

We can make the idea of social cooperation more specific by noting three of its elements:

1. Cooperation is distinct from merely socially coordinated activity, for example, from activity coordinated by orders issued by some central authority. Cooperation is guided by publicly recognized rules and procedures which those who are cooperating accept and regard as properly regulating their conduct.

2. Cooperation involves the idea of fair terms of cooperation: these are terms that each participant may reasonably accept, provided that everyone else likewise accepts them. Fair terms of cooperation specify an idea of reciprocity or mutuality: all who are engaged in cooperation and who do their part as the rules and procedures require are to benefit in some appropriate way as assessed by a suitable benchmark of comparison. A conception of political justice characterizes the fair terms of social cooperation. Since the primary subject of justice is the basic structure of society, this is accomplished in

justice as fairness by formulating principles that specify basic rights and duties within the main institutions of society, and by regulating the institutions of background justice over time so that the benefits produced by everyone's efforts are fairly acquired and divided from one generation to the next.

3. The idea of social cooperation requires an idea of each participant's rational advantage, or good. This idea of good specifies what those who are engaged in cooperation, whether individuals, families, or associations, or even nation-states, are trying to achieve, when the scheme is viewed from their own standpoint.

Now consider the idea of the person.[15] There are, of course, many aspects of human nature that can be singled out as especially significant depending on our point of view. This is witnessed by such expressions as *homo politicus, homo oeconomicus, homo faber*, and the like. Justice as fairness starts from the idea that society is to be conceived as a fair system of cooperation and so it adopts a conception of the person to go with this idea. Since Greek times, both in philosophy and law, the concept of the person has been understood as the concept of someone who can take part in, or who can play a role in, social life, and hence exercise and respect its various rights and duties. Thus, we say that a person is someone who can be a citizen, that is, a fully cooperating member of society over a complete life. We add the phrase "over a complete life" because a society is viewed as a more or less complete and self-sufficient scheme of cooperation, making room within itself for all the necessities and activities of life, from birth until death. A society is not an association for more limited purposes; citizens do not join society voluntarily but are born into it, where, for our aims here, we assume they are to lead their lives.

Since we start within the tradition of democratic thought, we also think of citizens as free and equal persons. The basic intuitive idea is that in virtue of what we may call their moral powers, and the powers of reason, thought, and judgment connected with those powers, we say that persons are free. And in virtue of their having these powers to the requisite degree to be fully cooperating members of society, we say that persons are equal.[16] We can elaborate this conception of the person as follows. Since persons can be full participants in a fair system of social cooperation, we ascribe to them the two moral powers connected with the elements in the idea of social cooperation noted above: namely, a capacity for a sense of justice and a capacity for a conception of the good. A sense of justice is the capacity to understand, to apply, and to act from the public conception of justice which characterizes the fair terms of social cooperation. The capacity for a conception of the good is the capacity to form, to revise, and rationally to pursue a conception of one's rational advantage, or good. In the case of social cooperation, this good must not be understood narrowly but rather as a conception of what is valuable in human life. Thus, a conception of the good normally consists of a more or less determinate scheme of final ends, that is, ends we want to realize for their own sake, as well as of attachments to other persons and loyalties to various groups and associations. These attachments and loyalties give rise to affections and devotions, and therefore the flourishing of the persons and associations who are the objects of these sentiments is also part of our conception of the good. Moreover, we must also include in such a conception a view of our relation to the world – religious, philosophical, or moral – by reference to which the value and significance of our ends and attachments are understood.

In addition to having the two moral powers, the capacities for a sense of justice and a conception of the good, persons also have at any given time a particular conception of the good that they try to achieve. Since we wish to start from the idea of society as a fair system of cooperation, we assume that persons as citizens have

all the capacities that enable them to be normal and fully cooperating members of society. This does not imply that no one ever suffers from illness or accident; such misfortunes are to be expected in the ordinary course of human life; and provision for these contingencies must be made. But for our purposes here I leave aside permanent physical disabilities or mental disorders so severe as to prevent persons from being normal and fully cooperating members of society in the usual sense.

Now the conception of persons as having the two moral powers, and therefore as free and equal, is also a basic intuitive idea assumed to be implicit in the public culture of a democratic society. Note, however, that it is formed by idealizing and simplifying in various ways. This is done to achieve a clear and uncluttered view of what for us is the fundamental question of political justice: namely, what is the most appropriate conception of justice for specifying the terms of social cooperation between citizens regarded as free and equal persons, and as normal and fully cooperating members of society over a complete life. It is this question that has been the focus of the liberal critique of aristocracy, of the socialist critique of liberal constitutional democracy, and of the conflict between liberals and conservatives at the present time over the claims of private property and the legitimacy (in contrast to the effectiveness) of social policies associated with the so-called welfare state.

IV

I now take up the idea of the original position.[17] This idea is introduced in order to work out which traditional conception of justice, or which variant of one of those conceptions, specifies the most appropriate principles for realizing liberty and equality once society is viewed as a system of cooperation between free and equal persons. Assuming we had this purpose in mind, let's see why we would introduce the idea of the original position and how it serves its purpose.

Consider again the idea of social cooperation. Let's ask: how are the fair terms of cooperation to be determined? Are they simply laid down by some outside agency distinct from the persons cooperating? Are they, for example, laid down by God's law? Or are these terms to be recognized by these persons as fair by reference to their knowledge of a prior and independent moral order? For example, are they regarded as required by natural law, or by a realm of values known by rational intuition? Or are these terms to be established by an undertaking among these persons themselves in the light of what they regard as their mutual advantage? Depending on which answer we give, we get a different conception of cooperation.

Since justice as fairness recasts the doctrine of the social contract, it adopts a form of the last answer: the fair terms of social cooperation are conceived as agreed to by those engaged in it, that is, by free and equal persons as citizens who are born into the society in which they lead their lives. But their agreement, like any other valid agreement, must be entered into under appropriate conditions. In particular, these conditions must situate free and equal persons fairly and must not allow some persons greater bargaining advantages than others. Further, threats of force and coercion, deception and fraud, and so on, must be excluded.

So far so good. The foregoing considerations are familiar from everyday life. But agreements in everyday life are made in some more or less clearly specified situation embedded within the background institutions of the basic structure. Our task, however, is to extend the idea of agreement to this background framework itself. Here we face a difficulty for any political conception of justice that uses the idea of a contract, whether social or otherwise. The difficulty is this: we must find some point of view, removed from and not distorted by the particular features and circumstances of the all-encompassing background framework, from which a fair agreement between free and equal persons can be reached.

The original position, with the feature I have called "the veil of ignorance," is this point of view.[18] And the reason why the original position must abstract from and not be affected by the contingencies of the social world is that the conditions for a fair agreement on the principles of political justice between free and equal persons must eliminate the bargaining advantages which inevitably arise within background institutions of any society as the result of cumulative social, historical, and natural tendencies. These contingent advantages and accidental influences from the past should not influence an agreement on the principles which are to regulate the institutions of the basic structure itself from the present into the future.

Here we seem to face a second difficulty, which is, however, only apparent. To explain: from what we have just said it is clear that the original position is to be seen as a device of representation and hence any agreement reached by the parties must be regarded as both hypothetical and non-historical. But if so, since hypothetical agreements cannot bind, what is the significance of the original position?[19] The answer is implicit in what has already been said: it is given by the role of the various features of the original position as a device of representation. Thus, that the parties are symmetrically situated is required if they are to be seen as representatives of free and equal citizens who are to reach an agreement under conditions that are fair. Moreover, one of our considered convictions, I assume, is this: the fact that we occupy a particular social position is not a good reason for us to accept, or to expect others to accept, a conception of justice that favors those in this position. To model this conviction in the original position the parties are not allowed to know their social position; and the same idea is extended to other cases. This is expressed figuratively by saying that the parties are behind a veil of ignorance. In sum, the original position is simply a device of representation: it describes the parties, each of whom are responsible for the essential interests of a free and equal person, as fairly situated and as reaching an agreement subject to appropriate restrictions on what are to count as good reasons.[20]

Both of the above-mentioned difficulties, then, are overcome by viewing the original position as a device of representation: that is, this position models what we regard as fair conditions under which the representatives of free and equal persons are to specify the terms of social cooperation in the case of the basic structure of society; and since it also models what, for this case, we regard as acceptable restrictions on reasons available to the parties for favoring one agreement rather than another, the conception of justice the parties would adopt identifies the conception we regard — *here and now* — as fair and supported by the best reasons. We try to model restrictions on reasons in such a way that it is perfectly evident which agreement would be made by the parties in the original position as citizens' representatives. Even if there should be, as surely there will be, reasons for and against each conception of justice available, there may be an overall balance of reasons plainly favoring one conception over the rest. As a device of representation the idea of the original position serves as a means of public reflection and self-clarification. We can use it to help us work out what we now think, once we are able to take a clear and uncluttered view of what justice requires when society is conceived as a scheme of cooperation between free and equal persons over time from one generation to the next. The original position serves as a unifying idea by which our considered convictions at all levels of generality are brought to bear on one another so as to achieve greater mutual agreement and self-understanding.

To conclude: we introduce an idea like that of the original position because there is no better way to elaborate a political conception of justice for the basic structure from the fundamental intuitive idea of society as a fair system of cooperation between citizens as free and equal persons. There are, however, certain hazards. As a device of representation the original position is likely to seem somewhat abstract and hence open to misunderstanding. The description of the parties may seem to presuppose some metaphysical conception of the person, for example, that the essential nature of persons is independent of and prior to their contingent attributes, including their final ends and attachments, and indeed, their character as a whole. But this is an illusion caused by not seeing the original position as a device of representation. The veil of ignorance, to mention one prominent feature of that position, has no metaphysical implications concerning the nature of the self; it does not imply that the self is ontologically prior to the facts about persons that the parties are excluded from knowing. We can, as it were, enter this position any time simply by reasoning for principles of justice in accordance with the enumerated restrictions. When, in this way, we simulate being in this position, our reasoning no more commits us to a metaphysical doctrine about the nature of the self than our playing a game like Monopoly commits us to thinking that we are landlords engaged in a desperate rivalry, winner take all.[21] We must keep in mind that we are trying to show how the idea of society as a fair system of social cooperation can be unfolded so as to specify the most appropriate principles for realizing the institutions of liberty and equality when citizens are regarded as free and equal persons.

V

I just remarked that the idea of the original position and the description of the parties may tempt us to think that a metaphysical doctrine of the person is presupposed. While I said that this interpretation is mistaken, it is not enough simply to disavow reliance on metaphysical doctrines, for despite one's intent they may still be involved. To rebut claims of this nature requires discussing them in detail and showing that they have no foothold. I cannot do that here.[22]

I can, however, sketch a positive account of the political conception of the person, that is, the conception of the person as citizen (discussed in Section III), involved in the original position as a device of representation. To explain what is meant by describing a conception of the person as political, let's consider how citizens are represented in the original position as free persons. The representation of their freedom seems to be one source of the idea that some metaphysical doctrine is presupposed. I have said elsewhere that citizens view themselves as free in three respects, so let's survey each of these briefly and indicate the way in which the conception of the person used is political.[23]

First, citizens are free in that they conceive of themselves and of one another as having the moral power to have a conception of the good. This is not to say that, as part of their political conception of themselves, they view themselves as inevitably tied to the pursuit of the particular conception of the good which they affirm at any given time. Instead, as citizens, they are regarded as capable of revising and changing this conception on reasonable and rational grounds, and they may do this if they so desire. Thus, as free persons, citizens claim the right to view their persons as independent from and as not identified with any particular conception of the good, or scheme of final ends. Given their moral power to form, to revise, and rationally to pursue a conception of the good, their public identity as free persons is not affected by changes over time in their conception of the good. For example, when citizens convert from one religion to another, or no longer affirm an established religious faith, they do not cease to be, for questions of political justice, the same persons they were before. There is no loss of what we may call their public identity, their identity as a matter of basic law. In general, they still have the same basic rights and duties; they own the same property and can make the same claims as before,

except insofar as these claims were connected with their previous religious affiliation. We can imagine a society (indeed, history offers numerous examples) in which basic rights and recognized claims depend on religious affiliation, social class, and so on. Such a society has a different political conception of the person. It may not have a conception of citizenship at all; for this conception, as we are using it, goes with the conception of society as a fair system of cooperation for mutual advantage between free and equal persons.

It is essential to stress that citizens in their personal affairs, or in the internal life of associations to which they belong, may regard their final ends and attachments in a way very different from the way the political conception involves. Citizens may have, and normally do have at any given time, affections, devotions, and loyalties that they believe they would not, and indeed could and should not, stand apart from and objectively evaluate from the point of view of their purely rational good. They may regard it as simply unthinkable to view themselves apart from certain religious, philosophical, and moral convictions, or from certain enduring attachments and loyalties. These convictions and attachments are part of what we may call their "nonpublic identity." These convictions and attachments help to organize and give shape to a person's way of life, what one sees oneself as doing and trying to accomplish in one's social world. We think that if we were suddenly without these particular convictions and attachments we would be disoriented and unable to carry on. In fact, there would be, we might think, no point in carrying on. But our conceptions of the good may and often do change over time, usually slowly but sometimes rather suddenly. When these changes are sudden, we are particularly likely to say that we are no longer the same person. We know what this means: we refer to a profound and pervasive shift, or reversal, in our final ends and character; we refer to our different nonpublic, and possibly moral or religious, identity. On the road to Damascus Saul of Tarsus becomes Paul the Apostle. There is no change in our public or political identity, nor in our personal identity as this concept is understood by some writers in the philosophy of mind.[24]

The second respect in which citizens view themselves as free is that they regard themselves as self-originating sources of valid claims. They think their claims have weight apart from being derived from duties or obligations specified by the political conception of justice, for example, from duties and obligations owed to society. Claims that citizens regard as founded on duties and obligations based on their conception of the good and the moral doctrine they affirm in their own life are also, for our purposes here, to be counted as self-originating. Doing this is reasonable in a political conception of justice for a constitutional democracy; for provided the conceptions of the good and the moral doctrines citizens affirm are compatible with the public conception of justice, these duties and obligations are self-originating from the political point of view.

When we describe a way in which citizens regard themselves as free, we are describing how citizens actually think of themselves in a democratic society should questions of justice arise. In our conception of a constitutional regime, this is an aspect of how citizens regard themselves. That this aspect of their freedom belongs to a particular political conception is clear from the contrast with a different political conception in which the members of society are not viewed as self-originating sources of valid claims. Rather, their claims have no weight except insofar as they can be derived from their duties and obligations owed to society, or from their ascribed roles in the social hierarchy justified by religious or aristocratic values. Or to take an extreme case, slaves are human beings who are not counted as sources of claims, not even claims based on social duties or obligations, for slaves are not counted as capable of having duties or obligations. Laws that prohibit the abuse and maltreatment of slaves are not founded on claims made by slaves on their own behalf, but on claims originating either from slaveholders, or from the general interests of society (which does not include the interests of slaves). Slaves are, so to speak, socially dead: they are not publicly recognized as persons at all.[25] Thus, the contrast with a political conception, which allows slavery makes clear why conceiving of citizens as free persons in virtue of their moral powers and their having a conception of the good, goes with a particular political conception of the person. This conception of persons fits into a political conception of justice founded on the idea of society as a system of cooperation between its members conceived as free and equal.

The third respect in which citizens are regarded as free is that they are regarded as capable of taking responsibility for their ends and this affects how their various claims are assessed.[26] Very roughly, the idea is that, given just background institutions and given for each person a fair index of primary goods (as required by the principles of justice), citizens are thought to be capable of adjusting their aims and aspirations in the light of what they can reasonably expect to provide for. Moreover, they are regarded as capable of restricting their claims in matters of justice to the kinds of things the principles of justice allow. Thus, citizens are to recognize that the weight of their claims is not given by the strength and psychological intensity of their wants and desires (as opposed to their needs and requirements as citizens), even when their wants and desires are rational from their point of view. I cannot pursue these matters here. But the procedure is the same as before: we start with the basic intuitive idea of society as a system of social cooperation. When this idea is developed into a conception of political justice, it implies that, viewing ourselves as persons who can engage in social cooperation over a complete life, we can also take responsibility for our ends, that is, that we can adjust our ends so that they can be pursued by the means we can reasonably expect to acquire given our prospects and situation in society. The idea of responsibility for ends is implicit in the public political culture and discernible in its practices. A political conception of the person articulates this idea and fits it into the idea of society as a system of social cooperation over a complete life.

To sum up, I recapitulate three main points of this and the preceding two sections:

First, in Section III persons were regarded as free and equal in virtue of their possessing to the requisite degree the two powers of moral personality (and the powers of reason, thought, and judgment connected with these powers), namely, the capacity for a sense of justice and the capacity for a conception of the good. These powers we associated with two main elements of the idea of cooperation, the idea of fair terms of cooperation and the idea of each participant's rational advantage, or good.

Second, in this section (Section V), we have briefly surveyed three respects in which persons are regarded as free, and we have noted that in the public political culture of a constitutional democratic regime citizens conceive of themselves as free in these respects.

Third, since the question of which conception of political justice is most appropriate for realizing in basic institutions the values of liberty and equality has long been deeply controversial within the very democratic tradition in which citizens are regarded as free and equal persons, the aim of justice as fairness is to try to resolve this question by starting from the basic intuitive idea of society as a fair system of social cooperation in which the fair terms of cooperation are agreed upon by citizens themselves so conceived. In Section IV, we saw why this approach leads to the idea of the original position as a device of representation.

VI

I now take up a point essential to thinking of justice as fairness as a liberal view. Although this conception is a moral conception, it is not, as I have said, intended as a comprehensive moral doctrine. The conception of the citizen as a free and equal person is not a moral ideal to govern all of life, but is rather an ideal belonging to a conception of political justice which is to apply to the basic structure. I emphasize this point because to think otherwise would be incompatible with liberalism as a political doctrine. Recall that as such a doctrine, liberalism assumes that in a constitutional democratic state under modern conditions there are bound to exist conflicting and incommensurable conceptions of the good. This feature characterizes modern culture since the Reformation. Any viable political conception of justice that is not to rely on the autocratic use of state power must recognize this fundamental social fact. This does not mean, of course, that such a conception cannot impose constraints on individuals and associations, but that when it does so, these constraints are accounted for, directly or indirectly, by the requirements of political justice for the basic structure.[27]

Given this fact, we adopt a conception of the person framed as part of, and restricted to, an explicitly political conception of justice. In this sense, the conception of the person is a political one. As I stressed in the previous section, persons can accept this conception of themselves as citizens and use it when discussing questions of political justice without being committed in other parts of their life to comprehensive moral ideals often associated with liberalism, for example, the ideals of autonomy and individuality. The absence of commitment to these ideals, and indeed to any particular comprehensive ideal, is essential to liberalism as a political doctrine. The reason is that any such ideal, when pursued as a comprehensive ideal, is incompatible with other conceptions of the good, with forms of personal, moral, and religious life consistent with justice and which, therefore, have a proper place in a democratic society. As comprehensive moral ideals, autonomy and individuality are unsuited for a political conception of justice. As found in Kant and J. S. Mill, these comprehensive ideals, despite their very great importance in liberal thought, are extended too far when presented as the only appropriate foundation for a constitutional regime.[28] So understood, liberalism becomes but another sectarian doctrine.

This conclusion requires comment: it does not mean, of course, that the liberalisms of Kant and Mill are not appropriate moral conceptions from which we can be led to affirm democratic institutions. But they are only two such conceptions among others, and so but two of the philosophical doctrines likely to persist and gain adherents in a reasonably just democratic regime. In such a regime the comprehensive moral views which support its basic institutions may include the liberalisms of individuality and autonomy; and possibly these liberalisms are among the more prominent doctrines in an overlapping consensus, that is, in a consensus in which, as noted earlier, different and even conflicting doctrines affirm the publicly shared basis of political arrangements. The liberalisms of Kant and Mill have a certain historical preeminence as among the first and most important philosophical views to espouse modern constitutional democracy and to develop its underlying ideas in an influential way; and it may even turn out that societies in which the ideals of autonomy and individuality are widely accepted are among the most well-governed and harmonious.[29]

By contrast with liberalism as a comprehensive moral doctrine, justice as fairness tries to present a conception of political justice rooted in the basic intuitive ideas found in the public culture of a constitutional democracy. We conjecture that these ideas are likely to be affirmed by each of the opposing comprehensive moral doctrines influential in a reasonably just democratic society. Thus justice as fairness seeks to identify the kernel of an overlapping consensus, that is, the shared intuitive ideas which when worked up into a political conception of justice turn out to be sufficient to underwrite a just

constitutional regime. This is the most we can expect, nor do we need more.[30] We must note, however, that when justice as fairness is fully realized in a well-ordered society, the value of full autonomy is likewise realized. In this way justice as fairness is indeed similar to the liberalisms of Kant and Mill; but in contrast with them, the value of full autonomy is here specified by a political conception of justice, and not by a comprehensive moral doctrine.

It may appear that, so understood, the public acceptance of justice as fairness is no more than prudential; that is, that those who affirm this conception do so simply as a *modus vivendi* which allows the groups in the overlapping consensus to pursue their own good subject to certain constraints which each thinks to be for its advantage given existing circumstances. The idea of an overlapping consensus may seem essentially Hobbesian. But against this, two remarks: first, justice as fairness is a moral conception: it has conceptions of person and society, and concepts of right and fairness, as well as principles of justice with their complement of the virtues through which those principles are embodied in human character and regulate political and social life. This conception of justice provides an account of the cooperative virtues suitable for a political doctrine in view of the conditions and requirements of a constitutional regime. It is no less a moral conception because it is restricted to the basic structure of society, since this restriction is what enables it to serve as a political conception of justice given our present circumstances. Thus, in an overlapping consensus (as understood here), the conception of justice as fairness is not regarded merely as a *modus vivendi*.

Second, in such a consensus each of the comprehensive philosophical, religious, and moral doctrines accepts justice as fairness in its own way; that is, each comprehensive doctrine, from within its own point of view, is led to accept the public reasons of justice specified by justice as fairness. We might say that they recognize its concepts, principles, and virtues as theorems, as it were, at which their several views coincide. But this does not make these points of coincidence any less moral or reduce them to mere means. For, in general, these concepts, principles, and virtues are accepted by each as belonging to a more comprehensive philosophical, religious, or moral doctrine. Some may even affirm justice as fairness as a natural moral conception that can stand on its own feet. They accept this conception of justice as a reasonable basis for political and social cooperation, and hold that it is as natural and fundamental as the concepts and principles of honesty and mutual trust, and the virtues of cooperation in everyday life. The doctrines in an overlapping consensus differ in how far they maintain a further foundation is necessary and on what that further foundation should be. These differences, however, are compatible with a consensus on justice as fairness as a political conception of justice.

VII

I shall conclude by considering the way in which social unity and stability may be understood by liberalism as a political doctrine (as opposed to a comprehensive moral conception).[31]

One of the deepest distinctions between political conceptions of justice is between those that allow for a plurality of opposing and even incommensurable conceptions of the good and those that hold that there is but one conception of the good which is to be recognized by all persons, so far as they are fully rational. Conceptions of justice which fall on opposite sides of this divide are distinct in many fundamental ways. Plato and Aristotle, and the Christian tradition as represented by Augustine and Aquinas, fall on the side of the one rational good. Such views tend to be teleological and to hold that institutions are just to the extent that they effectively promote this good. Indeed, since classical times the dominant tradition seems to have been that there is but one rational

conception of the good, and that the aim of moral philosophy, together with theology and metaphysics, is to determine its nature. Classical utilitarianism belongs to this dominant tradition. By contrast, liberalism as a political doctrine supposes that there are many conflicting and incommensurable conceptions of the good, each compatible with the full rationality of human persons, so far as we can ascertain within a workable political conception of justice. As a consequence of this supposition, liberalism assumes that it is a characteristic feature of a free democratic culture that a plurality of conflicting and incommensurable conceptions of the good are affirmed by its citizens. Liberalism as a political doctrine holds that the question the dominant tradition has tried to answer has no practicable answer; that is, it has no answer suitable for a political conception of justice for a democratic society. In such a society a teleological political conception is out of the question: public agreement on the requisite conception of the good cannot be obtained.

As I have remarked, the historical origin of this liberal supposition is the Reformation and its consequences. Until the Wars of Religion in the sixteenth and seventeenth centuries, the fair terms of social cooperation were narrowly drawn: social cooperation on the basis of mutual respect was regarded as impossible with persons of a different faith; or (in the terminology I have used) with persons who affirm a fundamentally different conception of the good. Thus one of the historical roots of liberalism was the development of various doctrines urging religious toleration. One theme in justice as fairness is to recognize the social conditions that give rise to these doctrines as among the so-called subjective circumstances of justice and then to spell out the implications of the principle of toleration.[32] As liberalism is stated by Constant, de Tocqueville, and Mill in the nineteenth century, it accepts the plurality of incommensurable conceptions of the good as a fact of modern democratic culture, provided, of course, these conceptions respect the limits specified by the appropriate principles of justice. One task of liberalism as a political doctrine is to answer the question: how is social unity to be understood, given that there can be no public agreement on the one rational good, and a plurality of opposing and incommensurable conceptions must be taken as given? And granted that social unity is conceivable in some definite way, under what conditions is it actually possible?

In justice as fairness, social unity is understood by starting with the conception of society as a system of cooperation between free and equal persons. Social unity and the allegiance of citizens to their common institutions are not founded on their all affirming the same conception of the good, but on their publicly accepting a political conception of justice to regulate the basic structure of society. The concept of justice is independent from and prior to the concept of goodness in the sense that its principles limit the conceptions of the good which are permissible. A just basic structure and its background institutions establish a framework within which permissible conceptions can be advanced. Elsewhere I have called this relation between a conception of justice and conceptions of the good the priority of right (since the just falls under the right). I believe this priority is characteristic of liberalism as a political doctrine and something like it seems essential to any conception of justice reasonable for a democratic state. Thus to understand how social unity is possible given the historical conditions of a democratic society, we start with our basic intuitive idea of social cooperation, an idea present in the public culture of a democratic society, and proceed from there to a public conception of justice as the basis of social unity in the way I have sketched.

As for the question of whether this unity is stable, this importantly depends on the content of the religious, philosophical, and moral doctrines available to constitute an overlapping consensus. For example, assuming the public political conception to be justice as fairness, imagine citizens to affirm one of three views: the first view affirms justice as fairness because its religious beliefs and understanding of faith lead to a principle of toleration and underwrite the fundamental idea of society as a scheme of social cooperation between free and equal persons; the second view affirms it as a consequence of a comprehensive liberal moral conception such as those of Kant and Mill; while the third affirms justice as fairness not as a consequence of any wider doctrine but as in itself sufficient to express values that normally outweigh whatever other values might oppose them, at least under reasonably favorable conditions. This overlapping consensus appears far more stable than one founded on views that express skepticism and indifference to religious, philosophical, and moral values, or that regard the acceptance of the principles of justice simply as a prudent *modus vivendi* given the existing balance of social forces. Of course, there are many other possibilities.

The strength of a conception like justice as fairness may prove to be that the more comprehensive doctrines that persist and gain adherents in a democratic society regulated by its principles are likely to cohere together into a more or less stable overlapping consensus. But obviously all this is highly speculative and raises questions which are little understood, since doctrines which persist and gain adherents depend in part on social conditions, and in particular, on these conditions when regulated by the public conception of justice. Thus we are forced to consider at some point the effects of the social conditions required by a conception of political justice on the acceptance of that conception itself. Other things being equal, a conception will be more or less stable depending on how far the conditions to which it leads support comprehensive religious, philosophical, and moral doctrines which can constitute a stable overlapping consensus. These questions of stability I cannot discuss here.[33] It suffices to remark that in a society marked by deep divisions between opposing and incommensurable conceptions of the good, justice as fairness enables us at least to conceive how social unity can be both possible and stable.

Notes

1 Cambridge, MA: Harvard University Press, 1971.

2 A number of these changes, or shifts of emphasis, are evident in three lectures entitled "Kantian Constructivism in Moral Theory," *Journal of Philosophy* 77 (September 1980). For example, the account of what I have called "primary goods" is revised so that it clearly depends on a particular conception of persons and their higher-order interests; hence this account is not a purely psychological, sociological, or historical thesis. See pp. 526f. There is also throughout those lectures a more explicit emphasis on the role of a conception of the person as well as on the idea that the justification of a conception of justice is a practical social task rather than an epistemological or metaphysical problem. See pp. 518f. And in this connection the idea of "Kantian constructivism" is introduced, especially in the third lecture. It must be noted, however, that this idea is not proposed as Kant's idea: the adjective "Kantian" indicates analogy not identity, that is, resemblance in enough fundamental respects so that the adjective is appropriate. These fundamental respects are certain structural features of justice as fairness and elements of its content, such as the distinction between what may be called the Reasonable and the Rational, the priority of right, and the role of the conception of the persons as free and equal, and capable of autonomy, and so on. Resemblances of structural features and content are not to be mistaken for resemblances with Kant's views on questions of epistemology and metaphysics. Finally, I should remark that the title of those lectures, "Kantian Constructivism in Moral Theory," was misleading; since the conception of justice discussed is a political conception, a better title would have been "Kantian Constructivism in Political Philosophy." Whether constructivism is reasonable for moral philosophy is a separate and more general question.

3 *Theory*, Sec. 2, and see the index; see also "The Basic Structure as Subject," in *Values and Morals*, eds. Alvin Goldman and Jaegwon Kim (Dordrecht: Reidel, 1978), pp. 47–71.

4 See "Basic Structure as Subject," ibid., pp. 48–50.

5 This idea was introduced in *Theory*, pp. 387f., as a way to weaken the conditions for the reasonableness of civil disobedience in a nearly just democratic society. Here and later in Secs. VI and VII it is used in a wider context.

6 *Theory*, Preface, p. viii.

7 Ibid., pp. 582f. On the role of a conception of justice in reducing the divergence of opinion, see pp. 44f., 53, 314, and 564. At various places the limited aims in developing a conception of justice are noted: see p. 364 on not expecting too much of an account of civil disobedience; pp. 200f. on the inevitable indeterminacy of a conception of justice in specifying a series of points of view from which questions of justice can be resolved; pp. 89f. on the social wisdom of recognizing that perhaps only a few moral problems (it would have been better to say: problems of political justice) can be satisfactorily settled, and thus of framing institutions so that intractable questions do not arise; on pp. 53, 87ff, 320f. the need to accept simplifications is emphasized. Regarding the last point, see also "Kantian Constructivism," pp. 560–4.

8 The statement of these principles differs from that given in *Theory* and follows the statement in "The Basic Liberties and Their Priority," *Tanner Lectures on Human Values*, Vol. III (Salt Lake City: University of Utah Press, 1982), p. 5. The reasons for the changes are discussed at pp. 46–55 of that lecture. They are important for the revisions made in the account of the basic liberties found in *Theory* in the attempt to answer the objections of H.L.A. Hart; but they need not concern us here.

9 The idea of the worth of these guarantees is discussed ibid., pp. 40f.

10 *Theory*, pp. 20f., 48–51, and 120f.

11 Ibid, pp. 580–3.

12 Ibid., pp. 214f.

13 On Kantian constructivism, see especially the third lecture referred to in footnote 2 above.

14 Although *Theory* uses this idea from the outset (it is introduced on p. 4), it does not emphasize, as I do here and in "Kantian Constructivism," that the

basic ideas of justice as fairness are regarded as implicit or latent in the public culture of a democratic society.

15 It should be emphasized that a conception of the person, as I understand it here, is a normative conception, whether legal, political, or moral, or indeed also philosophical or religious, depending on the overall view to which it belongs. In this case the conception of the person is a moral conception, one that begins from our everyday conception of persons as the basic units of thought, deliberation and responsibility, and adapted to a political conception of justice and not to a comprehensive moral doctrine. It is in effect a political conception of the person, and given the aims of justice as fairness, a conception of citizens. Thus, a conception of the person is to be distinguished from an account of human nature given by natural science or social theory. On this point, see "Kantian Constructivism," pp. 534f.

16 *Theory*, Sec. 77.

17 Ibid., Sec. 4, Ch. 3, and the index.

18 On the veil of ignorance, see ibid., Sec. 24, and the index.

19 This question is raised by Ronald Dworkin in the first part of his very illuminating, and to me highly instructive, essay "Justice and Rights" (1973), reprinted in *Taking Rights Seriously* (Cambridge, MA: Harvard University Press, 1977). Dworkin considers several ways of explaining the use of the original position in an account of justice that invokes the idea of the social contract. In the last part of the essay (pp. 173–83), after having surveyed some of the constructivist features of justice as fairness (pp. 159–68) and argued that it is a right-based and not a duty-based or a goal-based view (pp. 168–77), he proposes that the original position with the veil of ignorance be seen as modeling the force of the natural right that individuals have to equal concern and respect in the design of the political institutions that govern them (p. 180). He thinks that this natural right lies as the basis of justice as fairness and that the original position serves as a device for testing which principles of justice this right requires. This is an ingenious suggestion but I have not followed it in the text. I prefer not to think of justice as fairness as a right-based view; indeed, Dworkin's

classification scheme of right-based, duty-based and goal-based views (pp. 171f.) is too narrow and leaves out important possibilities. Thus, as explained in Sec. II above, I think of justice as fairness as working up into idealized conceptions certain fundamental intuitive ideas such as those of the person as free and equal, of a well-ordered society and of the public role of a conception of political justice, and as connecting these fundamental intuitive ideas with the even more fundamental and comprehensive intuitive idea of society as a fair system of cooperation over time from one generation to the next. Rights, duties, and goals are but elements of such idealized conceptions. Thus, justice as fairness is a conception-based, or as Elizabeth Anderson has suggested to me, an ideal-based view, since these fundamental intuitive ideas reflect ideals implicit or latent in the public culture of a democratic society. In this context the original position is a device of representation that models the force, not of the natural right of equal concern and respect, but of the essential elements of these fundamental intuitive ideas as identified by the reasons for principles of justice that we accept on due reflection. As such a device, it serves first to combine and then to focus the resultant force of all these reasons in selecting the most appropriate principles of justice for a democratic society. (In doing this the force of the natural right of equal concern and respect will be covered in other ways.) This account of the use of the original position resembles in some respects an account Dworkin rejects in the first part of his essay, especially pp. 153f. In view of the ambiguity and obscurity of *Theory* on many of the points he considers, it is not my aim to criticize Dworkin's valuable discussion, but rather to indicate how my understanding of the original position differs from his. Others may prefer his account.

20 The original position models a basic feature of Kantian constructivism, namely, the distinction between the Reasonable and the Rational, with the Reasonable as prior to the Rational. (For an explanation of this distinction, see "Kantian Constructivism," pp. 528–32, and passim.) The relevance of this distinction here is that *Theory* more or less consistently speaks not of rational but of reasonable (or sometimes of fitting or appropriate)

conditions as constraints on arguments for principles of justice (see pp. 18f., 20f., 120f., 130f., 138, 446, 516f., 578, 584f.). These constraints are modeled in the original position and thereby imposed on the parties: their deliberations are subject, and subject absolutely, to the reasonable conditions the modeling of which makes the original position fair. The Reasonable, then, is prior to the Rational, and this gives the priority of right. Thus, it was an error in *Theory* (and a very misleading one) to describe a theory of justice as part of the theory of rational choice, as on pp. 16 and 583. What I should have said is that the conception of justice as fairness uses an account of rational choice subject to reasonable conditions to characterize the deliberations of the parties as representatives of free and equal persons; and all of this within a political conception of justice, which is, of course, a moral conception. There is no thought of trying to derive the content of justice within a framework that uses an idea of the rational as the sole normative idea. That thought is incompatible with any kind of Kantian view.

21 *Theory*, pp. 138f., 147. The parties in the original position are said (p. 147) to be theoretically defined individuals whose motivations are specified by the account of that position and not by a psychological view about how human beings are actually motivated. This is also part of what is meant by saying (p. 121) that the acceptance of the particular principles of justice is not conjectured as a psychological law or probability but rather follows from the full description of the original position. Although the aim cannot be perfectly achieved, we want the argument to be deductive, "a kind of moral geometry." In "Kantian Constructivism" (p. 532) the parties are described as merely artificial agents who inhabit a construction. Thus I think R. B. Brandt mistaken in objecting that the argument from the original position is based on defective psychology. See his *A Theory of the Good and the Right* (Oxford: Clarendon Press, 1979), pp. 239–42. Of course, one might object to the original position that it models the conception of the person and the deliberations of the parties in ways that are unsuitable for the purposes of a political conception of justice; but for these purposes psychological theory is not directly relevant. On the other hand, psychological theory is relevant for the account of the stability of a conception of justice, as discussed in *Theory*, Pt. III. See below, footnote 33. Similarly, I think Michael Sandel mistaken in supposing that the original position involves a conception of the self " . . . shorn of all its contingently-given attributes," a self that "assumes a kind of supra-empirical status, . . . and given prior to its ends, a pure subject of agency and possession, ultimately thin." See *Liberalism and the Limits of Justice* (Cambridge: Cambridge University Press, 1982), pp. 93–5. I cannot discuss these criticisms in any detail. The essential point (as suggested in the introductory remarks) is not whether certain passages in *Theory* call for such an interpretation (I doubt that they do), but whether the conception of justice as fairness presented therein can be understood in the light of the interpretation I sketch in this article and in the earlier lectures on constructivism, as I believe it can be.

22 Part of the difficulty is that there is no accepted understanding of what a metaphysical doctrine is. One might say, as Paul Hoffman has suggested to me, that to develop a political conception of justice without presupposing, or explicitly using, a metaphysical doctrine, for example, some particular metaphysical conception of the person, is already to presuppose a metaphysical thesis: namely, that no particular metaphysical doctrine is required for this purpose. One might also say that our everyday conception of persons as the basic units of deliberation and responsibility presupposes, or in some way involves, certain metaphysical theses about the nature of persons as moral or political agents. Following the method of avoidance, I should not want to deny these claims. What should be said is the following. If we look at the presentation of justice as fairness and note how it is set up, and note the ideas and conceptions it uses, no particular metaphysical doctrine about the nature of persons, distinctive and opposed to other metaphysical doctrines, appears among its premises, or seems required by its argument. If metaphysical presuppositions are involved, perhaps they are so general that they would not distinguish between the distinctive metaphysical views – Cartesian, Leibnizian, or Kantian; realist, idealist,

or materialist – with which philosophy traditionally has been concerned. In this case, they would not appear to be relevant for the structure and content of a political conception of justice one way or the other. I am grateful to Daniel Brudney and Paul Hoffman for discussion of these matters.

23 For the first two respects, see "Kantian Constructivism," pp. 544f. (For the third respect, see footnote 26 below.) The account of the first two respects found in those lectures is further developed in the text above and I am more explicit on the distinction between what I call here our "public" versus our "nonpublic or moral identity." The point of the term "moral" in the latter phrase is to indicate that persons' conceptions of the (complete) good are normally an essential element in characterizing their nonpublic (or nonpolitical) identity, and these conceptions are understood as normally containing important moral elements, although they include other elements as well, philosophical and religious. The term "moral" should be thought of as a stand-in for all these possibilities. I am indebted to Elizabeth Anderson for discussion and clarification of this distinction.

24 Here I assume that an answer to the problem of personal identity tries to specify the various criteria (for example, psychological continuity of memories and physical continuity of body, or some part thereof) in accordance with which two different psychological states, or actions (or whatever) which occur at two different times may be said to be states or actions of the same person who endures over time; and it also tries to specify how this enduring person is to be conceived, whether as a Cartesian or a Leibnizian substance, or as a Kantian transcendental ego, or as a continuant of some other kind, for example, bodily or physical. See the collection of essays edited by John Perry, *Personal Identity* (Berkeley, CA: University of California Press, 1975), especially Perry's introduction, pp. 3–30; and Sydney Shoemaker's essay in *Personal Identity* (Oxford: Basil Blackwell, 1984), both of which consider a number of views. Sometimes in discussions of this problem, continuity of fundamental aims and aspirations is largely ignored, for example, in views like H. P. Grice's (included in Perry's collection) which emphasizes continuity of memory. Of course, once

continuity of fundamental aims and aspirations is brought in, as in Derek Parfit's *Reasons and Persons* (Oxford: Clarendon Press, 1984), Pt. III, there is no sharp distinction between the problem of persons' nonpublic or moral identity and the problem of their personal identity. This latter problem raises profound questions on which past and current philosophical views widely differ, and surely will continue to differ. For this reason it is important to try to develop a political conception of justice which avoids this problem as far as possible.

25 For the idea of social death, see Orlando Patterson, *Slavery and Social Death* (Cambridge, MA: Harvard University Press, 1982), esp. pp. 5–9, 38–45, 337. This idea is interestingly developed in this book and has a central place in the author's comparative study of slavery.

26 See "Social Unity and Primary Goods," in *Utilitarianism and Beyond*, eds. Amartya Sen and Bernard Williams (Cambridge: Cambridge University Press, 1982), Sec. IV, pp. 167–70.

27 For example, churches are constrained by the principle of equal liberty of conscience and must conform to the principle of toleration, universities by what may be required to maintain fair equality of opportunity, and the rights of parents by what is necessary to maintain their children's physical well-being and to assure the adequate development of their intellectual and moral powers. Because churches, universities, and parents exercise their authority within the basic structure, they are to recognize the requirements this structure imposes to maintain background justice.

28 For Kant, see *The Foundations of the Metaphysics of Morals* and *The Critique of Practical Reason*. For Mill, see *On Liberty*, particularly Ch. 3 where the ideal of individuality is most fully discussed.

29 This point has been made with respect to the liberalisms of Kant and Mill, but for American culture one should mention the important conceptions of democratic individuality expressed in the works of Emerson, Thoreau, and Whitman. These are instructively discussed by George Kateb in his "Democratic Individuality and the Claims of Politics," *Political Theory* 12 (August 1984).

30 For the idea of the kernel of an overlapping consensus (mentioned above), see *Theory*, last par.

of Sec. 35, pp. 22f. For the idea of full autonomy, see "Kantian Constructivism," pp. 528ff.

31 This account of social unity is found in "Social Unity and Primary Goods," referred to in footnote 26 above. See esp. pp. 160f., 170–3, 183f.

32 The distinction between the objective and the subjective circumstances of justice is made in *Theory*, pp. 126ff. The importance of the role of the subjective circumstances is emphasized in "Kantian Constructivism," pp. 540–2.

33 Part III of *Theory* has mainly three aims: first, to give an account of goodness as rationality (Ch. 7) which is to provide the basis for identifying primary goods, those goods which, given the conception of persons, the parties are to assume are needed by the persons they represent (pp. 397, 433f.); second, to give an account of the stability of a conception of justice (Chs. 8–9), and of justice as fairness in particular, and to show that this conception is more stable than other traditional conceptions with which it is compared, as well as stable enough; and third, to give an account of the good of a well-ordered society, that is, of a just society in which justice as fairness is the publicly affirmed and effectively realized political conception of justice (Chs. 8–9 and culminating in Sec. 86). Among the faults of Part III, I now think, are these. The account of goodness as rationality often reads as an account of the complete good for a comprehensive moral conception; all it need do is to explain the list of primary goods and the basis of the various natural goods recognized by common sense and in particular, the fundamental significance of self-respect and self-esteem (which, as David Sachs and Laurence Thomas have pointed out to me, are not properly distinguished), and so of the social bases of self-respect as a primary good. Also, the account of the stability of justice as fairness was not extended, as it should have been, to the important case of overlapping consensus, as sketched in the text; instead, this account was limited to the simplest case where the public conception of justice is affirmed as in itself sufficient to express values that normally outweigh, given the political context of a constitutional regime, whatever values might oppose them (see the third view in the overlapping consensus indicated in the text). In view of the discussion in Secs. 32–5 of Ch. 4 of liberty of conscience, the extension to the case of overlapping consensus is essential. Finally, the relevance of the idea of a well-ordered society as a social union of social unions to giving an account of the good of a just society was not explained fully enough. Throughout Part III too many connections are left for the reader to make, so that one may be left in doubt as to the point of much of Chs. 8 and 9.

Chapter 20

Gerald Gaus

THE MORAL FOUNDATIONS OF LIBERAL NEUTRALITY

Gerald Gaus (1952–) is a professor of philosophy at the University of Arizona who has written widely on liberalism and the public justification of coercion. In this 2009 essay, Gaus clarifies and defends the concept of liberal neutrality, and argues that it is a more demanding standard than most previous theorists have recognized, so strong that it "raises the question of what, if anything, the officials of the state may do."

Section 1 of this essay explicates the concept of neutrality. Section 2 provides two arguments supporting a conception of *Liberal Moral Neutrality*. Given a certain understanding of moral and rational persons, I argue, moral neutrality is a fundamental and inescapable commitment. Section 3 shows how liberal moral neutrality leads to *Liberal Political Neutrality*. Fully grasping the nature of this liberal political neutrality, I argue in section 4, has radical implications for our understanding of the proper limits of government.

1. The Concept of Neutrality

For the last few decades political theorists have vigorously debated whether liberalism is committed to some doctrine of "neutrality," and whether neutrality provides a plausible constraint on legitimate laws and policies. In my view, this long-running controversy has been disappointing: theorists tend to stake their claim as advocates or critics of neutrality, yet the precise contours of the concept and its justification remain vague. To be sure, we have witnessed some important advances. Discussions of neutrality are now careful to distinguish: (i) the idea that a *justification* (say, of a policy) should be neutral; (ii) the claim that the *aims* of policy-makers should be neutral; (iii) the claim that the *effects* of policy should be neutral.[1] Yet interpretations of neutrality are far more diverse than most analyses recognize.[2] Neutrality is sometimes understood as a doctrine about: constraints on legislation or legislators,[3] the proper functions of the state,[4] the prohibition of the state "taking a stand" on some issues,[5] the prohibition of the state enforcing moral character,[6] or the requirement that the state take a stance of impartiality.[7] Alternatively, neutrality can be understood as a requirement of a theory of justice rather than state action.[8] There are also differences about whether neutral states (or theories of justice, or legislators) are supposed to be neutral between conceptions of the good,[9] controversial conceptions of the good,[10] conceptions of the good that citizens may rightfully adopt,[11] comprehensive doctrines and conceptions of the good,[12] particular sets of ends,[13] particular or substantive conceptions of the good,[14] ways of life,[15] or final ends.[16] And it is unclear whether every principle of neutrality is inherently one of liberal neutrality, or whether liberal neutrality is a specific sort of neutral principle.[17]

To make a start at clarifying just what the debate is about, I propose the following general definition-schema:

A's ϕ-ing is neutral between X and Y concerning X's and Y's difference D iff ϕ does not treat X and Y differently on the basis of D.

The definition-schema is, I think, fully general about claims concerning neutrality. It must be stressed that the definition-schema is not intended to resolve substantive disputes about the proper interpretation of neutrality; the aim is to get clearer about the variables around which controversy centers. Each conception of neutrality provides a different interpretation of the variables. The most familiar controversy, which I mentioned above, concerns the proper interpretation of "treatment." Varying conceptions proffer different explications: those who think that neutrality requires *neutrality of effect* hold that unless *A*'s ϕ-ing has the same effect on X and Y with respect to D, *A*'s ϕ-ing treats them differently; those who uphold *neutrality of justification* maintain that *A* treats X and Y the same when *A* has a justification for ϕ that does not appeal to D.

To better see how the definition-schema is to be applied, consider the classical case of a government that is neutral between two combatants. The government (*A*) is neutral between the combatants (X and Y) concerning the differences in their war aims (D) when *A*'s decision, say, about shipments of arms or war-related matters (ϕ) does not treat X and Y differently on the basis of their war aims, alliances, etc. Note a few points. (i) The range of ϕ – what sorts of actions must be neutral – is in dispute between different notions of state neutrality in war (just as it is in

liberal neutrality). In 1914 President Wilson insisted that:

The United States must be neutral in fact, as well as in name. . . . We must be impartial in thought, as well as action, must put a curb upon our sentiments, as well as upon every transaction that might be construed as a preference of one party to the struggle before another.[18]

But that is an extreme interpretation of ϕ (and was not lived up to). The Swedish Government in 1941 declared that:

Neutrality does not demand that nations not participating in an armed conflict should be indifferent to the issues of the belligerents. The sympathies of neutrals may well lie entirely with one side, and a neutral does not violate his duties as long as he does not commit any unneutral acts that might aid the side he favors.[19]

Adopting this, let us call ϕ such acts by the state. (ii) Notice that the Swedish doctrine explicitly allows that *A* (the neutral government) need not always refrain from different treatment of X and Y on the basis of their war aims (D): *A*'s public schools might still favor X's aims, and treat X and Y differently in its curriculum, but this would not impair *A*'s neutrality regarding ϕ – e.g., arms shipments or war materials. (iii) Note also that the definition-schema does not require a neutral *A* to always treat X and Y the same when ϕ-ing. Suppose *A* sells arms to both X and Y, but X has paid and Y has not (international law allows neutrals to sell arms). Then *A* may treat X differently than Y even regarding ϕ, because the difference in treatment is not grounded on D (their war aims), but on whether payment has been made.

Moving a little closer to our concern, think about a neutral umpire. The neutral umpire (*A*) does not treat the players (X and Y) differently with regard to what team they are on or whether she personally likes them (*D*), when making calls in the game (φ). But, of course, *A* does treat them differently in making calls in the game (φ) depending on whether one has violated the rules. And *A* can still be a neutral umpire if, when buying Christmas presents, she selects her hometown team's jersey, so does sometimes base her differential treatment on D (but not when φ-ing).[20]

Philosophy differs from mystery writing: in philosophy we can give the ending away without ruining the story. It may help to give a general description of the conceptions of neutrality that I defend here.

> *Liberal Moral Neutrality: A* [a free and equal reasonable moral person] making φ [a moral demand] addressed to Y [a free and equal reasonable moral person] must be neutral between X and Y [where *A is also person X; that is where A is one of the relevant parties*]: the justification of *A*'s moral demand must not treat Y and *A* differentially based on the differences (D) in their evaluative standards.

> *Liberal Political Neutrality: A* [an agent of the state] when φ-ing [exercising coercion on citizen X who is also a free and equal reasonable moral person, or participating in the authorization of such coercion] must be neutral between X and Y [where Y = any other rational citizen/moral person]: the justification of *A*'s coercion must not appeal to X's and Y's differences (D) in their evaluative standards.

Liberal Moral and Political Neutrality, as I explicate them, are not concerned with neutrality between conceptions of the good (or, more broadly, what I will call "evaluative standards"). Liberalism, I shall argue, is neutral between *persons*, and this neutrality requires not treating them differentially on the basis of their differing evaluative standards (or, loosely, conceptions of the good). Liberalism is not concerned with

neutrality between conceptions of the good, as if conceptions of the good themselves had claims to neutral treatment. It is only because citizens hold such conceptions that neutrality between citizens has consequences for the way conceptions of the good can enter into moral and political justification. This might seem to be a distressingly pedantic point, but, I think, it helps us avoid confusion. Suppose at time t_1 there are two conceptions of the good in society, C_1 and C_2 but at time t_2, everyone has come to embrace C_1. It would seem that, if liberalism is really committed to neutrality between conceptions of the good *per se*, then even at t_2, it must be neutral between C_1 and C_2. But this seems implausible. As I understand liberal neutrality, since it is a requirement to be neutral between persons, appealing at t_2 to C_1 does not run afoul of neutrality, since there are no differences between citizens on this matter. So it is not in itself non-neutral to appeal to conceptions of the good; it all depends on the differences that obtain among moral persons and citizens.

2. Liberal Moral Neutrality

2.1 Free and Equal Moral Persons

I take as my starting point the supposition that we conceive of ourselves and others as (i) moral persons who are (ii) free and equal. Although these features are assumed in this essay, we should not suppose that these assumptions cannot themselves be defended. John Rawls rightly argues that this general conception of moral persons is implicit in our public culture.[21] In much the same vein, I have argued that our commitment to the public justification of our moral demands on each other follows from our present conception of ourselves and others.[22] Let me briefly explain each of these two fundamental characteristics.

A moral person is one who makes, and can act upon, moral demands. Moral persons thus conceive of themselves as advancing moral claims on others. Alternatively, we can say that moral persons understand themselves to be owed certain restraints and acts.[23] Not all humans – not even all functioning adult humans – are moral persons: psychopaths do not appear to understand themselves as pressing moral claims on others that demand respect, nor do they see others as moral persons.[24] As well as advancing moral claims, moral persons have the capability to act on justified moral claims made on them. In this sense moral persons are not solely devoted to their own ends; they have a capacity to put aside their personal ends and goals to act on justified moral claims. Moral persons, then, are not simply instrumentally rational agents;[25] they possess a capacity for moral autonomy. Insofar as moral autonomy presupposes the ability to distinguish one's own ends from the moral claims of others, the idea of a moral person presupposes some cognitive skills.[26]

In the *Second Treatise* John Locke held that "The natural liberty of man is to be free from any superior power on earth, and not to be under the will or legislative authority of man, but to have only the law of Nature for his rule."[27] To conceive of oneself as morally free is to understand oneself as free from any natural moral authority that would accord others status to dictate one's moral obligations. This is not at all to say that one sees oneself as unbound by any morality; as Locke suggests, we may have the law of nature as our rule. Although we are by no means committed to a natural law conception of morality, the crucial point, again one in the spirit of Locke, is that free moral persons call on their own reason when deciding the dictates of moral law. A free person employs her own standards of evaluation when presented with claims about her moral liberties and obligations. A free person, we can say, has an interest in living in ways that accord with her own standards of rightness, value and goodness. At a minimum, to conceive of oneself as a morally free person is to see oneself as

bound only by moral requirements that can be validated from one's own point of view.[28] This conception of freedom has much in common with Rawls's notion of the rational autonomy of parties to the original position, according to which "there are no given antecedent principles external to their point of view to which they are bound."[29]

Now to say that moral persons are equal is to claim, firstly, that qua moral persons they possess the minimum requisite moral personality so that they are equal participants in the moral enterprise and, secondly, that each is morally free insofar as no one is subjected to the moral authority of others. The equality of moral persons is their equality qua free moral persons: it is not a substantive principle of moral equality but is a presupposition of the practice of moral justification insofar as it defines the status of the participants in moral justification. While a modest conception of moral equality, it rules out some conceptions of moral justification. Rawls not only conceives of moral persons as advancing claims on each other, but stresses that they view themselves as "self-authenticating sources of valid claims."[30] It would seem, and apparently Rawls agrees, that those who understand themselves as authenticating their own claims would not see themselves as bound to justify their claims on others – they would not suppose that only claims justified to others are valid.[31] But to advance a self-authenticating claim on others is not to respect their moral freedom, for others are bound only by moral claims that they can validate through their own reason: "there are no given antecedent principles external to their point of view to which they are bound." The supposition of equal moral freedom thus requires that one's moral claims can be validated by those to whom they are addressed.

Many have advanced stronger conceptions of moral equality. Some have claimed, for example, that the very practice of morality presupposes an "equal right of each to be treated only with justification."[32] In a similar vein S. I. Benn and R. S. Peters defended the principle that "The onus of justification rests on whoever would make distinctions. . . . Presume equality until there is a reason to presume otherwise."[33] Such a principle of moral equality does not simply require us to justify our moral claims to others: it requires us to justify all our actions that disadvantage some. Now, leaving aside whether some such presumptive egalitarian principle could be morally justified,[34] this conception of moral equality is not presupposed by the very idea of a justified morality among free and equal moral persons. If I accept this principle, I claim that others act wrongly if they disadvantage me without good justification. But unless this nondiscriminatory principle itself can be validated by others, I disrespect their moral freedom, as I am making a moral claim on them to nondiscriminatory action that is not validated by their own reason.

Validation from the rational and reflective perspective of another, however, is not the same as her actual consent. To treat another as a free and equal moral person is to accept that moral claims must be validated from her perspective when she employs her rational faculties in a competent manner and reflects upon them. Now, although as John Stuart Mill noted, there is a strong presumption that each knows her own perspective best, this is not necessarily so.[35] Just as others can make sound judgments about a person's beliefs and principles, and be correct even when the person disagrees, so can others be correct, and the moral agent wrong, about what is validated from her perspective when she reflects on it. Knowledge of oneself is generally superior to others' knowledge of one, but it is not indefeasible. People may withhold assent for a variety of reasons, including strategic objectives, pigheaded-ness, confusion, manifestly false beliefs, neurosis, and so on. Nevertheless, respect for the equal moral freedom of another requires that the presumption in favor of self-knowledge only be overridden given strong

reasons for concluding that she has misunderstood what is validated from her own point of view. Suppose that Alf and Betty reasonably disagree about whether some moral principle P is validated from Betty's rational and reflective perspective. Say that Alf has good reasons to conclude that Betty has misunderstood what is validated from her point of view: P, he says, really is validated from her point of view. Betty has reason to insist it isn't. For Alf to insist that his merely reasonable view of Betty's commitments override her own reasonable understanding of her moral perspective constitutes a violation of her moral freedom, for Alf is claiming authority to override her own reasonable understanding of her moral commitments with his merely reasonable view.[36] Crucial to moral freedom is that, over a wide range of deliberative competency, that one's moral deliberations lead you to conclude α authorizes you to believe α.[37]

2.2 Morality as Giving Others Reasons

We can reach much the same conclusion by a different route. Rather than relying directly on respecting the equal moral freedom of others, we can appeal to a theory of *moral reasons*. Morality is inherently a rational and practical enterprise insofar as addressing moral claims to others is to give them reasons to comply. To say that I have valid moral claims but these give others – even rational others – no reason to comply with them seems to undermine the point of advancing moral claims. If we are not simply concerned with calling others names – criticizing them for "doing wrong," "being guilty," "violating the rights of others," and so on – what is the point of advancing moral claims that do not appeal to their rational nature? To be sure, views of morality that attenuate its practical or rational nature in this way are often defended. Some see moral judgments as essentially descriptive and so not essentially practical ("ϕ is best described as a right action"). And some understand moral statements as a way to express disapproval at what others are doing, and so are not essentially rational ("Boo to φ!", "I disapprove of φ and you should too!"). Such views do not capture the crux of moral practice: it is a way for us to relate to each other as rational agents, who can give each other reasons to perform, or refrain from, actions of certain types.

If we accept that morality is necessarily about giving reasons to others, then our understanding of moral justification will be deeply influenced by our understanding of what constitutes a reason. We cannot enter here into the complexities of different accounts of reasons; consider, however, a plausible view. To give someone a reason is to give her a consideration to φ that, if she employs her rational faculties in an informed, careful, competent, and reflective way, she can see as counting in favor of φ. Suppose Alf claims that R is a reason for Betty to φ, but Alf admits that even were she to be fully informed about information that is relevant, and she carefully and competently reflects on R, she still could not see how R is a consideration in favor of φ-ing. It is hard to see in what way Alf can say that R is a reason for Betty to φ; he has admitted that it really cannot be grasped by her reflective deliberation, and given that, it cannot be a reason for her to do anything. The idea of a reason that is unable to play a role in deliberation is surely odd. Perhaps it would be good for Betty to φ, but it seems implausible to say that *she* has *any* considerations that count in favor of φ.

If we accept this plausible view of what it is to give another a reason, combined with our practical and rational conception of the moral enterprise, we are again led to the view that, for Alf to make a valid moral claim on Betty that she φs, this claim must be validated from Betty's perspective: there must be a reason *for her*.

2.3 Liberal Moral Neutrality

Given the requirements for treating others as free and equal moral persons and the requirements

of moral justification, the task of publicly justifying a moral principle P requires that P be validated from the perspective of each rational and reflective free and equal moral person. To publicly justify a moral principle is to justify it to all rational and reflective free and equal moral persons within some public, who confront each other as strangers.[38] I shall assume that the relevant public here is something like a society; we could also define the public in terms of all persons (a universalistic cosmopolitan morality) or a smaller community. As our main concern is with morality insofar as it relates to political justice, focus on the notion of a society's morality is appropriate.

Abstracting from the notions of goods, values, moral "intuitions" and so on, let us provisionally say that Σ is an evaluative standard for moral person Alf if and only if holding Σ, along with various sound beliefs about the world, is a reason for or against a purported moral principle, etc., from Alf's rational and reflective point of view.[39] So a person's evaluative standards are to be distinguished from justified moral requirements. Suppose, then, that Alf attempts to justify some moral principle P on the basis of his evaluative standard Σ_a, which is not shared by Betty. He clearly has not justified P. For P to be justified it must be validated from Betty's viewpoint. Thus, appealing to an evaluative standard about which Alf and Betty rationally and reflectively disagree cannot be justificatory: if Betty's careful and rational reflection cannot endorse Σ_a as a consideration in favor of P, then P has not yet been justified as a moral principle at all. Even if a careful, rational and reflective Betty can see Σ_a as a consideration in favor of P, this is still not enough to show that P is validated from her view. She might also have reason to embrace Σ_b and that may be a consideration against P; the matter then turns on which consideration defeats the other in her overall ranking of evaluative standards.

It is crucial to appreciate that this argument does not show that Alf has a moral obligation to justify his claims on Betty.[40] On such a view, although Alf may have a moral obligation not to insist on P without justification, he might have an overriding moral obligation to act on P even if it cannot be justified to her. On the account I have articulated here, unless P is validated from Betty's perspective, it is not a moral principle at all, and so cannot ground *any* moral reasons. Its status as a reason-giving moral principle applying to society depends on its validation from the public perspective. Morality supposes impartiality, and impartiality requires that the principle be validated by all members of the moral public.

If Alf is to respect others as free and equal moral persons and provide them with genuine moral claims, he is committed to:

Liberal Moral Neutrality: Alf's moral demands addressed to Betty must be neutral between his and Betty's evaluative standards: the justification of Alf's moral demands must not rely on relevant differences between his and Betty's evaluative standards.

Let us consider more carefully why Alf is committed to Liberal Moral Neutrality:

(i) We are supposing that Alf is committed to treating others as free and equal moral persons, and he is a moral person committed to making moral demands on others. If this is so, he must advance moral demands on others, and for these to be valid moral demands (i.e., to actually be moral demands) they must be justified to those others.

(ii) Liberal Moral Neutrality does not require that Alf present, or even be aware of, the justifications for his moral demands – he may be unable to articulate arguments about what others have reason to accept. But for his moral demands to be genuine, they must provide considerations for all reflective and rational others. Now given

this, it cannot be the case that their justification either favors his evaluative standards or theirs on a relevant difference between them. If there is a relevant difference (a difference that affects the justification of P), then if Alf is biased towards his own evaluative standards he will not be providing Betty with adequate reasons; should for some reason he favor Betty's, then the moral demand would not be validated from his view: it would not provide him with a sufficient reason. Note that if their evaluative standards converge on P, then the justification of the demand may be based in their different evaluative standards because it would not then be exploiting a difference between them, but appealing to their commonality. This is important. Public justifications may be based either on consensus or convergence of evaluative standards.[41] A consensus justification maintains that P is justified because everyone has grounds to endorse it on the basis of the same evaluative standard; a convergence justification maintains that P is justified because Alf has grounds to endorse it on the basis Σ_a, Betty on the basis of Σ_b, etc. Now a consensus justification is perfectly neutral: the justification does not rely on our disagreements about evaluative standards but, instead, on our agreement about the implications of our standards. Thus we must reject the plausible idea that liberal neutrality prohibits appeal to "controversial conceptions of the good"; we see here that in some cases such appeals treat all as free and equal moral persons to whom we owe reasons.

(iii) It should be clear why "treatment" is to be understood in terms of justification. The reason we are led to Liberal Moral Neutrality is a conception of free and equal moral persons who are committed to making moral demands on others that provide reasons from everyone's perspective. The grounding of morality is impartial treatment qua moral justification. Any more robust requirement of non-differential treatment – say, that every state policy should equally impact each conception of the good life – would have to be justified *within* the moral or political enterprises. Such robust conceptions of non-differential treatment are surely not presuppositions of the moral enterprise itself.

3. Liberal Political Neutrality

3.1 The Non-coercion Principle

I deem this conception of moral neutrality "liberal" because it starts from the quintessentially liberal conception of moral persons as free and equal, rational and reflective, agents. It is not, however, liberal in any more substantive sense. In order to move toward Liberal Political Neutrality we must first make a basic, and I think fairly uncontroversial, claim *within* morality. If any claim can be justified within the constraints of Liberal Moral Neutrality, it is surely:

> The Non-coercion Principle: (i) It is *prima facie* morally wrong for Alf to coerce Betty, or to employ force against her. (ii) With sufficient justification, Alf may have a moral right to use of coercion or force against Betty.

Almost every liberal political philosopher has understood the Non-coercion Principle as a basic moral commitment of liberal political philosophy. The principle's core claim is that, other things equal, the use of force or coercion against another is wrong. To show that other things are not equal, and so that the use of force and coercion is morally permissible, a moral justification is required.[42]

It is hard to see a plausible case against the Non-coercion Principle.[43] Whatever one's

evaluative standards, so long as one has any reason to act on them, and so be an agent, one must have strong reason to object when others exercise force or coercion to thwart one's agency. Someone who seeks to coerce you (without justification) to make you do as he wishes is attacking your fundamental interest in acting on your own evaluative standards. The wrongful coercer supplants your evaluative standards with his own as the grounds for your action. Jeffrey Reiman aptly describes this as a case of "subjugation": i.e., "the judgment of one person prevails over the contrary judgment of another simply because it can and without adequate justification for believing it should."[44] As Reiman suggests, the "suspicion of subjugation" can be dispelled – we can distinguish "might from right" – if there is adequate justification:[45] to say that coercion is "prima facie" wrong is to say that reasons can be provided to vindicate some instances of coercion. Suppose someone denies this: she says that coercion can never be justified: she accepts part (i) of the principle but denies (ii). Such an objector must, then, see self-defense as always wrong: in response to the wrongful force by another, it would still be wrong for her to employ force to resist. Though some have advanced such extreme pacifist views, the claim that one is never justified in employing any degree of coercion to repel any wrongful aggression against oneself is highly counterintuitive; I will not pause to consider it further. If our agency is of fundamental importance to us, then we must accept that, at least in some cases, we have reason to endorse a principle that allows coercion – at the very least, to counter coercion against us.

3.2 The Moral Claims of, and Constraint on, Liberal Governors

Government officials participate in the authorization of coercion; unjustified coercion is wrong, so if officials are not to act wrongly their coercion must be justified. Consider first the two-person case: official Alf is coercing citizen

Betty, say, by imposing a law. So, at a minimum, Alf must have a justified moral liberty to coerce Betty: it must be, morally, not wrong for him to coerce her.[46] And, of course, this justification must meet the demands of Liberal Moral Neutrality: he cannot favor his own evaluative standards. But for the same reason, the justification cannot favor the evaluative standards of some third party, Charlie, when coercing Betty. Now take any law that applies to both Betty and Charlie: in the justification of the law Alf cannot exploit differences in Betty's and Charlie's evaluative standards, since then one of them will have inadequate reason to accept that Alf has a moral right to impose the law. So Alf's act of imposing the law is only morally permissible if there is a justification for the imposition that meets Liberal Political Neutrality.[47]

This all supposes that the Non-coercion Principle applies to governments and its agents (qua agents). This is not entirely uncontroversial; a recurring view in the history of political philosophy insists that the "normal" moral restraints that apply to individual actors do not apply to the state; "the State, as such, certainly cannot be guilty of personal immorality, and it is hard to see how it can commit theft or murder in the sense in which these are moral offenses."[48] More generally, what has been called "political realism" insists that the constraints of "ordinary" morality are not applicable to politics. As Machiavelli famously observed, "A man who wishes to make a profession of goodness in everything must necessarily come to grief among so many who are not good."[49] If governors have a duty to protect the interests of their citizens, it has seemed to many that in the unpredictable and morally lax environment in which politicians often operate, they must ignore the normal precepts of everyday morality and look to promote the good of their people. As the realist sees it, to insist that the Non-coercion Principle applies to those in government fails to appreciate the distinctive character of the political.

We need to distinguish three different conceptions of the special nature of politics.[50] (i) The "realist" insists that there is an "ineluctable tension between the moral command and the requirements of successful political action."[51] On this conception successful politics requires immorality: one must often have morally "dirty hands" to be a successful politician. The liberal tradition in politics rejects such realism: politics is neither above nor outside the claims of morality. (ii) The first view is puzzling: why should the fact (if it be a fact) that political success requires immorality be a reason to ignore morality rather than to forgo political success? If a trade union official told us that success for the union requires immorality, we would hardly think that this excuses her immorality. A moral plausible view is that while morality applies to the government, it is an entirely different morality: the state, we are told by some, cannot be guilty of personal immorality – it is held accountable to a higher morality: "successful political action" is "itself inspired by the moral principle of national survival," and so politicians have no "moral right" to sacrifice their state in the pursuit of fidelity to the principles of individual morality.[52] This special "morality of the state" is also rejected by the liberal tradition: there is not one morality for persons and a different one for states, as if states were not composed of individuals with commitments to respect the moral personality of others. (iii) However, to deny that there is a special morality of the state is not to deny that that the special circumstances of politics may allow for justifying acts that otherwise would be wrong. Liberals (although not perhaps libertarians) accept that the conditions under which the agents of the state can justifiably employ coercion differ from the conditions under which private individuals may. This, of course, is the fundamental concern of political philosophy: how does the state come to be authorized to employ coercion (such as to punish) while private individuals are not so authorized? To accept that the agents of the state are justified in employing coercion when non-state agents are not does not mean that the Non-coercion Principle fails to apply to governors: the liberal claims that there are arguments that meet the test of Liberal Moral Neutrality that, in some cases, allow only agents of the state to justifiably coerce.

The upshot is that unless we wish to join the realist in withdrawing politics from the purview of morality, or allow that the state is subject to its own special morality of national interest, the actions of those who are agents of the state must conform to requirements of morality, specifically the Non-coercion Principle, and the only way to overcome the presumption against coercion is though a justification that conforms to the demands of Liberal Moral Neutrality. We thus have:

> *Liberal Political Neutrality*: An agent of the state, when coercing a citizen, or participating in the authorization of such coercion, must be neutral between that citizen and any other citizen: the justification of the state official's coercion must not treat differentially reasonable and reflective citizens' differences in their evaluative standards.

Notice that we have switched our focus from *moral persons* to *citizens*. For the most part, I shall leave open the relation between these two classes. We do need to suppose that all members of the class of citizens are also free and equal moral persons, since the moral foundations of Liberal Political Neutrality lie in Liberal Moral Neutrality. Perhaps *all* moral persons residing within a jurisdiction should be considered as citizens (I am certainly sympathetic to this proposal); however, I shall leave open the possibility that that some moral persons within a jurisdiction (i.e., resident aliens) might be excluded from the class of citizens. This is an important issue in political theory, but we cannot pause to discuss it here. Nothing I say in what follows turns on this point.

3.3 *The Coercive Nature of the State*

Does Liberal Political Neutrality apply to all, or only some, action by state officials? John Stuart Mill distinguished authoritative from non-authoritative interventions by government; while the former take the form of a command backed by enforcement, the latter give advice and information, or establish an agency to deal with a problem while allowing others to compete.[53] Although the government threatening drug users with prison sentences is indeed an act of coercion, drug education programs, on Mill's view, would not be coercive. George Sher makes much of this point. In order to promote certain aims, governments might offer rewards, engage in economic policies that favor the aim, fund educational programs, and so on.[54] If these policies are not coercive, then they do not fall under the Non-coercion Principle.

What is sometimes called the "libertarian" response must be right here: each of the supposedly non-coercive measures is only possible because of a prior act of coercion, be it threats associated with the tax code, threats that back up banking regulations (relevant, say, to setting interest rates), and so on. The action "conduct an educational program" presupposes the action "raise via taxation the revenues to conduct the program." Assuming the former is impossible without the latter, it is inappropriate to separately evaluate them. An act that depends on having certain resources or powers cannot be evaluated without consideration of the legitimacy of obtaining those resources or powers. Here at least is a case where the dictum that "He who wills the end must also will the means" is appropriate: to insist that there is nothing coercive about the end, when the only way to achieve the end is through a coercive means, is disingenuous. To say that it is not coercive to spend your money, even though I must use coercion to get my hands on it, hardly seems convincing. The object of evaluation should be the complex act (raise revenues through taxation and spend them on an educational program). That the complex should be the focus of evaluation is by no means simply a libertarian view: the American Civil Liberties Union sues public authorities that use tax money to advertise religion (say, by using public workers to erect signs saying "Jesus is Lord").[55] The idea is that this is not a mere educational measure that does not impose burdens on some; it does impose burdens that must be born by dissenting citizens because of threats of punishment by the taxation department.

It can, though, plausibly be maintained that some state actions are less coercive than others. Just as a threat of a short prison sentence is less coercive than threat of a long one, and threat of a small fine is less coercive than threat of a moderate jail term, so too the coercion involved in an extra one percent marginal tax rate is typically less coercive than the threat of jail.[56] Thus, if we concern ourselves with the strength of the justifications required to legitimate the coercion, then a distinction between stronger and milder forms of coercion will be relevant.[57] But that distinction is not relevant to the Non-coercion Principle, which concerns the set of actions that require justification.

4. The Implications of Liberal Political Neutrality

4.1 The Demanding Nature of Liberal Political Neutrality

To paraphrase Robert Nozick, so strong and far-reaching is Liberal Political Neutrality that it raises the question of what, if anything, the officials of the state may do.[58] It is unclear whether much in the way of public policy survives the neutrality test. Since we have seen that whenever state officials act they participate in a coercion-authorizing process, to implement any such policy would require a justification that does not exploit differences in the evaluative standards of reasonable and reflective citizens – i.e., is neutral between them. Some may think that this is not

terribly demanding. It is reasonable to suppose that, after all, citizens do share many evaluative standards. Although we may not have consensus on a full-fledged conception of the good, we might still identify "a public conception of the good": there might be substantive shared values that are a matter of overlapping consensus of everyone's conceptions of the good – say, health, security, and happiness.[59] Suppose, for example, that some evaluative standard Σ is shared by all. Then it would seem that an appeal to Σ in a justification for policy P would not run afoul of Liberal Political Neutrality: implementing policy P treats all citizens neutrally since the justification for it does not appeal to their reasonable differences in evaluative standards. But this moves too quickly, for we need to take account of different citizens' rankings of their evaluative standards. Reason R does not justify a policy consistent with neutrality unless it would be accepted by all fully rational and reflective citizens. Now although a rational Betty might reject R as a reason because it appeals to an evaluative standard that she does not share, she will also reasonably reject it as a good reason in favor of P when it appeals to a ranking of evaluative standards that she does not share; R may be *a* reason in favor of P, but it is overridden in her ranking by R*, which is a reason against P. According to Milton Rokeach, a psychologist, Americans agree in affirming a set of 36 values; what they differ on is "the way they organize them to form value hierarchies or priorities."[60] If so, our main disagreements are not about what is of value (what is an evaluative standard), but the relative importance of our evaluative standards. Even if everyone agrees, say, that smoking causes cancer and that this is *a* reason for a policy discouraging smoking, rational people clearly do disagree about whether the pleasures are worth the risk of death. Given that rational people weigh the relative values of pleasure and safety differently, coercive acts that can only be justified on the grounds that the pleasure does not outweigh the risk to health fail to provide a neutral case. Thus, although the badness of ill health caused by smoking can be invoked in a neutral justification, that its badness outweighs the goodness of the pleasure of smoking cannot; and without that, no state policies discouraging smoking will be justified. This has direct relevance to United States drug policy, which is based on certain middle-class value rankings, and which results in policies that place inordinate costs on the poor.[61]

This fundamental point deserves emphasis. Political philosophers are usually insensitive to what economists call "opportunity costs": the cost of getting one thing you value is that you must forgo something else you value.[62] It is often assumed that once we recognize a shared value, we have the basis for a neutral policy: but everything depends on whether achieving this shared value requires that some give up something of greater value. If it does, then for those citizens pursuing this shared value is irrational: they are giving up something more important for something they prize less. So it does no good to simply point to shared value: we must point to a shared ranking of values, so that all rational and reflective citizens will agree that achieving this value is more important than any other values that might be achieved. But this is a daunting task: rational and reflective, free and equal persons appear to disagree deeply on the rankings of their evaluative standards (what is a "conception of the good" but a scheme in which values are weighted?). It looks as if almost any collective pursuit of values will involve some citizens being coerced into pursuing a value than is less important to them than a value they had to give up (say, because they were taxed for the collectively pursued value).

Some try to blunt the radical implications of Liberal Political Neutrality by restricting the range of the neutrality principle (the class of cases covered by φ) to a small set of basic political matters.[63] Rawls, for example, appears to restrict φ to constitutional issues or matters of basic justice: unless an issue concerns a "constitutional essential" neutrality does not apply – apparently

non-neutral justifications can be employed in everyday (non-constitutional) politics. Can they? Suppose that we have a neutral justification of a constitution, and now are advocating policy P, which is not itself about a constitutional matter. There are two possibilities. It might be that the constitution, which is *ex hypothesi* neutrally justified, authorizes P. In this case P *does* have a neutral justification insofar as it is justified through the constitution which is neutrally justified. The issue, though, is whether a constitution with extensive authorizations of this sort *could* be neutrally justified. It seems doubtful indeed that, for example, a constitution that allows the government to use taxation to discourage smoking, encourage a healthy life-style, regulate drugs, fund the arts, go to war to spread democracy, seek to advance human flourishing, protect the family, or promote community, is capable of neutral public justification. Given what has been said above, there is a strong presumption that all coerced citizens could not be given impartial reasons of the requisite sort for granting the state authority over these matters. The other alternative is that the constitution is neutrally justified, but only the constitution; there is no indirect neutral justification via the constitution for policy P. The case for P is another matter entirely, outside of the scope of Liberal Political Neutrality. But this implies that P is a coercive act without adequate justification and so, wrong. Neutrality cannot be restricted to a certain "level" because the Non-coercion Principle is a fully general principle, applying to all coercive acts.

4.2 The Specter of Anarchism?

If Liberal Political Neutrality is *that* demanding, is any law justified? Do we end up with anarchism? Everything I have thus far said about public policies that seek to advance values such as health would seem to apply to matters of basic political justice, such as a regime of property rights. While every rational and reflective citizen may agree that some system of property rights is better than none (for then we avoid the state of nature, where there is no "mine and thine"), no argument for a specific system of property can function as a neutral justification of the requisite sort, as it will be rationally rejected by some. Some will, say, rank a libertarian system of property higher than a welfare state system, while others will have evaluative standards that lead them to the reverse ranking. The difference between the smoking case and the property rights case lies in where the option "no policy at all in this matter" is on each rational citizen's rankings. Suppose that all rational citizens endorse or prefer systems of property $\{Pr_1, Pr_2, Pr_3\}$ over no system of property rights, but some prefer no system of property rights over $\{Pr_4, Pr_5\}$. If so, there is a Liberal Political Neutralist justification for selecting from the set of $\{Pr_1, Pr_2, Pr_3\}$; our evaluative standards converge on the conclusion that any member of that set is better than no property regime at all. What is required next – and this is where democracy enters in – is a justified procedure to select from that set.[64] If we have such a procedure, then we will have a fully justified system of property rights despite the disagreements about what is the best system – disagreements on the relative merits of $\{Pr_1, Pr_2, Pr_3\}$. In contrast, in the typical public policy case, at least over a very wide range of issues, for *each and every* policy P in the set of options, a number of citizens rank P as inferior to "no policy at all on this matter." No policy whatsoever will be preferred, first, by those who prefer no policy to every policy, and so rank P and all other policies behind no policy at all (e.g., classical liberals regarding pornography regulation). Second, P will also be ranked worse than no policy at all by those who prefer some other policy P* to no policy at all, but prefer no policy at all to P.[65] Thus on issues where some rational citizens fall into one of these two groups no public justification of P can be advanced. Of course, if there is a public justification for *some policy* on this matter (for example, regarding a public good such as pollution control), and P is in the set of admissible policies, then we move

to a case like that of property rights. It is very likely, though, that once we take account of comparative judgments, Liberal Political Neutrality precludes a great deal of contemporary legislation.

4.3 Liberal Political Neutrality: Critical or Apologetic?

Liberal Political Neutrality is a radical principle: it expresses a suspicion that coercion threatens subjugation and, based on our understanding of others as free and equal moral persons, advances a demanding test to overcome this suspicion. *Pace* almost all contemporary advocates of Liberal Neutrality, I have argued that Liberal Political Neutrality is genuinely liberal in the sense that it is suspicious of all coercion and drastically limits the scope of government. Many of the things that contemporary states do fail the test of Liberal Political Neutrality – which is to say that contemporary states are not genuinely liberal. Some advocates of "liberal neutrality" see this conclusion as a *reductio ad absurdum*.[66] To these liberals, any adequate conception of liberal neutrality *must* show that most of what contemporary governments do is justified. Thus some tell us that if a conception of liberal neutrality excludes, say, public school classes in drama and music, it is shown to be an absurd conception.[67] This common view presupposes what liberals must question: that state coercion is justified. I see no good reason to accept what amounts to a conception of political philosophy as an apology for the current state. To appropriate a contemporary if not pellucid term, in the eyes of liberals the state is problematic. That is why the classic social contract theories begin with the state of nature – a condition without any government – and seek to show that construction of a limited government is consistent with moral principles. Current advocates of neutrality work the other way around: they start with government as we know it and test moral principles by showing that they justify it.

Even supposing it is true that "daily politics is irretrievably perfectionist" – that the aim of politics is to make people more autonomous, or healthier, or wiser, or more family-oriented, or more God-fearing – this would by no means show that anti-perfectionism is absurd or misguided.[68] If compelling moral claims show that most state coercion is unjust, then the loser is state coercion, not these fundamental moral convictions. Liberal moral principles are indeed "self-stultifying"[69] when what is being stultified is unjustified coercion of some by others. Morality stultifies a host of things that we may wish to do, including making others more perfect in our own eyes.

Notes

1 See Charles Larmore, *Patterns of Moral Complexity* (Cambridge: Cambridge University Press, 1987), pp. 43ff.; Will Kymlicka, "Liberal Individualism and Liberal Neutrality," *Ethics* 99 (Jul. 1989): 833–905; Simon Caney, "Consequentialist Defenses of Liberal Neutrality," *The Philosophical Quarterly* 41 (Jan. 1991): 457–77.

2 The most careful discussion is George Sher, *Beyond Neutrality: Perfectionism and Politics* (Cambridge: Cambridge University Press, 1997), Ch. 2.

3 See Jeremy Waldron, "Legislation and Moral Neutrality" in his *Liberal Rights* (Cambridge: Cambridge University Press, 1993), pp. 149ff.

4 Peter Jones, "The Ideal of the Neutral State" in Robert E. Goodin and Andrew Reeve, eds., *Liberal Neutrality* (London: Routledge, 1989), p. 9; Govert Den Hartogh, "The Limits of Liberal Neutrality," *Philosophica* 56 (1995): 59–89 at p. 61.

5 Colin M. MacLeod, "Liberal Neutrality or Liberal Tolerance?" *Law and Philosophy* 16 (Sep. 1997): 529–59 at p. 532; Paul Rosenberg, "Liberal Neutralism and the Social-Democratic Project," *Critical Review* 8 (1994): 217–34 at p. 218.

6 Wojciech Sadurski, "Theory of Punishment, Social Justice and Liberal Neutrality," *Law and Philosophy* 7 (1988–9): 351–74 at p. 371.

7 See Jones, "The Ideal of the Neutral State," p. 9.

8 See Philippe van Parijs, *Real Freedom for All* (Oxford: Oxford University Press, 1995), p. 28.

9 Bruce A. Ackerman, *Social Justice in the Liberal State* (New Haven, CT: Yale University Press, 1980), p. 11.

10 Larmore, *Patterns of Moral Complexity*, pp. 53ff.

11 Robert Talisse, *Democracy After Liberalism* (London: Routledge, 2005), p. 33.

12 See John Rawls, *Justice as Fairness: A Restatement*, ed. Erwin Kelly (Cambridge, MA: Belknap Press of Harvard University Press, 2001), p. 152.

13 Jones, "The Ideal of the Neutral State," p. 9.

14 See Brian Barry, *Justice as Impartiality* (Oxford: Clarendon Press, 1995), pp. 139–45; Ronald Dworkin, "Liberalism" in his *A Matter of Principle* (Cambridge, MA: Harvard University Press, 1985), p. 191; Roger Paden, "Democracy and Liberal Neutrality," *Contemporary Philosophy* 14 (1): 17–20.

15 Kymlicka, "Liberal Individualism and Liberal Neutrality," p. 886.

16 J. Donald Moon, *Constructing Community: Moral Pluralism and Tragic Conflicts* (Princeton, NJ: Princeton University Press, 1993), p. 55.

17 See Barry, *Justice as Impartiality*, pp. 125ff.; Robert E. Goodin and Andrew Reeve, "Liberalism and Neutrality" in their edited collection, *Liberal Neutrality*, pp. 1–8.

18 Woodrow Wilson, *Message to Congress*, 63rd Cong., 2d Session, Senate Doc. No. 566 (Washington, DC, 1914), pp. 3–4.

19 http://lawofwar.org/Neutrality.htm

20 This assumes that expressive stances are a form of treatment. On this see Christi Dawn Favor, "Expressive Desert and Deserving Compensation," in Julian Lamont, Christi Dawn Favor and Gerald Gaus, eds., *Essays on Philosophy, Politics and Economics* (Stanford, CA: Stanford University Press, 2009).

21 See John Rawls, "Kantian Constructivism in Moral Theory," in Samuel Freeman, ed., *John Rawls: Collected Papers* (Cambridge, MA: Harvard University Press, 1999), pp. 303–58, esp. 305ff. This is not to say that Rawls and I advance precisely the same conception of free and equal moral persons, as shall become clear in what follows.

22 See my *Value and Justification* (Cambridge: Cambridge University Press, 1990), pp. 278ff.

23 See here J. R. Lucas, *On Justice* (Oxford: Clarendon Press, 1980), p. 7. For a development of this conception of morality, see Thomas Scanlon, *What We Owe Each Other* (Cambridge, MA: Belknap Press of Harvard University Press, 1998), esp. pp. 177ff.

24   I argue this in *Value and Justification*, pp. 281ff.

25   See John Rawls, *Political Liberalism*, paperback edition (New York: Columbia University Press, 1996), p. 51.

26   I argue for this claim in "The Place of Autonomy in Liberalism," in John Christman and Joel Anderson, eds., *Autonomy and the Challenges to Liberalism* (Cambridge: Cambridge University Press, 2005), pp. 272–306.

27   John Locke, *Second Treatise of Government* in *Two Treatises of Government*, ed. Peter Laslett (Cambridge: Cambridge University Press, 1960), §22.

28   It also provides the basis for understanding morality as self-legislated. I develop this idea further in "The Place of Autonomy in Liberalism."

29   Rawls, "Kantian Constructivism," p. 334.

30   Rawls, *Justice as Fairness*, p. 23. The importance of the idea of self-authentication is easily overlooked in Rawls's thinking. It first appeared in his 1951 paper on an "Outline of a Decision Procedure for Ethics," which conceived of ethics as adjudicating the claims of individuals, which he clearly saw as self-authenticating. See section 5 of that paper in Rawls's *Collected Papers*, Ch. 1.

31   Hence, because of this, parties to Rawls's original position are not required to advance justifications for their claims. Rawls argues this in "Kantian Constructivism," p. 334.

32   Hadley Arkes, *First Things: An Inquiry into the First Principles of Moral and Justice* (Princeton, NJ: Princeton University Press, 1986), p. 70. Italics omitted.

33   S. I. Benn and R. S. Peters, *Social Principles and the Democratic State* (London: George Allen and Unwin, 1959), p. 110.

34   I argue that it cannot in *Justificatory Liberalism* (New York: Oxford University Press, 1996), pp. 162ff.

35   J. S. Mill, *On Liberty*, in *On Liberty and Other Essays*, ed. John Gray (New York: Oxford University Press, 1991), pp. 84–5 (ch. IV, para. 4). Mill also was aware that this assumption does not always hold true. See his *Principles of Political Economy*, in J. M. Robson, ed., *The Collected Works of John Stuart Mill* (Toronto: University of Toronto Press, 1963), vols. II and III, Book V, Ch. xi, § 9.

36   I deal with this complex question more formally in *Justificatory Liberalism*, Parts I and II.

37   Again, I recognize the complexities of this matter. I try to shed a little more light on it in "Liberal Neutrality: A Radical and Compelling Principle," in Steven Wall and George Klosko, eds., *Perfectionism and Neutrality: Essays in Liberal Theory* (Lanham, MD: Rowman & Littlefield, 2003), pp. 136–65, at pp. 150ff, and *Value and Justification*, pp. 399–404.

38   On the concept of the public, see S. I. Benn and G. F. Gaus, "The Liberal Conception of the Public and Private," in S. I. Benn and G. F. Gaus, eds., *Public and Private in Social Life* (New York: St. Martin's, 1983), pp. 31–66.

39   I leave aside here whether Σ is itself a belief about the world, as ethical naturalists would have it. It is important to stress that nothing in my account precludes moral realism as a meta-ethical or metaphysical thesis; the epistemic constraint on moral reasons is the crucial principle on which the analysis rests.

40   This interpretation is advanced by Christopher Eberle, *Religious Convictions in Liberal Politics* (Cambridge: Cambridge University Press, 2002), Ch. 3.

41   On convergence as a mode of justification, see Fred D'Agostino, *Free Public Reason: Making It Up As We Go* (New York: Oxford University Press, 1996), pp. 30–1.

42   In order to simplify, I will henceforth refer to "coercion" rather than the more cumbersome "force and coercion."

43   I have considered some possible objections in "Liberal Neutrality: A Radical and Compelling Principle."

44   Jeffrey Reiman, *Justice and Modern Moral Philosophy* (New Haven, CT: Yale University Press, 1990), p. 2.

45   Reiman, *Justice and Modern Moral Philosophy*, p. 2.

46   According to Wesley Hohfeld, Alf has a liberty to ϕ, if and only if Betty has no claim against Alf that he not ϕ. For Hohfeld's classic analysis, see his "Some Fundamental Legal Conceptions as Applied in Judicial Reasoning," *Yale Law Review* 23 (1913): 16–59.

47   Note that should the law not apply to some other party, the law would not have to be justified to him: a law might apply to only a "section of the public." Think, for example, of a law that regulates motorcycle use: it may not require justification to some class of citizens (say, those who do not drive). Stanley Benn and I explore the idea of a "section of the public" in "The Liberal Conception of the Public and Private."

48 Bernard Bosanquet, *The Philosophical Theory of the State* in *The Philosophical Theory of the State and Related Essays*, ed. Gerald F. Gaus and William Sweet (Indianapolis, IN: St. Augustine Press, 2001), p. 285. Even Bosanquet, however, insisted that, while the state as such could not be guilty of immorality, "if an agent, even under the order of his executive superior, commits a breach of morality, *bona fide* in order to do what he conceives to be a public end desired by the State, he and his superior are certainly blamable . . ." (p. 284).

49 Niccolò Machiavelli, *The Prince* in *The Prince and the Discourses* (New York: Modern Library, 1950 [1515]), p. 56.

50 I consider these issues in more detail in "Dirty Hands" in R. G. Frey and Kit Wellman, eds., *The Blackwell Companion to Applied Ethics* (Oxford: Basil Blackwell, 2003), pp. 169–79.

51 Hans J. Morganthau, *Politics Among Nations*, 5th edn (New York: Alfred A. Knopf, 1973), p. 10. See also Reinhold Niebuhr, *Moral Man and Immoral Society* (London: Student Christian Movement Press, 1963).

52 Morganthau, *Politics Among Nations*, p. 10. Note that Morganthau seems to advocate both positions (i) and (ii). It is often difficult to know whether "realists" are arguing against applying moral considerations to politics, or are arguing for a special political morality.

53 Mill, *Principles of Political Economy*, Book V, Ch. XI.

54 Sher, *Beyond Neutrality*, pp. 34–7.

55 *The Times-Picayune* (New Orleans), Sunday Feb. 24, 2002, Metro Section, p. 1.

56 See Daniel M. Weinstock, "Neutralizing Perfection: Hurka on Liberal Neutrality," *Dialogue* 38 (1999): 45–62.

57 I explore the problems of degrees of coercion and strength of justification in "Coercion, Ownership, and the Redistributive State," *Social Philosophy & Policy* (forthcoming 2010).

58 Nozick, *Anarchy, State and Utopia*, p. ix.

59 Weinstock, "Neutralizing Perfection," p. 55.

60 See Milton Rokeach, *The Nature of Human Values* (New York: The Free Press, 1973), p. 110; Milton Rokeach, "From Individual to Institutional Values," in his *Understanding Values* (London: Collier Macmillan, 1979), p. 208.

61 See J. Donald Moon, "Drugs and Democracy" in Pablo De Greiff, ed., *Drugs and the Limits of Liberalism* (Ithaca, NY: Cornell University Press, 1999), pp. 133–55.

62 George Klosko is something of an exception. He acknowledges that people disagree in their rankings, but he insists that somehow this is not a problem for justification. Thus he tells us that it is not "forbidden that government policy priorities reflect some conceptions more than others. Neutrality requires only that public policies be intended to realize nonsectarian values and that the relevant means be similarly defensible." ["Reasonable Rejection and Neutrality of Justification" in Steven Wall and George Klosko, eds., *Perfectionism and Neutrality: Essays in Liberal Theory* (Lanham, MD: Rowman & Littlefield, 2003), pp. 167–89 at p. 178.] Klosko's position seems to be that so long as policy is justified on "nonsectarian" grounds, it is neutrally justified, even if the policy "reflects" some citizens' ranking over others. I cannot see the motivation for restricting justification to the kinds of reasons advanced but not their importance; unless a more complicated account is offered, a person has no reason to accept a policy that is based on a ranking of evaluative criteria that she reasonably rejects. Klosko thus defends motorcycle helmet laws as "neutral" even though he admits that they presuppose rankings of values that are rationally rejected by some citizens. Klosko's main motivation, I think, is simply to ensure that liberal neutrality does not have radical implications; see §4.3 below.

63 Weinstock, "Neutralizing Perfection," p. 54.

64 I have argued that constitutional democracy is such a procedure in *Justificatory Liberalism*, Part III.

65 I explore this problem in much more depth in "The Legal Coordination Game," *American Philosophical Association's Newsletter on Philosophy and Law 1* (Spring 2002): 122–8.

66 See, e.g., Klosko, "Reasonable Rejection and Neutrality of Justification," pp. 175ff.; Weinstock, "Neutralizing Perfection," p. 47.

67 See Klosko, "Reasonable Rejection and Neutrality of Justification," p. 175. Klosko is reporting, but apparently concurring with, the views of Richard Kraut.

68 Den Hartogh, "The Limits of Liberal Neutrality," p. 59.

69 This term is Weinstock's.

PART 2

Government, the Economy, and Morality

2a. POLITICAL ECONOMY

IT IS HARD TO GET FAR IN THINKING about political philosophy without running into empirical claims. This is especially true when thinking about whether and to what extent the government ought to be involved in a nation's economy. For most of us, whether the government ought to mandate a legal minimum wage, regulate foreign imports, control monopolies, or tax citizens in order to provide for roads and clean air will depend at least in part on what the *consequences* of government's following or not following these policies will be. This is obviously true for those who are moral consequentialists like Mill, but even rights-based theorists like Nozick and Rawls will give some weight to pragmatic considerations.

To address these empirical considerations in a somewhat systematic way, we turn in this section to the field of political economy. Political economy, as its name suggests, is a field devoted to the study of the intersection of politics and the economy. Its primary question is how economic production and trade should be organized by the state. Historically, political economy became a major subject of study around the time of the publication of Adam Smith's *Inquiry into the Nature and Causes of the Wealth of Nations* (1776). In this text, excerpts from which appear in this section, Smith argued against the doctrine of mercantilism, which held that nations ought to seek to enhance their own wealth by tightly restricting the importation of foreign goods, and argued in favor of free trade both within and between nations. It was in this text that Smith famously claimed that under capitalism, individuals would be led by an "invisible hand" to promote the wealth of their society, since the only way that they could enrich themselves would be to provide others with goods or services that those others valued more than their money. Social wealth, on this view, is an unintended side-effect of the individual pursuit of self-interest.

For Smith, the division of labour was the key for the development of a nation's wealth. By allowing individuals to specialize in a skill, to save time moving between different tasks, and to develop technology to do the same task more easily, the division of labour greatly improves the productive power of labour. Smith saw that this principle applied just as well between nations as it did within a single nation, but it would be almost forty years before that insight was formalized by the British political economist, David Ricardo. In his *Principles of Political Economy and Taxation*, Ricardo set forth the principle of comparative advantage, which demonstrates that even when one country is more productive than another in absolute terms, it will benefit both countries to specialize and trade freely. This is because even less productive countries (or individuals — the principle holds for both) can have a *comparative* advantage in certain areas of production where their opportunity costs — what they have to give up in order to engage in one activity rather than another — are lower.

Thus, imagine Art and Betty living together on an island. Suppose Betty can produce either 100 fish or 200 apples with a week's work, while Art could only produce 50 fish or 50 apples. Even though Betty is more productive than Art in absolute terms, Art enjoys a comparative advantage in the production of fish, since in terms of his opportunity costs producing one fish only requires that he give up one apple, whereas for Betty to produce one fish she must give up *two* apples. Given that this is so, *both* Art and Betty will be better off if each specializes in producing that good for which they enjoy the greatest comparative advantage (fish for Art and apples for Betty), and then trades to ensure a balanced diet. Free trade will benefit not just super-productive Betty, but even moderately-productive Art. Contemporary defenders of globalization have argued that this principle provides strong support for outsourcing and other forms of trade between not just developed countries, but between developed and developing countries alike.

Not all political economists, however, have been so sanguine about the morally beneficial effects of the pursuit of self-interest. Karl Marx, for instance, argued that capitalism, just as much as the feudalism that preceded it, is a system of class conflict. The interests of the capital-owning class require them to extract as much value as possible from labourers at the lowest cost. Workers in a capitalist system are treated as little more than machines for the production of labour, and the interest of capitalists is to get that labour out of those machines as cheaply as possible. This leads to a system in which workers — on whose back the productivity of an economy depends — are systematically exploited. Further, Marx paints a picture of capitalism as a ravenous beast that must consume everything in its path — traditional ways of life, the dignity of the individual, foreign nations — or else die. Contemporary critics of globalization will find Marx's writings to be a prescient critique of the current spread of that system.

Marx's line of argument constitutes a radical critique of the paradigm of classical economics, and by extension the neoclassical economics that followed it. But it is possible to make a case for government intervention in the economy from within the neoclassical paradigm itself. For even if Smith was right that market forces *often* channel self-interest into socially beneficial outcomes, there are certain categories of cases in which what's good for the individual and what's good for society come apart. Economists refer to these cases as *market failures,* and define them more precisely as cases in which markets fail to produce economically efficient outcomes. In his essay in this section, Charles Wolf discusses some of the most common forms of market failure such as negative externalities, public goods, and monopolies. The concept of market failure has played a central role in most contemporary work in political economy. Indeed, many economists have viewed the existence of market failures as one of the fundamental justifications for political authority. Since roads, national defense, and even arguably the law and the capitalist market itself are all public goods that cannot adequately be provided for by voluntary exchange, some coercive mechanism such as the state is required in order to provide them. Government, the argument goes, is therefore justified because it helps individuals achieve goods that they want but cannot practically produce on their own.

But even as government solves some economic problems, it creates others of its own. The field of public choice, lying at the intersection of economics and political science, applies economic tools of analysis to political institutions. And, not surprisingly, if we assume government to be populated by the same rational self-interested agents that economics supposes to populate the market, it turns out that government policies will often be aimed more at promoting the interests of politicians, rather than the interest of the public at large. Randy Simmons' essay in this section discusses some of the kinds of "government failure" that the field of public choice has discovered. The lesson is that in deciding upon the proper roles of government and the economy, we must judge an admittedly imperfect market against a government that has serious shortcomings of its own.

This section is far too brief to decisively settle the contentious issues of political economy. My hope in including it, then, is rather that readers will come away with an appreciation of the various ways in which the claims of political philosophers often depend on empirical matters regarding the relationship between the economy and state, and that they have an understanding of some of the more important theories that have developed from such empirical investigation.

Further Reading

Buchanan, A. (1985). *Ethics, Efficiency, and the Market.* New York: Rowman and Littlefield.

Buchanan, J., and Tullock, G. (1962). *The Calculus of Consent.* Ann Arbor: University of Michigan Press.

Cowen, T. (1988). *The Theory of Market Failure: A Critical Examination.* Fairfax: George Mason University Press.

Friedman, M. (2002). *Capitalism and Freedom* (40th Anniversary ed.). Chicago: University of Chicago.

Keynes, J. M. (1997). *The General Theory of Employment, Interest, and Money.* New York: Prometheus Books.

Marx, K. (1992). *Capital.* New York: Penguin.

Mill, J. S. (2004). *Principles of Political Economy with Applications to Social Philosophy.* Indianapolis: Hackett.

Mitchell, W., and Simmons, R. T. (1994). *Beyond Politics: Markets, Welfare, and the Failure of Bureaucracy.* Boulder, CO: Westview Press.

Mueller, D. C. (2003). *Public Choice III.* Cambridge: Cambridge University Press.

Ricardo, D. (2004). *On the Principles of Political Economy and Taxation.* Indianapolis: Liberty Fund.

Samuelson, P., and Nordhaus, W. (1998). *Economics.* Boston: Irwin McGraw-Hill.

Schmidtz, D. (1991). *The Limits of Government: An Essay on the Public Goods Argument.* Boulder, CO: Westview Press.

Smith, A. (1982). *The Wealth of Nations.* Indianapolis: Liberty Fund.

Chapter 21

Karl Marx and Friedrich Engels

THE COMMUNIST MANIFESTO

Karl Marx (1818–83) and Friedrich Engels (1820–95) were German philosophers and social thinkers who were jointly responsible for the creation of the theory of communism. "The Communist Manifesto" (1848) sets out the basic tenets of communism, including its theory of class conflict and its materialist theory of history.

Manifesto of the Communist Party

A spectre is haunting Europe – the spectre of communism. All the powers of old Europe have entered into a holy alliance to exorcise this spectre: Pope and Csar, Metternich and Guizot, French Radicals and German police-spies.

Where is the party in opposition that has not been decried as communistic by its opponents in power? Where is the opposition that has not hurled back the branding reproach of communism, against the more advanced opposition parties, as well as against its reactionary adversaries?

Two things result from this fact:

I.   Communism is already acknowledged by all European powers to be itself a power.
II.   It is high time that Communists should openly, in the face of the whole world, publish their views, their aims, their tendencies, and meet this nursery tale of the Spectre of Communism with a manifesto of the party itself.

To this end, Communists of various nationalities have assembled in London and sketched the following manifesto, to be published in the English, French, German, Italian, Flemish and Danish languages.

I. Bourgeois and Proletarians[1]

The history of all hitherto existing society[2] is the history of class struggles.

Freeman and slave, patrician and plebeian, lord and serf, guild-master[3] and journeyman, in a word, oppressor and oppressed, stood in constant opposition to one another, carried on an uninterrupted, now hidden, now open fight, a fight that each time ended, either in a revolutionary reconstitution of society at large, or in the common ruin of the contending classes.

In the earlier epochs of history, we find almost everywhere a complicated arrangement of society into various orders, a manifold gradation of social rank. In ancient Rome we have patricians, knights, plebeians, slaves; in the Middle Ages, feudal lords, vassals, guild-masters, journeymen, apprentices, serfs; in almost all of these classes, again, subordinate gradations.

The modern bourgeois society that has sprouted from the ruins of feudal society has not done away with class antagonisms. It has but established new classes, new conditions of oppression, new forms of struggle in place of the old ones.

Our epoch, the epoch of the bourgeoisie, possesses, however, this distinct feature: it has simplified class antagonisms. Society as a whole is more and more splitting up into two great hostile camps, into two great classes directly facing each other – Bourgeoisie and Proletariat.

From the serfs of the Middle Ages sprang the chartered burghers of the earliest towns. From these burgesses the first elements of the bourgeoisie were developed.

The discovery of America, the rounding of the Cape, opened up fresh ground for the rising bourgeoisie. The East-Indian and Chinese markets, the colonization of America, trade with the colonies, the increase in the means of exchange and in commodities generally, gave to commerce, to navigation, to industry, an impulse never before known, and thereby, to the revolutionary element in the tottering feudal society, a rapid development.

The feudal system of industry, in which industrial production was monopolized by closed guilds, now no longer sufficed for the growing wants of the new markets. The manufacturing system took its place. The guild-masters were pushed on one side by the manufacturing middle class; division of labour between the different corporate guilds vanished in the face of division of labour in each single workshop.

Meantime the markets kept ever growing, the demand ever rising. Even manufacture no longer sufficed. Thereupon, steam and machinery revolutionized industrial production. The place of manufacture was taken by the giant, Modern Industry; the place of the industrial middle class by industrial millionaires, the leaders of the whole industrial armies, the modern bourgeois.

Modern industry has established the world market, for which the discovery of America paved the way. This market has given an immense development to commerce, to navigation, to communication by land. This development has, in its turn, reacted on the extension of industry; and in proportion as industry, commerce, navigation, railways extended, in the same proportion the bourgeoisie developed, increased its capital, and pushed into the background every class handed down from the Middle Ages.

We see, therefore, how the modern bourgeoisie is itself the product of a long course of development, of a series of revolutions in the modes of production and of exchange.

Each step in the development of the bourgeoisie was accompanied by a corresponding political advance of that class. An oppressed class under the sway of the feudal nobility, an armed and self-governing association in the medieval commune:[4] here independent urban republic (as in Italy and Germany); there taxable "third estate" of the monarchy (as in France); afterwards, in the period of manufacturing proper, serving either the semi-feudal or the absolute monarchy as a counterpoise against the nobility, and, in fact, cornerstone of the great monarchies in general, the bourgeoisie has at last, since the establishment of Modern Industry and of the world market, conquered for itself, in the modern representative State, exclusive political sway. The executive of the modern state is but a committee for managing the common affairs of the whole bourgeoisie.

The bourgeoisie, historically, has played a most revolutionary part.

The bourgeoisie, wherever it has got the upper hand, has put an end to all feudal, patriarchal, idyllic relations. It has pitilessly torn asunder the motley feudal ties that bound man to his "natural superiors," and has left remaining no other nexus between man and man than naked self-interest, than callous "cash payment." It has drowned the most heavenly ecstasies of religious fervour, of chivalrous enthusiasm, of philistine sentimentalism, in the icy water of egotistical calculation. It has resolved personal worth into exchange value, and in place of the numberless indefeasible chartered freedoms, has set up that single, unconscionable freedom — Free Trade. In one word, for exploitation, veiled by religious and political illusions, it has substituted naked, shameless, direct, brutal exploitation.

The bourgeoisie has stripped of its halo every occupation hitherto honoured and looked up to with reverent awe. It has converted the physician, the lawyer, the priest, the poet, the man of science, into its paid wage labourers.

The bourgeoisie has torn away from the family its sentimental veil, and has reduced the family relation to a mere money relation.

The bourgeoisie has disclosed how it came to pass that the brutal display of vigour in the Middle Ages, which reactionaries so much admire, found its fitting complement in the most slothful indolence. It has been the first to show what man's activity can bring about. It has accomplished wonders far surpassing Egyptian pyramids, Roman aqueducts, and Gothic cathedrals; it has conducted expeditions that put in the shade all former Exoduses of nations and crusades.

The bourgeoisie cannot exist without constantly revolutionizing the instruments of production, and thereby the relations of production, and with them the whole relations of society. Conservation of the old modes of production in unaltered form, was, on the contrary, the first condition of existence for all earlier industrial classes. Constant revolutionizing of production, uninterrupted disturbance of all social conditions, everlasting uncertainty and agitation distinguish the bourgeois epoch from all earlier ones. All fixed, fast-frozen relations, with their train of ancient and venerable prejudices and opinions, are swept away, all new-formed ones become antiquated before they can ossify. All that is solid melts into air, all that is holy is profaned, and man is at last compelled to face with sober senses his real conditions of life, and his relations with his kind.

The need of a constantly expanding market for its products chases the bourgeoisie over the entire surface of the globe. It must nestle everywhere, settle everywhere, establish connexions everywhere.

The bourgeoisie has through its exploitation of the world market given a cosmopolitan character to production and consumption in every country. To the great chagrin of Reactionists, it has drawn from under the feet of industry the national ground on which it stood. All old-established national industries have been destroyed or are daily being destroyed. They are dislodged by new industries, whose introduction becomes a life and death question for all civilized nations, by industries that no longer work up indigenous raw material, but raw material drawn from the remotest zones; industries whose products are consumed, not only at home, but in every quarter of the globe. In place of the old wants, satisfied by the production of the country, we find new wants, requiring for their satisfaction the products of distant lands and climes. In place of the old local and national seclusion and self-sufficiency, we have intercourse in every direction, universal interdependence of nations. And as in material, so also in intellectual production. The intellectual creations of individual nations become common property. National one-sidedness and narrow-mindedness become more and more impossible, and from the numerous national and local literatures, there arises a world literature.

The bourgeoisie, by the rapid improvement of all instruments of production, by the immensely facilitated means of communication, draws all, even the most barbarian, nations into civilization. The cheap prices of commodities are the heavy artillery with which it batters down all Chinese walls, with which it forces the barbarians' intensely obstinate hatred of foreigners to capitulate. It compels all nations, on pain of extinction, to adopt the bourgeois mode of production; it compels them to introduce what it calls civilization into their midst, i.e., to become bourgeois themselves. In one word, it creates a world after its own image.

The bourgeoisie has subjected the country to the rule of the towns. It has created enormous cities, has greatly increased the urban population as compared with the rural, and has thus rescued a considerable part of the population from the idiocy of rural life. Just as it has made the country dependent on the towns, so it has made barbarian and semi-barbarian countries dependent on the civilized ones, nations of peasants on nations of bourgeois, the East on the West.

The bourgeoisie keeps more and more doing away with the scattered state of the population, of the means of production, and of property. It has agglomerated population, centralized the means of production, and has concentrated property in a few hands. The necessary consequence of this was political centralization. Independent, or but loosely connected provinces, with separate interests, laws, governments, and systems of taxation, became lumped together into one nation, with one government, one code of laws, one national class-interest, one frontier, and one customs-tariff.

The bourgeoisie, during its rule of scarce one hundred years, has created more massive and more colossal productive forces than have all preceding generations together. Subjection of Nature's forces to man, machinery, application of chemistry to industry and agriculture, steam-navigation, railways, electric telegraphs, clearing of whole continents for cultivation, canalization of rivers, whole populations conjured out of the ground – what earlier century had even a presentiment that such productive forces slumbered in the lap of social labour?

We see then: the means of production and of exchange, on whose foundation the bourgeoisie built itself up, were generated in feudal society. At a certain stage in the development of these means of production and of exchange, the conditions under which feudal society produced and exchanged, the feudal organization of agriculture and manufacturing industry, in one word, the feudal relations of property became no longer compatible with the already developed productive forces; they became so many fetters. They had to be burst asunder; they were burst asunder.

Into their place stepped free competition, accompanied by a social and political constitution adapted in it, and the economic and political sway of the bourgeois class.

A similar movement is going on before our own eyes. Modern bourgeois society, with its relations of production, of exchange and of property, a society that has conjured up such gigantic means of production and of exchange, is like the sorcerer who is no longer able to control the powers of the nether world whom he has called up by his spells. For many a decade past the history of industry and commerce is but the history of the revolt of modern productive forces against modern conditions of production, against the property relations that are the conditions for the existence of the bourgeois and of its rule. It is enough to mention the commercial crises that by their periodical return put the existence of the entire bourgeois society on its trial, each time more threateningly. In these crises, a great part not only of the existing products, but also of the previously created productive forces, are periodically destroyed. In these crises, there breaks out an epidemic that, in all earlier epochs, would have seemed an absurdity – the epidemic of over-production. Society suddenly finds itself put back into a state of momentary barbarism; it appears as if a famine, a universal war of devastation, had cut off the supply of every means of subsistence; industry and commerce seem to be destroyed; and why? Because there is too much civilization, too much means of subsistence, too much industry, too much commerce. The productive forces at the disposal of society no longer tend to further the development of the conditions of bourgeois property; on the contrary, they have become too powerful for these conditions, by which they are fettered, and so soon as they overcome these fetters, they bring disorder into the whole of bourgeois society, endanger the existence of bourgeois property. The conditions of bourgeois society are too narrow to comprise the wealth created by them. And how does the bourgeoisie get over these crises? On the one hand by enforced destruction of a mass of productive forces; on the other, by the conquest of new markets, and by the more thorough exploitation of the old ones. That is to say, by paving the way for more extensive and more destructive crises, and by diminishing the means whereby crises are prevented.

The weapons with which the bourgeoisie felled feudalism to the ground are now turned against the bourgeoisie itself.

But not only has the bourgeoisie forged the weapons that bring death to itself; it has also called into existence the men who are to wield those weapons – the modern working class – the proletarians.

In proportion as the bourgeoisie, i.e., capital, is developed, in the same proportion is the proletariat, the modern working class, developed – a class of labourers, who live only so long as they find work, and who find work only so long as their labour increases capital. These labourers, who must sell themselves piecemeal, are a commodity, like every other article of commerce, and are consequently exposed to all the vicissitudes of competition, to all the fluctuations of the market.

Owing to the extensive use of machinery, and to the division of labour, the work of the proletarians has lost all individual character, and, consequently, all charm for the workman. He becomes an appendage of the machine, and it is only the most simple, most monotonous, and most easily acquired knack, that is required of him. Hence, the cost of production of a workman is restricted, almost entirely, to the means of subsistence that he requires for maintenance, and for the propagation of his race. But the price of a commodity, and therefore also of labour, is equal to its cost of production. In proportion, therefore, as the repulsiveness of the work increases, the wage decreases. Nay more, in

proportion as the use of machinery and division of labour increases, in the same proportion the burden of toil also increases, whether by prolongation of the working hours, by the increase of the work exacted in a given time or by increased speed of machinery, etc.

Modern Industry has converted the little workshop of the patriarchal master into the great factory of the industrial capitalist. Masses of labourers, crowded into the factory, are organized like soldiers. As privates of the industrial army they are placed under the command of a perfect hierarchy of officers and sergeants. Not only are they slaves of the bourgeois class, and of the bourgeois State; they are daily and hourly enslaved by the machine, by the overlooker, and, above all, by the individual bourgeois manufacturer himself. The more openly this despotism proclaims gain to be its end and aim, the more petty, the more hateful and the more embittering it is.

The less the skill and exertion of strength implied in manual labour, in other words, the more modern industry becomes developed, the more is the labour of men superseded by that of women. Differences of age and sex have no longer any distinctive social validity for the working class. All are instruments of labour, more or less expensive to use, according to their age and sex.

No sooner is the exploitation of the labourer by the manufacturer, so far, at an end, that he receives his wages in cash, than he is set upon by the other portions of the bourgeoisie, the landlord, the shopkeeper, the pawnbroker, etc.

The lower strata of the middle class – the small tradespeople, shopkeepers, and retired tradesmen generally, the handicraftsmen and peasants – all these sink gradually into the proletariat, partly because their diminutive capital does not suffice for the scale on which Modern Industry is carried on, and is swamped in the competition with the large capitalists, partly because their specialized skill is rendered worthless by new methods of production. Thus the proletariat is recruited from all classes of the population.

The proletariat goes through various stages of development. With its birth begins its struggle with the bourgeoisie. At first the contest is carried on by individual labourers, then by the workpeople of a factory, then by the operative of one trade, in one locality, against the individual bourgeois who directly exploits them. They direct their attacks not against the bourgeois conditions of production, but against the instruments of production themselves; they destroy imported wares that compete with their labour, they smash to pieces machinery, they set factories ablaze, they seek to restore by force the vanished status of the workman of the Middle Ages.

At this stage, the labourers still form an incoherent mass scattered over the whole country, and broken up by their mutual competition. If anywhere they unite to form more compact bodies, this is not yet the consequence of their own active union, but of the union of the bourgeoisie, which class, in order to attain its own political ends, is compelled to set the whole proletariat in motion, and is moreover yet, for a time, able to do so. At this stage, therefore, the proletarians do not fight their enemies, but the enemies of their enemies, the remnants of absolute monarchy, the landowners, the non-industrial bourgeois, the petty bourgeois. Thus, the whole historical movement is concentrated in the hands of the bourgeoisie; every victory so obtained is a victory for the bourgeoisie.

But with the development of industry, the proletariat not only increases in number; it becomes concentrated in greater masses, its strength grows, and it feels that strength more. The various interests and conditions of life within the ranks of the proletariat are more and more equalized, in proportion as machinery obliterates all distinctions of labour, and nearly everywhere reduces wages to the same low level. The growing competition among the bourgeois, and the resulting commercial crises, make the wages of the workers ever more fluctuating. The increasing improvement of machinery, ever more rapidly developing, makes their livelihood more and more precarious; the collisions between individual workmen and individual bourgeois take more and more the character of collisions between two classes. Thereupon, the workers begin to form combinations (Trades' Unions) against the bourgeois; they club together in order to keep up the rate of wages; they found permanent associations in order to make provision beforehand for these occasional revolts. Here and there, the contest breaks out into riots.

Now and then the workers are victorious, but only for a time. The real fruit of their battles lies, not in the immediate result, but in the ever expanding union of the workers. This union is helped on by the improved means of communication that are created by modern industry, and that place the workers of different localities in contact with one another. It was just this contact that was needed to centralize the numerous local struggles, all of the same character, into one national struggle between classes. But every class struggle is a political struggle. And that union, to attain which the burghers of the Middle Ages, with their miserable highways, required centuries, the modern proletarians, thanks to railways, achieve in a few years.

This organization of the proletarians into a class, and, consequently into a political party, is continually being upset again by the competition between the workers themselves. But it ever rises up again, stronger, firmer, mightier. It compels legislative recognition of particular interests of the workers, by taking advantage of the divisions among the bourgeoisie itself. Thus, the ten-hours' bill in England was carried.

Altogether collisions between the classes of the old society further, in many ways, the course of development of the proletariat. The bourgeoisie finds itself involved in a constant battle. At first with the aristocracy; later on, with those portions of the bourgeoisie itself, whose interests have become antagonistic to the progress of industry; at all times, with the bourgeoisie of foreign countries. In all these battles, it sees itself compelled to appeal to the proletariat, to ask for help, and thus, to drag it into the political arena. The bourgeoisie itself, therefore, supplies the proletariat with its own elements of political and general education, in other words, it furnishes the proletariat with weapons for fighting the bourgeoisie.

Further, as we have already seen, entire sections of the ruling class are, by the advance of industry, precipitated into the proletariat, or are at least threatened in their conditions of existence. These also supply the proletariat with fresh elements of enlightenment and progress.

Finally, in times when the class struggle nears the decisive hour, the progress of dissolution going on within the ruling class, in fact within the whole range of old society, assumes such a violent, glaring character, that a small section of the ruling class cuts itself adrift, and joins the revolutionary class, the class that holds the future in its hands. Just as, therefore, at an earlier period, a section of the nobility went over to the bourgeoisie, so now a portion of the bourgeoisie goes over to the proletariat, and in particular, a portion of the bourgeois ideologists, who have raised themselves to the level of comprehending theoretically the historical movement as a whole.

Of all the classes that stand face to face with the bourgeoisie today, the proletariat alone is a really revolutionary class. The other classes decay and finally disappear in the face of Modern Industry; the proletariat is its special and essential product.

The lower middle class, the small manufacturer, the shopkeeper, the artisan, the peasant, all these fight against the bourgeoisie, to save from extinction their existence as fractions of the middle class. They are therefore not revolutionary, but conservative. Nay more, they are reactionary, for they try to roll back the wheel of history. If by chance, they are revolutionary, they are only so in view of their impending transfer into the proletariat; they thus defend not their present, but their future interests, they desert their own standpoint to place themselves at that of the proletariat.

The "dangerous class," [*lumpenproletariat*] the social scum, that passively rotting mass thrown off by the lowest layers of the old society, may, here and there, be swept into the movement by a proletarian revolution; its conditions of life, however, prepare it far more for the part of a bribed tool of reactionary intrigue.

In the condition of the proletariat, those of old society at large are already virtually swamped. The proletarian is without property; his relation to his wife and children has no longer anything in common with the bourgeois family relations; modern industrial labour, modern subjection to capital, the same in England as in France, in America as in Germany, has stripped him of every trace of national character. Law, morality, religion, are to him so many bourgeois prejudices, behind which lurk in ambush just as many bourgeois interests.

All the preceding classes that got the upper hand sought to fortify their already acquired status by subjecting society at large to their conditions of appropriation. The proletarians cannot become masters of the productive forces of society, except by abolishing their own previous mode of appropriation, and thereby also every other previous mode of appropriation. They have nothing of their own to secure and to fortify; their mission is to destroy all previous securities for, and insurances of, individual property.

All previous historical movements were movements of minorities, or in the interest of minorities. The proletarian movement is the self-conscious, independent movement of the immense majority, in the interest of the immense majority. The proletariat, the lowest stratum of our present society, cannot stir, cannot raise itself up, without the whole superincumbent strata of official society being sprung into the air.

Though not in substance, yet in form, the struggle of the proletariat with the bourgeoisie is at first a national struggle. The proletariat of each country must, of course, first of all settle matters with its own bourgeoisie.

In depicting the most general phases of the development of the proletariat, we traced the more or less veiled civil war, raging within existing society, up to the point where that war breaks out into open revolution, and where the violent overthrow of the bourgeoisie lays the foundation for the sway of the proletariat.

Hitherto, every form of society has been based, as we have already seen, on the antagonism of oppressing and oppressed classes. But in order to oppress a class, certain conditions must be assured to it under which it can, at least, continue its slavish existence. The serf, in the period of serfdom, raised himself to membership in the commune, just as the petty bourgeois, under the yoke of feudal absolutism, managed to develop into a bourgeois. The modern labourer, on the contrary, instead of rising with the process of industry, sinks deeper and deeper below the conditions of existence of his own class. He becomes a pauper, and pauperism develops more rapidly than population and wealth. And here it becomes evident, that the bourgeoisie is unfit any longer to be the ruling class in society, and to impose its conditions of existence upon society as an over-riding law. It is unfit to rule because it is incompetent to assure an existence to its slave within his slavery, because it cannot help letting him sink into such a state, that it has to feed him, instead of being fed by him. Society can no longer live under this bourgeoisie, in other words, its existence is no longer compatible with society.

The essential conditions for the existence and for the sway of the bourgeois class is the formation and augmentation of capital; the condition for capital is wage-labour. Wage-labour rests exclusively on competition between the labourers. The advance of industry, whose involuntary promoter is the bourgeoisie, replaces the isolation of the labourers, due to competition, by the revolutionary combination, due to association. The development of Modern Industry,

therefore, cuts from under its feet the very foundation on which the bourgeoisie produces and appropriates products. What the bourgeoisie therefore produces, above all, are its own grave-diggers. Its fall and the victory of the proletariat are equally inevitable.

II. Proletarians and Communists

In what relation do the Communists stand to the proletarians as a whole?

The Communists do not form a separate party opposed to other working-class parties.

They have no interests separate and apart from those of the proletariat as a whole.

They do not set up any sectarian principles of their own, by which to shape and mould the proletarian movement.

The Communists are distinguished from the other working-class parties by this only: 1. In the national struggles of the proletarians of the different countries, they point out and bring to the front the common interests of the entire proletariat, independently of all nationality. 2. In the various stages of development which the struggle of the working class against the bourgeoisie has to pass through, they always and everywhere represent the interests of the movement as a whole.

The Communists, therefore, are on the one hand, practically, the most advanced and resolute section of the working-class parties of every country, that section which pushes forward all others; on the other hand, theoretically, they have over the great mass of the proletariat the advantage of clearly understanding the line of march, the conditions, and the ultimate general results of the proletarian movement.

The immediate aim of the Communists is the same as that of all other proletarian parties: formation of the proletariat into a class, overthrow of the bourgeois supremacy, conquest of political power by the proletariat.

The theoretical conclusions of the Communists are in no way based on ideas or principles that have been invented, or discovered, by this or that would-be universal reformer.

They merely express, in general terms, actual relations springing from an existing class struggle, from a historical movement going on under our very eyes. The abolition of existing property relations is not at all a distinctive feature of communism.

All property relations in the past have continually been subject to historical change consequent upon the change in historical conditions.

The French Revolution, for example, abolished feudal property in favour of bourgeois property.

The distinguishing feature of Communism is not the abolition of property generally, but the abolition of bourgeois property. But modern bourgeois private property is the final and most complete expression of the system of producing and appropriating products, that is based on class antagonisms, on the exploitation of the many by the few.

In this sense, the theory of the Communists may be summed up in the single sentence: Abolition of private property.

We Communists have been reproached with the desire of abolishing the right of personally acquiring property as the fruit of a man's own labour, which property is alleged to be the groundwork of all personal freedom, activity and independence.

Hard-won, self-acquired, self-earned property! Do you mean the property of petty artisan and of the small peasant, a form of property that preceded the bourgeois form? There is no need to abolish that; the development of industry has to a great extent already destroyed it, and is still destroying it daily.

Or do you mean the modern bourgeois private property?

But does wage-labour create any property for the labourer? Not a bit. It creates capital, i.e., that kind of property which exploits wage-labour, and which cannot increase except upon condition of begetting a new supply of wage-labour

for fresh exploitation. Property, in its present form, is based on the antagonism of capital and wage-labour. Let us examine both sides of this antagonism.

To be a capitalist, is to have not only a purely personal, but a social *status* in production. Capital is a collective product, and only by the united action of many members, nay, in the last resort, only by the united action of all members of society, can it be set in motion.

Capital is therefore not only personal; it is a social power.

When, therefore, capital is converted into common property, into the property of all members of society, personal property is not thereby transformed into social property. It is only the social character of the property that is changed. It loses its class character.

Let us now take wage-labour.

The average price of wage-labour is the minimum wage, i.e., that quantum of the means of subsistence which is absolutely requisite to keep the labourer in bare existence as a labourer. What, therefore, the wage-labourer appropriates by means of his labour, merely suffices to prolong and reproduce a bare existence. We by no means intend to abolish this personal appropriation of the products of labour, an appropriation that is made for the maintenance and reproduction of human life, and that leaves no surplus wherewith to command the labour of others. All that we want to do away with is the miserable character of this appropriation, under which the labourer lives merely to increase capital, and is allowed to live only in so far as the interest of the ruling class requires it.

In bourgeois society, living labour is but a means to increase accumulated labour. In Communist society, accumulated labour is but a means to widen, to enrich, to promote the existence of the labourer.

In bourgeois society, therefore, the past dominates the present; in Communist society, the present dominates the past. In bourgeois society capital is independent and has individuality, while the living person is dependent and has no individuality.

And the abolition of this state of things is called by the bourgeois, abolition of individuality and freedom! And rightly so. The abolition of bourgeois individuality, bourgeois independence, and bourgeois freedom is undoubtedly aimed at.

By freedom is meant, under the present bourgeois conditions of production, free trade, free selling and buying.

But if selling and buying disappears, free selling and buying disappears also. This talk about free selling and buying, and all the other "brave words" of our bourgeois about freedom in general, have a meaning, if any, only in contrast with restricted selling and buying, with the fettered traders of the Middle Ages, but have no meaning when opposed to the Communistic abolition of buying and selling, of the bourgeois conditions of production, and of the bourgeoisie itself.

You are horrified at our intending to do away with private property. But in your existing society, private property is already done away with for nine-tenths of the population; its existence for the few is solely due to its non-existence in the hands of those nine-tenths. You reproach us, therefore, with intending to do away with a form of property, the necessary condition for whose existence is the non-existence of any property for the immense majority of society.

In one word, you reproach us with intending to do away with your property. Precisely so; that is just what we intend.

From the moment when labour can no longer be converted into capital, money, or rent, into a social power capable of being monopolized, i.e., from the moment when individual property can no longer be transformed into bourgeois property, into capital, from that moment, you say, individuality vanishes. *eerie*

You must, therefore, confess that by "individual" you mean no other person than the bourgeois, than the middle-class owner of property. This person must, indeed, be swept out of the way, and made impossible.

Communism deprives no man of the power to appropriate the products of society; all that it does is to deprive him of the power to subjugate the labour of others by means of such appropriations.

It has been objected that upon the abolition of private property, all work will cease, and universal laziness will overtake us.

According to this, bourgeois society ought long ago to have gone to the dogs through sheer idleness; for those of its members who work, acquire nothing, and those who acquire anything do not work. The whole of this objection is but another expression of the tautology: that there can no longer be any wage-labour when there is no longer any capital.

All objections urged against the Communistic mode of producing and appropriating material products, have, in the same way, been urged against the Communistic mode of producing and appropriating intellectual products. Just as, to the bourgeois, the disappearance of class property is the disappearance of production itself, so the disappearance of class culture is to him identical with the disappearance of all culture.

That culture, the loss of which he laments, is, for the enormous majority, a mere training to act as a machine.

But don't wrangle with us so long as you apply, to our intended abolition of bourgeois property, the standard of your bourgeois notions of freedom, culture, law, &c. Your very ideas are but the outgrowth of the conditions of your bourgeois production and bourgeois property, just as your jurisprudence is but the will of your class made into a law for all, a will whose essential character and direction are determined by the economical conditions of existence of your class.

The selfish misconception that induces you to transform into eternal laws of nature and of reason, the social forms springing from your present mode of production and form of property – historical relations that rise and disappear in the progress of production – this misconception you share with every ruling class that has preceded you. What you see clearly in the case of ancient property, what you admit in the case of feudal property, you are of course forbidden to admit in the case of your own bourgeois form of property.

Abolition [*Aufhebung*] of the family! Even the most radical flare up at this infamous proposal of the Communists.

On what foundation is the present family, the bourgeois family, based? On capital, on private gain. In its completely developed form, this family exists only among the bourgeoisie. But this state of things finds its complement in the practical absence of the family among the proletarians, and in public prostitution.

The bourgeois family will vanish as a matter of course when its complement vanishes, and both will vanish with the vanishing of capital.

Do you charge us with wanting to stop the exploitation of children by their parents? To this crime we plead guilty.

But, you say, we destroy the most hallowed of relations, when we replace home education by social.

And your education! Is not that also social, and determined by the social conditions under which you educate, by the intervention direct or indirect, of society, by means of schools, &c.? The Communists have not invented the intervention of society in education; they do but seek to alter the character of that intervention, and to rescue education from the influence of the ruling class.

The bourgeois clap-trap about the family and education, about the hallowed co-relation of parents and child, becomes all the more disgusting, the more, by the action of Modern Industry, all the family ties among the proletarians are torn asunder, and their children transformed into simple articles of commerce and instruments of labour.

But you Communists would introduce community of women, screams the bourgeoisie in chorus.

The bourgeois sees his wife a mere instrument of production. He hears that the instruments of production are to be exploited in common, and, naturally, can come to no other conclusion that the lot of being common to all will likewise fall to the women.

He has not even a suspicion that the real point aimed at is to do away with the status of women as mere instruments of production.

For the rest, nothing is more ridiculous than the virtuous indignation of our bourgeois at the community of women which, they pretend, is to be openly and officially established by the Communists. The Communists have no need to introduce community of women; it has existed almost from time immemorial.

Our bourgeois, not content with having wives and daughters of their proletarians at their disposal, not to speak of common prostitutes, take the greatest pleasure in seducing each other's wives.

Bourgeois marriage is, in reality, a system of wives in common and thus, at the most, what the Communists might possibly be reproached with is that they desire to introduce, in substitution for a hypocritically concealed, an openly legalized community of women. For the rest, it is self-evident that the abolition of the present system of production must bring with it the abolition of the community of women springing from that system, i.e., of prostitution both public and private.

The Communists are further reproached with desiring to abolish countries and nationality.

The working men have no country. We cannot take from them what they have not got. Since the proletariat must first of all acquire political supremacy, must rise to be the leading class of the nation, must constitute itself the nation, it is, so far, itself national, though not in the bourgeois sense of the word.

National differences and antagonism between peoples are daily more and more vanishing, *abolish everything!*

owing to the development of the bourgeoisie, to freedom of commerce, to the world market, to uniformity in the mode of production and in the conditions of life corresponding thereto.

The supremacy of the proletariat will cause them to vanish still faster. United action, of the leading civilized countries at least, is one of the first conditions for the emancipation of the proletariat.

In proportion as the exploitation of one individual by another will also be put an end to, the exploitation of one nation by another will also be put an end to. In proportion as the antagonism between classes within the nation vanishes, the hostility of one nation to another will come to an end.

The charges against Communism made from a religious, a philosophical and, generally, from an ideological standpoint, are not deserving of serious examination.

Does it require deep intuition to comprehend that man's ideas, views, and conception, in one word, man's consciousness, changes with every change in the conditions of his material existence, in his social relations and in his social life?

What else does the history of ideas prove, than that intellectual production changes its character in proportion as material production is changed? The ruling ideas of each age have ever been the ideas of its ruling class.

When people speak of the ideas that revolutionize society, they do but express that fact that within the old society the elements of a new one have been created, and that the dissolution of the old ideas keeps even pace with the dissolution of the old conditions of existence.

When the ancient world was in its last throes, the ancient religions were overcome by Christianity. When Christian ideas succumbed in the eighteenth century to rationalist ideas, feudal society fought its death battle with the then revolutionary bourgeoisie. The ideas of religious liberty and freedom of conscience merely gave expression to the sway of free competition within the domain of knowledge.

"Undoubtedly," it will be said, "religious, moral, philosophical, and juridical ideas have been modified in the course of historical development. But religion, morality, philosophy, political science, and law, constantly survived this change."

"There are, besides, eternal truths, such as Freedom, Justice, etc., that are common to all states of society. But Communism abolishes eternal truths, it abolishes all religion, and all morality, instead of constituting them on a new basis; it therefore acts in contradiction to all past historical experience."

What does this accusation reduce itself to? The history of all past society has consisted in the development of class antagonisms, antagonisms that assumed different forms at different epochs.

But whatever form they may have taken, one fact is common to all past ages, viz. the exploitation of one part of society by the other. No wonder, then, that the social consciousness of past ages, despite all the multiplicity and variety it displays, moves within certain common forms, or general ideas, which cannot completely vanish except with the total disappearance of class antagonisms.

The Communist revolution is the most radical rupture with traditional property relations; no wonder that its development involved the most radical rupture with traditional ideas.

But let us have done with the bourgeois objections to Communism.

We have seen above, that the first step in the revolution by the working class is to raise the proletariat to the position of ruling class to win the battle of democracy.

The proletariat will use its political supremacy to wrest, by degree, all capital from the bourgeoisie, to centralize all instruments of production in the hands of the State, i.e., of the proletariat organized as the ruling class; and to increase the total productive forces as rapidly as possible.

Of course, in the beginning, this cannot be effected except by means of despotic inroads on the rights of property, and on the conditions of bourgeois production; by means of measures, therefore, which appear economically insufficient and untenable, but which, in the course of the movement, outstrip themselves, necessitate further inroads upon the old social order, and are unavoidable as a means of entirely revolutionizing the mode of production.

These measures will, of course, be different in different countries.

Nevertheless, in most advanced countries, the following will be pretty generally applicable:

1. Abolition of property in land and application of all rents of land to public purposes.
2. A heavy progressive or graduated income tax.
3. Abolition of all rights of inheritance.
4. Confiscation of the property of all emigrants and rebels.
5. Centralization of credit in the hands of the state, by means of a national bank with State capital and an exclusive monopoly.
6. Centralization of the means of communication and transport in the hands of the State.
7. Extension of factories and instruments of production owned by the State; the bringing into cultivation of waste-lands, and the improvement of the soil generally in accordance with a common plan.
8. Equal liability of all to work. Establishment of industrial armies, especially for agriculture.
9. Combination of agriculture with manufacturing industries; gradual abolition of all the distinction between town and country by a more equable distribution of the populace over the country.
10. Free education for all children in public schools. Abolition of children's factory labour in its present form. Combination of education with industrial production, &c, &c.

When, in the course of development, class distinctions have disappeared, and all production has been concentrated in the hands of a vast association of the whole nation, the public power will lose its political character. Political power, properly so called, is merely the organized power of one class for oppressing another. If the proletariat during its contest with the bourgeoisie is compelled, by the force of circumstances, to organize itself as a class, if, by means of a revolution, it makes itself the ruling class, and, as such, sweeps away by force the old conditions of production, then it will, along with these conditions, have swept away the conditions for the existence of class antagonisms and of classes generally, and will thereby have abolished its own supremacy as a class.

In place of the old bourgeois society, with its classes and class antagonisms, we shall have an association, in which the free development of each is the condition for the free development of all.

[. . .]

IV. Position of the Communists in Relation to the Various Existing Opposition Parties

[. . .]

Communists everywhere support every revolutionary movement against the existing social and political order of things.

In all these movements, they bring to the front, as the leading question in each, the property question, no matter what its degree of development at the time.

Finally, they labour everywhere for the union and agreement of the democratic parties of all countries.

The Communists disdain to conceal their views and aims. They openly declare that their ends can be attained only by the forcible overthrow of all existing social conditions. Let the ruling classes tremble at a Communistic revolution. The proletarians have nothing to lose but their chains. They have a world to win.

Working Men of All Countries, Unite!

Notes

1   By bourgeoisie is meant the class of modern Capitalists, owners of the means of social production and employers of wage-labour. By proletariat, the class of modern wage-labourers who, having no means of production of their own, are reduced to selling their labour power in order to live. [Engels, 1888 English edition]

2   That is, all written history. In 1847, the pre-history of society, the social organization existing previous to recorded history, was all but unknown. Since then, August von Haxthausen (1792-1866) discovered common ownership of land in Russia, Georg Ludwig von Maurer proved it to be the social foundation from which all Teutonic races started in history, and, by and by, village communities were found to be, or to have been, the primitive form of society everywhere from India to Ireland. The inner organization of this primitive communistic society was laid bare, in its typical form, by Lewis Henry Morgan's (1818-61) crowning discovery of the true nature of the *gens* and its relation to the *tribe*. With the dissolution of the primaeval communities, society begins to be differentiated into separate and finally antagonistic classes. I have attempted to retrace this dissolution in The Origin of the Family, Private Property, and the State, second edition, Stuttgart, 1886. [Engels, 1888 English Edition and 1890 German Edition (with the last sentence omitted)]

3   Guild-master, that is, a full member of a guild, a master within, not a head of a guild. [Engels, 1888 English Edition]

4   This was the name given their urban communities by the townsmen of Italy and France, after they had purchased or conquered their initial rights of self-government from their feudal lords. [Engels, 1890 German edition] "Commune" was the name taken in France by the nascent towns even before they had conquered from their feudal lords and masters local self-government and political rights as the "Third Estate." Generally speaking, for the economical development of the bourgeoisie, England is here taken as the typical country; for its political development, France. [Engels, 1888 English Edition]

Chapter 22

Karl Marx

CRITIQUE OF THE GOTHA PROGRAM

Karl Marx (1818–83) was a German philosopher and social thinker who was, with Friedrich Engels, responsible for the creation of the theory of communism. The "Critique of the Gotha Program" (1873) is mainly directed at criticizing a rival political movement, but is also notable for its expression of the Marxist doctrine of "from each according to his ability, to each according to his needs."

I

1. Labor is the source of wealth and all culture, and since useful labor is possible only in society and through society, the proceeds of labor belong undiminished with equal right to all members of society.

First part of the paragraph: "Labor is the source of all wealth and all culture."

Labor is *not the source* of all wealth. *Nature* is just as much the source of use values (and it is surely of such that material wealth consists!) as labor, which itself is only the manifestation of a force of nature, human labor power. The above phrase is to be found in all children's primers and is correct insofar as it is implied that labor is performed with the appurtenant subjects and instruments. But a socialist program cannot allow such bourgeois phrases to pass over in silence the *conditions* that alone give them meaning. And insofar as man from the beginning behaves toward nature, the primary source of all instruments and subjects of labor, as an owner, treats her as belonging to him, his labor becomes the source of use values, therefore also of wealth. The bourgeois have very good grounds for falsely ascribing *supernatural creative power* to labor; since precisely from the fact that labor depends on nature it follows that the man who possesses no other property than his labor power must, in all conditions of society and culture, be the slave of other men who have made themselves the owners of the material conditions of labor. He can only work with their permission, hence live only with their permission.

Let us now leave the sentence as it stands, or rather limps. What could one have expected in conclusion? Obviously this:

Since labor is the source of all wealth, no one in society can appropriate wealth except as the product of labor. Therefore, if he himself does not work, he lives by the labor of others and also acquires his culture at the expense of the labor of others.

Instead of this, by means of the verbal rivet "and since," a proposition is added in order to draw a conclusion from this and not from the first one.

Second part of the paragraph: "Useful labor is possible only in society and through society."

According to the first proposition, labor was the source of all wealth and all culture; therefore no society is possible without labor. Now we learn, conversely, that no "useful" labor is possible without society.

One could just as well have said that only in society can useless and even socially harmful labor become a branch of gainful occupation, that only in society can one live by being idle, etc., etc. – in short, once could just as well have copied the whole of Rousseau.

And what is "useful" labor? Surely only labor which produces the intended useful result. A savage – and man was a savage after he had ceased to be an ape – who kills an animal with a stone, who collects fruit, etc., performs "useful" labor.

Thirdly, the conclusion: "Useful labor is possible only in society and through society, the proceeds of labor belong undiminished with equal right to all members of society."

A fine conclusion! If useful labor is possible only in society and through society, the proceeds of labor belong to society – and only so much therefrom accrues to the individual worker as is not required to maintain the "condition" of labor, society.

In fact, this proposition has at all times been made use of by the champions of the *state of society prevailing at any given time*. First come the claims of the government and everything that sticks to it, since it is the social organ for the maintenance of the social order; then come the claims of the various kinds of private property, for the various kinds of private property are the foundations of society, etc. One sees that such hollow phrases are the foundations of society, etc. One sees that such hollow phrases can be twisted and turned as desired.

The first and second parts of the paragraph have some intelligible connection only in the following wording:

"Labor becomes the source of wealth and culture only as social labor," or, what is the same thing, "in and through society."

This proposition is incontestably correct, for although isolated labor (its material conditions presupposed) can create use value; it can create neither wealth nor culture.

But equally incontestable is this other proposition:

In proportion as labor develops socially, and becomes thereby a source of wealth and culture, poverty and destitution develop among the workers, and wealth and culture among the non-workers.

This is the law of all history hitherto. What, therefore, had to be done here, instead of setting down general phrases about "labor" and "society," was to prove concretely how in present capitalist society the material, etc., conditions have at last been created which enable and compel the workers to lift this social curse.

In fact, however, the whole paragraph, bungled in style and content, is only there in order to inscribe the Lassallean catchword of the "undiminished proceeds of labor" as a slogan at the top of the party banner. I shall return later to the "proceeds of labor," "equal right," etc., since the same thing recurs in a somewhat different form further on.

[. . .]

3. The emancipation of labor demands the promotion of the instruments of labor to the common property of society and the co-operative regulation of the total labor, with a fair distribution of the proceeds of labor.

"Promotion of the instruments of labor to the common property" ought obviously to read their "conversion into the common property;" but this is only in passing.

What are the "proceeds of labor?" The product of labor, or its value? And in the latter case, is it the total value of the product, or only that part of the value which labor has newly added to the value of the means of production consumed?

"Proceeds of labor" is a loose notion which Lassalle has put in the place of definite economic conceptions.

What is "a fair distribution?"

Do not the bourgeois assert that the present-day distribution is "fair?" And is it not, in fact, the only "fair" distribution on the basis of the present-day mode of production? Are economic relations regulated by legal conceptions, or do not, on the contrary, legal relations arise out of economic ones? Have not also the socialist sectarians the most varied notions about "fair" distribution?

To understand what is implied in this connection by the phrase "fair distribution," we must take the first paragraph and this one together. The latter presupposes a society wherein the instruments of labor are common property and the total labor is co-operatively regulated, and from the first paragraph we learn that "the proceeds of labor belong undiminished with equal right to all members of society."

"To all members of society"? To those who do not work as well? What remains then of the "undiminished" proceeds of labor? Only to those members of society who work? What remains then of the "equal right" of all members of society?

But "all members of society" and "equal right" are obviously mere phrases. The kernel consists in this, that in this communist society every worker must receive the "undiminished" Lassallean "proceeds of labor."

Let us take, first of all, the words "proceeds of labor" in the sense of the product of labor; then the co-operative proceeds of labor are the *total social product.*

From this must now be deducted: *First*, cover for replacement of the means of production used up. *Second*, additional portion for expansion of production. *Third*, reserve or insurance funds to provide against accidents, dislocations caused by natural calamities, etc.

These deductions from the "undiminished" proceeds of labor are an economic necessity, and their magnitude is to be determined according to available means and forces, and partly by computation of probabilities, but they are in no way calculable by equity.

There remains the other part of the total product, intended to serve as means of consumption.

Before this is divided among the individuals, there has to be deducted again, from it: *First*, the general costs of administration not belonging to production. This part will, from the outset, be very considerably restricted in comparison with present-day society, and it diminishes in proportion as the new society develops. *Second*, that which is intended for the common satisfaction of needs, such as schools, health services, etc. From the outset, this part grows considerably in comparison with present-day society, and it grows in proportion as the new society develops. *Third*, funds for those unable to work, etc., in short, for what is included under so-called official poor relief today.

Only now do we come to the "distribution" which the program, under Lassallean influence, alone has in view in its narrow fashion – namely, to that part of the means of consumption which is divided among the individual producers of the co-operative society.

The "undiminished" proceeds of labor have already unnoticeably become converted into the "diminished" proceeds, although what the producer is deprived of in his capacity as a private individual benefits him directly or indirectly in his capacity as a member of society.

Just as the phrase of the "undiminished" proceeds of labor has disappeared, so now does the phrase of the "proceeds of labor" disappear altogether.

Within the co-operative society based on common ownership of the means of production, the producers do not exchange their products; just as little does the labor employed on the products appear here as the *value* of these products, as a material quality possessed by them, since now, in contrast to capitalist society, individual labor no longer exists in an indirect fashion but directly as a component part of total labor. The phrase "proceeds of labor," objectionable also today on account of its ambiguity, thus loses all meaning.

What we have to deal with here is a communist society, not as it has *developed* on its own foundations, but, on the contrary, just as it *emerges* from capitalist society; which is thus in every respect, economically, morally, and intellectually, still stamped with the birthmarks of the old society from whose womb it emerges. Accordingly, the individual producer receives back from society – after the deductions have been made – exactly what he gives to it. What he has given to it is his individual quantum of labor. For example, the social working day consists of the sum of the individual hours of work; the individual labor time of the individual producer is the part of the social working day contributed by him, his share in it. He receives a certificate from society that he has furnished such-and-such an amount of labor (after deducting his labor for the common funds); and with this certificate, he draws from the social stock of means of consumption as much as the same amount of labor cost. The same amount of labor which he has given to society in one form, he receives back in another.

Here, obviously, the same principle prevails as that which regulates the exchange of commodities, as far as this is exchange of equal values. Content and form are changed, because under the altered circumstances no one can give anything except his labor, and because, on the other hand, nothing can pass to the ownership of individuals, except individual means of consumption. But as far as the distribution of the latter among the individual producers is concerned, the same principle prevails as in the exchange of commodity equivalents: a given amount of labor in one form is exchanged for an equal amount of labor in another form.

Hence, *equal right* here is still in principle – *bourgeois right*, although principle and practice are no longer at loggerheads, while the exchange of equivalents in commodity exchange exists only on the average and not in the individual case.

In spite of this advance, this equal right is still constantly stigmatized by a bourgeois limitation. The right of the producers is *proportional* to the labor they supply; the equality consists in the fact that measurement is made with an *equal standard*, labor.

But one man is superior to another physically, or mentally, and supplies more labor in the same time, or can labor for a longer time; and labor, to serve as a measure, must be defined by its duration or intensity, otherwise it ceases to be a standard of measurement. This *equal* right is an unequal right for unequal labor. It recognizes no class differences, because everyone is only a worker like everyone else; but it tacitly recognizes unequal individual endowment, and thus productive capacity, as a natural privilege. It is, therefore, a right of inequality, in its content, like every right. Right, by its very nature, can consist only in the application of an equal standard; but unequal individuals (and they would not be different individuals if they were not unequal) are measurable only by an equal standard insofar as they are brought under an equal point of view, are taken from one definite side only – for instance, in the present case, are regarded *only as workers* and nothing more is seen in them, everything else being ignored. Further, one worker is married, another is not; one has more children than another, and so on and so forth. Thus, with an equal performance of labor, and hence an equal share in the social consumption fund, one will in fact receive more than another, one will be richer than another, and so on. To avoid all these defects, right, instead of being equal, would have to be unequal.

But these defects are inevitable in the first phase of communist society as it is when it has just emerged after prolonged birth pangs from capitalist society. Right can never be higher than the economic structure of society and its cultural development conditioned thereby.

In a higher phase of communist society, after the enslaving subordination of the individual to the division of labor, and therewith also the antithesis between mental and physical labor, has vanished; after labor has become not only a means of life but life's prime want; after the productive forces have also increased with the all-around development of the individual, and all the springs of co-operative wealth flow more abundantly – only then then can the narrow horizon of bourgeois right be crossed in its entirety and society inscribe on its banners: From each according to his ability, to each according to his needs!

I have dealt more at length with the "undiminished" proceeds of labor, on the one hand, and with "equal right" and "fair distribution," on the other, in order to show what a crime it is to attempt, on the one hand, to force on our Party again, as dogmas, ideas which in a certain period had some meaning but have now become obsolete verbal rubbish, while again perverting, on the other, the realistic outlook, which it cost so much effort to instill into the Party but which has now taken root in it, by means of ideological nonsense about right and other trash so common among the democrats and French socialists.

Quite apart from the analysis so far given, it was in general a mistake to make a fuss about so-called distribution and put the principal stress on it.

Any distribution whatever of the means of consumption is only a consequence of the distribution of the conditions of production themselves. The latter distribution, however, is a feature of the mode of production itself. The capitalist mode of production, for example, rests on the fact that the material conditions of production are in the hands of non-workers in the form of property in capital and land, while

the masses are only owners of the personal condition of production, of labor power. If the elements of production are so distributed, then the present-day distribution of the means of consumption results automatically. If the material conditions of production are the co-operative property of the workers themselves, then there likewise results a distribution of the means of consumption different from the present one. Vulgar socialism (and from it in turn a section of the democrats) has taken over from the bourgeois economists the consideration and treatment of distribution as independent of the mode of production and hence the presentation of socialism as turning principally on distribution. After the real relation has long been made clear, why retrogress again?

[...]

II

Starting from these basic principles, the German workers' party strives by all legal means for the free state — and — socialist society: that abolition of the wage system together with the iron law of wages — and — exploitation in every form; the elimination of all social and political inequality.

I shall return to the "free" state later.

So, in future, the German Workers' party has got to believe in Lassalle's "iron law of wages!" That this may not be lost, the nonsense is perpetrated of speaking of the "abolition of the wage system" (it should read: system of wage labor), "together with the iron law of wages." If I abolish wage labor, then naturally I abolish its laws also, whether they are of "iron" or sponge. But Lassalle's attack on wage labor turns almost solely on this so-called law. In order, therefore, to prove that Lassalle's sect has conquered, the "wage system" must be abolished "together with the iron law of wages" and not without it.

It is well known that nothing of the "iron law of wages" is Lassalle's except the word "iron" borrowed from Goethe's "great, eternal iron laws". The word "iron" is a label by which the true believers recognize one another. But if I take the law with Lassalle's stamp on it, and consequently in his sense, then I must also take it with his substantiation for it. And what is that? As Lange already showed, shortly after Lassalle's death, it is the Malthusian theory of population (preached by Lange himself). But if this theory is correct, then again I cannot abolish the law even if I abolish wage labor a hundred times over, because the law then governs not only the system of wage labor but *every* social system. Basing themselves directly on this, the economists have been proving for 50 years and more that socialism cannot abolish poverty, which has its basis in nature, but can only make it *general*, distribute it simultaneously over the whole surface of society!

But all this is not the main thing. Quite apart from the false Lassallean formulation of the law, the truly outrageous retrogression consists in the following:

Since Lassalle's death, there has asserted itself in our party the scientific understanding that wages are not what they appear to be – namely, the *value*, or *price*, of *labor* – but only a masked form for the *value*, or *price*, of *labor power*. Thereby, the whole bourgeois conception of wages hitherto, as well as all the criticism hitherto directed against this conception, was thrown overboard once and for all. It was made clear that the wage worker has permission to work for his own subsistence – that is, *to live*, only insofar as he works for a certain time gratis for the capitalist (and hence also for the latter's co-consumers of surplus value); that the whole capitalist system of production turns on the increase of this gratis labor by extending the working day, or by developing the productivity — that is, increasing the intensity of labor power, etc.; that, consequently, the system of wage labor is a system of slavery, and indeed of a slavery which becomes more

severe in proportion as the social productive forces of labor develop, whether the worker receives better or worse payment. And after this understanding has gained more and more ground in our party, some return to Lassalle's dogma although they must have known that Lassalle *did not know* what wages were, but, following in the wake of the bourgeois economists, took the appearance for the essence of the matter.

It is as if, among slaves who have at last got behind the secret of slavery and broken out in rebellion, a slave still in thrall to obsolete notions were to inscribe on the program of the rebellion: Slavery must be abolished because the feeding of slaves in the system of slavery cannot exceed a certain low maximum!

Does not the mere fact that the representatives of our party were capable of perpetrating such a monstrous attack on the understanding that has spread among the mass of our party prove, by itself, with what criminal levity and with what lack of conscience they set to work in drawing up this compromise program!

Instead of the indefinite concluding phrase of the paragraph, "the elimination of all social and political inequality," it ought to have been said that with the abolition of class distinctions all social and political inequality arising from them would disappear of itself.

[. . .]

IV

I come now to the democratic section.

A. The free basis of the state.

First of all, according to II, the German Workers' party strives for "the free state."

Free state – what is this?

It is by no means the aim of the workers, who have got rid of the narrow mentality of humble subjects, to set the state free. In the German Empire, the "state" is almost as "free" as in

Russia. Freedom consists in converting the state from an organ superimposed upon society into one completely subordinate to it; and today, too, the forms of state are more free or less free to the extent that they restrict the "freedom of the state."

The German Workers' party – at least if it adopts the program – shows that its socialist ideas are not even skin-deep; in that, instead of treating existing society (and this holds good for any future one) as the *basis* of the existing state (or of the future state in the case of future society), it treats the state rather as an independent entity that possesses its own intellectual, ethical, and libertarian bases.

And what of the riotous misuse which the program makes of the words "present-day state," "present-day society," and of the still more riotous misconception it creates in regard to the state to which it addresses its demands?

"Present-day society" is capitalist society, which exists in all civilized countries, more or less free from medieval admixture, more or less modified by the particular historical development of each country, more or less developed. On the other hand, the "present-day state" changes with a country's frontier. It is different in the Prusso-German Empire from what it is in Switzerland, and different in England from what it is in the United States. The "present-day state" is therefore a fiction.

Nevertheless, the different states of the different civilized countries, in spite of their motley diversity of form, all have this in common: that they are based on modern bourgeois society, only one more or less capitalistically developed. They have, therefore, also certain essential characteristics in common. In this sense, it is possible to speak of the "present-day state" in contrast with the future, in which its present root, bourgeois society, will have died off.

The question then arises: What transformation will the state undergo in communist society? In other words, what social functions will remain in existence there that are analogous to present state functions? This question can only be answered scientifically, and one does not get a flea-hop nearer to the problem by a thousand-fold combination of the word "people" with the word "state."

Between capitalist and communist society there lies the period of the revolutionary transformation of the one into the other. Corresponding to this is also a political transition period in which the state can be nothing but *the revolutionary dictatorship of the proletariat*.

Now the program does not deal with this, nor with the future state of communist society.

Its political demands contain nothing beyond the old democratic litany familiar to all: universal suffrage, direct legislation, popular rights, a people's militia, etc. They are a mere echo of the bourgeois *People's party*, of the *League of Peace and Freedom*. They are all demands which, insofar as they are not exaggerated in fantastic presentation, have already been *realized*. Only the state to which they belong does not lie within the borders of the German Empire, but in Switzerland, the United States, etc. This sort of "state of the future" is a present-day state, although existing outside the "framework" of the German Empire.

But one thing has been forgotten. Since the German Workers' party expressly declares that it acts within "the present-day national state," hence within its own state, the Prusso-German Empire – its demands would indeed be otherwise largely meaningless, since one only demands what one has not got – it should not have forgotten the chief thing, namely, that all those pretty little gewgaws rest on the recognition of the so-called sovereignty of the people and hence are appropriate only in a *democratic republic*.

Since one has not the courage – and wisely so, for the circumstances demand caution – to demand the democratic republic, as the French workers' programs under Louis Philippe and under Louis Napoleon did, one should not have resorted, either, to the subterfuge, neither "honest" nor decent, of demanding things which have meaning only in a democratic republic from a state which is nothing but a police-guarded military despotism, embellished with parliamentary forms, alloyed with a feudal admixture, already influenced by the bourgeoisie, and bureaucratically carpentered, and then to assure this state into the bargain that one imagines one will be able to force such things upon it "by legal means."

Even vulgar democracy, which sees the millennium in the democratic republic, and has no suspicion that it is precisely in this last form of state of bourgeois society that the class struggle has to be fought out to a conclusion – even it towers mountains above this kind of democratism, which keeps within the limits of what is permitted by the police and not permitted by logic.

That, in fact, by the word "state" is meant the government machine, or the state insofar as it forms a special organism separated from society through division of labor, is shown by the words "the German Workers' party demands as the economic basis of the state: a single progressive income tax," etc. Taxes are the economic basis of the government machinery and of nothing else. In the state of the future, existing in Switzerland, this demand has been pretty well fulfilled. Income tax presupposes various sources of income of the various social classes, and hence capitalist society. It is, therefore, nothing remarkable that the Liverpool financial reformers – bourgeois headed by Gladstone's brother – are putting forward the same demand as the program.

B. The German Workers' party demands as the intellectual and ethical basis of the state:

1. Universal and equal elementary education by the state. Universal compulsory school attendance. Free instruction.

"Equal elementary education?" What idea lies behind these words? Is it believed that in present-day society (and it is only with this one has to deal) education can be *equal* for all classes? Or is it demanded that the upper classes also shall be compulsorily reduced to the modicum of education – the elementary school – that alone is compatible with the economic conditions not only of the wage-workers but of the peasants as well?

"Universal compulsory school attendance. Free instruction." The former exists even in Germany, the second in Switzerland and in the United States in the case of elementary schools. If in some states of the latter country higher education institutions are also "free," that only means in fact defraying the cost of education of the upper classes from the general tax receipts. Incidentally, the same holds good for "free administration of justice" demanded under A, 5. The administration of criminal justice is to be had free everywhere; that of civil justice is concerned almost exclusively with conflicts over property and hence affects almost exclusively the possessing classes. Are they to carry on their litigation at the expense of the national coffers?

This paragraph on the schools should at least have demanded technical schools (theoretical and practical) in combination with the elementary school.

"Elementary education by the state" is altogether objectionable. Defining by a general law the expenditures on the elementary schools, the qualifications of the teaching staff, the branches of instruction, etc., and, as is done in the United States, supervizing the fulfillment of these legal specifications by state inspectors, is a very different thing from appointing the state as the educator of the people! Government and church should rather be equally excluded from any influence on the school. Particularly, indeed, in the Prusso-German Empire (and one should not take refuge in the rotten subterfuge that one is speaking of a "state of the future"; we have seen how matters stand in this respect) the state has need, on the contrary, of a very stern education by the people.

But the whole program, for all its democratic clang, is tainted through and through by the Lassallean sect's servile belief in the state, or, what is no better, by a democratic belief in miracles; or rather it is a compromise between these two kinds of belief in miracles, both equally remote from socialism.

"Freedom of science" says a paragraph of the Prussian Constitution. Why, then, here?.

"Freedom of conscience"! If one desired, at this time of the *Kulturkampf* to remind liberalism of its old catchwords, it surely could have been done only in the following form: Everyone should be able to attend his religious as well as his bodily needs without the police sticking their noses in. But the Workers' party ought, at any rate in this connection, to have expressed its awareness of the fact that bourgeois "freedom of conscience" is nothing but the toleration of all possible kinds of religious freedom of conscience, and that for its part it endeavors rather to liberate the conscience from the witchery of religion. But one chooses not to transgress the "bourgeois" level.

Chapter 23

Adam Smith

THE WEALTH OF NATIONS

Adam Smith (1723–90) was a professor of moral philosophy at the University of Glasgow in Scotland, and one of the founding thinkers of modern economics. These excerpts, taken from his most famous work, *An Inquiry into the Nature and Causes of the Wealth of Nations* (1776), discuss the crucial importance of the division of labour in the generation of wealth, the relationship between self-interested individual behavior and beneficial social outcomes, the errors of mercantilism (protectionism), and Smith's own vision of the proper scope of government: "the obvious and simple system of natural liberty."

Book 1, Chapter I: Of the Division of Labour

The greatest improvements in the productive powers of labour, and the greater part of the skill, dexterity, and judgment, with which it is anywhere directed, or applied, seem to have been the effects of the division of labour. The effects of the division of labour, in the general business of society, will be more easily understood, by considering in what manner it operates in some particular manufactures. It is commonly supposed to be carried furthest in some very trifling ones; not perhaps that it really is carried further in them than in others of more importance: but in those trifling manufactures which are destined to supply the small wants of but a small number of people, the whole number of workmen must necessarily be small; and those employed in every different branch of the work can often be collected into the same workhouse, and placed at once under the view of the spectator.

In those great manufactures, on the contrary, which are destined to supply the great wants of the great body of the people, every different branch of the work employs so great a number of workmen, that it is impossible to collect them all into the same workhouse. We can seldom see more, at one time, than those employed in one single branch. Though in such manufactures, therefore, the work may really be divided into a much greater number of parts, than in those of a more trifling nature, the division is not near so obvious, and has accordingly been much less observed.

To take an example, therefore, from a very trifling manufacture, but one in which the division of labour has been very often taken notice of, the trade of a pin-maker: a workman not educated to this business (which the division of labour has rendered a distinct trade), nor acquainted with the use of the machinery employed in it (to the invention of which the same division of labour has probably given occasion), could scarce, perhaps, with his utmost industry, make one pin in a day, and certainly could not make twenty. But in the way in which this business is now carried on, not only the whole work is a peculiar trade, but it is divided into a number of branches, of which the greater part are likewise peculiar trades. One man draws out the wire; another straights it; a third cuts it; a fourth points it; a fifth grinds it at the top for receiving the head; to make the head requires two or three distinct operations; to put it on is a peculiar business; to whiten the pins is another; it is even a trade by itself to put them into the paper; and the important business of making a pin is, in this manner, divided into about eighteen distinct operations, which, in some manufactories, are all performed by distinct hands, though in others the same man will sometimes perform two or three of them. I have seen a small manufactory of this kind, where ten men only were employed, and where some of them consequently performed two or three distinct operations. But though they were very poor, and therefore but indifferently accommodated with the necessary machinery, they could, when they exerted themselves, make among them about twelve pounds of pins in a day. There are in a pound upwards of four thousand pins of a middling size. Those ten persons, therefore, could make among them upwards of forty-eight thousand pins in a day. Each person, therefore, making a tenth part of forty-eight thousand pins, might be considered as making four thousand eight hundred pins in a day. But if they had all wrought separately and independently, and without any of them having been educated to this peculiar business, they certainly could not each of them have made twenty, perhaps not one pin in a day; that is, certainly, not the two hundred and fortieth, perhaps not the four thousand eight hundredth, part of what they are at present capable of performing, in consequence of a proper division and combination of their different operations.

In every other art and manufacture, the effects of the division of labour are similar to what they are in this very trifling one, though, in many of them, the labour can neither be so much subdivided, nor reduced to so great a simplicity of operation. The division of labour, however, so far as it can be introduced, occasions, in every art, a proportionable increase of the productive powers of labour. The separation of different trades and employments from one another, seems to have taken place in consequence of this advantage. This separation, too, is generally carried furthest in those countries which enjoy the highest degree of industry and improvement; what is the work of one man, in a rude state of society, being generally that of several in an improved one. In every improved society, the farmer is generally nothing but a farmer; the manufacturer, nothing but a manufacturer. The labour, too, which is necessary to produce any one complete manufacture, is almost always divided among a great number of hands. How many different trades are employed in each branch of the linen and woollen manufactures, from the growers of the flax and the wool, to the bleachers and smoothers of the linen, or to the dyers and dressers of the cloth! The nature of agriculture, indeed, does not admit of so many subdivisions of labour, nor of so complete a separation of one business from another, as manufactures. It is impossible to separate so entirely the business of the grazier from that of the corn-farmer, as the trade of the carpenter is commonly separated from that of the smith. The spinner is almost always a distinct person from the weaver; but the ploughman, the harrower, the sower of the seed, and the reaper of the corn, are often the same. The occasions for those different sorts of labour returning with the different seasons of the year, it is impossible that one man should be constantly employed in any one of them. This impossibility of making so complete and entire a separation of all the different branches of labour employed in agriculture, is perhaps the reason why the improvement of the productive powers of labour, in this art, does not always keep pace with their improvement in manufactures. The most opulent nations, indeed, generally excel all their neighbours in agriculture as well as in manufactures; but they are commonly more distinguished by their superiority in the latter than in the former. Their lands are in general better cultivated, and having more labour and expense bestowed upon them, produce more in proportion to the extent and natural fertility of the ground. But this superiority of produce is seldom much more than in proportion to the superiority of labour and expense. In agriculture, the labour of the rich country is not always much more productive than that of the poor; or, at least, it is never so much more productive, as it commonly is in manufactures. The corn of the rich country, therefore, will not always, in the same degree of goodness, come cheaper to market than that of the poor. The corn of Poland, in the same degree of goodness, is as cheap as that of France, notwithstanding the superior opulence and improvement of the latter country. The corn of France is, in the corn-provinces, fully as good, and in most years nearly about the same price with the corn of England, though, in opulence and improvement, France is perhaps inferior to England. The corn-lands of England, however, are better cultivated than those of France, and the corn-lands of France are said to be much better cultivated than those of Poland. But though the poor country, notwithstanding the inferiority of its cultivation, can, in some measure, rival the rich in the cheapness and goodness of its corn, it can pretend to no such competition in its manufactures, at least if those manufactures suit the soil, climate, and situation, of the rich country. The silks of France are better and cheaper than those of England, because the silk manufacture, at least under the present high duties upon the importation of raw silk, does not so well suit the climate of England as that of France. But the hard-ware and the coarse woollens of England are beyond all comparison superior to those of France, and much cheaper, too, in the same degree of goodness. In Poland there are said to be scarce any manufactures of any kind, a few of those coarser household manufactures excepted, without which no country can well subsist.

This great increase in the quantity of work, which, in consequence of the division of labour, the same number of people are capable of performing, is owing to three different circumstances; first, to the increase of dexterity in every particular workman; secondly, to the saving of the time which is commonly lost in passing from one species of work to another; and, lastly, to the invention of a great number of machines which facilitate and abridge labour, and enable one man to do the work of many.

First, the improvement of the dexterity of the workmen, necessarily increases the quantity of the work he can perform; and the division of labour, by reducing every man's business to some one simple operation, and by making this operation the sole employment of his life, necessarily increases very much the dexterity of the workman. A common smith, who, though accustomed to handle the hammer, has never been used to make nails, if, upon some particular occasion, he is obliged to attempt it, will scarce, I am assured, be able to make above two or three hundred nails in a day, and those, too, very bad ones. A smith who has been accustomed to make nails, but whose sole or principal business has not been that of a nailer, can seldom, with his utmost diligence, make more than eight hundred or a thousand nails in a day. I have seen several boys, under twenty years of age, who had never exercised any other trade but that of making nails, and who, when they exerted themselves, could make, each of them, upwards of two thousand three hundred nails in a day. The making of a nail, however, is by no means one of the simplest operations. The same person blows the bellows, stirs or mends the fire as there is occasion, heats the iron, and forges every part of the nail: in forging the head, too, he is obliged to change his tools. The different operations into which the making of a pin, or of a metal button, is subdivided, are all of them much more simple, and the dexterity of the person, of whose life it has been the sole business to perform them, is usually much greater. The rapidity with which some of the operations of those manufactures are performed, exceeds what the human hand could, by those who had never seen them, be supposed capable of acquiring.

Secondly, the advantage which is gained by saving the time commonly lost in passing from one sort of work to another, is much greater than we should at first view be apt to imagine it. It is impossible to pass very quickly from one kind of work to another, that is carried on in a different place, and with quite different tools. A country weaver, who cultivates a small farm, must lose a good deal of time in passing from his loom to the field, and from the field to his loom. When the two trades can be carried on in the same workhouse, the loss of time is, no doubt, much less. It is, even in this case, however, very considerable. A man commonly saunters a little in turning his hand from one sort of employment to another. When he first begins the new work, he is seldom very keen and hearty; his mind, as they say, does not go to it, and for some time he rather trifles than applies to good purpose. The habit of sauntering, and of indolent careless application, which is naturally, or rather necessarily, acquired by every country workman who is obliged to change his work and his tools every half hour, and to apply his hand in twenty different ways almost every day of his life, renders him almost always slothful and lazy, and incapable of any vigorous application, even on the most pressing occasions. Independent, therefore, of his deficiency in point of dexterity, this cause alone must always reduce considerably the quantity of work which he is capable of performing.

Thirdly, and lastly, everybody must be sensible how much labour is facilitated and abridged by the application of proper machinery. It is unnecessary to give any example. I shall only observe, therefore, that the invention of all those machines by which labour is so much facilitated and abridged, seems to have been originally owing to the division of labour. Men are much more likely to discover easier and readier methods of attaining any object, when the whole attention of their minds is directed towards that single object, than when it is dissipated among a great variety of things. But, in consequence of the division of labour, the whole of every man's attention comes naturally to be directed towards some one very simple object. It is naturally to be expected, therefore, that some one or other of those who are employed in each particular branch of labour should soon find out easier and readier methods of performing their own particular work, whenever the nature of it admits of such improvement. A great part of the machines made use of in those manufactures in which labour is most subdivided, were originally the invention of common workmen, who, being each of them employed in some very simple operation, naturally turned their thoughts towards finding out easier and readier methods of performing it. Whoever has been much accustomed to visit such manufactures, must frequently have been shewn very pretty machines, which were the inventions of such workmen, in order to facilitate and quicken their own particular part of the work. In the first fire engines {this was the current designation for steam engines}, a boy was constantly employed to open and shut alternately the communication between the boiler and the cylinder, according as the piston either ascended or descended. One of those boys, who loved to play with his companions, observed that, by tying a string from the handle of the valve, which opened this communication, to another part of the machine, the valve would open and shut without his assistance, and leave him at liberty to divert himself with his play-fellows. One of the greatest improvements that has been made upon this machine, since it was first invented, was in this manner the discovery of a boy who wanted to save his own labour.

All the improvements in machinery, however, have by no means been the inventions of those who had occasion to use the machines. Many improvements have been made by the ingenuity of the makers of the machines, when to make them became the business of a peculiar trade; and some by that of those who are called philosophers, or men of speculation, whose trade it is not to do any thing, but to observe every thing; and who, upon that account, are often capable of combining together the powers of the most distant and dissimilar objects. In the progress of society, philosophy or speculation becomes, like every other employment, the principal or sole trade and occupation of a particular class of citizens. Like every other employment, too, it is subdivided into a great number of different branches, each of which affords occupation to a peculiar tribe or class of philosophers; and this subdivision of employment in philosophy, as well as in every other business, improves dexterity, and saves time. Each individual becomes more expert in his own peculiar branch, more work is done upon the whole, and the quantity of science is considerably increased by it.

It is the great multiplication of the productions of all the different arts, in consequence of the division of labour, which occasions, in a well-governed society, that universal opulence which extends itself to the lowest ranks of the people. Every workman has a great quantity of his own work to dispose of beyond what he himself has occasion for; and every other workman being exactly in the same situation, he is enabled to exchange a great quantity of his own goods for a great quantity or, what comes to the same thing, for the price of a great quantity of theirs. He supplies them abundantly with what they have occasion for, and they accommodate him as amply with what he has occasion for, and a general plenty diffuses itself through all the different ranks of the society.

Observe the accommodation of the most common artificer or daylabourer in a civilized and thriving country, and you will perceive that the number of people, of whose industry a part, though but a small part, has been employed in procuring him this accommodation, exceeds all computation. The woollen coat, for example, which covers the day labourer, as coarse and rough as it may appear, is the produce of the joint labour of a great multitude of workmen. The shepherd, the sorter of the wool, the wool-comber or carder, the dyer, the scribbler, the spinner, the weaver, the fuller, the dresser, with many others, must all join their different arts in order to complete even this homely production. How many merchants and carriers, besides, must have been employed in transporting the materials from some of those workmen to others who often live in a very distant part of the country? How much commerce and navigation in particular, how many ship-builders, sailors, sail-makers, rope-makers, must have been employed in order to bring together the different drugs made use of by the dyer, which often come from the remotest corners of the world? What a variety of labour, too, is necessary in order to produce the tools of the meanest of those workmen! To say nothing of such complicated machines as the ship of the sailor, the mill of the fuller, or even the loom of the weaver, let us consider only what a variety of labour is requisite in order to form that very simple machine, the shears with which the shepherd clips the wool. The miner, the builder of the furnace for smelting the ore, the feller of the timber, the burner of the charcoal to be made use of in the smelting-house, the brickmaker, the bricklayer, the workmen who attend the furnace, the mill-wright, the forger, the smith, must all of them join their different arts in order to produce them. Were we to examine, in the same manner, all the different parts of his dress and household furniture, the coarse linen shirt which he wears next his skin, the shoes which cover his feet, the bed which he lies on, and all the different parts which compose it, the kitchen-grate at which he prepares his victuals, the coals which he makes use of for that purpose, dug from the bowels of the earth, and brought to him, perhaps, by a long sea and a long land carriage, all the other utensils of his kitchen, all the furniture of his table, the knives and forks, the earthen or pewter plates upon which he serves up and divides his victuals, the different hands employed in preparing his bread and his beer, the glass window which lets in the heat and the light, and keeps out the wind and the rain, with all the knowledge and art requisite for preparing that beautiful and happy invention, without which these northern parts of the world could scarce have afforded a very comfortable habitation, together with the tools of all the different workmen employed in producing those different conveniencies; if we examine, I say, all these things, and consider what a variety of labour is employed about each of them, we shall be sensible that, without the assistance and co-operation of many thousands, the very meanest person in a civilized country could not be provided, even according to, what we very falsely imagine, the easy and simple manner in which he is commonly accommodated. Compared, indeed, with the more extravagant luxury of the great, his accommodation must no doubt appear extremely simple and easy; and yet it may be true, perhaps, that the accommodation of an European prince does not always so much exceed that of an industrious and frugal peasant, as the accommodation of the latter exceeds that of many an African king, the absolute masters of the lives and liberties of ten thousand naked savages.

Book 1, Chapter II: Of the Principle Which Gives Occasion to the Division of Labour

This division of labour, from which so many advantages are derived, is not originally the effect of any human wisdom, which foresees and intends that general opulence to which it gives occasion. It is the necessary, though very slow and gradual, consequence of a certain propensity in human nature, which has in view no such extensive utility; the propensity to truck, barter, and exchange one thing for another.

Whether this propensity be one of those original principles in human nature, of which no further account can be given; or whether, as seems more probable, it be the necessary consequence of the faculties of reason and speech, it belongs not to our present subject to inquire. It is common to all men, and to be found in no other race of animals, which seem to know neither this nor any other species of contracts. Two greyhounds, in running down the same hare, have sometimes the appearance of acting in some sort of concert. Each turns her towards his companion, or endeavours to intercept her when his companion turns her towards himself. This, however, is not the effect of any contract, but of the accidental concurrence of their passions in the same object at that particular time. Nobody ever saw a dog make a fair and deliberate exchange of one bone for another with another dog. Nobody ever saw one animal, by its gestures and natural cries signify to another, this is mine, that yours; I am willing to give this for that. When an animal wants to obtain something either of a man, or of another animal, it has no other means of persuasion, but to gain the favour of those whose service it requires. A puppy fawns upon its dam, and a spaniel endeavours, by a thousand attractions, to engage the attention of its master who is at dinner, when it wants to be fed by him. Man sometimes uses the same arts with his brethren, and when he has no other means of engaging them to act according to his inclinations, endeavours by every servile and fawning attention to obtain their good will. He has not time, however, to do this upon every occasion. In civilized society he stands at all times in need of the co-operation and assistance of great multitudes, while his whole life is scarce sufficient to gain the friendship of a few persons.

In almost every other race of animals, each individual, when it is grown up to maturity, is entirely independent, and in its natural state has occasion for the assistance of no other living creature. But man has almost constant occasion for the help of his brethren, and it is in vain for him to expect it from their benevolence only. He will be more likely to prevail if he can interest their self-love in his favour, and shew them that it is for their own advantage to do for him what he requires of them. Whoever offers to another a bargain of any kind, proposes to do this. Give me that which I want, and you shall have this which you want, is the meaning of every such offer; and it is in this manner that we obtain from one another the far greater part of those good offices which we stand in need of. It is not from the benevolence of the butcher, the brewer, or the baker that we expect our dinner, but from their regard to their own interest. We address ourselves, not to their humanity, but to their self-love, and never talk to them of our own necessities, but of their advantages. Nobody but a beggar chooses to depend chiefly upon the benevolence of his fellow-citizens. Even a beggar does not depend upon it entirely. The charity of well-disposed people, indeed, supplies him with the whole fund of his subsistence. But though this principle ultimately provides him with all the necessaries of life which he has occasion for, it neither does nor can provide him with them as he has occasion for them. The greater part of his occasional wants are supplied in the same manner as those of other people, by treaty, by barter, and by purchase. With the money which one man gives him he purchases food. The old clothes which another bestows upon him he exchanges for other clothes which suit him better, or for lodging, or for food, or for money, with which he can buy either food, clothes, or lodging, as he has occasion.

As it is by treaty, by barter, and by purchase, that we obtain from one another the greater part of those mutual good offices which we stand in need of, so it is this same trucking disposition which originally gives occasion to the division of labour. In a tribe of hunters or shepherds, a particular person makes bows and arrows, for example, with more readiness and dexterity than any other. He frequently exchanges them for cattle or for venison, with his companions; and he finds at last that he can, in this manner, get more cattle and venison, than if he himself went to the field to catch them. From a regard to his own interest, therefore, the making of bows and arrows grows to be his chief business, and he becomes a sort of armourer. Another excels in making the frames and covers of their little huts or moveable houses. He is accustomed to be of use in this way to his neighbours, who reward him in the same manner with cattle and with venison, till at last he finds it his interest to dedicate himself entirely to this employment, and to become a sort of house-carpenter. In the same manner a third becomes a smith or a brazier; a fourth, a tanner or dresser of hides or skins, the principal part of the clothing of savages. And thus the certainty of being able to exchange all that surplus part of the produce of his own labour, which is over and above his own consumption, for such parts of the produce of other men's labour as he may have occasion for, encourages every man to apply himself to a particular occupation, and to cultivate and bring to perfection whatever talent of genius he may possess for that particular species of business.

The difference of natural talents in different men, is, in reality, much less than we are aware of; and the very different genius which appears to distinguish men of different professions, when grown up to maturity, is not upon many occasions so much the cause, as the effect of the division of labour. The difference between the most dissimilar characters, between a philosopher and a common street porter, for example, seems to arise not so much from nature, as from habit, custom, and education. When they came in to the world, and for the first six or eight years of their existence, they were, perhaps, very much alike, and neither their parents nor play-fellows could perceive any remarkable difference. About that age, or soon after, they come to be employed in very different occupations. The difference of talents comes then to be taken notice of, and widens by degrees, till at last the vanity of the philosopher is willing to acknowledge scarce any resemblance. But without the disposition to truck, barter, and exchange, every man must have procured to himself every necessary and conveniency of life which he wanted. All must have had the same duties to perform, and the same work to do, and there could have been no such difference of employment as could alone give occasion to any great difference of talents.

As it is this disposition which forms that difference of talents, so remarkable among men of different professions, so it is this same disposition which renders that difference useful. Many tribes of animals, acknowledged to be all of the same species, derive from nature a much more remarkable distinction of genius, than what, antecedent to custom and education, appears to take place among men. By nature a philosopher is not in genius and disposition half so different from a street porter, as a mastiff is from a greyhound, or a grey hound from a spaniel, or this last from a shepherd's dog. Those different tribes of animals, however, though all of the same species are of scarce any use to one another. The strength of the mastiff is not in the least supported either by the swiftness of the greyhound, or by the sagacity of the spaniel, or by the docility of the shepherd's dog. The effects of those different geniuses and talents, for want of the power or disposition to barter and exchange, cannot be brought into a common stock, and do not in the least contribute to the better accommodation and conveniency of the species. Each animal is still obliged to support and defend itself, separately and independently, and derives no sort of advantage from that variety of talents with which nature has distinguished its fellows. Among men, on the contrary, the most dissimilar geniuses are of use to one another; the different produces of their respective talents, by

the general disposition to truck, barter, and exchange, being brought, as it were, into a common stock, where every man may purchase whatever part of the produce of other men's talents he has occasion for.

[. . .]

Book IV, Chapter II: Of Restraints Upon Importation from Foreign Countries of Such Goods as Can Be Produced at Home

By restraining, either by high duties, or by absolute prohibitions, the importation of such goods from foreign countries as can be produced at home, the monopoly of the home market is more or less secured to the domestic industry employed in producing them. Thus the prohibition of importing either live cattle or salt provisions from foreign countries, secures to the graziers of Great Britain the monopoly of the home market for butcher's meat. The high duties upon the importation of corn, which, in times of moderate plenty, amount to a prohibition, give a like advantage to the growers of that commodity. The prohibition of the importation of foreign woollen is equally favourable to the woollen manufacturers. The silk manufacture, though altogether employed upon foreign materials, has lately obtained the same advantage. The linen manufacture has not yet obtained it, but is making great strides towards it. Many other sorts of manufactures have, in the same manner obtained in Great Britain, either altogether, or very nearly, a monopoly against their countrymen. The variety of goods, of which the importation into Great Britain is prohibited, either absolutely, or under certain circumstances, greatly exceeds what can easily be suspected by those who are not well acquainted with the laws of the customs.

That this monopoly of the home market frequently gives great encouragement to that particular species of industry which enjoys it, and frequently turns towards that employment a greater share of both the labour and stock of the society than would otherwise have gone to it, cannot be doubted. But whether it tends either to increase the general industry of the society, or to give it the most advantageous direction, is not, perhaps, altogether so evident.

The general industry of the society can never exceed what the capital of the society can employ. As the number of workmen that can be kept in employment by any particular person must bear a certain proportion to his capital, so the number of those that can be continually employed by all the members of a great society must bear a certain proportion to the whole capital of the society, and never can exceed that proportion. No regulation of commerce can increase the quantity of industry in any society beyond what its capital can maintain. It can only divert a part of it into a direction into which it might not otherwise have gone; and it is by no means certain that this artificial direction is likely to be more advantageous to the society, than that into which it would have gone of its own accord.

Every individual is continually exerting himself to find out the most advantageous employment for whatever capital he can command. It is his own advantage, indeed, and not that of the society, which he has in view. But the study of his own advantage naturally, or rather necessarily, leads him to prefer that employment which is most advantageous to the society.

First, every individual endeavours to employ his capital as near home as he can, and consequently as much as he can in the support of domestic industry, provided always that he can thereby obtain the ordinary, or not a great deal less than the ordinary profits of stock.

Thus, upon equal, or nearly equal profits, every wholesale merchant naturally prefers the home trade to the foreign trade of consumption, and the foreign trade of consumption to the carrying trade. In the home trade, his capital is never so long out of his sight as it frequently is in the foreign trade of consumption. He can

know better the character and situation of the persons whom he trusts; and if he should happen to be deceived, he knows better the laws of the country from which he must seek redress. In the carrying trade, the capital of the merchant is, as it were, divided between two foreign countries, and no part of it is ever necessarily brought home, or placed under his own immediate view and command. The capital which an Amsterdam merchant employs in carrying corn from Koningsberg to Lisbon, and fruit and wine from Lisbon to Koningsberg, must generally be the one half of it at Koningsberg, and the other half at Lisbon. No part of it need ever come to Amsterdam. The natural residence of such a merchant should either be at Koningsberg or Lisbon; and it can only be some very particular circumstances which can make him prefer the residence of Amsterdam. The uneasiness, however, which he feels at being separated so far from his capital, generally determines him to bring part both of the Koningsberg goods which he destines for the market of Lisbon, and of the Lisbon goods which he destines for that of Koningsberg, to Amsterdam; and though this necessarily subjects him to a double charge of loading and unloading as well as to the payment of some duties and customs, yet, for the sake of having some part of his capital always under his own view and command, he willingly submits to this extraordinary charge; and it is in this manner that every country which has any considerable share of the carrying trade, becomes always the emporium, or general market, for the goods of all the different countries whose trade it carries on. The merchant, in order to save a second loading and unloading, endeavours always to sell in the home market, as much of the goods of all those different countries as he can; and thus, so far as he can, to convert his carrying trade into a foreign trade of consumption. A merchant, in the same manner, who is engaged in the foreign trade of consumption, when he collects goods for foreign markets, will always be glad, upon equal or nearly equal profits, to sell as great a part of them at home as he can. He saves himself the risk and trouble of exportation, when, so far as he can, he thus converts his foreign trade of consumption into a home trade. Home is in this manner the center, if I may say so, round which the capitals of the inhabitants of every country are continually circulating, and towards which they are always tending, though, by particular causes, they may sometimes be driven off and repelled from it towards more distant employments. But a capital employed in the home trade, it has already been shown, necessarily puts into motion a greater quantity of domestic industry, and gives revenue and employment to a greater number of the inhabitants of the country, than an equal capital employed in the foreign trade of consumption; and one employed in the foreign trade of consumption has the same advantage over an equal capital employed in the carrying trade. Upon equal, or only nearly equal profits, therefore, every individual naturally inclines to employ his capital in the manner in which it is likely to afford the greatest support to domestic industry, and to give revenue and employment to the greatest number of people of his own country.

Secondly, every individual who employs his capital in the support of domestic industry, necessarily endeavours so to direct that industry, that its produce may be of the greatest possible value.

The produce of industry is what it adds to the subject or materials upon which it is employed. In proportion as the value of this produce is great or small, so will likewise be the profits of the employer. But it is only for the sake of profit that any man employs a capital in the support of industry; and he will always, therefore, endeavour to employ it in the support of that industry of which the produce is likely to be of the greatest value, or to exchange for the greatest quantity either of money or of other goods.

But the annual revenue of every society is always precisely equal to the exchangeable value of the whole annual produce of its industry, or rather is precisely the same thing with that exchangeable value. As every individual, therefore, endeavours as much as he can, both to employ his capital in the support of domestic industry, and so to direct that industry that its produce maybe of the greatest value; every individual necessarily labours to render the annual revenue of the society as great as he can. He generally, indeed, neither intends to promote the public interest, nor knows how much he is promoting it. By preferring the support of domestic to that of foreign industry, he intends only his own security; and by directing that industry in such a manner as its produce may be of the greatest value, he intends only his own gain; and he is in this, as in many other cases, led by an invisible hand to promote an end which was no part of his intention. Nor is it always the worse for the society that it was no part of it. By pursuing his own interest, he frequently promotes that of the society more effectually than when he really intends to promote it. I have never known much good done by those who affected to trade for the public good. It is an affectation, indeed, not very common among merchants, and very few words need be employed in dissuading them from it.

What is the species of domestic industry which his capital can employ, and of which the produce is likely to be of the greatest value, every individual, it is evident, can in his local situation judge much better than any statesman or lawgiver can do for him. The statesman, who should attempt to direct private people in what manner they ought to employ their capitals, would not only load himself with a most unnecessary attention, but assume an authority which could safely be trusted, not only to no single person, but to no council or senate whatever, and which would nowhere be so dangerous as in the hands of a man who had folly and presumption enough to fancy himself fit to exercise it.

To give the monopoly of the home market to the produce of domestic industry, in any particular art or manufacture, is in some measure to direct private people in what manner they ought to employ their capitals, and must in almost all cases be either a useless or a hurtful regulation. If the produce of domestic can be brought there as cheap as that of foreign industry, the regulation is evidently useless. If it cannot, it must generally be hurtful. It is the maxim of every prudent master of a family, never to attempt to make at home what it will cost him more to make than to buy. The tailor does not attempt to make his own shoes, but buys them of the shoemaker. The shoemaker does not attempt to make his own clothes, but employs a tailor. The farmer attempts to make neither the one nor the other, but employs those different artificers. All of them find it for their interest to employ their whole industry in a way in which they have some advantage over their neighbours, and to purchase with a part of its produce, or, what is the same thing, with the price of a part of it, whatever else they have occasion for.

What is prudence in the conduct of every private family, can scarce be folly in that of a great kingdom. If a foreign country can supply us with a commodity cheaper than we ourselves can make it, better buy it of them with some part of the produce of our own industry, employed in a way in which we have some advantage. The general industry of the country being always in proportion to the capital which employs it, will not thereby be diminished, no more than that of the abovementioned artificers; but only left to find out the way in which it can be employed with the greatest advantage. It is certainly not employed to the greatest advantage, when it is thus directed towards an object which it can buy cheaper than it can make. The value of its annual produce is certainly more or less diminished, when it is thus turned away from producing commodities evidently of more value than the commodity which it is directed to produce. According to the supposition, that commodity could be purchased from foreign countries cheaper than it can be made at home; it could

therefore have been purchased with a part only of the commodities, or, what is the same thing, with a part only of the price of the commodities, which the industry employed by an equal capital would have produced at home, had it been left to follow its natural course. The industry of the country, therefore, is thus turned away from a more to a less advantageous employment; and the exchangeable value of its annual produce, instead of being increased, according to the intention of the lawgiver, must necessarily be diminished by every such regulation.
[...]

Book IV, Chapter IX: Of the Agricultural Systems, or of Those Systems of Political Economy which Represent the Produce of Land, as Either the Sole or the Principal Source of the Revenue and Wealth of Every Country

It is thus that every system which endeavours, either, by extraordinary encouragements to draw towards a particular species of industry a greater share of the capital of the society than what would naturally go to it, or, by extraordinary restraints, to force from a particular species of industry some share of the capital which would otherwise be employed in it, is, in reality, subversive of the great purpose which it means to promote. It retards, instead of accelerating the progress of the society towards real wealth and greatness; and diminishes, instead of increasing, the real value of the annual produce of its land and labour.

All systems, either of preference or of restraint, therefore, being thus completely taken away, the obvious and simple system of natural liberty establishes itself of its own accord. Every man, as long as he does not violate the laws of justice, is left perfectly free to pursue his own interest his own way, and to bring both his industry and capital into competition with those of any other man, or order of men. The sovereign is completely discharged from a duty, in the attempting to perform which he must always be exposed to innumerable delusions, and for the proper performance of which, no human wisdom or knowledge could ever be sufficient; the duty of superintending the industry of private people, and of directing it towards the employments most suitable to the interests of the society. According to the system of natural liberty, the sovereign has only three duties to attend to; three duties of great importance, indeed, but plain and intelligible to common understandings: first, the duty of protecting the society from the violence and invasion of other independent societies; secondly, the duty of protecting, as far as possible, every member of the society from the injustice or oppression of every other member of it, or the duty of establishing an exact administration of justice; and, thirdly, the duty of erecting and maintaining certain public works, and certain public institutions, which it can never be for the interest of any individual, or small number of individuals to erect and maintain; because the profit could never repay the expense to any individual, or small number of individuals, though it may frequently do much more than repay it to a great society.

Chapter 24

Charles Wolf, Jr.

MARKET FAILURE

Charles Wolf Jr. (1924–) is an economist and a senior economic adviser and corporate fellow in international economics with the RAND Corporation. This essay surveys the various kinds of market failure — cases where the market fails to provide an efficient allocation of goods and services. Such market failures are often thought to be a justification for using government policy to achieve a superior outcome.

The Inadequacies of Markets

The principal justification for public policy intervention lies in the shortcomings of market outcomes. Yet this rationale is only a necessary, not a sufficient, condition for policy formulation or for government intervention. The comment made a century ago by the British economist Henry Sidgwick can hardly be improved upon:

> It does not follow that whenever laissez faire falls short government interference is expedient; since the inevitable drawbacks of the latter may, in any particular case, be worse than the shortcomings of private enterprise.[1]

Policy formulation properly requires that the realized shortcomings of market outcomes be compared with the potential shortcomings of non-market efforts to provide remedies. The pathology of market shortcomings or failures provides only limited help in prescribing therapies for government success.

But how are we to judge the "success" or "failure" of market outcomes? Two broad criteria are usually and properly, though sometimes ambiguously, employed: efficiency and distributional equity.

Market outcomes can be termed efficient if the same level of total benefits which they generate cannot be obtained at lower cost or, alternatively, if greater benefits cannot be generated at the same level of costs; in either case, the resulting total benefits must exceed total costs if the outcomes are to be deemed efficient. Efficiency is thus like a contest among different ways of doing a job: If the market can accomplish the job at a lower cost than can other institutional arrangements, or can do a better job for the same costs, then the market is relatively efficient. On the other hand, if other institutional arrangements can accomplish the task at lower cost, or can do it better for the same cost, then the market is, in this respect, relatively inefficient.

This criterion defines *allocative,* or *static, efficiency*. It can be extended and refined in various ways to allow for other types of efficiency. For example, *dynamic efficiency* – especially emphasized in the writings of Joseph Schumpeter – relates to the capability of free markets, or of other institutional arrangements, to promote new technology that lowers costs, improves product quality, or creates new and marketable products, and to promote these things at lower cost than other ways of doing them.[2] "X-efficiency" – a term coined by Harvey Leibenstein – relates to the capability of free markets or of other institutional arrangements to lower costs and raise the productivity of any given technology by stimulating organizational improvements, increased worker and management motivation, and improvements in a wide range of business decisions, including hiring and firing, promotions, salaries and bonuses, allocation of space, furniture, telephones, parking facilities, and so on.[3]

Whether markets are more or less able to promote these outcomes than are other institutional arrangements determines whether markets are relatively more or less dynamically efficient, or X-efficient.

Although invoking the second criterion for judging market outcomes – distributional equity – goes beyond the conventional boundaries of microeconomics, it has profound significance with respect to the formulation, evaluation, and implementation of alternative public policies. Economists are generally less comfortable in grappling with the murkiness of distributional issues than with the relative precision of efficiency issues. Yet the treatment of tax incidence, for example, is central to the field of public finance, and tax incidence is quintessentially distributional in character. Moreover, in the real world of public policy – whether pertaining to education, energy, housing, foreign trade, or even defense policy – distributional issues are usually more influential than efficiency ones in shaping judgments about the success or shortcomings of market outcomes. As Jacob Viner observed, extensive government intervention in the free market has come about "... largely as

the result of dissatisfaction with the prevailing distribution of income. ... No modern people will have zeal for the free market unless it operates in a setting of 'distributive justice' with which they are tolerably content."[4]

Even when the central importance of distributional equity is acknowledged, the question remains, What standard should be used to evaluate it? The answer will be very different, and often ambiguous, depending on whether equity is interpreted in the sense of equality of outcome or equality of opportunity, or in the sense of "horizontal equity," or "vertical equity," or in the Marxian sense, or in the sense of the Old Testament, or in the sense of the New Testament, or in the sense of assuring that the least-favored have their lot improved before any further improvements are allowed for those who are more favored.[5]

That markets may fail to produce either economically optimal (efficient) or socially desirable (equitable) outcomes has been elaborated in a well-known and voluminous literature.[6] Although the last word has not been written, the essential points in the accepted theory of market failure are worth summarizing as background for the subsequent discussion of non-market failure.[7]

Types of Market Failure

There are four sources or types of market shortcomings or failures. I use the terms "shortcomings" and "failures" interchangeably; strictly speaking, "shortcomings" has a looser and more inclusive meaning. Most economists would confine "market failure" to departures from Pareto-efficient outcomes, thereby excluding distributional issues except to the extent that distribution affects efficiency. By contrast, many non-economists (and even some economists) argue that distribution has, or should have, priority over efficiency, and they fault the market precisely because of its failure to accord this priority.[8] The choice between disciplinary orthodoxy and practical relevance seems clear to me. I therefore consider distributional considerations to lie within the purview of market "shortcomings" or "failures."

Externalities and Public Goods

Where economic activities create "spillovers," whether benefits or costs, that are not, respectively, appropriable by or collectible from the producer, then market outcomes will not be efficient in the allocative sense defined above. Since these external benefits or costs do not enter the calculations upon which production decisions are based, too little will tend to be produced where the externalities are (net) benefits, and too much where they are (net) costs, compared with socially efficient output levels. Education is an example of an activity that putatively yields positive externalities (benefits) for society at large in addition to the benefits directly derived by the recipient. These externalities provide a rationale for government intervention – through subsidy or direct public sector production – to compensate for the tendency of the market, if it is not prodded, to produce insufficient output.

Other instances of positive externalities are the knowledge and technology resulting from activities and expenditures devoted to research and development. To the extent these benefits are external to, and non-appropriable by, the firms that bear the associated costs, these and other firms will invest too little in R & D. Once again, the market will fail according to the criterion of allocative efficiency, unless government intervenes by subsidizing or otherwise stimulating these activities. Moreover, to the extent that dynamic efficiency – the development of new products and processes – also depends on the creation of knowledge and technology, the unfettered market will fall short on this criterion as well.

Chemical and noise emissions from aircraft or other industrial activities are examples of negative externalities (costs). Their existence provides a rationale for government intervention – through taxing or direct regulation – to compensate for the market's tendency to produce excessive output in this instance, because the externalities are otherwise not taken into account.

"Private" goods that are associated with externalities can be distinguished from "public" goods: The former term applies where most of the benefits or costs associated with output are, respectively, collected or paid by the producer, although some are not; and the latter (public goods) applies where most of an activity's consequences consist of non-appropriable benefits (for example, national security, which is the classical example of a genuinely public good) or non-collectible costs (for example, crime, the classical public "bad").[9]

A powerful counter-argument to the market failure created by externalities has been made by Ronald Coase (1960). Coase contends that externalities do not necessarily lead to market failure. Those who are the victims of external costs (such as the external costs imposed by chemical or noise emissions) can make these costs tangible to their sources by offering to pay the latter to desist or diminish the culpable activities (for example, to refrain from or reduce the emissions). Once the offer has been made, continuance of the emissions becomes a tangible cost, because the perpetrator will forgo the offered payment unless he refrains from the objectionable activity. Consequently, in an effort to eat his cake and have it, a rational, cool, and calculating source of such negative externalities will seek to diminish them. Toward this end, he will consider, for example, using different chemical processes, or following different routes, or developing appropriate new technology enabling him to continue his production activities (which accounted for the emissions in the first place), without incurring the costs that have been made tangible by the victims' offer.

Unfortunately, Coase's powerful theoretical argument runs into a serious problem of implementation. The problem lies in the difficulty of bringing about the kind of bargain or contract he envisages between the sources and the victims of the negative externalities.[10] In practice, the difficulty (which implies costs) of accomplishing such transactions between perpetrators and victims, or between benefactors and beneficiaries, is likely to be so formidable as to preclude the bargain being struck at all. However, to the extent these formidable transaction costs can be avoided or surmounted, markets can overcome externalities and continue to function efficiently. In that event, the distribution of benefits that results from the adjusted, and now once-more efficient, market outcomes will be altered. Under the assumed bargain, the beneficiary or the victim of the prior externalities will have to part with some income in order to avoid the negative externalities or retain the positive ones, respectively. Thus, the efficiency of market outcomes will be preserved, while its distributional equity may be enhanced or diminished, depending on the equity criterion that is applied (see the discussion below on distributional equity).

Increasing Returns

Where economic activities are subject to increasing returns and decreasing marginal costs, markets will again fail to generate efficient outcomes. Under conditions of decreasing costs, the lowest cost mode of production would be achieved by a single producer. Consequently, a free market will result in monopoly. Assuming that the monopolist cannot discriminate in the prices charged to different buyers, and hence a single price prevails in the market (single-part pricing), the outcome will be inefficient, in both static and dynamic terms.

In static terms, the outcome will be inefficient because the quantity produced will be lower, and the profit-maximizing price charged by the monopolist will be higher, than warranted by the costs of production. In terms of dynamic efficiency, as defined earlier, the outcome will

also leave something to be desired because incentives for innovation by a secure and unchallenged monopolist will be weaker than would likely prevail under a more competitive regime.

Where increasing returns exist, various types of government intervention may be justified to alter the market outcome: (1) through direct operation or regulation of a "natural" monopoly (for example, public utilities), through setting prices or allowable rates of return on its capital, at levels closer to those which would prevail in a competitive environment; (2) through legal protection to prevent a single-firm takeover and to encourage competition (for example, through antitrust legislation). Such types of intervention depart from a theoretically efficient outcome, although they seek to approach it.[11]

A recent development in economics – the theory of "contestable markets" – suggests that, even in the face of increasing returns and the prevalence of monopoly, strong tendencies may persist for efficient, or nearly efficient, pricing and output decisions by monopolists, thereby avoiding or mitigating the impact of this source of market failure. The theory of contestable markets has been developed by William Baumol, and was foreshadowed several decades ago by the French economist François Perroux. Perroux suggested that, if markets are open to new entrants and there are few barriers and limited costs to entry, monopolists will be disciplined by the potential entry of competitors (the "potential rival"), who would contest the monopolized market unless profit margins are kept low and output is kept high.[12]

Thus, where barriers to entry are low, the production of a good or provision of a service by a monopolist does not necessarily signify that he will be able to exploit monopoly power. In the case of the airline industry, for example, even monopoly suppliers of service on thinly served routes have been unable to charge monopoly prices because the existence of potential entrants and competitors has discouraged such practices by the existing monopolists. Consequently,

dynamic efficiency = appropriate balance of short run concerns
(static efficiency) w/ concerns in long run.

following deregulation of the airlines, rates charged on thinly served routes have not been characterized by monopoly pricing or monopoly profits any more than have the heavily served and clearly competitive routes.[13]

Even for the Schumpeterian criterion of dynamic efficiency, increasing returns and monopolistic market structure may not stray as far from the desirable goal of innovation and rising productivity as has usually been assumed. Here again the influence of the contestability of the market by potential entrants ("rivals"), may enforce a strong discipline on monopolists, obliging them to maintain a high level of R&D and to sustain rapid innovation to protect their presently monopolized markets. Potential competition may thus have an effect similar to that of actual competition.

The recent breakup of AT&T, after lengthy litigation in which the huge corporation was found in violation of antitrust legislation, provides an interesting example of the conflict between the two preceding types of market failure: externalities and increasing returns. To remedy one source of market failure (increasing returns), the courts have perhaps created another (externalities). Perceiving a lack of effective competition in an industry subject to increasing returns (telecommunications), the courts have replaced it by a situation in which benefits from undertaking R&D and innovation, which formerly were largely "internalized" by the giant AT&T, are now largely external to the seven or eight regional firms into which the industry has been split. Hence, incentives may be weakened for the newly competing entities in the telecommunications industry to undertake as aggressive efforts in R&D and technological improvement as did AT&T in the past. The disincentives arise because of the externalities that R&D generates: Competitors can "free ride" on the R&D expenses incurred by any one firm. By contrast, when AT&T dominated the entire market, the results of R&D and innovation were internalized by the single firm that benefited from, as well as

generated, them. Hence, the "free rider" problem was avoided.

The AT&T case illustrates a frequent experience in the public policy arena. Public policy efforts motivated by the aim of remedying one type of shortcoming may well create a different one as a byproduct. It remains to be seen how the balance of advantage between these two sources of market failure – externalities and increasing returns – will work out under the new market structure established in the telecommunications industry.

Market Imperfections

Where the price, information, and mobility characteristics of "perfect" markets depart significantly from those prevailing in actual markets, the outcomes resulting from those markets will not be efficient. Once again, a rationale arises for government intervention. Where prices and interest rates, for one reason or another, do not indicate relative scarcities and opportunity costs, where consumers do not have equal access to information about products and markets, where information about market opportunities and production technology is not equally available to all producers, or where factors of production are restricted in their ability to move in response to such information, market forces will not allocate efficiently and the economy will produce below its capacity. These conditions abound in the economies of less developed countries, and they are surely not unfamiliar in the economies of more developed ones. Indeed, these imperfections apply to some extent in all markets and to a greater extent in some. In such circumstances, the implication for public policy is to reduce, if not remove, these imperfections: to facilitate availability of information, to lower barriers to entry and mobility, and so on.[14]

However, where many of the conditions required for efficient functioning of markets do not exist, improving some will not necessarily improve the efficiency of the market as a whole. Consequently, the policy implications of market imperfections may be ambiguous.[15] Legal protection of patents provides an example of how one type of market imperfection may even contribute to market efficiency. In this case the market imperfection is the restriction of access to technological information that is created by patents. A short-run loss of efficiency results because firms that do not hold the patent are restricted in their access to improved technological information because of the price (royalty) they have to pay to obtain and to use it. Consumers are thus deprived of benefits in the short run. However, the purpose of the patent restriction is to enhance incentives for technological improvement, thereby contributing to dynamic efficiency in the long run. The presumption is that the long-run gains, due to enhancement of incentives and the resulting impetus to dynamic efficiency, will exceed the short-term losses resulting from diminished allocative efficiency.

In less developed countries, the scale and pervasiveness of market imperfections – and sometimes even the apparent absence of functioning markets – is often adduced as a rationale for government dominance and control in the economy. A "big push" by government is presumed to be needed to compensate for the inadequacies of markets.

Certainly, market imperfections abound in these countries. They are characterized by restricted access to economically relevant information, by factor immobilities, price and interest rate distortions, and so on. Yet despite these characteristics, it is a striking fact that the few relatively successful developing countries – Korea, Hong Kong, Malaysia, Singapore, and Taiwan – have benefited hugely from decisions to limit the government's role in economic decision-making, and instead to allow markets – notwithstanding their imperfections and shortcomings – to exercise a decisive and increasing role in determining resource allocations.[16]

Distributional Equity

As already noted, most economists exclude distributional effects from judgments about the success or failure of markets. In textbook usage, the term "market failure" is usually confined to departures from competitive equilibrium and strictly efficient (Pareto-efficient) outcomes; as narrowly construed, then, "market failure" typically excludes departures from distributional equity. Nevertheless, this exclusion is usually accompanied by an acknowledgment that the distributional results of even well-functioning markets may not accord with socially accepted standards of equity, or with society's preferences for reducing excessive disparities in the distribution of income and wealth. It is also usually acknowledged that, where there is a tradeoff between efficiency and equity, social consensus in democratic systems often is prepared to forgo some of the one to realize more of the other.[17]

In welfare economics this tradeoff is usually dealt with by considering the relative efficiency of various redistributive measures (for example, income taxes, excises, subsidies, unemployment relief, and income transfers), in achieving a desired redistribution (that is, minimizing the allocative distortions resulting from the income and substitution effects of redistribution).

Nevertheless, from one perspective, it is theoretically correct to consider distributional inequity as an example of market failure. From this perspective, income distribution is a particular type of public good. An "equitable" redistribution does not result from freely functioning markets because philanthropy and charity yield benefits that are external to, and not appropriable by, the donors, but are instead realized by society as a whole. Left to its own devices, the market will therefore produce less redistribution than is "efficient" (that is, socially desirable), because of the usual "free-rider" problem associated with externalities, public goods, and incomplete markets.[18]

Another perspective for viewing distributional equity is quite unrelated to market failure in the strict sense. From this perspective, the equilibrium redistribution previously referred to may be quite inequitable in terms of one or another ethical norm. Even if the market could surmount the narrow type of "failure" discussed above, its distributional outcome might still be socially and ethically unacceptable from the standpoint of one or more such norms.[19] On these grounds, the distributional outcomes of even perfectly functioning markets can be justifiably criticized.

As noted earlier, Jacob Viner pointed out several decades ago that the decisive test of the acceptability of markets in modern democratic societies depends fundamentally on the extent to which such markets can co-exist within a general setting of "distributive justice" with which the electorate is "tolerably content."[20] Furthermore, most public policy decisions are usually even more concerned with distributional issues (namely, who gets the benefits and who pays the costs) than with efficiency issues (namely, how large are the benefits and costs). Since the principal aim of this book is to compare market shortcomings with the shortcomings of non-market remedies, distributional inequity will be included among the offenders.

Notes

1 See Sidgwick, Henry. *Principles of Political Economy*, Macmillan, London (1883), p. 414, and Cairncross, Alexander. "The Market and the State," in Thomas Wilson and A. S. Skinner (eds), *Essays in Honour of Adam Smith*, Oxford Clarendon Press, London (1976).

2 See, for example, Schumpeter, J. A. The Theory of Economic Development, Harvard University Press, Cambridge, MA (1934).

3 Leibenstein, Harvey. "Allocative Efficiency Versus X-Efficiency," *American Economic Review*, Vol. 56, No. 3 (1966), pp. 392–415.

4 See Viner, Jacob. "The Intellectual History of Laissez Faire," *Journal of Law and Economics*, Vol. 3 (1960), p. 68.

5 See Chap. 4 [not included in this volume] for a more extensive discussion of these several standards of equity.

6 See, for example, Reder, Melvin W. *Studies in the Theory of Welfare Economics*, AMS Press, New York (1947); Little, I. M. D. *A Critique of Welfare Economics*, 2nd ed., Clarendon Press, Oxford (1957); Samuelson, Paul A. "The Pure Theory of Public Expenditure," *Review of Economics and Statistics*, Vol. 36, No. 387 (1954); Lipsey, Richard G. and Kelvin Lancaster, "The General Theory of Second Best," *Review of Economic Studies*, Vol. 24, No. 11 (1956); Bator, Francis M. "The Anatomy of Market Failure," *Quarterly Journal of Economics*, Vol. 72, No. 351 (1958); Viner, "Intellectual History," (1960), pp. 45–69; Mishan, L. J. "The Relationship Between Joint Products, Collective Goods and External Effects," *Journal of Political Economy*, Vol. 77, No. 329 (1969); Arrow, Kenneth J. "Political and Economic Evaluation of Social Effects and Externalities," in Michael D. Intriligator (ed.), *Frontiers of Quantitative Economics*, North Holland Publ., Amsterdam (1971); Rawls, John. *A Theory of Justice*, Belknap Press, Cambridge, MA (1971); Davis, J. R. and J. R. Hewlett, *An Analysis of Market Failure: Externalities, Public Goods, and Mixed Goods*, University of Florida Press, Gainesville (1977); Thurow, Lester. "Psychic Income: A Market Failure," *Journal of Post-Keynsian Economics*, Winter (1981), pp. 183–93; and Tew, Bernard V., J. M. Broder, and W. M. Musser, "Market Failure in Multi-Phase Irrigation," *American Journal of Agricultural Economics*, Vol. 64, No.5 (1982), p. 1091.

7 As Arrow (1971) observes, "The clarification of these concepts [relating to market failure] is a long, historical process, not yet concluded."

8 See, for example, Rawls's "second principle" of a just society (Rawls, 1971).

9 Externalities are thus a more general concept than public goods. Stated another way, a public good is the limiting case of a "private" good with externalities: "Private" benefits approach zero, and all remaining benefits are external. More precisely, if v_{ij}^s is the valuation placed, or price paid, by the ith person for the jth unit of a good s, and mc_j^s is its marginal cost of production, then the condition for an allocatively efficient level of output for a private good with externalities is:

$$mc_j^s = v_{ij}^s + \sum_{m=1}^{k} v_{mj}^s,$$

where v_{ij} ·is the price paid by i and the $\sum v_{mj}^s$ are externalities (experienced by all other k individuals as a result of i's consumption of the jth unit of s), positive if the externalities are benefits and negative if costs.

For a "pure" public good, $v_{ij}^s = 0$. Consumption is collective, and no single unit is purchased by anybody. The optimum condition then is

$$mc_j^s = \sum_{m=1}^{k} v_{mj}^s .$$

Compare Mishan (1969): 329–48.), *supra*.

This condition is sometimes misstated as equivalent to a zero marginal cost of production. For example, the marginal cost of national defense in, say, the United States or NATO is *not* zero, although non-taxpayers, as well as citizens of other countries, receive the resulting benefits.

The generalized explanation for the existence of externalities and public goods is that markets do not exist for capturing some benefits or levying some costs. Non-existence of markets in these cases is explained by (1) the high cost or inability of excluding beneficiaries (for example, from the benefits of national defense or police expenditures), or of establishing property rights as a basis for claiming liability when they are infringed (for example, noise emissions in airport vicinities); and (2) the lack of information required for market transactions to be concluded (for example, ascertaining what the "true" v_{ij} are in the previous discussion), due at least in part to the free-rider problem associated with (1).

10 Coase, Ronald Harry. "The Problem of Social Cost," *Journal of Law & Economics*, 3 (1960): 1. It should be clear that Coase's line of argument can be applied to positive externalities (external benefits) as well as to negative externalities. In this case, the potential bargain would be one in which the source of the external benefits would try to extract a payment by threatening to eliminate or reduce the benefits unless the beneficiaries compensate him for these windfalls. However, in this case credibility of the threat may be impaired because the responsible source would very likely have to incur costs to carry it out: The beneficiaries must be persuaded that the threatener just might be willing to deprive himself of some gains in pursuit of larger ones.

11 Some discussions of market failure include increasing returns (for example, Francis M. Bator, *supra*), while others exclude it. Arrow, for example, contrasts increasing returns ("essentially a technological phenomenon") with market failure (which relates to "the mode of economic organization"), Kenneth J. Arrow, *supra*. I think this categorization leaves something to be desired. For example, improvements in technology can eliminate or at least reduce externalities (which Arrow considers market failures because they relate to the "mode of economic organization") by resolving the problems of exclusion and non-appropriability. As an illustration, electronic warning and protection devices may be an efficient means of lowering the risk of theft for households purchasing them. One can also imagine acoustical and air-filtration devices that would reduce the negative externalities represented by airport emissions, or identify their source as a basis for imposing and collecting costs. Conversely, Arrow's "technological" phenomenon of increasing returns can be reconciled with efficient pricing and output by suitable modes of economic organization, for example, through multipart pricing. (For a discussion of various pricing and market devices for reconciling increasing returns with efficient operation, see Wolf, Harris, Klitgaard, Nelson, Stein, and Baeza (1975). Increasing returns are a source of market inefficiency only as long as markets do not·exist for *separate* units of the same good. Allowing for enough subscripting, in the Arrow-Debreu sense, and hence separability of commodities, increasing returns are theoretically as compatible with competitive equilibrium as are externalities.

12 See Baumol, W. J., J. C. Panzer, and R. D. Willig. *Contestable Markets and the Theory of Industry Structure*, Harcourt Brace Jovanovich, San Diego, CA (1982), and Perroux, Francois. *Theorie Generale du Progres Economique*, Vol. II, Paris (1957), p. 18.

13 Federal Reserve Bank of San Francisco, *Airline Deregulation*, March 9 (1984), p. 2.

14 See the discussion in Chap. 8 [not included in this volume] of opportunities for government actions designed to improve the functioning of markets.

15 This is the essential message of second-best theory (Lipsey and Lancaster, 1956, *supra*). For example, changing a tariff that has applied equally to

imports from all countries, so that it applies instead only to a few countries, may reduce efficiency. Trade will be diverted as well as created, and the loss from the former may exceed the gains from the latter. (See Viner, Jacob. *The Customs Issues*, Carnegie Endowment for International Peace (1950)).

16 See Wolf, Charles Jr. "Economic Success, Stability and the 'Old' International Economic Order," *International Security*, Vol. 6, No. 1 (1981).

17 Little (1956). See also Scitovsky, Tibor. "The State of Welfare Economics," *American Economic Review*, Vol. 41, No.303 (1951), and Okun, Arthur. *Equality and Efficiency: The Big Trade-Off*, The Brookings Institution, Washington DC (1975).

18 The point can be formulated more precisely. Individual demands for redistribution can be defined in the same notional sense in which such demands can be defined for defense, or for law and order. For example, the demand for redistribution can be expressed as the desired *change* in current distribution (as measured, say, by the Gini coefficient); demand for redistribution is presumed to decline as the desired amount of voluntary individual philanthropy per dollar of earned income rises. Presumably, individual willingness to pay for redistribution declines as the price of achieving it rises. A cost function for redistribution can also be defined in terms of the same two variables. In principle, individual demands could be added, and the social equilibrium level of redistribution would be that for which the marginal optimization condition is satisfied (see note 9 *supra*). This equilibrium redistribution is not achieved because there is either no market or an incomplete market for philanthropy, just as there is an incomplete market for defense. In both cases, voluntary donations (unless motivated by special tax incentives) would be lacking due to the usual non-appropriability and non-excludability reasons.

19 See the discussion above concerning the different standards of equity, and the more extended discussion in Chap. 6 [not included in this volume].

20 See Viner (1960, p. 68).

Chapter 25

Randy Simmons

PATHOLOGICAL POLITICS
The Anatomy of Government Failure

Randy Simmons (1950–) is a professor of economics at Utah State University who has written widely in the field of public choice — a methodological approach in which the tools of economic analysis are brought to bear on the behavior of governmental actors and institutions. In this essay, taken from his book *Beyond Politics* (2011), he discusses the concept and causes of "government failure" — cases where institutional features of government lead predictably to inefficient outcomes — in order to question the idea that government policy is the best way of addressing market failures.

This essay completes the analysis of government failure by showing how and why the political process is defective and examines further whether these defects are inherent in politics or in particular institutions that might be altered and improved.

Citizen Sovereignty and Efficiency

A pathology of politics is meaningless without a normative foundation — in this case, efficiency, a much misunderstood and abused term among non-economists. Here it refers to a measure of how well society provides for the material wants of its members. This simple definition is in accord with the more precise one of Pareto, namely, whether a given policy, action, or allocation is able to improve the subjective well-being of anyone without diminishing that of others. Such a result is said to be a Pareto improvement. A polity or economy producing huge quantities of *unwanted* goods and services even at the lowest

cost is not Pareto efficient since no one would be made better off. Indeed, many would be worse off since the resources devoted to making unwanted goods could be allocated for goods people actually want. So, the chief concern is with *allocative* efficiency – improving people's subjective well-being. I am secondarily concerned with technical efficiency, which is producing something at the lowest cost. Efficiency in politics, then, is concerned with meeting individual preferences, while employing resources in their most valued uses.

Despite the importance of individual preferences in democracies, a number of otherwise attractive political features have the unhappy facility of violating Paretian efficiency. The two most prominent involve redistribution of income. Redistributive gains dominate efficiency considerations in policy discussions, and democratic institutions encourage this redistributive propensity. In addition, democracy has an unfortunate but a distinct penchant for enacting inefficient proposals – proposals that make some better off but at the expense of others or, even worse, making everyone worse off in the long run. By choosing policies and rules that produce greater costs than benefits and failing to enact those having greater benefits than costs, citizens are made worse off, if not absolutely then worse off than they might be otherwise.

Sources of inefficiency in the political process may be usefully categorized in seven ways: (1) perverted incentives; (2) collective provision of private wants; (3) deficient signaling mechanisms; (4) electoral rules and the distortion of preferences; (5) institutional myopia; (6) dynamic difficulties; and (7) policy symbolism.

Perverted Incentives

Adam Smith's greatest accomplishment was demonstrating the beneficence of the hidden hand of the market in converting self-interests into collective good. Just how the invisible hand operates has preoccupied economists for more than 200 years. The great accomplishment of modern public choice has been to demonstrate the pernicious workings of the visible hand of politics. The same decision makers operating under market and political rules produce quite different results. One of the major reasons pertains to the incentives governing choosers. Although both political and market participants are assumed to be self-interested, the incentives – objective rewards and penalties – differ profoundly. What the market and polity offer in the way of concrete awards, encouragements, discouragements, and costs contrast so much that people who have worked in both environments are puzzled at and sometimes exasperated by the variations. Businessmen in particular find working in the public sector frustrating.

In markets, the promise of profits fortified by the ever present risk of loss encourages entrepreneurs to improve their products and services, while lowering the cost of doing so. The wealth of customers and entrepreneurs is increased and

innovative ideas are provided by other competitors. By serving himself, the producer serves others; by serving others, he profits. It is, in short, an exchange system enabling mutual gains.

Some students of politics, including well-known economists and political scientists, see parallels and argue that politics ought to also be viewed as a vast exchange system. One such economist, Donald Wittman (1995) referred to "an invisible-hand theory of efficient democratic markets." According to Wittman, "vote maximization leads to wealth maximization in democratic markets in the same way that profit maximization leads to wealth maximization in economic markets" (p. 160). One trouble with Wittman's analysis is that politics and government do not offer a full range of profit making activities to its participants. In fact, the abuse of authority is feared so much that profit making (as distinct from self-seeking) in politics is prohibited by extraordinary constitutional, statutory, and ethical limitations on public officials. These rules circumscribe discretion and even goals. In this respect, the American Constitution is (and was designed to be) a distinctly negative document.

Government officials are not permitted to sell their official services or goods. And since they must offer their goods and services to all at zero or less-than-cost prices, we can never learn the precise values citizens place on these activities and goods. Without a market, value becomes impossible to ascertain and implement. Since everything in the market acquires a price, comparative efficiency judgments can be made by buyers and sellers enabling each to make ready, fairly accurate calculations on the right thing to do. Political actors have no such guidance and without it efficient choices become, as Mises and Hayek argued, impossible. A mayor might know how much it costs to construct a neighborhood park requested by citizens in the neighborhood, but there is no way to know the efficient amount of park to supply or if one ought to be supplied at all. The mayor's measure of demand is the number of citizens who sign a petition or show up at a city council meeting and the citizens' measure of cost is the opportunity cost of their time spent lobbying. Without prices and market forces, at best, government officials and citizens know what it costs them to purchase resources and products; but they cannot determine the values consumers place on the government services produced. Thus, it is next to impossible for even the most skilled government economist to construct a valid demand curve for politically provided goods.

When choosing public policies, politicians – who wish to remain in office – must rank the vote impact higher than the efficiency impact of alternative courses of action. Their calculations are at odds with those of businessmen, their market counterparts. Whereas the latter asks *how much* people want something, the equivalent of asking what they are willing to pay, the politician asks *how many* people want something. Politicians count majorities first, and intensity of preferences and beliefs second, and indirectly. A firm does not have to win majorities in order to do business; the politician, interest group, and voter do. Since a vote is weighted the same as any other vote, they are all equal. But some buyers have more dollar-votes than others and their voices, therefore, count for more. Since equal votes and unequal dollars are fundamental facts of the political economy they provide the crucial bases for debates and conflicts over the redistribution of income, wealth, status and power. Those who seek equality of outcomes wish to extend the realm of votes while those who prefer uncertain inequality tend to favor the market domain.

Separating Costs and Benefits

Perhaps *the* fundamental political fact – one characterized by inexpedient and untimely consequences – is the separation of cost and benefit considerations. The fact that few persons are forced to weigh them one against the other before making policy choices enables and encourages people to seek additional gains at collective expense.

As the number seeking favors from government increases, the government finds itself in the difficult position of having to cater to private desires rather than providing public goods, the goods governments are supposed to provide. The opportunity costs of devoting more time and resources to favor-seekers are that the provision of national defense, domestic law and order, and other genuine public goods is reduced. An analogy to government stretching to do more is the concept of "feature creep." As software programmers add more and more features to their products, the system becomes so overburdened that it cannot perform its basic and intended functions well. Recognition of feature creep has led several writers to worry about "governmental overload" and the consequent frustrations engendered by failure to provide basic services. Some writers claim that much of our alleged civic malaise and even cynicism results from governments attempting to do too many things and doing none well. The well-known conservative columnist George Will makes this a touchstone in his critiques of contemporary America. Although expressed in non-efficiency terms, his point is well taken.

More economically minded analysts would point out that citizens seeking collective provision of their private wants seek those goods for which they would not pay in the private market. So long as the goods come free, they demand more and, thereby, misallocate scarce resources from their higher valued uses. I spent six years as a city council member and four years as mayor of a small Utah city (yes, I understand the ironies) and saw such misallocations first hand. A nearby city of just 4,000 people, for example, received a road grant for $4 million. The money came because the city manager's daughter had served an internship in the U.S. House of Representatives and when spare, unexpected money showed up for road projects, the Congressional staff remembered her and called to see if her father's city could use the money. The city had planned and set aside money for a $1 million road but are quite happy to spend the $4 million instead to construct a four-lane road. The local officials most certainly would not have built four lanes if they had to spend their own restricted tax monies when other projects were more needed. And the local taxpayers would not have increased their taxes to build the road. But the four lanes were built not only because they did not burden local taxpayers but also because the expenditure of dollars from elsewhere provided a local contractor with additional work. They might as well have built pyramids or simply dug ditches and then filled them; the economic effects would have been the same. All the other mayors in the county were jealous of what they call the "lucky money" that came from the Congressional office and most are staying in close touch with Congressional offices in hopes of getting lucky money of their own.

The pervasiveness of this means of self-aggrandizement is saddening but understandable. How could it be otherwise when to sacrifice private goods in the public interest forces the sacrificer to pay all the costs while others enjoy the benefits? Divorcing costs from benefits induces not only a favor-seeking motive in each citizen but in the long run turns democracy into a constant search for a free lunch. But, as Milton Friedman (1962) reminded us, TANSTAAFL! – "There ain't no such thing as a free lunch!" since someone always pays. Milton's son David Friedman (1989) describes the political free-lunch-seeking process in the following parable:

> Special interest politics is a simple game. A hundred people sit in a circle, each with his pocket full of pennies. A politician walks around the outside of the circle, taking a penny from each person. No one minds; who cares about a penny? When he has gotten all the way around the circle, the politician

throws fifty cents down in front of one person, who is overjoyed at the unexpected windfall. The process is repeated, ending with a different person. After a hundred rounds, everyone is a hundred cents poorer, fifty cents richer, and happy (p. 107).

Divorcing costs from benefits is what happens in the familiar setting of a group dining together and agreeing to split the bill. The situation even has a name – *the unscrupulous diner's dilemma*. If the bill is being split evenly the selfish diner will order an exceptional dinner in the belief that her fellows will order normally. But if everyone orders more in the expectation that others will help pay the cost they each end up with a far higher bill individually and severally than if they had agreed at the outset to each pay their own portion of the bill. If friends are willing to do this to each other in face-to-face sitting around a table, think how much more citizen-taxpayers are willing to do it to anonymous, other taxpayers. And in politics we cannot say as did Phoebe in Season two, Episode five of the television series *Friends* when Ross tried to split the bill among them all, "No, uh uh, no way, I'm sorry, not gonna happen."

Political Signaling: Votes and Rhetoric

One of the greatest inventions is money, for it is a wonderfully convenient means of enabling persons with diverse interests to communicate in simple, precise, and rapid transactions. Without a monetary system, a modern society would soon dissolve into chaos. Without money we would not be able to avoid the double contingency problem of barter, that is, finding a trading partner who wants what you have and has what you want. Barter is extraordinarily cumbersome, imprecise, and inefficient. So are the substitutes for the pricing system that enable planners to play at market competition: price ceilings and floors, subsidies, tariffs, barriers to entry, quotas, make-work rules, rationing. Knowing these fundamental facts, however, has not dissuaded many political scientists from finding virtues in political systems that, in effect, employ barter and planning.

In democracies, the chief unit of account and medium of exchange is the vote. Now consider the vote itself as an analog to money. In the first place, everyone has but one vote and that vote is indivisible. Accordingly, the vote cannot express a voter's *intensity* of preferences. Without multiple votes or a weighted system of voting we cannot indicate to others just how much we prefer one candidate to another, or one policy over another. All we can say is that whomever or whatever we vote for is more preferred than the option not voted for. The vote, the mark, or "X" on the ballot can, therefore, convey little information and indeed when counted on Election Day, produces considerable ambiguity. What does the "X" mean? Both winners and losers can rationalize the outcomes. Is it a strong positive endorsement or merely a negative minimizing of a choice among bads? As guidance to policymakers the "X's" are highly ambiguous. Reducing the mystery and improving elections has inspired many formal theorists of public choice and other reformers to devise intricate reforms of the ballot, electoral rules, etc. Few of their suggestions are ever adopted.

The above problems can be reduced somewhat through the use of vote trading, a form of barter better known as logrolling in legislatures. (Logrolling is a term from the American frontier for reciprocity in rolling heavy logs to build a cabin or to clear a field – "I'll help you roll your logs if you'll help me roll mine.") Although a good case can be made that vote trading offers an improvement over non-trading, the argument usually breaks down in practice because the skewed distribution of diffused costs and concentrated benefits dominates the aggregate size of those results. Vote trading will, therefore, favor projects in which total costs exceed total benefits. If everyone votes on each project separately, all will be defeated. Voting on them

individually yet providing for vote trading will see them enacted into law and we will all be worse off.

An example will illustrate as well as demonstrate the logic of logrolling at its worst. Suppose three voters are confronted with two projects, a jail and a school. Each project is to be voted on independently of one another, and the decision is to be made by majority rule. If the voters estimate their respective costs and benefits as shown in Table 25.1, we expect that both projects would be voted down: in the case of the jail by voters A and C while in the case of the school by voters A and B. Since both projects are inefficient, that is, costs exceed total benefits, it is clear that the election produced the correct result.

But consider what might occur if the voters discovered and practiced logrolling. In such an event, voter B would agree to support voter C's school, if C will support B's jail. The result is that the three-member polity has now adopted two inefficient projects with a total loss of $200. Although B and C must help pay for each other's project, they still come out as gainers, but, of course, this is accomplished at the expense of A who must bear $400 of the total cost of $800. We can just as easily construct further simple situations showing the opposite results, but I believe in the real world, logrolling is more likely to confirm the blackboard illustration. While vote trading among ordinary voters is effectively discouraged by prohibitive transaction and monitoring costs, the politicians have managed, quite rationally, to impose a form of implicit trading on voters through the use of issue packaging. The practice is simply one of

Table 25.1 Inefficiency of Logrolling Voters' Net Benefit

Project	A	B	C
Jail	− $200	$300	− $200
School	− $200	− $200	$300
Net	− $400	$100	$100

combining individually popular proposals into a single package such as a party platform or, more commonly, through non-germane amendments to bills in legislature. The less popular proposals are attached as riders to popular ones; for a legislature and/or a President to reject the dubious rider entails rejecting all the good measures as well, and taxpayers are forced to suffer losses to support the gains of a few.

A variant on this form of vote trading is found in the strategy Anthony Downs (1957) termed a "coalition of minorities." Suppose that three issues are presented to voters with the division among them being 20 percent in favor of a particular subsidy and 80 percent opposed on each issue. One might superficially assume that political candidates would quickly announce their support of the overwhelming majorities on each issue and oppose all three subsidies. But they need not because supporting a combination of those 20 percent who favor each policy will garner a majority of 60 percent, a majority incidentally, that is much more likely to materialize and remain stable because the gains afforded individuals are apt to be greater than the individual losses suffered by those who oppose the subsidies. Realistically, we should also assume that some of the taxpayers/consumers who oppose subsidies other than their own will number among those who gain from one or more other subsidies. The Smoot-Hawley Tariff, generally credited with deepening and extending the Great Depression, was produced through just such a process. Members of Congress joined the coalition supporting the tariff by gaining some concession, usually a tariff on something manufactured in his district. Eventually enough members joined the coalition to pass the bill and there were so many products protected that international trade was reduced to a fraction of what it was before Smoot-Hawley. Everyone was made worse off, although all members of Congress acted, they believed, in the interest of their constituents. Thus, we get the term "paradox of vote trading" – each voter in a coalition, like the diners splitting the check at a restaurant, makes others, and sometimes themselves, worse off.

This problem does not arise in the private economy because coalitions and logrolling are irrelevant to making decisions. Each buyer and seller can and does act independently and normally without consideration of others; in fact, they compete not only across markets but on the same side of the market, consumer against consumer and seller against seller.

The signaling of intentions and communication more generally is conducted in polity and economy, alike, through the use of everyday language. The acquisition of a common language is a marvelous achievement, especially appreciated when one visits a foreign country, or attempts to communicate with babies and domesticated animals. But language, as English teachers know only too well, can be used with varying degrees of skill. Some people communicate better than others. Scientists and technicians, for example, are able to employ the languages of mathematics and science with extraordinary precision and economy.

Because voters are rationally ignorant (the costs of gaining particular information are greater than the benefits since one vote is essentially meaningless) politicians must employ a language designed to evoke emotion, enough emotion to motivate the right people to turn out and vote. Thus, politicians rarely speak with precise meanings, marginal calculations, or logical reasoning; instead they manipulate affect, raw emotions, group identifications, and even hatred, envy, and threats. Because premature commitment to an issue can cause one to end up in a minority position, successful politicians equivocate, hint, exaggerate, procrastinate, "straddle fences," adopt code words, and voice *non sequiturs*. Understanding the politician is, therefore, extremely frustrating for those who value precise statements. Note that this is not the fault of the politician; it is rooted in the rational ignorance of voters, distribution of conflicting sentiments among voters, and the nature of collective endeavor.

What all this means is clear: political communication is rarely conducive to rational or efficient allocation of scarce resources. This does not mean that the individual politicians are irrational in their choice of language and symbolic activities. Waving the flag and kissing babies are practiced because of their tactical value in an activity that is at once a rational game and a morality play, which is the endless fascination and frustration of politics.

Institutional Myopia

A primary accusation by critics of markets is an alleged indifference of markets to the needs of future generations. This criticism never fails to be made because it has a profound appeal among those who really care about the future. Since market agents are selfish and short-sighted, how could they possibly pursue conservation goals? "Cut and run" is their guiding precept. It is assumed and claimed that only the political process and governments have the incentive and the ability to serve the future. Horror stories about the exploitation of our Eastern and Northern woods, wanton killing of bison, and callous overfishing of streams and the ocean are cited as convincing examples and evidence of the failure.

The fact of the matter is that the historical examples are misunderstood, and the capacity of governments to enact protective laws is grossly overestimated. Markets are governed by persons, both buyers and sellers, constantly and necessarily engaged in comparing present and future values; if they did not make such comparisons we would have a difficult time explaining why many choose to make substantial investments during uncertain times. Profit maximizers serve themselves, but they do so by investing in uncertain future prospects. Thus, through their efforts to determine whether future generations of buyers will buy their wares, they may conserve

now and/or invest in producing more resources for future use. In order to do this they must make estimates of future demands for present and possibly new demands. If private Louisiana logging firms believe future sales of lumber products will increase (for whatever reasons), they will choose to harvest fewer trees now and even plant more for future harvest. Private timber firms are even preserving wildlife habitat and scenic vistas because of their expected future value and, as many close students of the oil industry have pointed out, oil companies do not pump oil twenty-four hours a day; market signals dictate the holding of vast inventories of oil in the ground. All resource holders operating in a private property, free market context are *forced to* consider inventory policy and the future.

What of the political possibilities? The conventional wisdom is that informed voters and dispassionate but professional public officials will be more far-sighted. Deprived of making profits, officials are assumed to place higher values on the future than would entrepreneurs, but just why remains something of a mystery since future voters are either unborn or have yet to register their preferences at the polls. Common sense suggests that a citizen-voter deprives herself of a great deal in casting support for, say, conservation measures when all benefits are conferred on unknown future voters with unknown tastes. Politicians seem to understand this dilemma because historically they have not been in the forefront of the environmental movement. If government is so omniscient, why did it take so long to protect our environment? Socialist countries it seems are even more negligent. We must not forget that for the politician a week is an eternity, especially around elections. The reason for politicians' myopia is simple: voters are also myopic. Voters are short-sighted because most public policies confer either long-run benefits with immediate costs or immediate gains with delayed costs. In the first instance, political systems produce inaction, delay, and caution; while in the second situation speedy action is undertaken, but the action is usually ill considered, excessive and enacted under the strains of crisis. Legislation enacted during increasing unemployment may create the illusion of action and accomplishment but always at considerable, real, long-run cost in the operation of free markets. Price controls enacted during inflation are a singular example of such illusory gains and real costs.

There seems to be no compelling reasons why voters, politicians, and bureaucrats should be more future-oriented than selfish buyers and sellers. Removing property rights and the profit motive does not enhance the future's prospects; it actually diminishes the time horizons of political beings.

Dynamics: Uncertainty, Innovation, and Welfare

Facing uncertainty, governments understandably behave in highly uncertain ways, making prediction of their behavior problematic. On the one hand we observe that bureaucracies seem lethargic while legislatures and chief executives seem, all too often, to bounce from inaction to hyper-action and back again. Private firms appear to be somewhat more stable in their responses. Perhaps the reason for the variances between government and private firms has to do with the existence of profit and its connection with uncertainty in markets, and the absence of profit but the presence of uncertainty in politics.

Students of international politics and public planning have long observed that governments are woefully underequipped with vital information and theory having practical value. Unlike private firms, governments do not have a single purpose or goal such as profit maximization. Instead they pursue conflicting objectives and make trade-offs. Relating conflicting ends and highly uncertain means is inherently difficult. Economists might phrase it by saying society does not have a "social welfare function" or a single "public interest." Public planners facing

this dilemma react with either excessive caution or haste. We see plentiful examples of both. Grandiose projects have been authorized overnight without much assurance of success, while promising programs are avoided and delayed. Few federal dam building programs, for instance, have positive cost-benefit ratios, yet they were enacted with disconcerting consistency. And we should expect such misallocations as long as politicians continue to spend taxpayers' money, especially when interest groups can gain private benefits at public expense.

Elected officials respond to changing voter preferences in predictable ways, usually erratic over-responses while the bureaucrats held responsible for the implementation of hastily conceived plans behave in less dramatic (but equally inappropriate) ways of inaction and delay. Among bureaucrats the costs of errors are thought to exceed the gains from risky choices so excessive caution or prudence is the norm. Regulation provides good examples. Inadequate resources, due-process requirements, competing claims among clients, and fear of legislators all contribute to maximizing time wasted in performance of regulatory goals.

Policies, once adopted, come to have the status of sacred cows even when they are manifestly inefficient. This paradox, like many others encountered in public choice, can be easily unraveled once we understand that inefficient policies can be enacted if benefits are highly concentrated and costs widely distributed. Beneficiaries enjoying benefits have little difficulty keeping their gains because abolishing those gains would do great damage and confer but small gains on millions of taxpayers. So the latter do not act, while the former can be certain to mobilize enormous resources in defense of privilege. Apparently we will fight harder to keep a certain gain than fight for a greater but uncertain gain.

Things may be even worse than the previous paragraph suggests. Bryan Caplan (2007) argues that concentrated benefits and dispersed costs may characterize most government programs, but the real reason those programs are adopted is that the voters want them. The average voter, according to Caplan, is motivated by biases against markets and in favor of government. Not only do voters have insufficient information about how markets and government work, they hold damaging and wrong-headed beliefs. No wonder the Social Security program remains with us. No wonder all the bankrupt farm programs are not only with us but grow. No wonder other subsidies hang on, and worse, multiply and increase.

Inefficient and even destructive policies continue to exist and grow because virtually every policy can be defended as having contributed some good to someone in need. Even those most disadvantaged by a certain institution or policy are often among those who defend practices such as minimum wages, equal opportunity laws, and rent control. Ironically, efficiency reforms have few constituents even during so-called conservative administrations. In fact, one might well contend that conservatives are particularly well suited to consolidate and legitimize past inefficiencies as well as serve the interests of the better off. None of the five Republican presidents since Lyndon Johnson's "Great Society" legislation started the escalation of the American welfare state have diminished its scope. Some wag has said "the Republican Party can only promise to do what the Democrats do, only do less of it." If so, innovation in the practical political sense is largely the prerogative of the political Left. Indeed, President Bill Clinton, a Democrat, proposed and got the Congress to enact welfare program reforms that are far more imaginative than any tried by Republicans since Richard Nixon proposed the Family Assistance plan, which would have been a negative income tax.

Once again Milton Friedman (1962) had some intriguing insights into the close connection between beliefs about the role of government, time perspective, and policy innovation.

The liberal in the original sense – the person who gives primacy to freedom and believes in limited government – tends to take the long view, to put major emphasis on the ultimate and permanent consequences of policies rather than on the immediate and possible transitory consequences. The modern liberal – the person who gives primacy to welfare and believes in greater governmental control – tends to take the short view, to put primary emphasis on the immediate effects of policy measures. This connection is one of reciprocal cause and effect. The man who has a short time perspective will be impatient with the slow workings of voluntary arrangements in producing changes in institutions. He will want to achieve changes at once, which requires centralized authority that can override objections. Hence he will be disposed to favor a greater role for government. But conversely, the man who favors a greater role for government will thereby be disposed to have a shorter time perspective. Partly, he will be so disposed because centralized government can achieve changes of some kinds rapidly; hence he will feel that if the longer-term consequences are adverse, he – through the government – can introduce new measures that will counter them, that he can have his cake and eat it. Partly, he will have a short time perspective because the political process demands it. In the market, an entrepreneur can experiment with a new innovation without first persuading the public. He need only have confidence that after he has made his innovation enough of the public will buy his product to make it pay. He can afford to wait until they do. Hence, he can have a long time perspective. In the political process, an entrepreneur must first get elected in order to be in a position to innovate. To get elected, he must persuade the public in advance. Hence he must look at immediate results that he can offer the public. He may not be able to take a very long time perspective and still hope to be in power (pp. 16–17).

Electoral Rules: Paradoxes and Impossibilities

Among the numerous properties of democracy, one of the most important is the impact of formal rules on group decision making and especially rules pertaining to elections in which we choose candidates and policies. According to such famous theorists as Kenneth Arrow, Duncan Black, Charles Plott, William H. Riker, and a host of lesser-known formal analysts, rules matter. Because their work is highly technical, accessibility is achieved only by considerable translation and oversimplification.

Much (but hardly all) of the formal, technical mathematical analysis of politics is based on the path-breaking work of Kenneth Arrow (1951) and Duncan Black (1958), the former a Nobel Laureate in Economics. This discussion is based mostly on their efforts. For those who see little fault in democracy, Arrow's results are earth-shaking because he proves that no democratic voting rule can satisfy five basic conditions – perfectly reasonable ones – simultaneously. One or more must be violated in the effort to arrive at collective results that are consistent with individual preferences. We learn that majority rule does not function well when voters have more than two options. If three options are offered and each voter is asked to rank the three, it is frequently the case that no one option will win a majority of first place rankings. And, if they were to consider their choices in pairs they would soon learn that voting cycles result in each option defeating all others and no one winning.

All this can be illustrated with the use of a simple table in which we suppose there are three voters and three options, which might be either policies or candidates. The voters rank their preferences as shown in Table 25.2.

If each option is paired or compared with each other, we clearly learn that a will beat b, and b will beat out c, but that c will in turn beat a. Thus, majority rule has some severe problems, for each option can beat every other option and

Table 25.2 The Voting Paradox

Ranking	Voters		
	A	*B*	*C*
1st	a	b	c
2nd	b	c	a
3rd	c	a	b

no determinate winner emerges that can claim to be the majority preference. Cycling is the name of this phenomenon. Of course, there are ways out of the dilemma or ways of preventing it, and there is no necessity that cycling will occur. But it is true that as the number of options increases relative to the number of voters that the cycle will occur with increasing frequency. For our purposes it is sufficient to note that cycles are real and while they do not prevent us from employing majority rule, they do create difficulties that should not and cannot be ignored. Majority rule is no panacea.

An alternative to majority rule is the plurality rule – the candidate who garners the most votes among all those the voters consider is elected. Of course that can mean the winner receives less than a majority of all the votes while the losers represent a majority of all voters. Abraham Lincoln and Bill Clinton won office not with a majority but with a plurality – a majority of voters voted for other candidates. George W. Bush did not even gain a plurality in 2000 as Al Gore received more of the popular vote. Another problem with plurality rules is that the existence of a third option can change the relative ranking of the first two options. That is, one's choices can be influenced by whether or not there are more than two options.

An effect of having more than two options is shown by the 2002 French presidential election. Incumbent president Jacques Chirac was the highest vote-getter in the three-person primary race between himself, Jean-Marie Le Pen, and Lionel Jospin. Le Pen was the next highest vote-getter and Jospin was third. Chirac and Le Pen then ran against each other to select the president and Chirac won. Polling data indicated that in a two-person race, Jospin would have defeated Le Pen and could have also defeated Chirac. Thus, Le Pen's presence in the race changed relative rankings for Chirac and Jospin (Dasgupta and Maskin, 2008).

Another problem with voting is how to count the votes. No one who studies elections will forget Florida's "hanging," "dimpled," and "pregnant" chads in the 2000 U.S. presidential election. The state of Florida certified the vote and declared George W. Bush the winner after the U.S. Supreme Court stopped recounts ordered by the Florida Supreme Court. Independent recounts showed that Bush won in all legally requested scenarios but a statewide recount with different counting rules would have resulted in Al Gore defeating Bush. Additionally, the National Opinion Research Center examined nine recount scenarios based on different methods of interpreting ballots and concluded that Gore would have won under five of them and Bush would have won under four of them (Keating, 2002). How we count votes matters.

Some students of elections have advanced a variety of weighted voting schemes designed to overcome some of the difficulties of political choice, but they do not solve all. The big problem is how to weigh the votes, for that will affect the totaling of the various scores. So, technical ingenuity has yet to resolve all of Arrow's reservations. Then there is the agenda problem or the order in which options are voted upon, a problem that can be solved, but only through manipulation.

Of course, the American system does not operate by any such direct voting as suggested by Arrow's criteria; instead we vote directly on a few policy issues and mostly confine our voting to elections in which candidates for public office are selected. In these latter choices we encounter specific forms of electoral institutions peculiar to different democracies. For example, Americans select their presidential candidates through the use of party conventions and primary elections in which delegates to a national convention are chosen. The nominated candidates then compete in a national election. In 48 of the states the winning candidate receives the state's entire electoral vote whether won by a substantial majority or but one vote; it is a winner-take-all result. As political scientists know so well, the strongest candidate in the primaries need not be strongest in the general election; that is the case because the more committed voters who attend the party primaries select the more extreme competitors. An additional result of our system is that candidates for the U.S. Presidency tend to devote more of their attention to states with more Electoral College votes and ignore those with fewer votes.

Another consequence of the American electoral system is the frequent honoring of the so-called median voter, that is, politicians tend to adopt positions departing from those favored by more extreme voters and converge instead on the preferences of median voter(s). The logic of appealing to the median voter is seen in Figure 25.1. In this figure, voters are normally distributed across a standard left–right continuum. Since the mass of voters is located at the center of the distribution, vote-maximizing candidates will propose policies that appeal to those voters. In Figure 25.1, Candidate A will move right and Candidate B will move left, if they want to reach the median voter – if they want to win. Unless Candidate B moves, A will win easily. If A expects B to move, she will move to position M in order to beat B to the median voter. By appealing to the voters at the very center of the distribution, the candidates divide the vote equally. If either candidate moves away from the middle, the other candidate captures the votes in the middle and wins the election.

Seeking the vote of the median voter is said to drive candidates to a "tweedle-dee-tweedle-dum" strategy in which the median voter is indifferent between the candidates. Of course, minority voters out on the far reaches of

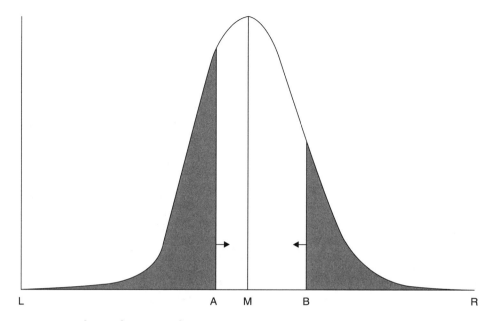

Figure 25.1 The Median Voter Theorem.

the normal unimodal preference distribution lose because they are minorities. At best they gain only vague rhetorical reassurances from the candidates. Since the median voter gets so much attention, it is to the advantage of concerned interest groups to shape voter preferences for one position or another. As Gordon Tullock (1967) argued, the name of the political game is shaping preferences and their distribution. That is why political advertising, even the uninformative, is such an important ingredient in the electoral process. At its worst, advertising tempts exaggeration, deception, and lies. Shaping the options and the agenda become additional subjects of intense scrutiny among activists – for on them depend the outcomes of the elections.

Earlier I alluded to the problem of the geographical distribution of voters suggesting that it might have something to do with final policy choices. Several studies have shown that majority voting does not necessarily reflect overall majority views if the voting is done in separate single member districts (a voting system in which only one person is elected from each electoral district). It is conceivable and quite likely under majority rule that the minority position will be underrepresented in a legislature or convention. For example, the overall minority position may win overwhelming majorities in a handful of districts, and lose by small margins in most other districts and end up placing few representatives in the legislature. Those who win bare majorities in the districts can, therefore, win a huge majority in the legislature. In California, for instance, after the 2000 Census, Congressional district boundaries were changed to preserve party strongholds. The results of this were demonstrated in 2004, 2006, and 2008 when only one sitting Democrat and one Republican lost their seats to the candidate from the other party (those two candidates were undergoing corruption investigations). Almost all candidates won with more than 65 percent of the vote (*Harvard Law Review* Staff, 2009). All this is accomplished under majority rule! It becomes clear why politicians have such fierce fights over geographical boundaries for legislative districts; their own interests are at stake and so are those of voters.

Since most voting is for candidates rather than issues, and most of policymaking takes place between elections, there may not be much significance to the median voter beyond the symbolic and a few generalized constraints on government to elections. It is risky to argue that the policies of the center voters prevail. Instead, both theory and empirical outcomes strongly support the notion that most of the distributive policies enacted by government would not be favored by sovereign majorities if the voters were directly confronted in referenda with issues involving tariffs, quotas, make-work rules, barriers to entry, or government loans. The only way in which they might be adopted would be to allow logrolling among voters, and that would be prohibitively expensive. As Robert Dahl (1956) wrote more than fifty years ago, the democratic political process is not, "a majestic march of median-voter majorities but rather the steady appeasement of minorities" (p. 80). If this is true, surely we have a major failure of the polity.

Even a cursory review of a vast and highly intricate, technical body of theory and empirical studies illustrates the extensive perversity of electoral institutions, the cornerstone of democracy. Even if voters, politicians, bureaucrats, and interest groups are all altruistic and informed, their individual policy preferences will be distorted through the workings of the basic rules themselves. These rules create winners and losers and seemingly have no particularly rational or consistent basis. If we are concerned that pervasive market imperfections and failures be properly handled and improved, we are apt to be disappointed. No set of rules can guarantee the achievement of fair and efficient policies. Nor should we assume that politicians and others are indifferent to manipulating the rules themselves; they cannot afford disinterest. While generations of political theorists have often suspected these results, we could not place much confidence in their suspicions until formal public choice enabled us to better understand the actual mechanisms.

Justice and Redistribution

Continual reference has been made to the problem of equity or justice in the context of both markets and democracy, but without any sustained analysis. I have alluded to the fact that although government in liberal societies is often expected to rectify "unjust" market distributions of wealth and income, such governments more often than not exacerbate inequalities. Although this problem is addressed in detail in Chapter 10 [not included in this volume] some preliminary discussion is warranted.

An efficient distribution of income and/or wealth may or may not be considered just or equitable. If, for example, most wealth were in the hands of a single family and a government proposed to take some away and redistribute to the less well off, such a proposal would have to be termed inefficient since the wealthy family would object. Whether another distribution is equitable depends on the criteria we employ in making such judgments, and there is no widespread agreement on the appropriate criteria.

Regardless of our feelings about distributive outcomes, there remains the positive problem of determining how various political processes will, in fact, decide such issues. Many members of the Left are inclined to believe that not only should greater equality prevail, but also that under majority rule it will prevail. A good case cannot be made in defense of the prediction. The reasoning is as follows.

Suppose that a simple majority of voters is required to pass a redistribution bill and that 100 voters, each with a different income, participate in the decision. Under this arrangement the two median voters (income recipients) will decide. Those persons could support the wealthier 49 or the less well-off 49 voters. If they bargain, they may quickly surmise that they can command more of the redistribution by supporting the upper income group than by joining the poorer folk. On the other hand, they may reason that there is more to tax from the rich than from the poor so they will stand to gain more from that redistribution. In either case, the median voters will have the power to decide the outcome and in this case they could exact an outcome that would maximize their share. According to this theory, first advanced independently by Stigler (1970) and Tullock (1988), the middle class profits most from redistributive efforts of democratic governments. Whether or not the facts of empirical life support this theory is still in doubt because it is not easy to test; furthermore, it is complicated by the fact that much redistribution takes place within each income class. We do know that adopting welfare programs for the poor requires the support of the middle class, who provide their support in exchange for having welfare benefits extended to themselves. More than one study has demonstrated this to be so in such fields as housing, education, transportation, environmental improvements, and health services. And, of course, much tax policy is so designed as to confer tax benefits on the middle class.

The point is this: the political process not only promotes inefficiency but is skewed to advance the interests of those who are better off. Those who do well in the marketplace also do well in the polity.

Policy Symbolism

As explained earlier, voting sends mixed messages and political arrangements separate decisions about costs from those about benefits. One result of these conditions is that politicians can engage in "policy symbolism," making grand policy statements whose objectives will not be accomplished. There are at least two forms: (1) statements of sentiment, such as congressional resolutions, that have no legal policy effect, and (2) decisions that legally establish real policy objectives and potentially could have effects, but that have been designed *not* to achieve their objectives (Lyons, 1999: 286).

Regulatory law provides many opportunities for policy symbolism. A common tactic is to create grand-sounding legislation but not provide funds sufficient to accomplish its objectives. In addition, Congress often provides policy objectives that are completely unrealistic or gives agencies "lengthy lists of actions to take and deadlines to achieve that the agency cannot even begin to accomplish" (Bryner, 1987: 207). This approach gives little direction since "if everything is a priority then nothing is." Sometimes, politicians know their policies are so strict that they will be unenforced, especially by state and local officials who are fearful of driving out industry and employment. Thus, Congress passes laws and creates policies in anticipation that enforcement will be spotty and easily circumvented.

There are understandable political reasons for engaging in such symbolism. One is because "enthusiastic support is much more likely to be generated by dramatic promises than by modest, incremental proposals" (Bryner, 1987: 207). Another is to be able to place blame for failures on the bureaucracy (Fiorina, 1977: 72–9). Symbolism may also be designed to placate idealistic interest groups and rationally uninformed voters.

Agencies obviously find unrealistic and often unfunded promises impossible to achieve. Requirements for zero pollution discharges into navigable waters, non-impairment of worker health, and zero cancer risks make good political statements, for example, but cannot be achieved. These requirements provide no guidance about how inevitable trade-offs are to be accomplished. Such rules deny that once policies have been implemented their marginal costs may outweigh their marginal benefits. Worse, they ignore the possibility that total costs may exceed total benefits. These policies are symbols meant to demonstrate to voters that their politicians are taking bold steps.

Some Conclusions

The unromantic and pathological properties of the democratic process have been explored. The picture is not a pretty one, but readers should not draw easy and superficial conclusions from the examination and comparisons of real and idealistic worlds. While markets and polities are both imperfect, we do have some choices, and those choices are important for our individual and collective well-being. The important caution is this: even imperfect democracies have far more to be said in their favor than do the non-democracies. Democracies honor individual sovereignty as a goal worth attaining. And whether we like a particular citizen's preferences in the market or polity makes no difference as compared to her opportunity to give voice to them. Even in this regard, obnoxious political preferences are more difficult to accept than are obnoxious market preferences. In short, the market has fewer externalities than does the polity. Nevertheless, I much prefer living in our flawed democracy to residing in any dictatorship. This must be thoroughly understood throughout my analysis of detailed policy imperfections in the following chapters.

[...]

References

Arrow, Kenneth J. *Social Choice and Individual Values.* New York: John Wiley and Sons, 1951, rev. ed. 1963.

Arrow, Kenneth, Amartya Sen, and Kotaru Sazumra. *Handbook of Social Choice and Welfare Volume 1* (Handbooks in Economics). 1st ed. Paris: North Holland, 2002.

Black, Duncan. *The Theory of Committees and Elections.* Cambridge: Cambridge University Press, 1958.

Bryner, Gary C. *Bureaucratic Discretion: Law and Policy in Federal Regulatory Agencies.* New York: Pergamon Books, Inc., 1987.

Caplan, Bryan. *The Myth of the Rational Voter: Why Democracies Choose Bad Policies.* Princeton: Princeton University Press, 2007.

Dahl, Robert A. *A Preface to Democratic Theory.* Chicago: University of Chicago Press, 1956, p. 24.

Doel, Hans van den and Ben van den Velthoven. *Democracy and Welfare Economics.* 2nd ed. New York: Cambridge University Press, 1993.

Downs, Anthony. *An Economic Theory of Democracy.* New York: Harper and Brothers, 1957, Chapters 4 and 9.

Fiorina, Morris P. *Congress: Keystone of the Washington Establishment.* New Haven, CT: Yale University Press, 1977.

Friedman, David. *The Machinery of Freedom.* La Salle, IL: Open Court, 1989.

Friedman, Milton. *Capitalism and Freedom.* Chicago: University of Chicago Press, 1962, pp. 16–17.

Friedman, Milton and Rose Friedman. *Free to Choose.* New York: Harcourt Brace Jovanovich, 1979, p. 19.

Gwartney, James D., David Macpherson, Russell S. Sobel, and Richard L. Stroup. *Economics: Private and Public Choice.* 13th ed. Mason, OH: South-Western, Cengage Learning, 2010.

Harvard Law Review Staff, "Political Gerrymandering 2000–2008: A Self-Limiting Enterprise?" *Harvard Law Review,* 122 (2009), pp. 1468–88.

Keating, Dan. "Democracy Counts: the Media Consortium Florida Ballot Project." Paper presented at the 2002 American Political Science Association annual meeting. http://www.aei.org/docLib/20040526_KeatingPaper.pdf.

Lyons, Michael. "Political Self Interest and U.S. Environmental Policy." *Natural Resources Journal,* 39 (2): (Spring 1999), pp. 271–94.

Moe, Terry M. *The Organization of Interests: Incentives and the Internal Dynamics of Political Interest Groups.* Chicago: University of Chicago Press, 1988.

Olson, Mancur. *The Logic of Collective Action.* Cambridge, MA: Harvard University Press, 1965.

Riker, William H. *Liberalism Against Populism: A Confrontation Between the Theory of Democracy and the Theory of Social Choice.* Long Grove, IL: Waveland Press, 1988.

Schumpeter, Joseph. *Capitalism, Socialism, and Democracy.* 1. Reprint, New York: Harper Perennial Modern Classics, 2008.

Stigler, George. "Director's Law of Public Income Redistribution," *Journal of Law and Economics* (April, 1970).

Tullock, Gordon. *Toward a Mathematics of Politics.* Ann Arbor: University of Michigan Press, 1967, p. 2.

Tullock, Gordon. *Wealth, Poverty, and Politics.* New York: Basil Blackwell, 1988.

Wittman, Donald. *The Myth of Democratic Failure.* Chicago: University of Chicago Press, 1995.

2b. PROPERTY RIGHTS

THE FACT THAT BILL GATES owns a lot of stuff has important normative implications. It means, for instance, that if I were to try to walk off with some of it without his permission, he could use a moderate level of physical violence to stop me. Or, more commonly, he could call the police who could either credibly threaten or administer such violence on his behalf. Even if the property in question is Bill's ten millionth loaf of bread and I am on the brink of starvation, the fact that I *need* the bread more than he does is irrelevant. Property rights, in this case, seem to trump other moral considerations such as need, desert, or merit.

How, then, can such property rights be justified? What kind of moral story can we tell that would legitimate someone claiming an object as *hers* and forcibly excluding all others from its use without her consent?

It might seem that it would be relatively easy to come up with such a story, at least when the object in question is something that someone has *made*. If I own two widgets, and put them together into some kind of super-widget, then my ownership claim to the super-widget simply follows from my ownership claims over its constituent parts — the two original widgets plus my labour.

But this story is *too* easy. For just as we may demand a story about how one came to legitimately own the super-widget, so can we ask a similar story about how one came to legitimately own its constituent parts. If the constituent parts were themselves made by somebody (or bought from somebody who made them), then we simply push our demand for justification back to *their* constituent parts. But eventually this story will have to stop. For eventually, everything that is made by someone is made out of things that were *not* made by anybody — the raw materials of the earth. And here we face an entirely different sort of problem. How can something that was once owned by nobody come to be owned by somebody?

Actually, not all philosophers would be happy with this way of stating the question. For it embodies an assumption that the raw materials of the earth are owned by nobody. But one might also plausibly hold that they are owned by *everybody* — that the raw materials of the earth are the collective property of humankind.

Whichever way we think of the raw materials of the earth, we face what has become known as the *problem of original appropriation*: how can one person or group of persons appropriate to themselves something which had not previously been appropriated? There are a variety of different responses one could make to this problem. One could, for instance, deny that *any* act of original appropriation is morally permissible, and that the earth that originally belonged to humankind in common still rightfully does. On this view, private property is a kind of theft—it is an instance of one person claiming for herself what rightfully belongs to everyone.

This claim seems more plausible for some types of property than for others. If I plant an apple tree on uncultivated and unoccupied land, and then harvest the apples myself, it seems implausible to suppose that I have stolen anything from the human race. *Land*, on the other hand, seems to pose a more difficult problem since it both exists in a fixed quantity and is not created by any human effort. One could conceivably then argue that the original appropriation of some property is justified while holding that the land itself belongs to humankind in common.

As the more attentive readers will have noticed, several of the examples I have given above are based on the implicit or explicit assumption that individuals own their own labour, and that this can help them to establish ownership rights in those things they create with their labour. This assumption is generally held as part of a broader assumption known as the *self-ownership thesis*. The self-ownership thesis holds that individuals own themselves and, since their labour is a part of themselves, own their labour as well. The most famous proponent of a self-ownership thesis was John Locke, who used it to justify private property by arguing that individuals can come to own previously unowned goods by "mixing their labour" with them, so long as certain conditions were met. The main contemporary defenders of the self-ownership thesis are libertarians and other defenders of private property such as Robert Nozick, but the claim is also sometimes endorsed by critics of private property. These critics agree that individuals own *themselves*, but deny that they can come to own external goods simply by mixing their labour with those goods. Philosophers who draw this line sometimes end up advocating a position known as *left-libertarianism* wherein individuals have a right to bodily integrity and the raw fruits of their labour, but have no correspondingly strong rights over external goods, which such theorists generally hold ought to be distributed in some egalitarian manner.

Of course, tracing current property claims back to a justified act of original appropriation is not the *only* way to justify property. One could also make the case for certain kinds of property on the grounds that such property promotes the value of freedom. Property — especially private property — allows individuals a domain in which they can make decisions without needing permission from others, and so provides them with the material goods necessary to carry out their plans of life. Or, one could justify property on utilitarian grounds, by arguing that private property provides individuals with an incentive to labour in a way that increases the wealth of society as a whole. What is important to note, though, is that the nature of the *moral justification* we give for property rights will affect the *form and content* those property rights ultimately have. If property rights are based on a kind of deontological respect for self-ownership, for instance, then criticisms of property rights based on consequentialist considerations (consider a city government that wishes to exercise the power of eminent domain to prevent a property owner from refusing to sell and thereby blocking a proposed development) will have considerably less traction, since rights are generally thought to trump consequences as a moral concern. On the other hand, if property rights are justified by the way in which they promote freedom, then those property rights will be probably limited in certain ways when they appear to conflict with freedom — as when they lead to monopolies or, arguably, the subjection of poor workers to wealthy capitalists.

Discussions about the origins of property rights might seem arcane. But they are of tremendous practical importance for several reasons. First, we sometimes have to make decisions about how to allocate property rights in previously unowned goods. Most of the land in the world has been claimed by now, but as of yet there is no private property on the moon. And property rights in the air, water, genes, and ideas are becoming increasingly important. Second, we sometimes have to decide whether existing property arrangements came about in a just way, and if not what we should do about it. Many advocates for the poor in Latin America, for instance, argue that some policy of land reform is necessary to rectify for past injustices, including the past unjust seizure of the land. Finally, we would like to know which existing or proposed government policies are compatible with a proper respect for property rights. In the United States, government can often seize private property which it views as "blighted" in order to turn it over to private industry so as to promote economic development. Does this count as an unjustifiable violation of individuals' property rights? What about zoning laws that prevent people from running certain kinds of business in certain neighborhoods? What about taxation? Is taxation, as Nozick and other libertarians have argued, morally on a par with forced labour? Given its connection to questions of governmental taxation and regulation, the issue of property rights will have important implications for our thinking about other issues of political philosophy — especially issues of distributive justice — as well.

Further Reading

Cohen, G. A. (1995). *Self-ownership, Freedom, and Equality*. Cambridge; New York: Cambridge University Press.

Ellickson, R. (1993). Property in Land. *Yale Law Journal, 102*, 1315–400.

Gaus, G. F. (1990). Are Property Rights Problematic? *Monist. 0, 90*, 483–503.

Lomasky, L. E. (1987). *Persons, Rights, and the Moral Community*. Oxford: Oxford University Press.

Moore, A. D. (1998). Intangible Property: Privacy, Power, and Information Control. *American Philosophical Quarterly, 35*(4), 365–78.

Munzer, S. R. (1990). *A Theory of Property*. Cambridge: Cambridge University Press.

Narveson, J. (1999). Property Rights: Original Acquisition and Lockean Provisos. *Public Affairs Quarterly, 13*(3), 205–27.

Nozick, R. (1974). *Anarchy, State, and Utopia*. New York: Basic Books.

Schmidtz, D. (1990). When is Original Appropriation Required? *Monist. 0, 90*, 504–18.

Sreenivasan, G. (1995). *The Limits of Lockean Rights in Property*. Oxford: Oxford University Press.

Verhaegh, M. (2004). Kant and Property Rights. *Journal of Libertarian Studies, 18*(3), 11–32.

Waldron, J. (1991). *The Right to Private Property*. Oxford: Oxford University Press.

Chapter 26

John Locke

PROPERTY

John Locke (1632–1704) was an English philosopher and revolutionary who was an influential supporter of the Glorious Revolution wherein King James II was overthrown and the relative balance of power swung toward Parliament. His *Second Treatise of Civil Government* (published in 1698) was an extended critique of authoritarianism and a defense of limited, representative government. In this excerpt, Locke argues that human beings can come to acquire property rights in external goods by "mixing their labour" with those goods, so long as enough and as good is left for others.

§ 25. Whether we consider natural reason, which tells us, that men, being once born, have a right to their preservation, and consequently to meat and drink, and such other things as nature affords for their subsistence; or revelation, which gives us an account of those grants God made of the world to Adam, and to Noah, and his sons; it is very clear, that God, as king David says, Psal. cvx. 16, "has given the earth to the children of men"; given it to mankind in common. But this being supposed, it seems to some a very great difficulty how any one should ever come to have a property in any thing: I will not content myself to answer, that if it be difficult to make out property, upon a supposition that God gave the world to Adam and his posterity in common, it is impossible that any man, but one universal monarch, should have any property, upon a supposition that God gave the world to Adam, and his heirs in succession, exclusive of all the rest of his posterity. But I shall endeavour to show how men might come to have a property in several parts of that which God gave to mankind in common, and that without any express compact of all the commoners.

§ 26. God, who hath given the world to men in common, hath also given them reason to make use of it to the best advantage of life and convenience. The earth, and all that is therein, is given to men for the support and comfort of their being. And though all the fruits it naturally produces, and beasts it feeds, belong to mankind in common, as they are produced by the spontaneous hand of nature; and nobody has originally a private dominion, exclusive of the rest of mankind, in any of them, as they are thus in their natural state: yet being given for the use of men, there must of necessity be a means to appropriate them some way or other before they can be of any use, or at all beneficial to any particular man. The fruit, or venison, which nourishes the wild Indian, who knows no enclosure, and is still a tenant in common, must be his, or so his, i.e. a part of him, that another can no longer have any right to it, before it can do him any good for the support of his life.

§ 27. Though the earth, and all inferior creatures, be common to all men, yet every man has a property in his own person: this nobody has any right to but himself. The labour of his body, and the work of his hands, we may say, are properly his. Whatsoever then he removes out of the state that nature hath provided, and left it in, he hath mixed his labour with, and joined to it something that is his own, and thereby makes it his property. It being by him removed from the common state nature hath placed it in, it hath by this labour something annexed to it that excludes the common right of other men. For this labour being the unquestionable property of the labourer, no man but he can have a right to what that is once joined to, at least where there is enough, and as good, left in common for others.

§ 28. He that is nourished by the acorns he picked up under an oak, or the apples he gathered from the trees in the wood, has certainly appropriated them to himself. Nobody can deny but the nourishment is his. I ask then, when did they begin to be his? when he digested? or when he ate? or when he boiled? or when he brought them home? or when he picked them up? and it is plain, if the first gathering made them not his, nothing else could. That labour put a distinction between them and common: that added something to them more than nature, the common mother of all, had done; and so they became his private right. And will any one say, he had no right to those acorns or apples he thus appropriated, because he had not the consent of all mankind to make them his? was it a robbery thus to assume to himself what belonged to all in common? If such a consent as that was necessary, man had starved, notwithstanding the plenty God had given him. We see in commons, which remain so by compact, that it is the taking any part of what is common, and removing it out of the state nature leaves it in, which begins the property; without which the common is of no use. And the taking of this or that part does

not depend on the express consent of all the commoners. Thus the grass my horse has bit; the turfs my servant has cut; and the ore I have digged in any place, where I have a right to them in common with others; become my property, without the assignation or consent of any body. The labour that was mine, removing them out of that common state they were in, hath fixed my property in them.

§ 29. By making an explicit consent of every commoner necessary to any one's appropriating to himself any part of what is given in common, children or servants could not cut the meat, which their father or master had provided for them in common, without assigning to every one his peculiar part. Though the water running in the fountain be every one's, yet who can doubt but that in the pitcher is his only who drew it out? His labour hath taken it out of the hands of nature, where it was common, and belonged equally to all her children, and hath thereby appropriated it to himself.

§ 30. Thus this law of reason makes the deer that Indian's who hath killed it; it is allowed to be his goods who hath bestowed his labour upon it, though before it was the common right of every one. And amongst those who are counted the civilized part of mankind, who have made and multiplied positive laws to determine property, this original law of nature, for the beginning of property, in what was before common, still takes place; and by virtue thereof, what fish any one catches in the ocean, that great and still remaining common of mankind; or what ambergris any one takes up here, is by the labour that removes it out of that common state nature left it in made his property who takes that pains about it. And even amongst us, the hare that any one is hunting is thought his who pursues her during the chase: for being a beast that is still looked upon as common, and no man's private possession; whoever has employed so much labour about any of that kind, as to find and pursue her, has thereby removed her from the state of nature, wherein she was common, and hath begun a property.

§ 31. It will perhaps be objected to this, that "if gathering the acorns, or other fruits of the earth, &c. makes a right to them, then any one may engross as much as he will." To which I answer, Not so. The same law of nature, that does by this means give us property, does also bound that property too. "God has given us all things richly," 1 Tim. vi. 17, is the voice of reason confirmed by inspiration. But how far has he given it us? To enjoy. As much as any one can make use of to any advantage of life before it spoils, so much he may by his labour fix a property in: whatever is beyond this, is more than his share, and belongs to others. Nothing was made by God for man to spoil or destroy. And thus, considering the plenty of natural provisions there was a long time in the world, and the few spenders; and to how small a part of that provision the industry of one man could extend itself, and engross it to the prejudice of others; especially keeping within the bounds, set by reason, of what might serve for his use; there could be then little room for quarrels or contentions about property so established.

§ 32. But the chief matter of property being now not the fruits of the earth, and the beasts that subsist on it, but the earth itself; as that which takes in, and carries with it all the rest; I think it is plain, that property in that too is acquired as the former. As much land as a man tills, plants, improves, cultivates, and can use the product of, so much is his property. He by his labour does, as it were, enclose it from the common. Nor will it invalidate his right, to say every body else has an equal title to it, and therefore he cannot appropriate, he cannot enclose, without the consent of all his fellow-commoners, all mankind. God, when he gave the world in common to all mankind, commanded man also to labour, and the penury of his condition required it of him. God and his reason commanded him to subdue the earth, i.e. improve it for the benefit of life, and therein lay out something upon it that was his own, his labour. He that, in obedience to this command

of God, subdued, tilled, and sowed any part of it, thereby annexed to it something that was his property, which another had no title to, nor could without injury take from him.

§ 33. Nor was this appropriation of any parcel of land, by improving it, any prejudice to any other man, since there was still enough, and as good left; and more than the yet unprovided could use. So that, in effect, there was never the less left for others because of his enclosure for himself: for he that leaves as much as another can make use of, does as good as take nothing at all. Nobody could think himself injured by the drinking of another man, though he took a good draught, who had a whole river of the same water left him to quench his thirst; and the case of land and water, where there is enough of both, is perfectly the same.

§ 34. God gave the world to men in common; but since he gave it them for their benefit, and the greatest conveniencies of life they were capable to draw from it, it cannot be supposed he meant it should always remain common and uncultivated. He gave it to the use of the industrious and rational (and labour was to be his title to it), not to the fancy or covetousness of the quarrelsome and contentious. He that had as good left for his improvement as was already taken up, needed not complain, ought not to meddle with what was already improved by another's labour: if he did, it is plain he desired the benefit of another's pains, which he had no right to, and not the ground which God had given him in common with others to labour on, and whereof there was as good left as that already possessed, and more than he knew what to do with, or his industry could reach to.

§ 35. It is true, in land that is common in England, or any other country, where there is plenty of people under government, who have money and commerce, no one can enclose or appropriate any part without the consent of all his fellow-commoners; because this is left common by compact, i.e. by the law of the land, which is not to be violated. And though it be common, in respect of some men, it is not so to all mankind, but is the joint property of this county, or this parish. Besides, the remainder, after such enclosure, would not be as good to the rest of the commoners as the whole was when they could all make use of the whole; whereas in the beginning and first peopling of the great common of the world it was quite otherwise. The law man was under was rather for appropriating. God commanded, and his wants forced him to labour. That was his property which could not be taken from him wherever he had fixed it. And hence subduing or cultivating the earth, and having dominion, we see are joined together. The one gave title to the other. So that God, by commanding to subdue, gave authority so far to appropriate: and the condition of human life, which requires labour and materials to work on, necessarily introduces private possessions.

§ 36. The measure of property nature has well set by the extent of men's labour and the conveniencies of life: no man's labour could subdue, or appropriate all; nor could his enjoyment consume more than a small part; so that it was impossible for any man, this way, to intrench upon the right of another, or acquire to himself a property, to the prejudice of his neighbour, who would still have room for as good and as large a possession (after the other had taken out his) as before it was appropriated. This measure did confine every man's possession to a very moderate proportion, and such as he might appropriate to himself, without injury to any body, in the first ages of the world, when men were more in danger to be lost, by wandering from their company, in the then vast wilderness of the earth, than to be straitened for want of room to plant in. And the same measure may be allowed still without prejudice to any body, as full as the world seems: for supposing a man, or family, in the state they were at first peopling of the world by the children of Adam, or Noah; let him plant in some inland, vacant places of America, we shall find that the possessions he

could make himself, upon the measures we have given, would not be very large, nor, even to this day, prejudice the rest of mankind, or give them reason to complain, or think themselves injured by this man's encroachment; though the race of men have now spread themselves to all the corners of the world, and do infinitely exceed the small number was at the beginning. Nay, the extent of ground is of so little value, without labour, that I have heard it affirmed, that in Spain itself a man may be permitted to plough, sow, and reap, without being disturbed, upon land he has no other title to, but only his making use of it. But, on the contrary, the inhabitants think themselves beholden to him, who, by his industry on neglected, and consequently waste land, has increased the stock of corn, which they wanted. But be this as it will, which I lay no stress on; this I dare boldly affirm, that the same rule of propriety, viz. that every man should have as much as he could make use of, would hold still in the world, without straitening any body; since there is land enough in the world to suffice double the inhabitants, had not the invention of money, and the tacit agreement of men to put a value on it, introduced (by consent) larger possessions, and a right to them; which, how it has done, I shall by and by show more at large.

§ 37. This is certain, that in the beginning, before the desire of having more than man needed had altered the intrinsic value of things, which depends only on their usefulness to the life of man; or had agreed, that a little piece of yellow metal, which would keep without wasting or decay, should be worth a great piece of flesh, or a whole heap of corn; though men had a right to appropriate, by their labour, each one to himself, as much of the things of nature as he could use: yet this could not be much, nor to the prejudice of others, where the same plenty was still left to those who would use the same industry. To which let me add, that he who appropriates land to himself by his labour, does not lessen, but increase the common stock of mankind: for the provisions serving to the support of human life, produced by one acre of enclosed and cultivated land, are (to speak much within compass) ten times more than those which are yielded by an acre of land of an equal richness lying waste in common. And therefore he that encloses land, and has a greater plenty of the conveniencies of life from ten acres, than he could have from an hundred left to nature, may truly be said to give ninety acres to mankind: for his labour now supplies him with provisions out of ten acres, which were by the product of an hundred lying in common. I have here rated the improved land very low, in making its product but as ten to one, when it is much nearer an hundred to one: for I ask, whether in the wild woods and uncultivated waste of America, left to nature, without any improvement, tillage, or husbandry, a thousand acres yield the needy and wretched inhabitants as many conveniencies of life as ten acres equally fertile land do in Devonshire, where they are well cultivated?

Before the appropriation of land, he who gathered as much of the wild fruit, killed, caught, or tamed, as many of the beasts, as he could; he that so employed his pains about any of the spontaneous products of nature, as any way to alter them from the state which nature put them in, by placing any of his labour on them, did thereby acquire a propriety in them: but if they perished, in his possession, without their due use; if the fruits rotted, or the venison putrefied, before he could spend it; he offended against the common law of nature, and was liable to be punished; he invaded his neighbour's share, for he had no right, farther than his use called for any of them, and they might serve to afford him conveniencies of life.

§ 38. The same measures governed the possession of land too: whatsoever he tilled and reaped, laid up and made use of, before it spoiled, that was his peculiar right; whatsoever he enclosed, and could feed, and make use of, the cattle and product was also his. But if either the grass of his enclosure rotted on the ground, or the fruit of his planting perished without

gathering and laying up; this part of the earth, notwithstanding his enclosure, was still to be looked on as waste, and might be the possession of any other.

[...]

§ 39. And thus, without supposing any private dominion and property in Adam, over all the world, exclusive of all other men, which can no way be proved, nor any one's property be made out from it; but supposing the world given, as it was, to the children of men in common, we see how labour could make men distinct titles to several parcels of it, for their private uses; wherein there could be no doubt of right, no room for quarrel.

§ 40. Nor is it so strange, as perhaps before consideration it may appear, that the property of labour should be able to overbalance the community of land: for it is labour indeed that put the difference of value on every thing; and let any one consider what the difference is between an acre of land planted with tobacco or sugar, sown with wheat or barley, and an acre of the same land lying in common, without any husbandry upon it, and he will find, that the improvement of labour makes the far greater part of the value. I think it will be but a very modest computation to say, that of the products of the earth useful to the life of man, nine-tenths are the effects of labour: nay, if we will rightly estimate things as they come to our use, and cast up the several expenses about them, what in them is purely owing to nature, and what to labour, we shall find, that in most of them ninety-nine hundredths are wholly to be put on the account of labour.

§ 41. There cannot be a clearer demonstration of any thing, than several nations of the Americans are of this, who are rich in land, and poor in all the comforts of life; whom nature having furnished as liberally as any other people with the materials of plenty, i.e. a fruitful soil, apt to produce in abundance what might serve for food, raiment, and delight; yet, for want of improving it by labour, have not one-hundredth part of the conveniencies we enjoy: and a king of a large and fruitful territory there feeds, lodges, and is clad worse than a day-labourer in England.

§ 42. To make this a little clear, let us but trace some of the ordinary provisions of life, through their several progresses, before they come to our use, and see how much of their value they receive from human industry. Bread, wine, and cloth, are things of daily use, and great plenty; yet notwithstanding, acorns, water, and leaves, or skins, must be our bread, drink, and clothing, did not labour furnish us with these more useful commodities: for whatever bread is more worth than acorns, wine than water, and cloth or silk than leaves, skins, or moss, that is wholly owing to labour and industry; the one of these being the food and raiment which unassisted nature furnishes us with; the other, provisions which our industry and pains prepare for us; which, how much they exceed the other in value, when any one hath computed, he will then see how much labour makes the far greatest part of the value of things we enjoy in this world: and the ground which produces the materials is scarce to be reckoned in as any, or, at most, but a very small part of it; so little, that even amongst us, land that is left wholly to nature, that hath no improvement of pasturage, tillage, or planting, is called, as indeed it is, waste; and we shall find the benefit of it amount to little more than nothing.

This shows how much numbers of men are to be preferred to largeness of dominions; and that the increase of lands, and the right of employing of them, is the great art of government: and that prince, who shall be so wise and godlike, as by established laws of liberty to secure protection and encouragement to the honest industry of mankind, against the oppression of power and narrowness of party, will quickly be too hard for his neighbours: but this is by the by. To return to the argument in hand.

§ 43. An acre of land, that bears here 20 bushels of wheat, and another in America, which, with the same husbandry, would do the like, are, without doubt, of the same natural intrinsic value: but yet the benefit mankind receives from the one in a year is worth 5l. and from the other possibly not worth a penny, if all the profit an Indian received from it were to be valued, and sold here; at least, I may truly say, not one thousandth. It is labour, then, which puts the greatest part of the value upon land, without which it would scarcely be worth any thing: it is to that we owe the greatest part of all its useful products; for all that the straw, bran, bread, of that acre of wheat, is more worth than the product of an acre of as good land, which lies waste, is all the effect of labour: for it is not barely the ploughman's pains, the reaper's and thresher's toil, and the baker's sweat, is to be counted into the bread we eat; the labour of those who broke the oxen, who digged and wrought the iron and stones, who felled and framed the timber employed about the plough, mill, oven, or any other utensils, which are a vast number, requisite to this corn, from its being seed to be sown to its being made bread, must all be charged on the account of labour, and received as an effect of that: nature and the earth furnished only the almost worthless materials, as in themselves. It would be a strange "catalogue of things, that industry provided and made use of, about every loaf of bread," before it came to our use, if we could trace them; iron, wood, leather, bark, timber, stone, bricks, coals, lime, cloth, dyeing, drugs, pitch, tar, masts, ropes, and all the materials made use of in the ship, that brought any of the commodities used by any of the workmen, to any part of the work: all which it would be almost impossible, at least too long, to reckon up.

§ 44. From all which it is evident, that though the things of nature are given in common, yet man, by being master of himself, and "proprietor of his own person, and the actions or labour of it, had still in himself the great foundation of property"; and that which made up the greater part of what he applied to the support or comfort of his being, when invention and arts had improved the conveniencies of life, was perfectly his own, and did not belong in common to others.

§ 45. Thus labour, in the beginning, gave a right of property wherever any one was pleased to employ it upon what was common, which remained a long while the far greater part, and is yet more than mankind makes use of. Men, at first, for the most part, contented themselves with what unassisted nature offered to their necessities: and though afterwards, in some parts of the world, (where the increase of people and stock, with the use of money, had made land scarce, and so of some value) the several communities settled the bounds of their distinct territories, and by laws within themselves regulated the properties of the private men of their society, and so, by compact and agreement, settled the property which labour and industry began: and the leagues that have been made between several states and kingdoms, either expressly or tacitly disowning all claim and right to the land in the others' possession, have, by common consent, given up their pretences to their natural common right, which originally they had to those countries, and so have, by positive agreement, settled a property amongst themselves, in distinct parts and parcels of the earth; yet there are still great tracts of ground to be found, which (the inhabitants thereof not having joined with the rest of mankind in the consent of the use of their common money) lie waste, and are more than the people who dwell on it do or can make use of, and so still lie in common; though this can scarce happen amongst that part of mankind that have consented to the use of money.

§ 46. The greatest part of things really useful to the life of man, and such as the necessity of subsisting made the first commoners of the world look after, as it doth the Americans now, are generally things of short duration; such as, if they are not consumed by use, will decay and perish of themselves: gold, silver, and diamonds, are things that fancy or agreement hath put the value on, more than real use, and the necessary support of life. Now of those good things which

nature hath provided in common, every one had a right (as hath been said) to as much as he could use, and property in all that he could effect with his labour; all that his industry could extend to, to alter from the state nature had put it in, was his. He that gathered a hundred bushels of acorns or apples, had thereby a property in them; they were his goods as soon as gathered. He was only to look that he used them before they spoiled, else he took more than his share, and robbed others. And indeed it was a foolish thing, as well as dishonest, to hoard up more than he could make use of. If he gave away a part to any body else, so that it perished not uselessly in his possession, these he also made use of. And if he also bartered away plums, that would have rotted in a week, for nuts that would last good for his eating a whole year, he did no injury; he wasted not the common stock; destroyed no part of the portion of the goods that belonged to others, so long as nothing perished uselessly in his hands. Again, if he would give his nuts for a piece of metal, pleased with its colour; or exchange his sheep for shells, or wool for a sparkling pebble or a diamond, and keep those by him all his life, he invaded not the right of others; he might heap as much of these durable things as he pleased; the exceeding of the bounds of his just property not lying in the largeness of his possession, but the perishing of any thing uselessly in it.

§ 47. And thus came in the use of money, some lasting thing that men might keep without spoiling, and that by mutual consent men would take in exchange for the truly useful, but perishable supports of life.

§ 48. And as different degrees of industry were apt to give men possessions in different proportions, so this invention of money gave them the opportunity to continue and enlarge them: for supposing an island, separate from all possible commerce with the rest of the world, wherein there were but an hundred families, but there were sheep, horses, and cows, with other useful animals, wholesome fruits, and land enough for corn for a hundred thousand times as many, but nothing in the island, either because of its commonness, or perishableness, fit to supply the place of money; what reason could any one have there to enlarge his possessions beyond the use of his family and a plentiful supply to its consumption, either in what their own industry produced, or they could barter for like perishable, useful commodities with others? Where there is not something, both lasting and scarce, and so valuable, to be hoarded up, there men will not be apt to enlarge their possessions of land, were it ever so rich, ever so free for them to take: for I ask, what would a man value ten thousand, or an hundred thousand acres of excellent land, ready cultivated, and well stocked too with cattle, in the middle of the inland parts of America, where he had no hopes of commerce with other parts of the world, to draw money to him by the sale of the product? It would not be worth the enclosing, and we should see him give up again to the wild common of nature, whatever was more than would supply the conveniencies of life to be had there for him and his family.

§ 49. Thus, in the beginning all the world was America, and more so than that is now; for no such thing as money was anywhere known. Find out something that hath the use and value of money amongst his neighbours, you shall see the same man will begin presently to enlarge his possessions.

§ 50. But since gold and silver, being little useful to the life of man in proportion to food, raiment, and carriage, has its value only from the consent of men, whereof labour yet makes, in great part, the measure; it is plain, that men have agreed to a disproportionate and unequal possession of the earth; they having, by a tacit and voluntary consent, found out a way how a man may fairly possess more land than he himself can use the product of, by receiving, in exchange for the overplus, gold and silver, which may be hoarded up without injury to any one; these metals not spoiling or decaying in the hands of the possessor. This partage of things in an inequality of private possessions, men have made practicable out of the bounds of society, and without compact; only by putting a value on gold and silver, and tacitly agreeing in the use of money: for in governments, the laws regulate the right of property, and the possession of land is determined by positive constitutions.

§ 51. And thus, I think, it is very easy to conceive, "how labour could at first begin a title of property" in the common things of nature, and how the spending it upon our uses bounded it. So that there could then be no reason of quarrelling about title, nor any doubt about the largeness of possession it gave. Right and conveniency went together; for as a man had a right to all he could employ his labour upon, so he had no temptation to labour for more than he could make use of. This left no room for controversy about the title, nor for encroachment on the right of others; what portion a man carved to himself was easily seen: and it was useless, as well as dishonest, to carve himself too much, or take more than he needed.

Chapter 27

Henry George

THE INJUSTICE OF PRIVATE PROPERTY IN LAND

Henry George (1839–97) was an American political economist best known for his advocacy of the Single Tax (land rent) movement. In this excerpt, taken from his *Progress and Poverty* (1879), George argues that while people fully own themselves and the products of their labor, there are no just grounds for full private property in natural resources, and hence government is justified in extracting from the current holders of resources a tax to be redistributed to society as a whole.

When it is proposed to abolish private property in land the first question that will arise is that of justice. Though often warped by habit, superstition, and selfishness into the most distorted forms, the sentiment of justice is yet fundamental to the human mind, and whatever dispute arouses the passions of men, the conflict is sure to rage, not so much as to the question "Is it wise?" as to the question "Is it right?"

This tendency of popular discussions to take an ethical form has a cause. It springs from a law of the human mind; it rests upon a vague and instinctive recognition of what is probably the deepest truth we can grasp. That alone is wise which is just; that alone is enduring which is right. In the narrow scale of individual actions and individual life this truth may be often obscured, but in the wider field of national life it everywhere stands out.

I bow to this arbitrament, and accept this test. If our inquiry into the cause which makes low wages and pauperism the accompaniments of material progress has led us to a correct conclusion, it will bear translation from terms of political economy into terms of ethics, and as the source of social evils show a wrong. If it will not do this, it is disproved. If it will do this, it is proved by the final decision. If private property in land be just, then is the remedy I propose a false one; if, on the contrary, private property in land be unjust, then is this remedy the true one.

What constitutes the rightful basis of property? What is it that enables a man justly to say of a thing, "It is mine!" From what springs the sentiment which acknowledges his exclusive right as against all the world? Is it not, primarily, the right of a man to himself, to the use of his own powers, to the enjoyment of the fruits of his own exertions? Is it not this individual right, which springs from and is testified to by the natural facts of individual organization – the fact that each particular pair of hands obey a particular brain and are related to a particular stomach; the fact that each man is a definite, coherent, independent whole – which alone justifies individual ownership? As a man belongs to himself, so his labor when put in concrete form belongs to him.

And for this reason, that which a man makes or produces is his own, as against all the world – to enjoy or to destroy, to use, to exchange, or to give. No one else can rightfully claim it, and his exclusive right to it involves no wrong to any one else. Thus there is to everything produced by human exertion a clear and indisputable title to exclusive possession and enjoyment, which is perfectly consistent with justice, as it descends from the original producer, in whom it vested by natural law. The pen with which I am writing is justly mine. No other human being can rightfully lay claim to it, for in me is the title of the producers who made it. It has become mine, because transferred to me by the stationer, to whom it was transferred by the importer, who obtained the exclusive right to it by transfer from the manufacturer, in whom, by the same process of purchase, vested the rights of those who dug the material from the ground and shaped it into a pen. Thus, my exclusive right of ownership in the pen springs from the natural right of the individual to the use of his own faculties.

Now, this is not only the original source from which all ideas of exclusive ownership arise – as is evident from the natural tendency of the mind to revert to it when the idea of exclusive ownership is questioned, and the manner in which social relations develop – but it is necessarily the only source. There can be to the ownership of anything no rightful title which is not derived from the title of the producer and does not rest upon the natural right of the man to himself. There can be no other rightful title, because (1st) there is no other natural right from which any other title can be derived, and (2d) because the recognition of any other title is inconsistent with and destructive of this.

For (1st) what other right exists from which the right to the exclusive possession of anything can be derived, save the right of a man to himself? With what other power is man by nature clothed, save the power of exerting his own faculties? How can he in any other way act upon or affect material things or other men? Paralyze the motor nerves, and your man has no more external influence or power than a log or stone. From what else, then, can the right of possessing and controlling things be derived? If it spring not from man himself, from what can it spring? Nature acknowledges no ownership or control in man save as the result of exertion. In no other way can her treasures be drawn forth, her powers directed, or her forces utilized or controlled. She makes no discriminations among men, but is to all absolutely impartial. She knows no distinction between master and slave, king and subject, saint and sinner. All men to her stand upon an equal footing and have equal rights. She recognizes no claim but that of labor, and recognizes that without respect to the claimant. If a pirate spread his sails, the wind will fill them as well as it will fill those of a peaceful merchantman or missionary bark; if a king and a common man be thrown overboard, neither can keep his head above water except by swimming; birds will not come to be shot by the proprietor of the soil any quicker than they will come to be shot by the poacher; fish will bite or will not bite at a hook in utter disregard as to whether it is offered them by a good little boy who goes to Sunday-school, or a bad little boy who plays truant; grain will grow only as the ground is prepared and the seed is sown; it is only at the call of labor that ore can be raised from the mine; the sun shines and the rain falls, alike upon just and unjust. The laws of nature are the decrees of the Creator. There is written in them no recognition of any right save that of labor; and in them is written broadly and clearly the equal right of all men to the use and enjoyment of nature; to apply to her by their exertions, and to receive and possess her reward. Hence, as nature gives only to labor, the exertion of labor in production is the only title to exclusive possession.

(2d) This right of ownership that springs from labor excludes the possibility of any other right of ownership. If a man be rightfully entitled to the produce of his labor, then no one can be rightfully entitled to the ownership of anything which is not the produce of his labor, or the labor of some one else from whom the right has passed to him. If production give to the producer the right to exclusive possession and enjoyment, there can rightfully be no exclusive possession and enjoyment of anything not the production of labor, and the recognition of private property in land is a wrong. For the right to the produce of labor cannot be enjoyed without the right to the free use of the opportunities offered by nature, and to admit the right of property in these is to deny the right of property in the produce of labor. When non-producers can claim as rent a portion of the wealth created by producers, the right of the producers to the fruits of their labor is to that extent denied.

There is no escape from this position. To affirm that a man can rightfully claim exclusive ownership in his own labor when embodied in material things, is to deny that any one can rightfully claim exclusive ownership in land. To affirm the rightfulness of property in land, is to affirm a claim which has no warrant in nature, as against a claim founded in the organization of man and the laws of the material universe.

What most prevents the realization of the injustice of private property in land is the habit of including all the things that are made the subject of ownership in one category, as property, or, if any distinction is made, drawing the line, according to the unphilosophical distinction of the lawyers, between personal property and real estate, or things movable and things immovable. The real and natural distinction is between things which are the produce of labor and things which are the gratuitous offerings of nature; or, to adopt the terms of political economy, between wealth and land.

These two classes of things are in essence and relations widely different, and to class them together as property is to confuse all thought when we come to consider the justice or the injustice, the right or the wrong of property.

A house and the lot on which it stands are alike property, as being the subject of ownership, and are alike classed by the lawyers as real estate. Yet in nature and relations they differ widely. The one is produced by human labor, and belongs to the class in political economy styled wealth. The other is a part of nature, and belongs to the class in political economy styled land.

The essential character of the one class of things is that they embody labor, are brought into being by human exertion, their existence or non-existence, their increase or diminution, depending on man. The essential character of the other class of things is that they do not embody labor, and exist irrespective of human exertion and irrespective of man; they are the field or environment in which man finds himself; the storehouse from which his needs must be supplied, the raw material upon which and the forces with which alone his labor can act.

The moment this distinction is realized, that moment is it seen that the sanction which natural justice gives to one species of property is denied to the other; that the rightfulness which attaches to individual property in the produce of labor implies the wrongfulness of individual property in land; that, whereas the recognition of the one places all men upon equal terms, securing to each the due reward of his labor, the recognition of the other is the denial of the equal rights of men, permitting those who do not labor to take the natural reward of those who do.

Whatever may be said for the institution of private property in land, it is therefore plain that it cannot be defended on the score of justice.

The equal right of all men to the use of land is as clear as their equal right to breathe the air – it is a right proclaimed by the fact of their existence. For we cannot suppose that some men have a right to be in this world and others no right.

If we are all here by the equal permission of the Creator, we are all here with an equal title to the enjoyment of his bounty – with an equal right to the use of all that nature so impartially offers.[1] This is a right which is natural and inalienable; it is a right which vests in every human being as he enters the world, and which during his continuance in the world can be limited only by the equal rights of others. There is in nature no such thing as a fee simple in land. There is on earth no power which can rightfully make a grant of exclusive ownership in land. If all existing men were to unite to grant away their equal rights, they could not grant away the right of those who follow them. For what are we but tenants for a day? Have we made the earth, that we should determine the rights of those who after us shall tenant it in their turn? The Almighty, who created the earth for man and man for the earth, has entailed it upon all the generations of the children of men by a decree written upon the constitution of all things – a decree which no human action can bar and no prescription determine. Let the parchments be ever so many, or possession ever so long, natural justice can recognize no right in one man to the possession and enjoyment of land that is not equally the right of all his fellows. Though his titles have been acquiesced in by generation after generation, to the landed estates of the Duke of Westminster the poorest child that is born in London to-day has as much right as has his eldest son.[2] Though the sovereign people of the state of New York consent to the landed possessions of the Astors, the puniest infant that comes wailing into the world in the squalidest room of the most miserable tenement house, becomes at that moment seized of an equal right with the millionaires. And it is robbed if the right is denied.

Our previous conclusions, irresistible in themselves, thus stand approved by the highest and final test. Translated from terms of political economy into terms of ethics they show a wrong as the source of the evils which increase as material progress goes on. The masses of men, who in the midst of abundance suffer want; who, clothed with political freedom, are condemned to the wages of slavery; to whose toil labor-saving inventions bring no relief, but rather seem to rob them of a privilege, instinctively feel that "there is something wrong." And they are right.

The wide-spreading social evils which everywhere oppress men amid an advancing civilization spring from a great primary wrong – the appropriation, as the exclusive property of some men, of the land on which and from which all must live. From this fundamental injustice flow all the injustices which distort and endanger modern development, which condemn the producer of wealth to poverty and pamper the non-producer in luxury, which rear the tenement house with the palace, plant the brothel behind the church, and compel us to build prisons as we open new schools.

There is nothing strange or inexplicable in the phenomena that are now perplexing the world. It is not that material progress is not in itself a good; it is not that nature has called into being children for whom she has failed to provide; it is not that the Creator has left on natural laws a taint of injustice at which even the human mind revolts, that material progress brings such bitter fruits. That amid our highest civilization men faint and die with want is not due to the niggardliness of nature, but to the injustice of man. Vice and misery, poverty and pauperism, are not the legitimate results of increase of population and industrial development; they only follow increase of population and industrial development because land is treated as private property – they are the direct and necessary results of the violation of the supreme law of justice, involved in giving to some men the exclusive possession of that which nature provides for all men.

The recognition of individual proprietorship of land is the denial of the natural rights of other individuals – it is a wrong which must show itself in the inequitable division of wealth. For as labor cannot produce without the use of land, the denial of the equal right to the use of land is necessarily the denial of the right of labor to its own produce. If one man can command the land upon which others must labor, he can appropriate the produce of their labor as the price of his permission to labor. The fundamental law of nature, that her enjoyment by man shall be consequent upon his exertion, is thus violated. The one receives without producing; the others produce without receiving. The one is unjustly enriched; the others are robbed. To this fundamental wrong we have traced the unjust distribution of wealth, which is separating modern society into the very rich and the very poor. It is the continuous increase of rent — the price that labor is compelled to pay for the use of land, which strips the many of the wealth they justly earn, to pile it up in the hands of the few, who do nothing to earn it.

Why should they who suffer from this injustice hesitate for one moment to sweep it away? Who are the land holders that they should thus be permitted to reap where they have not sown?

Consider for a moment the utter absurdity of the titles by which we permit to be gravely passed from John Doe to Richard Roe the right exclusively to possess the earth, giving absolute dominion as against all others. In California our land titles go back to the Supreme Government of Mexico, who took from the Spanish King, who took from the Pope, when he by a stroke of the pen divided lands yet to be discovered between the Spanish or Portuguese — or if you please they rest upon conquest. In the Eastern States they go back to treaties with Indians and grants from English Kings; in Louisiana to the Government of France; in Florida to the Government of Spain; while in England they go back to the Norman conquerors. Everywhere, not to a right which obliges, but to a force which compels. And when a title rests but on force, no complaint can be made when force annuls it. Whenever the people, having the power, choose

to annul those titles, no objection can be made in the name of justice. There have existed men who had the power to hold or to give exclusive possession of portions of the earth's surface, but when and where did there exist the human being who had the right? The right to exclusive ownership of anything of human production is clear. No matter how many the hands through which it has passed, there was, at the beginning of the line, human labor — some one who, having procured or produced it by his exertions, had to it a clear title as against all the rest of mankind, and which could justly pass from one to another by sale or gift. But at the end of what string of conveyances or grants can be shown or supposed a like title to any part of the material universe? To improvements, such an original title can be shown; but it is a title only to the improvements, and not to the land itself. If I clear a forest, drain a swamp, or fill a morass, all I can justly claim is the value given by these exertions. They give me no right to the land itself, no claim other than to my equal share with every other member of the community in the value which is added to it by the growth of the community. But it will be said: There are improvements which in time become indistinguishable from the land itself! Very well; then the title to the improvements becomes blended with the title to the land; the individual right is lost in the common right. It is the greater that swallows up the less, not the less that swallows up the greater. Nature does not proceed from man, but man from nature, and it is into the bosom of nature that he and all his works must return again.

Yet, it will be said: As every man has a right to the use and enjoyment of nature, the man who is using land must be permitted the exclusive right to its use in order that he may get the full benefit of his labor. But there is no difficulty in determining where the individual right ends and the common right begins. A delicate and exact test is supplied by value, and with its aid there is no difficulty, no matter how dense population may become, in determining and securing the exact rights of each, the equal rights of all. The value of land, as we have seen, is the price of monopoly. It is not the absolute, but the relative, capability of land that determines its value. No matter what may be its intrinsic qualities land that is no better than other land, which may be had for the using, can have no value. And the value of land always measures the difference between it and the best land that may be had for the using. Thus, the value of land expresses in exact and tangible form the right of the community in land held by an individual; and rent expresses the exact amount which the individual should pay to the community to satisfy the equal rights of all other members of the community. Thus, if we concede to priority of possession the undisturbed use of land, confiscating rent for the benefit of the community, we reconcile the fixity of tenure which is necessary for improvement with a full and complete recognition of the equal rights of all to the use of land. As for the deduction of a complete and exclusive individual right to land from priority of occupation, that is, if possible, the most absurd ground on which land owner-ship can be defended. Priority of occupation give exclusive and perpetual title to the surface of a globe on which, in the order of nature, countless generations succeed each other! Had the men of the last generation any better right to the use of this world than we of this? or the men of a hundred years ago? or of a thousand years ago? Had the mound-builders, or the cave-dwellers, the contemporaries of the mastodon and the three-toed horse, or the generations still further back, who, in dim æons that we can think of only as geologic periods, followed each other on the earth we now tenant for our little day?

Has the first comer at a banquet the right to turn back all the chairs and claim that none of the other guests shall partake of the food provided, except as they make terms with him? Does the first man who presents a ticket at the door of a theater, and passes in, acquire by his priority the right to shut the doors and have the performance go on for him alone? Does the first passenger who enters a railroad car obtain the right to scatter his baggage over all the seats and compel the passengers who come in after him to stand up?

The cases are perfectly analogous. We arrive and we depart, guests at a banquet continually spread, spectators and participants in an enter-tainment where there is room for all who come; passengers from station to station, on an orb that whirls through space – our rights to take and possess cannot be exclusive; they must be bounded everywhere by the equal rights of others. Just as the passenger in a railroad car may spread himself and his baggage over as many seats as he pleases, until other passengers come in, so may a settler take and use as much land as he chooses, until it is needed by others – a fact which is shown by the land acquiring a value – when his right must be curtailed by the equal rights of the others, and no priority of appro-priation can give a right which will bar these equal rights of others. If this were not the case, then by priority of appropriation one man could acquire and could transmit to whom he pleased, not merely the exclusive right to 160 acres, or to 640 acres, but to a whole township, a whole state, a whole continent.

And to this manifest absurdity does the recog-nition of individual right to land come when carried to its ultimate – that any one human being, could he concentrate in himself the indi-vidual rights to the land of any country, could expel therefrom all the rest of its inhabitants; and could he thus concentrate the individual rights to the whole surface of the globe, he alone of all the teeming population of the earth would have the right to live.

And what upon this supposition would occur is, upon a smaller scale, realized in actual fact. The territorial lords of Great Britain, to whom grants of land have given the "white parasols and elephants mad with pride," have over and over again expelled from large districts the native population, whose ancestors had lived on the land from immemorial times – driven them off to emigrate, to become paupers, or to starve. And on uncultivated tracts of land in the new state of California may be seen the blackened chimneys of homes from which settlers have been driven by force of laws which ignore natural right, and great stretches of land which might be populous are desolate, because the recognition of exclusive ownership has put it in the power of one human creature to forbid his fellows from using it. The comparative handful of proprietors who own the surface of the British Islands would be doing only what English law gives them full power to do, and what many of them have done on a smaller scale already, were they to exclude the millions of British people from their native islands. And such an exclusion, by which a few hundred thousand should at will banish thirty million people from their native country, while it would be more striking, would not be a whit more repugnant to natural right than the spectacle now presented, of the vast body of the British people being compelled to pay such enormous sums to a few of their number for the privilege of being permitted to live upon and use the land which they so fondly call their own; which is endeared to them by memories so tender and so glorious, and for which they are held in duty bound, if need be, to spill their blood and lay down their lives.

I refer only to the British Islands, because, land ownership being more concentrated there, they afford a more striking illustration of what private property in land necessarily involves. "To whomsoever the soil at any time belongs, to him belong the fruits of it," is a truth that becomes more and more apparent as population becomes denser and invention and improvement add to productive power; but it is everywhere a truth – as much in our new States as in the British Islands or by the banks of the Indus.

Notes

1 In saying that private property in land can, in the ultimate analysis, be justified only on the theory that some men have a better right to existence than others, I am stating only what the advocates of the existing system have themselves perceived. What gave to Malthus his popularity among the ruling classes – what caused his illogical book to be received as a new revelation, induced sovereigns to send him decorations, and the meanest rich man in England to propose to give him a living, was the fact that he furnished a plausible reason for the assumption that some have a better right to existence than others – an assumption which is necessary for the justification of private property in land, and which Malthus clearly states in the declaration that the tendency of population is constantly to bring into the world human beings for whom nature refuses to provide, and who consequently "have not the slightest right to any share in the existing store of the necessaries of life"; whom she tells as interlopers to begone, "and does not hesitate to extort by force obedience to her mandates," employing for that purpose "hunger and pestilence, war and crime, mortality and neglect of infantine life, prostitution and syphilis." And today this Malthusian doctrine is the ultimate defense upon which those who justify private property in land fall back. In no other way can it be logically defended.

2 This natural and inalienable right to the equal use and enjoyment of land is so apparent that it has been recognized by men wherever force or habit has not blunted first perceptions. To give but one instance: The white settlers of New Zealand found themselves unable to get from the Maoris what the latter considered a complete title to land, because, although a whole tribe might have consented to a sale, they would still claim with every new child born among them an additional payment on the ground that they had parted with only their own rights, and could not sell those of the unborn. The government was obliged to step in and settle the matter by buying land for a tribal annuity, in which every child that is born acquires a share.

Chapter 28

David Schmidtz

THE INSTITUTION OF PROPERTY

David Schmidtz (1955–) is a professor of philosophy and economics at the University of Arizona, and the founding director of their Freedom Center. In this essay, Schmidtz tackles the problem of how the original appropriation of unowned resources such as land can be justified, and argues that part of the justification can be found in the way in which property changes the zero-sum game of the Tragedy of the Commons into the positive-sum game of a system that allows for free exchange.

The evolution of property law is driven by an ongoing search for ways to internalize externalities: positive externalities associated with productive effort and negative externalities associated with misuse of commonly held resources. In theory, and sometimes in practice, costs are internalized over time. Increasingly, people pay for their own mistakes and misfortunes, and not for mistakes and misfortunes of others.

If all goes well, property law enables would-be producers to capture the benefits of productive effort. It also enables people to insulate themselves from negative externalities associated with activities around the neighborhood. Property law is not perfect. To minimize negative externalities that neighbors might otherwise impose on each other, people resort to nuisance and zoning laws. People turn to institutions like the Environmental Protection Agency for the same reasons they turn to central planners in other parts of the world; they think decentralized decision-making is chaos, and that with chaos comes a burgeoning of negative externalities.

What is the reality? The reality is that decentralization may or may not be chaos. It depends on institutional structure. An open-access commons decentralizes decision-making in one way; private property decentralizes it in another way, with systematically different results.

Philosophers speak of the ideal of society as a cooperative venture for mutual advantage. To be a cooperative venture for mutual advantage, though, society must first be a setting in which mutually advantageous interaction is possible. In the parlance of game theorists, society must be a positive-sum game. What determines the extent to which society is a positive-sum game? This essay explains how property institutions convert negative-sum or zero-sum games into positive-sum games, setting the stage for society's flourishing as a cooperative venture.

The term "property rights" is used to refer to a bundle of rights that could include rights to sell, lend, bequeath, and so on. In what follows, I use the phrase to refer primarily to the right of owners to exclude nonowners. Private owners have the right to exclude nonowners, but the right to exclude is a feature of property rights in general rather than the defining feature of private ownership in particular. The National Park Service claims a right to exclude. Communes claim a right to exclude nonmembers. This essay does not settle which kind or which mix of public and private property institutions is best. Instead, it asks how we could justify *any* institution that recognizes a right to exclude.

1. Original Appropriation: The Problem

The right to exclude presents a philosophical problem, though. Consider how full-blooded rights differ from mere liberties. If I am at liberty to plant a garden, that means my planting a garden is permitted. That leaves open the possibility of you being at liberty to interfere with my gardening as you see fit. Thus, mere liberties are not full-blooded rights. When I stake a claim to a piece of land, though, I claim to be changing other people's liberties – canceling them somehow – so that other people no longer are at liberty to use the land without my permission. To say I have a right to the land is to say I have a right to exclude.

From where could such rights have come? There must have been a time when no one had a right to exclude. Everyone had liberties regarding the land, but not rights. (Perhaps this does not seem obvious, but if no one owns the land, no one has a right to exclude. If no one has a right to exclude, everyone has liberties.) How, then, did we get from each person having a liberty to someone having an exclusive right to the land? What justifies original appropriation: that is, staking a claim to previously unowned resources?

To justify a claim to unowned land, people need not make as strong a case as would be needed to justify confiscating land already owned by someone else. Specifically, since there is no prior owner in original appropriation cases, there is no one from whom one can or needs to get consent. What, then, must a person do? Locke's idea seems to have been that any

residual (perhaps need-based) communal claim to the land could be met if a person could appropriate it without prejudice to other people, in other words, if a person could leave "enough and as good" for others. This so-called Lockean Proviso can be interpreted in many ways, but an adequate interpretation will note that this is its point: to license claims that can be made without making other people worse off. In the language of modern environmental economics, we might read it as a call for sustainable use.

We also should consider whether the "others" who are to be left with enough and as good include not just people currently on the scene but latecomers as well, including people not yet born. John Sanders asks, "What possible argument could at the same time require that the present generation have scruples about leaving enough and as good for one another, while shrugging off such concern for future generations?" (Sanders, 1987, p. 377). Most theorists accept the more demanding interpretation. It fits better with Locke's idea that the preservation of humankind (which includes future generations) is the ultimate criterion by which any use of resources is assessed. Aside from that, we have a more compelling defense of an appropriation (especially in environmental terms) when we can argue that there was enough left over not just for contemporaries but also for generations to come.

Of course, when we justify original appropriation, we do not in the process justify expropriation. Some say institutions that license expropriation make people better off; I think our histories of violent expropriation are ongoing tragedies for us all. Capitalist regimes have tainted histories. Communist regimes have tainted histories. Indigenous peoples have tainted histories. Europeans took land from native American tribes, and before that, those tribes took the same land from other tribes. We may regard those expropriations as the history of markets or governments or Christianity or tribalism or simply as the history of the human race. It makes little difference. This essay discusses the history of property institutions, not because their history can justify them, but rather because their history shows how some of them enable people to make themselves and the people around them better off without destroying their environment. Among such institutions are those that license original appropriation (and not expropriation).

2. Original Appropriation: A Solution

Private property's philosophical critics often have claimed that justifying original appropriation is the key to justifying private property, frequently offering a version of Locke's Proviso as the standard of justification. Part of the Proviso's attraction for such critics was that it seemingly could not be met. Even today, philosophers generally conclude that the Proviso is, at least in the case of land appropriation, logically impossible to satisfy, and thus that (private) property in land cannot possibly be justified along Lockean lines.

The way Judith Thomson puts it, if "the first labor-mixer must literally leave as much and as good for others who come along later, then no one can come to own anything, for there are only finitely many things in the world so that every taking leaves less for others" (Thomson, 1990 p. 330). To say the least, Thomson is not alone:

> We leave enough and as good for others only when what we take is not scarce.
>
> (Fried, p. 230n)

> The Lockean Proviso, in the contemporary world of overpopulation and scarce resources, can almost never be met.
>
> (Held, p. 6)

> Every acquisition worsens the lot of others – and worsens their lot in relevant ways.
>
> (Bogart, p. 834)

> The condition that there be enough and as good left for others could not of course be literally satisfied by any system of private property rights.
>
> (Sartorius, p. 210)

> If the "enough and as good" clause were a necessary condition on appropriation, it would follow that, in these circumstances, the only legitimate course for the inhabitants would be death by starvation . . . since *no* appropriation would leave enough and as good in common for others.
>
> (Waldron, p. 325)

And so on. If we take something out of the cookie jar, we *must* be leaving less for others. This appears self-evident. It has to be right.

2.1. *Appropriation Is Not a Zero-Sum Game*

But it is not right. First, it is by no means impossible – certainly not logically impossible – for a taking to leave as much for others. Surely we can at least imagine a logically possible world of magic cookie jars in which, every time you take out one cookie, more and better cookies take its place.

Second, the logically possible world I just imagined is the sort of world we actually live in. Philosophers writing about original appropriation tend to speak as if people who arrive first are luckier than those who come later. The truth is, first appropriators begin the process of resource creation; latecomers get most of the benefits. Consider America's first permanent English settlement, the Jamestown colony of 1607. (Or, if you prefer, imagine the lifestyles of people crossing the Bering Strait from Asia twelve thousand years ago.) Was their situation better than ours? How so? Was it that they never worried about being overcharged for car repairs? They never awoke in the middle of the night to the sound of noisy refrigerators, leaky faucets, or flushing toilets? They never had to change a light bulb? They never agonized over the choice of long-distance telephone companies?

Philosophers are taught to say, in effect, that original appropriators got the good stuff for free. We have to pay for ugly leftovers. But in truth, original appropriation benefits latecomers far more than it benefits original appropriators. Original appropriation is a cornucopia of wealth, but mainly for latecomers. The people who got here first never dreamt of things we latecomers take for granted. The poorest among us have life expectancies exceeding theirs by several decades. This is not political theory. It is not economic rhetoric. It is fact.

Original appropriation diminishes the stock of what can be originally appropriated, at least in the case of land, but that is not the same thing as diminishing the stock of what can be owned.[1] On the contrary, in taking control of resources and thereby removing those particular resources from the stock of goods that can be acquired by original appropriation, people typically generate massive increases in the stock of goods that can be acquired by trade. The lesson is that appropriation typically is not a zero-sum game. It normally is a positive-sum game. As Locke himself stressed, it creates the possibility of mutual benefit on a massive scale. It creates the possibility of society as a cooperative venture.

The argument is not merely that enough is produced in appropriation's aftermath to compensate latecomers who lost out in the race to appropriate. The argument is that the bare fact of being an original appropriator is not the prize. The prize is prosperity, and latecomers win big, courtesy of those who got here first. If anyone had a right to be compensated, it would be the first appropriators.

2.2. The Commons Before Appropriation Is Not Zero-Sum Either

The second point is that the commons before appropriation is not a zero-sum game either. Typically it is a negative-sum game. Let me tell two stories. The first comes from the coral reefs of the Philippine and Tongan Islands (Chesher, 1985; Gomez, Alcala, and San Diego, 1981). People once fished those reefs with lures and traps, but have recently caught on to a technique called bleach-fishing, which involves dumping bleach into the reefs. Fish cannot breath sodium hypochlorite. Suffocated, they float to the surface where they are easy to collect.[2]

The problem is, the coral itself is composed of living animals. The coral suffocates along with the fish, and the dead reef is no longer a viable habitat. (Another technique, blast-fishing, involves dynamiting the reefs. The concussion produces an easy harvest of stunned fish and dead coral.) You may say people ought to be more responsible. They ought to preserve the reefs for their children.

That would miss the point, which is that individual fishermen lack the option of saving the coral for their children. Individual fishermen obviously have the option of not destroying it themselves, but what happens if they elect not to destroy it? What they want is for the reef to be left for their children; what is actually happening is that the reef is left for the next blast-fisher down the line. If a fisherman wants to have anything at all to give his children, he must act quickly, destroying the reef and grabbing the fish himself. It does no good to tell fishermen to take responsibility. They are taking responsibility – for their children. Existing institutional arrangements do not empower them to take responsibility in a way that would save the reef.

Under the circumstances, they are at liberty to not destroy the reef themselves, but they are not at liberty to do what is necessary to save the reef for their children. To save the reef for their children, fishermen must have the power to restrict access to the reef. They must claim a right to exclude blast-fishers. Whether they stake that claim as individuals or as a group is secondary, so long as they actually succeed in restricting access. But one way or another, they must claim and effectively exercise a right to restrict access.

The second story comes from the Cayman Islands.[3] The Atlantic Green Turtle has long been prized as a source of meat and eggs. The turtles were a commonly held resource and were being harvested in an unsustainable way. In 1968, when by some estimates there were as few as three to five thousand left in the wild, a group of entrepreneurs and concerned scientists created Cayman Turtle Farm and began raising and selling captive-bred sea turtles. In the wild, as few as one tenth of one percent of wild hatchlings survive to adulthood. Most are seized by predators before they can crawl from nest to sea. Cayman Farm, though, boosted the survival rate of captive-bred animals to well over fifty percent. At the peak of operations, they were rearing in excess of a hundred thousand turtles. They were releasing one percent of their hatchlings into the wild at the age of ten months, an age at which hatchlings had a decent chance of surviving to maturity.

In 1973, commerce in Atlantic Green Turtles was restricted by CITES (the Convention on International Trade in Endangered Species) and, in the United States, by the Fish and Wildlife Service, the Department of Commerce, and the Department of the Interior. Under the newly created Endangered Species Act, the U.S. classified the Atlantic Green Turtle as an endangered species, but Cayman Farm's business was unaffected, at first, because regulations pertaining to commerce in Atlantic Green Turtles exempted commerce in captive-bred animals. In 1978, however, the regulations were published in their final form, and although exemptions were granted for trade in captive-bred animals of other species, no exemption was made for trade in turtles. The company could no longer do business in the U.S. Even worse, the company no longer could ship its products through American ports, so it no longer had access via Miami to world markets. The Farm exists today only to serve the population of the Cayman Islands themselves.

What do these stories tell us? The first tells us we do not need to justify failing to preserve the commons in its pristine, original, unappropriated form, because preserving the commons in pristine original form is not an option. The commons is not a time capsule. Leaving our environment in the commons is not like putting our environment in a time capsule as a legacy for future generations. In some cases, putting resources in a time capsule might be a good idea. However, the second story reminds us: there are ways to take what we find in the commons and preserve it — to put it in a time capsule — but before we can put something in a time capsule, we have to appropriate it.[4]

2.3. Justifying the Game

Note a difference between justifying institutions that regulate appropriation and justifying particular acts of appropriation. Think of original appropriation as a game and of particular acts of appropriation as moves within the game. Even if the game is justified, a given move within the game may have nothing to recommend it. Indeed, we could say (for argument's sake) that any act of appropriation will seem arbitrary when viewed in isolation, and some will seem unconscionable. Even so, there can be compelling reasons to have an institutional framework that recognizes property claims on the basis of moves that would carry no weight in an institutional vacuum. Common law implicitly acknowledges morally weighty reasons for not requiring original appropriators to supply morally weighty reasons for their appropriations. Carol Rose (1985) argues that a rule of first possession, when the world is notified in an unambiguous way, induces discovery (and future productive activity) and minimizes disputes over discovered objects. Particular acts of appropriation are justified not because they carry moral weight but because they are permitted moves within a game that carries moral weight.

Needless to say, the cornucopia of wealth generated by the appropriation and subsequent mobilization of resources is not an unambiguous benefit. The commerce made possible by original appropriation creates pollution, and other negative externalities as well. (I will return to this point.) Further, there may be people who attach no value to the increases in life expectancy and other benefits that accompany the appropriation of resources for productive use. Some people may prefer a steady-state system that indefinitely supports their lifestyles as hunter-gatherers, untainted by the shoes and tents and safety matches of Western culture. If original appropriation forces such people to participate in a culture they want no part of, then from their viewpoint, the game does more harm than good.

Here are two things to keep in mind, though. First, as I said, the commons is not a time capsule. It does not preserve the status quo. For all kinds of reasons, quality of life could drop after appropriation. However, pressures that drive waves of people to appropriate are a lot more likely to compromise quality of life when those waves wash over an unregulated commons. In an unregulated commons, those who conserve pay the costs but do not get the benefits of conservation, while overusers get the benefits but do not pay the costs of overuse. Therefore, an unregulated commons is a prescription for overuse, not for conservation.

Second, the option of living the life of a hunter-gatherer has not entirely disappeared. It is not a comfortable life. It never was. But it remains an option. There are places in northern Canada and elsewhere where people can and do live that way. As a bonus, those who opt to live as hunter-gatherers retain the option of participating in Western culture on a drop-in basis during medical emergencies, to trade for supplies, and so on. Obviously, someone might respond, "Even if the hunter-gatherer life is an option now, that option is disappearing as expanding populations equipped with advancing technologies claim the land for other purposes." Well, probably so. What does that prove? It proves that, in the world as it is, if hunter-

gatherers want their children to have the option of living as hunter-gatherers, then they need to stake a claim to the territory on which they intend to preserve that option. They need to argue that they, as rightful owners, have a right to regulate access to it. If they want a steady-state civilization, they need to be aware that they will not find it in an unregulated commons. They need to argue that they have a right to exclude oil companies, for example, which would love to be able to treat northern Canada as an unregulated commons.

When someone says appropriation does not leave enough and as good for others, the reply should be "compared to what?" Compared to the commons as it was? As it is? As it will be? Often, in fact, leaving resources in the commons does not leave enough and as good for others. The Lockean Proviso, far from forbidding appropriation of resources from the commons, actually requires appropriation under conditions of scarcity. Moreover, the more scarce a resource is, the more urgently the Proviso requires that it be removed from the negative-sum game that is the unregulated commons. Again, when the burden of common use exceeds the resource's ability to renew itself, the Proviso comes to require, not merely permit, people to appropriate and regulate access to the resource. Even in an unregulated commons, some fishermen will practice self-restraint, but something has to happen to incline the group to practice self-restraint in cases where it already has shown it has no such inclination in an unregulated commons.

Removing goods from the commons stimulates increases in the stock of what can be owned and limits losses that occur in tragic commons. Appropriation replaces a negative-sum with a positive-sum game. Therein lies a justification for social structures enshrining a right to remove resources from the unregulated commons: when resources become scarce, we need to remove them if we want them to be there for our children. Or anyone else's.

3. What Kind of Property Institution Is Implied?

I have defended appropriation of, and subsequent regulation of access to, scarce resources as a way of preserving (and creating) resources for the future. When resources are abundant, the Lockean Proviso permits appropriation; when resources are scarce, the Proviso requires appropriation. It is possible to appropriate without prejudice to future generations. Indeed, when resources are scarce, it is leaving them in the commons that is prejudicial to future generations.

Private property enables people (and gives them an incentive) to take responsibility for conserving scarce resources. It preserves resources under a wide variety of circumstances. It is the preeminent vehicle for turning negative-sum commons into positive-sum property regimes. However, it is not the only way. Evidently, it is not always the best way, either. Public property is ubiquitous, and it is not only rapacious governments and mad ideologues who create it. Sometimes it evolves spontaneously as a response to real problems, enabling people to remove a resource from an unregulated commons and collectively take responsibility for its management. The following sections discuss research by Martin Bailey, Harold Demsetz, Robert Ellickson, and Carol Rose, showing how various property institutions help to ensure that enough and as good is left for future generations.

3.1. The Unregulated Commons

An unregulated commons need not be a disaster. An unregulated commons will work well enough so long as the level of use remains within the land's carrying capacity. However, as use nears carrying capacity, there will be pressure to shift to a more exclusive regime. As an example of an unregulated commons evolving into something else as increasing traffic begins to exceed carrying capacity, consider Harold Demsetz's account of how property institutions evolved among indigenous tribes of the Labrador peninsula. As Demsetz tells the story, the region's people had, for generations, treated the land as an open-access commons. The human population was small. There was plenty to eat. Thus, the pattern of exploitation was within the land's carrying capacity.[5] The resource maintained itself. In that situation, the Proviso, as interpreted above, was satisfied. Original appropriation would have been permissible, other things equal, but it was not required.

With the advent of the fur trade, though, the scale of hunting and trapping activity increased sharply. The population of game animals began to dwindle. The unregulated commons had worked for a while, but now the tribes were facing a classic tragedy. The benefits of exploiting the resource were internalized but the costs were not, and the arrangement was no longer viable. Clans began to mark out family plots. The game animals in question were small animals like beaver and otter that tend not to migrate from one plot to another. Thus, marking out plots of land effectively privatized small game as well as the land itself. In sum, the tribes converted the commons in nonmigratory fur-bearing game to family parcels when the fur trade began to spur a rising demand that exceeded the land's carrying capacity. When demand began to exceed carrying capacity, that was when the Proviso came not only to permit but to require original appropriation.

One other nuance of the privatization of fur-bearing game: although the fur was privatized, the meat was not. There was still plenty of meat to go around, so tribal law allowed trespass on another clan's land to hunt for meat. Trespassers could kill a beaver and take the meat, but had to leave the pelt displayed in a prominent place to signal that they had eaten and had respected the clan's right to the pelt. The new customs went to the heart of the matter, privatizing what had to be privatized, leaving intact liberties that people had always enjoyed with respect to other resources where unrestricted access had not yet become a problem.

3.2. The Communal Alternative[6]

We can contrast the unregulated or open-access commons with communes. A commune is a restricted-access commons. In a commune, property is owned by the group rather than by individual members. People as a group claim and exercise a right to exclude. Typically, communes draw a sharp distinction between members and nonmembers, and regulate access accordingly. Public property tends to restrict access by time of day or year. Some activities are permitted; others are prohibited.

Ellickson believes a broad campaign to abolish either private property or public and communal property would be ludicrous. Each kind of property serves social welfare in its own way. Likewise, every ownership regime has its own externality problems. Communal management leads to overconsumption and to shirking on maintenance and improvements, because people receive only a fraction of the value of their labor, and bear only a fraction of the costs of their consumption. To minimize these disincentives, a commune must intensively monitor people's production and consumption activities.

In practice, communal regimes can lead to indiscriminate dumping of wastes, ranging from piles of unwashed dishes to ecological disasters that threaten whole continents. Privately managed parcels also can lead to indiscriminate dumping of wastes and to various other uses that ignore spillover effects on neighbors. One advantage of private property is that owners can buy each other out and reshuffle their holdings in such a way as to minimize the extent to which their activities bother each other. But it does not always work out so nicely, and the reshuffling itself can be a waste. There are transaction costs. Thus, one plausible social goal would be to have a system that combines private and public

property in a way that reduces the sum of transaction costs and the cost of externalities.

4. Local versus Remote Externalities

Is it generally best to convert an unregulated commons to smaller private parcels or to manage it as a commune with power to exclude nonmembers? It depends on what kind of activities people tend to engage in. Ellickson separates activities into three categories: small (like cultivating a tomato plant), medium (like damming part of a river to create a pond for ducks), and large (like using an industrial smokestack to disperse noxious fumes). The distinction is not meant to be sharp. As one might expect, it is a matter of degree. It concerns the relative size of the area over which externalities are worth worrying about. The effects of small events are confined to one's own property. Medium events affect people in the immediate neighborhood. Their external effects are localized. Large events affect people who are more remote.

Ellickson says private regimes are clearly superior as methods for minimizing the costs of small and medium events. Small events are not much of a problem for private regimes. When land is parceled out, the effects of small events are internalized. Neighbors do not care much when we pick tomatoes on our own land; they care a great deal when we pick tomatoes on the communal plot. In the former case, we are minding our own business; in the latter, we are minding theirs.

In contrast, the effects of medium events tend to spill over onto one's neighbors, and thus can be a source of friction. Nevertheless, privatization has the advantage of limiting the number of people having to be consulted about how to deal with the externality, which reduces transaction costs. Instead of consulting the entire community of communal owners, each at liberty with respect to the affected area, one consults a handful of people who own parcels in the immediate area of the medium event. A further virtue of privatization is that disputes arising from medium events tend to be left in the hands of people in the immediate vicinity, who tend to have a better understanding of local conditions and thus are in a better position to devise resolutions without harmful unintended consequences. They are in a better position to foresee the costs and benefits of a medium event.

When it comes to large events, though, there is no easy way to say which mix of private and public property is best. Large events involve far-flung externalities among people who do not have face-to-face relationships. The difficulties in detecting such externalities, tracing them to their source, and holding people accountable for them are difficulties for any kind of property regime. It is no easy task to devise institutions that encourage pulp mills to take responsibility for their actions while simultaneously encouraging people downstream to take responsibility for their welfare, and thus to avoid being harmed by large-scale negative externalities. Ellickson says there is no general answer to the question of which regime best deals with them.

A large event will fall into one of two categories. Releasing toxic wastes into the atmosphere, for example, may violate existing legal rights or community norms. Or, such laws or norms may not yet be in place. Most of the problems arise when existing customs or laws fail to settle who (in effect) has the right of way. That is not a problem with parceling land per se but rather with the fact that key resources like air and waterways remain in a largely unregulated commons.

So, privatization exists in different degrees and takes different forms. Different forms have different incentive properties. Simply parceling out land or sea is not always enough to stabilize possession of resources that make land or sea valuable in the first place. Suppose, for example, that fish are known to migrate from one parcel to another. In that case, owners have an incentive to grab as many fish as they can whenever the school passes through their own territory. Thus, simply dividing fishing grounds into parcels may not be enough to put fishermen in a position collectively to avoid exceeding sustainable yields. It depends on the extent to which the sought-after fish migrate from one parcel to another, and on conventions that are continuously evolving to help neighbors deal with the inadequacy of their fences (or other ways of marking off territory). Clearly, then, not all forms of privatization are equally good at internalizing externalities. Privatization per se is not a panacea, and not all forms of privatization are equal. There are obvious difficulties with how private property regimes handle large events. The nature and extent of the difficulties depends on details. So, for purposes of comparison, Ellickson looked at how communal regimes handle large events.

5. Jamestown and Other Communes

The Jamestown Colony is North America's first permanent English settlement. It begins in 1607 as a commune, sponsored by London-based Virginia Company. Land is held and managed collectively. The colony's charter guarantees to each settler an equal share of the collective product regardless of the amount of work personally contributed. Of the original group of one hundred and four settlers, two thirds die of starvation and disease before their first winter. New shiploads replenish the population, but the winter of 1609 cuts the population from five hundred to sixty. In 1611, visiting Governor Thomas Dale finds living skeletons bowling in the streets, waiting for someone else to plant the crops. Their main food source consists of wild animals such as turtles and raccoons, which settlers hunt and eat by dark of night before neighbors can demand equal shares. In 1614, Governor Dale has seen enough. He assigns three-acre plots to individual settlers, which reportedly increases productivity seven-fold. The colony converts the rest of its land holdings to private parcels in 1619.

Why go communal in the first place? Are there advantages to communal regimes? One advantage is obvious. Communal regimes can help people spread risks under conditions where risks are substantial and where alternative risk-spreading mechanisms, like insurance, are unavailable. But as communities build up capital reserves to the point where they can offer insurance, they tend to privatize, for insurance lets them secure a measure of risk-spreading without having to endure the externalities that afflict a communal regime.

A communal regime might also be an effective response to economies of scale in large-scale public works that are crucial in getting a community started. To build a fort, man its walls, dig wells, and so on, a communal economy is an obvious choice as a way of mobilizing the teams of workers needed to execute these urgent tasks. But again, as these tasks are completed and community welfare increasingly comes to depend on small events, the communal regime gives way to private parcels. At Jamestown, Plymouth, the Amana colonies, and Salt Lake, formerly communal settlers "understandably would switch to private land tenure, the system that most cheaply induces individuals to undertake small and medium events that are socially useful" (Ellickson, p. 1342). (The legend of Salt Lake says the sudden improvement in the fortunes of once-starving Mormons occurred in 1848 when God sent seagulls to save them from plagues of locusts, at the same time as they coincidentally were switching to private plots. Similarly, the Jamestown tragedy sometimes is attributed to harsh natural conditions, as if those conditions suddenly changed in 1614, multiplying productivity seven-fold while Governor Dale coincidentally was cutting the land into parcels.)

Of course, the tendency toward decentralized and individualized forms of management is only a (strong) tendency and, in any case, there are tradeoffs. For example, what would be a small event on a larger parcel becomes a medium event under more crowded conditions. Loud music is an innocuous small event on a ranch but an irritating medium event in an apartment complex. Changes in technology or population density affect the scope or incidence of externalities. The historical trend, though, is that as people become aware of and concerned about a medium or large event, they seek ways of reducing the extent to which the event's cost is externalized. Social evolution is partly a process of perceiving new externalities and devising institutions to internalize them.

Historically, the benefits of communal management have not been enough to keep communes together indefinitely. Perhaps the most enduring and successful communes in human memory are the agricultural settlements of the Hutterites, dating in Europe back to the sixteenth century. There are now around 28,000 people living in such communities. Hutterites believe in a fairly strict sharing of assets. They forbid the possession of radio or television sets, to give one example of how strictly they control contact with the outside world.

Ellickson says Hutterite communities have three special things going for them: 1. A population cap: when a settlement reaches a population of 120, a portion of the community must leave to start a new community. The cap helps them retain a close-knit society; 2. Communal dining and worship: people congregate several times a day, which facilitates a rapid exchange of information about individual behavior and a ready avenue for supplying feedback to those whose behavior deviates from the norm; 3. A ban on birth control: the average woman bears nine children, which more than offsets the trickle of emigration. We might add that Hutterite culture and education leave people ill-prepared to live in anything other than a Hutterite society, which surely accounts in part for the low emigration rate.

Ellickson discusses other examples of communal property regimes. But the most pervasive example of communal ownership in America, Ellickson says, is the family household. American suburbia consists of family communes nested within a network of open-access roadways. Family homes tacitly recognize limits to how far we can go in converting common holdings to individual parcels. Consider your living room. You could fully privatize, having one household member own it while others pay user fees. The fees could be used to pay family members or outside help to keep it clean. In some respects, it would be better that way. The average communal living room today, for example, is notably subject to overgrazing and shirking on maintenance. Yet we put up with it. No one charges user fees to household members. Seeing the living room degraded by communal use may be irritating, but it is better than treating it as one person's private domain.

Some institutions succeed while embodying a form of ownership that is essentially collective. History indicates, though, that members of successful communes internalize the rewards that come with that collective responsibility. In particular, they reserve the right to exclude nonmembers. A successful commune does not run itself as an open-access commons.

6. Governance By Custom

Many commons (such as our living rooms) are regulated by custom rather than by government, so saying there is a role for common property and saying there is a role for government management of common property are two different things. As Ellickson notes, "Group ownership does not necessarily imply government ownership, of course. The sorry environmental records of federal land agencies and Communist regimes are a sharp reminder that governments are often particularly inept managers of large tracts." Carol Rose tells of how, in the nineteenth century, public property was thought to be owned by society at large. The idea of public property often was taken to imply no particular role for government beyond whatever enforcement role is implied by private property. Society's right to such property was held to precede and supersede any claim by government. Rose says, "Implicit in these older doctrines is the notion that, even if a property should be open to the public, it does not follow that public rights should necessarily vest in an active governmental manager" (Rose, 1986 p. 720). Sometimes, rights were understood to be held by an "unorganized public" rather than by a "governmentally organized public" (Rose, 1986 p. 736).

Along the same lines, open-field agricultural practices of medieval times gave peasants exclusive cropping rights to scattered thin strips of arable land in each of the village fields. The strips were private only during the growing season, after which the land reverted to the commons for the duration of the grazing season. Thus, ownership of parcels was usufructuary in the sense that once the harvest was in, ownership reverted to the common herdsmen without negotiation or formal transfer. The farmer had an exclusive claim to the land only so long as he was using it for the purpose of bringing in a harvest. The scattering of strips was a means of diversification, reducing the risk of being ruined by small or medium events: small fires, pest infestations, etc. The post-harvest commons in grazing land exploited economies of scale in fencing and tending a herd.

According to Martin Bailey, the pattern observed by Rose and Ellickson also was common among aboriginal tribes. That is, tribes that practiced agriculture treated the land as private during the growing season, and often treated it as a commons after the crops were in. Hunter-gatherer societies did not practice agriculture, but they too tended to leave the land in the commons during the summer when game was plentiful. It was during the winter, when food was most scarce, that they privatized. The rule among hunter-gatherers is that where group hunting's advantages are considerable, that factor dominates. But in the winter, small game is relatively more abundant, less migratory, and evenly spread. There was no "feast or famine" pattern of the sort one expects to see with big-game hunting. Rather, families tended to gather enough during the course of the day to get themselves through the day, day after day, with little to spare.

Even though this pattern corroborates my own general thesis, I confess to being a bit surprised. I might have predicted that it would be during the harshest part of the year that families would band together and throw everything into the common pot in order to pull through. Not so. It was when the land was nearest its carrying capacity that they recognized the imperative to privatize.

Customary use of medieval commons was hedged with restrictions limiting depletion of resources. Custom prohibited activities inconsistent with the land's ability to recover (Rose, 1986 p. 743). In particular, the custom of "stinting" allowed the villagers to own livestock only in proportion to the relative size of their (growing season) land holdings. Governance by custom enabled people to avoid commons tragedies.[7]

Custom is a form of management unlike exclusive ownership by either individuals or governments. Custom is a self-managing system for according property rights (Rose, 1986 p. 742). For example, custom governs the kind of rights-claims you establish by taking a place in line at a supermarket checkout counter. Rose believes common concerns often are best handled by decentralized, piecemeal, and self-managing customs that tend to arise as needed at the local level. So, to the previous section's conclusion that a successful commune does not run itself as an open-access commons, we can add that a successful commune does not entrust its governance to a distant bureaucracy.

7. The Hutterite Secret

I argued that the original appropriation of (and subsequent regulation of access to) scarce resources is justifiable as a mechanism for preserving opportunities for future generations. There are various means of exclusive control, though. Some internalize externalities better than others, and how well they do so depends on the context. My argument does not presume there is one form of exclusive control that uniquely serves this purpose. Which form is best depends on what kind of activities are most prevalent in a community at any given time. It also depends on the extent to which public ownership implies control by a distant bureaucracy rather than by local custom.

As mentioned earlier, I have heard people say Jamestown failed because it faced harsh natural conditions. But communal (and non-communal) settlements typically face harsh natural conditions. Jamestown had to deal with summer in Virginia. Hutterites dealt with winter on the Canadian prairie. It is revealing, not misleading, to compare Jamestown to settlements that faced harsher conditions more successfully. It also is fair to compare the two Jamestowns: the one before and the one immediately following Governor Dale's mandated privatization. What distinguished the first Jamestown from the second was not the harshness of its natural setting but rather the thoroughness with which it prevented people from internalizing externalities.

Sociologist Michael Hechter considers group solidarity to be a function of (a) the extent to which members depend on the group and (b) the extent to which the group can monitor and enforce compliance with expectations that members will contribute to the group rather than free ride upon it (Hechter, p. 21). On this analysis, it is unsurprising that Hutterite communal society has been successful. Members are extremely dependent, for their upbringing leaves them unprepared to live in a non-Hutterite culture. Monitoring is intense. Feedback is immediate. But if that is the secret of Hutterite success, why did Jamestown fail? They too were extremely dependent on each other. They too had nowhere else to go. Monitoring was equally unproblematic. Everyone knew who was planting crops (no one) and who was bowling (everyone). What was the problem?

The problem lay in the guarantee embedded in the Jamestown colony's charter. Jamestown's charter entitled people to an equal share regardless of personal contribution, which is to say it took steps to ensure that individual workers would be maximally alienated from the fruits of their labors. The charter ensured that workers would think of their work as disappearing into an open-access commons.

Robert Goodin says, "Working within the constraints set by natural scarcity, the greatest practical obstacle to achieving as much justice as resources permit is, and always has been, the supposition that each of us should cultivate his own garden" (Goodin, 1985, p. 1).[8] However, Jamestown's charter did not suppose each of us should cultivate his own garden. It supposed the opposite. Colonists abided by the charter, and even while they suffered, people in other colonies were tending their own gardens, and thriving.

We should applaud institutions that encourage people to care for each other. But telling people they are required to tend someone else's garden rather than their own does not encourage people to care for each other. It does the opposite. It encourages spite. The people of Jamestown reached the point where they would rather die, bowling in the street, than tend the gardens of their free-riding neighbors, and die they did.

Notes

1 Is it fair for latecomers to be excluded from acquiring property by rules allowing original appropriation? Sanders (1987, p. 385) notes that latecomers "are *not* excluded from acquiring property by these rules. They are, instead, excluded from being the first to own what has not been owned previously. Is *that* unfair?"

2 Nash (1996) says fishermen currently pump 330,000 pounds of cyanide per year into Philippine reefs.

3 I thank Peggy Fosdick at the National Aquarium in Baltimore for correspondence and documents. See also Fosdick and Fosdick (1994).

4 A private non profit organization, The Nature Conservancy, is pursuing such a strategy. Although not itself an original appropriator, it has acquired over a billion dollars' worth of land in an effort to preserve natural ecosystems. Note that this includes habitat for endangered species that have no market value.

5 This was not true everywhere. I have seen places where tribes hunted bison by stampeding whole herds over the edge of a cliff. (The Blackfoot name for one such place translates as "head-smashed-in buffalo jump.") So I accept Dukeminier and Krier's warning against forming "an unduly romantic image of Native American culture prior to the arrival of 'civilization.' There is considerable evidence that some American Indian tribes, rather than being natural ecologists who lived in respectful harmony with the land, exploited the environment ruthlessly by overhunting and extensive burning of forests" (1993, p. 62).

6 This essay discusses Ellickson's article in some detail. While I take little credit for the ideas in the next few sections, any errors are presumably mine.

7 Of course, no one thinks governance by custom automatically solves commons problems. Custom works when local users can restrict outsider access and monitor insider behavior, but those conditions are not always met, and tragedies like those discussed in section 2.2 continue to occur.

8 Goodin and I debate the issue at length in Schmidtz & Goodin (1998).

References

Bailey, Martin J. 1992. Approximate Optimality of Aboriginal Property Rights. *Journal of Law and Economics* 35: 183–98.

Bogart, J. H. 1985. Lockean Provisos and State of Nature Theories. *Ethics* 95: 828–36.

Chesher, R. 1985. Practical Problems in Coral Reef Utilization and Management: a Tongan Case Study. *Proceedings of the Fifth International Coral Reef Congress* 4: 213–24.

Demsetz, Harold. 1967. Toward a Theory of Property Rights. *American Economic Review* (Papers & Proceedings) 57: 347–59.

Dukeminier, Jesse, and James E. Krier. 1993. *Property.* 3rd edn. Boston: Little, Brown.

Ellickson, Robert C. 1993. Property in Land. *Yale Law Journal* 102: 1315–400.

Fosdick, Peggy, and Fosdick, Sam. 1994. *Last Chance Lost?* York, PA: Irvin S. Naylor Publishing.

Fried, Barbara. 1995. Wilt Chamberlain Revisited: Nozick's "Justice in Transfer" and the Problem of Market-Based Distribution. *Philosophy and Public Affairs* 24: 226–45.

Gomez, E., A. Alcala and A. San Diego. 1981. Status of Philippine Coral Reefs – 1981. *Proceedings of the Fourth International Coral Reef Symposium* 1: 275–85.

Goodin, Robert E. 1985. *Protecting the Vulnerable: Toward a reanalysis of Our Social Responsibilities.* Chicago: University of Chicago Press.

Hardin, Garrett. 1977. The Ethical Implications of Carrying Capacity. In G. Hardin and J. Baden, eds., *Managing the Commons.* San Francisco: W. H. Freeman.

Hechter, Michael. 1983. A Theory of Group Solidarity. In Hechter, ed., *Microfoundations of Macrosociology.* Philadelphia: Temple University Press. 16–57.

Held, Virginia. 1980. Introduction. In Held, ed., *Property, Profits, & Economic Justice.* Belmont: Wadsworth.

Hohfeld, Wesley. 1919. *Fundamental Legal Conceptions.* New Haven: Yale University Press.

Locke, John. 1690. *Second Treatise of Government.* ed. P. Laslett. Cambridge: Cambridge University Press (reprinted 1960).

Nash, J. Madeleine. 1996. Wrecking the Reefs. *Time* (September 30): 60–2.

Rose, Carol. 1985. Possession as the Origin of Property. *University of Chicago Law Review* 52: 73–88.

Rose, Carol. 1986. The Comedy of the Commons: Custom, Commerce, and Inherently Public Property. *University of Chicago Law Review* 53: 711–87.

Sanders, John T. 1987. Justice and the Initial Acquisition of Private Property. *Harvard Journal of Law and Public Policy* 10: 367–99.

Sartorius, Rolf. 1984. Persons and Property. In Ray Frey, ed., *Utility and Rights.* Minneapolis: University of Minnesota Press.

Schmidtz, David, and Robert E. Goodin. 1998. *Social Welfare and Individual Responsibility.* Cambridge: Harvard University Press.

Thomson, Judith Jarvis. 1990. *The Realm of Rights.* Cambridge: Harvard University Press.

Waldron, Jeremy. Enough and As Good Left For Others. *Philosophical Quarterly* 29 (1976) 319–28.

2c. DISTRIBUTIVE JUSTICE

THERE JUST AREN'T ENOUGH good things to go around. Land, money, health care, opportunities, education and romantic partners (to name just a few) are all limited in the sense that demand for them will always exceed supply. How, then, should we determine who gets what? This is the basic question of distributive justice.

Generally, philosophers attempt to answer this question by appealing to some more basic value. A just distribution, one might say, is one that promotes freedom. Or, another might claim, perhaps a just distribution is one that in some way respects people as equals. We will look at both of these values in more detail in subsequent chapters. In this chapter, our concern will be with the concept of distributive justice more generally, rather than its relation to one particular value.

In fact, part of the task of this chapter will be to examine the legitimacy of the very subject of distributive justice itself. For, the concept is one that has come under severe criticism from certain libertarian theorists such as Robert Nozick and Friedrich Hayek. Such theorists argue that the notion of distributive justice is appropriate only when there is some *agent* making a choice about how to distribute certain goods. A parent, for instance, who allocates allowance money amongst her children, or a teacher who assigns grades to the various students in his class. But in a market economy, such theorists argue, there is no single agent responsible for the distribution of goods among persons. Who gets what is a result of a complicated series of decisions by many, many different decision makers whose choices cannot be captured in any single principle. Parents give money and other gifts to their children out of love and obligation, bosses give raises to workers as a reward for merit or as an incentive for future performance, consumers give money to Routledge in exchange for stimulating books on political philosophy, etc. The point is that as long as individuals are free to do what they want with their possessions — including transfer some of those possessions to others — there can be no guarantee that the overall results of their decisions will conform to any single principle of just distribution, nor can it be said that the distribution resulted from the application of some single principle.

Nozick thus argues that the only meaningful sense in which we can talk about the justice of a distribution is as an essentially *historical* matter — the justice of a distribution is a function of the way in which that distribution comes about, and not in the value it promotes or the pattern in which it falls. Distributions are just if they arise as a result of people acting justly, and since Nozick believes that voluntary "capitalist acts between consenting adults" are just, then any distribution that results from a series of such capitalist acts is itself just.

In one sense, this sort of move avoids some potential difficulties for the libertarian. Rawls, in an earlier chapter, argued that individuals in a market economy (or elsewhere) cannot be said to deserve their wealth, since they did nothing to deserve the social or natural endowments of which that wealth was a product. Other critics of capitalism have argued that markets often fail to reward those with the greatest talent, or that they tend to promote material inequality, or fail to meet people's basic needs. But Nozick's position is, in a sense, immune to these sorts of criticisms. For his position is not that markets are good because they get people what they need, deserve, or merit. His position is that they are good because they allow people to do what they choose with what they own. That some people will choose to do things that do not promote equality, merit, or whatever, is not an embarrassment to the theory — it is, rather, the virtually inevitable result of allowing people to act freely.

Still, adopting this position requires the libertarian to bite a fairly sizable bullet. For, as the readings by Cohen and Van Parijs forcefully argue, we care deeply about values like desert and equality and are inclined to view it as a failure of a social system if it creates distributions which fail to realize them. In making this argument, they recall Marx's famous critique of capitalism which charged that markets promote the freedom of some only at the expense of others.

Low-skill workers seem forced to spend the greater part of their day engaged in grueling, unpleasant, and sometimes demeaning work in order to make enough money to provide for their basic needs. Their freedom appears to be curtailed both in the concrete sense in that they are told what to wear, what to do, how to speak and so on, and in the more general sense in that the economic system is set up so that they must accept these more concrete limitations on their freedom in order to make ends meet. Can a market system that is indifferent to, and arguably promotes, such inequalities of power really be justified?

G. A. Cohen doubts that it can, and in his essay in this section, he argues that while "socialism" has become something of a dirty word in American politics, it is actually more responsive to the values of community and equality that most of us hold dear than a capitalist economy. It is an ideal to which we should aspire, and the practical obstacles that stand in the way of it are ones that can and should be surmounted. Philippe Van Parijs, on the other hand, argues that a capitalist economy could be made just, but only if all persons are guaranteed by the state a basic income sufficient for sustenance. Interestingly, while Van Parijs probably has more in common politically with a socialist like G. A. Cohen, his proposal for a universal basic income is one that has been endorsed by libertarians like Milton Friedman and conservatives like Charles Murray. It thus represents a fascinating (and rare!) instance of an important policy enjoying broad support across the political spectrum.

Moral theorists have long argued that utilitarianism is inadequate as a moral philosophy because in its single-minded concern with maximizing *total* utility, it utterly neglects the issue of how that utility is distributed among separate persons. A utilitarian seems committed to saying that enslaving a minority of the population would be morally permissible (indeed, required!) if it created greater overall utility than allowing everyone freedom. But most of us share Rawls' intuition that justice guarantees each individual a certain kind of inviolability — there are certain things that you can't do to me no matter *how* much you, or society as a whole for that matter, would benefit.

Showing that capitalism is a just social system, then, will require more than simply showing that it creates a great amount of wealth *in the aggregate*. Like utility, we care not just about how much wealth is created, but how that wealth is distributed among separate persons. And this means that we need to settle on moral principles to distinguish just from unjust distributions. It is to that task that the readings in this section are devoted.

Further Reading

Cohen, G. A. (1997). Where the Action is: On the Site of Distributive Justice. *Philosophy and Public Affairs, 26*(1), 3–30.

Feinberg, J. (1963). "Justice and Personal Desert" in *Nomos VI: Justice*, C. J. Friedrich and J. W. Chapman (Eds), 69–97. New York: Atherton Press.

Fleischacker, S. (2004). *A Short History of Distributive Justice*. Cambridge: Harvard University Press.

Goodin, R. E. (1995). *Utilitarianism as a Public Philosophy*. Cambridge: Cambridge University Press.

Hayek, F. A. (1976). *Law, Legislation and Liberty, Vol. 2: The Mirage of Social Justice*. London: Routledge & Kegan Paul.

Lamont, J. (1994). The Concept of Desert in Distributive Justice. *Philosophical Quarterly, 44*(174), 45–64.

Miller, D. (1976). *Social Justice*. Oxford: Oxford University Press.

Miller, D. (1999). *Principles of Social Justice*. Cambridge: Harvard University Press.

Murray, C. (2006). *In Our Hands: A Plan to Replace the Welfare State*. Washington, D.C.: The AEI Press.

Nozick, R. (1974). *Anarchy, State, and Utopia*. New York: Basic Books.

Rawls, J. (1971). *A Theory of Justice* (1st ed.). Cambridge: Belknap Press.

Roemer, J. E. (1996). *Theories of Distributive Justice*. Cambridge: Harvard University Press.

Sen, A., & Williams, B. (1982). *Utilitarianism and Beyond*. Cambridge: Cambridge University Press.

Tomasi, J. (2012). *Free Market Fairness*. Princeton: Princeton University Press.

Van Parijs, P. (1995). *Real Freedom for All: What (if Anything) Can Justify Capitalism?* Oxford: Oxford University Press.

Chapter 29

Robert Nozick

THE ENTITLEMENT THEORY OF JUSTICE

Robert Nozick (1938–2002) was a professor of philosophy at Harvard University for almost his entire professional career. He wrote widely in such areas as epistemology and decision theory, but his best known work is *Anarchy, State, and Utopia* (1974), a book-length exploration of libertarian political theory. In this excerpt, Nozick sets forth his "entitlement theory" of justice, which holds that the justice of a distribution of wealth is entirely determined by the historical process by which it came about. Non-historical, patterned principles, Nozick argues, require continual interference in people's liberty to maintain and should therefore be rejected.

The minimal state is the most extensive state that can be justified. Any state more extensive violates people's rights. Yet many persons have put forth reasons purporting to justify a more extensive state. It is impossible within the compass of this book to examine all the reasons that have been put forth. Therefore, I shall focus upon those generally acknowledged to be most weighty and influential, to see precisely wherein they fail. In this chapter we consider the claim that a more extensive state is justified, because necessary (or the best instrument) to achieve distributive justice; in the next chapter we shall take up diverse other claims.

The term "distributive justice" is not a neutral one. Hearing the term "distribution," most people presume that some thing or mechanism uses some principle or criterion to give out a supply of things. Into this process of distributing shares some error may have crept. So it is an open question, at least, whether redistribution should take place; whether we should do again what has already been done once, though poorly. However, we are not in the position of children who have been given portions of pie by someone who now makes last minute adjustments to rectify careless cutting. There is no central distribution, no person or group entitled to control all the resources, jointly deciding how they are to be doled out. What each person gets, he gets from others who give to him in exchange for something, or as a gift. In a free society, diverse persons control different resources, and new holdings arise out of the voluntary exchanges and actions of persons. There is no more a distributing or distribution of shares than there is a distributing of mates in a society in which persons choose whom they shall marry. The total result is the product of many individual decisions which the different individuals involved are entitled to make. Some uses of the term "distribution," it is true, do not imply a previous distributing appropriately judged by some criterion (for example, "probability distribution"); nevertheless, despite the title of this chapter, it would be best to use a terminology that clearly is neutral. We shall speak of people's holdings; a principle of justice in holdings describes (part of) what justice tells us (requires) about holdings. I shall state first what I take to be the correct view about justice in holdings, and then turn to the discussion of alternate views.[1]

Section I

The Entitlement Theory

The subject of justice in holdings consists of three major topics. The first is the original acquisition of holdings, the appropriation of unheld things. This includes the issues of how unheld things may come to be held, the process, or processes, by which unheld things may come to be held, the things that may come to be held by these processes, the extent of what comes to be held by a particular process, and so on. We shall refer to the complicated truth about this topic, which we shall not formulate here, as the principle of justice in acquisition. The second topic concerns the transfer of holdings from one person to another. By what processes may a person transfer holdings to another? How may a person acquire a holding from another who holds it? Under this topic come general descriptions of voluntary exchange, and gift and (on the other hand) fraud, as well as reference to particular conventional details fixed upon in a given society. The complicated truth about this subject (with place-holders for conventional details) we shall call the principle of justice in transfer. (And we shall suppose it also includes principles governing how a person may divest himself of a holding, passing it into an unheld state.)

If the world were wholly just, the following inductive definition would exhaustively cover the subject of justice in holdings.

1.   A person who acquires a holding in accordance with the principle of justice in acquisition is entitled to that holding.

2.   A person who acquires a holding in accordance with the principle of justice in transfer, from someone else entitled to the holding, is entitled to the holding.

3.   No one is entitled to a holding except by (repeated) applications of 1 and 2.

The complete principle of distributive justice would say simply that a distribution is just if everyone is entitled to the holdings they possess under the distribution.

A distribution is just if it arises from another just distribution by legitimate means. The legitimate means of moving from one distribution to another are specified by the principle of justice in transfer. The legitimate first "moves" are specified by the principle of justice in acquisition.[2]

Whatever arises from a just situation by just steps is itself just. The means of change specified by the principle of justice in transfer preserve justice. As correct rules of inference are truth-preserving, and any conclusion deduced via repeated application of such rules from only true premises is itself true, so the means of transition from one situation to another specified by the principle of justice in transfer are justice-preserving, and any situation actually arising from repeated transitions in accordance with the principle from a just situation is itself just. The parallel between justice-preserving transformations and truth-preserving transformations illuminates where it fails as well as where it holds. That a conclusion could have been deduced by truth-preserving means from premises that are true suffices to show its truth. That from a just situation a situation could have arisen via justice-preserving means does not suffice to show its justice. The fact that a thief's victims voluntarily could have presented him with gifts does not entitle the thief to his ill-gotten gains. Justice in holdings is historical; it depends upon what actually has happened. We shall return to this point later.

Not all actual situations are generated in accordance with the two principles of justice in holdings: the principle of justice in acquisition and the principle of justice in transfer. Some people steal from others, or defraud them, or enslave them, seizing their product and preventing them from living as they choose, or forcibly exclude others from competing in exchanges. None of these are permissible modes of transition from one situation to another. And some persons acquire holdings by means not sanctioned by the principle of justice in acquisition. The existence of past injustice (previous violations of the first two principles of justice in holdings) raises the third major topic under justice in holdings: the rectification of injustice in holdings. If past injustice has shaped present holdings in various ways, some identifiable and some not, what now, if anything, ought to be done to rectify these injustices? What obligations do the performers of injustice have toward those whose position is worse than it would have been had the injustice not been done? Or, than it would have been had compensation been paid promptly? How, if at all, do things change if the beneficiaries and those made worse off are not the direct parties in the act of injustice, but, for example, their descendants? Is an injustice done to someone whose holding was itself based upon an unrectified injustice? How far back must one go in wiping clean the historical slate of injustices? What may victims of injustice permissibly do in order to rectify the injustices being done to them, including the many injustices done by persons acting through their government? I do not know of a thorough or theoretically sophisticated treatment of such issues.[3] Idealizing greatly, let us suppose theoretical investigation will produce a principle of rectification. This principle uses historical information about previous situations and injustices done in them (as defined by the first two principles of justice and rights against interference), and information about the actual course of events that flowed from these injustices, until the present, and it yields a description (or descriptions) of holdings in the society. The principle of rectification presumably will make use of its best estimate of subjunctive information about what would have occurred (or a probability distribution over what might have occurred, using the expected value) if the injustice had not taken place. If the actual description of holdings turns out not to be one of the descriptions yielded by the principle, then one of the descriptions yielded must be realized.[4]

The general outlines of the theory of justice in holdings are that the holdings of a person are just if he is entitled to them by the principles of justice in acquisition and transfer, or by the principle of rectification of injustice (as specified by the first two principles). If each person's holdings are just, then the total set (distribution) of holdings is just. To turn these general outlines into a specific theory we would have to specify the details of each of the three principles of justice in holdings: the principle of acquisition of holdings, the principle of transfer of holdings, and the principle of rectification of violations of the first two principles. I shall not attempt that task here. (Locke's principle of justice in acquisition is discussed below.)

Historical Principles and End-Result Principles

The general outlines of the entitlement theory illuminate the nature and defects of other conceptions of distributive justice. The entitlement theory of justice in distribution is historical; whether a distribution is just depends upon how it came about. In contrast, current time-slice principles of justice hold that the justice of a distribution is determined by how things are distributed (who has what) as judged by some structural principle(s) of just distribution. A utilitarian who judges between any two distributions by seeing which has the greater sum of utility and, if the sums tie, applies some fixed equality criterion to choose the more equal distribution, would hold a current time-slice principle of justice. As would someone who had a fixed schedule of trade-offs between the sum of happiness and equality.

According to a current time-slice principle, all that needs to be looked at, in judging the justice of a distribution, is who ends up with what; in comparing any two distributions one need look only at the matrix presenting the distributions. No further information need be fed into a principle of justice. It is a consequence of such principles of justice that any two structurally identical distributions are equally just. (Two distributions are structurally identical if they present the same profile, but perhaps have different persons occupying the particular slots. My having ten and your having five, and my having five and your having ten are structurally identical distributions.) Welfare economics is the theory of current time-slice principles of justice. The subject is conceived as operating on matrices representing only current information about distribution. This, as well as some of the usual conditions (for example, the choice of distribution is invariant under relabeling of columns), guarantees that welfare economics will be a current time-slice theory, with all of its inadequacies.

Most persons do not accept current time-slice principles as constituting the whole story about distributive shares. They think it relevant in assessing the justice of a situation to consider not only the distribution it embodies, but also how that distribution came about. If some persons are in prison for murder or war crimes, we do not say that to assess the justice of the distribution in the society we must look only at what this person has, and that person has, and that person has . . . at the current time. We think it relevant to ask whether someone did something so that he *deserved* to be punished, deserved to have a lower share. Most will agree to the relevance of further information with regard to punishments and penalties. Consider also desired things. One traditional socialist view is that workers are entitled to the product and full fruits of their labor; they have earned it; a distribution is unjust if it does not give the workers what they are entitled to. Such entitlements are based

upon some past history. No socialist holding this view would find it comforting to be told that because the actual distribution A happens to coincide structurally with the one he desires D, A therefore is no less just than D; it differs only in that the "parasitic" owners of capital receive under A what the workers are entitled to under D, and the workers receive under A what the owners are entitled to under D, namely very little. This socialist rightly, in my view, holds onto the notions of earning, producing, entitlement, desert, and so forth, and he rejects current time-slice principles that look only to the structure of the resulting set of holdings. (The set of holdings resulting from what? Isn't it implausible that how holdings are produced and come to exist has no effect at all on who should hold what?) His mistake lies in his view of what entitlements arise out of what sorts of productive processes.

We construe the position we discuss too narrowly by speaking of *current* time-slice principles. Nothing is changed if structural principles operate upon a time sequence of current time-slice profiles and, for example, give someone more now to counterbalance the less he has had earlier. A utilitarian or an egalitarian or any mixture of the two over time will inherit the difficulties of his more myopic comrades. He is not helped by the fact that *some* of the information others consider relevant in assessing a distribution is reflected, unrecoverably, in past matrices. Henceforth, we shall refer to such unhistorical principles of distributive justice, including the current time-slice principles, as *end-result principles* or *end-state principles*.

In contrast to end-result principles of justice, historical principles of justice hold that past circumstances or actions of people can create differential entitlements or differential deserts to things. An injustice can be worked by moving from one distribution to another structurally identical one, for the second, in profile the same, may violate people's entitlements or deserts; it may not fit the actual history.

Patterning

The entitlement principles of justice in holdings that we have sketched are historical principles of justice. To better understand their precise character, we shall distinguish them from another subclass of the historical principles. Consider, as an example, the principle of distribution according to moral merit. This principle requires that total distributive shares vary directly with moral merit; no person should have a greater share than anyone whose moral merit is greater. (If moral merit could be not merely ordered but measured on an interval or ratio scale, stronger principles could be formulated.) Or consider the principle that results by substituting "usefulness to society" for "moral merit" in the previous principle. Or instead of "distribute according to moral merit," or "distribute according to usefulness to society," we might consider "distribute according to the weighted sum of moral merit, usefulness to society, and need," with the weights of the different dimensions equal. Let us call a principle of distribution patterned if it specifies that a distribution is to vary along with some natural dimension, weighted sum of natural dimensions, or lexicographic ordering of natural dimensions. And let us say a distribution is patterned if it accords with some patterned principle. (I speak of natural dimensions, admittedly without a general criterion for them, because for any set of holdings some artificial dimensions can be gimmicked up to vary along with the distribution of the set.) The principle of distribution in accordance with moral merit is a patterned historical principle, which specifies a patterned distribution. "Distribute according to I.Q." is a patterned principle that looks to information not contained in distributional matrices. It is not historical, however, in that it does not look to any past actions creating differential entitlements to evaluate a distribution; it requires only distributional matrices whose columns are labeled by I.Q. scores. The distribution in a society, however, may be composed of such simple patterned distributions, without itself being simply patterned. Different sectors may operate different patterns, or some combination of patterns may operate in different proportions across a society. A distribution composed in this manner, from a small number of patterned distributions, we also shall term "patterned." And we extend the use of "pattern" to include the overall designs put forth by combinations of end-state principles.

Almost every suggested principle of distributive justice is patterned: to each according to his moral merit, or needs, or marginal product, or how hard he tries, or the weighted sum of the foregoing, and so on. The principle of entitlement we have sketched is not patterned.[5] There is no one natural dimension or weighted sum or combination of a small number of natural dimensions that yields the distributions generated in accordance with the principle of entitlement. The set of holdings that results when some persons receive their marginal products, others win at gambling, others receive a share of their mate's income, others receive gifts from foundations, others receive interest on loans, others receive gifts from admirers, others receive returns on investment, others make for themselves much of what they have, others find things, and so on, will not be patterned. Heavy strands of patterns will run through it; significant portions of the variance in holdings will be accounted for by pattern-variables. If most people most of the time choose to transfer some of their entitlements to others only in exchange for something from them, then a large part of what many people hold will vary with what they held that others wanted. More details are provided by the theory of marginal productivity. But gifts to relatives, charitable donations, bequests to children, and the like, are not best conceived, in the first instance, in this manner. Ignoring the strands of pattern, let us suppose for the moment that a distribution actually arrived at by the operation of the principle of entitlement is random with respect to any pattern. Though the resulting set of holdings will be unpatterned, it will not be incomprehensible, for it can be seen as arising from the operation of a small number of principles. These principles specify how an initial distribution may arise (the principle of acquisition of holdings) and how distributions may be transformed into others (the principle of transfer of holdings). The process whereby the set of holdings is generated will be intelligible, though the set of holdings itself that results from this process will be unpatterned.

The writings of F. A. Hayek focus less than is usually done upon what patterning distributive justice requires. Hayek argues that we cannot know enough about each person's situation to distribute to each according to his moral merit (but would justice demand we do so if we did have this knowledge?); and he goes on to say, "our objection is against all attempts to impress upon society a deliberately chosen pattern of distribution, whether it be an order of equality or of inequality."[6] However, Hayek concludes that in a free society there will be distribution in accordance with value rather than moral merit; that is, in accordance with the perceived value of a person's actions and services to others. Despite his rejection of a patterned conception of distributive justice, Hayek himself suggests a pattern he thinks justifiable: distribution in accordance with the perceived benefits given to others, leaving room for the complaint that a free society does not realize exactly this pattern. Stating this patterned strand of a free capitalist society more precisely, we get "To each according to how much he benefits others who have the resources for benefiting those who benefit them." This will seem arbitrary unless some acceptable initial set of holdings is specified, or unless it is held that the operation of the system over time washes out any significant effects from the initial set of holdings. As an example of the latter, if almost anyone would have bought a car from Henry Ford, the supposition that it was an arbitrary matter who held the money then (and so bought) would not place Henry Ford's earnings under a cloud. In any event, his coming to hold it is not arbitrary. Distribution according to benefits to others is a major patterned strand in a free capitalist society, as Hayek correctly points out, but it is only a strand and does not constitute the whole pattern of a system of entitlements (namely, inheritance, gifts for arbitrary reasons, charity, and so on) or a standard that one should insist a society fit. Will people tolerate for long a system yielding distributions that they believe are unpatterned?[7] No doubt people will not long accept a distribution they believe is unjust. People want their society to be and to look just. But must the look of justice reside in a resulting pattern rather than in the underlying generating principles? We are in no position to conclude that the inhabitants of a society embodying an entitlement conception of justice in holdings will find it unacceptable. Still, it must be granted that were people's reasons for transferring some of their holdings to others always irrational or arbitrary, we would find this disturbing. (Suppose people always determined what holdings they would transfer, and to whom, by using a random device.) We feel more comfortable upholding the justice of an entitlement system if most of the transfers under it are done for reasons. This does not mean necessarily that all deserve what holdings they receive. It means only that there is a purpose or point to someone's transferring a holding to one person rather than to another; that usually we can see what the transferrer thinks he's gaining, what cause he thinks he's serving, what goals he thinks he's helping to achieve, and so forth. Since in a capitalist society people often transfer holdings to others in accordance with how much they perceive these others benefiting them, the fabric constituted by the individual transactions and transfers is largely reasonable and intelligible.[8] (Gifts to loved ones, bequests to children, charity to the needy also are non-arbitrary components of the fabric.) In stressing the large strand of distribution in accordance with benefit to others, Hayek shows the point of many transfers, and so shows that the system of transfer of entitlements is not just spinning its gears aimlessly. The system of entitlements is defensible when constituted by the individual aims of individual transactions. No overarching aim is needed, no distributional pattern is required.

To think that the task of a theory of distributive justice is to fill in the blank in "to each according to his _____" is to be predisposed to search for a pattern; and the separate treatment of "from each according to his _____" treats production and distribution as two separate and independent issues. On an entitlement view these are not two separate questions. Whoever makes something, having bought or contracted for all other held resources used in the process (transferring some of his holdings for these cooperating factors), is entitled to it. The situation is not one of something's getting made, and there being an open question of who is to get it. Things come into the world already attached to people having entitlements over them. From the point of view of the historical entitlement conception of justice in holdings, those who start afresh to complete "to each according to his _____" treat objects as if they appeared from nowhere, out of nothing. A complete theory of justice might cover this limit case as well; perhaps here is a use for the usual conceptions of distributive justice.[9]

So entrenched are maxims of the usual form that perhaps we should present the entitlement conception as a competitor. Ignoring acquisition and rectification, we might say:

> From each according to what he chooses to do, to each according to what he makes for himself (perhaps with the contracted aid of others) and what others choose to do for him and choose to give him of what they've been given previously (under this maxim) and haven't yet expended or transferred.

This, the discerning reader will have noticed, has its defects as a slogan. So as a summary and great simplification (and not as a maxim with any independent meaning) we have:

> *From each as they choose, to each as they are chosen.*

How Liberty Upsets Patterns

It is not clear how those holding alternative conceptions of distributive justice can reject the entitlement conception of justice in holdings. For suppose a distribution favored by one of these non-entitlement conceptions is realized. Let us suppose it is your favorite one and let us call this distribution D_1; perhaps everyone has an equal share, perhaps shares vary in accordance with some dimension you treasure. Now suppose that Wilt Chamberlain is greatly in demand by basketball teams, being a great gate attraction. (Also suppose contracts run only for a year, with players being free agents.) He signs the following sort of contract with a team: In each home game, 25 cents from the price of each ticket of admission goes to him. (We ignore the question of whether he is "gouging" the owners, letting them look out for themselves.) The season starts, and people cheerfully attend his team's games; they buy their tickets, each time dropping a separate 25 cents of their admission price into a special box with Chamberlain's name on it. They are excited about seeing him play; it is worth the total admission price to them. Let us suppose that in one season one million persons attend his home games, and Wilt Chamberlain winds up with $250,000, a much larger sum than the average income and larger even than anyone else has. Is he entitled to this income? Is this new distribution, D_2, unjust? If so, why? There is no question about whether each of the people was entitled to the control over the resources they held in D_1; because that was the distribution (your favorite) that (for the purposes of argument) we assumed was acceptable. Each of these persons *chose* to give 25 cents of their money to Chamberlain. They could have spent it on going to the movies, or on candy bars, or on copies of *Dissent* magazine, or of *Monthly Review*. But they all, at least one million of them, converged on giving it to Wilt Chamberlain in exchange for watching him play basketball. If D_1 was a just distribution, and people voluntarily moved from it to D_2, transferring parts of their shares they were given under D_1 (what was it for if not to do something with?), isn't D_2 also just? If the people were entitled to dispose of the resources to which they were entitled (under D_1), didn't this include their being entitled to give it to, or exchange it with, Wilt Chamberlain? Can anyone else complain on grounds of justice? Each other person already has his legitimate share under D_1. Under D_1, there is nothing that anyone has that anyone else has a claim of justice against. After someone transfers something to Wilt Chamberlain, third parties *still* have their legitimate shares; *their* shares are not changed. By what process could such a transfer among two persons give rise to a legitimate claim of distributive justice on a portion of what was transferred, by a third party who had no claim of justice on any holding of the others *before* the transfer?[10] To cut off objections irrelevant here, we might imagine the exchanges occurring in a socialist society, after hours. After playing whatever basketball he does in his daily work, or doing whatever other daily work he does, Wilt Chamberlain decides to put in *overtime* to earn additional money. (First his work quota is set; he works time over that.) Or imagine it is a skilled juggler people like to see, who puts on shows after hours.

Why might someone work overtime in a society in which it is assumed their needs are satisfied? Perhaps because they care about things other than needs. I like to write in books that I read, and to have easy access to books for browsing at odd hours. It would be very pleasant and convenient to have the resources of Widener Library in my back yard. No society, I assume, will provide such resources close to each person who would like them as part of his regular allotment (under D_1). Thus, persons either must do

without some extra things that they want, or be allowed to do something extra to *get* some of these things. On what basis could the inequalities that would eventuate be forbidden? Notice also that small factories would spring up in a socialist society, unless forbidden. I melt down some of my personal possessions (under D_1) and build a machine out of the material. I offer you, and others, a philosophy lecture once a week in exchange for your cranking the handle on my machine, whose products I exchange for yet other things, and so on. (The raw materials used by the machine are given to me by others who possess them under D_1, in exchange for hearing lectures.) Each person might participate to gain things over and above their allotment under D_1. Some persons even might want to leave their job in socialist industry and work full time in this private sector. I shall say something more about these issues in the next chapter. Here I wish merely to note how private property even in means of production would occur in a socialist society that did not forbid people to use as they wished some of the resources they are given under the socialist distribution D_1.[11] The socialist society would have to forbid capitalist acts between consenting adults.

The general point illustrated by the Wilt Chamberlain example and the example of the entrepreneur in a socialist society is that no end-state principle or distributional patterned principle of justice can be continuously realized without continuous interference with people's lives. Any favored pattern would be transformed into one unfavored by the principle, by people choosing to act in various ways; for example, by people exchanging goods and services with other people, or giving things to other people, things the transferrers are entitled to under the favored distributional pattern. To maintain a pattern one must either continually interfere to stop people from transferring resources as they wish to, or continually (or periodically) interfere to take from some persons resources that others for some reason chose to transfer to them. (But if some time limit is to be set on how long people may keep resources others voluntarily transfer to them, why let them keep these resources for *any* period of time? Why not have immediate confiscation?) It might be objected that all persons voluntarily will choose to refrain from actions which would upset the pattern. This presupposes unrealistically (1) that all will most want to maintain the pattern (are those who don't to be "reeducated" or forced to undergo "self-criticism"?), (2) that each can gather enough information about his own actions and the ongoing activities of others to discover which of his actions will upset the pattern, and (3) that diverse and far-flung persons can coordinate their actions to dovetail into the pattern. Compare the manner in which the market is neutral among persons' desires, as it reflects and transmits widely scattered information via prices, and coordinates persons' activities.

It puts things perhaps a bit too strongly to say that every patterned (or end-state) principle is liable to be thwarted by the voluntary actions of the individual parties transferring some of their shares they receive under the principle. For perhaps some *very* weak patterns are not so thwarted.[12] Any distributional pattern with any egalitarian component is overturnable by the voluntary actions of individual persons over time; as is every patterned condition with sufficient content so as actually to have been proposed as presenting the central core of distributive justice. Still, given the possibility that some weak conditions or patterns may not be unstable in this way, it would be better to formulate an explicit description of the kind of interesting and contentful patterns under discussion, and to prove a theorem about their instability. Since the weaker the patterning, the more likely it is that the entitlement system itself satisfies it, a plausible conjecture is that any patterning either is unstable or is satisfied by the entitlement system.

[...]

Redistribution and Property Rights

Apparently, patterned principles allow people to choose to expend upon themselves, but not upon others, those resources they are entitled to (or rather, receive) under some favored distributional pattern D_1. For if each of several persons chooses to expend some of his D_1 resources upon one other person, then that other person will receive more than his D_1 share, disturbing the favored distributional pattern. Maintaining a distributional pattern is individualism with a vengeance! Patterned distributional principles do not give people what entitlement principles do, only better distributed. For they do not give the right to choose what to do with what one has; they do not give the right to choose to pursue an end involving (intrinsically, or as a means) the enhancement of another's position. To such views, families are disturbing; for within a family occur transfers that upset the favored distributional pattern. Either families themselves become units to which distribution takes place, the column occupiers (on what rationale?), or loving behavior is forbidden. We should note in passing the ambivalent position of radicals toward the family. Its loving relationships are seen as a model to be emulated and extended across the whole society, at the same time that it is denounced as a suffocating institution to be broken and condemned as a focus of parochial concerns that interfere with achieving radical goals. Need we say that it is not appropriate to enforce across the wider society the relationships of love and care appropriate within a family, relationships which are voluntarily undertaken?[13] Incidentally, love is an interesting instance of another relationship that is historical, in that (like justice) it depends upon what actually occurred. An adult may come to love another because of the other's characteristics; but it is the other person, and not the characteristics, that is loved.[14] The love is not transferrable to someone else with the same characteristics, even to one who "scores" higher for these characteristics. And the love endures through changes of the characteristics that gave rise to it. One loves the particular person one actually encountered. Why love is historical, attaching to persons in this way and not to characteristics, is an interesting and puzzling question.

Proponents of patterned principles of distributive justice focus upon criteria for determining who is to receive holdings; they consider the reasons for which someone should have something, and also the total picture of holdings. Whether or not it is better to give than to receive, proponents of patterned principles ignore giving altogether. In considering the distribution of goods, income, and so forth, their theories are theories of recipient justice; they completely ignore any right a person might have to give something to someone. Even in exchanges where each party is simultaneously giver and recipient, patterned principles of justice focus only upon the recipient role and its supposed rights. Thus discussions tend to focus on whether people (should) have a right to inherit, rather than on whether people (should) have a right to bequeath or on whether persons who have a right to hold also have a right to choose that others hold in their place. I lack a good explanation of why the usual theories of distributive justice are so recipient oriented; ignoring givers and transferrers and their rights is of a piece with ignoring producers and their entitlements. But why is it *all* ignored?

Patterned principles of distributive justice necessitate redistributive activities. The likelihood is small that any actual freely-arrived-at set of holdings fits a given pattern; and the likelihood is nil that it will continue to fit the pattern as people exchange and give. From the point of view of an entitlement theory, redistribution is a serious matter indeed, involving, as it does, the violation of people's rights. (An exception is those takings that fall under the principle of the rectification of injustices.) From other points of view, also, it is serious.

Taxation of earnings from labor is on a par with forced labor.[15] Some persons find this claim

obviously true: taking the earnings of n hours labor is like taking n hours from the person; it is like forcing the person to work n hours for another's purpose. Others find the claim absurd. But even these, if they object to forced labor, would oppose forcing unemployed hippies to work for the benefit of the needy.[16] And they would also object to forcing each person to work five extra hours each week for the benefit of the needy. But a system that takes five hours' wages in taxes does not seem to them like one that forces someone to work five hours, since it offers the person forced a wider range of choice in activities than does taxation in kind with the particular labor specified. (But we can imagine a gradation of systems of forced labor, from one that specifies a particular activity, to one that gives a choice among two activities, to . . .; and so on up.) Furthermore, people envisage a system with something like a proportional tax on everything above the amount necessary for basic needs. Some think this does not force someone to work extra hours, since there is no fixed number of extra hours he is forced to work, and since he can avoid the tax entirely by earning only enough to cover his basic needs. This is a very uncharacteristic view of forcing for those who *also* think people are forced to do something *whenever* the alternatives they face are considerably worse. However, *neither* view is correct. The fact that others intentionally intervene, in violation of a side constraint against aggression, to threaten force to limit the alternatives, in this case to paying taxes or (presumably the worse alternative) bare subsistence, makes the taxation system one of forced labor and distinguishes it from other cases of limited choices which are not forcings.[17]

The man who chooses to work longer to gain an income more than sufficient for his basic needs prefers some extra goods or services to the leisure and activities he could perform during the possible non-working hours; whereas the man who chooses not to work the extra time prefers the leisure activities to the extra goods or services he could acquire by working more. Given this, if it would be illegitimate for a tax system to seize some of a man's leisure (forced labor) for the purpose of serving the needy, how can it be legitimate for a tax system to seize some of a man's goods for that purpose? Why should we treat the man whose happiness requires certain material goods or services differently from the man whose preferences and desires make such goods unnecessary for his happiness? Why should the man who prefers seeing a movie (and who has to earn money for a ticket) be open to the required call to aid the needy, while the person who prefers looking at a sunset (and hence need earn no extra money) is not? Indeed, isn't it surprising that redistributionists choose to ignore the man whose pleasures are so easily attainable without extra labor, while adding yet another burden to the poor unfortunate who must work for his pleasures? If anything, one would have expected the reverse. Why is the person with the non-material or non-consumption desire allowed to proceed unimpeded to his most favored feasible alternative, whereas the man whose pleasures or desires involve material things and who must work for extra money (thereby serving whomever considers his activities valuable enough to pay him) is constrained in what he can realize? Perhaps there is no difference in principle. And perhaps some think the answer concerns merely administrative convenience. (These questions and issues will not disturb those who think that forced labor to serve the needy or to realize some favored end-state pattern is acceptable.) In a fuller discussion we would have (and want) to extend our argument to include interest, entrepreneurial profits, and so on. Those who doubt that this extension can be carried through, and who draw the line here at taxation of income from labor, will have to state rather complicated patterned *historical* principles of distributive justice, since end-state principles would not distinguish *sources* of income in any way. It is enough for now to get away from end-state principles and to make clear how various patterned principles are dependent upon particular views about the sources or the illegitimacy or the lesser legitimacy of profits, interest, and so on; which particular views may well be mistaken.

What sort of right over others does a legally institutionalized end-state pattern give one? The central core of the notion of a property right in X, relative to which other parts of the notion are to be explained, is the right to determine what shall be done with X; the right to choose which of the constrained set of options concerning X shall be realized or attempted.[18] The constraints are set by other principles or laws operating in the society; in our theory, by the Lockean rights people possess (under the minimal state). My property rights in my knife allow me to leave it where I will, but not in your chest. I may choose which of the acceptable options involving the knife is to be realized. This notion of property helps us to understand why earlier theorists spoke of people as having property in themselves and their labor. They viewed each person as having a right to decide what would become of himself and what he would do, and as having a right to reap the benefits of what he did.

This right of selecting the alternative to be realized from the constrained set of alternatives may be held by an *individual* or by a *group* with some procedure for reaching a joint decision; or the right may be passed back and forth, so that one year I decide what's to become of X, and the next year you do (with the alternative of destruction, perhaps, being excluded). Or, during the same time period, some types of decisions about X may be made by me, and others by you. And so on. We lack an adequate, fruitful, analytical apparatus for classifying the *types* of constraints on the set of options among which choices are to be made, and the *types* of ways decision powers can be held, divided, and amalgamated. A *theory* of property would, among other things, contain such a classification of constraints and decision modes, and from a small number of principles would follow a host of interesting statements about the *consequences* and effects of certain combinations of constraints and modes of decision.

When end-result principles of distributive justice are built into the legal structure of a society, they (as do most patterned principles) give each citizen an enforceable claim to some portion of the total social product; that is, to some portion of the sum total of the individually and jointly made products. This total product is produced by individuals laboring, using means of production others have saved to bring into existence, by people organizing production or creating means to produce new things or things in a new way. It is on this batch of individual activities that patterned distributional principles give each individual an enforceable claim. Each person has a claim to the activities and the products of other persons, independently of whether the other persons enter into particular relationships that give rise to these claims, and independently of whether they voluntarily take these claims upon themselves, in charity or in exchange for something.

Whether it is done through taxation on wages or on wages over a certain amount, or through seizure of profits, or through there being a big *social pot* so that it's not clear what's coming from where and what's going where, patterned principles of distributive justice involve appropriating the actions of other persons. Seizing the results of someone's labor is equivalent to seizing hours from him and directing him to carry on various activities. If people force you to do certain work, or unrewarded work, for a certain period of time, they decide what you are to do and what purposes your work is to serve apart from your decisions. This process whereby they take this decision from you makes them a *part-owner* of you; it gives them a property right in you. Just as having such partial control and power of decision, by right, over an animal or inanimate object would be to have a property right in it.

End-state and most patterned principles of distributive justice institute (partial) ownership by others of people and their actions and labor. These principles involve a shift from the classical liberals' notion of self-ownership to a notion of (partial) property rights in *other* people.

Considerations such as these confront end-state and other patterned conceptions of justice with the question of whether the actions necessary to achieve the selected pattern don't themselves violate moral side constraints. Any view holding that there are moral side constraints on actions, that not all moral considerations can be built into end states that are to be achieved (see Chapter 3, pp. 28–30 [pp. 174–5 of this volume]), must face the possibility that some of its goals are not achievable by any morally permissible available means. An entitlement theorist will face such conflicts in a society that deviates from the principles of justice for the generation of holdings, if and only if the only actions available to realize the principles themselves violate some moral constraints. Since deviation from the first two principles of justice (in acquisition and transfer) will involve other persons' direct and aggressive intervention to violate rights, and since moral constraints will not exclude defensive or retributive action in such cases, the entitlement theorist's problem rarely will be pressing. And whatever difficulties he has in applying the principle of rectification to persons who did not themselves violate the first two principles are difficulties in balancing the conflicting considerations so as correctly to formulate the complex principle of rectification itself; he will not violate moral side constraints by applying the principle. Proponents of patterned conceptions of justice, however, often will face head-on clashes (and poignant ones if they cherish each party to the clash) between moral side constraints on how individuals may be treated and their patterned conception of justice that presents an end state or other pattern that *must* be realized.

May a person emigrate from a nation that has institutionalized some end-state or patterned distributional principle? For some principles (for example, Hayek's) emigration presents no theoretical problem. But for others it is a tricky matter. Consider a nation having a compulsory scheme of minimal social provision to aid the neediest (or one organized so as to maximize the position of the worst-off group); no one may opt out of participating in it. (None may say, "Don't compel me to contribute to others and don't provide for me via this compulsory mechanism if I am in need.") Everyone above a certain level is forced to contribute to aid the needy. But if emigration from the country were allowed, anyone could choose to move to another country that did not have compulsory social provision but otherwise was (as much as possible) identical. In such a case, the person's *only* motive for leaving would be to avoid participating in the compulsory scheme of social provision. And if he does leave, the needy in his initial country will receive no (compelled) help from him. What rationale yields the result that the person be permitted to emigrate, yet forbidden to stay and opt out of the compulsory scheme of social provision? If providing for the needy is of overriding importance, this does militate against allowing internal opting out; but it also speaks against allowing external emigration. (Would it also support, to some extent, the kidnapping of persons living in a place without compulsory social provision, who could be forced to make a contribution to the needy in your community?) Perhaps the crucial component of the position that allows emigration solely to avoid certain arrangements, while not allowing anyone internally to opt out of them, is a concern for fraternal feelings within the country. "We don't want anyone here who doesn't contribute, who doesn't care enough about the others to contribute." That concern, in this case, would have to be tied to the view that forced aiding tends to produce fraternal feelings between the aided and the aider (or perhaps merely to the view that the knowledge that someone or other voluntarily is not aiding produces unfraternal feelings).

Notes

1 The reader who has looked ahead and seen that the second part of this chapter [not included in this volume] discusses Rawls' theory mistakenly may think that every remark or argument in the first part against alternative theories of justice is meant to apply to, or anticipate, a criticism of Rawls' theory. This is not so; there are other theories also worth criticizing.

2 Applications of the principle of justice in acquisition may also occur as part of the move from one distribution to another. You may find an unheld thing now and appropriate it. Acquisitions also are to be understood as included when, to simplify, I speak only of transitions by transfers.

3 See, however, the useful book by Boris Bittker, *The Case for Black Reparations* (New York: Random House, 1973).

4 If the principle of rectification of violations of the first two principles yields more than one description of holdings, then some choice must be made as to which of these is to be realized. Perhaps the sort of considerations about distributive justice and equality that I argue against play a legitimate role in *this* subsidiary choice. Similarly, there may be room for such considerations in deciding which otherwise arbitrary features a statute will embody, when such features are unavoidable because other considerations do not specify a precise line; yet a line must be drawn.

5 One might try to squeeze a patterned conception of distributive justice into the framework of the entitlement conception, by formulating a gimmicky obligatory "principle of transfer" that would lead to the pattern. For example, the principle that if one has more than the mean income one must transfer everything one holds above the mean to persons below the mean so as to bring them up to (but not over) the mean. We can formulate a criterion for a "principle of transfer" to rule out such obligatory transfers, or we can say that no correct principle of transfer, no principle of transfer in a free society will be like this. The former is probably the better course, though the latter also is true.

   Alternatively, one might think to make the entitlement conception instantiate a pattern, by using matrix entries that express the relative strength of a person's entitlements as measured by some real-valued function. But even if the limitation to natural dimensions failed to exclude this function, the resulting edifice would *not* capture our system of entitlements to *particular* things.

6   F. A. Hayek, *The Constitution of Liberty* (Chicago: University of Chicago Press, 1960), p. 87.

7   This question does not imply that they will tolerate any and every patterned distribution. In discussing Hayek's views, Irving Kristol has recently speculated that people will not long tolerate a system that yields distributions patterned in accordance with value rather than merit. (" 'When Virtue Loses All Her Loveliness' – Some Reflections on Capitalism and 'The Free Society,' " *The Public Interest*, Fall 1970, pp. 3–15.) Kristol, following some remarks of Hayek's, equates the merit system with justice. Since some case can be made for the external standard of distribution in accordance with benefit to others, we ask about a weaker (and therefore more plausible) hypothesis.

8   We certainly benefit because great economic incentives operate to get others to spend much time and energy to figure out how to serve us by providing things we will want to pay for. It is not mere paradox mongering to wonder whether capitalism should be criticized for most rewarding and hence encouraging, not individualists like Thoreau who go about their own lives, but people who are occupied with serving others and winning them as customers. But to defend capitalism one need not think businessmen are the finest human types. (I do not mean to join here the general maligning of businessmen, either.) Those who think the finest should acquire the most can try to convince their fellows to transfer resources in accordance with *that* principle.

9   Varying situations continuously from that limit situation to our own would force us to make explicit the underlying rationale of entitlements and to consider whether entitlement considerations lexicographically precede the considerations of the usual theories of distributive justice, so that the *slightest* strand of entitlement outweighs the considerations of the usual theories of distributive justice.

10   Might not a transfer have instrumental effects on a third party, changing his feasible options? (But

what if the two parties to the transfer independently had used their holdings in this fashion?) I discuss this question below, but note here that this question concedes the point for distributions of ultimate intrinsic non-instrumental goods (pure utility experiences, so to speak) that are transferrable. It also might be objected that the transfer might make a third party more envious because it worsens his position relative to someone else. I find it incomprehensible how this can be thought to involve a claim of justice. On envy, see Chapter 8 [not included in this volume].

Here and elsewhere in this chapter, a theory which incorporates elements of pure procedural justice might find what I say acceptable, if kept in its proper place; that is, if background institutions exist to ensure the satisfaction of certain conditions on distributive shares. But if these institutions are not themselves the sum or invisible-hand result of people's voluntary (non-aggressive) actions, the constraints they impose require justification. At no point does *our* argument assume any background institutions more extensive than those of the minimal night-watchman state, a state limited to protecting persons against murder, assault, theft, fraud, and so forth.

11   See the selection from John Henry MacKay's novel, *The Anarchists*, reprinted in Leonard Krimmerman and Lewis Perry, eds., *Patterns of Anarchy* (New York: Doubleday Anchor Books, 1966), in which an individualist anarchist presses upon a communist anarchist the following question: "Would you, in the system of society which you call 'free Communism' prevent individuals from exchanging their labor among themselves by means of their own medium of exchange? And further: Would you prevent them from occupying land for the purpose of personal use?" The novel continues: "[the] question was not to be escaped. If he answered 'Yes!' he admitted that society had the right of control over the individual and threw overboard the autonomy of the individual which he had always zealously defended; if on the other hand, he answered 'No!' he admitted the right of private property which he had just denied so emphatically. . . . Then he answered 'In Anarchy any number of men must have the right of forming a voluntary association, and so realizing their ideas

in practice. Nor can I understand how any one could justly be driven from the land and house which he uses and occupies . . . every serious man must declare himself: for Socialism, and thereby for force and against liberty, or for Anarchism, and thereby for liberty and against force.' " In contrast, we find Noam Chomsky writing, "Any consistent anarchist must oppose private ownership of the means of production," "the consistent anarchist then . . . will be a socialist . . . of a particular sort." Introduction to Daniel Guerin, *Anarchism: From Theory to Practice* (New York: Monthly Review Press, 1970), pages xiii, xv.

12 Is the patterned principle stable that requires merely that a distribution be Pareto-optimal? One person might give another a gift or bequest that the second could exchange with a third to their mutual benefit. Before the second makes this exchange, there is not Pareto-optimality. Is a stable pattern presented by a principle choosing that among the Pareto-optimal positions that satisfies some further condition C? It may seem that there cannot be a counterexample, for won't any voluntary exchange made away from a situation show that the first situation wasn't Pareto-optimal? (Ignore the implausibility of this last claim for the case of bequests.) But principles are to be satisfied over time, during which new possibilities arise. A distribution that at one time satisfies the criterion of Pareto-optimality might not do so when some new possibilities arise (Wilt Chamberlain grows up and starts playing basketball); and though people's activities will tend to move then to a new Pareto-optimal position, *this* new one need not satisfy the contentful condition C. Continual interference will be needed to insure the continual satisfaction of C. (The theoretical possibility of a pattern's being maintained by some invisible-hand process that brings it back to an equilibrium that fits the pattern when deviations occur should be investigated.)

13 One indication of the stringency of Rawls' difference principle, which we attend to in the second part of this chapter [not included in this volume], is its inappropriateness as a governing principle even within a family of individuals who love one another. Should a family devote its resources to maximizing the position of its least well off and least talented child, holding back the other children or using resources for their education and development only if they will follow a policy through their lifetimes of maximizing the position of their least fortunate sibling? Surely not. How then can this even be considered as the appropriate policy for enforcement in the wider society? (I discuss below what I think would be Rawls' reply: that some principles apply at the macro level which do not apply to micro-situations.)

14 See Gregory Vlastos, "The Individual as an Object of Love in Plato" in his *Platonic Studies* (Princeton: Princeton University Press, 1973), pp. 3–34.

15 I am unsure as to whether the arguments I present below show that such taxation merely *is* forced labor; so that "is on a par with" means "is one kind of." Or alternatively, whether the arguments emphasize the great similarities between such taxation and forced labor, to show it is plausible and illuminating to view such taxation in the light of forced labor. This latter approach would remind one of how John Wisdom conceives of the claims of metaphysicians.

16 Nothing hangs on the fact that here and elsewhere I speak loosely of *needs*, since I go on, each time, to reject the criterion of justice which includes it. If, however, something did depend upon the notion, one would want to examine it more carefully. For a skeptical view, see Kenneth Minogue, *The Liberal Mind*, (New York: Random House, 1963), pp. 103–12.

17 Oppression will be less noticeable if the background institutions do not prohibit certain actions that upset the patterning (various exchanges or transfers of entitlement), but rather prevent them from being done, by nullifying them.

18 On the themes in this and the next paragraph, see the writings of Armen Alchian.

Chapter 30

Friedrich Hayek

THE ATAVISM OF SOCIAL JUSTICE

Friedrich Hayek (1899–1992) was an Austrian economist and social theorist, and winner of the Nobel prize in economics in 1974. He is best known for his work on the knowledge-generating function of a free-market price system, but also produced very influential work in jurisprudence and cognitive science. In this essay (published in 1976), Hayek criticizes the notion of "social justice" as a doctrine that was appropriate to the small primitive groups of our distant ancestral past, but not to a modern society governed by abstract rules.

1

To discover the meaning of what is called "social justice" has been one of my chief preoccupations for more than ten years. I have failed in this endeavor – or, rather, have reached the conclusion that, with reference to a society of free men, the phrase has no meaning whatever. The search for the reason why the word has nevertheless for something like a century dominated political discussion, and has everywhere been successfully used to advance claims of particular groups for a larger share in the good things of life, remains, however, a very interesting one. It is this question with which I shall here chiefly concern myself.

But I must at first briefly explain, as I attempt to demonstrate at length in volume 2 of my *Law, Legislation and Liberty*, about to be published, why I have come to regard "social justice" as nothing more than an empty formula, conventionally used to assert that a particular claim is justified without giving any reason. Indeed that volume, which bears the sub-title *The Mirage of Social Justice,*

is mainly intended to convince intellectuals that the concept of "social justice," which they are so fond of using, is intellectually disreputable. Some of course have already tumbled to this; but with the unfortunate result that, since "social" justice is the only kind of justice they have ever thought of, they have been led to the conclusion that all uses of the term justice have no meaningful content. I have therefore been forced to show in the same book that rules of just individual conduct are as indispensable to the preservation of a peaceful society of free men as endeavors to realize "social" justice are incompatible with it.

The term "social justice" is today generally used as a synonym of what used to be called "distributive justice." The latter term perhaps gives a somewhat better idea of what can be meant by it, and at the same time shows why it can have no application to the results of a market economy: there can be no distributive justice where no one distributes. Justice has meaning only as a rule of human conduct, and no conceivable rules for the conduct of individuals supplying each other with goods and services in a market economy would produce a distribution which could be meaningfully described as just or unjust. Individuals might conduct themselves as justly as possible, but as the results for separate individuals would be neither intended nor foreseeable by others, the resulting state of affairs could neither be called just nor unjust.

The complete emptiness of the phrase "social justice" shows itself in the fact that no agreement exists about what social justice requires in particular instances; also that there is no known test by which to decide who is right if people differ, and that no preconceived scheme of distribution could be effectively devised in a society whose individuals are free, in the sense of being allowed to use their own knowledge for their own purposes. Indeed, individual moral responsibility for one's actions is incompatible with the realization of any such desired overall pattern of distribution.

A little inquiry shows that, though a great many people are dissatisfied with the existing pattern of distribution, none of them has really any clear idea of what pattern he would regard as just. All that we find are intuitive assessments of individual cases as unjust. No one has yet found even a single general rule from which we could derive what is "socially just" in all particular instances that would fall under it – except the rule of "equal pay for equal work." Free competition, precluding all that regard for merit or need and the like, on which demands for social justice are based, tends to enforce the equal pay rule.

2

The reason why most people continue firmly to believe in "social justice," even after they discover that they do not really know what the phrase means, is that they think if almost everyone else believes in it, there must be something in the phrase. The ground for this almost universal acceptance of a belief, the significance of which people do not understand, is that we have all

inherited from an earlier different type of society, in which man existed very much longer than in the present one, some now deeply ingrained instincts which are inapplicable to our present civilization. In fact, man emerged from primitive society when in certain conditions increasing numbers succeeded by disregarding those very principles which had held the old groups together.

We must not forget that before the last 10,000 years, during which man has developed agriculture, towns and ultimately the "Great Society," he existed for at least a hundred times as long in small food-sharing hunting bands of 50 or so, with a strict order of dominance within the defended common territory of the band. The needs of this ancient primitive kind of society determined much of the moral feelings which still govern us, and which we approve in others. It was a grouping in which, at least for all males, the common pursuit of a perceived physical common object under the direction of the alpha male was as much a condition of its continued existence as the assignment of different shares in the prey to the different members according to their importance for the survival of the band. It is more than probable that many of the moral feelings then acquired have not merely been culturally transmitted by teaching or imitation, but have become innate or genetically determined.

But not all that is natural to us in this sense is therefore necessarily in different circumstances good or beneficial for the propagation of the species. In its primitive form the little band indeed did possess what is still attractive to so many people: a unitary purpose, or a common hierarchy of ends, and a deliberate sharing of means according to a common view of individual merits. These foundations of its coherence, however, also imposed limits on the possible development of this form of society. The events to which the group could adapt itself, and the opportunities it could take advantage of, were only those of which its members were directly aware. Even worse, the individual could do little of which others did not approve. It is a delusion to think of the individual in primitive society as free. There was no natural liberty for a social animal, while freedom is an artifact of civilization. The individual had in the group no recognized domain of independent action; even the head of the band could expect obedience, support and understanding of his signals only for conventional activities. So long as each must serve that common order of rank for all needs, which present-day socialists dream of, there can be no free experimentation by the individual.

3

The great advance which made possible the development of civilization and ultimately of the Open Society was the gradual substitution of abstract rules of conduct for specific obligatory ends, and with it the playing of a game for acting in concert under common indicators, thus fostering a spontaneous order. The great gain attained by this was that it made possible a procedure through which all relevant information widely dispersed was made available to ever-increasing numbers of men in the form of the symbols which we call market prices. But it also meant that the incidence of the results on different persons and groups no longer satisfied the age-old instincts.

It has been suggested more than once that the theory explaining the working of the market be called catallactics from the classical Greek word for bartering or exchanging – *katallattein*. I have fallen somewhat in love with this word since discovering that in ancient Greek, in addition to "exchanging," it also meant "to admit into the community" and "to change from enemy into friend." I have therefore proposed that we call the game of the market, by which we can induce the stranger to welcome and serve us, the "game of catallaxy."

The market process indeed corresponds fully to the definition of a game which we find in *The Oxford English Dictionary*. It is "a contest played according to rules and decided by superior skill,

strength or good fortune." It is in this respect both a game of skill as well as a game of chance. Above all, it is a game which serves to elicit from each player the highest worthwhile contribution to the common pool from which each will win an uncertain share.

The game was probably started by men who had left the shelter and obligations of their own tribe to gain from serving the needs of others they did not know personally. When the early neolithic traders took boatloads of flint axes from Britain across the Channel to barter them against amber and probably also, even then, jars of wine, their aim was no longer to serve the needs of known people, but to make the largest gain. Precisely because they were interested only in who would offer the best price for their products, they reached persons wholly unknown to them, whose standard of life they thereby enhanced much more than they could have that of their neighbors by handing the axes to those who no doubt could also have made good use of them.

4

As the abstract signal-price thus took the place of the needs of known fellows as the goal towards which men's efforts were directed, entirely new possibilities for the utilization of resources opened up – but this also required wholly different moral attitudes to encourage their exploitation. The change occurred largely at the new urban centers of trade and handicrafts, which grew up at ports or the crossroads of trade routes, where men who had escaped from the discipline of tribal morals established commercial communities and gradually developed the new rules of the game of catallaxy.

The necessity to be brief forces me here somewhat to over-simplify and to employ familiar terms where they are not quite appropriate. When I pass from the morals of the hunting band in which man spent most of his history, to the morals which made possible the market order of the open society, I am jumping over a long intermediate stage, much shorter than man's life in the small band, but still of much greater length than the urban and commercial society has enjoyed yet, and important because from it date those codifications of ethics which became embodied in the teaching of the monotheistic religions. It is the period of man's life in tribal society. In many ways it represents a transitional stage between the concrete order of the primitive face-to-face society, in which all the members knew each other and served common particular ends, and the open and abstract society, in which an order results from individuals observing the same abstract rules of the game while using their own knowledge in the pursuit of their own ends.

While our emotions are still governed by the instincts appropriate to the success of the small hunting band, our verbal tradition is dominated by duties to the "neighbor," the fellow member of the tribe, and still regarding the alien largely as beyond the pale of moral obligation.

In a society in which individual aims were necessarily different, based on specialized knowledge, and efforts came to be directed towards future exchange of products with yet unknown partners, common rules of conduct increasingly took the place of particular common ends as the foundations of social order and peace. The interaction of individuals became a game, because what was required from each individual was observation of the rules, not concern for a particular result, other than to win support for himself and his family. The rules which gradually developed, because they made this game most effective, were essentially those of the law of property and contract. These rules in turn made possible the progressive division of labor, and that mutual adjustment of independent efforts, which a functioning division of labor demands.

5

The full significance of this division of labor is often not appreciated, because most people think of it — partly because of the classical illustration given by Adam Smith — as a designed intra-mural arrangement in which different individuals contribute the successive steps in a planned process for shaping certain products. In fact, however, co-ordination by the market of the endeavors of different enterprises in supplying the raw materials, tools and semi-finished products which the turning out of the final commodity requires is probably much more important than the organized collaboration of numerous specialist workers.

It is in a great measure this inter-firm division of labor, or specialization, on which the achievement of the competitive market depends, and which that market makes possible. Prices the producer finds on the market at once tell him what to produce and what means to use in producing it. From such market signals he knows that he can expect to sell at prices covering his outlays, and that he will not use up more resources than are necessary for the purpose. His selfish striving for gain makes him do, and enables him to do, precisely what he ought to do in order to improve the chances of any member of his society, taken at random, as much as possible — *but only if* the prices he can get are determined solely by market forces and not by the coercive powers of government. Only prices determined on the free market will bring it about that demand equals supply. But not only this. Free market prices also ensure that all of a society's dispersed knowledge will be taken into account and used.

The game of the market led to the growth and prosperity of communities who played it because it improved the chances for all. This was made possible because remuneration for the services of individuals depended on objective facts, all of which no one could know, and not on someone's opinions about what they ought to have.

But it also meant that while skill and industry would improve each individual's chances, they could not guarantee him a specified income; and that the impersonal process which used all that dispersed knowledge set the signals of prices so as to tell people what to do, but without regard to needs or merits. Yet the ordering and productivity enhancing function of prices, and particularly the prices of services, depends on their informing people where they will find their most effective place in the overall pattern of activities – the place in which they are likely to make the greatest contribution to aggregate output. If, therefore, we regard *that* rule of remuneration as just which contributes as much as possible to increasing the chances of any member of the community picked out at random, we ought to regard the remunerations determined by a free market as the just ones.

6

But they are inevitably very different from the relative remunerations which assisted the organization of the different type of society in which our species lived so much longer, and which therefore still governs the feelings which guide us. This point has become exceedingly important since prices ceased to be accepted as due to unknown circumstances, and governments came to believe they could determine prices with beneficial effects. When governments started to falsify the market price signals, whose appropriateness they had no means of judging (governments as little as anyone else possessing all the information precipitated in prices), in the hope of thereby giving benefits to groups claimed to be particularly deserving, things inevitably started to go wrong. Not only the efficient use of resources, but, what is worse, also the prospects of being able to buy or sell as expected through demand equaling supply were thereby greatly diminished.

It may be difficult to understand, but I believe there can be no doubt about it, that we are led to utilize more relevant information when our remuneration is made to depend indirectly on circumstances we do not know. It is thus that, in the language of modern cybernetics, the feedback mechanism secures the maintenance of a self-generating order. It was this which Adam Smith saw and described as the operation of the "invisible hand" – to be ridiculed for 200 years by uncomprehending scoffers. It is indeed *because* the game of catallaxy disregards human conceptions of what is due to each, and rewards according to success in playing the game under the same formal rules, that it produces a more efficient allocation of resources than any design could achieve. I feel that in any game that is played because it improves the prospects of all beyond those which we know how to provide by any other arrangements, the result must be accepted as fair, so long as all obey the same rules and no one cheats. If they accept their winnings from the game, it is cheating for individuals or groups to invoke the powers of government to divert the flow of good things in their favor – whatever we may do outside this game of the market to provide a decent minimum for those for whom the game did not supply it. It is not a valid objection to such a game, the outcome of which depends partly on skill and particular individual circumstances and partly on pure chance, that the initial prospects for different individuals, although they are all improved by playing that game, are very far from being the same. The answer to such an objection is precisely that one of the purposes of the game is to make the fullest possible use of the inevitably different skills, knowledge and environment of different individuals. Among the greatest assets which a society can use in this manner for increasing the pool from which the earnings of individuals are drawn are the different moral, intellectual and material gifts parents can pass on to their children – and often will acquire, create or preserve only in order to be able to pass them on to their children.

7

The result of this game of catallaxy, therefore, will necessarily be that many have much more than their fellows think they deserve, and even more will have much less than their fellows think they ought to have. It is not surprising that many people should wish to correct this by some authoritative act of redistribution. The trouble is that the aggregate product which they think is available for distribution exists only *because* returns for the different efforts are held out by the market with little regard to deserts or needs, and are needed to attract the owners of particular information, material means and personal skills to the points where at each moment they can make the greatest contribution. Those who prefer the quiet of an assured contractual income to the necessity of taking risks to exploit ever-changing opportunities feel at a disadvantage compared with possessors of large incomes, which result from continual redisposition of resources.

High actual gains of the successful ones, whether this success is deserved or accidental, is an essential element for guiding resources to where they will make the largest contribution to the pool from which all draw their share. We should not have as much to share if *that* income of an individual were not treated as *just*, the prospects of which induced him to make the largest contribution to the pool. Incredibly high incomes may thus sometimes be just. What is more important, scope for achieving such incomes may be the necessary condition for the less enterprising, lucky, or clever to get the regular income on which they count.

The inequality, which so many people resent, however, has not only been the underlying condition for producing the relatively high incomes which most people in the West now enjoy. Some people seem to believe that a lowering of this general level of incomes – or at least a slowing down of its rate of increase – would not be too high a price for what they feel would be a juster distribution. But there is an even greater obstacle

to such ambitions today. As a result of playing the game of catallaxy, which pays so little attention to justice but does so much to increase output, the population of the world has been able to increase so much, without the income of most people increasing very much, that we can maintain it, and the further increases in population which are irrevocably on the way, only if we make the fullest possible use of that game which elicits the highest contributions to productivity.

8

If people in general do not appreciate what they owe to catallaxy and how far they are even dependent on it for their very existence, and if they often bitterly resent what they regard as its injustice, this is so because they have never designed it and therefore do not understand it. The game rests on a method of providing benefits for others in which the individual will accomplish most if, within the conventional rules, he pursues solely his own interests – which need not be selfish in the ordinary sense of the word, but are in any case his own.

The moral attitude which this order demands not only of the entrepreneur but of all those, curiously called "self-employed," who have constantly to choose the directions of their efforts, if they are to confer the greatest benefit on their fellows, is that they compete honestly according to the rules of the game, guided only by the abstract signals of prices and giving no preferences because of their sympathies or views on the merits or needs of those with whom they deal. It would mean not merely a personal loss, but a failure in their duty to the public, to employ a less efficient instead of a more efficient person, to spare an incompetent competitor, or to favor particular users of their product.

The gradually spreading new liberal morals, which the Open or Great Society demanded, required above all that the same rules of conduct should apply to one's relation to all other members of society – except for natural ties to the members of one's family. This extension of old moral rules to wider circles, most people, and particularly the intellectuals, welcome as moral progress. But they apparently did not realize, and violently resented when they discovered it, that the equality of rules applicable to one's relationship to all other men necessarily implied not only that new obligations were extended to people who formerly had no such claims, but also that old obligations which were recognized to some people but could not be extended to all others had to disappear.

It was this unavoidable attenuation of the content of our obligations, which necessarily accompanied their extension, that people with strongly ingrained moral emotions resented. Yet these are kinds of obligations which are essential to the cohesion of the small group but which are irreconcilable with the order, the productivity, and the peace of a great society of free men. They are all those demands which under the name of "social justice" assert a moral claim on government that it give us what it can take by force from those who in the game of catallaxy have been more successful than we have been. Such an artificial alteration of the relative attractiveness of the different directions of productive efforts can only be counter-productive.

If expected remunerations no longer tell people where their endeavors will make the greatest contribution to the total product, an efficient use of resources becomes impossible. Where the size of the social product, and no longer their contributions to it, gives individuals and groups a moral claim to a certain share of that product, the claims of what deserve really to be described as "free riders" become an unbearable drag on the economy.

9

I am told that there arc still communities in Africa in which able young men, anxious to adopt modern commercial methods, find it impossible thereby to improve their position, because tribal customs demand that they share the products of their greater industry, skill or luck with all their kin. An increased income of such a man would merely mean that he had to share it with an ever-increasing number of claimants. He can, therefore, never rise substantially above the average level of his tribe.

The chief adverse effect of "social justice" in our society is that it prevents individuals from achieving what they could achieve – through the means for further investment being taken from them. It is also the application of an incongruous principle to a civilization whose productivity is high, *because* incomes are very unequally divided and thereby the use of scarce resources is directed and limited to where they bring the highest return. Thanks to this unequal distribution the poor get in a competitive market economy more than they would get in a centrally directed system.

All this is the outcome of the, as yet merely imperfect, victory of the obligatory abstract rule of individual conduct over the common particular end as the method of social co-ordination – the development which has made both the open society and individual freedom possible, but which the socialists now want to reverse. Socialists have the support of inherited instincts, while maintenance of the new wealth which creates the new ambitions requires an acquired discipline which the non-domesticated barbarians in our midst, who call themselves "alienated," refuse to accept although they still claim all its benefits.

10

Let me, before I conclude, briefly meet an objection which is bound to be raised because it rests on a very widespread misunderstanding. My argument, that in a process of cultural selection we have built better than we understood, and that what we call our intelligence has been shaped concurrently with our institutions by a process of trial and error, is certain to be met by an outcry of "social Darwinism." But such a cheap way of disposing of my argument by labeling it would rest on an error. It is true that during the latter part of the last century some social scientists, under the influence of Darwin, placed an excessive stress on the importance of natural selection of the most able individuals in free competition. I do not wish to underrate the importance of this, but it is not the main benefit we derive from competitive selection. This is the competitive selection of cultural institutions, for the discovery of which we did not need Darwin, but the growing understanding of which in fields like law and language rather helped Darwin to his biological theories. My problem is not genetic evolution of innate qualities, but cultural evolution through learning — which indeed leads sometimes to conflicts with near-animal natural instincts. Nevertheless, it is still true that civilization grew not by the prevailing of that which man thought would be most successful, but by the growth of that which turned out to be so, and which, precisely because he did not understand it, led man beyond what he could ever have conceived.

Chapter 31

G. A. Cohen

WHY NOT SOCIALISM?

G. A. Cohen (1941–2009) was a professor of social and political theory at Oxford, best known for his explication and defense of Marxist theory from the perspective of analytical philosophy. In this piece (published in 2009), Cohen shows how socialism embodies values of community and equality through a short story about a camping trip. He then argues for the feasibility and desirability of extending those principles across society as a whole.

I The Camping Trip

You and I and a whole bunch of other people go on a camping trip. There is no hierarchy among us; our common aim is that each of us should have a good time, doing, so far as possible, the things that he or she likes best (some of those things we do together; others we do separately). We have facilities with which to carry out our enterprise: we have, for example, pots and pans, oil, coffee, fishing rods, canoes, a soccer ball, decks of cards, and so forth. And, as is usual on camping trips, we avail ourselves of those facilities collectively: even if they are privately owned things, they are under collective control for the duration of the trip, and we have shared understandings about who is going to use them when, and under what circumstances, and why. Somebody fishes, somebody else prepares the food, and another person cooks it. People who hate cooking but enjoy washing up may do all the washing up, and so on. There are plenty of differences, but our mutual under-standings, and the spirit of the enterprise, ensure that there are no inequalities to which anyone could mount a principled objection.

It is commonly true on camping trips, and, for that matter, in many other non-massive contexts, that people cooperate within a common concern that, so far as is possible, everybody has a roughly similar opportunity to flourish, and also to relax, on condition that she contributes, appropriately to her capacity, to the flourishing and relaxing of others. In these contexts most people, even most antiegalitarians, accept, indeed, take for granted, norms of equality and reciprocity. So deeply do most people take those norms for granted that no one on such trips questions them: to question them would contradict the spirit of the trip.

You could imagine a camping trip where everybody asserts her rights over the pieces of equipment, and the talents that she brings, and where bargaining proceeds with respect to who is going to pay what to whom to be allowed, for example, to use a knife to peel the potatoes, and how much he is going to charge others for those now-peeled potatoes that he bought in an unpeeled condition from another camper, and so on. You could base a camping trip on the principles of market exchange and strictly private ownership of the required facilities.

1. Now, most people would hate that. Most people would be more drawn to the first kind of camping trip than to the second, primarily on grounds of fellowship, but also, be it noted, on grounds of efficiency. (I have in mind the inordinate transaction costs that would attend a market-style camping trip. Too much time would be spent bargaining, and looking over one's shoulder for more lucrative possibilities.) And this means that <u>most people are drawn to the socialist ideal, at least in certain restricted settings.</u>

To reinforce this point, here are some conjectures about how most people would react in various imaginable camping scenarios:

a. Harry loves fishing, and Harry is very good at fishing. Consequently, he catches, and provides, more fish than others do. Harry says: "It's unfair, how we're running things. I should have better fish when we dine. I should have only perch, not the mix of perch and catfish that we've all been having." But his fellow campers say: "Oh, for heaven's sake, Harry, don't be such a shmuck. You sweat and strain no more than the rest of us do. So, you're very good at fishing. We don't begrudge you that special endowment, which is, quite properly, a source of satisfaction to you, but why should we *reward* your good fortune?"

b. Following a three-hour time-off-for-personal-exploration period, an excited Sylvia returns to the campsite and announces, "I've stumbled upon a huge apple tree, full of perfect apples." "Great," others exclaim, "now we can all have applesauce, and apple pie, and apple strudel!" "Provided, of course," so Sylvia rejoins, "that you reduce my labor burden, and/or furnish me with more room in the tent, and/or with more bacon at breakfast." Her claim to (a kind of) ownership of the tree revolts the others.

c. The trippers are walking along a bridle path on which they discover a cache of nuts that some squirrel has abandoned. Only Leslie, who has been endowed from birth with many knacks and talents, knows how to crack them, but she wants to charge for sharing that information. The campers see no important difference between her demand and Sylvia's.

d. Morgan recognizes the campsite. "Hey, this is where my father camped thirty years ago. This is where he dug a special little pond on the other side of that hill, and stocked it with specially good fish. Dad knew I might come camping here one day, and he did all that so that I could eat better when I'm here. Great. Now I can have better food than you guys have." The rest frown, or smile, at Morgan's greed.

Of course, not everybody likes camping trips. I do not myself enjoy them much, because I'm not outdoorsy, or, at any rate, I'm not outdoorsy overnight-without-a-mattress-wise. There's a limit to the outdoorsiness to which some academics can be expected to submit: I'd rather have my socialism in the warmth of All Souls College than in the wet of the Catskills, and I love modern plumbing. But the question I'm asking is not: wouldn't you like to go on a camping trip? but: isn't this, the socialist way, with collective property and planned mutual giving, rather obviously the *best* way to run a camping trip, whether or not you actually *like* camping?

The circumstances of the camping trip are multiply special: many features distinguish it from the circumstances of life in a modern society. One may therefore not infer, from the fact that camping trips of the sort that I have described are feasible and desirable, that society-wide socialism is equally feasible and equally desirable. There are too many major differences between the contexts for that inference to carry any conviction. What we urgently need to know is precisely *what* are the differences that matter, and how can socialists address them? Because of its contrasts with life in the large, the camping trip model serves well as a reference point for purported demonstrations that socialism across society is not feasible and/or desirable, since it seems eminently feasible and desirable on the trip.

II The Principles Realized on the Camping Trip

Two principles are realized on the camping trip, an egalitarian principle, and a principle of community. The community principle constrains the operation of the egalitarian principle by forbidding certain inequalities that the egalitarian principle permits. (The egalitarian principle in question is, as I shall explain, one of radical equality of opportunity: it is therefore consistent with certain inequalities of outcome.)

There are, in fact, a number of potentially competing egalitarian principles with which the camping trip, as I have described it, complies, because the simple circumstances of the trip, unlike more complex ones, do not force a choice among them. But the only egalitarian principle realized on the trip that I shall bring into focus is the one that I regard as the correct egalitarian principle, the egalitarian principle that justice endorses, and that is a radical principle of equality of opportunity, which I shall call "socialist equality of opportunity."

Now, equality of opportunity, whether moderate or radical, removes obstacles to opportunity from which some people suffer and others don't, obstacles that are sometimes due to the enhanced opportunities that the more privileged people enjoy. Importantly, the removal of blocks to the opportunity of some people does not always leave the opportunities of the initially better placed intact: sometimes it reduces the opportunities of those who benefit from inequality of opportunity. I underline this point because it means that promoting equality of opportunity is not only an *equalizing*, but also a *redistributing*, policy. Promoting equality of opportunity, in all of its forms, is not merely giving to some what others had and continue to enjoy.

We can distinguish three forms of equality of opportunity and three corresponding obstacles to opportunity: the first form removes one obstacle, the second form removes that one and a second, and the third form removes all three.

First, there is what might be called *bourgeois* equality of opportunity, by which I mean the equality of opportunity that characterizes (at least in aspiration) the liberal age. Bourgeois equality of opportunity removes socially constructed status restrictions, both formal and informal, on life chances. An example of a formal status restriction is that under which a serf labors in a feudal society; an example of an informal status restriction is that from which a person whose skin is the wrong color may suffer in a society that is free of racist law but that nevertheless possesses a racist consciousness that generates racial disadvantage. This first form of equality of opportunity widens people's opportunities by removing constraints on opportunity caused by rights assignments and by bigoted and other prejudicial social perceptions.

Left-liberal equality of opportunity goes beyond bourgeois equality of opportunity. For it also sets itself against the constraining effect of social circumstances by which bourgeois equality of opportunity is undisturbed, the constraining effect, that is, of those circumstances of birth and upbringing that constrain not by assigning an inferior *status* to their victims, but by nevertheless causing them to labor and live under substantial disadvantages. The disadvantage targeted by left-liberal equality of opportunity derives immediately from a person's circumstances and does not depend for its constraining power on social perceptions or on assignments of superior and inferior rights. Policies promoting left-liberal equality of opportunity include head-start education for children from deprived backgrounds. When left-liberal equality of opportunity is fully achieved, people's fates are determined by their native talent and their choices, and, therefore, not at all by their social backgrounds.

Left-liberal equality of opportunity corrects for *social* disadvantage, but not for native, or *inborn*, disadvantage. What I would call *socialist* equality of opportunity treats the inequality that arises out of native differences as a further source of injustice, beyond that imposed by unchosen social backgrounds, since native differences are equally unchosen. (Hence the similarity of the campers' attitudes to Sylvia's good luck and Leslie's, in scenarios b. and c. on p. 415 above.) Socialist equality of opportunity seeks to correct for *all* unchosen disadvantages, disadvantages, that is, for which the agent cannot herself reasonably be held responsible, whether they be disadvantages that reflect social misfortune or disadvantages that reflect natural misfortune. When socialist equality of opportunity prevails, differences of outcome reflect nothing but difference of taste and choice, not differences in natural and social capacities and powers.

So, for example, under socialist equality of opportunity income differences obtain when they reflect nothing but different individual preferences, including income/leisure preferences. People differ in their tastes, not only across consumer items, but also between working only a few hours and consuming rather little on the one hand, and working long hours and consuming rather more on the other. Preferences across income and leisure are not in principle different from preferences across apples and oranges, and there can be no objection to differences in people's benefits and burdens that reflect nothing but different preferences, *when* (which is not always) *their satisfaction leads to a comparable aggregate enjoyment of life.* Such

differences in benefits and burdens do not constitute *inequalities* of benefits and burdens.

Let me spell out the analogy at which I have just gestured. A table is before us, laden with apples and oranges. Each of us is entitled to take six pieces of fruit, with apples and oranges appearing in any combination to make up that six. Suppose, now, I complain that Sheila has five apples whereas I have only three. Then it *should* extinguish my sense of grievance, a sense of grievance that is here totally inappropriate, when you point out that Sheila has only one orange whereas I have three, and that I could have had a bundle just like Sheila's had I forgone a couple of oranges. So, similarly, under a system where each gets the same income per hour, but can choose how many hours she works, it is not an intelligible complaint that some people have more take-home pay than others. The income/leisure trade-off is relevantly like the apples/oranges trade-off: that I have more income than you do no more shows, just as such, that we are unequally placed than my having four apples from the table when you have two represents, just as such, an objectionable inequality. (Of course, some people love working, and some hate it, and that could be thought to [and I think it does] induce an injustice in the contemplated scheme, since those who love work will, *ceteris paribus*, relish their lives more than those who hate work do. But the same goes for some people enjoying *each* of apples and oranges more than others do; yet, even so, the apple/orange regime is a giant step toward equality [compared, for example, to a capitalist market society], and so, too, is equal pay for every hour worked, with each choosing the number of hours that she works.

Accordingly, and for that reason, and also because this is a short book, I ignore, henceforth, the complication that is exposed within these parentheses. I assume the fulfillment of the condition that was italicized above.)

Now, you might think that I have misused the term "socialist" in the phrase "socialist equality of opportunity," for the simple reason that it is a familiar socialist policy to insist on equality of both income and hours of work: haven't kibbutzim, those paradigms of socialism, worked that way?

I would draw attention, in reply, to the distinction between socialist principles and socialist modes of organization, the first, of course, being the putative justifications of the second. What I call "socialist equality of opportunity" is, as expounded here, a principle, one, so I say, that is satisfied on the camping trip, but I have not said what modes of organization would, and would not, satisfy it in general. And, although the suggested strictly equal work/wage regime would indeed contradict it, I acknowledge that socialists have advocated such regimes, and I have no wish, or need, to deny that those regimes can be called *socialist* work/wage regimes. What I do need to insist is that such systems contradict the fundamental principles animating socialists, when those principles are fully thought through. No defensible fundamental principle of equality or, indeed, of community, taken by itself, warrants such a system, which may nevertheless be amply justified as an appropriate "second best" in light of the constraints of a particular place and time, and also in light of general constraints on the gathering and use of information about the tastes and powers of individuals, and, indeed, on their capacity to supply that information. Although justice might favor sensitivity to how happy or otherwise people are in similar circumstances – see the parenthetical remarks two paragraphs above – it is in general not possible, or even desirable, to fine-tune equality in that way.

What I have called *socialist* equality of opportunity is consistent with three forms of inequality, the second and third forms being subtypes of one type. Accordingly, I designate the three forms of inequality as (i), (ii-a), and (ii-b). The first form of inequality is unproblematic, the second form is a bit problematic, and the third is very problematic.

(i) The first type, or form, of inequality is unproblematic because it does not constitute an inequality, all things considered. Variety of preference and choice across lifestyle options means that some people will have more goods of a certain sort than others do, but that is no inequality in the relevant sense, where comparable aggregate enjoyment obtains. That was the lesson of the apples/oranges example, and of its application to income/leisure choices.

(ii) The second type of inequality is problematic, since it does involve an inequality in aggregate benefit. For socialist equality of opportunity tolerates inequality of benefit, where the inequality reflects the genuine choices of parties who are initially equally placed and who may therefore reasonably be held responsible for the consequences of those choices. And this type of inequality takes two forms: inequality that is due to *regrettable choice* and inequality that is due to differences in *option luck.*

(ii-a) To illustrate the first of these forms, imagine that one apple/orange chooser (but not the other) carelessly waits so long that, by the time he picks up the fruit to which he's entitled, it has lost its full savor: the resulting inequality of benefit raises no grievance. And the same goes for someone in a work/pay regime whose ultimate fortune is inferior because she did not bother to examine her job opportunities properly.

These inequalities of aggregate benefit are justified by differential exercises of effort and/or care by people, who are, initially, absolutely equally placed, and who are equal even in their *capacities* to expend effort and care. A stock example is that of the grasshopper and the ant, who must be presumed to be equal in those capacities for the story to carry its customary moral. A mark of the fact that grasshopper/ant presents an inequality of benefit is that the homeless grasshopper retrospectively *regrets* his choice. He does so because he knows that, had he chosen as the ant did, his situation would now be comparable to the ant's, instead of inferior in total benefit (including the benefits of idleness) to that of the ant.

Now you may be a skeptic about the grasshopper/ant story. You may believe (against the grain, I wager, of your reactions to people in ordinary life: see the paragraph that follows) that there is no such thing, ultimately, as being "truly responsible," or "choosing to be idle"; you may believe that greater negligence, for example, can reflect nothing but a smaller capacity for self-application, in the given circumstances, than others have, which should not be penalized. And if that is what you believe, then you will not countenance this second form of inequality. But even if, like me, you are not firmly disposed to disallow it, the question remains, how *large* is this inequality likely to be? Well, that is a very difficult question, and my own view, or hope, is that, under an intelligent institutionalization of the relevant principle, it wouldn't be very large, *on its own*: it can, however, contribute to very high degrees of inequality when it's in synergy with the third and truly problematic form of inequality, that is, ii-b, which is consistent with socialist equality of opportunity.

I said that believing that no inequality could truly reflect real freedom of choice would contradict your reactions to people in day-to-day life, and that I lack that belief. I lack that belief because I am not convinced that it is true *both* that all choices are causally determined *and* that causal determination obliterates responsibility. If you are indeed so convinced, then do not *blame* me for thinking otherwise, do not *blame* right-wing politicians for reducing welfare support (since, in your view, they can't help doing so), do not, indeed, blame, or praise, anyone for choosing to do anything, and therefore live your life, henceforth, differently from the way that we both know that you have lived it up to now.

(ii-b) The truly problematic inequality in overall benefit, the substantial inequality that is consistent with socialist equality of opportunity, is inequality that reflects differences in what philosophers call option luck. The paradigm case of option luck is a deliberate gamble. We start out equally placed, with $100 each, and we are relevantly identical in all respects, in character, in talents, and in circumstances. One of the features that we share is a penchant for gambling, so we flip a coin on the understanding that I give you $50 if it comes up heads, and you give me $50 if it comes up tails. I end up with $150 and you end up with $50, and with no extra anythings to offset that monetary shortfall.

This inequality is consistent with socialist equality of opportunity; you and I simply used our radically similar opportunities, and, moreover, in exactly the same way. And unlike the grasshopper, the losing gambler, while of course regretting his loss, need not regret his decision to gamble in the way the grasshopper regrets his decision to be idle. The losing gambler can say: "Faced afresh with the same options, I would have made the same choice; it was a reasonable gamble."

Now this form of inequality does not occur only as a result of gambling narrowly so called. There is also an element of option luck in the generation of market inequalities, which partly reflect gambles about where to put one's money or one's labor. Accordingly, some market-generated inequalities are partly compatible with, and, indeed, partly congruent with, socialist equality of opportunity. But one must not exaggerate the extent to which market inequalities have their genesis in pure market luck: market gambling differs significantly from standard gambling. Standardly, one has a choice whether or not to gamble: gambling is avoidable. But the market is hardly avoidable in a market society: even the means of exiting any particular market society consist of resources that are accessible only on terms set by that market society. The market, one might say, is a casino from which it is difficult to escape, and the inequalities that it produces are tainted with injustice for that reason. Whatever else is true, it is certainly safe to say that the yawning gulf between rich and poor in capitalist countries is not largely due to luck and the lack of it in optional gambling, but is rather a result of unavoidable gambling and straightforward brute luck, where no kind of gambling is involved. To be sure, avoidable option luck may figure in the explanation of cases where one entrepreneur prospers and another fails, but that is not, of course, the sort of inequality that exercises socialists.

Although inequalities of forms (ii-a) and (ii-b) are not condemned by justice, they are nevertheless repugnant to socialists when they obtain on a sufficiently large scale, because they then contradict community: community is put under strain when large inequalities obtain. The sway of socialist equality of opportunity must therefore be tempered by a principle of community, if society is to display the socialist character that makes the camping trip attractive.

"Community" can mean many things, but the requirement of community that is central here is that people care about, and, where necessary and possible, care for, one another, and, too, care that they care about one another. There are two modes of communal caring that I want to discuss here. The first is the mode that curbs some of the inequalities that result from socialist equality of opportunity. The second mode of communal caring is not strictly required for equality, but it is nevertheless of supreme importance in the socialist conception.

We cannot enjoy full community, you and I, if you make, and keep, say, ten times as much money as I do, because my life will then labor under challenges that you will never face, challenges that you could help me to cope with, but do not, because you keep your money. To illustrate: I am rich, and I live an easy life, whereas you are poor, because of regrettable choices and/or bad option luck, and not, therefore, because of any lack of equality of opportunity. You have to ride the crowded bus every day, whereas I pass you by in my comfortable car. One day, however, I must take the bus, because my wife needs the car. I can reasonably complain about that to a fellow car-driver, but not to you.

I can't say to you: "It's awful that I have to take the bus today." There is a lack of community between us of just the sort that naturally obtains between me and the fellow car-driver. And it will show itself in many other ways, for we enjoy widely different powers to care for ourselves, to protect and care for offspring, to avoid danger, and so on.

I believe that certain inequalities that cannot be forbidden in the name of socialist equality of opportunity should nevertheless be forbidden, in the name of community. But is it an injustice to forbid the transactions that generate those inequalities? Do the relevant prohibitions merely define the terms within which justice will operate, or do they sometimes (justifiably?) contradict justice? I do not know the answer to that question. (It would, of course, be a considerable pity if we had to conclude that community and justice were potentially incompatible moral ideals.)

So, to return to the camping trip, suppose that we eat pretty meagerly, but you have your special high-grade fish pond, which you got neither by inheritance nor by chicanery nor as a result of the brute (that is, non-option) luck of your superior exploratory talent, but as a result of an absolutely innocent option luck that no one can impugn from the point of view of justice: you got it through a lottery that we all entered. Then, even so, even though there is no injustice here, your luck cuts you off from our common life, and the ideal of community condemns that, and therefore also condemns the running of any such lottery.

The other expression of communal caring that is instantiated on the camping trip is a communal form of reciprocity, which contrasts with the market form of reciprocity, as I shall presently explain. Where starting points are equal, and there are independent (of equality of opportunity) limits put on inequality of outcome, then communal reciprocity is not required for equality, but it is nevertheless required for human relationships to take a desirable form.

Communal reciprocity is the antimarket principle according to which I serve you not because of what I can get in return by doing so but because you need or want my service, and you, for the same reason, serve me. Communal reciprocity is not the same thing as market reciprocity, since the market motivates productive contribution not on the basis of commitment to one's fellow human beings and a desire to serve them while being served by them, but on the basis of cash reward. The immediate motive to productive activity in a market society is (not always but) typically some mixture of greed and fear, in proportions that vary with the details of a person's market position and personal character. It is true that people can engage in market activity under other inspirations, but the motives of greed and fear are what the market brings to prominence, and that includes greed on behalf of, and fear for the safety of, one's family. Even when one's concerns are thus wider than those of one's mere self, the market posture is greedy and fearful in that one's opposite-number marketeers are predominantly seen as possible sources of enrichment, and as threats to one's success. These are horrible ways of seeing other people, however much we have become habituated and inured to them, as a result of centuries of capitalist civilization. (Capitalism did not, of course, invent greed and fear: they are deep in human nature. But, unlike its predecessor feudal civilization, which had the [Christian or other] grace to condemn greed, capitalism celebrates it.)

I said that, within communal reciprocity, I produce in a spirit of commitment to my fellow human beings: I desire to serve them while being served by them, and I get satisfaction from each side of that equation. In such motivation, there is indeed an expectation of reciprocation, but it differs critically from the reciprocation expected in market motivation. If I am a marketeer, then I am willing to serve, but only in order to be served: I would not serve if doing so were not a means to get service. Accordingly, I give as little service as I can in exchange for as much service as I can get: I want to buy cheap and sell dear. I serve others *either* in order to get something that I desire – that is the greed motivation; *or* in order to ensure that something that I seek to avoid is avoided – that is the fear motivation. A marketeer, considered just as such, does not value cooperation with others for its own sake: she does not value the conjunction, *serve-and-be-served*, as such.

A non-market cooperator relishes cooperation itself: what I want, as a non-marketeer, is that we serve each other; and when I serve, instead of trying to get whatever I can get, I do not regard my action as, all things considered, a sacrifice. To be sure, I serve you in the expectation that (if you are able to) you will also serve me. My commitment to socialist community does not require me to be a sucker who serves you regardless of whether (if you are able to do so) you are going to serve me, but I nevertheless find value in both parts of the conjunction – I serve you *and* you serve me – and in that conjunction itself: I do not regard the first part – I serve you – as simply a means to my real end, which is that you serve me. The relationship between us under communal reciprocity is not the market-instrumental one in which I give because I get, but the non-instrumental one in which I give because you need, or want, and in which I expect a comparable generosity from you.

For ease and vividness of exposition, I characterized communal reciprocity in the foregoing paragraphs in two-person (I–you) terms. But communal reciprocity can link chains of people no pair of whom directly give to one another: in a spirit of communal reciprocity that encompasses us all, I can serve you and you her and she him and he me. Communal networks that are in some ways structurally like market networks can form, under a different animating motivation. They are like them only in some ways because in a market network no one does anything for anyone without getting something from *that* person.

Because motivation in market exchange consists largely of greed and fear, a person typically does not care *fundamentally*, within market interaction, about how well or badly anyone other than herself fares. You cooperate with other people not because you believe that cooperating with other people is a good thing in itself, not because you want yourself *and* the other person to flourish, but because *you* seek to gain and you know that you can do so only if you cooperate with others. In every type of society people perforce provision one another: a society *is* a network of mutual provision. But, in market society, that mutuality is only a by-product of an unmutual and fundamentally *non*-reciprocating attitude.

III Is the Ideal Desirable?

It is the aspiration of socialists to realize the principles that structure life on the camping trip on a national, or even on an international, scale. Socialists therefore face two distinct questions, which are often not treated as distinctly as they should be. The first is: would socialism, if feasible, be desirable? The second is: is socialism feasible?

Some might say that the camping trip is itself unattractive, that, as a matter of principle, there should be *scope* for much greater inequality and instrumental treatment of other people, even in small-scale interaction, than the ethos of the camping trip permits. These opponents of the camping trip ethos would not, of course, recommend society-wide equality and community *as* extensions to the large of what is desirable in the small, and they are unlikely to recommend for the large what they disparage even in the small.

The opponents in question do not say that there *should* be more inequality and treating of people as mere means on a camping trip, but just that people have a *right* to make personal choices, even if the result is inequality and/or instrumental treatment of people, and, so they say, that right is not honored on the camping trip. But this criticism seems to me to be misplaced. For there *is* a right to personal choice

on the camping trip, and there are plenty of private choices on it, in leisure, and in labor (where there is more than one reasonable way of distributing it), under the voluntarily accepted constraint that those choices must blend fairly with the personal choices of others. Within market society, too, the choices of others massively confine each individual's pursuit of her own choices, but that fact is masked in market society, because, unlike what's true on the camping trip, in market society the unavoidable mutual dependence of human beings is not brought into common consciousness, as a datum for formal and informal planning. A particular person in a market society may face a choice of being a building laborer or a carer or starving, his set of choices being a consequence of everybody else's choices. But nobody designed things that way, and his restricted options consequently misappear as mere facts of life.

Although few would take the line that I have just opposed, which says that it is all right for camping trips *themselves* to be run on market lines, many would point to features special to the camping trip that distinguish it from the normal mill of life in a modern society and that consequently cast doubt on the desirability and/or the feasibility of realizing camping trip principles in such a society. Such people might grant that I have displayed the attractiveness, and the feasibility, of socialist values, but only in the course of a substantially recreational activity, in which there are no competing social groups, in which everyone to whom you relate is known to you personally and observed by you daily, and in which an individual's family ties exert no counter-pull to his sense of social obligation. To what extent do these differences render the ideal un-, or less, desirable? And to what extent do they render it, im-, or less, practicable?

I do not see that the stated differences undermine the desirability of the spread across society of camping trip values. I do not think that the cooperation and unselfishness that the trip displays are appropriate only among friends, or within a small community. In the mutual provisioning of a market society, I am essentially indifferent to the fate of the farmer whose food I eat: there is no or little community between us, as that value was articulated in Part II above. In the next Part I address the question whether it is feasible to proceed otherwise. But it does seem to me that all people of goodwill would welcome the news that it had become possible to proceed otherwise, perhaps, for example, because some economists had invented clever ways of harnessing and organizing our capacity for generosity to others. I continue to find appealing the sentiment of a left-wing song that I learned in my childhood, which begins as follows: "If we should consider each other, a neighbor, a friend, or a brother, it could be a wonderful, wonderful world, it could be a wonderful world." The point is often made, in resistance to the sentiment of the song, that one cannot be friends with the millions of people who compose a large society: that idea is at best impossible to realize, and, so some add, it is even incoherent, because of the exclusivity that goes with friendship. But the song need not be interpreted in that overambitious fashion. It suffices that I treat everyone with whom I have any exchange or other form of contact as someone toward whom I have the reciprocating attitude that is characteristic of friendship. And general social friendship, that is, community, is, like friendship, not an all-or-nothing thing. It is surely a welcome thing when more rather than less community is present in society.

But whatever we may wish to conclude about the *desirability* of socialism, we must also address the independent question of its *feasibility*, to which I now turn.

IV Is the Ideal Feasible? Are the Obstacles to it Human Selfishness, or Poor Social Technology?

Whether or not the socialist relations of the camping trip are attractive, and whether or not it would also be desirable for such relations to spread across society as a whole, many people who have thought about the matter have judged socialism to be *infeasible* for society as a whole. "Socialism in one short camping trip, maybe. But socialism across society, all the time? You gotta be kidding! The camping trip is a happy recreational context, in which people are removed from the complexity of everyday life and willing to suspend their normal operating principles. It is almost by *definition* special. Nothing in it reduces the implausibility of the idea of socialism on a grand scale."

It is worth pointing out, to begin with, that it is not only in happy contexts, but also in much less benign ones, that camping trip attitudes tend to prevail. People regularly participate in emergencies like flood or fire on camping trip principles. But let us look at the question about the feasibility of socialism more closely.

There are two contrasting reasons why society-wide socialism might be thought infeasible, and it is very important, both intellectually and politically, to distinguish them. The first reason has to do with the limits of human nature, and the second has to do with the limits of social technology. The first putative reason why socialism is infeasible is that people are, so it is often said, by nature insufficiently generous and cooperative to meet its requirements, however ① generous and cooperative they may be within the frame of limited time and special intimacy in which the camping trip unrolls. The second putative reason why socialism is infeasible is that, even if people are, or could become, in the ② right culture, sufficiently generous, we do not know how to harness that generosity; we do not know how, through appropriate rules and stimuli, to make generosity turn the wheels of the economy. Contrast human selfishness, which we know how to harness very well.

Of course, even if neither of these problems, and no comparable ones, obtained, socialism might still be unattainable, because political and ideological forces – including the enormous practical force of the belief that socialism is infeasible – that would resist a movement toward socialism are too strong. But the question about feasibility that I am addressing here is *not* whether socialism is straightforwardly *accessible*, whether we can get to it from where we are, and burdened as we are with a massive legacy of capitalism and with all the other contingencies that compose our current social condition. The present feasibility question is about whether socialism would work, and be stable, if we were indeed in a position to institute it. And an important aspect of that question is whether the working of a socialist society would reinforce, or, rather, undermine, the communal and egalitarian preferences that are required for socialism's stability. (We must, moreover, also ask a question that I shall not pursue here, which is whether socialism is consistent not only with the springs of human nature but also with human nature as it has been shaped by capitalism; the forces that might block the installation of socialism might also operate so as to foil its efficient working.)

In my view, the principal problem that faces the socialist ideal is that we do not know how to design the machinery that would make it run. Our problem is not, primarily, human selfishness, but our lack of a suitable organizational technology: our problem is a problem of *design*. It may be an *insoluble* design problem, and it is a design problem that is undoubtedly exacerbated by our selfish propensities, but a design problem, so I think, is what we've got.

Both selfish and generous propensities reside, after all, in (almost?) everyone. Our problem is that, while we know how to make an economic system work on the basis of the development, and, indeed, the hypertrophy, of selfishness, we do not know how to make it work by developing and exploiting human generosity. Yet even in the real world, in our own society, a great deal depends on generosity, or, to put it more generally and more negatively, on non-market incentives. Doctors, nurses, teachers and others do not, or do not comprehensively, gauge what they do in their jobs according to the amount of money they're likely to get as a result, in the way that capitalists and workers in non-caring occupations do. (The aforementioned carers won't, of course, work for nothing, but that is like the fact that you need to eat on the camping trip: it does not follow, and it is false, that carers tailor their work to expected monetary return.) And the reason for the difference is not that carers are made of morally superior clay, but, in good part, the more cognitive reason that their conception of what is to be produced is guided by a conception of human need: market signals are not necessary to decide what diseases to cure or what subjects to teach, nor are they efficient means of deciding that. But, once we pass out of the sphere of need, or, more generally, of goods that everyone can be expected to want, to the wide sphere of optional commodities, and we pass increasingly to that as economies progress and as life therefore becomes easier and more elegant, it also becomes more difficult to know what to produce, and how to produce it, without the device of market signals: very few socialist economists would now dissent from that proposition. One reason why the camping trip can readily do without market exchange is that the information that the campers need to plan their activities is modest in extent, and comparatively easy to obtain and to aggregate.

Now, market prices serve two logically distinguishable functions: an information function and a motivation function. First, they make known how much people would be willing to sacrifice to obtain given goods and services: they show how valuable goods are to people, and thereby reveal what is worth producing. But, distinctly, market prices serve as a motivation to provide people with the goods in question: the marketeer seeks to capture, for her own gain, what people are prepared to pay. The two functions are not only logically separable: sometimes the first operates without the second, as when an official who acts, for example, on behalf of a charity, seeks to maximize the revenue from its endowment, but transparently not in order to line her own pockets: she does not keep the money that accrues, and, at least in certain cases, her own income is unaffected by how well the fund she manages performs.

In the light of the infirmities of comprehensive planning on the one hand and of the injustice of market results and the moral shabbiness of market motivation on the other, it is natural to ask whether it might be practically feasible to preserve the information function of the market, to continue to get the benefits it provides of information generation and processing with respect to what should be produced, while extinguishing its normal motivational presuppositions and distributive consequences. Can we have market efficiency in production without market incentives, and, hence, without a market distribution of rewards?

Precisely that distinction is the center of a groundbreaking book by Joseph Carens, who works in the Political Science Department at the University of Toronto. The book, published by the University of Chicago Press in 1981, was called *Equality, Moral Incentives, and the Market,* and its significant subtitle was *An Essay in Utopian Politico-Economic Theory.* Carens described a society in which what looks like a standard capitalist market organizes economic activity, but the tax system cancels the disequalizing results of that market by redistributing income to complete equality. There are (pretax) profit-seeking capitalists, and workers who own no capital, but people acknowledge an obligation to serve others, and the extent to which they discharge that obligation is measured by how close their pretax income is to what it would be in the most remunerative (and therefore, on standard assumptions, the most socially contributing) activity available to them, while taxation effects a fully egalitarian posttax distribution of income. Here, then, producers aim, in an immediate sense, at cash results, but they do not keep (or otherwise benefit from) the money that accrues, and they seek it out of a desire to contribute to

society: a market mechanism is used to solve the social technology problem, in the service of equality and community.

There are plenty of problems with the Carens scheme, but it seems to me to be one that is amply worth refining, and the principle of the scheme enjoys a modest measure of realization whenever better-off people do not decide to reduce their labor input in the face of adverse redistributive taxation because they approve of the purpose to which the taxation is put.

The Carens scheme is Utopian partly in that it relies entirely on non-self-interested choice. But there are ways of introducing strong elements of community and equality into an economic system in which self-interested choice nevertheless continues to obtain, but now with confined scope. One familiar such way is through the institution of a welfare state, which takes a great deal of provision for need out of the market system. A less familiar way is through the institution of *market* socialism, on which more in a moment. Each of these systems works only if people are un-self-interested *enough* to accept the constraints that the systems put on the pursuit of self-interest.

Whereas many socialists have recently put their faith in market socialism, nineteenth-century socialists were, by contrast, for the most part opposed to market organization of economic life. The mainstream socialist pioneers favored something that they thought would be far superior, to wit, comprehensive central planning, which, it was hoped, could realize the socialist ideal of a truly sharing society. And the pioneers' successors were encouraged by what they interpreted as victories of planning, such as the industrialization of the Soviet Union and the early institution of educational and medical provision in the People's Republic of China. But central planning, at least as practiced in the past, is, we now know, a poor recipe for economic success, at any rate once a society has provided itself with the essentials of a modern productive system.

Now, since, historically, the idea of socialism was strongly linked to that of central planning, economists of socialist persuasion did not, until recently, study non-central planning ways of organizing what would remain in one key respect a socialist economy, in that the assets used to produce things are shared. Market socialism is called "socialist" because it abolishes the division between capital and labor: there is, in market socialism, no class of capitalists facing workers who own no capital, since workers themselves, that is, the whole population, own the capital of firms (though not necessarily of the very firms that they work in, as will be illustrated two paragraphs on). Economic inequality is thereby substantially diminished. And there now exist various designs for workers' ownership, for different forms of semi-public ownership, for example, at a municipal level, and other attempts to formulate a realization of the principle of collective ownership in the absence of central state direction of all economic activity.

Market socialism is, however, unlike traditionally conceived socialism in that its worker or publicly owned firms confront one another, and consumers, in market-competitive fashion; and market socialism is also, and relatedly, unlike traditionally conceived socialism in that it reduces, even though it does not entirely eliminate, the traditional socialist emphasis on economic equality. Equality is prejudiced because market competition leads to inequality between winners and losers. And community, too, is prejudiced, under market socialism, because exchange under market socialism is no less market exchange than it is under capitalism: it is not, as it is in the Carensian economy described above, only superficially market exchange. True reciprocity, express rather than merely implicit reciprocity (see pp. 420–421 above), does not prevail at the heart of market socialism's economic transactions. But it lies in the background of the system: the values of equality and reciprocity justify the constraints under which the socialist market functions, and all of that is true, too, of the welfare state, and of

the proposal that the state ensure that all of its citizens have a substantial market-independent *basic income*.

A particularly careful design of market socialism can be found in the book *A Future for Socialism*, by the Yale economist John Roemer, which was published in 1994 by Harvard University Press. In Roemer's scheme, each citizen enjoys a birthright entitlement to a per capita share of her country's total capital assets. She is free to trade the vouchers that represent her share on the stock market, and thereby, with skill and luck, to obtain more stock and/or more dividend income than others, but she may not realize her stock so as to convert it into such goods as mansions, yachts, Dior gowns, and so forth: shares in firms are inconvertible into ordinary money, nor can they be bought with ordinary money, but only with other shares. And, on her demise, a person's shares return to the treasury so that new birthrights to capital assets can be formed. The labor market, on the other hand, is not otherwise changed, so its inequalities remain, but not, now, in inflating synergy with the capital/labor divide.

In brief, the system is like a traditional capitalist market economy except that one market is closed: the one on which exchanges can be made of firm stock for money that buys consumption goods. The capitalist class is liquidated, but the efficiency results of the capitalist market are, Roemer claims, achieved, by different means.

To illustrate the latter point. Large shareholders in given firms standardly discipline those firms into efficient operation in a capitalist economy: their shares are large enough for them to have an immediate and substantial stake in how well the firm functions. But in Roemer's market socialism the dynamic of stock transactions will spread each individual's portfolio across many firms, with no individual having enough stock, or, therefore, stake, in any given firm, to undertake the required disciplining role. That role is therefore assigned to banks and other financial institutions, as prefigured by what actually now happens in the Japanese *Keiretsu* system, and in Germany.

Being an economist, Roemer is concerned to show that his system is not less efficient than capitalism. But suppose he is wrong. Suppose his scheme, or any comparable socialist or semi-socialist scheme, is somewhat less efficient than standard capitalism. The right inference from that need not be that we should keep capitalism: efficiency is, after all, only one value, and it would show a lack of balance to insist that even small deficits in that value should be eliminated at whatever cost to the values of equality and community. For efficiency, in the relevant sense, only means providing the goods and services that you want when you do not take into account (other aspects of) the quality of your life, and the quality of your relations to your fellow citizens. Why should we make *no* sacrifice of the former for the sake of the latter?

Market socialism does not fully satisfy socialist standards of distributive justice, but it scores far better by those standards than market capitalism does, and is therefore an eminently worthwhile project, from a socialist point of view. Market socialism nevertheless remains deficient from that point of view, because, by socialist standards, there is injustice in a system that confers high rewards on people who happen to be unusually talented and who form highly productive cooperatives. Market socialism is also a deficient socialism because the market exchange that lies at its heart tends against the value of community.

But could we go further than Roemer in a non-market direction? I do not know whether the needed refinements are possible, nor do I know, speaking more generally, whether the full socialist ideal is feasible, in the Carensian, or in some other form. We socialists don't *now* know how to replicate camping trip procedures on a nationwide scale, amid the complexity and variety that comes with nationwide size. We don't *now* know how to give collective ownership and equality the real meaning that it has in

the camping trip story but which it didn't have in the Soviet Union and in similarly ordered states. The camping trip's confined temporal, spatial, and population scale mean that, within its confines, the right to personal choice can be exercised, without strain, consistently with equality and community. But while that can happen in the small, we do not know how to honor personal choice, consistently with equality and community, on a large social scale. But I do not think that we now know that we will never know how to do these things: I am agnostic on that score.

The technology for using base motives to productive economic effect is reasonably well understood. Indeed, the history of the twentieth century encourages the thought that the easiest way to generate productivity in a modern society is by nourishing the motives of which I spoke earlier, namely, those of greed and fear. But we should never forget that greed and fear are repugnant motives. Who would propose running a society on the basis of such motives, and thereby promoting the psychology to which they belong, if they were not known to be effective, if they did not have the instrumental value which is the only value that they have? In the famous statement in which Adam Smith justified market relations, he pointed out that we place our faith not in the butcher's generosity but in his self-interest when we rely on him to provision us. Smith thereby propounded a wholly instrumental justification of market motivation, in face of what he acknowledged to be its unattractive intrinsic character. Old-style socialists often ignore Smith's point, in a moralistic condemnation of market motivation that fails to address its instrumental justification. Certain contemporary overenthusiastic market socialists tend, contrariwise, to forget that the market is intrinsically repugnant, because they are blinded by their belated discovery of the market's instrumental value. It is the genius of the market that it (1) recruits low-grade motives to (2) desirable ends; but (3) it also produces undesirable effects, including significant unjust inequality. In a balanced view, all three sides of that proposition must be kept in focus, but many market socialists now self-deceptively overlook (1) and (3). Both (1) and (2) were kept in focus by the pioneering eighteenth-century writer Bernard Mandeville, whose market-praising *Fable of the Bees* was subtitled *Private Vices, Public Benefits*. Many contemporary celebrants of the market play down the truth in the first part of that subtitle.

V Coda

Any attempt to realize the socialist ideal runs up against entrenched capitalist power and individual human selfishness. Politically serious people must take those obstacles seriously. But they are not reasons to disparage the ideal itself. Disparaging the ideal because it faces those obstacles leads to confusion, and confusion generates disoriented practice: there are contexts where the ideal *can* be advanced, but is pushed forward less resolutely than it might be, because of a lack of clarity about what the ideal is.

The socialist aspiration is to extend community and justice to the whole of our economic life. As I have acknowledged, we now know that we do not now know how to do that, and many think that we now know that it is impossible to do that. But community conquests in certain domains, such as health care and education, have sustained viable forms of production and distribution in the past, and it is imperative, now, to defend community, since it is a value that is currently under aggressive threat from the market principle. The natural tendency of the market is to increase the scope of the social relations that it covers, because entrepreneurs see opportunities at the edge to turn what is not yet a commodity into one. Left to itself, the capitalist dynamic is self-sustaining, and socialists therefore need the power of organized politics to oppose it: their capitalist opponents, who go with the grain of the system, need that power less (which is not to say that they lack it!).

I agree with Albert Einstein that socialism is humanity's attempt "to overcome and advance beyond the predatory phase of human development." Every market, even a socialist market, is a system of predation. Our attempt to get beyond predation has thus far failed. I do not think the right conclusion is to give up.

Chapter 32

Philippe Van Parijs

A BASIC INCOME FOR ALL

Philippe Van Parijs (1951–) is a philosopher and political economist at the Université Catholique de Louvain in Belgium. He is best-known for his defense of a universal basic income (UBI), which would pay a fixed sum to every adult regardless of their other income or ability or willingness to work. In this essay, originally published in the *Boston Review* in 2000, Parijs explains the UBI, lays out several lines of reasoning in support of it, and defends it against some common objections.

Entering the new millennium, I submit for discussion a proposal for the improvement of the human condition: namely, that everyone should be paid a *universal basic income* (UBI), at a level *sufficient for subsistence*.

In a world in which a child under five dies of malnutrition every two seconds, and close to a third of the planet's population lives in a state of "extreme poverty" that often proves fatal, the global enactment of such a basic income proposal may seem wildly utopian. Readers may suspect it to be impossible even in the wealthiest of OECD nations.

Yet, in those nations, productivity, wealth, and national incomes have advanced sufficiently far to support an adequate UBI. And if enacted, a basic income would serve as a powerful instrument of social justice: it would promote real freedom for all by providing the material resources that people need to pursue their aims. At the same time, it would help to solve the policy dilemmas of poverty and unemployment, and serve ideals associated with both the feminist and green movements. So I will argue.

I am convinced, along with many others in Europe, that – far from being utopian – a UBI makes common sense in the current context of the European Union.[1] As Brazilian senator Eduardo Suplicy has argued, it is also relevant to less developed countries – not only because it helps keep alive the remote promise of a high level of social solidarity without the perversity of high unemployment, but also because it can inspire and guide more modest immediate reforms.[2] And if a UBI makes sense in Europe and in less developed countries, why should it not make equally good (or perhaps better) sense in North America?[3] After all, the United States is the only country in the world in which a UBI is already in place: in 1999, the Alaska Permanent Fund paid each person of whatever age who had been living in Alaska for at least one year an annual UBI of $1,680. This payment admittedly falls far short of subsistence, but it has nonetheless become far from negligible two decades after its inception. Moreover, there was a public debate about UBI in the United States long before it started in Europe. In 1967, Nobel economist James Tobin published the first technical article on the subject, and a few years later, he convinced George McGovern to promote a UBI, then called "demogrant," in his 1972 presidential campaign.[4]

To be sure, after this short public life the UBI has sunk into near-oblivion in North America. For good reasons? I believe not. There are many relevant differences between the United States and the European Union in terms of labor markets, educational systems, and ethnic make-up. But none of them makes the UBI intrinsically less appropriate for the United States than for the European Union. More important are the significant differences in the balance of political forces. In the United States, far more than in Europe, the political viability of a proposal is deeply affected by how much it caters to the tastes of wealthy campaign donors. This is bound to be a serious additional handicap for any proposal that aims to expand options for, and empower, the least wealthy. But let's not turn necessity into virtue, and sacrifice justice in the name of increased political feasibility. When fighting to reduce the impact of economic inequalities on the political agenda, it is essential, in the United States as elsewhere, to propose, explore, and advocate ideas that are ethically compelling and make economic sense, even when their political feasibility remains uncertain. Sobered, cautioned, and strengthened by Europe's debate of the last two decades, here is my modest contribution to this task.

UBI Defined

By *universal basic income* I mean an income paid by a government, at a uniform level and at regular intervals, to each adult member of society. The grant is paid, and its level is fixed, irrespective of whether the person is rich or poor, lives alone or with others, is willing to work or not.

In most versions – certainly in mine – it is granted not only to citizens, but to all permanent residents.

The UBI is called "basic" because it is something on which a person can safely count, a material foundation on which a life can firmly rest. Any other income – whether in cash or in kind, from work or savings, from the market or the state – can lawfully be added to it. On the other hand, nothing in the definition of UBI, as it is here understood, connects it to some notion of "basic needs." A UBI, as defined, can fall short of or exceed what is regarded as necessary to a decent existence.

I favor the highest sustainable such income, and believe that all the richer countries can now afford to pay a basic income above subsistence. But advocates of a UBI do not need to press for a basic income at this level right away. In fact, the easiest and safest way forward, though details may differ considerably from one country to another, is likely to consist of enacting a UBI first at a level below subsistence, and then increasing it over time.

The idea of the UBI is at least 150 years old. Its two earliest known formulations were inspired by Charles Fourier, the prolific French utopian socialist. In 1848, while Karl Marx was finishing off the Communist Manifesto around the corner, the Brussels-based Fourierist author Joseph Charlier published *Solution of the Social Problem*, in which he argued for a "territorial dividend" owed to each citizen by virtue of our equal ownership of the nation's territory. The following year, John Stuart Mill published a new edition of his *Principles of Political Economy*, which contains a sympathetic presentation of Fourierism ("the most skillfully combined, and with the greatest foresight of objections, of all the forms of Socialism") rephrased so as to yield an unambiguous UBI proposal: "In the distribution, a certain minimum is first assigned for the subsistence of every member of the community, whether capable or not of labour. The remainder of the produce is shared in certain proportions, to be determined beforehand, among the three elements, Labour, Capital, and Talent."[5]

Under various labels – "state bonus," "national dividend," "social dividend," "citizen's wage," "citizen's income," "universal grant," "basic income," etc. – the idea of a UBI was repeatedly taken up in intellectual circles throughout the twentieth century. It was seriously discussed by left-wing academics such as G. D. H. Cole and James Meade in England between the World Wars and, via Abba Lerner, it seems to have inspired Milton Friedman's proposal for a "negative income tax."[6] But only since the late 1970s has the idea gained real political currency in a number of European countries, starting with the Netherlands and Denmark. A number of political parties, usually green or "left-liberal" (in the European sense), have now made it part of their official party program.

UBI and Existing Programs

To appreciate the significance of this interest and support, it is important to understand how a UBI differs from existing benefit schemes. It obviously differs from traditional social-insurance based income-maintenance institutions (such as Social Security), whose benefits are restricted to wage workers who have contributed enough out of their past earnings to become eligible. But it also differs from West European or North American conditional minimum-income schemes (such as welfare).

Many, indeed most, West European countries introduced some form of guaranteed minimum-income scheme at some point after World War II.[7] But these schemes remain conditional: to receive an income grant a beneficiary must meet more or less stringent variants of the following three requirements: if she is able to work, she must be willing to accept a suitable job, or to undergo suitable training, if offered; she must pass a means test, in the sense that she is only entitled to the benefit if there are grounds to believe that she has no access to a

sufficient income from other sources; and her household situation must meet certain criteria – it matters, for example, whether she lives on her own, with a person who has a job, with a jobless person, etc. By contrast, a UBI does not require satisfaction of any of these conditions.

Advocates of a UBI may, but generally do not, propose it as a full substitute for existing conditional transfers. Most supporters want to keep – possibly in simplified forms and necessarily at reduced levels – publicly organized social insurance and disability compensation schemes that would supplement the unconditional income while remaining subjected to the usual conditions. Indeed, if a government implemented an unconditional income that was too small to cover basic needs – which, as I previously noted, would almost certainly be the case at first – UBI advocates would not want to eliminate the existing conditional minimum-income schemes, but only to readjust their levels.

In the context of Europe's most developed welfare states, for example, one might imagine the immediate introduction of universal child benefits and a strictly individual, noncontributory basic pension as full substitutes for existing means-tested benefit schemes for the young and the elderly. Indeed, some of these countries already have such age-restricted UBIs for the young and the elderly. Contributory retirement insurance schemes, whether obligatory or optional, would top up the basic pension.

As for the working-age population, advocates of a universal minimum income could, in the short term, settle for a "partial" (less-than-subsistence) but strictly individual UBI, initially pitched at, say, half the current guaranteed minimum income for a single person. In US terms, that would be about $250 per month, or $3,000 a year. For households whose net earnings are insufficient to reach the socially defined subsistence level, this unconditional and individual floor would be supplemented by means-tested benefits, differentiated according to household size and subjected, as they are now, to some work requirements.

UBI and Some Alternatives

While the UBI is different from traditional income maintenance schemes, it also differs from a number of other innovative proposals that have attracted recent attention. Perhaps closest to a UBI are various negative income tax (NIT) proposals.[8]

NIT

Though the details vary, the basic idea of a negative income tax is to grant each citizen a basic income, but in the form of a refundable tax credit. From the personal tax liability of each household, one subtracts the sum of the basic incomes of its members. If the difference is positive, a tax needs to be paid. If it is negative, a benefit (or negative tax) is paid by the government to the household. In principle, one can achieve exactly the same distribution of post-tax-and-transfer income among households with a UBI or with an NIT. Indeed, the NIT might be cheaper to run, since it avoids the to-and-fro that results from paying a basic income to those with a substantial income and then taxing it back.

Still, a UBI has three major advantages over an NIT. First, any NIT scheme would have the desired effects on poverty only if it was supplemented by a system of advance payments sufficient to keep people from starving before their tax forms are examined at the end of the fiscal year. But from what we know of social welfare programs, ignorance or confusion is bound to prevent some people from getting access to such advance payments. The higher rate of take-up that is bound to be associated with a UBI scheme matters greatly to anyone who wants to fight poverty.

Second, although an NIT could in principle be individualized, it operates most naturally and is usually proposed at the household level. As a result, even if the inter-household distribution of income were exactly the same under an NIT and the corresponding UBI, the intra-household distribution will be far less unequal under the UBI. In particular, under current circumstances, the income that directly accrues to women will be considerably higher under the UBI than the NIT, since the latter tends to ascribe to the household's higher earner at least part of the tax credit of the low- or non-earning partner.

Third, a UBI can be expected to deal far better than an NIT with an important aspect of the "unemployment trap" that is stressed by social workers but generally overlooked by economists. Whether it makes any sense for an unemployed person to look for or accept a job does not only depend on the difference between income at work and out of work. What deters people from getting out to work is often the reasonable fear of uncertainty. While they try a new job, or just after they lose one, the regular flow of benefits is often interrupted. The risk of administrative time lags — especially among people who may have a limited knowledge of their entitlements and the fear of going into debt, or for people who are likely to have no savings to fall back on — may make sticking to benefits the wisest option. Unlike an NIT, a UBI provides a firm basis of income that keeps flowing whether one is in or out of work. And it is therefore far better suited to handle this aspect of the poverty trap.

The Stakeholder Society

UBI also differs from the lump-sum grant, or "stake," that Thomas Paine and Orestes Brownson — and, more recently, Bruce Ackerman and Anne Alstott — have suggested be universally awarded to citizens at their maturity in a refashioned "stakeholder society."[9] Ackerman and Alstott propose that, upon reaching age 21, every citizen, rich or poor, should be awarded a lump-sum stake of $80,000. This money can be used in any way its recipient wishes — from investing in the stock market or paying for college fees to blowing it all in a wild night of gambling. The stake is not conditioned on recipients being "deserving," or having shown any interest in contributing to society. Funding would be provided by a two percent wealth tax, which could be gradually replaced over time (assuming a fair proportion of recipients ended their lives with enough assets) by a lump-sum estate tax of $80,000 (in effect requiring the recipient to pay back the stake).

I am not opposed to a wealth or estate tax, nor do I think it is a bad idea to give everyone a little stake to get going with their adult life. Moreover, giving a large stake at the beginning of adult life might be regarded as formally equivalent – with some freedom added – to giving an equivalent amount as a life-long unconditional income. After all, if the stake is assumed to be paid back at the end of a person's life, as it is in the Ackerman/Alstott proposal, the equivalent annual amount is simply the stake multiplied by the real rate of interest, say an amount in the (very modest) order of $2,000 annually, or hardly more than Alaska's dividend. If instead people are entitled to consume their stake through life – and who would stop them? – the equivalent annual income would be significantly higher.

Whatever the level, given the choice between an initial endowment and an equivalent life-long UBI, we should go for the latter. Endowments are rife with opportunities for waste, especially among those less well equipped by birth and background to make use of the opportunity the stake supplies. To achieve, on an ongoing basis, the goal of some baseline income maintenance, it would therefore be necessary to keep a means-tested welfare system, and we would be essentially back to our starting point – the need and desirability of a UBI as an alternative to current provisions.

Why a UBI?

So much for definitions and distinctions. Let us now turn to the central case for a UBI.

Justice

The main argument for UBI is founded on a view of justice. Social justice, I believe, requires that our institutions be designed to best secure *real freedom* to all.[10] Such a real-libertarian conception of justice combines two ideas. First, the members of society should be formally free, with a well-enforced structure of property rights that includes the ownership of each by herself. What matters to a real libertarian, however, is not only the protection of individual rights, but assurances of the real value of those rights: we need to be concerned not only with liberty, but, in John Rawls's phrase, with the "worth of liberty." At first approximation, the worth or real value of a person's liberty depends on the resources the person has at her command to make use of her liberty. So it is therefore necessary that the distribution of opportunity – understood as access to the means that people need for doing what they might want to do – be designed to offer the greatest possible real opportunity to those with least opportunities, subject to everyone's formal freedom being respected.

This notion of a just, free society needs to be specified and clarified in many respects.[11] But in the eyes of anyone who finds it attractive, there cannot but be a strong presumption in favor of UBI. A cash grant to all, no questions asked, no strings attached, at the highest sustainable level, can hardly fail to advance that ideal. Or if it does not, the burden of argument lies squarely on the side of the challengers.

Jobs and Growth

A second way to make the case for UBI is more policy-oriented. A UBI might be seen as a way to solve the apparent dilemma between a European-style combination of limited poverty and high unemployment and an American-style combination of low unemployment and widespread poverty. The argument can be spelled out, very schematically, as follows.

For over two decades, most West European countries have been experiencing massive unemployment. Even at the peak of the jobs cycle, millions of Europeans are vainly seeking work. How can this problem be tackled? For a while, the received wisdom was to deal with massive unemployment by speeding up the rate of growth. But considering the speed with which technological progress was eliminating jobs, it became apparent that a fantastic rate of growth would be necessary even to keep employment stable, let alone to reduce the number of unemployed. For environmental and other reasons, such a rate of growth would not be desirable. An alternative strategy was to consider a substantial reduction in workers' earnings. By reducing the relative cost of labor, technology could be redirected in such a way that fewer jobs were sacrificed. A more modest and therefore sustainable growth rate might then be able to stabilize and gradually reduce present levels of unemployment. But this could only be achieved at the cost of imposing an unacceptable standard of living on a large part of the population, all the more so because a reduction in wages would require a parallel reduction in unemployment benefits and other replacement incomes, so as to preserve work incentives.

If we reject both accelerated growth and reduced earnings, must we also give up on full employment? Yes, if by full employment we mean a situation in which virtually everyone who wants a *full-time* job can obtain one that is both affordable for the employer *without any subsidy* and affordable for the worker *without any additional benefit*. But perhaps not, if we are willing to redefine full employment by either shortening the working week, paying subsidies to employers, or paying subsidies to employees.

A first option, particularly fashionable in France at the moment, consists in a social redefinition of "full time" – that is, a reduction in maximum working time, typically in the form of a reduction in the standard length of the working week. The underlying idea is to ration

jobs: because there are not enough jobs for everyone who would like one, let us not allow a subset to appropriate them all.

On closer scrutiny, however, this strategy is less helpful than it might seem. If the aim is to reduce unemployment, the reduction in the work week must be dramatic enough to more than offset the rate of productivity growth. If this dramatic reduction is matched by a proportional fall in earnings, the lowest wages will then fall – unacceptably – below the social minimum. If, instead, total earnings are maintained at the same level, if only for the less well paid, labor costs will rise. The effect on unemployment will then be reduced, if not reversed, as the pressure to eliminate the less skilled jobs through mechanization is stepped up. In other words, a dramatic reduction in working time looks bound to be detrimental to the least qualified jobs – either because it kills the supply (they pay less than replacement incomes) or because it kills the demand (they cost firms a lot more per hour than they used to).

It does not follow that the reduction of the standard working week can play no role in a strategy for reducing unemployment without increasing poverty. But to avoid the dilemma thus sketched, it needs to be coupled with explicit or implicit subsidies to low-paid jobs. For example, a reduction of the standard working week did play a role in the so-called "Dutch miracle" – the fact that, in the last decade or so, jobs expanded much faster in the Netherlands than elsewhere in Europe. But this was mainly as a result of the standard working week falling below firms' usual operating time and thereby triggering a restructuring of work organization that involved far more part-time jobs. But these jobs could not have developed without the large implicit subsidies they enjoy, in the Netherlands, by virtue of a universal basic pension, universal child benefits, and a universal health care system.

Any strategy for reducing unemployment without increasing poverty depends, then, on some variety of the *active* welfare state – that is, a welfare state that does not subsidize passivity (the unemployed, the retired, the disabled, etc.) but systematically and permanently (if modestly) subsidizes productive activities. Such subsidies can take many different forms. At one extreme, they can take the form of general subsidies to employers at a level that is gradually reduced as the hourly wage rate increases. Edmund Phelps has advocated a scheme of this sort, restricted to full-time workers, for the United States.[12] In Europe, this approach usually takes the form of proposals to abolish employers' social security contributions on the lower earnings while maintaining the workers' entitlements to the same level of benefits.

At the other extreme we find the UBI, which can also be understood as a subsidy, but one paid to the employee (or potential employee), thereby giving her the option of accepting a job with a lower hourly wage or with shorter hours than she otherwise could. In between, there are a large number of other schemes, such as the US Earned Income Tax Credit and various benefit programs restricted to people actually working or actively looking for full-time work.

A general employment subsidy and a UBI are very similar in terms of the underlying economic analysis and, in part, in what they aim to achieve. For example, both address head-on the dilemma mentioned in connection with reductions in work time: they make it possible for the least skilled to be employed at a lower cost to their employer, without thereby impoverishing workers.

The two approaches are, however, fundamentally different in one respect. With employer subsidies, the pressure to take up employment is kept intact, possibly even increased; with a UBI, that pressure is reduced. This is not because permanent idleness becomes an attractive option: even a large UBI cannot be expected to secure a comfortable standard of living on its own. Instead, a UBI makes it easier to take a break between two jobs, reduce working time, make room for more training, take up

self-employment, or to join a cooperative. And with a UBI, workers will only take a job if they find it suitably attractive, while employer subsidies make unattractive, low-productivity jobs more economically viable. If the motive in combating unemployment is not some sort of work fetishism – an obsession with keeping everyone busy – but rather a concern to give every person the possibility of taking up gainful employment in which she can find recognition and accomplishment, then the UBI is to be preferred.

Feminist and Green Concerns

A third piece of the argument for a UBI takes particular note of its contribution to realizing the promise of the feminist and green movements. The contribution to the first should be obvious. Given the sexist division of labor in the household and the special "caring" functions that women disproportionately bear, their labor market participation, and range of choice in jobs, is far more constrained than those of men. Both in terms of direct impact on the interindividual distribution of income and the longer-term impact on job options, a UBI is therefore bound to benefit women far more than men. Some of them, no doubt, will use the greater material freedom UBI provides to reduce their paid working time and thereby lighten the "double shift" at certain periods of their lives. But who can sincerely believe that working subject to the dictates of a boss for forty hours a week is a path to liberation? Moreover, it is not only against the tyranny of bosses that a UBI supplies some protection, but also against the tyranny of husbands and bureaucrats. It provides a modest but secure basis on which the more vulnerable can stand, as marriages collapse or administrative discretion is misused.

To discuss the connection between UBI and the green movement, it is useful to view the latter as an alliance of two components. Very schematically, the *environmental* component's central concern is with the *pollution* generated by industrial society. Its central objective is the establishment of a society that can be sustained by its physical environment. The *green-alternative* component's central concern, on the other hand, is with the *alienation* generated by industrial society. Its central objective is to establish a society in which people spend a great deal of their time on "autonomous" activities, ruled by neither the market nor the state. For both components, there is something very attractive in the idea of a UBI.

The environmentalists' chief foe is productivism, the obsessive pursuit of economic growth. And one of the most powerful justifications for fast growth, in particular among the working class and its organizations, is the fight against unemployment. The UBI, as argued above, is a coherent strategy for tackling unemployment without relying on faster growth. The availability of such a strategy undermines the broad productivist coalition and thereby improves the prospects for realizing environmentalist objectives in a world in which pollution (even in the widest sense) is not the only thing most people care about.

Green alternatives should also be attracted to basic income proposals, for a UBI can be viewed as a general subsidy financed by the market and state spheres to the benefit of the autonomous sphere. This is in part because the UBI gives everyone some real freedom – as opposed to a sheer right – to withdraw from paid employment in order to perform autonomous activities, such as grass-roots militancy or unpaid care work. But part of the impact also consists in giving the least well endowed greater power to turn down jobs that they do not find sufficiently fulfilling, and in thereby creating incentives to design and offer less alienated employment.

Some Objections

Suppose everything I have said thus far is persuasive: that the UBI, if it could be instituted, would be a natural and attractive way of ensuring a fair distribution of real freedom, fighting unemployment without increasing poverty, and promoting the central goals of both the feminist and the green movements. What are the objections?

Perhaps the most common is that a UBI would cost too much. Such a statement is of course meaningless if the amount and the scale is left unspecified. At a level of $150 per month and per person, a UBI is obviously affordable in some places, since this is the monthly equivalent of what every Alaskan receives as an annual dividend. Could one afford a UBI closer to the poverty line? By simply multiplying the poverty threshold for a one-person household by the population of a country, one soon reaches scary amounts – often well in excess of the current level of total government expenditure.

But these calculations are misleading. A wide range of existing benefits can be abolished or reduced once a UBI is in place. And for most people of working age, the basic income and the increased taxes (most likely in the form of an abolition of exemptions and of low tax rates for the lowest income brackets) required to pay for it will largely offset each other. In a country such as the United States, which has developed a reasonably effective revenue collection system, what matters is not the gross cost but its distributive impact – which could easily work out the same for a UBI or an NIT.

Estimates of the net budgetary cost of various UBI and NIT schemes have been made both in Europe and the United States.[13] Obviously, the more comprehensive and generous existing means-tested minimum-income schemes are, the more limited the net cost of a UBI scheme at a given level. But the net cost is also heavily affected by two other factors. Does the scheme aim to achieve an effective rate of taxation (and hence of disincentive to work) at the lower end of the distribution of earnings no higher than the tax rates higher up? And does it give the same amount to each member of a couple as to a single person? If the answer is positive on both counts, a scheme that purports to lift every household out of poverty has a very high net cost, and would therefore generate major shifts in the income distribution, not only from richer to poorer households, but also from single people to couples.[14] This does not mean that it is "unaffordable," but that a gradual approach is required if sudden sharp falls in the disposable incomes of some households are to be avoided. A basic income or negative income tax at the household level is one possible option. A strictly individual, but "partial" basic income, with means-tested income supplements for single adult households, is another.

A second frequent objection is that a UBI would have perverse labor supply effects. (In fact, some American income maintenance experiments in the 1970s showed such effects.) The first response should be: "So what?" Boosting the labor supply is no aim in itself. No one can reasonably want an overworked, hyperactive society. Give people of all classes the opportunity to reduce their working time or even take a complete break from work in order to look after their children or elderly relatives. You will not only save on prisons and hospitals. You will also improve the human capital of the next generation. A modest UBI is a simple and effective instrument in the service of keeping a socially and economically sound balance between the supply of paid labor and the rest of our lives.

It is of the greatest importance that our tax-and-transfer systems not trap the least skilled, or those whose options are limited for some other reason, in a situation of idleness and dependency. But it is precisely awareness of this risk that has been the most powerful factor in arousing public interest for a UBI in those European countries in which a substantial means-tested guaranteed minimum income had been operating for some time. It would be absurd to deny that such schemes depress in undesirable ways workers' willingness to accept low-paid jobs and stick with them, and therefore also employers'

interest in designing and offering such jobs. But reducing the level or security of income support, on the pattern of the United States 1996 welfare reform, is not the only possible response. Reducing the various dimensions of the unemployment trap by turning means-tested schemes into universal ones is another. Between these two routes, there cannot be much doubt about what is to be preferred by people committed to combining a sound economy and a fair society – as opposed to boosting labor supply to the maximum.

A third objection is moral rather than simply pragmatic. A UBI, it is often said, gives the undeserving poor something for nothing. According to one version of this objection, a UBI conflicts with the fundamental principle of reciprocity: the idea that people who receive benefits should respond in kind by making contributions. Precisely because it is unconditional, it assigns benefits even to those who make no social contribution – who spend their mornings bickering with their partner, surf off Malibu in the afternoon, and smoke pot all night.

One might respond by simply asking: How many would actually choose this life? How many, compared to the countless people who spend most of their days doing socially useful but unpaid work? Everything we know suggests that nearly all people seek to make some contribution. And many of us believe that it would be positively awful to try to turn all socially useful contributions into waged employment. On this background, even the principle "To each according to her contribution" justifies a modest UBI as part of its best feasible institutional implementation.

But a more fundamental reply is available. True, a UBI is undeserved good news for the idle surfer. But this good news is ethically indistinguishable from the undeserved luck that massively affects the present distribution of wealth, income, and leisure. Our race, gender, and citizenship, how educated and wealthy we are, how gifted in math and how fluent in

English, how handsome and even how ambitious, are overwhelmingly a function of who our parents happened to be and of other equally arbitrary contingencies. Not even the most narcissistic self-made man could think that he fixed the parental dice in advance of entering this world. Such gifts of luck are unavoidable and, if they are fairly distributed, unobjectionable. A minimum condition for a fair distribution is that everyone should be guaranteed a modest share of these undeserved gifts.[15] Nothing could achieve this more securely than a UBI.

Such a moral argument will not be sufficient in reshaping the politically possible. But it may well prove crucial. Without needing to deny the importance of work and the role of personal responsibility, it will save us from being overimpressed by a fashionable political rhetoric that justifies bending the least advantaged more firmly under the yoke. It will make us even more confident about the rightness of a universal basic income than about the rightness of universal suffrage. It will make us even more comfortable about everyone being entitled to an income, even the lazy, than about everyone being entitled to a vote, even the incompetent.

Notes

1 Many academics and activists who share this view have joined the Basic Income European Network (BIEN). Founded in 1986, BIEN holds its eighth congress in Berlin in October 2000. It publishes an electronic newsletter (bien@etes.ucl.ac.be), and maintains a web site that carries a comprehensive annotated bibliography in all EU languages (http://www.etes.ucl.ac.be/BIEN/bien.html). For a recent set of relevant European essays, see Loek Groot and Robert Jan van der Veen, eds., *Basic Income on the Agenda: Policy Objectives and Political Chances* (Amsterdam: Amsterdam University Press, 2000).

2 Federal senator for the huge state of Sao Paulo and member of the opposition Workers Party (PT), Suplicy has advocated an ambitious guaranteed minimum income scheme, a version of which was approved by Brazil's Senate in 1991.

3 Two North American UBI networks were set up earlier this year: the United States Basic Income Guarantee Network, c/o Dr Karl Widerquist, The Jerome Levy Economics Institute of Bard College, Annandale-on-Hudson, NY 12504-5000, USA (http://www.usbig.net); and Basic Income/ Canada, c/o Prof. Sally Lerner, Department of Environment and Resource Studies, University of Waterloo, Waterloo, Ontario, Canada N2L 3G1 (http://www.fes.uwaterloo.ca/Research/FW).

4 See James Tobin, Joseph A. Pechman, and Peter M. Mieszkowski, "Is a Negative Income Tax Practical?" *Yale Law Journal* 77 (1967): 1–27. See also a recent conversation with Tobin in BIEN's newsletter ("James Tobin, the Demogrant and the Future of U.S. Social Policy," in *Basic Income* 29 (Spring 1998), available on BIEN's web site).

5 See Joseph Charlier, *Solution du problème social ou constitution humanitaire* (Brussels: Chez tous les libraires du Royaume, 1848); John Stuart Mill, *Principles of Political Economy*, 2nd ed. [1849] (New York: Augustus Kelley, 1987).

6 See the exchange between Eduardo Suplicy and Milton Friedman in *Basic Income* 34 (June 2000).

7 The latest countries to introduce a guaranteed minimum income at national level were France (in 1988) and Portugal (in 1997). Out of the European Union's 15 member states, only Italy and Greece have no such scheme.

8 In the United States, one recent proposal of this type has been made in Fred Block and Jeff Manza, "Could We End Poverty in a Postindustrial Society? The Case for a Progressive Negative Income Tax," *Politics and Society* 25 (December 1997): 473–511.

9 Bruce Ackerman and Anne Alstott, *The Stakeholder Society* (New Haven: Yale University Press, 1999). Their proposal is a sophisticated and updated version of a proposal made by Thomas Paine to the French Directoire. See "Agrarian Justice" [1796], in *The Life and Major Writings of Thomas Paine*, P. F. Foner, ed., (Secaucus, N.J.: Citadel Press, 1974), pp. 605–623. A similar program was proposed, independently, by the New England liberal, and later arch-conservative, Orestes Brownson, in the *Boston Quarterly Review* of October 1840. If the American people are committed to the principle of "equal chances," he argued, then they should

make sure that each person receives, on maturity, an equal share of the "general inheritance."

10 For a more detailed discussion, see Philippe Van Parijs, *Real Freedom for All* (New York: Oxford University Press, 1995).

11 One can think of alternative normative foundations. For example, under some empirical assumptions a UBI is also arguably part of the package that Rawls's difference principle would justify. See, for example, Walter Schaller, "Rawls, the Difference Principle, and Economic Inequality," in *Pacific Philosophical Quarterly* 79 (1998) 368–91; Philippe Van Parijs, "Difference Principles," in *The Cambridge Companion to John Rawls*, Samuel Freeman, ed., (Cambridge: Cambridge University Press, forthcoming). Alternatively, one might view a UBI as a partial embodiment of the Marxian principle of distribution according to needs. See Robert J. van der Veen and Philippe Van Parijs, "A Capitalist Road to Communism," *Theory and Society* 15 (1986): 635–55.

12 See Edmund S. Phelps, *Rewarding Work* (Cambridge, Mass.: Harvard University Press, 1997).

13 In the U.S. case, for example, the fiscally equivalent negative-income-tax scheme proposed by Block and Manza, which would raise all base incomes to at least 90 percent of the poverty line (and those of poor families well above that), would, in mid-1990s dollars, cost about $60 billion annually.

14 To fund this net cost, the personal income tax is obviously not the only possible source. In some European proposals, at least part of the funding comes from ecological, energy, or land taxes; from a tax on value; from non-inflationary money creation; or possibly even from Tobin taxes on international financial transactions (although it is generally recognized that the funding of a basic income in rich countries would not exactly be a priority in the allocation of whatever revenues may be collected from this source). But none of these sources could realistically enable us to dispense with personal income taxation as the basic source of funding. Nor do they avoid generating a net cost in terms of real disposable income for some households, and thereby raising an issue of "affordability."

15 Along the same lines, Herbert A. Simon observes "that any causal analysis explaining why American GDP is about $25,000 per capita would show that at least 2/3 is due to the happy accident that the income recipient was born in the U.S." He adds, "I am not so naive as to believe that my 70% tax [required to fund a UBI of $8,000 p.a. with a flat tax] is politically viable in the United States at present, but looking toward the future, it is none too soon to find answers to the arguments of those who think they have a solid moral right to retain all the wealth they earn." See Simon's letter to the organizers of BIEN's seventh congress in *Basic Income* 28 (Spring 1998).

2d. FREEDOM

MOST POLITICAL PHILOSOPHERS AGREE that freedom is an important value, and that protecting or promoting this value is one of the chief tasks of governments. But what exactly *is* freedom, and what governmental policies are truly consistent with it? The answers to these questions are of crucial importance for political philosophy.

Suppose you've always wanted to climb Mt. Shasta in California. You have the equipment, you've read the books, and you've even hired yourself a guide. Your boss has given you the time off from work, and no one is stopping you from fulfilling your dream. The only problem is that you suffer from a crippling acrophobia — the thought of standing on a high, exposed mountainside leaves you unable to take a single step. Are you free to climb the mountain, or not?

In a sense, of course, you are. There is no law against your climbing the mountain, and no person or external obstacle is standing in your way of your doing so. But then again, *something* is standing in your way. Even if you truly and fully want to climb the mountain, your disease prevents you from doing so. And what difference does it make to you whether what stops you from doing what you want is a person with a gun telling you "no" or your own disabling mental condition?

The problem is that we use the word "freedom" in at least two different senses. One sense — which has been called *negative freedom* — characterizes freedom as the lack of external obstacles, especially those caused by other human beings. The other sense of freedom is generally referred to as *positive freedom*, and has more to do with self-mastery — with being able to direct one's own actions in accordance with one's own truly autonomous desires. Since nobody is stopping you from climbing Mt. Shasta, you are free to do so in the negative sense. But because your acrophobia prevents you from acting as you truly wish to act (the condition controls your behavior, not your autonomous desires), you lack freedom in the positive sense.

To say that one values freedom, then, is not enough to give a clear indication of the kind of governmental policies one would support. One must also say what *kind* of freedom one values. For one who values freedom in the negative sense, all that is generally required of governments is to get out of the way — "*laissez faire et laissez passez; le monde va de lui même.*"[1] Governments can enhance individuals' freedom by preventing them from forcibly interfering with each other through laws against robbery, assault and the like. But apart from that, government activity should be severely constrained, lest government *itself* become an impediment to liberty by restricting what people can say or read, what they can trade on the market, or what they can do with their bodies or property. This classical liberal emphasis on the importance of negative freedom is to be found both in John Stuart Mill's defense of the "harm principle" as the sole standard for legitimate interference with individual liberty, and in Isaiah Berlin's insistence on the importance of negative liberty, and the dangers of tyranny inherent in its confusion with positive liberty.

Many, however, have found classical liberalism's exclusive focus on negative freedom to be unsatisfying. For some of these critics, such as the nineteenth century conservative James Fitzjames Stephen, the main problem is the classical liberal's failure to *balance* a concern for negative liberty with other important social values. For Stephen, religion and morality are essential to the maintenance of social order, and to the instruction of those masses of humanity who are too "selfish, sensual, frivolous, [and] idle" to govern themselves by the light of their own individual reason. But both religion and morality rely essentially upon *coercion* for their operation, and thus run afoul of the strict Millian principle of negative liberty.

For others, the problem with classical liberalism is not that it focuses *too much* on liberty, but that it focuses on the *wrong kind* of liberty. Consider Anatole France's quip that "The law, in its majestic equality, forbids rich and poor alike to sleep under bridges, beg in the streets or steal bread." His point, of course, is that the rich and poor only enjoy the same freedoms under the law in a *formal* sense. Sure, the law doesn't forbid the rich from sleeping under bridges, any more than it forbids the poor from dining on caviar and champagne. But the fact that the law doesn't forbid these things is not really what matters. What matters is the *substantive* freedom that people actually enjoy — the activities that they are actually free in a *positive* sense to engage in. An exclusive focus on negative liberty not only obscures the inequality of formal liberty between rich and poor, but exacerbates that inequality by condemning redistributive transfers of wealth and limits on economic power as violations of the only kind of freedom that really matters.

It was precisely this sort of concern that led Franklin Delano Roosevelt to include "freedom from want" in his "Four Freedoms" speech. Roosevelt gave this speech at a time when the U.S. Supreme Court was striking down numerous economic regulations as unconstitutional on the grounds that they violated freedom of contract. In the famous 1905 case *Lochner v. New York*, for instance, the Court struck down as unconstitutional a New York law limiting the number of hours a baker could work per week, on the grounds that the number of hours worked per week was properly a matter to be decided on by an agreement between a worker and their employer. For Roosevelt and others in the progressive movement, this insistence on defending the (negative) liberty of contract merely privileged the economically powerful at the expense of the (positive) liberty of the economically disadvantaged to work reasonable hours in a safe environment for a fair wage. Freedom from want, Roosevelt thought, should be considered a basic human right along with freedom of speech, and not a privilege of the well-off.

The debate between advocates of negative liberty and advocates of positive liberty dominated philosophical discussion for much of the last half of the twentieth century. But in recent decades, a new approach has emerged. Ironically, it might also be the *oldest* approach to freedom, drawing as it does on a rich tradition of thought dating back to Cicero and the Roman Republic. This "republican" conception of liberty sees the essence of freedom as consisting in the absence of *domination*, where domination is understood as the capacity to interfere arbitrarily with another person's activities.

Slavery, on the republican view, is a paradigmatic case of domination, and the antithesis of freedom. But a life of poverty can subject one to domination too, especially in a capitalist society like the United States where poverty might mean that one is subject to the arbitrary dictates of one's employer, landlord, etc. The republican conception will thus have some overlap with both the negative and the positive approaches to freedom, but its focus on the *capacity* for interference (rather than actual interference), and on *arbitrary* interference (rather than interference as such) renders it an importantly distinct view.

Our widespread agreement on the value of freedom, then, masks a tremendous disagreement regarding the *meaning* of freedom, regarding the comparative value of different types of freedom, and regarding the comparative value of freedom and other distinct values. It is to these difficult questions that the readings in this section are addressed.

Note

1 "Leave things alone, let them pass; the world runs by itself," a saying attributed to the eighteenth century French economist and head of the Physiocrats, Vincent de Gournay.

Further Reading

Carter, I. (2004). *A Measure of Freedom*. Oxford: Oxford University Press.

Carter, I., Kramer, M., and Steiner, H. (2007). *Freedom: An Anthology*. New York: Wiley-Blackwell.

Cohen, G. A. (1995). *Self-ownership, Freedom, and Equality*. New York: Cambridge University Press.

Constant, B. (1988). The Liberty of the Ancients Compared with That of the Moderns. In B. Fontana (Ed.), *Constant: Political Writings* (pp. 309–28). New York: Cambridge University Press.

Green, T. H. (2006). Liberal Legislation and Freedom of Contract. In D. Miller (Ed.), *The Liberty Reader* (pp. 21–32). Boulder, CO: Paradigm Publishers.

Hayek, F. A. (1960). *The Constitution of Liberty*. Chicago: University of Chicago Press.

MacCallum, G. (2006). Negative and Positive Freedom. In D. Miller (Ed.), *The Liberty Reader* (pp. 100–22). Boulder, CO: Paradigm Publishers.

Mack, E., and Gaus, G. (2004). Classical Liberalism and Libertarianism: The Liberty Tradition. In G. Gaus and C. Kukathas (Eds.), *Handbook of Political Theory* (pp. 115–30). London: Sage.

Nozick, R. (1974). *Anarchy, State, and Utopia*. New York: Basic Books.

Pettit, P. (2006). The Republican Ideal of Freedom. In D. Miller (Ed.), *The Liberty Reader* (pp. 223–43). Boulder, CO: Paradigm Publishers.

Skinner, Q. (2006). A Third Concept of Liberty. In D. Miller (Ed.), *The Liberty Reader* (pp. 243–54). Boulder, CO: Paradigm Publishers.

Stephen, J. F. (1992). *Liberty, Equality, and Fraternity*. Chicago: University of Chicago Press.

Taylor, C. (2006). What's Wrong with Negative Liberty? In D. Miller (Ed.), *The Liberty Reader* (pp. 141–62). Boulder, CO: Paradigm Publishers.

Wertheimer, A. (2006). *Coercion*. Princeton: Princeton University Press.

Chapter 33

John Stuart Mill

ON LIBERTY

John Stuart Mill (1806–73) was a British philosopher and, with Jeremy Bentham, one of the most historically influential proponents of the moral philosophy known as utilitarianism. In these excerpts from his enormously influential *On Liberty* (1859), Mill sets forth his "harm principle"—the claim that the only legitimate grounds for interfering with an individual's liberty is to prevent harm to others—and explains the way in which a consistent recognition of that principle would severely limit the authority of society over the individual.

Chapter I

Introductory

The subject of this Essay is not the so-called Liberty of the Will, so unfortunately opposed to the misnamed doctrine of Philosophical Necessity; but Civil, or Social Liberty: the nature and limits of the power which can be legitimately exercised by society over the individual. A question seldom stated, and hardly ever discussed, in general terms, but which profoundly influences the practical controversies of the age by its latent presence, and is likely soon to make itself recognized as the vital question of the future. It is so far from being new, that, in a certain sense, it has divided mankind, almost from the remotest ages; but in the stage of progress into which the more civilized portions of the species have now entered, it presents itself under new conditions, and requires a different and more fundamental treatment.

The struggle between Liberty and Authority is the most conspicuous feature in the portions of history with which we are earliest familiar, particularly in that of Greece, Rome, and England. But in old times this contest was between subjects, or some classes of subjects, and the Government. By liberty, was meant protection against the tyranny of the political rulers. The rulers were conceived (except in some of the popular governments of Greece) as in a necessarily antagonistic position to the people they ruled. They consisted of a governing One, or a governing tribe or caste, who derived their authority from inheritance or conquest, who, at all events, did not hold it at the pleasure of the governed, and whose supremacy men did not venture, perhaps did not desire, to contest, whatever precautions might be taken against its oppressive exercise. Their power was regarded as necessary, but also as highly dangerous; as a weapon which they would attempt to use against their subjects, no less than against external enemies. To prevent the weaker members of the community from being preyed upon by innumerable vultures, it was needful that there should be an animal of prey stronger than the rest, commissioned to keep them down. But as the king of the vultures would be no less bent upon preying on the flock than any of the minor harpies, it was indispensable to be in a perpetual attitude of defence against his beak and claws. The aim, therefore, of patriots was to set limits to the power which the ruler should be suffered to exercise over the community; and this limitation was what they meant by liberty. It was attempted in two ways. First, by obtaining a recognition of certain immunities, called political liberties or rights, which it was to be regarded as a breach of duty in the ruler to infringe, and which if he did infringe, specific resistance, or general rebellion, was held to be justifiable. A second, and generally a later expedient, was the establishment of constitutional checks, by which the consent of the community, or of a body of some sort, supposed to represent its interests, was made a necessary condition to some of the more important acts of the governing power. To the first of these modes of limitation, the ruling power, in most European countries, was compelled, more or less, to submit. It was not so with the second; and, to attain this, or when already in some degree possessed, to attain it more completely, became everywhere the principal object of the lovers of liberty. And so long as mankind were content to combat one enemy by another, and to be ruled by a master, on condition of being guaranteed more or less efficaciously against his tyranny, they did not carry their aspirations beyond this point.

A time, however, came, in the progress of human affairs, when men ceased to think it a necessity of nature that their governors should be an independent power, opposed in interest to themselves. It appeared to them much better that the various magistrates of the State should be their tenants or delegates, revocable at their pleasure. In that way alone, it seemed, could they have complete security that the powers of government would never be abused to their

disadvantage. By degrees this new demand for elective and temporary rulers became the prominent object of the exertions of the popular party, wherever any such party existed; and superseded, to a considerable extent, the previous efforts to limit the power of rulers. As the struggle proceeded for making the ruling power emanate from the periodical choice of the ruled, some persons began to think that too much importance had been attached to the limitation of the power itself. *That* (it might seem) was a resource against rulers whose interests were habitually opposed to those of the people. What was now wanted was, that the rulers should be identified with the people; that their interest and will should be the interest and will of the nation. The nation did not need to be protected against its own will. There was no fear of its tyrannizing over itself. Let the rulers be effectually responsible to it, promptly removable by it, and it could afford to trust them with power of which it could itself dictate the use to be made. Their power was but the nation's own power, concentrated, and in a form convenient for exercise. This mode of thought, or rather perhaps of feeling, was common among the last generation of European liberalism, in the Continental section of which it still apparently predominates. Those who admit any limit to what a government may do, except in the case of such governments as they think ought not to exist, stand out as brilliant exceptions among the political thinkers of the Continent. A similar tone of sentiment might by this time have been prevalent in our own country, if the circumstances which for a time encouraged it, had continued unaltered.

But, in political and philosophical theories, as well as in persons, success discloses faults and infirmities which failure might have concealed from observation. The notion, that the people have no need to limit their power over themselves, might seem axiomatic, when popular government was a thing only dreamed about, or read of as having existed at some distant period of the past. Neither was that notion necessarily disturbed by such temporary aberrations as those of the French Revolution, the worst of which were the work of a usurping few, and which, in any case, belonged, not to the permanent working of popular institutions, but to a sudden and convulsive outbreak against monarchical and aristocratic despotism. In time, however, a democratic republic came to occupy a large portion of the earth's surface, and made itself felt as one of the most powerful members of the community of nations; and elective and responsible government became subject to the observations and criticism which wait upon a great existing fact. It was now perceived that such phrases as "self-government," and "the power of the people over themselves," do not express the true state of the case. The "people" who exercise the power are not always the same people with those over whom it is exercised; and the "self-government" spoken of is not the government of each by himself, but of each by all the rest. The will of the people, moreover, practically means the will of the most numerous or the most active *part* of the people; the majority, or those who succeed in making themselves accepted as the majority; the people, consequently *may* desire to oppress a part of their number; and precautions are as much needed against this as against any other abuse of power. The limitation, therefore, of the power of government over individuals loses none of its importance when the holders of power are regularly accountable to the community, that is, to the strongest party therein. This view of things, recommending itself equally to the intelligence of thinkers and to the inclination of those important classes in European society to whose real or supposed interests democracy is adverse, has had no difficulty in establishing itself; and in political speculations "the tyranny of the majority" is now generally included among the evils against which society requires to be on its guard.

Like other tyrannies, the tyranny of the majority was at first, and is still vulgarly, held in dread, chiefly as operating through the acts of the public authorities. But reflecting persons perceived that when society is itself the tyrant – society collectively over the separate individuals who compose it – its means of tyrannizing are not restricted to the acts which it may do by the hands of its political functionaries. Society can and does execute its own mandates: and if it issues wrong mandates instead of right, or any mandates at all in things with which it ought not to meddle, it practices a social tyranny more formidable than many kinds of political oppression, since, though not usually upheld by such extreme penalties, it leaves fewer means of escape, penetrating much more deeply into the details of life, and enslaving the soul itself. Protection, therefore, against the tyranny of the magistrate is not enough: there needs protection also against the tyranny of the prevailing opinion and feeling; against the tendency of society to impose, by other means than civil penalties, its own ideas and practices as rules of conduct on those who dissent from them; to fetter the development, and, if possible, prevent the formation, of any individuality not in harmony with its ways, and compels all characters to fashion themselves upon the model of its own. There is a limit to the legitimate interference of collective opinion with individual independence: and to find that limit, and maintain it against encroachment, is as indispensable to a good condition of human affairs, as protection against political despotism.

But though this proposition is not likely to be contested in general terms, the practical question, where to place the limit – how to make the fitting adjustment between individual independence and social control – is a subject on which nearly everything remains to be done. All that makes existence valuable to any one, depends on the enforcement of restraints upon the actions of other people. Some rules of conduct, therefore, must be imposed, by law in the first place, and by opinion on many things which are not fit subjects for the operation of law. What these rules should be is the principal question in human affairs; but if we except a few of the most obvious cases, it is one of those which least progress has been made in resolving.

[. . .]

The object of this Essay is to assert one very simple principle, as entitled to govern absolutely the dealings of society with the individual in the way of compulsion and control, whether the means used be physical force in the form of legal penalties, or the moral coercion of public opinion. That principle is, that the sole end for which mankind are warranted, individually or collectively, in interfering with the liberty of action of any of their number, is self-protection. That the only purpose for which power can be rightfully exercised over any member of a civilized community, against his will, is to prevent harm to others. His own good, either physical or moral, is not a sufficient warrant. He cannot rightfully be compelled to do or forbear because it will be better for him to do so, because it will make him happier, because, in the opinions of others, to do so would be wise, or even right. These are good reasons for remonstrating with him, or reasoning with him, or persuading him, or entreating him, but not for compelling him, or visiting him with any evil in case he do otherwise. To justify that, the conduct from which it is desired to deter him must be calculated to produce evil to some one else. The only part of the conduct of any one, for which he is amenable to society, is that which concerns others. In the part which merely concerns himself, his independence is, of right, absolute. Over himself, over his own body and mind, the individual is sovereign.

It is, perhaps, hardly necessary to say that this doctrine is meant to apply only to human beings in the maturity of their faculties. We are not speaking of children, or of young persons below the age which the law may fix as that of manhood or womanhood. Those who are still in a state to require being taken care of by others, must be protected against their own actions as well as against external injury. For the same reason, we may leave out of consideration those backward states of society in which the race itself may be considered as in its nonage. The early difficulties in the way of spontaneous progress are so great, that there is seldom any choice of means for overcoming them; and a ruler full of the spirit of improvement is warranted in the use of any expedients that will attain an end, perhaps otherwise unattainable. Despotism is a legitimate mode of government in dealing with barbarians, provided the end be their improvement, and the means justified by actually effecting that end. Liberty, as a principle, has no application to any state of things anterior to the time when mankind have become capable of being improved by free and equal discussion. Until then, there is nothing for them but implicit obedience to an Akbar or a Charlemagne, if they are so fortunate as to find one. But as soon as mankind have attained the capacity of being guided to their own improvement by conviction or persuasion (a period long since reached in all nations with whom we need here concern ourselves), compulsion, either in the direct form or in that of pains and penalties for non-compliance, is no longer admissible as a means to their own good, and justifiable only for the security of others.

It is proper to state that I forego any advantage which could be derived to my argument from the idea of abstract right, as a thing independent of utility. I regard utility as the ultimate appeal on all ethical questions; but it must be utility in the largest sense, grounded on the permanent interests of a man as a progressive being. Those interests, I contend, authorize the subjection of individual spontaneity to external control, only in respect to those actions of each, which concern the interest of other people. If any one does an act hurtful to others, there is a *prima facie* case for punishing him, by law, or, where legal penalties are not safely applicable, by general disapprobation. There are also many positive acts for the benefit of others, which he may rightfully be compelled to perform; such as to give evidence in a court of justice; to bear his fair share in the common defence, or in any other joint work necessary to the interest of the society of which he enjoys the protection; and to perform certain acts of individual beneficence, such as saving a fellow-creature's life, or interposing to protect the defenceless against ill-usage, things which whenever it is obviously a man's duty to do, he may rightfully be made responsible to society for not doing. A person may cause evil to others not only by his actions but by his inaction, and in either case he is justly accountable to them for the injury. The latter case, it is true, requires a much more cautious exercise of compulsion than the former. To make any one answerable for doing evil to others is the rule; to make him answerable for not preventing evil is, comparatively speaking, the exception. Yet there are many cases clear enough and grave enough to justify that exception. In all things which regard the external relations of the individual, he is *de jure* amenable to those whose interests are concerned, and, if need be, to society as their protector. There are often good reasons for not holding him to the responsibility; but these reasons must arise from the special expediencies of the case: either because it is a kind of case in which he is on the whole likely to act better, when left to his own discretion, than when controlled in any way in which society have it in their power to control him; or because the attempt to exercise control would produce other evils, greater than those which it would prevent. When such reasons as these preclude the enforcement of responsibility, the conscience of the agent himself should step into the vacant judgment seat, and protect those interests of others which have no external protection; judging himself all the more rigidly, because the case does not admit of his being made accountable to the judgment of his fellow-creatures.

But there is a sphere of action in which society, as distinguished from the individual, has, if any, only an indirect interest; comprehending all that portion of a person's life and conduct which affects only himself, or if it also affects others, only with their free, voluntary, and undeceived consent and participation. When I say only himself, I mean directly, and in the first instance; for whatever affects himself, may affect others through himself; and the objection which may be grounded on this contingency, will receive consideration in the sequel. This, then, is the appropriate region of human liberty. It compromises, first, the inward domain of consciousness; demanding liberty of conscience in the most comprehensive sense; liberty of thought and feeling; absolute freedom of opinion and sentiment on all subjects, practical or speculative, scientific, moral, or theological. The liberty of expressing and publishing opinions may seem to fall under a different principle, since it belongs to that part of the conduct of an individual which concerns other people; but, being almost of as much importance as the liberty of thought itself, and resting in great part on the same reasons, is practically inseparable from it. Secondly, the principle requires liberty of tastes and pursuits; of framing the plan of our life to suit our own character; of doing as we like, subject to such consequences as may follow: without impediment from our fellow-creatures, so long as what we do does not harm them, even though they should think our conduct foolish, perverse, or wrong. Thirdly, from this liberty of each individual, follows the liberty, within the same limits, of combination among individuals; freedom to unite, for any purpose not involving harm to others: the persons combining being supposed to be of full age, and not forced or deceived.

No society in which these liberties are not, on the whole, respected, is free, whatever may be its form of government; and none is completely free in which they do not exist absolute and unqualified. The only freedom which deserves the name, is that of pursuing our own good in our own way, so long as we do not attempt to deprive others of theirs, or impede their efforts to obtain it. Each is the proper guardian of his own health, whether bodily, or mental and spiritual. Mankind are greater gainers by suffering each other to live as seems good to themselves, than by compelling each to live as seems good to the rest.

Though this doctrine is anything but new, and, to some persons, may have the air of a truism, there is no doctrine which stands more directly opposed to the general tendency of existing opinion and practice.

[. . .]

Apart from the peculiar tenets of individual thinkers, there is also in the world at large an increasing inclination to stretch unduly the powers of society over the individual, both by the force of opinion and even by that of legislation; and as the tendency of all the changes taking place in the world is to strengthen society, and diminish the power of the individual, this encroachment is not one of the evils which tend spontaneously to disappear, but, on the contrary, to grow more and more formidable. The disposition of mankind, whether as rulers or as fellow-citizens, to impose their own opinions and inclinations as a rule of conduct on others, is so energetically supported by some of the best and by some of the worst feelings incident to human nature, that it is hardly ever kept under restraint by anything but want of power; and as the power is not declining, but growing, unless a strong barrier of moral conviction can be raised against the mischief, we must expect, in the present circumstances of the world, to see it increase.

Chapter IV

Of the Limits to the Authority of Society over the Individual

What, then, is the rightful limit to the sovereignty of the individual over himself? Where does the authority of society begin? How much of human life should be assigned to individuality, and how much to society?

Each will receive its proper share, if each has that which more particularly concerns it. To individuality should belong the part of life in which it is chiefly the individual that is interested; to society, the part which chiefly interests society.

Though society is not founded on a contract, and though no good purpose is answered by inventing a contract in order to deduce social obligations from it, every one who receives the protection of society owes a return for the benefit, and the fact of living in society renders it indispensable that each should be bound to observe a certain line of conduct towards the rest. This conduct consists, first, in not injuring the interests of one another; or rather certain interests, which, either by express legal provision or by tacit understanding, ought to be considered as rights; and secondly, in each person's bearing his share (to be fixed on some equitable principle) of the labours and sacrifices incurred for defending the society or its members from injury and molestation. These conditions society is justified in enforcing, at all costs to those who endeavour to withhold fulfillment. Nor is this all that society may do. The acts of an individual may be hurtful to others, or wanting in due consideration for their welfare, without going to the length of violating any of their constituted rights. The offender may then be justly punished by opinion, though not by law. As soon as any part of a person's conduct affects prejudicially the interests of others, society has jurisdiction over it, and the question whether the general welfare will or will not be promoted by interfering with it, becomes open to discussion. But there is no room for entertaining any such question when a person's conduct affects the interests of no persons besides himself, or needs not affect them unless they like (all the persons concerned being of full age, and the ordinary amount of understanding). In all such cases, there should be perfect freedom, legal and social, to do the action and stand the consequences.

It would be a great misunderstanding of this doctrine to suppose that it is one of selfish indifference, which pretends that human beings have no business with each other's conduct in life, and that they should not concern themselves about the well-doing or well-being of one another, unless their own interest is involved. Instead of any diminution, there is need of a great increase of disinterested exertion to promote the good of others. But disinterested benevolence can find other instruments to persuade people to their good than whips and scourges, either of the literal or the metaphorical sort. I am the last person to undervalue the self-regarding virtues; they are only second in importance, if even second, to the social. It is equally the business of education to cultivate both. But even education works by conviction and persuasion as well as by compulsion, and it is by the former only that, when the period of education is passed, the self-regarding virtues should be inculcated. Human beings owe to each other help to distinguish the better from the worse, and encouragement to choose the former and avoid the latter. They should be for ever stimulating each other to increased exercise of their higher faculties, and increased direction of their feelings and aims towards wise instead of foolish, elevating instead of degrading, objects and contemplations. But neither one person, nor any number of persons, is warranted in saying to another human creature of ripe years that he shall not do with his life for his own benefit what he chooses to do with it. He is the person most interested in his own well-being: the interest which any other person, except in cases of strong personal attachment, can have in it, is trifling, compared with that which he himself has; the interest which society has in him individually (except as to his conduct to others) is fractional, and altogether indirect; while with respect to his own feelings and circumstances, the most ordinary man or woman has means of knowledge immeasurably surpassing those that can be possessed by any one else. The

interference of society to overrule his judgment and purposes in what only regards himself must be grounded on general presumptions; which may be altogether wrong, and even if right, are as likely as not to be misapplied to individual cases, by persons no better acquainted with the circumstances of such cases than those are who look at them merely from without. In this department, therefore, of human affairs, Individuality has its proper field of action. In the conduct of human beings towards one another it is necessary that general rules should for the most part be observed, in order that people may know what they have to expect: but in each person's own concerns his individual spontaneity is entitled to free exercise. Considerations to aid his judgment, exhortations to strengthen his will, may be offered to him, even obtruded on him, by others: but he himself is the final judge. All errors which he is likely to commit against advice and warning are far outweighed by the evil of allowing others to constrain him to what they deem his good.

I do not mean that the feelings with which a person is regarded by others ought not to be in any way affected by his self-regarding qualities or deficiencies. This is neither possible nor desirable. If he is eminent in any of the qualities which conduce to his own good, he is, so far, a proper object of admiration. He is so much the nearer to the ideal perfection of human nature. If he is grossly deficient in those qualities, a sentiment the opposite of admiration will follow. There is a degree of folly, and a degree of what may be called (though the phrase is not unobjectionable) lowness or depravation of taste, which, though it cannot justify doing harm to the person who manifests it, renders him necessarily and properly a subject of distaste, or, in extreme cases, even of contempt: a person could not have the opposite qualities in due strength without entertaining these feelings. Though doing no worse to any one, a person may so act as to compel us to judge him, and feel to him, as a fool, or as a being of an inferior order: and since this judgment and feeling are a fact which he would prefer to avoid, it is doing him a service to warn him of it beforehand, as of any other disagreeable consequence to which he exposes himself. It would be well, indeed, if this good office were much more freely rendered than the common notions of politeness at present permit, and if one person could honestly point out to another that he thinks him in fault, without being considered unmannerly or presuming. We have a right, also, in various ways, to act upon our unfavourable opinion of any one, not to the oppression of his individuality, but in the exercise of ours. We are not bound, for example, to seek his society; we have a right to avoid it (though not to parade the avoidance), for we have a right to choose the society most acceptable to us. We have a right, and it may be our duty, to caution others against him, if we think his example or conversation likely to have a pernicious effect on those with whom he associates. We may give others a preference over him in optional good offices, except those which tend to his improvement. In these various modes a person may suffer very severe penalties at the hands of others for faults which directly concern only himself; but he suffers these penalties only in so far as they are the natural and, as it were, the spontaneous consequences of the faults themselves, not because they are purposely inflicted on him for the sake of punishment. A person who shows rashness, obstinacy, self-conceit – who cannot live within moderate means – who cannot restrain himself from hurtful indulgences – who pursues animal pleasures at the expense of those of feeling and intellect – must expect to be lowered in the opinion of others, and to have a less share of their favourable sentiments; but of this he has no right to complain, unless he has merited their favour by special excellence in his social relations, and has thus established a title to their good offices, which is not affected by his demerits towards himself.

What I contend for is, that the inconveniences which are strictly inseparable from the unfavourable judgment of others, are the only ones to which a person should ever be subjected for that portion of his conduct and character which concerns his own good, but which does not affect the interest of others in their relations with him. Acts injurious to others require a totally different treatment. Encroachment on their rights; infliction on them of any loss or damage not justified by his own rights; falsehood or duplicity in dealing with them; unfair or ungenerous use of advantages over them; even selfish abstinence from defending them against injury – these are fit objects of moral reprobation, and, in grave cases, of moral retribution and punishment. And not only these acts, but the dispositions which lead to them, are properly immoral, and fit subjects of disapprobation which may rise to abhorrence. Cruelty of disposition; malice and ill-nature; that most anti-social and odious of all passions, envy; dissimulation and insincerity, irascibility on insufficient cause, and resentment disproportioned to the provocation; the love of domineering over others; the desire to engross more than one's share of advantages (the πλεονεξία of the Greeks); the pride which derives gratification from the abasement of others; the egotism which thinks self and its concerns more important than everything else, and decides all doubtful questions in its own favour – these are moral vices, and constitute a bad and odious moral character: unlike the self-regarding faults previously mentioned, which are not properly immoralities, and to whatever pitch they may be carried, do not constitute wickedness. They may be proofs of any amount of folly, or want of personal dignity and self-respect; but they are only a subject of moral reprobation when they involve a breach of duty to others, for whose sake the individual is bound to have care for himself. What are called duties to ourselves are not socially obligatory, unless circumstances render them at the same time duties to others. The term duty to oneself, when it means anything more than prudence, means self-respect or self-development, and for none of these is any one accountable to his fellow-creatures, because for none of them is it for the good of mankind that he be held accountable to them.

The distinction between the loss of consideration which a person may rightly incur by defect of prudence or of personal dignity, and the reprobation which is due to him for an offence against the rights of others, is not a merely nominal distinction. It makes a vast difference, both in our feelings and in our conduct towards him, whether he displeases us in things in which we think we have a right to control him, or in things in which we know that we have not. If he displeases us, we may express our distaste, and we may stand aloof from a person as well as from a thing that displeases us; but we shall not therefore feel called on to make his life uncomfortable. We shall reflect that he already bears, or will bear, the whole penalty of his error; if he spoils his life by mismanagement, we shall not, for that reason, desire to spoil it still further: instead of wishing to punish him, we shall rather endeavour to alleviate his punishment, by showing him how he may avoid or cure the evils his conduct tends to bring upon him. He may be to us an object of pity, perhaps of dislike, but not of anger or resentment; we shall not treat him like an enemy of society: the worst we shall think ourselves justified in doing is leaving him to himself, if we do not interfere benevolently by showing interest or concern for him. It is far otherwise if he has infringed the rules necessary for the protection of his fellow-creatures, individually or collectively. The evil consequences of his acts do not then fall on himself, but on others; and society, as the protector of all its members, must retaliate on him; must inflict pain on him for the express purpose of punishment, and must take care that it be sufficiently severe. In the one case, he is an offender at our bar, and we are called on not only to sit in judgment on him, but, in one shape or another, to execute our own sentence: in the other case, it is not our part to inflict any suffering on him, except what may incidentally follow from our using the same liberty in the regulation of our own affairs, which we allow to him in his.

The distinction here pointed out between the part of a person's life which concerns only himself, and that which concerns others, many persons will refuse to admit. How (it may be asked) can any part of the conduct of a member of society be a matter of indifference to the other members? No person is an entirely isolated being; it is impossible for a person to do anything seriously or permanently hurtful to himself, without mischief reaching at least to his near connections, and often far beyond them. If he injures his property, he does harm to those who directly or indirectly derived support from it, and usually diminishes, by a greater or less amount, the general resources of the community. If he deteriorates his bodily or mental faculties, he not only brings evil upon all who depended on him for any portion of their happiness, but disqualifies himself for rendering the services which he owes to his fellow-creatures generally; perhaps becomes a burthen on their affection or benevolence; and if such conduct were very frequent, hardly any offence that is committed would detract more from the general sum of good. Finally, if by his vices or follies a person does no direct harm to others, he is nevertheless (it may be said) injurious by his example; and ought to be compelled to control himself, for the sake of those whom the sight or knowledge of his conduct might corrupt or mislead.

And even (it will be added) if the consequences of misconduct could be confined to the vicious or thoughtless individual, ought society to abandon to their own guidance those who are manifestly unfit for it? If protection against themselves is confessedly due to children and persons under age, is not society equally bound to afford it to persons of mature years who are equally incapable of self-government? If gambling, or drunkenness, or incontinence, or idleness, or uncleanliness, are as injurious to happiness, and as great a hindrance to improvement, as many or most of the acts prohibited by law, why (it may be asked) should not law, so far as is consistent with practicability and social convenience, endeavour to repress these also? And as a supplement to the unavoidable imperfections of law, ought not opinion at least to organize a powerful police against these vices, and visit rigidly with social penalties those who are known to practise them? There is no question here (it may be said) about restricting individuality, or impeding the trial of new and original experiments in living. The only things it is sought to prevent are things which have been tried and condemned from the beginning of the world until now; things which experience has shown not to be useful or suitable to any person's individuality. There must be some length of time and amount of experience after which a moral or prudential truth may be regarded as established: and it is merely desired to prevent generation after generation from falling over the same precipice which has been fatal to their predecessors.

I fully admit that the mischief which a person does to himself may seriously affect, both through their sympathies and their interests, those nearly connected with him and, in a minor degree, society at large. When, by conduct of this sort, a person is led to violate a distinct and assignable obligation to any other person or persons, the case is taken out of the self-regarding class, and becomes amenable to moral disapprobation in the proper sense of the term. If, for example; a man, through intemperance or extravagance, becomes unable to pay his debts, or, having undertaken the moral responsibility of a family, becomes from the same cause incapable of supporting or educating them, he is deservedly reprobated, and might be justly punished; but it is for the breach of duty to his family or creditors, not for the extravagance. If the resources which ought to have been devoted to them, had been diverted from them for the most prudent investment, the moral culpability would have been the same. George Barnwell murdered his uncle to get money for his mistress, but if he had done it to set himself up in business, he would equally have been hanged. Again, in the frequent case of a man who causes grief to his family by addiction to bad habits, he deserves reproach for his unkindness or ingratitude; but so he may for cultivating habits not in themselves vicious, if they are painful to those with whom he passes his life, or who from personal ties are dependent on him for their comfort. Whoever fails in the consideration generally due to the interests and feelings of others, not being compelled by some more imperative duty, or justified by allowable self-preference, is a subject of moral disapprobation for that failure, but not for the cause of it, nor for the errors, merely personal to himself, which may have remotely led to it. In like manner, when a person disables himself, by conduct purely self-regarding, from the performance of some definite duty incumbent on him to the public, he is guilty of a social offence. No person ought to be punished simply for being drunk; but a soldier or a policeman should be punished for being drunk on duty. Whenever, in short, there is a definite damage, or a definite risk of damage, either to an individual or to the public, the case is taken out of the province of liberty, and placed in that of morality or law. But with regard to the merely contingent, or, as it may be called, constructive injury which a person causes to society, by conduct which neither violates any specific duty to the public, nor occasions perceptible hurt to any assignable individual except himself; the inconvenience is one which society can afford to bear, for the sake of the greater good of human freedom. If grown persons are to be punished for not taking proper care of themselves, I would rather it were for their own sake, than under pretence of preventing them from impairing their capacity or rendering to society benefits which society does not pretend it has a right to exact.

[. . .]

But the strongest of all the arguments against the interference of the public with purely personal conduct is that, when it does interfere, the odds are that it interferes wrongly, and in the wrong place. On questions of social morality, of duty to others, the opinion of the public, that is, of an overruling majority, though often wrong, is likely to be still oftener right; because on such questions they are only required to judge of their own interests; of the manner in which some mode of conduct, if allowed to be practised, would affect themselves. But the opinion of a similar majority, imposed as a law on the minority, on questions of self-regarding conduct, is quite as likely to be wrong as right; for in these cases public opinion means, at the best, some people's opinion of what is good or bad for other people; while very often it does not even mean that; the public, with the most perfect indifference, passing over the pleasure or convenience of those whose conduct they censure, and considering only their own preference. There are many who consider as an injury to themselves any conduct which they have a distaste for, and resent it as an outrage to their feelings; as a religious bigot, when charged with disregarding the religious feelings of others, has been known to retort that they disregard his feelings, by persisting in their abominable worship or creed. But there is no parity between the feeling of a person for his own opinion, and the feeling of another who is offended at his holding it; no more than between the desire of a thief to take a purse, and the desire of the right owner to keep it. And a person's taste is as much his own peculiar concern as his opinion or his purse. It is easy for any one to imagine an ideal public which leaves the freedom and choice of individuals in all uncertain matters undisturbed, and only requires them to abstain from modes of conduct which universal experience has condemned. But where has there been seen a public which set any such limit to its censorship? or when does the public trouble itself about universal experience? In its interferences with personal conduct it is seldom thinking of anything but the enormity of acting or feeling differently from itself; and this standard of judgment, thinly disguised, is held up to mankind as the dictate of religion and philosophy, by nine-tenths of all moralists and speculative writers. These teach that things are right because they are right; because we feel them to be so. They tell us to search in our own minds and hearts for laws of conduct binding on ourselves and on all others. What can the poor public do but apply these instructions, and make their own personal feelings of good and evil, if they are tolerably unanimous in them, obligatory on all the world?

The evil here pointed out is not one which exists only in theory; and it may perhaps be expected that I should specify the instances in which the public of this age and country improperly invests its own preferences with the character of moral laws. I am not writing an essay on the aberrations of existing moral feeling. That is too weighty a subject to be discussed parenthetically, and by way of illustration. Yet examples are necessary to show that the principle I maintain is of serious and practical moment, and that I am not endeavouring to erect a barrier against imaginary evils. And it is not difficult to show, by abundant instances, that to extend the bounds of what may be called moral police, until it encroaches on the most unquestionably legitimate liberty of the individual, is one of the most universal of all human propensities.

As a first instance, consider the antipathies which men cherish on no better grounds than that persons whose religious opinions are different from theirs do not practice their religious observances, especially their religious abstinences. To cite a rather trivial example, nothing in the creed or practice of Christians does more to envenom the hatred of Mahomedans against them than the fact of their eating pork. There are few acts which Christians and Europeans regard with more unaffected disgust than Mussulmans regard this particular mode of satisfying hunger. It is, in the first place, an offence against their religion; but this circumstance by no means explains either the degree or the kind of their repugnance; for wine also is forbidden by their religion, and to partake of it is by all Mussulmans accounted wrong, but not disgusting. Their aversion to the flesh of the "unclean beast" is, on the contrary, of that peculiar character, resembling an instinctive antipathy, which the idea of uncleanness, when once it thoroughly sinks into the feelings, seems always to excite even in those whose personal habits are anything but scrupulously clean and of which the sentiment of religious impurity, so intense in the Hindoos, is a remarkable example. Suppose now that in a people, of whom the majority were Mussulmans, that majority should insist upon not permitting pork to be eaten within the limits of the country. This would be nothing new in Mahomedan countries. Would it be a legitimate exercise of the moral authority of public opinion? and if not, why not? The practice is really revolting to such a public. They also sincerely think that it is forbidden and abhorred by the Deity. Neither could the prohibition be censured as religious persecution. It might be religious in its origin, but it would not be persecution for religion, since nobody's religion makes it a duty to eat pork. The only tenable ground of condemnation would be that with the personal tastes and self-regarding concerns of individuals the public has no business to interfere.

To come somewhat nearer home: the majority of Spaniards consider it a gross impiety, offensive in the highest degree to the Supreme Being, to worship him in any other manner than the Roman Catholic; and no other public worship is lawful on Spanish soil. The people of all Southern Europe look upon a married clergy as not only irreligious, but unchaste, indecent, gross, disgusting. What do Protestants think of these perfectly sincere feelings, and of the attempt to enforce them against non-Catholics? Yet, if mankind are justified in interfering with each other's liberty in things which do not concern

the interests of others, on what principle is it possible consistently to exclude these cases? or who can blame people for desiring to suppress what they regard as a scandal in the sight of God and man? No stronger case can be shown for prohibiting anything which is regarded as a personal immorality, than is made out for suppressing these practices in the eyes of those who regard them as impieties; and unless we are willing to adopt the logic of persecutors, and to say that we may persecute others because we are right, and that they must not persecute us because they are wrong, we must beware of admitting a principle of which we should resent as a gross injustice the application to ourselves.

The preceding instances may be objected to, although unreasonably, as drawn from contingencies impossible among us: opinion, in this country, not being likely to enforce abstinence from meats, or to interfere with people for worshipping, and for either marrying or not marrying, according to their creed or inclination. The next example, however, shall be taken from an interference with liberty which we have by no means passed all danger of. Wherever the Puritans have been sufficiently powerful, as in New England, and in Great Britain at the time of the Commonwealth, they have endeavoured, with considerable success, to put down all public, and nearly all private, amusements: especially music, dancing, public games, or other assemblages for purposes of diversion, and the theatre. There are still in this country large bodies of persons by whose notions of morality and religion these recreations are condemned; and those persons belonging chiefly to the middle class, who are the ascendant power in the present social and political condition of the kingdom, it is by no means impossible that persons of these sentiments may at some time or other command a majority in Parliament. How will the remaining portion of the community like to have the amusements that shall be permitted to them regulated by the religious and moral sentiments of the stricter Calvinists and Methodists? Would they not, with considerable peremptoriness, desire these intrusively pious members of society to mind their own business? This is precisely what should be said to every government and every public, who have the pretension that no person shall enjoy any pleasure which they think wrong. But if the principle of the pretension be admitted, no one can reasonably object to its being acted on in the sense of the majority, or other preponderating power in the country; and all persons must be ready to conform to the idea of a Christian commonwealth, as understood by the early settlers in New England, if a religious profession similiar to theirs should ever succeed in regaining its lost ground, as religions supposed to be declining have so often been known to do.

To imagine another contingency, perhaps more likely to be realized than the one last mentioned. There is confessedly a strong tendency in the modern world towards a democratic constitution of society, accompanied or not by popular political institutions. It is affirmed that in the country where this tendency is most completely realized – where both society and the government are most democratic – the United States – the feeling of the majority, to whom any appearance of a more showy or costly style of living than they can hope to rival is disagreeable, operates as a tolerably effectual sumptuary law, and that in many parts of the Union it is really difficult for a person possessing a very large income to find any mode of spending it which will not incur popular disapprobation. Though such statements as these are doubtless much exaggerated as a representation of existing facts, the state of things they describe is not only a conceivable and possible, but a probable result of democratic feeling, combined with the notion that the public has a right to a veto on the manner in which individuals shall spend their incomes. We have only further to suppose a considerable diffusion of Socialist opinions, and it may become infamous in the eyes of the majority to possess more property than some

very small amount, or any income not earned by manual labour. Opinions similar in principle to these already prevail widely among the artisan class, and weigh oppressively on those who are amenable to the opinion chiefly of that class, namely, its own members. It is known that the bad workmen who form the majority of the operatives in many branches of industry, are decidedly of opinion that bad workmen ought to receive the same wages as good, and that no one ought to be allowed, through piecework or otherwise, to earn by superior skill or industry more than others can without it. And they employ a moral police, which occasionally becomes a physical one, to deter skilful workmen from receiving, and employers from giving a larger remuneration for a more useful service. If the public have any jurisdiction over private concerns, I cannot see that these people are in fault, or that any individual's particular public can be blamed for asserting the same authority over his individual conduct which the general public asserts over people in general.

But, without dwelling upon suppositious cases, there are, in our own day, gross usurpations upon the liberty of private life actually practised, and still greater ones threatened with some expectation of success, and opinions propounded which assert an unlimited right in the public not only to prohibit by law everything which it thinks wrong, but, in order to get at what it thinks wrong, to prohibit a number of things which it admits to be innocent.

Under the name of preventing intemperance, the people of one English colony, and of nearly half the United States, have been interdicted by law from making any use whatever of fermented drinks, except for medical purposes: for prohibition of their sale is in fact, as it is intended to be, prohibition of their use. And though the impracticability of executing the law has caused its repeal in several of the States which had adopted it, including the one from which it derives its name, an attempt has notwithstanding been commenced, and is prosecuted with considerable zeal by many of the professed philanthropists, to agitate for a similar law in this country. The association, or "Alliance" as it terms itself, which has been formed for this purpose, has acquired some notoriety through the publicity given to a correspondence between its secretary and one of the very few English public men who hold that a politician's opinions ought to be founded on principles. Lord Stanley's share in this correspondence is calculated to strengthen the hopes already built on him, by those who know how rare such qualities as are manifested in some of his public appearances unhappily are among those who figure in political life. The organ of the Alliance, who would "deeply deplore the recognition of any principle which could be wrested to justify bigotry and persecution," undertakes to point out the "broad and impassable barrier" which divides such principles from those of the association. "All matters relating to thought, opinion, conscience, appear to me," he says, "to be without the sphere of legislation; all pertaining to social act, habit, relation, subject only to a discretionary power vested in the State itself, and not in the individual, to be within it." No mention is made of a third class, different from either of these, viz., acts and habits which are not social, but individual; although it is to this class, surely, that the act of drinking fermented liquors belongs. Selling fermented liquors, however, is trading, and trading is a social act. But the infringement complained of is not on the liberty of the seller, but on that of the buyer and consumer; since the State might just as well forbid him to drink wine as purposely make it impossible for him to obtain it. The secretary, however, says, "I claim, as a citizen, a right to legislate whenever my social rights are invaded by the social act of another." And now for the definition of these "social rights":

> If anything invades my social rights, certainly the traffic in strong drink does. It destroys my primary right of security, by constantly creating and stimulating social disorder. It invades my right of equality, by deriving a profit from the creation of a misery I am taxed to support. It impedes my right to free moral and intellectual development, by surrounding my path with dangers, and by weakening and demoralising society, from which I have a right to claim mutual aid and intercourse.

A theory of "social rights" the like which probably never before found its way into distinct language: being nothing short of this – that it is the absolute social right of every individual, that every other individual shall act in every respect exactly as he ought; that whosoever fails thereof in the smallest particular violates my social right, and entitles me to demand from the legislature the removal of the grievance. So monstrous a principle is far more dangerous than any single interference with liberty; there is no violation of liberty which it would not justify; it acknowledges no right to any freedom whatever, except perhaps to that of holding opinions in secret, without ever disclosing them: for, the moment an opinion which I consider noxious passes any one's lips, it invades all the "social rights" attributed to me by the Alliance. The doctrine ascribes to all mankind a vested interest in each other's moral, intellectual, and even physical perfection, to be defined by each claimant according to his own standard.

Another important example of illegitimate interference with the rightful liberty of the individual, not simply threatened, but long since carried into triumphant effect, is Sabbatarian legislation. Without doubt, abstinence on one day in the week, so far as the exigencies of life permit, from the usual daily occupation, though in no respect religiously binding on any except Jews, is a highly beneficial custom. And inasmuch as this custom cannot be observed without a general consent to that effect among the industrious classes, therefore, in so far as some persons by working may impose the same necessity on others, it may be allowable and right that the law should guarantee to each the observance by others of the custom, by suspending the greater operations of industry on a particular day. But this justification, grounded on the direct interest which others have in each individual's observance of the practice, does not apply to the self-chosen occupations in which a person may think fit to employ his leisure; nor does it hold good, in the smallest degree, for legal restrictions on amusements. It is true that the amusement of some is the day's work of others; but the pleasure, not to say the useful recreation, of many, is worth the labour of a few, provided the occupation is freely chosen, and can be freely resigned. The operatives are perfectly right in thinking that if all worked on Sunday, seven days' work would have to be given for six days' wages; but so long as the great mass of employments are suspended, the small number who for the enjoyment of others must still work, obtain a proportional increase of earnings; and they are not obliged to follow those occupations if they prefer leisure to emolument. If a further remedy is sought, it might be found in the establishment by custom of a holiday on some other day of the week for those particular classes of persons. The only ground, therefore, on which restrictions on Sunday amusements can be defended, must be that they are religiously wrong; a motive of legislation which can never be too earnestly protested against. "Deorum injuriæ Diis curæ." It remains to be proved that society or any of its officers holds a commission from on high to avenge any supposed offence to Omnipotence, which is not also a wrong to our fellow-creatures. The notion that it is one man's duty that another should be religious, was the foundation of all the religious persecutions ever perpetuated, and, if admitted, would fully justify them. Though the feeling which breaks out in the repeated attempts to stop railway travelling on Sunday, in the resistance to the opening of Museums, and the like, has not the cruelty of the old persecutors, the state of mind indicated by it is

fundamentally the same. It is a determination not to tolerate others in doing what is permitted by their religion, because it is not permitted by the persecutor's religion. It is a belief that God not only abominates the act of the misbeliever, but will not hold us guiltless if we leave him unmolested.

I cannot refrain from adding to these examples of the little account commonly made of human liberty, the language of downright persecution which breaks out from the press of this country whenever it feels called on to notice the remarkable phenomenon of Mormonism. Much might be said on the unexpected and instructive fact that an alleged new revelation, and a religion founded on it, the product of palpable imposture, not even supported by the *prestige* of extraordinary qualities in its founder, is believed by hundreds of thousands, and has been made the foundation of a society, in the age of newspapers, railways, and the electric telegraph. What here concerns us is, that this religion, like other and better religions, has its martyrs: that its prophet and founder was, for his teaching, put to death by a mob; that others of its adherents lost their lives by the same lawless violence; that they were forcibly expelled, in a body, from the country in which they first grew up; while now that they have been chased into a solitary recess in the midst of a desert, many in this country openly declare that it would be right (only that it is not convenient) to send an expedition against them, and compel them by force to conform to the opinions of other people. The article of the Mormonite doctrine which is the chief provocative to the antipathy which thus breaks through the ordinary restraints of religious tolerance, is its sanction of polygamy; which, though permitted to Mahomedans, and Hindoos, and Chinese, seems to excite unquenchable animosity when practised by persons who speak English and profess to be a kind of Christian. No one has a deeper disapprobation than I have of this Mormon institution; both for other reasons, and because, far from being in any way countenanced by the principle of liberty, it is a direct infraction of that principle, being a mere riveting of the chains of one half of the community, and an emancipation of the other from reciprocity of obligation towards them. Still, it must be remembered that this relation is as much voluntary on the part of the women concerned in it, and who may be deemed the sufferers by it, as is the case with any other form of the marriage institution; and however surprising this fact may appear, it has its explanation in the common ideas and customs of the world, which teaching women to think marriage the one thing needful, make it intelligible that many a woman should prefer being one of several wives, to not being a wife at all. Other countries are not asked to recognize such unions, or release any portion of their inhabitants from their own laws on the score of Mormonite opinions. But when the dissentients have conceded to the hostile sentiments of others far more than could justly be demanded; when they have left the countries to which their doctrines were unacceptable, and established themselves in a remote corner of the earth, which they have been the first to render habitable to human beings; it is difficult to see on what principles but those of tyranny they can be prevented from living there under what laws they please, provided they commit no aggression on other nations, and allow perfect freedom of departure to those who are dissatisfied with their ways. A recent writer, in some respects of

considerable merit, proposes (to use his own words) not a crusade, but a *civilizade*, against this polygamous community, to put an end to what seems to him a retrograde step in civilization. It also appears so to me, but I am not aware that any community has a right to force another to be civilized. So long as the sufferers by the bad law do not invoke assistance from other communities, I cannot admit that persons entirely unconnected with them ought to step in and require that a condition of things with which all who are directly interested appear to be satisfied, should be put an end to because it is a scandal to persons some thousands of miles distant, who have no part or concern in it. Let them send missionaries, if they please, to preach against it; and let them, by any fair means (of which silencing the teachers is not one), oppose the progress of similar doctrines among their own people. If civilization has got the better of barbarism when barbarism had the world to itself, it is too much to profess to be afraid lest barbarism, after having been fairly got under, should revive and conquer civilization. A civilization that can thus succumb to its vanquished enemy, must first have become so degenerate, that neither its appointed priests and teachers, nor anybody else, has the capacity, or will take the trouble, to stand up for it. If this be so, the sooner such a civilization receives notice to quit the better. It can only go on from bad to worse, until destroyed and regenerated (like the Western Empire) by energetic barbarians.

Chapter 34

Isaiah Berlin

TWO CONCEPTS OF LIBERTY

Sir Isaiah Berlin (1909–97) was a political philosopher at Oxford University, known for his defense of value pluralism and individual liberty. In this essay (from 1958), Berlin introduces the distinction between negative and positive liberty, and argues that the latter concept is ripe for abuse at the hands of tyrants. Because there is no single correct way of judging the relative importance of competing plural values, Berlin argues, a great deal of individual freedom is necessary so that each person may choose a life embodying those values of his or her own choosing.

I

To coerce a man is to deprive him of freedom – freedom from what? Almost every moralist in human history has praised freedom. Like happiness and goodness, like nature and reality, it is a term whose meaning is so porous that there is little interpretation that it seems able to resist. I do not propose to discuss either the history of this protean word or the more than two hundred senses of it recorded by historians of ideas. I propose to examine no more than two of these senses – but they are central ones, with a great deal of human history behind them, and, I dare say, still to come. The first of these political senses of freedom or liberty (I shall use both words to mean the same), which (following much precedent) I shall call the "negative" sense, is involved in the answer to the question "What is the area within which the subject – a person or group of persons – is or should be left to do or be what he is able to do or be, without interference by other persons?" The second, which I shall call the "positive" sense, is involved in the answer to the question "What, or who, is the source of control or interference that can determine someone to do, or be, this rather than that?" The two questions are clearly different, even though the answers to them may overlap.

The Notion of Negative Freedom

I am normally said to be free to the degree to which no man or body of men interferes with my activity. Political liberty in this sense is simply the area within which a man can act unobstructed by others. If I am prevented by others from doing what I could otherwise do, I am to that degree unfree; and if this area is contracted by other men beyond a certain minimum, I can be described as being coerced, or, it may be, enslaved. Coercion is not, however, a term that covers every form of inability. If I say that I am unable to jump more than ten feet in the air, or cannot read because I am blind, or cannot understand the darker pages of Hegel, it would be eccentric to say that I am to that degree enslaved or coerced. Coercion implies the deliberate interference of other human beings within the area in which I could otherwise act. You lack political liberty or freedom only if you are prevented from attaining a goal by human beings.[1] Mere incapacity to attain a goal is not lack of political freedom.[2] This is brought out by the use of such modern expressions as "economic freedom" and its counterpart, "economic slavery." It is argued, very plausibly, that if a man is too poor to afford something on which there is no legal ban – a loaf of bread, a journey round the world, recourse to the law courts – he is as little free to have it as he would be if it were forbidden him by law. If my poverty were a kind of disease which prevented me from buying bread, or paying for the journey round the world or getting my case heard, as lameness prevents me from running, this inability would not naturally be described as a lack of freedom, least of all political freedom. It is only because I believe that my inability to get a given thing is due to the fact that other human beings have made arrangements whereby I am, whereas others are not, prevented from having enough money with which to pay for it, that I think myself a victim of coercion or slavery. In other words, this use of the term depends on a particular social and economic theory about the causes of my poverty or weakness. If my lack of material means is due to my lack of mental or physical capacity, then I begin to speak of being deprived of freedom (and not simply about poverty) only if I accept the theory.[3] If, in addition, I believe that I am being kept in want by a specific arrangement which I consider unjust or unfair, I speak of economic slavery or oppression. The nature of things does not madden us, only ill will does, said Rousseau.[4] The criterion of oppression is the part that I believe to be played by other human beings, directly or indirectly, with or without the intention of doing so, in frustrating my wishes. By being free in this sense I mean not being interfered with by others. The wider the area of non-interference the wider my freedom.

This is what the classical English political philosophers meant when they used this word.[5] They disagreed about how wide the area could or should be. They supposed that it could not, as things were, be unlimited, because if it were, it would entail a state in which all men could boundlessly interfere with all other men; and this kind of "natural" freedom would lead to social chaos in which men's minimum needs would not be satisfied; or else the liberties of the weak would be suppressed by the strong. Because they perceived that human purposes and activities do not automatically harmonize with one another, and because (whatever their official doctrines) they put high value on other goals, such as justice, or happiness, or culture, or security, or varying degrees of equality, they were prepared to curtail freedom in the interests of other values and, indeed, of freedom itself. For, without this, it was impossible to create the kind of association that they thought desirable. Consequently, it is assumed by these thinkers that the area of men's free action must be limited by law. But equally it is assumed, especially by such libertarians as Locke and Mill in England, and Constant and Tocqueville in France, that there ought to exist a certain minimum area of personal freedom which must on no account be violated; for if it is overstepped, the individual will find himself in an area too narrow for even that minimum development of his natural faculties which alone makes it possible to pursue, and even to conceive, the various ends which men hold good or right or sacred. It follows that a frontier must be drawn between the area of private life and that of public authority. Where it is to be drawn is a matter of argument, indeed of haggling. Men are largely interdependent, and no man's activity is so completely private as never to obstruct the lives of others in any way. "Freedom for the pike is death for the minnows";[6] the liberty of some must depend on the restraint of others. Freedom for an Oxford don, others have been known to add, is a very different thing from freedom for an Egyptian peasant.

This proposition derives its force from something that is both true and important, but the phrase itself remains a piece of political claptrap. It is true that to offer political rights, or safeguards against intervention by the State, to men who are half-naked, illiterate, underfed and diseased is to mock their condition; they need medical help or education before they can understand, or make use of, an increase in their freedom. What is freedom to those who cannot make use of it? Without adequate conditions for the use of freedom, what is the value of freedom? First things come first: there are situations in which — to use a saying satirically attributed to the nihilists by Dostoevsky — boots are superior to Pushkin; individual freedom is not everyone's primary need. For freedom is not the mere absence of frustration of whatever kind; this would inflate the meaning of the word until it meant too much or too little. The Egyptian peasant needs clothes or medicine before, and more than, personal liberty, but the minimum freedom that he needs today, and the greater degree of freedom that he may need tomorrow, is not some species of freedom peculiar to him, but identical with that of professors, artists and millionaires.

What troubles the consciences of Western liberals is, I think, the belief, not that the freedom that men seek differs according to their social or economic conditions, but that the minority who possess it have gained it by exploiting, or, at least, averting their gaze from, the vast majority who do not. They believe, with good reason, that if individual liberty is an ultimate end for human beings, none should be deprived of it by others; least of all that some should enjoy it at the expense of others. Equality of liberty; not to treat others as I should not wish them to treat me; repayment of my debt to those who alone have made possible my liberty or prosperity or enlightenment; justice, in its simplest and most universal sense — these are the foundations of liberal morality. Liberty is not the only goal of men. I can, like the Russian critic Belinsky, say

that if others are to be deprived of it — if my brothers are to remain in poverty, squalor and chains — then I do not want it for myself, I reject it with both hands and infinitely prefer to share their fate. But nothing is gained by a confusion of terms. To avoid glaring inequality or widespread misery I am ready to sacrifice some, or all, of my freedom: I may do so willingly and freely; but it is freedom that I am giving up for the sake of justice or equality or the love of my fellow men. I should be guilt-stricken, and rightly so, if I were not, in some circumstances, ready to make this sacrifice. But a sacrifice is not an increase in what is being sacrificed, namely freedom, however great the moral need or the compensation for it. Everything is what it is: liberty is liberty, not equality or fairness or justice or culture, or human happiness or a quiet conscience. If the liberty of myself or my class or nation depends on the misery of a number of other human beings, the system which promotes this is unjust and immoral. But if I curtail or lose my freedom in order to lessen the shame of such inequality, and do not thereby materially increase the individual liberty of others, an absolute loss of liberty occurs. This may be compensated for by a gain in justice or in happiness or in peace, but the loss remains, and it is a confusion of values to say that although my "liberal," individual freedom may go by the board, some other kind of freedom — "social" or "economic" — is increased. Yet it remains true that the freedom of some must at times be curtailed to secure the freedom of others. Upon what principle should this be done? If freedom is a sacred, untouchable value, there can be no such principle. One or other of these conflicting rules or principles must, at any rate in practice, yield: not always for reasons which can be clearly stated, let alone generalized into rules or universal maxims. Still, a practical compromise has to be found.

Philosophers with an optimistic view of human nature and a belief in the possibility of harmonizing human interests, such as Locke or Adam Smith or, in some moods, Mill, believed that social harmony and progress were compatible with reserving a large area for private life over which neither the State nor any other authority must be allowed to trespass. Hobbes, and those who agreed with him, especially conservative or reactionary thinkers, argued that if men were to be prevented from destroying one another and making social life a jungle or a wilderness, greater safeguards must be instituted to keep them in their places; he wished correspondingly to increase the area of centralized control and decrease that of the individual. But both sides agreed that some portion of human existence must remain independent of the sphere of social control. To invade that preserve, however small, would be despotism. The most eloquent of all defenders of freedom and privacy, Benjamin Constant, who had not forgotten the Jacobin dictatorship, declared that at the very least the liberty of religion, opinion, expression, property must be guaranteed against arbitrary invasion. Jefferson, Burke, Paine, Mill compiled different catalogues of individual liberties, but the argument for keeping authority at bay is always substantially the same. We must preserve a minimum area of personal freedom if we are not to "degrade or deny our nature."[7] We cannot remain absolutely free, and must give up some of our liberty to preserve the rest. But total self-surrender is self-defeating. What then must the minimum be? That which a man cannot give up without offending against the essence of his human nature. What is this essence? What are the standards which it entails? This has been, and perhaps always will be, a matter of infinite debate. But whatever the principle in terms of which the area of non-interference is to be drawn, whether it is that of natural law or natural rights, or of utility, or the pronouncements of a categorical imperative, or the sanctity of the social contract, or any other concept with which men have sought to clarify and justify their convictions, liberty in this sense means liberty from; absence of interference beyond the shifting, but always recognizable, frontier. "The only

freedom which deserves the name, is that of pursuing our own good in our own way," said the most celebrated of its champions.[8] If this is so, is compulsion ever justified? Mill had no doubt that it was. Since justice demands that all individuals be entitled to a minimum of freedom, all other individuals were of necessity to be restrained, if need be by force, from depriving anyone of it. Indeed, the whole function of law was the prevention of just such collisions: the State was reduced to what Lassalle contemptuously described as the functions of a night-watchman or traffic policeman.

What made the protection of individual liberty so sacred to Mill? In his famous essay he declares that, unless the individual is left to live as he wishes in "the part [of his conduct] which merely concerns himself,"[9] civilization cannot advance; the truth will not, for lack of a free market in ideas, come to light; there will be no scope for spontaneity, originality, genius, for mental energy, for moral courage. Society will be crushed by the weight of "collective mediocrity."[10] Whatever is rich and diversified will be crushed by the weight of custom, by men's constant tendency to conformity, which breeds only "withered" capacities, "pinched and hidebound," "cramped and dwarfed" human beings. "Pagan self-assertion" is as worthy as "Christian self-denial."[11] "All errors which [a man] is likely to commit against advice and warning, are far outweighed by the evil of allowing others to constrain him to what they deem his good."[12] The defence of liberty consists in the "negative" goal of warding off interference. To threaten a man with persecution unless he submits to a life in which he exercises no choices of his goals; to block before him every door but one, no matter how noble the prospect upon which it opens, or how benevolent the motives of those who arrange this, is to sin against the truth that he is a man, a being with a life of his own to live. This is liberty as it has been conceived by liberals in the modern world from the days of Erasmus (some would say of Occam) to our own. Every plea for civil liberties and individual rights, every protest against exploitation and humiliation, against the encroachment of public authority, or the mass hypnosis of custom or organized propaganda, springs from this individualistic, and much disputed, conception of man.

Three facts about this position may be noted. In the first place Mill confuses two distinct notions. One is that all coercion is, in so far as it frustrates human desires, bad as such, although it may have to be applied to prevent other, greater evils; while non-interference, which is the opposite of coercion, is good as such, although it is not the only good. This is the "negative" conception of liberty in its classical form. The other is that men should seek to discover the truth, or to develop a certain type of character of which Mill approved – critical, original, imaginative, independent, non-conforming to the point of eccentricity, and so on – and that truth can be found, and such character can be bred, only in conditions of freedom. Both these are liberal views, but they are not identical, and the connection between them is, at best, empirical. No one would argue that truth or freedom of self-expression could flourish where dogma crushes all thought. But the evidence of history tends to show (as, indeed, was argued by James Stephen in his formidable attack on Mill in his *Liberty, Equality, Fraternity*) that integrity, love of truth and fiery individualism grow at least as often in severely disciplined communities, among, for example, the puritan Calvinists of Scotland or New England, or under military discipline, as in more tolerant or indifferent societies; and if this is so, Mill's argument for liberty as a necessary condition for the growth of human genius falls to the ground. If his two goals proved incompatible, Mill would be faced with a cruel dilemma, quite apart from the further difficulties created by the inconsistency of his doctrines with strict utilitarianism, even in his own humane version of it.[13]

In the second place, the doctrine is comparatively modern. There seems to be scarcely any discussion of individual liberty as a conscious political ideal (as opposed to its actual existence) in the ancient world. Condorcet had already remarked that the notion of individual rights was absent from the legal conceptions of the Romans and Greeks; this seems to hold equally of the Jewish, Chinese and all other ancient civilizations that have since come to light.[14] The domination of this ideal has been the exception rather than the rule, even in the recent history of the West. Nor has liberty in this sense often formed a rallying cry for the great masses of mankind. The desire not to be impinged upon, to be left to oneself, has been a mark of high civilization on the part of both individuals and communities. The sense of privacy itself, of the area of personal relationships as something sacred in its own right, derives from a conception of freedom which, for all its religious roots, is scarcely older, in its developed state, than the Renaissance or the Reformation.[15] Yet its decline would mark the death of a civilization, of an entire moral outlook.

The third characteristic of this notion of liberty is of greater importance. It is that liberty in this sense is not incompatible with some kinds of autocracy, or at any rate with the absence of self-government. Liberty in this sense is principally concerned with the area of control, not with its source. Just as a democracy may, in fact, deprive the individual citizen of a great many liberties which he might have in some other form of society, so it is perfectly conceivable that a liberal-minded despot would allow his subjects a large measure of personal freedom. The despot who leaves his subjects a wide area of liberty may be unjust, or encourage the wildest inequalities, care little for order, or virtue, or knowledge; but provided he does not curb their liberty, or at least curbs it less than many other regimes, he meets with Mill's specification.[16]

Freedom in this sense is not, at any rate logically, connected with democracy or self-government. Self-government may, on the whole, provide a better guarantee of the preservation of civil liberties than other regimes, and has been defended as such by libertarians. But there is no necessary connection between individual liberty and democratic rule. The answer to the question "Who governs me?" is logically distinct from the question "How far does government interfere with me?" It is in this difference that the great contrast between the two concepts of negative and positive liberty, in the end, consists.[17] For the "positive" sense of liberty comes to light if we try to answer the question, not "What am I free to do or be?" but "By whom am I ruled?" or "Who is to say what I am, and what I am not, to be or do?" The connection between democracy and individual liberty is a good deal more tenuous than it seemed to many advocates of both. The desire to be governed by myself, or at any rate to participate in the process by which my life is to be controlled, may be as deep a wish as that for a free area for action, and perhaps historically older. But it is not a desire for the same thing. So different is it, indeed, as to have led in the end to the great clash of ideologies that dominates our world. For it is this, the "positive" conception of liberty, not freedom from, but freedom to – to lead one prescribed form of life – which the adherents of the "negative" notion represent as being, at times, no better than a specious disguise for brutal tyranny.

II

The Notion of Positive Freedom

The "positive" sense of the word "liberty" derives from the wish on the part of the individual to be his own master. I wish my life and decisions to depend on myself, not on external forces of whatever kind. I wish to be the instrument of my own, not of other men's, acts of will. I wish to be a subject, not an object; to be moved by reasons, by conscious purposes, which are my own, not by causes which affect me, as it were, from outside. I wish to be somebody, not nobody; a doer – deciding, not being decided

for, self-directed and not acted upon by external nature or by other men as if I were a thing, or an animal, or a slave incapable of playing a human role, that is, of conceiving goals and policies of my own and realizing them. This is at least part of what I mean when I say that I am rational, and that it is my reason that distinguishes me as a human being from the rest of the world. I wish, above all, to be conscious of myself as a thinking, willing, active being, bearing responsibility for my choices and able to explain them by reference to my own ideas and purposes. I feel free to the degree that I believe this to be true, and enslaved to the degree that I am made to realize that it is not.

The freedom which consists in being one's own master, and the freedom which consists in not being prevented from choosing as I do by other men, may, on the face of it, seem concepts at no great logical distance from each other – no more than negative and positive ways of saying much the same thing. Yet the "positive" and "negative" notions of freedom historically developed in divergent directions, not always by logically reputable steps, until, in the end, they came into direct conflict with each other.

One way of making this clear is in terms of the independent momentum which the, initially perhaps quite harmless, metaphor of self-mastery acquired. "I am my own master;" "I am slave to no man"; but may I not (as Platonists or Hegelians tend to say) be a slave to nature? Or to my own "unbridled" passions? Are these not so many species of the identical genus "slave" – some political or legal, others moral or spiritual? Have not men had the experience of liberating themselves from spiritual slavery, or slavery to nature, and do they not in the course of it become aware, on the one hand, of a self which dominates, and, on the other, of something in them which is brought to heel? This dominant self is then variously identified with reason, with my "higher nature," with the self which calculates and aims at what will satisfy it in the long run, with my "real," or "ideal," or "autonomous" self, or with my self "at its best"; which is then contrasted with irrational impulse, uncontrolled desires, my "lower" nature, the pursuit of immediate pleasures, my "empirical" or "heteronomous" self, swept by every gust of desire and passion, needing to be rigidly disciplined if it is ever to rise to the full height of its "real" nature. Presently the two selves may be represented as divided by an even larger gap; the real self may be conceived as something wider than the individual (as the term is normally understood), as a social "whole" of which the individual is an element or aspect: a tribe, a race, a Church, a State, the great society of the living and the dead and the yet unborn. This entity is then identified as being the "true" self which, by imposing its collective, or "organic," single will upon its recalcitrant "members," achieves its own, and therefore their, "higher" freedom. The perils of using organic metaphors to justify the coercion of some men by others in order to raise them to a "higher" level of freedom have often been pointed out. But what gives such plausibility as it has to this kind of language is that we recognize that it is possible, and at times justifiable, to coerce men in the name of some goal (let us say, justice or public health) which they would, if they were more enlightened, themselves pursue, but do not, because they are blind or ignorant or corrupt. This renders it easy for me to conceive of myself as coercing others for their own sake, in their, not my, interest. I am then claiming that I know what they truly need better than they know it themselves. What, at most, this entails is that they would not resist me if they were rational and as wise as I and understood their interests as I do. But I may go on to claim a good deal more than this. I may declare that they are actually aiming at what in their benighted state they consciously resist, because there exists within them an occult entity – their latent rational will, or their "true" purpose – and that this entity, although it is belied by all that they overtly feel and do and say, is their "real" self, of which the poor empirical self in space and time may know nothing or little; and that this inner spirit is the only self that deserves to have its wishes taken into account.[18] Once I take this view, I am in a position to ignore the actual wishes of men or societies, to bully, oppress, torture them in the name, and on behalf, of their "real" selves, in the secure knowledge that whatever is the true goal of man (happiness, performance of duty, wisdom, a just society, self-fulfilment) must be identical with his freedom – the free choice of his "true," albeit often submerged and inarticulate, self.

This paradox has been often exposed. It is one thing to say that I know what is good for X, while he himself does not; and even to ignore his wishes for its – and his – sake; and a very different one to say that he has *eo ipso* chosen it, not indeed consciously, not as he seems in everyday life, but in his role as a rational self which his empirical self may not know – the "real" self which discerns the good, and cannot help choosing it once it is revealed. This monstrous impersonation, which consists in equating what X would choose if he were something he is not, or at least not yet, with what X actually seeks and chooses, is at the heart of all political theories of self-realization. It is one thing to say that I may be coerced for my own good, which I am too blind to see: this may, on occasion, be for my benefit; indeed it may enlarge the scope of my liberty. It is another to say that if it is my good, then I am not being coerced, for I have willed it, whether I know this or not, and am free (or "truly" free) even while my poor earthly body and foolish mind bitterly reject it, and struggle with the greatest desperation against those who seek, however benevolently, to impose it.

This magical transformation, or sleight of hand (for which William James so justly mocked the Hegelians), can no doubt be perpetrated just as easily with the "negative" concept of freedom, where the self that should not be interfered with is no longer the individual with his actual wishes and needs as they are normally conceived, but the "real" man within, identified with the pursuit of some ideal purpose not dreamed of by his empirical self. And, as in the case of the "positively" free self, this entity may be inflated into some super-personal entity — a State, a class, a nation, or the march of history itself, regarded as a more "real" subject of attributes than the empirical self. But the "positive" conception of freedom as self-mastery, with its suggestion of a man divided against himself, has in fact, and as a matter of history, of doctrine and of practice, lent itself more easily to this splitting of personality into two: the transcendent, dominant controller, and the empirical bundle of desires and passions to be disciplined and brought to heel. It is this historical fact that has been influential. This demonstrates (if demonstration of so obvious a truth is needed) that conceptions of freedom directly derive from views of what constitutes a self, a person, a man. Enough manipulation of the definition of man, and freedom can be made to mean whatever the manipulator wishes. Recent history has made it only too clear that the issue is not merely academic.

The consequences of distinguishing between two selves will become even clearer if one considers the two major forms which the desire to be self-directed — directed by one's "true" self — has historically taken: the first, that of self-abnegation in order to attain independence; the second, that of self-realization, or total self-identification with a specific principle or ideal in order to attain the selfsame end.

III

The Retreat to the Inner Citadel

I am the possessor of reason and will; I conceive ends and I desire to pursue them; but if I am prevented from attaining them I no longer feel master of the situation. I may be prevented by the laws of nature, or by accidents, or the activities of men, or the effect, often undesigned, of human institutions. These forces may be too much for me. What am I to do to avoid being crushed by them? I must liberate myself from desires that I know I cannot realize. I wish to be master of my kingdom, but my frontiers are long and insecure, therefore I contract them in order to reduce or eliminate the vulnerable area. I begin by desiring happiness, or power, or knowledge, or the attainment of some specific object. But I cannot command them. I choose to avoid defeat and waste, and therefore decide to strive for nothing that I cannot be sure to obtain. I determine myself not to desire what is unattainable. The tyrant threatens me with the destruction of my property, with imprisonment, with the exile or death of those I love. But if I no longer feel attached to property, no longer care whether or not I am in prison, if I have killed within myself my natural affections, then he cannot bend me to his will, for all that is left of myself is no longer subject to empirical fears or desires. It is as if I had performed a strategic retreat into an inner citadel — my reason, my soul, my "noumenal" self — which, do what they may, neither external blind force, nor human malice, can touch. I have withdrawn into myself; there, and there alone, I am secure. It is as if I were to say: "I have a wound in my leg. There are two methods of freeing myself from pain. One is to heal the wound. But if the cure is too difficult or uncertain, there is another method. I can get rid of the wound by cutting off my leg. If I train myself to want nothing to which the possession of my leg is indispensable, I shall not feel the lack of it."This is the traditional self-emancipation of ascetics and quietists, of stoics or Buddhist sages, men of various religions or of none, who have fled the world, and escaped the yoke of society or public opinion, by some process of deliberate self-transformation that enables them to care no longer for any of its values, to remain, isolated and independent, on its edges, no longer vulnerable to its weapons.[19] All political isolationism, all economic autarky, every form of autonomy, has in it some element of this attitude. I eliminate the obstacles in my path by abandoning the path; I retreat into my own sect, my own planned economy, my own deliberately insulated territory, where no voices from outside need be listened to, and no external forces can have effect. This is a form of the search for security; but it has also been called the search for personal or national freedom or independence.

From this doctrine, as it applies to individuals, it is no very great distance to the conceptions of those who, like Kant, identify freedom not indeed with the elimination of desires, but with resistance to them, and control over them. I identify myself with the controller and escape the slavery of the controlled. I am free because, and in so far as, I am autonomous. I obey laws, but I have imposed them on, or found them in, my own uncoerced self. Freedom is obedience, but, in Rousseau's words, "obedience to a law which we prescribe to ourselves,"[20] and no man can enslave himself. Heteronomy is dependence on outside factors, liability to be a plaything of the external world that I cannot myself fully control, and which *pro tanto* controls and "enslaves" me. I am free only to the degree to which my person is "fettered" by nothing that obeys forces over which I have no control; I cannot control the laws of nature; my free activity must therefore, *ex hypothesi*, be lifted above the empirical world of causality. This is not the place in which to discuss the validity of this ancient and famous doctrine; I only wish to remark that the related notions of freedom as resistance to (or escape from) unrealizable desire, and as independence of the sphere of causality, have played a central role in politics no less than in ethics.

For if the essence of men is that they are autonomous beings – authors of values, of ends in themselves, the ultimate authority of which consists precisely in the fact that they are willed freely – then nothing is worse than to treat them as if they were not autonomous, but natural objects, played on by causal influences, creatures at the mercy of external stimuli, whose choices can be manipulated by their rulers, whether by threats of force or offers of rewards. To treat men

in this way is to treat them as if they were not self-determined. "Nobody may compel me to be happy in his own way," said Kant. Paternalism is "the greatest despotism imaginable."[21] This is so because it is to treat men as if they were not free, but human material for me, the benevolent reformer, to mould in accordance with my own, not their, freely adopted purpose. This is, of course, precisely the policy that the early utilitarians recommended. Helvétius (and Bentham) believed not in resisting, but in using, men's tendency to be slaves to their passions; they wished to dangle rewards and punishments before men – the acutest possible form of heteronomy – if by this means the "slaves" might be made happier.[22] But to manipulate men, to propel them towards goals which you – the social reformer – see, but they may not, is to deny their human essence, to treat them as objects without wills of their own, and therefore to degrade them. That is why to lie to men, or to deceive them, that is, to use them as means for my, not their own, independently conceived ends, even if it is for their own benefit, is, in effect, to treat them as subhuman, to behave as if their ends are less ultimate and sacred than my own. In the name of what can I ever be justified in forcing men to do what they have not willed or consented to? Only in the name of some value higher than themselves. But if, as Kant held, all values are made so by the free acts of men, and called values only so far as they are this, there is no value higher than the individual. Therefore to do this is to coerce men in the name of something less ultimate than themselves – to bend them to my will, or to someone else's particular craving for (his or their) happiness or expediency or security or convenience. I am aiming at something desired (from whatever motive, no matter how noble) by me or my group, to which I am using other men as means. But this is a contradiction of what I know men to be, namely ends in themselves. All forms of tampering with human beings, getting at them, shaping them against their will to your own pattern, all thought-control and conditioning,[23] is, therefore, a denial of that in men which makes them men and their values ultimate.

Kant's free individual is a transcendent being, beyond the realm of natural causality. But in its empirical form – in which the notion of man is that of ordinary life – this doctrine was the heart of liberal humanism, both moral and political, that was deeply influenced both by Kant and by Rousseau in the eighteenth century. In its a priori version it is a form of secularized Protestant individualism, in which the place of God is taken by the conception of the rational life, and the place of the individual soul which strains towards union with him is replaced by the conception of the individual, endowed with reason, straining to be governed by reason and reason alone, and to depend upon nothing that might deflect or delude him by engaging his irrational nature. Autonomy, not heteronomy: to act and not to be acted upon. The notion of slavery to the passions is – for those who think in these terms – more than a metaphor. To rid myself of fear, or love, or the desire to conform is to liberate myself from the despotism of something which I cannot control. Sophocles, whom Plato reports as saying that old age alone has liberated him from the passion of love – the yoke of a cruel master – is reporting an experience as real as that of liberation from a human tyrant or slave owner. The psychological experience of observing myself yielding to some "lower" impulse, acting from a motive that I dislike, or of doing something which at the very moment of doing I may detest, and reflecting later that I was "not myself," or "not in control of myself," when I did it, belongs to this way of thinking and speaking. I identify myself with my critical and rational moments. The consequences of my acts cannot matter, for they are not in my control; only my motives are. This is the creed of the solitary thinker who has defied the world and emancipated himself from the chains of men and things. In this form the doctrine may seem primarily an ethical creed, and scarcely political at all; nevertheless its political implications are clear, and it enters into the tradition of liberal individualism at least as deeply as the "negative" concept of freedom.

It is perhaps worth remarking that in its individualistic form the concept of the rational sage who has escaped into the inner fortress of his true self seems to arise when the external world has proved exceptionally arid, cruel or unjust. "He is truly free," said Rousseau, "who desires what he can perform, and does what he desires."[24] In a world where a man seeking happiness or justice or freedom (in whatever sense) can do little, because he finds too many avenues of action blocked to him, the temptation to withdraw into himself may become irresistible. It may have been so in Greece, where the Stoic ideal cannot be wholly unconnected with the fall of the independent democracies before centralized Macedonian autocracy. It was so in Rome, for analogous reasons, after the end of the Republic.[25] It arose in Germany in the seventeenth century, during the period of the deepest national degradation of the German States that followed the Thirty Years War, when the character of public life, particularly in the small principalities, forced those who prized the dignity of human life, not for the first or last time, into a kind of inner emigration. The doctrine that maintains that what I cannot have I must teach myself not to desire, that a desire eliminated, or successfully resisted, is as good as a desire satisfied, is a sublime, but, it seems to me, unmistakable, form of the doctrine of sour grapes: what I cannot be sure of, I cannot truly want.

This makes it clear why the definition of negative liberty as the ability to do what one wishes – which is, in effect, the definition adopted by Mill – will not do. If I find that I am able to do little or nothing of what I wish, I need only contract or extinguish my wishes, and I am made free. If the tyrant (or "hidden persuader") manages to condition his subjects (or customers) into losing their original wishes and embracing ("internalizing") the form of life he has invented for them, he will, on this definition, have succeeded in liberating them. He will, no doubt, have made them *feel* free – as Epictetus feels freer than his master (and the proverbial good man is said to feel happy on the rack). But what he has created is the very antithesis of political freedom.

Ascetic self-denial may be a source of integrity or serenity and spiritual strength, but it is difficult to see how it can be called an enlargement of liberty. If I save myself from an adversary by retreating indoors and locking every entrance and exit, I may remain freer than if I had been captured by him, but am I freer than if I had defeated or captured him? If I go too far, contract myself into too small a space, I shall suffocate and die. The logical culmination of the process of destroying everything through which I can possibly be wounded is suicide. While I exist in the natural world, I can never be wholly secure. Total liberation in this sense (as Schopenhauer correctly perceived) is conferred only by death.[26]

I find myself in a world in which I meet with obstacles to my will. Those who are wedded to the "negative" concept of freedom may perhaps be forgiven if they think that self-abnegation is not the only method of overcoming obstacles; that it is also possible to do so by removing them: in the case of non-human objects, by physical action; in the case of human resistance, by force or persuasion, as when I induce somebody to make room for me in his carriage, or conquer a country which threatens the interests of my own. Such acts may be unjust, they may involve violence, cruelty, the enslavement of others, but it can scarcely be denied that thereby the agent is able in the most literal sense to increase his own freedom. It is an irony of history that this truth is repudiated by some of those who practise it most forcibly, men who, even while they conquer power and freedom of action, reject the "negative" concept of it in favour of its "positive" counterpart. Their view rules over half our world; let us see upon what metaphysical foundation it rests.

IV

Self-realization

The only true method of attaining freedom, we are told, is by the use of critical reason, the understanding of what is necessary and what is contingent. If I am a schoolboy, all but the simplest truths of mathematics obtrude themselves as obstacles to the free functioning of my mind, as theorems whose necessity I do not understand; they are pronounced to be true by some external authority, and present themselves to me as foreign bodies which I am expected mechanically to absorb into my system. But when I understand the functions of the symbols, the axioms, the formation and transformation rules – the logic whereby the conclusions are obtained – and grasp that these things cannot be otherwise, because they appear to follow from the laws that govern the processes of my own reason,[27] then mathematical truths no longer obtrude themselves as external entities forced upon me which I must receive whether I want to or not, but as something which I now freely will in the course of the natural functioning of my own rational activity. For the mathematician, the proof of these theorems is part of the free exercise of his natural reasoning capacity. For the musician, after he has assimilated the pattern of the composer's score, and has made the composer's ends his own, the playing of the music is not obedience to external laws, a compulsion and a barrier to liberty, but a free, unimpeded exercise. The player is not bound to the score as an ox to the plough, or a factory worker to the machine. He has absorbed the score into his own system, has, by understanding it, identified it with himself, has changed it from an impediment to free activity into an element in that activity itself.

What applies to music or mathematics must, we are told, in principle apply to all other obstacles which present themselves as so many lumps of external stuff blocking free self-development. That is the programme of enlightened rationalism from Spinoza to the latest (at times unconscious) disciples of Hegel. *Sapere aude.* What you know, that of which you understand the necessity – the rational necessity – you cannot, while remaining rational, want to be otherwise. For to want something to be other than what it must be is, given the premises – the necessities that govern the world – to be *pro tanto* either ignorant or irrational. Passions, prejudices, fears, neuroses spring from ignorance, and take the form of myths and illusions. To be ruled by myths, whether they spring from the vivid imaginations of unscrupulous charlatans who deceive us in order to exploit us, or from psychological or sociological causes, is a form of heteronomy, of being dominated by outside factors in a direction not necessarily willed by the agent. The scientific determinists of the eighteenth century supposed that the study of the sciences of nature, and the creation of sciences of society on the same model, would make the operation of such causes transparently clear, and thus enable individuals to recognize their own part in the working of a rational world, frustrating only when misunderstood. Knowledge liberates, as Epicurus taught long ago, by automatically eliminating irrational fears and desires.

Herder, Hegel and Marx substituted their own vitalistic models of social life for the older, mechanical, ones, but believed, no less than their opponents, that to understand the world is to be freed. They merely differed from them in stressing the part played by change and growth in what made human beings human. Social life could not be understood by an analogy drawn from mathematics or physics. One must also understand history, that is, the peculiar laws of continuous growth, whether by "dialectical" conflict or otherwise, that govern individuals and groups in their interplay with each other and with nature. Not to grasp this is, according to these thinkers, to fall into a particular kind of error, namely the belief that human nature is static, that its essential properties are the same everywhere and at all times, that it is governed by

unvarying natural laws, whether they are conceived in theological or materialistic terms, which entails the fallacious corollary that a wise lawgiver can, in principle, create a perfectly harmonious society at any time by appropriate education and legislation, because rational men, in all ages and countries, must always demand the same unaltering satisfactions of the same unaltering basic needs. Hegel believed that his contemporaries (and indeed all his predecessors) misunderstood the nature of institutions because they did not understand the laws – the rationally intelligible laws, since they spring from the operation of reason – that create and alter institutions and transform human character and human action. Marx and his disciples maintained that the path of human beings was obstructed not only by natural forces, or the imperfections of their own characters, but, even more, by the workings of their own social institutions, which they had originally created (not always consciously) for certain purposes, but whose functioning they systematically came to misconceive, in practice even more than in theory, and which thereupon became obstacles to their creators' progress. Marx offered social and economic hypotheses to account for the inevitability of such misunderstanding, in particular of the illusion that such man-made arrangements were independent forces, as inescapable as the laws of nature. As instances of such pseudo-objective forces, he pointed to the laws of supply and demand, or the institution of property, or the eternal division of society into rich and poor, or owners and workers, as so many unaltering human categories. Not until we had reached a stage at which the spells of these illusions could be broken, that is, until enough men reached a social stage that alone enabled them to understand that these laws and institutions were themselves the work of human minds and hands, historically needed in their day, and later mistaken for inexorable, objective powers, could the old world be destroyed, and more adequate and liberating social machinery substituted.

We are enslaved by despots — institutions or beliefs or neuroses — which can be removed only by being analysed and understood. We are imprisoned by evil spirits which we have ourselves — albeit not consciously — created, and can exorcize them only by becoming conscious and acting appropriately: indeed, for Marx understanding *is* appropriate action. I am free if, and only if, I plan my life in accordance with my own will; plans entail rules; a rule does not oppress me or enslave me if I impose it on myself consciously, or accept it freely, having understood it, whether it was invented by me or by others, provided that it is rational, that is to say, conforms to the necessities of things. To understand why things must be as they must be is to will them to be so. Knowledge liberates not by offering us more open possibilities amongst which we can make our choice, but by preserving us from the frustration of attempting the impossible. To want necessary laws to be other than they are is to be prey to an irrational desire — a desire that what must be X should also be not-X. To go further, and believe these laws to be other than what they necessarily are, is to be insane. That is the metaphysical heart of rationalism. The notion of liberty contained in it is not the "negative" conception of a field (ideally) without obstacles, a vacuum in which nothing obstructs me, but the notion of self-direction or self-control. I can do what I will with my own. I am a rational being; whatever I can demonstrate to myself as being necessary, as incapable of being otherwise in a rational society — that is, in a society directed by rational minds, towards goals such as a rational being would have — I cannot, being rational, wish to sweep out of my way. I assimilate it into my substance as I do the laws of logic, of mathematics, of physics, the rules of art, the principles that govern everything of which I understand, and therefore will, the rational purpose, by which I can never be thwarted, since I cannot want it to be other than it is.

This is the positive doctrine of liberation by reason. Socialized forms of it, widely disparate

and opposed to each other as they are, are at the heart of many of the nationalist, Communist, authoritarian, and totalitarian creeds of our day. It may, in the course of its evolution, have wandered far from its rationalist moorings. Nevertheless, it is this freedom that, in democracies and in dictatorships, is argued about, and fought for, in many parts of the earth today. Without attempting to trace the historical evolution of this idea, I should like to comment on some of its vicissitudes.

V

The Temple of Sarastro

Those who believed in freedom as rational self-direction were bound, sooner or later, to consider how this was to be applied not merely to a man's inner life, but to his relations with other members of his society. Even the most individualistic among them — and Rousseau, Kant and Fichte certainly began as individualists — came at some point to ask themselves whether a rational life not only for the individual, but also for society, was possible, and if so, how it was to be achieved. I wish to be free to live as my rational will (my "real self") commands, but so must others be. How am I to avoid collisions with their wills? Where is the frontier that lies between my (rationally determined) rights and the identical rights of others? For if I am rational, I cannot deny that what is right for me must, for the same reasons, be right for others who are rational like me. A rational (or free) State would be a State governed by such laws as all rational men would freely accept; that is to say, such laws as they would themselves have enacted had they been asked what, as rational beings, they demanded; hence the frontiers would be such as all rational men would consider to be the right frontiers for rational beings.

But who, in fact, was to determine what these frontiers were? Thinkers of this type argued that if moral and political problems were genuine — as surely they were – they must in principle be soluble; that is to say, there must exist one and only one true solution to any problem. All truths could in principle be discovered by any rational thinker, and demonstrated so clearly that all other rational men could not but accept them; indeed, this was already to a large extent the case in the new natural sciences. On this assumption the problem of political liberty was soluble by establishing a just order that would give to each man all the freedom to which a rational being was entitled. My claim to unfettered freedom can prima facie at times not be reconciled with your equally unqualified claim; but the rational solution of one problem cannot collide with the equally true solution of another, for two truths cannot logically be incompatible; therefore a just order must in principle be discoverable – an order of which the rules make possible correct solutions to all possible problems that could arise in it. This ideal, harmonious state of affairs was sometimes imagined as a Garden of Eden before the Fall of Man, an Eden from which we were expelled, but for which we were still filled with longing; or as a golden age still before us, in which men, having become rational, will no longer be "other-directed," nor "alienate" or frustrate one another. In existing societies justice and equality are ideals which still call for some measure of coercion, because the premature lifting of social controls might lead to the oppression of the weaker and the stupider by the stronger or abler or more energetic and unscrupulous. But it is only irrationality on the part of men (according to this doctrine) that leads them to wish to oppress or exploit or humiliate one another. Rational men will respect the principle of reason in each other, and lack all desire to fight or dominate one another. The desire to dominate is itself a symptom of irrationality, and can be explained and cured by rational methods. Spinoza offers one kind of explanation and remedy, Hegel another, Marx a third. Some of these theories may perhaps, to some degree, supplement each other, others are not combinable. But they all assume

that in a society of perfectly rational beings the lust for domination over men will be absent or ineffective. The existence of, or cravings for, oppression will be the first symptom that the true solution to the problems of social life has not been reached.

This can be put in another way. Freedom is self-mastery, the elimination of obstacles to my will, whatever these obstacles may be – the resistance of nature, of my ungoverned passions, of irrational institutions, of the opposing wills or behaviour of others. Nature I can, at least in principle, always mould by technical means, and shape to my will. But how am I to treat recalcitrant human beings? I must, if I can, impose my will on them too, "mould" them to my pattern, cast parts for them in my play. But will this not mean that I alone am free, while they are slaves? They will be so if my plan has nothing to do with their wishes or values, only with my own. But if my plan is fully rational, it will allow for the full development of their "true" natures, the realization of their capacities for rational decisions, for "making the best of themselves" – as a part of the realization of my own "true" self. All true solutions to all genuine problems must be compatible: more than this, they must fit into a single whole; for this is what is meant by calling them all rational and the universe harmonious. Each man has his specific character, abilities, aspirations, ends. If I grasp both what these ends and natures are, and how they all relate to one another, I can, at least in principle, if I have the knowledge and the strength, satisfy them all, so long as the nature and the purposes in question are rational. Rationality is knowing things and people for what they are: I must not use stones to make violins, nor try to make born violin-players play flutes. If the universe is governed by reason, then there will be no need for coercion; a correctly planned life for all will coincide with full freedom – the freedom of rational self-direction – for all. This will be so if, and only if, the plan is the true plan – the one unique pattern which alone fulfils the claims of reason. Its laws will be the rules which reason prescribes: they will only seem irksome to those whose reason is dormant, who do not understand the true "needs" of their own "real" selves. So long as each player recognizes and plays the part set him by reason – the faculty that understands his true nature and discerns his true ends – there can be no conflict. Each man will be a liberated, self-directed actor in the cosmic drama. Thus Spinoza tells us that children, although they are coerced, are not slaves, because they obey orders given in their own interests, and that the subject of a true commonwealth is no slave, because the common interests must include his own.[28] Similarly, Locke says "Where there is no law there is no freedom," because rational law is a direction to a man's "proper interests" or "general good"; and adds that since law of this kind is what "hedges us in only from bogs and precipices" it "ill deserves the name of confinement,"[29] and speaks of desires to escape from it as being irrational, forms of "licence," as "brutish,"[30] and so on. Montesquieu, forgetting his liberal moments, speaks of political liberty as being not permission to do what we want, or even what the law allows, but only "the power of doing what we ought to will,"[31] which Kant virtually repeats. Burke proclaims the individual's "right" to be restrained in his own interest, because "the presumed consent of every rational creature is in unison with the predisposed order of things."[32]

The common assumption of these thinkers (and of many a schoolman before them and Jacobin and Communist after them) is that the rational ends of our "true" natures must coincide, or be made to coincide, however violently our poor, ignorant, desire-ridden, passionate, empirical selves may cry out against this process. Freedom is not freedom to do what is irrational, or stupid, or wrong. To force empirical selves into the right pattern is no tyranny, but liberation.[33] Rousseau tells me that if I freely surrender all the parts of my life to society, I create an entity which, because it has been built by an equality of sacrifice of all its members, cannot wish to

hurt any one of them; in such a society, we are informed, it can be in nobody's interest to damage anyone else. "In giving myself to all, I give myself to none,"[34] and get back as much as I lose, with enough new force to preserve my new gains. Kant tells us that when "the individual has entirely abandoned his wild, lawless freedom, to find it again, unimpaired, in a state of dependence according to law," that alone is true freedom, "for this dependence is the work of my own will acting as a lawgiver."[35] Liberty, so far from being incompatible with authority, becomes virtually identical with it. This is the thought and language of all the declarations of the rights of man in the eighteenth century, and of all those who look upon society as a design constructed according to the rational laws of the wise lawgiver, or of nature, or of history, or of the Supreme Being. Bentham, almost alone, doggedly went on repeating that the business of laws was not to liberate but to restrain: every law is an infraction of liberty[36] – even if such infraction leads to an increase of the sum of liberty.

If the underlying assumptions had been correct – if the method of solving social problems resembled the way in which solutions to the problems of the natural sciences are found, and if reason were what rationalists said that it was – all this would perhaps follow. In the ideal case, liberty coincides with law: autonomy with authority. A law which forbids me to do what I could not, as a sane being, conceivably wish to do is not a restraint of my freedom. In the ideal society, composed of wholly responsible beings, rules, because I should scarcely be conscious of them, would gradually wither away. Only one social movement was bold enough to render this assumption quite explicit and accept its consequences – that of the Anarchists. But all forms of liberalism founded on a rationalist metaphysics are less or more watered-down versions of this creed.

In due course, the thinkers who bent their energies to the solution of the problem on these lines came to be faced with the question of how in practice men were to be made rational in this way. Clearly they must be educated. For the uneducated are irrational, heteronomous, and need to be coerced, if only to make life tolerable for the rational if they are to live in the same society and not be compelled to withdraw to a desert or some Olympian height. But the uneducated cannot be expected to understand or co-operate with the purposes of their educators. Education, says Fichte, must inevitably work in such a way that "you will later recognize the reasons for what I am doing now."[37] Children cannot be expected to understand why they are compelled to go to school, nor the ignorant – that is, for the moment, the majority of mankind – why they are made to obey the laws that will presently make them rational. "Compulsion is also a kind of education."[38] You learn the great virtue of obedience to superior persons. If you cannot understand your own interests as a rational being, I cannot be expected to consult you, or abide by your wishes, in the course of making you rational. I must, in the end, force you to be protected against smallpox, even though you may not wish it. Even Mill is prepared to say that I may forcibly prevent a man from crossing a bridge if there is not time to warn him that it is about to collapse, for I know, or am justified in assuming, that he cannot wish to fall into the water. Fichte knows what the uneducated German of his time wishes to be or do better than he can possibly know this for himself. The sage knows you better than you know yourself, for you are the victim of your passions, a slave living a heteronomous life, purblind, unable to understand your true goals. You want to be a human being. It is the aim of the State to satisfy your wish. "Compulsion is justified by education for future insight."[39] The reason within me, if it is to triumph, must eliminate and suppress my "lower" instincts, my passions and desires, which render me a slave; similarly (the fatal transition from individual to social concepts is almost imperceptible) the higher elements in society – the better educated,

the more rational, those who "possess the highest insight of their time and people"[40] – may exercise compulsion to rationalize the irrational section of society. For – so Hegel, Bradley, Bosanquet have often assured us – by obeying the rational man we obey ourselves: not indeed as we are, sunk in our ignorance and our passions, weak creatures afflicted by diseases that need a healer, wards who require a guardian, but as we could be if we were rational; as we could be even now, if only we would listen to the rational element which is, *ex hypothesi*, within every human being who deserves the name.

The philosophers of "Objective Reason," from the tough, rigidly centralized, "organic" State of Fichte, to the mild and humane liberalism of T. H. Green, certainly supposed themselves to be fulfilling, and not resisting, the rational demands which, however inchoate, were to be found in the breast of every sentient being.

But I may reject such democratic optimism, and turning away from the teleological determinism of the Hegelians towards some more voluntarist philosophy, conceive the idea of imposing on my society – for its own betterment – a plan of my own, which in my rational wisdom I have elaborated; and which, unless I act on my own, perhaps against the permanent wishes of the vast majority of my fellow citizens, may never come to fruition at all. Or, abandoning the concept of reason altogether, I may conceive myself as an inspired artist, who moulds men into patterns in the light of his unique vision, as painters combine colours or composers sounds; humanity is the raw material upon which I impose my creative will; even though men suffer and die in the process, they are lifted by it to a height to which they could never have risen without my coercive – but creative – violation of their lives. This is the argument used by every dictator, inquisitor and bully who seeks some moral, or even aesthetic, justification for his conduct. I must do for men (or with them) what they cannot do for themselves, and I cannot ask their permission or consent, because they are in no condition to know what is best for them; indeed, what they will permit and accept may mean a life of contemptible mediocrity, or perhaps even their ruin and suicide. Let me quote from the true progenitor of the heroic doctrine, Fichte, once again: "No one has . . . rights against reason." "Man is afraid of subordinating his subjectivity to the laws of reason. He prefers tradition or arbitrariness."[41] Nevertheless, subordinated he must be.[42] Fichte puts forward the claims of what he called reason; Napoleon, or Carlyle, or romantic authoritarians may worship other values, and see in their establishment by force the only path to "true" freedom.

The same attitude was pointedly expressed by August Comte, who asked why, if we do not allow free thinking in chemistry or biology, we should allow it in morals or politics.[43] Why indeed? If it makes sense to speak of political truths – assertions of social ends which all men, because they are men, must, once they are discovered, agree to be such; and if, as Comte believed, scientific method will in due course reveal them; then what case is there for freedom of opinion or action – at least as an end in itself, and not merely as a stimulating intellectual climate – either for individuals or for groups? Why should any conduct be tolerated that is not authorized by appropriate experts? Comte put bluntly what had been implicit in the rationalist theory of politics from its ancient Greek beginnings. There can, in principle, be only one correct way of life; the wise lead it spontaneously, that is why they are called wise. The unwise must be dragged towards it by all the social means in the power of the wise; for why should demonstrable error be suffered to survive and breed? The immature and untutored must be made to say to themselves: "Only the truth liberates, and the only way in which I can learn the truth is by doing blindly today what you, who know it, order me, or coerce me, to do, in the certain knowledge that only thus will I arrive at your clear vision, and be free like you."

We have wandered indeed from our liberal beginnings. This argument, employed by Fichte in his latest phase, and after him by other defenders of authority, from Victorian schoolmasters and colonial administrators to the latest nationalist or Communist dictator, is precisely what the Stoic and Kantian morality protests against most bitterly in the name of the reason of the free individual following his own inner light. In this way the rationalist argument, with its assumption of the single true solution, has led by steps which, if not logically valid, are historically and psychologically intelligible from an ethical doctrine of individual responsibility and individual self-perfection to an authoritarian State obedient to the directives of an élite of Platonic guardians.

What can have led to so strange a reversal – the transformation of Kant's severe individualism into something close to a pure totalitarian doctrine on the part of thinkers some of whom claimed to be his disciples? This question is not of merely historical interest, for not a few contemporary liberals have gone through the same peculiar evolution. It is true that Kant insisted, following Rousseau, that a capacity for rational self-direction belonged to all men; that there could be no experts in moral matters, since morality was a matter not of specialized knowledge (as the Utilitarians and *philosophes* had maintained), but of the correct use of a universal human faculty; and consequently that what made men free was not acting in certain self-improving ways, which they could be coerced to do, but knowing why they ought to do so, which nobody could do for, or on behalf of, anyone else. But even Kant, when he came to deal with political issues, conceded that no law, provided that it was such that I should, if I were asked, approve it as a rational being, could possibly deprive me of any portion of my rational freedom. With this the door was opened wide to the rule of experts. I cannot consult all men about all enactments all the time. The government cannot be a continuous plebiscite. Moreover, some men are not as well attuned to the voice of their own reason as others: some seem singularly deaf. If I am a legislator or a ruler, I must assume that if the law I impose is rational (and I can consult only my own reason) it will automatically be approved by all the members of my society so far as they are rational beings. For if they disapprove, they must, *pro tanto*, be irrational; then they will need to be repressed by reason: whether their own or mine cannot matter, for the pronouncements of reason must be the same in all minds. I issue my orders and, if you resist, take it upon myself to repress the irrational element in you which opposes reason. My task would be easier if you repressed it in yourself; I try to educate you to do so. But I am responsible for public welfare, I cannot wait until all men are wholly rational. Kant may protest that the essence of the subject's freedom is that he, and he alone, has given himself the order to obey. But this is a counsel of perfection. If you fail to discipline yourself, I must do so for you; and you cannot complain of lack of freedom, for the fact that Kant's rational judge has sent you to prison is evidence that you have not listened to your own inner reason, that, like a child, a savage, an idiot, you are either not ripe for self-direction, or permanently incapable of it.[44]

If this leads to despotism, albeit by the best or the wisest – to Sarastro's temple in *The Magic Flute* – but still despotism, which turns out to be identical with freedom, can it be that there is something amiss in the premises of the argument? That the basic assumptions are themselves somewhere at fault? Let me state them once more: first, that all men have one true purpose, and one only, that of rational self-direction; second, that the ends of all rational beings must of necessity fit into a single universal, harmonious pattern, which some men may be able to discern more clearly than others; third, that all conflict, and consequently all tragedy, is due solely to the clash of reason with the irrational or the insufficiently rational – the immature and undeveloped elements in life, whether individual or communal – and that such clashes are,

in principle, avoidable, and for wholly rational beings impossible; finally, that when all men have been made rational, they will obey the rational laws of their own natures, which are one and the same in them all, and so be at once wholly law-abiding and wholly free. Can it be that Socrates and the creators of the central Western tradition in ethics and politics who followed him have been mistaken, for more than two millennia, that virtue is not knowledge, nor freedom identical with either? That despite the fact that it rules the lives of more men than ever before in its long history, not one of the basic assumptions of this famous view is demonstrable, or, perhaps, even true?

VI

The Search for Status

[. . .]

No doubt every interpretation of the word "liberty," however unusual, must include a minimum of what I have called "negative" liberty. There must be an area within which I am not frustrated. No society literally suppresses all the liberties of its members; a being who is prevented by others from doing anything at all on his own is not a moral agent at all, and could not either legally or morally be regarded as a human being, even if a physiologist or a biologist, or even a psychologist, felt inclined to classify him as a man. But the fathers of liberalism – Mill and Constant – want more than this minimum: they demand a maximum degree of non-interference compatible with the minimum demands of social life. It seems unlikely that this extreme demand for liberty has ever been made by any but a small minority of highly civilized and self-conscious human beings. The bulk of humanity has certainly at most times been prepared to sacrifice this to other goals: security, status, prosperity, power, virtue, rewards in the next world; or justice, equality, fraternity, and many other values which appear wholly, or in part, incompatible with the attainment of the greatest degree of individual liberty, and certainly do not need it as a precondition for their own realization. It is not a demand for *Lebensraum* for each individual that has stimulated the rebellions and wars of liberation for which men have been ready to die in the past, or, indeed, in the present. Men who have fought for freedom have commonly fought for the right to be governed by themselves or their representatives – sternly governed, if need be, like the Spartans, with little individual liberty, but in a manner which allowed them to participate, or at any rate to believe that they were participating, in the legislation and administration of their collective lives. And men who have made revolutions have, as often as not, meant by liberty no more than the conquest of power and authority by a given sect of believers in a doctrine, or by a class, or by some other social group, old or new. Their victories certainly frustrated those whom they ousted, and sometimes repressed, enslaved or exterminated vast numbers of human beings. Yet such revolutionaries have usually felt it necessary to argue that, despite this, they represented the party of liberty, or "true" liberty, by claiming universality for their ideal, which the "real selves" of even those who resisted them were also alleged to be seeking, although they were held to have lost the way to the goal, or to have mistaken the goal itself owing to some moral or spiritual blindness. All this has little to do with Mill's notion of liberty as limited only by the danger of doing harm to others. It is the non-recognition of this psychological and political fact (which lurks behind the apparent ambiguity of the term "liberty") that has, perhaps, blinded some contemporary liberals to the world in which they live. Their plea is clear, their cause is just. But they do not allow for the variety of basic human needs. Nor yet for the ingenuity with which men can prove to their own satisfaction that the road to one ideal also leads to its contrary.

[...]

VIII

The One and the Many

One belief, more than any other, is responsible for the slaughter of individuals on the altars of the great historical ideals – justice or progress or the happiness of future generations, or the sacred mission or emancipation of a nation or race or class, or even liberty itself, which demands the sacrifice of individuals for the freedom of society. This is the belief that somewhere, in the past or in the future, in divine revelation or in the mind of an individual thinker, in the pronouncements of history or science, or in the simple heart of an uncorrupted good man, there is a final solution. This ancient faith rests on the conviction that all the positive values in which men have believed must, in the end, be compatible, and perhaps even entail one another. "Nature binds truth, happiness and virtue together by an indissoluble chain," said one of the best men who ever lived, and spoke in similar terms of liberty, equality and justice.[45]

But is this true? It is a commonplace that neither political equality nor efficient organization nor social justice is compatible with more than a modicum of individual liberty, and certainly not with unrestricted *laissez-faire*; that justice and generosity, public and private loyalties, the demands of genius and the claims of society can conflict violently with each other. And it is no great way from that to the generalization that not all good things are compatible, still less all the ideals of mankind. But somewhere, we shall be told, and in some way, it must be possible for all these values to live together, for unless this is so, the universe is not a cosmos, not a harmony; unless this is so, conflicts of values may be an intrinsic, irremovable element in human life. To admit that the fulfilment of some of our ideals may in principle make the fulfilment of others impossible is to say that the notion of total human fulfilment is a formal contradiction, a metaphysical chimera. For every rationalist metaphysician, from Plato to the last disciples of Hegel or Marx, this abandonment of the notion of a final harmony in which all riddles are solved, all contradictions reconciled, is a piece of crude empiricism, abdication before brute facts, intolerable bankruptcy of reason before things as they are, failure to explain and to justify, to reduce everything to a system, which "reason" indignantly rejects.

But if we are not armed with an a priori guarantee of the proposition that a total harmony of true values is somewhere to be found – perhaps in some ideal realm the characteristics of which we can, in our finite state, not so much as conceive – we must fall back on the ordinary resources of empirical observation and ordinary human knowledge. And these certainly give us no warrant for supposing (or even understanding what would be meant by saying) that all good things, or all bad things for that matter, are reconcilable with each other. The world that we encounter in ordinary experience is one in which we are faced with choices between ends equally ultimate, and claims equally absolute, the realization of some of which must inevitably involve the sacrifice of others. Indeed, it is because this is their situation that men place such immense value upon the freedom to choose; for if they had assurance that in some perfect state, realizable by men on earth, no ends pursued by them would ever be in conflict, the necessity and agony of choice would disappear, and with it the central importance of the freedom to choose. Any method of bringing this final state nearer would then seem fully justified, no matter how much freedom were sacrificed to forward its advance.

It is, I have no doubt, some such dogmatic certainty that has been responsible for the deep, serene, unshakeable conviction in the minds of some of the most merciless tyrants and persecutors in history that what they did was fully justified by its purpose. I do not say that the ideal of self-perfection – whether for individuals or nations or Churches or classes – is to be condemned in itself, or that the language which was used in its defence was in all cases the result of a confused or fraudulent use of words, or of moral or intellectual perversity. Indeed, I have tried to show that it is the notion of freedom in its "positive" sense that is at the heart of the demands for national or social self-direction which animate the most powerful and morally just public movements of our time, and that not to recognize this is to misunderstand the most vital facts and ideas of our age. But equally it seems to me that the belief that some single formula can in principle be found whereby all the diverse ends of men can be harmoniously realized is demonstrably false. If, as I believe, the ends of men are many, and not all of them are in principle compatible with each other, then the possibility of conflict – and of tragedy – can never wholly be eliminated from human life, either personal or social. The necessity of choosing between absolute claims is then an inescapable characteristic of the human condition. This gives its value to freedom as Acton conceived of it – as an end in itself, and not as a temporary need, arising out of our confused notions and irrational and disordered lives, a predicament which a panacea could one day put right.

I do not wish to say that individual freedom is, even in the most liberal societies, the sole, or even the dominant, criterion of social action. We compel children to be educated, and we forbid public executions. These are certainly curbs to freedom. We justify them on the ground that ignorance, or a barbarian upbringing, or cruel pleasures and excitements are worse for us than the amount of restraint needed to repress them. This judgment in turn depends on how we determine good and evil, that is to say, on our moral, religious, intellectual, economic and aesthetic values; which are, in their turn, bound up with our conception of man, and of the basic demands of his nature. In other words, our solution of such problems is based on our vision, by which we are consciously or unconsciously guided, of what constitutes a fulfilled human life, as contrasted with Mill's "cramped and dwarfed," "pinched and hidebound" natures.[46]

To protest against the laws governing censorship or personal morals as intolerable infringements of personal liberty presupposes a belief that the activities which such laws forbid are fundamental needs of men as men, in a good (or, indeed, any) society. To defend such laws is to hold that these needs are not essential, or that they cannot be satisfied without sacrificing other values which come higher – satisfy deeper needs – than individual freedom, determined by some standard that is not merely subjective, a standard for which some objective status – empirical or a priori – is claimed.

The extent of a man's, or a people's, liberty to choose to live as he or they desire must be weighed against the claims of many other values, of which equality, or justice, or happiness, or security, or public order are perhaps the most obvious examples. For this reason, it cannot be unlimited. We are rightly reminded by R. H. Tawney that the liberty of the strong, whether their strength is physical or economic, must be restrained. This maxim claims respect, not as a consequence of some a priori rule, whereby the respect for the liberty of one man logically entails respect for the liberty of others like him; but simply because respect for the principles of justice, or shame at gross inequality of treatment, is as basic in men as the desire for liberty. That we cannot have everything is a necessary, not a contingent, truth. Burke's plea for the constant need to compensate, to reconcile, to balance; Mill's plea for novel "experiments in living"[47] with their permanent possibility of error – the knowledge that it is not merely in practice but in principle impossible to reach clear-cut and certain answers, even in an ideal world of wholly good and rational men and wholly clear ideas – may madden those who seek for final solutions and single, all-embracing systems, guaranteed to be eternal. Nevertheless, it is a conclusion that cannot be escaped by those who, with Kant, have learnt the truth that "Out of the crooked timber of humanity no straight thing was ever made."[48]

There is little need to stress the fact that monism, and faith in a single criterion, has always proved a deep source of satisfaction both to the intellect and to the emotions. Whether the standard of judgment derives from the vision of some future perfection, as in the minds of the *philosophes* in the eighteenth century and their technocratic successors in our own day, or is rooted in the past – *la terre et les morts* – as maintained by German historicists or French theocrats, or neo-Conservatives in English-speaking countries, it is bound, provided it is inflexible enough, to encounter some unforeseen and unforeseeable human development, which it will not fit; and will then be used to justify the a priori barbarities of Procrustes – the vivisection of actual human societies into some fixed pattern dictated by our fallible understanding of a largely imaginary past or a wholly imaginary future. To preserve our absolute categories or ideals at the expense of human lives offends equally against the principles of science and of history; it is an attitude found in equal measure on the right and left wings in our days, and is not reconcilable with the principles accepted by those who respect the facts.

Pluralism, with the measure of "negative" liberty that it entails, seems to me a truer and more humane ideal than the goals of those who seek in the great disciplined, authoritarian structures the ideal of "positive" self-mastery by classes, or peoples, or the whole of mankind. It is truer, because it does, at least, recognize the fact that human goals are many, not all of them commensurable, and in perpetual rivalry with one another. To assume that all values can be graded on one scale, so that it is a mere matter of inspection to determine the highest, seems to me to falsify our knowledge that men are free agents, to represent moral decision as an operation which a slide-rule could, in principle, perform. To say that in some ultimate, all-reconciling yet realizable synthesis duty *is* interest, or individual freedom *is* pure democracy or an authoritarian State, is to throw a metaphysical blanket over either self-deceit or deliberate hypocrisy. It is more humane because it does not (as the system-builders do) deprive men, in the name of some remote, or incoherent, ideal, of much that they have found to be indispensable to their life as unpredictably self-transforming human beings.[49] In the end, men choose between ultimate values; they choose as they do because their life and thought are determined by fundamental moral categories and concepts that are, at any rate over large stretches of time and space, and whatever their ultimate origins, a part of their being and thought and sense of their own identity; part of what makes them human.

It may be that the ideal of freedom to choose ends without claiming eternal validity for them, and the pluralism of values connected with this, is only the late fruit of our declining capitalist civilization: an ideal which remote ages and primitive societies have not recognized, and one which posterity will regard with curiosity, even sympathy, but little comprehension. This may be so; but no sceptical conclusions seem to me to follow. Principles are not less sacred because their duration cannot be guaranteed. Indeed, the very desire for guarantees that our values are eternal and secure in some objective heaven is perhaps only a craving for the certainties of childhood or the absolute values of our primitive past. "To realise the relative validity of one's convictions," said an admirable writer of our time, "and yet stand for them unflinchingly is what distinguishes a civilised man from a barbarian."[50] To demand more than this is perhaps a deep and incurable metaphysical need; but to allow such a need to determine one's practice is a symptom of an equally deep, and more dangerous, moral and political immaturity.

Notes

1 I do not, of course, mean to imply the truth of the converse.

2 Helvétius made this point very clearly: "The free man is the man who is not in irons, not imprisoned in a gaol, nor terrorised like a slave by the fear of punishment." It is not lack of freedom not to fly like an eagle or swim like a whale. *De l'esprit*, first discourse, chapter 4.

3 The Marxist conception of social laws is, of course, the best-known version of this theory, but it forms a large element in some Christian and utilitarian, and all socialist, doctrines.

4 *Émile*, book 2: vol. 4, p. 320, in *Oeuvres complètes*, ed. Bernard Gagnebin and others (Paris, 1959–95).

5 "A free man," said Hobbes, "is he that . . . is not hindered to do what he has a will to." *Leviathan*, chapter 21: p. 146 in Richard Tuck's edition (Cambridge, 1991). Law is always a fetter, even if it protects you from being bound in chains that are heavier than those of the law, say some more repressive law or custom, or arbitrary despotism or chaos. Bentham says much the same.

6 R. H. Tawney, *Equality* (1931), 3rd ed. (London, 1938), chapter 5, section 2, "Equality and Liberty," p. 208 (not in previous editions).

7 Constant, *Principes de politique*, chapter 1: p. 318 in op. cit.

8 J. S. Mill, *On Liberty*, chapter 1: vol. 18, p. 226, in op. cit.

9 ibid., p. 224.

10 ibid., chapter 3, p. 268.

11 ibid., pp. 265–6. The last two phrases are from John Sterling's essay on Simonides: vol 1, p. 190, in his *Essays and Tales*, ed. Julius Charles Hare (London, 1848).

12 ibid., chapter 4, p. 277.

13 This is but another illustration of the natural tendency of all but a very few thinkers to believe that all the things they hold good must be intimately connected, or at least compatible, with one another. The history of thought, like the history of nations, is strewn with examples of inconsistent, or at least disparate, elements artificially yoked together in a despotic system, or held together by the danger of some common enemy. In due course the danger passes, and conflicts between the allies arise, which often disrupt the system, sometimes to the great benefit of mankind.

14 See the valuable discussion of this in Michel Villey, *Leçons d'histoire de la philosophie du droit* (Paris, 1957), chapter 14, which traces the embryo of the notion of subjective rights to Occam (see p. 272).

15 Christian (and Jewish or Muslim) belief in the absolute authority of divine or natural laws, or in the equality of all men in the sight of God, is very different from belief in freedom to live as one prefers.

16 Indeed, it is arguable that in the Prussia of Frederick the Great or in the Austria of Joseph II men of imagination, originality and creative genius, and, indeed, minorities of all kinds, were less persecuted and felt the pressure, both of institutions and custom, less heavy upon them than in many an earlier or later democracy.

17 "Negative liberty" is something the extent of which, in a given case, it is difficult to estimate. It might, prima facie, seem to depend simply on the power to choose between at any rate two alternatives. Nevertheless, not all choices are equally free, or free at all. If in a totalitarian State I betray my friend under threat of torture, perhaps even if I act from fear of losing my job, I can reasonably say that I did not act freely. Nevertheless, I did, of course, make a choice, and could, at any rate in theory, have chosen to be killed or tortured or imprisoned. The mere existence of alternatives is not, therefore, enough to make my action free (although it may be voluntary) in the normal sense of the word. The extent of my freedom seems to depend on (*a*) how many possibilities are open to me (although the method of counting these can never be more than impressionistic; possibilities of action are not discrete entities like apples, which can be exhaustively enumerated); (*b*) how easy or difficult each of these possibilities is to actualize; (*c*) how important in my plan of life, given my character and circumstances, these possibilities are when compared with each other; (*d*) how far they are closed and opened by deliberate human acts; (*e*) what value not merely the agent, but the general sentiment of the society in which he lives, puts on the various possibilities. All these magnitudes must be "integrated," and a conclusion, necessarily never precise, or indisputable, drawn from this process. It may well be that there are many incommensurable kinds and degrees of freedom, and that they cannot be drawn up on any single scale of magnitude. Moreover, in the case of societies, we are faced by such (logically absurd) questions as "Would arrangement X increase the liberty of Mr A more than it would that of Messrs B, C and D between them, added together?" The same difficulties arise in applying utilitarian criteria. Nevertheless, provided we do not demand precise measurement, we can give valid reasons for saying that the average subject of the King of Sweden is, on the whole, a good deal freer today [1958] than the average citizen of Spain or Albania. Total patterns of life must be compared directly as wholes, although the method by which we make the comparison, and the truth of the conclusions, are difficult or impossible to demonstrate. But the vagueness of the concepts, and the multiplicity of the criteria involved, are attributes of the subject-matter itself, not of our imperfect methods of measurement, or of incapacity for precise thought.

18 "[T]he ideal of true freedom is the maximum of power for all members of human society alike to make the best of themselves," said T. H. Green in 1881: op. cit., p. 200. Apart from the confusion of freedom with equality, this entails that if a man chose some immediate pleasure – which (in whose view?) would not enable him to make the best of himself (what self?) – what he was exercising was not "true" freedom: and if deprived of it, he would not lose anything that mattered. Green was a genuine liberal: but many a tyrant could use this formula to justify his worst acts of oppression.

19 "A wise man, though he be a slave, is at liberty, and from this it follows that though a fool rule, he is in slavery," said St Ambrose. It might equally well have been said by Epictetus or Kant. *Corpus scriptorum ecclesiasticorum latinorum*, vol. 82, part 1, ed. Otto Faller (Vienna, 1968), letter 7, §24 (p. 55).

20 *Social Contract*, book 1, chapter 8: vol. 3, p. 365 in *Oeuvres complètes*.

21 op. cit., vol. 8, p. 290, line 27, and p. 291, line 3.

22 "Proletarian coercion, in all its forms, from executions to forced labour, is, paradoxical as it may sound, the method of moulding communist humanity out of the human material of the capitalist period." These lines by the Bolshevik leader Nikolay Bukharin, especially the term "human material," vividly convey this attitude. Nikolay Bukharin, *Ekonomika perekhodnogo perioda* ['Economics in the Transitional Period'] (Moscow, 1920), chapter 10, p. 146.

23 Kant's psychology, and that of the Stoics and Christians too, assumed that some element in man – the "inner fastness of his mind" – could be made secure against conditioning. The development of the techniques of hypnosis, "brainwashing," subliminal suggestion and the like has made this a priori assumption, at least as an empirical hypothesis, less plausible.

24 op. cit., p. 309.

25 It is not perhaps far-fetched to assume that the quietism of the Eastern sages was, similarly, a response to the despotism of the great autocracies, and flourished at periods when individuals were apt to be humiliated, or at any rate ignored or ruthlessly managed, by those possessed of the instruments of physical coercion.

26 It is worth remarking that those who demanded – and fought for – liberty for the individual or for the nation in France during this period of German quietism did not fall into this attitude. Might this not be precisely because, despite the despotism of the French monarchy and the arrogance and arbitrary behaviour of privileged groups in the French State, France was a proud and powerful nation, where the reality of political power was not beyond the grasp of men of talent, so that withdrawal from battle into some untroubled heaven above it, whence it could be surveyed dispassionately by the self-sufficient philosopher, was not the only way out? The same holds for England in the nineteenth century and well after it, and for the United States today.

27 Or, as some modern theorists maintain, because I have, or could have, invented them for myself, since the rules are man-made.

28 Tractatus Theologico-Politicus, chapter 16: p. 137 in Benedict de Spinoza, The Political Works, ed. A. G. Wernham (Oxford, 1958).

29 Two Treatises of Government, second treatise, § 57.

30 ibid., §§ 6, 163.

31 De l'esprit des lois, book 11, chapter 3: p. 205 in Oeuvres complètes de Montesquieu, ed. A. Masson (Paris, 1950–5), vol. 1 A.

32 Appeal from the Old to the New Whigs (1791): pp. 93–4 in The Works of the Right Honourable Edmund Burke (World's Classics edition), vol. 5 (London, 1907).

33 On this Bentham seems to me to have said the last word: "The liberty of doing evil, is it not liberty? If it is not liberty, what is it then? . . . Do we not say that liberty should be taken away from fools, and wicked persons, because they abuse it?" The Works of Jeremy Bentham, ed. John Bowring (Edinburgh, 1843), vol. 1, p. 301. Compare with this the view of the Jacobins in the same period, discussed by Crane Brinton in "Political Ideas in the Jacobin Clubs," Political Science Quarterly 43 (1928), 249–64, esp. 257: "no man is free in doing evil. To prevent him is to free him." This view is echoed in almost identical terms by British Idealists at the end of the following century.

34 Social Contract, book 1, chapter 6: vol 3, p. 361, in Oeuvres complètes.

35 op. cit., vol. 6, p. 316, line 2.

36 op. cit., ibid.: "every law is contrary to liberty."

37 Johann Gottlieb Fichte's sämmtliche Werke, ed. I. H. Fichte (Berlin, 1845–6), vol. 7, p. 576.

38 ibid., p. 574.

39 ibid., p. 578.

40 ibid., p. 576.

41 ibid., pp. 578, 580.

42 "To compel men to adopt the right form of government, to impose Right on them by force, is not only the right, but the sacred duty of every man who has both the insight and the power to do so." ibid., vol. 4, p. 436.

43 loc. cit.

44 Kant came nearest to asserting the "negative" ideal of liberty when (in one of his political treatises) he declared that "The greatest problem of the human race, to the solution of which it is compelled by nature, is the establishment of a civil society universally administering right according to law. It is only in a society which possesses the greatest liberty . . . – and also the most exact determination and guarantee of the limits of [the] liberty [of each individual] in order that it may co-exist with the liberty of others – that the highest purpose of nature, which is the development of all her capacities, can be attained in the case of mankind." "Idee zu einer allgemeinen Geschichte in weltbürgerlicher Absicht" (1784), in op. cit., vol. 8, p. 22, line 6. Apart from the teleological implications, this formulation does not at first appear very different from orthodox liberalism. The crucial point, however, is how to determine the criterion for the "exact determination and guarantee of the limits" of individual liberty.

Most modern liberals, at their most consistent, want a situation in which as many individuals as possible can realize as many of their ends as possible, without assessment of the value of these ends as such, save in so far as they may frustrate the purposes of others. They wish the frontiers between individuals or groups of men to be drawn solely with a view to preventing collisions between human purposes, all of which must be considered to be equally ultimate, uncriticizable ends in themselves. Kant, and the rationalists of his type, do not regard all ends as of equal value. For them the limits of liberty are determined by applying the rules of "reason," which is much more than the mere generality of rules as such, and is a faculty that creates or reveals a purpose identical in, and for, all men. In the name of reason anything that is non-rational may be condemned, so that the various personal aims which their individual imaginations and idiosyncrasies lead men to pursue − for example, aesthetic and other non-rational kinds of self-fulfilment − may, at least in theory, be ruthlessly suppressed to make way for the demands of reason. The authority of reason and of the duties it lays upon men is identified with individual freedom, on the assumption that only rational ends can be the "true" objects of a "free" man's "real" nature.

I have never, I must own, understood what "reason" means in this context; and here merely wish to point out that the a priori assumptions of this philosophical psychology are not compatible with empiricism: that is to say, with any doctrine founded on knowledge derived from experience of what men are and seek.

45 Condorcet, from whose *Esquisse* these words are quoted, declares that the task of social science is to show "by what bonds nature has united the progress of enlightenment with that of liberty, virtue and respect for the natural rights of man; how these ideals, which alone are truly good, yet so often separated from each other that they are even believed to be incompatible, should, on the contrary, become inseparable, as soon as enlightenment has reached a certain level simultaneously among a large number of nations." He goes on to say that "Men still preserve the errors of their childhood, of their country and of their age long after having recognized all the truths needed for destroying them." ibid., pp. 9, 10. Ironically enough, his belief in the need for and possibility of uniting all good things may well be precisely the kind of error he himself so well described.

46 loc. cit.

47 loc. cit.

48 loc. cit.

49 On this also Bentham seems to me to have spoken well: "Individual interests are the only real interests . . . Can it be conceived that there are men so absurd as to . . . prefer the man who is not, to him who is; to torment the living, under pretence of promoting the happiness of those who are not born, and who may never be born?" op. cit., p. 321. This is one of the infrequent occasions when Burke agrees with Bentham; for this passage is at the heart of the empirical, as against the metaphysical, view of politics.

50 Joseph A. Schumpeter, *Capitalism, Socialism, and Democracy* (London, 1943), p. 243.

Chapter 35

Franklin Delano Roosevelt

THE FOUR FREEDOMS
Annual Message to Congress, January 6, 1941

Franklin Delano Roosevelt (F.D.R.) (1882–1945) was the thirty-second president of the United States, famous for his "New Deal" which sought to relieve the economic depression of the country through a variety of government and social programs. In this excerpt from one of his more famous speeches (1941), Roosevelt draws a connection between the classical freedoms of the American founding (freedom of speech and religion) and other freedoms which would later become hallmarks of twentieth-century American liberalism (freedom from want and from fear).

M*r. President, Mr. Speaker, Members of the Seventy-seventh Congress:*

I address you, the Members of the Seventy-seventh Congress, at a moment unprecedented in the history of the Union. I use the word "unprecedented," because at no previous time has American security been as seriously threatened from without as it is today.

[...]

As men do not live by bread alone, they do not fight by armaments alone. Those who man our defenses, and those behind them who build our defenses, must have the stamina and the courage which come from unshakable belief in the manner of life which they are defending. The mighty action that we are calling for cannot be based on a disregard of all things worth fighting for.

The Nation takes great satisfaction and much strength from the things which have been done to make its people conscious of their individual stake in the preservation of democratic life in America. Those things have toughened the fiber of our people, have renewed their faith and strengthened their devotion to the institutions we make ready to protect.

Certainly this is no time for any of us to stop thinking about the social and economic problems which are the root cause of the social revolution which is today a supreme factor in the world. For there is nothing mysterious about the foundations of a healthy and strong democracy. The basic things expected by our people of their political and economic systems are simple. They are:

Equality of opportunity for youth and for others.
Jobs for those who can work.
Security for those who need it.
The ending of special privilege for the few.
The preservation of civil liberties for all.
The enjoyment of the fruits of scientific progress in a wider and constantly rising standard of living.

These are the simple, basic things that must never be lost sight of in the turmoil and unbelievable complexity of our modern world. The inner and abiding strength of our economic and political systems is dependent upon the degree to which they fulfill these expectations.

Many subjects connected with our social economy call for immediate improvement. As examples:

We should bring more citizens under the coverage of old-age pensions and unemployment insurance.

We should widen the opportunities for adequate medical care.

We should plan a better system by which persons deserving or needing gainful employment may obtain it.

I have called for personal sacrifice. I am assured of the willingness of almost all Americans to respond to that call.

A part of the sacrifice means the payment of more money in taxes. In my Budget Message I shall recommend that a greater portion of this great defense program be paid for from taxation than we are paying today. No person should try, or be allowed, to get rich out of this program; and the principle of tax payments in accordance with ability to pay should be constantly before our eyes to guide our legislation.

If the Congress maintains these principles, the voters, putting patriotism ahead of pocketbooks, will give you their applause.

In the future days, which we seek to make secure, we look forward to a world founded upon four essential human freedoms.

The first is freedom of speech and expression – everywhere in the world.

The second is freedom of every person to worship God in his own way – everywhere in the world.

The third is freedom from wan – which, translated into world terms, means economic understandings which will secure to every nation a healthy peacetime life for its inhabitants – everywhere in the world.

The fourth is freedom from fear – which, translated into world terms, means a world-wide reduction of armaments to such a point and in such a thorough fashion that no nation will be in a position to commit an act of physical aggression against any neighbor – anywhere in the world.

That is no vision of a distant millennium. It is a definite basis for a kind of world attainable in our own time and generation. That kind of world is the very antithesis of the so-called new order of tyranny which the dictators seek to create with the crash of a bomb.

To that new order we oppose the greater conception – the moral order. A good society is able to face schemes of world domination and foreign revolutions alike without fear.

Since the beginning of our American history, we have been engaged in change – in a perpetual peaceful revolution – a revolution which goes on steadily, quietly adjusting itself to changing conditions – without the concentration camp or the quick-lime in the ditch. The world order which we seek is the cooperation of free countries, working together in a friendly, civilized society.

This nation has placed its destiny in the hands and heads and hearts of its millions of free men and women; and its faith in freedom under the guidance of God. Freedom means the supremacy of human rights everywhere. Our support goes to those who struggle to gain those rights or keep them. Our strength is our unity of purpose. To that high concept there can be no end save victory.

Chapter 36

Philip Pettit

REPUBLICAN POLITICAL THEORY

Philip Pettit (1945–) is a philosopher and political theorist at Princeton University. In political philosophy, he is best known for his work developing and revitalizing the republican tradition of liberty, in which the essence of freedom is understood as non-domination, and domination is understood as a condition of being subject to the arbitrary interference of others. This essay (published in 1997) explains the republican conception of liberty, contrasts it with the more currently popular notion of negative liberty, and explores its implications for policies involving the redistribution of wealth.

R epublican political theory takes its starting point from a long-established tradition of thinking about politics (Pocock 1975). The republican tradition is associated with Cicero at the time of the Roman republic; with a number of writers, pre-eminently Machiavelli – "the divine Machiavel" of the *Discourses* – in the Renaissance Italian republics; with James Harrington, Algernon Sydney and a host of lesser figures in and after the period of the English Civil War and commonwealth; and with the many theorists of republic or common-wealth in eighteenth-century England, the United States and France. These theorists – the commonwealthmen (Robbins 1959) – were greatly influenced by John Locke and, later, the Baron de Montesquieu; indeed they claimed Locke and Montesquieu, with good reason, as their own. They are well represented in docu-ments like *Cato's Letters* (Trenchard and Gordon 1971) and, on the American side of the Atlantic, the *Federalist Papers* (Madison et al. 1987).

The commonwealthmen helped to shape habits of political reflex and thought that still survive today. Their distinctive refrain had two parts: the cause of freedom rests squarely with the law and the state – it is mainly thanks to the constitution under which they live that people enjoy freedom; but the authorities are also an inherent threat and people have to strive to "keep the bastards honest." The price of liberty is civic virtue, then, where that includes both a willingness to participate in government and a determination to exercise eternal vigilance in regard to the governors. The common-wealthmen tended to advocate the removal of the monarchy in America, but in England most were content to see the king constitutionally fettered. England was "a nation," in Montesquieu's (1989: 70) unmistakeable reference, "where the republic hides under the form of monarchy" (Rahe 1992: 524).

I find the republican tradition of thought a wonderful source of ideas and ideals, and in this chapter I hope to communicate why (see Pettit 1997). But I should mention that I am not alone in finding the tradition inspirational. Historians like John Pocock (1975) and Quentin Skinner (1978; 1983; 1984) have not only made the republican way of thinking visible to us in the past couple of decades: they have also shown how it can give us a new perspective on contemporary politics. Skinner in particular has argued that it can give us a new understanding of freedom, and my own argument builds on this. Legal thinkers like Cass Sunstein (1990; 1993a; 1993b), on the other hand, have gone back to the republican tradition in its distinctively American incarnation in the late 1800s and have made a strong case for the claim that the tradition suggests a distinctive way of interpreting the U.S. Constitution and, more generally, that it gives us an insightful overview of the role of government. Criminologists and regulatory theorists like John Braithwaite, with whom I have actively collaborated (Braithwaite and Pettit 1990), find in the republican tradition a set of compelling ideas; it enables us to articulate both the demands that we should place on a regulatory system – say, the criminal justice system – and the expectations that we should hold out for how those demands can be best met (Ayres and Braithwaite 1992). And these are just a few thinkers among many commentators who have begun to chart republican connections, and sometimes to draw actively on republican ideas, in recent years.[1]

My own approach to republican political theory is to give centre place to the notion of freedom that was shared among republican thinkers generally, and to derive other republican claims from the commitment to this ideal. In this chapter I will present the republican ideal of freedom in the first section and then try to illustrate, in the second, the way in which that ideal has significance for contemporary political thought.

The Republican Ideal of Freedom

The Constant Connection

Early in the nineteenth century Benjamin Constant (1988) delivered a famous lecture entitled "The Liberty of the Ancients and the Liberty of the Moderns." He depicted the liberty of the moderns, in the familiar negative or liberal fashion, as the absence of interference. I am free in this sense "to the degree to which no human being interferes with my activity" (Berlin 1958: 7). Constant depicted the liberty of the ancients, on the other hand, as the liberty associated, ideally, with being a direct participant in a self-governing democracy. I am free in this sense, not through being uncontrolled by others, but through sharing with others the power to control all. The liberty of the ancients is the most prominent form of what Isaiah Berlin (1958) later called positive freedom.

The most important observation in introducing the republican conception of freedom is to recognize Constant's image of the liberty of the ancients as a caricature that served to hide the true republican way of thinking, only recently so prominent, from his contemporaries' eyes. Constant may not have been consciously propagandizing, but what he achieved was to mesmerize later generations into thinking that the only feasible, perhaps the only sensible, notion of freedom was the liberal idea of freedom as non-interference. The liberty of the ancients is no match for freedom as non-interference – even if it is thought desirable, it must be judged to be unattainable. The effect of setting up the two as the only relevant alternatives was to give victory, inevitably, to the liberal ideal.

The republican way of thinking about freedom, effectively suppressed by Constant, represents it as non-domination, not as direct democratic standing. And the difference between freedom as non-interference and freedom as non-domination is easily explained. Assume that one person dominates another to the extent that they have the capacity to interfere arbitrarily – to interfere on an arbitrary basis – in some or all of the other's choices (Pettit 1996; 1997). Freedom as non-interference makes the absence of interference sufficient for freedom; in contrast, freedom as non-domination requires the absence of a capacity on the part of anyone else – any individual or corporate agent – to interfere arbitrarily in their life or affairs. The difference between the two ways of conceiving of liberty may seem slight, but a little reflection will reveal hidden dimensions to the contrast.

Interference and Arbitrary Interference

The two conceptions of freedom both invoke the notion of interference, and we may begin our exploration of the contrast between the two ways of conceiving liberty with a comment on this. The first thing to note is that, on almost all accounts, the intrusions that count as interference have to be intentional acts, or at least acts for which the agent can be held responsible (Miller 1990: 35): they have to be intentional or quasi-intentional. The reason for this stipulation is that freedom under most accounts is a condition defined in relation to other intentional agents, not a condition defined by reference to favours bestowed by nature: not a condition defined by how far a person escapes various brute, non-intentionally imposed limitations (see Spitz 1995: 382–3).

The intrusions that constitute interference may be restricted to acts that make certain options impossible for the agent; or they may be extended to include acts that coerce or manipulate the agent in choosing between options. I shall assume that, for both conceptions of freedom, interference is to be understood in the broader fashion. Under this way of taking them, acts of interference include any acts that worsen the agent's situation – or least worsen it significantly – either by reducing the alternatives available in choice, or by raising the actual or expected costs associated with some of the alternatives. Thus the agent may be stopped from

doing something; the agent may be threatened with some extra cost, say some penalty, in the event of doing it; or the agent may simply be penalized for having done the act in question.

Freedom as non-interference invokes the notion of interference; freedom as non-domination goes further and invokes arbitrary interference: interference on an arbitrary basis. What makes an act of interference arbitrary, then, in the sense of being perpetrated on an arbitrary basis? An act is perpetrated on an arbitrary basis, we can say, if it is subject only to the *arbitrium*, the decision or judgment, of the agent; the agent was in a position to choose it or not choose it, at their pleasure. When we say that an act of interference is perpetrated on an arbitrary basis, then, we imply that like any arbitrary act it is chosen or not chosen at the agent's pleasure. And in particular, since interference with others is involved, we imply that it is chosen or rejected without reference to the interests, or the opinions, of those affected. The choice is not forced to track what the interests of those others require according to their own judgments.[2]

Under this conception of arbitrariness, then, an act of interference is non-arbitrary to the extent that it is forced to track the interests and ideas of the person suffering the interference. Since the interests and ideas of the person involved may make inconsistent demands, non-arbitrariness consists in recognition of the relevant ones. I may have an interest in the state imposing certain taxes or in punishing certain offenders, for example, and the state may pursue these ends according to procedures that conform to my ideas about appropriate means. But I may still not want the state to impose taxes on me – I may want to be an exception – or I may think that I ought not to be punished in the appropriate manner, even though I have been convicted of an offence. In such a case, my relevant interests and ideas are those that are shared in common with others, not those that treat me as exceptional, since the state is meant to serve others as well as me. And so, in these cases, the interference of the state in taxing or punishing me is not conducted on an arbitrary basis and does not represent domination.

The republican tradition of thinking took a distinctive view of what is required for an act of interference – in particular, an act of legal or government interference – to be non-arbitrary, and I follow that tradition in giving this account. Consider the complaint of Tom Paine (1989: 168) against monarchy: "It means arbitrary power in an individual person; in the exercise of which, *himself*, and not the *res-publica*, is the object" (cf. Sydney 1996: 199–200). What is required for non-arbitrary state power, as this comment makes clear, is that the power be exercised in a way that tracks, not the power-holder's personal welfare or world-view, but rather the welfare and world-view of the public. The acts of interference perpetrated by the state must be triggered by the shared interests of those affected; and the interpretation of what those interests require must be shared, at least at the procedural level, by those affected.

Thus there are two antonyms for freedom: one opposes freedom directly to interference, but the second varies this opposition in two ways. The second autonym of freedom involves not interference as such, only interference on an arbitrary basis. Moreover, this second antonym of freedom does not require actual arbitrary interference, only vulnerability to someone with the capacity for such interference.

The second autonym has the effect of making it harder for someone to lose their freedom or to have their freedom reduced. For if an agent interferes non-arbitrarily in their choices, that does not offend as such against their freedom; whatever damage is done by the interference, the non-arbitrariness is enough to ensure that their freedom is not compromised. But the second antonym also has the contrary effect of making it easier, not harder, for someone to suffer a loss of freedom. For if an agent has the capacity to interfere arbitrarily in any of their choices, then that in itself compromises their freedom;

they suffer a loss of freedom even if the other person does not actually exercise the capacity for interference.

The Harder-to-lose-freedom Effect

The harder-to-lose-freedom effect makes for a difference in the law's impact on liberty under the two conceptions. Under freedom as non-interference, a regime of law, being necessarily coercive, systematically compromises people's freedom, even if the consequence of putting the regime into operation is that less interference takes place overall. Subjection to the law, in and of itself, represents a loss of liberty. Under the second conception, however, subjection to the law need not represent a loss of liberty for anyone who lives under it, provided – and of course it is a big proviso – that the making, interpretation and implementation of the law are not arbitrary: provided that the legal coercion involved is constrained to track the interests and ideas of those affected. The proviso, intuitively expressed, is that the legal regime represents a fair rule of law.

A regime of legal coercion and restraint, while not itself constituting a compromise of liberty, may have the same effect as a natural obstacle in limiting the choices available to people or in making them more costly; in defining the range over which people enjoy undominated choice. Proponents of freedom as non-interference do not count natural obstacles as factors that compromise liberty – because they are in no way intentional – but they do admit that such obstacles affect the range of choice over which freedom as non-interference may be exercised; the obstacles condition freedom, as we might put the distinction, but they do not compromise it.[3] Proponents of freedom as non-domination move the locus of this boundary between compromising and conditioning factors. For them, the interference associated with a fair rule of law, like the natural obstacle, conditions people's liberty but does not in itself compromise it: the law does not in itself count as infringing or violating or reducing or offending against people's liberty.[4]

Hobbes and Bentham are the great advocates of the idea that law in itself represents a compromise of liberty. "As against the coercion applicable by individual to individual, no liberty can be given to one man but in proportion as it is taken away from another. All coercive laws, therefore, and in particular all laws creative of liberty, are as far as they go abrogative of liberty" (Bentham 1843). Or as Hobbes had put it: "The Liberty of a Subject, lyeth therefore only in those things, which in regulating their actions, the Soveraign hath praetermitted" (Hobbes 1968: 264).

But Hobbes and Bentham were consciously breaking with a longer tradition of thought – the republican or commonwealthman tradition – in taking this line (Skinner 1983). That tradition was defended in the first instance by James Harrington (1992: 20), who argued that Hobbes was confusing freedom from the law with freedom proper: freedom by the law. John Locke look Harrington's side, embracing "freedom from Absolute, Arbitrary Power" as the essential thing and presenting law as essentially on liberty's side: "that ill deserves the Name of Confinement which serves to hedge us in only from Bogs and Precipices . . . the end of Law is not to abolish or restrain, but to preserve and enlarge Freedom" (1965: 325, 348). William Blackstone (1978: 126) represents the eighteenth-century orthodoxy when he follows the same line; "laws, when prudently framed, are by no means subversive but rather introductive of liberty; for (as Mr Locke has well observed) where there is no law there is no freedom."

The difference between the two conceptions of liberty in their altitude to the law was of great significance from the point of view of Hobbes and Bentham. The view that all law compromises people's liberty enabled Hobbes to withstand the criticism that he anticipated from republicans, that his Leviathan was utterly inimical to freedom, constituting an arbitrary rule as distinct from a rule of law: an arbitrary rule as distinct from the republican vision of an "empire of laws, and not of men" (Harrington 1992: 8). And the same view enabled Bentham and those friends of his who opposed the American cause in the 1770s to argue against the colonists' main complaint. This was that, since the British parliament was not constrained in the laws that it passed for the governance of the American colonies – since it was not constrained in the same way that it was constrained in Britain itself – those laws represented an arbitrary interference with Americans and compromised their liberty (Lind 1776). Hobbes could argue that Leviathan did no worse than commonwealths in respect of the liberty of its subjects, since all law compromises liberty. And Bentham and his friends could argue on the same grounds that, in regard to liberty, Americans fared no worse under the law imposed by the British parliament than those in Britain itself.

So much for the harder-to-lose-freedom effect of opposing freedom to non-domination, not non-interference. But what of the easier-to-lose-freedom effect of shifting the antonym?

The Easier-to-lose-freedom Effect

This effect comes of the fact that someone loses freedom, not just to the extent that another person interferes on an arbitrary basis in their choices, but to the extent that another agent has the capacity to do this. With freedom as non-domination, a person loses freedom to the extent that they live under the thumb of another, even if that thumb is never used against them. Suppose that, under the existing laws and mores, a wife may be abused on an arbitrary basis by her husband, at least in certain areas and in a certain measure. Even if her husband is a loving and caring individual, such a wife cannot count as fully free under the construal of freedom as non-domination. And neither can the employee who lives under the thumb of an employer, nor the member of a minority who lives under the thumb of a majority coalition, nor the debtor who lives under the thumb of a creditor, nor anyone in such a subservient position.

Where the first effect of shifting the antonym shows up particularly in the assessment of law and liberty, the second relates to the association between law and slavery. As it became a matter of common assumption after Bentham that law represents a compromise of liberty, albeit a compromise that may be for the good overall, so it became impossible to maintain that to be unfree is always, in some measure, to be enslaved (Patterson 1991); no one was prepared to say that the law makes slaves of those who live under it. But before Bentham, when freedom was opposed first and foremost to domination, the association between unfreedom and slavery was complete. To be unfree was to live at the mercy of another; and that was, to live under a condition of enslavement to them.

Thus, Algernon Sydney (1990: 17) could write in the 1680s: "liberty solely consists in an independency upon the will of another, and by the name of slave we understand a man, who can neither dispose of his person nor goods, but enjoys all at the will of his master." And in the following century, the authors of *Cato's Letters* could give a characteristically forceful statement to the theme. "Liberty is, to live upon one's own Terms; Slavery is, to live at the mere Mercy of another; and a Life of Slavery is, to those who can bear it, a continual State of Uncertainty and Wretchedness, often an Apprehension of Violence, often the lingering Dread of a violent Death" (Trenchard and Gordon 1971, vol 2: 249–50).

The easier-to-lose-freedom effect of opposing liberty to domination connects with the slavery theme, because one of the striking things about a slave is that they remain a slave even if their master is entirely benign and never interferes with them. As Algernon Sydney (1990: 441) put it, "he is a slave who serves the best and gentlest man in the world, as well as he who serves the worst." Or as it was put by Richard Price (1991: 77–8) in the eighteenth century: "Individuals in private life, while held under the power of masters, cannot be denominated free, however equitably and kindly they may be treated. This is strictly true of communities as well as of individuals." There is domination, and there is unfreedom, even if no actual interference occurs.

I mentioned that the first effect of opposing freedom to domination provided an argument for the defenders of the American cause: while those in Britain were not made unfree by the law, given that the law could not be arbitrarily imposed there, those in America did not enjoy a similar status under the law. I should add that the second effect enabled them to sheet this argument home. They were in a position to argue that, even though the British parliament did not interfere much in American affairs – even though it levied only a small tax – still, because it could levy whatever tax it wished, without any serious restraint on its will, it related to the American colonists as master to slave.

Joseph Priestley (1993: 140) offers a nice example of this line of argument.

Q. What is the great grievance that those people complain of? A. It is their being taxed by the parliament of Great Britain, the members of which are so far from taxing themselves, that they ease themselves at the same time. If this measure takes place, the colonists will be reduced to a state of as complete servitude, as any people of which there is an account in history. For by the same power, by which the people of England can compel them to pay *one penny*, they may compel them to pay the *last penny* they have. There will be nothing but arbitrary imposition on the one side, and humble petition on the other.

Three Further Remarks

My comments on the two main differences associated with opposing freedom to domination rather than to interference should serve to make the notion intelligible. I want to add three further remarks, however, in order to underline some points that are important for understanding it fully.

First, although domination is constituted by one agent's having the capacity to interfere on an arbitrary basis in the affairs of another, some plausible empirical assumptions link it with a shared awareness on the part of the individuals or groups involved that this capacity exists. The question of whether you are undominated is bound to be of interest to anyone. The facts that make you undominated, if indeed you are such – the facts about your comparative resources, for example, and about the degree to which you are protected by legal and other means – are bound to be salient to all involved. Under standard assumptions as to people's inductive and inferential abilities, it follows that the fact of non-domination will be a matter of common recognition among the individuals in question (Lewis 1969: 56). And that is something of the greatest significance. For it means that under standard ways of achieving it, freedom as non-domination is intimately linked with the ability to look others in the eye, without having to defer to them or fear them. Montesquieu (1989: 157) emphasizes this theme when he writes: "Political liberty in a citizen is that tranquillity of spirit which comes from the opinion each one has of his security, and in order for him to have this liberty the government must be such that one citizen cannot fear another citizen."

The second remark that I want to make is also about domination. If someone is to enjoy freedom as non-domination, it is not enough that the other people are unlikely to exercise arbitrary interference; those other people must lack the capacity to interfere arbitrarily in that person's life, not just be unlikely to interfere. Suppose that you are subject to interference on an arbitrary basis from someone who, as it happens, really likes you and is extremely unlikely to interfere. If it still remains the case

that, by the ordinary standards of free-will attribution, they have a capacity to interfere or not to interfere, and this on a more or less arbitrary basis, then you are dominated in some measure by them and are thus far unfree. This is not a hard line to take, since you clearly suffer to the extent that the person has the capacity to interfere arbitrarily with you: you suffer to the extent that such interference is accessible to them as an agent, however improbable it is that they will exercise it. Their capacity for arbitrary interference means, for example, that you lack grounds for the subjective state of mind that goes with freedom as non-domination; you have reason to defer to the person in question and to look for their continued favour.

The third and last point is the most important. When Bentham and his associates came to reject the notion of freedom as non-domination, freedom as non-slavery, one theme in their reflections was that this sort of freedom did not come in degrees and so, unlike the rival conception, lent itself to "panegyric and careless declamation" (Paley 1825: 359–60; Long 1977: ch. 4). John Lind (1776: 25) expressed the criticism strongly in his attack on Richard Price's talk of the American colonists as slaves. "Things must be always at the maximum or minimum; there are no intermediate gradations: what is not white must be black." The third point I want to make is that this perception is mistaken. Freedom as non-domination is not an all-or-nothing matter.

The point should be obvious on a little reflection. Agents may have a more or less ready capacity to interfere. And the interference for which they have a capacity may be more or less serious, and may be available more or less without cost: say, without risk of retaliation. Thus the freedom as non-domination of those they are in a position to affect may be more or less intense; the weaker the agents, the greater the freedom of those they may affect.

Intensity, I should add, is only one dimension in which freedom as non-domination may vary.

As it is more or less intense, so freedom as non-domination may also be of one or another extent: it may be available for a smaller or larger number of choices, for choices that are more or less costly, and for choices of intuitively lesser or greater significance. Even if we have attained the highest possible intensity of non-domination for people in a society, there may be room for improving the range of undominated choice that is available to them: we may make the range of choice larger, or less costly, or intuitively more significant. Even if we remove all compromising influences on freedom as non-domination, it may still be possible to remove conditioning influences as well.

Thus, freedom as non-domination may be increased in either of two broad dimensions, intensity or extent; and we must decide how those dimensions are to be weighed against one another (Pettit 1997: ch. 3). Indeed, a similar problem arises with freedom as non-interference: it increases in intensity so far as interference is blocked, and increases in extent so far as the range of unobstructed choice is expanded, say, by providing people with extra resources. But I can overlook such problems of weighting here, as I shall he concerned with the promotion of these values only in the dimension of intensity. The question I address in the next section bears only on what is required for maximizing equal non-domination in the dimension of intensity.

The Significance of the Republican Ideal

The Paley Connection

Perhaps the most important figure in the demise of the republican ideal – someone more important even than Constant – is William Paley. Paley may have been the only writer in his time to recognize clearly the shift that was taking place – indeed, he argued for it. This was the shift from the received notion of freedom as non-domination, freedom as security against interference on an arbitrary basis, to freedom as non-interference. He sets out his view with admirable clarity in *The Principles of Moral and Political Philosophy*, which was first published in 1785 and was continually reprinted throughout the nineteenth century (Paley 1825).

Paley recognizes in this work that the usual notion of civil liberty, the one that agrees with "the usage of common discourse, as well as the example of many respectable writers" (357), is that of freedom as non-domination. "This idea places liberty in security; making it to consist not merely in an actual exemption from the constraint of useless and noxious laws and acts of dominion, but in being free from the *danger* of having such hereafter imposed or exercised" (357; original emphasis). But Paley argues against this received notion, and in favour of a Benthamite version of freedom as non-interference, on an extraordinary basis. He argues that the ideal in question, however well-established, is excessively demanding on the state: "those definitions of liberty ought to be rejected, which, by making that essential to civil freedom which is unattainable in experience, inflame expectations that can never be gratified, and disturb the public content with complaints, which no wisdom or benevolence of government can remove" (Paley 1825: 359).

How could Paley have thought that freedom as non-domination was the received ideal of freedom and yet that it was too demanding on the state? My hunch is that for Paley, as for most progressive thinkers of the late eighteenth century, it was no longer possible to think that political citizenship and consideration could be restricted, as traditional republicans had taken it to be restricted, to propertied males: women and servants could not be systematically and permanently excluded from concern. "Everybody to count for one, nobody for more than one," in the slogan ascribed to Bentham by John Stuart Mill (1969: 257). Thus, whereas traditional republicans could think that everyone relevant to the state's concern – every propertied male – might aspire to be free in the sense of not being subject to anyone's domination, egalitarians like Paley could not say this without seeming to embrace a wholly revolutionary doctrine: a doctrine that would require the upturning of relations between men and women, masters and servants. Their response was to deflate the ideal of freedom – to reduce it from non-domination to non-interference – at the same time that they argued that the constituency of political concern should be expanded. What they gave with the one hand, they took away with the other.

Why is the republican conception of liberty politically significant for the modern state? In a word, because it would recall the state to performing, in relation to citizens generally, the service that a republic – even a republic hidden under the form of a monarchy – was expected to perform for traditional elites. It may indeed have been impossible for someone like Paley or Bentham or Constant to envisage a state that would liberate servants as well as masters, women as well as men. But this is no longer an obviously infeasible ideal, even if it is obviously unattained. The limits on what we can envisage the state doing, and the limits on what we can imagine civil society allowing the state to do, have shifted dramatically over the last couple of centuries or so. Republicanism went underground at the time when the state began to become inclusivist, thereby permitting the state to become simultaneously more or less minimalist.[5] It is high time that the doctrine was restored to prominence, allowing us to consider the direction that an inclusive republic – a republic dedicated to the general promotion of freedom as non-domination – would have to take.

I have tried to display the significance of the republican perspective elsewhere, examining the impact of the republican ideal on our notions of equality and community; on the policy commitments that we prescribe for the modern state; on the way we conceive of constitutional and democratic values and institutions; on the approach that we take to issues of regulation and control; and on the image we have of how the state should relate to civil society (Pettit 1997). In order to illustrate the way in which the republican perspective can affect our thinking, I will concentrate here on its significance for issues of redistribution. This theme is particularly relevant, because it is at the centre of contemporary political discussions, and it also connects with the hostile reaction of Paley and others like him to the republican ideal.

Freedom as Non-interference, and Redistribution

How far is the maximal equal distribution of freedom as non-interference consistent with inequalities in other dimensions? How far is it consistent, for example, with different levels of provision in basic goods like food and shelter, modes of transport and media of reliable information; in basic services like medical care, legal counsel and accident insurance; in human capital of the kind associated with training and education; in social capital of the sort that consists in being able to call with confidence on others; in political capital such as office and authority confer; and in the material capital that is necessary for production? How far is it likely to require putting inequalities in these matters right or at least alleviating their effects: in particular, coercively putting them right, or coercively alleviating their effects, under state initiatives? How far is it likely to require what I shall describe, in a word, as redistribution?

The common wisdom on this question is that the maximal equal distribution of freedom as non-interference would leave a lot to be desired in regard to redistribution: it would fall short, under most conceptions, of achieving distributive justice (Rawls 1971). I think that wisdom is well placed and I wish to argue that, in this respect, freedom as non-domination represents a sharply contrasted ideal: the maximal equal distribution of such freedom requires a much more substantial commitment to redistribution.

Before coming to that argument, however, it will be useful to see why the connection between freedom as non-interference and distributive justice is so loose. Two questions arise from the viewpoint of freedom as non-interference, when any such issue of redistribution is considered. First, how far will redistribution entail interference in people's lives by the state? And second, how far will redistribution lower the probability of interference by other agents?

The answer to the first question is that redistribution always entails a degree of interference by the state. For even the most basic form of redistribution involves taxing some to give to others, and that in itself constitutes interference; it deprives those who are taxed of a choice in how to use their money. Besides tax, most forms of redistribution also require inspectors and other officials to oversee the operation. Thus the redistributive measures involve the creation of new possibilities of interference in people's lives.

The answer to the first question means that the onus of proof always lies, from the perspective of freedom as non-interference, with those who counsel redistribution. Whether redistribution in any area is to be supported, then, depends on whether the answer to the second question shows clearly that the margin whereby redistribution will reduce interference in a society is greater than the margin whereby it introduces interference itself. The margin of projected improvement will have to be large enough to ensure that even when we discount for the less-than-certain nature of the projection, the argument squarely favours redistribution.

Nevertheless, it is not easy to find grounds to defend the required answer to the second question. It is always possible for the opponent to argue that, so long as we do not think of the relatively advantaged as downright malicious, we must expect them not to be generally disposed to harm the disadvantaged, and not to be generally in need of curtailment by the redistributive state. Perhaps employers are in a position under the status quo to interfere in various

ways with their employees. But why expect them to interfere rather than striving for good and productive relationships? Perhaps husbands are able, given their greater strength and greater cultural backing, to abuse their wives. But why expect them to practise such abuse rather than remaining faithful to their affections and commitments? Perhaps those who lack medical care and legal counsel are prey to the unscrupulous. But why expect doctors and lawyers to be unwilling to provide essential services *pro bono*, especially when they can make good publicity of providing such services?

I sympathize with the drift of these rhetorical questions, believing that it is a mistake to demonize the relatively advantaged and see them always as potential offenders (Pettit 1995). But the effect of the questions in the context of endorsing an ideal of freedom as non-interference is what concerns me now, not the propriety of raising them. The effect is to lead those who take the ideal as the only relevant yardstick of social performance not to require much in the way of redistribution: not to require much in the way of what we intuitively describe as distributive justice. It is quite possible to believe that the regime under which freedom as non-interference is equally distributed at maximal levels is a regime that allows great inequalities in other regards.

Freedom as Non-domination, and Redistribution

We can begin to recognize the significance of the republican ideal of freedom when we notice that its connection with redistribution is different from that of freedom as non-interference. We have seen that the project of equalizing freedom as non-interference at the maximal possible level is hostile to redistribution in two ways. First, it introduces a presumption against redistribution; it casts the onus on the side of anyone who wants to argue for redistribution. And second, it ensures that any argument for redistribution must be probabilistic in a manner that is bound to make it easy to resist. I wish to argue that the ideal of maximizing freedom as non-domination at the maximal level possible differs from the associated ideal of freedom as non-interference in both these respects.

Freedom as non-interference introduces a presumption against redistribution, because redistribution is itself a species of the evil of interference. But no corresponding argument is available with freedom as non-domination. For if the redistributive measures adopted can be pursued under a fair rule of law, and are so pursued, then they do not themselves introduce any form of domination. I assume that many of the redistributive measures contemplated in discussions of distributive justice can be pursued under a fair rule of law. Freedom as non-domination, then, does not introduce any presumption against redistribution of the kind associated with freedom as non-interference. If redistributive measures are used in the promotion of non-domination, the good at which they are directed does not have to be balanced against a violation of that very good in the process of production; the process of production need not itself represent a form of domination.

The process is not entirely innocent, of course. As we mentioned, any rule of law, and certainly any redistributive rule of law, is going to remove certain choices or raise the costs of pursuing them. But this way of restricting choice, this way of conditioning people's freedom as non-domination, falls far short of compromising such freedom on their part. If it succeeds in reducing the extent to which the poor or the sick or the needy have their freedom compromised, then this cost in the conditioning of the freedom of people generally is well worth paying.

Here is another way of thinking about the point. Redistribution under a fair rule of law counts in the republican ledger-book as a form of conditioning of liberty on a par with the conditioning effected by factors like poverty or disability or illness or whatever. Redistribution

involves moving around the factors that serve as conditioning influences on freedom: and this, without itself dominating anyone; without itself compromising anyone's freedom as non-domination. If that reshuffling of freedom-relevant factors can itself increase the degree of equal freedom in the society, then there is little or no question to raise about it. There is no reason to have a presumption against it.

This argument, I hasten to emphasize, is advanced under the assumption that the redistribution effected is achieved under a fair rule of law. And that assumption remains plausible only up to a certain level, and only under a certain kind, of redistribution by a state. Suppose that the redistribution allowed involves the exercise of unconstrained discretion by individual agents of the state; the discretion may arise in the way goods are taken from some, for example, or in the way goods are given to others. Or suppose that the redistribution is so extensive, or subject to such frequent adjustments, that people hardly know where they stand relative to the state. Under any such suppositions, the prospect of redistribution looks very unattractive from a republican point of view.

The republican tradition of thinking has always put the state under severe scrutiny, for fear that state authorities will ever become, or ever support, relatively arbitrary powers. In arguing that the ideal of freedom as non-domination is not hostile to redistribution, in particular not hostile in the manner of freedom as non-interference, I do not mean to reject that tradition. I think that, if we treasure freedom as non-domination, then we have to be vigilant about not allowing the state certain sorts of power; we have to be careful to see that it is subject to all sorts of constitutional and other constraints. My point has been only that, provided a state can be sufficiently constrained – and that may be a very big proviso – there is nothing inherently objectionable about allowing it to use redistributive means for promoting antipower.[6]

The second point that we noticed about the redistributive significance of equalizing non-interference was that the question of whether any redistributive measure increased people's freedom as non-interference remained inevitably a probabilistic matter. Perhaps we can interfere with employers to ensure that they do not interfere in certain ways with their employees. Perhaps we can interfere with husbands to ensure that they do not interfere in certain ways with their wives. But before we think of practising interference, we have to convince ourselves that some shaky arithmetic comes out right. We have to convince ourselves that there is a suitably high probability of a suitably large reduction in the practice of interference by employers and husbands. That thought may well give pause to any projects of redistribution that the ideal of freedom as non-interference is otherwise likely to sponsor.

Like the matter of the presumption against redistribution, however, the ideal of freedom as antipower, freedom as non-domination, has quite a different impact here. Suppose that an employer has the capacity in some measure to interfere arbitrarily in the affairs of an employee. Employment is so scarce and the prospect of unemployment so repellent, that the employer can alter agreed conditions of work, make life much tougher for employees, or even practise some illegal interference in their affairs, with relative ease. And suppose now that we contemplate introducing a system of unemployment benefits, or a set of health and safety regulations, or an arrangement for arbitrating workplace disputes, that would improve the lot of employees. Do we have to do a range of probabilistic sums before we can be sure of the benefits of such a redistributive regime?

Assuming that the regime is consistent with a fair rule of law, and does not itself introduce an independent source of domination – provided it does not have any dominational side-effects – it should be clear that no such sums are necessary. Just the existence of reasonable unemployment benefits is bound to reduce the extent to which an employee is willing to tolerate arbitrary interference by an employer, and by the same token reduces the capacity of the employer to interfere at will and with impunity in the lives of employees. There is no uncertainly plaguing the connection. Or at least there is no uncertainty of the kind that makes the connection with freedom as non-interference so problematic.

Similar points go through on a number of fronts. The fact that people are poor or illiterate or ignorant or unable to get legal counsel or uninsured against illness or incapable of getting around – the fact that they lack basic capabilities in any of these regards (Sen 1985) – makes them subject to a certain sort of exploitation and manipulation. Other things being equal, then, any improvement in their lot is bound to reduce the capacity of others to interfere more or less arbitrarily in their lives. And that means that, other things being equal – dominational side-effects being absent – any such improvement is bound to increase their freedom as non-domination.

The crucial difference in this second respect between the ideals of freedom as non-interference and freedom as non-domination comes of the fact that the first ideal is compromised only by actual interference, the second by the capacity for interference, in particular the capacity for arbitrary interference. It may be unclear whether a given measure will actually reduce the overall level of interference practised by the more advantaged, while it is absolutely certain that the measure will reduce their capacity for interference.

Suppose that the employer in our earlier example is actually benign, or actually committed to a smooth and productive workplace, and thus is unlikely ever to interfere in the affairs of employees. The introduction of employment benefits, or health and safety regulations, or arbitration procedures, will not significantly reduce the probability of interference in such a scenario; that probability is already negligible.

But still, the introduction of any such scheme will certainly reduce the employer's capacity for arbitrary interference. For whether the employer interferes or not will no longer be dependent on their good grace; it will be substantially determined by factors outside the employer's will.

Some will retort at this point that there is no reason why we should want to reduce the capacity of an employer to interfere with employees, especially given the cost of doing so, when it is certain that no interference will actually occur. But that is to shift the issue from the matter of what the ideal of freedom as non-domination would require – and, in particular, from the observation that it would require, other things being equal, that the employer is constrained – to the issue of whether it is an attractive ideal. My aim here is not to argue that it is an attractive ideal (on this issue see Pettit 1997), only that it is a redistributively demanding one.

We saw earlier that freedom as non-interference may be maximized, and maximized under the constraint of more or less equal distribution, without any significant redistribution of resources being required. What we have now seen is that, in this respect, as in so many others, freedom as non-domination is quite different. The republican ideal, just in itself, may be capable of encoding the redistributive measures that many of us would think it reasonable to require of the modern state. While remaining an ideal of liberty, it may give adequate expression to the more demanding aspirations that the non-libertarians amongst us find compelling.

Notes

I am most grateful to Geoffrey Brennan and Michael Smith for helpful discussions of the material. I was enormously helped by comments received when the paper was presented to a meeting in New Orleans organised by the Murphy Institute of Political Economy, Tulane University, and the International Society for Economics and Philosophy.

1 For example, Michelman 1986, Elkin 1987, Pagden 1987, Taylor 1989, Oldfield 1990, Fontana 1994, Hutton 1995, Blom 1995, Spitz 1995, Viroli 1995.

2 Notice that an act of interference can he arbitrary in the procedural sense intended here – it may occur on an arbitrary basis – without being arbitrary in the substantial sense of actually going against the interests or judgments of the persons affected. An act is arbitrary, in this usage, by virtue of the controls – specifically, the lack of controls – under which it materializes, not by virtue of the particular consequences to which it gives rise. The usage I follow means that there is no equivocation involved in speaking, as I do, either of a power of arbitrary interference or of an arbitrary power of interference. What is in question in each case is a power of interfering on an arbitrary, unchecked basis.

3 When proponents of this ideal speak of making freedom as non-interference effective, not just leaving it as a formal freedom, I assume that they often have in mind removing or reducing the obstacles that condition the exercise of freedom as non-domination: extending the range of choice available to people. See Van Parijs 1995.

4 The extreme case of legal interference is punishment for an offence. Such punishment will always condition people's freedom as non-domination: removing the capacity for undominated choice (capital punishment); restricting the range over which such choice may be exercised (prison); or raising the costs of making certain undominated choices (fines). But it need not result in the person punished having their liberty compromised through subjection to the arbitrary will of another. This remark is not meant to make legal punishment seem any more tolerable, only to articulate a perhaps surprising corollary of the conception of freedom as non-domination.

5 Liberalism can be identified as the movement that took freedom as the primary ideal and that construed it as non-interference. In this case, then short of taking on a secondary ideal – something like the second principle of justice proposed by Rawls (1971) – or of insisting on making freedom more and more effective – see Van Parijs (1993) – it will tend to support a minimal state. Left-leaning

liberals, of course, generally want to follow the sorts of lines represented by Rawls and Van Parijs. For more, see Pettit (1997, Introduction).

6 Libertarians often say that they are against big government. Republicans are also against big government, but in a different sense. They object, not necessarily to government's having redistributive rights and responsibilities, but rather to the government's having power to act arbitrarily in the pursuit of redistributive ends; the pursuit must always be governed by a fair rule of law.

References

Ayres, Ian, and Braithwaite, John. 1992. *Responsive Regulation*. New York: Oxford University Press.

Bentham, Jeremy. 1843. "Anarchical Fallacies," in *The Works of Jeremy Bentham*, ed. J. Bowring. vol. 2. Edinburgh.

Berlin, Isaiah. 1958. *Four Essays on Liberty*. Oxford: Oxford University Press.

Blackstone, William. 1978 [1783]. *Commentaries on the Laws of England*, 9th edn. New York: Garland (facsimile).

Blom, Hans W. 1995. *Causality and Morality in Politics: The Rise of Naturalism in Dutch Seventeenth-Century Political Thought*. The Hague: CIP-Gegevens Koninklijke Bibliotheek.

Braithwaite, John, and Pettit, Philip. 1990. *Not Just Deserts: A Republican Theory of Criminal Justice*. Oxford: Oxford University Press.

Constant, Benjamin. 1988. *Constant: Political Writings*, ed. B. Fontana. Cambridge: Cambridge University Press.

Dworkin, Ronald. 1978. *Taking Rights Seriously*. London: Duckworth.

Elkin, Stephen L. 1987. *City and Regime in the American Republic*. Chicago: Chicago University Press.

Fontana, Biancamaria, ed. 1994. *The Invention of the Modern Republic*. Cambridge: Cambridge University Press.

Harrington, James. 1992. *The Commonwealth of Oceana, and A System of Politics*, ed. J. G. A. Pocock. Cambridge: Cambridge University Press.

Hobbes, Thomas. 1968. *Leviathan*, ed. C. B. MacPherson. Harmondsworth, Mddx: Penguin.

Hutton, Will. 1995. *The State We're In*. London: Jonathan Cape.

Lewis, David. 1969. *Convention*. Cambridge, Mass.: Harvard University Press.

Lind, John. 1776. *Three Letters to Dr Price*. London: T. Payne.

Locke, John. 1965. *Two Treatises of Government*, ed. Peter Laslett. New York: Mentor.

Long, Douglas C. 1977. *Bentham on Liberty*. Toronto: University of Toronto Press.

Madison, James, Hamilton, Alexander, and Jay, John. 1987. *The Federalist Papers*, ed. Isaac Kramnik. Harmondsworth, Mddx: Penguin.

Michelman, Frank. 1986. "The Supreme Court 1985 Term," *Harvard Law Review*, 100.

Mill, J. S. 1969. *Essays on Ethics, Religion and Society (Collected Works*, vol. 10). London: Routledge.

Miller, David. 1990. *Market, State and Community*. Oxford: Oxford University Press.

Montesquieu, Charles de Secondat. 1989. *The Spirit of the Laws*, trans. and ed. A. M. Cohler, B. C. Miller and H. S. Stone. Cambridge: Cambridge University Press.

Oldfield, Adrian. 1990. *Citizenship and Community: Civic Republicanism and the Modern World*. London: Routledge.

Pagden, Anthony, ed. 1987. *The Languages of Political Theory in Early Modern Europe*. Cambridge: Cambridge University Press.

Paine, Tom. 1989. *Political Writings*, ed. Bruce Kuklick. Cambridge: Cambridge University Press.

Paley, William. 1825. *The Principles of Moral and Political Philosophy (Collected Works*, vol. 4). London: C. and J. Rivington.

Patterson, Orlando. 1991. *Freedom in the Making of Western Culture*. New York: Basic Books.

Pettit, Philip. 1995. "Institutional Design and Rational Choice," in R. E. Goodin, ed., *The Theory of Institutional Design*. Cambridge: Cambridge University Press.

Pettit, Philip. 1996. "Freedom as Antipower," *Ethics*, 106.

Pettit, Philip. 1997. *Republicanism: A Theory of Freedom and Government*. Oxford: Oxford University Press.

Pocock, J. G. A. 1975. *The Machiavellian Moment: Florentine Political Theory and the Atlantic Republican Tradition*. Princeton, NJ: Princeton University Press.

Price, Richard. 1991. *Political Writings*, ed. D. O. Thomas. Cambridge: Cambridge University Press.

Priestley, Joseph. 1993. *Political Writings*, ed. P. N. Miller. Cambridge: Cambridge University Press.

Rahe, Paul Anthony. 1992. *Republics, Ancient and Modern: Classical Republicanism and the American Revolution*. Chicago: University of Chicago Press.

Rawls, John. 1971. *A Theory of Justice*. Oxford: Oxford University Press.

Robbins, Caroline. 1959. *The Eighteenth Century Commonwealthman*. Cambridge, Mass.: Harvard University Press.

Sen, Amartya. 1985. *Commodities and Capabilities*. Amsterdam: North-Holland.

Skinner, Quentin. 1978. *The Foundations of Modern Political Thought*, 2 vols. Cambridge: Cambridge University Press.

Skinner, Quentin. 1983. "Machiavelli on the Maintenance of Liberty," *Politics*, 18.

Skinner, Quentin. 1984. "The Idea of Negative Liberty" in R. Rorty, J. B. Schneewind and Q. Skinner, eds, *Philosophy in History*. Cambridge: Cambridge University Press.

Spitz, Jean-Fabien. 1995. *La Liberté Politique*. Paris: Presses Universitaires de France.

Sunstein, Cass R. 1990. *After the Rights Revolution: Reconceiving the Regulatory State*. Cambridge, Mass.: Harvard University Press.

Sunstein, Cass R. 1993a. *The Partial Constitution*. Cambridge, Mass.: Harvard University Press.

Sunstein, Cass R. 1993b. *Democracy and the Problem of Free Speech*. New York: Free Press.

Sydney, Algernon. 1990. *Discourses Concerning Government*, ed. T. G. West. Indianapolis: Liberty Classics.

Sydney, Algernon. 1996. *Court Maxims*, ed. H. W. Blom, E. H. Muller and Ronald Janse. Cambridge: Cambridge University Press.

Taylor, Charles. 1989. "Cross-Purposes: The Liberal-Communitarian Debate," in N. L. Rosenblum, ed., *Liberalism and the Moral Life*. Cambridge, Mass.: Harvard University Press.

Trenchard, John, and Gordon, Thomas. 1971. *Cato's Letters*. 6th (1755) edn. New York: Da Capo.

Van Parijs, Philippe. 1995. *Real Freedom for All*. Oxford: Oxford University Press.

Viroli, Maurizio. 1995. *For Love of Country*. Oxford: Oxford University Press.

2e. EQUALITY

THERE IS A SENSE in which any moral theory whatsoever must presuppose equality as a fundamental value. Morality, after all, is largely about justifying the ways in which we treat one another. And in justifying our actions, the assumption is that we will treat like cases alike. If, for instance, someone were to claim that *his* interests deserved greater consideration than yours in some context, you would naturally want to know *why*. And the answer you would expect him to give would involve him pointing to some feature of his person or situation that justifies that greater consideration, *and that would justify a similarly greater consideration for anyone else* who possessed that same feature. If he cannot or is unwilling to point to such a feature — if he is simply demanding greater consideration for his interests *just because* they are his — then he is arguably not making a *moral* argument at all. He is simply being a bully.

Equality, then, is arguably an inescapable commitment of our moral thinking. And for good reason. After all, as both Hobbes and Locke recognized, there doesn't seem to be any sense in which some persons are naturally superior to all others in the sense that their interests are worthy of greater respect than everyone else's. Particular occasions may call for unequal treatment — as when we pay an employee who does superior work more than another. But in those cases where unequal treatment is warranted, it is because we think that unequal *treatment* is compatible with equal *respect*. Equality is the default position, departures from which stand in need of justification.

Why, then, do our political institutions tolerate so much inequality? To be sure, things are not as bad as they used to be. The feudal system in which some persons were born to the aristocracy and some to the peasantry — social classes that were virtually inescapable and which largely determined the rights and responsibilities of those who lived in them — has largely been eliminated from the face of the planet. And in most developed countries, formal discrimination against women, religious, and ethnic minorities has greatly diminished. But even countries that proclaim fidelity to the ideal of "equality before the law" still tolerate tremendous inequalities in income, wealth, access to education and health care, and other important goods. Given the central role of equality in moral thought, it might seem as though these outcomes are morally objectionable. Are they? And if so, what should be done about it?

Surprisingly, very few contemporary philosophers — even those who are very politically liberal — advocate strict equality in the distribution of resources. The reason is that strict egalitarianism of this sort faces several serious problems.

The first problem is what has come to be known as the "leveling down objection," and is presented in fictional form in the short story by Kurt Vonnegut. Generally we think that the way to correct inequality is to give the person who has less of a good more of it. But, strictly speaking, this is not necessary. One who valued equality above all else could also achieve her goal by taking goods away from the person who has more. Even if nothing is done with the goods — they are simply destroyed — the resulting distribution will be superior in terms of equality. To many, however, the idea that the resulting distribution could be better all-things-considered is absurd. Take a situation where initially A has 100 units of a good and B has 75, and 25 units of A's goods are seized and burned. Who is better off as a result of our doing this? Not A, who has lost 25 units of his good. But not B, either — for B is just as well off (in terms of possession of the good in question) as he was before. How, then, can the overall distribution be better if there is no person *for whom* it is better? The only plausible way in which the situation can be described as an improvement for any person is that B doesn't have to feel upset about A's greater holdings anymore. But do we really want a theory of justice that takes *envy* as a legitimate ground for making social change?

The second problem, developed in a famous essay by Harry Frankfurt, can be seen as drawing on insights gleaned from the first. What the leveling down objection appears to show us is that how much we have *relative* to other people is sometimes secondary in importance — or perhaps not important at all — compared to how much we have in absolute terms. A society in which A has 100 units of a good and B has 85 is a society of greater inequality than one in which A has 10 and B has 9. But it is also a world in which both A and B are much, much better off. Should we nevertheless conclude that the society with greater inequality is a *worse* society? It depends. In the real world, our concern about inequality often gets mixed up with our concern about other things. Part of the reason that global inequality is troubling (see section 3c, below), for example, is that many people in the world stand in desperate need of help while others live lives of luxury. But is what is troubling about this situation the fact that some people have *more* than others? Or is it that some people don't have *enough* to live decent lives, and that others who could help are failing to do so? The fact that inequality of material resources among a nation composed exclusively of multi-billionaires would not be troubling suggests that often our real moral concern is to see that people have *sufficient* resources, not that they have *equal* resources.

The third problem is developed in this section by Richard Arneson, and has to do with our belief that at least sometimes, people are *responsible* for having more or less than others because of the choices they make. In such cases, we tend to think, it is not plausible to claim that the individuals who do poorly have a *right* to be brought back up to an equal level with everyone else. A prudent person who works hard and saves *deserves* to wind up with more money, we think, than a profligate person who lives fast and works little. But still, even if some inequalities are the result of voluntary choice, clearly not all are. I did nothing to deserve being born into a middle-class family in one of the wealthiest nations on earth, people born with severe mental retardation did nothing to deserve their condition, etc. For Arneson, then, egalitarianism demands not equality of outcome but equality of opportunity — rectifying those inequalities that are a result of brute luck, but allowing those which are the result of voluntary choice.

Ultimately, then, we may wish to conclude with David Schmidtz that the kind of egalitarianism required by morality is equal *respect*, not necessarily equal *shares* of resources. Schmidtz argues that the circumstances in which respecting others as equals require distributing things equally are severely limited. If resources fell to the earth like manna from heaven, with no one having a greater claim upon them than anyone else, then equal distribution would be a natural solution. But in the real world, most goods are already "attached" in some way to some person or group of persons. And to view goods over which others already claim ownership as up for (re-)distribution in the same way that manna from heaven would be is not to treat those owners with respect, nor would be likely to create a society where people are secure in their plans and welcoming of newcomers.

Even if we agree that equal respect does not always require equal distribution, however, this still leaves less than fully clear what equal respect *does* require. One especially significant example of this difficulty arises in the context of gender equality. What does it mean for a society to treat men and women as equals? As Catharine MacKinnon notes in her contribution to this section, law in the United States has defined equality in terms of equivalence — "equal pay for equal work," and the like — and this has meant that women could only expect equal treatment if they could show that they were the *same* as men. But why should men be the benchmark by which women are measured? For MacKinnon, respecting women as equals is not a matter of treating them *the same* as men, it is a matter of freeing them from domination. And because women are different than men, this might require treating women in ways that are different from the ways we treat men. Policies that recognize and accommodate the fact that women, and not men, can become pregnant and unable to perform certain types of work are not "special protection" at all, but a basic requirement of respecting women as equals.

Equality, like liberty, is a value to which almost everyone claims to adhere. And perhaps everyone does. But, like liberty, it is probably better understood not as a single value but as a cluster of loosely related values. And much of our practical disagreement results not because some people value equality and some people don't, but because different people value different *kinds* of equality. This section explores and illuminates some of those differences, without purporting to settle them.

Further Reading

Anderson, E. (1999). What is the Point of Equality? *Ethics, 109,* 287–337.

Arneson, R. (1997). Egalitarianism and the Undeserving Poor. *Journal of Political Philosophy, 5,* 327–50.

Cohen, G. A. (1993). Equality of what? On Welfare, goods, and capabilities. In M. Nussbaum, and Sen, Amartya (Ed.), *The Quality of Life.* Oxford: Oxford University Press.

Cohen, G. A. (1995). *Self-ownership, Freedom, and Equality.* Cambridge; New York: Cambridge University Press.

Daniels, N. (1990). Equality of What: Welfare, Resources or Capabilities? *Philosophy and Phenomenological Research, 50,* 273–306.

Dworkin, R. (1981a). What Is Equality?: Part I, Equality of Welfare. *Philosophy and Public Affairs, 10,* 185–246.

Dworkin, R. (1981b). What Is Equality?: Part 2, Equality of Resources. *Philosophy and Public Affairs, 10,* 283–345.

Frankfurt, H. (1987). Equality as a Moral Ideal. *Ethics,* 21–43.

Nagel, T. (1991). *Equality and Partiality.* Oxford: Oxford University Press.

Parfit, D. (1997). Equality and Priority. *Ratio, 10,* 202–221.

Pojman, L., and Westmoreland, R. (1996). *Equality: Selected Readings.* Oxford: Oxford University Press.

Scanlon, T. M. (1996). The Diversity of Objections to Inequality. In A. C. Williams, M. (Ed.), *The Ideal of Equality.*

Sen, A. (1987). "Equality of What?" in Liberty, Equality, and Law, McMurrin, Sterling M (Ed.), 137–162. Salt Lake City: University of Utah Press.

Temkin, L. (1993). *Inequality.* Oxford: Oxford University Press.

Chapter 37

Kurt Vonnegut

HARRISON BERGERON

Kurt Vonnegut (1922–2007) was a prolific novelist and writer of short stories, whose works often blended social satire, science fiction, and dark humor. This story, taken from his *Welcome to the Monkey House* (1968) tells the story of a future society in which a certain kind of equality has been realized — and is ruthlessly enforced by the state.

The year was 2081, and everybody was finally equal. They weren't only equal before God and the law. They were equal every which way. Nobody was smarter than anybody else. Nobody was better looking than anybody else. Nobody was stronger or quicker than anybody else. All this equality was due to the 211th, 212th, and 213th Amendments to the Constitution, and to the unceasing vigilance of agents of the United States Handicapper General.

Some things about living still weren't quite right, though. April for instance, still drove people crazy by not being springtime. And it was in that clammy month that the H-G men took George and Hazel Bergeron's fourteen-year-old son, Harrison, away.

It was tragic, all right, but George and Hazel couldn't think about it very hard. Hazel had a perfectly average intelligence, which meant she couldn't think about anything except in short bursts. And George, while his intelligence was way above normal, had a little mental handicap radio in his ear. He was required by law to wear it at all times. It was tuned to a government transmitter. Every twenty seconds or so, the transmitter would send out some sharp noise to keep people like George from taking unfair advantage of their brains.

George and Hazel were watching television. There were tears on Hazel's cheeks, but she'd forgotten for the moment what they were about.

On the television screen were ballerinas.

A buzzer sounded in George's head. His thoughts fled in panic, like bandits from a burglar alarm.

"That was a real pretty dance, that dance they just did," said Hazel.

"Huh," said George.

"That dance — it was nice," said Hazel.

"Yup," said George. He tried to think a little about the ballerinas. They weren't really very good — no better than anybody else would have been, anyway. They were burdened with sash-weights and bags of birdshot, and their faces were masked, so that no one, seeing a free and graceful gesture or a pretty face, would feel like something the cat drug in. George was toying with the vague notion that maybe dancers shouldn't be handicapped. But he didn't get very far with it before another noise in his ear radio scattered his thoughts.

George winced. So did two out of the eight ballerinas.

Hazel saw him wince. Having no mental handicap herself, she had to ask George what the latest sound had been.

"Sounded like somebody hitting a milk bottle with a ball peen hammer," said George.

"I'd think it would be real interesting, hearing all the different sounds," said Hazel a little envious. "All the things they think up."

"Um," said George.

"Only, if I was Handicapper General, you know what I would do?" said Hazel. Hazel, as a matter of fact, bore a strong resemblance to the Handicapper General, a woman named Diana Moon Glampers. "If I was Diana Moon Glampers," said Hazel, "I'd have chimes on Sunday – just chimes. Kind of in honor of religion."

"I could think, if it was just chimes," said George.

"Well – maybe make 'em real loud," said Hazel. "I think I'd make a good Handicapper General."

"Good as anybody else," said George.

"Who knows better then I do what normal is?" said Hazel.

"Right," said George. He began to think glimmeringly about his abnormal son who was now in jail, about Harrison, but a twenty-one-gun salute in his head stopped that.

"Boy!" said Hazel, "that was a doozy, wasn't it?"

It was such a doozy that George was white and trembling, and tears stood on the rims of his red eyes. Two of the eight ballerinas had collapsed to the studio floor, were holding their temples.

"All of a sudden you look so tired," said Hazel. "Why don't you stretch out on the sofa, so's you can rest your handicap bag on the pillows, honeybunch." She was referring to the forty-seven pounds of birdshot in a canvas bag,

which was padlocked around George's neck. "Go on and rest the bag for a little while," she said. "I don't care if you're not equal to me for a while."

George weighed the bag with his hands. "I don't mind it," he said. "I don't notice it any more. It's just a part of me."

"You been so tired lately – kind of wore out," said Hazel. "If there was just some way we could make a little hole in the bottom of the bag, and just take out a few of them lead balls. Just a few."

"Two years in prison and two thousand dollars fine for every ball I took out," said George. "I don't call that a bargain."

"If you could just take a few out when you came home from work," said Hazel. "I mean – you don't compete with anybody around here. You just set around."

"If I tried to get away with it," said George, "then other people'd get away with it – and pretty soon we'd be right back to the dark ages again, with everybody competing against everybody else. You wouldn't like that, would you?"

"I'd hate it," said Hazel.

"There you are," said George. "The minute people start cheating on laws, what do you think happens to society?"

If Hazel hadn't been able to come up with an answer to this question, George couldn't have supplied one. A siren was going off in his head.

"Reckon it'd fall all apart," said Hazel.

"What would?" said George blankly.

"Society," said Hazel uncertainly. "Wasn't that what you just said?"

"Who knows?" said George.

The television program was suddenly interrupted for a news bulletin. It wasn't clear at first as to what the bulletin was about, since the announcer, like all announcers, had a serious speech impediment. For about half a minute, and in a state of high excitement, the announcer tried to say, "Ladies and Gentlemen."

He finally gave up, handed the bulletin to a ballerina to read.

"That's all right —" Hazel said of the announcer, "he tried. That's the big thing. He tried to do the best he could with what God gave him. He should get a nice raise for trying so hard."

"Ladies and Gentlemen," said the ballerina, reading the bulletin. She must have been extraordinarily beautiful, because the mask she wore was hideous. And it was easy to see that she was the strongest and most graceful of all the dancers, for her handicap bags were as big as those worn by two-hundred pound men.

And she had to apologize at once for her voice, which was a very unfair voice for a woman to use. Her voice was a warm, luminous, timeless melody. "Excuse me —" she said, and she began again, making her voice absolutely uncompetitive.

"Harrison Bergeron, age fourteen," she said in a grackle squawk, "has just escaped from jail, where he was held on suspicion of plotting to overthrow the government. He is a genius and an athlete, is under-handicapped, and should be regarded as extremely dangerous."

A police photograph of Harrison Bergeron was flashed on the screen — upside down, then sideways, upside down again, then right side up. The picture showed the full length of Harrison against a background calibrated in feet and inches. He was exactly seven feet tall.

The rest of Harrison's appearance was Halloween and hardware. Nobody had ever born heavier handicaps. He had outgrown hindrances faster than the H-G men could think them up. Instead of a little ear radio for a mental handicap, he wore a tremendous pair of earphones, and spectacles with thick wavy lenses. The spectacles were intended to make him not only half blind, but to give him whanging headaches besides.

Scrap metal was hung all over him. Ordinarily, there was a certain symmetry, a military neatness to the handicaps issued to strong people, but Harrison looked like a walking junkyard. In the race of life, Harrison carried three hundred pounds.

And to offset his good looks, the H-G men required that he wear at all times a red rubber ball for a nose, keep his eyebrows shaved off, and cover his even white teeth with black caps at snaggle-tooth random.

"If you see this boy," said the ballerina, "do not — I repeat, do not — try to reason with him."

There was the shriek of a door being torn from its hinges.

Screams and barking cries of consternation came from the television set. The photograph of Harrison Bergeron on the screen jumped again and again, as though dancing to the tune of an earthquake.

George Bergeron correctly identified the earthquake, and well he might have — for many was the time his own home had danced to the same crashing tune. "My God —" said George, "that must be Harrison!"

The realization was blasted from his mind instantly by the sound of an automobile collision in his head.

When George could open his eyes again, the photograph of Harrison was gone. A living, breathing Harrison filled the screen.

Clanking, clownish, and huge, Harrison stood — in the center of the studio. The knob of the uprooted studio door was still in his hand. Ballerinas, technicians, musicians, and announcers cowered on their knees before him, expecting to die.

"I am the Emperor!" cried Harrison. "Do you hear? I am the Emperor! Everybody must do what I say at once!" He stamped his foot and the studio shook.

"Even as I stand here," he bellowed, "crippled, hobbled, sickened — I am a greater ruler than any man who ever lived! Now watch me become what I can become!"

Harrison tore the straps of his handicap harness like wet tissue paper, tore straps guaranteed to support five thousand pounds.

Harrison's scrap-iron handicaps crashed to the floor.

Harrison thrust his thumbs under the bar of the padlock that secured his head harness. The bar snapped like celery. Harrison smashed his headphones and spectacles against the wall.

He flung away his rubber-ball nose, revealed a man that would have awed Thor, the god of thunder.

"I shall now select my Empress!" he said, looking down on the cowering people. "Let the first woman who dares rise to her feet claim her mate and her throne!"

A moment passed, and then a ballerina arose, swaying like a willow.

Harrison plucked the mental handicap from her ear, snapped off her physical handicaps with marvelous delicacy. Last of all he removed her mask.

She was blindingly beautiful.

"Now —" said Harrison, taking her hand, "shall we show the people the meaning of the word dance? Music!" he commanded.

The musicians scrambled back into their chairs, and Harrison stripped them of their handicaps, too. "Play your best," he told them, "and I'll make you barons and dukes and earls."

The music began. It was normal at first — cheap, silly, false. But Harrison snatched two musicians from their chairs, waved them like batons as he sang the music as he wanted it played. He slammed them back into their chairs.

The music began again and was much improved.

Harrison and his Empress merely listened to the music for a while — listened gravely, as though synchronizing their heartbeats with it.

They shifted their weights to their toes.

Harrison placed his big hands on the girl's tiny waist, letting her sense the weightlessness that would soon be hers.

And then, in an explosion of joy and grace, into the air they sprang!

Not only were the laws of the land abandoned, but the law of gravity and the laws of motion as well.

They reeled, whirled, swiveled, flounced, capered, gamboled, and spun.

They leaped like deer on the moon.

The studio ceiling was thirty feet high, but each leap brought the dancers nearer to it.

It became their obvious intention to kiss the ceiling. They kissed it.

And then, neutralizing gravity with love and pure will, they remained suspended in air inches below the ceiling, and they kissed each other for a long, long time.

It was then that Diana Moon Glampers, the Handicapper General, came into the studio with a double-barreled ten-gauge shotgun. She fired twice, and the Emperor and the Empress were dead before they hit the floor.

Diana Moon Glampers loaded the gun again. She aimed it at the musicians and told them they had ten seconds to get their handicaps back on.

It was then that the Bergerons' television tube burned out.

Hazel turned to comment about the blackout to George. But George had gone out into the kitchen for a can of beer.

George came back in with the beer, paused while a handicap signal shook him up. And then he sat down again. "You been crying," he said to Hazel.

"Yup," she said.

"What about?" he said.

"I forget," she said. "Something real sad on television."

"What was it?" he said.

"It's all kind of mixed up in my mind," said Hazel.

"Forget sad things," said George.

"I always do," said Hazel.

"That's my girl," said George. He winced. There was the sound of a riveting gun in his head.

"Gee — I could tell that one was a doozy," said Hazel.

"You can say that again," said George.

"Gee —" said Hazel, "I could tell that one was a doozy."

Chapter 38

Richard J. Arneson

EQUALITY AND EQUAL OPPORTUNITY FOR WELFARE

Richard J. Arneson (1945–) is a professor of philosophy at the University of California, San Diego, who has written widely in political philosophy and ethics, especially on consequentialism and egalitarianism. This essay (published in 1989) surveys various forms that a morally defensible egalitarianism could take, and winds up advocating a view called "equality of opportunity for welfare" on the grounds that such a view minimizes the extent to which individuals' fates are governed by brute luck, but nevertheless holds them responsible for those outcomes which are the products of their voluntary choices.

Insofar as we care for equality as a distributive ideal, what is it exactly that we prize? Many persons are troubled by the gap between the living standards of rich people and poor people in modem societies or by the gap between the average standard of living in rich societies and that prevalent in poor societies. To some extent at any rate it is the gap itself that is troublesome, not just the low absolute level of the standard of living of the poor. But it is not easy to decide what measure of the "standard of living" it is appropriate to employ to give content to the ideal of distributive equality. Recent discussions by John Rawls[1] and Ronald Dworkin[2] have debated the merits of versions of equality of welfare and equality of resources taken as interpretations of the egalitarian ideal. In this paper I shall argue that the idea of equal opportunity for welfare is the best interpretation of the ideal of distributive equality.

Consider a distributive agency that has at its disposal a stock of goods that individuals want to own and use. We need not assume that each good is useful for every person, just that each good is useful for someone. Each good is homogeneous in quality and can be divided as finely as you choose. The problem to be considered is: How to divide the goods in order to meet an appropriate standard of equality. This discussion assumes that some goods are legitimately available for distribution in this fashion, hence that the entitlements and deserts of individuals do not predetermine the proper ownership of all resources. No argument is provided for this assumption, so in this sense my article is addressed to egalitarians, not their opponents.

I. Equality of Resources

The norm of equality of resources stipulates that to achieve equality the agency ought to give everybody a share of goods that is exactly identical to everyone else's and that exhausts all available resources to be distributed. A straightforward objection to equality of resources so

Smith + Jones situation.

understood is that if Smith and Jones have similar tastes and abilities except that Smith has a severe physical handicap remediable with the help of expensive crutches, then if the two are accorded equal resources, Smith must spend the bulk of his resources on crutches whereas Jones can use his resource share to fulfill his aims to a far greater extent. It seems forced to claim that any notion of equality of condition that is worth caring about prevails between Smith and Jones in this case.

At least two responses to this objection are worth noting. One, pursued by Dworkin,[3] is that in the example the cut between the individual and the resources at his disposal was made at the wrong place. Smith's defective legs and Jones's healthy legs should be considered among their resources, so that only if Smith is assigned a gadget that renders his legs fully serviceable in addition to a resource share that is otherwise identical with Jones's can we say that equality of resources prevails. The example then suggests that an equality of resources ethic should count personal talents among the resources to be distributed. This line of response swiftly encounters difficulties. It is impossible for a distributive agency to supply educational and technological aid that will offset inborn differences of talent so that all persons are blessed with the same talents. Nor is it obvious how much compensation is owed to those who are disadvantaged by low talent. The worth to individuals of their talents varies depending on the nature of their life plans. An heroic resolution of this difficulty is to assign every individual an equal share of ownership of everybody's talents in the distribution of resources.[4] Under this procedure each of the N persons in society begins adult life owning a tradeable 1/N share of everybody's talents. We can regard this share as amounting to ownership of a block of time during which the owner can dictate how the partially owned person is to deploy his talent. Dworkin himself has noticed a flaw in this proposal, which he has aptly named "the slavery of the talented."[5] The flaw is that

under this equal distribution of talent scheme the person with high talent is put at a disadvantage relative to her low-talent fellows. If we assume that each person strongly wants liberty in the sense of ownership over his own time (that is, ownership over his own body for his entire lifetime), the high-talent person finds that his taste for liberty is very expensive, as his time is socially valuable and very much in demand, whereas the low-talent person finds that his taste for liberty is cheap, as his time is less valuable and less in demand. Under this version of equality of resources, if two persons are identical in all respects except that one is more talented than the other, the more talented will find she is far less able to achieve her life plan than her less talented counterpart. Again, once its implications are exhibited, equality of resources appears an unattractive interpretation of the ideal of equality.

A second response asserts that given an equal distribution of resources, persons should be held responsible for forming and perhaps reforming their own preferences, in the light of their resource share and their personal characteristics and likely circumstances.[6] The level of overall preference satisfaction that each person attains is then a matter of individual responsibility, not a social problem. That I have nil singing talent is a given, but that I have developed an aspiration to become a professional opera singer and have formed my life around this ambition is a further development that was to some extent within my control and for which I must bear responsibility.

The difficulty with this response is that even if it is accepted it falls short of defending equality of resources. Surely social and biological factors influence preference formation, so if we can properly be held responsible only for what lies within our control, then we can at most be held to be partially responsible for our preferences. For instance, it would be wildly implausible to claim that a person without the use of his legs should be held responsible for developing a full set of aims and values toward the satisfaction of which leglessness is no hindrance. Acceptance of the claim that we are sometimes to an extent responsible for our preferences leaves the initial objection against equality of resources fully intact. For if we are sometimes responsible we are sometimes not responsible.

The claim that "we are responsible for our preferences" is ambiguous. It could mean that our preferences have developed to their present state due to factors that lay entirely within our control. Alternatively, it could mean that our present preferences, even if they have arisen through processes largely beyond our power to control, are now within our control in the sense that we could now undertake actions, at greater or lesser cost, that would change our preferences in ways that we can foresee. If responsibility for preferences on the first construal held true, this would indeed defeat the presumption that our resource share should be augmented because it satisfies our preferences to a lesser extent than the resource shares of others permit them to satisfy their preferences. However, on the first construal, the claim that we are responsible for our preferences is certainly always false. But on the second, weaker construal, the claim that we are responsible for our preferences is compatible with the claim that an appropriate norm of equal distribution should compensate people for their hard-to-satisfy preferences at least up to the point at which by taking appropriate adaptive measures now, people could reach the same preference satisfaction level as others.

The defense of equality of resources by appeal to the claim that persons are responsible for their preferences admits of yet another interpretation. Without claiming that people have caused their preferences to become what they are or that people could cause their preferences to change, we might hold that people can take responsibility for their fundamental preferences in the sense of identifying with them and regarding these preferences as their own, not as alien intrusions on the self. T. M. Scanlon has suggested the

example of religious preferences in this spirit.[7] That a person was raised in one religious tradition rather than another may predictably affect his lifetime expectation of preference satisfaction. Yet we would regard it as absurd to insist upon compensation in the name of distributive equality for having been raised fundamentalist Protestant rather than atheist or Catholic (a matter that of course does not lie within the individual's power to control). Provided that a fair (equal) distribution of the resources of religious liberty is maintained, the amount of utility that individuals can expect from their religious upbringings is "specifically not an object of public policy."[8]

The example of compensation for religious preferences is complex, and I will return to it in section II below. Here it suffices to note that even if in some cases we do deem it inappropriate to insist on such compensation in the name of equality, it does not follow that equality of resources is an adequate rendering of the egalitarian ideal. Differences among people including sometimes differences in their upbringing may render resource equality nugatory. For example, a person raised in a closed fundamentalist community such as the Amish who then loses his faith and moves to the city may feel at a loss as to how to satisfy ordinary secular preferences, so that equal treatment of this rube and city sophisticates may require extra compensation for the rube beyond resource equality. Had the person's fundamental values not altered, such compensation would not be in order. I am not proposing compensation as a feasible government policy, merely pointing out that the fact that people might in some cases regard it as crass to ask for indemnification of their satisfaction-reducing upbringing does not show that in principle it makes sense for people to assume responsibility (act as though they were responsible) for what does not lie within their control. Any policy that attempted to ameliorate these discrepancies would predictably inflict wounds on innocent parents and guardians far out of proportion to any gain that could be realized for the norm of distributive equality. So even if we all agree that in such cases a policy of compensation is inappropriate, all things considered, it does not follow that so far as distributive equality is concerned (one among the several values we cherish), compensation should not be forthcoming.

Finally, it is far from clear why assuming responsibility for one's preferences and values in the sense of affirming them and identifying them as essential to one's self precludes demanding or accepting compensation for these preferences in the name of distributive equality. Suppose the government has accepted an obligation to subsidize the members of two native tribes who are badly off, low in welfare. The two tribes happen to be identical except that one is strongly committed to traditional religious ceremonies involving a psychedelic made from the peyote cactus while the other tribe is similarly committed to its traditional rituals involving an alcoholic drink made from a different cactus. If the market price of the psychedelic should suddenly rise dramatically while the price of the cactus drink stays cheap, members of the first tribe might well claim that equity requires an increase in their subsidy to compensate for the greatly increased price of the wherewithal for their ceremonies. Advancing such a claim, so far as I can see, is fully compatible with continuing to affirm and identify with one's preferences and in this sense to take personal responsibility for them.

In practice, many laws and other public policies differentiate roughly between preferences that we think are deeply entrenched in people, alterable if at all only at great personal cost, and very widespread in the population, versus preferences that for most of us are alterable at moderate cost should we choose to try to change them and thinly and erratically spread throughout the population. Laws and public policies commonly take account of the former and ignore the latter. For example, the law caters to people's deeply felt aversion to public nudity but does not cater to people's aversion to the sight of tastelessly dressed strollers in public spaces. Of course, current American laws and policies are not designed to achieve any strongly egalitarian ideal, whether resource-based or not. But in appealing to common sense as embodied in current practices in order to determine what sort of equality we care about insofar as we do care about equality, one would go badly astray in claiming support in these practices for the contention that equality of resources captures the ideal of equality. We need to search further.

II. Equality of Welfare

According to equality of welfare, goods are distributed equally among a group of persons to the degree that the distribution brings it about that each person enjoys the same welfare. (The norm thus presupposes the possibility of cardinal interpersonal welfare comparisons.) The considerations mentioned seven paragraphs back already dispose of the idea that the distributive equality worth caring about is equality of welfare. To bring this point home more must be said to clarify what "welfare" means in this context.

I take welfare to be preference satisfaction. The more an individual's preferences are satisfied, as weighted by their importance to that very individual, the higher her welfare.

The preferences that figure in the calculation of a person's welfare are limited to self-interested preferences – what the individual prefers insofar as she seeks her own advantage. One may prefer something for its own sake or as a means to further ends; this discussion is confined to preferences of the former sort. The preferences that most plausibly serve as the measure of the individual's welfare are hypothetical preferences. Consider this familiar account: The extent to which a person's life goes well is the degree to which his ideally considered preferences are satisfied.[9] My ideally considered preferences are those I would have if I were to engage in thoroughgoing deliberation about my preferences with full pertinent information, in a calm mood, while thinking clearly and making no reasoning errors. (We can also call these ideally considered preferences "rational preferences.")

To avoid a difficulty, we should think of the full information that is pertinent to ideally considered preferences as split into two stages corresponding to "first-best" and "second-best" rational preferences. At the first stage one is imagined to be considering full information relevant to choice on the assumption that the results of this ideal deliberation process can costlessly correct one's actual preferences. At the second stage one is imagined to be considering also information regarding (a) one's actual resistance to advice regarding the rationality of one's preferences, (b) the costs of an educational program that would break down this resistance, and (c) the likelihood that anything approaching this educational program will actually be implemented in one's lifetime. What it is reasonable to prefer is then refigured in the light of these costs. For example, suppose that low-life preferences for cheap thrills have a large place in my actual conception of the good, but no place in my first-best rational preferences. But suppose it is certain that these low-life preferences are firmly fixed in my character. Then my second-best preferences are those I would have if I were to deliberate in ideal fashion about my preferences in the light of full knowledge about my actual preferences and their resistance to change. If you are giving me a birthday present, and your sale goal is to advance my welfare as much as possible, you are probably advised to give me, say, a bottle of jug wine rather than a volume of Shelley's poetry even though it is the poetry experience that would satisfy my first-best rational preference.[10]

On this understanding of welfare, equality of welfare is a poor ideal. Individuals can arrive at different welfare levels due to choices they make for which they alone should be held responsible. A simple example would be to imagine two persons of identical tastes and abilities who are assigned equal resources by an agency charged to maintain distributive equality. The two then voluntarily engage in high-stakes gambling, from[11] which one emerges rich (with high expectation of welfare) and the other poor (with low welfare expectation). For another example, consider two persons similarly situated, so they could attain identical welfare levels with the same effort, but one chooses to pursue personal welfare zealously while the other pursues an aspirational preference (e.g., saving the whales), and so attains lesser fulfillment of self-interested preferences. In a third example, one person may voluntarily cultivate an expensive preference (not cognitively superior to the preference it supplants), while another person does not. In all three examples it would be inappropriate to insist upon equality of welfare when welfare inequality arises through the voluntary choice of the person who gets lesser welfare. Notice that in all three examples as described, there need be no grounds for finding fault with any aims or actions of any of the individuals mentioned. No imperative of practical reason commands us to devote our lives to the maximal pursuit of (self-interested) preference satisfaction. Divergence from equality of welfare arising in these ways need not signal any fault imputable to individuals or to "society" understood as responsible for maintaining distributive equality.

This line of thought suggests taking equal opportunity for welfare to be the appropriate norm of distributive equality.

In the light of the foregoing discussion, consider again the example of compensation for one's religious upbringing regarded as affecting one's lifetime preference satisfaction expectation. This example is urged as a reductio ad absurdum of the norm of equality of welfare, which may seem to yield the counterintuitive implication that such differences do constitute legitimate grounds for redistributing people's resource shares, in the name of distributive equality. As I mentioned, the example is tricky; we should not allow it to stampede us toward resource-based construals of distributive equality. Two comments on the example indicate something of its trickiness.

First, if a person changes her values in the light of deliberation that bring her closer to the ideal of deliberative rationality, we should credit the person's conviction that satisfying the new values counts for more than satisfying the old ones, now discarded. The old values should be counted at a discount due to their presumed greater distance from deliberative rationality. So if I was a Buddhist, then become a Hindu, and correctly regard the new religious preference as cognitively superior to the old, it is not the case that a straight equality of welfare standard must register my welfare as declining even if my new religious values are less easily achievable than the ones they supplant.

Secondly, the example might motivate acceptance of equal opportunity for welfare over straight equality of welfare rather than rejection of subjectivist conceptions of equality altogether. If equal opportunity for welfare obtains between Smith and Jones, and Jones subsequently undergoes religious conversion that lowers his welfare prospects, it may be that we will take Jones's conversion either to be a voluntarily chosen act or a prudentially negligent act for which he should be held responsible. (Consider the norm: Other things equal, it is bad if some people are worse off than others through no voluntary choice or fault of their own.) This train of thought also motivates an examination of equal opportunity for welfare.

III. Equal Opportunity for Welfare

An opportunity is a chance of getting a good if one seeks it. For equal opportunity for welfare to obtain among a number of persons, each must face an array of options that is equivalent to every other person's in terms of the prospects for preference satisfaction it offers. The preferences involved in this calculation are ideally considered second-best preferences (where these differ from first-best preferences). Think of two persons

entering their majority and facing various life choices, each action one might choose being associated with its possible outcomes. In the simplest case, imagine that we know the probability of each outcome conditional on the agent's choice of an action that might lead to it. Given that one or another choice is made and one or another outcome realized, the agent would then face another array of choices, then another, and so on. We construct a decision tree that gives an individual's possible complete life histories. We then add up the preference satisfaction expectation for each possible life history. In doing this we take into account the preferences that people have regarding being confronted with the particular range of options given at each decision point. Equal opportunity for welfare obtains among persons when all of them face equivalent decision trees – the expected value of each person's best (= most prudential) choice of options, second-best, . . . nth-best is the same. The opportunities persons encounter are ranked by the prospects for welfare they afford.

The criterion for equal opportunity for welfare stated above is incomplete. People might face an equivalent array of options, as above, yet differ in their awareness of these options, their ability to choose reasonably among them, and the strength of character that enables a person to persist in carrying out a chosen option. Further conditions are needed. We can summarize these conditions by stipulating that a number of persons face effectively equivalent options just in case one of the following is true: (1) the options are equivalent and the persons are on a par in their ability to "negotiate" these options, or (2) the options are nonequivalent in such a way as to counterbalance exactly any inequalities in people's negotiating abilities, or (3) the options are equivalent and any inequalities in people's negotiating abilities are due to causes for which it is proper to hold the individuals themselves personally responsible. Equal opportunity for welfare obtains when all persons face effectively equivalent arrays of options.

Whether or not two persons enjoy equal opportunity for welfare at a time depends only on whether they face effectively equivalent arrays of options at that time. Suppose that Smith and Jones share equal opportunity for welfare on Monday, but on Tuesday Smith voluntarily chooses or negligently behaves so that from then on Jones has greater welfare opportunities. We may say that in an extended sense people share equal opportunity for welfare just in case there is some time at which their opportunities are equal and if any inequalities in their opportunities at later times are due to their voluntary choice or differentially negligent behavior for which they are rightly deemed personally responsible.

When persons enjoy equal opportunity for welfare in the extended sense, any actual inequality of welfare in the positions they reach is due to factors that lie within each individual's control. Thus, any such inequality will be non-problematic from the standpoint of distributive equality. The norm of equal opportunity for welfare is distinct from equality of welfare only if some version of soft determinism or indeterminism is correct. If hard determinism is true, the two interpretations of equality come to the same.

In actual political life under modern conditions, distributive agencies will be staggeringly ignorant of the facts that would have to be known in order to pinpoint what level of opportunity for welfare different persons have had. To some extent it is technically unfeasible or even physically impossible to collect the needed information, and to some extent we do not trust governments with the authority to collect the needed information, due to worries that such authority will be subject to abuse. Nonetheless, I suppose that the idea is clear in principle, and that in practice it is often feasible to make reliable rough-and-ready judgments to the effect that some people face very grim prospects for welfare compared to what others enjoy.

In comparing the merits of a Rawlsian conception of distributive equality as equal shares of primary goods and a Dworkinian conception of equality of resources with the norm of equality of opportunity for welfare, we run into the problem that in the real world, with imperfect information available to citizens and policymakers, and imperfect willingness on the part of citizens and officials to carry out conscientiously whatever norm is chosen, the practical implications of these conflicting principles may be hard to discern, and may not diverge much in practice. Familiar information-gathering and information-using problems will make us unwilling to authorize government agencies to determine people's distributive shares on the basis of their preference satisfaction prospects, which will often be unknowable for all practical purposes. We may insist that governments have regard to primary good share equality or resource equality as rough proxies for the welfarist equality that we are unable to calculate. To test our allegiance to the rival doctrines of equality we may need to consider real or hypothetical examples of situations in which we do have good information regarding welfare prospects and opportunities for welfare, and consider whether this information affects our judgments as to what counts as egalitarian policy. We also need to consider cases in which we gain new evidence that a particular resource-based standard is a much more inaccurate proxy for welfare equality than we might have thought, and much less accurate than another standard now available. Indifference to these considerations would mark allegiance to a resourcist interpretation of distributive equality in principle, not merely as a handy rough-and-ready approximation.

IV. Straight Equality Versus Equal Opportunity; Welfare Versus Resources

The discussion to this point has explored two independent distinctions: (1) straight equality versus equal opportunity and (2) welfare versus resources as the appropriate basis for measuring

[handwritten at top: Slavery of the talented = excessive redistribution]

distributive shares. Hence there are four positions to consider. On the issue of whether an egalitarian should regard welfare or resources as the appropriate standard of distributive equality, it is important to compare like with like, rather than, for instance, just to compare equal opportunity for resources with straight equality of welfare. (In my opinion Ronald Dworkin's otherwise magisterial treatment of the issue in his two-part discussion of "What Is Equality?" is marred by a failure to bring these four distinct positions clearly into focus.[12])

The argument for equal opportunity rather than straight equality is simply that it is morally fitting to hold individuals responsible for the foreseeable consequences of their voluntary choices, and in particular for that portion of these consequences that involves their own achievement of welfare or gain or loss of resources. If accepted, this argument leaves it entirely open whether we as egalitarians ought to support equal opportunity for welfare or equal opportunity for resources.

For equal opportunity for resources to obtain among a number of persons, the range of lotteries with resources as prizes available to each of them must be effectively the same. The range of lotteries available to two persons is effectively the same whenever it is the case that, for any lottery the first can gain access to, there is an identical lottery that the second person can gain access to by comparable effort. (So if Smith can gain access to a lucrative lottery by walking across the street, and Jones cannot gain a similar lottery except by a long hard trek across a desert, to this extent their opportunities for resources are unequal.) We may say that equal opportunity for resources in an extended sense obtains among a number of persons just in case there is a time at which their opportunities are equal and any later inequalities in the resource opportunities they face are due to voluntary choices or differentially negligent behavior on their part for which they are rightly deemed personally responsible.

[handwritten in left margin: a cross the street > across the divoert]

I would not claim that the interpretation of equal opportunity for resources presented here is the only plausible construal of the concept. However, on any plausible construal, the norm of equal opportunity for resources is vulnerable to the "slavery of the talented" problem that proved troublesome for equality of resources. Supposing that personal talents should be included among the resources to be distributed (for reasons given in section I), we find that moving from a regime of equality of resources to a regime that enforces equal opportunity for resources does not change the fact that a resource-based approach causes the person of high talent to be predictably and (it would seem) unfairly worse off in welfare prospects than her counterpart with lesser talent.[13] If opportunities for resources are equally distributed among more and less talented persons, then each person regardless of her native talent endowment will have comparable access to identical lotteries for resources that include time slices of the labor power of all persons. Each person's expected ownership of talent, should he seek it, will be the same. Other things equal, if all persons strongly desire personal liberty or initial ownership of one's own lifetime labor power, this good will turn out to be a luxury commodity for the talented, and a cheap bargain for the untalented.

A possible objection to the foregoing reasoning is that it relies on a vaguely specified idea of how to measure resource shares that is shown to be dubious by the very fact that it leads back to the slavery of the talented problem. Perhaps by taking personal liberty as a separate resource this result can be avoided. But waiving any other difficulties with this objection, we note that the assumption that any measure of resource equality must be unacceptable if applying it leads to unacceptable results for the distribution of welfare amounts to smuggling in a welfarist standard by the back door.

Notice that the welfare distribution implications of equal opportunity for resources will count as intuitively unacceptable only on the assumption that people cannot be deemed to have chosen voluntarily the preferences that are frustrated or satisfied by the talent pooling that a resourcist interpretation of equal opportunity enforces. Of course it is strictly non voluntary that one is born with a particular body and cannot be separated from it, so if others hold ownership rights in one's labor power one's individual liberty is thereby curtailed. But in principle one's self-interested preferences could be concerned no more with what happens to one's own body than with what happens to the bodies of others. To the extent that you have strong self-interested hankerings that your neighbors try their hand at, say, farming, and less intense desires regarding the occupations you yourself pursue, to that extent the fact that under talent pooling your own labor power is a luxury commodity will not adversely affect your welfare. As an empirical matter, I submit that it is just false to hold that in modern society whether any given individual does or does not care about retaining her own personal liberty is due to that person's voluntarily choosing one or the other preference. The expensive preference of the talented person for personal liberty cannot be assimilated to the class of expensive preferences that people might voluntarily cultivate.[14] On plausible empirical assumptions, equal opportunity for welfare will often find tastes compensable, including the talented person's taste for the personal liberty to command her own labor power. Being born with high talent cannot then be a curse under equal opportunity for welfare (it cannot be a blessing either).

V. Sen's Capabilities Approach

The equal opportunity for welfare construal of equality that I am espousing is similar to a "capabilities" approach recently defended by Amartya Sen.[15] I shall now briefly sketch and endorse Sen's criticisms of Rawls's primary social goods standard and indicate a residual welfarist

disagreement with Sen. Rawls's primary social goods proposal recommends that society should be concerned with the distribution of certain basic social resources, so his position is a variant of a resource-based understanding of how to measure people's standard of living. Sen holds that the distribution of resources should be evaluated in terms of its contribution to individual capabilities to function in various ways deemed to be objectively important or valuable. That is, what counts is not the food one gets, but the contribution it can make to one's nutritional needs, not the educational expenditures lavished, but the contribution they make to one's knowledge and cognitive skills. Sen objects to taking primary social goods measurements to be fundamental on the ground that persons vary enormously from one another in the rates at which they transform primary social goods into capabilities to function in key ways. Surely we care about resource shares because we care what people are enabled to be and do with their resource shares, and insofar as we care about equality it is the latter that should be our concern.

So far, I agree. Moreover, Sen identifies a person's well-being with the doings and beings or "functionings" that he achieves, and distinguishes these functionings from the person's capabilities to function or "well-being freedom."[16] Equality of capability is then a notion within the family of equality of opportunity views, a family that also includes the idea of equal opportunity for welfare that I have been attempting to defend. So I agree with Sen to a large extent.

But given that there are indefinitely many kinds of things that persons can do or become, how are we supposed to sum an individual's various capability scores into an overall index? If we cannot construct such an index, then it would seem that equality of capability cannot qualify as a candidate conception of distributive equality. The indexing problem that is known to plague Rawls's primary goods proposal also afflicts Sen's capabilities approach.[17]

Sen is aware of the indexing problem and untroubled by it. The grand theme of his lectures on "Well-being, Agency and Freedom" is informational value pluralism: We should incorporate in our principles all moral information that is relevant to the choice of actions and policies even if that information complicates the articulation of principles and precludes attainment of a set of principles that completely rank-orders the available alternative actions in any possible set of circumstances. "Incompleteness is not an embarrassment," Sen declares.[18] I agree that principles of decision should not ignore morally pertinent matters but I doubt that the full set of my functioning capabilities does matter for the assessment of my position. Whether or not my capabilities include the capability to trek to the South Pole, eat a meal at the most expensive restaurant in Omsk, scratch my neighbor's dog at the precise moment of its daily maximal itch, matters not one bit to me, because I neither have nor have the slightest reason to anticipate I ever will have any desire to do any of these and myriad other things. Presumably only a small subset of my functioning capabilities matter for moral assessment, but which ones? We may doubt whether there are any objectively decidable grounds by which the value of a person's capabilities can be judged apart from the person's (ideally considered) preferences regarding those capabilities. On what ground do we hold that it is valuable for a person to have a capability that she herself values at naught with full deliberative rationality? If a person's having a capability is deemed valuable on grounds independent of the person's own preferences in the matter, the excess valuation would seem to presuppose the adequacy of an as yet unspecified perfectionist doctrine the like of which has certainly not yet been defended and in my opinion is indefensible.[19] In the absence of such a defense of perfectionism, equal opportunity for welfare looks to be an attractive interpretation of distributive equality.

Postscript (1995)

My 1989 essay contains an unclear presentation of the norm of equal opportunity for welfare and hence might convey the impression to the reader that the idea is inherently confused. It is not. For the sake of clarity it might be of use to restate the idea in several stages.

Roughly, we can say that equal opportunity for welfare obtains among a group of persons at a time just in case the highest level of expected welfare that each person could gain if she were to behave with perfect prudence is the same for all persons. But it would be implausible for the norm of equal opportunity for welfare to require that people have equal opportunity throughout their lives, because people who are initially equally favorably situated can make choices that result in some having diminished opportunities for welfare compared to the opportunities enjoyed by the rest. The intuitive idea that lies behind the equal opportunity norm is that each individual makes choices that affect her life prospects, and it is morally legitimate that each should bear the consequences of her choices, at least when society has provided a fair menu of options from which to choose. So the equal opportunity norm may provisionally be formulated so: equal opportunity for welfare obtains among a group of persons just in case at the onset of adulthood each person can choose among a set of life strategies, and if the person chooses prudently from this set, her expected welfare over the course of her life is the same as everyone else's.

One further refinement is needed to capture the equal opportunity norm. Two people may have equal opportunity as defined above even though their abilities to make use of these opportunities efficiently to advance their welfare are quite different. For example, suppose that in order to choose prudently one must carry out a mathematical calculation. One person can do it easily, a second cannot do it, a third can do it only with great difficulty, or with acute discomfort. In order to carry out the prudent choice, one must resist a certain temptation, and again we may imagine that people differ markedly in their native "choice-following" talents. I will say that *true equal opportunity for welfare* obtains among a number of persons when society compensates and adjusts for individuals' different abilities to negotiate options, so that if from the onset of adulthood each person behaved as prudently as could reasonably be expected in the light of her choice-making and choice-following abilities, she would have the same expected welfare over the course of her life as anyone else.

Society might compensate for differential choice-making and choice-following ability by providing extra resources to those with lesser abilities. Such compensation can take many forms besides provision of money. Guardrails and warning signs in front of obvious cliff edges at national parks provide no benefit to alert and prudently cautious park visitors but may prevent some injuries to the dull-witted, inattentive, and negligent. Compulsory government programs that require savings for old age tend to equalize opportunities for welfare among myopic and far-sightedly prudent citizens. In some cases paternalistic restrictions of liberty such as bans on dangerous recreational drugs serve a similar function. Since there are various dimensions of personal decision-making talent, and given the difficulty of separating a person's native endowment of prudential talent from the part of a person's present disposition to prudence that is due to her own hard-earned efforts at character transformation for which she should be given credit, it may be unclear what constitutes the level of prudent conduct that it is reasonable to expect of someone. In the simplest case, imagine that individuals differ only in their native willpower, so that individuals who make equal good faith efforts to be prudent may via unequal willpower end up behaving with different degrees of prudence. In this case compensation and adjustment produce equal opportunity for welfare when it is the case that if each person

made good faith efforts to be prudent, all would have equal expected welfare.

In 1989 I wrote that when people enjoy equal opportunity for welfare as characterized just above, "any actual inequality of welfare in the positions they reach is due to factors that lie within each individual's control." But this is obviously false. Equality of opportunity for welfare obtains between Smith and Jones if their expected welfare given reasonably prudent conduct is the same. Facing these equal prospects. Smith and Jones may make exactly the demanded reasonably prudent choices, yet one enjoys better luck, and Smith ends up leading a miserable existence, while Jones lives well. Equal prospects prior to choice are compatible with unequal welfare as individuals lead their lives that comes about through sheer brute luck. (A lightning bolt strikes Smith and misses Jones, who is standing next to her.) Hence equal opportunity for welfare can obtain among a group of persons even though it also turns out to be the case that some of these persons are worse off than others through no fault or voluntary choice of their own.

This discussion suggests an alternate ideal of equal opportunity, call it *equal opportunity for welfare in the strict sense*. Strict equal opportunity obtains among a number of people just in case at the onset of adulthood they face option sets such that if each behaves as prudently as could reasonably be expected, all will attain the same level of welfare over the course of their lives. When strict equal opportunity obtains, no one is worse off than others through no fault or voluntary choice of her own.

Which version of the equal opportunity for welfare norm is ethically more appealing? This is a tricky matter. One might object to strict equal opportunity on the ground that it is violated if two individuals have identical initial prospects and identical tastes and abilities, then engage voluntarily in high-stakes gambling, a game of sheer chance, from which one emerges with high welfare prospects and the other with low welfare prospects. Even though strict equal opportunity is violated here, one might argue that in the morally relevant sense, these two individuals did have equal opportunities for welfare, because the eventual differences in their welfare prospects came about only through a process that both mutually agreed to undergo under conditions of full information against a background of equal initial prospects.

On the other hand, equal opportunity as I characterized it in 1989 (what I am calling here *true equal opportunity for welfare*) can be fully satisfied in circumstances in which some people become worse off than others through processes that entirely bypass their own choice. This difficulty is described three paragraphs back. A vivid illustration of the possibility is provided by an example suggested by Brian Barry: Imagine that in a class-stratified capitalist society marked by great inequalities in life prospects social science researchers discover that for many years nurses in hospitals have been conspiring to switch babies randomly just after birth so that at birth each person faces equal lifetime prospects of welfare, which resolve into very unequal prospects as soon as the nurses' lottery is concluded and you are placed either with a poor family or a rich family. After discovering this odd fact, would we then say that we had thought the society was terribly unjust, but now we see that since everyone had initially equal prospects, the society was just in its distributive practices after all? The inegalitarian society adjusted by the nurses' conspiracy seems to me far from just in its distributive practices, but more nearly just than an otherwise similar society minus the nurses' conspiracy. The implication of this story does not carry over in a completely smooth way to a society regulated by the norm of what I am calling "true" equal opportunity for welfare, because of the wrinkle about requiring equal prospects at the onset of adulthood. But it would be easy to invent a similar story about true equal opportunity for welfare that shows it vulnerable to Barry's criticism. As mentioned above, the point is that in a society in which the norm of

true equal opportunity for welfare is perfectly satisfied, it may yet be the case that some people end up worse off than others through no fault or voluntary choices of their own. The ethical imperative of undoing the effects of unchosen luck on the quality of human lives is only incompletely satisfied in a society that fully satisfies true equal opportunity for welfare.

Up to this point I have been engaged in an intramural dispute among rival versions of equal opportunity for welfare. This family of equal opportunity for welfare norms has been subjected to attack, and the question arises to what extent the criticisms discredit the norm. One criticism charges that the ideal of equal opportunity for welfare is utopian. We could not actually design and operate a society that would fulfill it. This criticism inflicts no significant damage. The ideal that everyone in the world should enjoy good health and longevity is also utopian, but this does not gainsay the desirability of the state of affairs posited as ideal. If a goal is worthwhile but unattainable, but we can approach it to greater or lesser extent, then a utopian ideal may dictate the eminently practical imperative that we ought to act so that we come as close to achieving the goal as is feasible.

A more significant worry is that given that some unfortunate persons could not be fully compensated for bad luck in their genetic endowments by any means, a serious attempt to attain equal life prospects for all would involve channeling all available resources to a few extremely unfortunate individuals, leaving these resource basin individuals still very badly off and the rest of the human race scarcely better off. The world being as it is, the average level of human welfare prospects would plummet if we tried to make welfare prospects as close to equal for all as possible. This point indicates that the norm of equal opportunity for welfare is one value among other values and that in practice many of these values conflict, so that more of one value means less of the others, and it is arguable that no single value should be given unqualified priority. At least, no version of the value of distributive equality is a likely candidate for the role of the single fundamental value to which all other values are to be subordinated. Any norm of equality, including equal opportunity for welfare, competes with other values and should sometimes lose the competition. My aim in my 1989 essay was not to gauge how important distributive equality is as it competes with other values, but to provide a plausible interpretation of the norm of distributive equality.

Some objections against equal opportunity for welfare are really objections against subjectivist conceptions of welfare. Consider Tiny Tim, the cripple in Charles Dickens's story *A Christmas Carol*. Being extremely cheerful and prone to appreciate small blessings, Tiny Tim can attain a high level of welfare construed as satisfaction despite his grave handicap and poverty. Yet we may judge he is one of society's unfortunates, entitled to compensation to offset his imposed poverty and physical disability. If equal opportunity for welfare cannot ratify this judgment, so much the worse for this ideal (so runs the objection). In this example there is an implicit appeal to objectivist convictions about human welfare or well-being. We believe that there are some goods that are important constituents of a good human life and that if one lacks too many of these constitutive elements one does not enjoy a good life, whatever one's level of preference satisfaction. With respect to this worry, my 1989 essay could have been more clear by stating that the conception of welfare I employed in formulating the equal opportunity norm is an objectivist conception – one according to which the measure of the welfare level that a person reaches is not fixed by that very individual's actual beliefs, desires, and values. After all, the individual could be dead wrong about these matters. At any rate, the issue of whether an objectivist or a subjectivist conception of welfare is more adequate does not impugn the ideal of equal opportunity for welfare as such. This is merely an issue about how best to interpret the ideal.

A more direct challenge to equal opportunity for welfare challenges the normative plausibility of any conception of distributive equality. Perhaps distributive justice is not concerned with equality at all, beyond the formal equality that requires that whatever the rules in place, they should be applied equally and impartially to all persons within their jurisdiction. Insofar as we are committed to distributive justice, perhaps instead of trying to make everyone's condition the same in any sense we should be trying to make the condition of the worst-off person in society as favorable as it can be made. Or perhaps justice requires arranging social practices so that each person is kept above some minimally acceptable threshold of well-being and beyond this floor, human well-being in the aggregate is maximized. Or, to mention an alternative that strikes me as plausible, perhaps justice requires that practices be set so as to maximize some function of aggregate human well-being that gives extra weight to improving the welfare of those who are badly off and that also gives extra weight to securing improvements for more deserving individuals. To suggest a quite different line, perhaps justice is simply refraining from violating anyone's individual rights understood in a neo-Lockean fashion. None of the ideas of social justice just mentioned includes any distributive equality requirement – that all persons' conditions be kept equally desirable. The issues raised here are delicate, complex, tangled, and fundamental. I would note only that the issue of the moral weight of the value of distributive equality is independent of the issue of how best to interpret the ideal of distributive equality. My 1989 essay explores the latter issue.

Notes

1 John Rawls, "Social Unity and Primary Goods," in Amartya Sen and Bernard Williams, eds., *Utilitarianism and Beyond* (Cambridge: Cambridge University Press, 1982), pp. 159–85.

2 Ronald Dworkin, "What Is Equality? Part 1: Equality of Welfare," *Philosophy and Public Affairs* 10 (1981): 185–246; and "What Is Equality? Part 2: Equality of Resources," *Philosophy and Public Affairs* 10 (1981): 283–345. See also Thomas Scanlon, "Preference and Urgency," *Journal of Philosophy* 72 (1975): 655–69.

3 Dworkin, "Equality of Resources."

4 Hal Varian discusses this mechanism of equal distribution, followed by trade to equilibrium, in "Equity, Envy, and Efficiency," *Journal of Economic Theory* 9 (1974): 63–91. See also John Roemer, "Equality of Talent," *Economics and Philosophy* 1 (1985): 151–86; and "Equality of Resources Implies Equality of Welfare," *Quarterly Journal of Economics* 101 (1986): 751–84.

5 Dworkin, "Equality of Resources," p. 312. It should be noted that the defender of resource-based construals of distributive equality has a reply to the slavery of the talented problem that I do not consider in this paper. According to this reply, what the slavery of the talented problem reveals is not the imperative of distributing so as to equalize welfare but rather the moral inappropriateness of considering all resources as fully alienable. It may be that equality of resources should require that persons be compensated for their below-par talents, but such compensation should not take the form of assigning individuals full private ownership rights in other people's talents, which should be treated as at most partially alienable. See Margaret Jane Radin, "Market-Inalienability," *Harvard Law Review* 100 (1987): 1849–937.

6 Rawls, "Social Unity and Primary Goods," pp. 167–70.

7 Thomas Scanlon, "Equality of Resources and Equality of Welfare: A Forced Marriage?", *Ethics* 97 (1986): 111–18; see esp. pp. 115–7.

8 Scanlon, "Equality of Resources and Equality of Welfare," p. 116.

9 See, e.g., John Rawls, *A Theory of Justice* (Cambridge, MA: Harvard University Press, 1971), pp. 416–24; Richard Brandt, *A Theory of the Good and the Right* (Oxford: Oxford University Press, 1979), pp. 110–29; David Gauthier, *Morals by Agreement* (Oxford: Oxford University Press, 1986), pp. 29–38; and Derek Parfit, *Reasons and Persons*

(Oxford: Oxford University Press, 1984), pp. 493–9.

10 In this paragraph I attempt to solve a difficulty noted by James Griffin in "Modern Utilitarianism," *Revue Internationale de Philosophie* 36 (1982): 331–75; esp. pp. 334–5. See also Amartya Sen and Bernard Williams, "Introduction" to *Utilitarianism and Beyond*, p. 10.

11 Here the most prudent choice cannot be identified with the choice that maximizes lifelong expected preference satisfaction, due to complications arising from the phenomenon of preference change. The prudent choice as I conceive it is tied to one's actual preferences in ways I will not try to describe here.

12 See the articles cited in note 2. Dworkin's account of equality of resources is complex, but without entering into its detail I can observe that Dworkin is discussing a version of what I call "equal opportunity for resources." By itself, the name chosen matters not a bit. But confusion enters because Dworkin neglects altogether the rival doctrine of equal opportunity for welfare. For a criticism of Dworkin's objections against a welfarist conception of equality that do not depend on this confusion, see my "Liberalism, Distributive Subjectivism, and Equal Opportunity for Welfare."

13 Roemer notes that the person with high talent is cursed with an involuntary expensive preference for personal liberty. See Roemer, "Equality of Talent."

14 As Rawls writes, ". . . those with less expensive tastes have presumably adjusted their likes and dislikes over the course of their lives to the income and wealth they could reasonably expect; and it is regarded as unfair that they now should have less in order to spare others from the consequences of their lack of foresight or self-discipline." See "Social Unity and Primary Goods," p. 169.

15 Amartya Sen, "Well-being, Agency and Freedom: The Dewey Lectures 1984," *Journal of Philosophy* 82 (1985): 169–221; esp. pp. 185–203. See also Sen, "Equality of What?", in his *Choice, Welfare and Measurement* (Oxford: Basil Blackwell, 1982), pp. 353–69.

16 Sen, "Well-being, Agency and Freedom," p. 201.

17 See Allan Gibbard, "Disparate Goods and Rawls' Difference Principle: A Social Choice Theoretic

Treatment," *Theory and Decision* 11 (1979): 267–88; see esp. pp. 268–9.

18 Sen, "Well-being, Agency and Freedom," p. 200.

19 However, it should be noted that filling out a preference-satisfaction approach to distributive equality would seem to require a normative account of healthy preference formation that is not itself preference-based. A perfectionist component may thus be needed in a broadly welfarist egalitarianism. For this reason it would be misguided to foreclose too swiftly the question of the possible value of a capability that is valued at naught by the person who has it. The development and exercise of various capacities might be an important aspect of healthy preference formation, and have value in this way even though this value does not register at all in the person's preference satisfaction prospects.

Chapter 39

David Schmidtz

EQUAL RESPECT AND EQUAL SHARES

David Schmidtz (1955–) is a professor of philosophy and economics at the University of Arizona, and the founding director of their Freedom Center. In this essay (published in 2002), Schmidtz examines the nature of a morally attractive egalitarianism, and argues that while equality in terms of equal respect for and equal treatment of all persons is desirable, it does not except in a narrow range of cases entail equal distribution of resources.

I. Introduction

We are all equal, sort of. We are not equal in terms of our physical or mental capacities. Morally speaking, we are not all equally good. Evidently, if we are equal, it is not in virtue of our actual characteristics, but despite them. Our equality is of a political rather than metaphysical nature. We do not expect people to be the same, but we expect differences to have no bearing on how people ought to be treated as citizens. Or when differences do matter, we expect that they will not matter in the sense of being a basis for class distinction. We admire tenacity, talent, and so on, but do not take such features to entitle their bearers to be treated as "upper class." Neither are people who are relatively lacking in these features obliged to tolerate being treated as "lower class." As a society, we have made moral progress. Such progress consists in part of progress toward political and cultural equality.

Have we also made progress toward *economic* equality? If so, does that likewise count as moral progress? Some people have more than others.

Some earn more than others. Do these things matter? In two ways, they could. First, we may care about differences in wealth and income on humanitarian grounds; that is, we may worry about some people having less not because less is less but because less sometimes is not enough. Second, we may care on grounds of justice; that is, we may think people would not have less if some injustice had not been done.[1]

What provokes such concerns? One provocation is conceptual: philosophical thought experiments, and so on. We imagine how the world would be in some idealized hypothetical situation, and then ask whether departures from the ideal are unjust, and if so, how they might be redressed. A second provocation is empirical: statistical reports on income inequality, and so on. Statistics paint a picture of how the world actually is, and how unequal it is. We are left wondering whether such inequality is acceptable, and if not, what to do about it.

This essay examines these two provocations. In response to concerns of a conceptual nature, Section II offers a limited defense of distribution according to a principle of "equal shares," explaining how and why even non-egalitarians can and should respect egalitarian concerns and make room for them even in otherwise non-egalitarian theories of justice. As Section III notes, though, "equal shares" is only one way of expressing egalitarian concern. The connection between equal treatment and justice may be essential, but the connection between equal treatment and equal shares is not. Sections IV and V reflect on why the rule of first possession limits attempts to distribute according to principles (not only egalitarian principles) of justice. Finally, in response to empirical concerns, Section VI examines recent studies of income distribution in the United States.

Undoubtedly, egalitarians will think I have not made *enough* room for egalitarian concern. After all, if an egalitarian is someone who thinks many economic goods should be distributed equally, and redistributed as often as needed so that shares remain equal, then at the end of the day, I am not an egalitarian. I am, however, a kind of pluralist. Justice is about giving people their due; if we are not talking about what people are due, then we are not talking about justice. On the other hand, what people are due is a complex, multifaceted, context-sensitive matter. There is a place for equal shares.

II. On Behalf of Equal Shares

Political theorist Bruce Ackerman's essay "On Getting What We Don't Deserve" is a short, engaging dialogue that captures the essence of egalitarian concern about the justice of differences in wealth and income.[2] Ackerman imagines you and he are in a garden. As Ackerman tells the story, you see two apples on a tree and swallow them in one gulp while an amazed Ackerman looks on. Ackerman then asks you, as one human being to another, shouldn't I have gotten one of those apples?

Should he? If so, why? Why only one? What grounds our admittedly compelling intuition that Ackerman should have gotten one – exactly one – of those apples? Notably, Ackerman explicitly rejects the idea that his claim to an apple is based on need, signaling that his primary concern is not humanitarian. Instead, Ackerman's view is that the point of getting one apple is that one apple would have been an equal share. Equal shares is a moral default. Morally speaking, distribution by equal shares is what we automatically go to if we cannot justify anything else. As Ackerman sees it, to give Ackerman an equal share is to treat him with respect. In Ackerman's garden, at least, to say he does not command an equal share is to say he does not command respect.

Is Ackerman right? Looking at the question dispassionately, there are several things to say on behalf of equal shares as an allocation rule, even if we reject Ackerman's presumption in favor of it. In Ackerman's garden, equal shares has the virtue of not requiring further debate about who gets the bigger share. No one has reason to envy anyone else's share. When we arrive all at once, equal shares is a cooperative, mutually advantageous, mutually respectful departure from the status quo (in which none of us yet has a share of the good to be distributed). In short, equal shares is easy. We call it "splitting the difference," and often it is a pleasant way of solving our distributional problem. In the process, we not only solve the problem, but offer each other a kind of salute. In Ackerman's garden, it is an obvious way to divide things and get on with our lives – with no hard feelings at worst, and at best with a sense of having been honored by honorable people.

These ideas may not be equality's foundation, but they are among equality's virtues. Crucially, even non-egalitarians can appreciate that they are virtues. Thus, while critics may say Ackerman is assuming the egalitarianism for which he is supposed to be arguing, the virtues just mentioned beg no questions. Even from non-egalitarian perspectives, then, there is something to be said for equal shares. Therefore, whatever conception of justice we ultimately entertain, we can agree there is a place in a just society for dividing certain goods into equal shares. In particular, when we arrive at the bargaining table more or less at the same time, for the purpose of dividing goods to which no one has made a prior claim, we are in a situation where equal shares is a way of achieving a just distribution.

It may not be the only way. For example, we could flesh out the thought experiment in such a way as to make bargainers' unequal needs more salient than their equality as citizens. But it is one way.

III. An Egalitarian Critique of Equal Shares

Yet there are times when following the equal-shares principle – paying people the same wage, say – would fail to show others equal respect. Suppose an employer routinely expects more work, or more competent work, from one employee than from another, but sees no reason to pay them differently. In such cases, the problem is not raw wage differentials so much as a lack of proportion in the relations between contribution and compensation. The lack of proportion is one kind of unequal treatment. And unequal treatment, and the lack of respect it signals, is what people resent.

Children often are jealous when comparing their shares to those of their siblings – or, a bit more precisely, when comparing shares doled out by their parents. Why? Because being given a lesser share by their parents signals to them that they are held in lower esteem. They tend to feel differently about having less than their richest neighbor, because so long as no one is deliberately assigning them smaller shares, no one is sending a signal of unequal esteem.[3] Here, too, the problem is departures from equal respect rather than from equal shares. Equal shares is not the same as equal respect, and is not always compatible with it.[4] "Unequal pay for equal work" is offensive, but so is "equal pay for unequal work."

Intuitively, we all believe some people deserve more than others. This belief, though, is ambiguous. If I have better opportunities than you do, and as a result acquire more than you do, do I deserve more? Egalitarians will say no. The ambiguity is this: I do not deserve "more than you do" *under this description* because there never was a fair competition between us to determine which of us deserves more. Therefore, I do not deserve to have a central distributor maintain any particular ratio between your reward and mine. Nevertheless, notice what this leaves open. I may well deserve X while you deserve Y, on the basis of my working hard for X and your working hard for Y as we live our separate lives, with nothing in this story even suggesting that X = Y. Therefore, even if we were right to suppose that a central distributor would have no basis for judging us to be of unequal merit, and thus could be denounced for deliberately assigning unequal shares, we could still be wrong to infer that the shares we respectively deserve are equal.

Accordingly, there is a difference between unequal treatment and unequal shares. Unequal treatment presupposes treatment; unequal shares do not. If we are being *treated* unequally, then there is someone whom we can ask to justify treating us unequally. It would make sense for an egalitarian such as Ackerman to insist on this. Moreover, in Ackerman's garden, your grabbing both apples arguably is a token of unequal treatment. But what if Ackerman arrives several years after you have grabbed both apples and turned the garden into an orchard? Non-simultaneous arrival complicates the case, making it harder to see the grab as a token of treatment at all, unequal or otherwise. Suffice it to say, we can be committed to denouncing unequal treatment without being committed to denouncing every unequal outcome as if it were a result of unequal treatment. Ackerman presumes the moral default (in a very general way) is equal shares. Even if, as seems likely, Ackerman is wrong, this is no reason to give up on the idea that the moral default is equal *treatment*.

A. Equal Worth and Equal Treatment

Suppose we have a certain moral worth that is not affected by our choices. That is, although we may live in a morally heroic way or a morally depraved way, how we live makes no difference as far as this moral worth is concerned: there is nothing we can do to make ourselves more or less worthy. If this were true, then we might all, as it happens, be of equal worth.

Now suppose instead that along certain dimensions our moral worth can be affected by our choices. In certain respects, that is, some of our choices make us more or less worthy. In this case, if in certain respects our choices affect our worth over time, it is unlikely that there will ever be a time when we are all of equal worth in those respects.

None of this is a threat to egalitarianism, because only a caricature of egalitarianism would presume that all of us are equally worthy along all dimensions. Instead, part of the point of the liberal ideal of political equality is to foster conditions under which we will tend to make choices that augment rather than diminish our worth along dimensions where worth depends on choice. Liberal political equality is not premised on the false hope that under ideal conditions, we all turn out to be equally worthy. It presupposes only a classically liberal optimism regarding the kind of society that results from putting people (all people, so far as this is realistically feasible) in a position to choose worthy ways of life.

B. Equality and Oppression

Humanitarianism is concerned with how people fare. Egalitarianism is concerned with how people fare relative to each other. So says philosopher Larry Temkin. Humanitarians, he says:

favor equality *solely* as a means to helping the worse off, and given the choice between redistribution from the better off to the worse off, and identical gains for the worse off with equal, or even greater, gains for the better off, they would see no reason to favor the former over the latter.... But such people are not egalitarians in my sense if their concerns would be satisfied by a system in which the poor had access to quality care, but the rich had even greater access to much better care.[5]

Accordingly, what distinguishes egalitarianism from humanitarianism is that a humanitarian would never compromise the care offered to the poor merely to greatly worsen the care offered to the rich, whereas an egalitarian at least sometimes would.[6] Temkin, himself an egalitarian, says the problem with humanitarianism is that it is not concerned with equality.[7] In Temkin's words, "As a plausible analysis of what the egalitarian really cares about, . . . humanitarianism is a nonstarter."[8]

Philosopher Elizabeth Anderson responds, "Those on the left have no less reason than conservatives and libertarians to be disturbed by recent trends in academic egalitarian thought."[9] Academic egalitarians, she thinks, have lost sight of why equality matters.[10] Thus, she criticizes philosopher Richard Arneson for saying, "The concern of distributive justice is to compensate individuals for misfortune.... Distributive justice stipulates that the lucky should transfer some or all of their gains due to luck to the unlucky."[11] Along with Arneson, Anderson classifies Gerald Cohen and John Roemer as welfare egalitarians.[12] She contrasts this group with those who advocate equalizing resources rather than welfare, such as Ronald Dworkin, Eric Rakowski, and Philippe Van Parijs.[13] Despite differences between these thinkers, what their works collectively show, Anderson says, is that "[r]ecent egalitarian writing has come to be dominated by the view that the fundamental aim of equality is to compensate people for undeserved bad luck."[14] Anderson, though, thinks that "[t]he proper negative aim of egalitarian justice is not to eliminate the impact of brute luck from human affairs, but to end oppression."[15] Egalitarianism's proper aim, she claims, is to enable us "to live together in a democratic community, as opposed to a hierarchical one."[16]

Anderson says that:

> democratic equality's principles of distribution neither presume to tell people how to use their opportunities nor attempt to judge how responsible people are for choices that lead to unfortunate outcomes. Instead, it avoids bankruptcy at the hands of the imprudent by limiting the range of goods provided collectively and expecting individuals to take personal responsibility for the other goods in their possession.[17]

In contrast, Anderson argues, academic egalitarianism gains some undeserved credibility because we assume anything calling itself egalitarian must also be humanitarian. But although she is an egalitarian herself, Anderson says we cannot assume this connection.[18] Moreover, the academic egalitarian's reasons for granting aid are disrespectful. When redistribution's purpose is to make up for someone's being less capable than others (due to bad luck in the natural lottery), the result in practice is that "[p]eople lay claim to the resources of egalitarian redistribution in virtue of their inferiority to others, not in virtue of their equality to others."[19] Political equality has no such consequence. In the nineteenth century, when women began to present themselves as having a right to vote, they were presenting themselves not as needy inferiors but as autonomous equals – not as having a right to equal shares but as having a right to equal treatment.

We can draw two conclusions from all this. First, egalitarianism cannot afford to define itself by contrast with humanitarianism. No

conception of justice can afford that. Second, egalitarians and non-egalitarians can agree that a kind of political equality is called for even when equal shares as a distributive principle is not. Thus, to the conclusion that a pluralistic theory of justice can make some room for equal shares, we can add that a pluralistic theory can make room for a second kind of equality as well, a specifically political kind.

C. Equality and Meritocracy

Very roughly, a regime is meritocratic to the extent that people are judged on the merits of their performance. A pure meritocracy is hard to imagine, but any regime is bound to have meritocratic elements. A corporation is meritocratic insofar as it ties promotions to performance, and departs from meritocracy insofar as it ties promotions to seniority. A society is meritocratic insofar as, within it, people are paid what their work is worth. In short, in meritocracies, rewards track performance. The important point is that rewards actually track performance; it is neither necessary nor sufficient that anyone *intends* for them to do so. A corporation's culture of meritocracy is often partially a product of deliberate design, but a corporation (or especially, a whole society) can be meritocratic in some ways without anyone deciding it ought to be.

The idea of meritocracy is vague, to be sure, yet precise enough for academic egalitarians to see conflict between equality and meritocracy. Thus, philosopher Norman Daniels says that claims of merit derive from considerations of efficiency and cannot support stronger notions of desert.[20] Furthermore, regarding job placement, "the meritocrat is committed, given his concern for productivity, to distributing at least some goods, the jobs themselves, in accordance with a morally arbitrary distribution of abilities and traits."[21] Daniels concludes:

> Unfortunately, many proponents of meritocracy have been so concerned with combating

the lesser evil of non-meritocratic job placement that they have left unchallenged the greater evil of highly inegalitarian reward schedules. One suspects that an elitist infatuation for such reward schedules lurks behind their ardor for meritocratic job placement.[22]

Daniels's view exemplifies what Anderson calls academic egalitarianism, but liberalism also has an older, non-academic tradition within which equal respect and meritocracy go hand in hand.[23] We see people as commanding equal respect qua citizens or human beings, but not as commanding equal respect in every respect. Egalitarians and non-egalitarians alike appreciate that genuine respect has meritocratic elements, and thus to some extent tracks how people distinguish themselves as they develop their differing potentials in different ways.[24]

Daniels says the "abilities and traits" that individuate people are "morally arbitrary," but I say that if we care about what people contribute to our society, then traits that enable people to contribute are not arbitrary. Those traits make people who they are and define what people aspire to be, at least in societies that respect those traits. We encourage people to work hard and contribute to society by truly respecting people who work hard, not by insisting that hard work is morally arbitrary while conceding a need to fake respect in hope of conditioning people to work harder. Incentive structures work better when we see them not merely as incentive structures but also as structures that recognize merit.

For practical purposes, certain kinds of egalitarian and meritocratic elements often go together. As a broad empirical generalization, wherever we find a substantial degree of political equality, we also find a substantial degree of economic meritocracy. Far from being antithetical, the two ideas are symbiotic. A central facet of the traditional liberal ideal of equal opportunity is a call for removing arbitrary political or cultural barriers to economic mobility. After the fact, we need not and do not attach the same

value to what people produce. (Obviously, people themselves are not indifferent to whether their plans pan out one way rather than another. If our inventions work, we attach more value to them than we would have if they had not, and we expect the market to do likewise.) Before the fact, though, traditional liberals want people – all people – to be as free as possible to pursue their dreams. That is to say, the equal-opportunity element of liberal tradition placed the emphasis on improving opportunities, not equalizing them.[25] The ideal of "equal pay for equal work," within the tradition from which that ideal emerged, has more in common with the ideal of meritocracy, and with the kind of equal respect built into the concept of meritocracy, than with equal shares per se.

In passing, note that meritocracy is not a synonym for market society. Meritocrats could say the marketplace's meritocratic tendencies are too weak; great talent too often goes unrecognized and unrewarded. Egalitarians could say such tendencies are too strong; Daniels seems to worry that rewards for satisfying millions of customers are larger than they should be. Underlying both complaints is the more fundamental fact that markets react to performance only in the form in which said performance is *brought to market.* So long as Emily Dickinson kept her poetry secret, the marketplace had no opinion about its merits. The marketplace tends to reward a particular kind of performance – namely, wealth-creating performance – and tends to reward that kind of performance in a particular way – namely, with wealth, or sometimes with fame and glory.[26] Markets create time and space within which people can afford hobbies; they can write poetry, if that is what pleases them, without having to worry about whether that particular activity is putting dinner on the table. But the marketplace generally does not judge, and does not reward, what people do with the space they reserve for non-market activities.

Let me stress that my remarks about the consistency of, and even synergy between, equality and meritocracy are offered in defense of the proposition that there is room within a pluralistic conception of justice for elements of egalitarianism. If, contrary to fact, it really were true that we had to make a choice between equality and meritocracy, it would be like choosing between egalitarianism and humanitarianism. When egalitarianism allows itself to be contrasted with humanitarianism, it begins to look monstrous. It likewise would be monstrous to reject a system not because it fails to recognize and reward merit, but precisely because it succeeds.

D. Pure Distribution is Rare

In the real world, almost nothing we do is purely distributive. To take from one and give to another does not only alter a distribution. It also alters the degree to which products are controlled by their producers. To redistribute under real-world conditions, we must alienate producers from their products. This alienation was identified as a problem by Marx, and ought to be regarded as a problem from any perspective.

In a world bound to depart systematically from egalitarian ideals, egalitarian philosophy can encourage these alienated and alienating attitudes, although egalitarian philosophy is not unique in this respect. As noted by Anderson, academic egalitarians tend to see luck as a moral problem. A purist meritocrat, though, would agree, saying success should not be mere luck, but ought to be earned. So, if meritocratic ideals had the actual effect of encouraging feelings of alienation in a world bound to depart systematically from meritocratic ideals, that would be regrettable. The general point here is that even when an uncompromisingly radical philosophy is attractive on its face, the psychological baggage that goes with it need not be. A theory of justice can deafen us to the cost of alienating producers from their product. It deafens us by telling us what we want to hear: that the product should be distributed in accordance with our dream, not the producers'.

Defenders of redistribution sometimes try to justify ignoring this cost. A familiar move is to deny that people are producers. On this account, natural endowments produce. Characters produce. Persons do not. A person's character "depends in large part upon fortunate family and social circumstances for which he can claim no credit,"[27] and therefore, at least theoretically, there is a form of respect we can have for people even while giving them no credit for the effort and talent they bring to the table.

So the story goes. One basic problem with it is that the form of respect it posits is not the kind that brings producers to the table, and therefore that form of respect is, from any perspective, deficient. It is not the kind of respect that human beings value; it is not the kind that makes societies work.

Anderson notes, as many have noted, that egalitarians "regard the economy as a system of cooperative, joint production," in contrast with "the more familiar image of self-sufficient Robinson Crusoes, producing everything all by themselves until the point of trade."[28] She goes on to say that we ought to "regard every product of the economy as jointly produced by everyone working together."[29] By way of response, we all understand that Anderson's article is the product of a system of cooperative, joint production. We all know she did not produce it by herself. Yet we also understand that it is her article, and we would be furious were we to learn that Ackerman had walked into her office one day and said, "Shouldn't I get half of that article?" We do not start "from scratch." Rather, we build upon work already done. We weave our contribution into an existing fabric of contributions. We contribute at the margin (as an economist would put it) to the system of cooperative production, and, within limits, we are seen as owning our contributions, however humble they may be. This is why people continue to contribute, and this in turn is why we continue to have a system of cooperative production.

The most crucial point, perhaps, is that there is something necessarily and laudably ahistorical about simply respecting the abilities that people bring to the table. We need not always dig around for evidence (or worse, stipulate) that people are products of nature and nurture and therefore ineligible for moral credit. Neither must we think of our trading partners as Robinson Crusoes. Often, we simply give them credit, and often simply giving them credit is the essence of treating them as persons rather than as mere confluences of historical forces.

When we do choose to reflect on the historical background of any particular ongoing enterprise, it is appropriate to feel grateful to Thomas Edison and all those people who actually did help to make the current enterprise possible. It would be inappropriate (that is, disrespectful to people like Edison) to feel similarly grateful to people who did not actually do anything to help make the current enterprise possible. (To my mind, one of the most perfectly incredible facts about political philosophy is that, given the premise that thousands of people contribute to the tide of progress that puts individuals in a position to do what they do, we go on to debate whether the appropriate response is to honor those who did contribute or to take their money and give it to those who did not.) When particular people literally contribute to joint projects, they ought to feel grateful to each other and collectively proud of their joint achievement. However, they need not feign agnosticism about the specifics of each partner's contribution in cases where (as it usually works) they are keenly aware of the nature and value of what particular partners have contributed.

Of course, there is much to be said for acknowledging how lucky we are to live within this particular "system of cooperative, joint production" and for respecting what makes it work. My point is only (and my guess is that Anderson would agree) that the room we make for these attitudes must leave room for acknowledging complementary considerations: the kind that bring producers to the table, and the kind involved in treating individual flesh-and-blood workers with genuine respect.

IV. Equal Shares Versus First Possession

In Section II, I attributed to Ackerman the view that "equal shares" is a moral default, the distribution rule we automatically go to if we cannot justify anything else. Needless to say, that is not how we actually do it. For various resources in the real world, the principle we go to if we cannot justify anything else is one invoking first possession. If you walk into the cafeteria carrying two apples, we do not begin to discuss how to allocate them. If the apples are in your hand, their allocation normally is not our business.

Ackerman, though, rejects the rule of first possession. He says that "the only liberty worthy of a community of rational persons is a liberty each is ready and willing to justify in conversation with his fellow questioners. To ground rights on first possession is at war with this ideal."[30] But if this is so, why is first possession ubiquitous? In Ackerman's garden, we are offended when you grab both apples. Why is the real world so different – so different that if Ackerman were to walk up to you in the cafeteria and say, "Shouldn't I get half of your lunch?" we would be offended by Ackerman's behavior, not yours?

Evidently, there is some difficulty in generalizing from Ackerman's thought experiment. Why? The main reason why Ackerman's point does not generalize is that in the real world we do not begin life by dividing a sack of apples that somehow, on its own, made its way to the bargaining table. Instead, we start with resources that some people have helped to produce and others have not, resources already possessed and in use by some people as others arrive on the scene. Contractarian frameworks like Ackerman's depict everyone as getting to the bargaining table at the same time; it is of fundamental moral importance that the world is not like that.

In a world where virtually everything at the table is there because someone brought it to the table, it is easy for equal respect and equal shares to come apart. In a world like that – a world like ours – to respect people is to acknowledge what they bring to the table, to respect the talent and effort manifest in what they bring, and to respect the hopes and dreams that lead them to bring what they do. But to respect them in this way is to respect their contributions as *theirs*.

A. Respect in a World of Non-simultaneous Arrival

Why do property regimes around the world and throughout history consistently operate on a principle of first possession rather than one of equal shares? The reason, I suppose, starts with the fact that in the real world people arrive at different times. When people arrive at different times, equal shares no longer has the intuitive salience it had in the case of simultaneous arrival. When someone has gotten there first and is peacefully trying to put his or her discovery to use, trying to grab a piece of the action, even if only an equal piece, is not a peaceful act. It is not a respectful act. If Ackerman were to enter a corner grocery and begin discussing how to allocate whatever he can find in the cash register, as if the shopkeeper were merely another party to the discussion, he would not be treating the shopkeeper with respect. Here is a thought experiment: in a world where Ackerman was not obliged to respect prior possession, how long would shops remain open for business?

Academic lawyer Carol Rose says that a legal rule that confers the status of owner upon the first person unambiguously taking possession of a given object induces discovery.[31] By inducing discovery, the rule induces future productive activity. A second virtue of such a rule is that it minimizes disputes over discovered objects.[32] In short, it enables shopkeepers to make a living in peace.[33]

Recall Ackerman's previous claim: "[T]he only liberty worthy of a community of rational persons is a liberty each is ready and willing to justify in conversation with his fellow questioners. To ground rights on first possession is at war with this ideal." Simply dismissing the other side as at war with the ideal of rational conversation, as Ackerman does here, is itself at war with the ideal of rational conversation. The truth, for millennia, has been that failing to respect prior possession is the stuff of war in an absolutely literal way. Moreover, the central place of prior possession is not a cultural artifact. Virtually any animal capable of locomotion understands at some level that if you ignore the claim of an animal that got there first, you are not treating it with respect.

B. Xenophobia

An overlooked virtue of first possession is that it lets us live together without having to view newcomers as a threat, whereas a rule of equal shares does not. If we were to regard every newcomer as having a claim to an equal share of our holdings, the arrival of newcomers would be inherently threatening. Imagine another thought experiment: A town has one hundred people. Each has a lot that is one hundred feet wide. Every time someone new shows up, we redraw property lines. Each lot shrinks by the amount needed to make room for the new person's equal share. Question: how friendly will this town be? Even now, in our world, people who see the world in zero-sum terms tend to despise immigrants. The point is not that xenophobia has moral weight, of course, but rather that it is real, a variable we want to minimize if we can. Recognizing first possession helps, compared to redistributing according to an equal-shares principle. To say the least, it would not help to tell people that newly arriving immigrants have a right to an equal share. At first, members of the community would clamor for a wall to stop people from getting in. Eventually, the point of the wall would be to stop people from getting out.

Likewise, apropos Ackerman's assertion that a liberty is worthy only if we are each ready and willing to justify it in conversation, imagine a world in which the title to your property was perpetually contingent on your ability to defeat all challengers in debate. In any remotely successful community, quite a lot of the structure of daily life literally goes without saying and needs no argument; this enables people to take quite a lot for granted and allows them to pour their energy into production rather than self-defense, verbal or otherwise.

The central role played by prior possession in any viable culture, across human history, is a problem for egalitarianism, although not uniquely for egalitarianism. Meritocracy is equally in a position of having to defer somewhat to a norm of respecting prior possession. A viable culture is a web of positive-sum games, but a game is positive-sum only if players are willing to take what they have as their starting point and carry on from there. A viable conception of justice takes this (along with other prerequisites of positive-sum games) as its starting point.

V. The Zero-Sum Perspective

The obvious moral problem with first possession, of course, is that those who arrive later do not get an equal share. Is that fair? It depends. Exactly how bad is it to be a latecomer? Egalitarian thought experiments such as Ackerman's are zero-sum games. In such models, first possession leaves latecomers with nothing. When you, the first appropriator, grab both apples (or even one, for that matter), you leave less for Ackerman or anyone else who comes along later. Your grab is a preface to pure consumption. Thus, as philosopher Hillel Steiner has noted, in the same way that first-comers would see newcomers as a threat under an equal-shares regime, newcomers would see first-comers as a threat under a regime of first possession.[34] Or at least, newcomers would see first-comers as a threat if it really were true that in a first-possession regime it is better to arrive early than late.

But this is not true. One central fact about a regime of first possession is that over time, as a rule, it is far better to arrive late than early. It would be unusual to meet people in a developed nation who are not substantially more wealthy than their grandparents were at a comparable age. We have unprecedented wealth today precisely because our ancestors got here first, cleared the land, and began the laborious process of turning society into a vast network of cooperative ventures for mutual advantage. In the real world, original appropriation typically is a preface to production, and then to mutually advantageous commerce with widely dispersed benefits. It is not a zero-sum game. First possessors pay the price of converting resources to productive use. Latecomers reap the benefits.[35] We occasionally should remind ourselves that in the race to appropriate, the chance to be a first appropriator is not the prize. The prize is prosperity, and latecomers win big, courtesy of the toil of those who got there first.

So, when someone asks why entrepreneurs should get to keep the whole value of what they produce, the answer is that they don't. To some people, this will seem obvious. Yet there are some who really do see the world in zero-sum terms. To them, when you grab an apple in Ackerman's garden and start planting apple seeds, it is analytic that no one else will ever benefit from all those future harvests.

A. Structural Unemployment

The zero-sum perspective is most tempting when viewing the labor market. Thus, philosopher Robert Goodin can say:

> If there are a thousand people looking for work and only one job, one can get work only on condition that the remainder do not. That one person succeeds in getting a job, far from proving that all could, actually precludes others from doing so.[36]

Goodin admits labor markets are not really like that, yet he does not retract the claim. Citing philosopher G. A. Cohen, Goodin says, "Marxian economics provides reasons for believing that precisely that is true of the proletarian in any capitalist economy."[37] That is, "If the structure of the situation is such that one can succeed only on condition that not all do, then the freedom of the one is perfectly consistent with the 'unfreedom' of the many."[38] This is what has come to be called "structural" unemployment.

Some will see Goodin as stating a necessary truth: when two people apply for the same job, it is as if there were only one apple in Ackerman's garden. Others will say that in developed economies, the salient ratio is not (or not only) the number of jobs per job-seeker but the number of jobs per month. The former ratio leads people to misinterpret the supply of jobs as a stock rather than as a flow. If the unemployment rate is 10 percent, that does not mean one-tenth of the population is doomed to unemployment. For many, what it means is that their number is called less often than it would be if the rate were lower – unless there is genuine structural unemployment, as in countries where, for example, women are legally or culturally barred from working. But what creates structural unemployment is structure, not the rate of flow in the labor market.

B. *Markets are not Auctions*

If society were a zero-sum game, then the only way for some to have more would be for others to have less. When we see society as actually like this, we are tempted to believe the argument that when some people have more dollars, they bid up prices of whatever is available for purchase, thereby outcompeting cash-poor people and making them worse off. This is an interesting and rhetorically powerful idea. It would even be true in a society where people acquire paper dollars from a central distributor without having done anything to create the stock of wealth for

which those paper dollars are supposed to be a receipt. But now contrast this zero-sum picture with a generally more realistic picture of market society. If I acquire more dollars by contributing more goods and services to the economy, then my participation in the economy is not inflationary. On the contrary, insofar as people give me paper dollars in exchange for goods and services I bring to market, the process by which I acquire dollars has a deflationary impact, for the result of my contribution is that there now are more goods and services in circulation with no corresponding increase in the number of paper dollars in circulation. The net impact of the process by which I amass paper dollars is that *prices fall*, unless the money supply is increased to keep pace with the increased volume of goods and services in circulation.

Many people, though, continue to be swayed (if not downright blinded) by arguments premised on the assumption that for some to have more, others must have less. For some reason, this assumption is unshaken by everyday observation of people acquiring wealth not by subtracting it from a fixed stock, but by adding goods and services to the economy.

C. Sexism

Goodin's odd picture of what it is like to participate in an economy is implicit in arguments of theorists who occasionally propose, as a way of redressing our society's sexist bias, that mothers be paid a wage simply for being mothers. This too begins with an interesting and rhetorically powerful idea: When men go to the factory and women stay home to manage the household, they both work really hard. The men get paid. Why don't the women?

Here is one answer. The problem is not that the market does not recognize *women*, but that it does not recognize what is *not brought to market*. Suppose a farmer raises a crop while his wife raises children. Is it sexist that only the man's labor earns money? To test the hypothesis, imagine a farmer saying to prospective customers, "My wife and I have two things for sale: first, the fact that we are growing a crop, and second, the fact that we are raising six kids." Would prospective customers volunteer to pay the farmer for raising crops, but not for raising children?

If they would, that might suggest a sexist bias. But they would not. Their response would be:

> Just show us what you have for sale. If your crop or your day-care services are for sale, we're interested. When your kids have goods of their own for sale, we'll be interested. But if what you want is to be paid to consume your own crop and raise your own kids, then in all seriousness, we have children of our own to feed. By the way, would you be better off if the king took your money to feed our kids and took our money to feed yours? Would your daughters be better off if women were expected to maximize their family's slice of the redistributive pie by having more babies than they otherwise would want? Would that end sexism?

When people say women should be paid to raise their own children, it is as if a farmer demanded to be paid for raising a crop without actually having brought anything to market. It is to fail to grasp what is involved in exchanging value for value. It is a mistake to criticize markets for failing to commodify children. Commodifying children would be catastrophic for everyone, but especially for women. If we want to keep making progress toward the kind of society in which men and women can flourish as political equals, we need to find another way.

VI. About Empirical Studies

I close with observations about the other major source of provocation mentioned at the outset — namely, empirical studies of income inequality.[39] Although I am a professor of economics by joint appointment, I am at heart a philosopher. I trust conceptual arguments. I do not want to win arguments I do not deserve to win, and when the terrain is conceptual, I trust myself to know where I stand. I do not feel this way about statistics. This section's main purpose is not to settle some empirical issue, but simply to show how easily numbers create false impressions.

For example, studies of income distribution typically separate populations into quintiles according to household income. While each quintile for household income contains 20 percent of all households by definition, as of 1997 the United States's bottom quintile contained only 14.8 percent of individual persons, whereas the top quintile contained 24.3 percent. Households in the bottom quintile averaged 1.9 persons and 0.6 workers, compared to 3.1 persons and 2.1 workers in the top.[40] So, one major source of income inequality among households is that some contain more wage-earners than others. If we look at raw data comparing household incomes in the top and bottom quintiles, we will not see this, and will be misled.

We can be misled in another way when studying changes in household income in a society where the number of wage-earners per household is falling. When the number of wage-earners per household falls, average *household* income can fall even as *individual* incomes rise. If two people live in a typical college-student household today versus three in a household a generation ago, this will show up in our statistics as a fall in the bottom quintile's average income. Yet in such cases, household income falls because the individuals are more wealthy, not less, which is why they now can afford to split the rent with fewer people.[41]

It is easy to dig up a study showing that average wages fell by, say, 9 percent between 1975 and 1997, if that is what we want to hear. If not, it is equally easy to verify that such studies are based upon a discredited way of correcting for inflation (in addition, these studies ignore factors such as the burgeoning of fringe benefits) and that when we use more currently accepted ways of correcting for inflation, the corrected numbers show average wages rising 35 percent between 1975 and 1997.[42] In 1996, a panel of five economists, commissioned by the Senate Finance Committee and chaired by Michael Boskin, concluded that the consumer price index overstates inflation by about 1.1 percent per year (perhaps as little as 0.8 percent; perhaps as much as 1.6 percent).[43] If the figure of 1.1 percent is correct, then "instead of the stagnation recorded in official statistics, a lower inflation measure would mean that *real* median family income grew from 1973 to 1995 by 36 percent."[44]

If there is one thing I would like readers to take away as the message of this section, it would not be a number. It would be the following picture. An income distribution is a bunch of people occupying steps on a staircase.[45] Pessimists use numbers to show that the bottom step is where it always has been. Even worse, they claim, the staircase has begun to stretch. The top now climbs higher than it once did, thereby increasing the gap between the top and bottom steps, that is, between the rich and poor. Optimists use the same numbers to show that people who once stood on the lower steps have moved up. While there are still people at the bottom, many belong to a younger generation whose time to move up is still coming. From a "snapshot" perspective, the picture is one of stagnation, but to people actually living these lives, the staircase is a moving escalator, lifting people to heights that did not exist when their grandparents were children. This perspective – which treats life in the way people actually live it – is a picture of incremental improvement.

I am not asking you to be an optimist. The message, instead, is that the pessimistic perspective is, at very best, only one way of being realistic. At bottom, the profound truth of the matter may be, as philosopher Richard Miller once remarked to me, that there is a place for a Democratic sort of emphasis on complaining about where some of us had to start, and also a place for a Republican sort of emphasis on accepting our starting point as a starting point and making the best of it.

A. Inequality and Age in the United States

Statistics seem to indicate that the rich are getting richer. The income gap between the top quintile and other quintiles has, by some measures, been growing. What does this mean? For the sake of reference, when we divide households into income quintiles, the income cutoffs as of 1999 are as follows:

> Lowest quintile: Zero to $17,262;
> Second quintile: $17,263 to $32,034;
> Third quintile: $32,035 to $50,851;
> Fourth quintile: $50,852 to $79,454;
> Top quintile: $79,455 and up.[46]

Household income at the 80th percentile is thus 4.6 times household income at the 20th percentile. Compare this to the median household incomes of different age groups, as of 1999:

> $24,031 when the head of the household is under 25;
> $43,309 when the head of the household is between ages 25 and 34;
> $54,993 when the head of the household is between ages 35 and 44;
> $65,303 when the head of the household is between ages 45 and 54;
> $54,249 when the head of the household is between ages 55 and 64.[47]

Like the gaps between the quintiles, gaps between age groups appear to be increasing. Where earnings had once begun to trail off as workers entered their forties, earnings now continue to rise as workers reach their fifties, only then beginning to drop as early retirements start to cut into average earnings. Economist

Michael Cox and journalist Robert Alm report that:

> ... [i]n 1951, individuals aged 35 to 44 earned 1.6 times as much as those aged 20 to 24, on average. By 1993, the highest paid age group had shifted to the 45 to 54-year-olds, who earned nearly 3.1 times as much as the 20 to 24-year-olds.[48]

The numbers seem to say that the top quintile cannot be characterized as a separate caste of aristocrats. To some extent, the quintiles appear to be constituted by ordinary median people at different ages.[49] So, when we read that median income at the 80th percentile has jumped by 46 percent in real dollar terms between 1967 and 1999,[50] we should entertain the likelihood that for many people living at the 20th percentile, that jump represents increasing opportunity for them, not just for some separate elite. It represents what many reasonably hope to earn as they reach the age when people like them take their turn composing the top quintile. Again, the fact that 45 to 54-year-olds are doing much better today, thereby widening the gaps between income quintiles, appears to be good news for a lot of people, not only for people currently in that age group.[51]

Even if the lowest quintile has not been getting richer over time, this does not mean that the group of people flipping burgers a generation ago is still today stuck flipping burgers. Rather, the implication is that when this year's crop of high school graduates flips burgers for a year, they will get paid roughly what their parents were paid when they were the same age, doing the same things. (What else would we expect?) Again, if today's bottom 20 percent is no richer than the bottom 20 percent was a generation ago, the upshot is that the lowest-paying *jobs* do not pay much more than they ever did, not that the people who once held those jobs still hold them today.

Although the lowest-paying jobs may not pay much more now than they ever did, we know many low-pay workers did not remain low-pay workers. "Individuals in the lowest income quintile in 1975 saw, on average, a $25,322 rise in their real income over the sixteen years from 1975 to 1991. Those in the highest income quintile had a $3,974 increase in real income, on average."[52] How could people who had been in the bottom quintile gain over six times as much as people who had been in the top one? Assuming the numbers indicate something real, my conjecture would be that, again, what we call income quintiles are, to some extent, different age groups. Over sixteen years, people who had in 1975 made up a large part of the top quintile edged into retirement while younger people who had made up a large part of the bottom quintile in 1975 hit their peak earning years. This is only a conjecture, but it would explain why those who had composed the bottom quintile gained substantially more over sixteen years than those who had composed the top did.

B. *While the Rich Get Richer*

Ideally, we want to know two things. First, are people doing better than their parents were doing at the same age? Second, do people do better as they get older? The answer to each of these crucial questions appears to be yes in general, although obviously I do not mean to suggest everyone is doing well. Still, in general, the numbers seem to say that it is not only the already rich who are getting richer. There are many more people *getting* rich. In 1967, only 3.2 percent of U.S. households were making the equivalent of $100,000 in 1999 dollars. By 1999, the number had risen to 12.3 percent. For whites, the increase was from 3.4 to 12.9 percent; for blacks, the increase was from 1.0 to 6.1 percent.[53] So, if we ask why the top quintile made further gains between 1967 and 1999, it apparently would be incorrect to explain the change by saying that a small cadre of people had a lot of money in 1967 and that by 1999 that same cadre had pulled even farther ahead.

On the contrary, what seems to explain the burgeoning wealth of the top quintile is that millions upon millions of people joined the ranks of the rich. These people were not rich when they were younger. Their parents were not rich. But they are rich today.

In "America's Rags-to-Riches Myth," journalist Michael M. Weinstein says Americans "cling to the conceit that they have unrivaled opportunity to move up."[54] But the conceit, Weinstein says, is merely that. Yet Weinstein is aware that the U.S. Treasury Department's Office of Tax Analysis found that of people in the bottom income quintile in 1979, 65 percent moved up two or more quintiles by 1988. Eighty-six percent jumped at least one quintile.[55] Are these findings unique? There is room for skepticism, here as elsewhere. But no, the finding is not unique. Using independent data from the Michigan Panel Study of Income Dynamics, Cox and Alm's study tracked a different group occupying the lowest quintile in 1975, and saw 80.3 percent of the group move up two or more quintiles by 1991. Ninety-five percent moved up at least one quintile. Furthermore, 29 percent moved from the bottom quintile to the top quintile between 1975 and 1991.[56] In absolute terms (that is, in terms of income gains in real dollar terms), the improvement is even larger. In absolute terms, 39.2 percent of those in the bottom quintile in 1975 had, by 1991, moved to where the top quintile *had been* in 1975. Only 2.3 percent remained at a living standard equal to that of 1975's lowest quintile.[57]

These studies do *not* show us to be a nation of people lifting ourselves out of poverty "by our own bootstraps," though, because not everyone with a low income is from a poor background. Many low-income people are students who receive substantial family support. We should not infer from Cox and Alm's study that family background does not matter.[58] Researchers Daniel McMurrer, Mark Condon, and Isabell Sawhill say:

Overall, the evidence suggests that the playing field is becoming more level in the United States. Socioeconomic origins today are less important than they used to be. Further, such origins have little or no impact for individuals with a college degree, and the ranks of such individuals continue to increase. This growth in access to higher education represents an important vehicle for expanding opportunity. Still, family background continues to matter. While the playing field may be becoming more level, family factors still significantly shape the economic outcomes of children.[59]

A related issue: we have looked at the upward mobility of individuals, but we find less mobility in studies tracking households. Researchers Greg Duncan, Johanne Boisjoly, and Timothy Smeeding estimate that if we were to look at household rather than individual mobility, we would see that 47 percent of those in the bottom quintile in 1975 were still there in 1991. (Actually, they refer to the bottom quintile as "the poor," which is an increasingly untenable equation as the percentage of households officially in poverty continues to drop.) Twenty percent moved to the distribution's top half, and 6 percent moved to the top quintile.[60]

These numbers suggest household mobility is quite substantial; nevertheless, there apparently is a big difference between individual upward mobility and household upward mobility. Why would that be? Imagine a household with two teenagers, circa 1975. Two studies track this household. One study tracks household members as individuals, and finds that sixteen years later the teenagers' incomes have risen several quintiles. A second study tracking the original household as a household finds that the household lost the summer wages the now-departed teenagers earned while living at home and attending college. When the teenagers left home, they disappeared from the second study because the households they went on to form did not exist when the study began in 1975. That is, a longitudinal study tracking 1975 house-holds ignores individuals who grow up, move out, form new households, and move up after 1975. Given the same data, a longitudinal study of circa-1975 households paints a picture of modest progress while a longitudinal study of circa-1975 individuals suggests volcanic upward mobility. Which picture is more realistic?

Duncan et al. do not reveal the basis of their estimates. I have no reason to doubt them, but it is interesting that Duncan et al. mention later in their article that their data set, drawn from the Michigan Panel Study, "is designed to be contin-uously representative of the non-immigrant population as a whole."[61] I presume they have reasons for excluding immigrants, yet I would wager that immigrant households are more upwardly mobile than non-immigrant house-holds. Immigrant and non-immigrant individ-uals may not differ much, relatively speaking, since they all start with teenage incomes and then move up. Households, though, are another matter, since if we exclude immigrant house-holds, we are excluding households that are not established but are instead in a position like that of individual teenagers: they have little wealth and little income, for now, but they came here to work and make a major move up as a household. A focus on households already lends itself to an understatement of income mobility, compared to studies that focus on tracking individuals. Excluding immigrant households presumably increases the magnitude of that relative understatement.

Again, I do not mean to say that the study by Duncan et al. is especially flawed. On the contrary, it is not. Like any other study, it is potentially informative, and potentially misleading. It offers not simply numbers, but interpretations of numbers. Any study of income mobility begins with key decisions about what the researchers are looking for. Different studies measure different things, and no one is to blame for that.

Weinstein simply dismisses Cox and Alm's study of individuals on the ground that many people who moved up were people who were students when the study began. Of course students make up a big part of the bottom quin-tile, and of course they move up, Weinstein says, but so what? "This upward mobility of students hardly answers the enduring question: How many grown-ups are trapped in low-paying jobs?" Weinstein answers his own question by saying, "The answer is, a lot."[62] Oddly, though, the only evidence he offers that "a lot" of grown-ups are trapped is a study of poverty among children. To that study we now turn.

C. Children

In their study, economists Peter Gottschalk and Sheldon Danziger separated children into quin-tiles according to family income.[63] Their data, Weinstein reports, shows that "[a]bout 6 in 10 of the children in the lowest group – the poorest 20 percent – in the early 1970's were still in the bottom group 10 years later ... No conceit about mobility, real or imagined, can excuse that unconscionable fact."[64]

Since Weinstein relies solely on Gottschalk and Danziger, I checked the original study. Gottschalk and Danziger were studying American children that were five years old or younger when their ten-year studies began – ten years later, the children were still children.[65] What we appear to have, then, is a cohort of mostly young couples with babies, about 40 percent of whom had moved into higher quintiles ten years later. Is this percentage bad? Out of context, it looks neither bad nor good. Has any society ever done better?

Yes. It turns out at least one society has done better: the United States itself. The figure cited by Weinstein is the result from the first decade of a two-decade study. Weinstein presents the figure from the 1970s (only 43 percent moving up) as an indictment of America today, neglecting to mention that the study's corresponding figure from the 1980s was 51 percent. Although the two figures come from the same table in

Gottschalk and Danziger's paper, Weinstein evidently felt the more up-to-date number and the upward trend were not worth mentioning.

A further thought: At the end of the Gottschalk–Danziger studies, the parents of the studied children are (generally) in their early thirties, still ten years away from the time when they become most upwardly mobile. And of course, the kids are still thirty years away from the time when they become most upwardly mobile. So, the Gottschalk–Danziger studies end at a point where I would have predicted it would be too soon for there to be much evidence of upward mobility.

I myself would have been one of those kids they are talking about. I grew up on a farm in Saskatchewan. We sold the farm when I was 11 and moved to the city, where Dad became a janitor and Mom became a cashier in a fabric shop. Even before we left the farm, we had already moved up in absolute terms – we got indoor plumbing when I was about three years old – but we would still have been in the bottom quintile. Even after we got a flush toilet, water had to be delivered by truck, and it was so expensive that we flushed the toilet only once a day – and it served a family of eight. Thirty-five years later, my household income is in the top five percent of the overall distribution. Had I been part of Gottschalk and Danziger's study, though, Weinstein would have been professing to be outraged by the "unconscionable" fact that when I was 10 years old, I had not yet made my move.

In my case, the problem with childhood poverty was not lack of money. Money was never a problem. Even the toilet was not really a problem. Lack of knowledge was a problem. Lack of educated role models was a problem. (My parents received sixth-grade educations. I did not know what a university was until we moved to the city.) I suspect that the Internet notwithstanding, the big obstacles I faced continue to be big obstacles for poor kids today.

Let us return to the study. As I said, I would have predicted that we would see precious little evidence of upward mobility in a study that ends before subjects reach their mid-teens. But let us take a look. According to Gottschalk and Danziger, among children in bottom-quintile families that received welfare payments in the early 1970s, 2.3 percent were in households that rose beyond the second quintile by the early 1980s. Bottom-quintile children living in single-parent families had a 6.4 percent chance of being in a household that moved beyond the second quintile.[66] Unsurprisingly, one-adult households brought in less income than two-adult households at both points in time, and therefore we find them in the bottom two quintiles. How bad is that? The poverty rate in the United States continues to fall and was most recently measured at 11.8 percent,[67] which means that being in the bottom two quintiles – the bottom 40 percent – is not the synonym for "being poor" that it once was.[68]

If there is a problem here, it appears to have less to do with differences in income and wealth per se and more to do with single parenthood (and I do not pretend to know how to solve that problem). Economist Robert Lerman estimates that half the increase in income inequality observed in the late 1980s and early 1990s was due to an increase in the number of single-parent households.[69] According to Gottschalk and Danziger, there is a big difference between being poor and white and being poor and black: blacks are more likely to stay in the bottom quintile. I am reluctant to quarrel with Gottschalk and Danziger here, and yet, according to their own numbers, the result of their ten-year study begun in 1971 is that "black children had a *higher* chance than white children of escaping poverty if they made the transition from a single-parent family to a 2-parent family by the end of the decade (67.9 versus 42.6 percent)."[70] Looking at results of the second study, begun in 1981, we find the chance of a child escaping poverty (actually, the bottom quintile) upon moving from a single-parent to a two-parent family improving to 87.8 percent for blacks and 57.6 percent for whites.[71]

The numbers seem to say that race is not the problem; again, coming from a single-parent family is the problem. However, in the 1980s, whites were nearly three times as likely as blacks to make that move from single-parent to two-parent families (which represents a closing of what had been a fourfold gap in the 1970s).[72] Furthermore, black children are more likely to be in a single-parent setting in the first place. As of 1998, the percentage of out-of-wedlock births was 21.9 percent for non-Hispanic whites and 69.3 percent for blacks.[73] I trust even hard-core egalitarians will agree that what is bad about these numbers is how high they are, not how unequal they are.

In the 1980s, Gottschalk and Danziger say, the overall probability that a child would escape poverty was higher than it was in the 1970s, although the improvement was not significant.[74] For the record – using their numbers – the chance of escaping poverty improved from 43.2 percent to 51.2 percent.[75] Oddly, when Gottschalk and Danziger say that an eight-point swing is not significant, they do not hasten to clarify what this means. What they do not say is that although the change appears huge, they did not collect enough data to be able to call the improvement *statistically* significant.[76] Uncritical readers such as Weinstein are left to infer that there was no improvement.

Gottschalk and Danziger say that "only one demographic group (children in two parent families) shows a significant decline in the prob-ability of remaining poor."[77] (What a discour-aging thought – that we have reached a point where children in two-parent families are "only one demographic group.") Within that group, the chance of escaping poverty improved from 47 percent in the 1970s to 65 percent in the 1980s. Again, there is something so odd here that I am left not knowing what to think: the authors acknowledge the massively improved prospects of "children of two parent families" parenthetically, as if that class were a small anomaly that does not bear on their contention

that the probability of escaping poverty has not significantly improved.

Finally, recall that we are talking about the chance of escaping poverty (more accurately, the bottom quintile) before leaving the 10–15 age bracket. If we sought deliberately to design an experiment guaranteed to show no evidence of vertical mobility, we could hardly do better. Yet what Gottschalk and Danziger's numbers say is that nearly two-thirds of poor kids in unbroken homes escape poverty before earning their first paycheck. If Gottschalk and Danziger's numbers are right, then it is fact, not myth: these kids live in a land of opportunity.

Are growing differences in wealth and income a problem? Maybe so, in some respects. Nothing said here proves otherwise. The truly obvious problem, though, is more specific. In general, in the United States, poor people not only can but typically do move up – it is kids from broken homes who have a problem.

D. The Political Problem

One might argue that the problem of inequality is fundamentally caused by a lack of political will to "soak" the rich. We can imagine asking young poor people whether it is to their advantage for us to raise marginal rates on the tax brackets they are hoping to move into. It is possible they will say yes, but it is equally possible that the tax hike would take a bigger bite out of their ambitions than out of rich people's wallets. (This last claim may be very hard to imagine for people who grew up in middle-class homes and never saw working-class life as an option, but a "What's the point?" sentiment was common among people with whom I grew up at a time when marginal tax rates were higher.)

Would "soaking the rich" lead to greater equality? The answer, obviously, is that it depends on how the tax revenues would be distributed. The current U.S. federal budget is 1.7 trillion dollars. If we were to distribute that kind of money among the 14.8 percent of people who make up the poorest 20 percent of American households – roughly forty million people – we would already have enough to give a little over $40,000 to each person. A family of four would receive over $160,000. Of course, nothing remotely like that is happening. Why not? At least a part of the story is that the federal government has other priorities, and always will. We might suspect the problem cannot be solved by giving the government more money. After all, gaps between rich and poor apparently widened in tandem with rising federal budgets.

We can hope that as the rich get richer, more money will trickle down to the poor. We can also hope that as federal budgets grow, money will trickle down to the poor. But the rich have been getting richer, and federal budgets have grown. So, if the trickle down is not working now, perhaps it never will. In particular, as federal budgets grow, we would expect to reach a point (if we have not already done so) where the trickle down would come to a halt, or even reverse itself. The reason is that as budgets grow, it becomes increasingly worthwhile for special interest groups to fight for control of those budgets at the expense of the politically disenfranchised. If unequal concentrations of political power can be thought of as a beast, then government budgets are part of what feeds that beast and gives it reason to live. Although it is beyond the scope of this essay, my guess is that an effective coalescing of will and ability to help people avoid or at least cope with single parenthood and other pressing problems is more likely to occur in those local non-governmental organizations whose budgets are small enough and whose governance is transparent enough to be less inviting to political opportunists.[78]

VII. Summary

As economist Amartya Sen says, "[E]very normative theory or social arrangement that has at all stood the test of time seems to demand equality of *something*."[79] It is worth adding, though, that by the same token every theory, including egalitarian theories, countenances inequality as well. An egalitarian is a person who embraces one kind of unequal treatment as the price of securing equality of (what he or she considers) a more important kind.

There is a place for equal shares. Paradigmatically, there is a place for the principle of equal shares when we arrive simultaneously at the bargaining table to distribute goods to which no one has any prior claim. It would be a thankless task to try to construct a complete catalog of cases where equal shares is most salient. Suffice it to say that we can ask what the virtues of equal shares would be in a given context, were we to assess the principle without begging the question; that is, were we to assess the principle by reference to moral considerations that do not presuppose the principle. This is how we can try to make room for any given principle of justice within a pluralist theory.[80]

Equal respect is among the most basic of moral desiderata. Equal respect or equal treatment may be analytically built into the concept of justice even if equal shares is not. The idea of giving people their due is the basic concept of justice, not merely a contested conception. And the idea of giving people their due is hard to separate (at least at the most abstract level) from an ideal of equal treatment.

However, it would be a mistake to think that a commitment to treat people with equal respect entails a *general* commitment to make sure they have equal shares. In the marketplace, at least, meritocracy can embody one way of implementing a conception of equal treatment. Historically, "equal pay for equal work" has been seen this way within the liberal tradition.

First possession arguably is not a principle of justice at all, yet it plays a central role in any viable society. It is one of the signposts by which we navigate in a social world. We can question the principle in theory (and in theory it probably is easier to attack than to defend), but we do not and cannot question the principle in our daily practice. We would be lost without it.

Empirically, it can be hard to know what to make of recent income trends. We are barraged by numbers, or by interpretations thereof, and people skilled at gathering numbers are not always so skilled at interpreting them. If I were to do serious empirical work, I would ask why people today generally look forward to standards of living almost beyond the imagination of their ancestors from a century ago. (Life expectancy, for example, has nearly doubled.) I would ask who has been left behind by this burgeoning of real prosperity and why, and what can be done about it. I would not assume that all problems have solutions, nor that all solutions are worth their costs. Optimist that I am, I assume we can do better. Realist that I am, I know we could do worse.

Notes

1 Some worry about differences in wealth because they believe such differences eventually become differences in political power. (Whether such concerns justify increasing or decreasing the amount of political power that eventually gets put up for sale is a separate question, touched on at the end of this essay.) This worry could be made to fit quite nicely into either of the above two reasons for concern about inequality, or we could call it a third, separate reason.

2 Bruce A. Ackerman, "On Getting What We Don't Deserve," *Social Philosophy and Policy* 1, no. 1 (1983): 60–70. My discussion of Ackerman borrows from David Schmidtz, "Finders, Keepers?" *Advances in Austrian Economics* 5 (1998): 277–89; and David Schmidtz and Robert Goodin, *Social Welfare and Individual Responsibility* (New York: Cambridge University Press, 1998). For a skeptical response to Ackerman's thought-experiment methodology from an egalitarian perspective, see James K. Galbraith, "Raised on Robbery," *Yale Law and Policy Review* 18, no. 2 (2000): 387–404.

3 As children grow up, we expect them to resent their siblings less rather than resent their neighbors more, but this expectation is not always met. A

well-known philosopher once complained to me about airline deregulation, not because of safety or quality of service or anything like that, but because it made her unsure of whether she was getting the lowest possible price. She had paid $300 for her ticket, and for all she knew the person beside her paid $200 for the same ticket. I speculated that before deregulation, both tickets would have cost $700. She answered, in a passionate voice, "But at least you knew!" Knew what? Obviously, there was nothing humanitarian in this kind of egalitarianism. This philosopher is not alone. A neighbor of mine recently said she would rather pay $20 for a blanket at K-Mart than pay $8 for the same blanket in the nearby border town of Nogales, because at K-Mart you know everyone is paying the same price, whereas in Nogales, someone else might be getting the same blanket for $6.

4 As David Gauthier expresses a related point, "impartial practices respect people as they are, the inequalities among them as well as the equalities." See David Gauthier, *Morals by Agreement* (Oxford: Oxford University Press, 1986), 270.

5 Larry S. Temkin, *Inequality* (New York: Oxford University Press, 1993), 8.

6 One of Temkin's contributions to the literature is his discussion of what he calls "the Slogan": "One situation cannot be better than another unless there is someone for whom it is better" (ibid., 248). The Slogan's point is to separate true egalitarians (who would say a more equal distribution can be better even when there is no one for whom it is better) from true humanitarians (who would deny this). Temkin, an egalitarian, says the Slogan is false (ibid., 249).

7 Ibid., 246.

8 Ibid., 247.

9 Elizabeth S. Anderson, "What Is the Point of Equality?" *Ethics* 109, no. 2 (1999): 288.

10 Terry L. Price reaches a similar conclusion in Terry L. Price, "Egalitarian Justice, Luck, and the Costs of Chosen Ends," *American Philosophical Quarterly* 36, no. 4 (1999): 267–78.

11 Richard J. Arneson, "Rawls, Responsibility, and Distributive Justice," in Maurice Salles and John A. Weymark, eds., *Justice, Political Liberalism, and Utilitarianism: Themes from Harsanyi* (Cambridge: Cambridge University Press, in press), quoted in

Anderson, "What Is the Point of Equality?" 290. For a later work in which Arneson abandons egalitarianism in favor of what he calls sufficientarianism, see Richard J. Arneson, "Why Justice Requires Transfers to Offset Income and Wealth Inequalities".

12 For a sustained and circumspect — yet uncompromising — defense of a related kind of egalitarianism, see the more recent Tom Christiano, "Arguing for Equality of Condition" (manuscript).

13 Anderson, "What Is the Point of Equality?" 293.

14 Ibid., 288.

15 Ibid.

16 Ibid., 313.

17 Ibid., 289.

18 Ibid.

19 Ibid., 306.

20 Norman Daniels, "Merit and Meritocracy," *Philosophy and Public Affairs* 7, no. 3 (1978): 207.

21 Ibid., 222.

22 Ibid.

23 I mean to be speaking here of the liberal tradition in a quite general way, rather than of classical or modern variations on the theme. To put it in terms of stylized history, I mean liberalism as it developed in Europe and America in reaction to monarchy in particular and to social hierarchy in general. For that matter, even the socialist tradition once was in part a meritocratic reaction to a social hierarchy that prevented working classes from being able to earn fair wages.

24 For a good discussion of this issue, see Richard J. Arneson, "What, if Anything, Renders All Humans Morally Equal?" in Dale Jamieson, ed., *Singer and His Critics* (Oxford: Blackwell Publishers, 1999), 103–28. Temkin too makes room for merit, saying, "I think deserved inequalities are not bad *at all*. Rather, what is objectionable is some being worse off than others *through no fault of their own*" (Temkin, *Inequality*, 17). Unfortunately, the sort of room Temkin tries to make has an awkward consequence. If Bill has more than me because he does better work, then according to the quotation's first sentence the inequality is deserved and therefore not bad at all; at the same time, though, I am worse off through no fault of my own, which is objectionable according to the quotation's second sentence.

25 Interestingly, Richard Miller says "people are pervasively victimized by social barriers to advancement in any reasonably efficient capitalist economy. . . . On the other hand, in an advanced industrial setting, some reasonably efficient capitalist system is best for everyone who is constrained by justice" as Miller conceives of it. There is nothing inconsistent about this, although it "depends on facts that would sadden most observers of the modern industrial scene, saddening different observers for different reasons: Central planning does not work, yet traditional socialists were right in most of their charges of capitalist inequality." Richard Miller, "Justice as Social Freedom," in Rodger Beehler, David Copp, and Béla Szabados, eds., *On the Track of Reason: Essays in Honor of Kai Nielsen* (Boulder, CO: Westview, 1992), 38.

26 On this topic, I regard as essential reading Tyler Cowen, *In Praise of Commercial Culture* (Cambridge, MA: Harvard University Press, 1998); and Tyler Cowen, *What Price Fame?* (Cambridge, MA: Harvard University Press, 2000).

27 John Rawls, *A Theory of Justice* (Cambridge, MA: Harvard University Press, 1971), 104. No one has done more than Rawls in recent generations to rekindle philosophical interest in liberal egalitarianism. Rawls's approach is to set aside as morally arbitrary everything that makes people unequal: that they have unequal talents, that some have better characters than others, that they have differing hopes and dreams, and so on. Crucially, and rather incredibly, he sets aside that some people have done more than others. All of these things, he says, are arbitrary from a moral point of view (ibid., sec. 17). Having done all this, it could hardly be news if the resulting conclusion turned out to have an egalitarian flavor. Many of Rawls's moderate and mainstream readers have been offended by Rawls's apparent denigration of everything that makes a person a person, and by what they see as egalitarianism taken to absurd extremes. But I think these reactions miss the fundamental point. The Rawlsian exercise does not surprise readers by coming to extreme yet plausible egalitarian conclusions. On the contrary, what is newsworthy is that the result is not a strict form of egalitarianism. Even if we resolve to ignore everything that

makes people unequal, and indeed everything that individuates them as persons, the door remains wide open for unequal shares. This is Rawls's signature contribution. If we understand Rawls in this way, then this essay's objective is complementary to Rawls's. That is, where Rawls argues that even if we stack the deck in favor of egalitarianism, we still find substantial room for unequal shares, I argue that even for beings as unequal in morally non-arbitrary ways as we are, there remains significant room within a pluralistic theory of justice for important elements of egalitarianism.

28 Anderson, "What Is the Point of Equality?" 321. In passing, the Crusoe image is indeed familiar, even if only in the works of liberalism's communitarian critics. In fact, the classical liberal view is that the legacy of free association is community, not atomic isolation. Humans have been organizing themselves into communities since long before there was any such thing as what we now call the state. See Loren Lomasky, "Nozick on Utopias," in David Schmidtz, ed., Robert Nozick (New York: Cambridge University Press, 2001); and Christopher Morris, An Essay on the Modern State (Cambridge: Cambridge University Press, 1998).

29 Anderson, "What Is the Point of Equality?" 321.

30 Ackerman, "On Getting What We Don't Deserve," 63.

31 Carol Rose, "Possession As the Origin of Property," University of Chicago Law Review 52, no. 1 (1985): 73–88.

32 Note that the person who establishes first possession need not acquire unconditional permanent ownership. The kind of ownership one establishes by being the first to register a patent, for example, is temporally limited. Alternatively, a usufructuary right is a particular kind of ownership that lasts only so long as the owned object is being used for its customary purpose. Thus, for example, the first person to grab a particular park bench acquires a right to use that seat for its customary purpose, but only so long as he or she occupies the bench. When the person gets up and leaves the park, the bench reverts to its previous unclaimed status.

33 Needless to say, history is filled with irreparable injustices, which often boil down to failures to respect claims of those who were there first. The ubiquitous phenomenon of respect for prior possession is mostly an in-group phenomenon. Human groups tend not to respect claims of other groups unless those other groups are capable of defending their claims in battle. So, nothing said by Rose or by me is meant to imply that prior possession has in fact been consistently respected. On the contrary, aboriginal peoples around the world consistently have been brutally subjugated. Had prior possession been respected, many of human history's most tragic episodes would not have happened.

34 Hillel Steiner, conversation with author, September 24, 2000.

35 For a state-of-the-art discussion of this issue, see John T. Sanders, "Projects and Property," in Schmidtz, ed., Robert Nozick. See also David Schmidtz, "The Institution of Property," Social Philosophy and Policy 11, no. 2 (1994): 42–62.

36 Schmidtz and Goodin, Social Welfare and Individual Responsibility, 126.

37 Ibid., 126 n.

38 Ibid., 126. Cohen considers the proletariat free to remain or not remain proletarian workers in the following sense: The proletariat is like a group of people locked in a room. There is a key, but it will work only for the first person who uses it. "Each is free to seize the key and leave. But note the conditional nature of his freedom. He is free not only because none of the others tries to get the key, but on condition that they do not (a condition which, in this story, is fulfilled)." G. A. Cohen, "The Structure of Proletarian Unfreedom," Philosophy and Public Affairs 12, no. 1 (1983): 11. Cohen's article is wonderfully provocative. It is easy to see how someone could see it as realistically describing the kind of "key to success" we have when seeking work, although I am not sure whether Cohen himself meant it this way.

39 See Tyler Cowen, "Does the Welfare State Help the Poor?" for a discussion of the relatively more accurate picture painted when we measure inequality of consumption rather than income.

40 Robert Rector and Rea S. Hederman, Income Inequality: How Census Data Misrepresent Income Distribution (Washington, DC: Heritage Foundation, 1999).

41 Edward Wolff notes that it is easy to contrive size-adjusted family-income equivalents. But my point

is that Census Bureau data — the standard source for almost any study you will read on U.S. income inequality — is not in fact corrected in this way.

42 Both figures are in Floyd Norris, "Sorry, Wrong Numbers: So Maybe It Wasn't the Economy," New York Times, December 1, 1996, sec. 4, p. 1. The first number is based on the standard consumer price index at the time. The second number was supplied by Leonard Nakamura, an economist with the Federal Reserve Bank of Philadelphia. Recent reports from the U.S. Census Bureau and the Bureau of Labor Statistics contain punishingly technical discussions of alternative ways of calculating inflation.
    Edward Wolff provides the first, negative number in Edward Wolff, "The Stagnating Fortunes of the Middle Class". In a conversation in September 2000 regarding a draft of that essay, Wolff admitted that his numbers were based upon a discredited method of adjusting for inflation. He rejected the idea that he should adjust his numbers, though, because, as he put it, "we can debate endlessly about the exact nature of the required adjustment, but it wouldn't be productive." When I noted that all he needed to do was correct his data by whatever measure he considered reasonable, and that his own best judgment would thereby be shown to be incompatible with his thesis that the middle class is stagnating, Wolff appeared indifferent.

43 "Statistical Guessing Game," Economist, December 7, 1996, 25.

44 David Gergen, "Flying in an Economic Fog," U.S. News and World Report, September 8, 1997, 104 (emphasis added). See also Michael Boskin et al., Toward a More Accurate Measure of the Cost of Living: Final Report to the Senate Finance Committee, available on-line at http://www.ssa.gov/history/reports/boskinrpt.html.

45 I borrow this metaphor from Stephen Rose, "Is Mobility in the United States Still Alive?" International Review of Applied Economics 13, no. 3 (1999): 417–36.

46 This data is from U.S. Census Bureau, Money Income in the United States: 1999 (Washington, DC: U.S. Government Printing Office, 2000), table 13.

47 This data is from ibid., table 4.

48 Michael Cox and Robert Alm, "By Our Own Bootstraps" (annual report of the Federal Reserve Bank of Dallas, published in 1995).

49 Richard Miller has referred me to a study estimating that the proportion of income inequality that is due to age inequality is 28 percent for men and 14 percent for women. See Gary Burtless, A Future of Lousy Jobs? The Changing Structure of U.S. Wages (Washington, DC: Brookings Institution, 1990). That is a substantial proportion, although I am a bit surprised, given the income statistics for 1999 just cited in the text. Given that average income for household heads aged 45 to 54 is now 2.7 times that for household heads under 25, I might guess the proportion of income inequality due to age inequality in 1999 was higher than the numbers cited by Burtless.

50 U.S. Census Bureau, Money Income in the United States: 1999, table C.

51 Martin Feldstein lists several reasons for rapid rises in income at the top of the distribution: there are more people with advanced educations; there has been an increase in entrepreneurial activity, with many new businesses being created; highly paid professionals are working longer hours; and the cost of capital is declining, reducing perceived risks of investment and entrepreneurial activity. See Martin Feldstein, "Overview" (comments delivered at symposium on income inequality hosted by the Federal Reserve Bank of Kansas City, Jackson Hole, WY, August 1998), available on-line at http://www.kc.frb.org/PUBLICAT/SYMPOS/1998/S98feldstein.pdf.

52 Cox and Alm, "By Our Own Bootstraps," 8, citing Institute for Social Research, A Panel Study of Income Dynamics (Ann Arbor, MI: Institute for Social Research, 1989). The numbers are in 1993 dollars.

53 This data is from U.S. Census Bureau, Money Income in the United States: 1999, table B–2.

54 Michael M. Weinstein, "America's Rags-to-Riches Myth," New York Times, February 18, 2000, A28.

55 U.S. Department of the Treasury, Office of Tax Analysis, "Household Income Changes over Time: Some Basic Questions and Facts," Tax Notes, August 24, 1992.

56 Cox and Alm, "By Our Own Bootstraps," 8, citing Institute for Social Research, A Panel Study of Income Dynamics.

57 Cox and Alm, "By Our Own Bootstraps," 8, citing Institute for Social Research, A Panel Study of Income Dynamics.

58 I thank Richard Miller for a helpful discussion and references, including Thomas L. Hungerford, "U.S. Income Mobility in the Seventies and Eighties," *Review of Income and Wealth* 39, no. 4 (1993): 403–17. As we would expect, Hungerford finds less movement in his seven-year studies than we see in the nine-year and sixteen-year studies by the U.S. Treasury Department and U.S. Federal Reserve Bank. Hungerford also finds that between his 1969–76 and 1979–86 studies, upward mobility decreased somewhat for the bottom five deciles, while increasing somewhat for the sixth, seventh, and eighth (ibid., 407). Isabel V. Sawhill and Daniel P. McMurrer compare several studies on income mobility and find a rough consensus that about 40 percent of those in the bottom quintile at a given point in time move up in ten years; after twenty years, about 50 percent have moved up. Isabell V. Sawhill and Daniel P. McMurrer, "Economic Mobility in the United States" (report published by the Urban Institute, December 1996), available on-line at http://www.urban.org/oppor/opp_031b.html.

59 Daniel P. McMurrer, Mark Condon, and Isabel V. Sawhill, "Intergenerational Mobility in the United States" (report published by the Urban Institute, May 1997), available on-line at http://www.urban.org/oppor/opp_4b.htm.

60 Greg Duncan, Johanne Boisjoly, and Timothy Smeeding, "How Long Does It Take for a Young Worker to Support a Family?" *NU Policy Research* 1, no. 1 (1996). *NU Policy Research* is an on-line journal; the essay is available at http://www.northwestern.edu/IPR/publications/nupr/nuprv01n1/duncan.html.

61 Ibid.

62 Weinstein, "America's Rags-to-Riches Myth."

63 Peter Gottschalk and Sheldon Danziger, "Income Mobility and Exits from Poverty of American Children, 1970–1992" (study prepared for UNICEF's International Child Development Centre, 1999), available on-line at http://ideas.uqam.ca/ideas/data/Papers/bocbocoec430.html. The paper is also in Bruce Bradbury, Stephen P. Jenkins, and John Micklewright, eds., *The Dynamics of Child Poverty in Industrialized Nations* (Cambridge: Cambridge University Press, 2001).

64 Weinstein, "America's Rags-to-Riches Myth."

65 Gottschalk and Danziger, "Income Mobility and Exits from Poverty," 4.

66 Ibid., 8.

67 U.S. Census Bureau, *Poverty in the United States: 1999* (Washington, DC: U.S. Government Printing Office, 2000), table A. The poverty threshold varies with the size of the household (and, less intuitively, with the age of the household's members). For 1999, the official poverty threshold for a household consisting of two adults under age 65 was $11,214. U.S. Census Bureau, "Poverty Thresholds: 1999," in U.S. Census Bureau, *March Current Population Survey: 1999* (Washington, DC: U.S. Government Printing Office, 2000).

68 Furthermore, being officially below the poverty threshold does not entail material hardship. There are truly suffering people out there, but in the United States they are a small percentage of the total population. According to a U.S. Department of Agriculture survey, only one-third of 1 percent of U.S. households reported a child skipping a meal due to lack of food in 1994–95. Of households *below the poverty level*, only 3.5 percent reported having a child who needed medical care or surgery but did not get it. The original sources of this data are U.S. Department of Agriculture, *Household Food Security in the United States in 1995: Summary Report of the Food Security Measurement Project* (Washington, DC: U.S. Department of Agriculture, 1997); and Centers for Disease Control, National Center for Health Statistics, *Access to Health Care* (Washington, DC: U.S. Government Printing Office, 1997). See also Robert E. Rector, Kirk A. Johnson, and Sarah E. Youssef, "The Extent of Material Hardship and Poverty in the United States," *Review of Social Economy* 57, no. 3 (1999): 351–87.

69 Robert I. Lerman, "The Impact of the Changing U.S. Family Structure on Child Poverty and Income Inequality," *Economica* 63, no. 250 (1996): 119–39.

70 Gottschalk and Danziger, "Income Mobility and Exits from Poverty," 11.

71 Ibid., table 6.

72 Ibid., table 7.

73 National Center for Health Statistics, "Births: Final Data for 1998," available on-line at http://www.cdc.gov/nchs/data/nvsr/nvsr48/nvs48_3.pdf.

74 Gottschalk and Danziger, "Income Mobility and Exits from Poverty," 9.

75 Ibid., table 4.

76 For the classic warning against equating statistical significance with significance in the ordinary sense of the term, see Deirdre N. McCloskey, *The Rhetoric of Economics*, 2d ed. (Madison: University of Wisconsin Press, 1998).

77 Ibid., 10.

78 But see the chapter on mutual aid in Schmidtz and Goodin, *Social Welfare and Individual Responsibility*.

79 Amartya Sen, *Inequality Reexamined* (Cambridge, MA: Harvard University Press, 1992), 12–13.

80 Or so I argue in the larger work (David Schmidtz, *The Elements of Justice*) of which this essay will be a part.

Chapter 40

Jean-Jacques Rousseau

DISCOURSE ON THE ORIGINS
OF INEQUALITY

Jean-Jacques Rousseau (1712–78) was a philosopher of the French Enlightenment who was influential both on Kant's development of his ethical theory and on the French Revolution. In these excerpts from his *Discourse on Inequality* (1754), Rousseau distinguishes between what he calls "natural" and "political" inequality, and argues that the latter is produced and reinforced by the structures of civil society, and in no way reflects anything natural or innate in humankind. Far from being necessary to the establishment of justice, Rousseau argues, the state and its laws "gave new fetters to the weak and new power to the rich; irretrievably destroyed natural liberty, fixed forever the laws of property and inequality; changed an artful usurpation into an irrevocable right; and for the benefit of a few ambitious individuals subjected the rest of mankind to perpetual labor, servitude, and misery."

A Dissertation on the Origin and Foundation of the Inequality of Mankind

It is of man that I have to speak; and the question I am investigating shows me that it is to men that I must address myself: for questions of this sort are not asked by those who are afraid to honour truth. I shall then confidently uphold the cause of humanity before the wise men who invite me to do so, and shall not be dissatisfied if I acquit myself in a manner worthy of my subject and of my judges.

I conceive that there are two kinds of inequality among the human species; one, which I call natural or physical, because it is established by nature, and consists in a difference of age, health, bodily strength, and the qualities of the mind or of the soul: and another, which may be called moral or political inequality, because it depends on a kind of convention, and is established, or at least authorized by the consent of men. This latter consists of the different privileges, which some men enjoy to the prejudice of others; such as that of being more rich, more honoured, more powerful or even in a position to exact obedience.

It is useless to ask what is the source of natural inequality, because that question is answered by the simple definition of the word. Again, it is still more useless to inquire whether there is any essential connection between the two inequalities; for this would be only asking, in other words, whether those who command are necessarily better than those who obey, and if strength of body or of mind, wisdom or virtue are always found in particular individuals, in proportion to their power or wealth: a question fit perhaps to

554 Jean-Jacques Rousseau

be discussed by slaves in the hearing of their masters, but highly unbecoming to reasonable and free men in search of the truth.

The subject of the present discourse, therefore, is more precisely this. To mark, in the progress of things, the moment at which right took the place of violence and nature became subject to law, and to explain by what sequence of miracles the strong came to submit to serve the weak, and the people to purchase imaginary repose at the expense of real felicity.

[...]

The First Part

[...]

If we strip this being, thus constituted, of all the supernatural gifts he may have received, and all the artificial faculties he can have acquired only by a long process; if we consider him, in a word, just as he must have come from the hands of nature, we behold in him an animal weaker than some, and less agile than others; but, taking him all round, the most advantageously organised of any. I see him satisfying his hunger at the first oak, and slaking his thirst at the first brook; finding his bed at the foot of the tree which afforded him a repast; and, with that, all his wants supplied.

While the earth was left to its natural fertility and covered with immense forests, whose trees were never mutilated by the axe, it would present on every side both sustenance and shelter for every species of animal. Men, dispersed up and down among the rest, would observe and imitate their industry, and thus attain even to the instinct of the beasts, with the advantage that, whereas every species of brutes was confined to one particular instinct, man, who perhaps has not any one peculiar to himself, would appropriate them all, and live upon most of those different foods which other animals shared among themselves; and thus would find his subsistence much more easily than any of the rest.

Accustomed from their infancy to the inclemencies of the weather and the rigour of the seasons, inured to fatigue, and forced, naked and unarmed, to defend themselves and their prey from other ferocious animals, or to escape them by flight, men would acquire a robust and almost unalterable constitution. The children, bringing with them into the world the excellent constitution of their parents, and fortifying it by the very exercises which first produced it, would thus acquire all the vigour of which the human frame is capable. Nature in this case treats them exactly as Sparta treated the children of her citizens: those who come well formed into the world she renders strong and robust, and all the rest she destroys; differing in this respect from our modern communities, in which the State, by making children a burden to their parents, kills them indiscriminately before they are born.

The body of a savage man being the only instrument he understands, he uses it for various purposes, of which ours, for want of practice, are incapable: for our industry deprives us of that force and agility, which necessity obliges him to acquire. If he had had an axe, would he have been able with his naked arm to break so large a branch from a tree? If he had had a sling, would he have been able to throw a stone with so great velocity? If he had had a ladder, would he have been so nimble in climbing a tree? If he had had a horse, would he have been himself so swift of foot? Give civilized man time to gather all his machines about him, and he will no doubt easily beat the savage; but if you would see a still more unequal contest, set them together naked and unarmed, and you will soon see the advantage of having all our forces constantly at our disposal, of being always prepared for every event, and of carrying one's self, as it were, perpetually whole and entire about one.

Hobbes contends that man is naturally intrepid, and is intent only upon attacking and fighting. Another illustrious philosopher holds the opposite, and Cumberland and Puffendorf also affirm that nothing is more timid and fearful than man in the state of nature; that he is always in a tremble, and ready to fly at the least noise or the slightest movement. This may be true of things he does not know; and I do not doubt his being terrified by every novelty that presents itself, when he neither knows the physical good or evil he may expect from it, nor can make a comparison between his own strength and the dangers he is about to encounter. Such circumstances, however, rarely occur in a state of nature, in which all things proceed in a uniform manner, and the face of the earth is not subject to those sudden and continual changes which arise from the passions and caprices of bodies of men living together. But savage man, living dispersed among other animals, and finding himself betimes in a situation to measure his strength with theirs, soon comes to compare himself with them; and, perceiving that he surpasses them more in adroitness than they surpass him in strength, learns to be no longer afraid of them. Set a bear, or a wolf, against a robust, agile, and resolute savage, as they all are, armed with stones and a good cudgel, and you will see that the danger will be at least on both sides, and that, after a few trials of this kind, wild beasts, which are not fond of attacking each other, will not be at all ready to attack man, whom they will have found to be as wild and ferocious as themselves. With regard to such animals as have really more strength than man has adroitness, he is in the same situation as all weaker animals, which notwithstanding are still able to subsist; except indeed that he has the advantage that, being equally swift of foot, and finding an almost certain place of refuge in every tree, he is at liberty to take or leave it at every encounter, and thus to fight or fly, as he chooses. Add to this that it does not appear that any animal naturally makes war on man, except in case of self-defence or excessive hunger, or betrays any of those violent antipathies, which seem to indicate that one species is intended by nature for the food of another.

[...]

With respect to sickness, I shall not repeat the vain and false declamations which most healthy people pronounce against medicine; but I shall ask if any solid observations have been made from which it may be justly concluded that, in the countries where the art of medicine is most neglected, the mean duration of man's life is less than in those where it is most cultivated. How indeed can this be the case, if we bring on ourselves more diseases than medicine can furnish remedies? The great inequality in manner of living, the extreme idleness of some, and the excessive labour of others, the easiness of exciting and gratifying our sensual appetites, the too exquisite foods of the wealthy which overheat and fill them with indigestion, and, on the other hand, the unwholesome food of the poor, often, bad as it is, insufficient for their needs, which induces them, when opportunity offers, to eat voraciously and overcharge their stomachs; all these, together with sitting up late, and excesses of every kind, immoderate transports of every passion, fatigue, mental exhaustion, the innumerable pains and anxieties inseparable from every condition of life, by which the mind of man is incessantly tormented; these are too fatal proofs that the greater part of our ills are of our own making, and that we might have avoided them nearly all by adhering to that simple, uniform and solitary manner of life which nature prescribed. If she destined man to be healthy, I venture to declare that a state of reflection is a state contrary to nature, and that a thinking man is a depraved animal. When we think of the good constitution of the savages, at least of those whom we have not ruined with our spirituous liquors, and reflect that they are troubled with hardly any disorders, save wounds and old age, we are tempted to believe that, in following the history of civil society, we shall be telling also that of human sickness.

Being subject therefore to so few causes of sickness, man, in the state of nature, can have no need of remedies, and still less of physicians: nor is the human race in this respect worse off than other animals, and it is easy to learn from hunters whether they meet with many infirm animals in the course of the chase. It is certain they frequently meet with such as carry the marks of having been considerably wounded, with many that have had bones or even limbs broken, yet have been healed without any other surgical assistance than that of time, or any other regimen than that of their ordinary life. At the same time their cures seem not to have been less perfect, for their not having been tortured by incisions, poisoned with drugs, or wasted by fasting. In short, however useful medicine, properly administered, may be among us, it is certain that, if the savage, when he is sick and left to himself, has nothing to hope but from nature, he has, on the other hand, nothing to fear but from his disease; which renders his situation often preferable to our own.

We should beware, therefore, of confounding the savage man with the men we have daily before our eyes. Nature treats all the animals left to her care with a predilection that seems to show how jealous she is of that right. The horse, the cat, the bull, and even the ass are generally of greater stature, and always more robust, and have more vigour, strength and courage, when they run wild in the forests than when bred in the stall. By becoming domesticated, they lose half these advantages; and it seems as if all our care to feed and treat them well serves only to deprave them. It is thus with man also: as he becomes sociable and a slave, he grows weak, timid and servile; his effeminate way of life totally enervates his strength and courage. To this it may be added that there is still a greater difference between savage and civilized man, than between wild and tame beasts: for men and brutes having been treated alike by nature, the several conveniences in which men indulge themselves still more than they do their beasts, are so many additional causes of their deeper degeneracy.

[. . .]

I see nothing in any animal but an ingenious machine, to which nature hath given senses to wind itself up, and to guard itself, to a certain degree, against anything that might tend to disorder or destroy it. I perceive exactly the same things in the human machine, with this difference, that in the operations of the brute, nature is the sole agent, whereas man has some share in his own operations, in his character as a free agent. The one chooses and refuses by instinct, the other from an act of free-will: hence the brute cannot deviate from the rule prescribed to it, even when it would be advantageous for it to do so; and, on the contrary, man frequently deviates from such rules to his own prejudice. Thus a pigeon would be starved to death by the side of a dish of the choicest meats, and a cat on a heap of fruit or grain; though it is certain that either might find nourishment in the foods which it thus rejects with disdain, did it think of trying them. Hence it is that dissolute men run into excesses, which bring on fevers and death; because the mind depraves the senses, and the will continues to speak when nature is silent.

Every animal has ideas, since it has senses; it even combines those ideas in a certain degree; and it is only in degree that man differs, in this respect, from the brute. Some philosophers have even maintained that there is a greater difference between one man and another than between some men and some beasts. It is not, therefore, so much the understanding that constitutes the specific difference between the man and the brute, as the human quality of free-agency. Nature lays her commands on every animal, and the brute obeys her voice. Man receives the same impulsion, but at the same time knows himself at liberty to acquiesce or resist: and it is particularly in his consciousness of this liberty that the spirituality of his soul is displayed. For physics may explain, in some measure, the mechanism of the senses and the formation of ideas; but in the power of willing or rather of choosing, and in the feeling of this power, nothing is to be found but acts which are purely spiritual and wholly inexplicable by the laws of mechanism.

However, even if the difficulties attending all these questions should still leave room for difference in this respect between men and brutes, there is another very specific quality which distinguishes them, and which will admit of no dispute. This is the faculty of self-improvement, which, by the help of circumstances, gradually develops all the rest of our faculties, and is inherent in the species as in the individual: whereas a brute is, at the end of a few months, all he will ever be during his whole life, and his species, at the end of a thousand years, exactly what it was the first year of that thousand. Why is man alone liable to grow into a dotard? Is it not because he returns, in this, to his primitive state; and that, while the brute, which has acquired nothing and has therefore nothing to lose, still retains the force of instinct, man, who loses, by age or accident, all that his *perfectibility* had enabled him to gain, falls by this means lower than the brutes themselves? It would be melancholy, were we forced to admit that this distinctive and almost unlimited faculty is the source of all human misfortunes; that it is this which, in time, draws man out of his original state, in which he would have spent his days insensibly in peace and innocence; that it is this faculty, which, successively producing in different ages his discoveries and his errors, his vices and his virtues, makes him at length a tyrant both over himself and over nature. It would be shocking to be obliged to regard as a benefactor the man who first suggested to the Oroonoko Indians the use of the boards they apply to the temples of their children, which secure to them some part at least of their imbecility and original happiness.

Savage man, left by nature solely to the direction of instinct, or rather indemnified for what he may lack by faculties capable at first of supplying its place, and afterwards of raising him much above it, must accordingly begin with purely animal functions: thus seeing and feeling must be his first condition, which would be common to him and all other animals. To will, and not to will, to desire and to fear, must be the first, and almost the only operations of his soul, till new circumstances occasion new developments of his faculties.

Whatever moralists may hold, the human understanding is greatly indebted to the passions, which, it is universally allowed, are also much indebted to the understanding. It is by the activity of the passions that our reason is improved; for we desire knowledge only because we wish to enjoy; and it is impossible to conceive any reason why a person who has neither fears nor desires should give himself the trouble of reasoning. The passions, again, originate in our wants, and their progress depends on that of our knowledge; for we cannot desire or fear anything, except from the idea we have of it, or from the simple impulse of nature. Now savage man, being destitute of every species of intelligence, can have no passions save those of the latter kind: his desires never go beyond his physical wants. The only goods he recognizes in the universe are food, a female, and sleep: the only evils he fears are pain and hunger. I say pain, and not death: for no animal can know what it is to die; the knowledge of death and its terrors being one of the first acquisitions made by man in departing from an animal state.

[. . .]

But be the origin of language and society what they may, it may be at least inferred, from the little care which nature has taken to unite mankind by mutual wants, and to facilitate the use of speech, that she has contributed little to make them sociable, and has put little of her own into all they have done to create such bonds of union. It is in fact impossible to conceive why, in a state of nature, one man should stand more in need of the assistance of another, than a monkey or a wolf of the assistance of another of its kind: or, granting that he did, what motives could induce that other to assist him; or, even then, by what means they could agree about the conditions. I know it is incessantly repeated that man would in such a state have been the most miserable of creatures; and indeed, if it be true, as I think I have proved, that he must have lived many ages, before he could have either desire or an opportunity of emerging from it, this would only be an accusation against nature, and not against the being which she had thus unhappily constituted. But as I understand the word *miserable*, it either has no meaning at all, or else signifies only a painful privation of something, or a state of suffering either in body or soul. I should be glad to have explained to me, what kind of misery a free being, whose heart is at ease and whose body is in health, can possibly suffer. I would ask also, whether a social or a natural life is most likely to become insupportable to those who enjoy it. We see around us hardly a creature in civil society, who does not lament his existence: we even see many deprive themselves of as much of it as they can, and laws human and divine together can hardly put a stop to the disorder. I ask, if it was ever known that a savage took it into his head, when at liberty, to complain of life or to make away with himself. Let us therefore judge, with less vanity, on which side the real misery is found. On the other hand, nothing could be more unhappy than savage man, dazzled by science, tormented by his passions, and reasoning about a state different from his own. It appears that Providence most wisely determined that the faculties, which he potentially possessed, should develop themselves only as occasion offered to exercise them, in order that they might not be superfluous or perplexing to him, by appearing before their time, nor slow and useless when the need for them arose. In instinct alone, he had all he required for living in the state of nature; and with a developed understanding he has only just enough to support life in society.

It appears, at first view, that men in a state of nature, having no moral relations or determinate obligations one with another, could not be either good or bad, virtuous or vicious; unless we take these terms in a physical sense, and call, in an individual, those qualities vices which may be injurious to his preservation, and those virtues which contribute to it; in which case, he would have to be accounted most virtuous, who put least check on the pure impulses of nature. But without deviating from the ordinary sense of the words, it will be proper to suspend the judgment we might be led to form on such a state, and be on our guard against our prejudices, till we have weighed the matter in the scales of impartiality, and seen whether virtues or vices preponderate among civilized men; and whether their virtues do them more good than their vices do harm; till we have discovered, whether the progress of the sciences sufficiently indemnifies them for the mischiefs they do one another, in proportion as they are better informed of the good they ought to do; or whether they would not be, on the whole, in a much happier condition if they had nothing to fear or to hope from any one, than as they are, subjected to universal dependence, and obliged to take everything from those who engage to give them nothing in return.

Above all, let us not conclude, with Hobbes, that because man has no idea of goodness, he must be naturally wicked; that he is vicious because he does not know virtue; that he always refuses to do his fellow-creatures services which he does not think they have a right to demand; or that by virtue of the right he truly claims to everything he needs, he foolishly imagines himself the sole proprietor of the whole universe. Hobbes had seen clearly the defects of all the modern definitions of natural right: but the consequences which he deduces from his own show that he understands it in an equally false sense. In reasoning on the principles he lays down, he ought to have said that the state of nature, being that in which the care for our own preservation is the least prejudicial to that of others, was consequently the best calculated to promote peace, and the most suitable for mankind. He does say the exact opposite, in consequence of having improperly admitted, as a part of savage man's care for self-preservation, the gratification of a multitude of passions which are the work of society, and have made laws necessary. A bad man, he says, is a robust child. But it remains to be proved whether man in a state of nature is this robust child: and, should we grant that he is, what would he infer? Why truly, that if this man, when robust and strong, were dependent on others as he is when feeble, there is no extravagance he would not be guilty of; that he would beat his mother when she was too slow in giving him her breast; that he would strangle one of his younger brothers, if he should be troublesome to him, or bite the arm of another, if he put him to any inconvenience. But that man in the state of nature is both strong and dependent involves two contrary suppositions. Man is weak when he is dependent, and is his own master before he comes to be strong. Hobbes did not reflect that the same cause, which prevents a savage from making use of his reason, as our jurists hold, prevents him also from abusing his faculties, as Hobbes himself allows: so that it may be justly said that savages are not bad merely because they do not know what it is to be good: for it is neither the development of the understanding nor the restraint of law that hinders them from doing ill; but the peacefulness of their passions, and their ignorance of vice: *tanto plus in illis proficit vitiorum ignoratio, quam in his cognitio virtutis.*[1]

There is another principle which has escaped Hobbes; which, having been bestowed on mankind, to moderate, on certain occasions, the impetuosity of egoism, or, before its birth, the desire of self-preservation, tempers the ardour with which he pursues his own welfare, by an innate repugnance at seeing a fellow-creature suffer.[2] I think I need not fear contradiction in holding man to be possessed of the only natural virtue, which could not be denied him by the most violent detractor of human virtue. I am speaking of compassion, which is a disposition suitable to creatures so weak and subject to so many evils as we certainly are: by so much the more universal and useful to mankind, as it comes before any kind of reflection; and at the same time so natural, that the very brutes themselves sometimes give evident proofs of it.

[...]

It is reason that engenders self-respect, and reflection that confirms it: it is reason which turns man's mind back upon itself, and divides him from everything that could disturb or afflict him. It is philosophy that isolates him, and bids

him say, at sight of the misfortunes of others: "Perish if you will, I am secure." Nothing but such general evils as threaten the whole community can disturb the tranquil sleep of the philosopher, or tear him from his bed. A murder may with impunity be committed under his window; he has only to put his hands to his ears and argue a little with himself, to prevent nature, which is shocked within him, from identifying itself with the unfortunate sufferer. Uncivilized man has not this admirable talent; and for want of reason and wisdom, is always foolishly ready to obey the first promptings of humanity. It is the populace that flocks together at riots and street-brawls, while the wise man prudently makes off. It is the mob and the market-women, who part the combatants, and hinder gentle-folks from cutting one another's throats.

It is then certain that compassion is a natural feeling, which, by moderating the violence of love of self in each individual, contributes to the preservation of the whole species. It is this compassion that hurries us without reflection to the relief of those who are in distress: it is this which in a state of nature supplies the place of laws, morals and virtues, with the advantage that none are tempted to disobey its gentle voice: it is this which will always prevent a sturdy savage from robbing a weak child or a feeble old man of the sustenance they may have with pain and difficulty acquired, if he sees a possibility of providing for himself by other means: it is this which, instead of inculcating that sublime maxim of rational justice, *Do to others as you would have them do unto you,* inspires all men with that other maxim of natural goodness, much less perfect indeed, but perhaps more useful; *Do good to yourself with as little evil as possible to others.* In a word, it is rather in this natural feeling than in any subtle arguments that we must look for the cause of that repugnance, which every man would experience in doing evil, even independently of the maxims of education. Although it might belong to Socrates and other minds of the like craft to acquire virtue by reason, the human race would long since have ceased to be, had its preservation depended only on the reasonings of the individuals composing it.

[...]

The Second Part

The first man who, having enclosed a piece of ground, bethought himself of saying *This is mine*, and found people simple enough to believe him, was the real founder of civil society. From how many crimes, wars and murders, from how many horrors and misfortunes might not any one have saved mankind, by pulling up the stakes, or filling up the ditch, and crying to his fellows, "Beware of listening to this impostor; you are undone if you once forget that the fruits of the earth belong to us all, and the earth itself to nobody." But there is great probability that things had then already come to such a pitch, that they could no longer continue as they were; for the idea of property depends on many prior ideas, which could only be acquired successively, and cannot have been formed all at once in the human mind. Mankind must have made very considerable progress, and acquired considerable knowledge and industry which they must also have transmitted and increased from age to age, before they arrived at this last point of the state of nature. Let us then go farther back, and endeavour to unify under a single point of view that slow succession of events and discoveries in the most natural order.

Man's first feeling was that of his own existence, and his first care that of self-preservation. The produce of the earth furnished him with all he needed, and instinct told him how to use it. Hunger and other appetites made him at various times experience various modes of existence; and among these was one which urged him to propagate his species – a blind propensity that, having nothing to do with the heart, produced a merely animal act. The want once gratified, the two sexes knew each other no more; and even the offspring was nothing to its mother, as soon as it could do without her.

Such was the condition of infant man; the life of an animal limited at first to mere sensations, and hardly profiting by the gifts nature bestowed on him, much less capable of entertaining a thought of forcing anything from her. But difficulties soon presented themselves, and it became necessary to learn how to surmount them: the height of the trees, which prevented him from gathering their fruits, the competition of other animals desirous of the same fruits, and the ferocity of those who needed them for their own preservation, all obliged him to apply himself to bodily exercises. He had to be active, swift of foot, and vigorous in fight. Natural weapons, stones and sticks, were easily found: he learnt to surmount the obstacles of nature, to contend in case of necessity with other animals, and to dispute for the means of subsistence even with other men, or to indemnify himself for what he was forced to give up to a stronger.

In proportion as the human race grew more numerous, men's cares increased. The difference of soils, climates and seasons, must have introduced some differences into their manner of living. Barren years, long and sharp winters, scorching summers which parched the fruits of the earth, must have demanded a new industry. On the seashore and the banks of rivers, they invented the hook and line, and became fishermen and eaters of fish. In the forests they made bows and arrows, and became huntsmen and warriors. In cold countries they clothed themselves with the skins of the beasts they had slain. The lightning, a volcano, or some lucky chance acquainted them with fire, a new resource against the rigours of winter: they next learned how to preserve this element, then how to reproduce it, and finally how to prepare with it the flesh of animals which before they had eaten raw.

This repeated relevance of various beings to himself, and one to another, would naturally give rise in the human mind to the perceptions of certain relations between them. Thus the relations which we denote by the terms, great, small, strong, weak, swift, slow, fearful, bold, and the like, almost insensibly compared at need, must have at length produced in him a kind of reflection, or rather a mechanical prudence, which would indicate to him the precautions most necessary to his security.

The new intelligence which resulted from this development increased his superiority over other animals, by making him sensible of it. He would now endeavour, therefore, to ensnare them, would play them a thousand tricks, and though many of them might surpass him in swiftness or in strength, would in time become the master of some and the scourge of others. Thus, the first time he looked into himself, he felt the first emotion of pride; and, at a time when he scarce knew how to distinguish the different orders of beings, by looking upon his species as of the highest order, he prepared the way for assuming pre-eminence as an individual.

Other men, it is true, were not then to him what they now are to us, and he had no greater intercourse with them than with other animals; yet they were not neglected in his observations. The conformities, which he would in time discover between them, and between himself and his female, led him to judge of others which were not then perceptible; and finding that they all behaved as he himself would have done in like circumstances, he naturally inferred that their manner of thinking and acting was altogether in conformity with his own. This important truth, once deeply impressed on his mind, must have induced him, from an intuitive feeling more certain and much more rapid than any kind of reasoning, to pursue the rules of conduct, which he had best observe towards them, for his own security and advantage.

Taught by experience that the love of well-being is the sole motive of human actions, he found himself in a position to distinguish the few cases, in which mutual interest might justify him in relying upon the assistance of his fellows; and also the still fewer cases in which a conflict of interests might give cause to suspect them. In the former case, he joined in the same herd with

them, or at most in some kind of loose association, that laid no restraint on its members, and lasted no longer than the transitory occasion that formed it. In the latter case, every one sought his own private advantage, either by open force, if he thought himself strong enough, or by address and cunning, if he felt himself the weaker.

In this manner, men may have insensibly acquired some gross ideas of mutual undertakings, and of the advantages of fulfilling them: that is, just so far as their present and apparent interest was concerned: for they were perfect strangers to foresight, and were so far from troubling themselves about the distant future, that they hardly thought of the morrow. If a deer was to be taken, every one saw that, in order to succeed, he must abide faithfully by his post: but if a hare happened to come within the reach of any one of them, it is not to be doubted that he pursued it without scruple, and, having seized his prey, cared very little, if by so doing he caused his companions to miss theirs.

[. . .]

Everything now begins to change its aspect. Men, who have up to now been roving in the woods, by taking to a more settled manner of life, come gradually together, form separate bodies, and at length in every country arises a distinct nation, united in character and manners, not by regulations or laws, but by uniformity of life and food, and the common influence of climate. Permanent neighbourhood could not fail to produce, in time, some connection between different families. Among young people of opposite sexes, living in neighbouring huts, the transient commerce required by nature soon led, through mutual intercourse, to another kind not less agreeable, and more permanent. Men began now to take the difference between objects into account, and to make comparisons; they acquired imperceptibly the ideas of beauty and merit, which soon gave rise to feelings of preference. In consequence of seeing each other often, they could not do without seeing each other constantly. A tender and pleasant feeling insinuated itself into their souls, and the least opposition turned it into an impetuous fury: with love arose jealousy; discord triumphed, and human blood was sacrificed to the gentlest of all passions.

As ideas and feelings succeeded one another, and heart and head were brought into play, men continued to lay aside their original wildness; their private connections became every day more intimate as their limits extended. They accustomed themselves to assemble before their huts round a large tree; singing and dancing, the true offspring of love and leisure, became the amusement, or rather the occupation, of men and women thus assembled together with nothing else to do. Each one began to consider the rest, and to wish to be considered in turn; and thus a value came to be attached to public esteem. Whoever sang or danced best, whoever was the handsomest, the strongest, the most dexterous, or the most eloquent, came to be of most consideration; and this was the first step towards inequality, and at the same time towards vice. From these first distinctions arose on the one side vanity and contempt and on the other shame and envy: and the fermentation caused by these new leavens ended by producing combinations fatal to innocence and happiness.

As soon as men began to value one another, and the idea of consideration had got a footing in the mind, every one put in his claim to it, and it became impossible to refuse it to any with impunity. Hence arose the first obligations of civility even among savages; and every intended injury became an affront; because, besides the hurt which might result from it, the party injured was certain to find in it a contempt for his person, which was often more insupportable than the hurt itself.

Thus, as every man punished the contempt shown him by others, in proportion to his opinion of himself, revenge became terrible, and men bloody and cruel. This is precisely the state reached by most of the savage nations known to us: and it is for want of having made a proper distinction in our ideas, and see how very far

they already are from the state of nature, that so many writers have hastily concluded that man is naturally cruel, and requires civil institutions to make him more mild; whereas nothing is more gentle than man in his primitive state, as he is placed by nature at an equal distance from the stupidity of brutes, and the fatal ingenuity of civilized man. Equally confined by instinct and reason to the sole care of guarding himself against the mischiefs which threaten him, he is restrained by natural compassion from doing any injury to others, and is not led to do such a thing even in return for injuries received. For, according to the axiom of the wise Locke, *There can be no injury, where there is no property*.

[. . .]

In this state of affairs, equality might have been sustained, had the talents of individuals been equal, and had, for example, the use of iron and the consumption of commodities always exactly balanced each other; but, as there was nothing to preserve this balance, it was soon disturbed; the strongest did most work; the most skilful turned his labour to best account; the most ingenious devised methods of diminishing his labour: the husbandman wanted more iron, or the smith more corn, and, while both laboured equally, the one gained a great deal by his work, while the other could hardly support himself. Thus natural inequality unfolds itself insensibly with that of combination, and the difference between men, developed by their different circumstances, becomes more sensible and permanent in its effects, and begins to have an influence, in the same proportion, over the lot of individuals.

[. . .]

Behold then all human faculties developed, memory and imagination in full play, egoism interested, reason active, and the mind almost at the highest point of its perfection. Behold all the natural qualities in action, the rank and condition of every man assigned him; not merely his share of property and his power to serve or injure others, but also his wit, beauty, strength or skill, merit or talents: and these being the only qualities capable of commanding respect, it soon became necessary to possess or to affect them.

It now became the interest of men to appear what they really were not. To be and to seem became two totally different things; and from this distinction sprang insolent pomp and cheating trickery, with all the numerous vices that go in their train. On the other hand, free and independent as men were before, they were now, in consequence of a multiplicity of new wants, brought into subjection, as it were, to all nature, and particularly to one another; and each became in some degree a slave even in becoming the master of other men: if rich, they stood in need of the services of others; if poor, of their assistance; and even a middle condition did not enable them to do without one another. Man must now, therefore, have been perpetually employed in getting others to interest themselves in his lot, and in making them, apparently at least, if not really, find their advantage in promoting his own. Thus he must have been sly and artful in his behaviour to some, and imperious and cruel to others; being under a kind of necessity to ill-use all the persons of whom he stood in need, when he could not frighten them into compliance, and did not judge it his interest to be useful to them. Insatiable ambition, the thirst of raising their respective fortunes, not so much from real want as from the desire to surpass others, inspired all men with a vile propensity to injure one another, and with a secret jealousy, which is the more dangerous, as it puts on the mask of benevolence, to carry its point with greater security. In a word, there arose rivalry and competition on the one hand, and conflicting interests on the other, together with a secret desire on both of profiting at the expense of others. All these evils were the first effects of property, and the inseparable attendants of growing inequality.

Before the invention of signs to represent riches, wealth could hardly consist in anything but lands and cattle, the only real possessions men can have. But, when inheritances so increased in number and extent as to occupy the whole of the land, and to border on one another, one man could aggrandize himself only at the expense of another; at the same time the supernumeraries, who had been too weak or too indolent to make such acquisitions, and had grown poor without sustaining any loss, because, while they saw everything change around them, they remained still the same, were obliged to receive their subsistence, or steal it, from the rich; and this soon bred, according to their different characters, dominion and slavery, or violence and rapine. The wealthy, on their part, had no sooner begun to taste the pleasure of command, than they disdained all others, and, using their old slaves to acquire new, thought of nothing but subduing and enslaving their neighbors; like ravenous wolves, which, having once tasted human flesh, despise every other food and thenceforth seek only men to devour.

Thus, as the most powerful or the most miserable considered their might or misery as a kind of right to the possessions of others, equivalent, in their opinion, to that of property, the destruction of equality was attended by the most terrible disorders. Usurpations by the rich, robbery by the poor, and the unbridled passions of both, suppressed the cries of natural compassion and the still feeble voice of justice, and filled men with avarice, ambition and vice. Between the title of the strongest and that of the first occupier, there arose perpetual conflicts, which never ended but in battles and bloodshed. The new-born state of society thus gave rise to a horrible state of war; men thus harassed and depraved were no longer capable of retracing their steps or renouncing the fatal acquisitions they had made, but, labouring by the abuse of the faculties which do them honour, merely to their own confusion, brought themselves to the brink of ruin.

Attonitus novitate mali, divesque miserque,
Effugere optat opes; et quæ modo voverat odit.[3]

It is impossible that men should not at length have reflected on so wretched a situation, and on the calamities that overwhelmed them. The rich, in particular, must have felt how much they suffered by a constant state of war, of which they bore all the expense; and in which, though all risked their lives, they alone risked their property. Besides, however speciously they might disguise their usurpations, they knew that they were founded on precarious and false titles; so that, if others took from them by force what they themselves had gained by force, they would have no reason to complain. Even those who had been enriched by their own industry, could hardly base their proprietorship on better claims. It was in vain to repeat, "I built this well; I gained this spot by my industry." Who gave you your standing, it might be answered, and what right have you to demand payment of us for doing what we never asked you to do? Do you not know that numbers of your fellow-creatures are starving, for want of what you have too much of? You ought to have had the express and universal consent of mankind, before appropriating more of the common subsistence than you needed for your own maintenance. Destitute of valid reasons to justify and sufficient strength to defend himself, able to crush individuals with ease, but easily crushed himself by a troop of bandits, one against all, and incapable, on account of mutual jealousy, of joining with his equals against numerous enemies united by the common hope of plunder, the rich man, thus urged by necessity, conceived at length the profoundest plan that ever entered the mind of man: this was to employ in his favour the forces of those who attacked him, to make allies of his adversaries, to inspire them with different maxims, and to give them other institutions as favourable to himself as the law of nature was unfavourable.

With this view, after having represented to his neighbours the horror of a situation which armed every man against the rest, and made their possessions as burdensome to them as their wants, and in which no safety could be expected either in riches or in poverty, he readily devised plausible arguments to make them close with his design. "Let us join," said he:

> to guard the weak from oppression, to restrain the ambitious, and secure to every man the possession of what belongs to him: let us institute rules of justice and peace, to which all without exception may be obliged to conform; rules that may in some measure make amends for the caprices of fortune, by subjecting equally the powerful and the weak to the observance of reciprocal obligations. Let us, in a word, instead of turning our forces against ourselves, collect them in a supreme power which may govern us by wise laws, protect and defend all the members of the association, repulse their common enemies, and maintain eternal harmony among us.

Far fewer words to this purpose would have been enough to impose on men so barbarous and easily seduced; especially as they had too many disputes among themselves to do without arbitrators, and too much ambition and avarice to go long without masters. All ran headlong to their chains, in hopes of securing their liberty; for they had just wit enough to perceive the advantages of political institutions, without experience enough to enable them to foresee the dangers. The most capable of foreseeing the dangers were the very persons who expected to benefit by them; and even the most prudent judged it not inexpedient to sacrifice one part of their freedom to ensure the rest; as a wounded man has his arm cut off to save the rest of his body.

Such was, or may well have been, the origin of society and law, which bound new fetters on the poor, and gave new powers to the rich; which irretrievably destroyed natural liberty, eternally fixed the law of property and inequality, converted clever usurpation into unalterable right, and, for the advantage of a few ambitious individuals, subjected all mankind to perpetual labour, slavery and wretchedness. It is easy to see how the establishment of one community made that of all the rest necessary, and how, in order to make head against united forces, the rest of mankind had to unite in turn. Societies soon multiplied and spread over the face of the earth, till hardly a corner of the world was left in which a man could escape the yoke, and withdraw his head from beneath the sword which he saw perpetually hanging over him by a thread. Civil right having thus become the common rule among the members of each community, the law of nature maintained its place only between different communities, where, under the name of the right of nations, it was qualified by certain tacit conventions, in order to make commerce practicable, and serve as a substitute for natural compassion, which lost, when applied to societies, almost all the influence it had over individuals, and survived no longer except in some great cosmopolitan spirits, who, breaking down the imaginary barriers that separate different peoples, follow the example of our Sovereign Creator, and include the whole human race in their benevolence.

But bodies politic, remaining thus in a state of nature among themselves, presently experienced the inconveniences which had obliged individuals to forsake it; for this state became still more fatal to these great bodies than it had been to the individuals of whom they were composed. Hence arose national wars, battles, murders, and reprisals, which shock nature and outrage reason; together with all those horrible prejudices which class among the virtues the honour of shedding human blood. The most distinguished men hence learned to consider cutting each other's throats a duty; at length men massacred their fellow-creatures by thousands without so much as knowing why, and committed more murders in a single day's fighting, and more violent outrages in the sack of a single town, than were committed in the state of nature during whole ages over the whole earth. Such were the first effects which we can see to have followed the division of mankind into different communities. But let us return to their institutions.

[. . .]

I have endeavoured to trace the origin and progress of inequality, and the institution and abuse of political societies, as far as these are capable of being deduced from the nature of man merely by the light of reason, and independently of those sacred dogmas which give the sanction of divine right to sovereign authority. It follows from this survey that, as there is hardly any inequality in the state of nature, all the inequality which now prevails owes its strength and growth to the development of our faculties and the advance of the human mind, and becomes at last permanent and legitimate by the establishment of property and laws. Secondly, it follows that moral inequality, authorized by positive right alone, clashes with natural right, whenever it is not proportionate to physical inequality; a distinction which sufficiently determines what we ought to think of that species of inequality which prevails in all civilized, countries; since it is plainly contrary to the law of nature, however defined, that children should command old men, fools wise men, and that the privileged few should gorge themselves with superfluities, while the starving multitude are in want of the bare necessities of life.

Notes

1 Justin, Hist. ii. 2. So much more does the ignorance of vice profit the one sort than the knowledge of virtue the other.
2 http://www.constitution.org/jjr/ineq_03.htm#03
3 Ovid, *Metamorphoses*, xi. 127.
   Both rich and poor, shocked at their new-found ills,
   Would fly from wealth, and lose what they had sought.

Chapter 41

Catharine MacKinnon

DIFFERENCE AND DOMINANCE

Catharine MacKinnon (1946–) is a feminist lawyer, activist, and professor of law at the University of Michigan, known especially for her work on sexual harassment and pornography. In this essay (from 1984), MacKinnon criticizes what she calls the "difference approach" to thinking about gender inequality, and argues that we should understand inequality instead in terms of power and dominance.

What is a gender question a question of? What is an inequality question a question of? These two questions underlie applications of the equality principle to issues of gender, but they are seldom explicitly asked. I think it speaks to the way gender has structured thought and perception that mainstream legal and moral theory tacitly gives the same answer to them both: these are questions of sameness and difference. The mainstream doctrine of the law of sex discrimination that results is, in my view, largely responsible for the fact that sex equality law has been so utterly ineffective at getting women what we need and are socially prevented from having on the basis of a condition of birth: a chance at productive lives of reasonable physical security, self-expression, individuation, and minimal respect and dignity. Here I expose the sameness/difference theory of sex equality, briefly show how it dominates sex discrimination law and policy and underlies its discontents, and propose an alternative that might do something.

According to the approach to sex equality that has dominated politics, law, and social perception, equality is an equivalence, not a distinction, and sex is a distinction. The legal mandate of equal treatment – which is both a systemic norm and a specific legal doctrine – becomes a matter of treating likes alike and unlikes unlike; and the sexes are defined as such by their mutual unlikeness. Put another way, gender is socially constructed as difference epistemologically; sex discrimination law bounds gender equality by difference doctrinally. A built-in tension exists between this concept of equality, which presupposes sameness, and this concept of sex, which presupposes difference. Sex equality thus becomes a contradiction in terms, something of an oxymoron, which may suggest why we are having such a difficult time getting it.

Upon further scrutiny, two alternate paths to equality for women emerge within this dominant approach, paths that roughly follow the lines of this tension. The leading one is: be the same as men. This path is termed gender neutrality doctrinally and the single standard philosophically. It is testimony to how substance gets itself up as form in law that this rule is considered formal equality. Because this approach mirrors the ideology of the social world, it is considered abstract, meaning transparent of substance; also for this reason it is considered not only to be the standard, but *a* standard at all. It is so far the leading rule that the words "equal to" are code for, equivalent to, the words "the same as" − referent for both unspecified.

To women who want equality yet find that you are different, the doctrine provides an alternate route: be different from men. This equal recognition of difference is termed the special benefit rule or special protection rule legally, the double standard philosophically. It is in rather bad odor. Like pregnancy, which always calls it up, it is something of a doctrinal embarrassment. Considered an exception to true equality and not really a rule of law at all, this is the one place where the law of sex discrimination admits it is recognizing something substantive. Together with the Bona Fide Occupational Qualification (BFOQ), the unique physical characteristic exception under Employment Rights Act (ERA, 1996) policy, compensatory legislation, and sex-conscious relief in particular litigation, affirmative action is thought to live here.[1]

The philosophy underlying the difference approach is that sex *is* a difference, a division, a distinction, beneath which lies a stratum of human commonality, sameness. The moral thrust of the sameness branch of the doctrine is to make normative rules conform to this empirical reality by granting women access to what men have access to: to the extent that women are no different from men, we deserve what they have. The differences branch, which is generally seen as patronizing but necessary to avoid absurdity, exists to value or compensate women for what we are or have become distinctively as women (by which is meant, unlike men) under existing conditions.

My concern is not with which of these paths to sex equality is preferable in the long run or more appropriate to any particular issue, although

most discourse on sex discrimination revolves about these questions as if that were all there is. My point is logically prior: to treat issues of sex equality as issues of sameness and difference *is to take a particular approach*. I call this the difference approach because it is obsessed with the sex difference. The main theme in the fugue is "we're the same, we're the same, we're the same." The counterpoint theme (in a higher register) is "but we're different, but we're different, but we're different." Its underlying story is: on the first day, difference was; on the second day, a division was created upon it; on the third day, irrational instances of dominance arose. Division may be rational or irrational. Dominance either seems or is justified. Difference is.

There is a politics to this. Concealed is the substantive way in which man has become the measure of all things. Under the sameness standard, women are measured according to our correspondence with man, our equality judged by our proximity to his measure. Under the difference standard, we are measured according to our lack of correspondence with him, our womanhood judged by our distance from his measure. Gender neutrality is thus simply the male standard, and the special protection rule is simply the female standard, but do not be deceived: masculinity, or maleness, is the referent for both. Think about it like those anatomy models in medical school. A male body is the human body; all those extra things women have are studied in obstetrics and gynecology. It truly is a situation in which more is less. Approaching sex discrimination in this way − as if sex questions are difference questions and equality questions are sameness questions − provides two ways for the law to hold women to a male standard and call that sex equality.

Having been very hard on the difference answer to sex equality questions, I should say that it takes up a very important problem: how to get women access to everything we have been excluded from, while also valuing everything that women are or have been allowed to become or have developed as a consequence of our struggle either not to be excluded from most of life's pursuits or to be taken seriously under the terms that have been permitted to be our terms. It negotiates what we have managed in relation to men. Legally articulated as the need to conform normative standards to existing reality, the strongest doctrinal expression of its sameness idea would prohibit taking gender into account in any way.

Its guiding impulse is: we're as good as you. Anything you can do, we can do. Just get out of the way. I have to confess a sincere affection for this approach. It has gotten women some access to employment[2] and education,[3] the public pursuits, including academic,[4] professional,[5] and blue-collar work;[6] the military;[7] and more than nominal access to athletics.[8] It has moved to change the dead ends that were all we were seen as good for and has altered what passed for women's lack of physical training, which was really serious training in passivity and enforced weakness. It makes you want to cry sometimes to know that it has had to be a mission for many women just to be permitted to do the work of this society, to have the dignity of doing jobs a lot of other people don't even want to do.

The issue of including women in the military draft[9] has presented the sameness answer to the sex equality question in all its simple dignity and complex equivocality. As a citizen, I should have to risk being killed just like you. The consequences of my resistance to this risk should count like yours. The undercurrent is: what's the matter, don't you want me to learn to kill . . . just like you? Sometimes I see this as a dialogue between women in the afterlife. The feminist says to the soldier, "we fought for your equality." The soldier says to the feminist, "oh, no, *we* fought for *your* equality."

Feminists have this nasty habit of counting bodies and refusing not to notice their gender. As applied, the sameness standard has mostly gotten men the benefit of those few things women have historically had – for all the good

they did us. Almost every sex discrimination case that has been won at the Supreme Court level has been brought by a man.[10] Under the rule of gender neutrality, the law of custody and divorce has been transformed, giving men an equal chance at custody of children and at alimony.[11] Men often look like better "parents" under gender-neutral rules like level of income and presence of nuclear family, because men make more money and (as they say) initiate the building of family units.[12] In effect, they get preferred because society advantages them before they get into court, and law is prohibited from taking that preference into account because that would mean taking gender into account. The group realities that make women more in need of alimony are not permitted to matter, because only individual factors, gender-neutrally considered, may matter. So the fact that women will live their lives, as individuals, as members of the group women, with women's chances in a sex-discriminatory society, may not count, or else it is sex discrimination. The equality principle in this guise mobilizes the idea that the way to get things for women is to get them for men. Men have gotten them. Have women? We still have not got equal pay,[13] or equal work,[14] far less equal pay for equal work,[15] and we are close to losing separate enclaves like women's schools through this approach.[16]

Here is why. In reality, which this approach is not long on because it is liberal idealism talking to itself, virtually every quality that distinguishes men from women is already affirmatively compensated in this society. Men's physiology defines most sports,[17] their needs define auto and health insurance coverage, their socially designed biographies define workplace expectations and successful career patterns, their perspectives and concerns define quality in scholarship, their experiences and obsessions define merit, their objectification of life defines art, their military service defines citizenship, their presence defines family, their inability to get along with each other – their wars and rulerships – defines history, their image defines god, and their genitals define sex. For each of their differences from women, what amounts to an affirmative action plan is in effect, otherwise known as the structure and values of American society. But whenever women are, by this standard, "different" from men and insist on not having it held against us, whenever a difference is used to keep us second class and we refuse to smile about it, equality law has a paradigm trauma and it's crisis time for the doctrine.

What this doctrine has apparently meant by sex inequality is not what happens to us. The law of sex discrimination that has resulted seems to be looking only for those ways women are kept down that have *not* wrapped themselves up as a difference – whether original, imposed, or imagined. Start with original: what to do about the fact that women actually have an ability men still lack, gestating children in utero. Pregnancy therefore is a difference. Difference doctrine says it is sex discrimination to give women what we need, because only women need it. It is not sex discrimination not to give women what we need because then only women will not get what we need.[18] Move into imposed: what to do about the fact that most women are segregated into low-paying jobs where there are no men. Suspecting that the structure of the marketplace will be entirely subverted if comparable worth is put into effect, difference doctrine says that because there is no man to set a standard from which women's treatment is a deviation, there is no sex discrimination here, only sex difference. Never mind that there is no man to compare with because no man would do that job if he had a choice, and of course he has because he is a man, so he won't.[19]

Now move into the so-called subtle reaches of the imposed category, the de facto area. Most jobs in fact require that the person, gender neutral, who is qualified for them will be someone who is not the primary caretaker of a preschool child.[20] Pointing out that this raises a concern of sex in a society in which women are expected to care for the children is taken as day one of taking gender into account in the structuring of jobs. To do that would violate the rule against not noticing situated differences based on gender, so it never emerges that day one of taking gender into account was the day the job was structured with the expectation that its occupant would have no child care responsibilities. Imaginary sex differences – such as between male and female applicants to administer estates or between males aging and dying and females aging and dying[21] – I will concede, the doctrine can handle.

I will also concede that there are many differences between women and men. I mean, can you imagine elevating one half of a population and denigrating the other half and producing a population in which everyone is the same? What the sameness standard fails to notice is that men's differences from women are equal to women's differences from men. There is an *equality* there. Yet the sexes are not socially equal. The difference approach misses the fact that hierarchy of power produces real as well as fantasied differences, differences that are also inequalities. What is missing in the difference approach is what Aristotle missed in his empiricist notion that equality means treating likes alike and unlikes unlike, and nobody has questioned it since. Why should you have to be the same as a man to get what a man gets simply because he is one? Why does maleness provide an original entitlement, not questioned on the basis of *its* gender, so that it is women – women who want to make a case of unequal treatment in a world men have made in their image (this is really the part Aristotle missed) – who have to show in effect that they are men in every relevant respect, unfortunately mistaken for women on the basis of an accident of birth?

The women that gender neutrality benefits, and there are some, show the suppositions of this approach in highest relief. They are mostly women who have been able to construct a biography that somewhat approximates the male norm, at least on paper. They are the qualified, the least of sex discrimination's victims. When they are denied a man's chance, it looks the most like sex bias. The more unequal society gets, the fewer such women are permitted to exist. Therefore, the more unequal society gets, the *less* likely the difference doctrine is to be able to do anything about it, because unequal power creates both the appearance and the reality of sex differences along the same lines as it creates its sex inequalities.

The special benefits side of the difference approach has not compensated for the differential of being second class. The special benefits rule is the only place in mainstream equality doctrine where you get to identify as a woman and not have that mean giving up all claim to equal treatment – but it comes close. Under its double standard, women who stand to inherit something when their husbands die have gotten the exclusion of a small percentage of the inheritance tax, to the tune of Justice Douglas waxing eloquent about the difficulties of all women's economic situation.[22] If we're going to be stigmatized as different, it would be nice if the compensation would fit the disparity. Women have also gotten three more years than men get before we have to be advanced or kicked out of the military hierarchy, as compensation for being precluded from combat, the usual way to advance.[23] Women have also gotten excluded from contact jobs in male-only prisons because we might get raped, the Court taking the viewpoint of the reasonable rapist on women's employment opportunities.[24] We also get protected out of jobs because of our fertility. The reason is that the job has health hazards, and somebody who might be a real person some day and therefore could sue – that is, a fetus – might be hurt if women, who apparently are not real persons and therefore can't sue either for the hazard to our health or for the lost employment opportunity, are given jobs that subject our bodies to possible harm.[25] Excluding women is always an option if equality feels in tension with

the pursuit itself. They never seem to think of excluding men. Take combat.[26] Somehow it takes the glory out of the foxhole, the buddiness out of the trenches, to imagine us out there. You get the feeling they might rather end the draft, they might even rather not fight wars at all than have to do it with us.

The double standard of these rules doesn't give women the dignity of the single standard; it also does not (as the differences standard does) suppress the gender of its referent, which is, of course, the female gender. I must also confess some affection for this standard. The work of Carol Gilligan on gender differences in moral reasoning[27] gives it a lot of dignity, more than it has ever had, more, frankly, than I thought it ever could have. But she achieves for moral reasoning what the special protection rule achieves in law: the affirmative rather than the negative valuation of that which has accurately distinguished women from men, by making it seem as though those attributes, with their consequences, really are somehow ours, rather than what male supremacy has attributed to us for its own use. For women to affirm difference, when difference means dominance, as it does with gender, means to affirm the qualities and characteristics of powerlessness.

Women have done good things, and it is a good thing to affirm them. I think quilts are art. I think women have a history. I think we create culture. I also know that we have not only been excluded from making what has been considered art; our artifacts have been excluded from setting the standards by which art is art. Women have a history all right, but it is a history both of what was and of what was not allowed to be. So I am critical of affirming what we have been, which necessarily is what we have been permitted, as if it is women's, ours, possessive. As if equality, in spite of everything, already ineluctably exists.

I am getting hard on this and am about to get harder on it. I do not think that the way women reason morally is morality "in a different voice."[28] I think it is morality in a higher register, in the feminine voice. Women value care because men have valued us according to the care we give them, and we could probably use some. Women think in relational terms because our existence is defined in relation to men. Further, when you are powerless, you don't just speak differently. A lot, you don't speak. Your speech is not just differently articulated, it is silenced. Eliminated, gone. You aren't just deprived of a language with which to articulate your distinctiveness, although you are; you are deprived of a life out of which articulation might come. Not being heard is not just a function of lack of recognition, not just that no one knows how to listen to you, although it is that; it is also silence of the deep kind, the silence of being prevented from having anything to say. Sometimes it is permanent. All I am saying is that the damage of sexism is real, and reifying that into differences is an insult to our possibilities.

So long as these issues are framed this way, demands for equality will always appear to be asking to have it both ways: the same when we are the same, different when we are different. But this is the way men have it: equal and different too. They have it the same as women when they are the same and want it, and different from women when they are different and want to be, which usually they do. Equal and different too would only be parity.[29] But under male supremacy, while being told we get it both ways, both the specialness of the pedestal and an even chance at the race, the ability to be a woman and a person, too, few women get much benefit of either.

There is an alternative approach, one that threads its way through existing law and expresses, I think, the reason equality law exists in the first place. It provides a second answer, a dissident answer in law and philosophy, to both the equality question and the gender question. In this approach, an equality question is a question of the distribution of power. Gender is also a question of power, specifically of male supremacy and female subordination. The question of equality, from the standpoint of what it is going to take to get it, is at root a question of hierarchy, which – as power succeeds in constructing social perception and social reality – derivatively becomes a categorical distinction, a difference. Here, on the first day that matters, dominance was achieved, probably by force. By the second day, division along the same lines had to be relatively firmly in place. On the third day, if not sooner, differences were demarcated, together with social systems to exaggerate them in perception and in fact, *because* the systematically differential delivery of benefits and deprivations required making no mistake about who was who. Comparatively speaking, man has been resting ever since. Gender might not even code as difference, might not mean distinction epistemologically, were it not for its consequences for social power.

I call this the dominance approach, and it is the ground I have been standing on in criticizing mainstream law. The goal of this dissident approach is not to make legal categories trace and trap the way things are. It is not to make rules that fit reality. It is critical of reality. Its task is not to formulate abstract standards that will produce determinate outcomes in particular cases. Its project is more substantive, more jurisprudential than formulaic, which is why it is difficult for the mainstream discourse to dignify it as an approach to doctrine or to imagine it as a rule of law at all. It proposes to expose that which women have had little choice but to be confined to, in order to change it.

The dominance approach centers on the most sex-differential abuses of women as a gender, abuses that sex equality law in its difference garb could not confront. It is based on a reality about which little of a systematic nature was known before 1970, a reality that calls for a new conception of the problem of sex inequality. This new information includes not only the extent and intractability of sex segregation into poverty, which has been known before, but the range of issues termed violence against women, which has not been. It combines women's material desperation, through being relegated to categories of jobs that pay nil, with the massive amount of rape and attempted rape – 44 percent of all women – about which virtually nothing is done;[30] the sexual assault of children – 38 percent of girls and 10 percent of boys – which is apparently endemic to the patriarchal family;[31] the battery of women that is systematic in one-quarter to one-third of our homes;[32] prostitution, women's fundamental economic condition, what we do when all else fails, and for many women in this country, all else fails often;[33] and pornography, an industry that traffics in female flesh, making sex inequality into sex to the tune of eight billion dollars a year in profits largely to organized crime.[34]

These experiences have been silenced out of the difference definition of sex equality largely because they happen almost exclusively to women. Understand: for this reason, they are considered *not* to raise sex equality issues. Because this treatment is done almost uniquely to women, it is implicitly treated as a difference, the sex difference, when in fact it is the socially situated subjection of women. The whole point of women's social relegation to inferiority as a gender is that for the most part these things aren't done to men. Men are not paid half of what women are paid for doing the same work on the basis of their equal difference. Everything they touch does not turn valueless because they touched it. When they are hit, a person has been assaulted. When they are sexually violated, it is not simply tolerated or found entertaining or defended as the necessary structure of the family, the price of civilization, or a constitutional right.

Does this differential describe the sex difference? Maybe so. It does describe the systematic relegation of an entire group of people to a condition of inferiority and attribute it to their nature. If this differential were biological, maybe biological intervention would have to be considered. If it were evolutionary, perhaps men would

have to evolve differently. Because I think it is political, I think its politics construct the deep structure of society. Men who do not rape women have nothing wrong with their hormones. Men who are made sick by pornography and do not eroticize their revulsion are not under-evolved. This social status in which we can be used and abused and trivialized and humiliated and bought and sold and passed around and patted on the head and put in place and told to smile so that we look as though we're enjoying it all is not what some of us have in mind as sex equality.

This second approach – which is not abstract, which is at odds with socially imposed reality and therefore does not look like a standard according to the standard for standards – became the implicit model for racial justice applied by the courts during the sixties. It has since eroded with the erosion of judicial commitment to racial equality. It was based on the realization that the condition of Blacks in particular was not fundamentally a matter of rational or irrational differentiation on the basis of race but was fundamentally a matter of white supremacy, under which racial differences became invidious as a consequence.[35] To consider gender in this way, observe again that men are as different from women as women are from men, but socially the sexes are not equally powerful. To be on the top of a hierarchy is certainly different from being on the bottom, but that is an obfuscatingly neutralized way of putting it, as a hierarchy is a great deal more than that. If gender were merely a question of difference, sex inequality would be a problem of mere sexism, of mistaken differentiation, of inaccurate categorization of individuals. This is what the difference approach thinks it is and is therefore sensitive to. But if gender is an inequality first, constructed as a socially relevant differentiation in order to keep that inequality in place, then sex inequality questions are questions of systematic dominance, of male supremacy, which is not at all abstract and is anything but a mistake.

If differentiation into classifications, in itself, is discrimination, as it is in difference doctrine, the use of law to change group-based social inequalities becomes problematic, even contradictory. This is because the group whose situation is to be changed must necessarily be legally identified and delineated; yet to do so is considered in fundamental tension with the guarantee against legally sanctioned inequality. If differentiation is discrimination, affirmative action, and any legal change in social inequality, is discrimination — but the existing social differentiations which constitute the inequality are not? This is only to say that, in the view that equates differentiation with discrimination, changing an unequal status quo is discrimination, but allowing it to exist is not.

Looking at the difference approach and the dominance approach from each other's point of view clarifies some otherwise confusing tensions in sex equality debates. From the point of view of the dominance approach, it becomes clear that the difference approach adopts the point of view of male supremacy on the status of the sexes. Simply by treating the status quo as "the standard," it invisibly and uncritically accepts the arrangements under male supremacy. In this sense, the difference approach is masculinist, although it can be expressed in a female voice. The dominance approach, in that it sees the inequalities of the social world from the standpoint of the subordination of women to men, is feminist.

If you look through the lens of the difference approach at the world as the dominance approach imagines it — that is, if you try to see real inequality through a lens that has difficulty seeing an inequality as an inequality if it also appears as a difference — you see demands for change in the distribution of power as demands for special protection. This is because the only tools that the difference paradigm offers to comprehend disparity equate the recognition of a gender line with an admission of lack of entitlement to equality under law. Since equality questions are primarily confronted in this approach as matters of empirical fit[36] — that is, as matters of accurately shaping legal rules (implicitly modeled on the standard men set) to the way the world is (also implicitly modeled on the standard men set) — any existing differences must be negated to merit equal treatment. For ethnicity as well as for gender, it is basic to mainstream discrimination doctrine to preclude any true diversity among equals or true equality within diversity.

To the difference approach, it further follows that any attempt to change the way the world actually is looks like a moral question requiring a separate judgment of how things ought to be. This approach imagines asking the following disinterested question that can be answered neutrally as to groups: against the weight of empirical difference, should we treat some as the equals of others, even when they may not be entitled to it because they are not up to standard? Because this construction of the problem is part of what the dominance approach unmasks, it does not arise with the dominance approach, which therefore does not see its own foundations as moral. If sex inequalities are approached as matters of imposed status, which are in need of change if a legal mandate of equality means anything at all, the question whether women should be treated unequally means simply whether women should be treated as less. When it is exposed as a naked power question, there is no separable question of what ought to be. The only real question is what is and is not a gender question. Once no amount of difference justifies treating women as subhuman, eliminating that is what equality law is for. In this shift of paradigms, equality propositions become no longer propositions of good and evil, but of power and powerlessness, no more disinterested in their origins or neutral in their arrival at conclusions than are the problems they address.

There came a time in Black people's movement for equality in this country when slavery stopped being a question of how it could be justified and became a question of how it could be ended. Racial disparities surely existed, or racism would have been harmless, but at that point – a point not yet reached for issues of sex – no amount of group difference mattered anymore. This is the same point at which a group's characteristics, including empirical attributes, become constitutive of the fully human, rather than being defined as exceptions to or as distinct from the fully human. To one-sidedly measure one group's differences against a standard set by the other incarnates partial standards. The moment when one's particular qualities become part of the standard by which humanity is measured is a millennial moment.

To summarize the argument: seeing sex equality questions as matters of reasonable or unreasonable classification is part of the way male dominance is expressed in law. If you follow my shift in perspective from gender as difference to gender as dominance, gender changes from a distinction that is presumptively valid to a detriment that is presumptively suspect. The difference approach tries to map reality; the dominance approach tries to challenge and change it. In the dominance approach, sex discrimination stops being a question of morality and starts being a question of politics.

You can tell if sameness is your standard for equality if my critique of hierarchy looks like a request for special protection in disguise. It's not. It envisions a change that would make possible a simple equal chance for the first time. To define the reality of sex as difference and the warrant of equality as sameness is wrong on both counts. Sex, in nature, is not a bipolarity; it is a continuum. In society it is made into a bipolarity. Once this is done, to require that one be the same as those who set the standard – those which one is already socially defined as different from – simply means that sex equality is concep-tually designed never to be achieved. Those who most need equal treatment will be the least similar, socially, to those whose situation sets the standard as against which one's entitlement to be

equally treated is measured. Doctrinally speaking, the deepest problems of sex inequality will not find women "similarly situated"[37] to men. Far less will practices of sex inequality require that acts be intentionally discriminatory.[38] All that is required is that the status quo be maintained. As a strategy for maintaining social power first structure reality unequally, then require that entitlement to alter it be grounded on a lack of distinction in situation; first structure perception so that different equals inferior, then require that discrimination be activated by evil minds who *know* they are treating equals as less.

I say, give women equal power in social life. Let what we say matter, then we will discourse on questions of morality. Take your foot off our necks, then we will hear in what tongue women speak. So long as sex equality is limited by sex difference, whether you like it or don't like it, whether you value it or seek to negate it, whether you stake it out as a grounds for feminism or occupy it as the terrain of misogyny, women will be born, degraded, and die. We would settle for that equal protection of the laws under which one would be born, live, and die, in a country where protection is not a dirty word and equality is not a special privilege.

Notes

1 The Bona Fide Occupational Qualification (BFOQ) exception to Title VII of the Civil Rights Act of 1964, 42 U.S.C. § 2000 e-(2)(e), permits sex to be a job qualification when it is a valid one. The leading interpretation of the proposed federal Equal Rights Amendment would, pursuing a similar analytic structure, permit a "unique phys-ical characteristic" exception to its otherwise abso-lute embargo on taking sex into account. Barbara Brown, Thomas I. Emerson, Gail Falk, and Ann E. Freedman, "The Equal Rights Amendment: A Constitutional Basis for Equal Rights for Women," 80 *Yale Law Journal* 893 (1971).

2 Title VII of the Civil Rights Act of 1964, 42 U.S.C. § 2000 e; Phillips v. Martin-Marietta, 400 U.S. 542 (1971). Frontiero v. Richardson, 411 U.S. 484

(1974) is the high-water mark of this approach. *See also* City of Los Angeles v. Manhart, 435 U.S. 702 (1978); Newport News Shipbuilding and Dry Dock Co. v. EEOC, 462 U.S. 669 (1983).

3 Title IX of the Education Amendments of 1972, 20 U.S.C. §1681; Cannon v. University of Chicago, 441 U.S. 677 (1981); Mississippi University for Women v. Hogan, 458 U.S. 718 (1982); *see also* De La Cruz v. Tormey, 582 F.2d 45 (9th Cir. 1978).

4 My impression is that women appear to lose most academic sex discrimination cases that go to trial, although I know of no systematic or statistical study on the subject. One case that won eventually, elevating the standard of proof in the process, is Sweeney v. Board of Trustees of Keene State College, 439 U.S. 29 (1979). The ruling for the plaintiff was affirmed on remand, 604 F.2d 106 (1st Cir. 1979).

5 Hishon v. King & Spalding, 467 U.S. 69 (1984).

6 *See*, e.g., Vanguard Justice v. Hughes, 471 F. Supp. 670 (D. Md. 1979); Meyer v. Missouri State Highway Commission, 567 F.2d 804, 891 (8th Cir. 1977); Payne v. Travenol Laboratories Inc., 416 F. Supp. 248 (N.D. Mass. 1976). *See also* Dothard v. Rawlinson, 433 U.S. 321 (1977) (height and weight requirements invalidated for prison guard contact positions because of disparate impact on sex).

7 Frontiero v. Richardson, 411 U.S. 484 (1974); Schlesinger v. Ballard, 419 U.S. 498 (1975).

8 This situation is relatively complex. *See* Gomes v. R.I. Interscholastic League, 469 F. Supp. 659 (D. R.I. 1979); Brenden v. Independent School District, 477 F.2d 1292 (8th Cir. 1973); O'Connor v. Board of Education of School District No. 23, 645 F.2d 578 (7th Cir. 1981); Cape v. Tennessee Secondary School Athletic Association, 424 F. Supp. 732 (E.D. Tenn. 1976), *rev'd*, 563 F.2d 793 (6th Cir. 1977); Yellow Springs Exempted Village School District Board of Education v. Ohio High School Athletic Association, 443 F. Supp. 753 (S.D. Ohio 1978); Aiken v. Lieuallen, 593 P.2d 1243 (Or. App. 1979).

9 Rostker v. Goldberg, 453 U.S. 57 (1981). *See also* Lori S. Kornblum, "Women Warriors in a Men's World: The Combat Exclusion," 2 *Law and Inequality: A Journal of Theory and Practice* 353 (1984).

10 David Cole, "Strategies of Difference: Litigating for Women's Rights in a Man's World," 2 *Law &* *Inequality: A Journal of Theory and Practice* 34 n.4 (1984) (collecting cases).

11 Devine v. Devine, 398 So. 2d 686 (Ala. Sup. Ct. 1981); Danielson v. Board of Higher Education, 358 F. Supp. 22 (S.D.N.Y. 1972); Weinberger v. Wiesenfeld, 420 U.S. 636 (1975); Stanley v. Illinois, 405 U.S. 645 (1971); Caban v. Mohammed, 441 U.S. 380 (1979); Orr v. Orr, 440 U.S. 268 (1979).

12 Lenore Weitzman, "The Economics of Divorce: Social and Economic Consequences of Property, Alimony and Child Support Awards," 28 *U.C.L.A. Law Review* 1118, 1251 (1982), documents a decline in women's standard of living of 73 percent and an increase in men's of 42 percent within a year after divorce.

13 Equal Pay Act, 29 U.S.C. § 206(d)(1) (1976) guarantees pay equality, as does case law, *but cf.* data on pay gaps, "Introduction," note 2.

14 Examples include Christenson v. State of Iowa, 563 F.2d 353 (8th Cir. 1977); Gerlach v. Michigan Bell Tel. Co., 501 F. Supp. 1300 (E.D. Mich. 1980); Odomes v. Nucare, Inc., 653 F.2d 246 (6th Cir. 1981) (female nurse's aide denied Title VII remedy because her job duties were not substantially similar to those of better-paid male orderly); Power v. Barry County, Michigan, 539 F. Supp. 721 (W.D. Mich. 1982); Spaulding v. University of Washington, 740 F.2d 686 (9th Cir. 1984).

15 County of Washington v. Gunther, 452 U.S. 161 (1981) permits a comparable worth-type challenge where pay inequality can be proven to be a correlate of intentional job segregation. *See also* Lemons v. City and County of Denver, 17 FEP Cases 910 (D. Colo. 1978), *aff'd*, 620 F.2d 228 (10th Cir. 1977), *cert. denied*, 449 U.S. 888 (1980); AFSCME v. State of Washington, 770 F.2d 1401 (9th Cir. 1985). *See generally* Carol Jean Pint, "Value, Work and Women," 1 *Law & Inequality: A Journal of Theory and Practice* 159 (1983).

16 Combine the result in Bob Jones University v. United States, 461 U.S. 547 (1983) with Mississippi University for Women v. Hogan, 458 U.S. 718 (1982), and the tax-exempt status of women-only schools is clearly threatened.

17 A particularly pungent example comes from a case in which the plaintiff sought to compete in boxing matches with men, since there were no matches

sponsored by the defendant among women. A major reason that preventing the woman from competing was found not to violate her equality rights was that the "safety rules and precautions [were] developed, designed, and tested in the context of all-male competition." Lafler v. Athletic Board of Control, 536 F. Supp. 104, 107 (W.D. Mich. 1982). As the court put it:

> In this case, the real differences between the male and female anatomy are relevant in considering whether men and women may be treated differently with regard to their partici- pating in boxing. The plaintiff *admits* that she wears a protective covering for her breasts while boxing. Such a protective covering ... would violate Rule Six, Article 9 of the Amateur Boxing Federation rules currently in effect. The same rule *requires* contestants to wear a protective cup, a rule obviously designed for the unique anatomical character- istics of men.
>
> Id. at 106 (emphasis added)

The rule is based on the male anatomy, therefore not a justification for the discrimination but an example of it. This is not considered in the opinion, nor does the judge discuss whether women might benefit from genital protection, and men from chest guards, as in some other sports.

18 This is a reference to the issues raised by several recent cases which consider whether states' attempts to compensate pregnancy leaves and to secure jobs on return constitute sex discrimina- tion. California Federal Savings and Loan Assn. v. Guerra, 758 F.2d 390 (9th Cir. 1985), *cert. granted* 54 U.S.L.W. 3460 (U.S. Jan. 13, 1986); *see also* Miller-Wohl v. Commissioner of Labor, 515 F. Supp. 1264 (D. Montana 1981), *vacated and dismissed,* 685 F.2d 1088 (9th Cir. 1982). The position argued in "Difference and Dominance" here suggests that if these benefits are prohibited under Title VII, Title VII is unconstitutional under the equal protection clause.

This argument was not made directly in either case. The American Civil Liberties Union argued that the provisions requiring pregnancy to be compensated in employment, without comparable coverage for men, violated Title VII's prohibition on pregnancy-based classifications and on sex. Montana had made it illegal for an employer to "terminate a woman's employment because of her pregnancy" or to "refuse to grant to the employee a reasonable leave of absence for such pregnancy." Montana Maternity Leave Act § 49-2-310(1) and (2). According to the ACLU, this provision:

> grants pregnant workers certain employment rights not enjoyed by other workers ... Legislation designed to benefit women has ... perpetuated destructive stereotypes about their proper roles and operated to deny them rights and benefits enjoyed by men. The [Montana provision] deters employers from hiring women who are or may become preg- nant, causes resentment and hostility in the workplace, and penalizes men.
>
> Brief of American Civil Liberties Union, *et al. amicus curiae,* Montana Supreme Court No. 84–172, at 7

The National Organization for Women argued that the California provision, which requires employers to give pregnant workers unpaid disability leave with job security for up to four months, would violate Title VII should Title VII be interpreted to permit it. Brief of National Organization for Women, *et al.,* United States Court of Appeals for the Ninth Circuit, 685 F.2d 1088 (9th Cir. 1982).

When Congress passed the Pregnancy Discrimination Act, amending Title VII, 42 U.S.C. § 2000 e(k), it defined "because of sex" or "on the basis of sex" to include "because of or on the basis of pregnancy, childbirth, or related medical condi- tions; and women affected by pregnancy, child- birth, or related medical conditions shall be treated the same for all employment-related purposes." In so doing, Congress arguably decided that one did not have to be the same as a man to be treated without discrimination, since it guaranteed freedom from discriminatory treatment on the basis of a condition that is not the same for men as it is for women. It even used the word "women" in the statute.

Further, Congress made this decision expressly to overrule the Supreme Court decision in General Electric v. Gilbert, 429 U.S. 125 (1976), which had held that failure to cover pregnancy as a disability was not sex discrimination because the line between pregnant and nonpregnant was not the line between women and men. In rejecting this logic, as the Court found it did expressly in Newport News Shipbuilding and Dry Dock Co. v. EEOC, 462 U.S. 669, 678 (1983), Congress rejected the implicit measuring of women's entitlement to equality by a male standard. Nor need all women be the same, that is, pregnant or potentially so, to have pregnancy-based discrimination be sex-based discrimination.

Upholding the California pregnancy leave and job security law, the Ninth Circuit opinion did not require sameness for equality to be delivered:

> The PDA does not require states to ignore pregnancy. It requires that women be treated equally . . . [E]quality under the PDA must be measured in employment opportunity, not necessarily in amounts of money expended – or in amounts of days of disability leave expended. Equality . . . compares coverage to actual need, not coverage to hypothetical identical needs.
>
> California Federal v. Guerra, 758 F.2d 390 (9th Cir. 1985) (Ferguson, J.)

"We are not the first court to announce the goal of Title VII is equality of employment opportunity, not necessarily sameness of treatment." Id. at 396 n.7.

19 Most women work at jobs mostly women do, and most of those jobs are paid less than jobs that mostly men do. *See,* e.g., Pint, note 15 above, at 162–3 nn.19, 20 (collecting studies). To the point that men may not meet the male standard themselves, one court found that a union did not fairly represent its women in the following terms:

> As to the yard and driver jobs, defendants suggest not only enormous intellectual requirements, but that the physical demands of those jobs are so great as to be beyond the capacity of any female. Again, it is noted that plaintiffs' capacity to perform those jobs was never tested, despite innumerable requests therefor. It is also noted that defendants have never suggested which of the innumerable qualifications they list for these jobs (for the

first time) the plaintiffs might fail to meet. The court, however, will accept without listing here the extraordinary catalogue of feats which defendants argue must be performed in the yard, and as a driver. That well may be. However, one learns from this record that one cannot be too weak, too sick, too old and infirm, or too ignorant to perform these jobs, *so long as one is a man.* The plaintiffs appear to the layperson's eye to be far more physically fit than many of the drivers who moved into the yard, over the years, according to the testimony of defense witnesses . . . In short, they were all at least as fit as the men with serious physical deficits and disabilities who held yard jobs.

> Jones v. Cassens Transport, 617 F. Supp. 869, 892 (1985) (emphasis in original)

20 Phillips v. Martin-Marietta, 400 U.S. 542 (1971).

21 Reed v. Reed, 404 U.S. 71 (1971) held that a statute barring women from administering estates is sex discrimination. If few women were taught to read and write, as used to be the case, the gender difference would not be imaginary in this case, yet the social situation would be even more sex discriminatory than it is now. Compare City of Los Angeles v. Manhart, 434 U.S. 815 (1978), which held that requiring women to make larger contributions to their retirement plan was sex discrimination, in spite of the allegedly proven sex difference that women on the average outlive men.

22 Kahn v. Shevin, 416 U.S. 351, 353 (1974).

23 Schlesinger v. Ballard, 419 U.S. 498 (1975).

24 Dothard v. Rawlinson, 433 U.S. 321 (1977); *see also* Michael M. v. Sonoma County Superior Court, 450 U.S. 464 (1981).

25 Doerr v. B.F. Goodrich, 484 F. Supp. 320 (N.D. Ohio 1979). Wendy Webster Williams, "Firing the Woman to Protect the Fetus: The Reconciliation of Fetal Protection with Employment Opportunity Goals Under Title VII," 69 *Georgetown Law Journal* 641 (1981). *See also* Hayes v. Shelby Memorial Hospital, 546 F. Supp. 259 (N.D. Ala. 1982); Wright v. Olin Corp., 697 F.2d 1172 (4th Cir. 1982).

26 Congress requires the Air Force (10 U.S.C. § 8549 [1983]) and the Navy (10 U.S.C. § 6015 [1983]) to exclude women from combat, with some exceptions. Owens v. Brown, 455 F. Supp. 291

(D.D.C. 1978), had previously invalidated the prior Navy combat exclusion because it prohibited women from filling jobs they could perform and inhibited Navy's discretion to assign women on combat ships. The Army excludes women from combat based upon its own policies under congressional authorization to determine assignment (10 U.S.C. § 3012 [e] [1983]).

27 Carol Gilligan, *In a Different Voice* (1982).

28 Id.

29 I argued this in Appendix A of my *Sexual Harassment of Working Women: A Case of Sex Discrimination* (1979). That book ends with "Women want to be equal and different, too." I could have added "Men are." As a standard, this would have reduced women's aspirations for equality to some corresponding version of men's actualities. But as an observation, it would have been true.

30 Diana Russell and Nancy Howell, "The Prevalence of Rape in the United States Revisited," 8 *Signs: Journal of Women in Culture and Society* 689 (1983) (44 percent of women in 930 households were victims of rape or attempted rape at some time in their lives).

31 Diana Russell, "The Incidence and Prevalence of Intrafamilial and Extrafamilial Sexual Abuse of Female Children," 7 *Child Abuse & Neglect: The International Journal* 133 (1983).

32 R. Emerson Dobash and Russell Dobash, *Violence against Wives: A Case against the Patriarchy* (1979); Bruno v. Codd, 90 Misc. 2d 1047, 396 N.Y.S. 2d 974 (Sup. Ct. 1977), rev'd, 64 A.D. 2d 582, 407 N.Y.S. 2d 165 (1st Dep't 1978), aff'd 47 N.Y. 2d 582, 393 N.E. 2d 976, 419 N.Y.S. 2d 901 (1979).

33 Kathleen Barry, *Female Sexual Slavery* (1979); Moira K. Griffin, "Wives, Hookers and the Law: The Case for Decriminalizing Prostitution," 10 *Student Lawyer* 18 (1982); Report of Jean Fernand-Laurent, Special Rapporteur on the Suppression of the Traffic in Persons and the Exploitation of the Prostitution of Others (a United Nations report), in *International Feminism: Networking against Female Sexual Slavery* 130 (Kathleen Barry, Charlotte Bunch, and Shirley Castley, eds.) (Report of the Global Feminist Workshop to Organize against Traffic in Women, Rotterdam, Netherlands, Apr. 6–15, 1983 [1984]).

34 Galloway and Thornton, "Crackdown on Pornography – A No-Win Battle," *U.S. News and World Report*, June 4, 1984, at 84. *See also* "The Place of Pornography," *Harper's*, November 1984, at 31 (citing $7 billion per year).

35 Loving v. Virginia, 388 U.S. 1 (1967), first used the term "white supremacy" in invalidating an anti-miscegenation law as a violation of equal protection. The law equally forbade whites and Blacks to intermarry. Although going nowhere near as far, courts in the athletics area have sometimes seen that "same" does not necessarily mean "equal" nor does "equal" require "same." In a context of sex inequality like that which has prevailed in athletic opportunity, allowing boys to compete on girls' teams may diminish overall sex equality. "Each position occupied by a male reduces the female participation and increases the overall disparity of athletic opportunity which generally exists." Petrie v. Illinois High School Association, 394 N.E. 2d 855, 865 (Ill. 1979). "We conclude that to furnish exactly the same athletic opportunities to boys as to girls would be most difficult and would be detrimental to the compelling governmental interest of equalizing general athletic opportunities between the sexes." Id.

36 The scholars Tussman and tenBroek first used the term "fit" to characterize the necessary relation between a valid equality rule and the world to which it refers. J. Tussman and J. tenBroek, "The Equal Protection of the Laws," 37 *California Law Review* 341 (1949).

37 Royster Guano Co. v. Virginia, 253 U.S. 412, 415 (1920): "[A classification] must be reasonable, not arbitrary, and must rest upon some ground of difference having a fair and substantial relation to the object of the legislation, so that all persons similarly circumstanced shall be treated alike." Reed v. Reed, 404 U.S. 71, 76 (1971): "Regardless of their sex, persons within any one of the enumerated classes ... are similarly situated ... By providing dissimilar treatment for men and women who are thus similarly situated, the challenged section violates the Equal Protection Clause."

38 Washington v. Davis, 426 U.S. 229 (1976) and Personnel Administrator of Massachusetts v. Feeney, 442 U.S. 256 (1979) require that intentional discrimination be shown for discrimination to be shown.

PART 3

Applied Political Philosophy

3a. DEMOCRATIC DELIBERATION AND VOTING

TO THE AVERAGE AMERICAN, democracy is an almost sacred political value. It was to defend democracy that the great wars of the first half of the twentieth century were fought, and those who defended war against Iraq in 2003 invoked the expansion of democracy as one of its chief justifications. Democracy, most people believe, is a system that recognizes the fundamental equality of human beings, and helps to guarantee the security of their basic human rights. It is a political system that promotes peace, tolerance, and mutual respect. It is the one thing, perhaps the only thing, that just about every politician of every political persuasion can agree is good.

But what exactly *is* democracy? And what about it, specifically, makes it so good? For most people, the defining feature of democracy is the fact that each person has a *vote*. Each person gets one, and only one vote, and so each person has an equal say in determining the policies of his or her political unit. But, on reflection, it's not obvious what's so great about *that*. A vote doesn't amount to much, in terms of actual political influence. The only case in which *your* vote makes a difference to the outcome of an election is that in which *everyone else's* votes are *exactly tied*. And in an election of any size, the chances of that happening are vanishingly small. In the 2008 presidential election, according to one estimate by stats wiz Nate Silver and his co-authors, the average American voter had about a 1 in 60 million chance of casting the decisive vote.[1] That hardly seems worth leaving one's home to drive to the polling booth for, let alone going to war for.

Moreover, the idea that equal votes amounts to equal political influence is hardly one that can stand up to even passingly close scrutiny. Larry Page, the CEO of Google, has one vote, just like I do. But that is where the similarity ends. I do not make multi-million dollar campaign contributions, nor am I responsible for the employment for tens of thousands of people. It strains credulity to suppose that politicians (who depend on dollars and votes for their continued employment) are unaware of this difference, or that it has no bearing on our relative influence over public policy.

Finally, it is worth pointing out that *nobody* thinks that *everything* should be decided by a majority vote. Some policies — such as those that violate basic human rights — are morally wrong. And they do not become any less wrong simply because a majority of the population votes in favor of them. Even in a democracy, then, not everything is or ought to be determined by majority vote, and so whatever value this method of decision-making has is obviously limited in its scope.

If the cherished status of democracy can be defended, then, it will not be on the basis the equal right to vote alone. What, then, is the alternative? One suggestion, articulated in defended by Deninis Thompson and Amy Guttman in their contribution to this section, is that the value of democracy lies in the *moral deliberation* it is capable of fostering. Because moral disagreement is a persistent feature of liberal societies (see the introduction to section 1d, above), we need some way or method for resolving disputes among reasonable persons in a way that is fair, mutually respectful, and relatively efficient. Democratic deliberation can do this in a way that confers legitimacy upon democratic outcomes, encourages individuals to take a perspective broader than their own on questions of public policy, clarifies the nature of moral conflict, and helps individuals to understand and rectify the incomplete understanding that often characterizes moral conflict.

Deliberative democrats point to these characteristics as ones that help to justify democratic institutions in their current form, but also show us how those institutions could be made even better in the future. Nobody forcibly *prevents* citizens from deliberating as much as they wish in democracies now. But democratic institutions, and the public understanding of democracy that currently gives pride of place to the private act of voting, could be reformed in ways that make deliberation more widespread, and more influential. Institutions of government could be made more transparent, for instance, and the role of experts diminished relative to the role of public dialogue and input.

Whether this is the right way to justify democracy, however, is far from clear. Indeed, it is not completely obvious that there is *any* way of justifying the immensely high regard with which democracy is held. In his contribution to this section, Jason Brennan examines a wide range of considerations that might be thought to render the political liberties characteristic of democracy valuable to the individuals who hold them. Those considerations include ones that appeal to the *instrumental* value of political liberties — that seek to show their value by demonstrating how they help individuals achieve *other* values that they hold, and those that appeal to the *intrinsic* value of political liberties — that hold them to be value for their own sake, apart from their consequences.

Ultimately, however, Brennan finds none of the seven considerations he canvasses to be convincing. Political liberties might possess a kind of *aggregate* value — i.e., it might be a valuable that *people in general* have them — and there might be good reason for holding that people are *entitled* to their political liberties. But it is difficult to show that political liberties are *valuable to the people who actually hold them* in the way that, say, the right to own personal property and to freely choose one's occupation clearly are.

There are a variety of other philosophical approaches to defending — and critiquing — democracy, a sample of which are represented in the bibliography below. And, of course, there is a large empirical literature on the performance of democracies compared to non-democracies on a number of different measures. As always, the purpose of the readings in this section is not to provide an exhaustive coverage of the debate, but merely to introduce readers to some of its most important elements.

Note

1 Andrew Gelman, Nate Silver, and Aaron Edlin, "What is the Probability Your Vote will Make a Difference?" *Economic Inquiry*, vol. 50, no. 2 (April 2012), pp. 321–26.

Further Reading

Brennan, G., and Lomasky, L. (Eds.). (1997). *Democracy and Decision: The Pure Theory of Electoral Preference*. Cambridge: Cambridge University Press.

Buchanan, J., and Tullock, G. (1965). *The Calculus of Consent: Logical Foundations of Constitutional Democracy*, Ann Arbor, MI: University of Michigan Press.

Caplan, B. (2011). *The Myth of the Rational Voter: Why Democracies Choose Bad Policies* (New Edition). Princeton: Princeton University Press.

Christiano, T. (1996). *The Rule of the Many: Fundamental Issues in Democratic Theory*, Boulder, CO: Westview Press.

Elster, J. (1998). *Deliberative Democracy* (Vol. 1). Cambridge: Cambridge University Press.

Gutmann, A., and Thompson, D. (2009). *Why Deliberative Democracy?*. Princeton: Princeton University Press.

Habermas, J. (1996). *Contributions to a Discourse Theory of Law and Democracy*. Cambridge: Polity Press.

Chapter 42

Amy Gutmann and Dennis Thompson

MORAL DISAGREEMENT IN A DEMOCRACY

Amy Gutmann (1949–) is a political theorist and currently President of the University of Pennsylvania. Dennis Thompson (1940–) is a professor of political philosophy at Harvard's Kennedy School of Government. In this essay (published in 1995), they argue that deep disagreement about significant moral issues is an intractable feature of our society, and that majority rule democracy provides the fairest way of dealing with these disagreements.

Moral disagreement about public policies – issues such as abortion, affirmative action, and health care – is a prominent feature of contemporary American democracy. Yet it is not a central concern of the leading theories of democracy. The two dominant democratic approaches in our time – procedural democracy and constitutional democracy – fail to offer adequate responses to the problem of moral disagreement. Both suggest some elements that are necessary in any adequate response, but neither one alone nor both together are sufficient. We argue here that an adequate conception of democracy must make moral deliberation an essential part of the political process. What we call "deliberative democracy" adds an important dimension to the theory and practice of politics that the leading conceptions of democracy neglect.

I. The Problem of Moral Disagreement

What makes a disagreement moral? No doubt there is disagreement about what should count as

moral disagreement itself, and this disagreement also has a place in deliberative democracy. It is nevertheless possible to identify some general features of morality, three characteristics that moral claims typically have in politics, which citizens and theorists of many different moral positions can acknowledge and to which any adequate conception of democracy should respond.[1]

First, although they are sometimes expressed as personal complaints, moral arguments are general rather than particular in form. They apply to anyone who is similarly situated in the morally relevant respect. The poor woman who seeks an abortion, the white male job applicant who opposes affirmative action, and the mother who needs prenatal care do not assert merely that they, or even only their friends, family, and associates, should receive the benefit; they maintain that all citizens, similarly situated, should receive it. The form of their claims, if fully developed, would impute rights and wrongs, or ascribe virtue and vice, to anyone who is similar in the respects that the argument assumes to be morally significant.

Second, the content of the argument reaches beyond the moral concerns of its maker. It appeals to values or principles that are shared or could be shared by fellow citizens. In politics, if not in morality in general, we try to base our claims on values or principles that no one, whatever his or her status, could reasonably reject.[2] Reaching in these ways for a common perspective, or at least for some shared standards, is of course not always successful. But it is a feature of moral argument that is especially important in politics. It enables us, for example, to recognize an argument as a moral one even if we disagree with its conclusions.

Third, moral arguments also take place in context: they implicitly rely on assumptions about matters of fact, common estimates of risks, suppositions about feasibility, and general beliefs about human nature and social processes. The assumptions may or may not be universally true, but whether they are does not usually affect a particular argument. Citizens who make the claims would not be moved if they learned that their moral claim would not be understood, let alone accepted, if they tried to make it in some remote village in Asia or among the Ick in Uganda.[3] Even those who rely on what they regard as universal moral principles do not presume that their practical conclusions are independent of facts about the society in which they live. The arguments begin from where we are, and appeal to those with whom we now live. This is why moral relativism is seldom an issue in practical political ethics.

These characteristics suggest correctly that moral claims seek some common ground. The claimants reach out to find principles or perspectives that others can accept. But even when the moral claimants seem to find some common principles, the disagreement persists. Citizens and officials who disagree with other citizens and officials, or who expect others to disagree with them, seek to justify or criticize political decisions and public policies or political actions more generally. The disagreements are often

deep. If they were not, there would be no need for argument. If they were too deep, there would be no point in argument. The disagreement lies in the range between simple misunderstanding and immutable irreconcilability.

What are these deeper sources of moral disagreement? This too may be a controversial question, but again we need to provide some general indication of those sources so that we can later assess how various forms of democracy respond to such disagreement. The temptation to try to turn moral disagreements into some simpler kind of conflict is great, especially in politics. Moral conflict seems slightly mysterious, dangerously subjective, and at once naive and complex. In a kind of reverse transmutation, some theorists attempt to reduce moral claims to self-interest and group interests.

Moral disagreements, these theorists assume, simply reflect the conflicting interests of individuals or groups. This familiar view has been around for a long time – finding its most systematic political statement in the theory of Thomas Hobbes. On this view, moral disagreements cannot properly be understood on their own terms. Moral terms are "inconstant names," referring to "things which please and displease us," which vary depending on what an individual sees to be in his or her interest.[4] The reduction of morality to self-interest cannot be sustained. We may disagree about precisely what is at stake in the debate over whether and when abortion should be legal, but even Hobbes, who thought his own birth traumatic, would not have supposed that the abortion controversy is best understood as a battle between the self-interest of women and fetuses.

It is of course possible to define self-interest so expansively that it subsumes all the interests citizens might have in fulfilling legitimate expectations, upholding rights, rewarding desert, and seeking fair treatment for themselves and people they care about. But only someone in the grip of a single-valued theory would try to do so. Such an expansive concept is misleading: it elides the distinction between interests exclusively in oneself and interests in other people and impersonal values. To criticize someone for being self-interested makes sense only if self-interest is understood as having interests only in oneself, and failing to demonstrate sufficient regard for the interests of others. If all human action is assumed to be a reflection of self-interest, the charge of self-interest loses its critical content, and the claim that moral disagreements can be reduced to conflicts of self-interest becomes a tautology.

Even if moral conflict cannot be meaningfully reduced to self-interest, some theorists insist that it can be reduced to a clash of group interests, another kind of nonmoral conflict. The effort to reduce moral conflict to group interest, exemplified in some Marxist theories and in a somewhat different way in pluralist political science, encounters problems analogous to those of the self-interest approach.[5] Consider the issue of distributing health care in the United States. Disagreements about what constitutes a just health-care policy abound, but they do not simply mirror the differences among groups, defined by income, age, ethnicity, gender, or profession. (Even when there is a correlation between certain group differences and political positions on health-care policy, there remains considerable moral disagreement within groups. The moral disagreement tends to be greater, moreover, before members of the group make any deliberative attempt to reach a consensus for political purposes.) Furthermore, if society were to become more egalitarian, moral conflict over the distribution of health care might shift its focus to different health-care issues, but it would surely not disappear.

Hume's account of the sources of moral conflict (or, as it has come to be known, the circumstances of justice)[6] begins to explain why we should not expect moral conflict to disappear with a more egalitarian society, even if the issues that create the most conflict change significantly over time. Moral conflicts of the kind in which

we are interested arise in conditions of scarcity[7] and limited generosity.[8] Hume is surely right that moral conflict is rooted not primarily in certain kinds of societies, but in more fundamental and more nearly universal features of societies. Hume is also convincing when he claims that among those features are scarcity of resources and the limited generosity of human nature. But Hume's account does not go far enough. There are at least two other sources of moral conflict that he ignores, and they make the problem of moral disagreement both more complex and more challenging than he implies.

Even totally benevolent individuals trying to decide on the morally best standards to govern a society of abundance would not be able to reconcile some moral conflicts. They would still face, for example, the problem of abortion. Nor is abortion a unique case. Similar moral conflicts characterize some aspects of the controversies over legalizing violent pornography, capital punishment, surrogate parenting, and many other contemporary issues over which moral opinion divides. These moral conflicts can be understood and experienced by one person taking a moral point of view, appreciating the competing claims of more than one fundamental value, and therefore struggling internally to resolve the conflict. The sources of moral disagreement lie partly within morality itself.[9]

The other circumstance we should add to Hume's account is incomplete understanding. Even if everyone were completely benevolent, some may reasonably give different weight to the many complex factors, moral and empirical, that affect the choice of public policies. Recognizing this human limitation does not imply moral skepticism, and is even compatible with believing that there are moral truths. It simply expresses a recognition that, at any particular moment in history, we cannot collectively resolve some moral dilemmas on their own terms.

If moral disagreement is so pervasive, how can we ever hope to resolve it? Some basis for hope of achieving some modest kind of resolution is to be found in the nature of moral claims themselves. Just as the problem of disagreement lies partly within morality itself, so does the basis for its resolution. The two primary characteristics of moral claims in politics – that they apply to everyone similarly situated and that they appeal to values each is assumed to share – support the possibility of resolution. If citizens make claims that they expect others would not reasonably reject, they are already engaged in a process of finding some common ground on which to resolve their conflicts.

In an important sense, however, we should not expect finally to resolve moral conflicts. The problem of moral disagreement should be considered a condition with which we must learn to live rather than an obstacle to be overcome on the way to a just society. We may reach some resolutions, but they are partial and tentative. They do not stand outside the process of moral argument, prior to it or protected from its provocations. We do not begin with a common morality, a substantial set of the principles or values that we assume we share, and then apply it to decisions and policies. Nor for that matter do we end with such a morality. Rather, the principles and values with which we live are provisional, formed and continually revised in the process of making and responding to moral claims in public life.

In its political aspect, this process embodies some form of democracy. Democracy seems a natural and reasonable way of coping with moral disagreement, since it is a conception of government that, at least in theory, accords equal respect to the moral claims of each citizen, and is therefore morally justifiable from the perspective of each citizen. If we have to morally disagree over matters of justice, it is better to do so in a democracy that as far as possible respects the moral status of each of us.[10]

The leading conceptions of democracy may be divided into two types: procedural and constitutional. Both in effect accept the goal of finding a common perspective for resolving moral disagreement: decisions and policies should in principle be acceptable to the people who are bound by them. Moral disagreements that are rooted in incomplete understanding, for example, should not be resolved by adopting policies or passing laws whose rationale citizens cannot reasonably accept. In this way, both forms of democracy seek a common perspective that is comprehensible to, and cannot reasonably be rejected by, the people bound by it. To what extent do they succeed?

II. The Response of Procedural Democracy

Procedural democracy defends popular rule as the fairest way of resolving moral conflicts.[11] The simplest form of popular rule is majoritarianism: members of a sovereign society agree to be governed by the will of a majority or their accountable representatives. The decision of a majority at any particular time is provisional, since it may always be revised by subsequent majorities; but what the majority decides resolves the moral conflict as a matter of law and policy at any particular time.

In the face of moral conflict (including disagreement about conceptions of democracy), majoritarianism commends itself as the default solution. It institutionalizes the premise, shared by all democrats, that each citizen should be respected as a political equal. If citizens cannot agree on the moral substance of policies and decisions, and no representative can be relied on to resolve substantive moral conflicts, then the claims of each citizen should be weighed equally, and the greatest number should prevail. Majority rule institutionalizes the idea that the claims of every person count equally in deciding which way the political community of which they are each a part should move.[12] The alternative is to impose the claims of the minority on the majority, and this assumes that the moral convictions of some citizens count for more than those of others. Such an assumption cannot be justified to people who consider themselves political equals.

Procedural democrats would argue that this rationale provides the common perspective we are seeking. The members of the losing minority, even if their position is morally correct, should not reasonably reject majoritarianism. Majority rule does not substantively resolve a moral conflict; it yields only a provisional procedural resolution. Majorities may of course believe that their view is right, but procedural democracy does not claim the majority's decision is morally right, only that the majority has the right to decide. Numerical might does not make moral right. Majorities have a right to govern only because minorities do not.

Some procedural democrats deny that there are any correct substantive moral conclusions in politics; there are no "fundamental values" that should be shared by all citizens.[13] But the moral skepticism that these denials imply is not required by procedural democracy, and in fact would undermine it. If there is no reason to believe that any moral claim is valid, then there is no reason to count any claim at all, and no reason therefore to defer to the claims of the greatest number.[14] Stronger justifications for majoritarianism do not rest on moral skepticism. They assume only that citizens cannot collectively agree, and should not be reasonably expected to do so, on the solutions to many moral conflicts. At the basis of this assumption lies a substantive moral value − political equality. The very basis for saying that the disagreement cannot be resolved (that citizens can reasonably reject its resolution) presumes that the (reasonable) moral claims of *each* citizen deserve respect.

Yet as soon as we recognize that proceduralism presumes this substantive value, we can ask whether majority rule adequately protects it. The answer, a simple example will make clear, is that it does not. Proceduralists, we shall see, need to qualify their majoritarianism in ways that

move procedural democracy in the direction of constitutional democracy.

Imagine five people who find themselves together in a railway car, some of whom wish to smoke and some of whom object to others smoking in their presence.[15] None of them can leave, and the car is not designated either smoking or nonsmoking. The passengers do not agree on any substantive principle such as "Everyone has a basic interest or right to smoke in each other's presence," or "Everyone has a basic interest or right not to inhale unwanted fumes." How should the conflict be resolved?

Brian Barry, who first described this hypothetical example, explains the appeal of letting majority preference determine the outcome:

> [Q]uite persuasive arguments can be made for saying that the decision should not simply reflect the number of people who want to smoke as against the number who dislike being in the presence of smokers. But, since opposing principles can be advanced, the existence of relevant principles does not seem to offer a sound basis for resistance to a majority decision.[16]

Barry imagines the Archbishop of Canterbury among the five passengers, claiming "the right to decide the smoking question on the basis either of his social position or on the basis of his presumptive expertise in casuistry." If the Archbishop's claim is accepted by all the other passengers, no decision-making problem arises, because there is agreement. If some of the passengers reject his claim, it again is difficult to see how the question can be settled except by a vote. If the Archbishop finds himself in the minority, it must be because he has failed to convince enough of his fellow passengers that he is right, or at least that he has the right to decide. He may continue to insist that his view should have been accepted, just as a believer in the natural right to smoke may continue to maintain that the others should have accepted his claim.

But, in the face of actual rejection of the minority views, the case for deferring to the majority decision looks strong.[17]

But the case looks different if we vary the example. Suppose that two of the passengers argue: "Nonsmokers should not be subject to the substantial health risks of passive smoking, and smokers are also harming themselves by smoking. So it is in no one's interest to smoke in this railway car." The vote is taken, and the two health-minded passengers lose, three to two. Does the case for deferring to the majority look as strong as before? Surely whether it does depends on the nature of the health risks. If we assume that the health risks are minor and uncertain, the case for majority rule still looks strong, though less so than it would be if there were no health risks at all. If we assume that the risks are likely to be great, however, the case weakens. Our confidence in the majority principle seems to decline as the health risks increase in severity and likelihood.

This simple example reveals that the appeal of majority rule depends on certain background assumptions, conditions that we implicitly take for granted in accepting it as the best way to deal with moral conflict. In the complex world of politics, these conditions can be quite complex and are rarely satisfied. When they are spelled out, majoritarianism looks less compelling, and proceduralism less satisfactory, as a way of resolving moral conflict.

Two conditions are most relevant for the moral conflicts in politics.[18] One is that the participants should have roughly equal chances of constituting the majority. As far as we could tell, none of the passengers in the railway car had any special relationships or history of prior associations; there were no voting blocs or ethnic or racial alliances that would interfere with a decision on the merits of the issue. Majority rule loses its moral appeal when there are "discrete and insular minorities"[19] in a democracy, citizens who systematically find themselves in the minority on most important decisions because

of the prejudices or distinctly different interests of majorities. In these circumstances, majoritarianism often works unfairly to the disadvantage of minorities, especially on issues of critical importance to them. Because the inspiration of procedural democracy is the ideal of citizens ruling themselves on equal terms rather than being ruled by an external power, the presence of discrete and insular minorities who consistently lose out undermines the moral appeal of majoritarian procedures. It is reasonable for discrete and insular minorities to reject majoritarianism on issues of critical importance to them if there is a procedural alternative that would better protect their legitimate interests.

Another condition qualifies the majority principle still further: the majority must not infringe the vital interests of individuals. If one of the passengers in the railway car is likely to suffer a severe asthma attack if he breathes tobacco smoke, he is surely not bound by a majority decision in favor of smoking.[20] More generally, we should want to say that decisions that violate the vital interests of any citizen cannot be justified simply by virtue of the fact that they result from a majoritarian or any other generally acceptable procedure.[21] Decisions that do not protect each citizen's basic liberty, as far as possible, can reasonably be rejected. Thus, even an otherwise acceptable procedural principle does not alone vindicate some substantive decisions.

Most procedural democrats accept that procedures should be constrained by some substantive values, but they try to restrict those values to those that are necessary to preserve the democratic process itself.[22] They agree that the majority must respect politically relevant rights such as freedom of speech, press, and association, the rule of law, and universal adult suffrage. But if our aim is to find a common perspective to resolve moral conflict, why limit ourselves to these procedural constraints? We have already seen that some decisions consistent with these procedural constraints – imposing life-threatening health risks on a few people for the sake of enhancing the pleasure of a greater number of people – cannot be justified. We have seen that the substance of the moral conflict may affect the justifiability of the procedure. If majoritarianism must be constrained by values internal to the democratic process, then it would seem that it should also be limited by values external to the process, such as those we have called vital interests. Indeed, some of these may also be necessary conditions of a fair democratic process. Procedure and substance are too intertwined to serve as markers for a distinction between constraints that should be part of a common perspective and those that should not. Neither kind of limit on majoritarianism can reasonably be rejected in general without considering the context of particular decisions and policies.

Acknowledging these limits of majority rule does not deny proceduralism a place in a common perspective for resolving moral conflicts. Some procedures are necessary for peacefully resolving moral conflicts, and no one has yet proposed a definitive decision-making procedure that is generally more justified than majority rule. Majoritarianism should not be dismissed, because, as Robert Dahl reminds us, "all the [procedural] alternatives to majority rule are also seriously flawed."[23]

Yet procedural democracy can never provide a completely adequate common perspective for resolving moral conflicts. In the absence of ideal conditions (such as those we identified in the example of the railway car), procedural democracy is incomplete in three respects.

First, it is indeterminate with respect to what it should know best – procedures.[24] Under some conditions (for example, permanent minorities), majority rule is not the uniquely right procedure for resolving moral conflicts. To decide whether majority rule or some other procedure is justified, we have to attend to the substantive values that are at stake in political decisions. Proceduralists therefore need to incorporate moral deliberation as a precondition for

adequately resolving many political disputes. This need undermines the original aim of proceduralism: to avoid substantive moral disagreement by less controversial procedural means. There is no way of realizing this aim without putting moral substance back into the procedure itself. This is one way in which deliberative democracy significantly revises proceduralism. Procedural indeterminacy opens the door for moral conflicts over procedures as well as substantive outcomes, and these conflicts cannot be resolved by invoking majority rule, interest-group bargaining, or any other procedural principle.[25] There is no substitute for substantive moral deliberation in resolving conflicts over procedures.

Even when it determines a correct procedure, procedural democracy remains incomplete in further ways, which also point to the need for deliberative democracy. One way is evident from our discussion of the modified railway-car example: even when otherwise justified, majority rule may not overrule vital interests (for example, serious and avoidable risks to health). The other way in which procedural democracy is incomplete can be brought out by modifying the example yet again. Suppose that one of the five passengers has specialized knowledge, gained by years of study, about the health risks of smoking. Another passenger, who has no strong views about whether smoking should be permitted in the car, wants to hear more about the pros and cons of the issue before she votes. No one objects to majority rule as the ultimate decision-making rule, but these two passengers object to the idea of simply taking a vote. They think it essential to discuss the substance of the question before anyone casts a vote.

This final variation of the example reminds us that any simple procedural principle such as majority rule is usually silent about an aspect of decision making that is of critical moral importance – the nature of the moral claims that are made before the vote is taken. To assess the justifiability of the procedure in particular instances, we need to know what kind of discussion took place, who participated, what arguments they presented, and how each responded to the claims of others. This is the moral deliberation that, we shall argue, is an essential part of any democratic process that seeks to resolve moral disagreement.

Procedural democracy does not so much reject as ignore deliberation. Proceduralists seek to resolve moral disagreement mainly by avoiding it: they make do with few substantive moral constraints, and they make little room for substantive moral discussion. Their silence about the content of political claims often accompanies a view of politics as the aggregation of individual or group interests. All claims come into the political process as expressions of preferences or interests. It is irrelevant, by proceduralist standards, whether these claims are supported by moral reasons or whether they can stand the test of public deliberation, as long as they are aggregated by the right procedure. The proceduralist view therefore naturally supports, and is in turn supported by, the well-known model of politics as interest-group bargaining, where the relative power of groups and their ability to take advantage of political procedures determines the outcome.

This model is inadequate as a moral understanding of politics for reasons that parallel the three ways in which proceduralism is incomplete. First, the procedures by which interest groups bargain are themselves not usually a product of interest-group bargaining. Nor should they be. Justifying procedures, as we have seen, requires attention to moral considerations. Second, interest-group bargaining cannot be justified if it violates the vital interests of individuals. Interest groups can constrain their own political demands by respect for the vital interests of others, but such self-constraint does not come naturally, nor is it guaranteed by any political procedure. To protect individual rights, a process of interest-group bargaining requires either self-constraint by interest groups or

external constraints. In either case, protecting the vital interests of individuals adds a missing nonprocedural element to the interest-group bargaining model. Third, at its best, interest-group bargaining is not well described as a process of merely asserting and aggregating interests. It is also a process of creating and modifying understandings of interests through collective discussion. Before they bargain, interest groups first deliberate internally to develop a morally defensible conception of their interests. In addition to bargaining with other groups, they also often appeal on moral grounds for public support.

Even at its best, however, interest-group bargaining cannot completely satisfy the demands of a common perspective. In every democratic society, some citizens are excluded from interest groups or included only in relatively weak ones, which cannot effectively represent the interests of their members. But even in an ideal society where interest groups had equal power, the three problems of proceduralism discussed above would still not be overcome. We have seen that even under the ideal conditions that proceduralists typically describe to justify interest-group bargaining, they find themselves under pressure to acknowledge more moral constraints and admit more moral discussion. Proceduralists are thus driven first in the direction of constitutional democracy and ultimately back toward deliberative democracy.

III. The Response of Constitutional Democracy

The critical difference between constitutional and procedural democrats is not that the former protect individual rights against majority rule, and the latter do not. Procedural democrats recognize two kinds of rights that limit majoritarianism: (1) rights such as voting equality that are *integral* to democratic procedures; and (2) rights such as a guaranteed minimum income that, though *external* to the democratic process, are *necessary* for its fair functioning.[26] They take notice of a third kind of right but deny it priority over majority rule: (3) rights that are *external* to the democratic process and *not necessary* for its fair functioning.[27] The view that this third kind of right should constrain any democratic procedure is what distinguishes constitutional from procedural democrats.[28]

We have already seen the intuitive appeal of constitutional democracy: some majority decisions are not acceptable because they violate vital or basic interests of individuals — for example, by posing serious health risks. From considering cases of this kind, we come to accept a general principle that holds that any legitimate decision-making procedure must respect a set of individual rights that protect the vital interests of individuals against the claims of majorities, pluralities, or minorities. A common perspective for resolving moral conflicts thus must make room for moral judgments not only of procedures but of their results. Constitutional democracy broadens the search for substantive values that can be included in a common perspective to resolve moral disagreements.

Broadening the search in this way, however, creates difficulties for constitutional democrats, parallel to the difficulties faced by procedural democrats. One difficulty is the same for both proceduralists and constitutionalists. Constitutional democrats insist, no less than procedural democrats, that citizens need morally justified processes for arriving at politically binding decisions. John Rawls, whose theory we take as a paradigm of constitutional democracy, writes:

> that some form of majority rule is justified as the best available way of insuring just and effective legislation. It is compatible with equal liberty . . . and possesses a certain naturalness; for if minority rule is allowed, there is no obvious criterion to select which one is to decide and equality is violated.[29]

Like proceduralists, constitutionalists also confront the problem of deciding what form of majority rule, if any, is the most justifiable way of securing just legislation.

Constitutional democrats face a further difficulty. Because they go further than procedural democrats in constraining democratic processes by substantive standards, the common perspective they propose becomes even more contestable. The substantive standards they offer seem compelling when stated abstractly: who would deny that majorities should not violate the vital interests of their fellow citizens? But the abstraction purchases reasonable agreement on the principles at the price of reasonable disagreement about their interpretation. The more abstract the constitutional standards, the more contestable their interpretation. For the purpose of assessing and resolving moral conflict in political life, the interpretation matters just as much as the principle. We must have a way of dealing with these interpretative disagreements before constitutional standards can establish a common perspective to inform not only the theory but also the practice of democratic politics.

To illustrate this problem of interpretation, consider Rawls's principle of equal liberty. Among the basic freedoms on Rawls's list are "the liberty and integrity of the person."[30] What does this liberty require in practice? Recall the railway car: would a majority decision to permit smoking count as a violation of basic liberty? More generally, would public policies permitting environmental pollution, or policies prohibiting it, contravene a basic liberty? The problem is not that we need more facts about the risks and the consequences: even with perfect information, we would still have to decide what risks to impose, and to what extent they violate this basic liberty. Giving priority to liberty in our common perspective, as constitutional democrats propose, scarcely begins to answer any of the specific questions that shape moral conflicts in everyday politics.

Constitutionalizing liberty still leaves wide differences of reasonable opinion about many important issues concerning individual liberty, such as legalizing violent pornography, prostitution, and abortion. Rawls does not, of course, offer his theory as a solution to such conflicts; he hopes that by focusing on the basic structure of society, he can avoid the indeterminacy of the conflicts posed by public policy. Perhaps a theory of justice is warranted in trying to avoid such conflicts, but theoretically informed practice that seeks a common perspective to resolve such conflicts is not.

Similar difficulties plague the constitutionalists' search for principles to govern social and economic inequalities. What policies would satisfy, for example, Rawls's principle of "fair equality of opportunity" or his "difference principle?" (The difference principle requires that social and economic inequalities "be to the greatest benefit of the least advantaged members of society."[31]) Does fair equality of opportunity demand, or permit, preferential hiring for African Americans, Native Americans, Hispanics, and women? Does the difference principle require universal access to health care? Constitutional democrats who insist on using these principles to constrain the democratic process have to provide answers to such questions, and at a level of specificity sufficient to resolve the conflicts they express. This seems more than a Herculean task.

In his more recent writing, Rawls in effect addresses this difficulty by suggesting that fair equality of opportunity and the difference principle should not be included among the elements of what we are calling a common perspective. "These matters are nearly always open to wide differences of reasonable opinion," he writes, and they "rest on complicated inferences and intuitive judgments that require us to assess complex social and economic information about topics poorly understood."[32] He concludes that "freedom of movement and free choice of occupation and a social minimum covering citizens'

basic needs count as constitutional essentials while the principle of fair opportunity and the difference principle do not."[33]

In this way Rawls escapes the problem of interpretation that plagues some constitutional democrats, at least as far as principles dealing with equal opportunity and social inequalities are concerned. But many, perhaps most, of the large questions of public policy fall within the territory that would be governed by the principles of fair equality of opportunity and the difference principle. The question therefore persists: on what basis should conflicts about these issues be resolved? Rawls relies on "established political procedures [being] reasonably regarded as fair" to resolve these substantive disagreements.[34] It appears that we have returned to proceduralism. The problem of resolving moral conflicts over social and economic inequalities becomes again the problem of justifying a set of political procedures. Yet, as we have seen, neither constitutional nor procedural democrats suggest how this can be done, or why we should even think it possible to resolve the remaining substantive disagreements over social and economic inequalities merely by procedural means.

Constitutional democrats do not ignore the importance of the democratic process. Rawls himself argues cogently for the value of citizenship and participation in politics. In the spirit of John Stuart Mill, he writes that democratic self-government enhances "the sense of political competence of the average citizen." Citizens are expected to vote and therefore "to have political opinions." He echoes Mill in declaring that the democratic citizen is "called upon to weigh interests other than his own, and to be guided by some conception of justice and the public good rather than by his own inclinations." Citizens must "appeal to principles that others can accept." Political liberty "is not solely a means," but also a valued way of life for citizens.[35] All of this suggests a morally robust political process.

Yet like other constitutional democrats, Rawls stops short of suggesting that a well-ordered democracy requires ordinary citizens and public officials to engage in extensive moral deliberation to resolve their moral disagreements. This is puzzling. One would think that if democratic citizens are to value political liberty not merely as a means, if they are to weigh the interests of others, and to be guided in their actions by a sense of justice, then democratic governments should encourage moral discussion about controversial political issues. Forums for moral deliberation should abound, and citizens and their representatives should continually confront their moral conflicts together. The lack of these forums both in theory and practice − what we might call the deliberative deficit − should be a matter of considerable concern to constitutional democrats.

When Rawls considers how to make the two principles of justice more specific, he does not propose that citizens discuss their disagreements in the public forum. Rather, he suggests that each of us alone perform an extended and intricate thought-experiment, a kind of private deliberation, incorporating a veil of ignorance that obscures our own personal interests and compels us to judge on a more impersonal basis. This process of reflection may be seen as a philosophical analogue of judicial deliberation. For some constitutional democrats, the U.S. Supreme Court performs the same function.

Here is how the solitary deliberation might go, as each of us alone tries to develop the common perspective by making the principles more specific.[36] Having agreed on the two principles of justice, we first enter a constitutional mode of thinking. We imagine ourselves as delegates at a constitutional convention trying to design institutions and procedures that will yield results in accord with the principles of justice. Having created the best possible constitution for our social circumstances, we recognize that it does not address most of the important issues of public policy, such as environmental pollution or preferential hiring. Lifting the veil of ignorance further so that we can know more about the current circumstances of society, we move to a legislative mode of thinking and try to decide what laws and policies would be just for our society. Even after we have gone through all the stages of thinking in this solitary process, we are likely to find that:

> this test is often indeterminate. . . . [W]hen this is so, justice is to that extent likewise indeterminate. Institutions within the permitted range are equally just, meaning that they could be chosen; they are compatible with all the constraints of the theory. . . . This indeterminacy in the theory of justice is not in itself a defect. It is what we should expect.[37]

Rawls is surely right that we should expect considerable indeterminacy in any theory of justice. He is also certainly right to suggest that each of us should think through the principles of justice on our own as best we can. But why should the indeterminacy of justice begin just where the determinacy of our solitary philosophical reflection leaves off? It appears that for Rawls and other constitutional democrats the point at which our solitary thinking about justice becomes indeterminate also marks the point at which social justice and our ability to find a common perspective on moral disagreements in politics becomes incapacitated. We might as well check our deliberative thinking at the door to the public forum; in any case we had better keep it to ourselves.

This conclusion fits uncomfortably within a theory that requires democratic citizens to achieve a high degree of moral and political competence and to maintain a stable commitment to principles of justice. The necessary competence and commitment are not likely to be sustained unless citizens consider together in public forums the meaning of constitutional principles and their implications for specific decisions and policies of government. Furthermore, it is premature to conclude that these principles are indeterminate over such a wide range of public policies. Just because we cannot in advance philosophically establish principles specific enough to constrain public policy, we should not conclude that we could not discover such principles through discussion with our fellow citizens in a process informed by the facts of political life, and inspired by the ideals of moral deliberation.

IV. The Need for Moral Deliberation

How far do procedural and constitutional democracy move toward a common moral perspective for resolving moral disagreements in politics? Both procedural and constitutional democrats rightly agree that the fundamental values of democratic institutions, such as equal political liberty, must be justified by moral arguments. They seek to show that democratic institutions protect the equal right of all citizens to participate in political processes and to enjoy basic freedoms. The justifications typically appeal to a moral conception of the person as a free and equal autonomous agent. At the foundation of democratic institutions, according to both proceduralists and constitutionalists, lie fundamental moral ideals that are or should be widely shared.

Procedural and constitutional democrats also agree that democratic institutions are not justified unless they generally produce morally acceptable results. Democratic institutions that produce policies that deprive some citizens of freedom of speech or religion, or deny others reasonable opportunities to live a decent life, would be rejected by both procedural and constitutional democrats. The precise content of the criticisms that proceduralists and constitutionalists make against such results may differ, but both have at their disposal the resources for a substantial moral appraisal of the laws and policies that emerge at the end of any democratic process.

Moral argument – justification from a common perspective – thus plays an important role in warranting both its foundations and its conclusions. It makes its appearance at both the beginning and the end of the democratic process. What role should it play *within* the ongoing processes of everyday politics – in what we might call "middle democracy"? If a common perspective for resolving moral disagreements must rely on moral arguments to justify the foundations and results of democracy, then should it not also require moral arguments within the ongoing processes of democracy? Yet on this question, on the place of moral argument *within* democratic politics, procedural and constitutional democrats are surprisingly silent. This is puzzling in a way that has not been sufficiently appreciated. If democracy must be moral in its structure and its outcomes, how can it remain amoral within its internal processes?

Middle democracy is the land of everyday politics, where legislators, executives, administrators, and judges make and apply policies and laws, sometimes arguing among themselves, sometimes explaining themselves to citizens. It is here that much of the moral life of a democracy, for good or for evil, is to be found. It is a land that democrats seeking a common moral perspective on democracy can scarcely afford to bypass. A democratic theory that is to remain faithful to its moral premises and aspirations for justice must take seriously the possibility of moral argument within these processes.

Given the limited generosity and incomplete understanding of both officials and citizens, what goes on in these processes generally falls far short of any moral ideal. Perhaps that is why so many democratic theorists seem to want to ignore the possibility of principled moral argument here. The everyday operation of the democratic process is imperfect, to be sure, but so are its structures and results. It is hard to see how we gain anything, morally speaking, by limiting ourselves to only some of its imperfect parts. It is more likely that neglecting the possibility of moral argument in any part will only multiply the imperfections in the whole. Amorality is rarely the weapon of choice in the battle against immorality. The amorality of a political process is surely more troubling than its imperfection. Imperfection is endemic to the human condition; amorality is not.

Many constitutional democrats recognize the importance of extensive moral deliberation within one of our democratic institutions – the Supreme Court.[38] They argue that judges cannot interpret constitutional principles without engaging in moral deliberation at least in order to fashion a coherent view from the many moral values that our constitutional tradition expresses. The fact that this process itself is imperfect – that judges disagree morally, even about the relevance of morality in the process – is not thought to be a reason to diminish the role of deliberation. On the contrary: the failures of moral argument in the judicial process are thought to make the quest for successes all the more urgent. Why is the same not true for the rest of the democratic process?

Moral argument is at least as important and no less frequent in other democratic institutions. Legislators, for example, make moral arguments regularly, and often quite capably, taking into account the conditions under which they work. Consider the way the U.S. Congress discussed the controversial issue of federal subsidies for abortion. In 1976, Congress adopted the so-called Hyde Amendment to the Medicaid provisions of the Social Security Act. The Medicaid provisions subsidize health care for citizens below the poverty line, and the amendment prohibited federal subsidies for Medicaid abortions except to save the life of the mother. A year later, rape and incest were added as exceptions. In 1980, the Supreme Court in a five-to-four decision upheld the constitutionality of the Hyde Amendment.[39] Congress recurrently debated the issue at length, while the Court has considered the case only once so far.

The controversy over subsidizing abortion for poor women has many of the features of the many moral disagreements that make their way through our imperfect legislative and judicial processes. The sources of the controversy include not only scarcity of resources and the limited generosity of citizens, but also incompatible values and incomplete understanding of how best to weigh the many factors that would help decide among the values. The issue is undeniably one in which moral principles are at stake, not merely personal preferences or group interests. Citizens and officials on both sides of the issue credibly invoke basic constitutional principles, in effect supporting the claim of constitutional democrats that decisions about fundamental moral values should be reviewed by authorities standing outside the ordinary political process, specifically the judiciary. But the controversy also provides evidence against the view that courts are the forum of principle in our democratic system, and that the legislatures are incapable, or demonstrably less capable, of considering moral principles in the making of law. Congressional debates over the Hyde Amendment have been replete with (good and bad) principled arguments – indeed, on this issue, more so than the opinions of the Supreme Court.

Even if moral deliberation in the wider democratic process is possible, it may not be desirable. We think that Congress reached the wrong conclusion on the question of subsidizing abortion. We cannot therefore locate the value of deliberation wholly in the justice of the policies it produces. (Those who agree with Congress on this issue should have no trouble in finding another case that would test their commitment to deliberation in the face of outcomes with which they disagree.) Extending the domain of deliberation may have other risks, too. Once the moral sensibilities of citizens and officials are engaged, they may be less willing to compromise. Issues come to be seen as matters of principle, creating occasions for high-minded statements, unyielding stands, and no-holds-barred opposition. Furthermore, once the forum admits reasonable moral claims, it cannot easily exclude the unreasonable ones. There are moral fanatics as well as moral sages, and in politics the former are likely to be more vocal than the latter.

These are real risks. It should be clear that no political process can avoid them completely, but more widespread deliberation is likely to decrease them. It is a hollow hope that any one institution, even the Supreme Court, could be relied on to reach the right conclusions, were it to do all our deliberating. Moral sensitivity, it is true, may sometimes make necessary political compromises more difficult, but its absence also makes unjustifiable ones more common. Moral argument can arouse moral fanatics, but it also combats their claims on their own terms. Furthermore, there is no reason to believe that the chief alternative to deliberation – bargaining among interests – protects us any better from moral extremism.[40] The extremists in the abortion debate neither deliberate nor bargain: they turn to violence outside the political process.

However we weigh these risks, we should also consider the positive value of moral deliberation in politics. The case for deliberation is best made by looking at specific issues of policy, noticing how it works in practice and how it might work better. But four general reasons – paralleling the four sources of moral disagreement – are worth emphasizing in general terms. Together they provide a compelling case on democratic grounds for extending the domain of deliberation within the democratic process, for granting it authority to deal with the moral conflicts that procedural and constitutional democracy fail to resolve.[41]

The first reason concerns the contribution that deliberation makes to the legitimacy of decisions and policies. Given scarce resources, some citizens will not get what they want, or even what they need, and sometimes none will. The hard choices that governments make in these circumstances should be more acceptable even to those who receive less than they deserve, if their claims have been considered on their merits, rather than on the basis of relative wealth, status, or power. Even among policies with which we disagree, we should take a different attitude toward those that are adopted after consideration of the relevant conflicting moral claims, and those that are adopted after only calculation of the relative strength of the competing political interests. Moral justifications do not, of course, make up for the material resources that we fail to receive. But they help sustain the political legitimacy that makes possible our collective efforts to secure more of those resources in the future, and to live with each other civilly in the meantime.

Second, deliberation responds to our limited generosity by creating forums in which we are encouraged to take a broader perspective on questions of public policy. John Stuart Mill presented one of the earliest and still most cogent accounts of such a process. Mill argued that when participating in political discussion, a citizen is:

> called upon ... to weigh interests not his own; to be guided, in case of conflicting claims, by another rule than his private partialities; to apply, at every turn, principles and maxims which have for their reason of existence the common good. ... .[42]

We do not need to make the optimistic assumption that most citizens will suddenly become public-spirited when they find themselves deliberating in the public forum. Much depends on the background conditions: the level of political competence (how well informed citizens are), the distribution of resources (how equally situated they are), and the nature of the political culture (what kind of arguments are taken seriously). All we need to assume is that citizens and their representatives are more likely to take a broader view of issues, to consider the claims of more of their fellow citizens, in a process in which moral arguments are taken seriously than in a process in which assertions of political power prevail.

The third reason for encouraging deliberation is that it can clarify the nature of a moral conflict. We are more likely to recognize what is morally at stake in a dispute if we employ moral reasoning in trying to resolve it. Deliberation helps sort out the self-interested from the public-spirited claims, and among the latter helps identify those that have greater weight. Through this kind of deliberative process, we can begin to isolate those conflicts that embody genuinely incompatible values. Those that do not may then turn out to be more easily resolvable: we might discover that they are the result of misunderstanding or lack of information, or we might now see ways to settle them by ordinary political processes of negotiation and compromise. For those conflicts that persist, those that represent moral conflict for which there is no reasonable resolution at present, deliberation can help citizens better understand the moral seriousness of the views they oppose, and better cooperate with their fellow citizens who hold these views. This potential for mutual respect is part of the common perspective that we seek.

In some situations, making democratic government more deliberative may increase political tensions and conflict, at least in the short run. Creating more deliberative forums may bring previously excluded voices into politics, and these voices are not likely to sing in harmony. We should count this as a virtue of deliberative democracy in bringing to light legitimate moral conflicts that are suppressed by political processes that are not sufficiently deliberative. The aim of deliberative democracy is not consensus per se but a morally justified consensus. Deliberative democracy strives for consensus not for its own sake but for the sake of finding a genuinely common perspective. No conception of democracy can justify the suppression of moral voices for the sake of producing political consensus in the short run. Deliberative

democracy decreases the risk of suppressing such conflict at the same time as it increases the chances of clarifying the values at stake in all our conflicts.

Finally, deliberation takes seriously the incomplete understanding that characterizes moral conflict. More than other kinds of political processes, it contains the means of its own correction. Through the give-and-take of argument citizens can learn from each other, come to recognize their individual and collective mistakes, and develop new views and policies that are more widely justifiable. When interest groups bargain and negotiate without deliberating, they may learn how better to get what they want, but they are not likely to learn that they should not try to get what they want. The main source of movement in this kind of politics is shifts in power, not changes of mind. Power shifts may bring improvement, but only accidentally. Changes of mind are responsive to reasons that at least direct our attention to improvement. When majorities are obligated to offer reasons to dissenting minorities, they expose their position to criticism and give minorities their most effective and fairest chance of persuading majorities of the justice of their position. We may even hope, encouraged by Aristotle, that views better than those held by either the majority or the minority will emerge from such a process. But even when deliberation fails to produce a satisfactory resolution of a moral conflict at any particular time, its self-correcting capacity remains our best hope – and our only democratic hope – for discovering such a resolution in the future.

For all these reasons, we should try to press deliberation beyond the boundaries that procedural and constitutional democracy now set. Both proceduralists and constitutionalists tend to neglect the importance of deliberation within the democratic process. Nevertheless, extending deliberation is consistent with the moral aspirations of constitutional and procedural democrats, and may even be required by them. As we have seen, procedural and constitutional democracy are indeterminate in a critical respect: both need, but neither provides, a way of arriving at provisionally justifiable resolutions of moral conflicts with sufficient specificity.

Furthermore, the conflict between these forms of democracy itself is not likely to be resolved without giving greater scope to deliberation in the political process than either now recognizes. Constitutional democrats tend to regard procedural democracy as dangerously amoral, and look to the judiciary for moral protection. Procedural democrats rightly point out that judicial processes, like legislative ones, are imperfect, and cannot be relied on for reaching morally right conclusions. Proceduralists ask: Why then make judges the arbiters of our fundamental moral conflicts? As long as procedural democrats neglect the need for deliberation, constitutional democrats have a powerful answer: An imperfectly deliberative judicial process is better than a consistently unprincipled legislative process. With all its imperfections, judicial deliberation comes closer to serving the ideal of a common perspective than does the interest-group bargaining to which the proceduralists give license.

We need not choose between proceduralism and constitutionalism, however, if we recognize the alternative of deliberative democracy, develop its principles, and pursue their practical implications. Our discussion has focused on developing a conception of deliberative democracy, an alternative to proceduralism and constitutionalism. That is, we believe, the most important step in restoring deliberation to its proper place in democracy.

Once we understand the conception of deliberative democracy, we can better develop the institutions that will realize it. Various forms of democratic government – including direct, participatory, and representative democracy – can all be designed in a way that is conducive to deliberation. The point of a conception of deliberative democracy is not to elevate one institutional form of democracy above the others, but rather to find ways of making each form more deliberative. Nor should deliberative democracy rely on one "master" deliberative forum, such as a judicial system, to convert power politics into a principled politics. Not only courts and legislatures, but administrative agencies, city councils, and local boards of education can and should deliberate. The practical task of deliberative democrats is to consider how each political institution can be designed to facilitate deliberation.

Some changes in political institutions will certainly be necessary. Deliberation requires, for example, that officials justify their actions in public, and that the reasons they give be accessible to citizens. This requirement may force some changes in the role of experts in policy making; at the least, they will have to find better ways to explain their recommendations in public forums. The requirement would also rule out some secret or confidential processes of policy making that now take place. Also, deliberative democracy would give preference to forums in which citizens with different moral perspectives could talk to each other, rather than the kind of forums that are now more common, in which citizens merely express their views to government. Congressional hearings, for example, would consist not merely of a procession of interest-group representatives giving testimony, but also of panels of citizens debating among themselves.

Deliberative democracy has implications for reform of not only political but also social institutions. Schools and other institutions of civic education, for example, must teach future citizens the skills and virtues of public deliberation.[43] Similarly, the many institutions in which citizens work and with which they interact – corporations, hospitals, the media – should provide opportunities for constructively engaging moral disagreement.

If all democratic institutions including judicial processes are imperfect, and all democratic institutions including legislative processes depend on the give-and-take of moral argument to correct their mistakes, then procedural and constitutional democrats can find some common ground. They can find it if each pays greater attention to the need for moral deliberation within all democratic forums.

[...]

Notes

1 These three characteristics may be seen as informal statements of criteria defining the moral point of view, or the formal conditions of right. See Kurt Baier, *The Moral Point of View* (Ithaca: Cornell University Press, 1958), pp. 187–213; and John Rawls, *A Theory of Justice* (Cambridge: Harvard University Press, 1971), pp. 130–6.

2 Our use of the standard of reasonable rejection owes most to T. M. Scanlon, "Contractualism and Utilitarianism," in *Utilitarianism and Beyond*, ed. Amartya Sen and Bernard Williams (Cambridge: Cambridge University Press, 1982), pp. 103–28.

3 Once the classic example of a people with an amoral if not immoral culture, the Ick, anthropologists now think, were unfairly maligned; they seem to be morally no worse in attitude and behavior than most cultures. See Robert Edgerton, *Sick Societies: Challenging the Myth of Primitive Harmony* (New York: Free Press, 1992), pp. 6–8.

4 Thomas Hobbes, *Leviathan*, ed. Michael Oakeshott (New York: Macmillan, 1962), ch. 4, pp. 39–40.

5 It is no longer plausible to claim as a matter of historical fact that "all moral theories have hitherto been the product of the economic conditions of society obtaining at the time.... [M]orality has always been class morality; it has (usually) justified the domination and the interest of the ruling class ..." (Friedrich Engels, "On Morality," in *The Marx-Engels Reader*, 2d ed., ed. Robert C. Tucker [New York: Norton, 1978], p. 726). One can, however, make these claims true by definition. The economic conditions of a society, for example, are an important part of what causally produces moral theorists and influences their consciousness, and therefore moral theories are, in this weak sense, the product of the economic conditions of society obtaining at any particular time.

6 David Hume, *A Treatise of Human Nature*, 2d ed., ed. L. A. Selby-Bigge (Oxford: Clarendon Press, 1978), Book III, part II, section ii, pp. 484–501.

7 Although Hume suggests that *extreme* scarcity would eliminate moral conflict, we should consider both moderate and extreme scarcity as sources of moral conflict. Extreme scarcity need not render disputes over justice beside the point. See D. Clayton Hubin's discussion in "The Scope of Justice," *Philosophy & Public Affairs*, vol. 9, no. 1 (Fall 1979), p. 18.

8 Although a society where people utterly lack generosity and fellow-feeling would be a strange society indeed, moral conflicts can also arise among complete egoists. Suppose that some of the egoists "work hard to create valuable objects from the moderate store of raw materials that nature provides." Genuine moral conflicts may break out among these ruffians, each of whom argues for his or her fair share. Even if they argue from self-interested motives, their arguments nonetheless can have genuine moral content. See Hubin, "The Scope of Justice," p. 10.

9 Philosophers who have developed versions of this view in recent years include Isaiah Berlin, "Two Concepts of Liberty," in *Four Essays on Liberty* (Oxford: Oxford University Press, 1969), pp. 118–72; Thomas Nagel, *Mortal Questions* (Cambridge: Cambridge University Press, 1979), pp. 128–41; Bernard Williams, "Ethical Consistency," in *Problems of the Self* (Cambridge: Cambridge University Press, 1973), pp. 166–86; and Michael Walzer, "Political Action: The Problem of Dirty Hands," *Philosophy & Public Affairs*, vol. 2 (Winter 1973), pp. 160–80. For a sample of views on both sides, see Christopher Gowan, ed., *Moral Dilemmas* (Oxford: Oxford University Press, 1987).

10 We do not attempt to argue for any general moral foundations for democracy here; we take it for granted that at least one of the moral justifications for democracy that political theorists have presented establishes its superiority over non-democracy. Our focus is on the comparative moral merits of different conceptions of democracy, and on only one aspect of that question: their comparative capacities for addressing moral conflict. Some

602 Amy Gutmann and Dennis Thompson

discussions of the general justification of democracy that we have found helpful include Robert A. Dahl, *Democracy and Its Critics* (New Haven: Yale University Press, 1989); David Held, *Models of Democracy* (Stanford: Stanford University Press, 1987); Jack Lively, *Democracy* (New York: St. Martin's Press, 1975); William Nelson, *Justifying Democracy* (London: Routledge and Kegan Paul, 1980); and J. Roland Pennock, *Democratic Political Theory* (Princeton: Princeton University Press, 1979). We also rely on our own earlier discussions of this topic: Amy Gutmann, *Liberal Equality* (Cambridge: Cambridge University Press, 1980); Dennis Thompson, *The Democratic Citizen* (Cambridge: Cambridge University Press, 1970); and Thompson, *John Stuart Mill and Representative Government* (Princeton: Princeton University Press, 1976).

11 We take Robert Dahl as a paradigmatic procedural democrat, in part because his subtle form of proceduralism recognizes that "the democratic process is . . . itself a rich bundle of substantive goods" (*Democracy and Its Critics*, p. 175). Other proceduralists who specifically defend majority rule include Elaine Spitz, *Majority Rule* (Chatham, NJ: Chatham House, 1984); and Douglas Rae, "Decision Rules and Individual Values in Constitutional Choice," *American Political Science Review*, vol. 63 (1969), pp. 40–56. More generally, the pluralist tradition in American political science, beginning most notably with the work of David Truman, provides numerous examples of proceduralism.

12 An assumption of political equality seems to lie behind Locke's defense of majority rule in the *Second Treatise*, ch. 8, section 96, in John Locke, *Two Treatises of Government*, ed. Peter Laslett (New York: New American Library, 1965), p. 375.

13 A prominent example is John Hart Ely, *Democracy and Distrust* (Cambridge: Harvard University Press, 1981).

14 For critiques of procedural democrats such as Ely, see Cass R. Sunstein, *The Partial Constitution* (Cambridge: Harvard University Press, 1993), esp. pp. 143–5; Jeremy Waldron, "A Right-based Critique of Constitutional Rights" (unpublished manuscript); and Ronald Dworkin, *A Matter of Principle* (Cambridge: Harvard University Press, 1985), pp. 57–65.

15 Brian Barry, "Is Democracy Special?" in *Democracy and Power, Essays in Political Theory I* (Oxford: Clarendon Press, 1991), p. 29, citing his early discussion in Barry, *Political Argument* (London: Routledge and Kegan Paul, 1965), p. 312.

16 Barry, "Is Democracy Special?" p. 30.

17 Ibid., p. 30.

18 Two other features of the railway-car example, and other cases in which majority rule seems the right solution, are worth noting not only because they are important in technical discussions but also because they are so rarely satisfied in real political circumstances. In such cases: (1) only one question is the subject of decision; and (2) the question offers only two, dichotomous alternatives (such as "smoking" or "no smoking"). When there are multiple decisions to be made or more than two alternatives ("smoking," "no smoking," "smoking at certain times only"), as there almost always are in political life, then there are also likely to be procedures other than simple majority rule that are reasonable ways of resolving the controversies. Plurality rule, for example, may be a reasonable way of resolving disagreements with more than two alternatives. See Barry, "Is Democracy Special?"

19 In his opinion for the Supreme Court in *United States v. Carotene Products Co.*, 304 U.S. 144, 152–3 n. 4 (1938), Justice Harlan Stone wrote that:

> prejudice against discrete and insular minorities may be a special condition, which tends seriously to curtail the operation of those political processes ordinarily to be relied upon to protect minorities, and . . . may call for a correspondingly more searching judicial inquiry.

20 Barry, "Is Democracy Special?" p. 37.

21 Ibid., p. 38.

22 Dahl, *Democracy and Its Critics*, p. 167. Stuart Hampshire, who in his most recent writings is a thoroughgoing proceduralist, may disagree, but he also may not think that democracy is necessary to justice; see Hampshire, *Innocence and Experience* (Cambridge: Harvard University Press, 1989). He argues for the need for procedural justice, but never claims that the procedures must be democratic to be just.

23 Dahl, *Democracy and Its Critics*, p. 162.

24 See William Riker, *Liberalism against Populism* (San Francisco: W. H. Freeman and Co., 1982); and

Kenneth Arrow, *Social Choice and IndividualValues*, 2d ed. (New York: Wiley, 1963).

25   David Miller discusses how deliberation can overcome the potential arbitrariness in democratic decision making that is revealed by social choice theorists, in Miller, "Social Choice and Deliberative Democracy," *Political Studies*, vol. 40 (1992), pp. 60–63.

26   Dahl, *Democracy and Its Critics*, p. 167.

27   Ibid.

28   We take John Rawls as the paradigmatic constitutional democrat; although obviously others have written more extensively about the legal and judicial basis for such a view, Rawls provides the most sophisticated and cogent defense of the rationale for constitutionalism. Furthermore, we find so much of his theory compelling that it is important for us to try to distinguish our own view from his. Other constitutional democrats we have found helpful include Laurence Tribe, *American Constitutional Law* (Minelo, NY: Foundation Press, 1978); Ronald Dworkin, *Taking Rights Seriously* (Cambridge: Harvard University Press, 1977); Dworkin, *A Matter of Principle*; and Dworkin, *Law's Empire* (Cambridge: Harvard University Press, 1986).

29   Rawls, *A Theory of Justice*, p. 356.

30   John Rawls, *Political Liberalism* (New York: Columbia University Press, 1993), p. 291.

31   Ibid.

32   Ibid., p. 229.

33   Ibid., p. 230.

34   Ibid.

35   Rawls, *A Theory of Justice*, p. 234.

36   The process we describe is a simplified version of the constitutional and legislative stages of the rarely discussed "four-stage sequence" in *A Theory of Justice*, pp. 195–201. The scheme, as Rawls outlines it, is intricate and elusive. We are less concerned with its details than with the general strategy of resolving specific moral conflicts that it represents.

37   Rawls, *A Theory of Justice*, p. 201.

38   See, e.g., Dworkin, *A Matter of Principle*, pp. 9–71, and *Law's Empire*, pp. 355–99.

39   *Harris v. Macrae*, 448 U.S. 297 (1980).

40   Bargaining among interests may be a morally appropriate way to resolve some political issues, where only competing interests are at stake and where resolving their differences should be primarily a matter of negotiation, but deliberation typically will be necessary to figure out when such bargaining is justified, and when it is not.

41   For other discussions of the basis of deliberative democracy, see Joshua Cohen, "Deliberation and Democratic Legitimacy," in *The Good Polity: Normative Analysis of the State*, ed. Alan Hamlin and Philip Pettit (Oxford: Basil Blackwell, 1989), pp. 17–34; James Fishkin, *Democracy and Deliberation* (New Haven: Yale University Press, 1971); Charles Larmore, *Patterns of Moral Complexity* (Cambridge: Cambridge University Press, 1987), esp. pp. 59–66; Bernard Manin, "On Legitimacy and Political Deliberation," *Political Theory*, vol. 15 (August 1987), pp. 338–68; Jane Mansbridge, "Motivating Deliberation in Congress," in *Constitutionalism in America*, vol. 2, ed. Sarah Baumgartner (New York: University Press of America, 1988), pp. 59–86; Cass R. Sunstein, *The Partial Constitution* (Cambridge: Harvard University Press, 1993), pp. 133–45; and Thompson, *The Democratic Citizen*, ch. 4, pp. 86–119.

42   John Stuart Mill, *Considerations on Representative Government*, in *Collected Writings*, vol. 19, ed. J. M. Robson (Toronto: University of Toronto Press; London: Routledge and Kegan Paul, 1977), ch. 3, p. 68. For discussion of empirical evidence that supports Mill, see Thompson, *John Stuart Mill and Representative Government*, pp. 38–43, 49–53.

43   For a defense of teaching deliberation and an examination of some of its institutional implications, see Amy Gutmann, *Democratic Education* (Princeton: Princeton University Press, 1987), pp. 50–52 and *passim*.

Chapter 43

Jason Brennan

POLITICAL LIBERTY
Who Needs It?

Jason Brennan (1979–) is Assistant Professor of Strategy, Economics, Ethics, and Public Policy in the McDonough School of Business, and Assistant Professor of Philosophy, at Georgetown University. He is the author of several important books in political philosophy, including *The Ethics of Voting* (Princeton, 2011). In this essay, he argues against the common view that political liberties like the right to vote and the right to run for elected office are among an individual's most valuable possessions. It might be good that all persons have such liberties, and every individual might have a *right* to such liberties. But for the individual who has them, political liberties don't do much good at all.

Most people accustomed to living in contemporary democracies believe that the political liberties, by which I specifically mean here the equal rights to vote and run for office, are especially important and valuable. Contemporary political philosophers and political theorists agree. These philosophers, including many deliberative democrats, Rawlsian "high liberals," civic republicans, and civic humanists have recently tended to endorse progressively stronger views about the value of the political liberties. They tend to hold that citizens' lives will be stunted, and their status as human beings will be diminished, unless they have equal rights to vote and run for office. It has become more common to hold that the political liberties – the rights to run for office and vote – are of special importance, even more important and valuable than the civil or economic liberties, such as the

right of free speech, or right to choose one's religion, or right to hold and use private property.[1]

In this essay, I challenge this trend. I think the political liberties are overvalued. Contrary to the mainstream view, I hold that the political liberties are much less important and valuable to us, as individuals, than the civic or economic liberties. I argue here that for most people the political liberties are of little value for the purposes of securing their social status, promoting their preferred political outcomes, acting autonomously, achieving enlightenment and bettering themselves, or expressing themselves.

The claim that the political liberties are not very valuable is easily confused with other claims. Note the distinction between the following two questions:

1. Are an individual's political liberties typically valuable to that individual?
2. Are the political liberties valuable in the aggregate?

Questions 1 and 2 ask different things. Question 2 might have a positive answer even if question 1 has a negative answer. After all, suppose democracy with universal suffrage produces the best expected consequences of any form of government. If so, then it would be valuable in the aggregate to imbue citizens with the rights to vote and run for office. However, it might still be that each individual's political liberties are of little value to her. Consider, in parallel, that each of us is free to pursue advances in physics. Most of us aren't clever enough to make much use of these scientific liberties. Yet, we benefit from living in a social system where everyone has these liberties. So, the scientific liberties are of little value to the typical person who holds them, even though they are valuable in the aggregate. So it might be with the political liberties. This essay concerns question 1, but not question 2.

Note also the distinction between these two questions:

1. Are an individual's political liberties typically valuable to that individual?
3. Does the typical individual value her political liberties?

Questions 1 and 3 are also distinct. Question 3 asks whether citizens subjectively value their political liberties. That's a psychological, not a philosophical, question. We could answer it with surveys. However, question 1 is philosophical. To ask whether the political liberties are valuable is to ask whether they *ought to be* valued, not whether people actually value them. Again, this essay concerns question 1.

Note finally the distinction between these two questions:

1. Are an individual's political liberties typically valuable to that individual?
4. Are all adult citizens entitled to the political liberties as a matter of justice?

In this paper, I am not asking question 4, which concerns whether citizens are entitled to the political liberties. The answer to question 4 might be positive even if the answer to question 1 is negative. A person might be entitled to a liberty even if is not valuable to her. After all, in general, whether someone is entitled to something is not decided by whether it is valuable to her. For instance, it would be disrespectful for someone to steal the unwanted junk out of my basement, even if that person knows I don't want the junk. There is no straightforward relationship between answers to question 1 and question 4. I take no stand here on what political liberties citizens are entitled to. I am not discussing whether anyone should be deprived of political liberty, but am instead asking how bad of a deprivation it would be. So, one way of framing this paper is as follows. Suppose we strip some random person of her political liberties. How bad for her is this? This question divides into two further questions. First, how *valuable* are the liberties we have taken away? Second, how *unjust* is it to take away these liberties? This paper concerns the first question, but not the second.

In this paper, I confine my use of the term "political liberties" to the right to vote and to run for public office. Some philosophers also include the rights of political speech, assembly, and to form political parties, but for the sake of this paper, I am classifying these as civil liberties, as instances of free speech and free association. I intend this to be a stipulation, not a point of conceptual analysis. I want to argue that the rights to run for office and vote are not particularly valuable, but I am neutral here as to whether the rights of political speech, assembly, and to form political parties and special interest groups are valuable. The reason I am interested in the rights to vote and run for office is that these rights — unlike the civil or economic liberties — are rights to exercise (or attempt to acquire) power over others. My right of free speech gives me power over myself; my right to vote gives me some power over everyone.

Philosophers and others have argued that the political liberties are needed or at least useful to:

A. have one's social status and the social bases of self-respect secured;
B. make the government responsive to one's interests and generate preferred political outcomes;
C. live autonomously as a member of society;
D. achieve education and enlightenment and take a broad view of the world and of others' interests;
E. and express oneself and one's attitudes about the political process and current states of affairs.

My strategy for this paper is to examine and challenge each of these reasons in favor of thinking that the political liberties are valuable. I know of no general non-value or not-of-much-value proof of the political liberties. However, if I can show that A through E fail to show the political liberties are valuable, this provides strong evidence that they are not. Thus, in effect, my argument is this:

1. Reasons A–E fail to show the political liberties are generally valuable.
2. There is probably no further reason, F, to think they are.
3. Therefore, the political liberties are not generally valuable.

I will examine each claim (A–E) in turn.

Before turning to reasons A–E, consider one argument for why the political liberties might be valuable:

The Justice Argument
1. Justice requires democracy.
2. Democracy requires that everyone have an equal right to vote and run for office.
3. For each individual, it is valuable to live in a just society.
4. Therefore, the political liberties are valuable.

This argument claims each individual has grounds for valuing her individual political liberties, because if even she alone lacked those liberties, this would suffice to make her society unjust. In the justice argument, the political liberties are not instrumentally or intrinsically valuable, but have constitutive value because they form part of something intrinsically valuable.[2] In this paper, I am putting aside questions of whether democracy is just, and looking only at arguments that do not rely upon premise 1 of the Justice Argument. If premise 1 turns out to be true, then I admit some version of the Justice Argument would succeed, and thus my thesis would have to be modified: the political liberties are not very valuable for most people except for the purposes of realizing justice. Note, however, that many people argue for premise 1 of the Justice Argument on the basis of some of the arguments I consider and rebut below. (For example, John Rawls defends premise 1 of the Justice Argument on the basis of what I call the Status Argument below.)

II. Status and Respect

One prominent, popular argument holds that if a person lacks the political liberties, this tends to undermine her self-respect and the respect others hold for her. The political liberties are thus valuable as means to achieving respect. Let's call this the *Status Argument*:

1. Social respect and self-respect are valuable.
2. Without the political liberties, citizens cannot (or are unlikely to) have social respect and self-respect.

3. Therefore, the political liberties are valuable.

John Rawls, among others, makes a version of this argument.[3]

Regarding the terms used in premise 1: A person has *social respect* when others view her in a favorable light, regarding her as valuable and of sufficiently high fundamental moral standing. A person has *self-respect* when she views herself in a favorable light, regarding herself as valuable and of sufficiently high fundamental moral standing.[4]

Premise 1 seems largely unobjectionable, so the success or failure of this argument depends on premise 2. In this section, I challenge this second premise. While I will not exactly refute this argument – and I take it to be the strongest argument on behalf of the personal value of the political liberties – I will still, in some sense, undermine it.

Premise 2 claims that citizens need the political liberties to have social respect and self-respect. One might be tempted to read premise 2 as stating something tautological: A person who lacks the political liberties by definition has a lower status than someone who holds them. They are things others may do that she may not. This is true, but it's true in the sense that a person who lacks a driver's, medical, hairdressing, or plumbing license has lower status than those who hold those licenses. All things equal, having a hairdressing license gives someone a higher legal status. Yet, no one thinks that lacking a hairdresser license (and thus lacking the liberty to practice hairdressing) lowers one's fundamental moral status, or removes the social bases for social and self-respect. For the Status Argument to succeed, it needs to interpret premise 2 in a robust way, as showing that lacking the political liberties is a great threat to one's fundamental moral status, in a way that lacking the hairdressing liberties is not.[5]

John Rawls holds that when some citizens lack the political liberties, this thereby encourages everyone to see those citizens as inferior. As Steven Wall (who rejects the Status Argument) summarizes Rawls's argument:

> The . . . argument begins with the plausible thought that political institutions established in a society bear importantly on the social component of self-respect. Some institutional arrangements do better than others in encouraging citizens to view one another as moral equals. . . . The public expression of . . . the fair value of political liberty is an affirmation of the equal status of all citizens.[6]

As a matter of fact, we human beings do tend to associate political power with a kind of majesty. We do tend to think that a person's fundamental moral standing in some way depends upon their political standing, and vice versa. Nation-states are like clubs, and we tend to treat the rights to vote and run for office as signifying full membership in the national club. People who lack these rights are junior members at best. When people lack the political liberties, we look down upon them. They might feel humiliated by their lesser status. And so, it seems true that the social bases of self-respect and social respect depend upon political power. But this is only contingently true – it's an artifact of how we happen to think. We don't need to think that way. And we shouldn't think that way, or so I will argue.

Imagine that in our culture, or in the human race in general, we tended to associate being given a red scarf by one's government as a mark of membership and status. You aren't fully in your national club until you get your scarf.

Now, suppose the government gives red scarves to everyone, except homosexuals. Homosexuals would rightly be upset – they would rightly claim that the government's refusal to grant them red scarves shows that homosexuals are considered second-class, inferior people. The government's behavior would tend to induce people (including homosexuals themselves) to regard homosexuals as having low status and being less valuable. Homosexuals and their sympathetic allies would have reason to take to the streets and demand that homosexuals be granted scarves. Given how everyone thinks about red scarves, it in some sense becomes crucial to have one.

However, at the same time, we can say, "There's no good reason to attach status and standing to red scarf ownership. Human dignity doesn't actually depend upon scarves. It's just a silly, contingent psychological or cultural fact that people think this way. And they shouldn't think this way." The red scarves aren't *really* valuable. They're valuable only as a result of a social construction, and a *bad* one at that.[7]

We can say the same thing about the political liberties and about associating moral standing with political power. (The political liberties are, after all, rights to political power.) There is no intrinsic or essential connection between status and political power. It's a contingent, psychological or cultural fact that people tend to associate human dignity with political power. But we shouldn't think that way.

I'm not just saying that we have no good reason to think this way. I want to go further: I think it's a vile, contemptible fact about human beings that we associate dignity with political power. The fact that we associate dignity with political power – even the tiny amount of power one gets with the right to vote – is a base, disgusting feature of human psychology, a feature which morally superior people would learn to overcome.

In the U.S., new parents sometimes say, "Who knows? Maybe my child will be president!" Implicit in such daydreams is the assumption that holding political power – and holding the most political power – is the most prestigious thing one can do.

Imagine a world otherwise like ours, in which people lacked these kinds of attitudes. Instead of viewing the president as majestic, or the office of presidency as deserving reverence, they just thought of the president as the chief public goods administrator. Instead of thinking of the rights to vote and run for office as possessing a lesser kind of majesty, and as signifying membership in the national club, they thought of them as licenses akin to hairdressing or plumbing licenses. Imagine if people did not associate national status with international political power, and did not associate personal status with power.

This would be a better world than ours. We tie esteem to political power. But we shouldn't; it has a terrible track record.[8] Just think of the abuses and injustices entire nations, kings, emperors, presidents, senators, district attorneys, police officers, and average voters have gotten away with throughout history, all because we attach standing, reverence, and status to political power, and we defer before such majestic standing. Moreover, one reason why kings, presidents, and district attorneys commit such abuses in the first place is that they associate status with power. For example, Henry VIII's wars had no chance of increasing his (or most of his subjects') personal wealth or comfort. He committed these atrocities in large part because he wanted the prestige and status that attach to increased political power. Most people revere power, more than they would admit to themselves. The romance of power and authority partly explains why people have so often willing to collaborate with government-sponsored injustices.

The tendency to tie status to political power has other bad effects. Because people tend to use political power – and the right to vote in particular – as a way of signifying who is a full member of the national club and who is inferior, political power has tended to be distributed for bad reasons. For example, many countries have denied voting rights to women and ethnic minorities in order to signify their lesser status. If people had divorced standing from power, perhaps they would not have denied others their political liberties on such bad grounds.

Also, many countries now give all adult citizens equal voting rights, in order to signify equal status. Perhaps unrestricted universal suffrage is just. Perhaps not – perhaps political liberties should be distributed on the basis of competence, or some other basis, rather than merely than on birth, citizenship, or permanent residency. After all, it might turn out, empirically, that doing so would produce substantively more just outcomes than a system with unrestricted universal suffrage. (Most voters have extremely low levels of political and economic knowledge, and so it's at least possible that allowing them to vote causes us all to suffer from the terrible consequences of bad government.[9]

However, we can barely entertain the question of whether there are better alternatives to democracy, because people associate power with status. So, associating power with status potentially nullifies improvements we could make in the quality of government.

Given our contingent attitudes, the political liberties confer status. We use these rights to signify who is in our club and whom we hold in high regard. We treat the political liberties as if they were red scarves from the thought experiment above. But we should stop using these rights to signify status. We should not regard political power as a sign of worth. It would be a better world if people did not attach such significance to political power.

Since we are doing normative theory in this paper, we needn't take contingent psychological or cultural facts about human beings as a given. One hundred years ago, it was a contingent psychological or cultural fact that people associated being male and white with standing, and so in that sense, it was valuable to be male and white. But a political philosopher could still say that being male and white aren't fundamentally valuable. They're valuable only as a result of a social construction (a construction that is perhaps rooted in our evolutionary past), and a *bad* one at that. Similarly, it's a contingent psychological or cultural fact that people associate political power (even the small amount conferred by the political liberties) with status. But a political philosopher can still say that political power

isn't fundamentally valuable. Political power is valuable only as a result of a social construction, and a *bad* one at that.

In some sense, my objections to the Status Argument leave its second premise intact. Political power is indeed conducive to obtaining valuable status. On the other hand, if my objections are sound, this also undermines the spirit of that argument. The political liberties are valuable as a means to securing one's status only in light of a disvaluable pattern of behavior.

III. Political Outcomes

In this section, I examine an argument that claims the political liberties are valuable, because each individual's exercise of political liberty has significant value in terms of its impact on the quality of government. This argument is deeply unsound.

The Outcomes Argument
1. The government will not be responsive to your interests unless you have the right to vote and to run for office.
2. It is valuable to have the government be responsive to your interests.
3. Therefore, it is valuable to have the right to vote and run for office.

Among many citizens in democracies, the Outcomes Argument is a common justification of the claim that the political liberties are valuable. Prima facie, it's the most obvious argument on behalf of the political liberties. The Outcomes Argument casts the political liberties as means to help ensure good behavior from government. Politicians want my vote. To get it, candidates compete in offering me the best package. Also, since I can run for office, politicians don't just need my vote. They need to behave well enough that I will not run against them.

This argument fails in part because individual votes in fact have vanishingly small instrumental value. The Outcomes Argument overstates the value of an individual's political liberties in terms of their ability to make government responsive to her interests.

If we want to know how valuable a vote is, it depends not only on how high stakes the election is, but also on whether the individual vote will make any difference. The right to vote is itself an opportunity to cast votes, and so the instrumental value of the right to vote is in part dependent on the instrumental value of the votes a citizen can cast.

For an individual voter, it makes no difference whether she votes or abstains. It is not as though the government will help you just in case you vote or ignore you just in case you abstain. As individuals, our single votes do not influence whether our elected leaders decide to help us, ignore us, or hurt us.[10] An individual's vote has an effect on political outcomes only if she changes the outcome of the election. Casting a vote is like playing the lottery – there is some small chance there will be a tie, and that your vote will decisively break that tie. When political scientists and economists estimate the probability that any one voter will be decisive, they usually conclude that the probability you will break a tie is vanishingly small.[11] Some think your chances are vanishingly small – they say you are more likely to win Powerball a few times in a row than break a tie.[12] The most optimistic estimates say you can have as high as a one in ten million chance of breaking a tie, but only if you live in New Mexico, New Hampshire, Virginia, or Colorado, and only if you vote Republican or Democrat.[13]

One might object that even if you have little chance of changing the outcome of an election, by voting, you can at least change the margin of victory (or loss), and then help determine whether a candidate enjoys a mandate.[14] However, the idea that candidates enjoy mandates that increase their political effectiveness is just a popular myth, a myth reinforced by uninformed journalists, but which has been roundly rejected by empirically-minded political scientists.[15]

Politicians rarely read the academic literature on the decisiveness of individual votes, but they generally are aware that individual votes do not count for much. A politician thus has little reason to cater to me. He needs votes, but he does not need my vote, and he knows it. My having the liberty to vote does little to ensure that politicians or the government will respond to my interests.

Similar remarks apply to the right to run for political office. The probability that a random American, if she tried, could secure a significant public office is low. In part, this is because there are few seats to go around.

There are over 1.7 million Americans for every seat in Congress. Even smaller, less important offices (such as town aldermen) tend at best to have ratios of 1 seat for every 2,000 citizens. If offices were distributed randomly at any given time, these would be bad odds. Of course, offices are not randomly distributed – rich, attractive, well-connected citizens have much better odds than others. I might decide to run for office, but politicians aren't cowering at the thought, and it isn't keeping them in line.

A weaker version of the Outcomes Argument might claim that the political liberties are necessary not to help me get preferred political outcomes, but to prevent me from being dominated by others. The worry is that unequal political liberties expose citizens to domination, and we can protect citizens from domination only by imbuing them each with strong political liberties.

There is a grain of truth to this argument. If we deprive all Snuvs of the right to vote and run for office, then this will help facilitate others in exploiting, dominating, and oppressing the Snuvs. However, this doesn't show that it's valuable for any individual Snuv to possess the political liberties. Instead, it shows that it's valuable to each Snuv that *enough* Snuvs possess the political liberties. A Snuv should be nearly indifferent between situations A and B:

A. All Snuvs *except her* have the political liberties.

B. All Snuvs have the political liberties.

If A isn't enough to stop the individual Snuv from being dominated, then neither is B.[16]

In the end, it's just not true that I need the political liberties to prevent others from dominating and exploiting me. What prevents me from being dominated is *other* citizens' restraint. If they decide to act badly, my rights to vote or run for office can't stop them. The moral majority stops the unjust minority, the courts stop them, or they stop themselves. Yet if tomorrow my country decides to dominate me, my political liberties provide me no more protection than a bucket provides against a flood.[17]

IV. Autonomy

Another closely related argument is the *Autonomy Argument*:

1. It is valuable for each person to be autonomous and self-directed, and to live by rules of her own making.
2. In order for each person living in a shared political environment to be autonomous and self-directed, and to live by rules of her own making, she needs to possess the political liberties and make use of them.
3. Therefore, each person living in a shared political environment needs to possess the political liberties and make use of them.[18]

This argument maintains that the political liberties are instrumental to, or perhaps even constitutive of, maintaining one's autonomy. If autonomy is valuable, then so are the political liberties.

If the Autonomy Argument is intended to show that a person needs the political liberties to be autonomous and self-directed over her own mind, it's clearly unsound. A person who lacks these rights might still be a self-controlled, self-legislating person, just as a person who has them might be slavish and blindly deferential.

If there is a connection between voting and autonomy, it must be something like this: By voting, a person is in part the author of the laws. If she abstains, then she has no partial authorship over the laws, and thus the laws are in some way imposed upon her.

Notice, however, that on this argument, voting confers autonomy on you only if your side wins. However, even then, the political liberties do not confer any significant autonomy. The Autonomy Argument appears to overstate the degree of autonomy that the rights to vote and run for office confer.

I've made quite a few autonomous decisions in my life. I've made autonomous decisions over petty things: what to wear each day, what to eat, what color toothbrush to have, what to watch on television. I've made autonomous decisions over important things: what to write about for my dissertation, where to go to college and graduate school, which job offers I would accept. I've made autonomous decisions over momentous things: whom to marry, whether to have a child, what to choose for a career.

Suppose these choices had been subject to democratic decision-making. We'd regard that as taking the choice away from me and giving it to the democratic body. Even if I had an equal vote in this body, it would be a severe loss of autonomy. Even if the democratic body didn't just vote, but actively deliberated over the best choices (and listened to me give my reasons), having it make the decisions would mean a severe loss of personal autonomy for me.

It's not just that I have more autonomy when I make decisions alone as opposed to when a democratic assembly (of which I am a member) makes the decisions. Rather, when a democratic assembly (of which I am a member) makes the decisions, I don't have much autonomy at all.

There is a sure-fire way to determine that you do not have autonomous control over a situation:

No matter what you choose, or what you decide, the same thing happens anyway. Your decisions make no difference. To illustrate: While writing this paragraph, I conducted an experiment. I decided that the sun would set early. While editing this paragraph later at night, I decided that the sun would rise early. Nothing happened. I repeated this experiment many times during subsequent editing. I conclude I lack autonomous control over the sun.

So it goes with voting. In every election, I choose not to be governed by a populist, warmongering, civil rights-violating, immigrant-excluding, child-murdering plutocrat. Yet, in every election, a populist, warmongering, civil rights-violating, immigrant-excluding, child-murdering plutocrat comes to power nonetheless. And so it goes with your votes, too, even when you vote for popular candidates. Regardless of whether you choose to vote or not, and regardless of how you, the same result will occur. We might as well be willing the sun to rise or set.

In contrast, today I also chose to eat tomato soup for lunch. After making the decision, I did in fact eat tomato soup. In later editing, I chose to eat different foods – and did in fact eat those different foods. My experiments allow to conclude that I have real autonomy over what I eat.

Robert Nozick illustrates this point with a story called the "Tale of the Slave." Nozick describes the changing conditions under which a slave lives and asks his readers to point out when the slave stops being a slave. Here's how the story goes. Let's say you are the slave. At first, you live under a cruel master, who beats you arbitrarily. Then the master posts a set of rules and only punishes you when you violate the rules. The master then starts allocating resources among all of his slaves on kindly grounds, considering their needs, merit, etc. The master then decides to allow the slaves to spend four days doing whatever they please and only requires them to work three days on his manor. The master then decides to allow the slaves to live in the city or wherever else they like,

provided they send the master three-sevenths of their income. The master also continues to regulate many of their activities and can call them back to the manor for defense. The master decides to allow his 10,000 slaves – other than you – to make decisions among themselves about how to regulate their behavior and how much of their income they must send the master. You are bound by their decision, but cannot vote or deliberate.

When the master dies, he leaves all of his slaves, including you, to each other as a collective body, except for you. That is, his 10,000 other slaves collectively own everyone, including you, but you own no one. The other 10,000 slaves decide to allow you to advise them about what rules they should pass. These rules govern both their behavior and yours. Eventually, as a reward for your service, they allow you to vote whenever they are evenly divided – 5,000 to 5,000 – over what to do. You cast a ballot in an envelope, which they agree to open whenever they are split. Finally, since they've never been evenly split, they just include your vote with theirs all the time.

At the end of the story, many readers think the slave never stopped being a slave. This is disturbing because by the end of the story, the situation very much resembles modern democracy. One thing we should learn from Nozick's story is that being a member of a rule-making body, especially a large one, does not give one much control. Each slave in the tale of the slave can legitimately claim that *everyone else makes all the decisions* and that *the decisions the body makes would have occurred without her input*. Even when democratic outcomes result from the equal input of all, there can be feeling of an utter lack of power. Our voices and votes are lost.

In parallel: I went to Mardi Gras one year. At night, the streets were so congested that I could lift my feet and be carried along by the crowd. It took serious effort to move against the current. Everyone in the crowd had the same predicament. We were all equals. Our individual movements equally decided the collective movement of the crowd. Yet, we were each powerless.[19]

One further point about autonomy: We can't control or have a say over everything that happens in our lives, so we have to choose where we make a stand, where we think it's important to be authentic. Politics is one place to make a stand, but it's not the only or obviously best place.

Consider an analogy. Chris was a punk rock kid who rode the bus with me in ninth grade. One day Chris complained about my manner of dress: "You wear the Gap just like everyone else. You don't try to be original or true to yourself." Chris, in contrast, had chosen to conform to the punk-rock subculture. I responded with something like this, "I don't care that much about how I dress. So, I go along with how others dress. It's not that important to me, and how they do it is good enough." (In contrast, it was very important to Chris to dress a certain way.) In this case, it's implausible to say that I was inauthentic or lacked self-control because I deferred to the crowd on how to dress. Sometimes this deference is a way of being authentic, or as authentic as it's reasonable to be, because deferring prevents one from wasting time on unimportant things.

There's no obvious reason why politics can't be like that. A self-controlled, authentic, autonomous individual might defer to others on politics because she recognizes that others will produce good enough outcomes, and within that range of likely outcomes, the outcomes just aren't that important to her. Or, she might defer because she accepts that she can't take control over everything, and she finds more important places to make her stand.

In summary, the Autonomy Argument fails for many of the same reasons the Outcomes Argument failed. To succeed, the Autonomy Argument would need citizens to have much more power than they in fact have. And one can develop autonomy and have satisfactory levels of self-control regardless of whether one possesses the political liberties.

V. Education and Enlightenment

If someone wishes to show that the political liberties are valuable, she will need to produce an argument compatible with the point that individual citizens have vanishingly little power over the political process. One such argument, the *Education Argument*, seems promising:

1. Civic and political activity requires citizens to take a broad view of others' interests, and to search for ways to promote the common good. This requires long-term thinking, and engagement with moral, philosophical, and social scientific issues.
2. If civic and political activity requires long-term thinking, and engagement with moral, philosophical, and social scientific issues, then civic and political activity serve a valuable educative function.
3. The political liberties are needed to engage in civic and political activity.
4. Therefore, the political liberties serve a valuable educative function.

Alexis de Tocqueville and John Stuart Mill advanced versions of the Education Argument.[20] Many contemporary political theorists, such as Richard Dagger, have advanced this argument as well.[21] The Education Argument holds that the political liberties are valuable because exercising these liberties tends to be enlightening.

If premise 1 is interpreted as a *descriptive* claim, it's plainly false. You can vote or run for office despite being narrow-minded, ignorant, and unenlightened. On the other hand, if premise 1 is interpreted as a *normative* claim, then this argument does not show that exercising the political liberties in fact tends to educate and enlighten citizens. At best, it would only show that the political liberties *could* do so, if citizens exercise their liberties the right way. Premise 1 is best replaced with this alternative:

> 1*: Citizens who make use of their political liberties will tend to take a broad view of others' interests, to search for ways to promote the common good, to engage in long-term thinking, and to engage with moral, philosophical and scientific issues.

Still, even with Premise 1*, this new argument is problematic.

Premise 3 is false. To engage in civic and political activities, you don't need to have the right to vote or run for office. You can debate politics with others, organize campaigns, donate to causes, write letters, and so on, even if you lack the political liberties. Instead, if citizens are enlightened, this results from deliberating, reading, debating, watching others deliberate, seeking evidence, and the like. Citizens can get all of these benefits without voting or running for office, and without having the right to vote or run for office.

Also, even if it were true that exercising the political liberties tends to enlighten citizens, that wouldn't show that the political liberties are uniquely or particularly valuable means to achieving enlightenment. There are other activities that tend to be enlightening. And perhaps these other activities do a superior job in enlightening citizens. In fact, even if participating in politics tends to educate and enlighten citizens, it's not as if what enlightens them are voting and running for office.

So, the Education Argument needs to be supplemented with the premise that citizens will tend not to deliberate, read, debate, etc., unless they have the political liberties. This is an empirical claim. Perhaps it's true, but anyone asserting it requires supporting empirical evidence. (To my knowledge, no one has any such evidence.)

Let's take a closer look at Premise 1*. Does engaging in politics really tend to educate and enlighten citizens? On the contrary, politics teaches enlightenment in much the same way that frat parties teach temperance. While politics provides an opportunity for enlightenment, it is more likely to stultify than enlighten.

People tend to be on some of their worst epistemic behavior when participating in politics. They display high levels of epistemic irrationality when discussing or participating in politics. In part, this is because our brains were designed more for winning arguments and forming coalitions than seeking truth. As psychologist Jonathan Haidt says:

> . . . reasoning was not designed to pursue the truth. Reasoning was designed by evolution to help us win arguments. That's why [Mercier and Sperber] call [their theory of why reasoning developed] The Argumentative Theory of Reasoning. So, as they put it . . ., "The evidence reviewed here shows not only that reasoning falls quite short of reliably delivering rational beliefs and rational decisions. It may even be, in a variety of cases, detrimental to rationality. Reasoning can lead to poor outcomes, not because humans are bad at it, but because they systematically strive for arguments that justify their beliefs or their actions. This explains the confirmation bias, motivated reasoning, and reason-based choice, among other things.[22]

Confirmation bias is the thesis that we tend to pay strong attention to and accept evidence in favor of beliefs we already hold, and tend to ignore, reject, or be bored by evidence against beliefs we hold. Motivated reasoning is the thesis that we have preferences over beliefs and that we tend to believe what we prefer to be true. E.g., I might prefer to think I am smart, I might prefer to think Democrats are good and Republicans are evil, or I might prefer to think God created the earth 6,000 years ago. Motivated reasoning occurs when the brain tries to arrive at beliefs that maximize good feelings and minimize bad feelings. "Reason-based choice" refers to the phenomenon of people confabulating or inventing reasons for their decisions when they in fact had no basis for decision.

Exercising the political liberties could be a way of making people more rational, self-directed, and deliberative, if only human beings were not the way they are. Actual human beings are wired not to seek truth and justice but to seek consensus. They are shackled by social pressure. They are overly deferential to authority. They cower before uniform opinion. They are swayed not so much by reason but by a desire to belong, by emotional appeal, and by sex appeal. We evolved as social primates who depended on tight in-group cooperative behavior. Unfortunately, this leaves us with a deep bent toward tribalism and conformity. Too much and too frequent democracy threatens to rob many of us of our autonomy and rationality.[23] Politics threatens to unenlighten at least as much as it promises to enlighten us.

Economist Bryan Caplan notes that average citizens have systematically different beliefs about basic economics than trained economists. (Note that laypeople tend to hold their economic views just as strongly, in fact, more strongly, than economists.) Even once we correct for possible demographic biases (since economists tend to be male, white, and upper-middle class), economists and laypeople still disagree about textbook economics.[24] According to Caplan, compared to economists, laypeople exhibit four basic biases: an anti-foreign bias, an anti-market bias, a pessimistic bias, and a make-work bias. That is, laypeople underestimate the value of trading with foreigners, underestimate the efficacy of markets, underestimate how good the future will be and overestimate how good the past was, and underestimate the value of labor-saving inventions and schemes. Now, since the available evidence strongly favors textbook economics, Caplan contends that average citizens most likely have systematically false beliefs about the economy and how it functions.[25]

Caplan claims that people are rationally irrational about politics. Rational irrationality is the thesis that it can be *instrumentally* rational to be *epistemically* irrational. That is, in the sphere of politics, it is not in most people's interest to collect and assess evidence properly, but instead to indulge in whatever beliefs they find flattering or emotionally appealing. If, despite the honking horns, you believe the street you're crossing is clear, you die. But if, despite overwhelming evidence that free trade is good and protectionism is bad, you believe protectionism is good and vote accordingly, nothing happens. So, if advocating trade restrictions helps to serve one's interests – such as feeling patriotic, forming in-groups and out-groups, sublimating racist attitudes, pretending to have solidarity with union workers or the poor – then a person will tend to endorse trade restrictions. For any given voter, the expected cost of maintaining her epistemic rationality in the sphere of politics is greater than the expected benefit.

The existence of rational irrationality is supported by many independent psychological studies. (Many studies on motivated reasoning are also studies in rational irrationality.) For an illustration, I will here recount one of psychologist Drew Westen's experiments on motivated reasoning.[26] Westen's subjects were loyal Republicans and Democrats. Subjects were shown a statement by a celebrity, followed by information potentially making the celebrity seem hypocritical. Then, subjects were presented with an "exculpatory statement." (A test run had a quote by Walter Cronkite saying he would never do TV work again after retiring, followed by footage showing he did work again after retiring, followed by an explanation saying it was a special favor.) In the experiment, the celebrities were identifiable as Republicans or Democrats. Democrat subjects strongly agreed that the famous Republicans contradicted themselves but only weakly agreed that the Democrats contradicted themselves. Republican subjects likewise readily accepted exculpatory statements from their favored party, but not the other party. Functional magnetic resonance imaging (fMRI) showed that subjects' pleasure centers were activated when condemning members of the other party, and activated again when subjects denied evidence against members of their own party.

Political scientist Diana Mutz's research provides evidence that politics tends to be stultifying, or, at least, that the people who tend to make the most use of their political liberties tend also to be unenlightened. Following Mutz, let's define a "deliberative citizen" as a citizen who has frequent cross cutting political discussion, who can intelligently articulate arguments both on behalf of her own views and on behalf of contrary views, and who has high levels of objective political knowledge. Let's define a "participatory citizen" as a citizen who engages heavily with politics, by voting, running for office, participating in political campaigns, joining causes, engaging in activism, and the like. Mutz's work shows that deliberation and participation do not come together. Deliberative citizens do not participate much, and participatory citizens do not deliberate much. The people who are most active in politics tend to be (in my words, not Mutz's) cartoon ideologues.[27] The people who are most careful in formulating their own political views and who spend the most time considering contrary views tend not to participate in politics.

Mutz's research indicates that active, participatory citizens tend not to engage in much deliberation and tend not to have much cross-cutting political discussion.[28] Instead, they seek out and interact only with others with whom they already agree. When asked why other people hold contrary points of view, participatory citizens tend to respond that others must be stupid or corrupt. Participatory citizens are often unable to give charitable explanations of why people might hold contrary views. (This is worrisome, I would add, because people who tend to demonize all contrary views tend to be unjustified in their own views.) In contrast, citizens who exhibit high degrees of the deliberative virtues are able to give charitable accounts of contrary viewpoints.

Many political theorists advocate "deliberative democracy." In the theory of deliberative democracy, citizens are supposed to come together to reason and deliberate. They are supposed to air their opinions in an open and honest way. They are supposed to make decisions together based on reasons everyone can appreciate. They are supposed to seek consensus.

However, when political scientists study real-world political deliberation, they find that deliberative democracy falls far short of its goals. Deliberation tends to reduce in-group/out-group biases only when the opposing sides have equal numbers. Otherwise, deliberation exacerbates these biases. Deliberation and group discussion tend to increase rather than decrease polarization. Emotional appeals and manipulative language tend to rule the day. Sometimes groups behave nicely and reach consensus, but that is usually just because they choose to avoid the controversial topics.[29] So, when we see non-empirically-minded political theorists saying that there is a need for deliberation in democracy, this is not really akin to them saying that aspirin cures headaches. Instead, this is closer to them saying that we need excess drinking cures headaches.

Getting people more involved in politics often causes greater conflict and increased polarization. It at least sometimes increases distrust. We can predict that all things equal, when people have happy feelings towards their government and each other, they participate more. But it does not follow that getting them to participate more would increase these happy feelings. On the contrary, more participation sometimes hurts.

In summary, the Education Argument seems unsound. If the Education Argument simply asserts that politics *can* serve an educational function, well, sure, it *can*. Lots of things – joining a street gang, taking heroin, dropping out of high school – *can* serve an educational function and help one achieve enlightenment. But if the Education Argument wants to assert that politics is *likely* to serve this function, our evidence points against this. An *Inverse* Education Argument seems more sound: the political liberties are bad because exercising them tends to be stultifying. However, this might be too strong. Some of the work mentioned above supports this claim, but some of it just shows that politically-engaged citizens tend not to be enlightened. Whether that is because politics makes them less enlightened or whether because enlightened people choose not to engage in politics isn't clear. In either case, though, the evidence on behalf of Premise 1* is weak, and so the Education Argument fails.

VI. Self-Expression

Another argument holds that the political liberties are important means of self-expression. Let's call this the *Expression Argument*:

1. Generally, it is a valuable to each citizen for that citizen to be able to express her opinions about her country is doing, what values should be promoted, what changes should be made, and so on.
2. The political liberties are valuable means for a citizen to express her opinion on these matters.
3. Therefore, generally, the political liberties are valuable to each citizen.

The Expression Argument suffers from many of the same flaws as the other arguments we've considered. First, exercising the political liberties is not a very good way to express oneself, and second, there are much better alternatives.[30]

The political liberties are ineffective ways to communicate our attitudes to others. A vote is not an expressive instrument. It's like a piano with only four keys and which breaks after playing one note. (We might add that the strings tend to be out-of-tune and rusty.) Suppose that in the last election, I voted for a certain

candidate, regarding him as the lesser of two warmongering, paternalistic, exploitative, plutocratic evils. Suppose a colleague voted for that same candidate, regarding him as a truly positive change he could believe in. Suppose someone else voted for that same candidate because he wanted to fit in with his friends. Suppose a fourth person cynically voted for that candidate because he wanted to hasten his country's demise. What did any of our votes express to others? Just by knowing whom someone voted for, you cannot infer what someone meant to express.

Or, suppose I run for office. What does that communicate? I might claim that I want to change the world for the better, but every politician says that. Regardless of my communicative intentions, running for office tends to communicate that I am power-and status-hungry.

So, exercising the political liberties is ineffective if we want to communicate with others. Still, sometimes we just want to express our attitudes to ourselves, rather than to others. In private, I might tear up photos of a recent ex-girlfriend. Here, the point is to express finality to myself, and to perform a closing ritual to help me move on. No doubt people can use their votes this way. The cynical voter can express his cynicism to himself by voting for the worst candidate. So, while the political liberties have little value in expressing our attitudes to others, they have some value in expressing our attitudes to ourselves.

Still, we have many other better outlets for self-expression. Even if someone wants to communicate his political attitudes to himself, he can usually best do so without exercising the political liberties. For example, the cynical citizen could donate money to the worst candidate, write a poem, or build and burn an effigy. And if someone wants to communicate with others, then writing letters, joining online forums, creating websites, making YouTube videos, and the like, are much more effective means of communicating than voting or running for office.

VII. Conclusion

We have examined a number of arguments in favor of the view that the political liberties generally are of high value to the people who hold them. These arguments have been found wanting. Unless there is some further argument in favor of the political liberties, we can conclude that they probably are not of much value to most people who hold them. The civil and economic liberties are likely to be more valuable to most people than their political liberties.

Again, I am not saying that people *do* value their political liberties than these other liberties, nor am I claiming that they in fact regard their political liberties as having little value. On the contrary, I suspect most people think their political liberties are quite valuable. Instead, in saying that the political liberties are not of much value, I am saying that they do not deserve to be valued highly.

However, I am arguing for only a general trend. Some people, given their needs, ends, abilities, and circumstances, will have grounds to value their political liberties highly. Since I am arguing for a general trend, to rebut my thesis, it will not be enough to show the political liberties are sometimes of high value to some people, but instead that they are generally of high value to most people.

Again, all of this leaves open whether the political liberties are valuable in the aggregate, or whether anyone is entitled to the political liberties. It might be that democracy is good and just, even if individuals do not usually have grounds for holding their political liberties are valuable. I take no stands on these issues here.

Notes

1 Consider, for instance, that most people believe political speech demands stronger protection than commercial speech.

2 Something is intrinsically valuable when it is valuable as an end in itself. Something is instrumentally valuable when it is valuable for the purpose of achieving some *other* end. Something is constitutively valuable when it is valuable as a *component* or piece of something valuable. So, for instance, if I have the final end of having an excellent philosophy career, then publishing papers is constitutively valuable to me as a component of that career. In section II, I examine an argument that holds that the political liberties have constitutive value because they are a component of the good life.

3 See John Rawls, *A Theory of Justice* (Cambridge, MA: Harvard University Press, 1971), 234; John Rawls, *Political Liberalism* (New York: Columbia University Press, 1993), 318-19; John Rawls, *Justice as Fairness: A Restatement* (Cambridge, MA: Harvard University Press, 2001), 131; Samuel Freeman, *Rawls* (New York: Routledge), 76. For an especially acute response to Rawls, see Steven Wall, "Rawls and the Status of Political Liberty," *Pacific Philosophical Quarterly* 87 (2006): 245–270, here pp. 257–61.

4 Different versions of the Status Argument could take different stances on what counts as "sufficiently high fundamental moral standing." For example, on Rawls's account, for citizens to have the right kind of status, they need to have a full range of liberal rights, their rights must be equal to others, and some of these rights (in particular, the political liberties) must have their fair value guaranteed. However, someone propounding the Status Argument could hold a less demanding view of what counts as sufficiently high standing.

5 Even libertarians, who regard such licensing as intrinsically unjust, stop short of saying that licenses threaten people's fundamental moral status.

6 Wall 2006, 257–8.

7 If it turned out these attitudes toward scarves resulted not from an arbitrary social practice, but from deep features in our evolved psychology, this argument would still stand. Our psychological tendencies would be lamentable, and scarves would be valuable only in light of these lamentable tendencies.

8 On this point, blogger Will Wilkinson has an excellent post from shortly after the 2008 U.S. presidential election. Wilkinson says that given that we tend to think of the presidency as "the highest peak, the top of the human heap," and given our

history of oppressing blacks, the fact that a black man won the presidency is momentous. At the same time, it would be better if we stopped thinking of the presidency as a majestic office and instead thought of it as the "chief executive of the national public goods administrative agency." Wilkinson continues, "I hope never to see again streets thronging with people chanting the glorious leader's name." See Will Wilkinson, "One Night of Romance," *The Fly Bottle*, http://www.willwilkinson.net/flybottle/2008/11/05/one-night-of-romance/.

9 See Jason Brennan, *The Ethics of Voting* (Princeton: Princeton University Press, 2011).

10 Some might claim that even if individual votes have almost no chance of changing the outcome of an election, individual votes can at least influence the mandate a candidate enjoys. However, the idea of mandate is just a popular myth. Hans Noel, in a review article, goes so far as to say that one thing political scientists know that laypeople do not, is "there is no such thing as a mandate." See Hans Noel, "Ten Things Political Scientists Know that You Don't," *The Forum* 8 (2010): 1–19, here p. 6. See also L. J. Grossback, D. A. M. Peterson, and J. A. Stimson: *Mandate Politics* (New York: Cambridge University Press, 2006); L. J. Grossbac., D. A. M. Peterson, and J. A. Stimson, "Electoral Mandates in American Politics" *British Journal of Political Science*. 37 (2007): 711–730. In fact, the US Advanced Placement Government exam sometimes asks students to answer the question, "Why are political scientists skeptical of the mandate theory of elections?"

11 See Geoffrey Brennan and Loren Lomasky, *Democracy and Decision* (New York: Cambridge University Press, 2003), pp. 56–7, 119.

12 Steven Landsburg, "Don't Vote. It Makes More Sense to Play the Lottery Instead." *Slate*, Sept. 29, 2004. URL= http://www.slate.com/articles/arts/everyday_economics/2004/09/dont_vote.html>

13 See Andrew Gelman, Nate Silver, and Aaron Edlin, "What is the Probability that Your Vote Will Make a Difference?" *Economic Inquiry* 50 (2012): 321–326.

14 See, for example, Gerry Mackie, "Why It's Rational to Vote," University of California, San Diego, 2009, unpublished manuscript.

15 See, for instance, R.A. Dahl, "The Myth of the Presidential Mandate," *Political Science Quarterly* 105 (1990): 355–372; Hans Noel, "10 Things Political Scientists Know that You Don't," *The Forum* 8 (2010): issue 3, article 12. The Advance Placement US Government exam routinely features the question, "Why are political scientists skeptical of the mandate theory of elections?"

16 One might try to argue that having the right to vote is, by the very definition of domination, a necessary condition for being non-dominated. However, this seems to render domination so defined of no obvious value.

17 One might try to argue that a citizen is dominated if and only if she lacks the vote. On this view, for a person to have a right to vote automatically means she is not dominated, regardless of what her country does to her. This seems too implausible to merit further discussion.

18 Versions of this argument can be found in Jean-Jacques Rousseau, *The Social Contract and Other Later Political Writings*, ed. Victor Gourevitch (New York: Cambridge University Press, 1997); Carol Gould, *Rethinking Democracy: Freedom and Social Cooperation in Politics, Economics, and Society* (New York: Cambridge University Press, 1988), 45–85. Gould argues that democracy is necessary for the good of autonomous self-government, and then argues that citizens are entitled to democracy.

19 Perhaps people who lived their whole lives this way would develop false consciousness and begin to regard the situation as empowering and free.

20 See Alexis de Tocqueville, *Democracy in America* (New York: Anchor Books, 1969), 243–4; John Stuart Mill, *Three Essays: "On Liberty," "Representative Government," and "The Subjection of Women,"* ed. Richard Wollheim (New York: Oxford University Press, 1975), 196–7.

21 Richard Dagger, *Civic Virtues* (New York: Oxford University Press, 1997), 102–4.

22 Jonathan Haidt, "The New Science of Morality," *Edge*, URL= http://www.edge.org/3rd_culture/morality10/morality.haidt.html. Haidt is summarizing research (which he endorses) by Hugo Mercier and Dan Sperber.

23 See David Schmidtz and Jason Brennan, *A Brief History of Liberty* (Boston: Wiley-Blackwell, 2010), 208–233, for empirical support of these claims.

24 By issuing surveys which ask citizens both about the their demographics and about their opinions on economics, we can determine using regressions how demographic factors correlate with economic beliefs.

25 See Bryan Caplan, *The Myth of the Rational Voter* (Princeton: Princeton University Press, 2007).

26 Drew Westen, Pavel S. Blagov, Keith Harenski, Clint Kilts, and Stephan Hamann, "The Neural Basis of Motivated Reasoning: An fMRI Study of Emotional Constraints on Political Judgment during the U.S. Presidential Election of 2004," *Journal of Cognitive Neuroscience* 18 (2007): 1947–58; Drew Westen, *The Political Brain: How We Make Up Our Minds without Using Our Heads* (New York: Perseus Books, 2008).

27 See Diana Mutz, *Hearing the Other Side: Deliberative versus Participatory Democracy* (New York, Cambridge University Press, 2006), 128.

28 Mutz 2006, 30. The more people join voluntary associations, the less they engage in crosscutting discussions. What demographic factors best predict that one will engage in crosscutting political discussion? Apparently, being non-white, poor, and uneducated. The reason for this is that white, rich, educated people have more control over the kinds of interactions they have with others. People generally do not enjoy having crosscutting political discussions. They enjoy agreement. So those with the most control over their lives choose not to engage in crosscutting discussions. See Mutz 2006, 27, 31, 46–47.

29 In support of all these claims, see Tali Mendelberg, "The Deliberative Citizen: Theory and Evidence," in *Research in Micropolitics, Volume 6: Political Decision Making, Deliberation, and Participation*, ed. Michael X. Delli Carpini, Leoni Huddy, and Robert Y. Shapiro (Amsterdam: Elsevier, 2002), pp. 151–193. Mendelberg reviews nearly every empirical study done on deliberation.

30 I am not here challenging the expressive theory of voting. The expressive theory of voting is a *descriptive* theory, which claims that many citizens vote in order to express attitudes. The expressive theory claims (roughly) that citizens know that their votes won't change the outcome of an election, and so they vote to express solidarity with certain causes. One person votes Democrat to express solidarity with the poor, while another votes Republican to express concern for personal responsibility. See Geoffrey Brennan and James Buchanan, "Voter Choice," *American Behavioral Scientist* 28, no. 2 (1984): 185–201; Brennan and Lomasky 1993; Geoffrey Brennan and Alan Hamlin, *Democratic Devices and Desires* (New York: Cambridge University Press, 2000).

3b. IMMIGRATION

DEBATES ABOUT IMMIGRATION POLICY often end up with one side accusing the other of bad faith. Advocates of open immigration accuse those who defend closed borders of being racists, fascists, or both. Those who argue in favor of tighter restrictions on immigration, on the other hand, often see immigrants and their advocates as threats to the survival of the cultural or economic way of life they hold dear. This degeneration into name-calling is unfortunate, however, because it ignores the fact that immigration is a complex and multifaceted moral issue, raising difficult questions to which neither side has entirely satisfying answers. Hopefully, philosophers can do better.

One of the key philosophical issues raised by the immigration debate is the moral significance of national borders. In a sense, the fact that national borders matter at all is surprising. After all, the general trend in moral philosophy since its beginning in Greece has been toward a kind of cosmopolitanism — the view that all human beings everywhere are of fundamentally equal moral value, and worthy of equal respect. But if this is the case, why should we think that we have a moral duty to pay taxes to provide for basic necessities and social services for those people who live on one side of an imaginary line, but not for those who live on the other? Or, to put the question somewhat less contentiously, if all persons everywhere are moral equals, then why should we set up political institutions to discharge our moral duties amongst each other in a way that leaves people with such *unequal* access to the benefits of those institutions?

The case for restrictions on immigration, then, will generally rest on establishing some justification for *nationalism* as opposed to *cosmopolitanism* — establishing, that is, the claim that we are morally justified in being especially concerned about, or giving special treatment to, our co-nationals as opposed to other persons with whom we do not share such a relation.

Surprisingly, the nationalist/cosmopolitan divide does not map well onto the standard left/right political division. It is true that the political "right" tends to be somewhat more hostile to increased immigration than the political "left." But the correlation is far from perfect, and it is not always clear that these positions are the result of the serious and consistent application of moral and political *principles*, rather than mere pragmatic politics. For instance, if the political right is as committed to free markets and free trade as its rhetoric suggests, then it is not clear why this shouldn't lead toward a strong presumption in support of relatively *open borders*. After all, if A wants to rent a home from B and work for C, then why should it matter that A is currently a citizen of a different country than B and C? What business does the state have in preventing A from engaging in voluntary labor and housing arrangements with B and C? If free markets are required by a respect for individual liberty, why isn't free migration too? Furthermore, the same efficiency arguments which support the right's defense of free trade across borders in goods such as cars and services would seem to support the free movement of persons.

On the other hand, those on the political left have some reason to oppose free immigration insofar as there is some evidence that increased immigration lowers wages for domestic unskilled labor — a group that the political left is often concerned to protect. There is also some empirical evidence to suggest that open immigration can make the maintenance of a generous social welfare state more difficult. It is easier to provide a robust social safety net when a) the people to whom that safety net is provided are ones with whom you can identify culturally and historically, rather than recent immigrants, and b) the number of people to whom the safety net is provided (and hence the cost of providing that safety net) is relatively small and stable.

Considerations of culture are another area in which the immigration issue cuts across standard political divides in surprising ways. It is not uncommon for people to argue in favor of restrictions on immigration on the grounds that such restrictions are necessary to preserve a nation's culture, perhaps especially its *political* culture. Such arguments seem to fit most naturally with a certain kind of conservative ideology, in which a premium is put on the preservation of a nation's traditions and values. But even a libertarian who believes that government should be tightly restricted to the protection of individual rights would have reason to worry if she believed that a large percentage of immigrants would be hostile to that vision of government, and would express that hostility at the voting booth. The same is true for liberals and communitarians who value cultural solidarity as an end in itself, or as a means toward the political solidarity of the welfare state. One need not think that these cultural considerations are *overridingly* important to recognize that they have *some* importance, and to realize that the various cross-cutting issues involved in the politics of immigration will often make for very strange bedfellows indeed!

But the question of how *much* immigration to allow is not the only question of philosophic interest surrounding this topic. For if we concede that *some* restrictions on immigration are permissible, then we must ask the further question of what *form* those restrictions will take. Specifically, is it morally permissible for a country to give preference to some sorts of immigrants over others? Should the decision of which immigrants to accept be guided by national economic self-interest alone (i.e. which immigrants can do the most good for *us*), or by humanitarian concern (i.e. which immigrants can we do the most good for), or by some mixture of both? What weight should be given to considerations of diversity and non-discrimination in immigration decisions? If selecting immigrants with high economic value adversely affects members of certain racial and ethnic groups, is this a problem? Or is adverse effect nothing to worry about so long as our policy is not *intentionally* discriminatory along racial lines, but only incidentally so in virtue of our concern with legitimate economic concerns?

The readings in this section will almost certainly not settle the contentious debate over the morality of immigration policy. That would be too much to ask. What is not too much to ask, I hope, is that readers come away with an appreciation of the strength of the arguments that the other side has to offer in this debate. On this issue, like so many others, there is much room for reasonable disagreement between well-meaning persons.

Further Reading

Blake, M. (2003). Immigration. In *A Companion to Applied Ethics: Blackwell Companions to Philosophy*, Frey, R G (ed.) (pp. 224–37). Malden, MA: Blackwell Publishing.

Block, W. (1998). A Libertarian Case for Free Immigration. *Journal of Libertarian Studies, 13*(2).

Carens, J. H. (1987). Aliens and Citizens: The Case for Open Borders. *The Review of Politics 49*: 251–73.

Cole, P. (2001). *Philosophies of Exclusion: Liberal Political Theory and Immigration*. Edinburgh: Edinburgh University Press.

Dummett, M. (2001). *On Immigration and Refugees*. New York: Routledge.

Hospers, J. (1998). A Libertarian Argument Against Opening Borders. *Journal of Libertarian Studies, 13*(2).

Huntington, S. (2004). *Who Are We?* New York: Simon and Schuster.

Kukathas, C. (2003). Immigration. In *The Oxford Handbook of Practical Ethics,* LaFollette, Hugh (ed.) (pp. 567–90). Oxford: Oxford University Press.

Kymlicka, W. (1996). Social Unity in a Liberal State. *Social Philosophy and Policy, 13*(1), 105–36.

Wellman, C.H., and Cole, P. (2011). *Debating the Ethics of Immigration: Is There a Right to Exclude?* Oxford: Oxford University Press.

Chapter 44

Michael Huemer

IS THERE A RIGHT TO IMMIGRATE?

Michael Huemer (1969–) is a professor of philosophy at the University of Colorado, Boulder, who works in metaethics, epistemology, ethics, and political philosophy. In this 2010 paper, Huemer argues that immigration restrictions are a "prima facie rights violation" insofar as such restrictions are coercive, impose extreme harms on would-be immigrants, and severely limit their freedoms. Huemer goes on to argue that immigration restrictions cannot be justified by economic, cultural, or other commonly invoked rationales.

1. The Immigration Question

Every year, close to one million individuals from foreign nations migrate to the United States legally. But many more are turned away. Individuals seeking to enter without the permission of the U.S. government are regularly barred at the border, and those discovered in the territory without authorization are forcibly removed. The government expels over one million people from the country each year.[1] Hundreds of thousands continue to try to smuggle themselves in, occasionally dying in the attempt.[2] On the face of it, this raises ethical questions. Is it right to forcibly prevent would-be immigrants from living in the United States? Those excluded seem, on the face of it, to suffer a serious harm. Why are we justified in imposing this harm?

Some reason that, just as a private club may exercise its discretion as to whom to admit or exclude, so a nation-state has the right to choose whom to admit or exclude. Some believe that we must exclude most would-be immigrants in order to maintain the integrity of our national culture. Others argue that immigrants cause economic hardship for existing citizens – that they take jobs from American workers, depress wages, and place an undue burden on social services provided by the state. Some go so far as to warn that unchecked immigration would bring on environmental, economic, and social catastrophes that would reduce the United States to the status of a Third World country.

Few would question the state's right to exclude at least some potential migrants. For example, the state may deny entry to international terrorists or fugitives from the law. The interesting question concerns the vast majority of other potential immigrants – ordinary people who are simply seeking a new home and a better life. Does the state have the right to exclude these ordinary people?

In the following, I argue that the answer to this question is no. I shall assume that we are considering ordinary, noncriminal migrants who wish to leave their country of origin for morally innocent reasons, whether to escape persecution or economic hardship, or simply to join a society they would prefer to live in. Though I shall conduct the discussion in terms of the situation of the United States, most of my arguments apply equally well to other countries.

My strategy is to argue, first, that immigration restriction is at least a prima facie violation of the rights of potential immigrants.[3] This imposes a burden on advocates of restriction to cite some special conditions that either neutralize or outweigh the relevant prima facie right. I then examine the most popular justifications offered for restricting immigration, finding that none of them offers a credible rationale for claiming either that such restriction does not violate rights or that the rights violation is justified. This leaves immigration restrictions ultimately unjustified.

A word about theoretical assumptions. In my view, most general theories or theoretical approaches in political philosophy – liberal egalitarianism, contractarianism, utilitarianism, and so on – are too controversial to form a secure basis for reasoning. It is not known which, if any, of those theories are correct. I have therefore sought to minimize the reliance on such theories. This does not mean that I assume that all such broad theories are false; I merely refrain from resting my arguments on them. Thus, I do not assume utilitarianism, contractarianism, libertarian rights theory, liberal egalitarianism, nor any general account of harm or rights. Nor do I assume the negation of any of those theories. Instead, I aim to rest conclusions on widely shared ethical intuitions about relatively specific cases. The method is to describe a case in which nearly everyone will share a particular, clear intuitive evaluation of some action, and then to draw a parallel from the case described to some controversial case of interest. This methodology follows a well-established tradition in applied ethics;[3] I propose that the approach be applied to the issue of immigration. The approach can, of course, be subjected to criticism, particularly for the weight placed on common ethical intuitions,

but this is not the place for a general discussion of the value of ethical intuition.[4] In any event, the intuitive premises I shall rely on are, I hope, much less controversial than the broad philosophical theories of the sort mentioned above, and much less initially controversial than the immigration issue itself.

2. Immigration Restriction as a Prima Facie Rights Violation

In this section, I aim to show that immigration restriction is a prima facie rights violation. A prima facie rights violation is an action of a sort that *normally* – that is, barring any special circumstances – violates someone's rights. For example, killing a human being is a prima facie rights violation: in normal circumstances, to kill someone is to violate his rights. But there are special circumstances that may alter this verdict: euthanasia and self-defense killings do not violate rights, for instance. Furthermore, even when an action violates rights, it may sometimes be justified nevertheless, because the victim's rights may be *outweighed* by competing moral considerations. Thus, killing one innocent person may be justified, though a violation of the victim's right to life, if it is necessary to prevent the deaths of one million others. Or so it seems to me.

The claim that an action is a prima facie rights violation, then, is not a very strong claim. It does not entail that the action is wrong all things considered, for there may be special circumstances that prevent the action from being an actual rights violation, or that render it justified despite its violation of rights. But nor is the claim entirely without force: to accept that an action is a prima facie rights violation has the effect of shifting a normative presumption. It becomes the burden of those who advocate the act in question to identify the special exculpatory or justificatory circumstances that make what tends to be a wrongful rights violation either not a rights violation in this case, or a justified rights violation. Those who oppose the act in question need only rebut such efforts.

Now before we turn to the case of immigration, consider the following scenario. Marvin is in desperate need of food. Perhaps someone has stolen his food, or perhaps a natural disaster destroyed his crops; whatever the reason, Marvin is in danger of starvation. Fortunately, he has a plan to remedy the problem: he will walk to the local marketplace, where he will buy bread. Assume that in the absence of outside interference, this plan would succeed: the marketplace is open, and there are people there who are willing to trade food to Marvin in exchange for something he has. Another individual, Sam, is aware of all this and is watching Marvin. For some reason, Sam decides to detain Marvin on his way to the marketplace, forcibly preventing him from reaching it. As a result, Marvin returns home empty-handed, where he dies of starvation.

What is the proper assessment of Sam's action? Did Sam harm Marvin? Did he violate Marvin's rights? Was Sam's action wrong?

It seems to me that there are clear answers to these questions. Sam's behavior in this scenario was both extremely harmful to Marvin and a severe violation of Marvin's rights. Indeed, if Marvin's death was reasonably foreseeable, then Sam's act was an act of murder. Unless there obtained some unusual circumstances not mentioned in the preceding description, Sam's behavior was extremely wrong.

Intuitively, Sam's behavior would still be wrong if the harm suffered by Marvin were less severe. Suppose that, rather than dying soon after returning home, Marvin foreseeably suffers from serious malnutrition. Again, assume that this misfortune would have been avoided had Marvin been able to trade in the marketplace, but Sam forcibly prevented him from doing so. In this case, again, it seems that Sam violates Marvin's rights and wrongfully harms Marvin.

What do these examples show? I think they show, to begin with, that individuals have a prima facie, negative right not to be subjected to seriously harmful coercion. Sam's behavior in the scenario was, by stipulation, coercive – it involved a use or threat of physical force against Marvin, significantly restricting his freedom of action. It was also extremely harmful, resulting in Marvin's starvation. These facts seem to explain why Sam's action was a violation of Marvin's rights, and why it was wrong.

How do we know that Sam harmed Marvin? A "harm" is commonly understood as a setback to someone's interests.[5] Marvin's death by starvation certainly sets back his interests. Moreover, in my view, no philosophical *theory* of harm is required in this case. Perhaps there are borderline cases in which one would need to appeal to a theory to determine whether an event counted as a harm or not. But the story of starving Marvin presents no such difficult case. Marvin's death is a paradigm case of a harm.

Still, there are some who draw a distinction between *harming* someone (making oneself the agent of harm) and merely *allowing a harm* to befall someone. And some believe that allowing harm is much less wrong than harming, perhaps not even wrong at all.[6] This view is controversial. Fortunately, we need not resolve that controversy here, because the case of Sam and Marvin is not a case of a mere allowing of harm. If Sam had merely stood by and refused to give Marvin food, then it could be said that Sam *allowed* Marvin to die. But that is not the story. The story is that Marvin is going to get some food, and Sam *actively and forcibly intervenes* to stop Marvin from getting it. This is a harming and, since the harm involved is death, it is a killing.[7] I take all this to be the judgment of common sense.

I am not claiming here that all acts of coercion are harmful. Paternalistic coercion, for instance, need not be harmful. Nor are all harmful actions coercive. One might harm a person, for instance, by spreading false rumors about her, without any exercise of physical force. I am only claiming that *this* action, Sam's forcible interference with Marvin's effort to reach the marketplace, was both harmful and coercive. Similarly, I am not claiming that all coercion violates rights, nor that all harmful acts violate rights. I claim only that, when an action is seriously harmful *and* coercive, it tends for that reason to be a rights violation, other things being equal – that is, it is a prima facie rights violation. Sam's behavior in the scenario described violates Marvin's rights, because it is an act of extremely harmful coercion, and there are no relevant extenuating circumstances. Sam's behavior could be justified if, for example, it was necessary to prevent the deaths of a million innocent persons; or, perhaps, if Marvin had for some reason contracted Sam to forcibly prevent Marvin from going to the marketplace. But assume that nothing like that is the case. The case is just as originally described, with no special circumstances. Few would doubt, then, that Sam's behavior is unacceptable.

How does all this relate to U.S. immigration policy? The role of Marvin is played by those potential immigrants who seek escape from oppression or economic hardship. The marketplace is the United States: were they allowed in, most immigrants would succeed in meeting their needs (to a greater extent, at least, than they will if they are not allowed in). The role of Sam is played by the government of the United States, which has adopted severe restrictions on entry. These restrictions are imposed by coercion: armed guards are hired to patrol the borders, physically barring unauthorized entry, and armed officers of the state forcibly detain and expel immigrants who are found residing in the country illegally. As in the case of Sam's detention of Marvin, the U.S. government's exclusion of undocumented immigrants is also very harmful to most of those excluded: many suffer from oppression or poverty that could and would be remedied if only they were able to enter the country of their choice. In view of this, the actions of the U.S. government, prima facie, constitute serious violations of the rights of potential immigrants – specifically, the government violates their prima facie right not to be harmfully coerced.

How might advocates of restriction object to this reasoning? Some might argue that the United States, in refusing entry to potential immigrants, merely fails to confer a benefit, or that it merely allows a harm to occur, rather than actually *harming* the potential immigrants. On some views, individuals have a right not to be harmed in certain ways, but no right to positive assistance.[8] There are at least two reasons why one might think that immigration restrictions merely allow harm. First, it might be thought that the United States is not the *cause* of the harms that potential immigrants suffer. Perhaps the harms are caused by natural disasters, or corrupt foreign governments. This claim is controversial;[9] nevertheless, I shall grant it for the sake of argument. Second, it might be thought that the U.S. does not harm potential immigrants by refusing them entry, because the good they are denied is only a good that would be provided by the United States itself, and it might be thought that a withholding of benefits that would be conferred by oneself – even if that withholding requires active agency – is a mere failure to benefit, rather than a harming.[10]

In response to the first point, we must recognize that it is possible to harm a person even when one is not the originating cause of the harm that person suffers: one can harm a person by preventing that person from averting or remedying a harm originated by someone or something else. That is the lesson of the Sam–Marvin case: Sam did not cause Marvin to be out of food to begin with. We may suppose that Marvin was initially in danger of starvation because a natural disaster destroyed his crops, or because thieves (entirely unconnected to Sam) stole his food. This initial situation would be no fault of Sam's. Nevertheless, when Sam actively and coercively interferes with Marvin's efforts to remedy the problem, Sam then becomes responsible for Marvin's misfortune.

In response to the second point, note that the agent to whom I am ascribing a wrong is not the United States (the society as a whole) but rather the U.S. government. In denying entry to potential immigrants, the U.S. government refuses to provide certain benefits to them, including all the social services that they would receive were they granted U.S. residence. But that is not the harm that I am claiming the government imposes on potential immigrants. (Perhaps that is a harm imposed by the state, perhaps not – but it is not what my argument rests upon.) The U.S. government also fails to provide assistance in the form of foreign aid to most of these would-be immigrants. But again, that is not the harm that I charge the U.S. government with imposing. The way the government harms potential immigrants is by excluding them from a certain physical area, and thereby effectively excluding them from interacting in important and valuable ways with people (other than the government itself) who are in that region. Many Americans would happily trade with or employ these would-be immigrants, in a manner that would enable the immigrants to satisfy their needs. The government does not merely refuse to give goods to the potential immigrants, nor does it merely refuse, itself, to trade with them. It expends great effort and resources on actively stopping Americans from trading with or employing them in the relevant ways.[11]

The point can be seen perhaps more clearly by returning to the case of Marvin. If Sam refuses to sell Marvin food, then Sam thereby fails to confer a benefit on Marvin. But when Sam actively stops Marvin from trading with anyone in the marketplace, when there are merchants present who would be glad to trade with Marvin, Sam thereby harms Marvin. He does not merely fail to benefit Marvin.

Sam's action might be justified if there were special circumstances not previously specified, circumstances that either cancelled the right that Marvin normally has not to be harmfully coerced, or that morally outweighed Marvin's

rights. Likewise, what we have said so far does not establish that the U.S. government's restrictions on immigration are wrong *tout court*, but only that those defending the policy incur a burden of providing a justification for these restrictions. In light of the seriousness of the harms involved in this case, the justification for immigration restrictions must be correspondingly clear and powerful.

3. Reasons for Restriction

Harmful coercion is sometimes justified. It may be justified when necessary to defend an innocent party against harmful coercion. It may be justified when necessary to prevent much worse consequences. It may be justified because of a prior agreement made by the coercee. And there may be other circumstances that justify harmful coercion as well.[12] Some believe, for instance, that harmful coercion may be justified because of a need to rectify severe economic inequality. The latter claim is controversial, as would be many other alleged justifications for harmful coercion. This illustrates one reason why a general theory of the conditions for justified harmful coercion would be difficult to devise and still more difficult to defend.

Fortunately, it may turn out that we do not need any such general theory. Some sorts of reasons, including some mentioned in the preceding paragraph, are generally accepted as legitimate justifications for harmful coercion. Equally, there are some sorts of reasons that we can see intuitively, even without a general theory, *not* to be legitimate justifications for harmful coercion. For instance, one is not justified in harmfully coercing a person simply because one wants the victim's shoes, or because one hates the race to which the victim belongs, or because one disagrees with the victim's philosophical beliefs. Whatever is the correct theory of justifications for harmful coercion, *those* reasons surely will not qualify. The task at hand is to determine whether there are any circumstances that justify the harmful coercion involved in immigration restrictions. Given that immigration restriction is a prima facie rights violation, the burden of proof falls on advocates of restriction. Thus, we may proceed by considering the reasons they have offered for restricting immigration. If it turns out that all of these reasons fall into the category of things that clearly do not count as valid justifications for harmful coercion, then it is fair to draw the conclusion that immigration restrictions are unjustified.

3.1. Immigration and Employment

In popular discourse, the most common sort of argument for limiting or eliminating immigration is economic. It is said that immigrants take jobs away from American workers, and that they cause a lowering of wage rates due to their willingness to work for lower wages than American workers.[13] At the same time, economists are nearly unanimous in agreeing that the overall economic effects of immigration on existing Americans are positive.[14] These claims are mutually consistent: there are certain industries in which immigrants are disproportionately likely to work. Preexisting workers in those industries are made worse off due to competition with immigrant workers. According to one estimate, immigration during the 1980s may have reduced the wages of native-born workers in the most strongly affected industries by about one to two percent (five percent for high school dropouts).[15] At the same time, employers in those industries and customers of their businesses are made better off due to lower production costs, and the economic gains to these latter groups outweigh the economic losses to the workers. Some economists have accused immigration opponents of overlooking the economic benefits of immigration due to a bias against foreigners or members of other races.[16]

Let us leave aside the question of the overall effects of immigration on the economy, and focus instead on the following question. Granted

that immigration makes some American workers economically worse off, does this show that immigration restriction does not violate the rights of would-be immigrants, or that if it does, the rights violation is nevertheless justified? More generally, does the following constitute a valid justification for harmful coercion: that the coercive action is necessary to prevent someone else from suffering slight to moderate economic disadvantage through marketplace competition?

It seems to me that it does not. Consider two related examples. In the first example, I am being considered for a particular job, for which I know that Bob is the only other candidate. I also know that Bob is willing to work for a lower salary than the salary that I could obtain if I were the only candidate. On the day Bob is scheduled to have his job interview, I accost him and physically restrain him from going to the interview. When confronted about my seemingly unacceptable conduct, I explain that my action was necessary to protect myself against Bob's taking the job that I would otherwise have, or my being forced to accept a lower salary in order to get the job. Does this provide an adequate justification for my behavior? Does it show that, contrary to initial appearances, my harmful coercion does not really violate Bob's rights? Alternatively, does it show that my action, though a rights violation, was an ethically justified rights violation?

Certainly not. The mere fact that Bob is competing with me for a job that I desire, or that Bob is willing to accept a lower salary than I could obtain if I did not have to compete with him, does not invalidate or suspend Bob's right not to be subjected to harmful coercion. Nor does my interest in having less economic competition *outweigh* Bob's right not to be coercively harmed. If my need for the job in question were very much greater than Bob's need, then some might argue that I would be justified in overriding Bob's rights. We need not decide exactly when a right may be overridden, nor whether a greater economic need could constitute an adequate basis for overriding a competitor's right to be free from harmful coercion; we need not decide these things here, because we can simply stipulate that Bob has at least as much need for the job for which we are competing as I do. In such a case, no one would say that Bob's right to be free from coercive harms is suspended or outweighed.

My second example is a modified version of the story of Sam and Marvin. As before, Marvin plans to walk to the local marketplace to obtain life-sustaining food. Due to his economic circumstances, Marvin will have to buy the cheapest bread available at the market. Sam's daughter, however, also plans to go to the market, slightly later in the day, to buy some of this same bread. This bread is often in short supply, so that the vendor may run out after Marvin's purchase. Sam's daughter could buy more expensive bread, but she would prefer not to. Knowing all this, Sam fears that if Marvin is allowed to go to the market, his daughter will be forced to pay a slightly higher price for bread than she would like. To prevent this from happening, he accosts Marvin on the road and physically restrains him from traveling to the market. Is Sam's action permissible?

Suppose Sam claims that his harmful coercion does not violate Marvin's rights, because it is necessary to protect his daughter from economic disadvantage. Certainly this defense falls flat. A person's right to be free from harmful coercion is not so easily swept aside. Likewise for the suggestion that Sam's action, though a rights violation, is justified because his daughter's interest in saving money outweighs Marvin's rights. No one would accept such feeble justifications.

Yet this seems analogous to the common economic argument for immigration restriction. The claim seems to be that we are justified in forcibly preventing individuals – many of whom are seeking escape from dire economic distress – from entering the American labor market, because American workers would suffer economic disadvantage through price competition. No one claims that American workers would be disadvantaged to anything like the degree that potential immigrants are disadvantaged by being forcibly excluded from the market. Nevertheless, the prospect of a modest lowering of American wages and narrowing of employment opportunities is taken to either suspend or outweigh the rights of needy foreigners. The ethical principle would have to be that a person's right to be free from extremely harmful coercion is sometimes held in abeyance simply by virtue of the fact that such coercion is necessary to protect third parties from modest economic disadvantage resulting from market-place competition. The implausibility of this principle is shown by the examples of Bob and Marvin above.

3.2. The State's Duty to its Citizens

Perhaps immigration restriction can be justified by reflection on the special obligations governments owe to their own citizens, as distinct from foreign nationals. Few doubt that there are such duties. States must provide their citizens protection from criminals and hostile foreign governments. A state does not have the same obligation to protect foreign citizens from criminals or other governments. Those who endorse a social contract theory of political authority may explain this by appeal to the idea that non-citizens of a given state are not party to the social contract with that state; the state therefore lacks the contractual obligations to non-citizens that it bears to citizens.

Perhaps this leads to a rationale for immigration restriction.[17] Perhaps the state has a general duty to serve the interests of its own citizens, including their economic interests, and no such duty, or no duty nearly as strong, to further the interests of foreign nationals. As a result, when the interests of American citizens come into conflict with those of foreigners, the American government must side with its own citizens, even when this results in a lowering of global social utility. Limitations on migration into the United States run contrary to the interests of would-be immigrants, but since those would-be immigrants are not presently U.S. citizens, the U.S. government has either no duty or a much weaker duty to consider their interests, as compared to the interests of its own citizens. Perhaps this gives some traction to the argument that American workers are disadvantaged because of competition with immigrants. Alternatively, one might argue that immigrants impose a financial burden on government providers of social services, such as health care, education, and law enforcement.[18] Since these social programs are financed through revenues collected from existing U.S. citizens, the government's consideration for the interests of its current citizens dictates that it limit the amount of immigration into the country.

Begin with the observation that immigration disadvantages American workers through labor market competition. There are two obstacles to regarding this as a justification for immigration restriction, even if we accept that the state has a much stronger obligation to protect the interests of its own citizens than it has to protect the interests of others. First, only some current citizens would be disadvantaged by increased immigration – those citizens who work in industries that immigrants are disproportionately likely to join. This is a relatively small portion of the population. All other current citizens would either fail to be significantly affected or actually be benefited by increased immigration. As mentioned earlier, most economists believe that the overall economic impact of immigration on current citizens is positive. Thus, if we consider only the interests of current citizens, it is at best unclear that immigration restrictions are beneficial. If we also give some weight to the interests of the immigrants themselves, it seems that the case for free immigration is clear.

Second, there are some obligations that any moral agent owes to other persons, merely in virtue of their status as persons. The

special obligations that governments owe to their citizens, whatever these obligations may consist in, do not eliminate the obligation to respect the human rights of non-citizens. In particular, the government's duty to give special consideration to its own citizens' interests cannot be taken to imply that the government is entitled to coercively impose grave harms on non-citizens for the sake of securing small economic benefits for citizens.

Consider again the case of starving Marvin. In the last version of the story, Sam coercively prevented Marvin from reaching the local marketplace, on the grounds that doing so was necessary to prevent his daughter from having to pay a higher than normal price for her bread. This action seems unjustified. Would Sam succeed in defending his behavior if he pointed out that, as a father, he has special obligations to his daughter, and that these imply that he must give greater weight to her interests than to the interests of non-family members? Certainly the premise is true – if anything, parents have even stronger and clearer duties to protect the interests of their offspring than a government has to protect its citizens' interests. But this does not negate the rights of non-family members not to be subjected to harmful coercion. One's special duties to one's offspring imply that if one must choose between giving food to one's own child and giving food to a non-family member, one should generally give the food to one's own child. But they do not imply that one may use force to stop non-family members from obtaining food, in order to procure modest economic advantages for one's own children.

Next, consider the charge that immigrants create a fiscal burden due to their consumption of social services. On the whole, immigrants pay slightly less in taxes than the cost of the social services they consume.[19] This is mainly because immigrants tend to have lower-than-average incomes, and thus pay relatively low taxes.[20] Some economists believe, however, that in the long run (over a period of decades), increased immigration would have a net positive fiscal impact.[21]

Assume that immigrants impose a net fiscal burden on government. Would this fact justify forcibly preventing a large number of potential immigrants from entering the country? To answer this, first we must ask whether the state presently has an obligation to provide social services to potential immigrants, even at a net cost to the state. On some theories of distributive justice, it could be argued that the state has such an obligation, even though these potential immigrants are not presently citizens.[22] If so, then the state obviously may not exclude potential immigrants for the purpose of shirking this duty.

Suppose, on the other hand, that the state has no such obligation to provide social services to potential immigrants, at least not without collecting from them sufficient revenues to cover the expenditure. If this is true, the state would perhaps be justified in denying social services to immigrants, raising taxes on immigrants, or charging special fees to immigrants for the use of social services. But it remains implausible that the state would be justified in excluding poten-tial immigrants from the territory entirely. It is not typically a satisfactory defense for a harmful act of coercion to say that because of a policy one has voluntarily adopted, if one did not coerce one's victim in this way, one would instead confer a benefit on the person that one does not wish to confer.

Suppose, for example, that Sam runs a charity organization. He has made a policy of offering free food to all poor people who enter the local marketplace. Unfortunately, the organization is running short on cash, so Sam is looking for ways to cut costs. When he learns that Marvin is heading to the market to buy some food, he decides to save money by forcibly preventing Marvin from reaching the market. Marvin would be better off being allowed into the marketplace, even without free food, since he could still buy some inexpensive food with his limited funds.

But Sam has already made a policy of offering free food to all poor people in the marketplace, so he would in fact offer free food to Marvin, were Marvin to make it there. Is it permissible for Sam to coercively inflict a serious harm on Marvin, in order to avoid having to either break his policy or give free food to Marvin?

Surely not. Perhaps Sam would be justified in altering his policy and refusing to give free food to Marvin when he arrives at the marketplace – this would be permissible, provided that Sam has no humanitarian obligation to assist Marvin. But whether or not Sam has any such humanitarian duties, he surely has no right to actively prevent Marvin from getting his own food. If Marvin had been coming to the market to *steal* Sam's food, perhaps then again Sam would be justified in excluding him. Even this claim would be controversial; if Marvin's condition of need were sufficiently urgent, some would say that Sam must let him take the food. But whatever one thinks about that question, surely Sam cannot justify barring Marvin from the opportunity to *buy* food from others, merely on the grounds that if Sam permits him to do so, then Sam will also voluntarily give him some food.

I have considered the possibilities both that the state owes potential immigrants a duty to help them satisfy their needs, and that the state owes them no such duty. But perhaps the situa-tion is more complex. Perhaps the state presently owes no duty to aid potential immigrants, but if and when they become residents in its territory, the state will *then* owe them a duty to provide the same level of services as it provides to native-born citizens. If so, the state could not, ethically, protect its financial interests by opening the borders and simply providing lower levels of social services to the mass of incoming immigrants.

In assessing this view, we must take account of the distinction between residents and citizens. It is much more plausible that states are obli-gated to help citizens satisfy their needs, than that states are obligated to help all *residents* do so.

So it is not clear that the suggestion of the preceding paragraph could justify preventing foreigners from residing in the United States, as opposed to justifying a refusal to grant citizenship. Nevertheless, let us assume that the state has a duty to offer equal levels of social services to all residents, once they are here. Even if mere residency somehow entitles one to equal levels of social services with native-born citizens, it is not plausible that this entitlement is *inalienable*, that is, that it cannot be voluntarily waived. The state therefore has at least one available strategy, apart from immigration restriction, for protecting its financial interests. This is to make a grant of legal residency or citizenship to potential immigrants contingent on the immigrants' agreement to waive their right to receive certain social services.[23] Alternatively, the state could require new immigrants to agree to pay a higher tax rate, sufficient to cover the government's expected costs. The availability of these alternatives undercuts any justification the state could plausibly be claimed to have, in virtue of its fiscal interests, for excluding most potential immigrants from the country.

It could be questioned whether the policy suggested in the preceding paragraph is permissible. If foreigners have a *right* to immigrate, one could argue, then the state must allow them to exercise that right, whether or not they agree to waive other rights (including rights that they may come to have in the future). This may be correct. But whether or not it is correct, my argument of the preceding paragraph stands. For my claim was not that the state in fact ought to require potential immigrants to waive their (future) right to receive social services. I claim only that the state ought *not* to prohibit potential immigrants from entering the country, given that there is an alternative method of achieving the same goal, and that this alternative is less coercive and less harmful. It may of course be that *neither* alternative is permissible. But in any event, the unnecessarily coercive alternative is not permissible. In general, whether one may

coercively harm innocent others to protect one's economic interests is open to debate. Perhaps there are circumstances in which one may do so. But even if one may do so, surely one may not employ *more* harmful coercion than is necessary to achieve one's goal.

3.3. Priority for the Least Advantaged

Some believe that the state ought to place greater weight on benefiting the least advantaged members of society than on benefiting other groups. Suppose this view (hereafter, "the Priority View") is correct.[24] What would it imply for the issue of immigration?

Joseph Carens believes that the Priority View provides further support for open borders. This is because Carens believes the Priority View should be applied internationally. Many of the globe's least advantaged inhabitants presently reside in foreign countries, and they could be helped by a policy of open borders.[25] Other thinkers argue, however, that a national government should apply the Priority View only within the borders of its own nation, thus prioritizing the interests of the least advantaged of its own citizens, rather than the least advantaged people on Earth.[26]

Why might the Priority View apply only to a government's own citizens? Michael Blake argues that obligations of distributive justice arise from the need to justify the *coercive* aspects of a social system. As a result, the Priority View applies only within the domain of those persons who are subject to the state's coercion, which he takes to mean the citizens of that state.[27] Stephen Macedo argues that a state has obligations of distributive justice only to those who are subject to a common system of laws. Considerations of distributive justice do not apply across borders, because individuals in different countries are not under a common legal system. Furthermore, according to Macedo, immigration causes economic disadvantage to those members of the native-born population who are already worst off. This is because immigrants often compete for the lowest-skilled jobs, thus further lowering the wage rates of the lowest-paid workers. The economic gain to consumers and employers may be greater than the economic loss to native-born workers, but, Macedo argues, the state should prioritize the interests of poor American workers over both the interests of wealthier Americans and the interests of would-be immigrants.[28] Thus, this version of the Priority View supports tight restrictions on immigration.

The Priority View itself is controversial.[29] But, even without challenging the general validity of the Priority View, there are still two things that may be said in response.

First, even if the Priority View is generally correct, it does not justify just *any* way in which the state might prioritize the interests of its least advantaged citizens. When the state has resources to spend, the Priority View tells us that the state ought, ceteris paribus, to spend its resources to help its poorest citizens. If the U.S. government is distributing food aid, it ought to give food to poor Americans before giving food to upper- or middle-class Americans. If Macedo and Blake are correct, the government ought also to give food to poor Americans before giving food to poor foreigners. But even those who are sympathetic to the Priority View would typically not, I think, hold that the state ought to promote the interests of its least advantaged citizens by *violating the rights* of foreigners. For example, suppose that the United States government were in a position to *steal* food from hungry people living in Afghanistan, ship the food to America, and give it to poor Americans. Very few, even among the most nationalistic egalitarians, would argue that the state was justified in doing so. Or suppose that the U.S. government could trick poor Afghans into giving the government money by offering to sell them food, but instead of giving them food, the government could just take the Afghans' money and give it to poor Americans. Or, finally, suppose the U.S. government could kill Afghan citizens, sell their organs, and use the

money to help poor Americans. In all of these cases, the U.S. government would be prioritizing the interests of its poorest citizens over those of foreigners. But presumably, these are not valid applications of the Priority View. A plausible account of why these applications of the Priority View are not valid is that the Priority View must be understood as operating under an implicit constraint: the state should promote the interests of its poorest citizens, but without violating the rights of others. If the argument of section 2 is correct, then restrictions on immigration are, prima facie, violations of the rights of foreigners; they thus could not be justified by appeal to the Priority View. Of course, we may yet find special circumstances that neutralize or override foreigners' prima facie rights in this case. The point here is simply that the Priority View does not point us to such a circumstance: as the examples discussed in this paragraph show, the fact that a particular action would promote the interests of the poorest Americans does not make what would otherwise be a violation of the rights of foreigners cease to be such.

A second response to Macedo and Blake is to argue that the Priority View, if correct, should after all apply to foreigners. This is clear when we consider Blake's view of the principles of distributive justice. Blake holds that such principles apply to all those who are subject to coercion by the state. *Pace* Blake, this group is not limited to the state's subjects. As I have been at pains to emphasize, immigration restrictions are coercive toward foreigners. Would-be immigrants are coercively prevented from immigrating. Therefore, by Blake's own lights, the state does after all owe these people a justification for its coercive activities.[30] If, as Blake believes, the justification for official coercion must derive from a hypothetical social contract among all parties subject to the state's coercion, then foreigners must be included in this contract. If the social contract demands a version of the Priority View, then it must be an internationalist Priority View.

Macedo's position is similar to Blake's: Macedo holds that the Priority View arises out of a social contract, to which the parties are all those subject to a common system of laws. Admittedly, foreigners are considerably less subject to U.S. law than U.S. citizens are. They are not, however, entirely exempt from American law. In particular, foreigners are subjected to U.S. *immigration* law, which prohibits most of them from migrating to the United States. Macedo might argue that their subjection to this relatively limited body of law, in contrast to the much larger body of laws from which they are exempt, is not enough to justify their inclusion in the hypothetical social contract. But this, it seems to me, is not a natural position. If legal systems require justification, perhaps because of the way in which they impose coercive restrictions on persons, and if, as a rule, they must be justifiable to all those on whom the laws are imposed, then the most natural view to take is that even limited bodies of law must be justifiable to all those on whom those limited bodies of law are imposed. Thus, immigration law should be justifiable to all those who are subjected to it, which is to say, to all potential immigrants. It seems unlikely that potential immigrants, if included in the hypothetical social contract, would agree in principle to being excluded from the country for the benefit of native-born citizens.

3.4. Cultural Preservation

In the views of some thinkers, states are justified in restricting the flow of immigration into their territories for the purposes of preserving the distinctive cultures of those nations.[31] Joseph Heath argues that citizens have an interest in preserving their culture because the culture helps them form values and decide how to live. If too many immigrants from other cultures arrive, they could disrupt our culture; thus, Heath believes, we have a right to restrict immigration.[32] David Miller argues that existing citizens have an interest in seeking to *control* how their culture does or does not develop, and this requires the ability to limit external influence; thus, again, we have a right to restrict immigration.[33]

To see this as a persuasive reason for restricting American immigration, we must accept two premises, one empirical and the other ethical. The empirical premise is that American culture is in danger of extinction or at least severe alteration if immigration is not restricted. The ethical premise is that the need to preserve one's culture constitutes a legitimate justification for harmful coercion of the sort involved in immigration restrictions.

Both premises are open to question. Empirically, it is doubtful whether apprehensions about the demise of American culture are warranted. Around the world, American culture, and Western culture more generally, have shown a robustness that prompts more concern about the ability of other cultures to survive influence from the West than vice versa. For example, Coca-Cola now sells its products in over 200 countries around the world, with the average human being on Earth drinking 4.8 gallons of Coke per year.[34] McDonald's operates more than 32,000 restaurants in over 100 countries.[35] The three highest grossing movies of all time, worldwide, were *Avatar, Titanic,* and *The Lord of the Rings: The Return of the King.* All three were made by American companies, but 70% of the box office receipts came from outside the United States.[36] The television show *Who Wants to Be a Millionaire?* has been franchised in over 100 countries worldwide, including such diverse places as Japan, Nigeria, Venezuela, and Afghanistan.[37] Whether one sees the phenomenon as desirable, undesirable, or neutral, Western culture has shown a remarkable ability to establish roots in a variety of societies around the world, including societies populated almost entirely by non-Western people. This robustness suggests that American culture is in no danger of being eradicated from America, even if America should drastically increase its rate of immigration. Other societies may have cause to fear the loss of their cultures due to foreign influence, but America does not.

Turning to the ethical premise of the argument for restriction, is the desire to preserve American culture a valid justification for immigration restriction? More generally, can one be justified in harmfully coercing others, solely because doing so is necessary to prevent those others from altering the culture of one's society? Miller is on plausible ground in maintaining that people have a strong interest in controlling their culture. But not everything in which one has an *interest* is something that one may, ethically, secure through harmful coercion of others, even if such coercion is required to protect one's interest. For instance, I have an interest in having my lawn mowed, but I may not force anyone to mow it, even if this is the only method I have available to secure the desired result. Even when one has a *right* to something, it is not always permissible to protect one's enjoyment of the right through coercion. Suppose that I am in need of a liver transplant, but there are no willing donors available. To preserve my life, I must take a liver by force from an unwilling donor. Even though I have both a strong interest in living and a right to life, this does not imply that I may coerce an unwilling donor.

Why, then, should we assume that our admittedly strong interest in preserving our culture entitles us to harmfully coerce others in the name of cultural preservation? Proponents of the cultural preservation argument have neglected this question. Two hypothetical examples, however, may help us to address it.

First, suppose that a number of your neighbors have been converting to Buddhism or selling their homes to Buddhists. Because of this, your neighborhood is in danger of being changed from a Christian to a Buddhist community. The Buddhists do not coercively interfere with your practice of your own religion, nor do they do anything else to violate your rights; still,

you object to the transformation, because you would prefer to live among Christians. If you catch on to what is happening in the early stages, are you ethically entitled to use force to stop your neighborhood from becoming Buddhist? Consider a few ways in which you might go about this. You might forcibly interfere with your neighbors' practice of their religion. You could go to their houses, destroy their Buddha statues, and replace them with crucifixes. You could force your neighbors to attend Christian churches. You could forcibly expel all Buddhists from the neighborhood. Or you could forcibly prevent any Buddhists from moving in. All of these actions seem unacceptable. Hardly anyone would accept the suggestion that your interest in preserving a Christian neighborhood either negates or outweighs your neighbors' rights not to be harmfully coerced by you.

A society's dominant religion is an important part of its culture, though not the only important part. But similar intuitions can be elicited with respect to other aspects of culture. You may not forcibly prevent your neighbors from speaking different languages, wearing unusual clothes, listening to unfamiliar music, and so on. This suggests that the protection of one's interest in cultural preservation is not a sufficient justification for harmful coercion against others.

Second, consider another variant of the story of Marvin. Again, imagine that Sam has coercively prevented Marvin from reaching the local marketplace, where he would have bought food needed to sustain his life. His earlier justifications for his behavior having fallen flat, Sam mentions that he had yet another reason. Marvin practices very different traditions from most of the other people in the marketplace. For instance, he wears unusual clothing, belongs to a minority religion, speaks a different language from most others (though he is able to get along well enough to purchase food), and admires very different kinds of art. Sam became concerned that, if Marvin went to the marketplace and interacted with the people gathered there, he might influence the thinking and behavior of others in the marketplace. He might convert others to his religion, for example, or induce more people to speak his language. Because Sam did not want these things to happen, he decided to forcibly prevent Marvin from reaching the marketplace.

Sam had a real interest in preventing the sort of changes that Marvin might have induced. The question is whether this interest is of such a kind that it justifies the use of harmful coercion against innocent others to protect that interest. Intuitively, the answer is no. Sam's desire to be surrounded by people who think and behave in ways similar to himself does not overrule Marvin's right to be free from harmful coercion.

Is this case a fair analogy to the case of immigration restriction? One difference is that Marvin is only one person, and it seems unlikely that he could single-handedly bring about a drastic change in the culture of Sam's society. In contrast, if the United States were to open its borders, *millions* of people would come across, making drastic cultural change a much more realistic possibility.

This difference between the two cases would invalidate my argument, if the reason why Sam's action was impermissible were that Marvin would not in fact have had the effects that Sam feared. But this is not the case. In both of my examples, it should be stipulated that the agent's fears are realistic: in the first example, you have well-founded fears that your neighborhood is becoming Buddhist; in the second example, Sam had well-founded fears that Marvin would have a large impact on the other people in the marketplace. (Perhaps the marketplace is small enough that a single person can significantly influence it.) My contention, with regard to these examples, is not that the cultural change would not happen, but that the avoidance of cultural change does not seem an adequate justification for harmful coercion against innocent others.

3.5. The Immigrant Flood and the Collapse of America

The last reason for restriction that we have to consider appeals to the catastrophic consequences that allegedly would result from the ocean of immigrants that would flood over America if the borders were opened. Brian Barry believes that at least one billion immigrants would pour into America if given the chance. The result would be severe overcrowding; the collapse of government social programs, including educational and health services; ethnic violence; the collapse of liberal democracy; environmental devastation; and a reduction of the U.S. standard of living to Third World levels.[38]

Each of these predictions merits a lengthy discussion on its own, but limitations of space preclude this. Here, I can make only a few observations about some of Barry's concerns. To begin with, consider Barry's prediction of one billion immigrants coming to the United States. Although he considers this "surely … quite a conservative estimate,"[39] the estimate seems to be the reverse of conservative. Barry bases the estimate on the assumption that a person will leave his home country whenever "there is at least one other place with a material standard of living higher enough to offset the cultural differences between the two places." Barry figures that there must be at least a billion people around the world whose material standard of living is much lower than what they would have in the U.S., sufficiently so to offset the disadvantage represented by the cultural differences between the two societies.

In practice, however, most people are much more reluctant to move than Barry's remarks would suggest. Even though migration among U.S. cities and states is legally unconstrained, 57 percent of Americans have never lived outside their current state of residence, and 37 percent have never lived outside the city in which they were born.[40] It seems unlikely that this is because such a large number of Americans were born in the city that offers them the greatest economic opportunities of any city in the country. This seems especially unlikely when one considers that those born in rural areas, which tend to have the most limited economic opportunities, are also those *least* likely to move. Nor would these Americans be likely to suffer cultural shock were they to leave their home towns or home states. Rather, those who have remained stationary most commonly cite family reasons for not moving. An individual who leaves his home town must generally leave behind his current neighbors, friends, and family (including extended family). This is extremely important to most people. In addition, most people feel an emotional attachment to the place in which they were born and raised. Most people also exhibit a kind of inertia: they do not survey all the alternative life paths possible to them at each moment, ready to switch paths whenever they identify one with greater expected utility; rather, they remain on their present path until something pushes them out of it. These are the main reasons why most Americans do not move within America. For foreigners, these same reasons would apply. In the case of people considering movement from one country to another, however, family considerations would be even more weighty than for people considering movement within the United States, because visiting family who live in another country is more difficult than visiting family who merely live in another city or state within the U.S. Foreigners also have additional reasons for not moving to America, deriving from language and other cultural barriers, as well as the sense of loyalty that most people feel to their native country.

There is some empirical evidence bearing on this issue. The U.S. State Department reportedly has about four million applicants on the waiting list for immigrant visas.[41] In addition, every year, the State Department conducts a lottery, known as the "Diversity Visa Lottery," to give away 50,000 green cards. Individuals from any country in the world, other than the twenty countries with the highest rates of emigration to the U.S., are eligible to apply (the purpose is to increase diversity in the group of incoming immigrants). In 2009, 9.1 million people applied. Anticipating that only some of those selected would actually come, the State Department selected about 100,000 people who were invited to pursue their applications further.[42] The 9.1 million applicants constituted approximately 0.3 percent of the total population of the eligible countries.[43] So there are presently about 13 million or so people living outside the United States who have made at least some effort towards moving to the U.S. legally. All of this gives us only a limited basis for guessing how many people would come to the United States if the borders were opened (among other things, there may be many who have refrained from trying to immigrate only because they believed they would not be permitted to do so). Nevertheless, these facts suggest that Barry has an overly liberal view of people's desire to move, and that his estimate of one billion immigrants may be off by one or two orders of magnitude.[44]

In addition to overestimating the supply of potential immigrants to the United States, Barry may have underestimated the capacity of the U.S. to assimilate immigrants. As a percentage of total population, the U.S. has coped with immigration rates far higher than the current rate.[45] Though Barry worries about overcrowding, the U.S. appears to have room for many more people. The population density of the United States in 2009 was about 34 persons per square kilometer. For comparison, the world average is 45 per square kilometer, and China has 144 per square kilometer, more than four times the American density.[46] This suggests that, at the least, we are not likely to soon run out of land.

In my view, Barry's speculations about the effects of open immigration are overly alarmist. For my part, however, I can offer little more than alternative speculation. No one knows what the full effects of a policy of open borders would be, since it has been a very long time since U.S. borders have been open. Perhaps Barry is correct that the result would be disastrous for American society. If so, this is the sort of extremely negative consequence that, it might be argued, outweighs the rights of potential immigrants to freedom of movement. As I have suggested above, it is not plausible that the rights of potential immigrants are outweighed by such relatively small considerations as modest economic disadvantages to American workers, or the aversion of some Americans to cultural change; it is, however, plausible that the rights of potential immigrants are outweighed by the need to preserve American society from the sort of devastation envisioned by Barry.

Therefore, I grant that it may be wise to move only gradually towards open borders. The United States might, for example, increase immigration by one million persons per year, and continue increasing the immigration rate until either everyone who wishes to immigrate is accommodated, or we start to observe serious harmful consequences. My hope and belief would be that the former would happen first. But in case the latter occurred, we could freeze or lower immigration levels at that time.

To summarize this section, we have examined the most popular reasons for immigration restriction. They include the concerns that immigrants harm poor Americans through labor market competition, that they burden government social welfare programs, that they threaten our culture, and that excessive numbers of immigrants could bring about the general collapse of American society. While each of these worries provides some reason for restriction, the question of interest is whether any of them provides a reason adequate to justify the harmful coercion entailed by such restrictions. In most cases, the answer is a clear no. This can best be seen by considering simpler, less controversial cases in which an individual engages in analogous

harmful coercion for similar reasons. Thus, it seems that Sam may not forcibly prevent Marvin from reaching the marketplace merely because Marvin would compete with Sam's daughter economically. This is true even though Sam has special duties to his daughter that require him, in many other circumstances, to put her interests before those of non-family members. Nor may Sam coerce Marvin to prevent Marvin from (peacefully) causing changes in the language spoken in the marketplace, or the religion practiced by the merchants there, or other social customs. The one concern that plausibly would, if well-founded, serve to justify immigration restriction is the worry that enormous numbers of immigrants would cause a virtual collapse of American society. This concern is also the most speculative and doubtful. Nevertheless, if the worry is valid, it would justify imposing some limits on the rate of immigration, albeit much looser limits than those currently in place. The conclusion is that for the most part, advocates of restriction have failed to satisfy the burden of justification created by the harmful, coercive nature of their favored policy, and that a far more liberal immigration policy is demanded by respect for individual rights. Those would-be immigrants who have been turned away from America have almost certainly suffered a serious violation of their rights.

4. The Right to Restrict: Club U.S.A.

We have now concluded the main argument for the right to immigrate. But some philosophers have advanced arguments, independent of any particular reasons in favor of restriction, for the conclusion that the state has a *right* to restrict immigration. The most popular argument of this kind is an argument based upon an analogy between citizenship and membership in other sorts of organizations.

In general, a private club may choose to exclude those whom it does not want as members, even if the club has no very strong reason for not wanting them. Suppose Sam, Betty, and Mike form a private club to discuss philosophy on the weekends. Marvin asks to join. For no particular reason, Sam, Betty, and Mike decide that they don't feel like having Marvin around, so they refuse. Though their behavior is unfriendly, the club members are within their rights. Marvin may attempt to persuade them to change their minds, but he cannot complain of an injustice or rights violation if he is not invited to the gatherings.

Some believe that a nation-state is similar to a private club in this respect: a nation may also, at its discretion, exclude unwanted members, even if the nation has no very strong reason for not wanting these prospective members.[47] Since most Americans do not want all the new members who would likely arrive if the nation's borders were opened, America is entitled to exclude most of those people.

There are at least two important objections to this reasoning. The first is that there are a number of important differences between a state and a private club of the sort envisioned above, and some of these differences may be morally significant enough to undermine the analogy.[48] In the case of states, everyone is compelled to be a citizen of at least one – no one has the option of simply not joining any country. In addition, these states provide extremely important services, but some states are much better than others, such that individuals who belong to the worse states are likely to suffer severe and lifelong deprivation or oppression. Finally, exclusion from a country generally also entails exclusion from any of a vast array of interactions with the citizens of a given country. None of these things is typically true of private clubs. No one, for example, is compelled to belong to a philosophy discussion club. Philosophy discussion clubs, while useful, do not provide services that everyone needs to have a decent life, nor are those who belong to inferior philosophy discussion clubs doomed to lifelong deprivation or oppression. Finally, those who

are excluded from a philosophy discussion club are not thereby effectively excluded from a vast array of business and social interactions with the members of the club. They may still visit the club members individually, hire or be hired by them, and so on.

In recognition of these important differences, we might devise another scenario that provides a closer analogy to governmental control over citizenship. Suppose there is an island, on which each individual belongs to one of several "water clubs." The water clubs procure water for their members, and all water on the island (including rain) is controlled by the clubs. Everyone is forced to belong to at least one club, and no one can obtain water except through a water club. Furthermore, some clubs are much better at managing their water, or simply have control of more and better-quality water, than others. As a result, many individuals on the island suffer from chronic thirst and water-borne illnesses. Many of these individuals attempt to join better water clubs, but the privileged members of the latter clubs refuse to admit them. *Some* members of the high-quality water clubs want to admit the less fortunate, thirstier people, but they are outvoted by other members. Furthermore, these privileged water clubs pass rules prohibiting any of their members from sharing water with thirsty people who do not belong to the club, and even from socializing with or doing business with such thirsty people. These rules are enforced through threats of violence.

This last scenario provides a closer analogy to the U.S. government's immigration policy than does the example of the weekend philosophy discussion club. In the water club story, the clubs in question have control over vital goods that everyone needs, everyone is compelled to belong to one, those who belong to inferior clubs thereby suffer serious deprivation, and those who are excluded from a club are also excluded from a wide array of business and social relations with any of that club's members. In all these respects, the water clubs are similar to governments, while the philosophy discussion club is not. And, whereas the philosophy discussion club seems within its rights in excluding unwanted members, it seems to me much more doubtful that the high-quality water clubs in the example are ethically permitted to exclude thirsty, less fortunate people.

That is one reason why the private club analogy fails to establish its intended conclusion. The second objection takes the form of a reductio ad absurdum: if the private club analogy succeeds in showing that foreign individuals have no right to immigrate to the United States and that states have the right to control their membership, then similar arguments can also be used to establish that individuals have hardly any rights at all, and that states have almost unlimited rights to coerce their members. The advocate of the club analogy will have to accept that a state may make demands of its citizens similar to those that a private club may make.

Of course, the advocate of the club analogy need not, initially, accept that states may do *all* things that private clubs may do. But he is committed to accepting that states have the same sort of rights to control the *conditions for citizenship* that private clubs have to control the conditions for membership, for that is the central point of the analogy. And the rights of private clubs are, in this regard, very extensive. A private club is within its rights even when it sets onerous, unwise, and unreasonable conditions (but not immoral conditions). Thus, I may if I wish start a club for people who refuse to eat vegetables and who flush $1,000 down the toilet every month (but I may not start a club for murderers). I may not compel anyone to join my club, but once they have joined, I do no wrong by requiring members to abstain from vegetables and flush money down the toilet. Whether I may *punish* members for failing to live up to the conditions of membership is more controversial, but I may at least demand that they either accept punishment or resign from the club. Similarly, the members of a club may (provided that this is

in accordance with the club's bylaws) vote to alter the membership conditions. A club initially started for philosophy discussion could become a club for people who eschew vegetables, provided that the change is made in accordance with club procedures. Again, the club could demand that all members either comply with the policy or resign their membership.

Following the analogy between clubs and states, then, a state could demand that all citizens refrain from eating vegetables (or else renounce their citizenship), provided that this policy was adopted in accordance with established legislative procedures. Some readers may not find this result especially disturbing. But now consider some of the other things that could be valid conditions for membership in a private club. I could, if I wished, start a club for people who cut off their left arms. Or for people who refrain from voting if female. Or for people who refrain from expressing political opinions. Again, I could not force anyone to join any of these clubs; I could, however, demand that anyone who belonged to the club either resign or follow the club's stated policies. If we rely on the analogy between states and clubs, then the state could require citizens to cut off their left arms, refrain from expressing political opinions, refrain from voting if they are female, and so on. Whatever the law requires, one could propose that abiding by that law is a condition on membership in the civil society. Thus, the state may demand that anyone who wishes to retain their citizenship should follow these laws.

Evidently, there is something wrong with that argument. The state does not have a right to require citizens to cut off their arms, or to prohibit women from voting, or to prohibit the expression of political opinions. The argument leading to those implausible results employed two main premises: one, that states have the same sort of rights of membership control that private clubs have; second, that a private club could impose the above conditions on membership. The first of these premises is the more doubtful and is the one we should reject. Perhaps the asymmetry between states and clubs derives from one of the differences noted earlier in this section between states and most private clubs. Or perhaps there is some other important difference not so far noticed. In any case, the fact that states do not have the same freedom in setting citizenship conditions that private clubs have in setting membership conditions undermines the argument for the claim that the state has a right to restrict immigration. The analogy to private clubs does not give us good reason to conclude that states have such a right.

5. Conclusion

The main argument of this paper ran as follows:

1. Individuals have a prima facie right to immigrate (that is, a right not to be prevented from immigrating). This is because:
   a. Individuals have a prima facie right to be free from harmful coercion.
   b. Immigration restrictions are harmful and coercive.
2. The prima facie right to immigrate is not overridden. In particular:
   a. It is not overridden because of immigrants' effects on the labor market.
   b. It is not overridden because of the fiscal burden of providing social services to immigrants.
   c. It is not overridden because of the state's special obligations to its citizens in general, nor its special obligations to its poorest citizens.
   d. It is not overridden because of the threat immigrants pose to the nation's culture.
3. Therefore, immigration restrictions are wrongful rights violations.

In this final section, I would like to comment, first, on how my argument compares with other

arguments on the subject, both in the popular discourse and in the academic literature; second, why the majority of citizens continue to support very restrictive immigration policies; and third, why the immigration issue is one of today's most important political issues.

In the popular discourse, most arguments surrounding immigration are restricted consequentialist ones: they are consequentialist arguments in which attention is restricted only to consequences for native-born citizens. Opponents of immigration typically claim that immigrants harm domestic workers, while advocates of more liberal immigration policies claim that immigrants are a boon to the domestic economy. Both sides commonly ignore the welfare of the immigrants themselves, as if they were of no concern, and further ignore any issues of rights and justice beyond economic consequentialism. In counterpoint to this depressingly shallow discourse, I have tried in this paper to draw attention to the rights of the potential immigrants, and to the moral significance of imposing harmful restrictions on people by force.

In the academic literature, many of the arguments in defense of restriction similarly overlook the rights of potential immigrants and the moral significance of coercion, in favor of a focus on the interests of native-born citizens.[49] This is true when, for example, advocates of restriction argue that citizens have an interest in controlling their society's culture, or that poor citizens have an interest in limiting labor market competition, without attending to the question of whether these interests are of the sort whose furtherance justifies harmful coercion of innocent others. Those who address the question of immigrants' rights most often frame the issue in terms of a right to freedom of movement and/or in terms of rights connected with distributive justice.[50] I have focused on a simpler, more general right: the right to be free from harmful coercion.

Most of the academic discussion is theory-centered: authors address the implications for immigration policy of some general philosophical theory or ideological orientation. Kershnar, for example, assumes a traditional social contract theory. Blake and Macedo each assume a Rawlsian hypothetical contract leading to the Difference Principle. Other authors examine the implications of liberal egalitarianism, liberalism in general, libertarianism, and utilitarianism.[51] As mentioned at the outset, I do not believe that any of these theories has been established. I have therefore sought to build a case upon generally acceptable intuitions about certain cases. These intuitions are not ideologically controversial – one would not, for example, expect liberals and conservatives to disagree over whether it was permissible to forcibly prevent a hungry person from traveling to a marketplace to buy food. The argument for free immigration ought to be persuasive to nearly everyone, regardless of ideological orientation.

Why, then, do most citizens of Western democratic countries oppose the opening of their borders? I believe the best explanation is that most of us suffer from a bias that makes it easy for us to forget about the rights and interests of foreigners. Racial bias once caused white persons to view members of their race as more important than those of other races, and to ignore the rights of members of other races. Sexist bias caused men to view themselves as more important than women and to ignore the rights of women. In modern times, great progress has been made in overcoming these biases. But some prejudices remain socially acceptable today, not even recognized by most as prejudices. Among these privileged prejudices is *nationalist bias*, the prejudice that causes us to view our countrymen as more important than citizens of other countries, and to ignore the rights of the foreign-born.[52]

When Americans today recall the unabashed racism of earlier generations, we may easily feel ashamed of our forebears. Most of us would cringe at the suggestion that our race is better than other races. We feel that we cannot understand what it would be like to be so prejudiced. How could one not see the injustice in slavery, or racial segregation? But most Americans, like most human beings around the world, in fact have easy access to what it was like to be an unabashed racist. It was to feel about one's race the way most of us now feel about our country. Today's Americans do not cringe when we hear the statement that America is the greatest country on Earth, any more than white people a century ago would have cringed to hear that whites were the best race. We do not cringe to hear that American businesses should hire native-born Americans rather than immigrants, any more than Americans three generations ago would have cringed to hear that white-owned businesses should hire white people in preference to blacks. Naturally, nationalists may attempt to devise explanations for why nationality is different from race, and why nationalism is really justified. This is not the place to attempt to argue that point. I would like simply to put forward for consideration the thought that perhaps we have no right to feel ashamed of our ancestors, and that our descendants may feel about us the way we feel about our ancestors.

Be that as it may, the question of immigration is surely underemphasized in contemporary philosophy, given its human importance. Literally *millions* of lives are affected in a serious and long-term manner by immigration restrictions. Were these restrictions lifted, millions of people would see greatly expanded opportunities and would take the chance to drastically alter their lives for the better. This makes immigration law a strong candidate for the most harmful body of law in America today. In view of this, it is particularly troubling that these restrictions appear to have so little justification.

[. . .]

Notes

1 U.S. Department of Homeland Security, *Yearbook of Immigration Statistics: 2007*, http://www.dhs.gov/

ximgtn/statistics/publications/yearbook.shtm (Washington, D.C.: U.S. Department of Homeland Security, Office of Immigration Statistics, 2008; accessed April 9, 2009), pp. 5, 95.

2 In 2005, a total of 472 people died while attempting to migrate illegally into the United States. Many died from exposure in the Arizona desert; other causes of death included drowning, motor vehicle accidents, and homicide (U.S. Government Accountability Office, "Illegal Immigration: Border-Crossing Deaths Have Doubled Since 1995; Border Patrol's Efforts to Prevent Deaths Have Not Been Fully Evaluated," http://www.gao.gov/new.items/d06770.pdf (Washington, D.C.: U.S. Government Accountability Office, August, 2006; accessed February 22, 2010), pp. 3–4, 59). Despite its efforts, the government estimates that 11.6 million people have succeeded in immigrating to the U.S. illegally (U.S. Department of Homeland Security, "Estimates of the Unauthorized Immigrant Population Residing in the United States: January 2008," http://www.dhs.gov/xlibrary/assets/statistics/publications/ois_ill_pe_2008.pdf (Washington, D.C.: U.S. Department of Homeland Security, Office of Immigration Statistics, 2009; accessed April 9, 2009)).

3 Think, for example, of Judith Thomson's violinist ("A Defense of Abortion," *Philosophy & Public Affairs* 1 (1971): 47–66, pp. 48–49), or Peter Singer's shallow pond (*Practical Ethics*, 2nd ed. (Cambridge: Cambridge University Press, 1993), p. 229).

4 See my *Ethical Intuitionism* (New York: Palgrave Macmillan, 2005) for a general defense of ethical intuition. See Peter Singer, "Ethics and Intuitions," *Journal of Ethics* 9 (2005): 331–52, for criticisms of the reliance on intuitions about cases.

5 Shelley Wilcox proposes to define harm in terms of "a human rights deficit": see "Immigrant Admissions and Global Relations of Harm," *Journal of Social Philosophy* 38 (2007): 274–91, p. 279. On this view, one must first determine whether a human right has been violated to determine whether someone has been harmed. This seems to me to put things the wrong way around. The notion of a human rights deficit is a more theoretical and controversial notion than that of a harm, and thus, one ought to be able to recognize

the existence of harms without recognizing human rights deficits. Utilitarians, for instance, may recognize that people are often harmed, even if (as they may also hold) there are no rights. Wilcox (p. 278) worries that a broader notion of harm may create difficulties if one also holds that it is generally wrong for a state to harm individuals. This problem may be avoided, however, by embracing only the weaker principle that it is prima facie wrong to *seriously and coercively* harm persons. This principle is uncontroversial, and yet it suffices, as we shall see, to make the case against immigration restriction.

6 See Jan Narveson, *Moral Matters* (Lewiston, N.Y.: Broadview, 1993), pp. 138–50.

7 Narveson (*Moral Matters*, p. 139) confirms this, characterizing a case of preventing someone from obtaining food as murder.

8 See Robert Nozick, *Anarchy, State, and Utopia* (New York: Basic Books, 1974), chaps. 3, 7; Narveson, *Moral Matters*, pp. 146–50.

9 Narveson (*Moral Matters*, pp. 153–55) suggests that most world poverty is caused by the governments of poor countries. Thomas Pogge, however, argues that the U.S. government is partly responsible for many harms suffered by inhabitants of less developed nations. See *World Poverty and Human Rights: Cosmopolitan Responsibilities and Reforms* (Cambridge: Polity Press, 2008), pp. 218–22.

10 See Jeff McMahan, "Killing, Letting Die, and Withdrawing of Aid," *Ethics* 103 (1993): 250–79. Particularly clear is Shelly Kagan's case in which an agent has written a check for famine relief and given it to a friend to mail (*The Limits of Morality* (Oxford: Oxford University Press, 1991), p. 107). The agent changes his mind and asks for the check back, before the friend mails it. Here, aid is withheld through active agency. Most would classify this as an allowing rather than a doing of harm (discussed in McMahan, "Killing, Letting Die," pp. 259–60).

11 The federal government spends almost $13 billion a year on actively excluding or expelling unauthorized immigrants (U.S. Office of Management and Budget, "Budget FY 2009, Department of Homeland Security," http://www.whitehouse.gov/omb/budget/fy2009/homeland.html; accessed April 9, 2009). Chandran Kukathas

explains the moral problem well: "It would be bad enough to meet such people with indifference and to deny them positive assistance. It would be even worse to deny them the opportunity to help themselves. To go to the length of denying one's fellow citizens the right to help those who are badly off, whether by employing them or by simply taking them in, seems even more difficult to justify – if, indeed, it is not entirely perverse." Chandran Kukathas, "The Case for Open Immigration," in Andrew I. Cohen and Christopher Heath Wellman (eds.), *Contemporary Debates in Applied Ethics* (Malden, Mass.: Blackwell, 2005), pp. 207–20, at p. 211.

12 Michael Blake argues that coercion may be justified by a hypothetical agreement, that is, by the circumstance that one would have agreed to the coercively imposed result under certain ideal circumstances. See "Distributive Justice, State Coercion, and Autonomy," *Philosophy & Public Affairs* 30 (2002): 257–96, p. 274.

13 See Susan Vroman, "Some Caveats on the Welfare Economics of Immigration Law," in Warren F. Schwartz (ed.), *Justice in Immigration* (Cambridge: Cambridge University Press, 1995), pp. 212–18; Roy Beck, *The Case Against Immigration* (New York: W.W. Norton, 1996), pp. 9–10.

14 Julian Simon and Stephen Moore surveyed a select group of twenty-seven highly respected economists, those who had been either presidents of the American Economic Association or members of the President's Council of Economic Advisors (reported in Julian Simon, *The Economic Consequences of Immigration* (Oxford: Blackwell, 1989), pp. 357–61). Twenty-two respondents said that the effect of twentieth-century immigration on the U.S. economy has been "very favorable." The remaining five characterized the effect as "slightly favorable." None found it unfavorable, and none said that he didn't know. Bryan Caplan discusses similar, though less extreme, results from the Survey of Americans and Economists on the Economy (*The Myth of the Rational Voter* (Princeton: Princeton University Press, 2007), pp. 58–59).

15 National Research Council, Panel on the Demographic and Economic Impacts of Immigration, *The New Americans: Economic, Demographic, and Fiscal Effects of Immigration*, ed. James P. Smith and Barry Edmonston (Washington, D.C.: National Academies Press, 1997), pp. 6–7. Stephen Macedo gives figures of 4% overall and 7.4% for high school dropouts, for the period from 1980–2000. See "The Moral Dilemma of U.S. Immigration Policy: Open Borders Versus Social Justice?" in Carol M. Swain (ed.), *Debating Immigration* (Cambridge: Cambridge University Press, 2008), pp. 63–81, at p. 66, citing George Borjas, *Heaven's Door: Immigration Policy and the American Economy* (Princeton: Princeton University Press, 1999).

16 Caplan, *The Myth of the Rational Voter*, pp. 58–59; Simon, *The Economic Consequences of Immigration*, pp. 11, 354–55.

17 See John Isbister, "A Liberal Argument for Border Controls: Reply to Carens," *International Migration Review* 34 (2000): 629–35.

18 Peter Brimelow, *Alien Nation: Common Sense about America's Immigration Disaster* (New York: Random House, 1995); Joseph Heath, "Immigration, Multiculturalism, and the Social Contract," *Canadian Journal of Law and Jurisprudence* 10 (1997): 343–61, pp. 347–48.

19 The National Research Council (*The New Americans*, p. 10) estimated that a 10% increase in immigration would impose an increased annual fiscal burden of $15 to $20 per household on existing Americans. As the Congressional Budget Office reports, the most costly government services used by immigrants are public school education, health care, and law enforcement ("The Impact of Unauthorized Immigrants on the Budgets of State and Local Governments," http://www.cbo.gov/doc.cfm?index=8711 (Washington, D.C.: Congressional Budget Office, 2007; accessed April 9, 2009)).

20 National Research Council, *The New Americans*, p. 11.

21 Ibid., pp. 11–12.

22 See below, section 3.3.

23 Kukathas ("The Case for Open Immigration," p. 213) suggests something like this arrangement. The U.S. federal government already bars legal resident immigrants from receiving means-tested federal assistance for five years after their arrival (Tanya Broder and Jonathan Blazer, "Overview of Immigrant Eligibility for Federal Programs," National Immigration Law Center, http://www.nilc.org/dc_conf/flashdrive09/

Access-to-Public-Benefits/pb1_overview-immeligfedprograms-2009-11-04.pdf (October 2009; accessed February 22, 2010)). However, the federal government generally requires state and local governments to provide social services to all residents, without regard to immigration status (U.S. Congressional Budget Office 2007).

24 John Rawls's Difference Principle is an extreme form of the Priority View (*A Theory of Justice*, revised ed. (Cambridge, Mass.: Harvard University Press, 1999), pp. 65–70). The term "Priority View" is from Derek Parfit, although Parfit uses the term to describe a general ethical view, rather than a view regarding the obligations of the state ("Equality or Priority?" 1991 Lindley Lecture, University of Kansas (published 1995), p. 19).

25 Joseph Carens, "Aliens and Citizens: The Case for Open Borders," *Review of Politics* 49 (1987): 251–73, pp. 255–62.

26 Isbister, "A Liberal Argument for Border Controls"; Blake, "Distributive Justice"; Macedo, "The Moral Dilemma of U.S. Immigration Policy."

27 Blake, "Distributive Justice," pp. 274–84; Michael Blake, "Immigration," in R.G. Frey and Christopher Heath Wellman (eds.), *A Companion to Applied Ethics* (Malden, Mass.: Blackwell, 2003), 224–37, at pp. 227–28.

28 Macedo, "The Moral Dilemma of U.S. Immigration Policy."

29 See Nozick, *Anarchy, State, and Utopia*, chap. 7, for influential criticisms of this kind of view.

30 Arash Abizadeh presses this argument in "Democratic Theory and Border Coercion: No Right to Unilaterally Control Your Own Borders," *Political Theory* 36 (2008): 37–65, pp. 44–48.

31 Brimelow, *Alien Nation*, pp. 178–81; Yael Tamir, *Liberal Nationalism* (Princeton: Princeton University Press, 1993), pp. 158–60; Michael Walzer, *Spheres of Justice: A Defense of Pluralism and Equality* (New York: Basic Books, 1983), pp. 38–41. Michael Dummett (*On Immigration and Refugees* (London: Routledge, 2001), pp. 50–52) recognizes a right to restrict immigration to prevent submersion of one's culture, but he believes very few countries have a valid concern about such submersion.

32 Heath ("Immigration, Multiculturalism," pp. 349–50) cites Will Kymlicka (*Liberalism, Community and Culture* (Oxford: Clarendon Press, 1989),

pp. 165–66) on the importance of culture, applying Kymlicka's thesis to the question of immigration control.

33 David Miller, "Immigration: The Case for Limits," in Cohen and Wellman (eds.), *Contemporary Debates in Applied Ethics*, 193–206, at pp. 200–201.

34 Daniel Workman, "Coca-Cola Global Sales: India Most Promising International Market," http://internationaltrade.suite101.com/article.cfm/coca_cola_global_sales (December 28, 2006; accessed March 30, 2009).

35 Daniel Workman, "McDonald's Global Sales: Big Mac's International Revenues Sizzle in 2006," http://internationaltrade.suite101.com/article.cfm/mcdonalds_global_ sales (October 24, 2006; accessed March 30, 2009).

36 Box Office Mojo, "All Time Worldwide Box Office Grosses," http://www.boxofficemojo.com/alltime/world/ (accessed February 22, 2010).

37 BBC News, "Millionaire Dominates Global TV," http://news.bbc.co.uk/2/hi/entertainment/4436837.stm (April 12, 2005; accessed March 30, 2009); Daily Mail Reporter, "Coming Soon to Afghanistan . . . Who Wants To Be A (Sort of) Millionaire?" http://www.dailymail.co.uk/news/article-1078294/Coming-soon-Afghanistan--Who-Wants-To-Be-A-sort-Millionaire.html (October 16, 2008; accessed March 30, 2009). *Who Wants to Be a Millionaire* originated in Britain. The web sites for the Nigerian, Venezuelan, and Japanese versions of the show can be viewed, respectively, at http://www.millionairenigeria.com/, http://www.rctv.net/Programacion/VerPrograma.aspx?ProgramacionId=24, and http://wwwz.fujitv.co.jp/quiz/index.html.

38 Brian Barry, "The Quest for Consistency: A Sceptical View," in Brian Barry and Robert E. Goodin (eds.), *Free Movement: Ethical Issues in the Transnational Migration of People and Money* (University Park: Pennsylvania State University Press, 1992), pp. 279–87.

39 Ibid., p. 281.

40 D'Vera Cohn and Rich Morin, "American Mobility: Movers, Stayers, Places and Reasons," Pew Research Center, http://pewresearch.org/pubs/1058/american-mobility-moversstayers-places-and-reasons (December 17, 2008; accessed April 2, 2009).

41 Doug Thompson, "Legal Immigration Waiting List Long, Records Show," *The Morning News*, http://www.nwaonline.net/articles/2007/05/09/news/051007arlegally.txt (May 9, 2007; accessed April 17, 2009).

42 U.S. Department of State, "Diversity Visa Lottery 2009 (DV-2009) Results," http://travel.state.gov/visa/immigrants/types/types_4317.html (accessed April 9, 2009). The countries *not* eligible for the Diversity Lottery were Brazil, Canada, China, Colombia, the Dominican Republic, Ecuador, El Salvador, Guatemala, Haiti, India, Jamaica, Mexico, Pakistan, Peru, the Philippines, Poland, Russia, South Korea, the United Kingdom, and Vietnam.

43 Population statistics are from CIA estimates (U.S. Central Intelligence Agency, "World Factbook," https://www.cia.gov/library/publications/the-world-factbook/index.html (accessed April 9, 2009)).

44 After writing the remarks in the text, I found polling data from Gallup indicating that the United States is the most desired destination country for migrants worldwide, with about 165 million people reporting that they would prefer to live in the United States rather than their present home country. See Neli Esipova and Julie Ray, "700 Million Worldwide Desire to Migrate Permanently," http://www.gallup.com/poll/124028/700-million-worldwide-desire-migrate-permanently.aspx (November 2, 2009; accessed February 19, 2010). Nevertheless, most of these individuals have not made an observable effort to migrate to the U.S.

45 Based on U.S. Census estimates, 2009 immigration was about 0.28% of the population (but note that this statistic omits illegal immigrants, an unknown number of whom entered the country in 2009) (U.S. Census Bureau, "Estimates of the Components of Resident Population Change for the United States, Regions, and States: July 1, 2008 to July 1, 2009 (NST-EST2008-05)," http://www.census.gov/popest/states/NST-comp-chg.html (released December, 2009; accessed February 22, 2010); U.S. Census Bureau, "Annual Estimates of the Resident Population for the United States, Regions, States, and Puerto Rico: April 1, 2000 to July 1, 2009 (NST-EST2009-01)," http://www.census.gov/popest/states/NST-ann-est.html (released December, 2009; accessed February 23, 2010)). In 1854, immigration was almost 2% of the population (Roger Daniels, *Coming to America: A History of Immigration and Ethnicity in American Life* (New York: HarperCollins, 1990), p. 124). In 1910, 14.7% of the U.S. population was foreign-born (Daniels, *Coming to America*, p. 125), compared with 7.3% in 2004, the latest year for which the Census Bureau has data available (U.S. Census Bureau, "Population by Sex, Age, and U.S. Citizenship Status: 2004," http://www.census.gov/population/www/socdemo/foreign/ppl-176.html (February 22, 2005; accessed April 2, 2009)).

46 All population density statistics have been calculated from U.S. Central Intelligence Agency ("World Factbook" (2009)) data. Population densities have been calculated using land areas only, excluding water-covered areas. Monaco, the world's most densely populated country, contains 16,767 people per square kilometer; however, as the country consists entirely of a single city, it is not to be expected that the U.S. could comfortably achieve a similar population density.

47 See Walzer, *Spheres of Justice*, pp. 39–41; Stephen Kershnar, "There Is No Moral Right to Immigrate to the United States," *Public Affairs Quarterly* 14 (2000): 141–58, p. 143; Christopher Heath Wellman, "Immigration and Freedom of Association," *Ethics* 119 (2008): 109–41, pp. 110–14. However, those who defend this view generally do not claim that the state may exclude immigrants for just any reason – for instance, the state may not exclude immigrants on racial grounds (Miller, "Immigration: The Case for Limits," p. 204; Wellman, "Immigration and Freedom of Association," pp. 139–40).

48 Phillip Cole rightly observes that Walzer has failed to show that political communities are relevantly similar to private clubs. See *Philosophies of Exclusion: Liberal Political Theory and Immigration* (Edinburgh: Edinburgh University Press, 2000), p. 72. Here, I go further by pointing out some relevant differences.

49 Blake ("Distributive Justice," p. 268) recognizes the moral import of coercion but seems to overlook the coercive nature of immigration restrictions.

50 On the alleged right to freedom of movement, see Joseph Carens, "Migration and Morality: A Liberal Egalitarian Perspective," in Barry and Goodin (eds.), *Free Movement*, pp. 25–47; Miller, "Immigration: The Case for Limits," pp. 194–97; Kershnar, "There Is No Right to Immigrate," pp. 151–53; Barry, "The Quest for Consistency," pp. 283–85. On distributive justice issues, see Wellman, "Immigration and Freedom of Association," pp. 121–30; Miller, "Immigration: The Case for Limits," pp. 197–99; Blake, "Distributive Justice"; Carens, "Aliens and Citizens," pp. 255–62; Veit Bader, "Citizenship and Exclusion: Radical Democracy, Community, and Justice. Or, What Is Wrong with Communitarianism?" *Political Theory* 23 (1995): 211–46, pp. 214–15.

Some authors have addressed the problem of harmful coercion (Abizadeh, "Democratic Theory and Border Coercion"; Kukathas, "The Case for Open Immigration," pp. 210–11).

51 Carens ("Migration and Morality") addresses liberal egalitarianism; Cole (*Philosophies of Exclusion*) and Isbister ("A Liberal Argument for Border Controls") address liberalism in general; Carens ("Aliens and Citizens") discusses libertarianism, utilitarianism, and Rawls's Difference Principle; Wellman ("Immigration and Freedom of Association," pp. 130–37) discusses libertarianism.

52 Caplan (*The Myth of the Rational Voter*, pp. 36–39, 58–59, 66, 69–71) discusses several manifestations of the bias against foreigners.

Chapter 45

David Miller

IMMIGRATION
The Case for Limits

David Miller (1946–) is a British professor of social and political theory at Nuffield College, best known for his work on nationalism and social justice. In this essay (published in 2005), Miller argues that existing defenses of a moral right of unlimited immigration fail, and claims that considerations regarding the preservation of culture and regarding the limitation of population growth support the right of states to limit immigration.

It is not easy to write about immigration from a philosophical perspective – not easy at least if you are writing in a society (and this now includes most societies in the Western world) in which immigration has become a highly charged political issue. Those who speak freely and openly about the issue tend to come from the far Right: they are fascists or racists who believe that it is wrong in principle for their political community to admit immigrants who do not conform to the approved cultural or racial stereotype. Most liberal, conservative, and social democratic politicians support quite strict immigration controls in practice, but they generally refrain from spelling out the justification for such controls, preferring instead to highlight the practical difficulties involved in resettling immigrants, and raising the spectre of a right-wing backlash if too many immigrants are admitted. Why are they so reticent? One reason is that it is not easy to set out the arguments for limiting immigration without at the same time projecting a negative image of those immigrants who have already been admitted, thereby playing directly into the hands of the far Right ideologues who would like to see such immigrants deprived of their full rights of citizenship and/or repatriated to their countries of origin. Is it possible *both* to argue that every member of the political community, native or immigrant, must be treated as a full citizen, enjoying equal status and the equal respect of his or her fellows, *and* to argue that there are good grounds for setting upper bounds both to the rate and the overall numbers of immigrants who are admitted? Yes, it is, but it requires dexterity, and always carries with it the risk of being misunderstood.

In this chapter, I shall explain why nation-states may be justified in imposing restrictive immigration policies if they so choose. The argument is laid out in three stages. First, I canvass three arguments that purport to justify an unlimited right of migration between states and show why each of them fails. Second, I give two reasons, one having to do with culture, the other with population, that can justify states in limiting immigration. Third, I consider whether states nonetheless have a duty to admit a special class of potential immigrants – namely refugees – and also how far they are allowed to pick and choose among the immigrants they do admit. The third section, in other words, lays down some conditions that an ethical immigration policy must meet. But I begin by showing why there is no general right to choose one's country of residence or citizenship.

Can There Be an Unlimited Right of Migration Between States?

Liberal political philosophers who write about migration usually begin from the premise that people should be allowed to choose where in the world to locate themselves unless it can be shown that allowing an unlimited right of migration would have harmful consequences that outweigh the value of freedom of choice (see, for instance, Carens, 1987; Hampton, 1995). In other words, the central value appealed to is simply freedom itself. Just as I should be free to decide who to marry, what job to take, what religion (if any) to profess, so I should be free to decide whether to live in Nigeria, or France, or the United States. Now these philosophers usually concede that in practice some limits may have to be placed on this freedom – for instance, if high rates of migration would result in social chaos or the breakdown of liberal states that could not accommodate so many migrants without losing their liberal character. In these instances, the exercise of free choice would become self-defeating. But the presumption is that people should be free to choose where to live unless there are strong reasons for restricting their choice.

I want to challenge this presumption. Of course there is always *some* value in people having more options to choose between, in this case options as to where to live, but we usually draw a line between *basic* freedoms that people should have as a matter of right and what we might call *bare* freedoms that do not warrant that kind of protection. It would be good from my point of

view if I were free to purchase an Aston Martin tomorrow, but that is not going to count as a morally significant freedom – my desire is not one that imposes any kind of obligation on others to meet it. In order to argue against immigration restrictions, therefore, liberal philosophers must do more than show that there is some value to people in being able to migrate, or that they often *want* to migrate (as indeed they do, in increasing numbers). It needs to be demonstrated that this freedom has the kind of weight or significance that could turn it into a right, and that should therefore prohibit states from pursuing immigration policies that limit freedom of movement.

I shall examine three arguments that have been offered to defend a right to migrate. The first starts with the general right to freedom of movement, and claims that this must include the freedom to move into, and take up residence in, states other than one's own. The second begins with a person's right to *exit* from her current state – a right that is widely recognized in international law – and claims that a right of exit is pointless unless it is matched by a right of entry into other states. The third appeals to international distributive justice. Given the huge inequalities in living standards that currently exist between rich and poor states, it is said, people who live in poor states have a claim of justice that can only be met by allowing them to migrate and take advantage of the opportunities that rich states provide.

The idea of a right to freedom of movement is not in itself objectionable. We are talking here about what are usually called basic rights or human rights, and I shall assume (since there is no space to defend the point) that such rights are justified by pointing to the vital interests that they protect (Griffin, 2001; Nickel, 1987; Shue, 1980). They correspond to conditions in whose absence human beings cannot live decent lives, no matter what particular values and plans of life they choose to pursue. Being able to move freely in physical space is just such a condition, as we can see by thinking about people whose legs are shackled or who are confined in small spaces. A wider freedom of movement can also be justified by thinking about the interests that it serves instrumentally: if I cannot move about over a fairly wide area, it may be impossible for me to find a job, to practice my religion, or to find a suitable marriage partner. Since these all qualify as vital interests, it is fairly clear that freedom of movement qualifies as a basic human right.

What is less clear, however, is the physical extent of that right, in the sense of how much of the earth's surface I must be able to move to in order to say that I enjoy it. Even in liberal societies that make no attempt to confine people within particular geographical areas, freedom of movement is severely restricted in a number of ways. I cannot, in general, move to places that other people's bodies now occupy (I cannot just push them aside). I cannot move on to private property without the consent of its owner, except perhaps in emergencies or where a special right of access exists — and since most land is privately owned, this means that a large proportion of physical space does not fall within the ambit of a right to free movement. Even access to public space is heavily regulated: there are traffic laws that tell me where and at what speed I may drive my car, parks have opening and closing hours, the police can control my movements up and down the streets, and so forth. These are very familiar observations, but they are worth making simply to highlight how hedged about with qualifications the existing right of free movement in liberal societies actually is. Yet few would argue that because of these limitations, people in these societies are deprived of one of their human rights. Some liberals might argue in favor of expanding the right — for instance, in Britain there has been a protracted campaign to establish a legal right to roam on uncultivated privately owned land such as moors and fells, a right that will finally become effective by 2005. But even the advocates of such a right would be hard-pressed to show that some vital interest was being injured by the more restrictive property laws that have existed up to now.

The point here is that liberal societies in general offer their members *sufficient* freedom of movement to protect the interests that the human right to free movement is intended to protect, even though the extent of free movement is very far from absolute. So how could one attempt to show that the right in question must include the right to move to some other country and settle there? What vital interest requires the right to be interpreted in such an extensive way? Contingently, of course, it may be true that moving to another country is the only way for an individual to escape persecution, to find work, to obtain necessary medical care, and so forth. In these circumstances the person concerned may have the right to move, not to any state that she chooses, but to *some* state where these interests can be protected. But here the right to move serves only as a remedial right: its existence depends on the fact that the person's vital interests cannot be secured in the country where she currently resides. In a world of decent states — states that were able to secure their citizens' basic rights to security, food, work, medical care, and so forth — the right to move across borders could not be justified in this way.

Our present world is not, of course, a world of decent states, and this gives rise to the issue of refugees, which I shall discuss in the final section of this chapter. But if we leave aside for the moment cases where the right to move freely across borders depends upon the right to avoid persecution, starvation, or other threats to basic interests, how might we try to give it a more general rationale? One reason a person may want to migrate is in order to participate in a culture that does not exist in his native land — for instance he wants to work at an occupation for which there is no demand at home, or to join a religious community which, again, is not represented in the country from which he comes. These might be central components in his plan of life, so he will find it very frustrating if he is not able to move. But does this ground a right to free movement across borders? It seems to me that it does not. What a person can legitimately demand access to is an *adequate* range of options to choose between – a reasonable choice of occupation, religion, cultural activities, marriage partners, and so forth. Adequacy here is defined in terms of generic human interests rather than in terms of the interests of any one person in particular – so, for example, a would-be opera singer living in a society which provides for various forms of musical expression, but not for opera, can have an adequate range of options in this area even though the option she most prefers is not available. So long as they adhere to the standards of decency sketched above, all contemporary states are able to provide such an adequate range internally. So although people certainly have an *interest* in being able to migrate internationally, they do not have a basic interest of the kind that would be required to ground a human right. It is more like my interest in having an Aston Martin than my interest in having access to *some* means of physical mobility.

I turn next to the argument that because people have a right to leave the society they currently belong to, they must also have a right to enter other societies, since the first right is practically meaningless unless the second exists – there is no unoccupied space in the world to exit *to*, so unless the right to leave society A is accompanied by the right to enter societies B, C, D, etc., it has no real force (Cole, 2000; Dummett, 1992).

The right of exit is certainly an important human right, but once again it is worth examining why it has the significance that it does. Its importance is partly instrumental: knowing that their subjects have the right to leave inhibits states from mistreating them in various ways, so it helps to preserve the conditions of what I earlier called "decency." However, even in the case of decent states the right of exit remains important, and that is because by being deprived

of exit rights individuals are forced to remain in association with others whom they may find deeply uncongenial – think of the militant atheist in a society where almost everyone devoutly practices the same religion, or the religious puritan in a society where most people behave like libertines. On the other hand, the right of exit from state A does not appear to entail an unrestricted right to enter any society of the immigrant's choice – indeed, it seems that it can be exercised provided that at least one other society, society B say, is willing to take him in. It might seem that we can generate a general right to migrate by iteration: the person who leaves A for B then has the right to exit from B, which entails that C, at least, must grant him the right to enter, and so forth. But this move fails, because our person's right of exit from A depended on the claim that he might find continued association with the other citizens of A intolerable, and he cannot plausibly continue making the same claim in the case of each society that is willing to take him in. Given the political and cultural diversity of societies in the real world, it is simply unconvincing to argue that only an unlimited choice of which one to join will prevent people being forced into associations that are repugnant to them.

It is also important to stress that there are many rights whose exercise is contingent on finding partners who are willing to cooperate in the exercise, and it may be that the right of exit falls into this category. Take the right to marry as an example. This is a right held against the state to allow people to marry the partners of their choice (and perhaps to provide the legal framework within which marriages can be contracted). It is obviously not a right to have a marriage partner provided – whether any given person can exercise the right depends entirely on whether he is able to find someone willing to marry him, and many people are not so lucky. The right of exit is a right held against a person's current state of residence not to prevent her from leaving the state (and perhaps aiding her in that endeavor by, say, providing a passport). But it does not entail an obligation on any other state to let that person in. Obviously, if no state were ever to grant entry rights to people who were not already its citizens, the right of exit would have no value. But suppose states are generally willing to consider entry applications from people who want to migrate, and that most people would get offers from at least one such state: then the position as far as the right of exit goes is pretty much the same as with the right to marry, where by no means everyone is able to wed the partner they would ideally like to have, but most have the opportunity to marry *someone*.

So once the right of exit is properly understood, it does not entail an unlimited right to migrate to the society of one's choice. But now, finally, in this part of the chapter, I want to consider an argument for migration rights that appeals to distributive justice. It begins from the assumption of the fundamental moral equality of human beings. It then points out that, in the world in which we live, a person's life prospects depend heavily on the society into which she happens to be born, so that the only way to achieve equal opportunities is to allow people to move to the places where they can develop and exercise their talents, through employment and in other ways. In other words, there is something fundamentally unfair about a world in which people are condemned to relative poverty through no fault of their own when others have much greater opportunities, whereas if people were free to live and work wherever they wished, then each person could choose whether to stay in the community that had raised him or to look for a better life elsewhere.

The question we must ask here is whether justice demands equality of opportunity at the global level, as the argument I have just sketched assumes, or whether this principle only applies *inside* societies, among those who are already citizens of the same political community (see, for instance, Caney, 2001). Note to begin with that embracing the moral equality of all human

beings – accepting that every human being is equally an object of moral concern – does not yet tell us what we are required to do for them as a result of that equality. One answer *might* be that we should attempt to provide everyone with equal opportunities to pursue their goals in life. But another, equally plausible, answer is that we should play our part in ensuring that their basic rights are respected, where these are understood as rights to a certain minimum level of security, freedom, resources, and so forth – a level adequate to protect their basic interests, as suggested earlier in this chapter. These basic rights can be universally protected and yet some people have greater opportunities than others to pursue certain aims, as a result of living in more affluent or culturally richer societies.

Is it nonetheless unfair if opportunities are unequal in this way? That depends upon what we believe about the *scope* of distributive justice, the kind of justice that involves comparing how well different people are faring by some standard. According to Michael Walzer, "the idea of distributive justice presupposes a bounded world within which distributions take place: a group of people committed to dividing, exchanging, and sharing social goods, first of all among themselves" (1983: 31). The main reason that Walzer gives for this view is that the very goods whose distribution is a matter of justice gain their meaning and value within particular political communities. Another relevant consideration is that the stock of goods that is available at any time to be divided up will depend on the past history of the community in question, including decisions about, for example, the economic system under which production will take place. These considerations tell against the view that justice at global level should be understood in terms of the equal distribution, at any moment, of a single good, whether this good is understood as "resources" or "opportunity" or "welfare" (Miller, 1999). The basic rights view avoids these difficulties, because it is plausible to think that whatever the cultural values of a particular society, and whatever its historical record, no human being should be allowed to fall below the minimum level of provision that protects his or her basic interests.

But what if somebody does fall below this threshold? Does this not give him the right to migrate to a place where the minimum level is guaranteed? Perhaps, but it depends on whether the minimum *could* be provided in the political community he belongs to now, or whether that community is so oppressive, or so dysfunctional, that escape is the only option. So here we encounter again the issue of refugees, to be discussed in my final section. Meanwhile, the lesson for other states, confronted with people whose lives are less than decent, is that they have a choice: they must either ensure that the basic rights of such people are protected in the places where they live – by aid, by intervention, or by some other means – or they must help them to move to other communities where their lives will be better. Simply shutting one's borders and doing nothing else is not a morally defensible option here. People everywhere have a right to a decent life. But before jumping to the conclusion that the way to respond to global injustice is to encourage people whose lives are less than decent to migrate elsewhere, we should consider the fact that this policy will do little to help the very poor, who are unlikely to have the resources to move to a richer country. Indeed, a policy of open migration may make such people worse off still, if it allows doctors, engineers, and other professionals to move from economically undeveloped to economically developed societies in search of higher incomes, thereby depriving their countries of origin of vital skills. Equalizing opportunity for the few may diminish opportunities for the many. Persisting global injustice does impose on rich states the obligation to make a serious contribution to the relief of global poverty, but in most instances they should contribute to improving conditions of life on the ground, as it were, rather than bypassing the problem by allowing (inevitably selective) inward migration.

Justifications for Limiting Immigration

I have shown that there is no general right to migrate to the country of one's choice. Does it follow that states have a free hand in choosing who, if anyone, to admit to membership? One might think that it does, using the analogy of a private club. Suppose that the members of a tennis club decide that once the membership roster has reached 100, no new members will be taken in. They do not have to justify this decision to would-be members who are excluded: if they decide that 100 members is enough, that's entirely their prerogative. But notice what makes this argument convincing. First, the benefit that is being denied to new applicants is the (relatively superficial) benefit of being able to play tennis. Second, it's a reasonable assumption that the rejected applicants can join another club, or start one of their own. It would be different if the tennis club occupied the only site within a 50-mile radius that is suitable for laying tennis courts: we might then think that they had some obligation to admit new members up to a reasonable total. In the case of states, the advantages that they deny to would-be immigrants who are refused entry are very substantial; and because states monopolize stretches of territory, and in other ways provide benefits that cannot be replicated elsewhere, the "go and start your own club" response to immigrants is not very plausible.

So in order to show that states are entitled to close their borders to immigrants, we have to do more than show that the latter lack the human right to migrate. Potential immigrants have a *claim* to be let in – if nothing else they usually have a strong *desire* to enter – and so any state that wants to control immigration must have good reasons for doing so. In this section, I shall outline two good reasons that states may have for restricting immigration. One has to do with preserving culture, the other with controlling population. I don't claim that these reasons will apply to every state, but they do apply to many liberal democracies that are currently having to decide how to respond to potentially very large flows of immigrants from less economically developed societies (other states may face larger flows still, but the political issues will be different).

The first reason assumes that the states in question require a common public culture that in part constitutes the political identity of their members, and that serves valuable functions in supporting democracy and other social goals. There is no space here to justify this assumption in any detail, so I must refer the reader to other writings where I have tried to do so (Miller, 1995 and 2000). What I want to do here is to consider how the need to protect the public culture bears upon the issue of immigration. In general terms we can say (a) that immigrants will enter with cultural values, including *political* values, that are more or less different from the public culture of the community they enter; (b) that as a result of living in that community, they will absorb some part of the existing public culture, modifying their own values in the process; and (c) that their presence will also change the public culture in various ways – for instance, a society in which an established religion had formed an important part of national identity will typically exhibit greater religious diversity after accepting immigrants, and as a consequence religion will play a less significant part in defining that identity.

Immigration, in other words, is likely to change a society's public culture rather than destroy it. And since public cultures always change over time, as a result of social factors that are quite independent of immigration (participation in the established religion might have been declining in any case), it doesn't on the face of it seem that states have any good reason to restrict immigration on that basis. They might

have reason to limit the *flow* of immigrants, on the grounds that the process of acculturation outlined above may break down if too many come in too quickly. But so long as a viable public culture is maintained, it should not matter that its character changes as a result of taking in people with different cultural values (Perry, 1995).

What this overlooks, however, is that the public culture of their country is something that people have an interest in controlling: they want to be able to shape the way that their nation develops, including the values that are contained in the public culture. They may not of course succeed: valued cultural features can be eroded by economic and other forces that evade political control. But they may certainly have good reason to try, and in particular to try to maintain cultural continuity over time, so that they can see themselves as the bearers of an identifiable cultural tradition that stretches backward historically. Cultural continuity, it should be stressed, is not the same as cultural rigidity: the most valuable cultures are those that can develop and adapt to new circumstances, including the presence of new subcultures associated with immigrants.

Consider the example of language. In many states today the national language is under pressure from the spread of international languages, especially English. People have an incentive to learn and use one of the international languages for economic and other purposes, and so there is a danger that the national language will wither away over the course of two or three generations. If this were to happen, one of the community's most important distinguishing characteristics would have disappeared, its literature would become inaccessible except in translation, and so forth. So the states in question adopt policies to insure, for instance, that the national language is used in schools and in the media, and that exposure to foreign languages through imports is restricted. What effect would a significant influx of immigrants who did not already speak the national language have in these circumstances? It is likely that their choice of second language would be English, or one of the other international languages. So their presence would increase the incentive among natives to defect from use of the national language in everyday transactions, and make the project of language-preservation harder to carry through. The state has good reason to limit immigration, or at least to differentiate sharply among prospective immigrants between those who speak the national language and those who don't, as the government of Quebec has done in recent years.

Language isn't the only feature to which the argument for cultural continuity applies. There is an internal relationship between a nation's culture and its physical shape – its public and religious buildings, the way its towns and villages are laid out, the pattern of the landscape, and so forth. People feel at home in a place in part because they can see that their surroundings bear the imprint of past generations whose values were recognizably their own. This doesn't rule out cultural change, but again it gives a reason for wanting to stay in control of the process – for teaching children to value their cultural heritage and to regard themselves as having a responsibility to preserve the parts of it that are worth preserving, for example. The "any public culture will do" position ignores this internal connection between the cultural and physical features of the community.

How restrictive an immigration policy this dictates depends on the empirical question of how easy or difficult it is to create a symbiosis between the existing public culture and the new cultural values of the immigrants, and this will vary hugely from case to case (in particular the experience of immigration itself is quite central to the public cultures of some states, but not to others). Most liberal democracies are now multicultural, and this is widely regarded as a source of cultural richness. But the more culturally diverse a society becomes, the greater need it has for a unifying public culture to bind its members

together, and this culture has to connect to the history and physical shape of the society in question – it can't be invented from scratch (Kymlicka, 2001: esp. part IV; Miller, 1995: ch. 4). So a political judgment needs to be made about the scale and type of immigration that will enrich rather than dislocate the existing public culture.

The second reason for states to limit immigration that I want to consider concerns population size.[1] This is a huge, and hugely controversial, topic, and all I can do here is to sketch an argument that links together the issues of immigration and population control. The latter issue really arises at two different levels: global and national. At the global level, there is a concern that the carrying capacity of the earth may be stretched to breaking point if the total number of human beings continues to rise as it has over the last half century or so. At national level, there is a concern about the effect of population growth on quality of life and the natural environment. Let me look at each level in turn.

Although there is disagreement about just how many people the earth can sustain before resource depletion – the availability of water, for example – becomes acute, it would be hard to maintain that there is no upper limit. Although projections of population growth over the century ahead indicate a leveling off in the rate of increase, we must also expect – indeed should welcome – increases in the standard of living in the developing world that will mean that resource consumption per capita will also rise significantly. In such a world it is in all our interests that states whose populations are growing rapidly should adopt birth control measures and other policies to restrict the rate of growth, as both China and India have done in past decades. But such states have little or no incentive to adopt such policies if they can "export" their surplus population through international migration, and since the policies in question are usually unpopular, they have a positive incentive not to pursue them. A viable population policy at global level requires each state to be responsible for stabilizing, or even possibly reducing, its population over time, and this is going to be impossible to achieve if there are no restrictions on the movement of people between states.

At national level, the effects of population growth may be less catastrophic, but can still be detrimental to important cultural values. What we think about this issue may be conditioned to some extent by the population density of the state in which we live. Those of us who live in relatively small and crowded states experience daily the way in which the sheer number of our fellow citizens, with their needs for housing, mobility, recreation, and so forth, impacts on the physical environment, so that it becomes harder to enjoy access to open space, to move from place to place without encountering congestion, to preserve important wildlife habitats, and so on. It's true, of course, that the problems arise not simply from population size, but also from a population that wants to live in a certain way – to move around a lot, to have high levels of consumption, and so on – so we could deal with them by collectively changing the way that we live, rather than by restricting or reducing population size (De-Shalit, 2000). Perhaps we should. But this, it seems to me, is a matter for political decision: members of a territorial community have the right to decide whether to restrict their numbers, or to live in a more ecologically and humanly sound way, or to do neither and bear the costs of a high-consumption, high-mobility lifestyle in a crowded territory. If restricting numbers is part of the solution, then controlling immigration is a natural corollary.

What I have tried to do in this section is to suggest why states may have good reason to limit immigration. I concede that would-be immigrants may have a strong interest in being admitted – a strong economic interest, for example – but in general they have no obligation-conferring *right* to be admitted, for reasons given in the previous section. On the other side, nation-states have a strong and legitimate interest in determining who comes in and who does

not. Without the right to exclude, they could not be what Michael Walzer has called "communities of character": "historically stable, ongoing associations of men and women with some special commitment to one another and some special sense of their common life" (1983: 62). It remains now to see what conditions an admissions policy must meet if it is to be ethically justified.

Conditions for an Ethical Immigration Policy

I shall consider two issues. The first is the issue of refugees, usually defined as people who have fled their home country as a result of a well-founded fear of persecution or violence. What obligations do states have to admit persons in that category? The second is the issue of discrimination in admissions policy. If a state decides to admit some immigrants (who are not refugees) but refuses entry to others, what criteria can it legitimately use in making its selection?

As I indicated in the first section of this chapter, people whose basic rights are being threatened or violated in their current place of residence clearly do have the right to move to somewhere that offers them greater security. Prima facie, then, states have an obligation to admit refugees, indeed "refugees" defined more broadly than is often the case to include people who are being deprived of rights to subsistence, basic healthcare, etc. (Gibney, 1999; Shacknove, 1985). But this need not involve treating them as long-term immigrants. They may be offered temporary sanctuary in states that are able to protect them, and then be asked to return to their original country of citizenship when the threat has passed (Hathaway and Neve, 1997). Moreover, rather than encouraging long-distance migration, it may be preferable to establish safety zones for refugees close to their homes and then deal with the cause of the rights-violations directly – whether this means sending in food and medical aid or intervening to remove a genocidal regime from power. There is obviously a danger that the temporary solution becomes semi-permanent, and this is unacceptable because refugees are owed more than the immediate protection of their basic rights – they are owed something like the chance to make a proper life for themselves. But liberals who rightly give a high moral priority to protecting the human rights of vulnerable people are regrettably often unwilling to countenance intervention in states that are plainly violating these rights.

If protection on the ground is not possible, the question then arises *which* state should take in the refugees. It is natural to see the obligation as shared among all those states that are able to provide refuge, and in an ideal world one might envisage some formal mechanism for distributing refugees among them. However, the difficulties in devising such a scheme are formidable (see Hathaway and Neve, 1997; Schuck, 1997). To obtain agreement from different states about what each state's refugee quota should be, one would presumably need to start with simple and relatively uncontroversial criteria such as population or per capita GNP. But this leaves out of the picture many other factors, such as population density, the overall rate of immigration into each state, cultural factors that make absorption of particular groups of refugees particularly easy or difficult, and so forth – all factors that would differentially affect the willingness of political communities to accept refugees and make agreement on a scheme very unlikely. Furthermore, the proposed quota system pays no attention to the choices of the refugees themselves as to where to apply for sanctuary, unless it is accompanied by a compensatory scheme that allows states that take in more refugees than their quota prescribes to receive financial transfers from states that take in less.

Realistically, therefore, states have to be given considerable autonomy to decide on how to respond to particular asylum applications: besides the refugee's own choice, they are entitled to consider the overall number of applications they face, the demands that temporary or longer-term accommodation of refugees will place on existing citizens, and whether there exists any special link between the refugee and the host community – for instance, similarities of language or culture, or a sense of historical responsibility on the part of the receiving state (which might see itself as somehow implicated among the causes of the crisis that has produced the refugees). If states are given this autonomy, there can be no guarantee that every bona fide refugee will find a state willing to take him or her in. Here we simply face a clash between two moral intuitions: on the one hand, every refugee is a person with basic human rights that deserve protection; on the other, the responsibility for insuring this is diffused among states in such a way that we cannot say that any particular state S has an obligation to admit refugee R. Each state is at some point entitled to say that it has done enough to cope with the refugee crisis. So the best we can hope for is that informal mechanisms will continue to evolve which make all refugees the *special* responsibility of one state or another (Miller, 2001).

The second issue is discrimination among migrants who are not refugees. Currently, states do discriminate on a variety of different grounds, effectively selecting the migrants they want to take in. Can this be justified? Well, given that states are entitled to put a ceiling on the numbers of people they take in, for reasons canvassed in the previous section, they need to select somehow, if only by lottery (as the United States began to do in 1995 for certain categories of immigrant). So what grounds can they legitimately use? It seems to me that receiving states are entitled to consider the benefit they would receive from admitting a would-be migrant as well as the strength of the migrant's own claim to move. So it is acceptable to give precedence to people whose cultural values are closer to those of the existing population – for instance, to those who already speak the native language.

This is a direct corollary of the argument in the previous section about cultural self-determination. Next in order of priority come those who possess skills and talents that are needed by the receiving community.[2] Their claim is weakened, as suggested earlier, by the likelihood that in taking them in, the receiving state is also depriving their country of origin of a valuable resource (medical expertise, for example). In such cases, the greater the interest the potential host country has in admitting the would-be migrant, the more likely it is that admitting her will make life worse for those she leaves behind. So although it is reasonable for the receiving state to make decisions based on how much the immigrant can be expected to contribute economically if admitted, this criterion should be used with caution. What cannot be defended in any circumstances is discrimination on grounds of race, sex, or, in most instances, religion – religion could be a relevant criterion only where it continues to form an essential part of the public culture, as in the case of the state of Israel.

If nation-states are allowed to decide how many immigrants to admit in the first place, why can't they pick and choose among potential immigrants on whatever grounds they like – admitting only red-haired women if that is what their current membership prefers? I have tried to hold a balance between the interest that migrants have in entering the country they want to live in, and the interest that political communities having in determining their own character. Although the first of these interests is not strong enough to justify a right of migration, it is still substantial, and so the immigrants who are refused entry are owed an explanation. To be told that they belong to the wrong race, or sex (or have hair of the wrong color) is insulting, given that these features do not connect to anything of real significance to the society they want to join. Even tennis clubs are not entitled to discriminate among applicants on grounds such as these.

Let me conclude by underlining the importance of admitting all long-term immigrants to full and equal citizenship in the receiving society (this does not apply to refugees who are admitted temporarily until it is safe to return to their country of origin, but it does apply to refugees as soon as it becomes clear that return is not a realistic option for them). Controls on immigration must be coupled with active policies to insure that immigrants are brought into the political life of the community, and acquire the linguistic and other skills that they require to function as active citizens (Kymlicka, 2001: ch. 8). In several states immigrants are now encouraged to take citizenship classes leading up to a formal admissions ceremony, and this is a welcome development insofar as it recognizes that becoming a citizen isn't something that just happens spontaneously. Precisely because they aim to be "communities of character," with distinct public cultures to which new immigrants can contribute, democratic states must bring immigrants into political dialogue with natives. What is unacceptable is the emergence of a permanent class of non-citizens, whether these are guest workers, illegal immigrants, or asylum seekers waiting to have their applications adjudicated. The underlying political philosophy which informs this chapter sees democratic states as political communities formed on the basis of equality among their members, and just as this gives such states the right to exclude, it also imposes the obligation to protect the equal status of all those who live within their borders.

Notes

1   For some reason this issue is rarely considered in philosophical discussions of immigration. An exception, albeit a brief one, is Barry (1992).

2   Another criterion that is often used in practice is having family ties to people who already have citizenship in the state in question, and this seems perfectly justifiable, but I am considering claims that have to do with features of the immigrants themselves.

References

Barry, Brian (1992). "The quest for consistency: a sceptical view." In B. Barry and R. E. Goodin (eds.), *Free Movement: Ethical Issues in the Transnational Migration of People and Money* (pp. 279–87). Hemel Hempstead: Harvester Wheatsheaf.

Caney, Simon (2001). "Cosmopolitan justice and equalizing opportunities." *Metaphilosophy*, 32: 113–34.

Carens, Joseph (1987). "Aliens and citizens: the case for open borders." *Review of Politics*, 49: 251–73.

Cole, Phillip (2000). *Philosophies of Exclusion: Liberal Political Theory and Immigration.* Edinburgh: Edinburgh University Press.

De-Shalit, Avner (2000). "Sustainability and population policies: myths, truths and half-baked ideas." In K. Lee, A. Holland, and D. McNeill (eds.), *Global Sustainable Development in the 21st Century* (pp. 188–200). Edinburgh: Edinburgh University Press.

Dummett, Ann (1992). "The transnational migration of people seen from within a natural law tradition." In B. Barry and R. E. Goodin (eds.), *Free Movement: Ethical Issues in the Transnational Migration of People and Money* (pp. 169–80). Hemel Hempstead: Harvester Wheatsheaf.

Gibney, Matthew J. (1999). "Liberal democratic states and responsibilities to refugees." *American Political Science Review*, 93: 169–81.

Griffin, James (2001). "First steps in an account of human rights." *European Journal of Philosophy*, 9: 306–27.

Hampton, Jean (1995). "Immigration, identity, and justice." In W. F. Schwartz (ed.), *Justice in Immigration* (pp. 67–93). Cambridge: Cambridge University Press.

Hathaway, J. C. and Neve, R. A. (1997). "Making international refugee law relevant again: a proposal for collectivized and solution-oriented protection." *Harvard Human Rights Journal*, 10: 115–211.

Kymlicka, Will (2001). *Politics in the Vernacular: Nationalism, Multiculturalism and Citizenship.* Oxford: Oxford University Press.

Miller, David (1995). *On Nationality.* Oxford: Clarendon Press.

Miller, David (1999). "Justice and global inequality." In A. Hurrell and N. Woods (eds.), *Inequality, Globalization, and World Politics* (pp. 187–210). Oxford: Oxford University Press.

Miller, David (2000). *Citizenship and National Identity.* Cambridge: Polity.

Miller, David (2001). "Distributing responsibilities." *Journal of Political Philosophy*, 9: 453–71.

Nickel, James (1987). *Making Sense of Human Rights.* Berkeley: University of California Press.

Perry, S. R. (1995). "Immigration, justice, and culture." In W. F. Schwartz (ed.), *Justice in Immigration* (pp. 94–135). Cambridge: Cambridge University Press.

Shacknove, Andrew (1985). "Who is a refugee?" *Ethics*, 95: 274–84.

Schuck, Peter A. (1997). "Refugee burden-sharing: a modest proposal." *Yale Journal of International Law*, 22: 243–97.

Shue, Henry (1980). *Basic Rights: Subsistence, Affluence, and US Foreign Policy.* Princeton, NJ: Princeton University Press.

Walzer, Michael (1983). *Spheres of Justice: A Defence of Pluralism and Equality.* Oxford: Martin Robertson.

3c. GLOBAL DISTRIBUTIVE JUSTICE

WITHIN A COUNTRY LIKE THE UNITED STATES, issues of distributive justice seem pressing enough. Vast inequalities in wealth and income (see section 2e) lead many to argue that some form of coercive redistribution is necessary to achieve justice. But when our focus is expanded from a national level to a global level, the problem seems even more pressing. For, as both Thomas Pogge and Peter Singer point out in their contributions to this section, not only are inequalities in the global distribution of wealth much more severe than those at the domestic level, but the problem of inequality is compounded by the problem of *absolute* poverty. It is not just that many of the world's poor have *less* than everyone else; it is that they do not have nearly *enough* to meet even the most basic of their needs.

The extremity of the situation makes for compelling intuitions. Peter Singer, for instance, suggests that those of us in wealthy countries who spend money on luxuries — decaf lattes, movie tickets, designer jeans, etc. — rather than sending that money to relief organizations like OXFAM who could use it to cheaply save the lives of desperate people, are morally on a par with someone who passively watches a child drown in a shallow pond in order to avoid muddying his expensive shoes. We are choosing to satisfy our own trivial desires rather than to save the life of another. In a very real sense, we are murderers — only we commit our murder through inaction, rather than through action.

What would it take for us to avoid being murderers, according to Singer? His answer is simple, yet challenging. We should give away what we have as long as we could prevent something very bad from happening by doing so without giving up anything of comparable significance. What this means in practice, however, is that we are essentially forbidden from spending any money ourselves beyond that necessary for bare survival so long as there are others in the world whose death or extreme suffering we could prevent with that money. And since the prospect of ending world starvation and malnutrition seems remote, this probably means that we will *always* be forbidden from spending money on "luxuries" for ourselves.

Singer is a utilitarian, so the claim that we should give our money away if doing so will create more good than harm comes naturally to him. But one needn't be a utilitarian to agree that when the choice is between allocating one's dollars toward saving a life or having an enjoyable night out at the theatre, the morally required decision is obvious. This is especially so when we cannot take full *responsibility* for our own favorable lot in life, nor can we assign responsibility to those who are less fortunate for theirs. The country into which we are born is entirely a matter of *luck*. And the country into which we are born has a tremendous influence on our life prospects. I have worked hard for my educational and professional accomplishments. But had I been born in Somalia instead of California, twice the amount of hard work would probably not have been sufficient to provide me with half the standard of living to which I am accustomed. Is it fair that some people should starve while others prosper if the difference between the two is caused by nothing more significant than a kind of cosmic lottery? And what if it's not *mere* luck? What if those in wealthy nations are in some way *causally responsible* for the poverty of those in the developing world, perhaps via military imperialism or economic exploitation?

There are many important philosophical questions about what each of us should do on a personal level to remedy this situation. Are we required, as Singer claims, to sacrifice for the greater good until we have given so much that we are no better off than those we are trying to help? Or are we allowed to spend a sizeable chunk of our money in the pursuit of our own personal hobbies and projects, no matter how insignificant these may be in terms of their contribution to global utility? Does it matter if other people are doing their share to alleviate the problem too?

Some of these questions are explored in the reading from Peter Singer, but since this is a text in *political* philosophy, our main concern will be with how political institutions—not individuals—should respond to the problem of global poverty. On this question there is wide and persistent disagreement among theorists. Some, like Thomas Pogge, call for a radical change in the global political and economic order, moving in the direction of greater egalitarianism. Others, like Loren Lomasky, are classical liberals who reject egalitarianism in favor of a commitment to negative liberty and the protection of property rights.

Yet even between these two very different theorists, there is surprising overlap. The most striking instance of which is their insistence that our priority in reforming global institutions should be the *avoidance of harm*, not the provision of aid. Both Pogge and Lomasky, for instance, point to the protectionist policies of wealthy nations as instances of unjust policies that dramatically set back the economic interests of those in the developing world (and, Lomasky notes, in the developed world too). As a general rule, workers in Guatemala cannot compete with workers in the United States in the production of semiconductors, automobiles, or cellphones. But it is possible for them to acquire a *comparative* advantage (if not an absolute advantage—see the introduction to section 2a for a discussion) in the production of certain agricultural goods. Protectionist laws prevent workers from taking advantage of that comparative advantage through specialization and trade, and so block one of their most natural and reliable roads out of poverty.

Between thinkers such as Pogge and Lomasky, however, there is ample room for debate regarding both the substantive content of principles of global justice—what they ultimately require of us—and the best institutional mechanisms to instantiate those principles. The kind of philosophical debate represented in this section will go some distance toward exploring the first question, but the first question can probably not be resolved entirely without addressing the second question, and the second question is more the province of disciplines such as economics and political science. Philosophy has much to say about the issue of global justice, but it can reasonably hope to contribute no more than a part of the overall story.

Further Reading

Beitz, C. R. (1975). Justice and International Relations. *Philosophy and Public Affairs, 4,* 360–89.

Cullity, G. (2006). *The Moral Demands of Affluence.* Oxford: Oxford University Press.

Lomasky, L. and Teson, F. (2014). *Justice at a Distance.* Oxford: Oxford University Press.

Mollendorf, D. (2002). *Cosmopolitan Justice.* New York: Westview Press.

Murphy, L. (2003). *Moral Demands in Nonideal Theory.* Oxford: Oxford University Press.

Nussbaum, M. (2000). *Women and Human Development: The Capabilities Approach.* Cambridge: Cambridge University Press.

Pogge, T. W. (2002). *World Poverty and Human Rights: Cosmopolitan Responsibilities and Reforms.* London: Polity Press.

Rawls, J. (1999). *The Law of Peoples.* Cambridge: Harvard University Press.

Risse, M. (2012). *On Global Justice.* Princeton, NJ: Princeton University Press.

Scheffler, S. (2003). *Boundaries and Allegiances: Problems of Justice and Responsibility in Liberal Thought.* Oxford: Oxford University Press.

Sen, A. (1999). *Development as Freedom.* New York: Random House.

Singer, P. (2002). *One World: The Ethics of Globalization.* New Haven: Yale University Press.

Teson, F. R. (1998). *A Philosophy of International Law.* Boulder, CO: Westview Press.

Zwolinski, M. (2007) Sweatshops, Choice, and Exploitation. *Business Ethics Quarterly 17* (4), pp. 689–727.

Chapter 46

Peter Singer

THE LIFE YOU CAN SAVE

Peter Singer (1946–) is an Australian philosopher who is currently the the Ira W. DeCamp professor of bioethics at Princeton University. His writings in defense of utilitarianism and animal liberation have been tremendously influential. In this excerpt from his 2009 book, *The Life You Can Save*, Singer argues that we have a moral obligation to do much more to help relieve extreme poverty in the developing world, and responds to various objections to this conclusion.

1. Saving a Child

On your way to work, you pass a small pond. On hot days, children sometimes play in the pond, which is only about knee-deep. The weather's cool today, though, and the hour is early, so you are surprised to see a child splashing about in the pond. As you get closer, you see that it is a very young child, just a toddler, who is flailing about, unable to stay upright or walk out of the pond. You look for the parents or babysitter, but there is no one else around. The child is unable to keep his head above the water for more than a few seconds at a time. If you don't wade in and pull him out, he seems likely to drown. Wading in is easy and safe, but you will ruin the new shoes you bought only a few days ago, and get your suit wet and muddy. By the time you hand the child over to someone responsible for him, and change your clothes, you'll be late for work. What should you do?

I teach a course called Practical Ethics. When we start talking about global poverty, I ask my students what they think you should do in this situation. Predictably, they respond that you should save the child. "What about your shoes? And being late for work?" I ask them. They brush that aside. How could anyone consider a pair of shoes, or missing an hour or two at work, a good reason for not saving a child's life?

In 2007, something resembling this hypothetical situation actually occurred near Manchester, England. Jordon Lyon, a ten-year-old boy, leaped into a pond after his stepsister Bethany slipped in. He struggled to support her but went under himself. Anglers managed to pull Bethany out, but by then Jordon could no longer be seen. They raised the alarm, and two police community support officers soon arrived; they refused to enter the pond to find Jordon. He was later pulled out, but attempts at resuscitation failed. At the inquest on Jordon's death, the officers' inaction was defended on the grounds that they had not been trained to deal with such situations. The mother responded: "If you're walking down the street and you see a child drowning you automatically go in that water. . . . You don't have to be trained to jump in after a drowning child."[1]

I think it's safe to assume that most people would agree with the mother's statement. But consider that, according to UNICEF, nearly 10 million children under five years old die each year from causes related to poverty. Here is just one case, described by a man in Ghana to a researcher from the World Bank:

> Take the death of this small boy this morning, for example. The boy died of measles. We all know he could have been cured at the hospital. But the parents had no money and so the boy died a slow and painful death, not of measles but out of poverty.[2]

Think about something like that happening 27,000 times everyday. Some children die because they don't have enough to eat. More die, like that small boy in Ghana, from measles, malaria, and diarrhea, conditions that either don't exist in developed nations, or, if they do, are almost never fatal. The children are vulnerable to these diseases because they have no safe drinking water, or no sanitation, and because when they do fall ill, their parents can't afford any medical treatment. UNICEF, Oxfam, and many other organizations are working to reduce poverty and provide clean water and basic health care, and these efforts are reducing the toll. If the relief organizations had more money, they could do more, and more lives would be saved.

Now think about your own situation. By donating a relatively small amount of money, you could save a child's life. Maybe it takes more than the amount needed to buy a pair of shoes – but we all spend money on things we don't really need, whether on drinks, meals out, clothing, movies, concerts, vacations, new cars, or house renovation. Is it possible that by choosing to spend your money on such things rather than

contributing to an aid agency, you are leaving a child to die, a child you could have saved?

Poverty Today

A few years ago, the World Bank asked researchers to listen to what the poor are saying. They were able to document the experiences of 60,000 women and men in seventy-three countries. Over and over, in different languages and on different continents, poor people said that poverty meant these things:

- You are short of food for all or part of the year, often eating only one meal per day, sometimes having to choose between stilling your child's hunger or your own, and sometimes being able to do neither.
- You can't save money. If a family member falls ill and you need money to see a doctor, or if the crop fails and you have nothing to eat, you have to borrow from a local moneylender and he will charge you so much interest as the debt continues to mount and you may never be free of it.
- You can't afford to send your children to school, or if they do start school, you have to take them out again if the harvest is poor.
- You live in an unstable house, made with mud or thatch that you need to rebuild every two or three years, or after severe weather.
- You have no nearby source of safe drinking water. You have to carry your water a long way, and even then, it can make you ill unless you boil it.

But extreme poverty is not only a condition of unsatisfied material needs. It is often accompanied by a degrading state of powerlessness. Even in countries that are democracies and are relatively well governed, respondents to the World Bank survey described a range of situations in which they had to accept humiliation without protest. If someone takes what little you have, and you complain to the police, they may not listen to you. Nor will the law necessarily protect you from rape or sexual harassment. You have a pervading sense of shame and failure because you cannot provide for your children. Your poverty traps you, and you lose hope of ever escaping from a life of hard work for which, at the end, you will have nothing to show beyond bare survival.[3]

The World Bank defines extreme poverty as not having enough income to meet the most basic human needs for adequate food, water, shelter, clothing, sanitation, health care, and education. Many people are familiar with the statistic that one billion people are living on less than one dollar per day. That was the World Bank's poverty line until 2008, when better data on international price comparisons enabled it to make a more accurate calculation of the amount people need to meet their basic needs. On the basis of this calculation, the World Bank set the poverty line at $1.25 per day. The number of people whose income puts them under this line is not one billion but 1.4 billion. That there are more people living in extreme poverty than we thought is, of course, bad news, but the news is not all bad. On the same basis, in 1981 there were 1.9 billion people living in extreme poverty. That was about four in every ten people on the planet, whereas now fewer than one in four are extremely poor.

South Asia is still the region with the largest number of people living in extreme poverty, a total of 600 million, including 455 million in India. Economic growth has, however, reduced the proportion of South Asians living in extreme poverty from 60 percent in 1981 to 42 percent in 2005. There are another 380 million extremely poor people in sub-Saharan Africa, where half the population is extremely poor – and that is the same percentage as in 1981. The most dramatic reduction in poverty has been in East Asia, although there are still more than 200 million extremely poor Chinese, and smaller numbers elsewhere in the region. The remaining

extremely poor people are distributed around the world, in Latin America and the Caribbean, the Pacific, the Middle East, North Africa, Eastern Europe, and Central Asia.[4]

In response to the "$1.25 a day" figure, the thought may cross your mind that in many developing countries, it is possible to live much more cheaply than in the industrialized nations. Perhaps you have even done it yourself, backpacking around the world, living on less than you would have believed possible. So you may imagine that this level of poverty is less extreme than it would be if you had to live on that amount of money in the United States, or any industrialized nation. If such thoughts did occur to you, you should banish them now, because the World Bank has already made the adjustment in purchasing power: Its figures refer to the number of people existing on a daily total consumption of goods and services – whether earned or home-grown – comparable to the amount of goods and services that can be bought in the United States for $1.25.

In wealthy societies, most poverty is relative. People feel poor because many of the good things they see advertised on television are beyond their budget – but they do have a television. In the United States, 97 percent of those classified by the Census Bureau as poor own a color TV. Three-quarters of them own a car. Three-quarters of them have air-conditioning. Three-quarters of them have a VCR or DVD player. All have access to health care.[5] I am not quoting these figures in order to deny that the poor in the United States face genuine difficulties. Nevertheless, for most, these difficulties are of a different order than those of the world's poorest people. The 1.4 billion people living in extreme poverty are poor by an absolute standard tied to the most basic human needs. They are likely to be hungry for at least part of each year. Even if they can get enough food to fill their stomachs, they will probably be malnourished because their diet lacks essential nutrients. In children, malnutrition stunts growth and can cause permanent brain damage. The poor may not be able to afford to send their children to school. Even minimal health care services are usually beyond their means.

This kind of poverty kills. Life expectancy in rich nations averages seventy-eight years; in the poorest nations, those officially classified as "least developed," it is below fifty.[6] In rich countries, fewer than one in a hundred children die before the age of five; in the poorest countries, one in five does. And to the UNICEF figure of nearly 10 million young children dying every year from avoidable, poverty-related causes, we must add at least another eight million older children and adults.[7]

Affluence Today

Roughly matching the 1.4 billion people living in extreme poverty, there are about a billion living at a level of affluence never previously known except in the courts of kings and nobles. As king of France, Louis XIV, the "Sun King," could afford to build the most magnificent palace Europe had ever seen, but he could not keep it cool in summer as effectively as most middle-class people in industrialized nations can keep their homes cool today. His gardeners, for all their skill, were unable to produce the variety of fresh fruits and vegetables that we can buy all year round. If he developed a toothache or fell ill the best his dentists and doctors could do for him would make us shudder.

But we're not just better off than a French king who lived centuries ago. We are also much better off than our own great-grandparents. For a start, we can expect to live about thirty years longer. A century ago, one child in ten died in infancy. Now, in most rich nations, that figure is less than one in two hundred.[8] Another telling indicator of how wealthy we are today is the modest number of hours we must work in order to meet our basic dietary needs. Today Americans spend, on average, only six percent of their income on buying food. If they work a

forty-hour week, it takes them barely two hours to earn enough to feed themselves for the week. That leaves far more to spend on consumer goods, entertainment, and vacations.

And then we have the superrich, people who spend their money on palatial homes, ridiculously large and luxurious boats, and private planes. Before the 2008 stock market crash trimmed the numbers, there were more than 1,100 billionaires in the world, with a combined net worth of $4.4 trillion.[9] To cater to such people, Lufthansa Technik unveiled its plans for a private configuration of Boeing's new 787 Dreamliner. In commercial service, this plane will seat up to 330 passengers. The private version will carry 35, at a price of $150 million. Cost aside, there's nothing like owning a really big airplane carrying a small number of people to maximize your personal contribution to global warming. Apparently, there are already several billionaires who fly around in private commercial-sized airliners, from 747s down. Larry Page and Sergey Brin, the Google cofounders, reportedly bought a Boeing 767 and spent millions fitting it out for their private use.[10] But for conspicuous waste of money and resources it is hard to beat Anousheh Ansari, an Iranian-American telecommunications entrepreneur who paid a reported $20 million for eleven days in space. Comedian Lewis Black said on Jon Stewart's *The Daily Show* that Ansari did it because it was "the only way she could achieve her life's goal of flying over every single starving person on earth and yelling 'Hey, look what I'm spending my money on!' "

While I was working on this book, a special advertising supplement fell out of my Sunday edition of *The New York Times*: a 68-page glossy magazine filled with advertising for watches by Rolex, Patek Philippe, Breitling, and other luxury brands. The ads didn't carry price tags, but a puff piece about the revival of the mechanical watch gave guidance about the lower end of the range. After admitting that inexpensive quartz watches are extremely accurate and functional, the article opined that there is "something engaging about a mechanical movement." Right, but how much will it cost you to have this engaging something on your wrist? "You might think that getting into mechanical watches is an expensive proposition, but there are plenty of choices in the $500–$5000 range." Admittedly, "these opening-price-point models are pretty simple: basic movement, basic time display, simple decoration and so on." From which we can gather that most of the watches advertised are priced upward of $5,000, or more than one hundred times what anyone needs to pay for a reliable, accurate quartz watch. That there is a market for such products — and one worth advertising at such expense to the wide readership of *The New York Times* — is another indication of the affluence of our society.[11]

If you're shaking your head at the excesses of the super rich, though, don't shake too hard. Think again about some of the ways Americans with average incomes spend their money. In most places in the United States, you can get your recommended eight glasses of water a day out of the tap for less than a penny, while a bottle of water will set you back $1.50 or more.[12] And in spite of the environmental concerns raised by the waste of energy that goes into producing and transporting it, Americans are still buying bottled water, to the tune of more than 31 billion liters in 2006.[13] Think, too, of the way many of us get our caffeine fix: You can make coffee at home for pennies rather than spending three dollars or more on a latte. Or have you ever casually said yes to a waiter's prompt to order a second soda or glass of wine that you didn't even finish? When Dr. Timothy Jones, an archaeologist, led a U.S. government-funded study of food waste, he found that 14 percent of household garbage is perfectly good food that was in its original packaging and not out of date. More than half of this food was dry-packaged or canned goods that keep for a long time. According to Jones, $100 billion of food is wasted in the United States every year.[14] Fashion designer Deborah Lindquist

claims that the average woman owns more than $600 worth of clothing that she has not worn in the last year.[15] Whatever the actual figure may be, it is fair to say that almost all of us, men and women alike, buy things we don't need, some of which we never even use.

Most of us are absolutely certain that we wouldn't hesitate to save a drowning child, and that we would do it at considerable cost to ourselves. Yet while thousands of children die each day, we spend money on things we take for granted and would hardly notice if they were not there. Is that wrong? If so, how far does our obligation to the poor go?

2. Is It Wrong Not to Help?

Bob is close to retirement. He has invested most of his savings in a very rare and valuable old car, a Bugatti, which he has not been able to insure. The Bugatti is his pride and joy. Not only does Bob get pleasure from driving and caring for his car, he also knows that its rising market value means that he will be able to sell it and live comfortably after retirement. One day when Bob is out for a drive, he parks the Bugatti near the end of a railway siding and goes for a walk up the track. As he does so, he sees that a runaway train, with no one aboard, is rolling down the railway track. Looking farther down the track, he sees the small figure of a child who appears to be absorbed in playing on the tracks. Oblivious to the runaway train, the child is in great danger. Bob can't stop the train, and the child is too far away to hear his warning shout, but Bob can throw a switch that will divert the train down the siding where his Bugatti is parked. If he does so, nobody will be killed, but the train will crash through the decaying barrier at the end of the siding and destroy his Bugatti. Thinking of his joy in owning the car and the financial security it represents, Bob decides not to throw the switch.

The Car or the Child?

Philosopher Peter Unger developed this variation on the story of the drowning child to challenge us to think further about how much we believe we should sacrifice in order to save the life of a child. Unger's story adds a factor often crucial to our thinking about real-world poverty: uncertainty about the outcome of our sacrifice. Bob cannot be certain that the child will die if he does nothing and saves his car. Perhaps at the last moment the child will hear the train and leap to safety. In the same way, most of us can summon doubts about whether the money we give to a charity is really helping the people it's intended to help.

In my experience, people almost always respond that Bob acted badly when he did not throw the switch and destroy his most cherished and valuable possession, thereby sacrificing his hope of a financially secure retirement. We can't take a serious risk with a child's life, they say, merely to save a car, no matter how rare and valuable the car may be. By implication, we should also believe that with the simple act of saving money for retirement, we are acting as badly as Bob. For in saving money for retirement, we are effectively refusing to use that money to help save lives. This is a difficult implication to confront. How can it be wrong to save for a comfortable retirement? There is, at the very least, something puzzling here.

Another example devised by Unger tests the level of sacrifice we think people should make to alleviate suffering in cases when a life is not at stake:

You are driving your vintage sedan down a country lane when you are stopped by a hiker who has seriously injured his leg. He asks you to take him to the nearest hospital. If you refuse, there is a good chance that he will lose his leg. On the other hand, if you agree to take him to hospital, he is likely to bleed onto the seats, which you have recently, and expensively, restored in soft white leather.

Again, most people respond that you should drive the hiker to the hospital. This suggests that when prompted to think in concrete terms, about real individuals, most of us consider it obligatory to lessen the serious suffering of innocent others, even at some cost (even a high cost) to ourselves.[16]

The Basic Argument

The above examples reveal our intuitive belief that we ought to help others in need, at least when we can see them and when we are the only person in a position to save them. But our moral intuitions are not always reliable, as we can see from variations in what people in different times and places find intuitively acceptable or objectionable. The case for helping those in extreme poverty will be stronger if it does not rest solely on our intuitions. Here is a logical argument from plausible premises to the same conclusion.

First premise: Suffering and death from lack of food, shelter, and medical care are bad.
Second premise: If it is in your power to prevent something bad from happening, without sacrificing anything nearly as important, it is wrong not to do so.
Third premise: By donating to aid agencies, you can prevent suffering and death from lack of food, shelter, and medical care, without sacrificing anything nearly as important.
Conclusion: Therefore, if you do not donate to aid agencies, you are doing something wrong.

The drowning-child story is an application of this argument for aid, since ruining your shoes and being late for work aren't nearly as important as the life of a child. Similarly, reupholstering a car is not nearly as big a deal as losing a leg. Even in the case of Bob and the Bugatti, it would be a big stretch to suggest that the loss of the Bugatti would come close to rivaling the significance of the death of an innocent person.

Ask yourself if you can deny the premises of the argument. How could suffering and death from lack of food, shelter, and medical care not be really, really bad? Think of that small boy in Ghana who died of measles. How you would feel if you were his mother or father, watching helplessly as your son suffers and grows weaker? You know that children often die from this condition. You also know that it would be curable, if only you could afford to take your child to a hospital. In those circumstances you would give up almost anything for some way of ensuring your child's survival.

Putting yourself in the place of others, like the parents of that boy, or the child himself, is what thinking ethically is all about. It is encapsulated in the Golden Rule, "Do unto others as you would have them do unto you." Though the Golden Rule is best known to most westerners from the words of Jesus as reported by Matthew and Luke, it is remarkably universal, being found in Buddhism, Confucianism, Hinduism, Islam, and Jainism, and in Judaism, where it is found in Leviticus, and later emphasized by the sage Hillel.[17] The Golden Rule requires us to accept that the desires of others ought to count as if they were our own. If the desires of the parents of the dying child were our own, we would have no doubt that their suffering and the death of their child are about as bad as anything can be. So if we think ethically, then those desires must count as if they were our own, and we cannot deny that the suffering and death are bad.

The second premise is also very difficult to reject, because it leaves us some wiggle room when it comes to situations in which, to prevent something bad, we would have to risk something *nearly* as important as the bad thing we are preventing. Consider, for example, a situation in which you can only prevent the deaths of other children by neglecting your own children. This standard does not require you to prevent the deaths of the other children.

"Nearly as important" is a vague term. That's deliberate, because I'm confident that you can do without plenty of things that are clearly and inarguably not as valuable as saving a child's life. I don't know what *you* might think is as important, or nearly as important, as saving a life. By leaving it up to you to decide what those things are, I can avoid the need to find out. I'll trust you to be honest with yourself about it.

Analogies and stories can be pushed too far. Rescuing a child drowning in front of you, and throwing a switch on a railroad track to save the life of a child you can see in the distance, where you are the only one who can save the child, are both different from giving aid to people who are far away. The argument I have just presented complements the drowning-child case, because instead of pulling at your heartstrings by focusing on a single child in need, it appeals to your reason and seeks your assent to an abstract bur compelling moral principle. That means that to reject it, you need to find a flaw in the reasoning.

3. Common Objections to Giving

Charity begins at home, the saying goes, and I've found that friends, colleagues, students, and lecture audiences express that resistance in various ways. I've seen it in columns, letters, and blogs too. Particularly interesting, because they reflect a line of thought prevalent in affluent America, were comments made by students taking an elective called Literature and Justice at Glenn view High (that's not its real name), a school in a wealthy Boston suburb. As part of the reading for the course, teachers gave students an article that I wrote for *The New York Times* in 1999, laying out a version of the argument you have just read, and asked them to write papers in response.[18] Scott Seider, then a graduate student at Harvard University researching how adolescents think about obligations to others, interviewed 38 students in two sections of the course and read their papers.[19]

Let's look at some of the objections raised by these varied sources. Perhaps the most fundamental objection comes from Kathryn, a Glennview student who believes we shouldn't judge people who refuse to give:

> There is no black and white universal code for everyone. It is better to accept that everyone has a different view on the issue, and all people are entitled to follow their own beliefs.

Kathryn leaves it to the individual to determine his or her moral obligation to the poor. But while circumstances do make a difference, and we should avoid being too black-and-white in our judgments, this doesn't mean we should accept that everyone is entitled to follow his or her own beliefs. That is moral relativism, a position that many find attractive only until they are faced with someone who is doing something really, really wrong. If we see a person holding a cat's paws on an electric grill that is gradually heating up, and when we vigorously object he says, "But it's fun, see how the cat squeals," we don't just say, "Oh, well, you are entitled to follow your own beliefs," and leave him alone. We can and do try to stop people who are cruel to animals, just as we stop rapists, racists, and terrorists. I'm not saying that failing to give is like committing these acts of violence, but if we reject moral relativism in some situations, then we should reject it everywhere.

After reading my essay, Douglas, another Glennview student, objected that I "should not have the right to tell people what to do." In one sense, he's correct about that. I've no right to tell you or anyone else what to do with your money, in the sense that that would imply that you *have* to do as I say. I've no authority over Douglas or over you. On the other hand, I do have the right of free speech, which I'm exercising right now by offering you some arguments you might consider before you decide what to do with your money. I hope that you will want to listen to a variety of views before making up your mind about such an important issue. If I'm wrong about that, though, you are free to shut the book now, and there's nothing I can do about it.

It's possible, of course, to think that morality is not relative, and that we should talk about it, but that the right view is that we aren't under any obligation to give anything at all. Lucy, another Glennview High student, wrote as follows:

> If someone wants to buy a new car, they should. If someone wants to redecorate their house, they should, and if they need a suit, get it. They work for their money and they have the right to spend it on themselves.

Lucy said that people have a right to spend the money they earn on themselves. Even if we agree with that, having a *right* to do something doesn't settle the question of what you *should* do. If you have a right to do something, I can't justifiably force you not to do it, but I can still tell you that you would be a fool to do it, or that it would be a horrible thing to do, or that you would be wrong to do it. You may have a right to spend your weekend surfing, but it can still be true that you ought to visit your sick mother. Similarly, we might say that the rich have a right to spend their money on lavish parties, Patek Philippe watches, private jets, luxury yachts, and space travel, or, for that matter, to flush wads of it down the toilet. Or that those of us with more modest means shouldn't be forced to forgo any of the less-expensive pleasures that offer us some relief from all the time we spend working. But we could still think that to choose to do these things rather than use the money to save human lives is wrong, shows a deplorable lack of empathy and means that you are not a good person.

Libertarians resist the idea that we have a duty to help others. Canadian philosopher Jan Narveson articulates that point of view:

> We are certainly responsible for evils we inflict on others, no matter where, and we owe those people compensation

. . . Nevertheless, I have seen no plausible argument that we owe something, as a matter of general duty, to those to whom we have done nothing wrong.[20]

There is, at first glance, something attractive about the political philosophy that says: "You leave me alone, and I'll leave you alone, and we'll get along just fine." It appeals to the frontier mentality, to an ideal of life in the wide-open spaces where each of us can carve out our own territory and live undisturbed by the neighbors. At first glance, it seems perfectly reasonable. Yet there is a callous side to a philosophy that denies that we have any responsibilities to those who, through no fault of their own, are in need. Taking libertarianism seriously would require us to abolish all state-supported welfare schemes for those who can't get a job or are ill or disabled, and all state-funded health care for the aged and for those who are too poor to pay for their own health insurance. Few people really support such extreme views. Most think that we do have obligations to those we can help with relatively little sacrifice – certainly to those living in our own country, and I would argue that we can't justifiably draw the boundary there. But if I have not persuaded you of that, there is another line of argument to consider: If we have, in fact, been at least in part a cause of the poverty of the world's poorest people – if we are harming the poor – then even libertarians like Narveson will have to agree that we ought to compensate them.

Some people imagine that the wealth of the world is a static quantity, like a pie that must be divided among a lot of people. In that model, the bigger the slice the rich get, the less there is for the poor. If that really were how the world works, then a relatively small elite would be inflicting a terrible injustice on everyone else, for just two percent of the world's people own half the world's wealth, and the richest 10 percent own 85 percent of the wealth. In contrast, half the world's people have barely 1 percent of the world's assets to split among them.[21] But the world's wealth is not fixed in size. The world is vastly richer now than it was, say, a thousand years ago. By finding better ways to create what people want, entrepreneurs make themselves rich, but they don't necessarily make others poorer. This book is about absolute poverty, not about being poor relative to how wealthy your neighbors are; in absolute terms, entrepreneurs increase the world's wealth. So the unequal distribution of the world's wealth – startling though it is – is not sufficient to show that the rich have harmed the poor.

There are many ways in which it is clear, however, that the rich *have* harmed the poor. Ale Nodye knows about one of them. He grew up in a village by the sea, in Senegal, in West Africa. His father and grandfather were fishermen, and he tried to be one too. But after six years in which he barely caught enough fish to pay for the fuel for his boat, he set out by canoe for the Canary Islands, from where he hoped to become another of Europe's many illegal immigrants. Instead, he was arrested and deported. But he says he will try again, even though the voyage is dangerous and one of his cousins died on a similar trip. He has no choice, he says, because "there are no fish in the sea here anymore." A European Commission report shows that Nodye is right: The fish stocks from which Nodye's father and grandfather took their catch and fed their families have been destroyed by industrial fishing fleets that come from Europe, China, and Russia and sell their fish to well-fed Europeans who can afford to pay high prices. The industrial fleets drag vast nets across the seabed, damaging the coral reefs where fish breed. As a result, a major protein source for poor people has vanished, the boats are idle, and people who used to make a living fishing or building boats are unemployed. The story is repeated in many other coastal areas around the world.[22]

Or consider how we citizens of rich countries obtain our oil and minerals. Teodoro Obiang, the dictator of tiny Equatorial Guinea, sells most of his country's oil to American corporations, among them Exxon Mobil, Marathon, and Hess.

Although his official salary is a modest $60,000, this ruler of a country of 550,000 people is richer than Queen Elizabeth II. He owns six private jets and a $35 million house in Malibu, as well as other houses in Maryland and Cape Town and a fleet of Lamborghinis, Ferraris, and Bentleys. Most of the people over whom he rules live in extreme poverty, with a life expectancy of forty-nine and an infant mortality of eighty-seven per one thousand (this means that more than one child in 12 dies before its first birthday).[23] Equatorial Guinea is an extreme case, but other examples are almost as bad. In 2005, the Democratic Republic of the Congo exported minerals worth $200 million. From this, its total tax revenues were $86,000. Someone was surely making money from these dealings, but not the people of the Congo.[24] In 2006, Angola made more than $30 billion in oil revenue, about $2,500 for each of its 12 million citizens. Yet the majority of Angolans have no access to basic health care; life expectancy is forty-one years; and one child in four dies before reaching the age of five. On Transparency International's corruption perception index, Angola is currently ranked 147th among 180 countries.

In their dealings with corrupt dictators in developing countries, international corporations are akin to people who knowingly buy stolen goods, with the difference that the international legal and political order recognizes the corporations not as criminals in possession of stolen goods but as the legal owners of the goods they have bought. This situation is, of course, profitable for corporations that do deals with dictators, and for us, since we use the oil, minerals, and other raw materials we need to maintain our prosperity. But for resource-rich developing countries, it is a disaster. The problem is not only the loss of immense wealth that, used wisely, could build the prosperity of the nation. Paradoxically, developing nations with rich deposits of oil or minerals are often worse off than otherwise comparable nations without

those resources. One reason is that the revenue from the sale of the resources provides a huge financial incentive for anyone tempted to overthrow the government and seize power. Successful rebels know that if they succeed, they will be rewarded with immense personal wealth. They can also reward those who backed their coup, and they can buy enough arms to keep themselves in power no matter how badly they rule. Unless, of course, some of those to whom they give the arms are themselves tempted by the prospect of controlling all that wealth . . . Thus the resources that should benefit developing nations instead become a curse that brings corruption, coups, and civil wars.[25] If we use goods made from raw materials obtained by these unethical dealings from resource-rich but money-poor nations, we are harming those who live in these countries.

One other way in which we in the rich nations are harming the poor has become increasingly clear over the past decade or two. President Yoweri Museveni of Uganda put it plainly, addressing the developed world at a 2007 meeting of the African Union: "You are causing aggression to us by causing global warming. . . . Alaska will probably become good for agriculture, Siberia will probably become good for agriculture, but where does that leave Africa?"[26]

Strong language, but the accusation is difficult to deny. Two-thirds of the greenhouse gases now in the atmosphere have come from the United States and Europe. Without those gases, there would be no human-induced global warming problem. Africa's contribution is, by comparison, extremely modest: less than three percent of the global emissions from burning fuel since 1900, somewhat more if land clearing and methane emissions from livestock production are included, but still a small fraction of what has been contributed by the industrialized nations. And while every nation will have some problems in adjusting to climate change, the hardship will, as Museveni suggests, fall disproportionately on the poor in the regions of the world closer to the equator. Some scientists believe that precipitation will decrease nearer the equator and increase nearer the poles. In any case, the rainfall upon which hundreds of millions rely to grow their food will become less reliable. Moreover, the poor nations depend on agriculture to a far greater degree than the rich. In the United States, agriculture represents only four percent of the economy; in Malawi it is 40 percent, and 90 percent of the population are subsistence farmers, virtually all of whom are dependent on rainfall. Nor will drought be the only problem climate change brings to the poor. Rising sea levels will inundate fertile, densely settled delta regions that are home to tens of millions of people in Egypt, Bangladesh, India, and Vietnam. Small Pacific Island nations that consist of low-lying coral atolls, like Kiribati and Tuvalu, are in similar danger, and it seems inevitable that in a few decades they will be submerged.[27]

The evidence is overwhelming that the greenhouse gas emissions of the industrialized nations have harmed, and are continuing to harm, many of the world's poorest people – along with many richer ones, too. If we accept that those who harm others must compensate them, we cannot deny that the industrialized nations owe compensation to many of the world's poorest people. Giving them adequate aid to mitigate the consequences of climate change would be one way of paying that compensation.

In a world that has no more capacity to absorb greenhouse gases without the consequence of damaging climate change, the philosophy of "You leave me alone, and I'll leave you alone" has become almost impossible to live by, for it requires ceasing to put any more greenhouse gases into the atmosphere. Otherwise, we simply are not leaving others alone.

America is a generous nation. As Americans, we are already giving more than our share of foreign aid through our taxes. Isn't that sufficient?

Asked whether the United States gives more, less, or about the same amount of aid, as a percentage of its income, as other wealthy countries, only one in twenty Americans gave the correct answer. When my students suggest that America is generous in this regard, I show them figures from the website of the OECD, on the amounts given by all the organization's donor members. They are astonished to find that the United States has, for many years, been at or near the bottom of the list of industrialized countries in terms of the proportion of national income given as foreign aid. In 2006, the United States fell behind Portugal and Italy, leaving Greece as the only industrialized country to give a smaller percentage of its national income in foreign aid. The average nation's effort in that year came to 46 cents of every $100 of gross national income, while the United States gave only 18 cents of every $100 it earned.

In four different surveys that asked Americans what portion of government spending (not national income) goes to foreign aid, the median answers ranged from 15 percent to 20 percent. The correct answer is less than one percent.

Asked what share of America's national income the United States gives in foreign aid, 42 percent of respondents believed that the nation gives more than four times as much as it actually

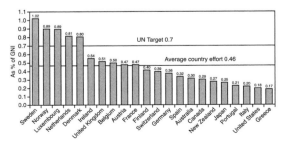

Figure 46.1 Official Aid as Percentage of Gross National Income (2006).[28]

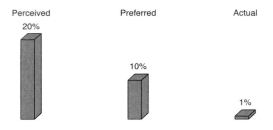

The columns represent the median responses to a survey carried out by the Program in International Policy Attitudes (PIPA) in 2000. Other surveys carried out by PIPA and by *The Washington Post* yielded similar results.

Figure 46.2 Foreign Aid as a Percentage of the Federal Budget.

gave, while eight percent of Americans thought that the United States gives more than 100 times the actual amount![29]

A majority of people in these surveys also said that America gives too much aid − but when they were asked how much America should give, the median answers ranged from five percent to 10 percent of government spending. In other words, people wanted foreign aid "cut" to an amount five to ten times greater than the United States actually gives!

Some contend that these figures for official aid are misleading because America gives much more than other countries in private aid. But although the United States gives more private aid than most rich nations, even its private giving trails that of Australia, Canada, Ireland, and Switzerland as a percentage of national income, and is on a par with giving by people in Belgium and New Zealand. Adding U.S. non-governmental aid, of seven cents per $100 earned, to U.S. government aid leaves America's total aid contribution at no more than 25 cents of every $100 earned, still near the bottom of the international aid league.[30]

Philanthropic responses undermine real political change.

If those on the right fear that I am encouraging the state to seize their money and give it to the world's poor, some on the left worry that encouraging the rich to donate to aid organizations enables them to salve their consciences while they continue to benefit from a global economic system that makes them rich and keeps billions poor.[31] Philanthropy, philosopher Paul Gomberg believes, promotes "political quietism," deflecting attention from the institutional causes of poverty − essentially, in his view, capitalism − and from the need to find radical alternatives to these institutions.[32]

Although I believe we ought to give a larger portion of our income to organizations combating poverty. I am open-minded about the best way to combat poverty.[33] Some aid agencies, Oxfam for example, are engaged in emergency relief, development aid, *and* advocacy work for a fairer global economic order. If, after investigating the causes of global poverty and considering what approach is most likely to reduce it, you really believe that a more revolutionary change is needed, then it would make sense to put your time, energy, and money into organizations promoting that revolution in the global economic system. But this is a practical question, and if there is little chance of achieving the kind of revolution you are seeking, then you need lo look around for a strategy with better prospects of actually helping some poor people.

Giving people money or food breeds dependency.

I agree that we should not be giving money or food directly to the poor, except in emergencies like a drought, earthquake, or flood, where food may need to be brought in to stop people from starving in the short term. In less dire situations, providing food can make people dependent. If the food is shipped in from a developed nation, for example the United States, it can destroy local markets and reduce incentives for local farmers to produce a surplus to sell. We need to make it possible for people to earn their own money, or to produce their own food and meet their other needs in a sustainable manner and by their own work. Giving them money or food won't achieve that. Finding a form of aid that will really help people is crucial, and not a simple task, but as we'll see, it can be done.

Cash is the seed corn of capitalism. Giving it away will reduce future growth.

Gaetano Cipriano contacted me after reading one of my articles because he thought that as an entrepreneurial capitalist, he could offer a helpful perspective. The grandson of immigrants to America, he owns and runs EI Associates, an engineering and construction firm based in Cedar Knolls, New Jersey, that has assets of around $80 million. "Cash is the seed corn of capitalism" is his phrase. Gaetano told me that he deploys his capital to the best of his ability to promote profits and enduring growth, and that giving more of it away would be "cutting my own throat." But he does not spend extravagantly. "I do not live in a splendid house," he told me, "I have no second home. I drive a 2001 Ford Explorer with 73,000 miles. I belong to a nice squash club, and have four suits and two pairs of black shoes. When I take vacations they are short and local. I do not own a boat or a plane." While he does give to charity, he does it "at a level which is prudent and balanced with sustainable growth." If he were to give much more money away, it would have to come out of sums that he now reinvests in his business. That, in turn, would reduce his future earnings and perhaps the number of people he is able to employ, or how well he can pay them. It would also leave him with less to give if, later in life, he decides that he wants to give more.

For similar reasons, we can agree that it's a good thing Warren Buffett did not give away the first million dollars he earned. Had he done so, he would not have had the investment capital he needed to develop his business, and would never have been able to give away the $31 billion that he has now pledged to give. It you are as skilled as Buffett in investing your money, I urge you to

keep it until late in life, too, and then give away most of it, as he has done. But people with less-spectacular investment abilities might do better to give it away sooner.
[. . .]

What if you took every penny you ever had and gave it to the poor of Africa . . .? What we would have is no economy, no ability to generate new wealth or help anybody.

This objection comes from Colin McGinn, a professor of philosophy at the University of Miami.[34] It isn't clear whether McGinn's "you" is you, the individual reader, or the group an American Southerner might refer to as "y'all." If you [insert your name], took every penny you ever had and gave it to the poor of Africa, our national economy would not notice. Even if every reader of this book did that, the economy would barely hiccup (unless the hook's sales exceed my wildest dreams). If *everyone* in America did it, the national economy would be ruined. But, at the moment, there is no cause for worry about the last possibility: there is no sign of it happening, and I am not advocating it.

Because so few people give significant amounts, the need for more to be given is great, and the more each one of us gives, the more lives we can save. If everyone gave significantly more than they now give, however, we would be in a totally different situation. The huge gulf between rich and poor means that if everyone were giving, there would be no need for them to take every penny they ever had and give it all to Africa. Quite a modest contribution from everyone who has enough to live comfortably, eat out occasionally, and buy bottled water, would suffice to achieve the goal of lifting most of the world's extremely poor people above the poverty line of $1.25 per day. If that modest contribution were given, we would no longer be in a situation in which 10 million children were dying from poverty every year. So whether a small number of people give a lot, or a large number of people give a little, ending large-scale extreme poverty wouldn't cripple our national economy. It leaves plenty of scope for entrepreneurial activity and individual wealth. In the long run, the global economy would be enhanced, rather than diminished, by bringing into it the 1.4 billion people now outside it, creating new markets and new opportunities for trade and investment.

> People do have special relationships with their families, their communities, and their countries. This is the standard equipment of humanity, and most people, in all of human history, have seen nothing wrong with it.[35]
>
> Alan Ryan, philosopher and warden of New College. Oxford

It is true that most of us care more about our family and friends than we do about strangers. That's natural, and there is nothing wrong with it. But how far should preference for family and friends go? Brendan, a Glennview High student, thought that instead of going to aid for the poor, money "can be better spent helping your family and friends who need the money as well." If family and friends really need the money, in anything remotely like the way those living in extreme poverty need it, it would be going too much against the grain of human nature to object to giving to them before giving to strangers. Fortunately, most middle-class people in rich nations don't have to make this choice. They can take care of their families in an entirely sufficient way on much less than they are now spending, and thus have money left over that can be used to help those in extreme poverty. Admittedly, saying just where the balance should be struck is difficult. I'll return to that question later in the book [not included in this volume].

Kiernan, another (Glennview High School student, made a point similar to Alan Ryan's:

> [Giving what we don't need to the poor] would make the world a better, more equal place. But it is like a little kid buying a pack of candy keeping one piece, and giving the rest away. It just doesn't happen.

The issue raised by all these remarks is the link between what we humans are (mostly) like, and what we *ought* to do. When Brendan O'Grady, a philosophy student at Queen's University in Ontario, posted a blog about this issue, he got the following response from another Canadian philosophy student, Thomas Simmons:

> Of course I do not want people to die, but I just feel generally unattached to them. I have no doubt that if I were to take a trip to places where people are starving then I might think diferently, but as it stands now they are just too far removed. In not making these donations, I am implicitly valuing the affluence of my own life over the basic sustenance of many others. And, well, I guess I do. Am I immoral for doing so? Maybe.[36]

When O'Grady queried this, Simmons clarified his position: "I don't intend to make a moral defense, but rather just reveal my personal feelings – that is, just to explain how I feel." The distinction between describing how things are and saying how they ought to be is also relevant to what Kiernan and Alan Ryan are saying. The fact that we tend to favor our families, communities, and countries may explain our failure to save the lives of the poor beyond those boundaries, but it does not justify that failure from an ethical perspective, no matter how many generations of our ancestors have seen nothing wrong with it. Still, a good explanation of why we behave as we do is an important first step toward understanding to what extent change is possible.

Notes

1   BBC News, September 21, 2007, http://news.bbc.co.uk/2/hi/uk_news/england/manchester/7006412.stm.

2   Deepa Narayan with Raj Patel, Kai Schafft, Anne Rademacher, and Sarah Koch-Schulte. *Voices of the Poor: Can Anyone Hear Us?* Published for the World

Bank by Oxford University Press (New York, 2000), p. 36.

3 This is a compilation of things said by the poor, cited in ibid., p. 28.

4 World Bank Press Release, "New Data Show 1.4 Billion Live on Less Than US$1.25 a Day, But Progress Against Poverty Remains Strong," August 26, 2008, http://go.worldbank.org/TOTEVOV4E0. The estimate is based on price data from 2005, and does not reflect increases in food prices in 2008, which are likely to have increased the number below the poverty line. For the research on which the press release is based, see Shaohua Chen and Martin Ravallion, "The Developing World Is Poorer Than We Thought, But No Less Successful in the Fight Against Poverty," Policy Research Working Paper 4073, World Bank Development Research Group, August 2008, www-wds.world-bank.org/external/default/WDSContentServer/IW3P/IB/2008/08/26/000158349_200808261 13239/Rendered/PDF/WPS4703.pdf.

   For further discussion of World Bank statistics, see Sanjay Reddy and Thomas Pogge, "How Not to Count the Poor," www.columbia.edu/~sr793/count.pdf, and Martin Ravallion, "How Not to Count the Poor: A Reply to Reddy and Pogge," www.columbia.edu/~sr793/wbreply.pdf.

5 Robert Rector and Kirk Anderson, "Understanding Poverty in America," Heritage Foundation Backgrounder #1713 (2004), www.heritage.org/Research/Welfare/bg1713.cfm. Rector and Anderson draw on data available from the 2003 U.S. Census Bureau report on poverty and on various other government reports.

6 United Nations, Office of the High Representative for the Least Developed Countries, Landlocked Developing Countries and the Small Island Developing States, and World Bank, World Bank Development Data Group, "Measuring Progress in Least Developed Countries: A Statistical Profile" (2006), tables 2 and 3, pp. 14–15. Available at www.un.org/ohrlls/.

7 United Nations Development Program, *Human Development Report 2000* (Oxford University Press, New York, 2000) p. 30; *Human Development Report 2001* (Oxford University Press, New York, 2001) pp. 9–12, p. 22; and World Bank, *World Development Report 2000/2001*, overview, p. 3, www.worldbank. org/poverty/wdrpoverty/report/overview.pdf, for the other figures. The *Human Development Reports* are available at http://hdr.undp.org.

8 James Riley, *Rising Life Expectancy: A Global History* (New York: Cambridge University Press, 2001); Jeremy Laurance, "Thirty Years: Difference in Life Expectancy Between the World's Rich and Poor Peoples," *The Independent* (UK), September 7, 2007.

9 "Billionaires 2008," *Forbes*, March 24, 2008, www.forbes.com/forbes/2008/0324/080.html.

10 Joe Sharkey, "For the Super-Rich, It's Time to Upgrade the Old Jumbo," *The New York Times*, October 17, 2006.

11 "Watch Your Time," Special Advertising Supplement to *The New York Times*, October 14, 2007. The passage quoted is on p. 40.

12 Bill Marsh, "A Battle Between the Bottle and the Faucet," *The New York Times*, July 15, 2007.

13 Pacific Institute, "Bottled Water and Energy: A Fact Sheet," www.pacinst.org/topics/water_and_sustainability/bottled_water/bottled_water_and_energy.html.

14 Lance Gay, "Food Waste Costing Economy $100 Billion, Study Finds," Scripps Howard News Service, August 10, 2005, www.knoxstudio.com/shns/story.cfm?pk=GARBAGE-08–10–05.

15 Deborah Lindquist, "How to Look Good Naked," Lifetime Network, Season 2, Episode 2, July 29, 2009. As relayed by Courtney Moran.

16 Peter Unger, *Living High and Letting Die* (New York: Oxford University Press, 1996).

17 For further discussion see Peter Singer, *The Expanding Circle*, (Oxford: Clarendon Press, 1981), pp. 136, 183. For further examples, see www.unification.net/ws/theme015.htm.

18 Peter Singer, "The Singer Solution to World Poverty," *The New York Times Sunday Magazine*, September 5, 1999.

19 Glennview High School is Seider's fictional name for the school, and the names of the students are also pseudonyms. Material about Glennview High School students is drawn from Scott Seider, "Resisting Obligation: How Privileged Adolescents Conceive of Their Responsibilities to Other," *Journal of Research in Character Education*, 6:1 (2008), pp. 3–19, and Scott Seider, *Literature, Justice and Resistance: Engaging Adolescents from Privileged Groups in Social Action*, unpublished doctoral dissertation, Graduate School of Education, Harvard University.

20 Jan Narveson, " 'We Don't Owe Them a Thing!' A Tough-minded but Soft-hearted View of Aid to the Faraway Needy," *The Monist*, 86:3 (2003), p. 419.

21 James B. Davies, Susanna Sandstrom, Anthony Shorrocks, and Edward N. Wolff, "The World Distribution of Household Wealth," Worldwide Institute for Development Economics Research of the United Nations University, Helsinki (December 2006), www.wider.unu.edu/research/2006-2007/2006-2007-l/wider-wdhw-launch-5-12-2006/wider-wdhw-report-5-12-2006.pdf.

22 Sharon Lafraniere, "Europe Takes Africa's Fish, and Boatloads of Migrants Follow," *The New York Times*, January 14, 2008, and Elizabeth Rosenthal, "Europe's Appetite for Seafood Propels Illegal Trade," *The New York Times*, January 15, 2008.

23 See Leif Wenar, "Property Rights and the Resource Curse," *Philosophy & Public Affairs* 36:1 (2008), pp. 2–32. A more detailed version is available on Wenar's website: www.wenar.staff.shef.ac.uk/PRRCwebpage.html.

24 Paul Collier, *The Bottom Billion* (New York: Oxford University Press, 2007).

25 See Leonard Wantchekon, "Why Do Resource Dependent Countries Have Authoritarian Governments?" *Journal of African Finance and Economic Development* 5:2 (2002), pp. 57–77; an earlier version is available at www.yale.edu/leitner/pdf/1999-11.pdf. See also Nathan Jensen and Leonard Wantchekon, "Resource Wealth and Political Regimes in Africa," *Comparative Political Studies*, 37 (2004), pp. 816–41.

26 President Museveni was speaking at the African Union summit, Addis Ababa, Ethiopia, February 2007, and the speech was reported in Andrew Revkin, "Poor Nations to Bear Brunt as World Warms," *The New York Times*, April 1, 2007.

27 Andrew Revkin, op. cit., and "Reports from Four Fronts in the War on Warming," *The New York Times*, April 3, 2007; Kathy Marks, "Rising Tide of Global Warming Threatens Pacific Island States," *The Independent* (UK), October 25, 2006.

28 Organisation for Economic Co-operation and Development (OECD), *OECD Journal on Development: Development Co-operation Report 2007*, p. 134, www.

oecd.org/dac/dcr. The table is reproduced by kind permission of OECD. See also *Statistical Annex of the 2007 Development Co-operation Report*, www.oecd.org/dataoecd/52/9/1893143.xls, Fig. 1e.

29 Program on International Policy Attitudes, www.worldpublicopinion.org/pipa/articles/home_page/383.php?nid=&id=&pnt=383&lb=hmpg1. The table is reproduced by kind permission of the Program on International Policy Attitudes, and is taken from "Americans on Foreign Aid and World Hunger: A Survey of U.S. Public Attitudes" (February 2, 2001), http://65.109.167.118/pipa/pdf.feb01/ForeignAid_Feb01_rpt.pdf.

30 Organisation for Economic Co-operation and Development (OECD), Statistical Annex of the 2007 Development Co-operation Report, www.oecd.org/dataoecd/52/9/1893143.xls, Table 7e. If we accept the much higher estimate of U.S. private philanthropy in the Hudson Institute's Index of Global Philanthropy, America's total aid contribution rises to 0.42 percent, which is more respectable, although still slightly below the average country effort for official aid. The Index of Global Philanthropy figures are not suitable for international comparisons, however, as we lack figures calculated on a similar basis for most other countries.

31 See, for example, Anthony Langlois, "Charity and Justice in the Singer Solution," in Raymond Younis (ed) *On the Ethical Life* (Newcastle upon Tyne: Cambridge Scholars, forthcoming); Paul Gomberg, "The Fallacy of Philanthropy," *Canadian Journal of Philosophy* 32:1 (2002), pp. 29–66.

32 Gomberg, *op. cit.*, pp. 30, 63–4.

33 See Andy Lamey's response to Anthony Langlois's paper in the volume referred to in n. 31, above.

34 Colin McGinn, as quoted by Michael Specter in "The Dangerous Philosopher," *The New Yorker*, September 6, 1999.

35 Alan Ryan, as quoted by Michael Specter in "The Dangerous Philosopher," *The New Yorker*, September 6, 1999.

36 http://www.muzakandpotatoes.com/2008/02/peter-singer-on-affluence.html.

Chapter 47

Thomas Pogge

WORLD POVERTY AND HUMAN RIGHTS

Thomas Pogge (1953–) is Leitner Professor of Philosophy and International Affairs at Yale University, widely known for his writings on global justice and health care. The following article is a revised version of an essay which first appeared in a symposium on his book, *World Poverty and Human Rights*. In it, he puts forward some data about the problem of world poverty, and argues that this poverty is a harm imposed on the developing world by the developed world. It is therefore a harm for which those in the developed world bear moral responsibility.

Despite a high and growing global average income, billions of human beings are still condemned to lifelong severe poverty, with all its attendant evils of low life expectancy, social exclusion, ill health, illiteracy, dependency, and effective enslavement. The annual death toll from poverty-related causes is around 18 million, or one-third of all human deaths, which adds up to approximately 400 million deaths since the end of the Cold War.[1]

This problem is hardly unsolvable, in spite of its magnitude. In 2010, the 2.94 billion people counted as living below the World Bank's more generous $2.50 per day international poverty line – though constituting 43 percent of the world's population – accounted for only about 1.4 percent of the global product, and would have needed only one percent more to escape poverty so defined.[2] By contrast, the high-income countries, with 1.1 billion citizens, had about 70 percent of the global product.[3] With our average per capita income some 134 times greater than that of the poor (at market exchange

rates), we could eradicate severe poverty world-wide if we chose to try – in fact, we could have eradicated it decades ago.

Citizens of the rich countries are, however, conditioned to downplay the severity and persistence of world poverty and to think of it as an occasion for minor charitable assistance. Thanks in part to the rationalizations dispensed by our economists, most of us believe that severe poverty and its persistence are due exclusively to local causes. Few realize that severe poverty is an ongoing harm we inflict upon the global poor. If more of us understood the true magnitude of the problem of poverty and our causal involvement in it, we might do what is necessary to eradicate it.

That world poverty is an ongoing harm we inflict seems completely incredible to most citizens of the affluent countries. We call it tragic that the basic human rights of so many remain unfulfilled, and are willing to admit that we should do more to help. But it is unthinkable to us that we are actively responsible for this catastrophe. If we were, then we, civilized and sophisticated denizens of the developed countries, would be guilty of the largest crime against humanity ever committed, the death toll of which exceeds, every three years, that of World War II with concentration camps and gulags included. What could be more preposterous?

But think about the unthinkable for a moment. Are there steps the affluent countries could take to reduce severe poverty abroad? It seems very likely that there are, given the enormous inequalities in income and wealth already mentioned. The common assumption, however, is that reducing severe poverty abroad at the expense of our own affluence would be generous on our part, not something we owe, and that our failure to do this is thus at most a lack of generosity that does not make us morally responsible for the continued deprivation of the poor.

I deny this popular assumption. I deny that the one billion citizens of the affluent countries are morally entitled to their 80 percent of the global product in the face of much larger numbers of people mired in severe poverty. Is this denial really so preposterous that one need not consider the arguments in its support? Does not the radical inequality between our wealth and their dire need at least put the burden on us to show why we should be morally entitled to so much while they have so little? In *World Poverty and Human Rights*,[4] I dispute the popular assumption by showing that the usual ways of justifying our great advantage fail. My argument poses three mutually independent challenges.

Actual History

Many believe that the radical inequality we face can be justified by reference to how it evolved, for example through differences in diligence, culture, and social institutions, soil, climate, or fortune. I challenge this sort of justification by invoking the common and very violent history

through which the present radical inequality accumulated. Much of it was built up in the colonial era, when today's affluent countries ruled today's poor regions of the world: trading their people like cattle, destroying their political institutions and cultures, taking their lands and natural resources, and forcing products and customs upon them. I recount these historical facts specifically for readers who believe that even the most radical inequality is morally justifiable if it evolved in a benign way. Such readers disagree about the conditions a historical process must meet for it to justify such vast inequalities in life chances. But I can bypass these disagreements because the actual historical crimes were so horrendous, diverse, and consequential that no historical entitlement conception could credibly support the view that our common history was sufficiently benign to justify today's huge inequality in starting places.

Challenges such as this are often dismissed with the lazy response that we cannot be held responsible for what others did long ago. This response is true but irrelevant. We indeed cannot inherit responsibility for our forefathers' sins. But how then can we plausibly claim the fruits of their sins? How can we have been entitled to the great head start our countries enjoyed going into the postcolonial period, which has allowed us to dominate and shape the world? And how can we be entitled to the huge advantages over the global poor we consequently enjoy from birth? The historical path from which our exceptional affluence arose greatly weakens our moral claim to it – certainly in the face of those whom the same historical process has delivered into conditions of acute deprivation. They, the global poor, have a much stronger moral claim to that one percent of the global product they may need to meet their basic needs than we affluent have to take 80 rather than 79 percent for ourselves. Thus, I write, "A morally deeply tarnished history should not be allowed to result in *radical* inequality" (p. 209).

Fictional Histories

Since my first challenge addressed adherents of historical entitlement conceptions of justice, it may leave others unmoved. These others may believe that it is permissible to uphold any economic distribution, no matter how skewed, if merely it *could* have come about on a morally acceptable path. They insist that we are entitled to keep and defend what we possess, even at the cost of millions of deaths each year, unless there is conclusive proof that, without the horrors of the European conquests, severe poverty worldwide would be substantially less today.

Now, *any* distribution, however unequal, *could* be the outcome of a sequence of voluntary bets or gambles. Appeal to such a fictional history would "justify" anything and would thus be wholly implausible. John Locke does much better, holding that a fictional history can justify the status quo only if the changes in holdings and social rules it involves are ones that all participants could have rationally agreed to. He also holds that in a state of nature persons would be entitled to a proportional share of the world's natural resources. Whoever deprives others of "enough and as good" – either through unilateral appropriations or through institutional arrangements, such as a radically unequal property regime – harms them in violation of a *negative* duty. For Locke, the justice of any institutional order thus depends on whether the worst-off under it are at least as well off as people would be in a state of nature with a proportional resource share.[5] This baseline is imprecise, to be sure, but it suffices for my second challenge: however one may want to imagine a state of nature among human beings on this planet, one could not realistically conceive it as involving suffering and early deaths on the scale we are witnessing today. Only a thoroughly organized state of civilization can produce such horrendous misery and sustain an enduring poverty death toll of 18 million annually. The existing distribution is then morally unacceptable on

Lockean grounds insofar as, I point out, "the better-off enjoy significant advantages in the use of a single natural resource base from whose benefits the worse-off are largely, and without compensation, excluded" (p. 208).

The attempt to justify today's coercively upheld radical inequality by appeal to some morally acceptable *fictional* historical process that *might* have led to it thus fails as well. On Locke's permissive account, a small elite may appropriate all of the huge cooperative surplus produced by modern social organization. But this elite must not enlarge its share even further by reducing the poor *below* the state-of-nature baseline in order to capture *more* than the entire cooperative surplus. The citizens and governments of the affluent states are violating this negative duty when we, in collaboration with the ruling cliques of many poor countries, coercively exclude the global poor from a proportional resource share and any equivalent substitute.

Present Global Institutional Arrangements

A third way of thinking about the justice of a radical inequality involves reflection on the institutional rules that sustain it. Using this approach, one can justify an economic order and the distribution it reproduces (irrespective of historical considerations) by comparing them to feasible alternative institutional schemes and the distributional profiles they would produce. Many broadly consequentialist and contractualist conceptions of justice exemplify this approach. They differ in how they characterize the relevant affected parties (groups, persons, time slices of persons, and so on), in the metric they employ for measuring how well off such parties are (in terms of social primary goods, capabilities, welfare, and so forth), and in how they aggregate such well-being information into one overall assessment (for example, by averaging, or in some egalitarian, prioritarian, or sufficientarian way). These conceptions consequently disagree about how economic institutions should best be shaped under modern conditions. But I can bypass such disagreements insofar as these conceptions agree that an economic order is unjust when it — like the systems of serfdom and forced labor prevailing in feudal Russia or France — foreseeably and avoidably gives rise to massive and severe human rights deficits. My third challenge, addressed to adherents of broadly consequentialist and contractualist conceptions of justice, is that we are preserving our great economic advantages by imposing a global economic order that is unjust in view of the massive and avoidable deprivations it foreseeably reproduces: "There is a shared institutional order that is shaped by the better-off and imposed on the worse-off," I contend. "This institutional order is implicated in the reproduction of radical inequality in that there is a feasible institutional alternative under which such severe and extensive poverty would not persist. . . . The radical inequality cannot be traced to extra-social factors (such as genetic handicaps or natural disasters) which, as such, affect different human beings differentially" (p. 205).

Three Notions of Harm

These three challenges converge on the conclusion that the global poor have a compelling moral claim to some of our affluence and that we, by denying them what they are morally entitled to and urgently need, are actively contributing to their deprivations. Still, these challenges are addressed to different audiences and thus appeal to diverse and mutually inconsistent moral conceptions.

They also deploy different notions of harm. In most ordinary contexts, the word "harm" is understood in a historical sense, either diachronically or subjunctively: someone is harmed when she is rendered worse off than she was at some earlier time, or than she would have been had

some earlier arrangements continued undisturbed. My first two challenges conceive harm in this ordinary way, and then conceive justice, at least partly, in terms of harm: we are behaving unjustly toward the global poor by imposing on them the lasting effects of historical crimes, or by holding them below any credible state-of-nature baseline. But my third challenge does not conceive justice and injustice in terms of an independently specified notion of harm. Rather, it relates the concepts of *harm* and *justice* in the opposite way, conceiving harm in terms of an independently specified conception of social justice: we are *harming* the global poor if and insofar as we collaborate in imposing an *unjust* global institutional order upon them. And this institutional order is definitely unjust if and insofar as it foreseeably perpetuates large-scale human rights deficits that would be reasonably avoidable through feasible institutional modifications.[6]

The third challenge is empirically more demanding than the other two. It requires me to substantiate three claims: Global institutional arrangements are causally implicated in the reproduction of massive severe poverty. Governments of our affluent countries bear primary responsibility for these global institutional arrangements and can foresee their detrimental effects. And many citizens of these affluent countries bear responsibility for the global institutional arrangements their governments have negotiated in their names.

Two Main Innovations

In defending the claims underlying my three challenges, my view on these more empirical matters is as oddly perpendicular to the usual empirical debates as my diagnosis of our moral relation to world poverty is to the usual moral debates.

The usual *moral* debates concern the stringency of our moral duties to help the poor abroad. Most of us believe that these duties are rather feeble, meaning that it isn't very wrong of us to give no help at all. Against this popular view, some (Peter Singer, Henry Shue, Peter Unger) have argued that our positive duties are quite stringent and quite demanding; and others (such as Liam Murphy) have defended an intermediate view according to which our positive duties, insofar as they are quite stringent, are not very demanding. Leaving this whole debate to one side, I focus on what it ignores: our moral duties not to harm. We do, of course, have positive duties to rescue people from life-threatening poverty. But it can be misleading to focus on them when more stringent negative duties are also in play: duties not to expose people to life-threatening poverty and duties to shield them from harms for which we would be actively responsible.

The usual *empirical* debates concern how developing countries should design their economic institutions and policies in order to reduce severe poverty within their borders. The received wisdom (often pointing to Hong Kong and, lately, China) is that they should opt for free and open markets with a minimum in taxes and regulations so as to attract investment and to stimulate growth. But some influential economists call for extensive government investment in education, health care, and infrastructure (as illustrated by the example of the Indian state of Kerala), or for some protectionist measures to "incubate" fledgling niche industries until they become internationally competitive (as illustrated by South Korea's growth spurt). Leaving these debates to one side, I focus once more on what is typically ignored: the role that the design of the *global* institutional order plays in the persistence of severe poverty.

Thanks to the inattention of our economists, many believe that the existing global institutional order plays no role in the persistence of severe poverty, but rather that national differences are the key factors. Such "explanatory nationalism" (pp. 145 ff.) appears justified by the dramatic performance differentials among

developing countries, with poverty rapidly disappearing in some and increasing in others. Cases of the latter kind usually display plenty of incompetence, corruption, and oppression by ruling elites, which seem to give us all the explanation we need to understand why severe poverty persists there.

But consider this analogy. Suppose there are great performance differentials among the students in a class, with some improving greatly while many others learn little or nothing. And suppose the latter students do not do their readings and skip many classes. Such performance differentials surely show that local, student-specific factors play a role in explaining academic success. But they decidedly *fail* to show that global factors (the quality of teaching, textbooks, classroom, and so forth) play no such role. For example, it remains possible that the teacher is uninspiring, and thereby dampens the performance of all students. And it remains possible that poor attendance and preparation arise from the teacher's efforts failing to engage the interests of many students or from his sexist comments de-motivating half his class. Analogues to these three possibilities obtain with regard to global institutional arrangements. Its design may be – and actually is, I argue – highly unfavorable for the poor and very supportive of corrupt and dictatorial government, especially in the resource-rich poor countries.

Once we break free from explanatory nationalism, global factors relevant to the persistence of severe poverty are easy to find. In the negotiations establishing the WTO, the affluent countries insisted on continued and asymmetrical protections of their markets through tariffs, quotas, anti-dumping duties, export credits, and huge subsidies to domestic producers. Such protectionism provides a compelling illustration of the hypocrisy of the rich states which insist and command that their own exports be received with open markets (pp. 20–23). And it greatly impairs export opportunities for the very poorest countries and regions. If the rich countries scrapped their protectionist barriers against imports from poor countries, the populations of the latter would benefit greatly: hundreds of millions would escape unemployment, wage levels would rise substantially, and incoming export revenues would be higher by hundreds of billions of dollars each year.

The same rich states also insist that their intellectual property rights − ever-expanding in scope and duration − must be vigorously enforced in the poor countries. Music and software, production processes, words, seeds, biological species, and medicines − for all these, and more, rents must be paid to the corporations of the rich countries as a condition for (still multiply restricted) access to their markets. Millions would be saved from diseases and death if generic producers could freely manufacture and market life-saving medicines in the poor countries (pp. 222–61).

While charging billions for their intellectual property, the rich countries pay nothing for the externalities they impose through their vastly disproportional contributions to global pollution and resource depletion. The global poor benefit least, if at all, from polluting activities, and also are least able to protect themselves from the impact such pollution has on their health and on their natural environment (such as flooding due to rising sea levels). It is true, of course, that we pay for the vast quantities of natural resources we import. But such payments cannot make up for the price effects of our inordinate consumption, which restrict the consumption possibilities of the global poor as well as the development possibilities of the poorer countries and regions (in comparison to the opportunities our countries could take advantage of at a comparable stage of economic development).

More important, the payments we make for resource imports go to the rulers (and affluent elites) of the resource-rich countries, with no concern about whether they are democratically elected or at least minimally attentive to the needs of the people whose resources they sell. It is on the basis of effective power alone that we recognize any such ruler as entitled to sell us the resources of "his" country and to borrow, to undertake treaty commitments, and to buy arms in its name. These international resource, borrowing, treaty, and arms privileges we extend to such rulers are highly advantageous to them, providing them with the money and arms they need to stay in power − often with great brutality and negligible popular support. These privileges are also quite convenient to us, securing our resource imports from poor countries irrespective of who may rule them and how badly. But these privileges have devastating effects on the global poor by enabling corrupt rulers to oppress them, to exclude them from the benefits of their countries' natural resources, and to saddle them with huge debts and onerous treaty obligations. By substantially augmenting the perks of governmental power, these same privileges also greatly strengthen the incentives to attempt to take power by force, thereby fostering coups, civil wars, and interstate wars in the poor countries and regions − especially in Africa, which has many desperately poor but resource-rich countries, where the resource sector constitutes a large part of the gross domestic product.

Reflection on the popular view that severe poverty persists in many poor countries because they govern themselves so poorly shows, then, that it is evidence not for but against explanatory nationalism. The populations of most of the countries in which severe poverty persists or increases do not "govern themselves" poorly, but *are* very poorly governed, and much against their will. They are helplessly exposed to such "government" because the rich states recognize their rulers as entitled to rule on the basis of effective power alone. We pay these rulers for their people's resources, often advancing them large sums against the collateral of future exports, and we eagerly sell them the weapons on which their continued rule all too often depends. Yes, severe poverty is fueled by local misrule. But such local misrule is fueled, in turn, by global rules that we impose and from which we benefit greatly.

Once this causal nexus between our global institutional order and the persistence of severe poverty is better understood, the injustice of that order, and of our imposition of it, becomes visible: "What entitles a small global elite – the citizens of the rich countries *and* the holders of political and economic power in the resource-rich developing countries – to enforce a global property scheme under which we may claim the world's natural resources for ourselves and can distribute these among ourselves on mutually agreeable terms?" I ask. "How, for instance, can our ever so free and fair agreements with tyrants give us property rights in crude oil, thereby dispossessing the local population and the rest of humankind?" (p. 148).

Notes

1 World Health Organization, *World Health Report 2004* (Geneva: WHO, 2004), Annex Table 2, pp. 120–5; available at www.who.int/whr/2004.

2 This estimate is based on the latest (2010) poverty statistics provided by the World Bank (iresearch. worldbank.org/PovalNet/index/htm?1, accessed July 9, 2013). The $2.50 per day poverty line is defined in terms of a monthly consumption expenditure equivalent to the purchasing power that $76 had in the US in 2005. To count as poor by this standard in the US today (2013), one would need to be compelled to live on less than $91 per person per month (www.bls.gov/data/inflation_calculator.htm, accessed July 9, 2013). The headcount figure provided, 50, gives the percentage of poor within the developing-country

population which, in 2010, was 5,889 million. The poverty gap figure provided, 21.64, gives the average shortfall from the poverty line in percent. Because this shortfall is zero for the non-poor, the average shortfall among the poor is the ratio of the poverty gap divided by the headcount. So the average poor person lives 43.3 percent below the poverty line. For all poor people together, this works out to an annual shortfall (poverty gap) of about $600 billion at market exchange rates. For a methodological critique of the World Bank's poverty statistics, see Thomas Pogge, *Politics as Usual: What Lies behind the Pro-Poor Rhetoric* (Cambridge: Polity Press 2010), chs. 3–4, as well as Sanjay Reddy and Thomas Pogge "How Not to Count the Poor," in Sudhir Anand, Paul Segal and Joseph Stiglitz, eds.: *Debates in the Measurement of Global Poverty* (Oxford: Oxford University Press 2010), also available at papers.ssrn.com/sol3/papers.cfm?abstract_id=893159 (accessed July 9, 2013).

3 World Bank, *World Development Report 2012* (Washington D.C.: World Bank, 2011), p. 393.

4 Thomas Pogge: *World Poverty and Human Rights: Cosmopolitan Responsibilities and Reforms*, second edition (Cambridge: Polity Press, 2008). All in-text citation references will be to this book.

5 For a fuller reading of Locke's argument, see Pogge, *World Poverty and Human Rights*, ch. 5.

6 One might say that the existing global order is not unjust if the only feasible institutional modifications that could substantially reduce the offensive deprivations would be extremely costly in terms of culture, say, or the natural environment. I preempt such objections by inserting the word "reasonably." Broadly consequentialist and contractualist conceptions of justice agree that an institutional order that foreseeably gives rise to massive severe deprivations is unjust if there are feasible institutional modifications that foreseeably would greatly reduce these deprivations without adding other harms of comparable magnitude.

Chapter 48

Loren Lomasky

LIBERALISM BEYOND BORDERS

Loren Lomasky (1947–) is a political philosopher at the University of Virginia. In this 2007 essay, Lomasky explores the implications of classical liberal political philosophy for international issues. He argues that a just international order would be marked by, among other characteristics, free trade and free migration, and explores questions surrounding cooperation with oppressive regimes and justified humanitarian intervention.

I. Introduction

Political philosophy is an anachronism. The institutional structure that provided its bearings – the *polis* – is more than two millennia defunct. Nonetheless, the discipline carries on, turning its attentions to the workings of empires, principalities, and forms in between. Its modern efflorescence coincides with and focuses on the development of the nation-state. With few exceptions, the subject matter of the preceding four centuries' political philosophy is the inner workings of the sovereign modern state. Those within its borders are clients to be served, and state institutions are assessed in terms of how effectively they vindicate individuals' rights, dispense justice, and promote overall well-being. Nowhere is this characterization more apt than in the theory of liberalism. From Thomas Hobbes and John Locke at one end to John Rawls at the other, the state is conceived as the self-contained object of analysis, whether in the mode of omnipotent leviathan or cooperative venture entered into at birth and exited only at death.

It now can be asked of modern liberal political theory whether it too has become an anachronism. Although the nation-state, unlike the *polis*, is still very much with us, no longer is it the unique juncture at which all political avenues meet. Rather, lines of influence and authority are diverse, including interstate, infra-state and nonstate entities. To do political theory as if the only noteworthy claims of justice are those resolvable within borders is to trade on an increasingly unrealistic conception. As communications and economics have gone global, so too must political philosophy. Otherwise, it risks not only anachronism but also obtuseness and irrelevance.

This should not produce an existential crisis among liberals. The deep structure of liberalism is friendly to a global outlook. Classic liberal manifestos are grounded on universal human rights, with the state and its privileged status derivative therefrom. But because everyone has valid claims on everyone, for noninterference if not for more, there is prima facie plausibility to the idea that a fully adequate model of political justice will have to incorporate bonds of obligation that extend beyond national borders.

That this universalist strand lies mostly latent in the tradition is explicable in terms of the context within which liberal philosophy emerged and evolved. First, its development coincided with the history of the burgeoning nation-state as it ascended to political dominance. Because this was the central problem of the seventeenth century (and beyond), it is entirely natural that philosophers would concentrate on the task of exploring its parameters and possibilities. Second, intensity of interaction was once a rapidly decreasing function of distance. In an era when most people lived their entire lives within the county, let alone country, in which they were born, relations across national borders were few and limited. Third, communication was no more rapid than the fastest boat or caravan could travel between population concentrations. Even where there existed a will to extend efficacy abroad, epistemic barriers made it difficult to do so. Fourth, to the extent that a theory of justice in international relations was pursued, it primarily addressed ramifications of traditional just war theory and hospitality to commercial travelers. Any prospect of more extended rule-governed interaction was thoroughly utopian.[1]

It is, perhaps, unnecessary to note that much has changed. The nation-state is mature (some would say verging on senescence),[2] markets for virtually all goods and many services are worldwide, communications across continents proceed at the pace of those conducted across the street, and populations in one country are profoundly affected by legislative enactments and stock-market fluctuations in another. Moreover, individuals are often subject to authority other than that of the sovereign nation-state via international treaties and multinational organizations such as the European Union and the United Nations. It is no longer the case that separate peoples occupy the world in a condition of general detachment from one another. Rather, John Donne's dictum that no man is an island now extends with equal force to communities, regions, nations, continents – and, for that matter, to islands. Along innumerable lines of influence, we affect each other for better and for worse. Because there are substantial gains (or losses) to be incurred through appropriately (or inappropriately) formulated rules of conduct, it seems impossible to deny, or even to ignore, the need to acknowledge principles of justice governing global transactions.

Another change is of special salience to political philosophers. In *A Theory of Justice*, John Rawls developed the theory of justice as fairness for a sovereign nation-state.[3] In that book, he offered only a promissory note concerning the requirements of justice beyond borders. That note was cashed in *The Law of Peoples*.[4] Although the inherent philosophical merits of the latter book are vigorously debated, it is incontrovertible that attention by Rawls to an issue amplifies its visibility many times over. Even prior to the publication of *The Law of Peoples*, philosophical allies of Rawls had endeavored to extend the theory of justice globally.[5] These treatments typically involved application of Rawls's difference principle (privileging the status of the least well-off members of society) to the entire world population, with massive wealth redistribution as the inescapable consequence. However, when Rawls himself decided to extend the theory of justice, his own take on its ramifications was substantially different. *The Law of Peoples* is only modestly redistributive, with the difference principle explicitly rejected as a basis for international cooperation.[6] Those who believe that the extraordinary disparity in access to primary goods between the world's haves and have-nots constitutes a massive injustice that demands rectification find little to cheer in the book. Therefore, the international-justice debate in the philosophical literature is being waged at least as much by Rawlsian against Rawlsian as by Rawlsian against anti-Rawlsian.

This is an essay in developing cross-border implications of liberalism. Both in motivation and in some of its findings it is in sympathy with *The Law of Peoples*. But as with the critics of Rawls, it proposes a theory of international justice that is continuous with national justice. Like those critics of Rawls, it argues that rich states impose grave and systematic injustices on the poorer peoples of the world. However, these are not attributed to insufficient zeal in applying the difference principle beyond borders. Rather, the flaw is rooted more deeply in a transgression against the grounding theory of liberalism: denial of equal liberty to those with whom one transacts.

Section II discusses the relationship between distance and the stringency of moral ties among persons. The world's peoples are strikingly diverse with regard to possession of the ingredients of well-being, and Section III examines some of the conditions that underlie these differences. Section IV is the most extended of the essay. Five guiding principles of a liberal theory of international justice are set out and defended. Section V offers a brief conclusion.

II. Moral Ties and Moral Claims

Many people believe that their obligations to co-nationals are weightier and more extensive than those owed to extra-nationals. This is, of course, a disputable proposition, but it is one of a family of claims that closeness, literal or figurative, matters for morality. Near kin and friends are due more consideration than distant relatives and casual acquaintances. The latter, however, take precedence over anonymous members of one's community, who in turn count for more than distant compatriots, who in turn count for more than residents of foreign lands. Such judgments are in tune with our uninstructed moral sentiments. They also are in tune with the basic precept of rationality that the greater the value one places on some item, the more cost one has reason to bear in order to safeguard that item.

Some theorists object that concern for personal interests is trumped by moral principles of impartial concern for the well-being of all persons, regardless of their connection to oneself.[7] Not only is that view counterintuitive, but it also forfeits any prospect of constructing an account of morality, including political morality, built on foundations of rational prudence.

Although there are respects in which it is accurate to characterize Rawls as an egalitarian, commitment to a thoroughgoing universal impartialism is not one of them. Rather, a founding assumption of his theory of justice is that persons possess distinct conceptions of the good that afford them individuated reasons to act on behalf of the ends that are distinctively their own. The possibility of reciprocal benefit prompts construction of principles of justice which, if generally adhered to, generate a cooperative surplus. It is in this respect that the theory of justice is said by Rawls to be "a part, perhaps the most significant part, of the theory of rational choice."[8]

How, then, is the Rawlsian difference principle to be understood? First, it does not annul the conception of justice as cooperation for mutual benefit but rather specifies how the cooperative surplus is to be distributed. Second, it applies only under tightly delimited circumstances. In a striking characterization of its range of applicability, Rawls declares, "In justice as fairness men agree to share one another's fate."[9] The implied corollary is that where dealings among people are too occasional or superficial to constitute the basis of any such fate-sharing agreement, the supposition that they could be obligated one to another by anything as strong as the difference principle lacks foundation. Instead, a basic order of live-and-let-live may be all that is rationally sustainable. How strong a spin should be given to the notion of "sharing fate" is open to debate, as is the feasible scope of application. Even to suppose that the citizens of a populous and diverse sovereign state are drawn together in so tight a circle is far-fetched;[10] it is all the more far-fetched to extend the perimeter to encompass all the peoples of the world. This explains, I believe, why when Rawls comes to write *The Law of Peoples*, he eschews grand principles of transnational redistribution in favor of considerably more modest articles mandating respect for the independence and sovereignty of other national units. Aid comes into the picture only to enable disfavored peoples to establish a minimally just and decent social order so that they then might proceed in their own preferred direction.[11] Somewhat surprisingly, such autonomy is accorded not only to liberal democratic regimes but also to old-fashioned autocracies (dubbed here "decent hierarchical peoples").

Rawls, then, is to be located among those theorists who hold that the weight of moral obligation is a decreasing function of distance. This helps to explain what some find a puzzling feature of his theory of international justice: the parties to the global original position are not the world's *people* but its *peoples*. One can, of course, imagine some sort of compact that a conclave of six billion souls might produce behind a veil of ignorance, but why on the other side of the veil they should acknowledge its terms as binding them in their subsequent dealings admits of no satisfactory answer. The qualitative and quantitative dimensions of their interactions are so slight that they can in only the most attenuated sense be described as cooperators for mutual advantage. Peoples, however, at least those that carry recognition as sovereign entities, do regularly interact as parties to treaties, members of international organizations, and transactors in commercial relationships. Therefore, they qualify as potentially reciprocating beneficiaries and so are subject to principles of justice that they would endorse as free and independent parties in a suitably characterized original position. Thus the structure of *The Law of Peoples*.

The preceding sketch is not intended to endorse Rawls's conclusions concerning the terms of international law. As I will argue in Section IV, the articles he presents are at best incomplete, holding for relations between states but silent concerning obligations of justice to individual foreign nationals. My sketch is, however, intended to endorse Rawls's method of attentiveness both to what may be called the supply side as well as the demand side of a theory of justice. Not much moral acuity is required to perceive the massive want and despair that disfigure the global arena. Questions expressing protest and indignation spontaneously follow: "What kind of world order is it in which some 2.8 billion people live on an income of less than two dollars a day, 1.2 billion of whom subsist on less than one dollar a day?" "When 30,000 children die *each day* from disease due to inadequate nutrition, doesn't that show that something is very wrong with the way resources are distributed?" As with other rhetorical questions, these do not invite extended reflection prior to ascertaining the indicated answer. Yet the phenomena adduced do not, as such, signify the existence of an injustice, let alone identify the offending party. Poverty, hunger, and disease naturally call forth instincts to compassion, but who, if anyone, are the parties accountable either for having brought about or for now addressing these circumstances is a further question, the answer to which is not obvious. The planet's poor, let us agree, no more deserve to bear their misery than do the citizens of rich nations of the West deserve to have been born to the affluence that they enjoy. This is lamentably bad fortune for one, good fortune for the other. On what grounds, though, can a claim for recompense be lodged by the former against the latter? If the better-off owe their wealth to unfair dealings with the worse-off, that would, of course, constitute the basis of a strong claim for reparations. However, the fact of inequality, even very great inequality, does not by itself amount to evidence of any prior injustice. Nor, absent a question-begging egalitarian premise, does it show that the wealthy have any duty to acquiesce in a transfer of some share of their resources to the poor. It may be *kind* of them to do so, a matter of laudable *charity* or *generosity*, but that is not equivalent to maintaining that they *must* (as a requirement of justice) do so. To put it slightly differently, that many people stand in urgent need of aid from those who might be able to provide assistance is unassailable. But why and how that need constitutes a valid claim on the actions of others is less clear. What people owe each other is, in the broadest sense, the subject matter of a theory of justice, and it is only within the framework of such a theory that global inequality and distress can accurately be translated into a language of rights and duties.

Parties intimately joined to each other by shared activities and aspirations are bound by a rich web of moral obligations. At the extreme, the bonds are encapsulated in the dictum "Love your neighbor as yourself." The key word in this injunction is, of course, "neighbor." The degree of neighborly closeness invoked to render the requirement comprehensible even as a counsel of perfection is extreme.[12] Although not quite so extreme, the degree of continuing care that would render it reasonable, in Rawls's words, "to share one another's fate" is high. Therefore, the circumstances under which anything approaching these conditions obtains are special and cannot be extrapolated into a general theory of morality, let alone a theory of justice. Instead, the proper starting point for an account of what human beings as such owe each other will presuppose no antecedent ties of affection or association. On what terms, then, is it reasonable for anonymous individuals to interact?

A plausible general morality is necessarily shaped by attention to *reciprocity*. Rational agents will reject any demand to sacrifice some share of their own good so as to confer benefits on moral strangers. Instead, they will put themselves under only those rules and institutional structures from which they deem themselves to be securing benefits that outweigh the costs they

are obliged to bear. The paradigmatic example of reciprocal transaction is trade. When Jones parts with x units of apples in order to secure from Smith y units of oranges, each party judges herself to be rendered better off. Jones need not care about what Smith will do with the apples or, indeed, about Smith's welfare at all. All she needs to know for the transaction to be well-judged from her point of view is that she herself has improved her prospects by agreeing to give up the apples for the oranges. Vice versa for Smith. Note that the parties need not concur with regard to the relative value of oranges to apples in order to fix a contract price for their transaction; indeed, it is precisely because their valuations differ that they transact.

Liberal theorists bring the contract model to their accounts of political association. In two respects, the social contract differs from trading wares: (1) the contract that grounds civil society is multiparty rather than pair-wise; (2) the transactors proffer to each other not some tangible commodity but rather their noninterference.[13] What renders the social contract recognizably contractual, however, is its exemplification of reciprocity understood as mutual benefit. That which each party forgoes is valued from that individual's perspective less than that which is secured. It is only because Jones values Smith's-noninterference-with-Jones more than she does Jones's-interference-with-Smith that it is rational from her perspective to give deference in exchange for getting deference. The result is generalizable.[14]

Although the social contract presents itself as grounding the sovereign state, reciprocal noninterference enjoys a wider, indeed universal, scope in theories of basic human rights. A right is properly basic if and only if it is a claim owed to everyone and held against everyone. Because the relationship in which rights-holders stand to each other is reciprocal, it is also symmetrical. There are no separate classes of givers and receivers, but rather what each gives to others is also received from them. For that reason, duties correlative to basic rights are all negative, refrainings rather than positive performances. Rights to life, liberty, and property are claims not to be killed, not to be imprisoned, not to be stolen from, rather than entitlements to receive life-, liberty-, or property-preserving bounty. The logic of reciprocity supporting universal human rights is identical to that underlying the social contract. That is why it is plausible to extend classical liberalism's regime of noninterference globally, while Rawlsian liberalism, especially its difference principle, does not travel comfortably across borders.

Wherever the further reaches of a theory of international justice lead, if the theory does not commence in an order of reciprocal noninterference, it goes nowhere at all. Perhaps just global institutions can evolve structures transcending noninterference in something like the way that the special relationships among citizens of a liberal regime generate claims and obligations that extend beyond respect for basic rights. However, the indicated analytical starting point is simple noninterference.

This is the method employed by Rawls in developing his law of peoples. At the center of this law are requirements of noninterference, with an additional requirement of fidelity to pacts made and a contingent duty of aid to distressed peoples. Whether the account is inadequate in virtue of lacking strongly egalitarian redistributionist principles is vigorously debated. More open to criticism, I believe, is the absence of principles governing the behavior of peoples toward individual foreign nationals. By his espousal of the case of respect for human rights, Rawls is committed to the seriousness of such principles. Thus, for example, a state/people may not take the life of a foreign national. To do so is not merely to wrong the people to which that individual belongs but, also and more fundamentally, to wrong the person. Similarly, foreigners may not be enslaved, may not be stolen from, and so on. All this may seem too obvious to bear repeating, but if developed in

parallel to intranational liberal theory, the consequences are far-reaching. Just as it is impermissible for Williams to interfere with Smith and Jones so as to prevent their transacting, so too is it a violation of liberty rights for the United States or France or Nigeria to block transactions between willing parties.[15] That holds true just as much for interactions across borders as within them. The noninterference requirement is modest, no more than a pro forma geographical extension of familiar principles of freedom of association within a state. However, if consistently put into practice it would force radical revision of the control that states exercise over their citizens' relations with foreign nationals. It would, in a word, be to establish a liberalism beyond borders.

III. Causes of the Wealth (and Woe) of Nations

Some time between the end of the religious wars of the seventeenth century and the present, human circumstances changed profoundly. Whereas wealth was heretofore very much the exception, now it is the rule. Or to be more precise: in selected locales it is the rule. But we can be more precise still. To oversimplify only slightly, the representative person's prospects for living a tolerably long, prosperous, and decent life are excellent in virtually every location in which there obtains robust protection of private property under the rule of law – that is, wherever liberal structures hold sway. (The only exceptions of which I am aware result from great natural disasters or war.) This result holds both for small island nations and for continental powers; it holds where natural resources are abundant and where they are scarce; it holds in the heart of the developed West and in recently impoverished corners of Asia. Social science is not physics, and the sort of precision exemplified by physical laws is not to be expected in mappings of social phenomena. Yet here if anywhere we have something approaching the status of a general law of societal achievement. The macro-problem of human misery has been solved – in theory but, in far too many venues, not in practice.

Whatever may have been the case some decades back when general prosperity was the special possession only of a small number of populations bordering the Atlantic, and when socialist fancies were the primary domain in which speculations about transformation of the human condition played themselves out, it is no longer credible to proceed on the assumption that poverty around the globe is a phenomenon to be understood in the first instance as the result of stinginess in transfer payments from the rich. If a people can provide for itself a basically liberal order, then its citizens will do well. Otherwise, they are in jeopardy. More effective than the transfer of financial assets from wealthy to poor lands is transfer of the institutional structures within which such assets are generated. One might imagine that accounts of international justice would automatically take this phenomenon as central to their analyses. Egalitarian theories, however, tend to resist or ignore this result. That calls for explanation.

If the dominant reason why poor countries[16] remain poor is because their own institutions are deficient, then the responsibility for the poverty of some is not the wealth of others. Children in America eat well, often too well for their own good, but in Somalia many starve. American plenty does not, however, explain African dearth. The world's wealth is not zero-sum, and thus to consume more is not to visit a harm on those who consume less. Disparities in holdings are, for the most part, explicable by noting how the rich have made themselves rich and the poor have made themselves poor. As Rawls observes, "the problem [of poor countries] is commonly the nature of the public political culture and the religious and philosophical traditions that underlie its institutions. The great social evils in poorer societies are likely to be oppressive government and corrupt

elites."[17] This is not to deny that gross inequalities among peoples are evidence of injustice, but it does strongly suggest that the claims of the world's poor are mostly to be addressed against their own governing institutions. However, in a moral environment in which the greatest of all offenses is to "blame the victim," stating this reasonably evident fact strikes some as indecent. Does it mean that the fortunate citizens of the West (and, increasingly, of other parts of the developed world) are at liberty to shrug off the plight of the world's destitute billions by saying, "That's their doing, not ours"? In a word, no. As I will argue, there is quite enough blame to go around, including blame ascribable to wealthy countries for committing injustices against their own citizens which simultaneously visit hardships on those in other countries who are least able to cope. The aim is not to let wealthy nations off the hook but to urge that they be pegged to the right one.

During the 1980s and 1990s, something on the order of 100 million Chinese were lifted above the dollar-a-day income threshold. This represents the single greatest rollback of abject poverty in the history of the world. That Chinese renaissance continues to accelerate, and alongside it a liftoff of comparable magnitude is occurring in India. Compared to these profound changes in the condition of poor peoples, the impact of foreign aid transfers has been minor. What has made the difference in China, as previously in smaller countries of southeast Asia, is security of property holdings coupled with openness to world markets. Conversely, those nations in which access to capital and enterprise formation are jealously controlled by ideological or kleptocratic state bureaucracies remain places in which prospects for leading decent lives have stagnated. Encouragingly, no Periclean exemplars of wise government have been needed to enable escape from general misery. China remains an undemocratic gerontocracy in which respect for human rights is patchy, especially for those entitlements that are deemed to challenge perquisites of the ruling political class. India, although firmly democratic, still has far to go in loosening the bureaucratic hobbles bequeathed by Fabian-inspired colonial overlords and its first generation of indigenous governors. The good news is that no more than a minimal level of political virtue, most especially the virtue of restraint, is needed to catalyze that initial jump into wealth-creation which then, barring backsliding, becomes self-sustaining.

The bad news, of course, is that too many regimes fall conspicuously short of even that minimal level. It seems hideously unfair that populations should suffer grievously from the failures of their domestic institutions, institutions over which they themselves have virtually no influence. Unfair indeed it is, but this is not an injustice readily addressable by well-meaning external donors. When tens of millions of Chinese citizens were class-struggle casualties of Mao's Great Leap Forward [sic] and then the misbegotten Cultural Revolution of the late 1960s, the injustices from which they suffered were almost entirely domestic in origin. And when they began to benefit from initial forays into the arena of global capitalism, melioration was also predominantly domestic. It is, therefore, misleading to characterize the gross wealth disparities that obtain in different sectors of the world as the subject matter of international (in)justice. These are far more the effect of depredations within borders than across them. That is not to say that poverty in other lands holds no moral relevance for the activities of well-off foreign agencies and individuals, but they are secondary respondents rather than primary instigators. In that restricted capacity, they can do some genuine good, but only if they realistically assess their efficacy.

It is much easier to transfer money than salutary social structures. In the extreme, dollar bills can be shoveled from helicopters to waft to waiting hands below. To the best of my knowledge, foreign aid has never been extended in such aerial form,[18] yet it would have one distinct advantage over formal intergovernmental transfers. Helicopter largesse, despite its windborne randomness, would find its way directly to primary beneficiaries, while aid extended via a stricken population's government passes first into just those hands that have shown themselves to be deficient. At best, funds extended may soften the edges of rough-hewn policies; at worst, they will strengthen the position of whichever thief or tyrant has lately taken up residence in the presidential palace. Because the natural interlocutors of a government are other governments, states are likely to have only limited facility in addressing the plight of distressed foreign populations. Even if there were a requirement of justice to alleviate misfortunes that are not of one's own making, direct foreign aid must be quite far down on the list of measures holding out a promise of efficacy.

A much stronger case can be made, in principle, for direct intervention to force maladroit or malevolent rulers to act on behalf of subject populations. That would be to address the proximate cause of distress rather than to apply financial salve in hit-or-miss fashion. The qualifier, however, looms large. Colonialist paternalism has been out of fashion for the last half-century, and the historical record does not make this a cause of regret. Western powers had their innings in Africa, the Middle East, and Asia; by and large, they did a sorry job of tending to the welfare of those over whom they ruled. There would be no reason at all to feel nostalgic for the reigns of viceroys and colonial governors were it not for the fact that home rule has, in many cases, shown itself to be even more sanguinary and corrupt. Nonetheless, it is now a firmly settled convention of international relations that sovereign states are, apart from exceptional circumstances, to be left alone to make their own way in the world. And when those exceptional circumstances have obtained – in Rwanda in 1994, in Srebrenica in 1995, and now in Darfur – the international community has shown itself to be less than adroit in stemming genocide, let alone establishing the underpinnings of benign social structures. That is not to conclude that foreign intervention is never justified on humanitarian grounds (see Section IV.E), but it is to suggest that this, too, is an uncertain device. America, it seems, did rather well for its client in postwar Japan, rather poorly in Somalia. The jury is still out in Iraq. However, the price of regime change is measured not only in dollars but also in blood. Reluctance on the part of democratic electorates to bear these costs for the sake of benefits that may or may not be bestowed on a distant people is neither surprising nor discreditable. Thus, the role of direct intervention to alter dysfunctional political and economic structures abroad will remain at most a small component of international justice.

IV. Precepts of Liberal International Justice

The preceding section should not be taken as a counsel of despair. The plight of the world's poor does not put them beyond hope. Almost without exception, they are but one step away from getting on the path to prosperity and decency. That step is replacement of malignant sociopolitical structures with tolerably humane and effective ones. With socialist nostrums now consigned to the dustbin of history and with the example of dozens of societies that have successfully made the leap from poverty to adequacy and then along to plenty, it is now well-known what such a transformation entails. It is also well-known what is not required: foreign aid packages, overgrown development bureaucracies, a "third way" that skirts the alleged excesses of both communism and capitalism. These are useless, worse than useless if they are seen as a substitute for commitment to robust property rights and free markets. But to say that embracing market institutions and the rule of law is "all" that is required to lift societies from abject want to increasing plenty is not a prediction that such progress will be widespread or rapid. Cooperation for mutual benefit is one way in which people

can seek to advance their interests, but another is predation by the strong on the weak. Where predatory structures are well-established, they can display depressing stability. Those on top are loath to give up their status to those on whom they fatten, and those on the bottom may have no aspiration burning more intensely in their breast than to turn the tables and despoil their despoilers. Predation is supported by ideologies of racial, national, and religious domination, and these are alive and well in the first decade of the twenty-first century. Moreover, many members of the intelligentsia of wealthy nations partake in esoteric rites of simulated self-flagellation in which they confess the culpability of their societies for the distress of the world's poor. (It is simulation because they exclude themselves from the strata of their societies who are blamed.) Even if not widely believed, they afford cover to those who are content to locate culpability closer to Washington, D.C., and London, say, than to Mogadishu and Damascus. Nor is it a sure thing that those who have leaped onto the train to increasing prosperity will not jump off. Over preceding centuries, peoples have shown a remarkable capacity to wed themselves to policies that lay themselves low; there is no reason except hubris to suppose that we have permanently lost the ability to imitate the lemmings as we jubilantly scramble toward the cliffs.

Nonetheless, and with all disclaimers duly noted, the proper attitude is one of optimism. For the first time in human history, it is at least possible for the entire world's population to live well. This is terrific news! Broadsides headlining wealth disparities between the wealthy 20 percent and the remainder should not be allowed to disguise the epochal significance of this alteration of the human condition. There are innumerable reasons why the world's poor suffer from hunger, disease, and the manifold brutalizations consequent on want and despair, but reluctance by the wealthy societies of the West to admit additional new members into their club is not among them.

If this essay is not a foray into pessimism, neither is it a rationalization of the conduct of the world's wealthy and powerful. To say that they are not the primary perpetrators of global distress is not to find them blameless. I have maintained that most so-called violations of international justice are in fact better understood as rooted in domestic failings, and that nearly all the world's peoples would enjoy lives of decency and prosperity if they were beneficiaries of tolerably adequate internal governance. It is only at the margin that external transactors make a difference – but when summed over billions of persons, these marginal effects are considerable.

Liberalism, especially in its classical version, is a theory about required omissions rather than commissions. To respect the rights of others is first and fundamentally to afford them noninterference. Positive provision of welfare goods is, if present at all, secondary. To extend the theory of liberalism across borders is to commend noninterference by both governments and private parties with foreign nationals. To the extent that this has not been forthcoming, there are justifiable complaints to be lodged against the members of the Organization for Economic Cooperation and Development (OECD) and their fortunate brethren. As with the practice of medicine, the primary and overriding requirement is, first, to do no harm. Insofar as the policies of some states impose harms on the nationals of others, a legitimate claim for redress can be made. This is not the occasion to prepare a comprehensive brief on behalf of the world's have-nots against the haves – or, for that matter, the haves against the have-nots – but the points made in the following five subsections convey a sense of the direction that a liberal account of justice across borders will take.

A. Noncooperation with Oppression

Both the state acting in its official capacity and citizens in their roles as private actors are to refrain from lending assistance to foreign oppressors. To facilitate the violation of rights is itself to be a rights-violator. This is true globally as well as locally. Murder and theft do not change their nature when committed across borders. They are strictly impermissible.

As a programmatic statement of liberal dicta, the foregoing is impeccable. However, application of the principle of nonfacilitation quickly becomes murky in a world of states that exercise authority in ways that deviate significantly from the paradigm of liberal democracies operating under an impersonal rule of law. Consider, for example, loans across state borders from rich to poor made either by governmental agencies, quasi-governmental instrumentalities such as the World Bank, or private lenders. On the one hand, resultant debt burdens fall on subject populations, sometimes weighing heavily for generations. Typically without any prior concurrence on their part, their meager income streams are encumbered to satisfy the demands of wealthy foreign note holders. On the other hand, access to capital is a necessary ingredient for lifting a people out of want and into contact with the markets in which wealth is generated. To decline to take on external debt is to acquiesce to continued poverty. What, then, is a conscientious lender to do? There exists no algorithm that yields answers satisfactory for all cases. Still, there are some general guidelines for respecting the interests of vulnerable populations. All else equal, loans that create only voluntarily assumed indebtedness are to be preferred to those that inflate tax burdens. Direct investment by foreign corporations or joint ventures with domestic parties satisfy this criterion unless they come attached to "guarantees" offered by the host state. Money extended directly to sovereign borrowers is more suspect, especially when there is no mechanism for containing it within national borders so that it does not take flight to nest in anonymous Swiss bank accounts. However, improvements in infrastructure – roads, education, health-care facilities – that are required for economic advancement and that will pay for themselves many times over in increased national productivity often can only be supplied through public funds. In such cases, it makes good economic and moral sense for responsible states to borrow and for conscientious dispensers of capital to lend. The problem is to tell these cases apart. Perhaps the fairest and most reliable means for getting situations like this right is to ensure that much or all of the risk of subsequent inability to repay falls on the lender. That way self-interest, if not a robust sense of justice, will lead lenders to do their homework before extending credit.

Similar considerations apply with regard to transnational corporations' access to labor and physical resources. For rulers who find vexingly slow the rate of cash flow into their coffers generated by taxes extracted from an impoverished citizenry, an occasion to secure personal emoluments from wealthy foreign firms in exchange for concessionary grants will be a welcome windfall. Between functionaries of the state and corporate buccaneers, not much may be left for those who do the laboring. But if exploitation of laborers by their own rulers is avoided, the entry of corporations from abroad affords welcome opportunities. Would-be Western well-wishers are wont to denounce as exploitative the low salaries and onerous working conditions that are offered to employees in developing countries, but those workers who find the terms of employment offered by branches of transnational corporations by far their best available opportunity will wish that they could bask yet more deeply in such "exploitation."[19]

Liberal principles of international justice, then, are friendly to cross-border economic transactions insofar as they do not incorporate coercion by local authorities. Transnational firms themselves do not threaten the rights of host populations, because it is almost never the case that businesses are in a position to exert undue pressure on their workers without the complicity of local authorities. If in pursuit of

accommodating labor relations, however, businesses accept authorities' offers of truncheons and prison cells so as to deny laborers an option of free exit, then they stand as co-perpetrators of injustice. Ultimately, estimations of where to draw lines with regard to acceptable lending, investment, and employment must avoid the opposed tendencies of utopianism and a cynicism that passes as realism. Transactional partners are rarely economic or moral paragons. Rejecting deals with parties tainted by oppressive, even murderous activities, would mean that even those states perched toward the high end of the spectrum of respect for individual rights would be barred from dealing with themselves! (Consider, for example, the 1993 killing of David Koresh and his followers by federal agents in Waco, Texas; or the systematic British humiliation of Irish prisoners.) Judgments must always be made at the margin: Is the proposed relationship more likely to nudge subject peoples toward decency and prosperity than to tighten the vise of their misery? Where money and power are at stake, honest responses are hard to come by, but, one must hope, not impossible.

B. Revising the Public/Private Aid Mix

Liberal international justice ought to be suspicious of government-to-government aid packages. Typically they come with strings attached. Superpowers shop for allies, and the foreign policy of mid-level states is often in the service of domestic commercial interests. On the recipient side, political elites who control aid distribution may be motivated by private interests that diverge from those of the populations they allegedly serve. States operate in a less ambiguous capacity, however, when they facilitate person-to-person aid between nongovernmental donors and targeted recipients. They are well-positioned to deploy their good offices to persuade rulers of host nations at least not to interfere with such aid arrangements. Simple state noninterference may be all that is needed to make a substantial difference. There is good reason to expect aid offered by private charitable agencies to be more effective and benevolent than that tendered politically. Because nongovernmental agencies are not able to secure funds through coercive extraction, and because they serve a simple agenda of doing some good abroad, they are apt to be more responsive than are state bureaus both to the donors who support their philanthropies and to the intended beneficiaries.

It may be asked whether enough assistance will be forthcoming under general privatization of the international assistance business. The question is ill-defined without some prior specification of what is meant by "enough." Even under the most optimistic forecast, it must be conceded that sums extended by charitable donors will not suffice to put impoverished peoples on a path to prosperity. That is not because individuals acting in a private capacity are less generous than governments, but because the necessary conditions for achieving general well-being are mostly domestic and only secondarily capable of being supplied by external grantors. Even if privatization of aid would result in smaller sums crossing borders, itself a speculative forecast, it is predictable that a much lesser fraction would be diverted to enrich corrupt authorities or be wasted on showy projects that better serve the interests of elites than those of needier segments of the population. Furthermore, private aid would have what from a liberal perspective must be the considerable advantage of being voluntarily tendered rather than coercively extracted. The interests of both givers and recipients count, and these interests are respected by an order of voluntary philanthropic relations.

Although anecdotes can take us only so far in reflecting on principles of international justice, it is worth observing that in response to disasters such as the December 2004 tsunami, individuals and charitable organizations across the world opened their pockets to assist devastated populations. Less spectacular, but no less estimable, are the continuing philanthropies of organizations such as Oxfam and the Bill and Melinda Gates Foundation. Governments and quasi-governmental agencies can genuinely contribute to the efficacy of those activities by quietly exerting influence on host governments not to block charitable transfers and to desist from siphoning off funds. They also can assist with transportation, communications, and accumulation of materiel in response to acute crises. But basically the role of the state should be secondary.[20] Moreover, it is to be expected that as governmental agencies gradually shed their role as leading players within the aid business, entrepreneurial charities would come up with innovative ways of occupying the territory ceded to them. "Crowding out" would be replaced by "crowding in." Critics will contend that the scenario depicted is rosily optimistic, that the actual accomplishments of an order of privatized aid are apt to fall short of these depictions. These critics may well be correct. However, it is not as if the practice of state-dominated aid that has obtained since the end of the Second World War has shown itself to be signally successful – else it would no longer be needed. Rather than calling for "more of the same," liberal principles of international assistance endorse substantial restructuring of the roles of private and public parties, according priority to the former.

C. Justice in Trade

Liberal support for loosening shackles that constrain trade across borders is more crucial than ever. Ready access to foreign markets is not merely an economic desideratum at the fringes of national economies but a necessary condition for lifting populations out of poverty. The argument for free trade has been thoroughly and consistently set out for more than two centuries. If intellectual merit sufficed to generate policy victories, protectionism would now be as defunct as the dodo. But impartial theorizing is apt to take a back seat to the play of interests, and those whose livelihoods depend on buying and selling rarely will oppose on principle measures that promise to shield them from some degree of competition. Thus, freeing up trade is not a battle that is won once and for all, but is rather an endless series of forays, each of which has to be fought anew. Today the campaign against open markets is waged most noticeably in the media and the streets by "anti-globalization" cadres, an ill-matched assortment from across the political spectrum who unite only on a platform of substituting political for economic parameters in governing production and exchange. One of the banners under which they march, "Fair trade, not free trade," explicitly represents the campaign as one for justice. Liberals will, of course, reject the implied opposition between freedom and fairness. The freedom of willing parties to transact on terms they find mutually agreeable is of the essence of fair dealing. Conversely, imposition of terms by third parties who foist their own interests and ideals on unwilling others is the epitome of injustice. But this is a very old tune that need not be rehearsed here.

However one interprets nuances of fairness and freedom, it is apparent that poor nations suffer from sins against both in the global marketplace. Extensive programs of tariffs, quotas, and subsidies distort markets for those primary commodities, especially agricultural goods, that are mainstays of the fledgling economies of these countries. Not only is it difficult for them to compete against the technological sophistication and efficiency of producers in the United States and Europe, but in addition they must contend with the subsidies these wealthy countries bestow on their own producers. These subsidies lead to underpricing of weaker competitors, which effectively bars them from international markets. The result is that wealthy corporate producers of crops such as cotton earn handsome profits while African workers of the land starve. In the postwar period, the various

installments of the General Agreement on Tariffs and Trade (GATT) and its successor, the World Trade Organization (WTO), have enjoyed signal success in lowering trade barriers. The result has been an unprecedented growth of international trade and the prosperity resulting therefrom. Not all parties, however, have benefited at this high level. Too many economies languish. That is not all to be laid at the door of the WTO, but it is presumptive evidence that the job of liberalizing the world market is far from complete.

Because economic activity is positive-sum, all parties are benefited by arrangements that afford them greater scope for undertaking beneficial transactions. Lowering trade barriers is not a "gift" to foreign entrants, but rather advances also the interests of domestic producers and consumers who thereby secure access to desired commercial relations. Therefore, each sovereign entity has self-interested reasons to liberalize markets regardless of what other states do. However, each does better still if those others also eschew protection. This is one reason why the game of trade negotiation often features states refusing to dismantle barriers unless other states reciprocate by offering corresponding relaxations.[21] It is possible, then, especially in a setting where the number of players is great and their interests diverse, that they remain indefinitely blocked from agreeing on measures that benefit everyone, each player holding out for terms that are yet more favorable from its own perspective. This is a fair characterization of recent stumbling at the 2004 WTO meetings in Doha, Qatar, in which rich countries demanded, among other provisions, enhanced protection for intellectual property rights, poor countries more welcoming markets for agricultural exports, never the twain managing to meet. Liberal theorists have no difficulty in characterizing such nonagreement for mutual disadvantage as ludicrously counterproductive and unjust. The theorists' expertise does not, however, extend to deriving tactics calculated to break such impasses. But as the diplomats continue to play their tortuous games, spectators on the sidelines ought to proclaim in a loud voice that while all protectionism perpetrates injustice, insult is added to injury by those barriers that especially disadvantage the poor. If it is impossible to brush away webs of restriction with one sweeping gesture, then first priority should be given to the elimination of those barriers most directly implicated in destitution and despair.

Some social philosophers, Thomas Pogge chief among them, have argued that deformities in international trade structures constitute actionable wrongs inflicted by the rich on the poor, and that these support a call for massive reparations to be made in the form of cash transfers.[22] For several reasons the call is misdirected. First, the timing is backwards. Before demanding of parties that they repair damages caused by their unjust policies, they must be persuaded that those policies are indeed wrong. In a world in which protection still carries (unmerited) respectability, demands for reparations are, at the very least, premature. Second, this is a thinly disguised plea for intergovernmental aid transfers, a less good medicine for the ills of poverty than is a grant of free access to markets. Third and most fundamentally, it confuses the nature of the harms done by the international trade regime. The OECD high-flyers are labeled culprits who unjustly enrich themselves at the expense of the world's poor. This is to buy into the protectionist fable that a country advances itself by erecting barriers to imports. From the early years of liberal theory, this conception has been put to the test and found wanting. What is objectionable about subsidies, quotas, and tariffs is not that these are techniques of hard-dealing via which the rich get richer and the poor get poorer. Rather, they are no less welfare-diminishing domestically than they are internationally. If, for example, cheap foreign textiles are not allowed into the United States, then would-be American consumers are made worse off for the advantage of American clothes

manufacturers. If African cotton cannot compete with American cotton because the latter benefits from substantial subsidies, then domestic cotton growers are being unfairly enriched at the expense of all other Americans – and, of course, at the expense of foreign producers. And so on with regard to the myriad gothic adornments of the world trade order. Their primary damage is intranational, not international.

The reason I focus on this point is because it spotlights with special clarity what is distinctive about the liberal understanding – an avowedly *classical liberal* understanding – of international justice advanced in this essay. Using some parties against their will as mere means for the ends of others is wrong wherever it is practiced. Crossing borders does not cleanse the practice. However, domestic forced redistributions that impose costs on some population segments so as to shower benefits on others are enthusiastically cheered by egalitarians of both liberal and anti-liberal persuasions. They accord to these redistributions the honorific rubric "social justice." But then when a practice warmly endorsed within states is seen to exacerbate hardships in distant lands, convoluted justificatory scrambling follows. Somehow, what is wrong with the European Union's Common Agricultural Policy has to be spelled out in a manner that does not impugn the EU's commitment to a sweeping range of internal controls and transfers.[23] Without recapitulating the entire social justice debate, starting with the first page of Rawls's *A Theory of Justice*, it is not possible to demonstrate in detail why this is a vain hope. Rawls himself bites the bullet of confining substantial redistribution within national borders, thus disappointing those followers who wish to extend the demands of (re)distributive justice into a seamless cosmopolitan theory.[24] They take the sharp difference between Rawls's theories of domestic and international justice to represent a debilitating inconsistency. Perhaps it does. But a more glaring inconsistency is to defend sacrifices imposed by a national politics of redistribution on some segments of the citizenry in order to benefit others while decrying the same when the victims are foreign nationals. A considerable advantage of the classical liberal theory of justice is that it exhibits greater continuity within and across borders than do any of the rival accounts.

D. Free Movement Across Borders

Most of the reasons supporting free movements of goods and services across borders also support free movement for individuals. The lines on a map that separate Mexicans from Americans or the European-Ins from the European-Outs are morally arbitrary, yet on which side one happens to have landed is liable to make an enormous difference for one's life prospects. To be blocked from buying and selling across borders is an unjustifiable restraint on liberty, but so also are general barriers against cross-border employment and residence agreements.[25]

There are two chief reasons why movement of persons across borders can be more problematic than movement of products: security concerns and financial entailments. A widget purchased from abroad is inert; it lies there until put to the service that widgets perform. But immigrants exercise agency. As no one needs to be reminded post–September 11, 2001, some intend harm to the country they have entered. Migrants who are utterly benign in their intentions need food, shelter, and occasional health services. They produce children who require these basic goods and educational services as well. For those who carry along with them a handsome asset portfolio or who are lucratively remunerated, meeting basic needs is not a problem. But the much greater number who are accompanied across borders only by their poverty may be deemed a significant potential drain on resources. As with the potentially hostile, their exclusion is justified on grounds of self-interest.

It is not possible to offer more than a cursory response to these two worries. Against the former, it is conceded that addressing security concerns is a legitimate function of the state, indeed its central function. The necessity of thwarting would-be malefactors, both domestic and external, should condition all state policies. Freedom of movement is a deeply held liberal principle, but it may permissibly be constrained by legitimate security concerns. Nonetheless, and with all due acknowledgment of the grim realities that have intruded into twenty-first century consciousness, it is simply not credible to maintain that the vast bulk of immigration poses any significant security threat. The tens of thousands of Mexicans who each year cross the Rio Grande, either legally or otherwise, do not enter the United States to do it harm. Their motives of self-advancement are transparent. So too for the vast majority of those who seek to work or study in Europe, Australia, and the other wealthy OECD countries. Reasonable persons will differ concerning the nature of immigration controls needed at entry points to address legitimate security concerns, but on even the most conservative reckoning, such measures will not exclude any large number of potential economic entrants.

The financial drain objection cuts more deeply. With a few dishonorable exceptions (e.g., restrictions on Chinese nationals), the United States throughout the nineteenth century and into the first two decades of the twentieth was, to its enduring credit, a land that threw open its borders to millions of individuals who wished to commence a new life under new skies. The United States is still one of the world's major recipients of immigration, but with many more restrictions on would-be entrants. What has changed in the interim? Prospects for personal advancement in America have not waned, nor has the ability of the economy to support increased numbers. The U.S. population has not become more insular in its vistas or more viciously nativist in its prejudices. Rather, the transformative process that most strikingly conditions immigration policy in the United States (and other traditional magnets for migrants) is the rise of the welfare state. To be on the lucky side of the border is to be in possession of a brass ring that entitles one to a wide variety of benefits, courtesy of the public treasury. It is no wonder that residents of well-off states in which taxation supports extensive welfare functions are disinclined to welcome impoverished entrants likely to be net subtractors from the pie to be carved up. Professionals and investors, yes; poor, tired, huddled masses, no.

Although some will cast blame on the greed of a grasping, inhospitable bourgeoisie, I do not share that assessment. A desire to possess and augment one's property is both honorable and the engine of economic advance. What is unfortunate is that in combination with the characteristic form of contemporary Western social democracies, this desire harshly damages the prospects of countless individuals who are stymied from relocating to where their lives would go better. I believe that the optimal resolution of this dilemma would be wholesale rolling back of the welfare state. That, of course, is utopian (others will say dystopian!) fantasy – if not forever, then at least for the foreseeable future. However, intermediate means are available for relaxing the firmness of borders while nonetheless maintaining politically popular redistributionist measures. For example, individuals could be allowed to enter at will, but with an express proviso that they and their families would not be permitted to avail themselves of any of the state's welfare services for a stipulated period. Although it is much preferable to current policies of exclusion, such a measure would almost certainly prove to be unsustainable.[26] To observe people sick from hunger and inadequate shelter, who are then denied health services for which they are unable to pay, and who lack the means to provide even basic education for their children, would be intolerable. Of course, such is the plight of vastly greater numbers of individuals living in destitution abroad, people whose prospects would skyrocket

if they were allowed to immigrate even under a no-welfare proviso, but not having actually to experience them close-up is wonderful balm to the conscience.

What may under current circumstances be the least bad policy would be to allow entry to all individuals who provide a surety that they are not likely to be a charge on the public.[27] This condition could, for example, be satisfied by posting a bond. The evident problem with this device is that penniless migrants are in no position to comply. However, others of like nationality, religion, or family connection (or charitable agencies) may choose to vouch for and provide surety for entrants. This has the great advantage of substantially privatizing immigration policy decisions. In addition, those immigrants in possession of a bona fide employment offer on terms such that they are thereby enabled to support themselves at a minimally decent level – where minimal decency is understood not as may be conceived by rich Westerners but relative to the standards that obtain in the countries from which the immigrants fled – would be deemed to have provided the requisite surety. Note that this policy is responsive not only to the interests of those desirous of entering the country but also to the rights of would-be employers to enter into mutually advantageous contractual relationships. To keep a tight lid on borders is to restrict the liberties not only of foreigners but also of citizens. Here again, the conclusions of international justice are congruent with those of intranational justice.

I do not deny that there are numerous complications that will have to be addressed in giving effect to these proposals. What happens when an immigrant loses her job or is exploited by a threat of being fired with deportation to follow? For how long a period must someone reside in the country and post a record of acceptable conduct before being accorded the full rights and privileges of residents? And so on. Without denying that these are legitimate concerns, and without having a grab-bag full of remedies on offer, I content myself with noting that in these considerations we are far from the world of ideal theory. The appropriate question to ask with regard to the desirability of any policy proposal is: Compared to what? Rendering borders less inimical to possibilities of human flourishing, if only at the margin, is a worthwhile aspiration of liberal theorizing.

Let me address two related matters before moving on. First, the principle propounded here radically revises current international legal practices that privilege refugees fleeing persecution over "mere" economic migrants. The former have a right against the host nation to be harbored (assuming that they are able to show their fear of persecution to be well-justified), while the latter do not, even if they can prove that they are escaping destitution. This I take to be backwards. Refugees ought indeed be accorded sanctuary, but the basis of their pull on our moral sensibilities is compassion or pity rather than justice in a strict sense. Observe that refugees must be sheltered even if doing so imposes significant costs on the receiver state. Economic migrants who are self-supporting or supported by willing private parties impose no direct costs on unwilling others, and thus their exclusion cannot be justified on grounds of defense of one's property. Why, then, the priority accorded refugees? I believe that the rationale is less a matter of concern for the persecuted than a handy pretext for barring the gates against all others. Is this belief cynical? Yes. Is it more accurate than not? Readers are invited to hazard a response. In saying that, from the perspective of justice, economic migrants possess the more substantial claim, I am not advocating withdrawal of sanctuary from refugees. To shield defenseless victims is admirable. Rather, the contention is that denying means of bettering their lot to those who do not satisfy the lawyers' criteria for being considered refugees is disgraceful.

Second, critics may contend that opening borders does not solve the problems of poor nations, and may indeed exacerbate them by allowing a brain-drain – and a labor-drain, and an ambition-drain – from venues where human as well as physical capital is in short supply. I concede the point. Relaxing border stringency will not erase those yawning inequalities and vast stretches of misery that are generated by the incompetence and brutality of the institutions of dysfunctional states. The problems that beset severely disadvantaged peoples are only slightly softened by the proposal. Unlike Rawls, however, I do not take the primary, let alone exclusive, focus of international justice to be *peoples*, but rather *people*. It is incompatible with basic liberal principles to hold individuals hostage to the collective entities, the "peoples," from which they would separate themselves. Hospitality to migrants is only a small component of international justice, but it is indispensable.

E. Humanitarian Intervention

On any given day, deliberate campaigns of murder and despoliation carried out by the powerful against the powerless generate mounds of corpses and crowds of displaced persons. As this paragraph is being composed, the Darfur region of Sudan is a notorious example. A few years earlier, the examples that would have come to mind were genocidal rampage in Rwanda, "ethnic cleansing" in the Balkans, Maoist slaughter of class enemies, and, paradigmatic for our time and perhaps all time, the Holocaust. If there has been any period of recent history in which these barbarisms have been absent, I am not aware of it. Certainly any theory of international justice has to take cognizance of such crimes against humanity. And yet . . .

Some problems do not admit of solution. Massacre is not one of them. Indeed, in virtually every such case the solution is transparently simple: let the perpetrators desist! The derivative problem is that they do not choose to do so, and to this there may indeed be no solution. More specifically, there may be no solution accessible to well-meaning external parties. What can be done about Darfur? Rephrase the question as: What can the United States/Europe/the United Nations/you-and-I do about Darfur? No doubt there are better and worse responses to each of these question-variations. The dispiriting fact of the matter may be, however, that against these greatest of injustices, no very good response is available to any party able and willing to make a difference. Perhaps sit-ins and public demonstrations are called for, not because they promise to alleviate the distress of those who are suffering, but because the alternative is to lend accommodation to evil by silence.

The best I am able to offer here are platitudes, but because not offering platitudes is offering nothing at all, platitudes it will be. Platitude number one is that those who are in a position effectively (and without imposing undue costs on non consenting others) to intervene should do so. This principle has extensive application to officials of those regimes that are superintending the killing, but may have limited scope for all others. The party most capable of addressing the ongoing misery of the North Korean masses is Kim Jong Il. The parties next most capable of taking action are North Korean military officers in a position to stage a coup or an assassination. Perhaps the Chinese government can exercise useful suasion, although even in these post–Tiananmen Square years, their hands are far from clean with regard to the practice of domestic oppression. But beyond these levels, the capacity of others to intervene effectively may be vanishingly small.

Platitude number two is that those unable to rectify the evil ought at least to try not to exacerbate it. Propping up great tyrants is to be avoided, even when those tyrants are useful allies in some international venture. Unfortunately, even this platitude is no better than a prima facie principle. During World War II, it was right and necessary for the Allied powers to lend support to Stalin in the fight against the Axis powers, even though Stalin remains high on the list of World's Greatest Despots. Nonetheless, and with all due acknowledgment of the manifold epistemic hurdles to be surmounted in determining whom to take on as an ally, not every crusade is as crucial for the maintenance of civilization as that against Hitler. There is a very strong presumption in favor of undermining rather than cooperating with tyrants. The leaders of liberal democracies have not always lent to that presumption the weight that it merits.

Platitude number three is that failure to intervene against murderous regimes can carry an exorbitantly high cost, but also that intervention itself can carry an exorbitantly high cost. Which of these is likely to be greater will often be unclear prospectively and even retrospectively. Without wishing to add fuel to contemporary debates, I note that the series of U.S. encounters with Saddam Hussein and Iraq – from initial support in Iraq's war against Iran, through the first Gulf War, the blockade and sanctions, the second Gulf War, and the subsequent reconstruction – has been such that at every stage reasonable persons can and do disagree about policy decisions. Issues of trade policy are (relatively) easy; issues surrounding relations with rogue regimes are excruciatingly difficult.

Platitude number four is that between forcibly intervening and refraining from intervention, there exists a standing presumption in favor of the latter. This may indeed be seen as nonplatitudinous, indeed erroneous, by those of a Wilsonian temperament. For them, the presumption is instead to seize opportunities where one finds them to make the world safe for democracy, or safe for whatever other ideal commands the day. The rationale for the platitude is not that Wilsonians are bound to do more harm than good, although I suspect that this may well be the case. Rather, the presumption against intervention appeals because of a very strong underlying presumption against pursuing valued ends by dragooning the lives and resources of others. The broken bodies of conscripts are as much battlefield fodder when the cause is just as when it is not. All-volunteer armies are funded by nonvoluntary taxation. In a world bearing marked affinities to the Hobbesian state of nature, coercive incursions on citizens are sometimes necessary, but they are to be kept to a minimum. That is why this principle is indeed a platitude within liberalism.

Platitude number five commends to all civilized states the task of seeking to devise fairer and more effective means of maintaining international order. There can be little disagreement with the observation that unilateral interventionary thrusts by superpowers for ostensibly humanitarian ends tend to work out rather less well than advertised in advance by their proponents. There can also be little disagreement with the observation that multilateral humanitarian operations also tend to work out less well than might be desired. And, of course, failures to intervene also may prove disastrous. The technology of international cooperation for humanitarian ends remains primitive. Certainly the United Nations as it is currently structured is a weak reed – although in some circumstances the strongest available. It may be that the various special interests of the several states thwarts all possibility of disinterested cooperation for the good of others. If so, then the need is to contrive some mechanism where, as in economic markets, an invisible hand transforms self-interest into the common good. Perhaps no such mechanism can be invented, but this cannot be known prior to serious, sustained attempts to achieve it.

V. Conclusion

Imagine the world as a board with many squares large and small. On some squares, chips are piled high, while others are almost vacant. The difference in size among piles is objectionable. The problem for a theory of justice can be conceived as devising a mechanism for transferring chips from where they are plentiful to where they are few. The viewpoint taken is external, that of a benevolent and impartial spectator rather than that of a square occupant. The viewpoint is also fundamentally prospective. Although some attention may be given to the historical record of how the piles grew or shrank, the aim of the exercise is not to evaluate the quality of preceding moves in the game as essayed by the various players, but rather to derive a strategy for moving toward pile equalization.

The checkerboard model is much too simplified to be pinned to any of the sophisticated philosophical theories of international justice that have been advanced over the more than three decades since the appearance of Rawls's *A Theory of Justice*. Nonetheless, both its inclusions and its exclusions provide a useful framework for assessing that literature. Certainly the model cannot be faulted for insisting that the absence in many locales of a minimally sufficient supply of goods constitutes a central issue for political morality, although perhaps it too exclusively assesses the moral imperative under the rubric of justice rather than generosity or compassion. Nor is the model to be faulted for observing that some wealth piles are many times larger than others. That observation is important if for no other reason than to identify these oases of plenty as objects of aspiration and potential emulation. If, however, the model then presumes that some piles are low *because* others are high, and that the well-endowed squares *act unjustly* unless they transfer some quantity of their chips to those that have little, it has taken a step too far. Why penury obtains where it does, which parties are obligated to act to alleviate it, and how that alleviation can be brought about are not data to be brought to the formulation of a theory of justice but rather theorems that are yielded by its construction. Both the externalism and the prospective reasoning of the checkerboard model must be modified by attention to how the occupants of the various squares appraise the trajectories that have landed them on their spots and the reasons they have from these various perspectives to respond to claims that might be lodged against them.

This essay has attempted to supply a framework for such investigations that is recognizably liberal and, thus, that propounds an account of international justice as continuous in the foundational principles it endorses with those of intranational justice. Rawls is frequently held by his critics to have failed to achieve such continuity. They propose to remedy that lapse by instituting a global difference principle or some similarly sweeping structure of cosmopolitan governance. By way of contrast, the account offered here derives from a more traditional liberalism of respect for persons' liberty and property. It contends that the persistence of poverty has much to do with the malformed domestic institutions of dysfunctional states, that hoped-for turnarounds will, therefore, mostly come from internal restructuring (if at all), and that wealthy peoples are obligated to support such efforts but are neither required nor in a position to be their primary engine. As that not-quite-liberal political theorist Deng Xiaoping observed, "To be wealthy is glorious!" – not a mark for recrimination. Acts of commission or omission that deprive others of opportunities to obtain wealth of their own are, however, injustices. Wealthy and powerful states have a duty not to lend assistance to despots who despoil subject populations, as well as duties to support (but not supplant) international philanthropies that directly address the needs of indigent persons as distinguished from their governors, to dismantle barriers to trade and migration, and to seek better international structures for precluding and responding to gross human rights violations.

One part of the program of international justice concerns the duties that peoples owe to each other. But another and arguably more fundamental part concerns obligations owed to individual persons both within and beyond national borders. To a much greater extent than is generally acknowledged, mandated transfers among citizens of a state and politically imposed restrictions on their liberty to transact with nonresidents foist burdens on non consenting others. Some of these burdens are local; others extend across the globe, with devastating effects on those least able to bear them. It is myopic to decry the latter while complacently accepting the former. I conclude by suggesting that the version of liberalism most suitable as a theoretical grounding for both internal and external dealings more closely resembles that of Adam Smith than that of John Rawls.

Notes

1 See Immanuel Kant, *Perpetual Peace*, in H. S. Reiss, ed., *Kant: Political Writings* (Cambridge: Cambridge University Press, 1970), 93–130.

2 See Christopher Morris, *An Essay on the Modern State* (New York: Cambridge University Press, 1998).

3 John Rawls, *A Theory of Justice* (Cambridge, MA: Harvard University Press, 1971).

4 John Rawls, *The Law of Peoples* (Cambridge, MA: Harvard University Press, 1999).

5 See, for example, Charles Beitz, *Political Theory and International Relations* (Princeton, NJ: Princeton University Press, 1979); and Thomas Pogge, *Realizing Rawls* (Ithaca, NY: Cornell University Press, 1990).

6 The difference principle is, of course, the principle that in a just society, social and economic inequalities are to be arranged so that they work to the greatest benefit of the least advantaged. See Rawls, *A Theory of Justice*, section 13.

7 See, for example, Peter Singer, "Famine, Affluence, and Morality," *Philosophy and Public Affairs* 1 (1972): 229–43; and Larry Temkin, "Thinking about the Needy: Justice and International Organizations," *Journal of Ethics* 8 (2004): 349–95.

8 Rawls, *A Theory of Justice*, 16. But see also John Rawls, *Political Liberalism* (New York: Columbia University Press, 1993), 53 n. 7, for a partial retraction of this characterization.

9 Rawls, *A Theory of Justice*, 102.

10 I make this objection in "Libertarianism at Twin Harvard," *Social Philosophy and Policy* 22, no. 1 (2005): 178–99. Rawls himself may have been implicitly reconsidering the applicability of this conception when, in the revised edition of *A Theory of Justice*

(Cambridge, MA: Harvard University Press, 1999), he omitted without explanation the "share one another's fate" sentence. Possibly, his own later work on international justice had persuaded him to moderate this aspect of the theory, but that is speculation.

11 Rawls, *The Law of Peoples*, 37.

12 "Good fences make good neighbors" stands at the opposite extreme.

13 A third respect in which they might differ is if the social contract is stipulated to be tacit or hypothetical, perhaps entered into behind a veil of ignorance. No further attention will be paid to these complications.

14 This is not a theorem of the abstract theory of rationality but rather presupposes a certain view of human nature. Only if people by and large place higher value on being left alone to advance their own projects than they do on meddling with the projects of others will they subscribe to an order of mutual forbearance. Classical social contract theories attempt in different ways to embed mutual and reciprocal willingness to forgo meddling into their accounts.

15 Strictly speaking, this claim should bear a *ceteris paribus* qualifier. If the transaction between A and B incorporates infliction of a material harm on C, then principles of self-defense legitimate C's acting so as to block the arrangement. In this respect, international transactions do not differ from domestic ones.

16 Selecting an appropriate term to refer to those states in which per-capita income hovers perilously close to the destitution line is difficult. Speaking of them as "developing countries" blissfully ignores the key problem that most are conspicuously failing to develop. "Third World nations" was lamentably vague when the Soviet Union pretended to be a functional regime and is just plain innumerate now. "Burdened society" seems to suggest an external burdener; "failed state" is pessimistic and abruptly final. I shall for the most part, then, unimaginatively speak of poor and wealthy countries.

17 Rawls, *The Law of Peoples*, 77.

18 The 1948–49 Berlin airlift comes close.

19 Denunciations of the degrading nature of working conditions abroad are especially suspect when offered by parties such as labor unions who stand as competitors to these foreign enterprises.

20 It might be objected that coercion by the state is needed to overcome what decision theorists call an "assurance problem." Citizens, it is claimed, might individually have some desire to act philanthropically, but they will contribute only if they are confident that others will also contribute. Without some mechanism affording assurance to each citizen of the similar compliance of the others, the philanthropic preference will go unrealized. Mandated tax contributions thus not only bring about a valuable result but also give effect to the predilections people already hold.

The story, although not impossible, is far-fetched. That many people really do strongly desire themselves and their compatriots to be taxed more heavily so as to swell foreign aid budgets seems to be confirmed neither by opinion polls nor by the observed politics of national budget-making. Nor is it evident that most people's charitable impulses are so strongly contingent on the behavior of others. It is an open question whether an order of privatized international aid would be hobbled by widespread tendencies to free-ride, and it is best answered by putting the hypothesis to the test.

21 Another important reason is that while economies as a whole will benefit from increased openness, there will always be some parties disadvantaged by widening the scope of competition. If they are politically potent, they may be able to block agreement.

22 See Thomas Pogge, "'Assisting' the Global Poor," in Deen K. Chatterjee, ed., *The Ethics of Assistance: Morality and the Distant Needy* (Cambridge: Cambridge University Press, 2004), 260–88.

23 French opponents of the proposed European Constitution successfully engineered its May 2005 referendum defeat in part by decrying its "extreme Anglo-Saxon liberalism." Despite whatever other grounds on which their appraisal of the proposed constitution was misjudged, they accurately diagnosed the intrinsic opposition between the welfare state's forced redistributions and the fundamental precepts of political and economic liberalism.

24 See, for example, the authors cited in note 5 above.

25 I develop a fuller response to the implications of morally arbitrary borders for trade and migration in "Toward a Liberal Theory of National Boundaries," in David Miller and Sohail Hashmi, eds., *Boundaries and Justice* (Princeton, NJ: Princeton University Press, 2001), 55–78.

26 Nor would it likely pass muster with courts either in the United States or in the European Union.

27 I say "not likely" because, for example, a net contributor may become a net subtractor by committing a crime and then consuming resources of the judicial and penal systems. This is true for both citizens and immigrants; in fact, citizens may be more likely to become net subtractors, insofar as one available cost-cutting sentence that can be employed against alien felons is deportation.

Glossary

Anarchism—As a philosophic doctrine, anarchism is the view that no state is justified; that all purported political authority is illegitimate.

Communitarianism—Refers to a family of political theories united by their rejection of liberalism's universalism and individualism, and their stress upon the importance of the social nature of the individual and political life in general.

Consequentialism—The moral doctrine that the consequences of an action (or policy) are the only criteria for its rightness or wrongness. Opposed to deontology.

Cosmopolitanism—The idea that all human beings, regardless of their political affiliation, belong to a common moral community. Cosmopolitans often believe that all individuals have the same basic moral status, and tend to downplay the importance or desirability of national political institutions. Opposed to nationalism.

Deontology—Refers to a family of moral theories that trace their roots to Immanuel Kant. Deontologists believe that morality is a matter of fulfilling duties and/or respecting rights, even when the effect of remaining committed to this principle are less than optimific. Opposed to consequentialism.

Difference Principle—The more widely discussed of Rawls' two principles of justice, this principle holds that social and economic equalities are to be tolerated only if the effect of allowing them is to benefit the least well-off members of society.

Distributive Justice—That area of philosophy concerned with the moral principles that ought to govern the allocation of benefits and burdens amongst individuals and groups.

Externalities—An economic term that refers to costs or benefits of an activity that are borne by persons not directly party to that activity. Negative (costly) externalities are often thought of as a market failure and a justification for corrective action by government.

Liberalism—Philosophically, liberalism refers not just to "left-wing" political positions, as it does in contemporary American politics, but to all political positions that share a commitment to the idea that political institutions are to be morally assessed by their effects on individuals, that are committed to the value of individual liberty, and that tend to favor (relatively) restricted government in order to secure this liberty.

Libertarianism—The doctrine that no more (or not much more) than a minimal state—one that provides police, military, and a court system — is morally legitimate; that government should be restricted to the protection of individual negative liberty; and that most functions currently provided by the state should be left to the market mechanism or other voluntary methods of provision.

Nationalism—The view that nations and national identity are deeply important values that ought to be protected by social norms and political institutions. This position bears some affinity with communitarianism and is most directly opposed to cosmopolitanism.

Natural Law—Natural law theorists trace their roots to St. Thomas Aquinas, and hold that there are objective moral truths that hold simply in virtue of human nature and the nature of the human world, and that these truths indicate a natural human good. Often, but not necessarily, these moral truths are held to derive their authority from God.

Natural Rights—The view that human beings have rights independent of and prior to the existence of government, and that these rights constrain the ways in which governments may legitimately treat individuals. Often connected with the natural law tradition, though the natural rights tradition tends to be less strictly tied with religious views.

Negative Liberty—Negative liberty is freedom from certain sorts of interference by others. Libertarians believe that negative liberty is the only sort of liberty we have, or that it is the only sort of liberty that may be politically enforced. Contrasted with positive liberty. One might have negative liberty to do something without actually being *able* to do it.

Negative Rights—Negative rights are claims against others that they refrain from engaging in certain types of activity. Libertarians believe that negative rights are the only sorts of rights we have, or that they are the only sorts of rights that may be politically enforced. Contrasted with positive rights.

Political Authority—That which renders a government morally legitimate — which justifies it in ruling over a population, exercising coercion upon them, and claiming a monopoly on the use of force.

Positive Liberty—A more nebulous concept than its cousin, negative liberty, positive liberty refers variously to the power to do what one desires (or might desire) to do, to realize one's true self, or to do what one morally ought to do. Having the positive liberty to do something may require more than non-interference from others.

Positive Rights—Claims against others which require them to perform some positive act for one's benefit, and not merely that they refrain from interfering. Rights to a state-provided education or to poverty relief are examples of positive rights.

Prioritarianism—The view that in matters of distributive justice, priority ought to be given to meeting the needs/desires of the least well-off.

Prisoner's Dilemma—A model of certain types of human interaction drawn from game theory. In the standard two-person Prisoner's Dilemma, each player has an incentive to defect against the other, even though mutual defection leaves both players worse off than they would have been with mutual cooperation.

Public Good—In economic terms, a public good is one which has the characteristics of non-rivalry (one person's consumption does not diminish the amount available for others) and non-excludability (it is impossible to exclude people from consuming the good). Because of these characteristics, rational and self-interested individuals will not choose to pay for public goods but to free-ride on the contributions of others, and markets will therefore tend to under-supply them. The provision of public goods such as clean air and national defense has been thought to be one of the chief justifications of government.

Social Contract—An agreement, sometimes thought to be a real historical event but more often hypothetical and heuristic in nature, by which individuals in the state of nature agree to the formation of government.

State of Nature—A state of affairs in which individuals are not subject to the authority of any government.

Utilitarianism—The moral view that holds that happiness/pleasure is the only intrinsic good, and that right actions are those that produce the greatest possible amount of happiness.

Index